A HISTORY OF
GREECE

I. THE MINOAN SNAKE-GODDESS (*c.* 1700–1600)
A statuette, fourteen inches high, of painted faience
found at Cnossus.
Heraklion Museum, Crete (see p. 30)

A HISTORY OF
GREECE
TO 322 B.C.

BY

N. G. L. HAMMOND

FORMERLY PROFESSOR OF GREEK
IN THE UNIVERSITY OF BRISTOL
AND FELLOW AND TUTOR OF
CLARE COLLEGE, CAMBRIDGE

THIRD EDITION

CLARENDON PRESS · OXFORD

Oxford University Press, Walton Street, Oxford OX2 6DP
Oxford New York
Athens Auckland Bangkok Bogota Bombay
Buenos Aires Calcutta Cape Town Dar es Salaam
Delhi Florence Hong Kong Istanbul Karachi
Kuala Lumpur Madras Madrid Melbourne
Mexico City Nairobi Paris Singapore
Taipei Tokyo Toronto
and associated companies in
Berlin Ibadan

Oxford is a trade mark of Oxford University Press

Published in the United States by
Oxford University Press Inc., New York

© Oxford University Press

First Edition 1959
Second Edition 1967
Third Edition 1986

British Library Cataloguing in Publication Data
Hammond, N. G. L.
A history of Greece to 332 B.C.—3rd ed.
1. Greece—History—To 146 B.C.
I. Title
t938 DF214
ISBN 0–19–873095–0 (pbk.)

Library of Congress Cataloging in Publication Data
Hammond, N. G. L. (Nicholas Geoffrey Lemprière), 1907–
A history of Greece to 332 B.C.
Bibliography : Includes index.
1. Greece—History—To 146 B.C. I. Title
DF214.H28 1986 938 86–5222
ISBN 0–19–873095–0 (pbk.)

9 10 8

Printed in Hong Kong

TO
MY PARENTS

PREFACE

THIS book has been written after careful consideration of the original sources on which our knowledge of Greek history is based. I have therefore chosen to make reference in the footnotes to the main parts of the original evidence, in the hope that some readers will be encouraged to study the ancient authorities in translation or in the original and form their own opinions. Limitations of space have not permitted me to refer also to the work of modern scholars, which has been an inspiration and a guide to me in interpreting events and tendencies; but reference to such work is available in commentaries on individual authors and in general histories. Many points in Greek history are controversial. I had intended to concentrate my studies on such points in a second volume, but it has seemed better to publish them as short appendixes here and as separate articles in classical journals, to which references are made in the footnotes. The general reader will find that no technical knowledge is required of him. There is no Greek script; ancient names are given in the traditional Latinized form (island names, for instance, end in -os and mainland names in -us), and modern place-names are transliterated and accented. A map reference will be found in the Index for almost every place which is mentioned in the book.

A knowledge of modern Greece has been of great value to me. It was acquired during many months of study and travel in Greek lands and two years of war-time service on the mainland and in Crete. I owe the opportunity of writing this book to the initiative of the Delegates of the Clarendon Press; they and their staff have shown great patience and thoroughness in bringing it to completion. While I was engaged upon it, the Master and Fellows of Clare College granted me a sabbatical year and the Council of Clifton College granted me a grace term. I am deeply grateful to them. The generosity of the Institute for Advanced Study, the Managing Committee of the British School of Archaeology at Athens, the Managers of the Leverhulme Research Fellowships, and the Fulbright Trustees enabled me to work under ideal conditions at Princeton and at Athens. So many scholars and pupils have helped me that I must be excused if I do not mention them all by name. I owe particular gratitude to Sir Frank Adcock, the late Professor A. J. B. Wace, and Professor H. A. Thompson for unfailing encouragement and assistance, and to the following scholars who have been most generous in reading and criticizing parts of the book: Professor A. Andrewes, Professor H. F. Cherniss, Professor J. M. Cook, Mr. R. M. Cook, the late Mr. T. J. Dunbabin, Professor C. F. Edson, Mr. G. T. Griffith, Mr. G. S. Kirk, Dr. A. H. McDonald, Mr. R. Meiggs, Professor B. D. Meritt, Professor D. L. Page, Professor A. E. Raubitschek, Dr. F. H. Stubbings, and Professor H. D.

Westlake. My wife helped me to compile the Index, and Mr. H. J. Crawfurd of Clifton College has read and corrected the proofs with so keen and scholarly an eye that any errors which remain are entirely due to me.

N. G. L. H.

Clifton College
Bristol

THE main changes in the second edition are as follows. I have rewritten entirely the opening part of Chapter 1 and the first two sections of Chapter 2 of Book I in the light of recent excavations and interpretations, with which my work as an editor of the revised *Cambridge Ancient History* I–II has kept me in touch. I have included mention of tumulus burials in Albania; the excavation reports have not been noted otherwise by scholars in western countries, and I give a fuller account of them in my forthcoming book *Epirus*. My knowledge of Albanian and my pen-friendship with one of the excavators, Professor Frano Prendi, have helped me in this matter. I have made changes in my account of the origins of the Athenian Alliance in sections 1 and 2 of Chapter 5 in Book III, and the arguments on which they are based will appear in a forthcoming article in *JHS* 87. A new section is added to Appendix 2; this refers to the cylinder seals found at Thebes. Otherwise the changes are small.

N. G. L. H.

The University
Bristol

The third edition takes account of some recent archaeological developments: the excavations at Thera, the discovery of more tumulus-burials in Albania and Greece, and the most spectacular Royal Tombs at Aegae in Macedonia. There is a new Appendix on the Date of the Earliest Coinages and some consequential changes in the text. The Decree of Themistocles was the subject of much controversy at the time of the second edition, and it is only recently that I published my own views (in *JHS* 102), which have led to some changes here. My work on Macedonian history, especially *HA*, has caused me to change some details in Book VI, Chapters 3 and 4. References to my *Studies in Greek History* have been added to some footnotes.

N.G.L.H.

Clare College
Cambridge

CONTENTS

INTRODUCTION

THE GEOGRAPHY OF THE GREEK PENINSULA AND ISLANDS

BOOK I

THE EARLY CIVILIZATIONS OF GREECE AND THE GREAT MIGRATIONS (*c.* 6000–850)

Contents

BOOK III

THE TRIUMPH OF GREECE (546–466)

Contents

BOOK V

THE PERIOD OF TRANSIENT HEGEMONIES (404-354)

BOOK VI

THE RISE AND EXPANSION OF MACEDON

APPENDIXES

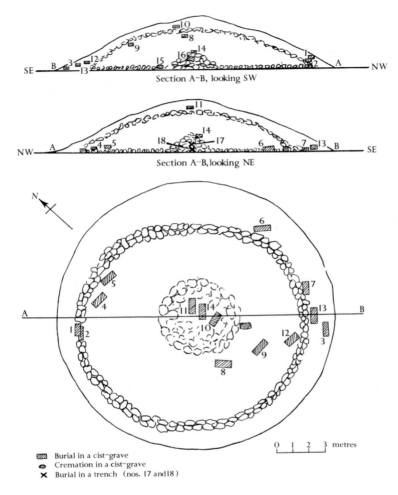

Section A-B, looking SW

Section A-B, looking NE

Burial in a cist-grave
Cremation in a cist-grave
Burial in a trench (nos. 17 and 18)

0 1 2 3 metres

Tumulus at Vodhinē in northern Epirus (*see p. 42*)

LIST OF FIGURES

List of Figures

LIST OF PLATES

ABBREVIATIONS

are those listed in Liddell-Scott-Jones *Lexicon*, ninth edition, except in the following cases:

AFD	*Athenian Financial Documents*, by B. D. Meritt, 1932.
ATL	*The Athenian Tribute Lists*, by B. D. Meritt, H. T. Wade-Gery, and M. F. McGregor, 1939–53.
DAT	*Documents on Athenian Tribute*, by B. D. Meritt, 1937.
DMG	*Documents in Mycenaean Greek*, by M. Ventris and J. Chadwick, 1956.
Ergon	*To ergon tēs arkhaeologikēs hetaireias*, Athens 1955–.
GC	*Greek Coins*, by C. Seltman, 1933.
GHI	*Greek Historical Inscriptions*, by M. N. Tod, 1946–9.
Gk. Lit. Pap.	*Greek Literary Papyri*, Loeb edition, 1950.
GMW	*Greek Mathematical Works*, by Ivor Thomas, Loeb edition, 1941.
HA	*Alexander the Great: King, Commander and Statesman*, by N. G. L. Hammond, 1980; 2nd edition, 1989.
HH. *GHI.*	*Greek Historical Inscriptions*, by E. L. Hicks and G. F. Hill, 1901.
IGA	*Inscriptiones Graecae Antiquissimae*, by H. Roehl, 1882.
MGM	*Manual of Greek Mathematics*, by Sir T. L. Heath, 1931.
Perachora	*Perachora*, by H. Payne and others, 1940–.
Plu. *GQ*	Plutarch, *Greek Questions*.
Richter, *AGA*	*Archaic Greek Art*, by G. M. A. Richter, 1949.
Richter, *Sc.*	*The Sculpture and Sculptors of the Greeks*, by G. M. A. Richter, 1930.
SEG	*Supplementum Epigraphicum Graecum*, Leyden, 1923–.
StGH	*Studies in Greek History*, by N. G. L. Hammond, 1973.
TAPA	*Transactions of the American Philological Association*, 1869–.

SHORT SELECTION OF TRANSLATIONS

Translations of almost all the works cited in this book will be found in the Loeb edition. The following is a list of cheap translations in England and America (Anchor = Anchor Books, Doubleday, 575 Madison Avenue, New York 22; Ev = Everyman's Library, Dent, 10 Bedford Street, London W.C. 2; Hafner Publishing Company, 31 E. 10th Street, New York 18; Lib = Liberal Arts Press, 153 W. 72nd Street, New York 23; MLCE = Modern Library College Editions, 457 Madison Avenue, New York 22; NAL = New American Library of World Literature, 501 Madison Ave., New York 22; Ox=Oxford University Press, Inc., 114 Fifth Ave., New York 11, N.Y.; P = Penguin Books).

A. Aeschylus. All plays (Ev), *Oresteian Trilogy* (P), *Persians* and *Prometheus Vinctus* (Ox).

Aesop, *Fables* (P; Ev).

Ar. Aristophanes. Eight plays (Ev), five comedies (Anchor).

Arist. Aristotle, *Ath. Pol. The Constitution of Athens and Related Texts* (Hafner).
Aristotle, *Poetics* (Ev; Lib).
Aristotle, *Politics* (Ev).

Arr. Arrian, *The Campaigns of Alexander* (P).

D. Demosthenes, *Crown and Other Orations* (Ev).

Demetr. Demetrius, *On Style* (Ev).

E. Euripides. All plays (Ev). *Alcestis and Other Plays* (P). *Bacchae and Other Plays* (P). *Alcestis, Bacchae, Electra, Hippolytus, Iphigeneia in Tauris, Medea, Supplices* (Ox).

Hdt. Herodotus. History (Ev; P).

Hes. Hesiod, *Theogony* (Lib).

Il. The Iliad (P; Ev; MLCE).

Longin. Longinus, *On the Sublime* (Ev).

Od. The Odyssey (P; Ev; NAL).

Pl. Plato, *Republic, Symposium, Protagoras, Meno, and Last Days of Socrates* (P). *Republic, Socratic Discourses, Ion and Other Dialogues* (Ev). *Great Dialogues of Plato* (NAL).

Plu. Plutarch, *Lives* (Ev; NAL).

S. Sophocles. All Plays (Ev). *The Theban Plays* (P; Ox). *Electra and Other Plays* (P). *Three Tragedies: Antigone, Oedipus the King, Electra* (Ox.).

Th. Thucydides, *The Peloponnesian War* (P; Ev; MLCE).

X. Xenophon, *The Persian Expedition* (P).

INTRODUCTION

THE GEOGRAPHY OF THE GREEK
PENINSULA AND ISLANDS

§ 1. *General characteristics*

THE climate of the Mediterranean area is temperate, being immune from the winter cold of Europe and from the summer heat of Africa. Its temperate character is due to the influence of the sea, which in winter attracts the mild rain-bearing westerly winds from the Atlantic and in summer the dry cooling north-easterly winds, the 'Etesians' of antiquity. The full Mediterranean climate is enjoyed by those areas in which the influence of the sea is strongest—the islands, peninsulas, and low-lying coastal fringes. As one proceeds inland away from the sea, the climate loses its Mediterranean quality of temperateness and approximates more closely to the continental climates of Europe or Africa. Consequently the incidence of the Mediterranean climate is not determined by latitude. In Greece, for example, a mainland peninsula such as Attica bears more resemblance in climate to Chalcidice and Argolis than to its inland neighbour Boeotia. So, too, within the Mediterranean area as a whole the coastal fringes of Spain, France, Italy, and Greece have more in common with those of Asia Minor, Syria, Palestine, Cyrenaica, and Carthage, than with their own adjacent hinterlands.

The pattern of the Mediterranean climate directed, and also limited, the spread of Mycenaean culture and later of Phoenician and Greek colonial settlements to the maritime areas of the Mediterranean Sea rather than to the continental parts of Macedonia and Syria. For in all these maritime areas the same mode of life can be practised. The summer drought, following on the winter rains and winter sunshine, permits the long period of germination and growth which is necessary for the olive, vine, and fig to mature, and facilitates the raising of cereals. The preponderance of sunshine, combined with the mildness of winter and the dry warmth of summer, stimulates the energy of the population and encourages an open-air life. Peoples accustomed to these conditions in the lowlands of Crete, Greece, and Phoenicia, when forced to seek new lands, naturally looked for them in areas which were blessed with the Mediterranean climate.

The greater part of the land-surface of the Greek mainland consists of mountainous tracts. The higher of them, extending as far south as the mountain plateaux of Arcadia in the Peloponnese, belong to the zone of continental climate. These tracts, which are usually covered with forest and scrub or else eroded into barren precipices of limestone and marble, are sparsely populated, but they nevertheless play an important part in the economy of Greece. Above all, they provide the pastures which the lowlands cannot yield

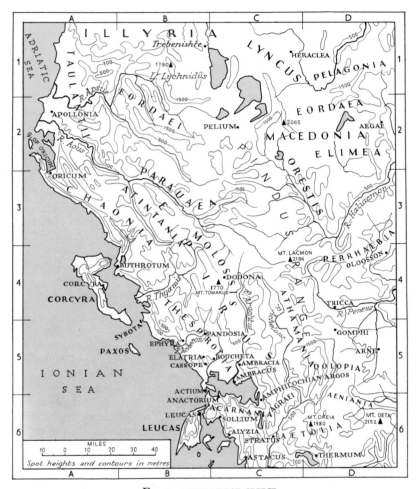

FIG. 1. NORTH–WEST GREECE

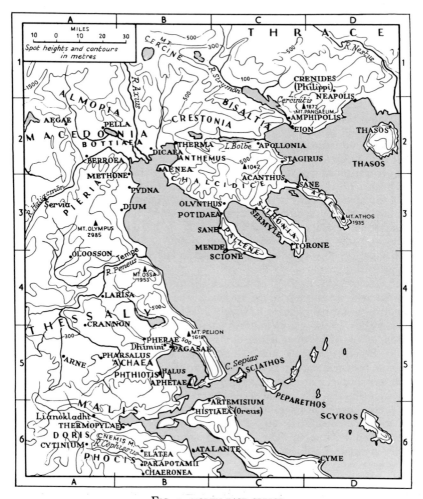

FIG. 2. NORTH-EAST GREECE

in the long summer drought. Large flocks of sheep migrate annually from the lowlands to the highlands in April and May, and return from the highlands to the lowlands in the autumn. The uplands, too, support cattle, goats, and swine. Thus the mountainous tracts provide the meat and the milk products, which combine with the cereals, olives, fruit, pulse, and vegetables of the lowlands to form a balanced diet. The mountains also supply timber for fuel and for building, including pine, cedar, and cypress for ship-construction and the valonea oak for dye, pig-fodder, and tanning extract. The highlanders, who live in the scattered villages and hamlets, retain a toughness of physique and a moral stability which tend to be bred out of their cousins in the lowlands by the softer conditions of climate and living.

The lowlands carry the bulk of the population, which lives in large villages or towns and gains a livelihood by agriculture, fishing, and trade. Fertile plains are numerous, but mostly small in extent, and the total area of cultivable land in Greece today is only 18 per cent. of the whole land-surface. In the earliest times it was even less. Consequently, arable land is and always has been in great demand; for the grain which it grows is vital. In comparison with the mountainous tracts of Greece the lowlands are rich in produce and population, enjoy a temperate climate and have ready access to the sea. Civilization developed there at times when the highland peoples were still backward. But whenever decadence set in among the lowland peoples, the highland races of Arcadia, Achaea, Aetolia, and north Greece proved superior in energy and vigour.

Throughout the history of Greece the peoples of the highlands have exerted pressure on those of the lowlands. The mountainous tracts shed continuously a surplus population which seeks employment and sustenance in the lowlands. From time to time the poorer peoples of the north drive southwards, attracted by the sunnier climate and the agricultural wealth of the plains. But the lowlands, being so small in extent, are themselves liable to become over-populated: their surplus peoples, being habituated to the Mediterranean climate and life, go overseas to settle in districts where similar conditions obtain. This cycle of movement has been fairly constant, though not continuous, in historical times. It operates today as it did in antiquity.

Within the Mediterranean Sea the Aegean basin is the most favoured in climate and in situation. The temperate summer lasts longest there and the winter months are mildest, and the sea breeds a rich variety of fish, the tunny being especially valuable to man. The Aegean is land-locked save on the south, where a string of islands separates it from the open Libyan Sea. Its waters are particularly favourable to the sailor in the summer months, when steady off-shore and on-shore winds blow along its coasts at morning and evening and the north-easterly Etesian winds are constant out at sea. In the archipelago of islands one rarely loses sight of land. Visibility is good by day, and the stars are lustrous by night; and innumerable islands and inlets afford shelter from storm. Tides are weak and currents rare, and small craft can be safely beached on shelving strands. Thus the summer seas of the Aegean formed the natural cradle for primitive seafaring. But the Greeks rightly regarded the sea as a fickle jade; for in a land-locked basin catabatic squalls swoop down without warning, and lee-shores may be rocky and steep-to. In the winter months, when storms are frequent, sailing is extremely hazardous. Even a modern caique, which is equipped with navigational aids and capable of tacking against a moderate wind, rarely sails in the winter.

The Ionian Sea, which washes the west coast of the Greek peninsula, possesses some of the advantages of the Aegean Sea. On the mainland the Gulfs of Corinth, Ambracia, and Oricum offer shelter, and the string of islands which runs parallel to the coast is rich in harbours. Here, too, during the summer months the off-shore and on-shore winds favour coastal sailing as far as the mouth of the Adriatic Sea. But the entry into that sea, or the crossing from Corcyra and the Gulf of Oricum to the heel of Italy, is often rendered dangerous by the north-easterly Etesian winds, which drive steep seas down the funnel-shaped Adriatic. Yet the direct passage from the Gulf of Corinth to Sicily or Italy was considered still more dangerous by ancient navigators. To the south the open sea is void of islands and liable to both calms and storms. Ancient ships rarely crossed this sea to Africa. They preferred to follow the island chain to Asia and coast past Syria and Palestine to Egypt.

As soon as seafaring was developed, it was inevitable that contacts between Mediterranean lands were made mainly by sea. Passage overland was in most cases circuitous and arduous. Under primitive conditions of sail the Ionian Sea and the Aegean basin formed the main channels for traffic between east and west and between north and south within the eastern Mediterranean; for their island chains and indented coasts offered safer routes than the wide seas of the southern Mediterranean. Within the Aegean area itself different centres have risen to pre-eminence at different periods in history, each in its turn owing its rise less to its own natural advantages than to the direction of contemporary currents of trade. When Egypt was the wealthiest state in the Mediterranean, Cyprus and Crete and southern Argolis were pre-eminent. When the area of trade expanded to comprise both the western Mediterranean and the Black Sea, the Isthmus became the bridge of traffic between West and East, and the adjacent states—Aegina, Corinth, and Athens—became the most important centres of exchange. In Hellenistic and Roman times, when the resources of the farther East were exploited, Alexandria and Cyprus and Rhodes came to the fore. In the dark age of Turkish domination the islanders of the central Aegean played the leading rôle. Thus, until the development of the steamship, the Aegean Sea was the focal point in the interchange of goods between Europe, Asia, and Egypt.

The main overland communications of Europe do not touch the Greek peninsula at all. Even when the products of northern and central Europe travel south to be exported across the Mediterranean Sea, they have always

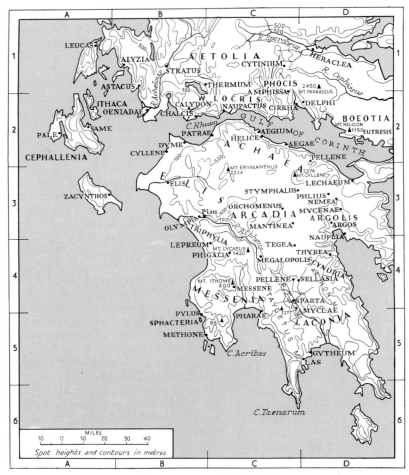

FIG. 3. SOUTH-WEST GREECE

FIG. 4. SOUTH-EAST GREECE

found more convenient points of departure at Marseilles and Venice or in the Black Sea and the Propontis. Within the Balkan peninsula the main route from central Europe, which follows the valleys of the rivers Morava and Axius, reaches the Aegean Sea on the shores of the Thermaic Gulf in Macedonia and does not proceed into the Greek peninsula. The best overland route from the eastern shore of the Adriatic Sea to the Propontis, having crossed the Balkan range near Lake Lychnidus, descends into Macedonia and follows the coast of Thrace to Byzantium. Thus the control of the overland communications in the Balkans and also of the Balkans' main outlet to the sea is concentrated in the grip of Macedonia. The potentialities of her position were realized by the great Macedonian kings and by the Romans of the Republican period. Then Macedonia lay athwart the landward communications of Greece. On the other hand, the Greek states never gained full control of Macedonia, and in consequence they never became a military power capable of dominating the Balkan peninsula. Instead they turned overseas in the pursuit of prosperity and power.

Within the Greek peninsula the greatest obstacle to overland communication is the southern extension of the main Balkan range. Whereas a single range forms the watershed between Macedonia and Albania, a wide belt of parallel mountain ranges separates east Greece from west Greece. Running southwards from Pindus to Oreia in the west and to Parnassus-Helicon in the east, it contains its own system of rivers. South of the Gulf of Corinth the belt continues in the high peaks of the Arcadian mountains (Mt. Erymanthus and Mt. Cyllene) and terminates in the three ranges of Aegaleos, Taygetus, and Parnon. To cross this mountain belt is extremely arduous. Passes are high and infrequent. The traveller is faced not by one watershed but by several as he travels from the east coast to the west coast. Consequently the overland routes from east to west are important only for local traffic and for the movement of armies. Goods are exchanged much more easily by sea.

Overland communications between north Greece and south Greece are drawn into a bottleneck at the Isthmus, where the passage is narrowed by the mass of Mt. Gerania. Setting out from the Eurotas valley in the Peloponnese one climbs over Mt. Parnon into the Argive plain, and then proceeds over a low pass near Nemea to Corinth and the Isthmus. Thence two main routes lead northwards. One follows the west side of Greece, where the mountain system runs parallel to the coast, by a fairly easy passage from Oeniadae to Oricum. The traveller follows a long sink (containing the lakes of Acarnania) to Limnaea and Amphilochian Argos, and then a narrow ridge above the Ambraciote Gulf to Ambracia in Epirus; from there he traverses the sides or floors of several long valleys, which run parallel to the coast, through Dodona and Atintania, and descends the Aous valley towards Apollonia or turns off westwards to the Gulf of Oricum. The other route to the north starts from the Isthmus and follows the east side of the peninsula, where the subsidiary ranges run not parallel but at right angles to the main range. These ranges divide east Greece into a series of cantons. They direct the rivers eastwards into the Aegean Sea, and they form a series of obstacles for the traveller as he proceeds northwards from the Isthmus on his way to Macedonia.

Of these two routes the eastern one is more arduous. But it is much more important than the western one because it connects two points of strategic value, the Isthmus and Macedonia. Neither route is easy for hauling or carrying goods. In general the soil is stony and the hills are rocky, so that the going is difficult for horses, which were unshod in ancient times. Pony and mule serve as pack-animals, and the ox is more in use for ploughing than the horse. Even in modern times wheeled vehicles are little used except on metalled roads and in the lowland plains. In ancient times road systems were developed in single cantons, such as Argolis, Attica, and Macedonia, and a main road ran through the Isthmus. But elsewhere goods were carried mainly by pack-animal, and any exchange over long distances was more quickly and more cheaply effected by sea.

The characteristics of Greece, which we have described, are common to almost all the cantons of the Greek mainland and to many of the islands. Each canton may be said to represent a cross-section of Greece, comprising highland, lowland, and coast. Laconia, Attica, and Acarnania, for example, possess arable plains and olive-growing lowlands as well as summer pastures and forest-clad highlands. The same is true of such islands, for example, as Cephallenia, Crete, and Rhodes. Within each canton and within many of the islands there are often several small plains, each surrounded with its own orbit of highland and lowland. Each canton or island, and even smaller units of territory within them, are self-sufficing in the primary products necessary for subsistence. This peculiarity favoured the growth of numerous states, which each possessed the first elements of self-sufficiency.

The cantons themselves are not homogeneous but strongly individual in character and scenery. This is partly due to climatic factors. The rain-bearing westerly winds precipitate most of their moisture on the west side of the main watershed which forms the central spine of the peninsula, so that Ambracia receives 42·6 inches of annual rainfall and Pagasae 21·6 inches, Patrae 26·5 and Athens 16·0, Elis 33·8 and Tiryns 20·0. West Greece is therefore more heavily forested, possesses better pasture, and has a less dazzling clarity of light than east Greece. In addition the lowlands of Greece become progressively warmer as one travels from north to south, until one reaches a climax in the southward-facing plains of Messenia, Crete, and Cyprus. Finally, the influence of the sea endows the peninsular districts of the mainland and the islands with a degree of temperateness which is not found in the other cantons of Greece.

Nor is the geological structure of Greece uniform. The high watershed of the mainland is composed partly of limestone and partly of volcanic rock, especially dark-green serpentine, which reappears sporadically in some Aegean islands, for instance Aegina, Melos, Thera, and Nisyros. The subsidiary ranges of west Greece are of limestone; and this formation sweeps in a semicircle through the outer Aegean islands along the line of Crete and Rhodes to the adjacent coast of Asia Minor. The subsidiary ranges of east Greece are partly limestone and partly crystalline, the latter containing marble and minerals; and the continuation of these ranges forms the islands of the central Aegean basin and the opposite coast of Asia Minor. Between these ranges and the alluvial plains beds of flysch intervene (flysch being a general term for sandstone, marl, slate, and conglomerate). The beds of flysch, which are hilly and provide a fertile detritus, are wider in east Greece than in west Greece and endow some Aegean islands with fertile tracts. The effects of these factors will be illustrated in the following survey of Greek lands.

§ 2. *Cantons and islands*

THE hinterland of *Epirus* is drained by the Aous and the Arachthus, which rise in the central knot of the Pindus range at Mt. Lacmon. This hinterland is continental in climate, and its population is robust. The high altitude and heavy rainfall make it rich in pasture and timber, but arable land is scarce; it was famous in antiquity for cattle, sheep, horses, and goats. The centre of the hinterland is the plateau of Dodona. Here the main route from Ambracia to Oricum joins the route eastwards over Mt. Lacmon to Thessaly. On the west side of the Pindus range there are four high limestone ranges, running parallel to the coastline, which shut off the hinterland from the Ionian Sea. Direct access to the sea is available only for the fertile plains of Buthrotum and the lower Acheron river, and for the smaller plain of the Thyamis river. These plains enjoy the Mediterranean climate and are rich in cereals and olives; as their produce finds a ready market in the hinterland, the people of these plains do not trade much by sea. The richest area in Epirus adjoins the north shore of the Gulf of Ambracia. It combines a high rainfall with a mild winter and abounds in cereals, olives, fruit, and pasture, as well as in fish-breeding lagoons. It is the natural outlet for the produce of central Epirus, and its ports are more active than any on the west coast.

On the east shore of the Ambraciote Gulf *Amphilochia* has a small coastal plain and densely-wooded sandstone hills which provide timber and shelter wild pig. It is of strategic importance, because it controls the route from Epirus to the south. *Acarnania*, being peninsular in outline and combining the Mediterranean climate with a heavy rainfall, has rich pasture-land and fertile plains round Stratus and Oeniadae. The structure of the limestone ranges resembles those of Epirus, so that its traffic is directed southwards to the Gulf of Corinth. The Acarnanians are not a seafaring people. Like the Epirotes, they have often tended to be backward in cultural and political development.

The frontiers of Upper *Macedonia* are formed by high mountain ranges. Its extensive plateaux of flysch are divided one from another by less high ranges, and drain either into lakes or into the rivers Axius, Lydias, and Haliacmon, which pierce the ring of mountains encircling the fertile plain of Lower Macedonia and then enter the Thermaic Gulf. The climate of Macedonia is continental; it is marked by bitter north winds in winter and by heavy heat in summer. Both in climate and in terrain Macedonia is more akin to the Balkan land-mass than to the Greek peninsula. Rich in timber, cattle, horses, sheep, cereals, and vines, it supports a larger population of hardy peasant stock than any canton of Greece. The trade-routes from the interior converge upon the coastal plain. The best harbours on the shore of the Gulf are possessed by the promontories of Chalcidice, which are Mediterranean in climate and produce olives, fruit, and timber suitable for ship-construction.

Separated from Macedonia by the towering peaks of Mt. Olympus and by the lower Cambunian range, *Thessaly* is entered from the north either through the Vale of Tempe, shaded by plane trees, or over the passes west of Mt. Olympus. The extensive plains of Thessaly are enclosed by a ring-wall of mountains; the lowest of these separates the plains from the sea and suffices to turn their drainage system northwards, where the river Peneus passes through the Vale of Tempe. The climate of the plains is continental, since the ranges of Ossa and Pelion shut out the influence of the sea, but the winter is less severe than that of Macedonia. The deep rich soil of the plains produces a surplus of cereals and supports fine herds of horses, cattle, and sheep, which find their main summer pastures on the flysch foothills and alpine slopes of north-west Thessaly. The plains are divided by foothills into four districts, centring on Larisa, Tricca, Arne, and Thebes. The crystalline ranges of Magnesia yield timber, pasture, olives, fruit, and nuts. The fertile coastal plains of Phthiotis are Mediterranean in climate and products; they face the land-locked Gulf of Pagasae and the Strait of Euboea. Although the mountains carry timber suitable for shipbuilding, the Thessalians of the classical period were an agricultural people whose exports were shipped by others.

The shortest route southwards climbs the high pass over Mt. Othrys. A longer route, starting from Halus, follows the coast. Both descend into the alluvial plain of *Malis*, which is soft in climate and fertile. The long valley of the Spercheus river is dominated by the pastoral peoples of the hill-country, Aeniania and Oetaea, and from its headwaters a difficult route crosses the mountainous belt westwards to Amphilochia.

The entry into central Greece is barred by the ranges of Oeta and Cnemis. The easiest route passes along the coast but is pinched at the narrows or 'gates' of Thermopylae; it then enters *Locris*, a narrow strip of hill-country with fertile plains at Thronium and Opus, which faces the Euboean Channel. An inland route climbs the high flank of Oeta to enter the small plateau of *Doris*, which collects the headwaters of the Cephissus. From this windy and wintry plateau there are two routes leading southward, one through Amphissa to the Corinthian Gulf and the other down the Cephissus valley into *Phocis*. There Mt. Parnassus is the dominant feature. It overlooks the narrow valley of Amphissa to the west and the long fertile valley of the Cephissus to the east. Its higher slopes are forested with conifers and afford summer pasture, but the lower slopes are barren or covered in prickly scrub. The southern face of Parnassus falls in sheer precipices into a rift running west and east, which contains the route from Lebadea to the Corinthian Gulf. On the north side of the rift and at the foot of the cliffs the sanctuary of Delphi commands the western exit of the route, before it descends through the rich olive-groves of Crisa to Itea. Between the rift and the Gulf there is an area of broken and intractable limestone. The richest part of Phocis is the well-watered Cephissus valley, possessing arable land and good pasture, with its towns set on the lowest spurs of Parnassus.

Boeotia, ringed with mountains except towards the south-east, is entered through the narrows of the Cephissus valley. Its extensive and fertile plain-lands, like those of Thessaly, are torrid in summer and raw in winter. There are two main plains, separated by a low range, which is an outlier of Mt. Helicon. On this ridge Thebes stands. The rich northern plain, of which Orchomenus is the centre, contains Lake Copaïs into which the Cephissus flows. In the bed of the lake there are funnels in the limestone; when these are kept clear, the waters of the lake drain away. The southern plain, with a fertile heavy soil, is traversed by the Asopus, which passes through Attica to enter the sea near Oropus. Boeotia was famous in antiquity for cereals, horses, cattle, and sheep. It was usually not a maritime state, although it possesses a coast on the Strait of Euboea and on the Corinthian Gulf.

Crossing the ranges of Cithaeron and Parnes one enters the full Mediterranean climate in the peninsula of *Attica*. Its thin arid soil is best suited to the production of the olive; the vine and the fig are of secondary importance. The central plain round Athens is bounded by three isolated mountains: Parnes, bearing coniferous forest and some summer pasture on its limestone summits, Pentelicus scarred with marble quarries, and Hymettus, barren on its western slopes save for thyme and other bee-nurturing herbs. From the central plain easy routes lead to the smaller plains of Eleusis, Marathon, and Mesogeia, of which the first grows wheat and the others barley. The lower slopes of the mountains and the hilly country of the coasts carry evergreen woods, especially the stunted Mediterranean pine which is tapped for resin. Poor in resources for agriculture and stock-raising, Attica is enriched by silver mines at Laurium and by the possession of natural harbours which face the Saronic Gulf and the Cyclades. A coastal route leads from Eleusis into *Megaris*. The small coastal plain below Megara (which is built on a barren limestone outcrop) produces cereals and vegetables. Its inland plain is rich in vines and olives, and its hill country affords scanty grazing and some timber. Its strategic position is important. The main road from Boeotia to the Peloponnese runs through its territory, and it has ports for small craft on the Saronic and Corinthian Gulfs.

The districts which we have described are bounded by natural frontiers.

Between the western and the eastern groups runs a mountainous tract, of which the central knot is formed by Mt. Lacmon. North of this point the high mountains are mainly of serpentine formation, rich in springs and soil-covered. Clad in virgin forests of beech, conifers, oak, and sweet chestnut, where the bear is extant and wolves numerous, these mountains afford wide areas of Alpine pasture which are grazed in summer by myriads of sheep from Epirus, Macedonia, and Thessaly. South of Mt. Lacmon there is a broad limestone belt which consists of a tangle of high ranges. Through them the Achelous, Euenus, and Daphnus cut their channels in a series of gorges towards the Gulf of Corinth. In this wild and wooded country scattered villages subsist on summer-sown cereals (mainly maize), livestock, nuts, and vegetables, and the uplands provide summer grazing for the sheep of the lowland areas farther east and west. The hardy hillmen form a reservoir of population which often overflows into the lowlands. Organized by tribes in ancient times, their habitats were known as *Athamania, Dolopia, Eurytania, Aperantia,* and *Agraea.* To the south the mountainous belt is cut by the Gulf of Corinth, on the coast of which lie the cantons of *Aetolia* and *Ozolian Locris.* Their hinterland is pastoral and continental in climate, while their lowlands, facing the sea, are Mediterranean in climate and products. The most fertile land lies west of Thermum in Aetolia and south of Amphissa in Locris. But both cantons are so split by mountain ranges that passage from west to east is extremely difficult.

The central mountainous area of the Peloponnese, *Arcadia,* is drained by the Alpheus river, which breaks its way westwards to the sea. High in elevation and remote from the sea, it is continental in climate and produces cattle, sheep, horses, asses, and pigs rather than cereals; the best arable land is in the basins of Tegea, Mantinea, Pheneus, and Stymphalus, which also afford rich pasture. The northern slopes of Mt. Erymanthus and Mt. Cyllene, falling steeply to the Corinthian Gulf, form the district *Achaea.* There vines, olives, and fruit flourish, but the pinched valleys have little arable land. The higher slopes carry fine forests of oak and conifer, and its long coast possesses a good harbour at Patrae, west of the narrows. Southwards from Arcadia run three parallel ranges which form the promontories of Acritas, Taenarum, and Malea. The central range, Taygetus, and the mountains of Arcadia divide the Peloponnese into two halves. The rainfall of the western half and also of the south shore of the Corinthian Gulf is almost double that of the eastern half; the western areas therefore have better pasture and more extensive forests, and the shore of the Gulf is particularly suited to growing the currant grape.

Messenia, combining a high rainfall with a southerly latitude, is very rich in vines, olives, figs, and pasture, while the alluvial plains of the west coast and of the Pamisus valley grow fine cereals. But its overland communications are difficult, and the value of its southern ports is impaired by the stormy promontories which enclose the Messenian Gulf. On its west coast Pylus possesses a well-sheltered harbour with sandy beaches; this forms an important station in the circumnavigation of the Peloponnese. To the north, *Elis* alone of the western areas has an extensive plain open to the sea, known as Coele Elis. Low-lying and swampy, this plain provides lush pasture for horses, cattle, and sheep and also raises cereals. On the foothills the currant grape is extensively grown, and the highlands of Mt. Erymanthus are clad with forests of oak and conifer. Between Elis and Messenia lie the cantons of *Pisatis*, watered by the lower Alpheus, beside which the sanctuary of Olympia is situated, and *Triphylia*, mountainous save for a narrow coastal plain. These western districts of the Peloponnese are rich in evergreen maquis woods (including laurel, myrtle, arbutus, ilex, and juniper), which give the hill country a fresher and softer appearance than elsewhere in Greece. Their overland communications to the east are poor. The shortest route through the mountain-belt climbs from the Messenian plain over Mt. Taygetus to Sparta; it can be traversed in one day, but is not easy for pack-animals. Less difficult but longer routes lead from Messenia and Elis to the plateau of Megalopolis, and thence southwards to Sparta or through Tegea to Argos.

In the eastern Peloponnese, *Corinthia* comprises the neck of the Isthmus and its southern approaches. It therefore commands not only the entry by land into the Peloponnese, but also the shortest haulage for cargoes and ships from Gulf to Gulf, which was facilitated in antiquity by the laying of rollers. The fertile plain of western Corinthia produces wheat and barley and above all the currant grape, but much of its territory is sparsely wooded limestone. Its access to both gulfs through the ports of Lechaeum and Cenchreae and its control of the Isthmus give it a unique position for trade by sea and land. Between Corinthia and Achaea, the small canton *Sicyonia* has a fertile coast and wooded hill country; its southern frontier is formed by a small upland canton *Phliasia*.

The peninsula of Argolis resembles Attica in outline and climate. It is strongly divided by Mt. Arachnaeus into two parts. The districts of *Epidauria*, *Troezenia*, and *Hermionis*, which produce vegetables, olives, and fruit, trade more readily with Aegina and Attica than with Argos. The fertile plain of *Argolis* and its hill country is a more self-sufficient unit. Autumn-sown cereals grow in the plain, olives, vines, and figs on the foothills, and summer vegetables and maize in the swampy land round Lerna and Tiryns, which also provides pasture for horses and cattle. The harbours of the plain, Nauplia and Asine, face the Cretan Sea. The coastal route to the south passes through the mountainous districts of *Thyreatis* and *Cynuria* to Sellasia, where it is joined by the southward route from Tegea, and descends thence into the central plain of *Laconia*, 'hollow Lacedaemon', set between the dark cliffs of Taygetus and the barren spurs of Parnon. In the arid summer the plain, watered by springs from Taygetus and ringed by olive-groves, has the fertility and charm of an oasis. It is separated by a broad limestone ridge from the swampy delta of the Eurotas, which provides pasture for horses but lacks good harbours. The south-western part of Laconia grows excellent olives; to the east the slopes of Parnon are barren except towards the coast, where woods of Mediterranean pine face the sea and pockets of arable land produce cereals and figs. The stormy promontories of Taenarum and Malea endanger the entry to the Laconian Gulf, and the harbours of east Laconia are remote from the inland plain, so that Laconia, like Messenia, is primarily an agricultural area.

The Ionian islands are the peaks of a submerged limestone range running parallel to the west coast of Greece. They combine a heavy rainfall with a temperate Mediterranean climate. Possessing better ports than the mainland coast, the islands attract sea-borne traffic and act as middlemen for the mainland. *Corcyra*, controlling the entry into Greek waters, has the highest rainfall and the densest rural population in Greece. Its rich soil produces a surplus of olives, vine, and fruit for export, and its forested highlands afford summer pasture for sheep. To maintain its large population it imports some cereals and winter-fodder for livestock. Corcyra harbour, facing east, commands the channel and attracts the trade of Epirus. *Paxos* and *Anti-Paxos*, lacking water but rich in olives, form stepping-stones on the route to *Leucas*, separated from Acarnania by a narrow channel which tends to silt up and become closed to shipping. This channel is used in rough weather to avoid rounding the white cliffs of Cape Leucate. Leucas produces sufficient cereals for its needs, and exports olives, wine, fish, and salt.

Ithaca, consisting of two peaks linked by a low isthmus, has little arable land and pasture but produces an export of olives. The population is mainly occupied in seafaring: its harbour on the east coast and its inner position among the islands enable it to control the entry into the Gulf of Corinth. *Cephallenia*, lying outside Ithaca, is primarily agricultural; it produces vines, cereals, olives, and fruit, and raises sheep, goats, and pigs. The main exports are wine and currant grapes. Little now remains of the forests of 'Cephallonian pine' and of the maquis woods which once covered its high mountains. To the south, *Zacynthos* is rocky but well watered. Its ports face Elis, which it resembles in terrain and products, namely wheat, wine, sheep, and goats. Here, too, there are remains of extensive woods.

Of the Aegean islands Aegina and Euboea are well placed to capture the trade of the adjacent mainland. *Aegina* holds a central position in the Saronic Gulf and controls the approaches; it possesses a small sheltered harbour facing west. Pigs, olives, and some cereals are products of the island. In contrast rocky *Salamis*, lying close off the ports of Megaris and Attica, is thinly populated and dependent on the mainland. *Euboea*, well forested with pine and sweet chestnut and rich in pastureland, produces cereals (mainly wheat), vines, and olives. Its richest land, the Lelantine plain, faces the narrows of the Euripus Channel, which is used by coasting vessels in order to avoid the rocky east coast of the long island. There are deposits of marble, lead, and zinc in the southern promontory.

Northwards of Euboea the promontory of Magnesia is continued in the *Northern Sporades*, limestone outcrops with little fertile land, some olives, and a seafaring tradition; Sciathos, Peparethos, and Scyros possess excellent harbours. Between them and the approaches to the Hellespont lie the islands of *Lemnos*, *Imbros*, and *Tenedos*. Lemnos and Imbros are mainly of fertile sandstone flysch; the former produces cereals and wine, the latter timber and cattle. Tenedos exports wine and raises some cereals. The best harbour in the group is that of Lemnos. *Thasos* and *Samothrace* lie towards the Thracian coast. Thasos is a wealthy island with temperate climate and considerable rainfall; its products are wine, fruit, olives, sheep, honey, and timber, and it contains silver mines. Its natural harbours and its position enable it to develop trade with Thrace. Samothrace, with its granite peak and sheer coast, is thickly forested and exports timber, cheese, and fruit.

The *Cyclades*, terminating to the south-east in Anaphe and Amorgos, form extensions of the ranges of Euboea and Attica, and provide ports of call on the short route from Greece to Samos and Asia Minor. The group from Andros to Naxos contains marble deposits, and the southerly islands are partly volcanic like southern Aegina. In antiquity gold and silver were mined at Siphnos. All the Cyclades are mountainous and resemble Attica in climate, in production of olives and wine, and in deficiency of cereals. Naxos and Melos alone have sufficient pasture to export cheese. At the centre of the group lie Delos and Syros, markets of exchange at different periods. To the south Melos and Thera are important stations on the direct route between the Peloponnese and the south-east Aegean. The outer Aegean islands form an extension of the west Greek limestone range, swinging in a semicircle to join the Carian coast in Asia Minor.

Cythera and *Anti-Cythera* lead from Laconia towards *Crete*, the largest Greek island. Crete is divided throughout its length by a high range, which in antiquity was forested with cypress, cedar, pine, and oak. The north coast of the island boasts the better ports; Crete therefore faces the Aegean archipelago rather than the open Libyan sea. The variety of its terrain and products makes the island self-sufficient, and even today its balance of trade is favourable, the main exports being currants, wine, olives, fruit, nuts, hides, and timber. The richest arable land is situated in the warm plain of Gortyn and Phaestus; north of this plain a gap in the range leads to the port of Herákleion and to the rolling hills in which Cnossus is situated. Land communications are difficult, whether to the upland plateaux, productive of cheese and cereals, or to the western plain of Cydonia and the eastern plain of Sitia. To the east of Crete, *Casos* and *Carpathos* lead towards *Rhodes*. This group enjoys a favoured climate, the heat of the long summer being alleviated by westerly winds. Casos lacks water and depends on fishing, while Carpathos exports olives, wine, and fruit but imports cereals. Rhodes raises a considerable quantity of cereals, and exports olives, wine, fruit, vegetables, and honey. Mt. Atabyris, a conspicuous landmark for mariners, was in the past forested with cypress and conifers which were used for ship-building. Its harbours, situated on the east coast, not only control the entry into the Aegean Sea but also form the meeting-point of the sea-routes which converge from the Greek peninsula and islands, from Phoenicia and the south-east, and from the Hellespont along the coast of Asia Minor.

This last route follows the chain of islands which girdle the coast of Asia Minor. Of these *Lesbos* and *Chios* are the richest, the former in olives, wine, figs, and timber, the latter in wine, figs, and mastic gum; both grow a considerable quantity of cereals and their mountains afford timber and pasture. *Samos* produces wine, olives, and fruit, and *Icaros* cattle and honey, while the small islands grouped round *Cos* win their living mainly from the sea. To the south-east *Cyprus* lies outside the Aegean. Its small harbours form important stations on the coasting route from Egypt to the Aegean, and dominate the approaches to the coasts of Cilicia and Phoenicia. Its intermediate position is reflected by the mixed origins of its population, which derives from Greece and from the adjacent coasts of Asia. The natural wealth of the island has always attracted settlers. Rich in copper and in timber suitable for ship-construction (especially cedar, cypress, and pine), the island grew sufficient cereals to export and was famous for its figs and fruit in antiquity. The plain inland of Salamis, like the plain of Phaestus in Crete, is subject to torrid heat in the summer months and approximates to the warmer climate of the Libyan coast.

§ 3. *Changes since antiquity*

THE modern traveller thinks of Greece as a rather bare and unproductive land. Throughout antiquity it was much more heavily wooded than it is to-day. The rainfall was then conserved by the forest cover and by man's skill in terracing the hillsides. Meat was much eaten by the Mycenaean peoples, and game was plentiful later even in the Peloponnese. When game declined, large cattle and fine horses were still bred in north Greece. The culture of the olive and the vine was widespread. From the fifth century B.C., when intensive agriculture developed in the plains, irrigation was probably conducted with more skill than it is today, and the population of Boeotia, for instance, was then more numerous. The great decline in productivity began in late Roman times and was most rapid under the Turkish Empire, when deforestation was uncontrolled, goats devoured young trees, and crude methods of agriculture were employed. Erosion proceeded apace. West Greece, facing the rain-bearing winds, suffered most, as its soil was washed away and the bare bones of limestone were revealed. Much of west Epirus and west Megaris, for example, which were once prosperous, are now almost uninhabited. Similar effects are visible in east Greece too, for example in southern Euboea and on Mt. Hymettus.

Rapid erosion has also altered parts of the coastline. Deltas, pushed forward by the fast-flowing rivers, have grown at the expense of the Thermaic

Gulf and the Maliac Gulf, and the gradual flow of soil from the hills has widened the coastal fringe at Thermopylae and Pegae. Rivers which were once navigable have filled up with boulders, so that Pella in Macedonia and Ambracia in Epirus can no longer be reached by boat. The outward push of the land in most parts has more than offset a rise in sea-level (or perhaps a land subsidence) of some five feet since the fifth century. The greatest changes in the prosperity of Greece came with the opening of the Far East and the 'New World' and the invention of the steamship. Then the Mediterranean Sea ceased to be the centre of world trade, and even within it the great sea-lanes from Alexandria to the Pillars of Heracles passed southwards of the Greek peninsula.

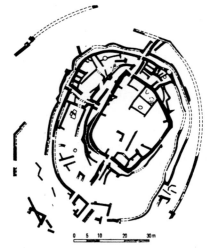

Fortified acropolis at Dhimíni in Thessaly in the
Late Neolithic Period (*see p. 37*)

BOOK I

THE EARLY CIVILIZATIONS OF GREECE AND THE GREAT MIGRATIONS
(*c.* 6000–850)

THE SOURCES OF KNOWLEDGE

OUR knowledge of the prehistoric period, extending from the origins of Minoan and Mycenaean civilization to the end of the Great Migrations, is due in a great degree to archaeological discovery, which has clothed in a material form the myths and sagas transmitted by Greek oral tradition. The bulk of the archaeologist's data is provided by excavation of sites on which a deep deposit of rubbish—building material, pottery, tools, &c.—has been formed by centuries of occupation. This deposit is stripped off by strata (or layers); objects found in each stratum are classified as a contemporary group. Thus from a well-stratified site a series of contemporary groups are obtained, which, like beads threaded on a string, lie in chronological sequence and provide material for reconstructing the history of the site. If, for example, the fifth stratum above virgin soil contains a widespread layer of ash and the sixth a new style of weapon, house-foundation, and pottery, one may conclude that the settlement underwent a critical change at this point. On such grounds one numbers the settlements at a given site, e.g. 'Troy I,' 'Troy II', &c.

When several stratified sites yield similar remains, the sites are grouped together as representing a common civilization. For example, a sequence of cultures was revealed by the excavation of Phylakopí in Melos, and objects characteristic of these cultures were found at other sites in the Cyclades. Thus the concept of a Cycladic civilization was formed. Other regional civilizations are known as Minoan (in Crete), Helladic (on the Greek mainland), Thessalian, Macedonian, and so forth. The history of a regional civilization may be divided on the same principle as the history of a single site into periods and subdivisions, for instance 'Early Minoan I' or 'Late Helladic III'. When objects characteristic of one regional civilization are discovered in the stratified sites of another regional civilization, a point of contact is made and a chronological correlation is established, such as, for instance, that Late

Minoan III and Late Helladic III began at the same time. In this way a structure of contemporaneity has been built up between and within the regional civilizations. This structure is defective in some places and insecure in others, sometimes because contact between regional civilizations was precluded for whatever reason, and sometimes because excavation has not yet been undertaken at a sufficient number of stratified sites. Even where conditions are best archaeology marks not a precise but an approximate degree on the scale of time. For it deals mainly with discarded objects; thus a tool or a jewel found in the same stratum as a broken pot is 'contemporary' only in the sense that it was deposited contemporaneously and not that it was produced contemporaneously.

When we pass beyond the regional civilizations to wider concepts, we meet the traditional framework of Neolithic, Bronze, and Iron Ages. They are so named after the material in which weapons were chiefly made—stone, bronze (or copper), and iron. But these Ages have no chronological limits of universal validity. Bronze weapons, for instance, were adopted at different times in different regions; some backward peoples today still use stone tools. Even within the area of Greek lands the Bronze Age did not begin simultaneously in all districts. There is also some latitude in interpretation when a regional civilization is passing from a stone-using to a copper-using economy, e.g. in the case of Thessaly. Nevertheless, this framework of Neolithic, Bronze, and Iron Ages has great convenience for the marshalling of the regional civilizations and is adopted in the following narrative.

In order to relate the whole structure of archaeological discovery to our own chronology, we turn to the records of Egypt, Babylonia, and Asia Minor, which preserve lists of kings' reigns datable in terms of our system. Thus Amenhotep III reigned in Egypt 1412–1376. A seal and a scarab of his consort, Queen Ty, were found in Crete with Late Minoan II pottery and at Mycenae with Late Helladic III pottery. In consequence (and other evidence being taken into account) the transition from Late Minoan II to Late Minoan III and from Late Helladic II to Late Helladic III was dated approximately to 1400 B.C. Such objects of Near Eastern origin and their counterpart, Aegean objects found in Near Eastern countries, are lynch-pins in the chronological structure. Their presence in Crete during the Minoan period provides a reasonably firm chronology, but their rarity on the mainland and especially in the north leaves chronology for the earliest periods elastic. Where they are lacking, as for instance in the Early Iron Age, one is left with a loosely knit group of regional civilizations and no external ruler affording a chronological scale. In such situations stylistic criteria are sometimes applied on the assumption that a stylistic development can be assessed in chronological terms. Here the margin of error is bound to be wide. It can only be narrowed by fresh discoveries. One of these, 'C-14', measuring the amount of carbon in wood, for instance, against a known rate of diminution, gives absolute dates but with an as yet uncertain margin of error. This margin will never disappear completely. The following table summarizes the present position, the dates serving as pointers to probability and being far from universally accepted:

		Crete	Cyclades	Mainland		Troy	
	NEOLITHIC	6100 Neolithic begins	3500 Neolithic begins	6200 Neolithic begins			
3000							3000
		Early Minoan	Early Cycladic	2800 — Neolithic still in Macedonia and Thessaly / Early Helladic		Troy I / Troy II	
2000						Troy III–V	2400 / 2000
1900	BRONZE AGE	Middle Minoan I and II	Middle Cycladic				1900
1800				Middle Helladic		Troy VI	1800
1700		Middle Minoan III					1700
1600							1600
1500		Late Minoan I and II*	Late Cycladic	Late Helladic I / Late Helladic II			1500
1400							1400
1300		Late Minoan III		Late Helladic III			1300
1200						Troy VII A	1200
1125		Sub-Minoan		Athens Sub-Myc.	Corinth	Laconia	1125
1075	IRON AGE			Proto-Geometric			1075
1000		Proto-Geometric	Proto-Geometric		Proto-Geometric	Proto-Geometric	1000
900				Geometric	Geometric		900
850							850

* Late Minoan II is a subdivision of Late Minoan I; it is peculiar to Cnossus and contemporary with the last 50 years of LM I.

The broadest aspects of ethnology are known to us from the study of language. Philologists can deduce that a non-Indo-European people occupied Greece before the arrival of the Indo-European Greek-speaking tribes. Archaeology and philology have determined in general terms that the centres of dispersion from which the two groups came to the Aegean were for the former probably upper Armenia and for the latter probably south Russia. In this narrative, which is concerned mainly with the Greek peninsula, the invading peoples are described as being of Mediterranean and of Nordic stock respectively.

Detailed conclusions about the movement of peoples in the prehistoric period are based to a great extent upon the interpretation of the archaeological evidence. Such interpretation is most hazardous. It is, for instance, difficult to determine whether the spread of objects characteristic of one regional civilization into the area of another civilization is due to the movement of trade or to a shift of population. In historical times trade was responsible for the hellenization of Macedonia, and invasion for the hellenization of Asiatic countries; yet if we relied exclusively on the archaeological evidence the distinction might be difficult to draw. There are, however, some criteria which indicate a change in the population of a site or region: new burial-customs, a new type of house-plan, a burnt layer followed by the use of different tools and weapons, and the appearance of a new physical type. By adhering strictly to such criteria as these, historians are generally agreed that Crete suffered no large-scale influx of population during the period 2700–1330, and that the eastern part of the Greek mainland suffered no large-scale invasion during the period 1700–1150. But small-scale movements and even the peaceful penetration of new peoples on a large scale are difficult to divine from the archaeological evidence, especially if the newcomers are backward in culture and quickly assimilate the civilization of the region they enter.

The consideration of climatic factors enables us to gauge what is probable. Primitive peoples are reluctant to move abruptly from one climatic zone into another, because their economy is thereby disrupted. If they do move, they are likely to settle *en route* in an area of transitional climate. Where mass-migration or colonization occurs, the migrants or colonists tend to seek a country similar in climate to their own. The migrations from the Greek mainland to the west coast of Asia Minor illustrate the point. The Aeolians chose the northern sector, the Dorians the southern, and the Ionians the central; their choice was clearly influenced by the climate and the character of the areas from which they came. So, too, Minoans, Mycenaeans, Phoenicians, and Greeks colonized only the coastal fringe of the Mediterranean area. Thus any suggestion that Mediterranean peoples settled in an area of cold climate such as the Macedonian or Serbian hinterland is discountenanced by the arguments of geographical probability and historical experience.

The oral tradition of the Greek peoples reached very far back into the past but is not on that account to be discredited. Its matter is known in part through the literary works of early classical writers, especially Homer, Hesiod, Herodotus, and Thucydides. At certain points oral tradition has been strikingly confirmed by archaeological discovery. Objects and situations described by Homer are now known to have existed at a period at least three centuries earlier than the lifetime of Homer. Traditions concerning the origins of the Greek peoples and of other races are found to be consistent with the archaeological evidence and with conclusions based on philological study of dialects, place-names, &c. There is, therefore, a strong presumption that the oral tradition generally contains an element of true historical fact.

It is clear that the reconstruction of the prehistoric period is and always will be tentative in character and approximate in detail. Nevertheless, the frontiers of established fact are becoming more precise and the approximations within them more limited in range. Any reconstruction is and will be not only premature, since new evidence is yet to come, but also personal, because it is based upon a personal assessment of various probabilities. The present author, in particular, places more credence in the traditions preserved by early Greek writers than many of his colleagues would do. This caveat should be noted now, because the narrative is unfolded without the frequent qualifications and modifications which caution might enjoin.

Portrait of a Prince or Priest-king
on a fresco at Cnossus *c.* 1400
(*see p. 30*)

CHAPTER 1

The Settlement of the Aegean Islands and Minoan Civilization

§ 1. *The origins of Minoan civilization*

THE earliest Neolithic settlement in the Aegean Islands was at Cnossus in Crete, with a C-14 date of approximately 6100. The settlers arrived with a well-established tradition of pottery-making and after a short period of camping they built in fired brick. Their houses had foundations of stone and brick, walls of fired brick, and flat roofs of clay on brushwood; food was prepared in cooking pits and in domed ovens, and stone querns and mortars were used for milling grain. They obtained stocks of obsidian probably from Melos; this vitreous lava, which flakes like flint into blades, was an important material for tools. And they made anthropomorphic figurines in clay and in stone. The origin of this early civilization is not known, but it seems to be unrelated to that of the Greek mainland and therefore not to have been derived from Asia Minor. After a considerable time the use of fired brick ceased, perhaps because the climate became less humid, and pounded clay took its place. Larger houses were built, usually with two rooms and an outer cobbled court, and greater numbers of figurines and also some mace-heads were found in the last stages of the Early Neolithic I period, which ended *c*. 5100. The next period, Early Neolithic II, was marked by the development of the site into a town with a regular plan, as indicated by the orientation of the walls, which continued to be the same throughout Middle and Late Neolithic times. Towards the end of the period large buildings with clusters of rooms, pebbled courtyards, and great hearths reveal a very advanced stage of neolithic development, unparalleled on the mainland or elsewhere in Crete, which had only a few late and small settlements. The Cyclades too were not occupied until late in the period, and even then only some of them by small groups. The uniqueness of neolithic Cnossus goes a long way towards explaining the unique nature of later 'Minoan' civilization, which was not produced elsewhere by Bronze Age immigrants from Asia Minor but did result from the fusion of those immigrants with the brilliant and mature neolithic people of Cnossus.

The Early Bronze Age (3000–2000) opened with waves of immigrants, who settled in the Cyclades and in east and central Crete. Their pottery shows that they had come from Asia Minor. In Crete they became fused with the earlier inhabitants, and skeletons found there show that the people were long-headed, narrow-faced, and short in stature, the men averaging 5 ft. 2 in. and the women 4 ft. 11 in. The newcomers chose sites by the sea, preferring east Crete, which is warmer, and soon abandoned the use of an indoor hearth which they had brought with them. Their large houses were made up of a cluster of rooms, like those of the Neolithic Age, and they buried their dead in tombs of two rooms, the inner room leading off the outer room. This type of house and tomb persisted with little change throughout a long period of civilization which lasted from 3000 to 1400 without any obvious break, except, perhaps, in the area of Phaestus. This civilization has been called 'Minoan', because the Greeks knew of a famous 'Minos', King of Crete, and the early Bronze Age settlers of Crete may therefore be styled the first Minoans.

A different people appeared later in the plain of Phaestus. They buried their dead in circular buildings, as much as 40 feet in diameter and roofed probably with thatch. Each building contains several hundred skeletons, and it is probable that they served as family or clan ossuaries. Since they resemble the much later *mapalia* of Libya, it may be that these intruders came from the African coast. In any event their culture did not affect Minoan civilization.

During the second phase of the Early Bronze Age copper was in common use for making daggers of triangular shape, saws, toilet instruments, and votive double-axes, the last being a feature of Minoan religion. Traces of the cultivation of the olive occur now for the first time, and longhorn cattle are imported. Jewellery and seals in gold, ivory, faience, and steatite, and fine stone vases reflect an influence from Egypt, which strengthens in the third phase of the Early Bronze Age.

Meanwhile in the Cyclades the Early Bronze Age settlers developed a distinct but related culture. Their villages consisted of houses more primitive than the Minoan houses, and they buried their dead in a contracted attitude in cist graves and at Syros in small walled chambers. Working in marble and stone they modelled vases and figurines (chiefly female) with great artistry. The obsidian of Melos was carried to all parts of the Aegean basin. A seagoing race, they portrayed their ships in little models of lead and in incised designs on their own individual types of pottery. Their occupation of the Cyclades appears to have been undisturbed during the period of Minoan civilization except for the expansion of Cretan power. Cyprus soon became important because of her deposits of copper, which were worked as early as 2300, and of her position as an intermediary between the Aegean and the East. The cylinder-seals, with which Babylonian merchants marked their wares, have been found in considerable numbers in Early Bronze Age settlements on Cyprus.

During the period from 2000 to 1600 Minoan civilization was growing towards its full stature. The development began in 2000–1750 when the centre of power moved from east Crete to central Crete and in particular to its north coast. A colony was planted at Cythera *c*. 2000 which shows that trade was developing westwards and northwards. During the same period the following innovations, later characteristic of Minoan civilization, made their first appearance: palace-buildings, a road system protected by guard-posts between Cnossus and the plain of Phaestus, shrines on mountain peaks and in caves, the smelting of bronze (which is an alloy of copper and tin), the rapier-sword with a medial rib, the wearing by men of the codpiece and the tight belt, and the pictographic form of writing. Cnossus and Phaestus developed a higher culture in the period 1900–1700. This culture was peculiar to them and indicates their joint sway over the island. Their craftsmen drew inspiration from Egypt then ruled by the XIIth dynasty; but they showed independence and originality in the naturalistic treatment of Egyptian motifs on their frescoes and pottery and in the evolution of the pictographic form of writing. Two severe earthquakes occurred c. 1700 and c. 1600. After each earthquake a number of new settlements were made on the north coast of the island, which lay within the orbit of Cnossus.

During the interval between the two earthquakes the palaces of Cnossus, Phaestus, and Mállia were rebuilt on a larger scale. The weapons of war improved. The rapier-sword lengthened to 3 feet and developed a tang, and the spear-head of bronze sheet was hammered into shape and fitted with a ring to prevent it splaying. The pictographic form of writing was abandoned in favour of a linear script, which was widely used within the island. This script —known as 'Linear Script A'—was probably a syllabary, the signs being written in ink on pottery and presumably on skin, papyrus, palm-leaves, or bark, and the characters were also incised on clay tablets and seals. Of the characters almost a third clearly derive from the earlier pictographs, but the origin of the remainder is unknown. Some of the pictographs and characters are illustrated in Fig. 8. The script was written from left to right. Only the symbols for numerals have been deciphered. They show that the decimal system was in use; for a unit is represented by a vertical stroke, a ten by a dot and later by a horizontal stroke, a hundred by a circle, a thousand by a circle with four short projecting strokes, and a fraction by 'L'. A clay disk from Phaestus, dating to the same period, bears another undeciphered script which is unrelated to the Minoan script. Its characters are suggestive of a warlike seafaring race; for they include a ship, an Asiatic bow, a plumed head-dress, and a round shield. This script may have come from the Aegean islands or the coastland of Asia Minor. The language of the Minoan Linear Script and also that of the Phaestus disk are not Greek, but belong most probably to the pre-Hellenic Mediterranean stock.[1]

In 1700–1600 Crete traded extensively with Byblus and Ugarit on the Syrian coast and also with the Cyclades. There Melos was a market of exchange, through which Minoan goods reached the Greek mainland and other

---

[1] Attempts have been made to define the language or languages of Linear Script A by transferring phonetic values from Linear Script B signs to Linear Script A signs where the signs are similar; but the values of B signs are not all known and the similarities are too uncertain for any positive conclusions to be drawn. See *CAH²* 2. 1. 595 f.

areas in the Aegean, and Crete herself was now becoming the cultural centre of the Aegean world.

§ 2. *Minoan civilization*

THE acme of Crete's prosperity was in 1600–1400. Volcanic eruptions destroyed Thera around 1500 but had only temporary effects in Crete. Another palace flourished at Zácro, overlooking the Kaso Strait. Two typical towns have been excavated at Goúrnia and Pseíra. The former, a market town situated on a low hill, is terraced with paved streets which run horizontally round the hill and are linked by stepped ascents. The houses, rising in tiers up the hill, are entered from the street by short flights of steps. These lead into the main-floor rooms, and underneath there are basement rooms. On the summit of the hill stands the mansion of the squire. It faces an open court and is built of squared masonry, whereas the other houses are constructed of small stones set in clay mortar. Pseíra, a seaside town on an island, is laid out in tiers of houses on terraced slopes which face a small harbour; all the houses are built of masonry and their floors are paved with slate. Both towns must have presented the same picturesque appearance as their successors of modern times in the Aegean islands. The best view of an ordinary house is afforded by faience plaques of an earlier period (Fig. 5*a*): the windows are mostly in the upper story or stories, the roofs are flat, and the upper projection is probably the head of a central light-well. The masonry, often set in clay, is bonded with beams of timber. In an upper-class house the entry passes through the light-well into the main reception-room on the ground floor, which also contains a pillar-crypt, bathroom, lavatory, hall, and interior staircases. These staircases lead to the basement with its store-rooms and to the first and second floors, where the private quarters and bedrooms are situated (Fig. 5*b*). The houses are drained by clay pipes, fitted together with narrow collars and cemented with clay.

The men generally wear a codpiece, a tight belt, and sometimes a short kilt, and the women a skirt, a tight belt, and sometimes a low bodice leaving the breasts exposed. The men are beardless. Both sexes are lithe and slim, wear their hair long, and mix freely in sport and at public functions. Male and female acrobats, similarly dressed in codpiece and belt, are shown in the Toreador frescoes somersaulting over the backs of charging longhorn bulls. Scenes of boxers wearing gloves, of harvesters revelling, of girls dancing, of youths drinking and of a mixed audience watching games and dances illustrate a gay open-air life of peaceful character. The exquisite portrayal of flowers, trees, animals, and fish in a wide range of delicate colours reveals the Minoans' joy in their natural surroundings. This is indeed the most frequent subject. Scenes of war, and even the representation of the human figure, are rare in comparison.

That the Minoans were devoutly religious is clear from the frequency with which the furniture of ritual is portrayed—the double-axe, the twin horns of

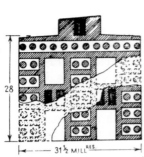

(a) Cretan house of Middle Minoan II period; from a faience plaque (showing the elevation)

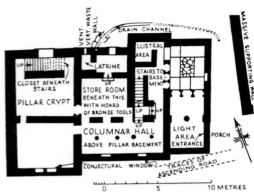

(b) Upper-class house at Cnossus c. 1600

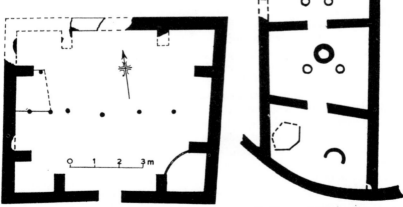

(c) Temple tomb at Cnossus, c. 1600

(d) House at Tsanglí, Thessaly, of the Middle Neolithic period

(e) House of 'Megaron' type at Dhimíni, Thessaly, of the Middle Neolithic period

FIG. 5 (a-e)

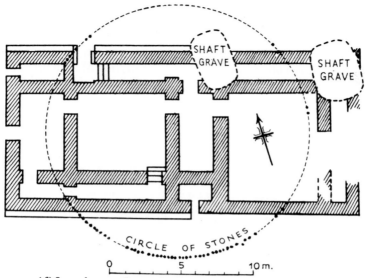

SHAFT GRAVE

SHAFT GRAVE

CIRCLE OF STONES

0   5   10 m.

(*f*) Large house at Lerna, Argolis, of Early Bronze Age period

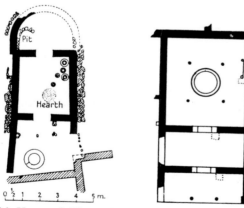

Pit

Hearth

0 ½ 1   2   3   4   5 m.

(*g*) House of 'Megaron' type at Eutresis, Boeotia, at the beginning of the Middle Bronze Age period

0   5   10   15   20 M.
0   5   10   15   20 YDS

(*h*) Throne-room, vestibule and porch in the centre of the Palace at Pylus, *c.* 1200

FIG. 5 (*f–h*)

consecration, and the three-legged table or altar, on which offerings were laid. The objects themselves have been found in numerous shrines, situated both within the house and in open-air places of worship. The centre of the Minoan cult was a female deity (Pl. I). Several exquisitely wrought statuettes represent her in human form, not naked but wearing Minoan dress. She is associated primarily with the snake but also with trees, birds, and animals, the bull and the dove taking priority. Her attendants are usually priestesses and animal-headed humans, who may be miming the animals associated with the cult in some ritual ceremony. The emphasis is on nature and on beauty, not on the fanciful and grotesque. The characteristic male deity is represented as a young boy. In addition to the chief goddess and the young god other goddesses and gods appear, the latter often holding a spear or shield, but in many cases it is difficult to distinguish god, priest, and votary.

Any attempt to reconstruct the inner meaning and significance of Minoan religion inevitably draws on later analogies and on speculations which may be misleading. Even the theories that the chief goddess is a Mother Goddess, Mistress of Animals and Goddess of Childbirth, and that the boy-god is her son and her lover, are mainly based on the well-known cults of Asia Minor in historical times. It is safe to conclude that Minoan religion was anthropomorphic in conception, and regarded the feminine rather than the masculine aspect of life as permeating the natural beauty of the physical world; and that Minoan worshippers, standing erect with upraised arms or hand to temple, felt awe and devotion rather than superstitious fear. Nor is there any conclusive evidence to prove that the Minoans worshipped their dead; rather, the simplicity of the common burials, where the corpse was trussed and thrust into a large jar or laid in a clay coffin, would suggest that they did not. Only the more well-to-do seem to have been interred in a rock-cut chamber, a simple shaft grave, or a tomb situated beside the foot of a shaft.

Throughout the zenith of Minoan civilization Cnossus was supreme in the island. The finest monument to her prosperity is the great palace with its state entrances and state halls, its spacious staircases and extensive storerooms, its delicate frescoes and superb masonry. The importance of its religious cult is indicated by the position of the pillared shrine in the central court. To the south of the palace the elaborate 'Temple Tomb' (Fig. 5*c*), with the pillared crypt giving access to the sepulchral chamber, suggests that some form of worship was paid to the dead rulers of Cnossus. Later Greek tradition named the ruler of Cnossus 'Minos'. He was said to be a son of Zeus and Europa; to hold converse with Zeus every ninth year; and to have as his consort Pasiphaë, the daughter of the sun. It seems probable that the reigning king and queen of Cnossus took these names as dynastic titles and were worshipped as divine beings, like the contemporary Pharaohs of Egypt. The so-called 'Priest-King' relief (p. 23) may portray a reigning Minos of the fifteenth century. The wealth of Cnossus is apparent from the abundance of precious metals and stones used by Minoan craftsmen and from the store-

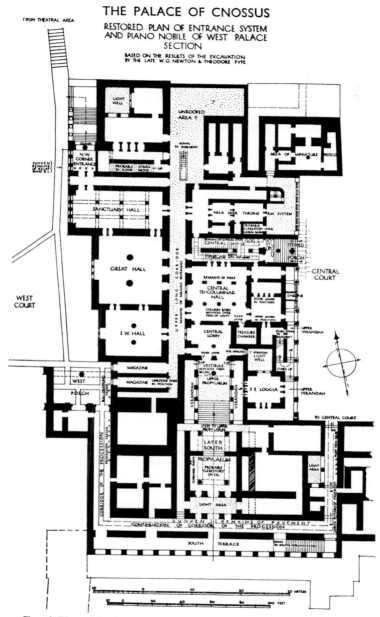

FIG. 6. Plan of the State-rooms in the Palace as they were *c.* 1550–1400

rooms of the Palace. Here the treasures of Minos, both in kind and in specie, were inventoried on clay tablets. Copper ingots, which have been found elsewhere in the islands, occur in the inventories (see p. 71). These ingots doubtless were valuable articles of trade and may have been a medium of exchange; there is, however, no indication of any fractional currency. The prosperity of Cnossus cannot be attributed solely to the exploitation of the natural resources of the island. It derived rather from overseas trade.

Crete was in very close contact with Egypt during the period 1600–1400. On a fresco in the tomb of Sennemut at Egyptian Thebes envoys are portrayed carrying gold and silver vessels of Minoan craftsmanship. Another fresco in the tomb of Rekhmire shows a reception of foreign envoys with their gifts, and some of them, to judge from the dress and the offerings, may be Minoans. On this fresco an inscription reads 'the coming in peace of the Great Ones of Keftiu and of the Isles in the midst of the sea'. Where Keftiu lay is disputed. It may have been Crete; for she was queen among the isles of the sea and certainly had diplomatic relations with Egypt. Cretan artists, too, gave their own independent treatment to motifs common in Egyptian art, such as the monkey and the cat in frescoes and the papyrus on pottery. Black troops, probably mercenaries from Libya or Egypt, form the subject of a fresco at Cnossus. Trade with Egypt ran mainly from Kómo near Phaestus to the Delta, either direct or via Libya, where an easterly current sets along the coast. In Egypt itself few objects of Cretan art, and in particular only a small quantity of pottery, whether Minoan or Mycenaean, have been found belonging to this period. It is therefore probable that Cretan exports to Egypt were mainly skins, meat, fruit, timber, and metals rather than the oil and wine which travelled in pots. Cyprus was probably a stage on the route. For a tablet at Énkomi in Cyprus, dating to c. 1500, is incised with a Cypriot Linear Script, which probably derives from the Minoan Linear Script. Minoan influence at Ugarit and Byblus on the Syrian coast was much weaker during this period than in 1700–1600.

Within the Aegean area Minoan trade expanded in 1600–1400. At Ialysus in Rhodes, which controls the entry into the Aegean, a Minoan colony was planted c. 1600 and flourished until c. 1425. A Minoan settlement was made at Miletus on the coast of Asia Minor, and another probably in Calymnos. The colony in Cythera was held until c. 1450. Thus Crete was in a fair position to control the sea-lanes which led southwards out of the Aegean Sea. The Cyclades passed strongly under the influence of Minoan civilization. Minoan fresco-painting excelled at Phylakopí in Melos and Thera until the eruption. The eastern and southern parts of the Greek mainland were strongly influenced by Minoan art, of which many typical characteristics survive in the frescoes at Tiryns, Mycenae, and Thebes. Minoan craftsmen probably settled on the mainland, and the common place-name 'Minoa' suggests that Minoan trading-stations were established at several points on the coast. In the west Minoan mariners may have sailed to Lipara, where Minoan pottery of the sixteenth century has been found, and perhaps to Malta and Ischia.

§ 3. *Cnossus 1450–1400*

DURING the zenith of Crete's prosperity a separate culture (known as Late Minoan II) developed at Cnossus and lasted *c.* 1450–1400. It did not extend beyond Cnossus to the rest of Crete, which continued as before. One mark of this cultural enclave was closer contact with the Mycenaean centres of main-land Greece. Cnossus now imported or imitated Mycenaean vases of the 'Palace' and 'Ephyrean' styles and Mycenaean alabastra (containers squat in shape). A militaristic spirit was discernible in the record of armaments, in-cluding war-chariots, and in the frescoes at Cnossus, and a shaft-grave and so-called 'warrior-graves' containing heavy spearheads and a bronze helmet have been found near Cnossus. More significant still was the use of a new Linear Script at the Palace of Cnossus and also at some palace centres on the mainland. The suggestion that Mycenaeans controlled this cultural enclave has been confirmed by the decipherment of the new Linear Script. It is now known that the language of this Linear Script, hitherto called Linear Script B, is Greek; whereas the language of Linear Script A is definitely not Greek and may be labelled 'Minoan', although the Minoan language is still un-deciphered. The change from the Minoan Linear Script to the Mycenaean Linear Script (as we may now call Linear Script A and Linear Script B) proves that the rulers of Cnossus from *c.* 1450 to 1400 spoke Greek.

The Mycenaean Linear Script adopted two thirds of its syllabic signs from the Minoan Linear Script and introduced new signs to express its own linguistic peculiarities. It was probably developed at Cnossus, where the Minoan Linear Script had long been in use, and not on the mainland which seems hitherto to have been without a script. The Mycenaeans changed the system of numerical notation and probably of weights and measures, and used new symbols, one of which may have represented the war-chariot. The Mycenaean Script, like its Minoan predecessor at Cnossus, was employed mainly to list the contents of the Palace store-rooms, which included an arsenal of weapons, and to record the payment of dues from the rest of Crete, which was evidently subject to the Mycenaean rulers of Cnossus. The script was incised on wet clay tablets (which served the purpose of labels in an in-ventory), and these clay tablets have only survived when they were baked hard in a fierce conflagration. Clay tablets which were not baked in this manner and other perishable materials, such as skin, papyrus, and bark, have long since disappeared without trace; but it is still remarkable that other objects which have survived, such as pottery, tombstones, metal utensils, and so on, are very rarely inscribed. So far as the present evidence goes, the Mycenaean script was used primarily, in some places exclusively to record property or transactions in property for the ruling class, and the scribes were skilled servants of the state or of the wealthy. On the mainland the script remained in use until *c.* 1200 at least, and its signs, 200 in number, were still static and unchanging, which implies that writing was a conservative skill devoted to a specialized function.

The Mycenaean Linear Script has not yet been fully deciphered, since no value has been attached to some of the syllabic signs. There is, therefore, still some degree of elasticity in the transcription and translation of the tablets, which is in part due also to the Script's lack of precision in expressing Greek. The syllabic signs convey syllables; there is one series of signs for the consonants l and r, one for p, ph, and b, one for k, kh, and g, and some consonants are omitted at the end of a syllable, while the quantities of vowels, such as epsilon and eta, are not given and diphthongs are marked only by their first vowel or sometimes (in au, eu, and ou) by their second vowel. We depend upon the context, where the syllabic signs for *ka-ko* can mean either 'bad' or 'bronze', and for Corcyra can equally well be for Crocyleia. The ideograms (signs which portray objects) and the symbols for numbers narrow the field of its interpretation somewhat, but much is left open to doubt. The substantial result of the decipherment is that the language is Greek, and the dialect may be related to classical Arcado-Cypriot or Aeolic or both. The tablets at Cnossus owe their survival to a fierce fire, which occurred *c.* 1400, and we may assume fifty years of past development for the script. The tablets probably supply some Greek personal names, mention Cnossus as *ko-no-so*, and give a number of names of places in Crete from which tribute was sent to the Palace. There is no indication of a name 'Minos' or any recognizable place-name overseas such as might suggest an Aegean empire, but the ruler of Cnossus had many slave-women labourers and exacted dues from the island as a whole.[1]

When Cnossus was taken over by Mycenaeans, other places were destroyed, presumably by raiders. Yet these destructions did not alter the culture of the rest of Crete, which continued to use the Minoan Script until 1400 and was not affected by the Mycenaean styles in pottery or writing. But the Greek rulers of Cnossus certainly controlled Crete by martial methods and maintained naval supremacy in the south Aegean. They did not follow the example of the Greek rulers of the Mycenaean world and build massive fortifications, no doubt because, like the warriors of classical Sparta, they trusted in their weapons, not in walls, and Crete was peaceful under their régime. Another Mycenaean enclave appeared *c.* 1450 in Rhodes and existed alongside a Minoan settlement there until *c.* 1425, when the Minoan settlement declined. It is probable that the Mycenaeans in Rhodes were independent of the Mycenaeans at Cnossus and were opening a new route for trade and piracy, which broke through the control of the southern Aegean hitherto exercised by Crete.

Crete did not derive her prosperity solely from the genius of her statesmen,

[1] *DMG*, 146–7 and nrs. 18–23.

sailors, and craftsmen in 1600–1400. She owed it also to her position within a wide complex of highly civilized states, which encircled the eastern Mediterranean Sea and tapped the resources of the hinterlands of Europe, Asia, and Africa. Of these states Egypt was the wealthiest; at this time, as later in the Hellenistic and Roman periods, she attracted the maritime trade of the Mediterranean area. The sea-lanes leading from the Aegean basin to Egypt passed through the ring of Minoan dependencies, which extended from Cythera to Rhodes. So long as Minoan sea power was supreme, the prosperity of Crete was assured.

On a spring day towards the close of the fifteenth century the unfortified palace of Cnossus was sacked and burnt to the ground. On the same occasion, or perhaps at a somewhat earlier date, a similar fate befell all the leading cities of Crete. Overseas the Minoan colonists probably abandoned Ialysus in Rhodes. This catastrophe broke the ring of Cretan power. Thereafter Crete remained prosperous and important. The western part of Crete was developed more thoroughly than in the previous period, and her genius in art, religion, and social life did not wither away. But her supremacy was at an end, and something of her inspiration disappeared for ever. The origin of the catastrophe is unknown. Some attribute it to a rising of the islanders against the Greek rulers of Cnossus; but Cnossus was not destroyed alone, and the extent of the disaster seems too great to have been caused by civil war among settled peoples. Others attribute it to an invasion by Mycenaean powers of the mainland. Yet the catastrophe was not followed at once by signs of Mycenaean colonization in Crete; nor does Greek folk-memory record such an invasion. It is more probable that the destruction of Cnossus and other Cretan sites, like the later destruction of Troy, Mycenae, and the Egyptian delta, was due to a great sea raid, in which the piratical powers of the eastern Mediterranean combined to overthrow the naval supremacy of Crete, to sack and pillage the island, and to withdraw with their loot. If so, it was the first disaster which heralded the gradual decline of the great Bronze Age civilization of the Mediterranean world.

A warship returns to Thera *c.* 1500.

CHAPTER 2

The Greek Mainland and Mycenaean Civilization

§ 1. *The peopling of the mainland*

THE earliest remains yet found on the mainland are those of Palaeolithic man, dating from Mousterian times at least and occurring mainly in Thessaly, Epirus, and Macedonia. Continuous occupation began much later with people of Neolithic culture in Thessaly who used stone tools but had no pottery; they lived in villages of small huts with a sunken or 'pit' floor, engaged in agriculture, herding, fishing, and hunting, and obtained obsidian from the island of Melos for making tools. They were succeeded, probably immediately at Sésklo, by pottery-using peoples who settled all down the eastern side of the mainland at sites accessible from the sea *c.* 6000–5500 B.C. The site which has yielded the earliest C-14 date (*c.* 6200 B.C.) is Nea Nikomedea, north of the Haliacmon river in the coastal plain of Macedonia. Its inhabitants lived in one- or two-roomed houses, walled with mud-brick on a timber frame and with some internal buttress-posts, clustered round a main building, some twelve metres square, which contained steatopygous female figurines of clay, axes of serpentine and clay, flint blades, and gourd-shaped clay vessels. The figurines here and elsewhere represent the Mother Goddess. They pursued the same activities as their aceramic predecessors, and we know from burials in storage-pits that some were tall and dolicho-cephalic and that nothing was placed with the dead, except meat for children. They excelled in the working of stone, particularly greenstone from northern Pindus, and made beautiful celts, axes, hammers, vessels, and figurines (for instance, of frogs). Their pottery, though simple at first, developed many shapes, and some of it was beautifully painted; clay was used also for other objects such as seals. This Early Neolithic civilization lasted about a thousand years—settled, peaceful, progressive, and engaging in sea communication. It originated in and maintained contacts with the older civilizations of Western Anatolia. Towards the end of the period an intrusive culture with 'barbotine' pottery, in which the clay was marked by the finger-nail, appeared in north Thessaly and in west Greece at Leucas; its source of origin is likely to have been Macedonia and Yugoslavia. This marked the first of many inter-actions in northern Greece between the central Balkans and Anatolia.

In the Middle Neolithic period, which extended over the fifth millennium, the intrusive element in north Thessaly disappeared and groups of new people kept settling at intervals of time in Thessaly, east central Greece, and eastern Peloponnese. Their cultures were derived now from one part and now from another part of Turkey, northern Syria, and Mesopotamia, and they maintained sea communication, as we see from their use of obsidian. Houses generally were rectangular, built on stone foundations with mud brick and often with internal buttresses as at Tsanglí (see Fig. 5*d*), and the 'megaron' type of house, long and narrow with an outer porch (see Fig. 5*e*), was in use by *c.* 4500, its prototype being found in the Konya plain of Turkey. Regional styles of pottery developed and a good standard of agricultural and pastoral life was maintained under peaceful conditions. The Late Neolithic period, covering the fourth millennium, saw the spread of matt-painted and polychrome wares of pottery, which were akin in fabric and decoration to the Ubaid ware of Cilicia and north Syria; coastal settlements with these wares have been found at Astacus, in Leucas, and in the hinterland of Oricum Gulf in northern Epirus; the settlers came probably from Corinthia and traded with southern Italy. The earliest settlements in Aegina, Ceos, and a few of the Cyclades occurred in the latter part of the period. The extreme limit of their pottery was at Sérvia in the bend of the Haliacmon river, but Macedonia and Thrace were occupied by people of a different culture, which in view of its incised and crusted wares and the use of spiraliform decoration had affinities with the central Balkans. The proximity of these peoples may explain the occurrence in north-east Thessaly of a specialized culture which is remarkable for a small acropolis at Dhimíni, fortified with rings of wall and containing megaron-type buildings (see Fig. on p. 18), and for spiraliform decoration on impressed and painted pottery. At the same time marble figurines seem to have been imported from the Cyclades. It is likely that the Dhimíni culture sprang from a fusion of elements which derived ultimately from Anatolia and from Europe. Thus the long Neolithic period, lasting some 3,000 to 4,000 years, was characterized almost entirely by the influences which came from the East. It was peaceful, agricultural, seafaring, and artistic, and its religious beliefs, if we may judge from the steatopygous female figurines, were focused on a mother goddess and may have been associated with a matriarchal society or at least with one which was not strongly patriarchal. But within these broad characterizations there was a wide range of variations, and the population of Greece was racially mixed and hybrid by the end of the Neolithic period. Outside the zone of Mediterranean climate, for instance in Macedonia and northern Epirus, there appeared cruder cultures which in some characteristics, as in climate, were related to those of Yugoslavia.

The Early Bronze Age extended over the third millennium. During the first two of its three phases (known as E.H. = Early Helladic, I, II, and III), which are dated by C-14 tests roughly to 2800–2500, 2500–2200, and 2200–1900 with regional overlaps, several waves of migrants from Turkey, especially from north-western Asia Minor, settled in the islands and on the eastern side of the Greek peninsula south of Mt. Othrys. A typical early site has been excavated at Eutresis in Boeotia, where the settlers in E.H. I had copper weapons and tools, red burnished pottery, and new vessel-shapes such as the sauceboat. The houses of the village were larger in E.H. II; one with three rooms contained storage-pits (*bothroi*) and a funnel-shaped cavity in the floor, which may indicate a belief in chthonian deities. In E.H. III sauceboats disappeared, new types of vessels and new forms of decoration appeared, and the period ended with the destruction of the site by peoples who came perhaps from the west rather than the north. A typical site in the Peloponnese at Lerna began its Early Bronze Age life in E.H. II, when new settlers fortified a high mound as an acropolis and built large houses inside it; their pottery included the sauceboat and they made beautiful clay seals. Towards the end of E.H. II the palace on the acropolis—'The House of Tiles' (Fig. 5*f*)—was destroyed by fire, and an entirely different town containing many apsidal houses grew up in E.H. III around the mound, which was levelled down until only a low circular tumulus, some 19 metres in diameter and bordered by a ring of stones, was left as a sacred area. These occupants of Lerna had some characteristics which appeared elsewhere first in the Middle Bronze period. Meanwhile in Thessaly the neolithic culture of Dhimíni persisted well into the E.H. period, presumably because its bearers were more warlike and resistant than their neighbours to the south, and Macedonia remained in the Neolithic phase of development except that some southern influences spread inland from trading-posts on the coastal route to Troy, for instance from Kritsaná in Chalcidice, where a hamlet of some twelve houses was defended by a rampart on the landward side. The native culture of central Macedonia was backward but it had characteristic features in the 'wishbone' handle and the bored battle-axe; and the horse appeared there *c.* 2200, earlier than at Troy and in Syria. In the last phase of the Bronze Age a crude form of the characteristic Macedonian pottery spread into inland Epirus, carried probably by shepherd families. Meanwhile the Bronze Age people of peninsular Greece who engaged in maritime trade had settled in Cephallenia, Ithaca, and Leucas and their influence reached Dodona in southern Epirus. There was also a reflex action from south-east Italy where there was an advanced Neolithic civilization at Molfetta in Apulia; seafaring people of this culture made transient settlements at Aphiona on the north-west coast of Corcyra and at Áyios Sotíra in Leucas.

Thus in the latest phase of the Early Bronze Age the accumulated layers of settlers from the East occupied the Greek peninsula south of Mt. Othrys, and their maritime interests had led some of them to settle in the north-west and at places like Kritsaná, where they were in touch with neighbouring peoples who had not come from the East. In the Middle and Late Bronze Age the tide of folk-movement turned and flowed from the northern areas into peninsular Greece. It is this turn of the tide which brought into the peninsula the first speakers of Greek, a language of the Indo-European group, whereas the Neolithic and Early Bronze Age inhabitants of Greece spoke non-Indo-European languages. Traces of the latter languages were preserved in place-names with non-Indo-European terminations in *-ssos* or *-ttos*, in

-inthos or *-indos* and in the plural *-enai* (e.g. Parnassos, Hymettos, Cnossos; Corinth, Tiryns; Athenai and Mycenai), and in names of Mediterranean flora and fauna (e.g. kissos, byssos, melissa; olynthos, terebinthos). Place-names with these terminations are found most thickly in western and southern Asia Minor, the Aegean islands, and eastern peninsular Greece, but rarely in Macedonia and Epirus. It is likely that this pattern of distribution is an indication of settlement. For instance, in Epirus such names occur in the hinterland of Oricum Gulf with the rivers Polyanthes and Celydnus, where Neolithic peoples settled, and in south Epirus (Assos and Mt. Perranthes), where Early Bronze peoples penetrated. Conversely the distribution of Indo-European place-names is thickest in northern Greece (e.g. the rivers Aeas or Aoös, Acheron, Acheloös, Inachos, Aphas, Apsos, Axios, Haliacmon) and thinner in eastern peninsular Greece and the Aegean islands. It is probable that these patterns of place-names existed already in the last phase of the Early Bronze Age.

Wherever the original home of the Indo-European group of languages was, it is clear from the evidence at present available that large groups of Indo-European peoples moved out of the Pontic regions in the period 2500–2000.[1] Their society was patriarchal, as their numerous words for agnatic relationships show; they were organized in tribes of kindred clans, each with its king, council, and meeting of freemen, features which are common to Hittites, Greeks, Macedonians, and Romans; and they were pastoral as well as agricultural but ignorant of the sea, and they worshipped male gods of the sky and not female deities such as the Mother Goddess and the Mistress of Animals. Those who moved out of the Ukraine used the battle-axe and the horse in war, and buried their chiefs under a barrow (*kurgan*) and their commoners in pit-graves. The earliest signs of such peoples arriving in the neighbourhood of peninsular Greece have been found in northern Macedonia, west Albania, and Leucas: a stone mace-head representing a horse's harnessed head, bored battle-axes, corded ware (cord being impressed on the wet clay), and burials in a circular pit, dug below ground level, which were then covered with a barrow—or to use a commoner term, a tumulus of soil. They are dated to E.H. II, around 2200. This archaeological evidence provides an all-important link with the linguistic and onomastic evidence.

Greek folk-tradition as crystallized by Hesiod took the form of a genealogy. Deucalion and Pyrrha, who ruled over Thessaly, begat Hellen and Thuia, Hellen being the eponymous ancestor of the Greek-speaking peoples. 'And from Hellen, the warloving king, were born Dorus, Xuthus, and Aeolus, who joys in horses, while Thuia brought forth two sons, Magnes and Macedon, who joys in horses, and they dwelt around Pieria and Olympus.'[2] The Greek gods too, especially Zeus the sky-god, were at home on Mt. Olympus and in Pieria, and the Zeus of Dodona derived his importance from the Bronze Age when he displaced a Mother Goddess and assimilated her as Aphrodite,

[1] Similar movements occurred in 400–350; see p. 576.   [2] Hes. *Fr.* 5 and 7.

daughter of Zeus and Dione.[1] The traditions and the localizations of the Greeks' gods show that their remote ancestors settled for a long period in Macedonia and Epirus, where the climate is still continental and life is mainly pastoral. On the present evidence those ancestors were there before the end of the Early Bronze Age. In the millennium which ensued three branches of the Greek-speaking peoples, defined by their pronounced dialects—Ionic, Aeolic, and West Greek (= Doric and north-west Greek)—and called descendants of Ion (son of Xuthus), Aeolus, and Dorus, carved out their claims in the Greek peninsula. It is probable that these dialects had begun to differentiate before the movement south from Macedonia or north Thessaly started in the last phase of the Early Bronze Age.

The Middle Bronze Age (1900–1600) was ushered in by violent destruction at many sites and by the desertion of others in the eastern part of Greece from Malis southwards. The succeeding culture was marked by some new house-types, by small cist-graves, and by a distinctive style of pottery which, being found at first at Orchomenus, the city of the Minyae, was christened 'Minyan ware'. The new house-types are well illustrated at Eutresis in Boeotia. The closely built Early Bronze Age village with flat-roofed square houses was burnt down and replaced by a more widely spaced and open village. This village had a number of apsidal and rectangular houses of the 'Megaron' type (Fig. 5g). Of these the apsidal houses were the earlier. They contained a circular hearth and shallow pits filled with ash (*bothroi*), which were used for baking. The rectangular houses which come later contained a circular hearth and a raised platform of beaten earth. The platform was probably the base of an oven. Apsidal houses together with Minyan pottery and stone battle-axes had appeared earlier at Lerna in the E.H. III period, and now, in the Middle Helladic period, bones of horses were found at Lerna also. Houses similar to those of Eutresis have been found in a contemporary setting at Tiryns and Korákou (near Lechaeum) in east Greece, and at Thermum and Olympia in west Greece.

The main styles of pottery in the Middle Bronze Age were two: 'matt-painted' ware, which may have evolved naturally from the Early Bronze Age style, and 'Minyan' ware. The latter is an innovation; for it is made on the potter's wheel and its shapes resemble those of vases made in metal. The grey variety of Minyan ware is the characteristic pottery of the stratum which follows the burnt layer; for instance at Eutresis. It is characteristic also of the beginning of Troy VI, where it coincided with the coming of new settlers. The distribution of grey and yellow Minyan ware covered most parts of peninsular Greece during the course of the Middle Bronze Age. It was in use also at the coastal sites in Chalcidice, and in large quantities at Troy VI. A pottery from which Minyan ware may have developed has been found in Macedonia, where it dates to the final phase of the Early Bronze Age.

Although some of the new elements in Middle Helladic culture may be

[1] *Il.* 5. 370.

attributed to Greek-speaking immigrants from the north, it must be remembered that these immigrants, though dominant, were very much in the minority and that the population into which they came was already very mixed. The qualities of Middle Helladic culture were thus due not only to Greek leadership but also to the abilities of the earlier and more civilized peoples of the land. As the period progressed, those qualities were enriched by increasing trade overseas. Trade with the Cyclades grew rapidly, and the islands served as centres of exchange between the eastern mainland and Crete. Trade with Troy was particularly strong and enlivened the coastal districts of Thessaly and Macedonia, especially Chalcidice. Trade with the north-west is revealed mainly by the discovery of weapons of Middle Minoan and Middle Helladic types at Plemmyrium near Syracuse, in south-eastern Italy, in the Mati and Devoli valleys in Albania, at Vajzë inland of Oricum Gulf, and in the Ionian islands. While civilization advanced in central and southern Greece, Macedonia and inland Thessaly lagged behind and Epirus, Acarnania, and Aetolia, and probably Corcyra, were being occupied by pastoral peoples, who retained the crudest form of Macedonian culture, marked by the wishbone handle, as they spread westwards and southwards. The ebb and flow of peoples brought local customs in its wake, and some of the burial customs are particularly interesting.

The most distinctive of the burial customs is tumulus burial. We have mentioned first examples of such burial in E.H. II, and we add other first examples at Tivat in the Gulf of Kotor and Belotić in western Serbia in E.H. III. If those who introduced this form of burial were Indo-European speakers, they were the founders of the Illyrian-speaking and the Greek-speaking peoples. The form of burial was as follows, in most cases. A first burial was made in a pit, circular or rectangular, dug below ground level, lined with stones and floored with pebbles, and originally roofed. This mortuary chamber represented a dwelling (or, to borrow the term from *Iliad* 23.254, a hut). Frequently a circle of stones was laid round but at some distance from the burial, and a mound of soil was raised over the circle to make a tumulus (hence the term 'Grave Circle'). Later burials were added by digging a shaft into the tumulus, making a mortuary chamber at the foot and refilling with soil. Many tumuli were used for more than a century, because burial was reserved for distinguished persons.

Tumuli multiplied in the Middle Helladic period. They have been found in Albania at seven places, ranging from Kukës in the north to Piskovë near Permet and Vodhinë in the south (see Fig., p. xviii). They are dated mainly by weapons of M.M. and M.H. types in warrior graves. The 'Royal Graves' at Leucas extended into the first phase of M.H., and were followed after a long gap by 'F Graves' in a tumulus which contained a rectangular structure built with orthostatic slabs and an annexe. Next, late in M.H., were the 'S Graves' within a tumulus surrounded by a circular stone wall. They all had some warrior graves. In Greece on the mainland tumulus burial appeared for the first time at many sites. There are examples for instance at Roupáki, Pýlos and Samikón in Elis, and at Voidhokoilía, Málthi, Papoúlia and Peristería in Messenia—some dating from the start of M.H. They have appeared in east central Greece at Elatea in Phocis and Aphidna and Marathon in Attica, and offshore on the island of Ceos; and in the Argolid at Mycenae, Argos and Asine. There are many features which connect the tumuli in Albania and Leucas with those on the Greek mainland. Thus the circular wall under the edge of the tumulus is common to Vodhinë, S tumulus at Leucas, Samikon, Peristeria, and Mycenae (Circle B). Orthostatic slabs formed a 'Grave Circle' at Pazhok (in central Albania), Arnissa (west Macedonia), Malthi (Messenia), and the commemorative Circle A at Mycenae. A tumulus covering a rectangular structure with an annexe was found at F tumulus at Leucas and at Marathon (T 2). Pairs of large tumuli were partly in contempory use, e.g. at Pazhok probably Vajzë (north Epirus), Leucas (R graves), and Mycenae. Weapons were found in many burials under the tumuli, wherever they were, and these show that they were burials of leading warriors.

Tumulus burial was clearly reserved, as in the *Iliad*, for distinguished members of ruling families. In Albania no settlements have been found in connection with M.H. tumuli, and it is apparent that the warriors buried there had led pastoral nomadic tribes. In mainland Greece the founders of the tumuli were often the forerunners of the Mycenaean dynasts: for example, at coastal Pylos (Voidhokoilía), Malthi, Marathon, Mycenae, Argos, and Asine. They brought with them the Greek language, military prowess and the will to dominate, and their successors created what we call Mycenaean civilization. But we must not forget the reservoir of Greek-speaking peoples who were living in Albania and no doubt feeling the pressure of the Illyrian-speaking peoples north of them. They moved south gradually, the last wave overthrowing Mycenaean civilization.

§ 2. The rise of Mycenaean civilization

THE name 'Mycenaean' was adopted from Mycenae, because Schliemann, the pioneer of excavation, first discovered this civilization at Mycenae; but it is also a correct title since Mycenae was the originator and centre of many new developments. While this civilization arose from a fusion of ideas and skills, deriving both from the indigenous peoples and from the Greek-speaking intruders, there is no doubt that the leaders came from the latter and possessed exceptional skill not only in war but also in administration. The cemeteries of the early rulers at Mycenae with their extravagant and almost barbaric splendour (described below) have therefore attracted much attention. The manner of burial is similar in the two Grave Circles, the earlier, 'B', being outside the later citadel, and the later, 'A', being inside it. The ground above Grave Circle B was levelled off at some subsequent date, and the excavator has suggested that each of the twenty-four graves inside the

Circle, which is 27·50 metres in diameter, originally had a small mound over it, but it is much more likely that one large tumulus covered them all. The Circle was marked by a peribolos of unworked stones, about two metres wide, such as occurred at Vodhinë in inland Epirus (see Fig. p. xviii). Grave Circle A, which is also some 27 metres in diameter, was rebuilt in its present monumental form *c.* 1300 and is likely in its original form to have resembled Grave Circle B. The earliest burials in both Circles were of late M.H. date, and the other burials covered the century 1600–1500. Some burials were in cist-graves, cut in the rock, and others were in shaft-graves, sunk one to five metres deep below the present surface and sometimes marked near the surface by stone *stelai*. Cist-graves were usual in the tumuli of E.H. II date and of M.H. date at Leucas and of L.H. date in inland Epirus, and it is obvious that originally the shaft-grave was sunk into a tumulus, three to five metres high, and then marked by a wooden or stone *stele*. At Lerna two shaft-graves of M.H. date were sunk one into the tumulus and the other alongside it in just this way. The tholos-tombs at Mycenae, built after 1500, were sometimes covered by a tumulus set over a circular wall, 20 to 25 metres in diameter, and even their concept of a dome over the grave was inherent in the dome of stones in the Vodhinë tumulus in Epirus (see Fig. p. xviii). The contents of the shaft-graves are equally striking. While they are far richer than those found in Albania and north Epirus, which were remote, backward areas, there is a remarkably close resemblance in the mixture of M.M. and M.H. weapons, for instance at Vajzë and Vodhinë, where rapiers, daggers, spearheads, and javelin-heads were found. So far then as the present evidence goes, the rulers of Mycenae and probably those of Lerna and Elatea came ultimately from an area in which central Albania lay—an area where, as we have seen, Indo-European peoples probably of Greek speech were living in the E.H. and M.H. periods.

Some of the shafts in the earlier Grave Circle B were quite small and had a single skeleton. Others were sunk nearly 3 metres into the soft conglomerate rock, and the grave at the foot of the shaft was roofed over with timber, reeds, and clay, and in one case with flagstones. Knives, daggers, spearheads, swords—some with ivory pommels and gold handles—gold, silver, and electrum ornaments, silver jugs and bronze and clay vases were buried with the dead, and a death-mask of electrum was found in a family grave with four skeletons. The workmanship of the metal objects is exquisite and far superior to anything of an earlier date which has been found on the mainland. Stone *stelai*, standing upright on a rectangular stone base, were set above some of the graves, and they were engraved with scenes of war and hunting. One, which was reused as a base, portrayed 'a warrior brandishing a broad sword against a fallen antagonist, and two lions apparently standing on their hind legs'. The shaft-graves and their contents are entirely different from anything known in Crete at this period, and the skeletons of persons who were between 5½ and 6 feet in height belong to a far taller race than the Minoans.

Grave Circle A was evidently made for a new dynasty which came into power *c.* 1600. Its members were buried in six deep shaft-graves. The earliest grave in this group followed closely on or even preceded the last of the burials in Grave Circle B, and the latest may be dated *c.* 1500. The graves were marked by sculptured *stelai*, and on some of them horse-drawn chariots were represented. The corpses were laid in a contracted attitude. Masks and breast-plates of gold, swords, daggers, gold and silver drinking cups, gold signet-rings, and vessels of metal, stone, and clay were buried with the men (Pl. II); gold frontlets, toilet-boxes, disks, and jewellery accompanied the women, and sheet-gold encased the two children. The delicate artistry and superb crafts-manship of their possessions reflect the influence and perhaps the hand of Minoan metal-workers. But the horse-drawn chariots, the preference for scenes of hunting and war on the inlays, the moustaches of the gold masks, the taste for amber in jewellery, and the presence of a boar's-tusk helmet show that these rulers, like their predecessors, were of mainland origin. For these features do not occur in contemporary Crete. Amber derives from the Baltic Sea and the earliest boar's-tusk helmet yet found comes from the Middle Bronze Age settlement at Eutresis (Fig. 10 *b*). The kings of the second dynasty at Mycenae are likely also to have been descendants of the Middle Bronze Age peoples who had invaded Corinthia and Argolis and established themselves as rulers of Mycenae and Lerna. Their residence was a fortified palace, which formed the citadel of Mycenae, and their realm seems to have comprised Argolis and Corinthia. Their wealth was probably based on con-trol of trade. The port at Korákou near Lechaeum on the Corinthian Gulf received the traffic from the west and north, while the ports of Tiryns and Asine now traded direct with Crete. They controlled also the overland route between the Peloponnese and central Greece. Similar dynasties were estab-lished at Thebes, Goulás, and Orchomenus; they, too, were influenced by Minoan art, for a fresco at Thebes shows women wearing Minoan dress. Their realm covered Boeotia and the Lelantine plain in Euboea, and their wealth was derived from the trade which passed by land through Boeotia and by sea through the Euripus channel towards the north-east.

The second shaft-grave dynasty at Mycenae was succeeded by the first period of the 'Tholos-Tomb' dynasty (*c.* 1500–1400). The approach to this type of tomb was by a cut or walled but unroofed passage-way (*dromos*), which ended in a massive doorway set in the wall of the tholos; the tomb within was circular in plan and the dome was conical in shape, having been excavated from the hillside, then faced with masonry, and finally covered with a tumulus inside a circular retaining wall. The blocks forming the dome were skilfully wedged and counter-weighted to carry the mass of earth and masonry. During the fifteenth century two groups of tholoi, distinguishable by the technique of the builders, were constructed at Mycenae. A prototype of the tholos-tomb and *dromos*, found near Pylus in Messenia, is dated to the end of the Middle Bronze Age; it occurred in one of the few areas where tumulus-burials were practised.

Mycenaean culture spread far and wide during this period. Numerous tholos-tombs have been discovered elsewhere in Argolis and Corinthia; in Messenia, Triphylia, and the Ionian islands to the west; in Laconia to the south; in Attica, Boeotia, Euboea, and Thessaly to the north. The expanding prosperity of the mainland drew much of its strength from Cnossus, which then stood supreme in the trade-circle of the Aegean area. The wealth of the mainland dynasts is shown by the magnificent Vaphió cups from Laconia, and by the so-called Palace style of pottery with its bold and luxuriant designs. The chamber-tombs of their dependants, who lived below the citadel, for instance at Mycenae, also reflect the growing prosperity of the age. In these tombs, which were cut in the rock and approached by an open *dromos*, members of the family in successive generations were laid to rest with their valuable possessions beside them.

A Greek dynasty established itself at Cnossus about 1450 and ruled over Crete, where the Mycenaean Linear Script was devised probably by Minoan clerks in order to express the Greek language.[1] The Script was soon employed at the mainland palaces for the same restricted purposes of recording property and transactions in property. The kings of Mycenae or Thebes evidently ruled over wide baronies, claiming tithes from their subjects and organizing an efficient bureaucratic service. The furniture of their tombs shows that they also engaged in trade overseas and began to rival the rulers of Cnossus and Minoan Crete in this field in 1450–1400. A Greek settlement was planted in Rhodes *c.* 1450 and another probably in Cos *c.* 1425; traders in Mycenaean goods settled in Miletus alongside Minoans; and more Mycenaean than Minoan objects have been discovered from this time in Egypt. In the West, Mycenaean pottery has been found at Lipara together with Minoan pottery of this period. Thus the mainland states emerged from their pupilage and took an independent place in the circle of prosperous powers.

The prosperity of Crete and the Greek mainland in the fifteenth century was due in a great degree to the general expansion of trade which marked the ripening of the Bronze Age civilization of the Near East. In this trade metal now played a very important part, whether in bulk or in the form of weapons, tools, and jewellery. Egypt was particularly rich in Nubian gold, which she exported for instance to Babylonia, while she imported silver mainly from Asia Minor. Copper was mined in the Sinai peninsula and was also imported from Cyprus and Syria. Farther east, the civilized centres in Mesopotamia drew their copper from the Arabian peninsula, from Transcaucasia and Asia Minor. From early times Crete played an important role in the development of copper weapons. The triangular-shaped dagger which she invented early in the Bronze Age travelled to Spain, Italy, and the Danube valley; there in turn the copper-ores of Spain, Elba, Etruria, Hungary, and Transylvania were exploited. Thus the interchange of metals and weapons between Europe, Africa, and Asia grew; from it Minoan Crete and Troy derived their wealth in gold, silver, and copper.

[1] I am not convinced by L. R. Palmer's later date in *On the Knossos Tablets* (1963).

The development and use of bronze, which is an alloy of copper and tin, may have first become general in Syria or in Asia Minor. Its adoption elsewhere gave added importance to the European area; for the richest deposits of tin were in Cornwall, Spain, Etruria, and Hungary. The earliest bronze weapons were brought from the eastern Mediterranean into Europe along three main lines of distribution: via Troy to the lower Danube basin, via Greece and the Adriatic to Italy and central Europe, and via Spain to northwest Europe. For example, the slim rapier of bronze, first produced in Crete *c.* 2000, travelled through Greece and Italy to the central Danube basin. Some centuries later the rapier evolved in Hungary into the broad slashing sword, which was gradually adopted in Italy and made its first appearance in Greece soon after 1375. Although the tempo of trade was slow, the areas which it traversed extended from the amber-producing shores of the Baltic Sea to the lowlands of Mesopotamia. The richest centres of exchange were in Egypt, Syria, and Asia Minor. Moreover, in the fifteenth century Egypt was at the height of her political power, dominating Palestine and Syria and allied with Babylonia and the Mitanni of north-east Syria; Cyprus recognized her suzerainty, and the Hittite kingdom in central Asia Minor respected her arms. In this century Egypt became the centre of the civilized world. Her navies and her armies controlled the trade-routes, which radiated into Abyssinia and Africa, into the Red Sea and the Indian Ocean, into the southern Mediterranean and the hinterland of Palestine and Syria.

Crete and the Greek mainland did not owe their prosperity in the fifteenth century to mineral wealth. Tin may have been mined at Cirrha near Delphi, but the copper-ores of Crete and the silver-deposits of Attica were probably not exploited. The Minoans and Mycenaeans were rather the intermediaries and beneficiaries of the trade which passed through the Mediterranean towards Egypt and the Near East, and their native craftsmen excelled in the production of weapons and jewellery. They also exported hides, timber, wine, olive oil, and purple dye to Egypt in exchange for precious metals, linen, papyrus, and rope. Crete occupied a particularly advantageous position on the trade-routes of the Mediterranean Sea at this time, when Egypt and Syria were the main centres of exchange. She and her dependencies commanded the entry into the south Aegean and the passage from Syria, Cyprus, and Rhodes towards the west, until the Mycenaean powers grew to maturity and claimed a place *c.* 1450. Then *c.* 1400 the naval supremacy of Cnossus was suddenly destroyed. The palaces and the treasuries of Crete were pillaged, and her political organization disrupted. This disaster did not impair the sources from which her prosperity had been derived, but it provided the opportunity for others to usurp the central position which she had enjoyed for many centuries.

§ 3. *The Mycenaean world 1400–1200*

THE Greek powers of the mainland were well qualified to inherit the leading position of Cnossus in the southern Aegean. Quickened by their contact with

Minoan civilization for two centuries, they had developed a fine Mycenaean style of pottery, in which the mainland tradition of formal design and technical skill was combined with the Minoan flair for decoration and shape. This pottery had been exported in considerable quantities before the sack of Cnossus, but after it the stream of Mycenaean exports greatly increased and set steadily through the intermediate stations of Melos, Thera, and Rhodes towards the Near East. Rhodes was strengthened by further settlements of Greek peoples and became an important centre of exchange. Greek settlements were also made on the southern and eastern coasts of Cyprus and subsequently in other parts of the island. In Cilicia Mycenaean remains have been found at Tarsus, Kazanli, and Mersin, and in Caria at Iasus. Ugarit received Greek traders, whose wares travelled up the Orontes valley as far as the cities of the Syrian plateau, and Mycenaean objects have recently been found at Poseidium in Syria. Mycenaean pottery also travelled inland from Ascalon into southern Palestine, and to a lesser extent from Haifa into northern Palestine. It was imported in larger quantities at Tell-el-Amarna, which replaced Thebes as the capital of Egypt *c.* 1374–1362, and then to a lesser extent at Gurob nearer to the Delta. Throughout the fourteenth century Mycenaean pottery had a general uniformity and was not marked by strong local characteristics, and Rhodes and Cyprus were exceedingly prosperous as main centres of exchange and probably also as manufacturers of pottery. In the latter part of the century a considerable number of mainlanders settled in Crete. They built houses of the Megaron type, and buried their dead in vaulted tombs with a *dromos*. They probably ruled over the Minoan population of the island, which had regained much of its prosperity and was well placed for trade with Egypt.

In the northern Aegean the Greek powers developed further the trade which they had already established with the rich city of Troy. At the end of the fourteenth century Troy VI was destroyed by earthquake, but its successor, Troy VII A, was equally wealthy and equally open to trade with the Greek mainland. This trade probably followed the coastal route along the shores of Thessaly, Macedonia, and Thrace, and accelerated the widespread adoption of Mycenaean culture in Thessaly and in lower Macedonia. In the Cyclades (apart from Melos and Thera) and in the northern Sporades small quantities of Mycenaean pottery have been found, most being at Delos; it is probable that the inhabitants of these islands and the coastal peoples of western Asia Minor (with the exception of Miletus) lay outside the main sphere of Mycenaean trade and culture.

Although Minoan and Mycenaean pottery reached Lipara and Ischia and liparite stone was brought to Crete from the Lipari isles, the first signs of settlement in the West came in the fourteenth century. Mycenaean pottery of this period and tholos-tombs have been found at Acragas and Syracuse in Sicily, and Mycenaean pottery in considerable quantities at Oria and Taras in south Italy. There were evidently Greek settlers in both areas, who had followed the trade-route towards Lipara and Ischia and established themselves at points of vantage, as their successors were to do some 600 years later.

The widening of the Mycenaean world and its immediate contacts with Egypt, Syria, Troy, Italy, and Sicily brought a growing prosperity to the peoples of the Greek mainland. In 1600–1400 the higher level of culture which was found at the palace-sites spread only gradually to their dependencies; but after 1400 a homogeneous Mycenaean culture grew rapidly, embraced all the mainland, except Epirus and inner Macedonia, and extended to the Ionian islands, except Corcyra, and to some Aegean islands. The tide turned *c.* 1300, when Greek trade with Egypt declined rapidly. Cyprus became an independent centre, which sent its own exports to Syria and Palestine; and fortifications were built to protect the copper workshops at its capital at Énkomi. The homogeneity of culture also began to break down, and Cyprus, for instance, developed its own local style of Mycenaean pottery. Thus the Greek mainland lost many markets in the East, perhaps to the Phoenicians of Byblus, who had not imported pottery from Greece in any quantity since the fifteenth century and were probably rivals in the carrying trade. Troy, too, imported less Mycenaean pottery after 1300, and in the West contact was broken off with Sicily, Lipara, and Ischia about 1300 (but maintained with the Greek settlements in south Italy). Gradually the prosperity of the Greek mainland declined, as conditions worsened for Greek trade overseas, and the comparative peace, which must have attended the full flowering of Mycenaean civilization, began to give way to an unsettled age, in which fortifications even more powerful than those of the past were built to protect the rulers of the palaces.

The palaces were the outstanding features of Greek culture throughout the Mycenaean period, and the Palace of Mycenae was the finest of them all. Soon after 1350 the citadel area was enlarged and enclosed within massive 'Cyclopean' walls, built of huge limestone and conglomerate blocks to a thickness of some 20 feet. The approach to the main entry was protected by a strong bastion. The entry itself consisted of a gateway 9 feet wide, formed of four great monoliths. The relieving triangle above the lintel was faced with the heraldic and religious emblem of Mycenae, two lionesses with their forepaws resting on the pedestal of a sacred pillar. A smaller postern gate with double doors gave entry from the north side of the circuit. Within the citadel a wide ramp led from the 'Lion Gate' to the palace of the king.

The central feature of the palace was an open and spacious court (Fig. 7 *a*). On the east side of the court a columned porch, paved with slabs of gypsum, gave access through a vestibule to the principal state-room, the 'Megaron', of which the painted stucco floor was edged with a row of gypsum slabs. In the centre of the Megaron four wooden columns, sheathed in bronze towards the base, surrounded a raised circular hearth (cf. Fig. 5 *h*). The walls of the room were decorated with frescoes representing chariots in battle, horses with their grooms, and ladies outside a palace. On the west side of the court a doorway

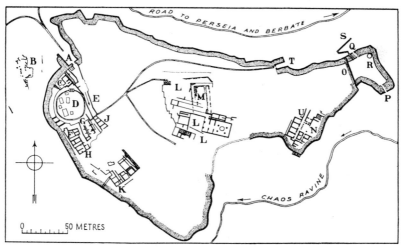

(a) Citadel of Mycenae, A. Lion Gate; B. Prehistoric cemetery outside walls; C. Granary; D. Grave Circle A; E. Ramp; F. House of Warrior Vase; G. Ramp House; H. South House; J. Hellenistic chambers; K. Tsountas' House; L. Palace; M. Temple foundations; N. House of Columns; O. Original north-east wall; P. Sally port; Q. Drain; R. Hellenistic cistern; S. Secret cistern; T. Postern Grate; U. Mycenaean terrace wall

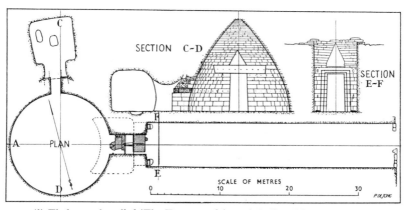

(b) Tholos-tomb, called 'The Treasury of Atreus', built at Mycenae c. 1330

FIG. 7

gave access to an ante-room separating the 'throne-room' from a grand stair-case, which descended to an entrance for state visitors. The domestic quarter of the palace lay on the north side of the court and also comprised the upper story; it was probably entered from the vestibule of the Megaron. Its rooms gave off two long corridors which ran parallel to the north and south walls of the court. In the northern and highest part of the palace a shrine contained round altars of painted stucco; near this an ivory group of two goddesses and a child was discovered. The flat clay roof of the palace, reinforced with reeds and laid on rafters, was carried by horizontal roof-beams. From the roof one gazed over the wide plain to the waters of the Argolic Gulf and beyond to the mountains of Arcadia and Laconia.

Below the citadel lay the extensive open quarters of the town, where wealthy merchants lived, the tholos-tombs of the kings, and the roads built with Cyclopean culverts and causeways which led to the fortresses of the Argive plain and northwards towards Corinth. Of the tholos-tombs the finest, 'the Treasury of Atreus' (Fig. 7 *b*), has a dome 40 feet high, and is most ad-mirable in its dignity and in its proportions. It was built *c.* 1330 as the resting-place of the king, for whom the citadel was fortified and the area of the court, the Megaron, and the throne room was laid out. The last of the great tholos-tombs was built *c.* 1300. During the thirteenth century the grand staircase was rebuilt, the circuit of Cyclopean walls was extended towards the north-east, and an underground passage was built down to a subterranean cistern which was fed by a spring outside the walls. It was also in the thirteenth century that massive fortifications were completed at Tiryns and storage galleries were inset in the great thickness of the walls.

Outside the Argolid the strongest centres of Mycenaean power lay in Boeotia. There the fertile alluvial plain round Lake Copaïs, which was drained by the Mycenaean people, lay under the control of the massive castle of Goulás. The citadel of Thebes, 'the Cadmea', stood on the ridge separating the main plains of Boeotia, and the rulers of Orchomenus were buried in a magnificent tholos-tomb, known as 'the Treasury of Minyas'. Attica was of less importance. The Cyclopean fortifications of the acropolis of Athens were perfected in the period 1250–1200, and a subterranean stair-way was then carried a hundred feet below ground-level to reach water. The other great centres of Mycenaean power were marked by fine tholos-tombs, citadels or prosperous towns, such as have been excavated at Iolcus in Thessaly, Las and Amyclae in Laconia, Pylus and Peristéria in Messenia, Kakóvatos in Triphylia, and Thermum in Aetolia; and there were centres in the islands of Aegina, Cephallenia, and Leucas.

The fortifications of the Mycenaean palaces and the preference for scenes of war and hunting testify to the martial spirit of the Greeks in this age. When Cnossus fell, Mycenae and her peers prospered by the power of the sword. Nor was the Mycenaean expansion overseas achieved without recourse to violent methods. For in this troubled age the guardian of trade was the sword. The Greek traders and settlers faced formidable rivals in the Sicels of the west, the islanders of the Cyclades, the coastal peoples of Asia Minor, and the Phoenicians of the Syrian coast. The Greek ships-of-war, like those of Minoan Crete, were built with a prolonged keel-beam, which was employed in ramming tactics, and sea-fights were portrayed in Minoan and Mycenaean art. Hitherto the weapons of the mainlanders, as of the Cretans, had been the rapier-sword, the thrusting spear, and the shield, which was suspended from the shoulder by a strap so as to leave both hands free. These cumbrous shields were used in hand-to-hand duels; but their main value may have been as a protection against missiles—the throwing-spear,[1] the arrow, and the sling-thrown pellet. The mainlanders generally wore the traditional 'boar's-tusk' helmet of conical shape (Fig. 10b); rare examples of a tight-fitting bronze helmet have been found in Crete and on the mainland. Towards the end of the fourteenth century a slashing-sword, which had originated in central Europe, appeared in the Aegean area. This deadly weapon led to the adoption of a smaller round shield, which was grasped in the hand, and of a fore-and-aft peaked or horned helmet, designed to divert a downward slash (see Fig. 10, p. 111). Such equipment was used throughout the Near East during the thirteenth century.

The use of the chariot in war was also widespread. Although the horse had served as a pack-animal on the Greek mainland from early times, it played no part in war until the chariot was introduced perhaps from the Near East during the sixteenth century. In Egypt and in Syria massed chariotry clashed in set charges; but we do not know whether the Greeks adopted the same tactics at the outset or employed the chariot as a mobile platform for casting missiles.

The Greeks of the Mycenaean period were only one of several powerful peoples in the eastern Mediterranean area, and they were certainly brought into touch with their neighbours by matters of trade or war. The Hittites and the Egyptians, who kept written records of diplomatic and military events, had good reason to mention the Greeks who visited Troy so often and controlled the southern Aegean. In their own saga the Greeks of later times referred to their ancestors of the Mycenaean period under the names of 'Akhaioi', 'Danaoi', and 'Argeioi', and such names may therefore be expected to occur in Hittite and Egyptian records.

In the fourteenth century, when the Hittite kingdom in Asia Minor controlled the trade-route through north Syria leading from Mesopotamia to the Mediterranean, the gods of the Hittites and the gods of the countries 'Ahhiyava' and 'Lazpa' were invoked in the reign of Mursil II (c. 1350–1320). In a letter of this or the next reign, which asked for help against invaders, a Hittite king's 'brother' (that is a king of similar standing), called 'Tavakavalas', was described as being an 'Ayavalash' king and a 'brother' of the king of 'Ahhiyava'. A later letter (c. 1300) speaks of the kings of 'Ahhiyava', Egypt, Babylonia, and Assyria.[2] The word 'Ahhiyava' (or in an earlier form

---

[1] *Il.* 15. 646.

[2] F. Sommer, *Die Ahhijava-Urkunden* (1932), 283 f., 9 f., 243 f. (in German). *BCH* 70 (1946), 58 f. (in French).

'Ahhayiva') is clearly a transcription of the Greek word 'Akhaïa', just as 'Ayavalash' (of which the ending is a Hittite ethnic) is a transcription of 'Akhaïos'. There were evidently two Achaean kings in the earlier letter: one being the king of Achaea *par excellence*, as in the later letter, and comparable in status to the kings of Egypt, &c., and the other some local Achaean king in Asia Minor. The former was evidently a king of the Greek mainland. The clue to the latter is probably given by Herodotus, who mentioned that the inhabitants of Pamphylia or Cilicia were once called 'Hyp-Akhaioi'.[1] 'Lazpa' was doubtless the island Lesbos, and 'Taroisa' (in another Hittite document) was Troy.

The records of Egypt in the fourteenth and thirteenth centuries give the names of many Aegean peoples. They were fighting either as mercenaries of Egypt or as allies of the Hittite empire. Among them figure the Shardana, Luka (or Lukki), Pidasa, Musa, Kalikisha, Dardenui, and Iliunna. The last two are to be identified with the 'Dardanoi' and 'Ilioi', who are named as the inhabitants of Troy in the Homeric poems. It is clear from these records that Troy sided with the Hittite empire during the thirteenth-century wars against Egypt.[2]

The next record of Aegean peoples comes in the late thirteenth century when conditions had changed for the worse. On the Greek mainland there were signs of serious warfare. The export of pottery from the mainland to Syria, Palestine, and Egypt ceased soon after *c.* 1230, and new Mycenaean settlements were established by violent methods at Énkomi in Cyprus and at Tarsus in Cilicia at about this time. Great raids were recorded in the Near East. Hittite records mention repeated attacks on Caria after 1250 and the ravaging of Cyprus *c.* 1225 by 'Attarissyas, the man of Ahhiyava', who should probably be identified with Atreus, King of Mycenae and father of Agamemnon, who sacked Troy about 1200. In 1221 a swarm of invaders entered the Delta from Libya and were defeated by the Pharaoh, whose victory-speech contained the following sentences.[3] 'They have repeatedly penetrated the fields of Egypt to the great river; they have halted, they have spent whole days and months . . . they spend their time fighting, going about the land to fill their bellies daily. They come to the land of Egypt to seek the necessities of their mouths.' These northerners from all lands are named Shakalsha, Akaiwasha, Tursha, Luka, and Shardana. The termination -sha being an ethnic suffix, the raiders are recognizable as Sagalassans (from Sagalassus on the coast of Palestine), Achaeans, Tursenoi, Lycians, and Sardinoi.

In the first decade of the twelfth century a large-scale attack by land and by sea was delivered on the western and the eastern approaches to the Delta. In 1194 the Egyptians repelled the attack from Libya. There were engaged in it the Peleset or Pulesat (Philistines), Thekel, Denyen (Danaoi), Sherden (Sardinoi), Weshesh, and Shekelesh (Sagalassans). In 1192 the Egyptian

---

[1] Hdt. 7. 91.
[2] Breasted, *Anc. Rec. of Egypt* (1906), 3, §§ 306, 309, 312, 349, 574, 579, 588, 601.
[3] Breasted, 3, § 580.

archers and mercenaries (including Tursha and Sherden) defeated the invaders from the east. This group, moving by land with their families in heavy two-wheeled ox-carts and by sea with a numerous fleet, had already raided Alasa (Cyprus) and the Syrian Coast. In the words of the Egyptian records[1] 'the countries which came from their isles in the midst of the sea, they advanced to Egypt, their hearts relying on their arms'. 'Their main support was Peleset, Thekel, Shekelesh, Denyen and Weshesh.' In 1187 another attack from Libya on the Delta was defeated. But the land-raids and sea-raids continued, until by the end of the century the kingdom of Egypt was cut off from the Mediterranean Sea.

Another pivot of prosperity in the Aegean area was Troy. The great city of Troy VI (*c.* 1900–1300) was founded by a people who were probably kindred of the Greek-speaking settlers of central Greece; they built a modified form of Megaron house, fortified the citadel, and brought the horse to Asia. When the city was destroyed by an earthquake, it was rebuilt again in a form similar to a Mycenaean stronghold, where the king and his entourage lived within a massive fortification wall. The latest phase of Troy VI was particularly rich, and trade relations and probably personal relations between Troy and Mycenaean Greece were very close. The Troad contains good agricultural land, and there is fine tunny-fishing in the Propontis; but Troy VI and Troy VII A owed their wealth primarily to the control which they were able to exert over the traffic between Asia and Europe. The city lay at the entry to the Hellespont, where navigation for primitive ships was difficult. They could not make headway up the straits against the strong northerly winds in the summer months and against the current running at two and a half knots. In order to enter the Propontis, primitive craft had to depend on towing, and perhaps portage as well for their cargoes. While the European shore was unsuitable for the purpose, the low-lying Asiatic coast with shallows inshore, which were less affected by the current, offered better facilities for towing and portage. There is, however, a limestone bluff which is the only obstacle to portage along the Asiatic coast, and to the south-west of this bluff lay Troy. The city was well placed to control the passage of the Hellespont. The Propontis provided the best crossing from Asia to Europe at a point where land-routes led to the Danube valley or the West. For the entry up the Bosporus into the Black Sea was made very difficult for the merchantmen of the Bronze Age by a four-knot current and by northerly winds in the summer months. The strength and the wealth of the seventh city of Troy suggest that it controlled the area both of the Hellespont and of the Propontis. The trade-routes radiating from this focal point by sea or land led to the lower Danube basin, to central Greece via the Thracian coast, to the southern Aegean and Cyprus along the Asiatic coast, and to the Hittite empire in central Asia Minor, where Assyrian traders had established a lively trade.

Excavation has revealed that Troy VII A and the settlement at Thermí in Lesbos were destroyed *c.* 1200; that at about the same time Mersin and

---

[1] Breasted, 4, § 77; § 64.

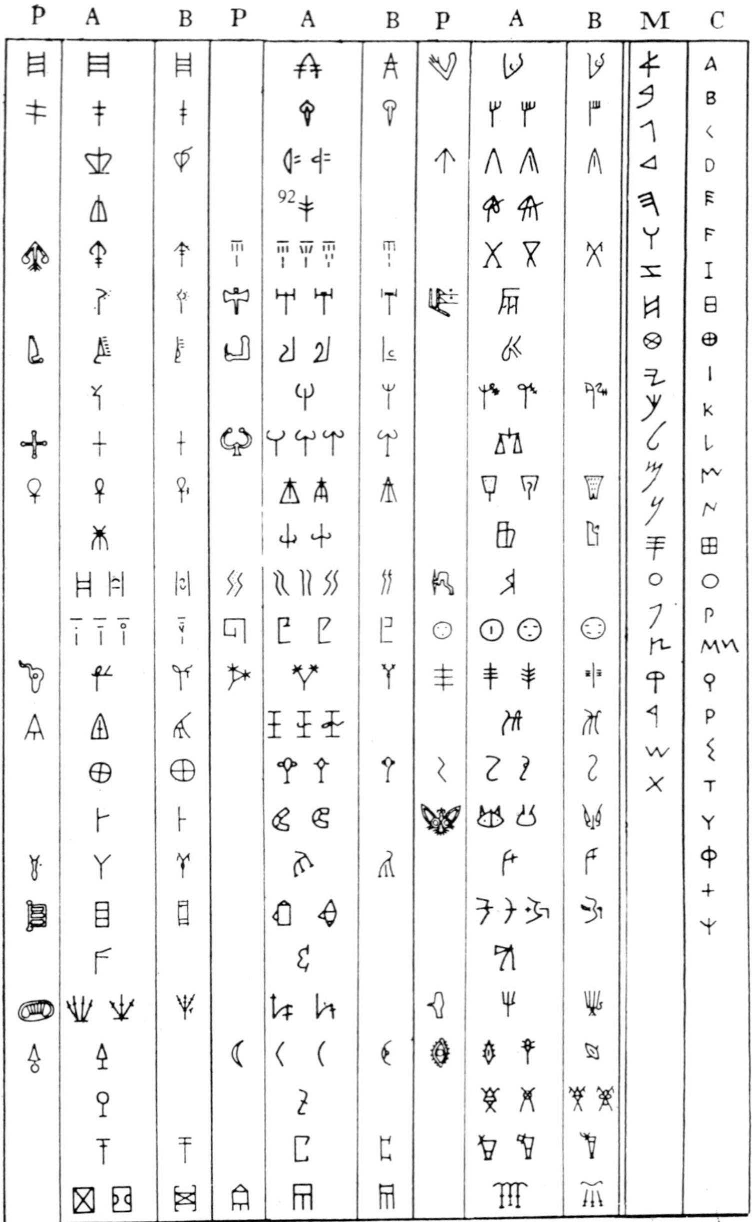

FIG. 8. Some signs of Minoan Pictographic writing (=P), Minoan Script (=A), and Mycenaean Script (=B), illustrating the central position of Minoan Script in development. Moabite and Chalcidian Alphabets (=M and C) derive from the Phoenician Alphabet

Tarsus in southern Asia Minor suffered this fate; and that the Hittite empire was completely overthrown by a barbarous power, which is probably to be identified with the Phrygian peoples. The next city of Troy (VII B) was impoverished; its remains contain at first some Mycenaean pottery and then a Danubian type of pottery, which indicates the occupation of Troy by invaders from Europe. The prosperity of Troy thus ended no less abruptly than that of the Hittite empire.

The tablets incised with the Mycenaean Linear Script, which have been found in burnt remains at Mycenae and Pylus, belong probably to the decades just before the fall of Troy. Although more than half the words so far deciphered are personal names, not one is the name of a hero recorded by Homer. Even at Pylus there is no sign of Neleus or Nestor. The syllables deciphered as *pu-ro* and identified as Pylus occur frequently on the tablets there. But this is rather puzzling; for *ko-no-so* is relatively infrequent on the tablets from Cnossus. The occurrence of the word *Pylus* would be more understandable, if it referred to the site at Peristéria rather than that at Ano Englianós, which archaeologists have identified with the Palace of Nestor. But the tablets show the accumulation of armaments, the fees and tribute paid by subjects in a feudal form of society, the large number of slave-women and the specialized occupations of the royal retainers. Offerings are made to the gods—Zeus, Hera, Poseidon, Hermes, and Athena Potnia. Ploughing-oxen have names like 'Dusky', and thirty oarsmen are dispatched on an expedition, perhaps to Pleuron in Aetolia. All this is of a piece with the conditions of society as they are described in the Homeric poems which relate the war at Troy and the return of the heroes. The discovery of sherds of local pottery with graffiti probably in Mycenaean Linear Script at Tarsus brings us close to Lycia, whither a message, says Homer, was sent in characters scratched on a tablet. Yet the tablets are only the labels of inventories at Pylus and Mycenae, recording the addition and withdrawal of stores, and they cannot be expected to rival the Egyptian and Hittite documents in their illustration of international affairs, such as the Trojan War or the movement of peoples.[1]

§ 4. *Language and traditions of the Mycenaean world*

The distribution of the Greek dialects in the classical period (see Fig. 9) has something to tell us of the Mycenaean world. When the Mycenaean sites were destroyed, central Greece and the Peloponnese were flooded by peoples who spoke dialects of the Doric group. However, some islands of earlier dialects survived in the classical period, and they provide clues for the state of affairs before the Dorians came.

The Aeolic dialect survived in a part of Thessaly and a part of Boeotia. It is therefore probable that the Late Bronze Age inhabitants of central Greece from Thessaly to Boeotia spoke the Aeolic dialect before the Doric-speaking peoples arrived. This probability is supported by the statements of Herodotus

---

[1] *DMG*, nrs. 6–16; *Il.* 6. 168. Similar graffiti in Mycenaean Linear Script have been found at Lipari.

and Thucydides, that Thessaly and Boeotia were previously 'Aeolic'. Corinth, too, and part of Aetolia were previously 'Aeolic' according to Thucydides, and Euboea according to Strabo.[1]

The Arcadian dialect survived in the centre of the Peloponnese, and Arcadian forms were present in the dialects of Elis and of south-east Laconia. We may, then, infer that the Late Bronze Age inhabitants of the Peloponnese were, at least in part, Arcadian-speaking before the Doric-speaking peoples arrived. Moreover, a form of Arcadian was spoken in Cyprus. The island must have been colonized at a time when Arcadian was spoken on the coast of the mainland. Such a time could only have been in the Bronze Age, and the occasion is shown by the archaeological evidence to have fallen in the Late Bronze Age *c.* 1350. At that date, therefore, Arcadian was a distinct and mature dialect. It is therefore highly probable that part of the eastern Peloponnese (south of 'Aeolic' Corinthia at least) was an Arcadian-speaking area in the fourteenth century.

The fact that the Achaean group of dialects subdivided into Aeolic and Arcadian suggests that two sections of the Achaean peoples had settled in separate geographical areas but had maintained some contact with one another over a considerable period of time. The appropriate conditions for this subdivision occurred also during the Late Bronze Age. Then the two leading centres of Mycenaean civilization lay respectively in Aeolic-speaking Boeotia and in Argolis, which was either Arcadian-speaking or adjacent to an Arcadian-speaking area. The dialects may have been closer to one another then than later; but that they were distinct is clear from the following case. In classical times a mixed Aeolic-Arcadian dialect was spoken in Pamphylia. The archaeological evidence from Mersin and Tarsus in Cilicia suggests that Mycenaean contact with the south coast of Asia Minor began about 1230. The colonists may have come from an area in which the two dialects, Aeolic and Arcadian, were spoken—perhaps from the realm of Mycenae, which extended over Aeolic-speaking Corinthia and probably over Arcadian-speaking areas. It is interesting that half the pottery of Mycenaean 'Granary' style at Tarsus was probably imported from the Argolid.

When we relate these conclusions to the evidence of archaeology, the following picture emerges. The first Greek-speaking peoples settled in Macedonia, Thessaly, and Epirus after *c.* 2500, and in these areas they developed different dialects. The first Greek-speaking peoples to enter Boeotia, Corinthia, and Argolis, after *c.* 1900, probably spoke Ionic. The main influx of Greek-speaking peoples entering Greece during the latter part of the Middle Bronze Age spoke the Achaean group of dialects. Of these the Aeolic-speaking branch occupied east Greece from Malis to Corinthia, driving the earlier Ionic-speaking peoples into Attica, while the Arcadian-speaking branch occupied most of the Peloponnese, driving the Ionic-speaking peoples into Achaea and Cynuria and overlaying them elsewhere.

[1] Hdt. 7. 176, 4; Th. 7. 57, 5; 4. 42, 2; 3, 102, 5; Str. 465; Plu. *GQ* 22.

It is doubtful if the incomplete decipherment of the Mycenaean Linear Script (see p. 34) has added much to our knowledge of the Greek dialects. The tablets at Cnossus date from *c.* 1400; at Mycenae from *c.* 1230; and at Pylus from *c.* 1200; and there are almost thirty fragments of inscribed jars from the Cadmea of Thebes, which are dated *c.* 1360. There are also some examples from Orchomenus, Eleusis, Tiryns, and Tarsus. The dialect seems to be neither northwest-Greek nor Doric, but may be related to Arcado-Cypriot or Aeolic. This is the general conclusion which we should expect on other grounds. But the local variations in the style of Mycenaean pottery, the analogy of classical times, and the evidence of Homer's language (which we shall consider next) make it unlikely that a uniform dialect was spoken from 1450 to 1200 at Cnossus, Thebes, Mycenae, and Pylus, even if its use by scribes was limited to court circles. When more tablets are found, a more precise transliteration of the Script may become possible and shed further light on the nature of the Mycenaean dialect or dialects.

These inferences from the distribution of dialects in the classical period are supported by a study of the dialect-forms in the earliest Greek literature. The epic poetry of Homer and Hesiod is written in an artificial language, which was formed by the accretion of different dialects during several centuries of transmission. The youngest stratum of dialect is Attic, and the main stratum is Ionic, reflecting the mature development of the epic saga in Ionia during the centuries after the collapse of the Mycenaean world. The earliest strata are Aeolic and, more rarely, Arcadian; these survive mainly in epithets and in participial forms, which could not be converted into Ionic without losing their metrical value. We are thus led to the conclusion that the origins of the epic language lie in the Mycenaean age at a time when Aeolic and Arcadian were the main dialects of the Greek world.

The oldest of the Greek dialects was Ionic. In the classical period it was spoken on the mainland in Attica alone, and in the L.H. III period in Attica[1] and at least in Achaea, Cynuria, and Boeotia[2] by the descendants probably of the first Greek-speaking settlers. In addition some non-Greek languages were spoken within the Greek area during the classical period. Pelasgian was spoken in the hinterland of Mt. Athos, in the islands of Lesbos, Imbros, and Samothrace, and in the neighbourhood of Cyzicus and Troy. It is probable that these Pelasgian-speakers were survivors of a pre-Hellenic people who had occupied the north Aegean area before the coming of the Greek-speaking peoples. In the Homeric poems Pelasgians appear in Crete and in the Troad; their name also occurs in connexion with Dodona in Epirus and with two cantons of Thessaly, 'Pelasgiotis' and 'Pelasgikon Argos'. Another non-Greek language was spoken by the Tyrseni, who were extant in the north-west Aegean; their language survives in a sixth-century inscription, which

---

[1] *Il.* 13. 685.   [2] Hdt. 1. 145; 5. 58; 8. 73. He puts 'Iones' in Boeotia when Cadmus came (*c.* 1350; see Appendix 2). A recent view, that the Ionic dialect developed after 1100, runs counter to the Greek tradition.

has been unearthed at Lemnos, and has affinities with Etruscan. At Praesus in Crete another non-Greek language occurs in fourth-century inscriptions. These undeciphered languages, like those of the Minoan Linear Script and the Phaestus disk, are probably to be regarded as relics of the pre-Hellenic peoples who entered the Greek peninsula and islands during the Neolithic and Early Bronze Ages.

Archaeological discovery has now provided a touchstone, by which the validity of Greek legend can be measured. The mythical tales of Cnossus, Mycenae, and Troy, once dismissed as fairy-stories, are found to rest on historical fact. As yet the range of archaeological discovery is limited; but its findings in certain cases confirm the assumption which Herodotus and Thucydides made, that Greek legend was set within a framework not of poetical fantasy but of historical reality. As Thucydides observed,[1] not all Greek tradition is to be believed. Elements of folk-lore were incorporated in early times, and rationalistic explanations were inserted later. But, when Homer and Hesiod canonized the Greek legends in literary form, they stood close to the springs of oral tradition and they were concerned in the true Greek manner with reality and not with fiction. Nor did oral tradition dry up with the development of literature. It was fully used in the fifth century by Herodotus, and Thucydides' convincing analysis of early Greek history demonstrates the value of oral tradition, when it is treated with historical insight.

Traditions of folk-movements were preserved not only by the Greek-speaking peoples but also by the survivors of other races, which had been in contact with the Aegean area in the Bronze Age. Thus Thucydides could state with confidence that the Pelasgians were once the most widespread people on the Greek mainland;[2] that the Tyrseni once occupied Athens and Lemnos;[3] that in the time of 'Minos' Carians and Phoenicians occupied most of the Aegean islands.[4] It is true that Herodotus, who sought to restrict the 'Hellenic' name to the Dorian branch of the Greek race, extended the Pelasgian name to embrace the other Greek-speaking peoples. Yet, if we discount this error in the method of Herodotus, he preserves many folk-traditions which are of importance. The Carians claimed that they were native to south-west Asia Minor and had expanded thence into the islands, and that they were related to the Mysians and the Lydians of Asia Minor.[5] The Leleges figure either as an alternative title for the Carians or as a neighbouring people in the islands. In later Greek tradition both peoples are said to have settled also on the Greek mainland. The Caunians claimed to have come from Crete to Asia Minor, and the Lycians likewise. The Phoenicians claimed to have migrated from the Erythraean Sea (that is, southern Arabia) to the Syrian coast, whence they expanded into the Aegean islands;[6] their occupation of Thera is stated to have extended over eight generations, of which five were anterior to the Trojan War. These traditions are certainly compatible with the broad

[1] 1. 20. 1.   [2] 1. 3. 2.   [3] 4. 109. 4.   [4] 1. 8. 1.   [5] 1. 171 f.   [6] 1. 1; 7. 89. 1.

deductions based on the archaeological evidence. Thus the Pelasgians may be represented for us by the Neolithic culture of Thessaly; the Carians, Tyrseni, and Leleges by the Early Helladic and Early Cycladic peoples; and the Caunians and Lycians by a diaspora from Crete after the sack of Cnossus. Recent excavation has revealed the presence of settlements at Byblus and Ugarit on the coast of Syria which are marked by a culture akin to the later Phoenician culture. Archaeologically the first coming of the Phoenicians to the Syrian coast has been dated to the middle of the third millennium, and this accords with the Phoenician dating of their arrival at Tyre to *c.* 2700. The arrival of Phoenicians at Thera and Cadmus at Thebes *c.* 1350 is supported by the cylinder-seals of King Burraburrias II (1367–1346), found in the palace at Thebes.[1]

Surviving traditions of the movements of the Greek-speaking peoples are mainly concerned with the period after the Trojan War. But Herodotus has preserved one interesting example of earlier folk-movement.[2] The Dorians, in a series of migrations, had settled in the areas of Phthiotis in south Thessaly, then of Histiaeotis below the mountains Ossa and Olympus, and then of Mt. Pindus where they were called 'Makednoi'. From there they moved to Dryopis between Malis and Phocis. Then, after the Trojan War, they penetrated into the Peloponnese. During the penultimate stage, in or near Dryopis, they joined forces with an Achaean clan, the Heracleidae, in an attempt to enter the Peloponnese in the generation before the Trojan War. The attempt failed; for Hyllus, their champion, was slain in single combat by Echemus, the champion of the Achaeans, Ionians, and Arcadians who then held the Peloponnese.

This account is credible; it shows a single tribe, the Dorians proper, being displaced from Thessaly and then pursuing a pastoral life in south-west Macedonia, Epirus, and Dryopis. When Mycenaean power was declining, they began to press southwards during the generation before the Trojan War. Their early migrations are defined by Herodotus in genealogical terms, the first stage being in the reign of Deucalion and the second in that of Dorus, son of Hellen. Now the traditional genealogies contain names of two kinds, personal names appropriate to individuals and eponymous names of a tribe or family. The latter may have once belonged to individuals; but they mark the formation of the tribe and probably lie beyond the range of chronological reckoning. This type of genealogical datum is valuable for its associating of related tribes and for its connexion with geographical localities. Thus the tradition, preserved by Hesiod,[3] that in Thessaly Deucalion's son, Hellen, begat Dorus, Xouthus (father of Ion), and Aeolus, places the origin of the Greek-speaking peoples in Thessaly; and it asserts the interrelationship of the Dorian, Ionian, and Aeolian branches of the Greek race.

Similarly, in the case of Troy, Homer[4] preserves the genealogy in which Dardanus, Tros, and Ilus figure as eponyms of the Dardanoi, Troes, and

[1] 2. 44; 4. 147. See Appendix 2.   [2] 1. 56; 9. 26.   [3] Hes. *Fr.* 7.   [4] *Il.* 20. 215.

Ilioi before the time when Laomedon built and fortified Troy (probably Troy VII A, *c.* 1300). This genealogy associates with Troy the peoples who appear in fourteenth-century Hittite records as 'Dardenui' and 'Iliunna' and may be presumed to be inhabitants of 'Taroisa'.

While the eponymous ancestor or the god at the head of a genealogy marks the back-stop of family tradition, the succeeding names in the pedigree of a dynasty may well be historical. The longest genealogies are located in Argos, Athens, Thebes, and Orchomenus, where archaeology reveals early settlements of Greek-speaking peoples. Of these, two derive from overseas: Epaphus founding a dynasty at Argos from Egypt nine generations before the Trojan War, and Cadmus founding a dynasty at Thebes from Phoenicia five generations before the Trojan War. If we assume an average of thirty years for a generation, these dynasties were founded very approximately *c.* 1470 and *c.* 1350, the former in the settled period before the sack of Cnossus and the latter after the collapse of Cretan sea-power. Although Epaphus and Cadmus were of foreign extraction, they seem not to have brought foreign peoples into Greece, and to have become hellenized themselves. The Argive dynasty includes the founders of Tiryns and Mycenae, Proetus *c.* 1350 and Perseus *c.* 1290. The dynasty of Athens is autochthonous; those of Orchomenus, Corinth, and Pylus derive their ancestors (Minyas, Sisyphus, and Neleus) from Thessaly *c.* 1380, 1320, and 1280. As these genealogies formed a background in the Homeric poems, they represented only fragmentary memories of the period before the Trojan War. For by 1200 these dynasties had mostly ceased to hold power.

On the other hand, the Homeric poems contain a number of short genealogies which represent the reigning dynasties at the time of the Trojan War. As the dynasties intermarried, they form a consistent framework, which has a claim to be historical. They show that the thirteenth century was a troubled period, in which new dynasties seized the chief centres of Mycenaean civilization, frequently marrying into the previous dynasty. Thus Tydeus, coming from Aetolia, won the throne of Argos; Atreus, whose father Pelops came from Asia, won the throne of Mycenae and his son Menelaus that of Sparta; Neleus, who came from Thessaly, won the throne of Pylus; and the dynasties of Achilles, Ajax, Idomeneus, and Odysseus reach back only two generations before the Trojan War. It is from these dynasties, established in the period *c.* 1280–1230, that the 'Heroic Age' of the Homeric poems takes its origin. Their figures are clear and defined, but their forerunners—Perseus, Minos, Sisyphus—are hazy and enveloped in the mists of folk-lore.

§ 5. *The Homeric poems and the Mycenaean background*

HESIOD interposed between the age of bronze and the age of iron 'a divine race of heroes, of whom a part were destroyed by evil war and dread battle, some beneath the walls of seven-gated Thebes in the land of Cadmus as they fought for the flocks of Oedipus, others at Troy whither they were borne on ships over the great gulf of the sea'.[1] Their exploits, falling in the period 1250–1150, formed the subject both of the epic saga, which reached its final form probably in the ninth and following centuries, and of Attic drama in the fifth century. The epics are assigned to three main cycles: the Theban cycle, covering the two generations before the Trojan war; the cycle of Heracles; and the Trojan cycle, which included the aftermath of the Trojan war. The analogy of Heroic Ages in other civilizations suggests that such ages were transitory, lasting only for three or four generations; that they originated in the introduction of less cultured but more virile warriors into a developed but declining civilization; and that they are marked by aggressive and pre-datory warfare, in which the princely class of warriors breaks away from the traditional bonds of national or tribal loyalties. In Greece the Heroic Age marks the final phase of the decline of the great Bronze Age civilization of the Aegean world. It may therefore have little affinity with the outlook of the preceding period, of which archaeology has revealed such noble remains. Thus the Homeric heroes may have been illiterate, whereas writing was em-ployed for drawing up inventories at Mycenaean palace-sites before and during the period of the Heroic Age. Likewise the heroes practised crema-tion, whereas the settled peoples of the Bronze Age inhumed their dead. In some cases the heroes used weapons which were no longer in vogue during the late Mycenaean period. So, too, their freshness of spirit and their freedom from social or religious restraint are the mark of newcomers rather than of the leaders of a slowly matured and ripe civilization.

The comparative study of heroic ages has shed light also upon the genesis and development of epic poetry. It appears to originate under the troubled conditions of a heroic age as oral poetry, composed and transmitted by min-strels, even though the art of writing survived from an earlier civilization. The earlier epic lays are usually short in length and deal with the exploits of one or more heroes. The later lays develop in length and in technique, are recited as court poetry, and deal with leaders of the princely class both male and female. In this later stage of epic poetry the interest of the poet tends to shift from the exploits of the heroes to the study of heroic character, and non-heroic themes such as religion or manticism or matters of general rather than personal scope may begin to intrude. Of Greek epic poetry the short lays, except the *Shield of Heracles*, are known to us only from late summaries of their contents. The *Iliad* and the *Odyssey* are elaborate lays of the later type and stand at the end of a long period of development; and most epics of the Hesiodic school are concerned with non-heroic themes. Although the short and the long lays, which have survived in full or in summarized form, were composed some centuries after the end of the Heroic Age, they appear to be derived from similar lays contemporary with the Heroic Age (such as Phemius is represented as reciting at the court of Ithaca);[2] for not only is the dialect of the epic language partly transmitted, as we have seen, from the

[1] Hes. *Op.* 161 f.   [2] *Od.* 1. 325 f.; 8. 62 f.

Mycenaean period but also the setting portrayed in the epic poems is true of the Mycenaean world and not of the subsequent age.

Clearly some parts of the *Iliad* and *Odyssey* are unhistorical, in that super-human exploits, divine intervention, folk-tales, and imaginary wanderings have been introduced by the epic poet. But the general situation and the civilization portrayed in the poems are historical. Certain objects which are described in the poems have been shown by the results of excavation to be characteristic of the Mycenaean age and to be absent in the early Iron Age. Such are the boar's-tusk helmet of Meriones,[1] the metal-inlay of Achilles' shield, the cup of Nestor, the cyanos-frieze in Alcinous' palace, and the spearhead of beaten bronze-sheet secured with a ring.[2] The same is true of such general usages in the poems as the predominance of bronze weapons, the lay-out of houses and palaces, the abundance of gold and ivory, and the use of the tower-shield. Although many of these examples are typical of the Late Bronze Age, certain aspects of the poems are particularly apposite to the period 1250–1150: the occurrence of iron tools and the knowledge of different methods of treating iron, the wearing of the fibula-brooch, the pre-dominance of the round shield, the corslet, and the helmet, and the use of the cutting as well as the thrusting sword. On the other hand, a few objects which are described in the poems are best paralleled by objects found usually, but not exclusively, in contexts later than the period 1250–1150: Odysseus' elaborate clasp, the snake on the cuirass sent by the King of Cyprus, the bear on the baldric of Heracles, and the temples built by Chryses and by Nausi-thous.[3] These may be anachronisms added by the poet; but it should be remembered that the participants in the Trojan War came from many parts of the Aegean world and that the evidence of archaeology is far from complete.

In the Homeric poems the earth is conceived as a flat body floating upon water. It is encircled by the stream of Ocean, where the sun has his rising and his setting. At the northern limits of the earth the Cimmerians live in mist and darkness, and the Laestrygonians shepherd their flocks during the long hours of daylight; at its southern limits the Pygmies live near Ocean's stream, whither the cranes migrate to escape the winter storms.[4] This idea of the world was not derived from the limited knowledge of the eastern Mediter-ranean which might have been gained during the early Iron Age. Rather it springs from acquaintance with the oceans beyond the Mediterranean Sea—the Atlantic, the Black Sea, and the Red Sea—an acquaintance which might well have been won by Minoan and Mycenaean sailors during the acme of the Bronze Age.

In the *Odyssey* the limits of the known world have already shrunk. Although the Sikeloi and Sikanie (Sicily) are mentioned, the Mediterranean

[1] *Il.* 10. 261.   [2] *Il.* 6. 320.
[3] *Od.* 19. 226; *Il.* 11. 20; *Od.* 11. 610; *Il.* 1. 39; *Od.* 6. 10.
[4] *Od.* 11. 14; 10. 82; *Il.* 3. 3; Hes. *Fr.* 43ᵃ, 45.

Sea west of Ithaca and Leucas is an area of fantasy. In the south Menelaus visits Cyprus, Phoenicia, Sidon, Egypt, Ethiopia, and Libya, and the wealth of Egyptian Thebes is remembered. But the Egyptian coast is visited rather for raids than peaceful intercourse, and the position of Pharos off the coast is incorrectly described.[1] This more limited knowledge and these troubled conditions correspond closely with the situation in the late thirteenth century, when contact with the Mycenaean settlements in Sicily had been cut and when a series of raids were delivered on the Delta. The Homeric heroes were warriors and raiders; thus Odysseus was deeply insulted when he was likened to a trader 'mindful of his cargo and alert for greedy gain'.[2] The carrying trade was in the hands of the Phoenicians. They traffic with Lemnos, voyage to Ithaca and (via Crete) to Libya, and are visited by the Taphians, a western people, who trade in precious metals with Temese (in Italy).[3] The Phoenicians usually go under the name 'Sidonians'; as Sidon was destroyed *c.* 1190 and thereafter Tyre outstripped Sidon in importance, it is probable that the Homeric account is based on the situation which existed before 1190.

Although the *Iliad* commences with the ninth year of the war, catalogues of the Achaean ship-captains and Trojan contingents which assembled at the beginning of the war are inserted in the second book of the poem. They serve no dramatic purpose where they stand. They were evidently traditional elements of the epic saga which were so important to the poet and his hearers that they had to be included. We may therefore assume that the catalogues were believed to describe a historical situation.

In the Trojan catalogue Priam, King of Troy, rules both sides of the Hellespont, and also the Asiatic coast from Mt. Ida to the south-east corner of the Propontis. His European allies extend as far as the Axius valley in Macedonia; his Asiatic allies as far as the Halizones in the north-east and as far as some isolated peoples in the areas of Sardis, Miletus, and Lycia in the south. The extent of Priam's realm and alliances is consistent with the wealth of Troy VII A (*c.* 1300–1200), but not at all with the poverty of its successors. Moreover, a number of names in the Trojan catalogue recur in Hittite and Egyptian documents of the fourteenth and thirteenth centuries: Ilioi (Iliunna), Dardanoi (Dardenui), Lukie and Lukioi (Luka), Pedasos (Pidasa), Asios (Asuva), Musoi (Musa), while Troia (Taroisa), Lesbos (Lazpa), and Kilikes (Kilikisha) occur elsewhere in the *Iliad*. Even the distant Halizones reappear in a seventh-century inscription as the 'Khalitu'. We are told that the father of old Priam, Laomedon, built the walls of Troy, and this refers to Troy VII A, built *c.* 1300. In the Trojan realm the sack of Lesbos and the later sack of Troy are confirmed by the excavations at Thermí and at Troy as dating to *c.* 1200. The fortified Mycenaean settlement at Miletus and settlements at sites in Cilicia were destroyed *c.* 1200. The leaders from Lycia, Sarpedon and Glaucus, are described as Achaeans, whose grandfather

---

[1] *Od.* 4. 83; *Il.* 9. 382; *Od.* 4, 354; 14. 258; 17. 427.
[2] *Od.* 8. 163.   [3] *Il.* 23. 744; *Od.* 14. 295 f.; 1. 184.

Bellerophon came from the Peloponnese.[1] Traces of Achaean activity in southern Asia Minor appear in the Aeolic-Arcadian dialect of Pamphylia; in the tradition preserved by Herodotus that the people of Cilicia were once called 'Hypachaeans'; and probably in the names 'Ahhiyava' and 'Akaiwasha' in Hittite and Egyptian records of the fourteenth and thirteenth centuries, and in the 'Danuna' who figure in eighth-century records at Karatepe in Cilicia.

The conclusion is unavoidable that the Trojan catalogue describes an historical situation which existed in the thirteenth century and not subsequently; in other words, Homer derived his Trojan catalogue from a catalogue composed during or soon after the Trojan War. It is a genuine record of Bronze Age conditions.

The case for the Achaean catalogue is no less strong. The distribution of power is quite unlike that of the archaic and classical periods. Mycenae, Tiryns, and Pylus are represented as the capitals of great states; later they became mere hamlets. It is therefore not a reflection of conditions in the Iron Age. Nor is it imaginary; for archaeological discoveries have proved beyond doubt that it corresponds in scope and in detail with the historical conditions of the Late Bronze Age. If we turn to the detailed contents of the catalogue, we can date its original composition to the generation of the Trojan War. For example, the lower town of Thebes (Hypothebai) is named in place of Thebes itself, which was destroyed by the expedition of the Epigoni one generation before the Trojan War;[2] and Tlepolemus, who leads his ships to Troy, is himself the founder of a new dynasty in Rhodes. Thus the Achaean catalogue of the *Iliad* is firmly based on an earlier lay which was composed during or soon after the Trojan War to describe the conditions of the time.

Some scholars have maintained that parts of the catalogue have been interpolated or altered by interested parties during the archaic and classical periods. The motive for such interpolation is not in dispute. When later Greek statesmen claimed the territory of their neighbours, they appealed to the catalogue with as much confidence as one might appeal to the Domesday Book. Yet this very confidence indicates that the Greeks did not believe it to be corrupted by interpolation. Moreover, the coincidence of the catalogue with the discoveries of archaeology shows that the catalogue has not suffered any widespread alteration; and the insignificance of Ionian Athens, of Dorian peoples, and even of Aeolians as such proves the absence of any considerable interpolation. One is apt to forget the great body of epic saga and of local legends which survived into classical times from the Bronze Age; these constituted many anchors, which prevented the catalogue, as enshrined in the *Iliad*, from drifting into the hands of the interpolator. Athens affords a good example. By virtue of her political and literary eminence she was uniquely placed for the game of interpolation. But her local legends proclaimed that her greatness lay in the generation of Theseus, and not in that of the Trojan

---

[1] *Il.* 6. 150 f.   [2] For the archaeological date see *AAA* 1970. 3. 327.

War. It was only when legend had lost its authority that Euripides, in the *Iphigeneia in Aulide*, could replace Homer's Menestheus, commander of Athens, by a son of Theseus and introduce other points in the interest of Athens; even so, these innovations never entered the Homeric catalogue. The passages athetized by Alexandrian scholars do not concern points of political significance, and the single line (said to have been interpolated by Solon or Peisistratus), which ranges the ships of Salamis alongside those of Athens,[1] did not figure at all in the texts of the Alexandrian scholars. This line was evidently a later interpolation like three lines in the Trojan catalogue.[2]

As a document of the Late Bronze Age, the Achaean catalogue contains interesting information. There is a wide variety in the organization and size of the contingents, and these represent the political units of the time. The contingent which came from eleven towns but was commanded by one man, Agamemnon, came from a well-knit realm; but the contingent of Buprasium and Elis, serving under four commanders, was drawn from a looser political organization. Athens provided only one contingent of fifty ships, while Thessaly provided nine contingents, totalling 280 ships. Such a disparity in strength between Athens and Thessaly, even in terms of landpower, was hardly found again until the Lamian War, when Athens had lost her vigour of the preceding centuries. The names of the peoples who provide the contingents are indicative of different stages of political development. 'Athenians', 'Cretans', and 'Rhodians', being named after a city or island, have become identified by lapse of time with their place of residence and act as a single people. Some peoples have no collective name at all; the followers, for instance, of Agamemnon, Diomede, or Protesilaus seem to owe their association only to the personality of a dynast and are too ephemeral to have evolved a common name. Other peoples are named as tribes, and their unity is dependent on race, not on locality.

These differences illustrate the diversity within the Mycenaean world, a diversity which is also shown elsewhere in the *Iliad* by the variety of armature and of genealogies in the Achaean army and its commanders.

The least civilized groups are formed by the tribal contingents. Boiotoi, Phoceeis, Lokroi, Abantes, Aitoloi, Enienes, Peraiboi, Magnetes, Myrmidones, Hellenes, and Akhaioi were located in central and north Greece; they occupied hilly and mountainous areas, with the exception of the Boiotoi who were recent invaders of the Boeotian plains. In the Peloponnese the Arkades took their name from mountainous Arcadia, the Epeioi occupied Elis and Doulikhion (Leucas) and the Kephallenes the southern Ionian islands with part of the adjacent mainland. The more advanced element is found in the Thessalian plain and in the areas which possess the full Mediterranean climate; there the population was named by town or island and not by tribe—Athenaioi, Argeioi, Pylioi, Kretes, Rhodioi, &c.—and more settled conditions of life are indicated by the numerous towns which are mentioned (23 in

[1] *Il.* 2. 558.   [2] *Il.* 2. 853–5.

the Thessalian plain, 31 in the Boeotian plain, 20 in the north-eastern Peloponnese, and 18 in the southern Peloponnese, while Crete is the island of a hundred towns). As excavation has shown, Attica also had its towns in Mycenaean times; but Athens alone is mentioned, 'the community of great-hearted Erechtheus', who is dated genealogically to *c.* 1350. This entry suggests that Athens had established a supremacy over the neighbouring towns to a greater extent than either Mycenae or Argos had done.

Although the contingents were diverse and individual, the army went under three general names—Akhaioi, Danaoi, and Argeioi. The most common term was Akhaioi. One of the three tribes led by Achilles (and in the *Odyssey* a tribe in Crete) was called 'Akhaioi',[1] but so unimportant a tribe cannot have given its name to the whole army. The term 'Akhaioi' seems rather to have been a traditional one harking back to the days when the Hittite kings had had diplomatic relations with the king of 'Ahhiyava'. The catalogue uses the term Danaoi; this may derive from the eponymous Danaus, whose dynasty at Argos was founded in the fifteenth century. The term Argeioi may derive from the same dynasty, or from the leadership imposed by Adrastus of Argos in the recent war of the Epigoni against Thebes. The order followed by the catalogue may also be traditional. The sequence is central Greece (Boeotia leading), the Peloponnese (Argos leading), the western isles and Aetolia (Dulichium leading), the south-eastern isles (Crete leading), and north-east Greece (the realm of Achilles leading). This grouping and the leading position in each group do not correspond with the relative strength and importance of the areas in the catalogue; they may reflect the spread of Mycenaean civilization or the importance of individual areas at an earlier period than the late thirteenth century, such as the period of the Labdacids before the fall of Oedipus.

Some degree of unity was imposed upon the army by Agamemnon's general command. He claimed a hereditary suzerainty 'to rule over many islands and all Argos';[2] this was symbolized by the divine sceptre of Pelops, handed down through the hands of Thyestes and Atreus to Agamemnon. Whether this wide suzerainty was exercised by Pelops, whose name survived in the name of the peninsula 'Peloponnesos', or by Atreus who probably appears in Hittite records as 'Attarissiyas' raiding Caria and Cyprus, the actual realm of Agamemnon included only Mycenae, Corinthia, and Achaea; for within the previous generation Adrastus and Tydeus had been independent rulers of Argos.[3] The superiority of Agamemnon's power depended rather on his contingents in Arcadia (to which he supplied ships) and in his brother Menelaus' rule over Lacedaemon; even so he could not order the other kingdoms to send contingents but either appealed in person or sent friendly kings as envoys to ask for aid.[4] Thus the forces for unity in the Greece of the *Iliad* are weak. The traditional suzerainties, once exercised by Thebes, Mycenae, and Argos, had broken down, while new and shifting

[1] *Il.* 2. 684; *Od.* 19. 175.   [2] *Il.* 2. 101 f.   [3] *Il.* 4. 376.   [4] *Il.* 11. 781 f.; 4. 376.

dynasties have entered many parts of the Greek world, and invading tribes such as the Boiotoi had occupied rich areas of the mainland. The Achaean catalogue depicts a world which stands already in the twilight between the long day of Bronze Age civilization and the darkness of the age of migrations.

The epic saga is concerned primarily with the members of the princely class. They were individualistic in outlook, and stood above many of the restraints which were normal in contemporary society. In the struggle for power they committed murder even within their own families, and many of them paid little heed to the claims of 'phratry' or 'tribe'. But the society in which they lived was certainly organized on a more conservative system. Nestor, the representative of an older generation, told Agamemnon to muster the host before Troy by phratry and tribe, 'that phratry may aid phratry and tribes tribes'. The commoners, rather than the princes, were loyal members of these 'brotherhoods' (phratries), which were based on kinship and formed together into tribes. Anyone who was not a member of a brotherhood (*aphretor*) was an outcast from society. He could not become a member of a tribe or attend an Assembly.

Anyone who entered this society from outside was without honour or right therein, unless he was a *demiourgos*, 'a worker for the public', such as a seer, doctor, shipbuilder, or minstrel.[1] There is no indication of any serf class in society; the term *thetes* is derived from an occupation, namely, working for hire on another's land. Slaves, however, were won in war or bought in the market for use in the home; in the palace of Odysseus male and female slaves numbered well over fifty. Family religion centred round the hearth (*hestia*), which occupied the central position in the Megaron at Mycenae and elsewhere, and family rights were controlled by the elders, who were deeply respected. Thus an outcast was defined as being 'without phratry, hearth or rights'.[2] There is no indication in the Homeric poems of hero-worship within the family; yet the royal dynasty of the shaft-graves at Mycenae seems to have received worship from its successors.

The town was a social rather than a political entity. Groups of towns with their territories were in the gift of the king, to reward a faithful follower,[3] even as the great king of Persia in later times rewarded Themistocles. The word *polis* was used of the high-town or citadel, on which the palace was set, while the open town was the *asty*; and sometimes the part stood for the whole in common usage. All political power was concentrated in the hands of the king. He was convener and leader of the Council and of the Assembly; he might consult them, but he alone decided. In war he exacted service, exercised command, and took the lion's share of the spoil; in peace he presided at the sacrifice and at the feast, and he was endowed with sacred lands. Although there was no appeal against his judgements, the king had obligations towards his people. As the shepherd of his people, he had to protect their wellbeing. If a king died and his son was a minor, the succession passed

---

[1] *Il.* 9. 648; *Od.* 17. 383 f.   [2] *Il.* 9. 63.   [3] *Il.* 9. 144 f.; 480 f.; *Od.* 4. 174 f.

through the queen to a second husband. As president of the banquet, the king had to give wine to the elders who formed his Council and to his retinue of companions, squires, and heralds.

The Councillors, too, had their rights. They enjoyed the title of 'elders' or of 'counsel-giving kings'; when they were convened as the Council in the king's megaron, their opinions were respected and they joined the king in receiving embassies and in addressing the Assembly. They ratified treaties with the 'oath of the elders'; they were arbiters in the blood feud; and they administered justice in the place of Assembly.[1] The elders were often kings in their own right; for they were probably the heads of phratries or family groups. The people (*demos*) were convened by the king as an Assembly in the assembly-place (*agora*) and as the army in time of war; they listened to the king and the elders, who spoke on the items of agenda—plagues, quarrels, division of spoil, policy, treaties, and so forth—but they had no vote and expressed their wishes only by silence or applause.[2] For a commoner like Thersites to speak was irregular. In the absence of any popular rights insurrection was a present danger.[3] This political system was maintained in the army before Troy, and in Troy, Ithaca, and Pylus.

In the *Odyssey* a fuller description was given of the Phaeacian state, which probably represented an ideal Ionian state. The king was attended by twelve kings who were 'sceptre-bearing' and 'counsel-giving' and met in the Hall of Thrones. In the place of assembly the 'elders', or 'leaders and rulers of the Phaeacian people' were addressed by the king, while the people watched. It is possible that the twelve 'sceptre-bearing' kings were the heads of the twelve phratries into which the four tribes of an Ionic state divided, and that the 'elders' were the heads of the constituent *gene* or family groups. In the *Iliad* the Athenians centring round Athens and Athena formed a closer unity than the people of Agamemnon or of Diomede. They were referred to as 'Iaones of the trailing robes', and they afford us an example of an Ionian state at the time of the Trojan War.[4] Moreover, the Athenians of the classical period preserved local traditions which reached back into the Bronze Age. This survival of tradition is natural; for the Athenians escaped the displacement which was the fate of most other Bronze Age peoples after the sack of Troy. Thucydides states that under the early kings there were separate settlements in Attica, each with its own council-hall and magistrates, which deliberated independently except in time of crisis and even fought against one another. Such settlements of the Mycenaean age are known, for instance, at Eleusis, Aphidna, Brauron, and Thoricus. In the reign of Theseus (that is *c.* 1250) the separate council-halls and magistracies were abolished, and one community was formed under a single council-hall and magistracy; from the time of Theseus onwards a state festival in memory of the 'living-together' was held in honour of the goddess Athena.[5] The unifying of Attica under one govern-

[1] *Il.* 22. 119; 18. 497; 1. 238; 16. 385 f.   [2] *Od.* 2. 6 f.
[3] *Il.* 2. 198; 12. 212; *Od.* 3. 137 f.; 24. 420 f.   [4] *Il.* 2. 546 f.; 13. 685.   [5] Th. 2. 15.

ment did not entail any large-scale movement of peoples to Athens from the countryside, where they maintained their traditional shrines and tombs and estates; but Attica had become one *polis*, that is one state in which the government was centralized at Athens and the citizens took their name from Athens.

Some early traditions of Attica are preserved in Aristotle's *Constitution of Athens*.[1] Before and after the time of Theseus the inhabitants of Attica were divided into four tribes, each under a tribal king; the tribes were divided each into three phratries, and each phratry into thirty family groups (*gene*), of which the members were styled *gennetai*. The community consisted of 'tillers of the soil' (*georgoi*) and 'workers for the public' (*demiourgoi*)—two groups defined by their occupations. Indeed the Athenian state of Theseus resembled the Phaeacian state; for the twelve phratriarchs corresponded to the twelve 'sceptre-bearing kings' and the heads of the gene to the 'elders'. There is thus good reason to believe that Athens derived not only her worship of Athena on the Acropolis but also the unification of Attica, as celebrated in the festival of 'living-together', from the Bronze Age period.

Another tradition of great antiquity ascribed to Minos of Crete the first law-giving or constitution-drafting.[2] The early authors followed Homer in regarding Minos as a historical person, who founded a dynasty at Cnossus two generations before the Trojan War. Herodotus expressly dated Minos to that generation and related his raids and his death in Sicily, and Thucydides implicitly referred to the same Minos in describing his seapower and his conquest of the islands.[3] The legend, that Athens once paid tribute of seven youths and seven maids to Minos, but was freed from this obligation when Theseus slew the Minotaur, is dated by the participation of Theseus to this same period. Some have seen in Minos a Cretan king of the fifteenth century and in the slaying of the Minotaur the sack of Cnossus *c.* 1400. But Greek saga contains no detailed memory of so remote a period, and the whole context of these traditions places them firmly in the thirteenth century. The name itself may have been a hereditary title from early times. But the Minos of Homer, Thucydides, and Herodotus is a Greek king who ruled in Crete. His lack of human ancestry implies that he had come from elsewhere to establish his dynasty. In the *Odyssey* the island of Crete was described as set in the midst of the wine-dark sea: 'there there is a diversity of tongues; therein are Akhaioi, great-hearted Eteokretes, Kudones, Doriees *trikhaikes*, and divine Pelasgoi; there is Knosos, a great city, where Minos ruled for spans of nine years in communion with great Zeus, Minos father of my father, great-hearted Deukalion'.[4] Of the peoples in Crete the Eteokretes were probably descendants of the 'Minoan' population, being of pre-Hellenic stock like the Kudones and Pelasgoi. The Akhaioi may be descendants of the first Greek-speaking people who entered the island, and the Doriees perhaps came with Minos in the thirteenth century. The epithet *trikhaikes*, in this

[1] Ar. *Ath.* 41, 2; *fr.* 5.   [2] Archil. *fr. ap.* Heraclid. Pont 3. (2); Ar. *Pol.* 1271[b].
[3] Th. 1. 4; Hdt. 1. 171; 7. 170.   [4] *Od.* 19. 175.

passage, was interpreted by Hesiod as meaning 'threefold' and understood as referring to their threefold division of the land,[1] which was probably due to the normal division of the Dorians into three tribes, Hylleis, Dymanes, and Pamphyloi. Another example of division into three tribes occurs at Rhodes where Tlepolemus, beloved of Zeus, ruled as a Heraclid,[2] and his followers, like those of other Heraclids, were probably Dorians, who overlaid the Achaean settlement in Rhodes as they had done in Crete. During the dark age the Dorians retained control of Crete, as the Ionians did of Attica. This continuity made it possible for some traditions of the Bronze Age legislators, Minos and Theseus, to be preserved into classical times.

The divine stage in the *Iliad* is a reflection of the human world. Zeus the King exercises as uneasy a suzerainty over the gods as Agamemnon does over his peers. They, too, have their individual rights, they sit in council, and they feast in the Great Hall of Zeus. The gods, like the princely class of heroes, are international or rather non-national. They demand service in the guise of ritual sacrifice from mankind; and they dispense success and failure to men as much from reasons of personal caprice as from any respect for justice. Their anthropomorphism is complete. They love, quarrel, and fight like men, they beget children in wedlock with women, and they suffer the indignities to which human flesh is exposed. Their power is greater than human power: their will controls human qualities and their intervention prompts human action. But the action of the gods is not co-ordinated, and their power is not omnivalent. Fate stands dimly in the background of divine and human life; it determines the life-span of man, his birth and his death, which even gods cannot avert.

The Homeric hero has no divinely revealed code of behaviour. He knows that he must respect the gods, his own parents, and the suppliants and strangers, whom Zeus himself protects. For the rest he follows his own conception of manliness, of which courage and wisdom are the cardinal virtues, and his highest reward is to earn renown among men. When Achilles stands victorious over the body of Hector, he cries out, 'Die—yet shall I meet my fate, whenever it pleases Zeus and the other immortal gods to determine'.[3] Death ends this life of glorious action. Once the body is burned or buried, the soul passes powerless into the underworld. Such concepts of divine and human nature seem to spring from the conditions of the Heroic Age. They differ from later thought and practice, in which spirits, demons, taboos, and cults of the dead play a part; and, however much may have been added to the epic saga by Homer in delicacy of feeling and in subtlety of character-drawing, it is most probable that he faithfully transmitted the fundamental beliefs of the Heroic Age.

Any attempt to discover elements of earlier religious belief, which may lie behind the civilization depicted in the Homeric poems, is extremely hazardous. In the Heroic Age itself religious practice probably varied in different classes of society and in different areas of the Aegean. While earlier practices

---

[1] Hes. *Fr.* 191.   [2] *Il.* 2. 668.   [3] *Il.* 22. 365.

may survive in the Homeric poems, we cannot exclude the possibility that such non-heroic themes as the visit of Odysseus to the underworld are later additions to the body of epic saga. Nevertheless, some tentative conclusions can be reached. The stock epithets 'owl-eyed' and 'cow-eyed' suggest that the goddesses Athena and Hera were associated or identified in earlier belief with the owl and the cow; such identifications are explicit in early Greek mythology, which derives to a great degree from the Minoan and the Mycenaean world. The oak tree of Zeus at Dodona and at Troy may recall worship of a deity represented in the form of a tree. Traces of sun-worship may survive in the Homeric account of the island and the herds sacred to Helios, the sun. Sacrifice is made to Helios, Ge, and Zeus in one passage which may represent a primitive worship of the sun, the earth, and the sky.[1]

Some of the gods have local associations; for example, Hera with Argos, Sparta, and Mycenae, Athena with Athens and Troy, Poseidon with Aegae, Hephaestus with Lemnos, Aphrodite with Paphus in Cyprus, and Ares with Thrace. Local cults also are mentioned, such as that of Pelasgic Zeus at Dodona, where the priests sleeping on the ground with unwashed feet interpret the oracles of the god.[2] These reflect the local origins of the gods, who are universally recognized in the Homeric poems; and the association of Zeus with Olympus and Dodona in Greece and with Ida in the Troad may indicate that the father of the gods was introduced by invading peoples from central Europe. The customs which attend the cremation of the Homeric hero include the burning of his weapons, the offering of hair and of gifts, lamentation, games, and banquets. In the Homeric poems these are marks of honour to the dead, but they survive from an age when the dead man was believed to need sustenance in the after-life and his spirit had to be placated, perhaps by human sacrifice as at the funeral of Patroclus.[3] These survivals serve to remind us that the religion of the Heroic Age is, like most religions, a synthesis of earlier beliefs. In its humanism and in its universality it rose superior to earlier beliefs of the Bronze Age. And, because it was essentially Greek in spirit, it proved an inspiration to the Greek peoples, when they emerged from the dark centuries of the early Iron Age. Of all the legacies bequeathed by the civilization of the Bronze Age the epic saga is paramount in beauty and in significance.

[1] *Od.* 12. 127 f.; *Il.* 3. 103.   [2] *Il.* 16. 233.   [3] *Il.* 23. 175.

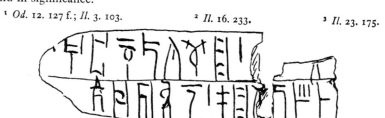

Clay tablet from Cnossus *c.* 1400 in Mycenaean Script deciphered as follows (*DMG* nr. 208): a-ta-na-po-ti-ni-ja 1 . . . e-nu-wa-ri-jo 1 pa-ja-wo [ne? 1] po-se-do [o-ne 1?] 'To Mistress Athena . . . to Enyalios, to Paian, to Poseidon' (see pp. 33 and 55)

CHAPTER 3

The Great Migrations

§ 1. *Invasions of the mainland*

THE migrations had begun on a small scale a century or more before the fall of Troy. The Trojans and the Achaeans had themselves broken their way into the circle of civilized Mediterranean powers, and they had proved unruly guardians of the peace. Their own realms had in turn been penetrated by Phrygians in the Hellespontine region, by Dorians in Crete and Rhodes, and by Boeotians in central Greece. On the mainland the generation of the Trojan War was marked by violence; for the outer town of Mycenae was burnt and the palace at Pylus was destroyed. The fall of Troy, however, was fraught with disastrous and far-reaching consequences. It is true that another city of Troy rose impoverished upon the ashes of Priam's city; but the military coalition, which under his leadership had repelled the invading Amazons at the Sangarius river,[1] was swept away for ever. The narrow gateway into Europe and Asia was now unguarded, and barbarian hordes immediately surged forward. A further influx of Phrygians from Thrace destroyed the ancient empire of the Hittites and occupied the central plains of Asia Minor. Lydia was overrun, and a new dynasty, claiming descent from Heracles, established itself.[2] The barbarian incursion drove forward the peoples of the coast and islands, who ravaged the prosperous cities in their path, such as Mersin, Tarsus, Ugarit, and Sidon, and pillaged the island of Cyprus. The Philistines seized and occupied the coast of Palestine. Repeated raids were delivered against the Delta of Egypt, and by the close of the twelfth century the Egyptian kingdom was cut off from the Mediterranean coast.

The devastation of the Near East in the decades after the fall of Troy brought worsening conditions to the Aegean islands and the Greek mainland. Here violence and *stasis* were widespread,[3] before migrating peoples broke into the peninsula *c.* 1150. Then central Macedonia, formerly protected by the western wing of Priam's coalition, was invaded by barbarians who penetrated into Epirus and Thessaly. Their attack initiated a great wave of migrations, which repeopled most of the Greek peninsula and drove forth many of the previous inhabitants. Thus throughout the Aegean area the process began which Thucydides so aptly described: 'migrations were of frequent occurrence, the several tribes readily abandoning their homes under the pressure of superior numbers.'[4] This process destroyed the civilization of the Bronze

---

[1] *Il.* 3. 184 f.   [2] Hdt. 1. 7.   [3] Th. 1. 12. 2.   [4] Th. 1. 2. 1.

Age. It resulted in three centuries of turmoil, during which even the art of writing may have died in the Greek mainland.

In periods of upheaval, when the arteries of trade are cut, the peoples of the Aegean islands and of the narrow sectors of the Asiatic coast feel the pinch of famine.[1] Poor in natural resources and dependent on the carrying trade for their livelihood, they resort to piracy or migration. At the time of the Trojan War the Achaeans and their kindred held Euboea, Aegina, and the southernmost chain of islands extending towards the south-west coast of Asia Minor. The other Aegean islands, which did not figure in the Achaean catalogue nor generally in early Greek legend, were probably occupied by Carians, Phoenicians, Leleges, Tursenoi, and Pelasgoi. The same peoples may have held parts of the coast of Asia Minor, where Lycians, Mysians, Achae-ans (in Pamphylia), and perhaps Philistines were also located. Many of these peoples appear among the raiders of the Delta: Tursha (Tursenoi), Luka (Lycians), Peleset (Philistines), Akaiwasha (Achaeans), and Denyen (Danaoi). The chaos in the eastern Mediterranean may have affected the West also; for the Meshwesh (a Libyan people) joined in the raids on the Delta.

The sea-raids were often accompanied by migrations. Some Tursenoi probably migrated to north-west Italy,[2] where they were named Etruscans by the Umbrians. Others passed through the straits of Gibraltar to found Tarshish (Tartessus) on the Atlantic coast of Spain. The Phoenicians of Tyre founded Utica, Hadrumetum, and finally Carthage on the African coast and Gades on the Spanish coast; and place-names on the African coast suggest that Carians and Mysians took part in the migrations. Trojans, too, may have settled in Chaonia[3] and at Eryx and Segesta in Sicily,[4] and landed on the coast of Latium to the south of Etruria. These peoples carried with them their skill in seafaring, trade, and art. When they had at last settled firmly in their new homes, they led a renaissance of culture in the western Mediterranean.

The returns (*nostoi*) of the Achaeans from Troy were recorded in the epic saga. During the sea-raids many chieftains with their heterogeneous follow-ing carved out new kingdoms for themselves. In Cyprus they established dynasties at Paphus, Salamis, Curium, Lapathus, and Soli, which traced their descent from leading families of Mycenaean Arcadia, Salamis, Argolis, Laconia and Attica.[5] Archaeological evidence of intrusion in the latest phase of the Bronze Age has recently been found at Sínda in central Cyprus. There they reinforced the earlier Mycenaean settlers, over whom Cinyras was king at the time of the Trojan War, and dynasties representing both waves of settlement survived into classical times, the Cinyradae at Paphus, for in-stance, and the Teucridae at Salamis.[6] On the south coast of Asia Minor Achaeans, Cilicians, and Pamphylians came from the Troad to found new settlements. The Achaean leaders, including Amphilochus of Argos, Calchas

[1] Hdt. 1. 94. 3; 7. 171. 2.　　　　　　　　　　　　　　　　　[2] Hdt. 1. 94.
[3] *FGrH* 4 (Hellanic.) F 31 and F 84; see Hammond, *Epirus*, pp. 412 f.
[4] Th. 6. 2. 3.　　[5] Hdt. 7. 90; Str. 683.　　[6] *Il.* 11. 20; Hsch. *Tamiradae*; Isoc. 3. 28.

of Mycenae, and Mopsus of Thebes, planted settlements at Phaselis, Olbia, Aspendus, Selge, Soli, Tarsus, Mallus, and on the Syrian coast at Poseidium.[1] Archaeological evidence of Mycenaean occupation at this time has appeared at Tarsus, and the eighth-century king 'Asitawandas' of Karatepe claimed descent from Mopsus. In Pamphylia, where the Aeolic-Arcadian dialect was already established, an admixture of Doric may have been due to the influx of Dorian settlers from Rhodes immediately after the Trojan War.[2] Other bands of Achaeans may have migrated to the West, where later tradition recorded settlements at Amphilochicum Argos, in south Illyria, and in south Italy.[3]

The violence of invasions in the Greek peninsula has left its mark in the archaeological evidence. The settlements of central Macedonia were destroyed by invaders, who came down the Axius valley and penetrated as far as Dodona in Epirus and the foothills of Mt. Ossa in Thessaly. The crude pottery which they brought has affinities with the pottery of the 'Lausitz' culture in the Danube valley. It appeared at this time also at Troy. Whether the invaders came from Europe or (less probably) from Asia, they broke down the northern defences of Mycenaean civilization and imparted momentum to other peoples who migrated southwards.[4] Most centres of Mycenaean power were looted and destroyed. At Mycenae all the buildings within the citadel were plundered and fired. At Tiryns the open town was razed and the ground used as a cemetery. The Mycenaean residence at Pelikáta in Ithaca became a cemetery.

The 'Lausitz' invasion and the sack of many Mycenaean centres are dated to the latter half of the twelfth century by the presence of the 'Granary' style of pottery in the burnt layers. The movement of the migrating peoples is not datable by any archaeological evidence. Its effects alone are apparent. Except at Athens and on the fringes of the Greek world in south Crete and in Cyprus, the standards of civilized life collapsed. Cities inhabited for centuries were suddenly deserted. Small settlements were made in high fastnesses, for instance in Crete, and in many fertile districts a hiatus in the archaeological evidence ensues. The intercommunication, which had been a feature of Mycenaean civilization, was completely broken and each district lived unto itself in isolation.

To the identity and origin of the migrants archaeology can offer scarcely any clue. During the dark age, which followed the first invasions, new features appeared sporadically and not synchronously. In warfare iron weapons, particularly the slashing-sword and the throwing-spear, came into vogue earliest at Athens and in Crete. The cavalryman, unknown to the epic saga, where riding was regarded as a peacetime accomplishment,[5] was important in archaic Greek warfare. The earliest portrayal of a cavalryman in Greek lands

[1] Hdt. 7. 91; *FGrH* 115 F 59, 103 (Theopompus); Str. 667 (Callinus), 672 f., 676 (Hesiod); Hdt. 3. 91.   [2] Str. 671.
[3] Th. 2. 68. 3; Paus. 5. 22. 4; Str. 263 f.   [5] *Il.* 15. 679
[4] *StGH* 36–46; Hammond, *Migrations*, pp. 135–49,

comes from Crete probably in the tenth century. Cremation of the dead was a rarity in Bronze Age Greece (occurring, for instance, at Leucas in the Middle Bronze Age, at the death of Heracles on Mt. Oeta, and at the obsequies of Achaean heroes at Troy), but it was practised regularly at some sites and not at all at others during the Early Iron Age. Athens and Crete afford the earliest examples of cremation. New types of fastenings for dress appeared.[1] Long pins, found in large numbers at Athens, were used to fasten the Doric *peplos* (a square woollen cloth folded round the body and pinned at the shoulders), which Herodotus[2] says was worn in early times by women throughout Greece and especially at Athens. Another type of fastening, the 'spectacle-fibula', which had been evolved in central Europe, was also used early in the Iron Age. In pottery the compass-drawn concentric circle as a decorative feature appeared earliest among the debris of the 'Lausitz' invaders of Macedonia and then on destroyed sites in Ithaca and Cephallenia.

From these innovations no positive conclusions can be drawn, the evidence being fragmentary and the chronology swinging with a variation of fifty years or more. Some negative conclusions are permissible. The invaders brought no distinctive painted pottery or other mark of a developed civilization. They did not take to urban life. They were probably nomadic at first, living in tents and huts, using wooden utensils, and worshipping wooden statues.[3] Their early village settlements were small. They showed no reverence for the standards of Mycenaean civilization, and therefore presumably came from outside the limits of the Mycenaean area. They must have been physically tough and ably led in order to overthrow the centres of Mycenaean power. They may have had some superior weapons, but in the arts they were inferior to those they conquered.

Greek tradition described the chief migrants as the Dorians, a Greek-speaking tribe, and their leaders as the Heracleidae, an Achaean clan descended from Heracles and living in exile. One early invasion ended in failure when Hyllus, son of Heracles, was killed in single combat at the Isthmus *c.* 1220, but Boiotoi from south-western Thessaly settled in 'Cadmeis'. Dorians settled in Crete and probably in Rhodes and the adjacent islands at this period; they were led thither by members of the Heracleidae, namely, Tlepolemus, who had been expelled from Ephyra (probably in Thesprotia), and the sons of Thessalus, who gave his name to the Thessaloi.[4] Sixty years after the sack of Troy, that is *c.* 1140, the Thessaloi, led by Heracleidae, migrated from Thesprotia in southern Epirus to enter the south-western canton of Thessaly, which was thenceforth called Thessaliotis. They ejected some Boiotoi, who migrated southwards to join the other branch of the same tribe in Cadmeis, thenceforth called Boeotia. Twenty years later (*c.* 1120) the Dorians, led by Heracleidae, migrated from Dryopis, a district of Doris, and reached the north shore of the Gulf of Corinth. Crossing thence by ship,

[1] For early examples in northern Epirus see Hammond, *Epirus*, p. 359.   [2] Hdt. 5. 87. 3.
[3] Plu. *Mor.* 478ª.   [4] Hdt. 9. 26; Th. 1. 12. 3; *Od.* 19. 177; *Il.* 2. 653 f.; 676 f.

in collusion with invaders from farther west in Aetolia, they gained a secure foothold on the north coast of the Peloponnese. After their initial success the two groups separated, the Dorians invading the Argolid and the others the northwestern area of the Peloponnese. Later still the Dorians swung north, defeated the Aeolic-speaking peoples of Corinthia, and occupied the Isthmus.[1] So far the tradition is precise and unanimous. Once the Peloponnese is invaded, the tradition ceases to be general and becomes peculiar to each locality. This change in the tradition marks the transition from the wider world of the Bronze Age to the local particularism of the Iron Age.

Before we enter the mists of the dark age which follows, we must consider the identity and the origin of the invading peoples. The Thessaloi and the Boiotoi brought their name with them. The former came from Thesprotia, and the latter from south-western Thessaly. The Dorians who invaded the Peloponnese were probably so named by the victims of the invasion. Hitherto they had been called 'Makednoi', having taken that name during their stay in northern Pindus.[2] They were now styled 'Dorieis', presumably because the first invading bands had set out from Doris, a district small in size but bordering on the Mycenaean world. On the other hand, the western group of invaders had no generic name. Led not by Heracleidae but by Aetolians of Bronze Age Aetolia, they later adopted the names of the localities in which they settled. These and further waves of invasion clearly flowed from the highland areas of north-west Greece, comprised between Doris, Thessaliotis, western Macedonia, and Thesprotia. Yet their leaders were already conversant with the sea. This is apparent from their earlier settlements in Crete, Rhodes, Nisyros, and other islands, and from the fact that in the Achaean catalogue the Boiotoi had larger ships than the Achaeans. Their seamanship may have been learnt in the gulf of Ambracia or on the western coast of Thesprotia, and it enabled them to undertake a sea-borne invasion of the Peloponnese.

In the Homeric poems there is no general name for the peninsula south of the Isthmus. The name Peloponnese, 'the island of Pelops', was probably given to it by the invading peoples. If they came by sea, they might regard the peninsula as an island; and their leaders, the Heracleidae, claimed that they were returning to win the realm of Pelops, from which the Pelopidae had expelled them. The name 'Hellēnes' came to be applied to all the invading peoples as distinct from their predecessors. In the Achaean catalogue only three tribes have a name ending in -*enes*: Enienes near Dodona, Kephallenes in the western isles and adjacent mainland, and Hellenes near Mt. Oeta. These three tribes were situated in or near north-west Greece, where in post-invasion times tribes with this ethnic termination were widespread. It is therefore probable that the Hellenes near Mt. Oeta, like the Boiotoi of Cadmeis, had come from north-west Greece in advance of the main body, and that

---

[1] Th. 1. 12. 3; Hdt. 7. 176. 4; 1. 56. 3; Tyrt. 2; Pi. *P.* 1. 66; Paus. 8. 5. 6 f.
[2] Hdt. 1. 56. 3.

their name was later applied to the whole concourse of their successors, whether they invaded Greece north or south of the Isthmus. In the end 'Hellenes' was used as the name of all Greek-speaking peoples. The word 'Hellas' has a similar history. The original home of the Hellenes was 'Hellas', the area round Dodona in Epirus, according to Aristotle. In the *Iliad* it was the home of Achilles' Hellenes; in the *Odyssey* Greece north of the Isthmus; and finally the whole peninsula of Greece.[1]

Once the centres of Mycenaean power were destroyed, the invaders settled on the best agricultural land. The Thessaloi spread their dominion from Thessaliotis over the main Thessalian plain. They replaced the nine Achaean realms with four large baronies, of which the centres were Larisa, Crannon, Pharsalus, and Pherae (only Pherae figured as a town in the Achaean catalogue). The strongest authority in Thessaly was wielded later by the Aleuadae of Larisa, who claimed descent from the Heracleidae, the original leaders of the invasion.[2] The Boiotoi in their southward thrust from Thessaliotis to Boeotia may have split the Locrians into two groups, after whom the separate areas, Opuntian Locris and Ozolian Locris, were named in later times. In northern Boeotia, the invaders first occupied Chaeronea and Coronea, the latter becoming the centre of the festival common to all Boeotians, the 'Pamboiotia' held in honour of Itonian Athena. The conquest and settlement of Boeotia was a slow process; Plataea was settled late, and Minyan Orchomenus retained its separate traditions into the classical period.[3] Here, as in Thessaly, the newcomers were led by strong clans, such as the Opheltiadae of Chaeronea and the Aegeidae of Thebes.

Within the Peloponnese the western group of invaders, led by the Aetolian Oxylus, occupied the rich plainland of 'hollow Elis'. The descendants of Oxylus, the Oxylidae, remained the leading clan in Elis and later were *Hellanodikai* (judges of the Hellenes) in the games at Olympia, where the cults of Zeus and Hera were established.[4] The eastern group of invaders, the Dorians led by the Heracleidae, occupied the richest areas in the eastern and southern Peloponnese. Tradition relates that, when lots were drawn by the leading Heracleidae *c.* 1120, Argolis fell to the eldest son Temenus, Messenia to Cresphontes, and Lacedaemonia to Aristodemus or his twin sons, Eurysthenes and Procles. At the outset they probably combined to destroy the Mycenaean strongholds which were capable of concerted resistance. But thereafter the conquest and the settlement of the three main areas demanded the efforts of several generations.

The grandsons of Temenus, inheriting Argos as their residence, reduced the towns of the Argive plain. At Epidaurus a son-in-law of Temenus, Deiphontes, maintained his independence from the Temenidae for a time. Troezen and Hermione received Dorian settlers from Argos. Aegina in the

[1] Arist. *Mete.* 1. 14 (352 a); *Il.* 2. 683; *Od.* 1. 344 (athetized); Hes. *ap.* Str. 370.
[2] Pi. *P.* 10. 1 f.
[3] Plu. *Cim.* 1; Str. 411; Th. 3. 61. 2.   [4] Str. 357; Pi. *O.* 3. 12.

Saronic Gulf was settled by Dorians from Epidaurus. On the Corinthian Gulf a son of Temenus founded Dorian Sicyon; his son in turn founded Dorian Phlius. Corinthia, however, was occupied by Dorians under the leadership of another Heraclid, Aletes, who was not one of the Temenidae. The occupation of Corinthia may have been later than the capture of Sicyon and Phlius.[1] Last of all, the Megarid was settled by Dorians who came from Corinthia, Messenia, and other Dorian areas of the Peloponnese.[2]

The invasion of Lacedaemonia was conducted under the leadership of Eurysthenes and Procles, and the period of conquest lasted for several generations. Amyclae, to the south of Sparta, fell only with the assistance of the Aegeidae, summoned from Thebes. The turmoil consequent upon the Dorian intrusion was more long-lived in Lacedaemonia than in any other area.[3] In Messenia the Heracleidae and the Dorians established themselves at Pylus on the coast. But inland the plain of Stenyclarus was ruled by the Aepytidae, a clan whose non-Dorian origin was glossed over in later traditions.[4] Thus after the irruption into the Peloponnese there was a long period of fighting and turmoil, during which some parts of the peninsula retained their independence.

While the main forces of the Dorians attacked the Mycenaean strongholds in Argolis, Lacedaemonia, and Messenia, other bands went overseas to invade the islands and join hands with their predecessors in Crete, Rhodes, Nisyros, and other islands. Cythera, Melos, and Thera were occupied by Dorians from Lacedaemonia. The invaders, led by Theras, a member of the Aegeidae clan, came to Thera in the generation of Eurysthenes and Procles; Melos, lying between the mainland and Thera, was probably occupied at the same time, according to Thucydides *c.* 1116.[5] Dorians from Lacedaemonia and Argolis under the leadership of Althaemenes, grandson of Temenus, whose *floruit* may be dated to *c.* 1050, occupied the rich plain in the centre of Crete, and later spread into other parts of the island. Dorians from the Argolid occupied the islands of Anaphe, Astypalaea, Casos, and Carpathos. Others joined the earlier Dorian settlers in Rhodes. There the cult of the original founder, Tlepolemus the Heraclid, was still observed in the fifth century. Argive influence, however, transferred his place of origin from Ephyra (probably in Thesprotia) to Tiryns in the Argolid. Nisyros, Cos, and Calydnae received settlers from Epidaurus.[6] On the neighbouring coast of Asia Minor Halicarnassus was founded by Dorians and Ionians from Troezen, Iasus by Dorians from the Argolid, and Cnidus by Dorians from Argolis and Lacedaemonia. These were the farthest outliers of the Dorian invasion. They held a cult of Triopian Apollo on the Cnidian promontory, to which only the Dorians of Cnidus,

---

[1] Paus. 2. 26. 2; 30. 10; Hdt. 8. 46. 1; Pi. *I.* fr. 1; Str. 389.

[2] Str. 393; Hdt. 5. 76; Scymn. 502.

[3] *FGrH* 4 F 116 (Hellanic.); Pi. *I.* 7. 15; Th. 1. 18. 1.

[4] Pi. *P.* 5. 70; E. *Fr.*, p. 497, s. *Cresphontes.*

[5] Th. 7. 57. 6; 5. 112. 2; Hdt. 4. 147.   [6] Str. 481; Th. 7. 57. 6; Pi. *O.* 7. 18 f.

Halicarnassus, Cos, and the three towns of Rhodes (Lindus, Ialysus, and Cameirus) were admitted. Thus the Dorians occupied all the islands of the Achaean catalogue, together with Melos, Thera, and Cythera. Their success was achieved by force of arms and at the expense of Achaeans, Carians, Phoenicians, and other Aegean peoples.[1] These islands had once formed the avenue of trade between the Greek mainland and the Orient. But in the dark age the flow of trade stopped.

§ 2. *The characteristics of the invaders*

THE invaders brought into the conquered areas two closely related dialects of the Greek language, Doric and north-west Greek. Doric was spoken during classical times in Aegina, Megaris, and the eastern Peloponnese from Sicyonia to Lacedaemonia; in Messenia, where its wide distribution may be partly due to the later conquest of Messenia by Sparta; in the southern Aegean islands; and on the adjacent coast of Asia Minor, except at Halicarnassus, where the settlers were of mixed stock and the Ionic dialect prevailed. North-west Greek was spoken in Elis and Achaea; in Ithaca, Cephallenia, and Zacynthos; and throughout the whole of central Greece from inland Acarnania and Amphilochia to southern Thessaly and parts of Boeotia.

The distribution of these dialects conforms with that of the invading peoples, as portrayed in the literary tradition. The pattern of Doric coincides precisely with the traditions of Dorian settlement. The pattern of north-west Greek enlarges on the meagre traditions which survive of the other invading peoples. It indicates that the Thessaloi, the Boiotoi, and the followers of Oxylus spoke the same dialect and therefore flowed from a common source into south-west Thessaly, Boeotia, and Elis. This common source can hardly have lain elsewhere than in southern Epirus. The distribution of north-west Greek shows also that the invaders of Thessaly, Boeotia, and Elis were followed by further peoples speaking the same dialect, who settled in other areas of Central Greece, in the southern islands of the Ionian Sea, and in Achaea in the Peloponnese. Other invaders, among them Phrygians, settled at Vergina in the Haliacmon valley and buried their dead in tumuli. The fact that north-west Greek and Doric are closely related dialects is explicable only on the hypothesis that before the time of the invasions the speakers of the two dialects had lived in contiguous areas. These areas were probably West Macedonia and Epirus. For, according to the literary tradition, the Dorians were situated first in south-west Macedonia and then in Doris, and the Thessaloi came from Thesprotia in Epirus.

That the Dorians differed from the other invading peoples is clear from subsequent history. The Dorians assumed and maintained the leading position in the Greek world. Their early states were more powerful, and their colonial enterprises were more ambitious than those of other Greeks. On the

[1] Hdt. 7. 99. 3; 1. 144; 1. 117. 5; 1. 174. 2; Plb. 16. 12; Str. 653; D.S. 5. 53.

FIG. 9. Dialects of the Greek Peninsula in classical times

other hand, the speakers of the north-west Greek dialect lagged behind in culture and in political development; engaging in agriculture rather than in seafaring, they played little or no part in the colonizing movement and in the development of Hellenic civilization.

The Dorians alone were brigaded in three tribes—Hylleis, Dymanes, and Pamphyloi. The fact that this tribal system was common to the first Dorian settlers of Crete and Rhodes and to the later Dorian states indicates that the division took place before the Dorian invasion of *c.* 1120. Its origin was probably racial; its perpetuation may have been due to a system of hereditary or caste occupations.[1] The invading Dorians fought in separate tribal regiments, and they divided up the land on a tribal basis. The Dorians of the Peloponnese observed the sacred month *Karneios* and the cult of Apollo Karneios; as *karnos* means a ram, it is probable that this Dorian god was originally the god of a pastoral people and later became identified with Apollo. The cult of Apollo Pythaeus was common to the Dorian states of the Peloponnese; it may have been adopted before the invasion, when the Dorians lived to the north of Delphi, the central shrine of Apollo. The other invading peoples did not share in these cults. The Thessalians and the Boeotians had a common worship in the cult of Athena Itonia, which probably dated from the beginning of the invasion.

Both groups of invading peoples were organized on a tribal basis with constituent phratries, which subdivided into clans or family groups. Annexing the best land in the plains, they lived in small open villages, which were called in the Dorian areas *komai* and in Elis *damoi*. Each village probably consisted of a family unit, and the head of the community held the title of king (*basileus*). To each family was allotted a holding of land (*klaros*), which was inalienable, and its possession constituted a right to membership of the free community. Such holdings varied widely in size in the non-Dorian areas; for instance in Thessaly, Boeotia, and Elis the owners of large holdings maintained cavalry and played a predominant part in politics. In the Dorian areas the holdings seem to have varied less in size. The holdings in Thessaly and in the Dorian areas were worked by serfs, who belonged to the community and had limited rights; this system may have been introduced by the Heracleidae who led the Thessalians and the Dorians, for it does not appear in Elis and in Boeotia or in the other areas of the north-west Greek dialect. The distribution of the land in such holdings did not mean the end of unsettled conditions. For village fought against village, and men went about their business wearing arms.[2]

The Dorians and the Thessalians proved hard masters to the peoples whom they conquered. In the plainlands they reduced them to serfdom, and in the hills to the tributary status of *perioikoi*. In both cases the earlier peoples were regarded as booty won by the spear, and their dialect sometimes influenced the speech of their masters. Thus Arcadian forms survived in Pisatis and in

[1] Hdt. 6. 60.   [2] Plu. 295[b] (*GQ* 17); Th. 1. 6. 1.

southern Laconia, and Aeolic forms in Elis and in some Corinthian colonies (probably reflecting the position in early Corinth). In Troezen the Ionic dialect survived long enough to be perpetuated in her colony Halicarnassus, but in Cynuria it succumbed to the Doric dialect. In Achaea, where there was probably a substratum of Ionic and Achaean inhabitants, the dialect in classical times was north-west Greek. In Crete the language of the early population, known as the Eteocretes, survived; in Carpathos the Eteocarpathioi adopted the Doric dialect.

The Boeotians and the other invaders of Central Greece did not reduce the earlier population to serfdom or to tributary status. In consequence the north-west Greek dialect of Phocis, of Opuntian Locris, and to a greater extent of Boeotia was influenced by the Aeolic dialect. Nor did the invaders necessarily exclude the earlier peoples from their own communities. The Heracleidae and their descendants, who formed the royal houses of Argos and of Sparta, were Achaeans; and the Aegeidae, who held the priesthood of Apollo Karneios at Thebes, Sparta, and Thera, were 'Cadmeans'. In some Dorian states the leaders of the earlier population were adopted into the franchized community and formed a fourth tribe. They entered the circle of privilege by deserting their compatriots.

§ 3. *The Aeolian and Ionian Migrations*

THE shock of invasion expelled many peoples from their homeland. Aeolians from Thessaly, Phocis, Locris, and Boeotia crossed the seas to find new territories. The first group, led by Penthilus, son of Orestes, gained a footing first on the Thracian coast, and in the course of the next two generations their descendants founded settlements on the north-west coast of Asia Minor and on the adjacent islands of Tenedos and Lesbos. Cyme was founded by a second group, and the total number of the settlements on the mainland rose to twelve; and from Cyme and Lesbos several towns were founded in the Troad.

The slow progress of the Aeolian migration is a measure of the resistance which was encountered. The settlers came in successive waves, mainly led by members of the Penthilidae, whose descendants held the hereditary title of 'king', for instance at Mitylene in Lesbos.[1] The emigrants from each district of the homeland did not form separate communities. They often mingled in a single community; for example, Methymna in Lesbos contained settlers from Erythrae, Phocis, and Scyros. They perpetuated their dialects and their cults, and they sought the conditions with which they were familiar, rich agricultural land and a climate raw in winter and hot in summer. With the renaissance of Greek literature, their genius in poetry and in music flowered again, but they played a small part in the political history of the classical period. If we reckon by the genealogy of the Penthilidae, the Aeolian migration began *c.* 1130 and lasted until *c.* 1000 or later.

[1] Hdt. 1. 149 f.; Str. 582, 622; Tz. ad Lyc. 1374.

Resistance to the invaders lasted for several generations in the mountainous country of the Peloponnese. The confused and sometimes inconsistent memories of this period, which survived in oral tradition and are known to us through the summary given by Pausanias, are not trustworthy in detail; but they give an indication of the bitter fighting which has characterized many similar periods of resistance in medieval and modern Greece.[1] The stronghold of resistance lay in Arcadia, which retained its Arcadian dialect and never succumbed. The mountainous country between Elis and Messenia, which forms the districts of Triphylia and Lepreatis, was held for centuries by Arcadians, Caucones, and Minyans. In the fourth century the Arcadians still laid claim to these areas, which were then under the control of Elis, and the local cults of Samian Poseidon and of Caucon were maintained.[2] The peaks and glens of Mt. Taygetus and its outrunners afforded sanctuary for refugees and bases for attack against the Dorians of Lacedaemonia and Messenia. Herodotus' tale, that camp-fires were kindled on the flanks of Mt. Taygetus by the Minyan refugees, may be accepted as typical of the guerilla warfare of this period.[3]

Achaea, too, with its mountainous interior and narrow valleys, formed an enclave between the followers of Oxylus in Elis and the Dorians of Sicyon. Here, tradition relates, the Achaeans from Argolis and Lacedaemonia sought refuge and named the country 'Achaea'. They established themselves at the expense of the Ionian inhabitants, who called the country 'Aegialus' and worshipped Poseidon at Helice. The Ionians in turn fled to Attica, whither the royal house of Pylus in Messenia, the Neleidae, had already found refuge after their expulsion by the Dorian invaders.[4] As the dialect of Achaea in classical times was north-west Greek, it is probable that the Achaeans themselves were overrun by speakers of north-west Greek during the turmoil of folk-movements within the Peloponnese. On the other hand, there are but few traces of emigration overseas by the non-Dorian peoples of the Peloponnese. The place-names 'Arkades' and 'Amyklaion' near Gortyn in Crete may derive from Arcadian and Achaean settlers, who preceded or perhaps accompanied the Dorian settlers. Epidaurians of Ionian stock, who migrated in the time of Deiphontes, settled in Samos where they established the cult of Hera, familiar to them in the Argolid. Emigrants from Cleonae and Phlius founded Clazomenae on the coast of Asia Minor.[5] The very paucity of such traditions suggests that the impact of the Dorians broke the chief centres of Mycenaean power and rendered most of the survivors incapable of winning new dominions overseas.

Attica was not attacked during the early phase of the invasions. The Boeotians made slow progress southwards, while the Dorians carried their advance into the Peloponnese and overseas. Thus Attica became a sanctuary for

---

[1] Paus. 3. 2; 4. 3.   [2] X. *HG.* 7. 1. 26; Hdt. 4. 148; Str. 343; 345.
[3] Hdt. 4. 145.   [4] Hdt. 1. 145; Paus. 7. 1; *FGrH* 4 F 125 (Hellanic.); Hdt. 5. 65.
[5] Paus. 7. 4. 2; 7. 3. 9; Str. 633.

refugees, among whom were the Neleidae from Pylus and the Ionians from Achaea. The literary tradition records that Melanthus the Neleid, who had been king at Pylus, represented the Athenians in a battle of champions against the Boeotians and later became King of Athens. In the list of the Athenian kings and in the genealogy of the Neleidae Melanthus stands in the fourth generation after the fall of Troy; his *floruit* may therefore be dated very approximately *c.* 1080. When the Dorians were occupying the Megarid and attacked the Athenians, Attica was defended by Codrus, son of Melanthus, whose *floruit* may be put very approximately at 1050. A younger son of Codrus, Neleus, was the leader of the so-called Ionian migration. In this manner the beginning of the migration may be dated very approximately to *c.* 1020. This date fits two other traditions: that the Ionian migration began four generations after the Aeolian migration, which itself commenced on genealogical reckoning *c.* 1130; and that members of the Dorian expedition which was defeated by Codrus migrated to Crete under the leadership of Althaemenes, the grandson of Temenus, whose *floruit* may be dated approximately at 1050.[1]

The ability of Athens to resist the last waves of invasion and to launch so large-scale a movement as the Ionian migration shows that she was a strongly organized state. Thucydides chose the Ionian migration to mark the close of the anarchic period on the mainland which followed the Dorian invasion. 'A long time elapsed before Hellas with difficulty achieved stability and was no longer subject to shifts of population; she then sent out colonies. Athens planted the Ionians and most of the islanders, and the Peloponnese mainly but also some other places in Greece colonised parts of Italy and Sicily.' Thucydides also analysed the sources of Athens' power: she had been free from internal strife, she had granted citizenship to the ablest of the refugees, and she had built up a still larger population.[2]

At this point archaeology offers some aid. The excavation of the cemetery at Kerameikós (the Potters' Quarter in Athens) has yielded a sequence of pottery styles, to which approximate dates have been given, namely, Sub-Mycenaean 1125–1075, Proto-Geometric 1075–950, and Geometric 950–710. Objects found with the pottery show that new customs came into Attica at this time. In the Sub-Mycenaean stratum three cremation-burials and some long pins (probably used to fasten the Doric *peplos*) were discovered. Two cremation-burials and a new type of fibula have been unearthed at Salamis, which may be a little earlier in date. Early in the Proto-Geometric period cremation was almost universal at the Kerameikós. From then on it predominated until *c.* 800, when inhumation came into fashion once more. Early in the Proto-Geometric period, too, iron swords and daggers were interred with the ashes, whereas in the preceding period no weapons had been buried with the dead at Athens. The new style of pottery known as Proto-Geometric

[1] *FGrH* 4 F 125 (Hellanic.); 3 F 155 (Pherecyd.); Hdt. 5. 76.
[2] Th. 1. 12. 4; 1. 2. 6.

commenced earlier at Athens (*c.* 1075) than elsewhere on the mainland. The finest period of this pottery started *c.* 1000. It was marked by a harmony between decoration and shape and a fine sense of proportion. At the same time (*c.* 1000) the cemetery doubled in extent, and great masses of pottery were deposited. Iron was then generally used for weapons, and the iron slashing-sword was common.

These changes in burial-customs, in dress, and in pottery-style were most probably due to the arrival of new people in Athens; and the gradual nature of the change suggests that they arrived in increasing numbers from 1100 to 1000. As there is no trace of influence from the East, the newcomers evidently came from the mainland and were no doubt refugees, such as those from Pylus and Achaea. The Kerameikós was their cemetery. For the native Athenians buried their dead in family tombs in the countryside, and they continued to do so until the Peloponnesian War. The refugees, on the other hand, who had left their traditional burial-grounds, cremated their dead in a strange country, as the Achaeans had done at Troy and the Athenians were later to do outside Syracuse; other migrating peoples were probably responsible for other early examples of cremation in Boeotia, Eretria, Crete, Thera, and Rhodes. The greatest influx of refugees came between 1050 and 1000, when the Kerameikós cemetery was extended and the finest Proto-Geometric pottery was made. No doubt they played their part in developing this style of Athenian pottery to its highest level, as the metics from Corinth did later in 530–490.

During the tenth century and probably in its early decades the Proto-Geometric style, developed and perfected at Athens, spread swiftly over much of the Aegean world. This spread appears to have been due not primarily to trade in pottery and the goods contained therein (for there is little or no sign of any exchange of pottery between Athens and other centres) but rather to a renewal of contacts within the Aegean area, which made known the vastly superior style of Athenian art. The centre of this zone of renewed contacts was the Cyclades; the fringes, so far as the evidence goes, were in north Crete, at Assarlik in Caria, at Smyrna in Ionia, in the Dodecanese and Lesbos, at Scyros and in Thessaly. There can be little doubt that those who led the way and in some cases carried the pottery were Ionians migrating from Athens. For they occupied the Cyclades and opened the seas to Greek and especially Athenian mariners. To a lesser extent the Proto-Geometric style affected the mainland areas near the Isthmus of Corinth and farther afield Phocis, Laconia, and Ithaca. Excavation at Lefkandi (between Chalcis and Eretria) has shown that it became a centre of maritime trade and produced a fine pottery in the tenth century. Its contacts reached Cyprus, which was itself in touch with the Levant and Egypt.

The Cyclades and the Asiatic coast, which the emigrants invaded, were occupied by civilized and warlike peoples. Foremost among them were the Carians, renowned as seamen and warriors, and their kith and kin, the

Mysians and the Lydians; in addition there were Leleges, Pelasgians, Phoenicians, and Tyrseni, and also emigrants from the Greek peninsula and from Crete, who had gained a footing on the islands and on the coast of Asia Minor. To eject these seafaring peoples from their possessions was no easy matter. The success which attended the Ionian migration must have been largely due to the seapower and the good leadership which Athens herself was able to supply. The emigrants were not native Athenians but enfranchised refugees and volunteers from other parts of Greece: Ionians from Achaea, Abantes from Euboea, Minyans from Orchomenus, Cadmeans from Boeotia, Dryopes, Phocians, Molossians, Arcadians, Dorians from Epidaurus, and many others.[1] Some unity was given to this motley host by the assistance of Athens and by the leadership of the Neleidae. Its progress was slow; successive waves of emigrants crossed the Aegean Sea for a century or more. The spirit of the settlers is admirably expressed in a poem by Mimnermus: 'We are they who left Pylus, the city of Neleus, and came in our ships to lovely Asia; with overmastering might we settled at beloved Colophon, pioneers of boisterous violence, and thence . . . by the grace of the gods we captured Aeolian Smyrna.'[2]

The traditions of Colophon aptly illustrate the nature of the migration. The first migrants, Ionians led by two members of the Neleidae clan, came to terms with the earlier inhabitants, Cretans and Cadmeans, who had themselves expelled the Carians. A second group, led by a Pylian Andraemon, captured Colophon and later entered a dispute for the possession of Smyrna, from which they ejected the Aeolian settlers.[3] In the hard fighting which inaugurated the planting of their settlements, the first Ionian conquerors of Miletus did not bring their families with them but took wives from the Carian inhabitants;[4] these Carians had themselves dispossessed the Minoan and Mycenaean settlers of the Bronze Age. From the turmoil of the tenth century the Ionians emerged triumphant with secure possession of twelve cities on the Asiatic coast and the neighbouring islands, which came to be known as the Ionian dodecapolis: Miletus, Myus, and Priene, which command the estuary and the valley of the river Maeander; Ephesus at the mouth of the river Caÿster and to the north Colophon, Lebedus, Teus, Clazomenae, and Erythrae; Phocaea on the coast westwards of the old outlet of the river Hermus; and the large islands, Chios and Samos.

Each city honoured its so-called founder, under whose leadership the first adventurers had arrived; his tomb was often revered, and his descendants held hereditary titles and offices. At Ephesus, for example, the descendants of Androcles, son of Codrus, still held the title of 'king' with the full insignia of kingship, the priesthood of Eleusinian Demeter and the presidency of the games as late as the beginning of the Christian era.[5] Since the settlers were often drawn from several parts of the Greek mainland, each city preserved

[1] Hdt. 1. 171; 1. 146; Th. 1. 12. 4; *FGrH* 3 F 155 (Pherecyd.).   [2] Mimn. *Fr.* 9.
[3] Paus. 7. 3; Str. 633–4; Hdt. 1. 150.   [4] Hdt. 1. 146. 2.   [5] Str. 633.

the traditions, the cults, and the dialect peculiar to the separate racial groups which constituted the citizen body. Thus Miletus, having been settled mainly by Ionians from Attica, retained the names of the four Ionic tribes which existed in Attica; the settlers from other parts of Greece were brigaded in two additional tribes, the Boreis and the Oenopes, of which the eponymous ancestors were associated with Thessaly and Boeotia. The important shrines of the Milesians were the temple of Athena at Assesus and the oracular shrine of Apollo at Didyma, served by an hereditary priesthood, the Branchidae.[1] At Samos, on the other hand, the settlers came mainly from Epidaurus under the leadership of Procles and maintained their worship of the Argive goddess Hera, while at Chios settlers from Euboea, Boeotia, and Thessaly were followed by Ionians from Attica, and the dialect of the island was Ionic with an admixture of Aeolic. But, of whatever stock the settlers were, they had many institutions in common: the gentilic organization by tribes, phratries, and *gene* (often under different names such as the 'thousands' and the 'hundreds' in Samos), the hereditary kingships and priesthoods, and the preservation of genealogies, which enabled Hecataeus of Miletus to claim that his sixteenth ancestor was a god.[2]

The Ionians occupied the finest sites on the littoral of Asia Minor. The indented coast afforded them the full Mediterranean climate and fine harbours, while Chios and Samos controlled the coasting route from north to south. At the same time the mainland cities, especially Ephesus and Miletus, controlled the exit of the main trade-routes from the interior down the valleys of the Caÿster and the Maeander. On the other hand, the Ionian cities were ill placed to defend themselves against the land powers of Asia Minor. Separated one from another by the mountain ranges, they did not even control a consecutive stretch of coast, let alone any depth of hinterland. Their common dangers encouraged them to combine in the worship of Poseidon Heliconius at the Panionium, a shrine situated on the promontory of Mycale. Diverse as they were in racial origin, they nevertheless adopted a common name 'Iaones' (later 'Iōnes'), which was extended by the Asiatic peoples in the form 'Javan' or 'Yawan' to include the whole Greek-speaking race. The chief bond between the Ionian cities lay in their aristocracies. Having set out from Attica under the leadership of the Codridae, the aristocrats brought with them the Athenian festival of the 'Apatouria' during which new members were admitted to the phratries.[3] This festival was probably observed by all members of the Ionian dodecapolis in the eighth century. It not only preserved the gentilic organization of society, but also emphasized the Ionian tie with Athens. Moreover, Ionian Attica had escaped invasion. It was, therefore, natural that the Ionians overseas looked to Attica as their homeland, and that Athens exercised her vote at the Delphic Amphictyony on behalf of the Ionians. Yet the tie was mainly one of religious sentiment; practical links,

[1] Hdt. 1. 19. 3; 1. 157. 3.   [2] Hdt. 2. 143. 4.
[3] Hdt. 1. 143. 3; 1. 147. 2.

such as existed between the later Greek colonies and their mother-cities, were never forged between the Ionian cities and Athens.

The Ionian Migration also ejected the non-Hellenic peoples, especially Carians, from the islands of the central Aegean and peopled them with emigrants from the Greek mainland. At Ceos, Seriphos, Siphnos, Naxos, Tenos, and Andros the emigrants were mainly Ionians from Attica, but the presence of people from Thessaly, Boeotia, and Locris is indicated by tribal names and cults. Athens supplied her four tribal names to the Ionians of Delos, two leaders for the settlement at Paros, and a member of the Neleidae as founder of Myconos. Cythnos was occupied by Dryopes, who came originally from the Spercheus valley. Although they were of diverse origin, the islanders soon came to regard themselves as a community. From the eighth century, and perhaps earlier, they assembled with their wives and children at Delos during the sacred month, when Apollo was honoured with dances and with contests in music, poetry, and athletics. In choosing Delos as their religious centre, the islanders followed the tradition of the Bronze Age peoples. They probably inherited there the cult of Anius and the worship of Eileithyia, Hecate, and Brizo. Of the mainland states Athens in particular had been associated with the sacred island in the legends which concerned Theseus and the tetrapolis of Marathon; and in the time of Solon, if not earlier, Athens, as the oldest land of Ionia, sent representatives to the Delian festival.[1]

§ 4. *The Ionians and the Homeric poems*

THE Ionians won and retained their footing on the islands and on the Asiatic coast by continuous warfare during the tenth and the ninth centuries. Material prosperity came later. Thus in fine pottery they lagged behind the leading peoples of the Greek mainland. At the same time the Ionians, having come from many parts of the mainland, were well qualified to collect and to transmit the epic lays of the Bronze Age; indeed by force of circumstances they still continued to live under the conditions of raiding and migrating which had given birth to epic. Athens and Cyprus also enjoyed a continuity of tradition; but neither had been leading states in the Heroic Age, and both had achieved settled conditions by the ninth century. The Aeolian emigrants, too, were survivors of the Bronze Age; but their preference for the agricultural way of life may have weakened their interest in the epic saga. It is therefore probable that during the migrations epics were recited in the courts of the Ionian kings and aristocrats, who, during their sojourn in Attica and their settlement of Ionia, looked back to the heyday of their former power.

In such a milieu the *Iliad* was composed. The traditional lays, from which the poem developed, were already sung in the Ionian dialect. The author was by general consent Homer. His descendants, the Homeridae, lived in Chios,

[1] Hdt. 8. 46 f.; Th. 7. 57; *h. Ap.* 146 f.; Th. 3. 104. 3 f.; *FGrH* 328 F 75 (Philoch.).

whether that island or Smyrna was his birthplace. The time of composition is hotly disputed. The date assigned by Herodotus, *c.* 850, may be accepted as approximately correct; for it stands at the end of the migratory period in Ionia and before the dawn of a new age, in which the Ionian states turned to colonial enterprise.[1]

The *Iliad* is remarkable for the objective conservatism with which the conditions of the Late Bronze Age are portrayed. Anachronisms are indeed so rare as to occasion surprise. This fidelity is due to the strength of the epic tradition rather than to the genius of Homer. Yet the *Iliad* is fundamentally different from the lays of the epic cycle in length, in characterization, and in art. Nothing reveals the personal genius of the author more clearly than the unity of plot, which centres a poem requiring five evenings for its full recitation round the theme of the wrath of Achilles. His skill in construction is equalled by his force in characterization. The lines of his characters are clean-cut and firm; and the light and shade of their changing moods owe their intensity to the poet's understanding of humanity. The art of his verse is unequalled in its speed and in its effects; however much the hexameter metre and the epic diction owed to the long centuries of earlier development, Homer employed them with a perfection to which no other composer of epic in Greek or in any other language has ever attained. These qualities in Homer's genius, working through the medium developed by centuries of tradition and set in the language of a gifted race, produced the finest epic poem of all literature. A masterpiece imbued with the directness and the delicacy inherent in all Greek poetry, the *Iliad* possesses some characteristics which were more highly developed in the Ionian than in the other branches of the Greek race: the sensitivity of touch, the candid expression of individualism, and the command of flowing narrative. These characteristics were probably more the qualities of Homer himself and of his Ionian milieu than of the earliest phases of the epic saga. If any scenes in the *Iliad* speak with the voice of Homer and of Ionia, they are those depicted on the shield of Achilles which show the pointless brutalities of war.

The effect of the poem was profound. So consummate an expression of the Greek outlook inspired the poets of the archaic period. Its mastery of plot and its concern with the realities of human life guided the tragedians in the development of Attic Drama. And its influence dominated the revival of epic poetry in the Hellenistic Age. Forming an essential part of education in all the Greek states, the poem established a canon of human ideals and of religious beliefs which constituted a force for unity in the diverse world of the Greek city-states. And even when philosophical speculation or secular materialism rendered Homer's conception of the gods unacceptable, the qualities of the heroes commanded the respect and challenged the emulation of successive generations.

Antiquity named Homer as the author also of the *Odyssey*. It resembles the

[1] Pi. *N.* 2. 1; Hdt. 2. 53. 2.

Iliad in grandeur of conception, subtlety of plot, power of characterization, and fidelity to the conditions of the Late Bronze Age. But the theme is entirely different. It treats not of war and warriors, but of the personal adventures and homecoming of Odysseus. Such a theme was indeed traditional in the epic saga, and both poems are to be regarded as the culmination of a long period of oral transmission. But the very nature of the theme permitted a more timeless approach and a less close adherence to the traditional lays; thus the *Odyssey* contains nothing analogous to the military catalogues, the funeral games, or the *aristeiai* of the *Iliad*, and admits such non-heroic topics as the distant wanderings of Odysseus and the descent into the underworld. For all its conservatism in detail the *Odyssey* moves with a more modern suppleness of mind than the *Iliad*. Even those who believed in a single authorship considered the *Odyssey* to be the later of the two poems and attributed its composition to the old age of Homer; thus the critic Longinus likened the Homer of the *Odyssey* to the setting sun, of which the grandeur remained without the intensity.[1]

Tempting as it is to attribute both poems to a single genius, the differences in the detail of language and in the sophistication of outlook are such that we should attribute the *Odyssey* to a different author who belonged to a separate school of bards and lived in a different part of the Greek world. The date of the *Odyssey* is also much disputed. Some scholars place it in the seventh century, but it is more likely to have been composed in the first half of the eighth century, before lyric poetry flowered in Ionia and Greek colonies were planted in the West. In the *Odyssey* other facets of the Greek outlook found immortal expression: capacity for wonder, regard for versatility, love of adventure, and directness in human relationships. If the *Iliad* foreshadowed the martial ideals of the Spartiate, the *Odyssey* foreshadowed the lovable qualities of the classical Athenian. Its literary influence extended to Herodotus, Menander, Lucian, and the Greek novelists, while its portrayal of the wine-dark sea in all her moods and of man's constancy and courage has never ceased to stir the imagination of posterity.

The *Iliad* and the *Odyssey* were the two masterpieces of the epic saga, but did not mark the end of the oral tradition. Small lays, or parts of lays, became attached to them as accretions, and many independent lays of the so-called epic cycle came to their final form. The *Cypria*, the *Aethiopis*, and the *Iliou Persis*, which formed prologues and epilogues to the theme of the *Iliad*, were composed probably in the eighth century and the *Ilias Parva* in the seventh; the *Nostoi*, similar in subject to the *Odyssey*, and the *Telegoneia* and the *Thesprotis*, which continued the theme of the *Odyssey*, were composed probably in the seventh and sixth centuries. Other lays, treating of the Theban myths, were probably composed in the eighth and seventh centuries —the *Thebais*, the *Oedipodeia*, and the *Epigoni*—and yet others, dealing with Heracles or with local legends, were composed within the limits of the archaic

[1] Longin. 9. 13.

period. The large number of these lays reflects the influence of the Homeric poems and the vitality of the epic saga. From this rich storehouse of legend the Greek poets of the classical period derived most of their material, and thereby acknowledged their debt to the civilizations which had preceded them.

Cyclops being blinded by the companions of Odysseus, from a Proto-Argive vase of the period 700–650 (comparison with *Odyssey* 9.382 shows the poem was known to the painter of this vase)

BOOK II

THE RENAISSANCE OF GREECE
(*c*. 850–546)

THE SOURCES OF KNOWLEDGE

WITHIN the period *c*. 850–546 the Greek states and the religious centres began to keep records. Olympic victors were listed from 776, and it is likely that lists of kings, priests, &c., were kept from earlier times. The Oracle of Delphi committed its responses to leather scrolls for safe keeping, and at Sparta and elsewhere these responses were guarded by state officials. Lists of annual magistrates were kept at Sparta, for instance, from 757 onwards. Nor should this year be regarded as the first date from which years were recorded; for an annual system was as essential as a calendar within the year for even the most primitive form of dealings within a society. From 750 onwards many of the Greek states held the lead in Mediterranean commerce; in these states writing was in such common use by 700 that people scribbled on potsherds. In 660, if not earlier, the compiling of legal archives began, and methods of publicizing the law quickly evolved. The literature of the period, apart from the Cyclic Epics, gave contemporary evidence of the life and thought of the times; of this literature a great amount survived throughout antiquity. The use of this material for historical purposes began with Eumelus of Corinth *c*. 725, and histories of considerable range were written during the late sixth century. In public life durable materials came into use. Some temples were built in stone from *c*. 750. Records, such as laws, decrees, or dedications, which had hitherto been written on leather or wood, were inscribed on bronze or stone; statues were sculptured in bronze or marble, and coins were engraved with state emblems. These developments began in the course of the seventh century. They provided material not only for the ancient writers but also for the modern archaeologist and scholar.

Of this wealth of material much has survived in the works of Herodotus, Thucydides, and Aristotle, and of other writers of less outstanding ability. The writings of poets who flourished between *c*. 850 and 546 and those of later historians have come down to us through the faithful and meticulous skill of clerks and scholars during our Middle Ages, who preserved the legacy of the classical period with a devotion similar to that of the epic bards in the dark age of the Mediterranean world. These writings are the basis of our inquiry into Greek history. As a supplement, and sometimes as a check, we have the aid of the modern archaeologist, epigraphist, numismatist, palaeographer, &c., who have applied a highly skilled technique to the problem of understanding the material objects which have survived from antiquity.

CHAPTER 1

A Period of Cultural and Political Revival (850–730)

§ 1. *The influence of the East and the religion of Hesiod*

DURING the migrations, which cut commercial communications and lowered the level of material culture throughout the Aegean area, a galaxy of small states in the Near East preserved and developed the legacy of Bronze Age civilization. A balance of power was maintained between these states, until in the course of the eighth century they were overrun by the Assyrian empire. Egypt, though stripped of her dependencies, remained a centre of civilization. In Palestine the independent kingdom of Philistia reached its zenith in the eleventh century, and that of Israel under David and Solomon in the tenth century. Phoenicia retained her primacy in seafaring and commerce throughout the period; her mariners sailed not only in the eastern but far into the west Mediterranean. Inland of Phoenicia the Syrian kingdoms of Hama and Damascus prospered, and to the north in south-eastern Asia Minor a neo-Hittite culture revived. Cyprus, too, where both Greeks and Phoenicians had settled, belonged to this group of small and independent states; she continued to trade, as she had done in the Late Bronze Age, with the coasts of Cilicia, Phoenicia, and Palestine.

In this oasis of culture the Phoenician alphabet was evolved from the hieroglyphic and the Linear Scripts, which had been in use during and since the Bronze Age. The invention of the alphabet was destined to revolutionize the means of communication and to make possible the art of writing, as we know it today; for the Roman, the Slavonic, and the Greek alphabets of modern Europe are all descended from the Phoenician alphabet. The Phoenicians and the peoples of Syria excelled also in the weaving and dyeing of embroidered tapestries, the working of bronze, the carving of ivory, and the manufacture of seals, scarabs, and faience. When the culture of the Near East began to spread once more into the Aegean basin, it was natural that Cyprus should play an important part as intermediary. Although intercourse with the Aegean area had been suspended during the dark age, the Greek element in Cyprus preserved many features of Minoan and Mycenaean civilization. A modified form of the Minoan Linear Script, adopted *c.* 1500, was in use *c.* 700–200 (no examples have survived from the period *c.* 1050–700, presumably because perishable materials were used). The Mycenaean style in fine pottery exerted a long-lasting influence, the tradition of epic saga culminated in the composition of the *Cypria* during the eighth century, and the Arcado-Cypriot dialect of the Greek language persisted. This outpost of the Greek race absorbed the rich influences of oriental art without losing its own identity. In this respect it was the forerunner of the Greek states.

During the ninth century contacts between the Near East and the Aegean area were gradually reopened. The main line of communication ran from Cyprus through Crete, Thera, and Melos towards the south-eastern coasts of the Greek mainland, following the path by which the culture of the East had spread in the course of the Middle Bronze Age. A route of secondary import-ance passed through Rhodes. At first contacts were irregular and infrequent, but they resulted in the spread of civilized ideas, which led a century later to a renaissance of Greek culture.

One of the earliest arrivals was the Phoenician alphabet, which was adapted to express Greek words. At first the signs for 'xi', 'phi', 'chi', and 'psi' were lacking, and examples of the alphabet at that stage have been found in Crete, Thera, and Melos. The date of its arrival in Greece is much disputed. Prob-ability points to a date about 825. A *terminus post quem* is given by the appear-ance of the Phoenician alphabet in a fully developed form in Cyprus *c.* 850, and a *terminus ante quem* by the use of a symbol for 'chi' in Attica in the period 750–700 and the occurrence of mature writing on a sherd from Aegina *c.* 720 and on an earlier bowl from Ischia which has a long inscription. An early date within the bracket 850–750 is suggested, because symbols very similar to those of the earliest Greek alphabet were being used in a Phoenician script in Moab *c.* 850. Knowledge of the alphabet spread quickly. Each state in turn devised its own symbols to express those vowels and consonants which were lacking in the Phoenician alphabet. Between 825 and 725 several Greek alphabets came into existence, and the peculiarities of each were re-peated in the colonies, which probably took them overseas in the latter half of the eighth century and onwards (see Fig. 8).

Precious objects from the Near East appeared sporadically in Greece *c.* 850–750. Carved ivories of Phoenician and Syrian craftsmanship, dating to the ninth and eighth centuries, have been found especially in Crete, Rhodes, Samos, Sparta, and Athens. Ivories of a different style, originating in the hinterland of Asia Minor, travelled via Ionia to Corinth. Phoenician in-fluence at Sparta led to the modelling of clay masks and the use of ivory needles for applying kohl to the eyelids. These objects were still rare and reached few mainland states, but they initiated an important traffic.

Such developments were possible because the conditions of life were be-coming less troubled in Crete, Rhodes, Sparta, Corinth, and Athens. The earliest temples which have survived from the Iron Age were built at Drerus in Crete, Sparta, and Perachóra (in south-west Megaris) between 850 and 750. The influences exerted by any one state on others worked slowly in the ninth century. Athenian Geometric pottery, for instance, affected Boeotia, Corinthia, and Argolis soon after 900, but a considerable time elapsed before it affected Sparta, Crete, and Rhodes. Thereafter each state developed its own style of Geometric pottery, Athens and Boeotia, for example, remaining distinct. Corinth had the widest influence, reaching Aegina and in the west Perachóra, Anticyra, and Ithaca; she was already beginning to traffic by sea, and some Corinthians probably settled on Ithaca *c*. 800. The Argive style in pottery extended to Tegea in Arcadia, and Sparta's wares resembled those of Crete and Thera.

In the latter half of the eighth century there was a great expansion of overseas contacts which caused a revolution in Greek ceramic art. The rich tapestries of the Near East with their bright colours and luxuriant designs inspired the potters to develop the 'Orientalizing' styles, in which the restrained linear ornamentation of the Geometric period was replaced by polychrome painting and by fanciful decoration. The new styles appeared first in Crete, Corinth, and Laconia, and later in Athens and Ionia. They represent not only the renaissance of Greek art but also the full establishment of intercourse with the Orient; and their first flourishing coincided with the beginnings of the colonial expansion which was to surpass the achievements of Minoan and Mycenaean colonization.

This new development in Greek art was due mainly to the genius of the Dorian states, Crete, Corinth, and Sparta; and in the ensuing period Corinth was to hold the primacy. If the Ionians fell behind in pottery, they were the pioneers in literary achievement. The *Iliad* and the *Odyssey* were indeed the fountain-head from which almost all forms of later Greek poetry flowed. But, what was more important in the late ninth and the eighth centuries, they revealed to the peoples of the mainland the full beauty of the Late Mycenaean civilization in its material achievements, its religious beliefs, its ideals of personal conduct, and its conception of the universe. The impact of these Ionian epics on the peoples of the mainland was more revolutionary and more lasting than the impact of Orientalizing art. Something of the difference between the Ionian outlook and that of the mainland in the late ninth century is apparent in the *Works and Days* of Hesiod, the Boeotian poet, whom Herodotus regarded as almost contemporary with Homer. Writing in the diction of Homer and using the hexameter in a pedestrian manner, Hesiod was concerned with the immediate problems of life in the poverty-stricken village of Ascra. The smallholder, with his yoke of oxen and a slave or two, must work hard for his subsistence. He must know the seasons and observe the calendar of lucky and unlucky days, to which superstitious taboos were attached. The occasion of the poem was personal; its purpose moral. Hesiod was admonishing his unjust brother, who intended with the collusion of 'bribe-devouring kings' to gain an unfair share of their inherited holding. He argued that human affairs are ruled by Zeus; therefore, justice prevails in the end and honest work alone brings lasting gains. So, too, in the life of a community the just city suffers neither war nor famine, and the unjust city is overwhelmed by disaster.[1] These simple and earnest beliefs were supported by the citation of fable, myth, and proverb, so dear to the heart of the peasant-farmer and so remote from the sophistication of Ionian epic.

In the *Theogony* Hesiod described the various generations of gods and their

[1] Hes. *Op.* 212–47.

wedlock with men and women (the latter being listed as a separate poem, the *Eoiae*); and in the *Catalogues* he set forth the genealogy of the Greek race from its human ancestors, Deucalion and Pyrrha. In these poems Hesiod presented a general and not a local picture of the gods and of the Greek race. We must suppose that he himself collected information about divine and human genealogies, in which the various branches of the Greek race believed; and that he could only have done so when travel and communication were generally possible in the Greek world. It is probable that Hesiod had to systematize the local traditions of folk-memory, where they were at variance one with another; but his own faith and credence, and the authority which was accorded to his work, suggest that he recorded the traditions accurately. In these poems he laid the foundations of theology and of history.

The outlook of the *Theogony* is more primitive than that of the Homeric poems (for it contains much cruder legends and advances a simpler belief in the supremacy of Zeus), but its cosmogony forms an indispensable background to the understanding of Greek religious thought. In the beginning was Chaos; out of Chaos Earth and Tartarus separated, and their offspring formed the material universe. Thereafter Earth and Heaven brought forth the gods, while Night brought forth Death and Fate whose ministers, the Moirae, 'pursue the transgressions of men and of gods'. Thereafter the gods created mankind.[1] According to this cosmogony the material universe is primary. The gods of Heaven and the powers of Tartarus are secondary; and neither group is stronger than the other, except in so far as the latter (for instance, Death and Fate) personify the conditions inherent in the material universe.

The guiding principle of the material universe is respect for order. If the separated elements encroach on one another, the universe will revert to chaos. The society of the gods observe the same principle: 'they divided their wealth and they shared out their powers', each receiving his or her apportionment (*moira*), which was henceforth safeguarded against transgression by the Moirae. The gods of Heaven were ruled by a hereditary monarchy, Cronus being the first monarch and Zeus the second. Within the span of their rule four races of mankind had passed away. The fifth was the contemporary race, the men of iron 'who never rest from labour and sorrow by day and from perishing by night'.[2] Man himself is subject to the conditions of the material universe, to the gods of Heaven and to the powers of Tartarus; and he will ultimately be destroyed by Zeus for his transgressions against the Justice of Zeus.

In Hesiod's poems there is no discord between the Justice of Zeus and man's own sense of justice. Hesiod was confident that the just man will prevail in the end, and the just city will suffer no disaster. This, he held, is the will of Zeus, and Zeus controls the events of human life. To later Greek thinkers this view was not always so acceptable. When they attempted to

---

[1] Hes. *Th.* 116 f.　　　　　　　　　　　[2] Hes. *Op.* 109 f.; *Th.* 176.

bring into harmony the Justice of Zeus and man's sense of justice, they had to modify the Hesiodic cosmogony.

The poems of Hesiod and the later poems of the Hesiodic school probably derived part of their subject-matter from the priests who tended the temple of Apollo at Delphi. The utterances of the Pythian priestess, the mouthpiece of the god, were partly based on the accumulated wisdom of the priests in both sacred and secular matters. The prestige of the oracle had been enhanced by its adherence to the Dorians at the time of their invasion, and the worship of Apollo Pythius was of great importance in the Dorian states. Sparta, in particular, attributed her dual kingship, her conquest of Amyclae with the help of the Aegeidae and her constitution to the oracular responses of Delphi; each king of Sparta was represented by two Spartans elected as 'Pythii', who consulted the oracle and preserved the oracular responses.[1] The fame of the oracle was already paramount on the mainland early in the eighth century. It supplied the orthodox version of religious and moral precepts, and it fostered the intercourse between the Greek states which arose from more settled conditions.

In the west of the Peloponnese another centre of religion arose at Olympia, the chief sanctuary of Zeus. For a time after the Dorian invasion the worship at this sanctuary was of only local importance, but the Olympic festival, founded in 776, soon attracted representatives from many states in Greece. Celebrated in every fourth year, the games were held in honour of Olympian Zeus. A religious truce protected the participants on their pilgrimage to and from the shrine. The list of victors, recorded from 776, is the earliest record of any inter-state significance on the mainland. It is probable that cults of regional importance were also observed at this period, such as the Amphictyony of northern Greek tribes meeting at Anthela near Thermopylae, the Pamboiotia celebrated near Coronea, and the worship of Poseidon at Calauria, in which several states adjacent to the Saronic Gulf and also Orchomenus participated.

Overseas the festival of Apollo at Delos was observed by the Ionians. A chorus was sent by the Messenians for the first time *c.* 750, Eumelus of Corinth composing the hymn for the occasion. In the *Hymn to Apollo* a rivalry between Delos and Delphi is apparent. The poem consists of two parts, originally independent, which are probably to be dated to the eighth century. The two parts of this Hymn and some of the other *Homeric Hymns* were probably composed to be sung in competitions at a festival rather than as preludes to recitations of epic poetry. In such a contest held at Chalcis in Euboea Hesiod competed and won the prize.[2]

§ 2. *The rise of City-states*

As intercourse was gradually resumed, a new political world began to emerge from the dark age of the migrations. With the exception of Attica, the great

[1] Hdt. 6. 57. 2.   [2] Hes. *Op.* 650 f.; Paus. 4. 4. 1.

states of the Mycenaean period had been destroyed for ever. During and after the migrations the Aeolians and the Ionians were incapable of reconstituting the extensive baronies and the large tribal states, comprising a number of inhabited centres, which had flourished on the Greek mainland at the time of the Trojan War. On the Asiatic coast each settlement was isolated, so that its settlers formed a single and self-contained entity; and they only maintained their hold by concentrating round a defensible city and staving off their enemies.

Under such conditions in Asia Minor a series of small city-states sprang into being, incapable at the outset of linking together and incapable, as the event proved, of conquering the hinterland to form a larger and unified state. For each settlement the defensible centre, the *polis* of the epic saga, took on a new significance: it became the focus of social and political life. In this sense the *polis* figures on the Shield of Achilles: there it is the scene of the wedding feast with music and dance and gazing women and of the elders judging a lawsuit in the presence of the assembled citizens. Such a description is more relevant to the conditions of Homer's own lifetime than to the citadel of Achilles' barony. For in the ninth century the Ionian and the Aeolian city-states of the Asiatic coast were firmly established. The islands, too, were small in extent, and most of them harboured a single community. A few contained several independent communities: Aeolian Lesbos, for instance, had five city-states and Ionian Ceos four. Their survival as independent states into classical times is a testimony to the spirit of particularism, which characterized all branches of the Hellenic race.

Such was the origin of the Aeolian and the Ionian form of the city-state. It was due initially to the fragmentation of the Mycenaean states, and it was fostered by the geographical conditions of the areas in which the migrants settled. Yet these city-states had much in common with the Mycenaean Age. They were racially tolerant, each comprising in its citizen body peoples of different origin. They perpetuated the cults, the dialects, and the tribal systems which their forefathers had developed on the mainland in the Late Bronze Age. For all their enterprise and vivacity they lacked the compact and exclusive solidarity which evolved under different conditions in the Dorian states of Crete and the Peloponnese.

On the mainland and in the south Aegean the period *c.* 850–750 was marked, as we have seen, by the renewal of contact with the civilization of the Near East and by the growing intercourse between the Greek states which arose from more settled conditions. Under these favourable circumstances the Dorian states attained a political form which assured them the leadership in the archaic period and in some cases survived throughout the classical period. Crete, the intermediary between the Near East and the mainland, was reputed in antiquity to have the most ancient *politeia*, a term which means both a community of citizens and a form of constitution. The Cretans maintained that the Dorian conquerors of Lyttus adopted there a constitution which had been instituted by Minos; and that this constitution was taken from Lyttus by the other Dorian communities in the island.[1] There, as elsewhere, the Dorian invaders had originally settled in villages (*komai*); they had reduced the earlier population to serfdom, and had maintained their own racial organization in the three Dorian tribes, which subdivided into *startoi* (equivalent to phratries) and into *gene*. By the end of the dark age the lines of a constitution common to all the Dorian communities in Crete were firmly drawn, and they persisted unchanged until the third century. The remarkable feature of these Cretan constitutions was the orientation of the citizens not towards their family group but towards the state alone.[2] On attaining the age of seventeen, the boys were recruited by the sons of leading houses into troops (*agelai*). These troops underwent a hard training in athletics, in hunting, and in mock-warfare to the accompaniment of the flute and lyre; discipline in each troop was maintained by the father of the boy who had recruited the members of his troop. Those who failed to gain admission were excluded from the political franchise and had lesser rights at law. Those who had acquitted themselves well in the troop were admitted at the age of nineteen to a men's mess, *andreion* or *hetairia*; the members of each mess fed together and campaigned together thereafter. The men were betrothed in marriage at the age of nineteen. The bride came to her husband when she reached maturity, and they set up house together; but from an early age the male children attended the mess to which their father belonged, and underwent a hard training as boarders before joining the *agela*.

Both the troops and the messes were maintained at public expense. The members of each mess received from the state sufficient means to support their family, and they were trained solely to serve the state in politics and in war. Family life was reduced to a minimum, the women being largely segregated from the men. The earlier racial system, with its tribes, phratries, and *gene*, lost all political significance in the community of citizens; but it persisted as a framework, within which the hereditary principle of citizenship was preserved. The sons jointly inherited the town-house, and an heiress was given in marriage to a fellow-tribesman, if close relatives were lacking. But any racial matter of political significance, such as adoption into a franchised family, had to be approved both in the mess and in the assembly.

In contrast to the franchised community, known as 'the warrior class' (*to machimon*), the non-franchised community, 'the land-working class' (*to georgoun*), comprised several grades of serfs and of slaves. The serfs were tied to the land, the *klarotai* probably to the *klaros* or original estate of a franchised family, the *mnoitai* to the common or state lands and the *aphamiotai* to other family estates. In addition, such peoples as had been conquered after the original settlement by the Dorians were called *perioikoi*, and they paid tribute to the conquerors. This class had some civil rights, such as those of owning and inheriting property. They were on a higher level than the bought slaves

[1] Arist. *Pol.* 1271ᵇ20. [2] Str. 480 f.

(*chrysonetoi*), who were their owners' personal property.[1] The citizens of military age in the average state were numbered only in hundreds, while their serfs and slaves were far more numerous. Therefore the citizens had a monopoly of all arms, military training, and political power, and they lived close together in the town-houses which formed their 'city'. Their position is admirably epitomized in the Cretan drinking song of Hybrias. 'My wealth is spear and sword, and the stout shield which protects my flesh; with this I plough, with this I reap, with this I tread the sweet wine from the grape, with this I am entitled master of the serfs.'[2]

These small privileged communities had need of a stable and conservative constitution. At the time of the invasion each group of Dorians had been governed by a hereditary kingship, which was supported by the elders, or heads of clans, who formed a council (*boule* or *gerousia*). When the kingship lapsed, the citizens elected from certain phratries (*startoi*) ten magistrates (*kosmoi*), who exercised the military command and other executive duties of the kingship. These magistrates were elected annually; they gave their name to the year, and they were liable to impeachment on concluding their year of office. The ten *kosmoi*, forming a committee with a secretary, maintained the social system of *agelai* and *andreia*. From the ex-magistrates the citizens elected a Council of thirty Elders, who held office for life, administered by edict and were not liable to audit. The Assembly, meeting in the town-centre (*agora*), elected the magistrates and the councillors. As a consultative body, the Assembly's function was simply to approve the agreed resolutions of the magistrates and the councillors; but if the magistrates and councillors disagreed, the assembly decided between any rival proposals.

In this constitution the executive and the Council possessed the widest powers. The Assembly had no right of initiating policy, and the electoral system was designed to maintain an oligarchy of administrative merit. The survival of the hereditary principle in the election of magistrates and councillors from certain phratries suggests that the constitution was evolved at an early stage of political development. The same constitution and the same organization of society were adopted in all the Dorian states in Crete, which numbered as many as a hundred; the adoption was probably gradual, and in one state at least the kingship still survived in the late seventh century. Crete thus became a society of small independent Dorian communities, which often went to war with one another but never raised their enemy's serfs in revolt; their common interest preserved them from the dangers which were ultimately to undermine the Dorian states on the mainland.[3]

The conditions of the dark age were probably responsible for the origin of the Dorian *polis* in Crete and elsewhere. At the time of the conquest the Dorian invaders had a wide tribal organization, similar to that of the peoples they dispossessed. But, as conditions deteriorated and intercourse declined,

[1] Arist. *Pol.* 1264[a]21; 1272[a]17; 1329[b]1.   [2] Ath. 695[f].
[3] Arist. *Pol.* 1272[a]; 1273[a]; 1269[a]39.

the wide horizons of the conquest vanished. Each group of conquerors, settled as an aggregate of related families in a village (*kome*), became an independent and isolated unit concerned with the problem of holding down its serfs. When conditions improved, the independent units were drawn together by common interests not into the earlier tribal organization but into small groups of adjacent villages. Such a group became the primitive *polis*. In the words of Aristotle 'the partnership of several villages is the full-grown *polis*, which already possesses the dimensions of virtually complete self-sufficiency'.[1]

The origin of the *polis* endowed it with pronounced characteristics. It inherited a strong sense of kinship from its constituent elements, the *komai*, so that citizenship was generally defined by hereditary descent on both sides. It perpetuated the distinction between master and serf and maintained the privilege of the citizen class in the community. It fostered the agricultural economy which was the source of its self-sufficiency, and it ensured for its citizen class an adequate degree of leisure to practise the arts of peace or war.

These characteristics persisted in many city-states for centuries; and they dominated the imagination of the political theorists of the fourth century. When the constituent villages were fully merged into the *polis*, a remarkably compact and almost indestructible community was created. Moreover, it generated an intense patriotism and dynamic energy. As compared with the unaggregated and independent *komai* on the one hand, and the looser Ionian and Arcadian states on the other hand, the Dorian city-state had superior strength. This was demonstrated most remarkably by the formation and the expansion of the Spartan state.

The Spartans of the fifth century believed that their institutions had been derived from the Cretan *politeia*. The similarity was indeed so close that their belief should not be doubted. The Spartan system of education was also designed to attach the child to the state rather than to the family.[2] From the age of seven the boys lived away from home. Organized into troops (*ilai, bouai,* and *agelai*), which were controlled by a state-superintendent (*paidonomos*) and led by a head-boy (*bouagor*), they became inured to physical hardship and to strict discipline, and their loyalty to the troop was fostered by contests with other troops. From eighteen to twenty they were trained for war and employed on secret service (*crypteia*) against the serfs. Then they lived in barracks under military discipline until the age of thirty, when they finally completed the course of education (*agoge*).

The members of the outgoing year were nominated for membership of a mess (*andreion* or *syssition*) and were admitted only if their election was unopposed. The successful candidate was a full citizen or 'equal' (*homoios*); the unsuccessful or 'inferior' (*hypomeion*) had no vote in politics and lesser rights in civil law. Marriage could be contracted at the age of twenty, but a man did not set up house until he was thirty years of age. Even so he continued to feed in his mess until the age of sixty. The girls, too, were organized in

[1] Arist. *Pol.* 1252^{b}28.   [2] Hdt. 1. 65. 4; Arist. *Pol.* 1271^{b}23; Plu. *Lyc.* 16 f.

troops. Although they lived and fed at home, they received a similar training in athletics, dancing, and music, and they mixed freely with the young men, until they assumed a veil on their marriage and lived at home. By this mode of life a high standard of physical perfection was achieved. New-born children were scrutinized by the elders of their tribe, and the sickly were exposed in a glen on Mt. Taygetus. At each stage in his long period of training the future citizen was closely supervised and tested. On its completion he was indelibly stamped in the Spartan mould, brave, disciplined, and loyal.

The earlier structure of racial tribe, phratry, and genos survived in such cults as the worship of Apollo Karneios, but it was devoid of any political significance. The hereditary principle remained a condition of citizenship, and only the sons of citizens could become citizens. But the solidarity of the family was weakened by a state-regulation which permitted the alienation of property by will and the free disposal of an heiress. For the Spartan state could tolerate no rival loyalties. The *élite* group of 'equals' must stand together in the task of controlling the subject-class. Each family owned a hereditary estate (*klaros*), which it was dishonourable to sell.[1] The estate was worked solely by Helots, who were tied to the land as state-serfs and could be emancipated or executed only by state-decree. Of the produce the Helots rendered a fixed amount annually to the owner and kept the residue. Despite their hard lot and limited rights the Helots were recruited as troops and rewarded by grants of freedom. But the danger of insurrection was always present. In order to avert it, the state declared war annually on the Helots and the 'secret service' disposed of any suspects without incurring blood-guilt.

This social system was not instituted at the time of the invasion. The early history of the Dorians at Sparta was marked by bitter strife, probably waged between racial groups; and in the course of it some non-Dorian peoples were enfranchised, in order to strengthen the free community.[2] Archaeology sheds a little light on that period. At Amyclae, where a shrine of Apollo had been instituted late in the Mycenaean period, there was no ostensible break in the cult and the transition from Mycenaean to Protogeometric pottery was gradual. In the area of Sparta itself new settlements and shrines were established; at these sites the earliest pottery was not uniform, and their outside contact was with Amyclae. But in the mid-ninth century the shrine of Artemis Orthia became an important centre with a continuous style of pottery, which was common to the Acropolis, the shrine of Athena Chalcioecus, the Heroon, Menelaion, and Amyclae. It is therefore probable that settled conditions were established in the mid-ninth century. At that time, too, Sparta was opening contact with Crete and so with the Near East.

The change from internal strife to an ordered society was attributed throughout antiquity to Lycurgus, the author of the reform known as the *Eunomia*, which embraced both the social system and the political constitu-

[1] Ath. 141^f; Arist. *Pol.* 1270^{a}20.
[2] Hdt. 1. 65. 2; Th. 1. 18. 1; Hdt. 4. 145. 5; Arist. *Pol.* 1270^{a}35.

tion. The date of the reform was and is disputed. Almost all the ancients placed it in the tenth or ninth century; modern scholars vary from the late ninth century to the sixth century. As it was believed that Lycurgus lived before the introduction of an annual dating-system in 757 he could only be dated in terms of a king's reign; but our earliest authorities give different reigns. In this dilemma the authority of Thucydides carries most weight: 'the Lacedaemonians enjoyed the same *politeia* for somewhat more than four hundred years up to the end of the war', that is in our reckoning from the last quarter of the ninth century.[1]

The general nature of the reform was not disputed in antiquity. It affected the social system and the political constitution, which show every indication of having been interrelated. The figure of Lycurgus is as shadowy as that of Homer. All we know, apart from his reform, is that a religious cult in his honour was observed at Sparta and that he was canonized in the oracular responses of Delphi. Some scholars have doubted whether a man Lycurgus ever existed, but the matter is relatively unimportant. Others have doubted whether one man could have been responsible for the reform; yet the fact that in a small community one statesman could carry a fundamental reform is amply demonstrated by the famous examples of Solon, Cleisthenes, Timoleon, and others. On such grounds it is sensible to accept the main conclusions of the ancient writers, based on local Spartan tradition, that a man, called Lycurgus, carried a sweeping reform in the period 825–800.

The aims of the constitutional reform were to diminish the rights of the double kingship (the two kings being, according to Spartan tradition, descended from the twins Eurysthenes and Procles); to change the membership of the Council (*Gerousia*); and to ensure the rights of the Assembly. The two kings retained their command in war and their importance in religious cult, as before, but they were now made ordinary members of the Council for all political purposes. The councillors in the past may have been the heads of the twenty-seven phratries. Their number was now raised to thirty, including the two kings. The councillors were elected in the Assembly by acclamation, only 'Equals' of sixty or more years of age being eligible for election, and they held office for life.[2] The Council alone had the right of proposing motions in the Assembly and of dismissing the Assembly. All the 'Equals' participated in the Assembly, which was henceforth to meet at a fixed place and at fixed times. Its electoral powers were defined, and its decision on the proposals submitted by the Council was binding. Lycurgus also instituted the Ephorate, the five Ephors being elected annually by the acclamation of the Assembly from the ranks of the Equals.[3] At this stage the Ephors did not hold a leading position in the political constitution. They supervised the working of the social system; they inspected the physical con-

---

[1] Th. 1. 18. 1; Hdt. 1. 65. 4; Plu. *Lyc.* 1; Arist. *Pol.* 1271[b]25. For the early date of Lycurgus' reform see *StGH* 85–103, and for 700–670 W. G. G. Forrest, *A History of Sparta*, pp. 41–60.
[2] Plu. *Lyc.* 5.
[3] Hdt. 1. 65. 5.

dition of the boys, judged cases of disobedience, and led the contingents at the Gymnopaediae (a national festival of music and athletics). On entering office the Ephors proclaimed an oath to the people 'to shave off the moustache and to obey the laws'—a true reflection of the Spartan's social and civic duties.[1] By these reforms Lycurgus overthrew all barriers of racial privilege and prejudice within the community of citizens. In the *agoge* and in the Assembly all Spartans were equal before the state, regardless of family lineage and of material wealth, and in the constitution, however strong the powers of the Gerousia might be, their voice was decisive in the cardinal issues of election and of ratification.

A summary statement of this constitutional reform has survived in the so-called Great Rhetra, which Aristotle copied and Plutarch transmitted. The Rhetra was an oracular response from Delphi, which thereby gave its blessing to the reform, and it was presumably preserved at Sparta by the Pythii. If we take into consideration Aristotle's commentary as recorded by Plutarch, we may translate this the earliest Greek document as follows. 'Found a sanctuary to Zeus Syllanius and Athena Syllania, form tribes and obes, set up a membership of thirty for the Gerousia including the kings, from season to season assemble between Babyka and Knakion; under these conditions (the Gerousia shall) introduce (proposals) and adjourn (the Assembly); the citizens shall be the Assembly and the decisive authority.'[2] The two opening sentences refer probably to the most important aspect of the reform. Zeus and Athena were associated very closely with the Spartan state in later times. They were, for instance, the deities who presided over the deliberations of the Council and the Assembly. The new shrine with the cult-title 'Syllanius' was probably dedicated to Zeus and Athena as protectors of the newly formed state. The tribes and the obes were evidently an innovation, replacing, for political purposes, the three racial tribes of the past and their subdivisions. In classical times the Spartan state consisted of five tribes and of five obes or local wards, which were four villages in the plain and the village of Amyclae. As the names of the tribes and the obes were the same, it seems that the original tribesmen of the new tribes were residents of the corresponding obes, and the qualification was one of residence. Their descendants continued to be members of a tribe by heredity, whether they lived in the original obe or not. These sentences probably record the act by which the Spartan state was formed from the franchised inhabitants of five villages, who were marshalled as citizens of Sparta in five tribes by their place of residence. It was from these divisions that the five regiments of the Spartan army were recruited as territorial units, and that the five Ephors may have been elected.[3]

By this fundamental reform the first *polis* or 'city-state' of the classical type on the Greek mainland came into existence. It was, as Aristotle so neatly ex-

[1] Arist. *Fr.* 539.   [2] Plu. *Lyc.* 6.
[3] *IG* 5. 1. 564. 4; 480. 9; Hsch. s.v. *Pitanates Stratos*; St. Byz. s.v. *Messoa*; Arist. *Fr.* 541.

pressed it, 'an association of several villages which achieves almost complete self-sufficiency'.[1] The association was political and not physical. No 'city' in an urban sense was created; for the separate villages retained their physical character. But a new and overriding citizenship was created, in which the political independence of the villages was submerged for ever. The result at Sparta was a strong and compact body of citizens, who owed full loyalty to the state and were distinct in privilege from the subject community of serfs and slaves. Citizenship was a hereditary prerogative. The state was in this respect an enlarged family group, proud and exclusive, but incapable of expanding save by an increase in the birth rate.

Sparta was not only the first *polis* of this type on the mainland. At one stroke she achieved a political maturity, which was to be emulated by other states in later centuries. Lycurgus had cut the strands of the racial nexus of tribe, phratry, and genos by instituting the *agoge* and creating new tribes based on residence. Other states preserved this racial nexus, which acted as a virus infecting the body politic. They were destined to pass through the stages of civil strife and of tyranny, before they placed loyalty to the state before loyalty to the clan and granted equal rights to all citizens. Thus in very early times Sparta received a well-ordered constitution. To it she owed her military power, her freedom from tyranny, and her influence in the Greek world.[2]

§ 3. *The expansion of Sparta*

THE Dorian inhabitants of Laconia lived in independent villages, a hundred in number, it was said, and were organized in six kingdoms.[3] But the kings of Sparta, as descendants of the Heracleidae who had first conquered Laconia, claimed a traditional suzerainty over them all as 'Lakedaimonioi'. When five villages had united to form the Spartan state, Sparta conquered the other villages *c.* 800–730 and reduced their inhabitants to vassaldom as *perioikoi*. The subject villages thenceforth administered their internal affairs under the supervision of a Spartan resident (*harmostes*), paid tithes on some of their land to the Spartan kings, and accepted the foreign policy of Sparta. They had no citizen rights or political representation at Sparta, but they were liable to conscription and to Spartan military law in time of war. Thus the whole of Laconia became the Lacedaemonian state, of which the control was entirely in Sparta's hands. She was now protected by a ring of subject communities, and her army was enlarged by their contingents.

The next step was the conquest of Messenia. The war, which lasted for twenty years, *c.* 740–720, ended in the annexation of the country, which was almost as large as Laconia. 'Spacious Messene, good to till and good to plant', was divided into lots (*klaroi*) for the Spartiates, and villages of Perioikoi were established in the hills. The Messenian stronghold, Ithome, was destroyed

---

[1] Arist. *Pol.* 1252[b]28.   [2] Th. 1. 18. 1.   [3] Str. 362; 364.

and the Messenian survivors were reduced to serfdom, 'toiling like asses under great burdens, and rendering half of the ploughlands' produce to their masters under bitter constraint'. By this conquest the agricultural resources and the labour-force of the Spartan state were doubled. Sparta was now potentially the richest and most powerful state in eighth-century Greece— potentially because the consolidation of her conquests in Laconia and Messenia was a gradual process. The first Dorian *polis* of the mainland had shown formidable strength in the first century of its existence.[1]

Under the strain of expansion Sparta's constitution was somewhat modified. During the reign of Polydorus and Theopompus, probably *c.* 757, a further sentence was added to the Great Rhetra with the blessing of Delphi: 'but, if the people declare wrongly, the Elders and Kings shall be adjourners'. The right of decision which Lycurgus had given to the Assembly was curtailed by this sentence; for, if its views were not to the taste of the Gerousia, it was simply dismissed. Thereafter, as in Crete, the function of the Assembly was merely to ratify the agreed proposals of the Gerousia. However, if the Gerousia was divided, then the choice between the rival proposals of its members still lay with the Assembly, whose decision was binding.[2] This modification of the constitution strengthened the hand of the Gerousia. When its members were unanimous, it could anticipate the Assembly's ratification, and therefore took secret but valid decisions, as, for example, in the prelude to the second Peloponnesian war.

The weakening of the democratic side of the constitution was to some extent made good by elevating the Ephorate to a position of constitutional importance. As elected representatives of the people, the Ephors each month received the oath of the kings to observe the laws, and they themselves gave the oath to respect the authority of the kings. Two of the Ephors accompanied a king on a campaign, and these were entitled to arrest and prosecute him on his return to Sparta. The judicial powers of the kings, save in matters of adoption and of inheritance, were transferred to the Ephors. Minor magistrates could be suspended from office and prosecuted by the Ephors, and any Spartan citizen could be summarily punished by their decree. They also pronounced the formal declaration of war against the Helots each year, and they could order the arrest of Perioeci. They were entitled to attend the meetings of the Gerousia, and they led the Assembly. Their powers were indeed so great that in later times, when the prestige of the kings sank low, they came to dominate the state 'like tyrants'.[3]

§ 4. *Other Dorian 'City-states'*

THE success of Sparta inspired other Dorians to follow her example. In the Megarid the Dorians, divided as usual into three racial tribes, had reduced the

---

[1] Tyrt. 4 and 5; Paus. 4. 4. 3 f.; E. *Fr.* 1083.
[2] Plu. *Lyc.* 6; Arist. *Pol.* 1272ª12; 1273ª6 f.
[3] Arist, *Pol.* 1270ᵇ; 1313ª25; Plu. *Lyc.* 7; X. *Lac.* 15. 7.

non-Dorian inhabitants to serfdom and lived themselves in five independent villages (*komai*). In the eighth century, probably *c.* 750, these villages coalesced politically, but not physically, to form the *polis* or city-state of Megara. The citizens were brigaded in five tribes, which were based on the five villages; they appointed five generals and five magistrates (*demiourgoi*), and each tribe provided a military contingent to the army of the state. The villages were left only with some powers of local government, and their political life was absorbed into the larger state of 'the Megarians', which soon showed its vigour in war with Corinth and in colonization overseas.[1]

In Corinthia the Dorians gave their franchise to some members of the non-Dorian nobility, who formed a tribe, called the Cynophali, alongside the usual three Dorian tribes. At first the Dorians lived probably in independent villages; for three inhabited sites, which are dated to the ninth and eighth centuries and are the remains of small villages, have been excavated within the area occupied later by Corinth. There was an ancient tradition that 'in accordance with an oracle Aletes made the Corinthians live together, creating eight tribes of citizens and eight divisions of the state'. As Aletes led the original invaders of Corinthia, he cannot be credited with this later development, but we may take the statement to mean that the *polis* or city-state of the Corinthians was created by a political union of eight village communities which provided the personnel of eight tribes. This step was taken probably in the eighth century, before 747 when the list of eponymous magistrates began. Corinth, like Sparta, prided herself on her *Eunomia*, and two Corinthians won fame as legislators. Pheidon, reputed to be one of the earliest Greek legislators, passed laws which were designed to keep the number of town houses (and thus the number of citizens) at a constant figure at Corinth, even though the original estates (*klaroi*) were unequal in size. He was evidently tackling a problem which Lycurgus solved at Sparta. Philolaus, who was active in 728, left Corinth for Thebes, where his regulations about adoption were designed to maintain the number of estates (*klaroi*) and therefore of citizens at Thebes, which may now have become a city-state.[2]

The energies of the new states, Megara and Corinth, were expended not only in planting powerful colonies but also in warring with one another. The bone of contention was southern Megaris, probably including Perachóra. Corinth annexed this area and reduced the inhabitants to serfdom *c.* 725, but a Megarian, Orsippus, who won a race at Olympia in 720, succeeded in a war of liberation. By the end of the century Corinth gained control of Perachóra and southern Megaris for good.[3]

The Dorian type of city-state, which arose in Crete, Sparta, Megara,

---

[1] Plu. *GQ.* 17; earliest mention of Megara in Hes. *Fr.* 96. 8 and of the ethnic Megarēs in the epigram recording the victory of Orsippus in 720 B.C. (*IG.* 7. 52).

[2] Suid. s.v. *Panta Okto*; Arist. *Pol.* 1265ᵇ12; 1274ᵃ32; Pi. *O.* 13. 6.

[3] Scholia to Pl. *Euthyd.* 292 e and to Pi. *N.* 7. 105; references in n. 1; see *BSA* 49. 93.

Corinth, and probably Thebes, had not been known in the Mycenaean world. It was created by Dorians and not by the Ionians, Aeolians, and Arcadians who were heirs of the Mycenaean traditions. It gave an initial superiority of power to the Dorian states, and it was to be the hallmark of Hellenic civilization.

Merchantman under sail, from an Attic Black Figure vase, *c.* 540

CHAPTER 2

The Colonial Expansion of the Greek City-states

§ 1. *The resources of Greece*

IN the field of practical affairs no achievement of the Greek city-states was more far-reaching and more lasting in its effects than the colonial movement. It provided the channel through which Hellenism reached the peoples of southern Europe, the countries surrounding the Black Sea, and the Libyan coast of Africa. The plantation of the colonies was a vital step in the development not only of Hellenic but also of European civilization. The agent of colonization was the city-state, and the effect of colonization was the city-state. Whether Corinth or Colophon was the foundress of a colony, that colony was itself a new city-state. As we have seen, the city-state was a diminutive unit in terms of world power. But it proved its potency just as signally in its colonizing activity as in its repulse of the Persian empire.

Greek colonization was sea-borne. Its limits were set by the rival sea powers of Phoenicia, Etruria, and Egypt. The colonies were planted on islands or on coastal strips, at the expense of peoples who were not as yet organized into strong states. When the colonies themselves expanded, they planted further colonies on similar sites and rarely ventured into the hinterland. For success they depended on their seamanship. The merchantman was, as it had been in the Bronze Age, a sailing vessel with broad beam, deep draught, curved hull, high stem and stern; small, slow, and seaworthy (see p. 108). The warship, however, underwent a new development during the late ninth century and the eighth century. It was then built with a low straight hull, of which the keel-beam was prolonged to form a thin ram. Its side-decks provided fighting-platforms for marines. Capable of moving under sail, the ship was propelled in action by single banks of oarsmen (Plate III *a*). Late in the eighth century a different type of warship is portrayed on a Corinthian vase: a long low vessel with a tapering ram, twenty-one rowing-ports piercing each side, and no decks. Both types of warship, the partly decked and the undecked, were in vogue during the seventh century. But the latter predominated in the sixth century; it was then standardized in two classes, the triaconter of thirty oars and the 90-foot penteconter of fifty oars. This development in ship construction accompanied a change in battle tactics from boarding to ramming. For the triaconter and the penteconter were eminently fast and manœuvrable weapons for ramming an enemy vessel (see p. 138 and Plate III*b*). In comparison with them the Phoenician warship of *c.* 705–686, with a double bank of oarsmen and a prominent ram, was clumsy and top-heavy.

During most of the eighth century the Ionian states probably held the lead; for at this time they were pioneers in exploration and in colonization. But the construction of the new type of warship, of which the standard examples were the triaconter and the penteconter (and much later the trireme), was due to a Dorian state, Corinth. Four warships of this type were built *c.* 705 for Samos by a Corinthian shipwright, Ameinocles. Paros and Miletus also possessed penteconters early in the seventh century.[1] This new development enabled Corinth and her colonies to establish a long-lasting supremacy in the waters between Greece and Sicily. Yet such a supremacy did not lead to a monopoly of the high seas. These small open vessels preferred to put into land at night and were less seaworthy in rough weather than the merchantmen, so that the imposition of a blockade was not practicable. Moreover, the city-state was itself small and numbered its war-fleet in tens rather than in hundreds; for instance, at Alalia *c.* 535 the Phocaeans manned sixty penteconters. Thus during the colonizing period no single state possessed an outright mastery of the seas, a 'thalassocracy' as it was to be called in the fifth century.[2]

For this reason among others it is doubtful whether, for the early period at least, any credence should be attached to a so-called 'List of Thalassocracies' which has come down to us in the text of Diodorus Siculus. The list purports to enumerate the Thalassocrats and the duration of each Thalassocracy from shortly after the sack of Troy down to the expedition of Alexander (sometimes emended to 'Xerxes').[3] Rather is it apparent from the large number of states which founded colonies in the west that the fleet of Corinth was little more than *prima inter pares*.

Sooner or later the colonies had to fight, in order to establish or maintain their colony against the local peoples and often against neighbouring colonists. Skill in warfare was of the greatest importance. In the mid-seventh century Ionians and Carians were employed in mercenary service by the Pharaoh Psammetichus I as the finest infantrymen of the Near East. They were named 'the men of bronze', because they wore protective body-armour of bronze—helmet, corslet, and greaves.[4] This armour was designed for use in close combat. The infantryman attacked with a thrusting spear and protected his exposed parts with a round shield, which was secured to the left forearm by a metal sheath. The invention of this equipment, coupled with the courage and skill of the Greek heavy-armed infantryman or 'hoplite' as he came to be called after his shield (*hoplon*), secured for Greek arms a supremacy which lasted until the rise of the Macedonian infantry. Its adoption can be dated approximately by the portrayal of its distinctive features in vase-paintings and in figurines: in Sparta, Corinth, Athens, Crete, and Chios *c.* 700–675, in Boeotia, Euboea, and the Cyclades *c.* 700–650, and in the cities of Asia Minor somewhat later. As this archaeological evidence only gives a *terminus ante quem*, it is probable that the hoplite equipment developed on the

---

[1] Th. 1. 13. 2–3; Archil. 51. 10 and 117.   [2] Hdt. 1. 166; 3. 122. 2.
[3] D.S. 7. 11.   [4] Hdt. 2. 152. 4.

mainland and pre-eminently in the Dorian city-states shortly before 700. Thus the Corinthian colonists, for instance, relied not only on their warships

(*a*) Gold signet-ring, from Shaft Grave iv at Mycenae, showing the use of the body shield, thrusting spear, rapier-sword, and dagger

(*c*) Bronze slashing sword from Moulianá in Crete, of late Minoan III period.

(*b*) Ivory head, from Myce-nae, showing a boar's tusk helmet

(*d*) Warrior-vase from Mycenae, of late Helladic III period, showing fore-and-aft helmet, smaller shield, and thrusting spear

FIG. 10 (see p. 51)

but also on their infantrymen, when they planted colonies. Nor were the Greeks of the colonizing period formidable only as heavy infantry; for they were also adept in the use of sword, bow, sling, and throwing javelin.[1]

[1] Callin. 1; Archil. 2 and 3.

These developments in seamanship and warfare were not alone responsible for the success of Greek colonization. The fundamental basis of the colonizing movement was, as Thucydides observed, the achievement of settled conditions in the homeland. Then the city-state, and especially the Dorian city-state, came to birth and possessed sufficient resources and organizing skill to plant colonies at the expense of less developed peoples. At this time, too, the world of Greek city-states was not embroiled in the Great Wars between rival coalitions which racked the fifth and fourth centuries and put an end to large-scale colonization. Wars occurred indeed between state and state in the seventh and sixth centuries, but they were local in extent and less catastrophic in their effect.[1]

§ 2. *The character of the colonies*

THE Greek colony was 'a settlement far from home' (*apoikia*). The colonists set out under the leadership of a 'colonizer' (*oikistes*), and they took from the hearth of their city the sacred fire which was to inaugurate the foundation of a new *polis*. They took, too, the religious and political institutions of their city cults: constitution, calendar, dialect, alphabet, &c. The new state became a replica of the old. Thus in the colonies of Miletus the eponymous official was the priest of Apollo, the *Stephanephoros*, and the chief magistrates were the *Prytaneis*; Cyzicus, for example, preserved the special worship of Apollo, the division into six tribes, the calendar, and the alphabet of Miletus. Epizephyrian Locri was governed by a Council of one thousand members, themselves descendants of the 'Hundred Houses' which formed the aristocracy of Opuntian Locris. Taras, a colony of Sparta, worshipped Apollo Hyacinthius and at first was ruled by a king. When the primary colonies themselves founded secondary colonies, they usually invited as *oikistes* a citizen of their home state and transplanted the same institutions. The Corcyraeans founded Epidamnus under the leadership of a Heraclid from Corinth; Heraclea, a colony of Taras, had a college of ephors; and Euesperides, a colony of Cyrene, both ephors and gerousia. Thus the sentimental attachment between foundress and colony was exceptionally strong. It derived from the indebtedness of the colonists to the state which had organized and launched the undertaking, and it was fostered by a strong sense of kinship with all its familial, religious, and political associations.

But once the colony was securely established, the cord between foundress and colony was cut. It was a symbol of the complete independence of the *apoikia* that it worshipped not its foundress but its *oikistes*, even if he was of alien origin.[2] In general the foundress seems to have claimed no political rights over her colony. A few exceptions are known. Corinth demanded precedence in joint ceremonies with colonies and sent annual magistrates to Potidaea; Zancle retained political control of Mylae, and Sinope exacted tribute from

[1] Th. 1. 12. 4; 1. 15. 2. [2] Hdt. 1. 168.

her own colonies in the fourth century.[1] It is not possible to determine whether these exceptions date from the colonizing period or came into being later. Privileges might indeed be granted voluntarily to the foundress, such as the immunity from taxation granted by Olbia to citizens of Miletus resident at Olbia. Or the foundress might be invited to arbitrate in a dispute between two of her colonies. But such privileges and invitations were extended also to states other than the foundress. Arbitration arose too from contacts which preceded the age of colonization; for instance, Argos arbitrated between Tylissus and Cnossus, which had been planted from the Argolid in the age of the migrations.[2] In general then the independence of the colonies was complete and untrammelled.

The authority exercised by the colonial city-state over its citizens was as absolute as in the homeland. At Leucas and at Locri the sale of the plots (*kleroi*), which had been allocated at the foundation of the colony and were transmitted within the family, was either entirely forbidden or permitted only under exceptional circumstances. The foundress also took steps to ensure that the colonists stayed in their colony. At Thera those selected by lot had to go to Cyrene, and no provision was made for them to return home and enjoy citizen rights unless the colony itself failed; at Eretria the returning settlers, who had been expelled from Corcyra by the Corinthians, were driven off with slings and went on to found Methone in Macedonia. Such provision may have been particularly necessary, when subsidiary colonists (*epoikoi*) were being dispatched. For these were often drawn in part from states other than the foundress, and it was important to impose a strict obligation upon them to remain in the colony.[3]

The dispatch of a colony was a deliberate act of policy by the foundress. It was solemnized by an official consultation of the divine will. The Ionians of the Asiatic coast consulted the oracle of Apollo at Didyma, while the mainlanders consulted the oracle of Apollo at Delphi and perhaps that of Zeus at Dodona. The god was himself regarded as the divine leader (*archegetes*) of the colony. Thus Apollo of Didyma played this role at Apollonia Rhyndacia, and Apollo of Delphi at Naxus in Sicily; cults in honour of Apollo Archegetes as divine founder and of the *oikistes* as human colonizer were faithfully observed, and contact with the oracular shrine was maintained by the appointment of sacred envoys (*theoroi*) in the colonies. Some of the responses from Apollo at Delphi have been preserved in an authentic form. The *oikistes* of the Parian colony at Thasos (*c.* 710) received the response 'Announce to the Parians, O Telesicles, that I bid you found a conspicuous city in the island of Eëria'. The *oikistai* of Gela, a colony of Crete and Rhodes, were instructed as follows: 'Entimus and cunning son of famous Craton, go you both to Sicily and inhabit that fair land, when you have built a town of Cretans and Rhodians together beside the mouth of the holy river Gela, and of the same

[1] Th. 1. 38. 3; 56. 2; Scholia ibid.; X. *An.* 5. 5. 7–10.　　　　[2] *GHI* 33.
[3] Arist. *Pol.* 1266ᵇ; Plu. 293ᵃ (*GQ* 11); Th. 1. 26.ː2 and 27.

name as the river.' It is clear from such examples that the colonists wished to receive the god's blessing on their choice of *oikistai* and on the site for the colony.

Once divine sanction was granted, they set forth to establish their new state. The settlers sometimes came in several waves (the later settlers usually being called *epoikoi*), but, as they intended from the outset to set up an independent and self-sufficient community, they included in their number members of different classes and trades. Many settlers at Syracuse came from inland Tenea in Corinthia; doubtless these were in part peasants, and they intended to acquire an allotment of land (*kleros*). In Thera a cross-section of the population was obtained by drawing lots between brothers from all parts of the island, perhaps with the object also of alleviating the demand for land in large families at home.[1] When opposition by the natives was expected, the first wave of settlers were fighting men. At Apollonia Illyrica, for instance, the original settlers from Corinth numbered 200, and the two penteconters dispatched to Platea off the Libyan coast can hardly have carried as many. To oppose a more redoubtable native population the Corinthians sent 1,000 men to Leucas, and the Milesians dispatched thirty ships to found Milesion Teichos in Egypt.[2] Many of the colonies were small from the outset and never expanded much. Anactorium, for instance, was situated on a small promontory and contributed only one ship to the Corinthian fleet in 433.

In choosing a site the colonists wanted enough arable land to become self-supporting, but their choice was often limited by such factors as their own small numbers and the need to occupy a defensible point. Small islands were a favourite choice, and from them new settlements were founded. In the west the earliest colonists occupied the island of Ischia, and later Cyme on the Italian coast; in the south the island of Platea, and later Cyrene on the Libyan coast; and on the west coast of the Black Sea the island of Istrus. Other typical colonies lay on the neck of a peninsula, such as Sinope, Leucas, and Mylae; or on higher ground in the delta of a great river, such as Oeniadae, Tyras, and Olbia. The occupation of a large or exposed site could only be undertaken by strong bodies of colonists, such as were dispatched by the powerful Dorian states, Sparta, Corinth, and Megara. Byzantium was occupied late for this reason, and not because the colonizers of Chalcedon were blind to the advantages offered by the site.[3]

§ 3. *The colonies in the North-east*

THE earliest colonies were founded in the first half of the eighth century by Miletus on the south shore of the Black Sea, at Sinope, Trapezus, and Amisus, the last with the aid of Phocaea.[4] They tapped the rich trade of the

---

[1] Str. 380; Hdt. 4. 153; *SEG* 9. 3 (decree on Cyrene).

[2] St. Byz. *Apollonia*; Hdt. 4. 153 and 156. 2; Scyl. 24.　　　　[3] Hdt. 4. 144.

[4] Archaeological evidence is still lacking to support this early date (see *Arch. Reports* 1962–63, 34). Recent excavations near Cyzicus show it was founded in the eighth century.

interior, especially in silver, iron, realgar, and ship-timber; Sinope was the main port of call on this coast for ships sailing to the Russian Crimea. Small settlements exposed to raids from nomadic peoples, Sinope and Amisus had to be refounded. Sinope subsequently planted daughter-colonies along this coast. The other shores of the Black Sea were exploited by Miletus during the seventh century. The earliest colonies there were placed on the estuaries of great rivers—Istrus on the Danube, Tyras on the Dniester, Olbia on the Bug, and Borysthenes on the Dnieper; they possessed excellent fisheries, and they exported the products of the hinterland. Further colonies were planted on these shores, notably Odessus and Tomis, during the sixth century. By that time Milesian enterprise had reached the Crimea and the east coast of the Black Sea, which had a harder climate. There Panticapaeum and her daughter-colony Theodosia derived their wealth from fish and above all from the wheat which passed through the Cimmerian Bosporus, while Phasis and Dioscurias were the outlets of a trade-route which ran from the Caspian Sea.

These colonies of Miletus with their satellites, numbering perhaps a hundred in all, were chiefly responsible for developing the trade of the Black Sea. Other Ionian states founded colonies in the Black Sea: Phocaea jointly with Miletus founded Apollonia Pontica *c.* 609, and Teus founded Phanagoria opposite Panticapaeum *c.* 540. Dorian colonies were planted by Megara during the sixth century at Heraclea Pontica and Mesembria, occupying strategic positions near the exit from the Black Sea; and Heraclea Pontica later drove out Ionians to settle Callatis and Chersonesus as her own colonies.

Miletus also was the first state to colonize the Propontis, a sea rich in fish and the centre of trade-routes leading from Asia to Europe and from the Mediterranean to the Black Sea. Cyzicus, founded in 756, was famous for its electrum and wool; destroyed by Cimmerian raiders early in the seventh century, it was refounded in 676. The Dorians of Megara soon appeared as rivals of the Milesians. They founded Chalcedon in 676, Byzantium in 660, and Selymbria in the Propontis. These colonies aimed at securing control of the Bosporus, where the entry into the Black Sea was rendered difficult by a strong current and the crossing from Asia to Europe was most convenient. The Ionians countered by concentrating on the southern Propontis and the Hellespont. Here Paros and Erythrae had founded Parium in 710. Miletus in 675 founded Abydus, which possessed gold-mines and controlled the shortest crossing of the Hellespont, and also several colonies in the southern Propontis. Phocaea founded Lampsacus in the Hellespont in 654. The island of Proconnesos was occupied by Miletus, perhaps with the aid of Samos, in 675, and the Samians founded Perinthus and other colonies on the Thracian coast of the Propontis. Colophon, too, planted a colony at Myrlea.

On the European side of the Hellespont small colonies with an agricultural economy were planted by the Aeolians of Lesbos, the least insignificant being Sestus which faced Abydus. Miletus founded Limnae on the west coast, and

Colophon Cardia on the neck of the Chersonese. The opening of the Black Sea attracted trade from the Greek mainland and increased the importance of the route along the Thracian coast. There the earliest colonies were founded *c.* 710 by Parians, who established themselves at Thasos, rich in gold, ship-timber, and wine. The colony at Thasos was threatened by the warlike Thracians of the mainland, and was reinforced *c.* 670 by further settlers from Paros, among them being the poet Archilochus, who served as commander of a mercenary force. Thereafter Thasos herself expanded and founded daughter-colonies on the mainland opposite, which was rich in gold, silver, and wheat.

Between Thasos and the Chersonese Chios founded Maronea, famous like its foundress for wine; Clazomenae founded Abdera in 654, but it was de-stroyed by Thracians and resettled from Teus; and Aeolians founded Aenus at the mouth of the Hebrus river. To the west of Thasos the three-pronged peninsula of Chalcidice grew olives, vines, cereals, and timber for shipbuild-ing; on the west it tapped the resources of Macedonia and on the east those of the Strymon valley, both areas possessing gold and silver.[1] The earliest colonies were founded *c.* 730 by Eretria at Mende in Chalcidice and at Me-thone and Dicaea in Macedonia, and *c.* 710 by Chalcis at Torone in Chal-cidice. Subsequently Chalcis founded some thirty colonies in this area; these were very small and eventually took into their ranks native non-Greek people. Scione was founded by Achaeans from Pellene in the Peloponnese, and Sane, Acanthus, Stagirus, and Argilus by Andros. But the strongest colony, Potidaea, was Dorian, being founded by Corinth *c.* 600. It was situated on the neck of the western peninsula and was well placed for trade with Macedonia. At the time of its foundation Corinthian colonies in Illyria controlled the western end of a trade-route which crossed the Balkan range from Illyria to Macedonia.

§ 4. *The colonies in the West and South*

THE earliest colonists in Italy and Sicily came from Chalcis and Eretria. On the route to the West the Eretrians planted a colony at Corcyra with holdings on the mainland opposite, which enabled them to control the straits of Cor-cyra.[2] Displaced thence by Corinthian colonists, some Eretrians settled at Oricum and in the district of south Illyria called Abantis, where Locrians joined them. The Corinthian colony planted at Corcyra in 733 was the first and the largest of several which ensured for Corinth the control of the western approaches. Probably about 700 Corinth founded colonies at Moly-crium, Macynia, Chalcis (perhaps at the expense of earlier Chalcidian colonists), and Oeniadae, all overlooking the entry into the Gulf of Corinth. To these she added colonies at Leucas and Ambracia and, jointly with Cor-cyra, at Anactorium near the mouth of the Gulf of Ambracia (*c.* 625). Farther north in Illyria, Corcyra founded Epidamnus in 627, and Corinth

---

[1] Hdt. 5. 23; 6. 46; 7. 112.
[2] Scholia A.R. 4. 1175; Th. 3. 85. 2; for pottery see *Arch. Rep.* 1968–69. 22.

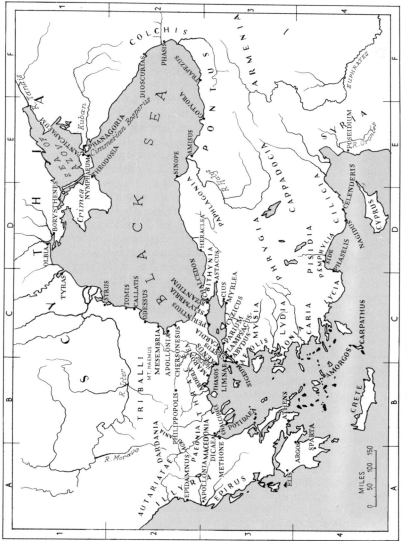

FIG. 11. The Black Sea and Eastern Mediterranean

founded Apollonia *c.* 600. This group of colonies showed the genius of Corinth as a colonizing state. She selected sites of strategic importance and controlled the export of silver, ship-timber, and pastoral products. In comparison the colonies of Elis—Boucheta, Elatria, and Pandosia, which were founded in south Epirus at an unknown date—remained unimportant. Early in the sixth century, when the Phocaeans sailed the upper Adriatic Sea in their warships, they founded no colonies themselves, but Cnidus with the help of Corcyra founded Corcyra Nigra.

The earliest colony in the West was planted by Chalcis, Eretria, and Cyme on the small fertile island of Pithecusae (Ischia), which had some deposits of gold. Later, in 757, Cyme or Cumae, as it is generally called, was founded on the adjacent coast, a defensible site with fairly good land and a sandy beach suitable for drawing up warships. Comparable in their position to the Eretrian colonies of Corcyra and the adjacent mainland, Pithecusae and Cumae were well placed to raid or tax the merchantmen which sailed to Etruria from the south and returned with cargoes of copper and iron ore from Elba and Campania. The settlers came from Pithecusae, Chalcis, Eretria, and Asiatic Cyme; together with them there came perhaps 'Graioi' from Boeotia, whose name is preserved in the Latin form 'Graeci' and in the modern form 'Greeks'. Samos founded Dicaearchia *c.* 531, and Cumae later founded Neapolis.

The Chalcidians also planted the earliest colony at the very toe of Italy, Rhegium *c.* 730–720. Among the settlers there were Messenians who had fled during the Messenian war with Sparta, and they formed the ruling class in the colony. The colonies of Achaea were also early—Sybaris, founded jointly with Troezen in 720, Croton, Metapontium, and Caulonia, which themselves planted daughter-colonies. They all possessed fertile land but inferior harbours. The finest harbour in south Italy was at Taras, founded by Sparta in 706. Taras herself founded Callipolis and Hydruntum on the heel of Italy, and she proved stronger than her Achaean neighbours. In the Gulf of Taras Colophon obtained a footing by founding Siris *c.* 680–670. The last port of call on the voyage to Sicily was at Epizephyrian Locri, founded in 673 by Locrians with the aid of Syracuse.

The earliest colony in Sicily was founded in 734 at Naxus, which was the first port of call from Italy but had little arable land. The colonists were Ionians from Chalcis, who was the foundress, and from the islands, especially Naxos. Although the colony remained small in size, sacrifice was made there to Apollo Archegetes by all Siceliote Greeks who sailed from Sicily on sacred missions. The *oikistes* of Naxus founded Leontini and Catana, which acquired the richest land in the island (729). A similar procedure was followed in the foundation of Zancle, which had little land but made good the deficiency by planting a daughter-colony at Mylae. Situated on the Sicilian side of the Straits of Messana, the site of Zancle was first occupied by pirates from Cumae in Italy; in 730 it was officially colonized by Cumae and Chalcis, the settlers coming from Chalcis and elsewhere in Euboea. When Zancle pro-

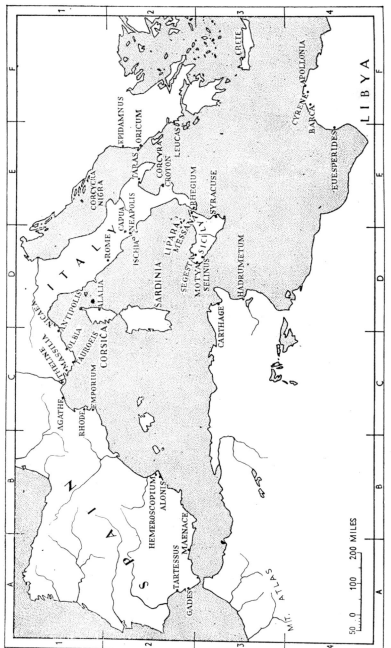

Fig. 12. The Far West

moted the foundation of Rhegium on the Italian coast, the two Chalcidian colonies exercised control of the passage through the straits. In 649 Zancle founded a daughter-colony, with the aid of exiles from Syracuse, at Himera which possessed good land and opened trade contacts with the Phoenician settlements of western Sicily.

While the Chalcidians thus secured north-east Sicily, the Dorians occupied the south-east angle of the island. Syracuse, founded in 733 by Corinth with the participation of other Dorians, possessed the finest harbour on the east coast and was from the outset a large colony, occupying the island of Ortygia and the mainland opposite. A strong force was therefore required to capture the site; yet this force was only a part of the original expedition, which during the voyage had founded Corcyra by expelling the Eretrians. Syracuse in turn planted Acrae, Casmenae, and Camarina. In founding Syracuse the Corinthians recruited some Dorians who had originally belonged to a force led by Megara and were operating in south Italy. This force encountered great difficulty in establishing a permanent foothold. After occupying Trotilum, an admirable base for piracy, the Megarians moved on to Leontini, whence they were later ejected. Settling for a short time on the small island of Thapsus, they were next invited by the native Sicels to the mainland nearby, where they founded Megara Hyblaea in 728. Pinched between the Chalcidian and the Syracusan spheres of influence, they expanded by founding a colony in 628 at Selinus, which was a neighbour of the Phoenician settlements in the south-west. Between Selinus and the Syracusan colonies another Dorian colony was founded in 688 by Cretans and Rhodians at Gela, rich in arable and grazing land. Gela herself planted a colony at Acragas in 580.

The first discovery of the Far West was accidental. In 638 Colaeus of Samos put in at the island of Platea off the Libyan coast with a merchant vessel, which was then driven by storms beyond the Straits of Gibraltar to Tartessus on the Atlantic coast of Spain. He returned with a fabulously rich cargo, which excited the cupidity of other adventurers.[1] The Phocaeans, who had already traded along the south coast of France, founded *c.* 600 the important colony of Massilia, famous for its harbour, olives, and vines. Massilia in turn founded colonies at points along the south coasts of France and Spain, which had already been visited by Greek traders: notably Nicaea, Antipolis, Olbia, Emporium, and Maenace. On the direct route from the Straits of Messana to Spain Phocaea founded a colony at Alalia in Corsica *c.* 560; and there may have been short-lived colonies of Phocaea in Sardinia and of Rhodes in the Balearic Isles. Finally, Cnidus founded in 580–576 a colony called Lipara in the small islands to the west of the Straits of Messana. The settlers were the survivors of an expedition of Cnidians and Rhodians, led by Pentathlus, which had been repulsed from western Sicily by the Phoenicians and Elymians.

The hostile reaction of the Phoenicians to Greek activity in the West was

[1] Hdt. 4. 152.

strengthened by the adherence of the Etruscans. The Phocaeans at Alalia, reinforced after the sack of Phocaea, defeated the fleets of Carthage and of Etruria *c.* 535, but suffered so heavily that they left Corsica and eventually settled at Elea in south Italy. After the loss of Alalia the range of Greek trade in the West contracted. For the Carthaginians soon closed the Straits of Gibraltar and destroyed Tartessus.

The Dorians of Thera opened the way to the Libyan coast by settling on the island of Platea, to which they were guided by a Cretan. After occupying Aziris on the mainland for six years, they were conducted by the Libyans to the site where Cyrene was founded *c.* 630.[1] Her wealth in corn, wool, dates, and the medicinal plant 'silphium' attracted further settlers from the Peloponnese and the islands *c.* 570, and daughter-colonies were founded on this coast, of which Barca and Euesperides were the most notable. Although Egypt employed Ionian mercenaries at an earlier date, the first Greek colony was established by Miletus at Milesion Teichos in the Delta during a civil war in Egypt towards the close of the seventh century.

Subsequently (*c.* 610) Naucratis was established on the western branch of the Nile for the benefit of Greek traders. Naucratis was indeed not a colony in the Greek sense but an *emporion*, a market for commercial business, in which the residence of foreigners was permitted by the Egyptian government.[2] A similar market for Greek traders was established in Syria at Poseidium close to the mouth of the Orontes. There Greek trade flourished from *c.* 750 to 600, then died and restarted *c.* 520. On the south coast of Asia Minor, where Greek settlers had established themselves during the age of migrations, it is probable that Phaselis was reinforced *c.* 690 by Rhodians, that Side was colonized by Aeolians from Cyme perhaps *c.* 750, and that Celenderis and Nagidus were founded by Samos probably in the sixth century. In the Aegean the small island of Amorgos was settled by Naxos, Samos, and Miletus. The Samian settlement was planted late in the seventh century, and the island was for long a dependency of Samos.

§ 5. *Aims, causes, and effects of colonization*

THE aims of the Greek city-states in founding their colonies varied from case to case. In the West, for instance, Greek products had already reached Sicily, Etruria, and France some time before the first colonists arrived there. That such products were carried in part by Greek merchantmen is probable in view of the voyages of Colaeus and the Phocaeans to Tartessus in Spain. There is indeed no doubt that colonies were planted for trade, especially in metals, at Sinope and Trapezus in the Black Sea, at Ischia[3] and Cumae in Italy, and at Naxus and Syracuse in Sicily. Closely allied to trade was the exploitation of trade by piracy or by the imposition of tolls. The sites chosen by the Megarians

[1] Hdt. 4. 150.   [2] Str. 801; Hdt. 2. 178.   [3] *Arch. Rep.* 1970–71. 66 f.

in Sicily and by the Cnidians at Lipara were suitable for piracy, and the famous voyages by Phocaean warships in the Adriatic Sea and to the West had piracy as well as exploration in mind. The imposition of tolls on transit trade was probably contemplated by the Megarians in settling on the approaches to the Bosporus, by the Eretrians and later the Corinthians in occupying Corcyra and points on the mainland, and by the Chalcidians in selecting Pithecusae and Cumae, and Zancle and Rhegium; for in the homeland Megara and Corinth exploited the transit-trade at the Isthmus, while Chalcis and Eretria controlled the narrows of the Euripus Channel. All colonies, of course, wanted a modicum of good land from which to support themselves. Some states aimed only at gaining control of exceptionally fertile land or fine fisheries. The Aeolians in the Chersonese, the Eleans in Epirus, and the Achaeans in Italy continued to pursue an agricultural way of life. The smaller Milesian and Phocaean colonies in the Black Sea, Propontis, and Gulf of Lyons were probably attracted by the richness of the tunny-fisheries.

Personal or general conditions at home sometimes encouraged men to emigrate. Poverty drove Archilochus to Thasos. Drought at Thera and dearth at Chalcis preceded the colonization of Cyrene and Rhegium.[1] Shortage of arable land was acute in all periods, and above all when settled conditions led to an increase in the birth rate; the surplus population then sought an outlet not only in colonization but also in mercenary service and later in imperialism. Thus the offer of land certainly tempted the *epoikoi* to join an established colony, both for its own sake and as a valuable form of property.[2] Man-made troubles also contributed. The Messenians at Rhegium and the 'natural sons' (*Partheniai*) at Taras sailed in consequence of the Messenian War, while the Phocaeans reinforced Alalia after the destruction of Phocaea.[3] But these were merely particular incentives to colonial enterprise; in other centuries the incentives were still operative, but colonization did not ensue.

The great age of colonization was due to general rather than particular causes. As we have seen, the Greek world had achieved not only settled conditions but also the political form, the diverse variety of city-states, which generated extraordinary energy and organizing ability. To this factor the amazing expansion of Corinth, Megara, Miletus, or Phocaea must be attributed no less than the expansion of the Spartan city-state in the southern Peloponnese. No doubt these states drew on the manpower of other states to people their colonies; but they initiated, organized, and controlled the development of the new colony. And it is a measure of the superior strength of the Dorian city-states that they planted the most powerful colonies, such as Syracuse, Taras, Corcyra, Byzantium, and Cyrene. The other important factor was not within the control of the Greek states. The outer Mediterranean world in the period 750–550 was ill-organized in comparison with the Greek society of city-states. The native tribes of the west and the north were

---

[1] Hdt. 4. 151; Str. 257.   [2] Th. 1. 15. 1; Hdt. 4. 159. 2–4.
[3] Str. 257; 278; Arist. *Pol.* 1306ᵇ30.

backward in political development. The Phoenicians and the Etruscans alone were comparable to the Greeks; and, when they combined, they arrested the progress of Greek expansion. In the east, where the continuity of Bronze Age traditions was less disturbed—in southern Asia Minor, Syria, Cyprus, Palestine, and Egypt—hardly any Greek colonies were planted. Here the Greek was invited to settle at Naucratis and Poseidium, because he was the expert in two fields of activity, commerce and warfare, which elsewhere were the means whereby he won or forced possession and planted colonies far and wide.

The pioneers were sometimes welcomed by the natives and took native wives. But, once a colony was established, it added to its territory by force of arms and became racially exclusive. Reinforcements of manpower were generally drawn from the homeland. Mixed colonies of Greeks and natives were rare. They occurred at the fringes of Ionian colonization, for instance at Crouni and Bizone in south Russia and at some small sites in Chalcidice. The Dorian colonists often reduced the natives to the position of serfs and *perioikoi*; Syracuse, Byzantium, and Heraclea Pontica possessed serfs, while Rhegium and Cyrene formed a system of *perioikoi*.[1] With the increase of prosperity the Greeks of the colonies came to own more private slaves, who were drawn in part from the native peoples of their locality. Wherever they were, the Greek colonies exercised a profound influence on the life and culture of the surrounding peoples. Greek art and Greek inventions gradually pervaded southern Europe from Spain to south Russia, and inspired even the mature civilization of Etruria. The tribes of Italy, for instance, adopted the Chalcidian form of the alphabet, while those of France learned to cultivate the olive and the vine. Such influences travelled along channels of trade, which radiated far inland from the Greek colonies on the coastal fringe.

The Greeks themselves adopted little from the native peoples. In Sicily and Italy the local system of weights and measures was indeed taken over by the Greek colonists, and the religious beliefs of Thrace and Scythia may have strengthened the cults of Ares and Zeus, for instance, at Tomis and Olbia. But, in general, closer acquaintance with the barbarian strengthened the confidence of the Greek in his own institutions; and this confidence created some unity of sentiment between the widely scattered city-states. More important was the stimulus imparted to Greek and especially Ionian thought by direct contact with a wide variety of cultures. Nowhere is this more evident than in the history of Herodotus, who inherited and transmitted the experience of the colonizing period. But most important of all was the expansion of trade which laid the economic basis for the second flowering of civilization in the Mediterranean area. As in the Late Bronze Age, so now Aegean merchants bartered tin from Britain, amber from the Baltic Sea, and gold from the Ural Mountains.[2] But there were now significant differences. The opening of the Black Sea and the advance to France and Spain offset the comparative decline of Egypt in

[1] Hdt. 7. 155. 2; 4. 159. 4; Str. 542; 257.
[2] Hdt. 3. 115; 4. 23–24.

the south. The main currents of trade now set along the northern shores and islands of the Mediterranean Sea. Thus until the Greco–Macedonian conquest of the East, the centre of balance in the movement of commerce was firmly fixed in the Greek peninsula and especially in its focal point, the narrow Isthmus separating the Saronic from the Corinthian Gulf.

Hoplites in action, from an Attic Black Figure vase by the C painter *c.* 575–550
(note the two grips inside the shields, and see p. 110)

CHAPTER 3

The Commercial Development of the Greek States
c. 750–550

§ 1. *The Eastern trade*

THE concert of small powers, extending from Cilicia to Egypt, was shattered by the advance of Assyria late in the eighth century. Thereafter, until the consolidation of Persia's power after 550, a series of wars and raids diminished the prosperity of Syria and Palestine. The Phoenicians suffered heavily, Sidon being sacked in 677 by the Assyrians and Tyre in 573 by the Babylonians. Cyprus was reduced in 709 by the Assyrians and again in the reign of Amasis (569–526) by the Egyptians. In Syria from 750 to 600 a Greek settlement at Poseidium maintained an active market of exchange; the main imports came initially from the Cyclades and later from 'East Greece' (comprising the Greek states of Asia Minor and the off-lying islands). Then from 600 to 520 this settlement ceased its activity.

Egypt had been closed to Greek enterprise since the Late Bronze Age. Intercourse was resumed when Psammetichus I (663–609) stiffened his army and navy with Ionian and Carian mercenaries. Permanent settlements for them were established at Stratopeda in the eastern Delta, and they served at frontier-posts such as Daphnae. His policy was continued by Apries (588–566), who concentrated a force of 30,000 at Sais in the western Delta, and by Amasis, who recruited his bodyguard from them.[1] An expedition by Greek mercenaries to the Second Cataract of the Nile *c.* 590 is recorded in an inscription 'cut by Archon son of Amoebichus and by Axe son of Nobody' on the leg of a colossal statue of Rameses II at Abu Simbel.[2] The names of Ionian mercenaries from Teus, Ialysus, and Colophon figure in the inscription. In the reign of Psammetichus a Milesian fleet of thirty ships succeeded in establishing a fortified post, called 'The Fort of the Milesians' (Milesion Teichos), on the western arm of the Nile. Later *c.* 610 during a revolt in Egypt they captured and founded Naucratis farther up the river. In the reign of Necho (609–593) relations with Miletus became friendly; for Necho made a dedication to the temple of Apollo in Milesian territory.[3]

From the outset the settlement at Naucratis imported large quantities of Greek pottery. Apries, who depended so extensively on Carian and Ionian mercenaries, probably granted a monopoly to Naucratis as the only port of entry for sea-borne trade. Amasis (569–526) adopted a philhellenic policy,

---

[1] Hdt. 2. 154; 163. [2] *GHI* 4. [3] Str. 801; Hdt. 2. 159.

granting to Greek immigrants a guarantee of permanent settlement at Naucratis and to passing traders land for the erection of Greek shrines. During his reign Egypt reached a high level of economic prosperity, reducing Cyprus to vassaldom and allying with Cyrene, but making no attempt to advance into Palestine or Syria. For her export trade Egypt turned now to the eastern Mediterranean and made close contact with the Greek states. Amasis himself married a Greek lady from Cyrene, dedicated statues at Cyrene, Rhodes, and Samos, and contributed 1,000 talents of alum towards the rebuilding of the temple at Delphi. The Greek traders and residents in Egypt came predominantly from 'East Greece'. Herodotus reports that their principal shrine, the *Hellenion*, was built by Chios, Teus, Phocaea, Clazomenae, Rhodes, Cnidus, Halicarnassus, Phaselis, and Mitylene; separate shrines were built by Samos and Miletus and from the western Aegean by Aegina. The account of Herodotus is supported by the evidence of the pottery found in Egypt at Naucratis and Tell Defenneh, the site of a garrison-post, perhaps Daphnae. The pottery is mainly East Greek, contact being especially close with Chios, famous for its wine. As at this period Poseidium on the Syrian coast was inactive, the main trade-route to Egypt from East Greece ran via Cyprus, Phaselis, and Rhodes. A less important trade-route ran via Cyrene towards Thera, Laconia, and the Saronic Gulf; for Attic and Corinthian pottery dating from 610 and Laconian pottery dating from 590 onwards has been found at Naucratis, and Attic pottery from 560 onwards at Tell Defenneh. From this intercourse with Egypt the Greeks derived the elements of geometry and chemistry and some aspects of Orphic religion.[1]

During the eighth century the centre of political power in Asia Minor lay far inland. But from *c.* 705, when Cimmerian raiders destroyed Midas and the Phrygian empire, the kingdom of Lydia became a powerful and immediate neighbour of the Greek states. After assassinating Candaules of Lydia, Gyges founded a new dynasty, which proved aggressive towards the Greek states. During his reign (*c.* 687–652) Gyges attacked individual states, such as Smyrna, Colophon, and Miletus, and raided Greek territory; similar raids by his successors and by the nomadic Cimmerians continued until *c.* 590. Then Alyattes made an alliance with Miletus, and this inaugurated a period of peaceful relations with the Greek states. Before 590 Ionian mercenaries had been employed by Lydia, and Greek trade had entered Sardis. After 590 Greek trade penetrated far inland, and the states of East Greece enjoyed great prosperity. Although Croesus, the successor of Alyattes, deprived the Asiatic Greeks of political independence, the period of prosperity continued until Persia conquered Lydia in 546.

In the eighth and seventh centuries the East Greek states were developing the resources of the Propontis and the Black Sea, where Ionian enterprise under the leadership of Miletus was in the ascendant. Elsewhere the trade of

[1] Hdt. 2. 177–82.

East Greece developed slowly. At Poseidium in Syria Cycladic wares were not ousted by East Greek wares until the seventh century, and Egypt provided little save employment for Ionian mercenaries. So, too, in the west Colophon and Rhodes alone planted colonies before the late seventh century. Thus until *c.* 610 East Greece was rather on the periphery of Greek trade in the Mediterranean area, and her influence on the Greek peninsula was small.

After *c.* 610 the position altered radically. New markets for East Greek trade opened in Egypt, in Lydia, and in the West as far as Tartessus. The Ionian states, and especially Miletus, now stood at the crossing of important trade-routes. An era of very great prosperity ensued. An example of the range of trade which the generality of the Ionian states in East Greece enjoyed is afforded by the exports of Chios; these have been found in considerable quantity in Naucratis, the Black Sea area, and Massilia, but with the exception of Aegina (which shared in the Egyptian market) rarely in the Greek peninsula, Sicily, and Italy. Miletus and Colophon, in particular, had close commercial relations with Sybaris and Siris, the wealthiest cities of south Italy. Phocaea was closely linked to Rhegium, which controlled the Straits of Messana. Through these contacts the plain ware produced for domestic use by East Greece reached the markets of the native Italian and Sicilian peoples in the sixth century, and Ionian sailors developed trade with Etruria, France, and Spain. The western market shrank considerably after the losses of the Phocaeans at Alalia in 535 and the sack of Sybaris in 510, when the citizens of Miletus went into mourning. Thus during the period 610–540 Ionia reached its highest level of prosperity. Ionian mercenaries were widely employed, and Ionian fleets, particularly those of Phocaea, Miletus, and Samos, controlled the coastal waters of Asia Minor and of the south-eastern Mediterranean, where Amasis granted them exceptional privileges. Hand in hand with her commercial expansion went developments in politics, poetry, and philosophy, the adoption of coinage, and the exercise of a strong influence on the Ionian homeland, Attica, and on the Dorian island, Rhodes.[1]

§ 2. *The islands as intermediaries*

In East Greece the Dorian states had a twofold advantage. They controlled the entry into the Aegean from the south-east and the terminal of the route from the West through the Dorian islands. Of these Crete was at first the most important. Absorbing the influences of the Near East via Cyprus and Rhodes, Crete developed the earliest orientalizing style of fine pottery and inaugurated the 'Daedalic' period, which made her an important centre in art from 750 to 650. Thereafter a gradual decline ensued until 600 and then a steep decline, Corinth and Rhodes forging ahead. Crete and the Dorian islands controlled the route south of the Peloponnese to the western Mediterranean. There Cretan pottery was imported until 700, when it was displaced by

[1] Th. 1. 13. 6; 16.

Corinthian pottery except at Gela, the joint colony of Crete and Rhodes, founded in 688. At the same time Crete and Rhodes extended their influence to the south-east by colonizing Phaselis on the route to Syria.

After 650 Rhodes outstripped Crete. She became second to Corinth in the West, and her terracottas enjoyed a wide vogue throughout the Greek world after 610. At Acragas, founded from Gela in 580, Rhodian influence predominated, and Rhodes founded short-lived colonies at Rhode, on the Balearic Isles, and on the Italian coast of the Adriatic. In this expansion Cnidus participated. Pentathlus, a Heraclid of Cnidus, led an expedition of Cnidians and Rhodians *c.* 580 to capture the south-western angle of Sicily. Repulsed thence, the Cnidians founded Lipara, where they evolved a way of life akin to communism and suited to piracy. Holding the land in common and living in *syssitia*, they devoted half of their manpower to agriculture and half to piracy at the expense of the Etruscans.[1] They also sailed the Adriatic Sea, where with the aid of Corcyra they founded a colony at Corcyra Nigra. Meanwhile trade grew with the south, where Cyrene and Naucratis had been founded. This trade enriched Rhodes as the intermediary between Ionia and Egypt. Thus Rhodes came to hold a central position on the trade-routes north and south and also east and west. In addition she was on good terms with Corinth, from which she imported pottery in 640–580, despite the fact that her trade with the West passed not through the Isthmus of Corinth but south of the Peloponnese. Her art, which had been characteristically Dorian, became infused with Ionian influences during the sixth century.

The Dorian route across the Aegean and to the West aided the development of Sparta and Thera. The Laconian style of fine pottery flourished from 700 to 550. In some respects it was second only to that of Corinth. Although Sparta founded Taras *c.* 710, the expansion of Laconian trade commenced *c.* 630, when Thera founded Cyrene and Rhodes prospered greatly. Laconian pottery in considerable quantity then reached most areas of the Greek mainland, Samos and Rhodes, Cyrene, Naucratis, and Etruria. In south Italy Laconian pottery, terracottas, and bronzes were imported to Taras after 600. Thus Laconia and to a lesser extent Thera gained from the trade of Cyrene and Egypt and from Rhodian and Cnidian enterprise in the West. Laconian art declined gradually after 550 and steeply after 500.

As the early products of Chalcis are not recognizable to the archaeologist, there is less evidence for the range of Chalcidian trade. But it may be presumed from the appearance of Cycladic pottery of the eighth century in Italy and Sicily, that Euboea as well as the Cyclades were rivals to Crete in the beginnings of the trade with the West. Moreover, Chalcis and Eretria together with Naxos, the richest of the Cyclades, founded all their important colonies in the West, and the Naxians probably explored the African coast before 700. Their colonies then controlled the Straits of Messana and the approaches to the important market of Etruria. During the eighth century

---

[1] D.S. 5. 9; Paus. 10. 11. 3.

Chalcis and Eretria colonized Chalcidice and Macedonia; Paros colonized Thasos and Parium; and Cycladic pottery was in the ascendant at Poseidium in Syria. Thus in the late eighth century the main trade-zone of the Cyclades and of Euboea covered the north Aegean and the western seas. In this zone the central point was Euboea. After 700 the trade from the Thracian coast increased, and further colonies were planted by Thasos and Andros. Vases of the period 550–500 which are attributable to Chalcis have been found in considerable quantities throughout the West, Rhegium probably being the centre for reshipment. The marble of Paros, too, was exported regularly to the western markets. Quite apart from their own trade contacts, it is probable that the Cycladic mariners acted as carriers of general Aegean trade in these as in other centuries.

§ 3. *The Isthmus markets*

THE keystone of Greek commerce was the Isthmus of Corinth. There the traffic from the Aegean Sea and the Black Sea, converging on the Saronic Gulf, and the traffic from the West, converging on the Corinthian Gulf, met at the great market of Corinth to be exchanged and distributed by land and by sea. Warships and small merchantmen as well as cargo were hauled along a stone runway (*diolkos*), which was laid across the narrow neck of the Isthmus. By 735 Corinth was already a powerful state, capable of launching the strongest colonizing expeditions. She evolved the finest 'orientalizing' style of pottery on the mainland, and she soon led the Greek world in naval construction. From 725 to 550 Corinth had an absolute predominance in the trade of the West. After the first trial of strength, when the Corinthians ejected the Eretrians from Corcyra, the Chalcidian colonies in Italy and Sicily seem to have co-operated with Corinth and her colony Syracuse. In exchange the Chalcidians presumably enjoyed favourable terms at the Isthmus for transit and at the Corinthian colonies of north-west Greece for harbourage. Corinth was also the centre of traffic between the Peloponnese and central Greece, and her pottery was widely imported into both areas after 700. Across the Aegean Corinthian pottery was imported by East Greece and by Poseidium in Syria from 700 onwards, and by the Black Sea colonies, Syria, Palestine, and Egypt after 630. Then, too, began the systematic exploitation of Epirus and Illyria, and after the foundation of Potidaea in 600 the development of trade with Macedonia. Carthage, too, imported Corinthian wares in the seventh and sixth centuries, reshipped perhaps from Etruria. Thus Corinth was the predominant commercial state of the Greek world, and her goods were sent to every market. Her grip relaxed only slightly when the fine pottery of Athens penetrated the West and began to displace that of Corinth there as elsewhere *c*. 550.

Megara, the neighbour of Corinth, possessed harbours on both Gulfs, but she had a less convenient route than Corinth for portage across the Isthmus. Her colonies, however, were planted early both in the West and in the East.

Although Megara Hyblaea in Sicily was pinched between the Corinthian and Chalcidian spheres, her secondary colony at Selinus was rich in wheat and well placed for trade with the Far West, Etruria, Carthage, and Rhodes. But the main source of Megarian trade flowed from the Black Sea, where her powerful colonies expanded steadily to control the Bosporus and its approaches. Despite the poverty of her territory, Megara remained independent of Corinth. This was in part due to her economic strength, which derived from her position on the Isthmus and from her colonial system.

Other states bordering the Corinthian Gulf and the Euripus Channel profited from the great development in colonization and commerce. Achaea sent her surplus population to south Italy and to Chalcidice, while Elis planted colonies in Epirus. Opuntian Locris joined in the ventures of Eretria, and Ozolian Locris enjoyed the favour of Corinth, when she founded Epizephyrian Locri. These districts, however, were not so much concerned with commerce as Sicyon. She planted no colonies, but, by virtue of her proximity to Corinth, she shared in the commercial results of western colonization. The oracle of Apollo at Delphi spread its influence as patron of colonization from the Far West to Cyrene in Libya and to the Parian colonies in the Hellespontine region. The sanctuary was enriched by grateful clients, and the states of Crisa and Delphi derived profit from the traffic of the pilgrims.

The other states of the homeland planted no colonies, although individual groups of their citizens joined the flow of colonists overseas. But they, too, benefited from the quickening pace of maritime commerce. Aegina served as a centre of exchange in the Saronic Gulf and had her own temple in Egypt after 610. Argolis was in close contact with Corinth; and the Argive school of art may have influenced some of the western colonies. Attica progressed less rapidly than Corinth in artistic development. Although she produced the finest pottery of the late Geometric style, only a few Attic vases dating to 750–700 have been found in the West. Late in the seventh century some Attic pottery began to appear as far afield as Etruria, Syria, and Egypt; and Egyptian scarabs were dedicated by mariners at Sunium in Attica. In 600–550 the range and the quantity of exports increased, until Attic replaced Corinthian after 550 as the leading pottery of the Greek world. In the West the rapid expansion of Attic trade after 580 was due to the close relations between Athens and Corinth, which enabled potters from Corinth to settle at Athens and Athenian goods to be exported via Perachóra on the Corinthian Gulf to the western markets. At Syracuse the Athenian penetration came late, *c.* 530, indicating that Corinthian ships did not carry Attic vases to Syracuse until Athens had finally outstripped Corinth in the manufacture of fine pottery.

§ 4. *Centres of exchange*

IN broad terms, then, the period 750–550 witnessed an amazing expansion of sea-borne commerce within the Mediterranean area. The lines of the main trade-routes are revealed to us chiefly by the distribution of the fine potteries which were manufactured in the homeland and not often in the colonies. Much of this pottery did not travel empty; it contained luxuries, such as unguents, oils, perfumes, and wines. The Corinthian aryballus, for instance, was a container for perfumes and unguents, and in these articles Corinth probably had a monopoly of export to the West. Other objects, which were perishable or of which the origin cannot now be identified, were exported by the homeland. Corinthian bronze-work, especially armour, had a wide vogue, and Chalcidian swords a great reputation. Corinthian shipwrights probably built ships for the colonial area as well as for Samos. Miletus exported woollen goods, and Megara may have done the same. In general, although the evidence at our disposal is patchy, we may conclude that the colonies exported raw material and foodstuffs—precious metals, timber, wool, hides, wheat, and dried fish—and imported finished articles from the homeland. The trade flowing along the main channels of communication was exploited by those states which provided centres of exchange. The principal bene-ficiaries were the Dorian states and the Dorian colonies. The traffic through the Isthmus enriched Corinth, Megara, Aegina, and Sicyon; and in the colonial areas Corcyra, Syracuse, Potidaea, Byzantium, and Chalcedon. The traffic on the southern route enriched Rhodes, Crete, Thera, and Laconia, with their colonies in Phaselis, Gela, Cyrene, and Taras. In comparison the Ionian states, despite their initiative in exploration and colonization and their development of the Black Sea, fared less well until the sixth century, when the opening of the Asiatic hinterland and of Egypt raised Ionia to its highest pitch of well-being. The richer centres of exchange also produced the finest potteries—Corinthian, Laconian, Cretan, and Rhodian—until the sixth century, when the art of Ionia and particularly of Athens began to rival Dorian art.

§ 5. *The invention and spread of coinage (see Plate XI)*

IN the trade of the Bronze Age and the early Iron Age barter was the means of exchange, and the most valuable article of barter was precious metal in the form of large ingots or small 'dumps' (bean-shaped pellets). It was from these dumps that coined money developed in three stages. First, the dump of metal was struck with the end of a metal rod to produce a deep 'incuse' mark, which showed whether the dump was of solid or plated metal. Then the dump was striated on the reverse side with tiny furrows, of which the ridges indicated the extent of wear and tear. Finally, the dump was struck with an emblem, which guaranteed its value and its origin, and thereby became the first true coin, that is a piece of metal 'sanctioned by usage' (*nomisma*). When smaller denominations were minted, this first coin was known as the standard coin of a specific weight (*stater*). The development took place during the seventh century in Lydia, where a special need arose. Here there were rich deposits of electrum, a natural alloy of gold and silver, in which the proportions of gold and silver content, and consequently the value, varied. Gyges, king of Lydia (*c.* 687–652), standardized the issues of electrum in different categories of paleness and darkness, and guaranteed the value of his electrum coins. After 650 the dumps were replaced by stamped coins, bearing the lion's head on the larger denominations and the lion's paw on the smaller ones. The weight of the different issues was probably regulated both by the degree of gold content and by its value in exchange for pure gold ingots.

The invention was adopted *c.* 625 by Miletus and Ephesus, which were in close contact with Lydia; they issued electrum coins stamped with their state emblems, a lion with head turned backwards and a bee or a stag. Phocaea, Chios, and Samos then followed suit. Chios and Samos soon issued coins in silver also. The electrum, or 'gold' as Herodotus called it, of Gyges became famous throughout the Greek world. But its fame was surpassed by the bimetallic currency of Croesus of Lydia (561–546). He issued staters of pure gold and pure silver; for these the gold was presumably extracted from the locally mined electrum. His staters were the prototype of the Persian gold coins and silver shekels (*sigloi*), the purest and finest currency of the ancient world until the rise of Philip of Macedon.

The Greek peninsula possessed no deposits of gold or electrum. Iron was mined in several places, especially Euboea and Laconia; copper in Euboea; and silver in Attica. Ingots and dumps of electrum, gold and silver were in use for exchange in the first half of the seventh century (see *JHS* 64.86). The value of the precious metals in relation to iron had to be regulated; the mainlanders bartered, and doubtless continued to barter, iron in the form of spits (*oboloi*), handfuls of spits (*drakhmai*), and large ingots. Hence dumps of varying weights took on the old names, 'obols' and 'drachmae', six obols making up one drachma. The adoption of the new medium of exchange was official at Argos, as in Lydia. Pheidon therefore dedicated iron spits to Hera, the state-goddess, and such iron spits together with an iron ingot have been found by the excavators of the Argive Heraeum. Around 625 a silver currency was established at Aegina, the centre of exchange, to which the silver was imported, perhaps from Siphnos. The coins themselves were struck with the emblem of a sea-turtle and bore a deep incuse mark. The intermediate stages, which we have seen in the Lydian coinage, did not occur. The Aeginetan coins were therefore derived ultimately from the coins of Lydia and began *c.* 625 (see Appendix 4). The Aeginetan turtles remained the standard coinage of the Peloponnese (except Olympia) for more than two centuries, and they were still in circulation much later. Thus the origins of coinage in Lydia and in Aegina illustrate the famous words of Aristotle: 'For the purpose of exchange men made a compact to give and accept a substance serviceable in itself and easy to handle in daily life, such as iron, silver, and other metals; at first it was defined simply by size and weight, but finally it was stamped to dispense with the need for measurement, since the stamp was established as the token of the amount.'[1]

The Lydian and Aeginetan coinages were based on different weights and regulated in relation to different metals. The bridge between them was formed by issuing a coin with a weight of silver related both to the Lydian system and to the Aeginetan system. This was first done by Samos and by Corinth, probably early in Periander's reign (*c.* 627–586). An inscription dated by the context to before 650–640, at the temple of Hera Limenia at Perachóra: 'O white-armed Hera, I, a drachma, [am deposited in thy forecourt]', may refer to the replacement of iron by silver as currency. The new coins, on the Euboic standard, circulated from *c.* 610 in the West, as well as on the mainland and in the Aegean; for Corinth was the greatest centre of exchange in the Mediterranean area.[2] As other states began to coin, each evolved its own standard of weight in accordance with local conditions. For all these coinages were valued at the real value of their silver, electrum, or gold content, and the cost price of silver, for example, varied from place to place and from time to time. Thus in Lydia and in Persia the relative value of gold to silver remained constant at $13\frac{1}{3}$:1; but in Thrace, where both gold and silver were mined, it fluctuated from 15:1 to 10:1; and the same must have been the case in states which had no local sources of supply. In consequence the precise weights of coins in different states varied.

Nevertheless, two main systems were prevalent in the period down to 550, the Aeginetic and the Euboic. To the former system belonged Aegina serving the Peloponnese, Megara, Athens until *c.* 593, Boeotia (coining first *c.* 550), and the southern Aegean islands between Aegina in the west and Rhodes in the east, together with Cnidus and Caunus on the adjacent mainland. To the Euboic system belonged Corinth, Athens after *c.* 593, Chalcis (coining first *c.* 550), Samos, and Cyrene (coining first *c.* 560); to this system that of Lydia, Miletus, Ephesus, Phocaea, and Chios was more closely related than to the Aeginetan system. These two systems reflect different orbits of trade, and the conversion of Athens from the Aeginetan to the Euboic system *c.* 593 indicated a change of policy in finance and in commerce.

In the West coinage was adopted in the sixth century. Previously barter had sufficed, probably because Corinth exercised almost a monopoly of exchange, including the export of bullion silver. The position altered when the Far West was opened by Ionian enterprise, and Spanish silver came into the market. From this source Himera, Selinus, and Zancle obtained silver. They coined on a separate standard of their own, and were later joined by Naxus. By 550 Taras, Sybaris, Metapontium, Caulonia, Croton, and Rhegium in Italy were coining on the Corinthian standard with Corinthian silver. On the route to Italy, Corcyra coined on a separate standard, which may have marked her emancipation from the control of Corinth. But Syracuse and the

---

[1] Arist. *Pol.* 1257ᵃ35; *GC* 25 f.; most scholars date coinage later. See Appendix 4.
[2] *GC* 38; *Perachora* 1. 258.

states of south-east Sicily did not issue coins until later, probably because they still traded mainly with Corinth. The relation between coinage and maritime commerce is seen clearly in the West. The early coins were all of large denominations. They were intended for large-scale transactions rather than for internal retail.[1]

Greek coinage was developed first at the main centres of international exchange by city-states which drew their revenues from commerce. They formed three groups: the Ionian led by Miletus and Ephesus, the Aeginetan comprising Aegina and her financial satellites, and the Corinthian, led by Corinth and Samos, and comprising later Athens and Euboea. As the use of coinage spread, secondary centres of exchange began to coin. Such were Himera, Taras, and Corcyra by 550, and Syracuse, Cyrene, Potidaea, and Thasos after 550. The Greek city-states avoided uniformity in coinage as in other respects, and from the outset the different standards and types of coinage were in competition. The primary function of coinage was to accelerate the movement of commercial exchange and to enrich the city-states by the accumulation of mobile capital. Coinage also had wide-reaching effects, because it stimulated the process of internal retail and introduced a novel form of property in the individual city-states. Some states resisted the spread of coinage, notably Sparta, Crete, and Byzantium. They preserved their social and political institutions at the cost of falling behind in the race for financial power.

Greek coins are amongst the finest examples of Greek art (Plates XI and XII). Purity of line and delicacy of detail are characteristics even of the early coins—the 'bees' of Ephesus, the 'turtles' of Aegina, the 'foals' of Corinth, and the 'owls' of Athens. The emblems were the official badges of the state, derived sometimes from a religious cult (for instance, the bee at Ephesus) and sometimes from a commercial product (for instance, the oil-amphora at Athens). The heraldic emblem of a ruler or of a ruling clan and the initial letters of a king or state were sometimes inscribed on the coinage (for example, the initial letters of Alyattes in Lydia and those of Athens and Chalcis), but the portraying of individual rulers was not customary in Greece until the Hellenistic period.

[1] *GC* 71 f.

CHAPTER 4

Warfare in the Period 750–550

§ 1. *Wars for frontiers and for hegemony*

THUCYDIDES described the land wars of the archaic period as domestic wars waged between individual neighbours and not in general productive of powerful groups such as coalitions and empires.[1] His description is correct but not comprehensive. As the new states grew up on the mainland and were planted overseas, they jostled for position, and they used their expanding resources in war against one another. The outcome was sometimes decisive, in that possession of disputed territory was securely established, but rarely catastrophic for one side and productive of power for the other. But by these wars the frontiers of the city-states were drawn, and the strength of each was circumscribed for the future.

The greatest and the most catastrophic of these land wars has already been described. Sparta, the first Dorian city-state on the mainland, subjugated the Messenian peoples and widened the basis of her own power by appropriating the territory and enslaving the population after a twenty-years' war (*c.* 740–720). Corinth, leader and beneficiary of the commercial expansion, deprived Megara of her southern territory in a war which probably ended *c.* 700 and was distinguished by the heroism of the Megarian Orsippus, the Olympic victor of 720.[2] Thereby the future of Corinth as the central market of exchange in the Greek world was assured; for henceforth she controlled the approaches by land and by sea to the shortest crossing of the Isthmus. Megara, robbed of territory which was rich in pasture and timber, relieved the pressure of over-population, at first by planting colonies overseas and then by subjugating the island of Salamis, which she secured towards 600 with Megarian settlers. Their presence threatened the approaches by sea to Eleusis and Athens. Inspired by the martial poems of Solon, the Athenians ejected the Megarians and in turn occupied the island. War continued between the two states; but by 560 Peisistratus secured lasting possession of this island, which was as vital to the future of Athens as the occupation of the southern Megarid was to Corinth.[3] Henceforth Megara remained a small but valiant state, depending for her survival upon astute diplomacy. Similar wars between neighbouring states were waged in Ionia and Aeolis with an occasional casualty, such as Smyrna and Arisbe.[4] In the colonial areas, where the

---

[1] Th. 1. 15. 2.
[2] HH. *GHI* 1; the date of Megara's loss is disputed, cf. *BSA* 49. 93.
[3] Paus. 1. 40. 5; Plu. *Sol.* 8; Arist. *Ath.* 17. 2; 14. 1. [4] Hdt. 1. 150–1.

states were less closely packed and had room to expand at the cost of weaker peoples, clashes occurred but not catastrophes; for new sites could be found, for instance, by the Milesians, when the Megarian colonists ejected them from Heraclea Pontica *c.* 560. More important for the future were the struggles for naval power and commercial exploitation in the western seas, where Corinth was embroiled with Corcyra *c.* 660 and Corcyra with Ambracia *c.* 620.[1] In the end Corinth asserted her control over her colonies but at the cost of a lasting animosity with Corcyra.

Coalitions arose when wider interests were involved. Thus the Lelantine war, waged before and after 700, began as a local dispute between Chalcis and Eretria for possession of the intervening Lelantine plain. The outcome, however, was a matter of general importance to the commercial and colonial powers of the Aegean. For Eretria ruled over Andros, Ceos, Tenos, and other islands, and Chalcis controlled the passage of the Euripus Channel; they shared the occupation of Chalcidice and the approaches to Etruria. Thucydides writes as if most of the Greek states participated in the Lelantine war. We know only that Samos sided with Chalcis and Miletus with Eretria, and we may conjecture that Corinth sided with the former and Megara with the latter. The decisive engagement was on land, when Thessalian cavalry won the day for Chalcis. Eretria, which boasted an army of 3,000 infantry, 600 cavalry, and 60 chariots, ceased to be a leading power. Andros celebrated her independence by planting colonies in Chalcidice *c.* 655. There Chalcis was now dominant, and Chalcis joined Corinth in exploiting the commerce of the West.[2]

In the Peloponnese the struggle began for military supremacy. The claims of Argos derived from the days of the conquest and were symbolized in the seniority of the Temenid royal family. She had played the leading part in founding Sicyon, Aegina, and Megara, and she aided Megara in a successful war against Corinth. Sparta challenged Argos by planting refugees from Asine (a city of the Argolid annexed by Argos) on the coast of Messenia. Argos took up the challenge and defeated Sparta decisively at Hysiae in 669.[3] The decline of Sparta's prestige and the success of Argos may have encouraged Pisa to revolt from Elis in 668 and gain control of the sanctuary at Olympia by 660. In 659 Sparta, campaigning against Phigalia, a canton of Arcadia which marched with Messenia, was repulsed by the Phigalians and the Oresthasians of Arcadia. Then *c.* 640 the Messenians revolted with the aid of Pisa, Arcadia, Argos, and Sicyon, and Sparta fought for her existence for nineteen years, receiving some aid from Corinth, Samos, and Lepreatis.[4] Sparta's victory was decisive. Her possession of Messenia was assured, her institutions vindicated, and her military prowess established. And in 546 she

---

[1] Th. 1. 13. 4; *GHI* 2.
[2] Str. 448; Th. 1. 15. 3; 1. 13. 3; Hdt. 5. 99; Arist. *Fr.* 98.
[3] Paus. 6. 19. 9; *FGrH* 115 F 383 (Theopompus); Paus. 2. 24. 7.
[4] Paus. 4. 14–24; Str. 362; Hdt. 3. 47.

defeated Argos in a battle which developed from a contest between 'Three Hundred Champions' on each side. This victory added Thyreatis permanently to her territory and made her the greatest military state in the Peloponnese.[1]

§ 2. *Military power in central Greece*

NORTH of the Peloponnese a local dispute between the Phocian states of Delphi and Crisa developed into the First Sacred War (595–586). Delphi, within whose territory the sanctuary of Apollo lay, had already become the centre of the so-called Delphic Amphictyony. The Amphictyons or 'dwellers-around' were the twelve tribes of north-east Greece—'Thessaloi, Perrhaiboi, Magnetes, Phthiotai, Dolopes, Malioi, Ainianes (or Oitaioi), Lokroi, Dorieis, Phoceeis, Iones, Boiotoi'—and the original centre of the Amphictyony had been at Thermopylae, close to the sanctuary of Demeter at Anthela. Each tribe had two votes on the Council of the Amphictyony, which was primarily concerned with religious ritual but could be harnessed to a political purpose. Crisa controlled the approaches from the north and from the coast towards Delphi; she was stronger than Delphi, and she may have profiteered at the expense of the pilgrims. Whatever the reason for the dispute, Delphi appealed to the Amphictyony. The Council obtained the blessing of the Pythian oracle and declared a sacred war on Crisa, which was formally excommunicated and sentenced to destruction. The secular power behind this decision was probably Thessaly, now united for purposes of war and ambitious to extend its influence. Under the general command of a Thessalian, Eurylochus, the Amphictyonic forces prevailed with the help of Sicyon and Athens in 591. They enslaved the survivors, dedicated the territory of Crisa to Apollo, and celebrated the victory by holding the first Pythian games in 582.[2] At these Eurylochus presided, and the Thessalians thereafter had precedence in the Amphictyony. The wrath of the god and the strength of the secular arm were vindicated. Crisa ceased to exist. Delphi, as a community, ministered to the sanctuary, and the Delphic priesthood conducted the ritual of the temple. The Amphictyonic Council charged itself with the protection of the shrine, the regulation of its finances and the conduct of its own members in matters of religious observance. The Sacred War enhanced the prestige of Apollo and Delphi, revealed the adaptability of the Amphictyonic machine for political purposes, and emphasized the military supremacy of Thessaly among the states north of the Isthmus.

This supremacy was put into operation after the Sacred War. Thessalian forces reduced Phocis and Locris and penetrated deep into Boeotia, before they suffered a defeat, approximately about 575. Later in the century the Phocians rebelled and secured their independence by defeating the Thessalian infantry in a night-attack and luring the Thessalian cavalry into a

[1] Hdt. 1. 82.
[2] *Marm. Par.* 37; Aeschin. 3. 107; Schol. Vet. Pi. *P. Hypothesis.*

camouflaged trap containing wine-jars.[1] Thus, before the time of the Persian invasion, the power of Thessaly had begun to decline.

§ 3. *The character of early warfare*

In the archaic period martial prowess was regarded as the noblest quality in a citizen. Tyrtaeus and Solon, as poets and statesmen, urged their fellow-citizens to valour with the resounding rhythm of their marching songs. 'To die, fallen in the front line, a brave man fighting for his fatherland, is honourable; but to leave one's city and its rich fields and live as a beggar is the depth of misery.' 'We march to Salamis to fight for that loved island and to cast off the burden of our shame.' Most wars were wars of extinction or survival. Messenia, Crisa, Smyrna, and Arisbe ceased to exist as states, and the enslavement of the survivors was normal. Such slaves were sometimes sold abroad and sometimes incorporated in the victor's territory in perpetuity. The Spartans and the Corinthians compelled the Messenians and the Megarians to send men and women to join in the mourning at the funeral of their masters, and the Spartans compelled the Messenians to take a solemn oath not to revolt, so that, should they revolt, they would have no right to religious asylum. When incorporation of conquered territory was not practicable, other methods were devised. Considerations of imperialism, not of humanity, prompted the Thessalians to install officers and tyrants in the Phocian cities. They had safeguards, too, against revolt; for they took civilian hostages, and they threatened rebels with unconditional warfare (*aspondos polemos*), which might entail massacre instead of enslavement.[2]

In the dark age warfare may have been decided by contests between champions, and a code of personal chivalry may have obtained, for instance, in a war within the Megarid. Then, too, members of the Delphic Amphictyony may have introduced the undertaking not to raze one another's city or cut off one another's water-supply in a secular war (as opposed to a sacred war).[3] But in the archaic period war involved more of the population and recognized fewer conventions. In battle wounded and disarmed men were dispatched, and the vanquished recovered only the dead, already stripped of their arms by the victors. Certain rules, carrying religious sanctions and probably of religious origin, were gradually accepted. Heralds and envoys were inviolable, the dead were not mutilated or denied burial, the truce covering such burial was sacrosanct, the oaths of a treaty were binding, and the altars of the gods offered sanctuary to the suppliant. In the archaic period these rules seem to have been generally observed.

The *élite* troops of the states were cavalry. The chariot of the Heroic Age was probably used in the Lelantine war, but otherwise it featured in Greece

[1] Plu. *Cam.* 19; Hdt. 8. 27.
[2] Tyrt. 6; Sol. 2; Paus. 4. 14. 4; Schol. Pi. *N.* 7. 155.
[3] Plu. 244[b]; 295[b] (*GQ* 17); Aeschin. 2. 115.

only in processions and races. Cavalry was the striking arm in the Lelantine War, and a cavalry engagement decided the issue; in Ionia, too, cavalry continued to be important in the Greek states and in Lydia.[1] But in the Peloponnese, although the prestige of cavalry persisted, the decisive arm was the infantry and the pitched battles after 700 were fought by lines of infantrymen, which could not be broken by cavalry assault. The hoplite had to be highly trained. He duelled with a six-foot spear against his opponent or opponents, maintained his position in the line and covered his neighbour's unshielded side; behind him line after line of infantrymen came into position and applied their weight and their steel in support (Plate IV *a*). Combat of this type demanded strength, spearmanship, and discipline, and in these qualities first the Argives and later the Spartans excelled. The prestige of Argos, perhaps early in the seventh century, is shown in a response by the oracle at Delphi. The men of Aegium, having captured a penteconter from the Aetolians, asked the god who were better than they, and he replied: 'Better are the fields of Pelasgicum Argos, the mares of Thessaly, the women of Sparta and the men who drink the water of fair Arethusa.[2] But better still are those that dwell between Tiryns and Arcadia rich in sheep, Argives of the linen corslet, pricks of war.' Those who could afford to equip themselves with helmet, cuirass, greaves, spear, and sword and to train for combat were themselves an *élite* in any state. When hoplite tactics became general, the importance of this *élite* grew; for a war was often decided in a pitched battle between the hoplite forces, and the verdict was accepted so long as the issue was of such limited scope as a frontier dispute. But in the archaic period set battles, except between Argos and Sparta, seem to have been rare. Few states had a sufficiency of hoplites, and the issues at stake were more fundamental. The 'battle of the trench' in the Messenian War and the capture of Crisa were not final; guerilla warfare persisted thereafter for eleven years in Messenia and for five on Mt. Parnassus. Thus wars were longlasting and sometimes more destructive of life and property, when every able-bodied man could take part as a light-armed skirmisher with sword, javelin, sling, or bow. These arms, too, were important, and certain states excelled in their use. Costly as these wars might be, they trained the Greeks in the prowess which won them colonies overseas and later defeated the Persian invasion.

[1] Str. 448; Polyaen. 7. 2. 2; Hdt. 1. 79.
[2] That is, the men of Chalcis; *AP* 14. 73.

Penteconter under sail, from an Attic Black Figure vase by Execias, *c.* 525–500 (the sail is not in the painting; see p. 110)

CHAPTER 5

Constitutional Developments (excluding Athens)

§ 1. *The decline of kingship*

THE kingship which prevailed during the Heroic Age and the Migrations was a particular type of kingship. It resembled constitutional kingship in that the king's privileges were defined, the king's authority was sanctioned by religion and usage, and the king's son had the right of succession. It resembled absolutism in that the king's powers were wellnigh absolute in war, religion, justice, and politics.[1] This type of kingship arose to meet the practical needs of warring and migrating peoples. The task of the king (*basileus*) was to hold together a number of racial groups, each group being built internally on racial kinship but the groups not necessarily being akin one to another. He had to weld them into unity by the force of his own personality and by virtue of his constitutional powers. The demands made upon kingship were exacting, but the services of the kings were proportionate to the needs of the times. Royal houses, such as the Heracleidae, Penthilidae, and Codridae, left a tradition of kingship which influenced later Greek thought.

As conditions changed, kingship became a rarity. The new states of the eastern Aegean developed an inner unity and soon dispensed with kingship. When the Athenians had secured their frontiers against the Dorians and had launched their fellow Ionians on the migration overseas, they abolished the kingship and became a republic. In the rest of the mainland the Dorian invasion was followed by a period of disintegration. The large groups of invaders, each held together by its king, separated out into their constituent elements—the small racial nuclei of diminutive size, which settled in village communities. Regional kingdoms thus gave way to local concentrations, and traditional kingships hardly operated beyond the borders of their quondam capitals. If towards the end of the dark age the villages had coalesced back into the old regional kingdoms, kingship might have survived. But in general the villages coalesced into smaller groups, city-states (*poleis*), which in Crete, for instance, replaced the realm of Idomeneus with a hundred political nuclei. This process rang the death-knell of kingship; for the Dorian *poleis* had an inner unity no less than the Ionian and Aeolian *poleis* overseas. Already when Aegina and Megara were founded, the god Apollo and not a king was the founder (*oikistes*) and the leader (*archegetes*). So, too, when the colonies were founded, the *oikistes* was generally not a king.

[1] Arist. *Pol.* 1284[b]35.

Kingship lasted longest either where its traditions were deep-rooted (in Argos; in Sparta, Thera and their colonies, Taras and Cyrene), or where the primitive conditions favourable to kingship continued (for instance in north-west Greece and in Macedonia). From Argos the senior branch of the Heracleidae, the sons of Temenus, had originally ruled the Argolid and founded Sicyon, Phlius, and Epidaurus. During the Dark Age disintegration ensued. New states formed; such were Tiryns, Nauplia, and Asine, which resisted to the death any attempt by the Temenidae to force them back into the kingdom. Pheidon alone achieved this task. Probably in the first half of the seventh century he reconstituted the traditional kingdom of the Temenidae, enhancing his prestige by defeating Sparta at Hysiae in 669 and by presiding over the Olympic festival with the compliance of Pisa.[1] His only lasting achievements were to issue the first coinage of peninsular Greece and to standardize the 'Pheidonian' system of weights and measures. For after his death the kingdom of the Temenidae collapsed, and about the end of the century kingship at Argos was defunct. Neither as a kingdom nor as a republic was Argos capable of uniting the other city-states of the Argolid into a close-knit and lasting unity. They were already hard-set in an irrefrangible political form.

Kingship survived at Sparta in a lasting form, because it had a most important function to perform. Sparta, as we have seen, was the first city-state on the mainland to form out of constituent villages, and in addition Sparta, like Argos, was the traditional capital of a Heraclid kingdom. She thus had the pretext and the power to reduce the separate villages piecemeal and re-assert the suzerainty of the Heraclid kings over all Laconia. The Spartan kings were the *fons et origo* of the new Lacedaemonian state, which comprised the Spartiates, the Perioeci, and the Helots of Laconia and later those of Messenia. The state funeral of a Spartan king was attended perforce by men and women representing all sections of the Lacedaemonian population, Spartiate, Perioecus, and Helot, and a ten days' period of official mourning was observed throughout the country. The kings declared war on behalf of the Lacedaemonian state, commanded the armed forces, which comprised Spartiates, Perioeci, and Helots, and sacrificed at the frontiers of Laconia before leading the army abroad. They held the priesthoods of Zeus Lacedaemon and Zeus Uranius, conducted all sacrifices on behalf of the community and nominated the state-delegates to consult the oracle of Apollo at Delphi. Their names appeared first on documents of the Lacedaemonian state, they took precedence in all state ritual and ceremony, and they were attended by a bodyguard of cavalry.[2] Indeed Spartan kingship had a function akin to that of the British Crown. It knit together not only the realm of Sparta but also the domains of Laconia and Messenia. Sparta itself was a city-state, formed by a political union of village-communities, and within the city-state constitution the powers of the kings were restricted, so that in the Gerousia,

[1] Str. 358; Paus. 6. 22. 2; Hdt. 6. 127.   [2] Th. 5. 24.

for instance, they were on an equal footing with the other members. Within the Lacedaemonian state the Spartan city-state was dominant and monopolized constitutional control. But the powers of the kings within the Lacedaemonian state were not restricted. For they formed the bridge between the Spartan state and the Lacedaemonian state, being kings of both.

In Thessaly there was a revival of kingly power in the form of a supreme military commander (*tagos*), who, like the original Heraclid kings of the conquest, claimed authority over all Thessaly. The first was probably Aleuas, head of the Heraclid clan at Larisa in the latter part of the seventh century, and he demanded a quota of forty cavalry and eighty infantry from each large estate (*kleros*).[1] The total forces were later reckoned at 6,000 cavalry and above 10,000 infantry, which are not impossible figures in view of Eretria's army in the Lelantine war. The cavalry were first class, but the infantry, being equipped with the light shield of goatskin or sheepskin (*pelte*), were not a match for hoplite forces. For a century or so the revival of the military powers of kingship made Thessaly the leading state north of the Isthmus. Thereafter the jealousy of the constituent elements within the military unit weakened its efficiency, and the office of *tagos* was insecurely held by any one baronial house against the intrigues of the others.

§ 2. *Aristocracy*

IN general kingship fell not by violence but by absorption into the next layer of authority, the aristocracy of the clan leaders, who had long formed the king's Council and the king's Court. The title was usually preserved, the 'king' becoming a magistrate at Argos, Athens, and Corinth, and a priest at Ephesus, Miletus, and Naxos, but the Council of Elders was now in control of the 'king' as *archon basileus*, one of several magistrates. The power of the aristocratic Council was more deeply entrenched than that of the king in the social structure of the city-state. For the aristocrats were the leaders of the racial groups—tribes, phratries, and clans—which had coalesced to make the city-states. In less developed areas such as Elis, where the small communities (*damoi*) had not yet coalesced, the kings were succeeded by a close aristocracy of the heads of the phratries and clans (*patriai* and *geneai*).[2] Their title-deeds were unchallenged in matters of religion, justice, and politics; for they were hallowed by centuries of tradition.

The central organ of aristocratic government in the city-states was the Council (*boule* or *gerousia*); its members were eligible for election at the ripe age, for example, of sixty at Sparta and fifty at Chalcis, retained membership for life, and were not held to audit for their acts. The Council was itself supported by the structure of phratry and clan, which conducted their affairs on the same system and enshrined the same principles. The magistrates, as the executive arm of the Council, were strictly controlled by the Council. In

---

[1] Arist. *Fr.* 497–8; X. *HG* 6. 1. 8.   [2] *Inscr. Olymp.* nr. 2; Arist. *Pol.* 1306ᵃ17.

some states, for example, only members of certain families were eligible for office; in others the Council had the power of scrutiny (*dokimasia*) and the right of rejecting a candidate. Tenure of office was normally limited to one year, and the magistrates' conduct was then reviewed by the Council; and in many cases the powers of office were divided among several magistrates, who formed a college and accepted the principle of a majority vote.

All aristocracies were oligarchical, rule being vested in the few, but the degree of oligarchy varied. In the narrowest aristocracies a monopoly of office was secured by the family in which the hereditary kingship had been vested. At Corinth, for instance, the Bacchiadae were descended from the royal house of the Heracleidae but more specifically from a distinguished king of Corinth, Bacchis. The immediate successors of Bacchis were kings, but from *c*. 747 the Bacchiadae ruled as a group, electing from itself an eponymous official of the year probably entitled *basileus* and intermarrying entirely within its own branches.[1] In such a clan the men of fifty years and above may have numbered some 200. At Mitylene the Penthilidae and at Erythrae and Ephesus the Basilidae held a similar monopoly of office.[2] A less narrow form of aristocracy was that in which office was restricted to certain phratries, for instance in the Cretan cities and in Locris where the members of 100 house-holds ruled, or to certain groups whose original privilege derived from the time of conquest or of foundation, such as the Hippobotae at Chalcis and the Gamoroi at Samos and Syracuse.[3]

The authority of the aristocracies rested not only upon religious and social tradition but also on economic and military strength. As the names Hippo-botae (horse-raisers) and Gamoroi (landowners) imply, the aristocrats owned the best land; from their hereditary estates (*kleroi*) they had accumulated great wealth at a time when seaborne trade was in its infancy and com-mercial profits small. In warfare, too, the aristocrats alone could provide the cavalry which was supreme in the leading city-states until 700 and in less developed areas after 700.[4] Their prestige and their power gave them the undisputed leadership also in the colonial field; for they organized the ex-peditions which planted the colonies, and they provided the founders, for instance, Archias at Syracuse and Chersicrates at Corcyra being members of the Bacchiad clan. Nor can it be denied that the aristocracies served their states well. To them must be attributed the great developments of the archaic period: the formation of the city-states, the blossoming of Greek art, and colonial expansion.

In most states aristocratic government had a high degree of stability. It was based upon the consent of the citizen community, which was itself organ-ized on the racial system and adhered to the same social and religious prin-ciples. Although initiation of policy and executive power were in the hands

[1] Hdt. 5. 92[b]; Str. 378; D.S. 7. 9.
[2] Arist. *Pol.* 1311[b]27; 1305[b]19; *FGrH* 268 F 3 (Baton).
[3] Polyb. 12. 5. 7.   [4] Arist. *Pol.* 1289[b]34.

of the aristocrats, there is no evidence that the Assembly of citizens was suppressed. The Assembly probably did no more than voice its opinion on major issues affecting foreign relations, colonial policy, land-tenure, and so forth, and elect candidates who had been nominated from a restricted class. But in these matters a serious clash was unlikely. For in the Dorian states the Assembly was as much concerned as the aristocrats to maintain the privileges of the citizens against the serfs and the perioeci, and in the states overseas against the slaves and the barbarians. Where the aristocracy held together and adapted itself to slowly changing conditions, it lasted into the fifth or fourth century.

Early lawgivers were often successful in prolonging the stable conditions of aristocratic government. The Corinthian lawgivers Pheidon and Philolaus maintained the numbers of the privileged class and the system of landed estates at Corinth and Thebes by modifying the laws of inheritance and adoption.[1] At Epizephyrian Locri c. 660 Zaleucus fixed the penalties for offences and regularized judicial procedure, and he may have been responsible for a law which forbade the sale of original *kleroi* and discouraged the sale of secondary estates. At Catana Charondas carried reforms in the administration of justice, and in Chalcidice Androdamas of Rhegium, who may have been inspired by the work of Charondas, reformed the laws governing murder trials and inheritances.[2] These lawgivers were concerned with three main problems. As citizenship depended upon the ownership of an estate (*kleros*), its alienation by sale or by bequest decreased the number of citizens and increased the landed property of rich citizens. In order to prevent this tendency, the number of estates was safeguarded, and laws permitting adoption and protecting heiresses were passed. The second problem sprang from the administration of justice in the courts of phratry and clan. Discontent was widespread against the 'crooked judgements of the corrupt kings',[3] that is the aristocrats who presided over these courts, and their control had to be modified. Thirdly, murder or homicide led to vendetta by the clan of the victim and brought pollution on the state; its effect could only be limited by the institution of a state court. Where the lawgivers solved these problems, the danger of revolution was averted.

Many states with an aristocratic government modified their institutions peacefully. At Heraclea Pontica and at Massilia, for instance, if the father was a member of the Council, the elder son could not become one, and similarly, if the elder brother was a member, not a younger brother; these prohibitions lapsed later, and the membership of the Council increased to 600 at Heraclea Pontica and probably at Massilia also.[4] In other cases the qualification for membership of the governing body changed from birth to wealth or military service. Such a change transformed an aristocracy into an oligarchy, if the technical term may be employed to avoid the phrases 'aristocratic oligarchy'

---

[1] Arist. *Pol.* 1265ᵇ12; 1274ᵃ31.   [2] Arist. *Pol.* 1266ᵇ18; 1274ᵇ6 and 23.
[3] Hes. *Op.* 221, 264; Thgn. 51.   [4] Arist. *Pol.* 1305ᵇ5.

and 'plutocratic oligarchy'. At Rhegium, for instance, the governing class were the descendants of the Messenian settlers; they were probably selected for office on principles of birth, but they were later elected on a property-qualification.[1] The Council at Rhegium numbered a thousand members, as did those of Epizephyrian Locri, Catana, and Croton and that of Opus in Epicnemidian Locris. In these cases there was probably an Assembly of all citizens, and its powers were as limited as they had been under an aristocracy. At Cyme in Aeolis and at Colophon in Ionia, where the governing body numbered one thousand, there was probably no Assembly at all.[2] In other states a close oligarchy ruled without reference to law or citizen body. Such an oligarchy (*dynasteia*) was in power at Thebes, and at Larisa, Pharsalus, and Crannon, where great wealth and high nobility were concentrated in single families.[3]

§ 3. *Tyranny on the mainland*

IN states which failed to solve these problems it often happened that power was seized by a single individual. His unconstitutional régime was called *monarchia* 'sole rule' or *tyrannis*, a Lydian word which came into general use. The origins of tyranny are obscured by a variety of factors. The tyrants themselves were at pains to whitewash and their opponents to blacken the tyrants' rise to power. The actions of the tyrants, when they were in power, accentuated the division within the state and drove opinion both for and against them to extremes. In the fourth century a second crop of tyrants arose for different reasons, and political thinkers of that century tended to project those reasons back to the sixth century, especially in the form that the tyrant grew out of the professional 'demagogue' (*demagogos*), the leader of a democratic faction. It is therefore important to be guided by the experience of those states which avoided tyranny in the seventh and sixth centuries, and by the views of early writers such as Solon, Theognis, Herodotus, and Thucydides.

'In general', wrote Thucydides, 'tyrannies were established in the city-states as revenues were increasing, when Greece was becoming more powerful and progressing in the acquisition of capital wealth.'[4] His view is supported by the fact that the earliest tyrannies arose at Sicyon, Corinth, and Megara, which were centres of commercial expansion. The rapid influx of wealth aggravated the problems which exercised many states in the seventh century. The competition of mobile wealth as opposed to landed property may have upset the system of *kleroi*, on which the aristocrats and the Dorian commons depended. It tended to widen the gap between rich and poor, and between

---

[1] *FHG* 2. 219. (Heracl. Pont. 25).

[2] *FHG* 2, 217 (Heracl. Pont. 11. 6); Ath. 526ᵃ and ᶜ.

[3] Thuc. 3. 62. 3; Hdt. 5. 79. 2 (where the Assembly was probably controlled by the oligarchy); Th. 4. 78. 3.   [4] Th. 1. 13. 1.

citizen and non-citizen, and it introduced a new factor into politics—a regard for wealth as a rival to regard for birth. To this new factor Alcaeus and Theognis refer in their epigrammatic comments. 'Money is the man, and no pauper is highborn or respectable.' 'Wealth confuses birth.'[1] Moreover, mobile wealth introduced a new means to power in the purchase of political support and of mercenary troops. There were certainly discontented elements in the population which could be raised in support of a successful tyrant, such as impoverished citizens, unprivileged citizens, perioeci, serfs, and slaves. But these elements were not organized, nor were they capable of overthrowing an aristocracy which was united in its own ranks. As Aristotle remarked and as the aristocratic lawgivers showed, 'a harmonious oligarchy does not easily cause its own destruction'.[2] The opportunity for tyranny usually arose when the aristocratic oligarchy split and the new means to power were exploited. This was expressed succinctly by Herodotus, who described the animosities and rivalries within an oligarchy, and continued: 'out of these arise factions, out of factions bloodshed, and from bloodshed the result is one-man-rule'. Solon and Theognis described the origin of tyranny in their own generation in similar terms: 'From the great men destruction comes to the state, and the people in its ignorance falls into servitude to the single ruler.' 'From corrupt judges arise factions and civil bloodshed and single rulers.'[3]

At Corinth Cypselus seized power from the Bacchiadae about 657. The son of a Bacchiad woman who had married into another noble house of Corinth, Cypselus probably became commander of the citizen army (*polemarchos*), killed the leader and exiled the remainder of the Bacchiad clan, and distributed their lands among his supporters. Ruling Corinth for some thirty years, he made rich dedications at Delphi and at Olympia, in order to win the blessing of the gods. It is probable that the oracle at Delphi recognized him as 'king' of Corinth, a title held in the past by the leader of the Bacchiadae. Of his internal policy we may conjecture that it brought an increasing prosperity at home which made his long tenure of the tyranny possible and ensured a peaceful succession by his son. In his foreign policy he hemmed in the Bacchiadae, who had taken refuge in Corcyra, by founding the three important colonies of Leucas, Anactorium, and Ambracia under the leadership of his three sons. In Syracuse his influence may have brought about the expulsion of a ruling clan, the Myletidae. In the latter part of his rule he may have come to terms with the Bacchiadae at Corcyra.[4]

Cypselus was succeeded by his legitimate son, Periander, who employed a bodyguard to secure his position. He endeavoured to sanctify his régime by rich offerings at Delphi and Olympia and by instituting the worship of Dionysus, building temples, and organizing the games at the Isthmus on a grand scale. He adopted coinage *c.* 610, and his revenues were provided by tolls

[1] Alc. 49; Thgn. 190.   [2] Arist. *Pol.* 1306ᵃ10.   [3] Hdt. 3. 82; Sol. 9; Thgn. 51.
[4] Hdt. 5. 92; *FGrH* 90 F 57 (Nic. Dam.); Polyaen. 5. 31.

on the traffic which passed through Corinthia. He enacted laws to discourage the drift of population towards the towns, to control local expenditure, and to limit extravagance, immorality, and the purchase of slaves.[1] During his tyranny, *c.* 627–586, Corinth reached the zenith of her prosperity and power. He laid a roadway (known as the *diolkos*) for hauling ships across the Isthmus and proposed also to cut a canal.[2] Her fleets sailed the two seas. Her colonial empire was completed by the reduction of Corcyra and by the planting of Apollonia Illyrica and Potidaea. Periander possessed a marriage alliance with Procles, tyrant of Epidaurus, a political alliance with Thrasybulus, tyrant of Miletus, and the friendship of Athens, Lydia, and probably Egypt. The poet Arion graced his court; and the artistic products of Corinth were in vogue throughout the Greek world. But Periander developed the proverbial vices of the tyrant. He killed his wife and banished his son Lycophron. When the Corcyraeans killed Lycophron, he planned to wreak vengeance by sending 300 sons of noble families to Alyattes of Lydia to serve as eunuchs at his court.[3]

His nephew and successor Psammetichus was assassinated *c.* 582. The corpse and the bones of his ancestors were cast beyond the borders of Corinthia, and the houses of the Cypselidae were razed to the ground.[4] No vestige was left of the hated tyranny, which had suppressed personal rights and political liberty. Even the priests at Delphi circulated a *vaticinium post eventum*, to the effect that the oracle had warned the Bacchiadae with reference to Cypselus' parents that disaster would come from any son they brought forth. In Ambracia, where a brother of Psammetichus was in power, the people rose and set up a democracy.[5] At Corinth an oligarchy came into power. The detail of its constitution is doubtful. There was probably a small board of magistrates with strong powers (*probouloi*), a Council (perhaps *Gerousia*) and an Assembly (*halia*); the eight wards of the state were represented in the board and in the Council, perhaps one ward in rotation electing members to the board and the other wards electing members to the Council.[6] The interesting feature at Corinth is that the aftermath of tyranny was not democracy. The tyrants had not favoured the concentration of citizens in the towns or enfranchised the perioeci.[7] The handicrafts and the retail trades were practised probably by foreigners, who were attracted to the prosperous ports and markets of Corinthia. Wealthy citizens certainly owned ships, and Corinthian sailors manned merchantmen as well as warships;[8] but the bulk of the citizens derived their revenues from landed estates, and they preserved the traditional exclusiveness of the Dorian state with its preference for ordered oligarchy. Pindar later sang the praises of Corinth as the state in

---

[1] *FHG* 2. 213 (Heracl. Pont. 5); coinage, see Plate XI *d*.
[2] Details of the *diolkos* reported in *Ergon* 1960, 117; D.L. 1. 99; *FGrH* 90 F 58.
[3] Hdt. 3. 48.　　　　　　[4] *FGrH* 90 F 60.　　　　　　[5] Arist. *Pol.* 1304ᵃ31.
[6] *FGrH* 90 F 60, of which the text is corrupt.
[7] Ibid. 59.　　　　　　　　　　　　　　[8] Dion. Hal. *AR.* 3. 46; Hdt. 1. 24.

which dwelt Orderliness, Justice, and Peace together with the sweet-singing Muse and the war-god strong in the spears of her young men.[1]

At Sicyon, the neighbour of Corinth, Orthagoras became tyrant in 655 and his dynasty lasted for a century. The tyrants endeavoured to obtain religious approval of their régime by dedicating rich offerings at Olympia and by supporting the Amphictyons of Delphi in the Sacred War. But upon their fall the priests at Delphi issued an oracle wherein the god had forewarned the Sicyonians that they would be 'scourged' for a hundred years; the detail that Orthagoras' father was a cook was built around this oracle and is not to be taken seriously. Orthagoras gained power after distinguishing himself in a frontier war and being appointed general.[2] At first the tyranny was moderate, but it became oppressive in the hands of Myron II, who was murdered by his brother Isodamus, and of Cleisthenes (*c.* 600–570) and Aeschines. The tyrants held the office of chief priest (*basileus*) and sacrificed on behalf of the state. Myron I, who won the chariot-race at Olympia in 648, dedicated a treasury at Olympia in the name of 'Myron and the people of Sicyon'. The tyrants thus tried to give a constitutional façade to their régime.[3] Within the state they did not revolutionize the social system; for during their régime one class of serfs (*katonakophoroi*) were excluded from the town, where the Dorian masters lived.[4] Artists were attracted to the court of Cleisthenes. In particular Dipoenus and Scyllis, who came from Crete, founded a leading school of sculpture in Parian marble, and Sicyonian painters and modellers were rivalled only by those of Corinth during the first half of the sixth century. Cleisthenes built a colonnade, which was named after him, and founded games at Sicyon in honour of Pythian Apollo, which added to the lustre of his house and the attractions of his state.[5]

In foreign policy Cleisthenes was the most distinguished of the Sicyonian tyrants. Disposing of a considerable army, he won allies by his offers of military aid, and he played a distinguished part in the Sacred War. His expenditure was lavish. He established his own Pythian games, won victories in the chariot-race at Olympia and at Delphi, and staged a competition for the wooing of his daughter Agariste. For at the end of the Olympic festival in 576 he invited suitors from all parts of Greece to compete at Sicyon for her hand. The field was strong. States in Italy as well as the mainland were represented. Agariste was awarded to Megacles, later head of the Alcmeonid clan at Athens; their son was the Athenian statesman Cleisthenes and their grand-daughter was Agariste the mother of Pericles. One state against which Cleisthenes waged war was Argos. To add insult to injury, he spoiled the cult of the Argive hero Adrastus at Sicyon by importing the relics of a rival

---

[1] Pi. *O.* 13.
[2] *FGrH* 105 F 2; for the chronology, which is disputed, see *CQ* 6. 45 f.
[3] Arist. *Pol.* 1315^{b}13; *FGrH* 90 F 61; Paus. 6. 19. 3.
[4] Pollux 7. 68; *FGrH* 115 F. 176 (Theopompus).
[5] Str. 382; Plin. 36. 4–5; Paus. 2. 9. 6.

Theban hero, Melanippus, and by transferring choral dances to a new festival of Dionysus. It was probably in connexion with the rump of the Adrastus cult and not with the political divisions of Sicyon that Cleisthenes coined the nicknames 'Pig-men, Ass-men, and Hog-men' for the traditional Hylleis, Dymanes, and Pamphyloi. These nicknames lasted for sixty years after Cleisthenes' death; their retention indicates that the political divisions at Sicyon were no longer the old racial tribes, Hylleis, Dymanes, and Pamphyloi, together with the non-Dorian Aegialeis, whom Cleisthenes had renamed 'Rulers'.[1]

For all his bravura Cleisthenes did not win the lasting favour of the Delphic priests. When he asked the god to bless the suppression of Adrastus, he received the tart response that Adrastus was the king of Sicyon and Cleisthenes a pebble-slinger. The days of the tyrants in the Dorian states were already numbered. Periander had overthrown the tyrant of Epidaurus, and Periander's successor had been expelled from Corinth. By 555 the tyrant Aeschines and the other members of Cleisthenes' family were driven out. Sicyon recovered her liberty, and Delphi denounced the brood of tyrants as scourges of the body politic.

As Procles, the tyrant of Epidaurus, was the father-in-law of Periander, his régime lay on both sides of 625. The information which we have concerning the constitution of Epidaurus probably dates to the period after and not before this early tyranny. The executive control was vested in a close oligarchy of 180 men. These evidently formed a Council, from which the citizens elected the 'directors' (*artynoi*), that is executive magistrates analogous to those at Argos (*artynai*). Of the common people the majority lived on the lands outside the city and were named the 'dusty-feet' (*konipodes*).[2] They may be identified with the unprivileged descendants of the perioeci or the serfs, analogous to the perioeci and *gymnesioi* at Argos. At Epidaurus, too, it appears that the tyranny had not altered the organization of society.

At Megara, the northern neighbour of Corinth, Theagenes arose as tyrant during the latter half of the seventh century. He managed to obtain a body-guard, slaughtered the cattle of the rich (presumably of his opponents only, for a wholesale destruction of stock would be absurd), built a famous aqueduct, and married his daughter to an influential noble, Cylon of Athens, who tried but failed with the aid of a Megarian force to establish himself as tyrant of his own state.[3] During the ensuing troubles at Athens the Megarians occupied Salamis and then cast out Theagenes. An aristocratic oligarchy returned to power but was overthrown by the poorer classes in the state. Under their democratic régime a law was passed whereby creditors had to return to debtors the interest already paid on the original loan; no doubt this law attended a cancellation of debts and a repeal of the law safeguarding creditors. The democrats fell foul of the Amphictyonic Council, when they

[1] Hdt. 6. 126; 5. 67; Schol. Pi. *N.* 9. 20.   [2] Plu. 291^e = *GQ* 1.
[3] Arist. *Rhet.* 1357^{b}32; *Pol.* 1305^{a}25; Paus. 1. 40. 1; Thuc. 1. 126. 3.

failed to punish an attack by Megarians on a group of pilgrims *en route* for Delphi. The Amphictyons then enforced the execution of some offenders and the banishment of others.[1]

It is probable that civil war between aristocrats and democrats became a struggle between rich and poor during the half-century ending about 555. Upon this period of internal strife some light is shed by a collection of verses, which are ascribed to Theognis of Megara but contain the work of several hands. Their bias is aristocratic and oligarchic. They resent the defeat of high birth in the political arena; they hate the wealthy *parvenu* as heartily as the enfranchised serf, who in the past lived like a hind outside the city's walls and now tills the aristocrat's lands. The fact that the poems do not refer to the tyranny of Theagenes shows that he did not upset the aristocratic privileges of the Dorian community. The revolution came with the democratic rising. In these poems we see for the first time the unmitigated evils which stemmed from civil war between rich and poor. 'Gone is Faith, goddess supreme, gone Moderation from mankind, and the Graces have deserted our land, my friend. Among men solemn oaths are no longer respected, and no one reveres the immortal gods. The generation of religious men is destroyed; they recognize no standards of law or of piety.' Hatred, treachery, and poverty prevail; man is at the mercy of gods whose will he cannot divine.[2]

The rule of the tyrants at Corinth, Sicyon, Megara, and Epidaurus coincided with the century of great commercial expansion. The tyrants were able men, who put the security of their own household first but pursued a policy of enlightened self-interest.[3] Once they had broken the ring of close aristocracy, they did not revolutionize the order of society but conciliated the Dorian communities, on which their military power rested. They fostered the arts and the trades, whence they drew their revenues, and the Cypselids expanded the colonial system of the Bacchiads. Their methods were aristocratic: they upheld religion, they competed in and organized athletic festivals, and they sought to marry into noble houses. They were no democrats: they did not liberate perioecus or serf and they had no wish to train the people for power. Their régime was rather an interlude in the evolution from aristocracy to oligarchy, which in fact followed their fall at Corinth, Sicyon, Megara, and Epidaurus. It is difficult to disassociate their achievement from the background of commercial prosperity, which they had not created but did not disrupt. By a process of natural selection they were the ablest of the aristocrats and the least scrupulous. At Corinth and at Sicyon they gave their states a long period of stable government over a century of transition and expansion. But there their services ended. Their disservices were greater. For they suppressed liberty among a people by whom liberty was cherished; this suppression split the state into two parties, the collaborators and the liberators, and fostered the growth of underground political clubs, ripe for

---

[1] Thgn. 41 f. with Plu. 295ᶜ = *GQ* 18; 304ᵉ = *GQ* 59.
[2] Thgn. 185; 53; 1200; 1137; 133.
[3] Th. 1. 7.

revolution. The full aftermath of tyranny became apparent at Megara, whence the use of the political society (*hetaireia*) spread with Cylon to Attica.[1] Its effects were such that the name of tyranny became an abomination in the Greek world.

§ 4. *Tyranny in the West and the East*

THE Greek colonies in Sicily and Italy were governed by aristocratic oligarchies, which retained firm control until the end of the sixth century. Only two tyrants arose before 550. They were probably aristocrats, and their régime was followed by the restoration of aristocratic oligarchy. Panaetius of Leontini exploited his position as general in a war against Megara Hyblaea and installed himself as tyrant *c.* 609. Phalaris of Acragas practised the arts of the proverbial tyrant. He assassinated leading citizens at the festival of the Thesmophoria, seized the Acropolis with the aid of a mercenary force, and disarmed the people; abroad he waged war successfully against Sicans and Phoenicians, and at home he suppressed opposition by terroristic methods. The bronze bull in which he roasted his victims alive was famous in the lifetime of Pindar. Neither tyranny revolutionized the structure of society. Rather they were interludes in the period of aristocratic government, which carried the colonial foundations forward to great prosperity.[2]

The late seventh century brought increased prosperity and political upheavals to the leading states of the eastern Aegean. Close aristocracies were overthrown by individual aristocrats, who exploited the opportunities of high office, or by the concerted rising of a military group, or by a general revolt of the people.[3] Some liberators turned tyrant. At Ephesus, for instance, Pythagoras plundered the rich, aided the poor, and violated sacred and secular laws. He sought the blessing of Delphi in vain. After him Melas became tyrant, married a daughter of Alyattes, and was succeeded by his son Pindarus, who saved Ephesus from subjugation by Croesus on the condition of his own withdrawal.[4] In other states individuals were appointed with dictatorial powers to arbitrate between the factions. Such were Tynnondas in Euboea and Pittacus in Mitylene. Pittacus was appointed arbiter (*aisymnetes*) to settle the civil war which had arisen after his assassination of a tyrant Melanchrus. The struggle was between three parties—a group of aristocrats, a democratic partly led by Myrsilus, and a party headed by the noble Cleanactidae. Pittacus achieved a settlement by banishing the first group, of which the poet Alcaeus was a member. His poems reveal the bitterness of the struggle. Whereas Theognis generalizes, Alcaeus proclaims his hatred for individuals. 'The low-born Pittacus was appointed tyrant of the spineless and ill-fated

---

[1] Thgn. 91 f.; Hdt. 5. 71; Sol. 3. 22.
[2] Arist. *Pol.* 1310^{b}29; 1316^{a}36; Polyaen. 5. 47; 5. 1. 1–2; *Pi. P.* 1. 95.
[3] Arist. *Pol.* 1305^{a}17; Plu. 303^e = *GQ* 57; Arist. *Pol.* 1305^{b}19.
[4] *FGrH* 268 F 3 (Baton); Ael. *VH* 3. 26.

state by one and all with shouts of praise.' 'Now Myrsilus is dead, one must make merry and drink deep.'¹ At Miletus, after the fall of the oppressive tyrant Thrasybulus, the state was torn by civil war for a period covering two generations, perhaps *c.* 580–520. During this time there probably arose the two extremist political clubs, named after the wealthy and the artisans, *Hetaireia Ploutis* and *Hetaireia Cheiromacha*, which lend meaning to the cry of the Milesian poet Phocylides 'better a small state set in order on a rock than frantic Nineveh'.²

In general the Ionian tyrants destroyed the old order but failed to build a stable government themselves; to that extent, they did more harm than the tyrants of the Dorian states in the homeland. The aftermath of tyranny, too, was worse, because the Ionians lacked both the self-restraint of the Dorian communities and the need to beware of a large unprivileged class. Racial loyalties were weaker and individualism stronger than on the mainland, so that the struggle was more directly in terms of oligarchy and democracy, wealth and poverty. Faction weakened the states politically; they fell piece-meal under the rule of Lydia and later of Persia. But their economic prosperity was not seriously affected. On the one hand Ionia held and exploited a favourable position in the expanding field of Greek commerce, and on the other political strife was probably confined to members of the political clubs. It was only under worsening economic conditions that the full effects of faction within the Greek states became apparent, and those days were far off.

The rapid development of economic prosperity gave added strength to the middle and lower classes in those Ionian states which engaged especially in seaborne commerce. Such a state was Chios early in the sixth century. Here the close aristocracy had been overthrown, and a moderate government with some democratic features was established. The people, probably voting in full assembly, issued ordinances of state. Citizens had the right of appeal to a people's Council, recruited by the election of fifty members from each tribe. This Council met once monthly, in full session, to conduct the business of the people and to complete the hearing of appeals, and its executive arm was formed by the people's magistrates (*demarchoi*). Beside the people's magis-trates, Council, and Assembly, there were state officials (*basileis*) and probably a second and older Council, which were legacies of the aristocratic constitu-tion of the state and stemmed from the tribal system. Our knowledge is derived from the discovery of an inscribed stone (found on a roadside near the modern town of Chios), which records enactments by the people con-cerning the administration of justice. This inscription gives us the first glimpse of a constitutional solution to which the genius of the Ionian peoples was particularly suited.³

¹ Arist. *Pol.* 1285ª31; Plu. *Sol.* 14. 4; Str. 617; Alc. 87; 39.
² Hdt. 1. 23; Plu. 298ᶜ = *GQ* 32; Phoc. 4.
³ Arist. *Pol.* 1306ᵇ5; *GHI* 1.

CHAPTER 6

Constitutional Developments at Athens and the Spartan Alliance

§ 1. *The Athenian state before 600*

D URING the tenth century Athens was the strongest state on the mainland. She had beaten off a concerted attack from the Dorians of the
Peloponnese, and she then launched the Ionian migration. Her pottery
in the late Protogeometric period was the finest in Greece, and its influence
was carried far afield. No Dorian state could rival these achievements. But
thereafter Athens fell back from her leading position, and in the period
735–625 her pottery, artistic as it was, only reached adjacent territories.[1] She
was now strikingly surpassed by the Dorian states, Corinth, Sparta, and even
Megara. It was not so much that she declined as that they developed. The
Dorians led in naval construction and in hoplite warfare; in great colonial
undertakings; in commercial expansion and in coinage; and even in the
'orientalizing' style of pottery. The explanation is to be sought in the political
field. The Dorian states had changed from the dismembered tribal kingdoms
of the tenth century into the new city-states, smaller indeed but more compact in organization and more dynamic in power. Athens remained essentially
a tribal state, much larger in citizen population than Corinth or Thebes but
looser in structure and less strong in action. To endow Athens with a comparable political form and to realize her potentialities in genius and in population was the task of two Athenian statesmen, Solon and Cleisthenes.

In extent Attica was similar to Boeotia. Whereas tens of city-states emerged
in Boeotia, Attica had been for centuries and remained a single state. The
Megarid was smaller in extent and much smaller in citizen population; for
the Megarians rested on a serf class, whereas Attica, like Boeotia, had no
serf system. The districts of Attica were three: 'the plain-land' (*pediake*), the
territory around Athens and Eleusis; 'the coast-land' (*paralia*), the sea-girt
promontory ending in Sunium; and 'the hill-land' (*diacria*), the northern
stretch dominated by the mountains Parnes and Pentelicus.[2] The whole
population was enrolled in four tribes, of which the names were common to
many of the Ionian states overseas. Each 'Ionic' tribe subdivided into three
'brotherhoods' (*phratriai*); as the land owned by members of a phratry was
specific and inalienable, a phratry was named in the geographical sense 'a
third' (*trittys*). There were thus twelve phratries and twelve trittyes in Attica.

---

[1] *BSA* 35. 165. [2] *AAP* (= Arist. *Ath.* in this chapter) 13. 4–5.

Upon them the constitution was built, until Cleisthenes carried his reforms in 508. The personnel of the phratry consisted of two groups, members of clans (*gene*) and members of guilds (*orgeones*). The broad distinction between them in terms of occupation was that clansmen worked (and owned) the land and guildsmen practised trades and handicrafts.[1]

The clan was a large familial group, comprising many households; among these some houses (*oikoi*) were nobler than others. Themistocles, for instance, was a member of the clan of the Lycomedae but not of the leading house, whereas Pericles was a member of the leading house of the Buzygae on his father's side and of the Alcmeonidae on his mother's side.[2] When the tribal state originally took shape, the number of clans was fixed; thereafter, as membership was hereditary, the number of clans did not increase. Before the time of Solon the estate of a family was vested in the family and, should the family die out, in the clan.[3] Land, the most important form of property, was thus inalienable. The guilds were a secondary development. When refugees came to Attica, they were often granted citizenship. At first they were adopted into clans. Later, probably in the period before the Ionian migration, they were formed into guilds, of which the membership could be swollen by new admissions or the numbers increased by new creations.[4] The guilds did not have their roots in the familial system and in the original allocation of lands to families; it is therefore to be supposed that the property of a guildsman was alienable by sale or by bequest.

When an Athenian reached maturity, he was enfranchised by being admitted to a phratry either as a clansman or as a guildsman; and he was then registered on the list of his phratry and of his clan or guild, as the case might be. If the legitimacy of an entrant was contested after the event, witnesses were called from his phratry and from his clan or guild.[5] The clans and the guilds did not have a merely social and political *raison d'être*. They were deeply rooted in the religious life of the state. The ceremony of admission was a religious occasion and entailed religious obligations. Phratores and orgeones observed corporate acts of worship. Clansmen were bound by even stronger religious ties. They possessed their own shrines and tombs in the countryside of Attica, and there they performed the funeral rites which were so often depicted on Attic vases of the early seventh century. Their attachment to the locality in which their age-old shrines and tombs stood was stronger than their attachment to the city of Athens. The clans had more social and political strength than the guilds. They were the racial *élite*, the numerical majority, and the holders of all fertile land in Attica. From the clans the state drew its hereditary priests, such as the Eumolpidae, Ceryces, and Eteobutadae. Within the phratry it was probably the *gennetai* proper, the elders of the clans, who conducted the administration of religion and of

---

[1] *AAP* fr. 5. See *StGH* 104f. for this section.   [2] Plu. *Them.* 1; *Per.* 3.
[3] *AAP* fr. 5; *PS* (= Plu. *Sol.* in this chapter) 21. 2.
[4] Th. 1. 2. 6; *FGrH* 328 F 35ᵃ (Philochorus).   [5] Is. 2. 14; 7. 13; D. 57. 67.

justice and the admission of new members. For each phratry and each clan in turn formed a state within the state.[1]

On the fall of the kingship, the religious duties of the royal office were conducted by the king-magistrate (*archon basileus*), the military duties by the military magistrate (*polemarchos*), and the civil duties by the eponymous *archon*, who gave his name to the year for the first time in 683, when tenure of the three archonships became annual. In later times the archon basileus still presided over the festivals and religious ceremonies of the state, judged disputes between clan and clan and between priest and priest, and tried certain cases of bloodshed. The polemarch's duties were military and religious, and, in regard to resident aliens, judicial. The eponymous archon organized the personnel and the finance for state festivals and gave judgement in cases affecting inheritance and family rights.[2] In judicial matters the magistrates gave final and not preliminary judgements. In secular matters their function was primarily to arbitrate between the clans and between the priests. Later a board of six 'recorders' (*thesmothetai*), who recorded but did not publish the law, was created. In all there were thus nine high magistrates, who were known as the archons. On relinquishing their office the archons became members for life of the Council which sat on the Areopagus hill.

The Areopagus Council scrutinized the incoming magistrates, supervised their conduct, and audited their acts on leaving office; controlled the administration of state affairs; safeguarded the constitution and the laws; inflicted penalties without the right of appeal; and transferred fines to the state treasury. It was thus the hub and centre of the constitution. The Assembly of all citizens (*ekklesia*) had elementary but important powers. It elected the magistrates and thereby the candidates for entry into the Areopagus Council. But candidature for election was defined in terms of 'birth and wealth', a double qualification which excluded the guildsmen. The Assembly doubtless deliberated and decided on some matters of state; but its competence was probably limited and the initiation of business lay solely with the Areopagus Council. Each citizen had the right of appeal to the Areopagus Council, naming the law in contravention of which he claimed to have been wronged.[3]

This constitution was hallowed by centuries of tradition. In the seventh century it had much the same merits and defects as the constitutions of other states. Its government faced similar problems, but its task was harder, inasmuch as it governed a large tribal state in which the power of the clans was intact. In 632 a young noble, Cylon, with Athenian accomplices and Megarian troops, seized the acropolis of Athens, hoping to establish himself as tyrant. The people rallied round their magistrates and blockaded the Acropolis. When Cylon escaped, his men took sanctuary at the altar of Athena, but many were executed on the spot. For this sacrilege the Alcmeonidae

---

[1] Th. 2. 16. 2; *AAP* fr. 5.   [2] *AAP* 3; 56–57.
[3] *AAP* 3; 4. 4; 8. 2; 8. 4; *FGrH* 324 F 4 (Androtion).

were held responsible. Their leader Megacles, as archon of the year, had been in charge of the blockade and had probably recruited the blockading force mainly from his own clansmen. This sacrilege brought pollution on the whole state. In the troubled times which followed the sense of guilt lay heavy on the people's conscience. About the turn of the century they set up a court to try the case, 300 jurors being elected on the qualification of birth alone. The Alcmeonidae were found guilty; the living were banished for all time, and the dead were exhumed and cast beyond the frontiers of Attica.[1] In this instance we can see the force of religious belief and the fear of state-pollution, the concept of clan responsibility for the acts of individuals, and the aristocratic principle in the selection of the court.

In 621, before the trial of the Alcmeonidae, Draco was appointed 'recorder' (*thesmothetes*) with special powers to publish the laws. Like Zaleucus and Charondas, he was concerned not with the working of the constitution[2] but with the administration of justice. His legal code was remarkable to later minds for its severity. The law of debt, for instance, entitled a creditor in certain cases to enslave, or to sell into slavery, an insolvent debtor and his dependents. The most urgent problem with which Draco dealt was the judicial procedure in cases of bloodshed. Such cases had probably been tried hitherto in the courts of the phratry or the tribe to which the parties belonged, or in an inter-tribal court when the parties belonged to different tribes. The inter-tribal court was named after the Prytaneum, where it met, and the judges were 'the kings', that is the four tribal kings (*phylobasileis*) and probably the archon basileus. But bloodshed might pollute the state as a whole. Draco therefore strengthened the position of the state by instituting a Court of Appeal, to which appeal could be made from the court of tribe or phratry. Its fifty-one judges were named 'judges of appeal' (*ephetai*), and they were elected *ad hoc* on the qualification of birth alone.

The Court of the Prytaneum and the Court of Appeal dealt only with cases arising from bloodshed and massacre. The supreme Court of the Areopagus dealt with offences against the state and in particular with treason. To these courts Solon referred in his law of amnesty. 'To those disfranchised before the archonship of Solon the franchise shall be restored, excepting such as were at the time of this law in banishment on conviction in the Court of the Areopagus, or on conviction in the Court of Appeal or in the Court of the Prytaneum under the kings on a charge of bloodshed or massacre, or on a charge of treason.'[3]

Draco's law of homicide is partly preserved in an accurate copy which was made in the late fifth century and preserved details then obsolete. This, the earliest legal document which has come down to us, is of great interest.

---

[1] Th. 1. 126; Hdt. 5. 71; *AAP* 1; *PS* 12.

[2] Arist. *Pol.* 1274^{b}15; *AAP* 4. 1–3 is anachronistic.

[3] Poll. 8. 125; *AAP* 57 fin.; *FGrH* 324 F 3; *PS* 18 (the order of the Greek words shows that the Areopagus tried treason cases).

If a man unintentionally kills another, he is to go into exile. The 'kings' inquire into the case, and the fifty-one judges of appeal make a preliminary verdict. Provision for the pardon of the offender is made in the event of *unanimous* consent by the following groups in widening circles: (1) immediate male relatives, (2) failing these, male relatives to the degree of cousin, (3) failing these, if the finding of the judges of appeal be homicide, ten phratry-members chosen by the judges on the qualification of birth. These provisions for pardon show the strength of the family and the clan organization, which must speak with one voice to grant pardon and thereby reverse the sentence of exile for life. The definition of group (3) covers the case where the dead man is not a member of a clan but of a guild. In that event his interests are represented not by the guild-members within his phratry but by the clan-members; for the phratry representatives are chosen on the qualification of birth alone. The law goes on to provide for the prosecution, which is similarly vested in groups, and the inscription then breaks off.[1]

Here and in the trial of the Alcmeonidae, the aristocratic principle was of paramount importance. The judges in both courts and the phratry representatives were elected expressly 'on the qualification of birth' (*aristinden*), the guild-members being thereby excluded, since they became eligible only 'on the qualification of wealth' (*ploutinden*). The right of prosecution and the right of pardon were restricted to the racial group—family, clan, or blood-members of the phratry. Control by the state was rudimentary. The state laid down procedure and the court gave its finding as between homicide and murder; but the state did not appropriate the rights of prosecution, sentence and pardon (as it does today). The privileges and the powers of the racial units, which made up the state, were respected rather than controlled by the state; and the guildsmen, who were equally citizens of the state, were excluded from participation in the procedure newly laid down by the state.

§ 2. *The legal and economic reforms of Solon*

DESPITE Draco's legislation and the banishment of the Alcmeonidae the faction worsened, and civil war threatened to destroy the state. The strains and stresses in the body politic were manifold:[2] rivalry between the leading clans, clashes of interest between district and district, political ambitions of oligarch and democrat, division between rich and poor and between clansmen and guildsmen. A most malignant evil arose from Draco's laws of debt. The precise nature of these laws and their application has long been a matter of dispute. The following explanation is based on the poems of Solon and the best commentary on them, Plutarch's *Life of Solon*.

Draco's laws dealt differently with the clansman, whose estate belonged to the clan and was inalienable, and with the guildsman, whose property was personal and alienable. When a clansman contracted a loan, he gave as a

[1] *GHI* 87.   [2] Sol. 4. 5–10; *PS* 12. 2; 13; *AAP* 2.

security not his estate, which he could not alienate, but the produce of his estate. If he became bankrupt, the law enjoined that he and his family should be tied to the estate and compelled to pay one-sixth of the produce *sine die* to the creditor. Such bankrupt clansmen were entitled 'Sixth-parters' (*hectemoroi*),[1] and their land was marked with a record-stone (*horos*). Their property did not pass to the creditor. It was 'enslaved' to the creditor, in the sense that the land and the family tied to it had lost their liberty, and its 'bondage' was marked by the record-stone. On the other hand, the guilds-man could pledge his property and his family, since no law forbade the selling of his wife or his child; if he became bankrupt, the law gave the creditor possession of the man and his family to sell into slavery either at home or abroad, as he willed.

These harsh laws of debt were exploited especially by the leading class. The opportunities which were offered by the introduction of mobile wealth, by commercial expansion, and by internal faction tempted men to practise usury and enrich themselves at the expense of clansmen and guildsmen alike. Within a short time 'all the poor were in debt to the rich. Either they worked their land under the title of *hectemorioi* and *thetes*, paying to the rich a sixth of the produce, or their persons being security for their debt they were seizable by the creditors, some serving as slaves in Attica, others being sold abroad.' Solon himself described the situation: 'Swiftly has the state fallen into a base slavery, which awakens into life contention and a civil war that has destroyed the fair manhood of many . . . such are our ills at home. . . . Many of the impoverished, sold and bound with shameful shackles, go to foreign lands.'[2]

To deal with this crisis Solon, eponymous archon of the year 594/3, was appointed 'arbiter' with full legislative powers. The middle class doubtless supported him. The extremists hoped to gain; the wealthy looked for greater profits, and the poor for land as well as liberty.[3] Later, when both groups were disappointed, Solon defended himself as follows. 'Should I stand before the bar of Time, witness on my behalf would best be given by black Earth, Mother supreme of the Olympian gods, from whose breast I took up the record-stones which were planted far and wide; she, hitherto in bondage, now is free. I restored to Athens, their god-built fatherland, many persons sold abroad—some justly, some unjustly—and others fled through stress of debt, who spoke no more the Attic tongue, and others here in Attica I liber-ated from a shameful slavery, wherein they trembled at their masters' ways.'[4] These words indicate the broad lines of his reforms. He abolished the system of 'sixth-parters', taking up the stones which recorded an obligation to pay

---

[1] *PS* 13. 2. The explanation in *AAP* 2 is confused and anachronistic; it implies that land could be alienated in the sixth century, but recent research has shown that this was so only in the late fifth or early fourth century. *PS* 21.2 gives a correct statement of the position in the matter of inheritance. See my article in *JHS* 81. 76 f.

[2] *PS* 13. 2–3; Sol. 3. 5 f. and 18–25.

[3] *PS* 14; Sol. 23. 13–21.

[4] Sol. 24. 3–15; Poll. 3. 85 (*horoi*).

produce to the creditors, and thereby liberating both the land itself and those tied to it. He restored the liberty of those sold into personal slavery, whether at home or abroad. He not only annulled the past contracts, which had reduced men to the status either of 'sixth-parters' or of slaves, but also cancelled current debts.

The reform was known as the 'disburdening' (*seisachtheia*); the disburdened were called 'debt-cutters' (*chreokopidai*), and in some cases the creditors were impoverished.[1] The implementation of Solon's reform needed time; for it was necessary to trace, purchase, and reinstate Athenians in slavery abroad and to register the cancellation of contracts and debts. For the future he enacted new laws of debt; in them he prohibited the making of loans on the terms which had created the 'sixth-parters', and on the security of the person. Henceforth clansmen and guildsmen were on an equal footing under the law of debt. The *habeas corpus* act was passed for both alike. 'I enacted laws in the spirit of equality for base-born and for high-born, according straight justice to each.'[2]

In preparation for this sweeping reform Solon had had the state cleansed of pollution by the Cretan seer Epimenides, and he had consulted the oracle at Delphi, which replied: 'Sit in the middle of the ship and steer a straight course; many Athenians are at thy side.' To allay the spirit of faction, he passed the law of amnesty, re-enfranchising all who had been deprived of the franchise, except those who had been exiled for 'bloodshed, massacre, or attempted tyranny'.[3] Therein he put state-interests before party-interests in a manner which was to be an inspiration to Athens in the dark days of 403. At the moment the Alcmeonids were excluded from the amnesty; for they had just been banished for 'massacre', albeit by a special court and not by one of those named in the fragment of the law which we possess. In order to relieve the distress caused by the cancellation of contracts and by the repatriation of liberated slaves, Solon placed a temporary ban on the export of any natural product save olive-oil, of which there was even at this crisis a surplus. He enacted laws dealing with the care of widows and orphans and with murder, these being urgent matters at the close of a civil war. Trials for premeditated murder were now transferred from the Court of Appeal to the Court of the Areopagus; we may conjecture that the arm of the state was thereby strengthened *vis-à-vis* the courts of tribe and of phratry.[4]

Solon had put the state back, as it were, to the pre-Draconian position in regard to debt; but he had done nothing to prevent the pauperization which had made borrowing necessary. With this object in view, he deliberately switched the economic policy of Attica from a purely agricultural to a primarily commercial programme. Athens at this time belonged to the 'Pheidonian' orbit in weights and measures and in coinage, which she issued first at the end of the seventh century. Within this orbit Aegina was chief

---

[1] *PS* 15. 3, 5, and 7; *AAP* 13, 3 and 5. [2] *AAP* 6. 1; Sol. 24. 18–20.
[3] *PS* 14. 4; 19. 3. [4] *PS* 24. 1; Harp. *sitos*; Poll. 8. 125.

exporter and importer, and Aegina's position in the Saronic Gulf dominated Athens. Solon therefore switched to the 'Euboic' system, placing Athens in the orbit of Samos and Corinth, in order that she might export more readily to the distant markets of East and West and not simply to Aegina, Boeotia, Megara, and Argolis. As the state owned the silver-mines at Laurium, silver was available for coining on the new standard, while the old currency was recalled at a fixed rate of exchange with the new.[1] The Solonian coinage (Plate XI *e*) bore the olive-oil amphora of Athens in place of the former emblem, the ox; its silver was of fine quality and secured the entry of Athenian merchants to many markets, and small denominations were minted to encourage its use for internal retail. From this expansion of commerce Solon could hope that the repatriated guildsmen would obtain a livelihood. But he was so confident of Athens' future that either now or during his second commission in 592/1 he not only put pressure on Athenians to enter a handicraft and to teach their sons one, but also offered citizenship to any foreigners who would settle with their families to ply a trade in Attica, or who were in permanent exile from their own state.[2] The offer of citizenship was a bold step. By it Athens no doubt drew from Corinth and Aegina many craftsmen who were denied the citizenship there through the Dorian policy of exclusiveness. By these reforms Solon laid the basis for Athens' future prosperity.

§ 3. *The constitutional reforms of Solon*

DURING the period when Solon's reforms in debt, law, and currency were being implemented, criticism flared up and died down again. It was probably for the Attic year 592/1 that he was appointed 'reformer of the constitution' with full legislative powers.[3] His first step was to change the qualification which governed candidature for office, from the double qualification of 'birth and wealth' to the single qualification of 'wealth'. In the past the well-to-do had been divided on a census of wealth into 'cavalrymen' (*hippeis*) and 'men of the line' (*zeugitai*); to these classes Solon added two more, the richest becoming the 'five-hundred bushellers' (*pentakosiomedimnoi*) and the poorest the 'labourers' (*thetes*). The census was based not on capital but on annual income assessed in terms of agricultural produce—cereals, oil, and wine— with which other forms of income were integrated. The lower limits of the top three classes were drawn at 500, 300, and 200 measures. Solon probably levied a special tax (*eisphora*) on these three classes, perhaps in the proportion of 6:3:1 and to a maximum of one talent, half a talent, and ten minae, in order to meet the state-expenditure required by his reforms. The fourth class paid no tax; this was just, for the annual wage of a poor thete was approximately one-sixtieth of the income of a five-hundred busheller.

Members of the first class were eligible for the office of state treasurer

---

[1] *AAP* 10; *PS* 15. 4; *FGrH* 328 F 200 (Philochorus).   [2] *PS* 24. 2.
[3] *PS* 16; *AAP* 10; 14. 1. The date is disputed, see *StGH* 145–169. Cf. *JHS* 60. 71; 68. 93.

(*tamias*); members of the first and second classes for the archonships and other high offices; and members of the first, second, and third classes for the minor offices. Members of the fourth class were ineligible for office.[1] The change in qualification for office was fundamental in principle, since it put clansmen and guildsmen on an equal footing. But its effect was limited in Solon's day; for the aristocratic landowners were in general the wealthiest men in Attica.

The method of election remained the same, direct election by a majority vote in the Assembly. The nine archons now met as a board in the office of the Thesmothetae with a view to co-ordinating their executive measures. Their powers were modified only in the matters of summary justice; for Solon instituted the right of appeal against magistrate's edict to a people's court, which we shall describe later. The lesser magistrates, so far as they are known to us from this time, had probably existed in the past: the *naukraroi*, financial officials in the forty-eight subdivisions into which the twelve trittyes were divided; the *poletai*, who let out state contracts and sold confiscated property; the 'eleven', the officers in charge of the state-police; and the *kolakretai*, who were concerned primarily with state sacrifices.[2]

The Council of the Areopagus continued, as before, to be recruited from ex-archons and to form the central organ in the state. It safeguarded the laws and the constitution, directed the executive, and had general control of the administration of state affairs. It was empowered to inflict summary punishment, against which there was no right of appeal. As a court of justice it now dealt with cases of premeditated murder, and its procedure in cases of treason was modernized.

Alongside the Council of the Areopagus, Solon instituted a 'Council of Four Hundred', 100 members from each tribe being nominated by him, probably with tenure for life. The main function of this Council was to prepare business for the Assembly. It not only considered beforehand but also recorded its recommendation on any business which went to the Assembly. As its recommendation was indispensable, the Council could in theory withhold a recommendation and prevent a matter being discussed by the Assembly. The effect of the two councils on the Assembly was described in a phrase drawn probably from Solon's poems: 'the ship of state, riding upon two anchors, will pitch less in the surf and make the people less turbulent.'[3]

Solon had already strengthened the position of the lowest class by vindicating their right to personal liberty, by emphasizing their place in the economy of the state, and by granting citizenship to incoming artisans and refugees. But he did not intend the Assembly, in which the lowest class probably held an outright majority, to rock the ship of state. As a deliberative body its competence was limited. The Areopagus Council interpreted the

---

[1] *AAP* 7. 3–4; *PS* 18. 1–2.
[2] Arist. *Pol.* 1274ª16 (preferable to *AAP* 8. 1); *AAP* 8. 3.
[3] *AAP* 8. 4; *PS* 19. 1–2.

constitution. The Council of Four Hundred sieved the agenda for discussion and appended a draft resolution to each agendum. The Assembly decided by voting for or against a resolution, but it could not frame a new resolution; that was the prerogative of the Council of Four Hundred. Even if a revolutionary resolution was made law by the Assembly, the Areopagus Council could annul the law, if it conflicted with the constitution. The Assembly was thus hedged in by safeguards. But within the safeguards its power was sovereign, and in it all citizens, irrespective of wealth and birth, sat as equals. As an elective body, it elected the magistrates from a list of candidates, who were restricted by qualification of wealth and were subject to a scrutiny conducted probably by the Areopagus Council.

Solon made the Assembly a judicial body under the title of the Heliaea. This was an important innovation. For the first time the people, or a panel of the people selected by lot, acted as jurors and judges. At first the Heliaea probably judged only cases of appeal and inflicted additional sentences. But it also heard appeals against the magistrates, and later it came to audit the acts of the magistrates at the end of their year of office, which were probably still scrutinized by the Areopagus Council in the time of Solon. But the principle was established that the magistrates were responsible to the people.[1] The Areopagus, however, was still exempt from interference by the Heliaea. Its members were not subject to audit, and their acts of summary justice and their judicial verdicts were not subject to appeal.

The Solonian constitution was later called oligarchic by oligarchs, democratic by democrats, and 'mixed' by Aristotle, who labelled the Areopagus Council as oligarchic, the election of magistrates as aristocratic, and the Heliaea as democratic.[2] As compared with the previous constitution, it had few innovations, but they were important. The aristocratic ring of Areopagus and magistrates, within which the final control of administration in all departments of policy, execution, and justice had been vested, was broken by the institution of the second Council and of the Heliaea. If they were effective, it would never again be possible for the aristocracy to reduce the Assembly to powerlessness and the poor to economic and personal slavery. This was the objective at which Solon aimed. He was neither a revolutionary nor a doctrinaire, but an impartial arbiter in a time of fierce political faction. He summarized his achievement as follows: 'I gave to the people the privilege sufficient unto the people, not diminishing its rights, nor demanding more, nor did I devise any unseemly position for those who held power and were respected for their wealth. I stood holding my stout shield over both parties, and I did not allow either party to prevail in despite of justice.'[3] The balance which Solon struck in his constitution was the balance which he judged appropriate to the abilities and the experience of the different classes in the state. Among them we must not forget the middle class, to which he gave its

[1] Arist. *Pol.* 1274ᵃ2 and 18; *AAP* 7. 3; 9. 1; *PS* 18. 2; Lys. 10. 16; D. 24. 105.
[2] *AAP* 29. 3; 41. 2; Arist. *Pol.* 1273ᵇ36.　　　　　　　　　　　　[3] Sol. 5. 1–6.

proportionate place in the magistrature, in the second Council, and in the Assembly and Heliaea. In this class lay the chief hope of stability in the future.

Solon established for the first time the right of any individual citizen to prosecute in person on behalf of himself or of an injured party. Thereby he emancipated all citizens alike from the control of clan or guild in this matter. The right of appeal to the people's court included appeal from the court of tribe, phratry, or clan, and an additional penalty could be given by the people's court. For instance, a law of Solon's runs 'if the Heliaea award a further sentence, he should be bound by the leg in the stocks for five days'. Solon also overhauled the legal code of the state. He abolished all the laws of Draco, except those governing trial by bloodshed. Of his new code we know only the few laws which were cited by lawyers and others in later times.[1] He legislated in the interest of the clans by safeguarding heiresses and orphans, even as he had safeguarded their land by liberating the sixth-parters. He regulated procedure and expenditure in regard to dowries and funerals, and he permitted bequests to persons outside the clan only in special circumstances and on condition of their adoption into the clan. In the interest of the guilds he made their contracts legally binding, if they did not conflict with the laws of the state; he left the rate of interest unfixed, and assessed penalties in coin as well as in kind. A number of social laws are known to us, such as those prohibiting the sale of females, except for unchastity, and the slander of the dead. The code was inscribed on stone columns, set up in the Royal Colonnade.

§ 4. *The principles of Solon and the rise of Peisistratus*

MORE important than the details are the principles implicit in Solon's reforms. He put the claims of the state above those of party or of clan, and he demanded the participation of all citizens in its affairs. He even enacted a law that in time of political faction everyone must take his stand on one side or the other. His laws were hallowed by religious sanctions: every citizen took an oath of obedience, and each archon and councillor vowed to dedicate a gold statue at Delphi, if he violated a law of Solon.[2] To each class in the state he gave responsibility in due measure, and he proclaimed the ideal of social justice between class and class. He appealed to reason, liberty, moderation, and humanity. Athens often fell short of Solon's standards, but she recognized those standards as her heritage for all time.

Solon was an important figure in the religious thought of his age. He believed in the lofty power of the gods and in the just decree of the supreme god, Zeus, that presumptuousness begets punishment. But divine justice, he realized, differs from human justice. Like a storm in spring, the wrath of Zeus descends upon a group, so that in a family the innocent children suffer and in a state the innocent citizens.[3] Man is master only of his internal affairs. An individual controls his own conduct, and a group controls its

---

[1] e.g. *PS* 20–21.   [2] *AAP* 8. 5; *PS* 20. 1; 25.   [3] Sol. 1. 16–32.

internal relations. The responsibility of the individual is to understand himself, and the responsibility of the group is to understand the harmonious relationship between its parts, which is 'justice', in the sense that we may speak of 'social justice'. When a society offends against that inner justice, chaos ensues, coincident with the will of Zeus, and affects every member in the society.[1] Neither state nor individual is master over outer circumstances, such as health or plague, prosperity or disaster. Despite all one's hopes merit and effort do not bring success; often a good worker fails and a bad worker succeeds. Merit is its own reward, and success is unpredictable. Solon himself was mocked for failing to exploit his position and secure wealth for himself. He replied, 'Many bad men are rich, many good men are poor; but we shall not exchange wealth for honour, for money flits from man to man but honour abides forever.'[2] He lived, as he preached, in the light of his reason and his ideals. He saw both the glory and the sadness of human life. Together with the *Iliad* and the *Odyssey*, the poems of Solon deserved to be, and were, an inspiration to Ionian Athens.

Having made his laws binding for one hundred years and urged each Athenian citizen to put his laws into effect, Solon withdrew from Attica for ten years. Thereupon faction started anew. The Alcmeonids returned to Athens, and Alcmeon commanded the Athenian contingent at the capture of Crisa. In 590 and in 586 constitutional government broke down, and in 581 the eponymous archon Damasias retained his office beyond the legal period of tenure. Upon his ejection in 580 ten archons were elected to represent the factions in the state and resume the powers of government. The aristocrats (*eupatridai*), who headed the strongest clans with their estates in the plainland and their houses in Athens, elected five of the ten archons. The 'countrymen' (*agroikoi*), who held the hill-country, as opposed to the *georgoi* of the plains, elected three. And the 'artisans' (*demiourgoi*), as opposed to those who made their living from the land, elected two. These parties were no doubt those which had split the state before Solon came into office. They coincided in general terms with the geographical divisions of 'plainland', 'hill-land', and 'coastland'. The aristocrats drew their support from the wealthy clans, the 'countrymen' in part from poor clans and in part from individual 'labourers' (*thetes*), and the 'artisans' from the guilds. The aristocrats aimed at oligarchy, wherein they would rule under the conditions of the pre-Solonian constitution; the 'countrymen' espoused democracy, which would entail a redistribution of land and the enrichment of the poor; and the 'artisans' upheld the 'middle' or Solonian constitution, under which the citizenship and the rights of the guildsmen were safeguarded.[3] The leaders of the groups were probably aristocrats, eager to win and exploit the office of eponymous archon.

The brief success of Damasias was emulated in 561 by Peisistratus, a noble whose family owned estates at Philaidae in the coastland area. In a war

[1] Sol. 3. 26 f.   [2] Sol. 1. 67; 4. 9–12.   [3] *AAP* 13. 2–5; *PS* 29. 1.

against Megara, Peisistratus distinguished himself and was elected pole-march. According to the popular tale he drove into the Agora at Athens, having inflicted wounds on himself and his mules, and said he had just escaped from an attack by his political opponents; the people in the Assembly voted him a bodyguard, and he seized the Acropolis. He had organized the democratic party in advance, and from it he drew his bodyguard of crook-carriers' (*korynephoroi*). His supporters were mainly the countrymen of the hill-land (*diakria*); to them were added two groups, those impoverished by the cancellation of debts and those recently admitted to the citizenship under Solon's laws. His opponents—the men of the plainland under Lycur-gus, head of the clan Eteobutadae, and the men of the coastland under Megacles, the head of the Alcmeonids—combined to expel him, but they then fell out among themselves. With the connivance of Megacles Peisistratus staged a return to Attica in a chariot on which a tall and beautiful girl stood dressed as the goddess Athena; the Athenians bowed down before her and admitted Peisistratus to Athena's Acropolis. The compact of the coalition between Megacles and Peisistratus was the marriage of Megacles' daughter to Peisistratus; but Peisistratus did not consummate the marriage, broke with Megacles, and set himself up as tyrant. After a few months he withdrew from Attica early in 555 and established himself in Thrace, where he prepared for another *coup d'état*.[1]

During these years of party strife Solon returned to Athens and con-demned the citizens for 'foxy ways and foolish wits'. 'Clouds shed thick snow and hail, bright lightning produces thunder; so the leading men destroy the state and the people in their folly fall into slavery under one-man-rule. Hard is it for one who sails far out to come inshore again; one should think of all things in good time.' That Solon's constitutional reform had not termin-ated political faction is in no way surprising. The aristocrats, and the clans on which their power rested, could be broken only by revolutionary force, which Solon refused to employ. That faction between the aristocrats led to civil war and to tyranny had been the common experience of other states on the mainland, and the Athenians should have been forewarned. Yet Athens was deeply indebted to Solon both directly and indirectly during the period 600–550. He won Salamis from Megara, and he gave the lead to the Amphic-tyons in the Sacred War; in the Hellespont Athens won her first foothold at Sigeum about 590.[2] In 566 the claims of the state were strengthened by the institution of the Panathenaic festival in honour of Athena, and about the same time by the institution of games at Eleusis.[3] His economic reforms bore fruit despite political strife. By 550 Attic pottery ousted Corinthian pottery from the leading position in the Greek world, and facilitated the export of Athenian goods. The coinage maintained its high standard of purity. The

---

[1] Hdt. 1. 59–61; *AAP* 13. 4. 15. 3; *PS* 29–30. The chronology of Peisistratus' career is controversial; for that given here see *CQ* 6. 51 (1956).   [2] *PS* 8–11; Hdt. 5. 95.
[3] *FGrH* 3 F 2 (Pherecyd.); *IG* i. 817.

fact that Athens was always able to offer this dependable silver coinage made her market exceptionally attractive to merchants from overseas. Craftsmen, attracted to Athens by the prospect of receiving citizenship, swelled the manpower and the resources of the state. By the middle of the century Athens was winning a place commensurate with her size and her traditions in the expanding world of Greek commerce.

§ 5. *The Spartan Alliance*

INTERSTATE relations developed first on the religious level. Oracles and shrines, festivals and games, pilgrimages and Amphictyonies were recognized universally and guaranteed against attack. The early sixth century saw an advance in this development. The Isthmian games were organized on a grand scale; the Pythian games and the Nemean games were instituted. The Delphic Amphictyony conducted a religious war, and the Amphictyony which centred probably on the Argive Heraeum arranged the terms and assessed the result of the contest between the Three Hundred Champions of Argos and Sparta.[1] On the commercial level interstate contacts increased. At Naucratis the Hellenium was founded by nine states—Aeolian, Dorian, and Ionian—and the market was controlled by their trade-representatives (*prostatai*).[2] Provision was made at Athens and no doubt elsewhere for resident or visiting aliens, and 'protectors' (*proxenoi*) were appointed to welcome members or to represent the interests of other states. On the political level interstate arbitration was employed *c.* 650 in Chalcidice, where a dispute between Andros and Chalcis was settled by arbiters from Erythrae, Paros, and Samos. Periander arbitrated between Athens and Mitylene on the possession of Sigeum, Sparta appointed five Spartiates to arbitrate between Athens and Megara on the possession of Salamis, and Demonax of Mantinea mediated in the internal affairs of Cyrene. A permanent settlement between two states was envisaged in the treaty of alliance made by Elis and Heraea in the early sixth century: 'for a hundred years . . . they shall stand by each other in all matters and especially in war'.[3]

When Sparta had won the Second Messenian War (*c.* 640–620), her prosperity and influence steadily increased. In art she reached her acme. The martial elegy of Tyrtaeus and the choral lyric of Alcman were outstanding, and Laconian pottery, figurines, and masks reached a high level in the period 625–550. The temple of Artemis Orthia was built *c.* 600; the Scias was adorned with sculpture by Theodorus of Samos *c.* 576, and the throne of Apollo at Amyclae by Bathycles of Magnesia after 550. She traded overseas, especially with Cyrene and Taras. The demands for redistribution of land, which had been made during the Messenian War, were quashed and the Spartan constitution was confirmed in its conservative stability. In her

---

[1] *FGrH* 287 F 2 (Chrysermus).   [2] Hdt. 2. 178.
[3] Plu. 298ᵃ = *GQ* 30; Hdt. 5. 95. 2; Plu. *Sol.* 10; Hdt. 4. 161; *GHI* 5.

foreign policy she deposed the last tyrant at Corinth *c.* 582, and probably helped Elis to gain control of the Olympic festival *c.* 570. In her frontier-wars she was successful except against Tegea in Arcadia. On consulting the oracle at Delphi, the Spartans were advised to acquire the bones of Orestes and then they would defeat Tegea. During a period of truce a Spartan performed this feat successfully; he stole the bones of a giant which had recently been un-earthed at Tegea, and declared them to be the bones of Orestes. Thereafter Sparta defeated Tegea, but instead of annexing Tegea's territory Sparta made a permanent settlement with her on the basis of a defensive alliance. The treaty probably contained a clause under which Tegea undertook to banish all Messenians from her territory.[1]

This alliance, concluded soon after 560, marked the transition to a new policy, of which the declared aims were liberation from tyranny and protection against Argos. These aims were welcome to the Greek states, and the declara-tion of them was well timed. The tyrants, denounced by Delphi, were already tottering and Argos had inspired alarm by her destruction, for in-stance, of Nauplia.[2] Sparta, on the other hand, was in favour with Delphi. She had liberated Corinth from tyranny. In contrast to the Argive policy of Dorian domination she had concluded a permanent alliance with the Arca-dians of Tegea and declared herself champion of the non-Dorian peoples by paying honour to their hero, Orestes. Her intention was to offer a permanent alliance and resist aggression by Argos or any other state. Such an alliance offered great advantages, and the military strength of Sparta was formidable.

The Spartan policy, initiated probably by her famous statesman Chilon, was brilliantly successful. Many states in central and northern Peloponnese accepted the offer of alliance. In the spring of 555 the Spartan king Anaxan-dridas and the ephor Chilon liberated Sicyon and perhaps Phlius and Megara from tyranny, and the presence of their army at the Isthmus may have prompted the withdrawal of the tyrant Peisistratus from Athens.[3] By these methods Sparta created a military coalition of great strength. Modern scholars have called it, rather misleadingly, 'the Peloponnesian League'. The ancient name 'the Lacedaemonians and their Allies' was literally and sub-stantially correct, and we shall, therefore, refer to it as the Spartan Alliance. It rested on separate defensive alliances, contracted in each case between Sparta and an individual state, and it therefore depended solely on Sparta for leadership. Although it was by contract a purely military alliance, which came into operation only in time of war, its existence had a marked political effect. By deposing tyrants in some states and by exerting a steady influence in others, Sparta so 'arranged the affairs' of the states that pro-Spartan oligarchies came into power.[4] In the Dorian states these oligarchies lasted long and gave stable government. They fostered Sparta's interests in general, and they kept the Messenians out of the Peloponnese, apart from Argolis.

---

[1] Hdt. 1. 65–68; Plu. 292^b = *GQ* 5.   [2] Paus. 4. 35. 2.
[3] *FGrH* 105 F 1 (cf. *CQ* 6. 49).   [4] Th. 1. 18. 1 and 19.

By her system of alliances Sparta insulated her own territories against outside interference and created a military cordon in the Peloponnese.

In 555 Croesus, king of Lydia, sent envoys to consult the oracle at Delphi, and on their return he learnt that Sparta was mistress of most of the Peloponnese. On the advice of the oracle, which had forewarned Sparta of its intentions, Croesus approached Sparta with the following message: 'The god has bidden me make the Greek my friend; I therefore invite you to become my friend and ally in all sincerity, since I learn that you hold the leadership in Greece'.[1] Lydia and Sparta then concluded a treaty of friendship and alliance. But Sparta's leadership was not secure, until she proved her superiority over Argos. In 546 she invaded the Argolid. By the arrangement of the Amphictyons of the Argive Heraeum a contest was held between 300 Argives and 300 Spartans. By nightfall two Argives survived; they returned to Argos to report their victory. But one Spartan was still alive. He reached the Spartan camp, bringing armour he had stripped from the Argive dead. Both sides claimed the victory and a general battle ensued with heavy losses on both sides. The result was a victory for Sparta. This confirmed her military supremacy and won lasting possession of Thyreatis and Cythera. To commemorate this battle the Spartans wore their hair long in triumph, and the Argives cut theirs short in mourning.[2] This was a decisive battle in the history of Greece. 'The Lacedaemonians and their Allies' were to play a leading part henceforth in Greek affairs and not least in the defeat of the great power which in the same year overthrew Croesus of Lydia and overshadowed the Aegean world.

---

[1] *FGrH* 239 A 41 (*Marm. Par.*); Hdt. 1. 69.
[2] Hdt. 1. 82; *FGrH* 287 F 2 (Chrysermus).

CHAPTER 7

Religion and Culture 850–546

DURING this period social organization and religious belief were in exceptionally close accord. Each family worshipped Hestia, goddess of the hearth, Zeus Herkeios, protector of the courtyard, and its own gods and heroes. If the members of the family maintained the proper relations towards one another, such as the tending of aged parents, they received protection from their gods; if they violated those relations, divine punishment fell on the whole family. So, too, each state worshipped Hestia, and its divine founder (Athena at Athens, Zeus at Sparta, Apollo at Megara, &c.)[1] and the gods and heroes personal to its history and locality. If the members of the state lived in concord, their gods aided them; but, if civil war or sacrilege ensued, pollution and retribution affected all members of the state. Important events in the life of the family, such as birth and death, were hallowed by religious ritual, and each rising generation recognized the obligation to bury its dead, avenge bloodshed, and maintain the cult of its ancestors. So, too, in the life of the state each meeting of Council and Assembly commenced with ritual, and acts of reform, such as the *Eunomia* at Sparta and the *Seisachtheia* at Athens, were occasions for public worship and thanksgiving.[2] The groups intermediate between family and state—namely, tribe, phratry, clan, and guild—were religious entities and performed their own acts of worship. When an Athenian submitted himself for office in the state, he had to give account of the Apollo of his ancestors, the Zeus of his courtyard, the position of these gods' shrines, the whereabouts of his family tombs, and his treatment of his parents. For only a man who had observed the religious obligations of the family was worthy to undertake the religious obligations of office in the state.[3]

While religion cemented family and state, it provided a looser bond between state and state. Regional Amphictyonies formed centres of common worship at Delphi, Argos, Delos, Triopium, and elsewhere. Ubiquitous influences flowed from the Oracles at Delphi, Dodona, and Didyma and from the festivals at Olympia, Delphi, Isthmus, and Nemea. As the Greek world expanded, the Oracles were recognized as the source of religious and political wisdom, and the festivals offered occasions of reunion. Their effect on interstate relations was small; for each state preserved its sovereignty in religious and in secular matters. When Elis and Heraea made an alliance, they agreed to pay to Zeus of Olympia the stipulated fine for any breach of its articles; but the alliance was not inaugurated or supervised by the priests at

---

[1] Sol. 3. 1–4; Tyrt. 2.   [2] Plu. *Lyc.* 6. 1; *Sol.* 16. 3.
[3] Poll. 8. 107; 111; Arist. *Ath.* 55. 3.

Olympia. Their effect on religious thought was considerable. They advised on questions of local worship. They also brought into prominence those elements which were common to religious beliefs of individual states. Thus the Greek states came to recognize an aristocracy among the gods, of which the membership was usually twelve, and worship was rendered in the state and at the festivals, for instance at Olympia,[1] to 'the twelve gods'. Yet 'the twelve' were not canonized; each state made its own selection.

From these festivals sprang a new genre of poetry, the Hymns in hexameter verse, which were ascribed in antiquity to early rhapsodes such as Olen, Homer, and Musaeus.[2] Hymns were composed for recitation in honour of a god, and prize Hymns were sung at successive festivals and became widely known. The Hymn to Apollo, which was probably composed by Cynaethus of Chios in the late eighth or early seventh century, acclaimed the universal worship of the god 'throughout the calf-raising mainland and throughout the isles' but concentrated on two main themes, the birth of the god at Delos and his coming to Delphi, where 'a precipice hangs overhead and a hollow rocky glen runs down below'. In this Hymn and also in those to Hermes, Aphrodite, and the Dioscuri, which probably belong to the seventh century, the local origin of the god was woven into his or her universal worship. The poems excelled in delicacy of description and in simplicity of thought, and they enshrined a religious belief which was completely anthropomorphic and anthropomorphically complete. For the washing and the swaddling of the newborn babe, Apollo, the ways and the wiles of golden Aphrodite, or the cunning and the craftsmanship of thieving Hermes were as integral to the life of the gods as they are to the life of men. In these Hymns, composed probably by Ionian poets, we can see an ebullient love of life and a warm affection for the natural world, which found devotional expression in thanksgiving to the gods of light and beauty.

Side by side with the communal religion of family or state and with the universal devotion to the Olympian gods, a personal religion developed from worship paid to Demeter and to Dionysus. The cult of Demeter was practised at Eleusis; it originated in the Bronze Age and it developed greatly during the late eighth and seventh centuries, when the shrine of the goddess and its precincts were rebuilt. The Hymn to Demeter, composed probably in the seventh century, narrated with great beauty the sacred story of the bringer of the seasons, Demeter. Her maiden daughter Persephone was abducted by Hades, the all-receiving god of death, and Demeter in her grief lived among mankind, drank of the symbolical cup of sorrow, and was consoled by the nursing of a human child. Then her grief broke all bounds. She sent a famine on the land, which lasted until the spring, when Zeus delivered Persephone from the underworld. But Persephone had eaten of the pomegranate offered by Hades. Therefore she had to spend a third of each year thereafter in the underworld. In this sacred story the mysteries of the chang-

[1] *GHI* 5; 8.   [2] Hdt. 4. 35; Th. 3. 104; Paus. 10. 5. 4.

ing seasons, of fertility and famine, of birth and death, were contained. They formed the essence of a communal worship which the women of Attica observed, and also of a personal worship which is mentioned in the Hymn to Demeter. 'Blessed among men on earth is he who has seen these sights; but he who is not initiated, and has no part in the holy ritual, never shares a like destiny, though he moulders beneath the dank darkness.'[1] Of this personal cult the secret was preserved by the initiates. The details are unknown to us, but it is clear that in the Eleusinian Mysteries a personal after-life was envisaged with conditions radically different from those in which the Homeric poems and orthodox belief placed the ghostly dead.

The origins of another mystery religion, Orphism, are more obscure. It evolved perhaps from an ecstatic frenzy, which Euripides was later to portray so vividly in the *Bacchae*; a frenzy in which a group of women became imbued with the wild spirit of natural life, tore up animals, and devoured the raw flesh. Dionysus, who inspired the frenzy, was himself devoured. This legend was not Greek in character, but otherwise Dionysus had many attributes which were akin to the general ideas of Greek religion. He was the god of wild animals and vegetation, the god of nature's fertility, and in the procession of his worshippers Satyrs and Sileni carried the emblem of the phallus.[2] The worship of Dionysus came from Thrace to Greece probably during the dark age, and it was assimilated by the priests of Delphi, who modified its ecstatic features. But it was also adopted into the cult of Orpheus, who, like Dionysus, was believed to have been torn to pieces by Thracian women. In the Orphic myth the Titans devoured the limbs of the god Dionysus and were destroyed by the lightning of Zeus. From the Titans' ashes mankind sprang, polluted by the Titans' act but containing a divine element which came from the devoured Dionysus. Hence arose a division of man into an impure body and a divine soul. Only a life lived in accordance with ritual purity could combat man's inherited impurity, and only death could part the living soul from the tomb of the body. In the after-life the souls of the good lived in bliss, but those of the unpurified endured terrible punishment. This cult, too, had its special rules, and it became assimilated in part to the Eleusinian mysteries.[3]

In the worship of the gods music and dance played an important part. The main instruments were oboe or flute (*aulos*) and lyre or cithara, invented by Apollo and Hermes[4] according to Greek belief but perhaps derived from Asia Minor. The types or modes (*nomoi*) of music were associated with moral qualities, the Dorian, for instance, with courage and the Lydian with softness. Musical competitions, with and without the accompaniment of the voice, were held at the Pythian games and in state festivals. Dance was closely allied with music, and the rhythms of dancing also bespoke moral qualities. In particular choric dances, akin perhaps to the folk-dances of modern Greece, played an essential part in ritual and in worship. The dancers mimed the

[1] *h. Cer.* 480.   [2] Hdt. 2. 48–49; *Vorsokr.* 22 B 15.
[3] Paus. 9. 30. 3–6.   [4] *h. Ap.* 131; *h. Merc.* 47.

narrative of the sacred story, and they portrayed the emotions which it excited. Music and dance were the partners of poetry, and the partnership was particularly close in this great age of lyric poetry.[1]

On the mainland Corinth and Sparta were the centres at which music, dance, and poetry evolved during this period. Processional songs (*prosodia*) were composed by Eumelus of Corinth, and choral songs in honour of Dionysus (*dithyramboi*) were set in artistic form by Arion of Lesbos, who lived at the court of Periander.[2] At Sparta the influences of Aeolian, Dorian, and Ionian musicians and poets, such as Terpander of Lesbos, Thaletas of Gortyn, and Polymnestus of Colophon, culminated in the choral lyric poetry of Alcman. The only considerable fragment which we possess comes from a maiden-song (*partheneion*), composed probably for a choir of ten maidens, who carried the sacred robe to the shrine of Artemis Orthia in the twilight between moonset and sunrise. The cadence of metre, the grace of diction, and the charm of sentiment in the poem enable us to envisage the beautiful setting of this religious ceremony. Alcman wrote also in the forms established by his predecessors, dance-song (*hyporchema*), triumph-song (*paian*), drinking-song (*skolion*), and hymn. Overseas Stesichorus developed the art of choral lyric at Himera early in the sixth century. He narrated the stories of Epic Saga and especially of the Hesiodic school in lyrical poems, which were famed for their imaginative colouring and dignity of style. He composed an *Oresteia* for performance probably at Sparta, the centre of the Dorian school, from which he drew much of his inspiration.

Ionia and Lesbos were the home of personal poetry. The oldest form, elegy, sung to the accompaniment of a flute, was used for a variety of topics—drinking-songs, camp-songs, love-songs, and political catches (*stasiotika*)—and later for narrative, dedication, and epitaph. During the seventh century Archilochus of Paros, Callinus of Ephesus, and Mimnermus of Smyrna composed in the elegiac metre. Closely allied to elegy was iambic poetry, of which the metre was close to the cadence of ordinary speech. The iambus was used by Archilochus and later by Simonides of Amorgos for satire and controversy. In expression of bitter feeling Archilochus was supreme. 'May the top-knotted Thracians take him, stripped of his kindly friends, where he will eat the bread of slavery and fill his cup with many ills. May they take him frozen stiff and strung with seaweed from the surge, his teeth chattering, his lips spewing the brine, his body sprawling doglike on his face by the edge of the surf. That is the sight I wish to see; for he wronged me and spurned his plighted oath, he that was my boon-companion.'[3]

The Aeolian school, established by Terpander and Arion in Lesbos, culminated at the turn of the seventh century in the personal lyric of Alcaeus and Sappho. Alcaeus wrote his lyrics on politics, love, and wine with the directness of Archilochus but with more beauty. His aristocratic scorn and passion in

---

[1] *Il.* 18. 491; 590; *Od.* 8. 260; Alcm. 67.
[2] Pi. *O.* 13. 19; Hdt. 1. 23; 2. 48.   [3] Archil. 79.

an age of faction were expressed in the vivid vernacular of the Lesbian dialect. Sappho drew her inspiration from the cult of Aphrodite and Aphrodite's attendant deities, the Graces and the Muses, to whose worship Sappho and the maidens of Lesbos were dedicated as a group. She felt the beauty of the maidens with the intensity which she devoted to her emotional and mystical adoration of Aphrodite. Her sensibility and her simplicity were unrivalled in the lyric poetry of her age and of later ages. When Anactoria, a girl she loved, left her company to be married, Sappho expressed her grief.

Some say the fairest thing on the black Earth is a company of horsemen, or of soldiers or of ships, but I say 'that which one loves'. To make this plain to everyone is so easy. For Helen, who far surpassed mankind in beauty, left the best of men and forgot child and dear parents to destroy the whole glory of Troy; for the Goddess of Love led her astray at first sight. Easily swayed is the heart of a bride and lightly fluttered by Desire, which even now reminds me of the absent Anactoria—her lovely tread and the shining sparkle of her eyes fain would I see rather than the chariots of Lydia and the soldiers in arms.[1]

Of the poetry of this period we possess only fragments. But they suffice to give us the measure of the poetical genius which was common to Aeolian, Ionian, and Dorian and flowered in numerous states from Sicily to Ionia. Lyric poetry found its inspiration in the glory of life, which drew the thoughts of men away from the heroic past to the delights of the present. Religious belief and religious practice prompted thanksgiving rather than fear, and the beauty inherent in its anthropomorphic mythology was in harmony with the spirit of an Alcman or a Sappho. Within this general framework of poetic achievement the individual qualities of the Greek states found their own expression. The nascent individualism of East Greece was already marked in the poems of Archilochus and Alcaeus. The corporate spirit and the religious seriousness of the mainland gave a different purport to elegiac and iambic poetry in the hands of Tyrtaeus, Solon, and Theognis. Different as the poets of the Greek states were in temperament and in outlook, they had one point in common. They were all aristocrats. The achievement of the aristocratic age was as remarkable in the field of poetry as in those of war and politics.

In art the Greek states showed an equal diversity of talent. The rich decoration of 'orientalizing' pottery achieved a mature brilliance at Corinth, Sparta, Athens, Boeotia, Rhodes, Chios, and elsewhere. A rapid mastery of technique and a precise taste were shown by engravers of dies, from which the varied coinages of the Greek states were struck. In the modelling of wood, clay, stone, and bronze a great number of states produced masterpieces before the end of this period. Statues, carved in wood and painted, were models for painted figures in stone, which were first sculptured in the middle of the seventh century. The style of the mainland, Crete, and the Cyclades

---

[1] Sapph. 27ᵃ.

was bold and strong in its attempt to portray the salient characteristics of human or animal form. Magnificent examples have been found at Corcyra, Perachora, Delphi, the Ptoan sanctuary in Boeotia, Tegea, Delos, Thera, and Prinias in Crete. At Athens the same vigour of expression was applied with more refinement of detail. In East Greece the style was less sturdy in conception and more soft in line.[1] By 550 the formalized stiffness of the earliest statues had evolved into a deeper understanding of anatomy and a more naturalistic representation of perfect physique.[2] Almost every site which has been excavated, from Selinus to Miletus, has yielded evidence of the creative vigour and the artistic taste which characterized the archaic states as a whole and were combined with individual qualities in each state. In subject, too, the artists had much in common. Mythological and animal scenes predominated in their painting and engraving, and the statues, massive or small, modelled in terracotta, marble, bronze, or gold and ivory, were dedicated in the service of the gods. The anthropomorphic concept of a divine being was the strongest inspiration of art.

The ideas of the period were essentially religious, in that men strove to understand the divine force which gave meaning to the natural world. Solon and Sappho no less than the Argive sculptor Polymedes penetrated the principles inherent in the state, in love, and in beauty. The same intellectual striving marked the beginnings of philosophy at Miletus, where Thales foretold a total eclipse of the sun[3] in the year 585 and Anaximander wrote the first prose work of which we know *c.* 546. Although Thales probably derived a knowledge of astronomy from Egypt and Babylon, his inquiry into the principles of the universe began from the assumptions of Greek religious thought.

The cosmogony of Hesiod, wherein Chaos separated out into a group of elements preserving their own internal balance or harmony, had been adapted by the Orphic movement for its own purpose. The Orphic doctrine was as follows. In the beginning water and a solid mingled with one another to form a slime, from which Time was born as an animate being. Time begot Air, Chaos, and Darkness, and then created in Air an egg, which split in two to bring forth Phanes, a bisexual god. He created the universe from within himself and with the aid of his daughter Night, who later succeeded Phanes as ruler of the Universe. A second act of creation occurred, when the sixth ruler Zeus swallowed Phanes. Zeus then became creator anew of the world and in particular of the Titans, from whose ashes man sprang.

We know little of Thales' philosophy save that he regarded water as the original substance of the universe, a substance possessing life and motion within itself. Anaximander began with 'the unlimited' (*to apeiron*), that is to say matter unlimited and undifferentiated in quantity and quality of ingredients. From 'the unlimited' the world or worlds emerged, and into it

---

[1] Richter *AGA*, figs. 19–23, 27, 32, 39, 47, 51, 52, 53, 56; 10–11; 62, 67, 69.
[2] Ibid. 92, 93, 141, 145, 149.　　　　　　　　　　　　　　　　[3] Hdt. 1. 74.

they return as they disintegrate in accordance with the rule of time.[1] The world or worlds were created by the action of opposite elements within the unlimited—the hot and the cold, the wet and the dry. Of these the cold elements and the wet elements coalesced into earth enwrapped in mist, while the hot elements and the dry elements formed into an outer sphere of flame, which, as it revolved, broke into wheels of fire visible through the mist as sun, moon, and stars. This outer fire dried the mass of earth, so that land became differentiated from water and life arose from the warmed slime. The first living beings were fishlike, and from them developed animals and man. Within the revolving sphere earth was cylindrical in shape and central in position, so that it stood stationary in equipoise.

The system of Anaximander was a triumph of human reason, proceeding to inquire into first principles from a basis of geographical, biological, and physical observations. His theory was carried an important step further by Anaximenes, who identified air as the first element, out of which mist, water, and solid matter evolved by condensation, and steam and fire evolved by rarefaction. Air in its purest form was literally the breath of life. A part of it was imprisoned within the body of animal or man, and was released finally by death.[2] Thus in Milesian philosophy the universe was explained as a group governed by its own immanent principle or elemental substance, even as the state appeared to Solon to be a group governed by its own immanent principle, *Eunomia*.

[1] *Vorsokr.* 12 A 9, B 1.

[2] *Vorsokr.* 13 B 1; 2.

BOOK III

THE TRIUMPH OF GREECE
(546–466)

CHAPTER 1

The Advance of Persia and the Growth of Athens

§ 1. *The power of Persia*

IN winter 546 Croesus of Lydia, ally of Sparta, Babylon, and Egypt, and master of many Greek states in Asia Minor, was overthrown by the military might of the Persian king, Cyrus (559–529). The Greek states, having rejected the request of Cyrus to revolt from Croesus, now offered to accept Persian rule on the terms they had received from Lydia. Cyrus refused, except in the case of Miletus. The other Ionian states, and with them the Aeolian states of the Asiatic coast, appealed for aid to Sparta. She had already incurred Persia's hostility by her alliance with Croesus; she now dispatched envoys, who claimed the right to protect the liberty of all Greek states and warned Cyrus not to intervene, but she sent no troops to Asia. Meanwhile, in the absence of any concerted action, Cyrus' deputies rapidly reduced the Greek states and the native peoples of Asia Minor, and added some of the adjacent islands to their realm. For the Greeks of Asia the choice was sub-mission or evacuation. The latter was recommended to the Ionians by Bias of Priene and was chosen by the people of Phocaea and Teus, who put to sea in their penteconters and settled in new lands. The Greek states which sub-mitted to Persia became liable to tribute and military service, were put under pro-Persian tyrants, and for a time lost the right to issue coinage. As the Persians advanced into Lycia and Caria, Ionian and Aeolian troops served in the victorious army. In 539 Babylon fell; the coast-towns of Phoenicia also passed into the Persian empire, and Cyprus transferred her allegiance from Egypt to Persia. In 525 Cambyses, the successor of Cyrus, reduced Egypt. Here Greek fought against Greek. For Egypt relied partly on Greek and Carian mercenaries, while the naval and military forces of Cambyses included ships and troops from Ionia and Cyprus as well as from Caria and Phoenicia.

Beyond Egypt the suzerainty of Cambyses was recognized by Cyrene and Barca, which henceforth paid tribute to Persia.[1]

The conquests of Cyrus and Cambyses were consolidated by Darius (522–486). The empire extended from Cyrenaica to the Indus, and from the Caucasus to the Persian Gulf. The administrative centre was at Susa, the capital of the Achaemenid dynasty; here was the court of the Great King, 'the King of the lands of all peoples'. The territories of Darius were divided into twenty provinces. Each was ruled by a Persian satrap with full military and civil power, and each paid tribute in specie and in kind to the King. The military strength of the empire was based on two components—the aristocratic cavalry and heavy infantry of Persia, and the contingents of the subject peoples which were commanded by Persian satraps or by native princes. In order to render these vast forces more mobile, Darius constructed a network of roads radiating from Susa; one of these, 'the Royal Road', reached the Aegean coast at Ephesus. The naval forces in the Mediterranean were supplied by the subject peoples and primarily by the Phoenicians, who had played a leading part in the conquest of Egypt.

In his financial policy Darius adopted the monetary system of Croesus and minted gold darics and silver shekels, which bore as device the Great King armed with bow and spear (Plate XI *g*). These coins, struck on the Babylonian standard, henceforth known as the Persian standard, were prized for their purity and served as a medium of international exchange from India to Sicily. A great reserve of the precious metals was formed by the royal treasury, where the excess revenue of the empire was hoarded. The Persians did not themselves engage in commerce; but Darius fostered the growth of seaborne trade by driving a canal from the Nile delta to the Red Sea and by sending out an expedition to circumnavigate from the mouth of the Indus to the Red Sea. The control of this vast empire was vested in the Great King, hereditary monarch of Persia, Media, and all lands, endowed with every temporal power and enthroned by divine right as King of Persia through grace of Ahura-Mazda, King of Babylon through choice of Marduk, and King of Egypt through adoption by Re. In the eyes of the Greeks he was 'The King' *par excellence*, a monarch absolute in religion, politics, and war, the antithesis of city-state liberalism and the anathema of Greek religious belief.[2]

The advance of the Persian empire affected the Greek states which had been overrun and those which might yet be overrun. The Asiatic Greeks suffered economically during the wars of Cyrus and Cambyses, and gradually regained some degree of prosperity from 520 onwards. But the golden age of East Greek trade did not return. Under Croesus and Amasis, who had looked to Greek states for trade, mercenaries, and oracular advice, the gold of Lydia and Egypt had flowed towards the Aegean. Under Cyrus and Darius, who were concerned with the expansion and consolidation of Persian rule, the

[1] Hdt. 1. 76–81; 84–85; 141; 151–3; 161–4; 168–76; 3. 1; 13; 19.
[2] Hdt. 3. 89–96; 4. 44; 5. 52–54; *GC* 62.

financial strength of the empire was built up in Persia and Babylonia. Thence the caravan routes ran to the Syrian coast, where the Greek trading post at Poseidium revived *c.* 520 but the main ports were in Phoenician hands. Cyprus was better placed to exploit this trade than any East Greek state, and the King of Salamis in Cyprus coined on the Persian standard. In Egypt the privileges extended by Amasis to the Greeks of Naucratis and Cyrene disappeared under Persian rule, and a decline in the volume of Greek trade resulted. But the Greek states were less concerned with the economic than the political aspects of the Persian empire. The states subject to Persia could not complain of Persian tolerance; for in general Persia did not interfere with local religion, customs, or trade, and in particular she soon permitted the Greek states to coin again in their own right. But Persia was tolerant only if her rule was accepted; the populations of disloyal or disobedient states, such as Priene, were enslaved or deported. In fact Persian dominance meant to a Greek city-state the loss of its most precious possession, political independence. In addition, it often meant the loss of internal freedom, because Persia favoured the installation of pro-Persian tyrants. The free states feared a further advance by Persia. But, until the advance began in earnest, individuals and parties were prepared to exploit this new factor in the political game. They did not take to heart the experience of Barca and of Samos. In Cyrenaica a feud between the Queen of Cyrene, Pheretima, and Cyrene's colony Barca led to the invocation of Persia; whereupon Barca was eliminated and Cyrene and Euesperides were incorporated in a Persian satrapy (*c.* 518). The Samian Syloson solicited Persia's help and was established as tyrant of Samos; the island then entered the satrapy of Otanes, but only after a widespread massacre (*c.* 518).[1]

The Persians explored as they conquered. The circumnavigation from India to the Red Sea was followed by the annexation of Arabia. Europe was the next objective for Darius. He sent an expedition of two triremes and a merchantman, equipped at Sidon and guided by a Greek doctor, Democedes of Croton, to explore the coasts of Greece and Italy, and at the same time he ordered the satrap of Cappadocia to sail across the Black Sea and raid the European Scythians.[2] He decided to attack the Scythians in strength. For, as they were related to the nomadic peoples who pressed upon his empire in Asia, he considered them to constitute a more immediate danger than the Greeks in Europe. While Darius mustered the contingents of all his subjects from the Sacae to the Greeks in Asia, a Samian engineer bridged the Bosporus with pontoons, and a fleet, which was mainly Greek, sailed two days' journey up the Danube and constructed a pontoon bridge there. His army, having defeated the Getae and received the submission of the eastern Thracians, crossed the Danube in 513 and pursued the nomadic Scythians deep into the Ukraine. There he was unable to force a decisive engagement. The Scythians destroyed the countryside in his path and their cavalry harassed his columns

[1] Hdt. 1. 161; 4. 165–7; 200–4; 3. 139–49.   [2] Hdt. 3. 135–8; Ctes. 16.

by day and night, until he outran his lines of supply and had to turn back, abandoning his sick and wounded. The retreat was hazardous as far as the Danube. There the Greek commanders, who had rejected the Scythians' offers of help if they would revolt, covered the crossing of the army into Thrace, but some of the Greek states in the Bosporus and the Hellespont had risen and threatened the crossing into Asia. Darius dealt with the rebels promptly and severely, burning Chalcedon and Abydus, and then returned to his capital at Susa.[1]

The defeat in Scythia meant the deferment and not the end of Darius' plans of conquest in Europe. It was essential to gain a firmer control of the Straits and extend the Persian satrapy in Europe, before another major campaign was set on foot. Darius, therefore, left a strong army in Europe under Megabazus and his successor Otanes. The Scythians realized their danger; the tribes united, approached Sparta as the leading Greek state in Europe for an alliance, and raided the Persian satrapy as far south as the Chersonese, probably in 511. Some Greek states near the Straits, led by Byzantium and Chalcedon, rose in sympathy, but Sparta and her allies made no move. The Persian commanders confirmed their control of the Straits by punishing the Greek rebels and conquering Imbros and Lemnos c. 509, and they extended their satrapy as far as the Strymon valley, from which a recalcitrant tribe of Paeonians was deported and sent to Asia. Beyond the Strymon Darius received the submission of Amyntas, king of Macedon, whose daughter was given in marriage to the son of Megabazus. The outstretched arm of the Persian empire now threatened peninsular Greece and southern Scythia, and Persian sea power ruled the waters of the Libyan coast and the eastern Aegean. In 500, when Persia received an invitation to intervene in the affairs of Naxos in the Cyclades, the time seemed ripe for an advance towards peninsular Greece, where the Greek states were known to be disunited.[2]

§ 2. *The tyrants at Athens*

WHEN Peisistratus withdrew from Athens with his party and his funds, he settled in the rich area between Macedonia and Thrace, at first at Rhaecelus (close to Aenea), which he founded, and then near Mt. Pangaeum. Like the Athenian noble Miltiades, who c. 556 became master of the Chersonese, and the Milesian tyrant Histiaeus, who after 510 founded Myrcinus in the Strymon valley,[3] Peisistratus was able to amass great wealth by exploiting the local resources of silver and of timber. In Thrace he coined Attic tetradrachms with the owl of Athena, similar to his coinages of 561 and 556, and he built the ships and transports which were necessary for the fulfilment of his plans. He was now able to buy political support and to hire mercen-

---

[1] Hdt. 4. 1; 83–144; Ctes. 17; Str. 305; 591; *IG* 14. 1297 for the date.
[2] Hdt. 5. 1; 12–32; 6. 84; Str. 591; for the dates in this paragraph see *CQ* 6. 119 f.
[3] Hdt. 6. 34–38; 5. 23.

aries. He collected money from friendly states, especially from the narrow oligarchy at Thebes, counted on the support of the oligarchy at Eretria, hired 1,000 mercenaries from Argos, where he had connexions by marriage, and received money and men from a Naxian adventurer, Lygdamis. He timed his attack cleverly in autumn 546, when his ally Argos was engaging the attention of the enemy of all tyrants, Sparta, and when the great conflict between Lydia and Persia lent uncertainty to the future. Landing at Marathon, where his partisans from the city and the villages joined him, Peisistratus defeated the Athenian forces at Pallene and urged the vanquished to return each to his own property. He then occupied the Acropolis, disarmed the people, seized as hostages the sons of the leading families, and established his tyranny securely on the basis of money, mercenaries, and alliances.[1] In fact Peisistratus had discovered a new avenue to power. Whereas Cypselus, Orthagoras, and Theagenes had exploited an internal situation, Peisistratus had used foreign troops and mercenaries to achieve his *coup d'état*. If Sparta could depose tyrants, other states could help to set them up; and Peisistratus did not scruple to employ their aid.

Until his death in 528/7 Peisistratus maintained his position as tyrant with outstanding ability. Since he levied a tenth part of all Attic produce and probably taxed all imports and exports, his personal wealth mounted in proportion to the productivity of the state. Fortunately for Peisistratus Athens had just outstripped Corinth in fine pottery, and the volume of trade was rising rapidly and steadily. Peisistratus favoured its flow by his foreign policy. On the north-eastern route to the Hellespont friendly ports now became available for Athenians at Eretria in Euboea, Rhaecelus on the Thermaic Gulf, his own base near Mt. Pangaeum, and also throughout the Chersonese, where Miltiades ruled as local dynast. To these Peisistratus added Sigeum in the Troad, where he displaced the Mityleneans and installed his son Hegesistratus as tyrant, no doubt with due recognition of the Persian satrap. In the central Aegean Peisistratus acquired strong allies. At Naxos he installed Lygdamis as tyrant and gave him custody of his Athenian hostages, and at Samos Lygdamis installed Polycrates as tyrant *c.* 533; Peisistratus also purified Delos in accordance with an oracle, hoping thereby to win prestige as patron of the Delian Amphictyony.[2] These operations certainly facilitated the growth of Athenian trade. Attic pottery reached new sites in the north-east, in Ionia, Cyprus, and Syria; the Euboic standard, which was common to Athens, Corinth, and Samos, was adopted *c.* 550–540 by Potidaea, Chalcis, and Delos for their first coinages. In the Aegean Athens, as one of several competing states, was aided by the fact that the Persian advance weakened many of the East Greek states. Even so, Polycrates of Samos outdid Peisistratus by conquering several islands and by dedicating Rhenea to Delian Apollo, while Lygdamis was already laying the foundations for the later eminence of Naxos.

---

[1] Arist. *Ath.* 15; 17. 1 and 4; Hdt. 1. 61–64.
[2] Hdt. 5. 94. 1; 1. 64; Th. 3. 104. 1; Polyaen. 1. 23.

Aegina, too, was stronger than Athens in the Aegean; her Pheidonian standard operated in Boeotia, most of the Peloponnese, Naxos, Paros, Tenos, and the southern isles of the Aegean. But Athens had the advantage, which accrued from good relations with Corinth, that her pottery was exported in great quantities to the West as far as Spain.[1] And, as 'the oldest land of Ionia', she offered a home to talented refugees from the ravaged states of Asia Minor.

Hippias and the other sons of Peisistratus, collectively styled 'the Peisistratidae', had to contend in 528–510 with worsening conditions, as Sparta's power and Persia's conquests expanded. By 522 the tyrants of Naxos and Samos had fallen, and by 519 Samos was held by a Persian governor, the tyrant Syloson.[2] In 514/13 Persia annexed the northern Aegean coast; thereafter the activities of Megabazus and the Scythian raiders must have diminished the flow of trade through the Hellespont and the Bosporus. While the skies were darkening around them, the Peisistratidae took an adventurous step. Miltiades I and his successors in the Chersonese had been the accepted rulers of the native Dolonci. When Miltiades, son of Cimon, went out to succeed his brother *c.* 516, the Peisistratids equipped him with a small but well-armed force. By treachery he trapped the local chieftains, hired 500 mercenaries, captured the Chersonese, and planted Athenian settlers at a number of points. He then went on with an Athenian force to capture Lemnos. But these attempts, the first of many, to seize and to occupy the approaches to the Black Sea were ruined by the Persian advance into Europe in 514–13. In 511 or so Miltiades departed from the Chersonese, and many Athenian settlers had probably left the Chersonese and Lemnos earlier.[3]

On the mainland the Peisistratids inherited friendly relations with Thebes, Argos, Thessaly, Eretria, and Sparta. But this network did not endure. Plataea, a small state in Boeotia near the Attic frontier, found itself hard pressed by Thebes to join the strong Boeotian League. In 519, when a Spartan force was operating in central Greece, the Plataeans turned to Sparta for aid; but the Spartans advised Plataea to turn to Athens, which promptly made an alliance. The object of the Spartans, to embroil Athens and Thebes, was achieved. A battle ensued between Athens and Thebes, in which Athens won a victory; she then advanced the boundaries of Plataea and her neighbour Hysiae.[4] This victory won for the Peisistratids the enmity of Thebes, hitherto their friend. At Delphi the oracle began to urge a willing Sparta to depose the tyrants; and behind the oracle were the Alcmeonid leaders, who were as ready to force a return with foreign aid in 511 as Peisistratus had been in 546. The Peisistratids could only hope for help from Argos, Thessaly, Plataea, and Hysiae; in the event they received some aid from Thessaly.

Peisistratus controlled all the internal means to power—mercenaries,

---

[1] Th. 1. 13. 6; 3. 104. 2; Hdt. 5. 28; *JHS* 60. 66; for coins see Plate XI*f* and *GC* 48 f.   [2] Hdt. 3. 44; 125.

[3] Hdt. 6. 39–40; 137–40; Nep. *Milt.* 1–2; for dates, &c., see *CQ* 6. 118 f.

[4] Hdt. 6. 108; Th. 3. 55; 68. 5; for dates cf. *Historia* 4. 393 f.

weapons, fleet, acropolis, executive posts, and regular revenues. Many of his opponents had been killed at Pallene. Some had gone with Miltiades to the Chersonese in 556; others fled with the Alcmeonids in 546. Peisistratus advised the survivors to return to their estates, which he did not confiscate but left as a condition for good behaviour;[1] in some cases their sons were held as hostages. It is possible that before his death in 528/7 he came to an understanding with some Athenian *émigrés* such as the Philaid Cimon, who returned under an agreement. His main aim was to win the goodwill of the rank and file of the citizens. He therefore respected the civil and constitutional laws of his country, even submitting to trial in the Court of the Areopagus.[2] But behind the scenes the tyrant held the strings. He tolerated no party and no policy save his own; candidates for major office were of his choosing, and on their election they administered his policy and in due course became members of the Areopagus.

In his attitude to the common people he was genial. In his policy he strengthened them, by making agricultural loans to the poor, by safeguarding the rights of the guildsmen, and by providing full employment for all citizens. His public works—roads, temples, water-supply, &c.—enhanced the splendour of his régime.[3] His patronage attracted artists to Athens, especially from the states subjugated by Persia. In dress and in art Ionian influence became marked, and on the fine red-figured Attic pottery scenes from Ionian mythology were frequent from 535 onwards. State cults—Panathenaea, Dionysia, and Eleusinia—were celebrated in a more lavish manner, and *c.* 534 a competition in tragic drama was instituted at the Dionysia.[4] By these means Peisistratus strengthened the appeal of state religion to all classes of the people, while he and his supporters manned the traditional priesthoods. In the judicial sphere he installed judges for the country divisions, who probably judged minor cases and perhaps heard appeals from the clan-courts. His rule gave peace, prosperity, and distinction to the Athenian state. He won the affection of a class which later became predominant, and his régime was remembered by many as a golden age, 'The age of Cronus'.

'As tyrants', wrote Thucydides, 'the sons of Peisistratus were to the greatest degree honourable in conduct and shrewd in policy; they beautified the city, excelled in war, and performed religious ritual.' This praise was not absolute but strictly relative to the records of other tyrants. In general the sons pursued their father's policy. They relied on mercenary troops and controlled the supply of weapons. Their financial reserves were such that they reduced direct taxation to one-twentieth of the natural produce of Attica. The arts received particular attention from Hipparchus.[5] He himself composed poems and snatches, which were inscribed on the 'Hermae' or milestones set up on his orders throughout Attica. He probably arranged for the removal to Athens from Persian-occupied Chios of the Homeric poems, which

---

[1] Hdt. 1. 63–64.   [2] Arist. *Pol.* 1315^b22.   [3] Arist. *Ath.* 16; Polyaen. 5. 14.
[4] *FGrH* 239 A 43 (*Marm. Par.*).   [5] Thuc. 6. 54. 5–6; Arist. *Ath.* 18.

had been long set down in writing and preserved by the Homeridae, and he made the recitation of the poems an integral part of the Panathenaic festival. He appointed one Onomacritus as recorder of the oracles which were housed on the Acropolis, and he invited the poets Anacreon and Simonides to the court.[1] The tyrants maintained the constitutional fiction, Hippias being eponymous archon in 526 and his son Peisistratus in 522. Altars to the Twelve Gods and to Apollo were dedicated by the young Peisistratus as archon, and the Panathenaic festival of 514 was conducted by Hippias and Hipparchus. If their father had not already done so, the Peisistratids recalled some members of leading clans from exile. In 525 Cleisthenes, a leading Alcmeonid, was eponymous archon and in 524 Miltiades, a Philaid.[2] The understanding with these powerful houses was evidently precarious; for Cleisthenes was soon an exile and returned to Delphi, and in 524, when Miltiades' father Cimon won his third successive victory in the chariot-race at Olympia, the Peisistratids being fearful of his popularity had him assassinated.[3] Their complicity was well concealed; in 516 they sent Miltiades to seize the Chersonese and later Lemnos, and his successes gave Athenians an opportunity to emigrate. But in 514/13 many colonists returned to Attica, and the loss of further Athenian footholds in the north Aegean and the arrival of refugees aggravated the problem of maintaining order in Athens. It was probably at this time that restrictions were placed on movement from the country into the town.[4]

The Peisistratids were afraid of the leading houses, at whose expense their father had established himself as tyrant—the Alcmeonids, the Eteobutads, and others, among whom were their own relatives, the Philaids. It is a striking fact that no ancient authority attributes to Peisistratus and his sons the confiscation of their enemies' estates. Cimon, indeed, when recalled from exile, 'returned under truce to his own estate', which suggests that he had not been expropriated.[5] Just as later an ostracized politician did not lose his property, so now it seems that the nobles in power respected the inalienable character of family property and did not break up the estates of their rivals. However that may be, the noble houses in exile maintained their wealth, as Peisistratus had done during his periods of exile. The Alcmeonids were ensconced at Delphi. Rallying the other exiles they made several attempts to return by force and in particular fortified a stronghold near the frontier at Leipsydrium, where they were joined by their partisans from the city. The tyrants, however, drove them out of Attica once more. In the political clubs of the city this event was celebrated by the drinking-song: 'alas, partisan-betraying Leipsydrium, how you did destroy the heroes, staunch in battle and noble in blood, who that day gave proof of their parentage!' This powerful opposition had its feelers not

---

[1] Ps–Pl. *Hipparch.* 228b; Hdt. 7. 6.
[2] Hdt. 6. 108. 4; Th. 6. 54; *Hesp.* 8 (1939) 59; *GHI* 8.
[3] Isoc. 15. 232; *FGrH* 328 F 115 (Philoch.); Hdt. 6. 103. 2; for the date see *CQ* 6. 117.
[4] Poll. 7. 68; *FGrH* 115 F 311 (Theopomp.).   [5] Hdt. 6. 103. 3.

only within Attica but also in other states. In particular the Alcmeonids gained the contract to rebuild the temple at Delphi, and won thereby not only financial profit but also the favour of the priests, who began to urge any Spartan that consulted the oracle to depose the Peisistratids.[1]

Between the expulsion from Leipsydrium and the gaining of the contract at Delphi, a stirring event occurred at the Panathenaic festival of the year 514—the assassination of Hipparchus by Harmodius and Aristogeiton, whose motives were personal and not political. These two 'tyrannicides' became thereafter the symbol of liberty to the Athenian people, which tended to attribute its liberation rather to them than to the coalition of Sparta and of the nobles under Alcmeonid leadership. They were honoured in the drinking-songs of those who opposed the nobles: 'I shall carry my sword in a myrtle branch, as did Harmodius and Aristogeiton, when they slew the tyrant and made Athens the land of equal rights.'[2]

After the assassination of Hipparchus, the Peisistratids executed many opponents, and their rule became more harsh. Hippias realized the danger of his position and married his daughter to the son of the tyrant of Lampsacus, who was influential at the Persian court. The attack came in 511/10 from Sparta, where the policy advocated by Delphi and inspired by the Alcmeonids was welcome in itself. The first Spartan force tried to effect a surprise by landing on the beach at Phalerum. But the Peisistratids, having been fore-warned, defeated the Spartans with the aid of 1,000 cavalry from Thessaly. A second Spartan force, commanded by the king Cleomenes and aided by the *émigré* nobles and their supporters in Attica, defeated the Thessalian cavalry and penned up the Peisistratids in the Acropolis. By a fortunate chance the sons of the Peisistratids were captured. Terms of capitulation were concluded in July 510. The Peisistratids withdrew intaçt to Sigeum in the Troad. Athens was free after thirty-six years of continuous tyranny.[3]

Although the tyrants probably did not confiscate the lands of the noble houses or impair the system of clan organization by any violence or legislation, their long tenure of power had a great effect on the evolution of the state. As the noble houses were mainly in exile, their claims on their followers were weakened by disuse and their prerogatives in the state were suspended. While this break in continuity encouraged men to think of a new system, the tyranny had vastly strengthened the other element in Attic society, the guildsmen, whose numbers had been swollen by immigration and whose importance had increased with the growing prosperity and maritime trade of Athens. The tyrants had always placed the interests of the state—as controlled by themselves—before those of the clans, and the buildings, festivals, and coins of the tyranny emphasized the fact. They had also fostered the interests of the small man the typical member of the people (*demos*), and

[1] Hdt. 5. 62–63; Arist. *Ath.* 19 and 20. 5; Ar. *Lys.* 665 cum Schol.
[2] Hdt. 6. 55; Th. 6. 54; Ath. 695ª. See Plate XII *d*.
[3] Hdt. 5. 63; Th. 6. 59. 3; Arist. *Ath.* 19; for dates see *Historia* 4. 389.

their own example set a value upon the individual as such. Thus, because the tyrants were enlightened and time did the work of reform, the Athenian state of 510 had a sense of unity and a trend of political thought which the faction-ridden state of 591 to 546 had lacked.

The tyranny fired Athenian ambitions in the Aegean, where Delos, Chersonesus, Lemnos, and Sigeum had been temporarily in their grip or under their influence, and in central Greece, where Plataea and Hysiae were added to the Athenian state after the defeat of Thebes. Athens gained also in prestige. She became a great centre of Ionian art and attracted Ionian poets. The removal of the Homeric poems to Athens had a political purpose; it marked Athens as the patroness of Ionian poetry, and at her Panathenaic festivals the poet of Ionia was honoured henceforth. The city of Athens was beautified by the tyrants (see p. 285). The security of their régime, the disarming of the people, and the general prosperity led to a more graceful and leisured life.[1] A greater mastery was achieved in art and sculpture. And in this age, when the rights of the individual competed with the claims of the group, the moment came for the birth of Attic Drama, the only form of poetry in which Athens was destined to excel.

§ 3. *The reform of Cleisthenes*

On the liberation of Athens in 510 Cleomenes withdrew. Athens probably joined the Spartan Alliance, and the nobles proceeded to form a government. They disfranchised many who were not Athenian by blood, and then began to struggle for personal supremacy. Two leading personalities emerged: Isagoras, probably a Philaid, related to the Peisistratids and a personal friend of Cleomenes; and Cleisthenes, the leader of the Alcmeonids, who had organized the exiles and instigated the intervention by Sparta. Isagoras gained the ascendancy in the political clubs and was elected archon in 508. Cleisthenes countered by canvassing those who were outside the clan-system, with the promise that he would ameliorate their position under the constitution. This class, so much strengthened by the policy of the tyrants, feared further acts of disfranchisement and therefore accorded its support to Cleisthenes, whose party already included the members of the Alcmeonid clan and related clans. Isagoras replied by invoking Cleomenes. He sent a herald to proclaim at Athens the banishment of Cleisthenes and many others on the ground that their families had incurred pollution during the conspiracy of Cylon.

When Cleisthenes and others had withdrawn, Cleomenes arrived with a small force. He banished as polluted persons the members of 700 households, designated to him by Isagoras. He endeavoured to disband 'the Council'—which was probably the Areopagus Council—and to establish in power a narrow oligarchy of three hundred men with Isagoras as president. The

---

[1] Th. 1. 6. 3 with Ath. 553ᵉ.

Council resisted. It raised the people against Cleomenes and Isagoras, who seized the Acropolis and found themselves besieged. After two days a safe-

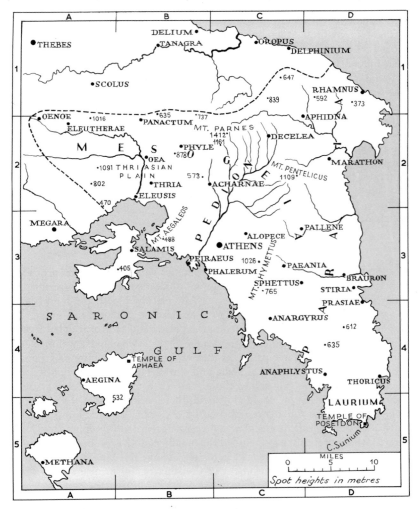

FIG. 13. Attica.

conduct was granted to Cleomenes and his force and to Isagoras with some of his supporters; the others were bound and executed. Having recalled Cleisthenes and the banished households, the Athenians sent envoys to Persia to sue for alliance and so gain protection against reprisals by Sparta. Persia demanded the tokens of submission. The envoys gave them, but the Athenians disowned their action.[1]

Meanwhile Cleisthenes was empowered to fulfil his promise and reform the constitution. He made a fundamental change in the electoral system of Attica. Hitherto the racial and geographical divisions of Attica had corresponded closely one to another. A single phratry owned land mainly in a single *trittys*; and within the phratry certain clans owned the land constituting a given *naucraria* within a trittys. Ownership was vested in the clan-members of the phratry and not in the guild-members; for the latter were only grafted on to the system at phratry level and might have no geographical affinity with naucrary or trittys. A noble house, such as the Alcmeonid house, exerted its influence both in the racial groups (clan and phratry) and in the geographical groups (naucrary and trittys) within which its estates lay. As the four tribes of Attica were racial tribes, composed each of related phratries, the influence of a noble house reached into the tribal units which constituted the state. Thus the noble houses formed pressure-points within widening groups, both racial and geographical, which were closely related one to another and derived their strength from the racial elements rather than from the engrafted guilds. The aim of Cleisthenes was to destroy the clans' influence in local and general elections and to place the guildsman on an equal footing with the clansman. He succeeded by dividing Attica into a new system of electoral wards.

Cleisthenes took as his basic unit the deme (*demos*), a small area analogous to an English parish. Many demes were already in existence; he added to their number by splitting up each heavily populated deme and creating two or more, notably in the town of Athens. These demes probably numbered some 170, and they were thus at least three times as numerous as the old naucraries. Citizenship was determined in the year of the reform by residence in a deme, and a citizen was then registered as 'A member of deme X'. Clansmen and guildsmen were thus registered on an equal footing; nothing in the register showed whether a citizen was of ancient descent or of recent adoption. The members of a deme were thus intermingled without distinction, and the qualification of residence may have enabled Cleisthenes to re-admit those who had been disfranchised and were regarded by the opposition as 'foreigners' or 'slaves'.[2]

The deme now displaced the naucrary as the unit of local administration for financial, electoral, and religious purposes. The demarch was president of the new unit, as the naucrarus had been of the old, and the demesmen had their own assembly and rites. In order to give to the deme a corporate spirit, Cleisthenes made membership of a deme from 507 onwards dependent on heredity and not on residence; subsequently, if a family moved elsewhere, it retained membership of the deme in which it had been living in 508/7.[3]

[1] Hdt. 5. 66; 69–74. 1; Arist. *Ath.* 13. 5; 20. For initiative by the Areopagus in a crisis see pp. 238 and 570.

[2] Arist. *Pol.* 1275ᵇ36. For the enclosure of the heroes see Fig. 14 (p. 188).

[3] Hdt. 5. 69; Arist. *Ath.* 21; *EM* s.v. *Eleeis*; Str. 396.

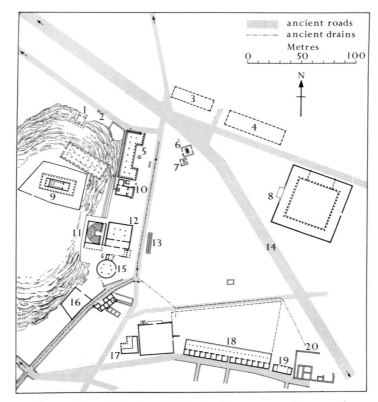

FIG. 14. Plan of the Agora in the fourth century B.C. (*see* p. 523)

1. Temple of Aphrodite Ourania
2. Sanctuary of Demos and Graces
3. Stoa of the Herms
4. Stoa Poikile
5. Stoa of Zeus
6. Altar of the Twelve Gods
7. Eschara
8. Leokorion
9. Temple of Hephaestus
10. Temple of Apollo Patroüs
11. Council House
12. Old Council House
13. Enclosure of the Ten Eponymous Heroes
14. Panathenaic Way
15. Tholos
16. Strategeion
17. South-west Fountain
18. Theseum
19. Enneakrounos
20. Mint

Cleisthenes divided Attica into three regions—the town with the surrounding territory (*asty*), the coastal region terminating in Sunium (*paralia*), and the interior (*mesogeion*)—so that each region had approximately the same number of inhabitants. These regions represented in a broad manner the divergent interests of Attica—handicrafts and capital, fishing and mining, pasture and timber—but they all had a common basis of agriculture. They did not coincide with the old divisions of plainland, coastland, and hill-land; for the contrast between town and interior had been substituted for that between plain and hill. Cleisthenes then grouped the demes within each region into ten 'trittyes' in such a way that the demes of a single trittys were in many cases contiguous, in others separate from one another; a 'trittys' was thus an aggregate of demes and not, as hitherto, a continuous piece of land. He then drew by lot one 'trittys' from each region and made up the three 'trittyes' or 'thirds' into a single unit, a tribe (*phyle*). He thus created ten tribes, the membership of which derived from membership of the deme and the Cleisthenic trittys, and not from membership of the phratry and its geographical parallel the old trittys. If an Athenian consulted the tribal register in 507, he found the entry 'A, member of deme X, trittys Y, tribe Z',[1] and this gave no indication whether A was a clansman or a guildsman.

Each tribe had equal representation from the three districts of Attica; no large geographical block existed within which local influence could exert pressure. Thus, if a naucrary had in the past been swayed by a noble house, the demes constituting that naucrary were likely to be distributed over several of the new tribes. For example, we find that later members of the Eumolpidae belonged to at least ten demes and several tribes. Membership of the tribe was from 507 onwards hereditary. The tribe had its own assembly and executive officers with electoral, religious, financial, and military functions. The eponymous heroes (*arkhegetai*) of the ten tribes were nominated by the Pythian priestess from 100 names elected by the tribes themselves. Thus the new tribal system was blessed by Delphi, and the tribal founders were 'selected from those elected' (*klerotoi ek prokriton*), the voice of the priestess being analogous to the use of the lot (*kleros*) in other cases.[2] The new tribal system cut clean across the old racial tribes and their subdivision into twelve racial phratries and twelve local trittyes.

The working of the new electoral system is clearest in the case of the Council of Five Hundred. Each deme elected a fixed number of representatives, who had to be over thirty years of age and of the zeugite property-class or above; the number was fixed in proportion to the population of each deme and therefore varied from deme to deme. From the representatives so elected by its demes each tribe selected by lot fifty representatives. Thus 500 representatives were 'selected from the elected' in such a manner that any group

---

[1] 'Son of B' must have been added sometimes to differentiate men of the same name, and this practice became general at a later time.

[2] Hdt. 5. 69; Arist. *Ath.* 21; *EM* s.v. *Eponymoi*; see Fig. 14, 13 opposite; Poll. 8. 110.

influence was likely to be eliminated. The 500 then underwent a scrutiny which now included the question 'from which deme?' It was initiated under the presidency of the Thesmothetae and judged by the Council in office; a rejected candidate had no appeal, and his place was filled from those not selected by lot. When 500 were accepted, they took the oath 'to advise what is best for the state' and entered upon office as Councillors at the beginning of the Attic year. The first Council did so for the Attic year 507, and the oath in the form which lasted for centuries was first used in 503. Ten tribal contingents were now commanded by *taxiarchoi*. In 501 ten *strategoi*, one from each tribe, elected by the people, probably took over operational command of the army from the *polemarchos*, who remained ceremonial commander or *hegemon*. The ten tribes perhaps became responsible for maintaining a certain number of ships in the navy.[1]

The electoral system gave to all Athenians, regardless of birth and wealth, an equality of political rights in the election of local and state officials, whether demarch, tribal general, or state Councillor. Cleisthenes' reform applied to the electoral sphere the equality of rights (*isonomia*) which Solon had established in regard to personal liberty and judicial procedure. Athenian citizens henceforth were equal in voting and in speaking (*isonomoi*). As distinct from a tyranny or a close oligarchy (*dynasteia*), the Athenian state was described as an equality in rights, in speech, or in power (*isonomia, isegoria*, or *isokratia*).[2]

This fundamental step was more important than any changes Cleisthenes made in the constitution; for it ensured to the individual citizens the right of voting as individuals free from outside pressure. In the constitution the Areopagus remained, as before, the most powerful single element. Its membership was still recruited from the ex-archons, and the archons were still elected by the people *en masse* and not in accordance with the new electoral system. The Areopagus and the election for the archonships remained aristocratic in character, and in fact the voters almost always returned aristocrats. The Council of Five Hundred assumed the functions which Solon's Council of Four Hundred had once held. In order to give continuity to its deliberations and to its control of routine administration, the Council was divided up by tribes into ten committees of fifty councillors, and one committee in turn, as decided by the lot, sat continually during one-tenth of the year (*prytaneia*). From the committeemen (*prytaneis*) a chairman (*epistates*) for the day was drawn by lot and a secretary (*grammateus*) was elected for the duration of the prytany. The *prytaneis* decided, for instance, whether or not to convene a special meeting of the Council; being in continual session they resided in a state-building, the Tholos, and received food from the state.[3] In this way

---

[1] Arist. *Ath.* 21; 22. 2; 55; 59. 4; *FGrH* 323 F 8 (Cleidemus). In the fourth century, when membership of a deme meant descent from the original residents, Acharnae had as many as 22 councillors while some demes had only one.

[2] Hdt. 3. 80. 6, cf. 142. 3; 5. 78; 5. 92a; Ath. 695b1.   [3] Arist. *Ath.* 43–44; 54. 3.

Cleisthenes prepared the Council for a more important position in the constitution. As a man could only be a Councillor twice and an *epistates* once between the age of thirty and sixty, a training in administration and in responsibility was extended during the next generation to a large proportion of the citizens, so that the people as a whole gained experience and understanding. But the Council did not occupy that more important position until 462. Cleisthenes left the constitution much as Peisistratus had found it. But he gave to the Council a full degree of responsibility and to the Assembly an electoral emancipation. These were later to make possible the rule of the majority in the state (*demokratia*).

Cleisthenes passed other laws, of which we know little. He may have reformed Solon's calendar to fit the rotating system of the prytanies. He may have banned a second tenure of the eponymous archonship, in order to avert the danger of tyranny, and some ancient authors thought he instituted ostracism with the same object in mind (see p. 221). In antiquity different party labels were attached to the constitution of Cleisthenes. It was described as 'aristocratic' in 462 and as 'not democratic but like that of Solon' in 411. To Herodotus and Isocrates it was 'democracy', but of an almost ideal type.[1] To an impartial observer the constitution was a balanced constitution, in which the powers given to Areopagus, magistrates, Council, and Assembly were appropriate to the experience of the different classes in the state after a long period of tyranny. Cleisthenes merits comparison with Solon, in that he united the classes by a just distribution of powers and established a true conception of a unified state, requiring the responsible co-operation of every individual citizen. 'The constitution', as Plutarch said, 'was admirably adapted to promote unanimity and preserve the state.' But Cleisthenes' vision extended also to the future. He realized the genius of the Athenian people. By his electoral reform and by his institution of Council and Prytanies he predetermined the role of the Demos in Athenian politics.[2] At the same time he left untouched and undisturbed the religious and moral structure of society, upon which ultimately the solidarity of the city-state turned. The four racial tribes, the twelve trittyes, the phratries, the clans, and the priesthoods continued to operate in the religious, moral, and social life of the community and to foster a corporate spirit and a loyal devotion, which, finding political expression under a liberal and progressive constitution, enabled the Athens of Cleisthenes to oppose a united front to Sparta and to Persia.

§ 4. *The successes of Athens*

UNDER the Peisistratids Athens had acquired control of Eleutherae, Plataea, and Hysiae, which were small states on the frontier between Athens and Thebes. Unwilling to be enrolled in the Boeotian League, they had put them-

---

[1] Plu. *Cim.* 15. 2; Arist. *Ath.* 29. 3; Hdt. 6. 131; Isoc. 7. 16.
[2] Plu. *Per.* 3; Arist. *Pol.* 1319ᵇ22; *Ath.* 21. 1.

selves in the hands of Athens. She gave them military alliance and some form of citizenship—perhaps a restricted 'isopolity', a reciprocal interchange of some citizen rights.[1] Eleutherae may have been acquired before 519, and Plataea and Hysiae in 519. As none of these figured in the electoral system of Attica, they were no more a part of the enfranchised community of Attica than the natives of Salamis and (later) of Oropus, who formed a subject community.[2]

In 506 Cleomenes organized a concerted attack on Athens from three sides. At the head of his Peloponnesian coalition he penetrated to Eleusis; the Boeotian army captured Oenoe and Hysiae; and that of Chalcis ravaged northern Attica. The Athenian army concentrated at Eleusis. When the Peloponnesian force withdrew, the Athenians turned to defeat the Boeotian army decisively and on the same day the Chalcidian army in Euboea. The numerous prisoners were ransomed by Boeotia and Chalcis; their fetters and a bronze chariot were dedicated on the Acropolis in commemoration of the double victory.[3] Athenian courage had been rewarded by brilliant success; moreover, the Peloponnesians did not return to the attack. The salvation of Athens confirmed the Cleisthenic constitution and gave her army great confidence. At the moment, too, it led to further commitments. By annexing part of Chalcis' territory and placing a garrison there, she threatened the flank of Boeotia and pressed on her from both sides. Thebes countered by allying with Aegina, which made no open declaration of war but plundered Phalerum and the Attic coast with a superior fleet. Athens now faced the enmity of Boeotia, Aegina, and Sparta. She sued again for Persian alliance. But, when Persia made the restoration of Hippias a condition, Athens broke off negotiations.[4] She had now emerged as an independent force in Aegean interstate politics.

On the richest land of Chalcis Athens settled 4,000 men of military age as smallholders (*kleroukhoi*). These cleruchs retained full Athenian citizenship, paying taxes, voting as demesmen, and serving in the tribal contingents. But they were bound by the obligation not to sell nor, save under special circumstances, to lease their holdings, so that in effect they became a standing garrison in Euboea. This was needed; for the Chalcidians were no doubt made subject to Athenian taxes and to Athenian policy, like the Boeotians of captured Oropus. Athens thus created the cleruchy as an extension of her own state and not as a separate entity. It was primarily a weapon of imperialism. Its secondary value was to relieve over-population; the refugees from the Chersonese and Lemnos, for example, could take up new lands. They were thereby assured of a position in the zeugite class, and the state was assured of a reservoir of hoplite troops.[5] This was not the earliest cleruchy. The system had probably originated in Salamis. There both Megara and Athens had settled cleruchs among the native Salaminians during the course of the sixth

---

[1] Hdt. 6. 108; Th. 3. 55; Paus. 1. 38. 8.   [2] Paus. 1. 35. 2; Th. 2. 23. 3.
[3] Hdt. 5. 74–78; *GHI* 12.   [4] Hdt. 5. 79–81; 89–90; 96.   [5] Hdt. 5. 77; 6. 100.

century; being so close to home, the cleruchs had naturally continued to be active citizens of their own state. A fragmentary inscription, dating perhaps to the Peisistratid period or perhaps later, records the conditions which governed the tenure of the holding and the military obligations of the cleruch. In Salamis a resident magistrate (*archon*) was appointed by Athens, perhaps to regulate affairs between the cleruchs and the natives.[1] In the Chersonese and in Lemnos *c.* 516–513 it is probable that colonies and not cleruchies were planted.[2] The reduction of neighbours to dependent status and the imposition of cleruchies were the first signs of imperialism in Athens.

[1] Paus. 1. 40. 4; *GHI* 11; *SEG* 10. 1; Schol. Pi. *N.* 2. 19; Arist. *Ath.* 54. 8.
[2] Hdt. 6. 140; Nep. *Milt.* 2.

CHAPTER 2

The Spartan Alliance and the Turbulence of the Greek States

§ 1. *The policy of Sparta*

SPARTA was consistently hostile to Persia. She aligned herself with the enemies of Persia—Croesus, Amasis, and the Scythians—and she attacked such friends of Persia as the tyrants at Samos and Athens. As Persia supported tyrants in the Greek states under her control, Sparta's hostility to tyrants coincided with her hostility to Persia. The aims of Sparta were to arrest the expansion of Persia and to strengthen her Alliance in Greece. About 524 Sparta took the initiative by attacking the pro-Persian tyrant, Polycrates of Samos, who possessed the leading fleet in the east Aegean and had been willing to aid Persia in the conquest of Egypt. The naval forces of Sparta, aided by Corinth, gained control of the Aegean. They secured the fall of tyrants at Naxos and at Thasos, whether now or later, but despite a month's siege failed to eject Polycrates. Shortlived though this activity was, it may have influenced Cambyses in his decision not to advance to the West. When Polycrates fell and the Samian fleet was captured by the Persians *c.* 518, Sparta refused the request of the refugee tyrant Maeandrius for help.[1] In Central Greece Spartan forces were operating in 519, when the Plataeans were advised to turn to Athens for aid; in 511/10, when two expeditions were sent to depose the pro-Persian Peisistratids; and again in 508 and in 506, when attempts were made to overthrow Cleisthenes and his government, then negotiating with Persia. Perhaps in 519 or in 510 Sparta deposed a tyrant Aulis of Phocis, and her defeat of the Thessalian cavalry in 510 strengthened her prestige in central Greece. By 510 her Alliance probably included Boeotia, Phocis, Athens, and perhaps Chalcis, and her influence with Delphi was at its height. And within the Peloponnese, too, the Spartan Alliance was dominant until the last decade of the century.

The vigorous policy of Sparta emanated from the Gerousia, the most experienced and influential organ in the constitution. It was merely executed by the ephors and the kings. Yet the latter, having full powers in the field, could affect policy seriously during a campaign. About 520 Anaxandrides was succeeded by Cleomenes, an ambitious and forceful king, whose genius proved to be akin to madness.[2] His diplomacy was apparent in 519, when he set Athens and Thebes against each other in regard to Plataea, and his liberation

---

[1] Hdt. 3. 46–48; 54–56; 148; Plu. 859d. [2] Hdt. 5. 42.

of Athens in 510 was achieved with military skill and political tact. In 508 Cleomenes, as a personal friend of Isagoras, may have influenced the Gerousia in the decision to intervene at Athens. The methods employed by Cleomenes—the announcement by herald, the wholesale banishments, the deposition of the Athenian Council—were on this occasion both foolish and foolhardy; for he showed a misunderstanding of Athens' libertarian spirit and a misconception of the military situation. In 506 Sparta acted to restore her damaged prestige and to subdue Athens. Both kings, Cleomenes and Demaratus, commanded the expeditionary force, which had been recruited from all Peloponnesian states save Argos. Cleomenes, however, kept the purpose of the campaign secret until the army reached Eleusis. When the Corinthians realized that Cleomenes intended to install Isagoras as tyrant, they withdrew from their position in the field. Demaratus then took his force out of the line, the allied contingents followed suit, and the army withdrew disconcerted. How the blame was apportioned at Sparta we do not know; but thenceforth the presence of two kings with equal powers of command on one campaign was forbidden by law.[1]

More serious for Sparta was the rift in her Alliance. At the start of this and perhaps earlier campaigns Sparta probably invoked her defensive alliance with each member of the Alliance and did not consult the members as a body. In 506 this procedure led to failure, partly induced by Cleomenes' cavalier methods. Probably in 505 it was replaced by one which was of great importance. Sparta convened representatives of the allied states to meet at Sparta and to be addressed by Spartan representatives on a matter of policy. At this meeting the Spartans doubtless claimed that the defensive alliance was invoked, because Athens had expelled Cleomenes in 508 and had attacked Boeotia and Chalcis in 506; and they proposed the policy of restoring Hippias to take control of Athens. The representative of Corinth spoke in opposition, protesting at the reversal of Sparta's policy of liberation, and obtained the unanimous support of the other allies.[2] Thereupon Sparta abandoned this policy not only for the purposes of the Alliance but also for herself, Boeotia, and Aegina, of which the combined forces could have reduced Athens.

Out of this meeting the regular procedure of the Spartan Alliance developed. Thenceforth the policy of 'the Lacedaemonians and their Allies' was decided by two equal and independent bodies: the assembly of Spartiates, representing the Lacedaemonian state as the executive head of the Alliance, and the Congress of Allies, each state sending one or more delegates and possessing one vote. In each body a majority vote was binding on all members. If both bodies voted alike on a matter of policy, then the whole Alliance was committed to the policy. But, if either body demurred, the policy lapsed. This machinery was practical and realistic. It revolved on the two points that without Sparta's leadership the Alliance had no existence and that without the Allies' support Sparta was unwise to act. Sparta's sub-

[1] Hdt. 5. 74-75. [2] Hdt. 5. 91-93.

mission to the will of the Congress in 505 afforded proof of a sincerity which ensured the success of the Spartan Alliance. Moreover, under the shadow of Persian aggression, Sparta had devised a fair method of reaching a common policy with a majority of Greek mainland states on a matter of general importance. In 505 the seed of the Hellenic Congress of 481 was sown.

In the last decade of the sixth century the influence of Argos revived. At Sicyon the nicknames of the tribes, which were offensive to Argos, were abolished.[1] At Argos the effects of the defeat in 546 had passed, and the refusal of the Spartan Alliance to act against Athens was encouraging to Argive ambitions. Persia, too, might offer aid. About 495, when Persia was engaged in putting down the Ionian revolt, Sparta took the initiative. She obtained ships and crews from Aegina and Sicyon by persuasion or force, and landed a Lacedaemonian army under Cleomenes on the Argive coast near Tiryns. In the ensuing battle at Sepeia, 6,000 Argives were slain. This was the bloodiest and most decisive battle of the series between Sparta and Argos. It confirmed Sparta's supremacy, and it kept Argos neutral throughout the Persian wars. For a time some perioeci and serfs were enfranchised to man the state, until the Argive boys grew to manhood and ejected them.[2] Tiryns, which was seized by the refugees, and Mycenae threw off Argive rule and showed their independence by taking part in the battle of Plataea in 479.

§ 2. *The beginnings of federalism*

THE unification of the Thessalian forces under a *tagos* had a military rather than a political aim, and it occurred only in time of war. The beginnings of political federation were instituted in central Greece, where the cantons had a geographical unity and a mixed North-West Greek and Aeolian population. In Phocis a federal state was formed by the individual city-states and by those tribes which were not settled in independent city-states. They styled themselves 'The Phocians'; they took joint military action and they issued a federal coinage, with the head of a bull as device, in the second half of the sixth century (Plate XI *h*). This federal unity preserved them against their neighbours and also against Thessaly.[3] Boeotia, however, was the leader of the federal movement. There all the members were city-states, and the Federal State was named 'The Boeotians'. The League issued a federal coinage before 550 with a shield as device. The shield was a symbol not only of military defence but also of religious unity; for it was associated with the goddess Athena Itonia, who presided over the Pamboeotian festival at Coronea. About 550 the letters 'BOI' were engraved on the federal coins, indicating the title of the federal state 'the Boiotoi', and on some issues the letters 'THEBA' were added to stress the position of Thebes as administrative centre of the League. In addition to the federal coinage six or seven member-states issued their own coins, bearing the federal emblem and also the initial letter of their own state. All

[1] Hdt. 5. 68.   [2] Hdt. 6. 76–83; 92; 7. 148; Arist. *Pol.* 1303a7; Paus. 3. 4. 1.
[3] Hdt. 8. 27; *GC* 159.

these coinages, being struck on the Pheidonian standard, reflected and favoured the community of economic interests. The Boeotian League was based not only on a common religious, economic, and political interest but also on the need for co-operation in defence against Thessaly and Athens. Each member contributed a contingent under its own commander, who became a federal official with the title 'Boeotarch'. When the League made an alliance with Chalcis against Athens in 507, it commemorated the occasion by striking coins with the Boeotian shield and the wheel of Chalcis as devices and the letters 'BOI' set within the wheel (Plate XI*i*).[1]

From the outset Thebes dominated the Boeotian League. She already possessed more territory and more manpower than any other member-state. Initially she had incorporated her smaller neighbours, such as Scolus, into the Theban state as equals, but at some time before the Persian wars she made them tributary to herself.[2] Thebes' treatment of her immediate neighbours did not inspire universal confidence among the other states of Boeotia. Orchomenus, for instance, remained aloof from the League and issued her own coinage; in 519 Plataea and Hysiae preferred to join Athens rather than yield to Theban coercion and join the League. But, if the dominance of Thebes limited the extent of the League, it gave a strong leadership and finally carried the Boeotians to a position of supremacy in Greece. The measure of Thebes' greatness proved to be the measure of the Boeotian League.

On the fringes of the Greek world new states were created by combining small communities around a new political centre. This sometimes involved the creation of a physical centre, such as Rhaecelus founded by Peisistratus and Myrcinus founded by Histiaeus,[3] and sometimes the establishment only of a political control, vested for instance in the Chersonese in a local Greek ruler. Such states showed the dynamic power of Greek ideas and Greek leadership; for many of the inhabitants were not Greek and yet they became fused into small but powerful states, capable of expanding territorially and of resisting larger groups such as the tribal kingdoms of Thrace. In the Chersonese Miltiades II created a state, entitled 'the Chersonesitae', in which the native tribe of the Dolonci, the colonial city-states of Ionian and Aeolian settlers, and the colonies founded by Miltiades I were all comprised. Over this conglomerate body Miltiades II and his hereditary successors ruled as kings or tyrants, from whichever standpoint they were viewed. Their state was powerful enough to resist its neighbours; its revenues enriched the rulers, who won chariot-races at Olympia and gained political influence in Athens. To Miltiades II the Chersonesitae paid posthumous honours, instituting athletic events and horse-races in his memory. In this state the Dolonci probably constituted the majority; for they invited Miltiades III, the son of Cimon, to return to the Chersonese in 496.[4]

[1] Hdt. 9. 15; *GC* 54.   [2] *Hell. Oxy.* 11. 3; Hdt. 9. 15. 2.
[3] Arist. *Ath.* 15. 2; Hdt. 5. 11 and 23.
[4] Hdt. 6. 34–41; see *CQ* 6. 113 f. for the family and dates of the Miltiadai.

§ 3. *The Aegean islands and Persia*

PEISISTRATUS set the example of seizing power by adroit use of mercenaries and money. Lygdamis at Naxos, Polycrates at Samos, and Miltiades III in the Chersonese employed the same means and consolidated their position by imprisoning, banishing, or massacring the leading men of the state and confiscating their property. Lygdamis, an aristocrat, overthrew the existing oligarchy by leading the popular party in a period of political strife and by winning election to the office of general; with the aid of Peisistratus he seized power and drove out his rivals.[1] His tyranny *c.* 545–524 broke the basis of aristocratic rule in Naxos; a democratic régime was in power *c.* 500, and wealthy aristocrats were then in exile. Polycrates, having established himself *c.* 535 by massacring many citizens of the hoplite class and by invoking Lygdamis' mercenaries, collected a mercenary force in support of his Samian corps of 1,000 archers, subdued some neighbouring states, and equipped a fleet of some 100 penteconters and forty triremes. When the Greek states on the Asiatic coast and the kingdom of Egypt were being disrupted by the Persian conquest, Polycrates' fleet and marines dominated the east Aegean and reaped an easy harvest by promiscuous piracy and widespread forays. He attacked Miletus and defeated the fleet of Lesbos; he kept on good terms with Egypt and then with Persia; and he survived the attack by Sparta and Corinth. Like Peisistratus, he affected leadership of the Ionians by dedicating Rhenea to Apollo of Delos, and he attracted Ionian poets to his court.[2] He built a famous tunnel for a watercourse, a mole protecting the harbour, and the last part of a temple of Hera—all three being more grandiose in scale than other undertakings in Greece. These and other works were executed probably by forced labour, slave, captive, or free.[3]

Polycrates used strong methods to preserve his power. He killed one brother and banished the other, named Syloson. When he sent forty triremes to aid Cambyses, he drafted the crews from malcontents and asked Cambyses to retain them. When they returned to attack him, Polycrates kept the Samians quiet by concentrating their wives and children in the boat-sheds, which were to be burnt in the event of an uprising. His ambition was boundless. He planned to establish a naval empire, comprising the islands and Ionia, in collaboration with the satrap Oroetes. But ambition was his downfall. Oroetes lured him to his court, mutilated him, and hung his corpse upon a cross.[4]

Polycrates impressed Herodotus as being 'incomparable in his magnificence with the other Greek tyrants'. His career showed what a ruthless individual could achieve by exploiting the accumulated resources of a prosperous maritime state. His success was due in great part to the elimination of many rivals by the power of Persia, which finally eliminated him. He battened on

---

[1] Arist. *Pol.* 1305ᵃ41; *Fr.* 558; *Ath.* 15; *Econ.* 1346ᵇ7; Hdt. i. 61 and 64.
[2] Polyaen. 1. 23; Hdt. 3. 39–44; Th. 1. 13. 6; 14. 1.
[3] Hdt. 3. 60; Arist. *Pol.* 1313ᵇ24.   [4] Hdt. 3. 120–5.

piracy, and his victims retaliated by piracy. While his external policy was disruptive, he failed to organize a new state to replace the old. With many Samians executed or exiled, Polycrates drew upon every form of manpower—mercenary, citizen, foreigner, or slave—in order to create an *entourage* which was attached less to the state than to its paymaster, the tyrant. A large number of Samians, headed by the crews of the forty triremes, were in exile. They were a pest wherever they went. They plundered Siphnos, exacted a hundred talents by blackmail, acquired Hydrea off the Argolic peninsula, and occupied by force Cydonia in north-west Crete. After five years of piracy they were defeated at sea and enslaved by a force of Aeginetans and Cretans.[1]

The power of Samos collapsed after the death of Polycrates. His deputy, Maeandrius, proclaimed 'an equality of rights' (*isonomia*) and invited the leading Samians to audit his accounts as sometime treasurer to Polycrates. Those who accepted the invitation were put in chains and were later executed in cold blood by his brother, Lycaretus. At this juncture Syloson, the exiled brother of Polycrates, was restored by the Persian satrap without any resistance from the Samians. Maeandrius sailed away with a safe conduct to Sparta, but he left a brother in charge of the mercenaries to attack the Persians and precipitate a massacre in the island. There his plan succeeded perfectly; but the Spartan authorities expelled him from Laconia. In Samos the massacre and Syloson's régime led to the caustic proverb 'plenty of room thanks to Syloson'. The island was repeopled on the orders of the Persian satrap Otanes, slaves being enfranchised for the purpose. The case of Samos was not unique. The Pelasgian population of Lemnos was exterminated by Lycaretus, whom the Persians set up as tyrant *c.* 509.[2]

When Persian control became organized and commercial relations were established, prosperity returned to the east Aegean and especially to Miletus and Naxos towards the last decade of the sixth century. Miletus had profited by its early settlement with Cyrus and lately by the arbitration of the leading citizens of Paros, who ended a period of party-faction by restricting full political rights to the large and small landholders.[3] Naxos under a democratic régime succeeded to the position once held by Samos. By the end of the century the forces of Naxos and her satellites were reckoned at 8,000 hoplites and a numerous fleet, and the island possessed great wealth in money and in slaves. Naxos thus became the object of Milesian and Persian ambition. In 500 the Naxian exiles invoked Aristagoras, who was acting as tyrant at Miletus; he secured the favour of the Persian satrap and the support of a Persian force which was commanded by a Persian of the royal family, Megabates, and comprised 200 triremes. In 499 the Milesian and Persian forces failed to take Naxos by surprise. After an unsuccessful siege, lasting four months, the Persians withdrew; and Aristagoras, instead of being Persian

[1] Hdt. 3. 45–46; 54–59.
[2] Hdt. 3. 142–9; Str. 638; Arist. *Fr.* 574–5; Hdt. 5. 27; for Lycaretus see *CQ* 6. 124.
[3] Hdt. 5. 29.

governor of Naxos, found himself the object of Persian disfavour.[1] The failure of the Persian force and the disgruntlement of Aristagoras were among the factors which led to the Ionian revolt.

§ 4. *Wars in the West*

IN the West the Greeks were faced by an increasing opposition. The Carthaginians held western Sicily, Sardinia, and the Balearic Isles, while the Etruscans controlled Corsica after the battle of Alalia *c.* 535. On the mainland the Etruscans and the local Italian peoples attacked Cumae in 524 with forces vastly superior in number but not in quality. By occupying a narrow defensive position the Cumaeans were able to inflict a heavy defeat on their enemies. In 509 Rome, having revolted from Etruria, made an alliance with Carthage, and *c.* 505 Cumae joined Aricia in an attack on the Etruscans of Campania.[2] On the African coast Dorieus, half-brother of the Spartan king Cleomenes, founded a colony at Cinyps in Tripolitania, with the help of Thera and Cyrene *c.* 514; but the Carthaginians and the local peoples combined to expel the colonists. Dorieus then led his force in 511 to Sicily, where Delphi prophesied success. He tried to plant a colony in west Sicily near Mt. Eryx, but the Phoenicians and the Segestans combined to kill Dorieus and most of his followers.[3] Yet the successes of Carthage did not impel the Greeks to unite. Rather, as in the case of Persia, individual parties and individual states had no scruples in invoking Carthaginian, Etruscan, or Campanian aid.

As the Greek colonies expanded, they came closer to one another and their ambitions clashed. Syracuse destroyed her daughter-colony Camarina *c.* 550; in Italy a coalition of Croton, Sybaris, and Metapontium destroyed Siris *c.* 530; Croton in turn suffered a severe defeat at the hands of Locri and Rhegium and *c.* 510 destroyed Sybaris, the richest state in the West, of which the total population numbered perhaps 500,000. The magnitude of these disasters did not deter the Greek states from pursuing their local rivalries. Unsettled conditions gave rise to a crop of tyrants at the turn of the century. At Gela *c.* 505 the ruling oligarchy was overthrown by Cleander, whose brother Hippocrates succeeded him as tyrant *c.* 498 and deprived Naxus, Callipolis, Zancle, and Leontini of their liberty. Campaigning with large mercenary forces and installing tyrants as governors, he built the first land-empire over Greek states. His methods were ruthless. In 493, when a force of Samian refugees seized Zancle during the absence of its tyrant Scythes on a campaign, Hippocrates recognized the Samian coup and imprisoned Scythes; he handed over 300 leading citizens to the Samians for execution and enslaved the remainder of the population. He defeated Syracuse in battle and refounded Camarina on territory wrested from Syracuse; the city itself was only saved by the mediation of Corinth and Corcyra. He was already the most powerful ruler in the West, when he fell in battle against the native Sicels *c.* 491.[4]

---

[1] Hdt. 5. 28–35.
[3] Hdt. 5. 42–48.
[2] D.H. 7. 3; Polyb. 3. 22.
[4] Hdt. 7. 154–5.

Other tyrants had meanwhile arisen in Sicily and Italy. Euryleon, one of Dorieus' officers, set himself up as tyrant of Selinus *c.* 505; and Anaxilas, a member of the Messenian aristocracy, seized power at Rhegium *c.* 494 and aided the Samians to seize Zancle. After the death of Hippocrates, he expelled the Samians and refounded Zancle as Messana, so that the control of the Straits was now in his hands.[1] At Cumae Aristodemus became tyrant *c.* 505. Having won a victory in support of Aricia against the Etruscans in Campania, he contrived with the help of his troops and the prisoners-of-war to seize power and execute the aristocrats. He gained popular support by proposing to set up a democracy with equal rights; but, once he had disarmed the people, he secured his own rule by reinforcing his bodyguard with liberated slaves and barbarian mercenaries and by currying favour with the Etruscans. He gave asylum to Tarquinius Superbus and detained Roman ships on the grounds that, as heir to the Tarquins, he was master of Rome. But soon after 490 he and his family were extirpated by the aristocratic refugees, who with the aid of Campanian mercenaries restored an oligarchic régime.[2] These tyrannies in the West resembled those of Polycrates and others in the East. Their methods were violent; they depended on large forces of mercenaries and had imperial ambitions. Compared with them, the tyrants of Athens were indeed men of moderation.

§ 5. *Developments in warfare*

GREEK mercenary troops, recruited in the past by Egypt, Babylonia, and Lydia, fell out of employment when the Persian empire advanced to the Mediterranean shore. They turned instead to the tyrants and dynasts, whether independent, such as Polycrates and Miltiades, or dependent on Persian favour, such as Histiaeus and Lycaretus. The Greek mercenary brought to the mainland a detailed knowledge of Persian infantry, cavalry, and siege-craft. The Scythian campaign of Darius revealed to Greek statesmen the value of amphibious operations and the scale of Persian might. From the West they had as yet little to learn; for the Greek hoplite was superior to the Italian soldier. In warfare on the Greek mainland the hoplite proved his superiority over all arms, and the Lacedaemonian hoplite over all opponents. Cleomenes achieved his victory at Sepeia *c.* 495 by a surprise assault and not by the traditional set battle, and the Phocians massacred the Thessalians in a bold night attack.[3] Thus Greek warfare was becoming less formal and more adaptable. Cleomenes, for instance, showed fine generalship in his synchronized attack on Attica from three sides in 506. It also became less scrupulous. In 506 the Aeginetans began an 'unheralded' or truceless war, and Cleomenes burnt the Argive troops at their sanctuary near Sepeia.

In Greek hands the art of wall-fortification developed rapidly. Miltiades I built a wall across the neck of the Chersonese to keep out the marauding

---

[1] Th. 6. 4. 6.　　　　[2] D.H. 7. 4–11; Liv. 2. 34. 4.　　　　[3] Hdt. 6. 78; 8. 27.

Apsinthians *c.* 555, and Polycrates' citadel was surrounded with a moat and strengthened with towers before the siege of *c.* 524. Usually the arts of defence were stronger than those of assault. Even after the victory at Sepeia *c.* 495 the Spartans could not capture the citadel of Argos. The Persians, who excelled in tunnelling and building ramps, failed in 499 to pierce the defences of Naxos; and when they withdrew, they left the outnumbered exiles to maintain themselves in small forts which they had built.[1] The walls of towns or citadels were usually over 6 feet thick, faced on both sides with cut masonry and filled with stone rubble; the blocks, being devoid of any mortar, were cut in the earliest style with curving sides and sometimes with convex and concave thicknesses, so that they fitted into one another precisely. In grandeur and in technique Greek fortifications approximate to the Crusader castles of the Levant.

In naval warfare the rivalry between Greek and Phoenician became more keen, when the Persian king adopted the Phoenician navy as the mainstay of his fleet. In ship construction, apart from a short-lived experiment in double-bank 'biremes', wherein one bank of oarsmen sat above another, rivalry in 550–500 turned on the development of the 'trireme' (Plate IV *b*). In this ship three men rowed their individual oars through one port; as compared with the penteconter of fifty oarsmen, the trireme carried 150 or more oars and gained superior speed and greater force in ramming. Because its construction required skill and its crew had to be expert, the trireme was far from displacing the penteconter as the standard Greek warship of the sixth century. The fleet of Polycrates *c.* 525 numbered 100 penteconters and 40 triremes, and a second-rate naval power such as Athens under the Peisistratids had but few triremes. In the East the Phoenicians manned 200 triremes against Naxos in 499, and in the West Corcyra and the Sicilian tyrants possessed large squadrons of triremes.[2] The states nearest to the Persian and Carthaginian navies seem to have adopted the trireme more quickly than the states of the Greek mainland.

The hoplite force of a leading military power numbered some 10,000 in this period, if we judge by exceptionally heavy losses suffered in battle— 7,000 hoplites of Cyrene in Libya, 6,000 of Argos at Sepeia, 4,000 of Thessaly in Phocis. The total force of infantry, including light-armed men, might be higher; for instance, Italian Cumae in 524 mustered some 13,000 infantry and 1,800 cavalry, and Sybaris in 510 probably a larger number. The number of hoplite troops was rather an index of prosperity than of total population. When Naxos and her satellites were at the zenith of prosperity, they mustered 8,000 hoplites and a considerable navy; in later times Naxos never raised such forces. A leading naval power, such as Polycrates' Samos in 525 with 100 penteconters and 40 triremes, needed crews totalling some 10,000 men, whereas the Phocaeans at Alalia probably mustered some 4,000 men to man

[1] Hdt. 6. 36. 2; 3. 39; 54; Polyaen. 7. 11. 5; 8. 33; Hdt. 5. 34. 3.
[2] Hdt. 3. 39; 44; 6. 39; Ael. *VH* 8. 2; Hdt. 5. 32; Th. 1. 14.

and fight their 60 penteconters. Athens in 500 boasted an adult male population of 30,000 citizens, and Sparta recruited little more than 5,000 hoplites from her citizen class.[1] As compared with the manpower available to the Persian empire or a single satrapy even a leading Greek state appeared puny. But the appearance was illusory. For the Greek hoplite phalanx and the Greek warship were choice weapons of war, highly trained and skilfully applied.

[1] Hdt. 5. 97. 2; 9. 10.

CHAPTER 3

The Ionian Revolt and Persia's Expedition against Athens and Eretria

§ 1. *The Ionian Revolt*

HISTIAEUS, irked by his honourable detention at the Persian court, decided to instigate a revolt in Ionia.[1] He shaved the head of a trusted slave, tattooed his orders on his scalp, and sent him to Miletus. There the orders were read by his son-in-law and deputy as tyrant of Miletus, Aristagoras, who had just returned from the unsuccessful expedition against Naxos. The orders of Histiaeus coincided with the wishes of Aristagoras; for Aristagoras realized that his days as a Persian agent were numbered. The motives of both men were self-interested. Histiaeus hoped that Darius might nominate him to quell the revolt, while Aristagoras saw in a revolt the means to continue his position of leadership and, if necessary, carve out a domain elsewhere.

At Miletus Aristagoras formed a group of conspirators. One of them, the historian Hecataeus, who had the interests of Ionia at heart, was opposed to the revolt. But he advised the conspirators, if they should revolt, to concentrate on winning the mastery of the seas.[2] This advice was well founded. The Ionian states of the mainland were exposed to the full strength of the Persian army, and they had no depth of territory within which to manœuvre. If they could enlist the help of the Aegean sea powers, their combined navies would outmatch the Persian fleet, of which the main component was the Phoenician squadron. Success at sea might cut off the Persian forces in Europe and render a Persian advance towards the Greek mainland impossible. It might even induce Darius to make terms which recognized the liberty of the Ionian states on the coastal fringe. But to sustain a naval war on this scale needed a coalition of Greek states and a large financial reserve. In the event Greek unity was not forthcoming. And Hecataeus' advice to use the temple-treasure of Apollo at Didyma in the cause of liberation was rejected.

The conspirators began by seizing the Ionian captains of the ships which had returned from Naxos, and by expelling the pro-Persian tyrants from the Ionian states. Aristagoras set the example at Miletus by proclaiming 'an equality of rights' (*isonomia*) as a constitutional form of government; other leaders followed suit and thereby enlisted popular support for the revolt.[3] The general uprising of the small Ionian states against the might of Persia is

---

[1] For the chronology of the revolt, which is controversial, see *Historia*, 4. 385.
[2] Hdt. 5. 35–36.   [3] 5. 37–38.

a remarkable instance of the courageous love of independence, which was one of the city-state's finest characteristics. For, while passivity brought economic prosperity to the states, war at such odds entailed heavy loss in men and means, and defeat was likely to be followed by massacre or deportation.

During the winter of 499–8 Aristagoras sailed to Greece. He sought aid first from Sparta, the state which had ordered Cyrus to respect the liberty of the Ionian states and had more recently been approached by Scythia for an alliance against Persia. But he failed to persuade the Spartan king Cleomenes to support his cause. The reason, according to Herodotus, was that Aristagoras told Cleomenes that the capital of the Persian empire was situated at a distance of three months' march from the coast.[1] This story reveals the logic of Sparta's refusal. Cleomenes saw, more clearly than Agesilaus a century later, that Sparta was above all a military power. Her army would be dissipated in the great expanses of Asia.

Disappointed at Sparta, Aristagoras then visited the motherland of the Ionian states, Athens, which was already embroiled with Persia; for she had revoked the act of submission which her envoys had made to Darius in 508/7, and she had courted the enmity of Persia by refusing to reinstate Hippias *c.* 505. The Athenian Assembly now decided to send to Ionia a squadron of twenty ships, a considerable part of their fleet which was faced by the hostile power of Aegina. This brave decision committed Athens to war with Persia, and made her popular for the moment with the Ionians. Eretria, too, which owed a debt of gratitude to Miletus, sent help, to the extent of five triremes.[2]

Apart from extricating the deported Paeonians and sending them home to Thrace, the Ionians took no action until the arrival of the ships from Greece. The assembled force, exploiting its mobility by sea, sailed to Ephesus, marched up the Caÿster valley, and delivered a surprise attack on Sardis. The buildings of the city, including the famous temple of the Lydian goddess, Cybele, were burnt to the ground; but the Persian garrison in the citadel, under the command of the satrap Artaphernes, and the Lydian townspeople drove the Ionians off. In the autumn of 498 the Persians, who had concentrated troops from all parts of Asia Minor, inflicted at Ephesus a severe defeat on the Ionian army, which then dispersed for the winter. The action of the Ionians in this campaign was justified not strategically but politically. For the burning of Sardis, although it increased the hostility of the Lydians, brought spectacular success in other quarters. For the revolt spread to the Greek states of the Bosporus and the Hellespont, which endangered the communications of the Persian forces in Thrace and safeguarded vital imports of corn from the Black Sea for the rebels; to the majority of the Carians, who ranked high as infantry; to the Dorian state Caunus on the Carian coast; and to the Greek states in Cyprus, which laid siege to Amathus, the largest city of the Phoenicians in the island.[3]

[1] 5. 49–51.   [2] 5. 97.   [3] 5. 98–104 (preferable to Plu. *Moralia* 861).

The revolt was now of serious proportions. Darius sent the artful Histiaeus to the coast, where his wiles did not deceive Artaphernes,[1] and prepared three army groups under the command of Daurises, Hymeas, and Artybius. Meanwhile the Athenians withdrew their aid, and Eretria probably followed their example. The Ionians failed to consolidate their allies or assume the initiative at sea; they took no steps, for instance, to secure Cyprus as an advanced base and so deny the Phoenician fleet entry into the Aegean. In the early summer of 497 Daurises and Hymeas captured and sacked some of the Ionian cities on the Asiatic coast.[2] In midsummer the main offensive was conducted by the army of Artybius and the fleet of Phoenicia against Cyprus. Here the Ionian fleet was already in position; but it did not contest the crossing of the enemy from Cilicia to north Cyprus. The Persian army proceeded to attack Salamis, and the Phoenician fleet rounded the north-east promontory to co-operate in the investment. Here the Greeks engaged on both elements. The Ionians proved superior to the Phoenicians. But, when the troops of Curium and the war-chariots of Salamis deserted to the Persians, the army of the Cyprians was routed. The reduction of Cyprus was now certain; by early 496 Soli, the last stronghold, capitulated in the fifth month of siege.[3]

During the campaign of Artybius in Cyprus, Daurises began to conquer the Greek states on the Asiatic shore of the Hellespont, and Hymeas reduced Cius in the Propontis. Towards the autumn of 497 Daurises marched south to Caria, where he defeated the Carians in two battles; in the second of these the Ionians participated with heavy loss. In the Hellespont Hymeas took over the area vacated by Daurises and subdued the peoples of the Troad. In 496 the circle was closing round the Ionian seaboard; for the army operating from the Troad captured Cyme and Clazomenae; but at this point the Carians ambushed the army of Daurises during a night-march, and annihilated it; their success drew the Persian offensive southwards.[4] A period of respite followed for the Ionians. Aristagoras, foreseeing the probable end of the revolt, sailed off to Thrace, where he was killed near Myrcinus.[5] Histiaeus meanwhile had fled from Artaphernes. He tried in vain to obtain the command at Miletus and then, with the aid of eight triremes from Lesbos, played the pirate in the Hellespont.[6] Here another adventurer had established himself; for in 496 Miltiades III, the son of Cimon, regained his position as tyrant of the Chersonese.[7]

For the final phase of operations in Asia Minor the Persian command recruited a fleet from Phoenicia, Cyprus, and Egypt, and directed its armies against Miletus, the leader of the revolt. Aware of the Persian preparations, the Ionian states sent their deputies (*probouloi*) to confer at a meeting, which was held at the Panionium. Their decision was to raise no army but to leave the defence of Miletus to its garrison, and to man every ship and station the

---

[1] 5. 105–7; 6. 1.   [2] 5. 116.   [3] 5. 108–15.   [4] 5. 117–23.
[5] 5. 124–6.   [6] 6. 2–5.   [7] 6. 40. 2; for the date see *CQ* 6. 119.

path was Thasos, which, after being attacked in 494 by Histiaeus, had devoted all surplus revenue from its gold-mines to the construction of warships. The Thasians submitted without a blow, and the Persian fleet advanced to Acanthus in 492. In rounding the sheer cliffs of Mt. Athos, the fleet met with disaster: a violent north wind dashed ships and men against the rocky coast, and the survivors were unfit to advance. At the same time the Brygi, a Thracian tribe, delivered a successful night-attack on the Persian army. Mardonius, however, was not daunted. He subjugated the Brygi and imposed the suzerainty of Persia on the coastal peoples as far as and including Macedonia. His objective achieved, he withdrew his main force to Asia in 491.[1]

With the European satrapy secure Darius prepared for an advance into Greece. Of this the preliminary stage was to be the punishment of Athens and Eretria for their part in the Ionian revolt. In summer 491 he ordered his subjects on the Mediterranean coast to equip a fleet of warships and prepare transports for infantry and cavalry, and he appointed Datis and Artaphernes, son of the satrap Artaphernes, to command the expeditionary force. As a seaborne invasion was intended, it was important to neutralize the navies of as many Greek states as possible. The Thasians were ordered to dismantle their fortifications and to send their fleet to Abdera on the Thracian coast, which they did without delay. The envoys of the king were dispatched to the states of the Aegean islands and of the Greek mainland to demand 'earth and water', the tokens of submission. To this demand many states acceded; important among them were the island states and not least the strong naval state of Aegina, which was at war with Athens.[2] In midsummer 491 it was apparent to Athens and Eretria that the Persian fleet, reinforced by its newly won adherents in the Aegean, would descend upon them next year and assault them in their isolation.

§ 3. *The situation in Greece*

IN 498 the Athenians had committed themselves wholeheartedly to support the Ionian Revolt, and their troops had participated in the burning of Sardis. Their withdrawal thereafter, by whatever reasons it was prompted, indicated a radical change of policy. The eponymous archon of the year 496/5 was Hipparchus; he may have been related to the family of the Peisistratidae, then in favour at the court of Darius, and his election may have been prompted by a desire to placate Persia. When Miletus fell in summer 494, the Athenians were deeply distressed by the fate of their fellow-Ionians. It formed the theme of a tragedy written by Phrynichus and produced at the Dionysia, probably in 493, which so moved the audience that the play was banned and the playwright fined. In the summer of 493 Miltiades returned from the Chersonese. He was impeached by his enemies. The overt charge concerned the tyranny which he had held in the Chersonese, but in a political

[1] Hdt. 6. 43–45.   [2] 6. 46–49.

trial of this nature his hostility to Persia and his support of the Ionian revolt were not irrelevant issues. His full acquittal was a triumph for those who were opposed to Persia. The eponymous archon for the year 493/2 was Themistocles. During his year of office he began the fortification of the Peiraeus, which with its three natural harbours afforded a much finer naval base than the open strand at Phalerum. His insistence on a naval policy for Athens was of great importance for the future; at the moment it strengthened her for the war against Aegina and for a possible war with Persia. These fragments of information[1] give us little insight into the internal politics of Athens during this decade, but they are sufficient to show that, although the policy towards Persia vacillated during the Ionian revolt, the Athenian people was resolved to meet the Persian menace not by appeasement but by war.

On the Greek mainland Athens was shackled by the legacy of the previous decade. The Boeotian states, particularly Thebes, were hostile. In Euboea, where the Athenian cleruchy at Chalcis gave her strength but not popularity, Eretria was an ally by her association in the Ionian Revolt and not by choice. Aegina was a bitter enemy; and, although there had probably been no major operations since 505, the 'unheralded' war still smouldered with intense hatred and might burst into flame at any moment. Sparta and her energetic king, Cleomenes, had been humiliated after the liberation of Athens from the tyrants and regarded the development of the Athenian constitution with antipathy. Nevertheless, the Persian menace encouraged a *rapprochement* between Sparta and Athens, different though they were in tradition and in outlook. Ever since 546 Sparta had been consistent and uncompromising in her opposition to Persia. The rising danger of recent years only stiffened her resolve, and the arrival of Persian envoys in Greece threatened her leadership of the Spartan Alliance. In summer 491, when Aegina recognized the suzerainty of Darius and tacitly withdrew from membership of the Spartan Alliance (for it was impossible to serve two masters), Athens immediately appealed to Sparta in the name of Greek freedom. Sparta's response was a worthy one. Cleomenes went in person to arrest the leaders of the oligarchic government in Aegina, who were responsible for the act of medism; when he was rebuffed, he and Leotychidas returned to the attack, probably in September, arrested ten responsible leaders and deposited them for custody at Athens.[2] Their prompt action not only strengthened Athens and neutralized Aegina for the moment. It also reaffirmed Sparta's control of her Alliance and gave a salutary warning to other states at a time when the agents of Persia were active in Greece.

Meanwhile at Sparta a grave constitutional crisis developed. The two kings, Cleomenes and Demaratus, had been at loggerheads since the unsuccessful invasion of Attica in 506. At that time the ancient law which required the presence of both kings as equal and joint commanders of the Lacedaemonian

---

[1] D. H. 6. 1. 1; 6. 34. 1; Hdt. 6. 21; 104; Th. 1. 93. 3; Paus. 1. 1. 2.

[2] Hdt. 6. 49–50; 73; for the chronology of the war with Aegina see *Historia* 4. 410.

forces on a campaign abroad had been rescinded, but the enmity between the kings disrupted other departments of state. In the Gerousia and in the Assembly the kings spoke with different voices on important questions of policy; Demaratus, for instance, opposed Cleomenes in the matter of Aegina and on the wider issue of relations with Persia. Even in the execution of state decisions their disunity was an impediment. When Cleomenes went alone to Aegina, he was rebuffed on the admittedly legal ground that a diplomatic intervention was only valid if both kings were present. It was imperative for Sparta to settle this domestic crisis immediately, before any further fiasco occurred and her policy towards Persia was undermined. On his return from Aegina Cleomenes instigated Leotychidas, whom he supported as a rival claimant to the throne, to arraign Demaratus on the ground that he was by birth a bastard and not the rightful king. As feeling ran high at Sparta, the case was referred to Pythian Apollo on the proposal of Cleomenes. When the sacred envoys reached Delphi, Cleomenes, working through a Delphian friend, had already inspired the voice of the Pythian priestess. Demaratus was pronounced illegitimate and was deposed forthwith. Cleomenes and Leotychidas, who became king in place of Demaratus, proceeded to Aegina and effected their purpose.[1] But thereafter the secret machinations of Cleomenes at Delphi became known. He therefore fled to Thessaly and moved from there to Arcadia, where he began to form a coalition of the Arcadian peoples against Sparta. The Spartan government then invited him back, and he returned home as king, probably in November 491. But his mind broke under the strain. He was placed in the stocks by his own family, persuaded a guard to give him a knife, and lacerated himself to death. He was succeeded by his brother Leonidas.[2]

The disgrace of Cleomenes cast a shadow upon the reputation of Leotychidas and upon the policy of resistance to Persia, which Cleomenes and Leotychidas had promoted. As soon as the death of Cleomenes was known, the Aeginetans sent envoys to Sparta and lodged a complaint against Leotychidas for his arrest of their ten leaders. He was put on trial, reprimanded, and sent with the Aeginetan envoys to demand the liberation of the ten men. The Athenians, availing themselves of the argument so recently used by the Aeginetans, refused to surrender the men on the grounds that both kings were not present. Leotychidas returned to Sparta to report his failure and his humiliation.[3] But, however low the reputation of Leotychidas sank, the policy of resistance to Persia prevailed at Sparta. In July 490 Demaratus fled under the taunts which Leotychidas heaped on him at a state-festival, and found a haven eventually at the court of Darius.[4] Thus Leotychidas carried through the enlightened policy of Cleomenes.

While Leotychidas was returning from Athens, the Aeginetans made a false move. A festival was being held in honour of Poseidon at Cape Sunium. The Aeginetans ambushed the sacred vessel and kidnapped a number of

[1] 6. 51; 61–66.   [2] 6. 74–75.   [3] 6. 85–86.   [4] 6. 67–70.

leading Athenians. This breach of international usage encouraged Athens to act on her conviction that Sparta would not now intervene on Aegina's behalf. After stimulating an unsuccessful rising by the democratic party in Aegina, Athens hired twenty ships at a nominal price from Corinth and manning seventy vessels in all defeated Aegina at sea. Fighting followed on the island, during which volunteers from Argos, a state which had already medized, were worsted by the Athenians. In the spring or early summer of 490 the Athenians withdrew after losing four ships in a naval engagement.[1] This phase of the 'unheralded' war, fought on the eve of the Persian invasion, had a salutary effect. It heightened the morale of Athens. It discouraged Aegina from placing her fleet and her harbour at the disposal of Persia. And it brought Corinth and Sparta into open sympathy with Athens. The unknown leaders of the Athenian state in this archon-year 491/90 had given proof of intelligence, courage, and determination.

§ 4. *The expedition against Eretria and Athens*

THE expeditionary force under the command of Datis and Artaphernes sailed from the Cilician coast in early summer 490. The fleet consisted of the squadrons supplied by subject peoples, Ionians and Aeolians included; the number of warships, although less than the conventional figure of 600, which Herodotus gave not only for this occasion but also for the attacks on Scythia and Miletus, was certainly sufficient to escort the transports for the infantry and cavalry and to outmatch the combined fleets of Athens and Eretria. The army, according to Herodotus, was 'numerous and well equipped'. It was an *élite* force of cavalry and infantry, recruited from the inland peoples of the empire and seasoned by training and experience. No number was given by Herodotus, and the numbers given by later authors were fantastic; but the exigencies of transportation probably limited the number of fighting troops to 25,000 at the most. The expedition was accompanied by Hippias, the head of the Peisistratidae, who counted on support in Athens and Attica.[2]

The immediate intention of Darius was to obtain control of the Cyclades and to punish Athens and Eretria for their part in the Ionian revolt. But his ultimate purpose, already revealed by the demand for 'earth and water', was to conquer and annex the Greek mainland; for without such annexation the Persian control of Thrace, Macedonia, and the Cyclades, and even of the Greek states in Asia Minor, could never be secure. In his plan of conquest the expedition of Datis and Artaphernes occupied an important place. Success would soften the will to resist and encourage those states and factions which already inclined towards submission. The fate not of Athens and Eretria alone but of the whole Greek world depended on the outcome.

The Persian force crossed the Aegean from Samos to Euboea in triumph. Naxos, which had defended itself so gallantly in 499, was punished by the

[1] 6. 87–93.   [2] 6. 94–95; Nep. *Milt.* 4; Just. 2. 9.

burning of the town and the temples and by the deportation of all who did not escape into the hills. In the other islands the Persians conscripted men for service and removed children as hostages. At Delos Datis made a dedication on the altar of Apollo and bade the Delians return from their refuge on Tenos; he hoped thereby to appease the religious sentiments of those islanders who had already submitted to Persia. On reaching the southern tip of Euboea, the Persians demanded troops and hostages from Carystus. With signal courage the Carystians refused. Their land was ravaged and their town besieged, until they yielded. This delay, when the Persian fleet lay at the mouth of the Euboic channel between Eretria and Athens, enabled Eretria to ask Athens for help. Athens promptly ordered her 4,000 cleruchs at Chalcis to reinforce Eretria. But there they found the citizens divided between resistance and submission, and on the advice of an Eretrian leader they crossed over to Attica. The Persian fleet then came to anchor off the Eretrian coast and disembarked the infantry and cavalry unopposed. The Eretrians had decided to defend their walls. For six days they withstood a violent assault, but on the seventh the city was betrayed from within. The temples were plundered and burnt, and the population was deported in accordance with the orders of Darius.[1]

A few days later the Persian fleet set sail for Attica. The Athenians may have expected the Persians to land in the bay of Phalerum, but the Persian command realized the difficulty of landing in small craft on an open coast which was defended by men and ships. The Persians, therefore, landed their troops unopposed in the bay of Marathon, which was close to their base of supply in Euboea and afforded excellent ground for cavalry action. Hippias may have played a part in this decision; for he had once defeated a Spartan landing in the bay of Phalerum, and his father had landed at Marathon and gained Athens in 546. The Persians now calculated that the plain would favour their cavalry, if the Athenian army marched out from Athens. If, however, it chose to defend the city—and this the Persian command may have expected after the example of Eretria—then the army would march into the plain of Athens, and the fleet, disencumbered of the transports, would be able to round Cape Sunium and engage any naval forces which might await them in the Saronic Gulf. At Athens the Assembly met and decided forthwith to advance to Marathon. At the same time a runner, Philippides, was dispatched to Sparta. He delivered the request for aid the next day, having travelled some 140 miles. The Spartans, however, were celebrating the festival of Apollo Carneius and a sacred law forbade any military operation until full moon, which was six days ahead. The Spartans replied that they would march from Laconia then but not before.[2]

When the Athenian army descended the foothills of Mt. Pentelicus towards the plain of Marathon, they saw the Persian troops bivouacked by the Oenoe stream, dry in September; the Persian camp to the north of the

---

[1] Hdt. 6. 96-101; *AP* 7. 256 (epitaph of the Eretrians).   [2] 6. 102-3; 105-6.

Great Marshes where springs provided abundant water; and the Persian
ships close inshore in the eastern part of the bay. The large force of Persian
cavalry dominated the plain. So long as it was present, no infantry line,
however resolute, could hope to cross the plain in the open; for its flanks and
its rear would be immediately exposed to attack by the massed squadrons of

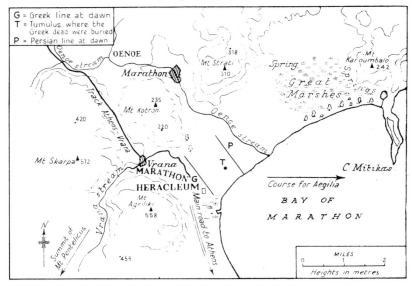

FIG. 16. Plan of Marathon

the Persian cavalry. The Persian infantry were already deployed. The length
of their line showed that they were superior in number, and they were
supported by a numerous corps of well-trained archers. The Athenians
positioned themselves in the western plain in defence of Marathon town;
their right wing, which extended to a precinct of Heracles, was defended by a
small marsh. They numbered some 10,000 hoplites, and they had brought
supplies with them; any further supplies that were necessary could be
brought in by light-armed troops. Cavalry, skirmishing troops, and archers had
not accompanied the army; for in these arms the Persians were in any case far
stronger. The Athenian army was thus simply a striking force of heavy-armed
infantry. The problem for the Athenian command was how best to strike.[1]

There was, however, no supreme commander. The decision lay with the
ten *strategoi* deliberating as a board. On this occasion the ten generals were
equally divided in their opinions. Five wished not to precipitate an en-

[1] Paus. 10. 20. 2; Nep. *Milt.* 5; Just. 2. 9; Arist. *Rh.* 1411ᵃ10; Schol. D. 19. 303.; Hdt.
6. 112. 2. See *StGH* 170–250 for the campaign and battle.

gagement. Their reasons were probably that the Athenian force was outnumbered, and that, if they delayed, the Spartan army might arrive; moreover, the ground had been chosen by the Persians and the Persian cavalry
were redoubtable. The other five wished to engage. They were headed by
Miltiades, who had himself proposed the motion in the Athenian Assembly
to march out to Marathon. He had had first-hand experience of the Persian
army during the Scythian campaign and subsequently during two periods of
rule in the Chersonese; and he was a determined and forceful personality.
Among his supporters was Aristides, a man respected for courage and integrity. The generals being equally divided, it was decided to summon the
polemarchos, Callimachus, who was of course not present at the meeting, and
to give him a vote in accordance with an earlier practice. Miltiades intercepted
Callimachus and won him over. The policy of engagement was adopted
through Callimachus' vote. Next, the operational command was held by each
general in turn for one day. Aristides now allocated his day of operational
command to Miltiades, and the three other supporting generals did likewise.
Thus, in effect, Miltiades became supreme commander, with the limitation
that he only held operational command on five days out of ten. He now waited,
hoping that the Persian cavalry would make a false move or some other
chance would enable him to attack. When the opportunity came, it happened
to fall on his own day of command. By that time the full force of the Plataeans, numbering about a thousand men of all arms, had arrived to reinforce
the Athenian army.[1]

Meanwhile the Persians maintained their position. They could afford to
do so, because supplies were easily ferried over from Euboea and the horses
could be watered and grazed at night in the northern part of the plain, where
there were strong springs and marshy ground. By day the cavalry, infantry,
and archers stood ready for any attack which the impetuous Greeks might
make on ground favourable to the Persians. While they were waiting, the
Greeks advanced their position to within a little less than a mile's distance
of the Persian line by felling trees and making rough stockades in the plain.
One night before dawn some Ionian soldiers, who were serving in the Persian
army, came to the stockades and passed a message to the Athenians: 'the
cavalry are away'.[2]

Miltiades acted at once. The Greek army was bivouacked at night in order
of battle, Athenians on the right and in the centre and Plataeans on the left.
As the men fell in, Miltiades extended the line, so as to equal the length
of the Persian line, and strengthened both wings with additional files of
men, thus thinning the centre. Callimachus made sacrifice to the gods.
The omens were favourable. As dawn was breaking the Greek line advanced
rapidly across the plain. When it came within range of the Persian arrows, the
men charged at the double and hurled themselves upon the Persian infantry.

[1] Hdt. 6. 109–10; Plu. *Arist.* 5; Hdt. 6. 108. 1.
[2] Hdt. 6. 108. 1; Nep. *Milt.* 5; Suid. *Khoris Hippeis*.

On the wings the greater depth of men, fighting with better defensive armour and with longer spears than the Persians, routed their opponents. In the centre the thinner line was broken and driven back by the Persians, who pursued their advantage. The Greek wings, however, wheeled and reformed to attack the Persian centre from the rear. A mêlée ensued, in which the Persian cavalry could not intervene effectively. The battle raged for long, but at last the Persians fled towards the Great Marshes, closely pursued by the Greeks. With the loss of seven ships the Persian fleet embarked the last of their men and stood out to sea. There they picked up the the Eretrian prisoners, who had been held on the island Aegilia, and set sail southwards for Cape Sunium and Athens.[1]

When the Persian fleet stood out to sea, Athenians on the battlefield noticed that a shield reflecting the rays of the morning sun was signalling to the Persians from a point inland. Such a signal meant treachery at Athens. Leaving part of his force to guard the spoil on the battlefield, Miltiades led his army in a forced march to Athens.[2] When the Persian fleet arrived off the strand at Phalerum, they saw the Athenian army already encamped in the precinct of Heracles at Cynosarges outside the walls. It was impossible now to land and surprise the city. The Persian seamen rested on their oars awhile, and then the fleet set sail for Asia. On the following day the vanguard of the Lacedaemonian army arrived, two thousand strong; they had marched some 140 miles in three days, leaving Sparta as soon as the moon had reached its full. They went on to Marathon to view the battlefield. There they saw the dead, the Athenians numbering 192 and the Persians 6,400, and noted the shorter spear and wicker shield of the Persian infantryman, clad not in bronze helmet, cuirass, and greaves like a Greek infantryman but in bonnet, tunic (protected sometimes with scales of iron), and close-fitting trousers. They studied, too, the lie of the land and the tactics of Miltiades. They then returned to Athens, congratulated the Athenian army on its action, and marched south for Laconia. No one in antiquity doubted the sincerity of the religious scruples which had prevented them from participating in the battle.[3]

To the student of ancient battles there always remain some unanswered problems. The battle of Marathon is no exception. For instance, our authorities give no reason for the absence of the Persian cavalry, which alone made it

---

[1] Hdt. 6. 111–15; Just. 2. 9.

[2] Plu. *Arist.* 5. Taking the direct route over Mt. Pentelicus, I walked fast from Athens to the mound at Marathon in 6 hours and returned the same day to Athens in 7 hours. The minimum time for the army's forced march and encamping at Cynosarges must have been 8 to 9 hours. Arriving before sundown at 6.30 on a September day, they therefore left Marathon between 9 and 10 a.m. The sun was then east of south, which was suitable for a shield-signal to reach the Persian fleet lying offshore to the east. As the battle was a long one and the embarkation was contested, the battle began probably about dawn, that is at about 5.30 in September. The Ionians, too, must have crossed the plain in the dark, so as to pass unobserved by the Persians; and what they had to say would have been obvious in daylight.   [3] Hdt. 6. 115–20; Pl. *Lg.* 698 c; *Mx.* 240 c.

possible for the Athenian infantry to advance across the plain. One authority states that Datis was absent with the cavalry, and another that he was present during the battle, presumably in the final phase when the battle was already lost.[1] But we know enough to realize the brilliance of Miltiades' generalship at every stage: his decision to march to Marathon, his determination to attack, his grasp of the suitable opportunity, and his tactical disposition of the infantry line. The charge by the infantry without opening a gap in the line and the wheeling of the wings to support the centre show a very high degree of skill and discipline in the Athenian hoplites. In hand-to-hand fighting their defeat of a more numerous enemy was due to their courage, spearmanship, and protective armour. At this crisis in her fate Athens produced the ablest general and the finest infantry force in her whole history.

The defeat of the Persians at Marathon, like the repulse of the Spanish Armada, was publicly commemorated in a noble work of art. A painting in the Poikile Stoa or 'Painted Colonnade' showed three phases of the battle: the charge at full speed by the Plataeans and Athenians and the first hand-to-hand fighting, then the enemy fleeing in disorder into the marsh, and finally the Greeks cutting down the Persians as they fled to the Phoenician ships. On the Greek side there were portraits of Callimachus, who fell fighting; Miltiades, cheering his men on; Cynegirus, whose arm was severed as he grasped the stern of an enemy ship; Epizelus, who was struck blind during the battle; and Aeschylus, the dramatist. On the Persian side there were portraits of Datis and Artaphernes. But the places of honour were taken by the gods and the heroes, who were believed to have appeared in person—Marathon, Theseus, Athena, and Heracles.[2]

The victory of Marathon did not avert the invasion of Greece by Persia. It keyed the fighting spirit of Athens to the highest pitch. It showed to Sparta the conditions under which Greek infantry could defeat Persian infantry. It inspired other Greek states with the will to resist. These three consequences were indispensable to the future salvation of Greece. In this sense the battle of Marathon was a decisive event in world history.

[1] Suid. loc. cit.; Ctes. 18. Many speculations have been made to account for the absence of the cavalry. It has been suggested, for instance, that the cavalry embarked on the transports; but, if the Persians intended to withdraw, they would have held the plain with their cavalry while the infantry embarked and then taken off the mobile force of cavalry elsewhere unmolested. The suggestion that the cavalry had gone ahead when the Persian army was about to march off southwards is equally unlikely; for the cavalry would have been used to hold the plain and give protection to the flank and rear of the army. It is more probable that the cavalry were grazing and watering their horses by the springs in the northern plain during the hours of darkness between moonset and sunrise, and that they were delayed or late for some reason not known to us. In that case the cavalry returned in the last phase of the battle, when the fighting was confused and the Persian infantry worsted; and the commander of the cavalry was in fact portrayed in the scene of the battle in the Poikile Stoa, and the ghostly echoes of the battle were the neighing of horses and the clashing of arms.

[2] Paus. 1. 15. 4; for epigrams see *The Aegean and the Near East* (Studies presented to H. Goldman), p. 268, and for coins see Plate XII *a*.

The Persian force brought back the prisoners from Naxos and Eretria. Darius settled the Eretrians near Susa, where they preserved their language and customs, and he received the report of the Persian command on the defeat at Marathon. It was clear that the conquest of Greece could not be achieved by a sea-borne expeditionary force. He therefore planned a full-scale invasion by military and naval forces. To this end he issued orders for the training of cavalry, infantry, and seamen conscripted from the different communities of the empire, for the provision of warships and transports, and for the accumulation of supplies. The planning and preparation covered three years, but the invasion was postponed. For in 487 Egypt rose in revolt. Darius proposed to deploy the great forces which he had mustered against both Egypt and Greece, but he died in the following year.[1] His successor, Xerxes, was urged by the Peisistratidae to proceed with the invasion of Greece, where the Aleuadae in Thessaly offered him their assistance. For the moment, however, he turned against Egypt, which was reduced to obedience in 485. In the following years Xerxes prepared to invade Greece. He already held many of the Greek islands and the whole of the north Aegean coast, along which he intended to march. In view of the Persian disaster off Mt. Athos in 492, a canal was driven through the neck of the peninsula, which was nearly a mile and a half wide and rose at the highest point some fifty feet above sea-level. The canal was dug in the years 483-1 by forced labour, and the Persian fleet, operating from its base at Elaeus in the Chersonese, afforded protection against attack from the sea. In these years the Greek states had ample warning of Xerxes' intentions.[2]

[1] Hdt. 6. 119; 7. 1; the heralds of Darius, who were killed at Athens and Sparta (Hdt. 7. 133), may have been sent at this time. The story is usually regarded as unhistorical, but Herodotus' informants seem to have been Spartans, who would hardly invent it.

[2] 7. 20-23.

CHAPTER 4

Xerxes' Invasion of Greece

§ 1. *The naval and political preparations of Athens*

IT was probably in 489 that Miltiades was given command of the Athenian navy, numbering seventy ships, and operated in the Cyclades. Through these islands Datis and Artaphernes had crossed from Samos; most of them had submitted to Persia and taken part willy-nilly in the attacks on Carystus, Eretria, and Athens. The intention of the Athenian Assembly was no doubt to punish those who had medized, perhaps by the exaction of fines, and to deprive Persia of her naval stations in the central Aegean. Paros, the richest and most powerful of the Cyclades since the destruction of her neighbour Naxos, resisted and was besieged. Miltiades offered peace on payment of 100 talents, but the Parians refused. On the twenty-sixth day Miltiades abandoned the siege and withdrew to Athens. There he was put on trial and condemned. Shortly afterwards he died from the effects of a wound sustained at Paros.[1] The audacious policy of following up the victory at Marathon, despite the fact that the Persian navy was intact and dominated the Aegean, may reasonably be ascribed to Miltiades. It certainly died with him. Thereafter Athens let the initiative revert to Persia.

The trial of Miltiades was political in character. At Athens the struggle for political power was not waged, as in a modern state, between organized parties with specific programmes but between leading personalities, whose attitude towards one another might vary with the question at issue. Except in the case of an outstanding individual such as Themistocles, these personalities were members of the wealthy and aristocratic clans, which had dominated Athenian politics throughout the sixth century.[2] For, although the electoral reform of Cleisthenes had put many departments of state beyond the reach of a clan's influence, the archons and the generals were appointed by direct election by the people as a whole.[3] As there were no preliminary elections by smaller units but the whole people voted outright, clan pressure could be effective and clan leaders be returned to office. The appointment of such leaders was not harmful in itself. For the aristocrats were able and experienced. Their leadership in politics and in war commanded respect, and they were answerable not only to the body of their peers, the Areopagus, but also to the people. But harmful consequences sprang from the fact that the aristocratic leaders fought between themselves for power. The rival groups into which they formed were impermanent, and the policy of individuals fluctuated.

[1] 6. 132–6; Nep. *Milt.* 7–8.   [2] Arist. *Ath.* 28.   [3] *St GH* 353 f.

Cleisthenes himself was an outstanding example. His family, the Alcmeonids, contracted a marriage alliance with Peisistratus and supported him in 556. They then opposed him and were banished in 546. Cleisthenes then joined the Peisistratidae and served as archon in 525. Banished by them, he enlisted the aid of Sparta. Ousted by Isagoras, he opposed Sparta and negotiated with Persia. In 510 he sought influence in the political clubs of the aristocrats, and in 508 his failure there led him to turn to the people. Such fluctuations were hazardous for the state, and the danger of a *coup d'état* by an ambitious aristocrat was always present. After Cleisthenes' reforms the struggle for power continued. But the conditions of the game were now altered. For, while the players for the highest stakes remained the same, the people sitting as the Ecclesia or the Heliaea became a strong and decisive umpire, capable of inflicting the severest penalties.

The career of Miltiades was almost as chequered as that of Cleisthenes. He had served as archon under the Peisistratidae in 524 and had opposed them thereafter, when it was believed that they were responsible for the murder of his father, Cimon. He had himself been tyrant in the Chersonese twice; he had served under Persia and against Persia. Now that he had failed at Paros, his rivals attacked him before the people, sitting in full Assembly. The charge was 'deception of the people', a form of treason. The prosecution demanded the death sentence, and the people were the jury and the judge. The prosecution was led by Xanthippus, an aristocrat of the Buzygae, who had married the Alcmeonid Agariste. The Buzygae and the Alcmeonidae had probably opposed Miltiades' clan, the Philaidae, before and during the campaign of Marathon. His trial in 493/2 on the charge of tyranny would come well from the family of Cleisthenes, the enemy of tyrants. When the generals at Marathon were equally divided, Miltiades argued that delay would result in dissension at Athens; and his argument was later upheld by the popular belief that the signal with the shield was made by his rivals, the Alcmeonids.[1] Whether the argument and the belief were correct, we cannot tell; but they illustrate political feeling on the eve of Miltiades' trial.

The defendant lay on a stretcher, unable to conduct his own defence. He was defended by his friends, the leaders probably of his own and other aristocratic clans. For Miltiades was known as 'the leader of the notables' in contrast to Xanthippus 'the leader of the people's faction'. The defence emphasized the services of Miltiades to Athens as conqueror of Lemnos and victor of Marathon. It was probably in recognition of these services that Miltiades was condemned not to death but to a fine of fifty talents, a huge sum, which was discharged later by his son, Cimon.[2] He was the first of many great statesmen whom the verdict of the Athenian people sentenced to disgrace, exile, or death.

Now that the dominant figure of Miltiades was removed, the field was open

[1] Hdt. 6. 109. 5; 115; for Miltiades' career, which is disputed, see *CQ* 6. 113.
[2] 6. 136; Arist. *Ath.* 28. 2; Nep. *Milt.* 8–9; Pl. *G.* 516 d.

for a struggle between the political leaders. But the threat of invasion, first by Darius and then by Xerxes, made a clear choice by the people imperative. In 488 a selective procedure, known as ostracism, was employed. The people cast their votes against any politician whom they wished to expel, by inscribing his name on a potsherd (*ostrakon*), and the man whose name appeared on most potsherds was expelled for ten years. Whether ostracism was invented by Cleisthenes *c.* 507 or by an unknown statesman in 488, is uncertain. The second alternative rests on stronger authority and corresponds better with the circumstances of its first application. In any event the aim and the effect of ostracism during the years 488 to 481 are not in doubt. Whoever proposed the law of ostracism intended to expel the leaders of the Peisistratid party and of clans related to the Peisistratidae by blood or marriage. Such were its first victims in 488 to 486: Hipparchus, son of Charmus, who was the leading Peisistratid in Athens; and Megacles, son of Hippocrates, and probably Callixenus, son of Aristonymus, who were leading members of the Alcmeonid clan. Ostracism then extended its scope: Xanthippus, the prosecutor of Miltiades, was ostracized in 485, and Aristides, the colleague of Miltiades at Marathon, was ostracized in 483 or 482.

Excavation at Athens has yielded hundreds of ostraka which date from this decade. Among them all the names occur which we have mentioned; and in addition ostraka were cast against Hippocrates, son of Anaxileus, and Callixenus, son of Cleisthenes, both probably being Alcmeonids, Boutalion of Marathon, and Themistocles of Phrearri. By this process of elimination the Athenian people chose as its leader for the war with Persia Themistocles of Phrearri. Once the choice was clear and the invasion imminent, a general amnesty was enacted and the victims of ostracism were recalled.[1] In 480 Athens was more united than in 490, and her chosen leader Themistocles was no less able than Miltiades had been.

In 487 a reform was carried in the method of appointing the nine archons. Hitherto they had been elected by the people. Now they were selected by lot from 500 candidates, who were themselves elected by their fellow-demesmen, each deme returning a number of candidates in proportion to its size.[2] The conditions of candidature were not changed. The candidates were still required to belong to one of the two highest property-classes, and the nine successful candidates were scrutinized by the Council of Five Hundred. This reform had several effects. It undermined the influence of the great clans; for the lot was impartial in its selection. It decreased the political importance of the archonships; for in the past an archon had commanded the publicly avowed support of a large section of the people, but now he rested on the votes of a single deme. It increased the political importance of the generalship (*strategia*). For the generalship remained elective. Ambitious men who

---

[1] *FGrH* 324 F 6 (Androtion); Arist. *Ath.* 22; Pi *P.* 7 (Megacles); And. 1. 77; 107; *Hesp.* Suppl. 8 (1949), 394; *Hesp.* 19 (1950), 376; 21 (1952), 1. For ostracism see further p. 263.
[2] Arist. *Ath.* 22. 5; the later procedure in 55. 1 is no guide for 487.

wished to obtain that public avowal of support which imparts political influence now stood as candidates not for the archonship but for the generalship. In consequence the generals tended to become political as well as military leaders. In course of time the reform affected the personnel and the prestige of the Areopagus Council, since the Council recruited its members from the ex-archons. The archons indeed continued to be efficient and experienced representatives of the two wealthier classes. But they were not, as they had generally been in the past, the leaders of the great clans, which occupied a central position not only in the political but also in the religious life of the state. In 487 the immediate aim of the reform was similar to that of ostracism. It limited the field of clan rivalry, and it threw additional emphasis on the fact that, if Athens was to survive the Persian invasion, she must concentrate on the election of a supreme commander.

In 483 the Persians began to cut the canal through the neck of the Athos peninsula. This showed that a large Persian fleet would accompany the army of invasion. In late 483 or early 482 a rich vein of silver was struck in the state-owned mines at Laurium, so that the state had at its disposal a sum of 100 talents. The disposal of this sum was debated in the Assembly. While some proposed to distribute it among the citizens, Themistocles urged that it be used to raise the fleet to a strength of 200 warships. The argument which chiefly swayed the Athenians was that Athens with her outmoded and smaller fleet could not defeat Aegina. For, although Aegina had taken no action during the expedition by Datis and Artaphernes, the two states were still at war and no doubt harried one another's shipping. Athens' hatred of her neighbour Aegina was stronger than her fear of a Persian invasion, which had already been deferred once by the death of Darius and might be deferred again. At the same time the danger of a Persian invasion must have been present in the minds of the people and of the speakers. Whether Athens would meet that invasion on land or at sea, or indeed on both elements, could not be foreseen; but, if the invaders came south and Aegina medized, Athens would be helpless at sea with a fleet inferior to that of Aegina.

The Athenians, therefore, approved the proposal of Themistocles. The keels of 100 triremes were laid early in 482. The timber may have been supplied by Alexander, king of Macedon, who combined nominal submission to Persia with friendship towards Athens; for the Persian fleet, operating between Mt. Athos and the Chersonese, would have prevented any export to Athens of Thracian or Thasian timber. And the training of crews for a larger fleet than Athens had had hitherto may have begun in these years. The proposal of Themistocles was in accord with his fortification of the Peiraeus in 493–2, the year of his archonship. His consistent policy was to make Athens a naval power as well as a land power. In this he met with opposition, led perhaps by Aristides. At about this time Aristides was ostracized, and Themistocles' ascendancy was confirmed. In the event this proved to be the salvation of Greece.[1]

[1] Hdt. 7. 144; 8. 79; 136. 1; Th. 1. 14. 3; Arist. *Ath.* 22. 7; Plu. *Them.* 4.

§ 2. *Sparta and the Greek Congress*

ALTHOUGH the Greek states of the mainland admired Athens for her victory at Marathon, they looked for leadership not to her but to Sparta. Athens had no following, and her neighbours were hostile. Sparta was the head of a great Alliance; among her followers she counted the neighbours of Athens—Megara, Aegina, and Thebes—and she had a practical and probably a formal alliance with Athens herself. Her influence was thus paramount among the Greek states. At the same time her prestige as a military power and as leader of a military Alliance stood very high since the crushing defeat of Argos at Sepeia. So far as the mainland states were concerned, military power had always counted for more than naval power; and, if Persia invaded by land, it was likely that only a military coalition would save their territories from being overrun. The whole problem of any organized resistance to the Persians therefore centred on Sparta. In this matter her own position was clear. She had consistently opposed Persia. Her desire to assist Athens in 490 had been genuine; for no one doubted the sincerity of Sparta's religious scruples. When Xerxes asked the Greek states for the tokens of submission, he did not approach Sparta and Athens. They were marked out as the object of his attack.[1]

For spiritual leadership the Greek states looked to the oracle of Apollo at Delphi in summer 481. They received no encouragement. Sparta was told that the will of Zeus was with the Persians, and that either Sparta town would be sacked or a Spartan king slain. Argos was bidden to sit still with her spear at the ready and guard her head. The envoys of Athens had hardly entered the sanctuary, when the Pythia bade them begone to the ends of the world. 'Unenviable is your lot; for the city is overwhelmed by fire and fierce Ares, who pursues in his Syrian chariot.' Afraid to return with this terrible prophecy, the envoys re-entered the sanctuary as suppliants and received a second response, which again described the fall of the city but continued with a less discouraging ambiguity:

> Safe shall the wooden wall continue for thee and thy children.
> Wait not the tramp of the horse, nor the footmen mightly moving
> Over the land, but turn your back to the foe and retire ye.
> Yet shall a day arrive when ye shall meet him in battle.
> Holy Salamis, thou shalt destroy the offspring of women,
> When men scatter the seed, or when they gather the harvest.

These oracles showed a consistent attitude. The city of Athens would be destroyed and, if the Athenians heeded the first oracle, they would migrate westwards like the Phocaeans in the past. The town of Sparta would be destroyed or else the state would suffer heavily in battle. As Xerxes had singled out these two states only for attack, Argos was advised to remain neutral.[2]

---

[1] Th. 1. 102. 4; 1. 18. 2; Hdt. 7. 133.   [2] Hdt. 7. 220; 148; 140.

The oracles were discussed by the Assembly at Athens in September 481. On the proposal of Themistocles 'the Athenians decided to receive the impending invasion of Greece by the barbarian with their full forces on their warships, in obedience to the god, together with any Greeks who were willing' (Hdt. 7. 144. 3). The corollary was the evacuation of Attica, ordered by the god in both oracles. The decision was courageous and epoch-making; for the victorious infantry of Marathon chose to become 'a naval people' (Thuc. 1. 18. 2). Action was to be taken immediately, 100 ships being sent to receive the impending invasion at Artemisium and the other 100 ships to lie in wait off Salamis for any attacking ships of Aegina, with whom Athens was still at war. The Decree of Themistocles set up at Troezen some two centuries later was based on the original decree of September 481 according to the present writer.[1] It provided for the property of the gods, the evacuation of Attica, and the call-up of 40,000 men for the fleet of 200 triremes. The Decree envisaged resistance 'together with Sparta, Corinth and [? Chalcis] and any state willing to share the danger'. Representatives of the willing states met at Sparta in October. They formed an alliance, made Sparta their commander, and ended wars among themselves, including the Athens–Aegina war.[2] They sent spies to Asia; these were caught and sent back by Xerxes with reports of enormous forces. They sent envoys to Argos, Crete, Corcyra, and Syracuse 'in the hope that the Greek world might become one' (Hdt. 7. 145). Meanwhile Xerxes had sent his envoys into Greece. They returned about January to report submission by many northern states and all Boeotia save Thespiae and Plataea (Hdt. 7. 131–2). By that time these states had been made to recant by the Greek allies.

At Argos the Council offered to join the alliance, if she received a truce with Sparta and an equal share in the command. The Spartans among the envoys offered a third share and proposed to refer the question of the truce to the Spartan Assembly. The Council rejected the offer.

Whether Argos entered into friendly relations with Persia was a matter of dispute in antiquity; but the allies knew that, if Xerxes passed the Isthmus, he would probably be joined by the army of Argos. In Crete the states consulted Delphi. The response of the oracle was such that they refused forthwith to aid the mainland Greeks. At Corcyra the envoys received promises of help. But, when the crisis came, the Corcyraean squadron of sixty ships had not yet rounded the Peloponnese; this delay caused the suspicion that they procrastinated deliberately, so as not to commit themselves against Persia.

From Corcyra the envoys went on to solicit the aid of Gelon, ruler of Syracuse. He offered large forces but on the condition that Sparta ceded the command to him. When the Spartan envoy refused, Gelon asked for the command by sea only; but the Athenian envoy refused on the ground that, if

---

[1] *JHS* 102 (1982) 75–93. The decree is in Meiggs-Lewis *GHI* no. 23. Other scholars refer it to some situation in 480.

[2] Paus. 3. 12. 6; Hdt. 7. 145. 1.

Sparta resigned the command by sea, it should pass to Athens. Gelon then withdrew his offer, and the envoys returned. As a neutral Gelon sent his own observer, Cadmus, with a large sum of money to the centre of neutrality, Delphi. There, if the Persians triumphed, Cadmus was to give the money to Xerxes and to tender the tokens of submission, earth and water.[1]

In the spring of 480 the Greek allies met at the Isthmus. Their organization had now taken shape. The nucleus of power around which it was built was the Spartan Alliance, 'the Lacedaemonians and their Allies'. This nucleus was emphasized twice by Herodotus: once when the envoys visited Gelon and discussed the command of the allies with him, and again when Athens was offered a separate peace and Sparta in the name of her Alliance promised sanctuary to the Athenian civilians.[2] As Sparta certainly held the initiative, she might have been tempted to use the existing framework of her own Alliance. This, however, she did not do. For the organization of the Greek allies, in which she played the leading part, was different in structure and in extent. Whereas the Spartan Alliance had two deliberative organs, the Spartan state and the congress of Sparta's allies, the Greek allies against Persia had a single Congress. In this Congress each allied state, Sparta included, was represented by its elected delegates (*probouloi*), cast a single vote, and was bound by a majority decision. After the preliminary meeting the Congress met not at Sparta but at the Isthmus. The command did not pass automatically, as in the Spartan Alliance, into the hands of Sparta; it was the subject of discussion by the delegates at the Congress.[3] The fact that Sparta did not seek to extend her own Alliance and assert her own supremacy, but preferred to treat as an equal with the other states and let them choose their leader, is an outstanding mark of her far-sighted statesmanship. The champion of freedom respected the full freedom of her associates in the cause of Greece.

The title of the new organization was 'The Greeks'.[4] It was now a League with a collective name—'The League of the Greeks' or the Greek League, as we shall call it—and with an administrative organ in its Congress. Potentially all Greeks were members; in actuality only those who had sworn to defend Greece against Persia. The functions of the Congress were wide. It decided the general strategy of the Greeks, allocated the command, and determined the contribution of troops and money.[5] It took the oath against medizing states, exacted punishment from them, and summoned individual medizers to face trial. It appointed envoys to negotiate with other states, and it made dedications in the name of 'The Greeks' from the spoils of victory. Thus the organization operated in the military, diplomatic, financial, judicial, and religious fields. If the Greek world had ever become one, the Greek League and its Congress might have served as models for the expression of Greek unity.[6]

[1] 7. 148–71.   [2] 7. 157. 1; 8. 142. 4.
[3] 7. 172. 1; D.S. 11. 1; Hdt. 8. 2–3.
[4] Hdt. 7. 173. 1 and generally; Th. 1. 132. 2; Plu. *Arist.* 21. 1; *Them.* 23 fin.
[5] Paus. 3. 12. 5; Hdt. 7. 173; Plu. *Arist.* 24. 1.
[6] Hdt. 7. 132; 9. 86; Plu. *Them.* 23 fin.; *Arist.* 21.

The number of states whose membership was recognized after the battle of Plataea was thirty-one, and their names were recorded, under the heading 'the following fought the war', on a bronze stand formed of three serpents and set up at Delphi. A golden tripod, which rested on the stand, was dedicated by the Greeks as firstfruits won from the Persians.[1] The order in which the names were inscribed is probably the order in which they joined the Greek League.[2] The list ran as follows: Lacedaemonians, Athenians, Corinthians, Tegeans, Sicyonians, Aeginetans, Megarians, Epidaurians, Orchomenians, Phliasians, Troezenians, Hermioneans, Tirynthians, Plataeans, Thespians, Mycenaeans, Ceans, Melians, Tenians, Naxians, Eretrians, Chalcidians, Styreans, Eleans, Potidaeans, Leucadians, Anactorians, Cythnians, Siphnians, Ambraciotes, and Lepreats. Of these some joined the cause late; there were also others who participated but were not accredited in 479.

The most influential states were Sparta at the head of her own Alliance; Athens, with her cleruchs from Chalcis and her close adherents, Plataea and Thespiae; and Corinth, with some of her colonies, Potidaea, Leucas, Anactorium, and Ambracia. The bulk of military strength came from within the Peloponnese, and the bulk of naval strength from the states of the Saronic Gulf. These facts had some bearing on the strategy of the Greeks as the campaign developed. The largest military force which the Greeks deployed came near to 40,000 heavy-armed infantry and 70,000 light-armed infantry; but, once Thessaly medized, their cavalry was negligible. The corresponding naval force came near to 400 triremes and a smaller number of penteconters. From the outset the Greeks knew that they would be outnumbered on both elements. They therefore intended to hold narrow positions, where the superior numbers of the enemy could not be brought into immediate effect; and, in addition, they had to choose such a position on land that, if it was turned, their forces would not be rounded up by the strong squadrons of Persian cavalry.

In planning its general organization the Congress of 'The Greeks' had recent experiences in mind. In arranging the system of command it showed that it had learnt the lessons of the Ionian revolt and of the campaign of Marathon. The supreme command on both elements was now vested in Sparta; it was exercised on each element by a single Spartan commander. Within the framework of strategy, which was imposed by the Congress of the Greeks, the Spartan commander made the operational decisions. His orders were issued to the allied contingents. Each contingent was led by a single native commander, such local peculiarities as the rotating command between ten generals at Athens being abrogated. The supreme commander, a Spartan general or admiral as the case might be, generally consulted the commanders of the allied contingents who sat in conference with him; but he did not have

---

[1] Th. 1. 132. 2–3; Hdt. 9. 81; Paus. 10. 13. 5; Plu. *Them.* 20; *GHI* 19.

[2] The Tenians were inserted later (Hdt. 8. 82); the Potidaeans may have joined before they revolted from Persian rule (Hdt. 8. 126).

to obtain their majority vote in favour of his tactics.[1] This system of command had great practical advantages. It made possible the co-ordination of amphibious operations, the conduct of a consistent strategy, and the taking of rapid decisions. That thirty states agreed to put their contingents unreservedly under the supreme command of a Spartan nominee gives some measure of their intelligence and of Spartan prestige.

When the Congress met at Corinth, Xerxes was advancing from Sardis towards the Hellespont. The Thessalian states which were opposed to the medizing policy of the Aleuadae of Larisa sent envoys to the Congress, and asked the allies to defend the pass of Tempe, leading from Macedonia to Thessaly. The Thessalians offered to co-operate in the defence; but if a strong force was not sent north they could not hold out and perforce would come to terms with Persia. The Congress agreed to the Thessalian request. A force of 10,000 hoplites, commanded by the Spartan Euaenetus and including Themistocles among its contingent commanders, was transported by sea to Halus in south Thessaly. Thence it marched through the plain to occupy the narrow vale of Tempe, where it was joined by the Thessalian cavalry—the strongest body of cavalry in Greece. There they learnt that the vale of Tempe could be turned by a pass through Perrhaebia. The coast, too, was unsuitable for any naval action in support of the army, since the waters were open and the coast southwards was dangerously rockbound and harbourless. Envoys, too, arrived from Alexander, the king of Macedon, who warned the Greeks to withdraw, before the large numbers of the Persian army and navy surrounded and destroyed them. The Greek force after a few days returned to the Isthmus.[2]

Strategically the decision was wise. The Greeks had not sufficient troops to hold the three or four passes which might be used by the enemy, and their navy could not prevent the landing of Persian troops to the south of Tempe. Politically the decision was unfortunate. North Greece was now exposed to the Persian onset. The states had little option but to submit, especially as they had already medized in autumn 481. Xerxes accepted the submission of the Thessalians and their neighbours (Dolopes, Aenianes, Perrhaebi, Magnetes, Achaeans of Phthiotis, and Malians), as he marched south, and he knew that there were strong pro-Persian parties in all the states north of Attica, with the exception of Phocis. Thus the first move by the Greeks was a mistaken one. If they had begun by occupying the position which they next adopted at Thermopylae, they might have retained the support of some of the peoples of central Greece and avoided the discouragement of retreating without any action. All that the allies could do was to reiterate the oath to dedicate to the god of Delphi every tenth man of any medizing state.[3]

[1] Hdt. 8. 2; 74–75; 79–81; 9. 21; 46; 51.
[2] 7. 172–4.
[3] 7. 132; D.S. 11. 3.

§ 3. *The Persians force the passage of Thermopylae*

THE host which Xerxes led into Greece was said by Herodotus to have exceeded 5,000,000 souls and consequently to have drunk many a river dry. The actual numbers cannot have been so great. Nevertheless, the total of combatants and non-combatants in the army and the navy was probably in the region of 500,000. The problem of supplying so great a force was serious. Foodstuffs were dumped in advance at points in Thrace and Macedonia, and further supplies were ferried over from Asia Minor.[1] By the time that the force reached Attica much of its manpower must have been engaged in guarding lines of communication and in bringing supplies forward for men and horses. In this service the fleet played its part. Under the protection of the warships convoys of merchantmen brought up supplies more rapidly than could be done by a baggage-train moving over the stony tracks. Because the army was dependent on the navy, they tended to advance together from one main position to the next. An equally serious problem was that of movement. Whereas during the Ionian revolt the three Persian armies had moved independently and rapidly, the host of Xerxes—both army and navy—advanced *en masse*. As it used porters, pack animals, and wagons to transport its gear, the speed of the general advance was that of the slowest animal. Despite the fact that bridges had been built over the Hellespont and the Strymon and the army was driven over under the lash, five months passed between leaving Abydus and invading Attica. During this period there were only three days of fighting. The very size and slowness of the Persian host contributed to its failure. For, when September came and wintry weather was in sight, it was clear that so great a host could not be maintained on the slender resources of central Greece for long.[2]

The composition of the Persian army was described by Herodotus on two occasions.[3] His narrative for the first occasion, when the army marched out of Sardis, may be derived ultimately from reliable eyewitnesses. The baggage-train went first and a mixed horde of many nations came next. Then after an interval the *élite* forces came marching before and behind the chariots of Ahura-Mazda, the supreme god of Persia, and of Xerxes, the king of kings. These picked troops were 2,000 cavalry and 2,000 spearmen. Behind them came 10,000 cavalry and 10,000 infantry, the latter known as 'the Immortals'. These troops were all Persian. After an interval the rest of the army followed in disorder. Among the horde of many nations there were certainly good fighting troops from Media, Bactria, India, the Caspian steppes, and other parts of the empire. For the second occasion, when Herodotus described the review of the army by Xerxes at Doriscus, he probably drew ultimately on a

---

[1] Hdt. 7. 184–6; 7. 25; the lowest figures for the fighting force in the army were 500,000 at Thermopylae (Ctes. 23 fin.; Just. 2. 11) and for the whole army 800,000 at Doriscus (Ctes. 23 init.; D.S. 11. 3. 7); the crews of 1,200 warships numbered about 240,000 men.

[2] Hdt. 7. 56; A. *Pers.* 790–4.   [3] 7. 40–41; 60–87.

Persian army-list, which gave not the forces on this expedition but the total forces of the Persian empire. This description is only valuable for our purpose in so far as it gives an account of equipment. The light cavalry were mainly armed with the javelin and the bow, which enabled them to harass the enemy infantry from a distance. The heavy cavalry were armed with the spear, which was intended for use at close quarters; they wore bronze or iron helmets and scaled breastplates, which withstood most blows. The former were probably mounted on small horses, similar to those bred in Greece. But the latter rode large warhorses, which were bred in Media and outpaced the swiftest horses of Greece. The heavy cavalry were able to engage Greek hoplites at close quarters.[1] The infantry of the line were armed with a short spear, a dagger, and a wicker shield; they generally wore a soft tiara or turban, quilted or scaled tunics, and trousers. In addition, they carried a larger bow than was usual in Greek warfare. Such infantry had already been outclassed in close fighting by the Greek hoplites at Marathon. But Xerxes also brought infantry from Asia Minor and recruited more in central and north Greece, who were equipped with the longer spear and sword of the Greek hoplite and with his protective armour of metal shield, helmet, cuirass, and greaves. Other infantry, such as the Sacae, fought at close quarters with the battle-axe or the scimitar, and there were many light infantry who served as archers, javelinmen, and slingers. The fighting forces were supported by sappers and pioneers, who were skilled in the construction of pontoon-bridges and of roads, and by a service corps, which was efficiently organized.

The fleet which Herodotus described[2] was probably that which mustered off Doriscus. There were 1,200 triremes, of which the fastest under oar or sail were the Phoenician. The largest squadrons came from Phoenicia, Egypt, and Cyprus; but some 300 vessels were supplied by those Greek states which had been reduced during and after the Ionian revolt. The crews were equipped for deck-fighting; many of them were armed in the Greek style, but the Phoenicians, Egyptians, and Cyprians wore less protective armour. The marines, which each trireme carried, were Persians, Medes, or Sacae; these were armed like infantrymen. The Phoenician triremes were probably larger and faster than the best Greek triremes. But they were less handy and less stoutly built for ramming. They were designed and equipped rather for boarding tactics.[3] The triremes were accompanied by smaller fighting or raiding ships—penteconters, triaconters, and light craft—and by numerous transports and supply-vessels. The aggregate of ships of all sorts at Doriscus, excluding the triremes, may have amounted to some 3,000. Their number was indeed so great that harbourage was often inadequate and fleet discipline was hard to maintain at sea.

The Persian command by land and by sea was in the hands of the king. He directed strategy and supervised operations. His military staff comprised

---

[1] 7. 40; 196; 9. 20–23.   [2] 7. 89–96; D.S. 11. 3. 7–9.
[3] 8. 10. 1; 60a; Plu. *Them.* 14.

six generals, each in command of an infantry group, Hydarnes, in command of the 10,000 Immortals, and three generals, each in command of a cavalry group. His naval staff numbered four, each being in command of a squadron. All these officers were Persians of high birth, some being members of the royal family. The infantry contingents of the various nations were commanded by Persian officers, but the naval contingents were commanded by their own officers. Such being the system of command, a great deal depended on the judgement of the king as commander-in-chief and on the abilities of his staff officers. The military staff had had wide experience of warfare against various peoples and in particular against Greek infantry in Ionia and at Marathon. The Persian admirals did not know the coastal waters of the Greek peninsula, and they were comparatively inexperienced in naval warfare; they therefore relied to a great extent on the leading native commanders in the battle-fleet.[1]

From Doriscus the Persian force marched and sailed without mishap to Therma, nowadays Saloníki, at the head of the Thermaic Gulf. From there, looking across the waters of the gulf, Xerxes saw the towering masses of Olympus and Ossa, the silent bastions of Greece. Leading a reconnaissance in full force he inspected the mouth of the Peneus river and the seaward end of the Vale of Tempe. Although the Greeks had long before withdrawn from Thessaly and his envoys reported the submission of the Thessalians and their neighbours, Xerxes decided to enter Greece not by the Vale of Tempe but by the passes west of Mt. Olympus. This decision involved a delay of some ten days, during which a road was cut through the forests and the fleet lay idle at Therma.[2] Possibly he wished to establish a line of communication which was less exposed to raiding forces than the Vale of Tempe, but it is surprising that he delayed the general advance for this purpose. A well-armed and mobile force might easily have been sent forward to secure key-points on the routes farther south.

While Xerxes delayed in Macedonia, the Greek Congress at the Isthmus was deliberating on strategy. The majority favoured the occupation of the pass of Thermopylae, which was narrower than the Vale of Tempe, and the stationing of the fleet at Artemisium, where it covered the entrance to the Euboic Channel (see Fig. 17). The two positions were sufficiently close to one another for the army and the fleet to keep in communication by smoke signal or dispatch boat. Each position had great merits. It was thought that the pass of Thermopylae could not be turned by any short détour. If it was carried by a frontal attack, the Greek army could withdraw over routes which were beyond the reach of the Persian cavalry. If it was not carried and Xerxes marched his army over the pass to Cytinium in Doris, he would have to overcome resistance in Phocis and Boeotia before he could rejoin his fleet. The Greek fleet at Artemisium had a friendly base in Euboea and a sheltered line of communication through the Euboic Channel. If the Greek fleet had to

[1] Hdt. 7. 81–83; 88; 97–99.   [2] 7. 128–32.

withdraw, it could do so between friendly coasts. If the Persian fleet wished to turn the Greek position, it would have to circumnavigate Euboea and operate independently of the Persian army. Thus the two positions, when held concurrently, would split the Persian advance. But if either fell, both would have to be abandoned.

The combined positions at Thermopylae and at Artemisium were very wisely chosen, but the choice had been made dangerously late. The appointed forces set off in haste by land and by sea to occupy the positions. When Xerxes pitched camp in the Trachinian plain, Thermopylae was held by six or seven thousand hoplites. The whole force was commanded by a Spartan king, Leonidas; it consisted of 4,100 Peloponnesians (of whom 300 were Spartiates and 1,000 Lacedaemonians), 700 Thespians, and 400 Thebans, and a levy of Phocians and Locrians of Opus, who had answered Leonidas' request for help. The force was intended to be the vanguard of the main army,[1] which would follow after celebrating the religious festivals at Sparta and Olympia. But, slow as Xerxes had been, the Greek allies had shown themselves to be even slower. The vanguard was destined to fight unaided the first and, as it proved, the only military engagement of the year 480.

The Greek fleet moved more rapidly into position. The Spartan Eurybiades had under his command 271 triremes and a few pentecenters. Of these 147 triremes were manned by Athens, Plataea, and her cleruchy at Chalcis; in consequence the Athenian commander, Themistocles, was the most influential member of Eurybiades' staff. During the advance of the Greek fleet, the people of Delphi consulted the oracle and sent the timely response to the Greeks: 'pray to the winds, for they will be staunch allies of Greece'. While the Persian fleet was still based at Therma, it sent a force of ten fast triremes ahead to reconnoitre. At the island of Sciathos three Greek triremes were on the lookout. When they saw the enemy, they fled, but despite their lead the Troezenian and the Aeginetan vessels were overhauled and captured; the Athenian ship escaped northwards and was abandoned at the mouth of the Peneus by its crew, who made their way homewards overland. The Persians then set up a stone pillar to mark a sunken rock in the channel between Sciathos and Cape Sepias, and signalled to the main fleet that their course was clear. Meanwhile the Greek fleet had been informed by fire-signals from Sciathos of the first contact with the enemy. It thereupon manned observation-posts on the heights of north Euboea and withdrew to the narrowest part of the Channel at Chalcis. This withdrawal left the way clear for the Persian fleet to enter the Gulf of Pagasae. Moreover, if the Greek fleet stayed at Chalcis, the position of the army at Thermopylae would become untenable; for the enemy fleet could land troops in its rear.[2]

At this critical moment the prayer to the winds was answered. The Persian fleet, moving with all its auxiliaries from Therma, was benighted off the

---

[1] 7. 175–7; 202–6; 228. 1; D.S. 11. 4. 5–6; Isoc. 4. 90; 6. 99.
[2] Hdt. 7. 178–83.

rocky coast of Magnesia. Throughout a calm night the ships lay eight lines deep and close inshore to a short beach, where only a few could find a mooring. At dawn an east wind, known locally as the Hellespontias, blew with gale strength and scattered the fleet, which was driven leewards by a raging sea on to the inhospitable coast. On the fourth day, when the storm abated, the Persian losses were estimated at 400 warships and a greater number of auxiliary vessels. Meanwhile the Greek fleet was lying in sheltered water at Chalcis. On learning of the Persian losses, the Athenians made sacrifice to Boreas, the god of the North Wind, and the Greeks as a whole to Poseidon the Saviour, the god of the sea. The Greek fleet then returned to Artemisium. When the sea had grown calm, the Persian fleet reassembled, rounded Cape Sepias, and entered the Gulf of Pagasae. The Greeks at Artemisium watched the enemy sail by and were dismayed at the huge number of vessels. Their morale was raised by a lucky chance. For fifteen Persian ships later rounded Cape Sepias, mistook the identity of the fleet across the channel, and sailed into the hands of the Greeks. After interrogation the prisoners were sent in chains to the Greek headquarters at the Isthmus.[1]

The opposed forces were now in position. Xerxes had intended his army and his fleet to arrive simultaneously. But the storm and the refitting in the Gulf of Pagasae delayed the fleet by four days.[2] During these days his army lay inactive in the Trachinian plain; for, although he regarded the Greek army at Thermopylae as contemptibly small, he did not proceed to the attack. His orders for the fifth day showed his purpose. A detachment of 200 triremes was to sail north of Sciathos, then pass unseen outside Euboea, and on the following day close the southern end of the Euboic Channel. The detachment had to elude the enemy observation-posts on north Euboea and complete its course of some 130 sea-miles to Cape Geraestus by dawn of the following day; it started therefore during the hours of darkness. In the early afternoon the main fleet was to move to Aphetae opposite Artemisium but not to engage. On the same day the assault by the Persian army was to begin at Thermopylae. On the next day, when it was expected the detachment of 200 triremes would be in position, the main fleet was to engage the Greek fleet and the assault was to continue at Thermopylae. The king's aim was to bottle up the whole Greek fleet between Aphetae and the narrows at Euripus, break through at Thermopylae and occupy the mainland coast, and destroy the Greek fleet so completely that not a sailor would survive. Success would be decisive. For the victorious Persian fleet could then turn any defensive positions which the Greek army might later adopt.[3]

---

[1] 7. 183. 2; 188-95.

[2] The sequence of events was given by Herodotus. The three days of fighting at Thermopylae and Artemisium were synchronous (8. 15). Before attacking at Thermopylae Xerxes waited in the plain for four days (7. 210). He entered the plain two days before the fleet rounded Cape Sepias (7. 196). Therefore two days passed while the fleet refitted in the Gulf of Pagasae; these days are necessary to account for the salvage work of the diver Scyllias, who could only operate when the sea was calm (8. 8. 1).   [3] Hdt. 8. 6-7.

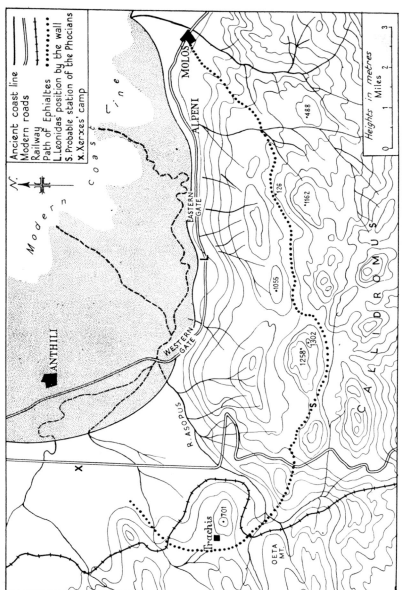

FIG. 17. The Pass of Thermopylae

During these days of delay the Greek army at Thermopylae and the navy at Artemisium maintained close communication by sea. The sight of the whole Persian army and navy filled the Greeks with such alarm that the majority were in favour of an immediate withdrawal from both positions. But Leonidas and Eurybiades held firm, the latter ably supported by Themistocles, who was afterwards believed to have indulged in bribery to the advantage of the Greek cause and his own pocket. On the fifth day a Greek diver, Scyllias of Scione, deserted to the Greek side; he was later credited with the impossible feat of having swum ten miles under water. But his exploit was of great importance. For he reported the full extent of the damage sustained by the Persian fleet and the sailing of the detachment of 200 triremes, which were already on their course off Euboea. At a meeting of the Greek naval staff the first proposal was to stay in position until midnight and then sail down the Channel to engage the detachment of 200 triremes next day near the Euripus. This proposal would have uncovered the position at Thermopylae and enabled the main Persian fleet to turn it. But later in the day, when the Persian fleet at Aphetae made no move, the Greek fleet decided to attack towards evening.[1]

Meanwhile the assault had begun at Thermopylae. Leonidas held the narrow passage between the cliffs and the sea, which was some 50 feet wide. Here an ancient wall of dry stone had been repaired by the army to protect their camp. In front of the wall the passage widened and then contracted again to a width of some 6 feet. In the space between the wall and the narrowest point Leonidas intended to fight; here he had a narrow strip of a mile or more in length, over which his men could advance or retire. Behind the wall and at about the same distance the passage narrowed again near the village of Alpeni, which was his base of supply.[2] On his arrival Leonidas had learnt of a mountain path by which his position could be turned; he had therefore detached the Phocian force, which volunteered to hold the path. Xerxes first sent out a mounted scout, who passed the narrowest point of Thermopylae and saw, on his side of the wall, only 300 Spartiates. Some were combing their hair, which they wore long since their defeat of the Argives at Sepeia, and others were doing gymnastic exercises. They took no notice of the horseman, who returned to tell the king what he had seen. Xerxes expressed his astonishment to Demaratus, the exiled Spartan king, who warned him that these were the bravest men in the world.

The warning was justified. Throughout the day waves of infantry—Median, Cassian, and the Persian Immortals themselves—passed through the narrow gap to be hewn down in serried ranks. They were outfought by the longer spear and heavier armour of the Greek hoplites and particularly by the Spartans, who retreated, wheeled, and charged with well-drilled precision. Xerxes could not bring his cavalry into action at all, but he hoped by the continued pressure of his infantry to wear down the defence.

[1] 8. 4–5; 8–9.   [2] 7. 176. 2–5.

Throughout the next day the assault continued without success, the Greek contingents taking turns in the front line. In the evening Ephialtes, a Greek of Malis, informed Xerxes of the mountain path. Under his guidance Hydarnes, in command of the Immortals, started out from the Persian camp about the time of the lighting of the lamps.[1]

During these two days the fleet had also been in action. When the Greek ships sailed out towards evening, the Persian fleet moved out into mid-channel. In face of superior numbers the Greek fleet formed into a circle, sterns inward and prows outward, so that they could not be attacked from the rear. As the Persian fleet enveloped them on all sides, the Greek ships rowed forward to ram and engage their opponents. The fighting was bitter and the outcome still in doubt when night fell and the fleets disengaged to return to their stations. Early in the night a storm broke over Mt. Pelion, with crashing thunder and lightning and teeming rain. A tempest blew from the south, driving the corpses and the wreckage from mid-channel into the Persian anchorage. The same storm smote the Persian detachment of 200 triremes, which was still in the open sea and sailing off the Hollows of south-east Euboea. In the darkness and tempestuous rain the ships were driven upon the rocky coast of Euboea and totally wrecked. Next day the news of the Persian disaster reached the Greek fleet at the same time as a reinforcement of fifty-three Athenian ships. These had probably been manned from the last reserves of Athenian manpower, entered the Euboic Channel, being unaware of the approach of the Persian detachment, and sheltered throughout the night near Chalcis. In the evening the Greek fleet attacked again and sank a number of Cilician vessels before nightfall. The Persian fleet, however, still outnumbered the Greek, and Xerxes ordered an attack next day at noon.[2]

On the third day dawn was beginning to break over the mountain path above Thermopylae, when the Phocians heard the rustle of oak leaves underfoot and sprang to arms. Harassed by showers of arrows they withdrew to higher ground up the mountainside and prepared to fight to the end. But Hydarnes and his Immortals passed on and descended rapidly towards Alpeni. In the plain below Leonidas had been informed by deserters, while it was still dark, that a Persian force was ascending the mountain path. When he called a conference of the contingent commanders, the news was confirmed by outposts who came running down from the heights at dawn. Counsel was divided. Leonidas ordered the other contingents to retire at once, for the position at Thermopylae was irretrievably turned; but the Spartan contingent and the Theban contingent were to stay. The Thespians and the seer, Megistias of Acarnania, refused to obey the order to retire. They stayed and died with Leonidas. The others made good their withdrawal up the mountainside.[3]

Knowing that he might be attacked in the rear by the Immortals, Leonidas

[1] Hdt. 7. 175. 2; 217. 2; 208–15; D.S. 11. 7. 2–3.
[2] Hdt. 8. 10–14; D.S. 11. 12. 4–13. 2.   [3] Hdt. 7. 216–22.

led his men forward to the narrowest point of the passage. An hour or two before noon, as the infantry of Xerxes were mustering for the attack, Leonidas deployed his men in the open ground in front of this defile and engaged the enemy, who were being driven on with whips by their officers. Those who were not killed outright by the Greeks were trampled to death by the succeeding files, and rank after rank was destroyed. Soon the spears of the Greeks were shivered and they fought with their swords. When Leonidas fell, the battle swayed thrice over his dead body, and then the Greeks carried it back. By now Hydarnes and the Immortals were approaching. The Greeks withdrew in a body through the narrowest point and then through the wall, to make their last stand on a hillock. There the Thebans drew away and, with upraised hands, surrendered, protesting their goodwill to the Persians. The remainder fought to the death, enveloped on all sides and overwhelmed by showers of missiles.

At the order of Xerxes the body of Leonidas was decapitated and hung on a cross. The rest of the dead were buried, and the Thebans were branded with the royal mark. When the days of danger had passed, the Amphictyons of Delphi set up a memorial to the Spartans, which bore the inscription 'Stranger, tell the Lacedaemonians that here we lie obedient to their words'.[1]

This same day at noon the Persian fleet sailed out to the attack. As the Greek fleet rode motionless off Artemisium, the Persians adopted a crescent formation, in order to envelop the wings of the enemy. The Greek fleet then advanced and engaged. In the press of ships the Persians often fell foul of one another; but the close fighting inflicted heavy loss in ships and men on both sides. Of the Persian force the Egyptians distinguished themselves and of the Greek the Athenians; among the latter the most dashing captain was the wealthy Clinias, the father of Alcibiades. By the evening, when the fleets disengaged and half of the Athenian ships were no longer battleworthy, the news of the fall of Thermopylae was brought to Eurybiades. The officers of the fleet met on the seashore. The decision was taken to withdraw. The fires were lit as usual; over them the crews roasted the cattle of the Euboean villagers. In the dark the fleet set sail, the Corinthians first and the Athenians last. At sunrise the Persians crossed over to find Artemisium deserted. As they sailed down the channel, sacking the villages on the coast, they saw a number of inscriptions which had been cut on the rocks by the order of Themistocles. These urged the Ionians and the Carians to desert or, if this was impossible, to fight faintheartedly in the Persian cause. By such deft propaganda Themistocles prepared the ground for the next engagement with the enemy.[2]

When Xerxes resumed his advance, some 20,000 of his best infantry lay on the field of battle. In the great storms and the three naval engagements half of his battle-fleet had been damaged or sunk. The Greeks had shown their

[1] 7. 223-8.   [2] 8. 15-22.

superiority man for man and ship for ship. At Thermopylae their dead numbered 4,000, of whom perhaps half were Helots, the attendants of the Spartan hoplites. From Artemisium the Greeks towed away their damaged ships and the enemy hulls, of which thirty had been captured on the first day. Their morale was high. For they knew now that the gods of sea and winds were on their side, and that with only a part of their naval forces they had withstood the Persian fleet. They awarded the prize of valour to the Athenians, who, in the words of Pindar, 'laid the bright foundation of liberty' at Artemisium.[1]

§ 4. *The battle of Salamis*

THE Persian army advanced by the inland route through Doris into Phocis, which was ravaged far and wide, the people taking refuge on the heights of Mount Parnassus. Descending into Boeotia, the Persians were welcomed by the states which had medized. The Plataeans, warned by their crews, which had disembarked at Chalcis and marched overland, made good their escape. But Plataea and Thespiae were burnt. A separate detachment of the Persian army headed for the sanctuary at Delphi. As the temples in Phocis had been plundered and burnt, the Delphians asked advice of the god and received the response that he was able to protect his own. They had hardly dispersed when the Persian force approached. It had probably been ordered to respect the temple; for from the Persian point of view the oracle had been neutral and even better than neutral, and the Persian policy, as Datis had shown at Delos, was to placate the chief centres at which Apollo was worshipped. As the Persians passed under the beetling cliffs and approached the silent sanctuary, a sudden storm broke over their heads. As thunder reverberated from crag to crag and lightning flashed through the gloom, two rocks were shattered from the cliffs above and fell amidst them, killing some of their number. The remainder fled.[2] For they, like the Greeks, believed the gods responsible for the storms which had sent so many of their ships and men to the bottom of the sea.

The Greek fleet meanwhile came to anchor in the bay of Salamis. The Greek Congress decided not to hold the entry at Parapotamii or Chaeronea into Boeotia, which had declared for Persia, nor the entries into Attica, which could be turned in any case by seaborne landings, but to build a wall across a narrow part of the Isthmus and hold it with their full strength. This task was entrusted to the peoples of Lacedaemonia, Arcadia, Elis, Corinth, Sicyon, Epidaurus, Phlius, Troezen, and Hermione; for the states of the Argolid and of Achaea maintained their doubtful neutrality. Conjointly with the holding of the Isthmus the Congress decided to station the full fleet in the bay of Salamis (see Fig. 18). This position was in one respect superior to that at

[1] 8. 24–25; 8. 11. 2; Pi. *Fr.* 77 ap. Plu. *Them.* 8.   [2] 8. 31–38; 50.

Artemisium; for the entries into the bay were so narrow that, if the Persians attacked, the greater numbers of their fleet could not be used to full effect. It was similar in other respects to the position at Artemisium. For the fleet had its shore base on an island, which the Greeks held, and it stood in advance of the Isthmus, so that it protected the Greek army from any seaborne landing by the enemy. The reserve fleet, which had mustered off Troezenia, now joined the main fleet at the bay of Salamis. The commander at the Isthmus was Cleombrotus, the brother of Leonidas, and the commander at Salamis was the Spartan Eurybiades. The latter was continued in his command, because the same qualities were likely to be needed at Salamis as at Artemisium —the determination to engage the enemy and the ability to lead the commanders of the contingents.[1]

Themistocles was one of Athens' representatives at the Congress. He doubtless pressed for the stationing of the Greek fleet at Salamis, partly in order to cover the evacuation of those who had not left Attica in autumn 481 or had returned since then, but mainly for strategic reasons. Moreover, he had persuaded the Athenians to take to their ships on the ground that 'Holy Salamis' in the oracle from Delphi (p. 223 above) portended a victory there. When the Greek fleet reached Salamis, the Generals issued a proclamation that persons still in Attica should save themselves as best they could.[2] They went mostly to Troezen, but others went to Salamis and Aegina. The Areopagus Council took charge in the emergency. It found the money to pay eight drachmae a head to men who would row in place of the Plataeans, who had returned to their city. The hulls were available to make up the loss and damage sustained at Artemisium; for the Assembly had decided in September 481 to build more triremes (7. 144. 2).

To desert their shrines and their homes filled the Athenians with the deepest grief and apprehension; for their religion as well as their affection was deeply rooted in the locality of Athens. The religious prestige of the Areopagus Council alleviated their fears. And its authority was fortified not only by the oracular response of Delphi but also by the priestess of Athena, who announced that the serpent of Athena on the Acropolis had not come out to eat its honeycake. Athena herself, then, had left the city. Even as the images of the Tyndaridae or Aeacidae accompanied the Spartans or Aeginetans on campaigns abroad, so Athena in person would aid her citizens in the bay of Salamis.

When Xerxes marched into Attica and the fleet joined him nine days after the last battle at Artemisium, the countryside was deserted. The Acropolis, however, was held by the treasurers of the temple and by a few supporters, who had set up a wooden barricade to form 'the wooden wall'. The Persians encamped on the Areopagus hill and ignited the barricade with incendiary arrows. Then they sent some Peisistratidae to offer terms of surrender. But the

---

[1] 8. 71–72; 40–42.
[2] 8. 41. 1–2; Arist. *Ath. Pol.* 23. 1; Plu. *Cim.* 5; *Them.* 10.

defenders refused any terms. They fought on until a group of Persian soldiers scaled the cliff and appeared on the summit of the Acropolis. Then some committed suicide, throwing themselves down from the wall, and others sought sanctuary in the temple, whence they were torn and massacred. The temple was plundered and the citadel fired. Xerxes now dispatched a messenger to Susa to proclaim his triumph.[1]

But Greece had yet to be won by force of arms and that without delay; for it was late in September and at the equinox stormy weather might confine the fleet to harbour and threaten the supplies of the entire Persian host. Yet rapid action was hazardous; for Xerxes appreciated the strength of the enemy positions. If he attacked the army, he would have to force an entry through the precipitous Scironian Way east of Mt. Gerania or through the difficult country to the west, before he came to grips with the main position at the Isthmus. On the other hand, if he attacked the fleet in the Strait of Salamis, he would be unable to take advantage of his superior numbers in the narrow waters. Faced by this dilemma, Xerxes decided to attack the fleet; for he thought that thus a quick success was more likely to be achieved. His decision was supported by his naval staff with the exception of Artemisia, Queen of Halicarnassus. The fleet was ready for action; for the losses in ships and men had been made good by drawing on the Greek islands. Xerxes relied on superior numbers, and he hoped that the Greek allies might fall out among themselves.[2]

The pall of smoke rising from the Acropolis was seen by the Greeks at Salamis. Terror fell upon the fleet. At a conference of the naval captains the majority wished to withdraw to the Isthmus, and some captains left before the final decision, in order to hoist sail on their vessels. Eurybiades was overborne and gave the order for withdrawal. This meant disaster for the Athenians on Salamis and an Athenian fleet without a base. Themistocles prevailed upon Eurybiades to convene another conference. He explained the advantages to the Greek fleet and to the Greek cause of fighting at Salamis and, when he was taunted as 'a man without a city' by the Corinthian commander, he threatened to sail away with the Athenian fleet of 200 ships and plant a colony in the West. His arguments prevailed over the opposition. Eurybiades cancelled his order, and the fleet kept its station in the Strait of Salamis. The two conferences took place on either side of midday on September 28th, the Acropolis having been captured that morning. The date is calculated from the eclipse of October 2nd (Hdt. 9. 10. 3).[3] On the 28th at midday the Persian fleet put out to sea from Phalerum and posted itself in order of battle between the Peiraeus and Salamis. As the enemy made no move, the Persians withdrew to land in the late afternoon. Meanwhile in the Greek fleet the discontent came to a head. They were afraid that they might be surrounded and cut off on the island, and their fears were heightened towards nightfall, when the Persian army was seen moving along

[1] 8. 51–54.
[2] 8. 67–69.
[3] 8. 56–63. For the date see *CAH²* 4. Chapter 11, Note 1, and for the course of the battle which follows *StGH* 251–310.

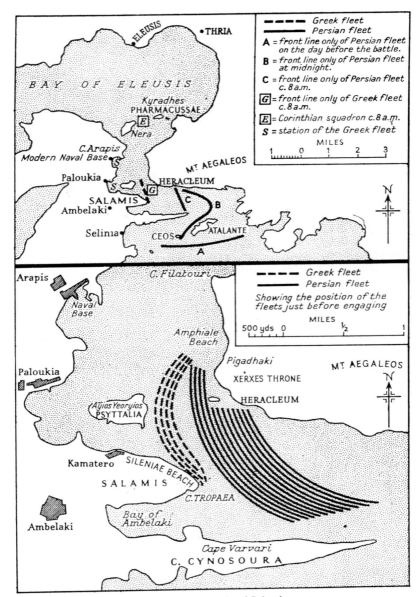

Top map labels:

Greek fleet
Persian fleet
A = front line only of Persian fleet on the day before the battle.
B = front line only of Persian fleet at midnight.
C = front line only of Persian fleet c. 8 a.m.
G = front line only of Greek fleet c. 8 a.m.
E = Corinthian squadron c. 8 a.m.
S = station of the Greek fleet

MILES
1 0 1 2 3

ELEUSIS
•THRIA
BAY OF ELEUSIS
Kyradhes
PHARMACUSSAE
E
Nera
C. Arapis
Modern Naval Base
Paloukia
S
MT AEGALEOS
HERACLEUM
SALAMIS
G
C
B
Ambelaki•
Selinia
CEOS
ATALANTE
A
N

Bottom map labels:

Greek fleet
Persian fleet
Showing the position of the fleets just before engaging

500 yds 0
MILES
½ 1

Arapis
C. Filatouri
Naval Base
Amphiale Beach
Pigadhaki
XERXES THRONE
MT AEGALEOS
Paloukia
Ἅγιος Γεώργιος PSYTTALIA
HERACLEUM
Kamatero
SILENIAE BEACH
SALAMIS
C. TROPAEA
Ambelaki
Bay of Ambelaki
Cape Varvari
C. CYNOSOURA
N

FIG. 18. The Battle of Salamis

the coast towards the Peloponnese. The Peloponnesians at once wished to withdraw and aid their comrades at the Isthmus; the Athenians, Aeginetans, and Megarians wished to stand firm. A conference was called by Eurybiades. Realizing that Eurybiades might be overborne again by the Peloponnesians, Themistocles sent a trusted slave, Sicinnus, to make contact with the Persian fleet and inform the Persian command that the Greeks were demoralized and would sail away on the morrow and that Themistocles intended to aid the Persians henceforth.[1] The Persian admirals were convinced by Sicinnus. That night they moved a strong force of infantry from the Attic coast to the island Psyttalia in mid-channel, and about midnight put to sea again and advanced their right wing silently in order to close the eastern exit from the bay of Salamis. Meanwhile they dispatched a squadron round the island to block the western exit between Salamis and Megara.[2]

The news that Sicinnus had been successful was brought by Aristides. While crossing from Aegina to Salamis, he had passed close to the enemy squadron sailing in the dark off Megara. He called Themistocles out of the conference. There an animated and acrimonious discussion in the Greek manner still continued through the small hours of the morning. Themistocles sent Aristides into the conference to make his report. All doubts were removed when a trireme of Tenos, deserting under cover of darkness, gave full information of the Persian dispositions. An engagement was now certain. The triremes were stripped for action. The marines were marshalled on the beach and harangued by the captains, and notably by Themistocles, before they embarked in the growing light of dawn.[3]

The Greek fleet numbered 380 ships. Of these a detachment, led by the Corinthians, was detailed to hold the channel against attack from the north. It rejoined the main fleet later during the action. The 310 triremes which were to meet the onslaught of a force more than three times as numerous[4] excelled in oarsmanship and in the tactics of ramming and boarding. For the low-built Greek trireme was stoutly made to stand the shock of ramming an enemy vessel, and the heavily armed marines, who manned its side-decks, were ready to board a disabled ship and work execution with spear and sword. But, in order to ram, the trireme had to strike at the enemy's broadside. The problem for the Greek command was to create a situation in which the Greek ships had some room to manœuvre and the enemy were likely to expose their broadsides. The solution seems to have been due to Themistocles.

As dawn broke, the whole Greek fleet moved off into the northern part of the strait out of sight of the enemy. There they formed into several columns, facing south and headed by the ten fastest ships of the fleet, which were

---

[1] 8. 70–75; Aesch. *Pers.* 355–60; D.S. 11. 16 fin.–17. 1; Plu. *Them.* 12.
[2] 8. 76; Aesch. *Pers.* 361–83; D.S. 11. 17. 2; Plu. loc. cit.
[3] 8. 78–83; Plu. loc. cit.
[4] Aesch. *Pers.* 338–43; Hdt. 8. 43–48; 82; 94; *GHI* 16.

Aeginetans. Next to them came Lacedaemonians, Megarians, and others under Eurybiades' command; then 'Chalcidians' and Athenians, totalling 200 in all, under Themistocles' command. These dispositions were made with full knowledge of Xerxes' plan and order of battle at sea.

The Persian fleet numbered some 1,200 vessels, of which a squadron had been detached to hold the exit off Megara. The Phoenician triremes were the finest; they were faster, larger, and higher than the Greek triremes. They were equipped for ramming but were less stoutly built. They therefore preferred to overbear an opponent and to discharge arrows and javelins from their higher decks on to the more open Greek trireme. Most of the other squadrons were equipped likewise, but the Ionian ships resembled the Greeks in build and armament. The plan of Xerxes was simplified by his belief that the Greek fleet was demoralized, as it had been at the battle of Lade. If it had fled into the bay of Eleusis, he would advance to hold both exits by sea, land troops at Salamis town, capture the enemy's shore base, and force the Greeks to surrender. If the Greek fleet fought and the Athenian squadron was disaffected, the task of his admirals appeared to be simple. The fleet, already marshalled in dense array, was to bear down the channel like a tidal wave and swamp the smaller Greek vessels. The leading ships would present a solid and closely packed front, being head on to the enemy and therefore not exposed to the enemy's rams, and the Persian archers and javelinmen would break down resistance with their fire. He was confident that the action, if there were an action at all, would take place in the northern part of the strait. With this in mind he had occupied Psyttalia, and he had ordered his *entourage* to establish his golden throne on a high point opposite Psyttalia on the Attic coast.[1]

At dawn Xerxes mounted his throne to survey the scene. At the eastern mouth of the channel the dense array of his ships spanned the glassy sea from the tip of Cape Cynosoura to the Attic coast. The front line numbered perhaps ninety ships in close order, Phoenicians on the right, Ionians on the left, and the others in the centre. Behind it the supporting files of each nationality, numbering some ten ships a file, stretched away into the distance. Defined in terms of nationality, the armada consisted of three main groups in column, tight-packed against one another and commanded each by a Persian admiral.[2] As the armada began to row ahead, the left wing fell into confusion. For, in passing between Atalante and Cynosoura and in rounding the tip of the promontory, the formation became congested and the ships fell foul of one another.[3] The result was that the Phoenicians on the right wing advanced much more rapidly than the Ionians on the left wing.

Seeing no sign of the enemy, the Phoenicians advanced confidently when, to their dismay, a trumpet sounded and a battle cry echoed from the crags of

---

[1] Ctes. 26; Str. 395; Hdt. 8. 90. 4; Aesch. *Pers.* 466; D.S. 11. 18. 3; Plu. *Them.* 13; the 'Chalcidians' were probably the Athenian cleruchs from Chalcis.

[2] Aesch. *Pers.* 364–7; Hdt. 8. 85. 1; D.S. 11. 17. 2–3.   [3] D.S. 11. 18. 4.

Salamis. From the northern part of the strait the Greek fleet emerged in several columns, the Aeginetans leading and the Athenians at the rear.[1] The Aeginetans headed at full speed for Cape Tropaea. The long columns then swung left into line of battle, facing prow on towards the Persian fleet. As the Phoenician squadron rowed on quickly under the eyes of the king, the Athenian squadron backed water steadily and drew the Phoenicians onwards into the narrows between Psyttalia and the mainland.[2]

By this bold manœuvre the Athenians dictated the tactics of the battle. The Greek formation now lay extended in the shape of a crescent. Its front consisted of some seventy-five ships; there were perhaps four lines in depth; and the left wing had sea-room, in which to manœuvre. On the other hand, the Phoenician squadron had been drawn forward *en échelon* into narrowing waters, so that the full supporting files of the right wing and right centre could not come up into action. The bulk of the Persian fleet, numbering at least 1,000 vessels, was now congested and ship collided with ship.[3] The moment seemed to have come for the Greeks to attack. But Themistocles, in command of the Athenian squadron of 180 ships, still bided his time, until a swell set through the channel and rolled the high-decked Phoenician galleys off their bearing. As their broadsides swung round, the low-built Athenian triremes, which were less affected by the swell, rowed in to the charge and rammed their opponents, shearing their oars or holing their sides.[4] As the ships lay locked together, the heavy-armed Athenian marines led the boarding-parties and swept their light-armed enemy into the scuppers or the sea. This was the signal for the whole Greek line to engage with vigour.

During the bitter fighting on the left wing, the Greeks on the shore of Salamis noticed for the first time that Psyttalia was occupied by Persian infantry. Aristides at once collected a force of hoplites by Salamis town, crossed in auxiliary vessels, stormed the island of Psyttalia, and held it as a haven for damaged shipping.[5] The Phoenician squadron fought hard but finally broke in disorder. Many ships were wrecked on the coast of Attica. Some Phoenician captains reported to Xerxes, and were decapitated for their pains. Others, trying to escape down the channel, were blocked by the ships of their own fleet. The Athenian squadron then wheeled to aid the Greek centre and right, which were faced by much greater numbers. Here, too, the Greeks broke down the resistance of the enemy. As the shattered fleet of Persia fell back, a west wind came down the channel and the Persians hoisted sail to fly before it to the open waters and to Phalerum. The Aeginetans on the Greek right now stood out into the channel and rammed the last files of the fugitives, which were formed by the remnants of the Phoenician squadron.[6]

---

[1] Aesch. *Pers.* 384–401.   [2] Hdt. 8. 84; cf. Th. 3. 78. 3 for ships backing water.
[3] Aesch. *Pers.* 412–16.
[4] Plu. *Them.* 14.
[5] Plu. *Arist.* 9; Aesch. *Pers.* 447–67; Hdt. 8. 95.
[6] D.S. 11. 19. 1–3; Hdt. 8. 90. 1; 91; Aesch. *Pers.* 480–1.

A great victory had been won by tactical skill, by the use of the ram, and by the fighting quality of the Greek marines. The first prize for valour was awarded to the Aeginetans, who had held the most exposed position on the right of the Greek line; and the second prize to the Athenians, who had first swung the battle towards victory. Trophies were set up on Psyttalia, at Salamis town and probably on Cape Cynosoura to commemorate the scene of the victory.

The danger, however, was not past. The Greek fleet had suffered severely. The loss of life was probably small, for the crews had swum ashore to Salamis, but many ships were damaged beyond repair. Most of the enemy hulls had been swept out of reach by the west wind, so that the Greeks could not make good their loss in vessels. The diminished fleet reassembled in readiness for a further engagement. The Persian fleet was still far superior in numbers. But Xerxes had seen too much of the battle for his liking. He reverted to an earlier plan, to build out a mole into the channel and protect it with a breakwater of merchant ships lashed together. While the preparations for this difficult feat of engineering were being made, it became apparent that the season was already too far advanced. Xerxes ordered his fleet to withdraw under cover of dark and sail to the Hellespont. He then marched with his whole army to Thessaly, where a large force was left to winter under the command of Mardonius. With the rest of his army, which was still the greater part, Xerxes marched on to the Hellespont in forty-five days, during which his men suffered heavily from famine, pestilence, and cold. As the bridge over the Hellespont had been carried away by a storm, the army was ferried across the Straits and given a period of rest at Abydus. Thence a remnant of the great host made the entry into Sardis. Xerxes rode in pomp and splendour, but the sacred chariot of Ahura-Mazda, the supreme god of Persia, was missing. It, too, had been lost in Europe.[1]

The Greek fleet sailed as far as Andros without sighting the enemy fleet. Eurybiadès and the Peloponnesian captains decided to proceed no farther; and Themistocles, who had voiced the wish of the Athenian captains to sail to the Hellespont and destroy the bridge, yielded to the decision of the Peloponnesians. But he made the most of the situation. He sent Sicinnus and other messengers to tell Xerxes that the Athenian commander, Themistocles, had restrained the Greeks from destroying the bridge over the Hellespont. From Andros and other islands which had aided Persia the Greek fleet demanded indemnities in money. Andros refused and was besieged without success. Others acceded, and some were believed to have paid money to Themistocles for his protection of their interests. Reassembled at Salamis, the victors paid due honour to the gods of Greece. From the spoil they dedicated at Delphi a colossal statue of Apollo, holding the prow of a trireme in his hand; and from the prizes a Phoenician trireme each to Ajax of Salamis, Poseidon of the Isthmus, and Athena of Sunium.[2]

[1] 8. 97–117; Aesch. *Pers.* 482–512.
[2] Hdt. 8. 108–12; 121–3. See Plate VI for the statue of Zeus at Artemisium.

§ 5. *The Greek victories at Plataea and Mycale*

THE campaign of 480 had been far from decisive. The Persian army was un-defeated. Mardonius had under his command in Thessaly the best cavalry and infantry of the Persian empire, and he was rejoined by the detachment which had escorted Xerxes to the Hellespont. His army was indeed more dangerous than the army of Xerxes; for, being disencumbered of a large number of inferior troops, it gained in mobility and in ease of supply. Mace-donia, Thessaly, and Boeotia provided not only fodder and foodstuffs but also fighting troops, especially in the cavalry arm. The Greek army as a whole had made no trial of the Persian strength, and was almost devoid of cavalry. The Peloponnesian commanders naturally preferred to hold their prepared position at the Isthmus, where the Persian cavalry could not operate. On the other hand, the Persian navy had suffered a signal defeat at Salamis. The loss of life had been heavy, for most of the Asiatic troops could not swim. The loss in ships had only reduced the margin of its superiority, and during the winter more crews and ships could be conscripted. Nevertheless Xerxes lingered on at Sardis into the summer, and his fleet remained inactive and disheartened at Cyme and at Samos. The initiative at sea thus passed to the Greeks. But, as their main concern was with the army of Mardonius, they mustered only 110 ships at Aegina in spring 479 and advanced no farther than Delos.[1] The fate of Greece was thus to be decided on the mainland.

During the winter the Persians gave an example of their methods in dealing with rebels. When Potidaea revolted and survived a siege of three months, Artabazus seized Olynthus, which he suspected of infidelity, and massacred the entire population in a marsh near the town. This act of terrorism stopped further risings. Resistance dwindled to guerrilla activities by the Phocians, who operated from the heights of Mt. Parnassus. The first aim of Mardonius in spring 479 was to detach Athens from the Greek cause. His envoy, Alex-ander, the king of Macedonia, offered alliance, independence, and repara-tions on behalf of Persia, but his offer was refused.[2] In early July, when the harvest was gathered and supplies greater, Mardonius invaded Attica. He sent another envoy with the same offer to the Athenians, who had withdrawn again to Salamis under the protection of their fleet. Even when they refused, he took no action in the hope that they would change their minds. When the Argives reported that the Greeks were moving out from the Peloponnese, Mardonius razed and burnt every building that still stood at Athens, and ravaged the countryside, as he withdrew by Decelea into Boeotia, where the terrain was better suited for cavalry and the population was loyal to the Per-sian cause.[3] Although he had not overcome the determination of Athens, he had prised the Peloponnesians out of their defensive position at the Isthmus; he had created some disharmony among the Greek allies; and he hoped to force a decisive battle under conditions of his own choosing.

[1] 8. 130–1.   [2] 8. 126–9; 9. 31. 5; 8. 136; 140–4.   [3] 9. 1–5; 12–15.

The danger of a split within the Greek League had been apparent before the battle of Salamis, when Themistocles had threatened to withdraw the Athenians, if the Peloponnesians insisted on holding the Isthmus. After the victory the Spartans entertained Themistocles, giving him a crown of olive leaves, a chariot, and an escort.[1] But the Athenians now chose Aristides and Xanthippus as their leaders. When the Spartans heard of the mission of Alexander of Macedon, they sent envoys to Athens and offered to receive and support the Athenian civilians—an offer which made it clear that Sparta did not intend to defend Attica. In the presence of the Persian envoy and the Spartan envoys Athens made her choice. Aristides declared that, so long as the sun continued in his course, the Athenians would attack the Persians with the aid of the gods and the heroes whose shrines the Persians had outraged; and that what Athens wanted was not the succour of their civilians but the defence of Attica by Greek forces operating in Boeotia. When a second Persian envoy came to the Athenian Council, then sitting in Salamis, the only Councillor who suggested referring his offer to the people was stoned to death. On the proposal of Aristides the Athenians sent an embassy to Sparta. They threatened to make separate arrangements, if the Spartans did not come to the aid of Athens. Envoys from Megara and Plataea supported the Athenians. The Spartans meanwhile proceeded with the Hyacinthian festival, which they happened to be celebrating. At last, when the exasperated envoys threatened to depart from Sparta and to return as allies of the Persian army, the Ephors replied that the Spartan infantry was already a night's march on its way towards Attica. There may have been method in Sparta's long delay. When their soldiers marched in late July, the defensive line at the Isthmus had been completed and could be held in the event of defeat in the field. But the price of the delay was the second devastation of Attica and the rising resentment of the Athenian people.[2]

Mardonius encamped in the southern plain of Boeotia by the river Asopus, facing the foothills of Mt. Cithaeron (see Fig. 19). He cleared the ground of trees and built a wooden stockade round his camp. His cavalry could now scour the plain and protect his line of supply from Thebes. The force under his command was estimated by the Greeks at some 300,000 men. The cavalry included the heavy-armed cuirassiers, commanded by Masistius; 1,000 household guards, formerly attendant on the king; light-armed cavalry from Persia, Media, Sacan Scythia, Bactria, and India; and the Greek horse of Boeotia, Thessaly, and Macedonia. The infantry included the 10,000 Immortals, the best troops which Xerxes had conscripted from the empire, and the hoplites of central Greece. The Phocians had not sent troops to Attica, but under compulsion they now supplied 1,000 hoplites. Their arrival gave Mardonius a chance to demonstrate the effectiveness of his cavalry in the plain. Encircled by the swarm of cavalry, the hoplites were brought to a halt and formed a square, facing outwards and prepared to endure the arrows and

[1] 8. 124; Plu. *Them.* 17.   [2] 8. 143–4; 9. 6–11; Plu. *Arist.* 10.

javelins of the horsemen. Mardonius then sent a herald to welcome the Phocians and to warn them to be diligent in the Persian cause. He now waited for the Greek army to attack him on his own ground or, if it refused to attack, to disintegrate under its own animosities. For his Greek allies and the oracles, which he had consulted, believed that in the end dissension would undermine Greek resistance.[1]

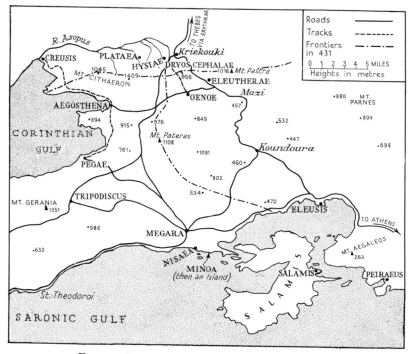

FIG. 19. Routes from Megara to Boeotia and Attica

The army of the Greek League was under the command of Pausanias, nephew of Leonidas, who was regent for the young king of Sparta, Pleistarchus. The largest and finest force came from Laconia: 5,000 Spartiates, 5,000 Lacedaemonian perioeci, and 35,000 Helots, the last being well-equipped skirmishers. The next largest contingents were 8,000 Athenians, commanded by Aristides, to whom the left wing of the battle-line was allocated, and 5,000 Corinthians who were placed next to 1,500 Tegeans and the Spartans on the right wing. The contingents of the other states formed the centre; those linking with the Athenians on the left were 600 Plataeans,

[1] 8. 113; 9. 15; 17–18.

3,000 Megarians, and 500 Aeginetans. The total of hoplites, drawn from twenty-four states, was 38,700; and the total of light-armed infantry some 70,000, of whom the Helots formed half. Cavalry there were none worthy of mention. When this great force collected at Plataea, the problem of supply soon became acute, for all foodstuffs had to be carried over the Cithaeron passes. It became worse when, eight days after their arrival, the Persian cavalry raided a pass and slaughtered a convoy of 500 pack-animals and their guards. Thereafter some devious routes had to be used. For this reason alone Pausanias and his staff desired an immediate engagement. But he was in the same position as Miltiades had been at Marathon—a position which the Spartans had studied after the battle. Now, too, the Greek infantry could not face the Persian cavalry in the plain, and were therefore unable to strike at the Persian infantry. Pausanias therefore posted his army in order of battle along the foothills and waited on the defensive.[1]

Both generals now played a waiting game. The Greeks suffered incessantly from the attentions of the Persian cavalry, irregularity of supplies, and inadequate sources of water. Their morale was raised for a day or two, when a picked force of 300 Athenians with supporting archers managed to kill Masistius and drive off the cuirassiers. His corpse was placed on a cart and carried past the troops of the Greek line; and that night the plain resounded with the wailing of the Asiatics, who cut the manes of their chargers and pack-animals in mourning. But the effect was short-lived. The attacks by the cavalry continued for a period of three weeks, during which both generals made abortive changes of disposition and received adverse omens from their seers.

Then late in the night a horseman approached the Athenian outposts and was passed back to the Athenian commanders. He was Alexander, the king of Macedonia. He reported that Mardonius would attack at dawn, and he probably gave the information that the best Persian infantry had·moved from their post opposite the Spartans to a post opposite the Athenians. Alexander then rode off. By dawn Pausanias had changed the posts of the Spartans and Athenians likewise. Mardonius then abandoned his plan, and both sides adopted their former dispositions. The Persian cavalry then attacked and drove back the Spartans from their chief source of water, the spring Gargaphia, which was efficiently blocked and fouled. This made the Greek position wellnigh untenable. Pausanias called a conference, at which it was agreed to move during the next night to a fresh position nearer Plataea.[2]

At dusk, when another day of incessant attacks by the Persian cavalry had added to the strain on the Greek infantry, the large force began its night-march. The contingents of the centre were already somewhat demoralized. In their fear of the Persian cavalry they pushed ahead to Plataea itself. Meanwhile Pausanias was having trouble with an obstinate Spartan officer, Amom-

---

[1] 9. 19; 28–30; 39; *BSA* 49. 112 = *StGH* 431 for routes.
[2] 9. 20–25; 36–37; 40–51.

pharetus, who had not attended the conference and now refused to obey the order to withdraw, which he regarded as tantamount to flight in the face of the enemy. Informed by Pausanias that the Spartans and Tegeans had not moved, the Athenians also stayed at their post. As dawn began to break, the general gave the order to move and left Amompharetus and his company behind. While the Athenians crossed the plain, Pausanias led his force along the foothills. Amompharetus and his company then followed at a leisurely pace, and Pausanias halted in order that they might join him.

The Persian cavalry, galloping to the attack at dawn and finding the Greek lines deserted, now assaulted and checked the combined forces of Pausanias and Amompharetus. To the eye of Mardonius the Greek army seemed to have disintegrated. He immediately ordered his whole line of infantry to advance at full speed. His Greek allies on the right cut off the Athenians, recalled in vain by Pausanias, and the Persian infantry led a general assault on the Lacedaemonians and Tegeans, now alone and unsupported. The Persians did not close at once. They made a rampart of their large wicker shields, to afford cover from the missiles of the Greek skirmishers, and poured their arrows into the ranks of the hoplites. Pausanias held his hoplites firm until the enemy ranks became congested. The omens were declared to be favourable. Then, with the slope in their favour, the hoplites charged in good order, swept aside the rampart, and closed with the enemy. Their deadly spears, their line of shields, and their weight of armour gradually overwhelmed the Persians, who fought bravely, even seizing the spearheads in their bare hands, but lacked shields, breastplates, and long weapons. The fighting was particularly severe where Mardonius, mounted on a white charger, led the royal bodyguard of infantry, a thousand strong. But these, too, were beaten down, and Mardonius was slain. Then the Persian infantry broke and fled in disorder, accompanied by the general mass of Medes, Bactrians, and others. The pursuit was so hot that the cavalry could not cut the Greeks off from the fugitives, as they ran towards the stockaded camp.

During the close fighting the troops of the Greek centre had rushed down from Plataea, some following the foothills, others crossing the plain. The latter were attacked by a squadron of Theban cavalry, lost 600 men, and were driven back to the slopes of Mt. Cithaeron. The Athenians on the left fought a pitched battle with the Boeotians; when the best Theban troops—a band of 300—were annihilated, the Boeotians withdrew to Thebes. Of the Persians some infantry of the centre under Artabazus and the squadrons of cavalry made off in good order towards the north. The Athenians then joined the Lacedaemonians, who had failed to carry the stockade. By determined and skilful attacks the Athenians opened a breach, and the Greeks poured in and butchered the Asiatics like sheep in a fold. For Pausanias, alarmed at the great number of the enemy and mindful perhaps of the massacres the enemy had committed, ordered his army to take no prisoners. When the slaughter ended, the main infantry force of the Persian army was no more. The threat of conquest by the Persian army was dispersed, for ever as it proved, by the superb spirit and skill of the Spartan hoplites, who proved themselves to be the finest infantrymen not of Greece alone but of the civilized world.[1]

The campaign of Plataea was the finest achievement of Greek unity. For three weeks more than 100,000 Greeks had stood together and resisted the attacks of the Persian horse. They had remained loyal to Zeus Hellenios, the god of the Greeks, whom the Athenians had once invoked in the allied cause. They had fulfilled the oath, to which they solemnly pledged themselves before crossing Mt. Cithaeron: 'I shall fight to the death, I shall put freedom before life, I shall not desert colonel or captain alive or dead, I shall carry out the generals' commands, and I shall bury my comrades-in-arms where they fall and leave none unburied'.[2] During the manœuvres before the battle the Plataeans had lifted their border-stones on the Attic frontier, in order to conform with a Delphic oracle, which promised a victory on Attic soil. After the battle the victors paid special honours to the Plataeans, in whose territory the Greek dead were buried. The member-states of the Greek League entered into a covenant, that on every anniversary of the victory the political and the religious representatives of 'The Greeks' should meet at Plataea to offer thanksgiving to Zeus the Liberator and to conduct the Games held in honour of Liberation; that the Plataeans should be dedicated to Zeus as an inviolable and sacred people; and that the Plataeans should offer sacrifice to Zeus and Hermes on behalf of the Greek dead. These ceremonies were maintained for many centuries, the chief magistrate of Plataea ending the sacrifice with the words 'I drink to the men who died for the freedom of the Greeks'.[3]

Since much of Greece was still under the Persian yoke, the victors bound themselves under the covenant of the Greek League to continue the struggle, and to levy regularly a Greek force of 10,000 hoplites, 1,000 cavalry, and 100 warships. Success brought new adherents to their cause. Already Samos had revolted from Persia and joined the League. Before the year was out, the Ionians and the Aeolians of the islands took the oaths of alliance and sent their representatives to the Congress of the Greeks. The oath taken before the battle at Plataea had probably repeated the original undertaking of the allies to 'tithe' the medizing states. They now resolved to march on Thebes and demand the surrender of the medizers. The Thebans withstood a siege for twenty days and then surrendered any medizers who had not escaped. They were taken to the allied headquarters at the Isthmus to stand their trial before

---

[1] 9. 52–70; Plu. *Arist.* 17–19; D.S. 11. 31–32.

[2] Hdt. 9. 7ª2; *GHI* 204. 23 f.; Lycurg. 1. 81; D.S. 11. 29. 3; *FGrH* 115 F 153 (Theopompus). The last stated that the Athenian version of the oath—and perhaps the Athenian claim to have supplied the original—was false. The inscription contains some Spartan terms, which Athenians are unlikely to have put in a false version. This oath was as famous then as is today the song of Rhígas, 'finer is one day of freedom than forty years of servitude and bondage'.

[3] Plu. *Arist.* 11; Hdt. 9. 85; Plu. *Arist.* 19 and 21 (the proposal being paraphrased and not cited verbatim); Th. 3. 58; D.S. 11. 29. 1.

the court of the Greek League. But Pausanias disbanded the allied army and put the medizers to death without delay.[1]

The same September day witnessed the battle of Plataea and a Greek victory at Mycale on the coast of Asia Minor. The latter event opened a new chapter in the relations between the mainland Greeks and the Persian empire. For, apart from the shortlived intervention of Athens and Eretria during the Ionian Revolt, the Greeks had not carried war into the territory of the Great King. The Greek navy undertook this offensive in 479, less to liberate the Greeks of Asia Minor than to prevent troops joining Mardonius by sea and protect Greece from a renewed invasion on the scale of the previous year. For, if the Greek fleet could worst the Persian fleet and control the Aegean basin, then Xerxes would hardly be able to maintain a larger army in Europe than he had left in the autumn of 480.

When the Greek fleet of 110 sail mustered at Aegina in spring 479, six refugees came from Chios to the headquarters of the commander, Leotychidas, king of Sparta. After failing to assassinate the pro-Persian tyrant of Chios, they had visited Sparta and asked the Spartan authorities ·to liberate Ionia. They now repeated their request to the commander of the Greek fleet. In both cases the request was refused. By August the strength of the fleet had risen to some 250 warships. Three men then arrived from a resistance group in Samos, the base of the enemy fleet. They reported that the Persian ships were in poor condition; that the Samian people would rise against the pro-Persian tyrant, Theomestor; and that the sight of the allied fleet off the coast would raise the Ionians in revolt. Leotychidas required the men to give pledges of good faith, and led the Greek fleet forward to engage at Samos. The enemy, however, dismissed the fast-sailing Phoenician ships and crossed with the remainder of the fleet to Mycale on the mainland, where the vessels were beached and a stockade built around them. At this place a Persian army of 60,000 men, which did garrison duty in Ionia, was already encamped, so that the total force at Mycale, including the marines and the crews, numbered some 100,000 men. Of these a considerable part was formed by Greeks and other subject peoples of doubtful loyalty. The Greek fleet, being equipped for boarding tactics, carried a complement of some 5,000 heavy-armed marines in addition to 45,000 sailors, who were armed for close combat. Leotychidas therefore sailed to Mycale and offered battle at sea, but the Persians made no move.[2]

Leotychidas decided to exploit the possibility of dissension in the enemy camp. Sailing his flagship close inshore, he made a proclamation to the Ionians in Persian service: let them be mindful of Freedom and spread the password 'Hera' among their friends. He then landed his whole force farther down the coast. The Persian commander, alarmed by the proclamation, as Leotychidas had intended, disarmed his Samian troops and posted the Mile-

[1] For 10,000 hoplites in the levy cf. Hdt. 7. 173; 9. 86–88

[2] 8. 132; D.S. 11. 34; Hdt. 9. 90–97. For these events see my article in *JHS* 86.

sians on the paths which led inland. His infantry then made a rampart with their tall wicker shields and strung their bows for action. As the Greeks under Leotychidas took up their posts, an unfounded rumour spread through the ranks that their kinsmen in Greece had won a great victory. In good heart the army advanced, the Athenians leading one wing over level ground by the sea-shore and forcing their way through the rampart of wicker shields. The hoplites in close order then drove back the Persian infantry and pursued the fugitives so closely that the troops of Athens, Corinth, Sicyon, and Troezen broke into the stockaded camp. There the rest of the army, led by the Lacedaemonians, who had been delayed by difficult ground, came up for the final onslaught, during which the Ionians in Persian service attacked their masters. The Persian infantrymen in small and isolated groups fought on to the death, while most of their subjects fled inland, where the Milesian troops set upon them. When the fighting ended, the dead numbered some 40,000, and the ships were burnt on the beaches. This decisive victory gave the Greeks a clear supremacy in the Aegean Sea. If Xerxes returned to the attack, he would rely only on the fleets of Phoenicia, Cyprus, and Egypt. For the Ionians and the Aeolians were again ready to revolt.[1]

The victory brought the Greeks face to face with a political and military problem of great importance. The Greek Congress at Corinth had no doubt ordered Leotychidas to hold or attack the Persian fleet and to avail himself of any aid which the Ionians might offer. It is probable that the Congress had appointed plenipotentiaries to the staff of Leotychidas, who were empowered to accept new members into the Greek League and determine policy in the east Aegean. Before the battle of Mycale Leotychidas had negotiated with Samian agents and more or less accepted the obligation to defend Samos against Persia. Should the same obligation be undertaken in regard to the Ionians and the Aeolians of the Asiatic mainland? The answer of Sparta to this question had always been clear: she would extend diplomatic protection but not military assistance. A land power, deficient in cavalry, she considered herself unable to defend the coastal strip against the military resources of the Persian empire. On this occasion, when the staff of Leotychidas debated the question, the Spartan opinion was the same and it was shared by the Peloponnesian members. They therefore advised the Ionians and Aeolians to leave the Asiatic coast—a course which Bias of Priene had once advocated and some states had adopted—and they proposed to settle them on territories with a commercial seaboard at the expense of the medizing states.

The Athenian representatives, however, vigorously opposed the proposal of the Spartans and the Peloponnesians. They did not wish Ionia to be evacuated; and in deference to their wishes the Spartans and Peloponnesians desisted. The allies then admitted as members of the Greek League Chios, Lesbos, and other island states, which were co-operating with the Greeks, but no Greek state of the Asiatic mainland.[2] With this arrangement the Spar-

---

[1] 9. 98–106; D.S. 11. 34–36. [2] 1. 152; 5. 49–51; 1. 170; 9. 106; D.S. 11. 37.

tans and the Peloponnesians might have rested content; for it would have given the *modus vivendi* with Persia which Sparta arranged almost a century later. At the moment it left the Greeks of Asia Minor unprotected by any treaty.

After the victory at Mycale the allied fleet sailed to Abydus. Leotychidas intended to destroy the bridge over the Hellespont, but it had already been washed away. As the season was late, he sailed home to disband the fleet. But Xanthippus and the Athenian commanders decided to conduct an independent operation. With the support of Ionian and Hellespontine Greeks who had been admitted into the Greek League, they laid siege to Sestus, the main Persian base in the Chersonese. When the siege dragged on into the winter, the Athenian troops grew restive, but their commanders refused to depart, unless orders were received from the Athenian state: for they were acting in the interests of the Greek League but under the orders of Athens. Before the winter ended, the Persians made a successful sortie from Sestus, but the rearguard, including many leading Persians, were captured. Artaÿctes, the commander, and his son were done to death on the orders of Xanthippus, and the others were ransomed by their kinsmen for large sums of money. In spring 478 Xanthippus sailed home with rich booty and with the cables of Xerxes' bridge, which were probably dedicated by the Athenian state to Apollo at Delphi and to Athena at Athens.[1]

With this operation Herodotus closed his history of the Persian War. There was, indeed, something symbolical in the capture of the bridge cables; but the real factors which prevented Xerxes from mounting another large-scale invasion were the battles of Plataea and Mycale. War with Persia, however, was not concluded in 478. Persian garrisons were maintained in Europe until about 465, and a Persian naval offensive was often possible until as late as 448, when Athens finally concluded peace with Persia. In 478 the threat of a second invasion loomed very large and impelled some Greek states to undertake further military and naval action against Persia.

[1] 9. 106 fin.; 114–21; Th. 1. 89. 2; *GHI* 18 with *Fouilles de Delphes* 2. 110 f. (*Le Portique d'Athéniens* by P. Amandry and *Charisterion Orlandou* 155 ('Two monuments on the Athenian Acropolis' by W. B. Dinsmoor).

CHAPTER 5

The Growth of the Athenian Alliance

§ 1. *Athens' relations with Sparta*

WITH the siege of Sestus in the winter of 479–478 Thucydides began his account of Athens' rise to power. Since 491 Sparta and Athens had acted in unison despite differences of opinion. Their soldiers and sailors, fighting side by side at Artemisium, Salamis, Plataea, and Mycale, had carried the Greeks on to victory over the Persians. The leadership of Sparta by land and by sea had been unquestioned. Athens, despite the bitter loss of her territory, had remained loyal to Sparta and to the Greek League. But in the siege of Sestus she acted without Sparta and the Peloponnesians and with some Ionian and Hellespontine Greeks, whose enthusiastic loyalty she now gained for herself. Her action gave encouragement also to the Aeolians and the Ionians of the Asiatic coast. In particular she was tied by sentiment and by interest to the Ionians of the Asiatic coast. She claimed to be their foundress and protectress, and with their aid she could strengthen her naval and commercial position in the Aegean. Moreover, the war had given Athens the means of separate action. She was now the leading naval power and the second military power in Greece; her courage and her endurance had inspired her citizens with confidence and filled others with admiration, and her fight for freedom rallied the Ionians to her side.

The separate action of Athens was a tacit challenge to the hegemony of Sparta. Yet it was within the framework of allied interest; for a vigorous naval offensive would do more than anything else to avert the danger of a renewed offensive by land. Sparta therefore did not seek to hinder it. But during the same winter months, when Sestus was under siege, a further cause of friction between Sparta and Athens arose. The victory at Plataea had enabled the Athenians to return to their devastated country and undertake the rebuilding of their defences. Sparta, however, asked the Athenian government to desist. She argued that all fortifications in central and northern Greece should be razed, so that the Persians would have no fortified base of operations in the event of a renewed invasion, and that the Peloponnese should be regarded as the haven and base of all the mainland Greeks. But Sparta's request was really a thinly veiled threat to the independence of Athens; for it was made at the very moment when Athens was weakened financially by the devastation of her territory and was exposed to attack as an open city. Athens' response to this challenge was immediate. She instructed Xanthippus to continue operations at Sestus, and she sent her ablest diplomat, Themistocles, to Sparta.

At this critical stage in Athenian affairs Themistocles was in control. He prompted the orders of Xanthippus and arranged that he should go ahead of the other members of the Athenian embassy to Sparta. There he took advantage of his popularity to procrastinate and lulled Spartan suspicions with bland assurances. The other envoys left Athens only when the walls were of defensible height. Meanwhile rumours reached Sparta that the walls were being rebuilt. Themistocles professed disbelief. He persuaded the Spartans to send a mission of their own to Athens, and secretly instructed the Athenians to hold the members of the Spartan mission as hostages. Meanwhile the other Athenian envoys arrived and Themistocles laid his cards upon the table. Athens, he said, was already defensible and would defend herself. In the perils of war she had shown herself capable of choosing a course of action which was in the interest both of herself and of the allied cause. Such a course she had chosen now in rebuilding her walls, and she asked Sparta to recognize the choice as that of an equal and sovereign state. The *fait accompli* was accepted, and both missions returned home. Later, when Themistocles went on to fortify the Peiraeus, he anticipated any Spartan protests by issuing a statement that the Peiraeus would be the base of the Greek navy in resisting any attack by the Persian navy.[1]

The differences between Sparta and Athens were overshadowed by the common danger, Persia. In summer 478, when the Peloponnesians had reaped the harvest, two expeditionary forces of the Greek League were dispatched by the Greek Congress. The first, commanded by Leotychidas, king of Sparta, was to punish the medizers of north Greece, especially the Aleuadae of Thessaly, and to secure the area against Persian intrigue. The army and the fleet advanced as far as Pagasae, but failed to oust the Aleuadae from Larisa. After this failure Leotychidas was haled before a court at Sparta and found guilty of corruption. The victor of Mycale was exiled for life from Sparta. It was probably in the same year that Sparta proposed in the Amphictyonic Council to expel all members who had been neutral in the war. The proposal was thwarted by the influence of Themistocles, who warned the other members that the Spartan Alliance would then dominate the Council.[2] The second force, commanded by Pausanias, the Spartan regent and victor of Plataea, followed up the victory of Mycale by reducing most of Cyprus and capturing Byzantium from the Persians. These important successes bottled up the Phoenician fleet and cut the second line of communication between Europe and Asia. But at this point Sparta suffered another humiliation. Dictatorial behaviour by Pausanias gave deep offence to the Greek captains and encouraged some Ionians and Aeolians, led by the Chians, Lesbians, and Samians, to approach Aristides and his captains with the proposal that Athens should take over the command as the foundress of Ionia.

[1] Th. 1. 89. 3-92; D.S. 11. 39-40; 43. 2; Plu. *Them.* 19.
[2] Hdt. 6. 72; Plu. *Them.* 20.

Aware of this intrigue, Sparta recalled Pausanias and put him on trial. He was acquitted on most of the charges, which concerned the abuse of his powers as supreme commander, but the evidence that he had intrigued with Persia seemed to be indisputable. The Spartan government therefore relieved Pausanias of his command and sent out a successor, Dorcis, who took with him a staff and a small force. But meanwhile all the allies in the Hellespont, except the marines and crews from the Peloponnese, had placed themselves under the command of Athens. Late in 478 Dorcis and his company withdrew, and Sparta made no further attempt to impose her command on the fleet.[1]

§ 2. *Organization and success of the Athenian Alliance*

DURING the winter of 478–7 Athens organized the system of command to her liking. She enjoyed the goodwill of the island and maritime states. Her fleet had given proof of its prowess, and her conduct had justified her claim to be the champion of liberation. These states were particularly in need of protection; for, if Persia returned to the attack, she would first try to reduce the Hellespont, Ionia, and the islands. They were therefore willing to give Athens favourable conditions of command. But at the same time Athens had no wish to break with Sparta or disassociate herself from the Greek League, to which she and some of the island states were bound by solemn oaths. The covenant of alliance, which formed the basis of the Greek League, was therefore left intact; indeed it remained effective until 462–1 and was not formally renounced until 457. Meanwhile within the Greek League Athens set out to form an Alliance, known later as 'The Athenians and their Allies', which was analogous in title and in constitution to the Spartan Alliance. The first step was an alliance between Athens and 'The Ionians'. They exchanged oaths with one another 'to have the same friend and enemy', and they cast lumps of red-hot iron into the sea to indicate that, until the iron rose to the surface, their oaths would be irrevocable. The terms of the undertaking 'to have the same friend and enemy' show that it was an offensive and defensive alliance against any aggressor. Athens then made separate alliances with Mitylene and other states. Finally Aristides, representing Athens, and delegates of the allied states exchanged oaths and brought into being the contract of alliance between Athens and 'The Greeks'. Their aims included liberation from and reprisals against Persia.[2]

The constitution of the new Alliance was bicameral, the Athenian state forming one chamber and the Synod of the Allies (known at first as 'The Greeks') the other. The Athenian state was what the Greeks called 'hegemon';

[1] Th. 1. 94–95; D.S. 11. 44–46; Plu. *Arist.* 23.
[2] Th. 1. 102. 4; Arist. *Ath.* 23. 5; Th. 1. 96. 1; 3. 10. 3; Hdt. 8. 143. 2; Plu. *Arist.* 25. See StGH 311–45 = *JHS* 87. 41 ff, for the organization of the Athenian Alliance, which is very controversial.

she commanded the confederate navy, brought in the contributions of ships and of money, and appointed 'treasurers of the Greeks' (*Hellenotamiai*) to receive the allied funds. She provided a considerable part of the allied fleet; and in compensation she took a half-share of all booty. The Allies were autonomous, their independence being guaranteed by Athens. Each Allied state, whether represented by one or more delegates, had a single vote on the Synod and the decision of the majority was binding on all members. The function of the Synod was deliberative; it considered all matters of policy such as war and peace and the admission of new members. The place of meeting was in the temple of Apollo and Artemis at Delos, the traditional centre of Ionian religion, and here the allied treasury was under the protection of the god and goddess.[1] Athens had no vote in the Synod; but for purposes of deliberation and liaison her representatives may on occasion have been present at its meetings. The two chambers, the Athenian state and the Synod of Allies, were equal in power: either chamber could initiate or reject an agendum for deliberation, and policy was adopted only if both chambers were in agreement. This constitution was less developed in the direction of federalism than that of the Greek League; but for the purposes of war it had the same strength as that of the Spartan Alliance, in that the hegemon held a permanent and powerful position. It was based partly on the experience of the Greek mainland and partly on that of the Ionians in the revolt of 499–493. They had then formed a political unit, 'The Ionians', with a council of delegates, a rate of contribution, and even an allied coinage; but they had had no hegemon, a weakness in practice which was now made good.

From the outset the Athenian Alliance worked promptly and decisively. The Athenian state had initiative and courage, and the Ionians had experience of allied deliberation through appointed delegates. In addition to the original allies, other states—Aeolian at first and Dorian later—entered the Alliance and took the same oaths. The first assessment of contributions was made in 478–7. The Synod of the Allies promised 460 talents for the coming year and invited Aristides to fix the contribution of each ally. He did this so impartially that he was acclaimed 'Aristides the Just'. Athens decided (on this occasion alone) which allies should make their contribution in ships and which in money. Thus ships and money together made up the first *phoros*, which meant 'contribution'; it was only later that *phoros* meant 'tribute in money' with political overtones. Athens undertook to supply ships, perhaps half of a combined fleet of at least 300 triremes, but not money, as she was exhausted by war and devastation. Many scholars hold a different view, namely that the 460 talents was the total of monetary contributions alone. The objection to this view is that after 454 very many more states contributed less than 400 talents a year and that therefore the burden on money-paying states in 477 would have been excessive. The objection is not decisive, because enthusiasm and necessity went hand in hand in 477 and Athens alone had

[1] Th. 1. 96–97; cf. 98. 4 and 3. 10. 4 on autonomy; Plu. *Cim.* 9 on booty.

spent 100 talents on her navy in 483–2; but it tips the scale in favour of the interpretation which is adopted here. In 477 and thereafter each member-state was under an obligation to provide troops which served under the command of the 'hegemon', Athens. These troops were distinct from the crews which were supplied by the ship-contributing states.[1] Thus the Athenian Alliance provided itself with a large fleet, fully manned, properly financed and ably commanded by Athens, the strongest naval state in the Greek world.

Of the early actions of the Athenian Alliance we know only a few. Thucydides mentions first the capture of Eïon from the Persians and the enslavement of the inhabitants, and then the capture of Scyros, from which the piratical inhabitants, the Dolopes, were expelled and sold as slaves. In Scyros the bones of Theseus, the great Athenian and Ionian hero, were discovered and brought in ceremony to Athens; for just as Sparta had claimed the leadership of all Peloponnesian peoples by acquiring the sacred relics of Orestes, so Athens fortified her claim to lead the Ionians. Both Eïon and Scyros were occupied by Athenian settlers; the former was soon lost, but the latter remained an Athenian cleruchy. These operations in the north-west Aegean fell in the archon year 476/5. They were probably preceded by the second capture of Byzantium, this time from Pausanias, who had gone there from Sparta as a private individual and set himself up as tyrant to intrigue further with Persia. Sestus, too, was probably captured again from the Persians, who were making every effort to reopen communications with their forces in Europe. Sometime after 476/475 Carystus in Euboea was forced to enter the Alliance, and Naxos, having seceded, was reduced by siege and compelled to rejoin under less favourable conditions.[2] Both states had resisted Persia and supported Persia in the past. We do not know whether at this time there was any justification for Athens' intervention.

Thucydides' list of incidents at Eïon, Scyros, Carystus, and Naxos is intended to illustrate the steps in Athens' rise to power and not the successes of the Athenian Alliance. He was aware of the imperial position to which Athens later raised herself by subjugating her allies and planting cleruchies, and he therefore attached a significance to these incidents which was not apparent at the time. To the eye of a contemporary Athens was pursuing a policy which was in the interest both of herself and of her allies, and used rather than abused the powers conceded to her as hegemon. For in time of war neutrality was not far removed from medism and might prove infectious; and in any case Naxos' secession probably constituted a breach of the oath of alliance. Against these incidents we must set a large number of successes by the Athenian Alliance which are unknown to us in detail but explain the triumphant campaign of the Eurymedon c. 467.

The Persians based a large army and a fleet of some 350 ships in Pam-

---

[1] Th. 1. 96. 2; 99. 1; Plu. *Arist.* 24; D.S. 11. 47 gives 560 talents; Eupolis fr. 232.

[2] Th. 1. 98; Hdt. 7. 107; 9. 105; *FGrH* 70 F 191 (Ephorus); Plu. *Cim.* 6–9; *Thes.* 36; D.S. 11. 60.

phylia *c.* 467, intending probably to advance into the Aegean. But Cimon, the Athenian commander, moved first with the forces of the Athenian Alliance. His battle-fleet numbered 300 ships, of which 200 triremes were provided and manned by Athens; these had the quickness of manœuvre which had been important at Salamis, but they were broader in the beam and the side-decks were joined at some points to provide passage for the marines from bulwark to bulwark. This change in design from the time of Themistocles to that of Cimon was in line with the change from defence to offence. At Salamis ramming was important; but Cimon commanded an assault force, which might need to fight on land as well as at sea and was therefore fitted to carry a larger complement of marines. His Athenian squadron probably carried some 5,000 hoplites. The 100 triremes of Athens' allies carried marines and also some archers.

The fleet of Cimon mustered at Cnidus and then sailed along the coast, winning over the maritime cities by diplomacy or force. At Phaselis, facing the Persian base on the Eurymedon river, Cimon at first assaulted the fortifications, but his Chian allies persuaded the citizens to pay ten talents and provide troops. With Phaselis as his base of operations, Cimon went in to the attack. The Persian fleet was not yet fully mustered; for eighty further Phoenician galleys were expected from Cyprus. Even so the Persians had more ships and a large army in support. But they withdrew their fleet into the basin of the Eurymedon to avoid an engagement at sea. Cimon, however, advanced into the basin. The Persians then put out in order of battle, but they kept close inshore. At the first contact the Persian ships fled shorewards. Some were sunk, some captured, and others shattered their timbers on the beach. The demoralization of the Persian navy was complete. In this engagement and in a later one with the expected Phoenician squadron off Cyprus, 200 vessels were sunk in action or captured intact.

As the Persian army came down to the beach to cover the fugitives, Cimon boldly forced a landing, and his hoplites charged the Persian infantry. The fighting was severe, and many distinguished Athenians fell, before the enemy were broken and the camp was taken. Cimon then sailed at once to surprise and destroy the Phoenician squadron off Cyprus. These remarkable victories reaffirmed the verdict of Mycale, that Greek ships and marines were superior to the coastal forces of the Persian empire, and justified the bold policy of Athens in 479–8 when she encouraged the Ionians to stay in Asia Minor. Her own soldiers and sailors, forming the spearhead of the Athenian Alliance and in this campaign outnumbering the troops of her allies by two to one, had indeed protected the liberty of the East Greeks from the imperial power of Persia. Soon after the battle Cimon cleared some Persians out of the Chersonese and won the peninsula for Athens. This action probably marked the end of the Persian satrapy which Darius had formed in 513. The triumph of Europe over Asia, of the small Greek states over the great state of Persia, was complete. Those who died at the Eurymedon guaranteed the freedom of the

Greeks. Their epitaph had a dignity worthy of the occasion. 'These are they who laid down the splendour of their manhood beside the Eurymedon; on land and on the swift-sailing ships alike they fought with their spears against the foremost of the bow-bearing Medes. They are no more, but they have left the fairest memorial of valour.'[1]

§ 3. *The troubles of Sparta*

THE Persian War enhanced Sparta's reputation but strained her institutions. Her armed forces, Spartiates and Perioeci and Helots alike, had fought superbly and imperturbably; her generals as the supreme commanders of the Greek armies and navies—Leonidas, Eurybiades, Pausanias, and Leotychidas—had succeeded brilliantly in handling a staff of many nationalities and in organizing victory. Her resolution had inspired others; even her slowness had sometimes had a steadying effect, and her military strength at Plataea, totalling 45,000 men, was far greater than that of any other Greek state. On the other hand, her losses were larger than those of any state except Athens, and the loss in Spartiates—perhaps 500 killed in action and many wounded—was more serious, in that the privileged class was already so heavily outnumbered by the unprivileged. The institutions of Sparta were admirably designed to maintain the traditional order in Laconia and Messenia, beyond which the inhabitants rarely moved. In the Persian War Spartiates, Perioeci, and Helots campaigned abroad and mixed with Greeks of different outlook and experience; they were exposed to the temptations of wealth and luxury, especially when the spoil was divided among the victorious troops, and in the higher ranks also to the temptations of a military command which was not constantly supervised by the civilian authorities. The effects were most conspicuous in the two royal families. The careers of Cleomenes, Demaratus, Leotychidas, and Pausanias ended in a degree of corruption or ambition which did not shrink from treason and medism, and their examples must have had a damaging influence on the loyalties of many Spartiates. Their excesses and their arrogance alienated the allies and in particular the Ionians; they cost Sparta the hegemony by sea in 478, and they caused the Spartan government to resign that hegemony without a struggle.[2]

These events affected the internal stability of Sparta and her leadership of the Spartan Alliance. In the Spartan constitution the dual Kingship had usually been counterbalanced by the Ephorate. As the prestige of the royal families sank and the crowns passed to two minors, Pleistarchus and Archidamus, the power of the Ephorate rose and resulted in a less adventurous policy. At the same time the Gerousia became emancipated from the influence of the kings and controlled the conduct of the state. Its members, being over sixty years of age (apart from the young kings), viewed the institutions of

---

[1] Th. 1. 100. 1; Plu. *Cim.* 12–14; D.S. 11. 60–62; *AP* 7. 258.
[2] Hdt. 9. 80–82; Th. 1. 95. 7; 130. 2.

Sparta with a conservative eye and tended to repress any individualism which service abroad had stimulated. The result was a tightening up of the Spartan system, which became more oppressive towards the Perioeci and the Helots and sealed the country off from the liberalizing tendencies of commerce and art. As leader of the Spartan Alliance Sparta exercised a more authoritative form of hegemony than she had done as leader of the Greek League. During the war the members of the Spartan Alliance had formed a majority in the Greek League, and they had had more opportunity to sway Sparta and to observe the defects of her leadership. So far as appearances went, Sparta had been forced by Athens to fight at Salamis and to campaign in Boeotia, at a time when the Peloponnesian members of the Spartan Alliance would have preferred to defend the Peloponnese. Sparta's leaders had been disgraced; her government had been outwitted by Themistocles; and a new and formidable power had arisen in Athens and her Alliance. The very success of Sparta in the cause of Greece had damaged the interests of Aegina, Corinth, and Thebes, and had evoked opposition in Elis and Mantinea, which sent their contingents late for the battle of Plataea.[1]

In 478 Sparta accepted her discomfiture in north Greece and the Aegean at the hands of Athens. Perhaps in 475 the Gerousia and the Assembly debated their future relations with Athens. In both bodies many favoured a war to depose Athens and reinstate Sparta as leader of the Greek League by sea. But a member of the Gerousia, Hetoemaridas, dissuaded the Spartans from this course on the grounds that the exercise of sea power was not expedient for Sparta.[2] He was certainly right in the sense that sea power was incompatible with the traditional institutions of Sparta. In consequence a period of dual leadership ensued, during which Sparta and Athens at the head of their respective Alliances were in league with one another (*homaikhmia*) and a balance of power resulted in the world of Greek states.

The alliance of Sparta and Athens had developed with the Greek League, and to its principles both were loyal. When Pausanias fled from Byzantium to Colonae in the Troad and intrigued with Persia, it is probable that Athens reported his activities to Sparta, whither he was recalled by the Ephors and imprisoned. Pausanias engineered his own release, and then offered himself for trial, but the Ephors lacked incontrovertible evidence, even when informers reported that he was organizing a rising of the Helots. At last a servant of Pausanias, who had been entrusted with a letter to the Great King, went to the Ephors and gave them the letter. Pausanias was then lured into a conversation with his servant, which was overheard by the Ephors and gave proof of his guilt. When they came to arrest him, he escaped into the temple of Athena of the Brazen House, where he was shut in and left to starve. Just before he died, the Ephors brought him out of the temple. For their sacrilegious behaviour the oracle at Delphi laid a curse on Sparta. At the same time Sparta asked Athens to join in arresting Themistocles, who was implicated

---

[1] Hdt. 9. 77. [2] D.S. 11. 50.

by the letter of Pausanias, and Athens agreed to do so. In this year, perhaps 471, Themistocles had already been ostracized from Athens and was living at Argos. He managed to escape from the emissaries of Sparta and Athens, before they could present him for trial before the court of the Greek League.[1]

While Sparta preserved her alliance with Athens, she made every effort to maintain her leadership of the Spartan Alliance. It was probably at her prompting that Elis and Mantinea banished their generals, when the contingents returned from Plataea. The governments of these states were loyal to Sparta when the next trial of strength came with Argos, perhaps in 472. Whereas Sparta had suffered losses in the Persian War, Argos had recovered from the effects of her defeat at Sepeia *c.* 495. Argos now enlisted the support of Tegea, whose hoplites were renowned for their valour. A decisive battle was fought at Tegea and resulted in a Spartan victory. In 471, perhaps under the influence of Themistocles who was active in the Peloponnese, the small communities of Elis (*damoi*) coalesced into a single city (*synoikismos*), which became the capital of a more strongly centralized state and probably adopted a democratic form of government. This development was viewed with distrust by Sparta, the champion of oligarchy in the Peloponnese.[2]

In 469 the Messenians rose in revolt, and maintained their resistance in the mountainous country of Ithome until 460. During the early years of the so-called Third Messenian War the morale of Sparta was shaken by a number of earthquakes, which were regarded as acts of retribution by the god Poseidon; for the Ephors of Sparta had recently torn suppliants from the altar of Poseidon in Cape Taenarum and put them to death. The embarrassment of Sparta gave an opportunity to her enemies. In 468 Argos, Cleonae, and Tegea annihilated the famous city of Mycenae. Tegea, too, was supported by all the Arcadian states except Mantinea in her secession from the Spartan Alliance. A decisive battle was fought at Dipaea, perhaps in 466. The Spartans, compelled to deploy their reserves against the Messenians at Ithome, were so heavily outnumbered by the Arcadians that they fought in a thin line. Once again the prowess of the Spartan hoplite won the day. In the difficult years which were to come the Arcadians remained loyal to Sparta, and Argos, having failed to support the Arcadians, began to lose her influence. The advice of Hetoemaridas, not to challenge the hegemony of Athens at sea, was justified by these events. For Sparta's strength was fully engaged in maintaining her position on land against the rebel Messenians and the Peloponnesian states.[3]

---

[1] Th. 1. 18. 2–3; 128–35; D.S. 11. 55. 4; Plu. *Them.* 23 fin.

[2] Hdt. 9. 77; 35; D.S. 11. 54. 1; Str. 337.

[3] D.S. 11. 63; 65; Str. 377; Isoc. 6. 99. The chronology of the Third Messenian War, the sack of Mycenae, and the battle of Dipaea are disputed. See *Historia* 4. 371 f. for the view adopted in the text.

§ 4. *Politics at Athens 479–466*

ATHENS emerged from the Persian War with added confidence in her institutions. The equality of rights (*isonomia*), which Cleisthenes had inaugurated, had given to the state a unity and concord which were heightened by the trials of evacuation and confirmed by the achievements of her armed forces. In these all classes in the state had had their share, the hoplites at Marathon and Plataea and the thetes as sailors at Artemisium, Salamis, and Mycale. There was as yet little contrast between the hoplites and the thetes in their services to the state; for in naval operations the hoplites played an important part as marines in boarding enemy vessels or leading assaults on shore. Thus both groups gained in self-confidence. Nor were they divided by sectional interests during the immediate aftermath of the Persian War. They worked together to rebuild the fortifications of Attica, and they fought side by side to develop the Athenian Alliance and to win the great victory at the Eurymedon. Nevertheless, the seeds of a later division within the state were sown during this period. The upper and middle classes generally owned land in Attica, in defence of which they fought as cavalry and hoplites and swayed the foreign policy of the state; to them relations with Sparta and her Alliance were as important as the conflict with Persia. The lower class owned no land. They found a new and more congenial field of employment in the fleet; for they built and rowed the triremes. Their future was tied up with naval expansion and with Athens' naval coalition. To them Themistocles appealed, when he urged his countrymen to develop their power at sea, and, if need arose, to fight from the Peiraeus and the ships against all comers.

During the emergency greater powers had been granted to the executive magistrates. After 487, the board of generals became more influential than the college of archons, and the commander elected to the staff of the Greek League wielded the highest authority, probably as a *strategos ex hapanton*. Such generals as Miltiades, Themistocles, Aristides, Xanthippus, and Cimon reached high position as much through political as military talents; in this respect they were the forerunners of Pericles and Alcibiades. But the greater their powers became, the more strict was the control exerted over them by the Assembly of the state. Ostracism was a more ruthless weapon than the annual audit of an outgoing magistrate (*euthyne*); for the victim of ostracism could not defend himself in court. In January of each year the Assembly voted whether or not to hold a casting of ostraca (*ostrakophoria*). If it decided to do so, a casting of ostraca was held without debate at a subsequent meeting, and provided that 6,000 or more votes were cast, an Athenian citizen was ostracized. He went into exile for ten years, without losing his property; and, if he returned before his time, he could be put to death with impunity. After 480 an ostracized person had to live 'within' the northernmost and southernmost points of the Saronic Gulf (where he could not intrigue with Athens' enemies overseas), or else be an outcast with no rights. By such means the Assembly asserted its authority over leading states-men, and its victims included Themistocles, Aristides, Xanthippus, and Cimon.[1]

During ten months and more in 480–479, when Attica was totally or parti-ally evacuated and Athenian manpower was under arms, the Areopagus Council, which organized the first evacuation, was the most powerful organ of state. It wielded its discretionary powers with such skill and gained such prestige in political and religious matters that thereafter until *c.* 463 it held a central position in the administration of the state. To its influence we may attribute the steady policy which the state pursued. When the people re-turned to Attica in 479, there was at first some agitation in favour of the poorer class. Aristides, for instance, proposed to abolish the property qualification for office and make every citizen eligible for candidature. Themistocles ad-vocated the development of overseas commerce and proposed to abolish the tax on resident aliens, so that artisans would be attracted to the Peiraeus and the economic basis be laid for a great maritime state. Neither of these pro-posals was adopted. To some extent these proposals were linked with ques-tions of foreign policy; for both statesmen wished to win a naval hegemony in the Aegean, and Themistocles was prepared to break with Sparta. Their diplomatic talents were of great service to the state. For Themistocles covered the refortification of Athens and resisted Sparta's influence in the Amphic-tyonic Council, while Aristides gained the confidence of the Ionians and launched the Athenian Alliance. But Themistocles' policy of opposing Sparta and attacking Persia, which envisaged the possibility of war on both fronts, was not accepted by the Athenian people. The alliance with Sparta was observed, and *c.* 475 Sparta decided not to intervene in the Aegean. Then or later, perhaps in 472, Themistocles was ostracized. When he was implicated in the accusations against Pausanias, he fled from Argos.[2]

Pursued by the agents of Athens and Sparta, Themistocles crossed from Corcyra to Epirus, where he was sheltered as a suppliant by Admetus, king of the Molossi, and later by Alexander, king of Macedon. When he was crossing the Aegean in a merchant ship, a storm drove him to Naxos, where an Athenian fleet was besieging the town. He revealed his identity to the captain and told him that, if he reached Asia, he would give him a reward; but that, if he was betrayed, he would say the captain had been bribed to take him across. The captain preferred the reward, and Themistocles finally reached the court of Xerxes' successor, Artaxerxes, *c.* 465, where he served the king

---

[1] Arist. *Ath.* 22. 8; 43. 5; *FGrH* 328 F 30 (Philochorus); Plu. *Arist.* 7. Philochorus and Plutarch describe different procedures. According to the former 6,000 votes had to be cast against an individual to make his ostracism valid; according to the latter a total of 6,000 votes had to be cast and, if the total was not reached, the ostraca were not read. The period of ostracism is described as sometimes ten years and sometimes five years. These differences probably represent modifications in the law of ostracism during seventy years of use. For ostracism see also p. 221 above.

[2] Arist. *Pol.* 1304[a]20; *Ath.* 23; 25. 1; Plu. *Arist.* 22; *Them.* 20 fin.; D.S. 11. 43. 3.

well and was given the revenues of Magnesia, Lampsacus, and Myus. He died a natural death. His bones were brought to Attica and buried in secret; for he had been outlawed by his city on a charge of treason.[1]

Themistocles lacked the moral fibre, or at least the reputation for moral fibre, which the Athenian people of this period demanded in their greatest statesmen. Stories of corruption surrounded his name, whether at Artemisium or Paros or Carystus or Ialysus; his overriding ambition made men fear the possibility of a *coup d'état*; and his secret communications with the enemy left a suspicion of ambidexterity, which was heightened by the medism of his friend Pausanias. His intellectual gifts won the highest praise from Thucydides. His prescience, his resourcefulness, and his quickness were unrivalled in the sphere of strategy, tactics, and politics. He imposed his will upon Athens before and during Xerxes' invasion, upon the Greek and Persian commanders alike at Salamis, and upon the Ephors at Sparta in 479. He foresaw the potentiality and the weakness of Athens in the arena of power politics: the capacity of her citizens, resident aliens, and ports for exercising naval and commercial supremacy in the Aegean, the value of her prestige with the Ionians for winning hegemony and forming a coalition, and the danger of encirclement on land and of assault by Sparta. In the lifetime of Thucydides Themistocles was proved correct.[2] Athens developed as he had predicted. In consequence she found herself at war simultaneously with Sparta and Persia not once but thrice. With other statesmen in power the result for Athens was disaster. With Themistocles in power it might have been otherwise.

The trust which Athens denied to Themistocles was granted to Cimon, son of Miltiades, sometime tyrant in the Chersonese and victor of Marathon, who died at Athens disgraced, imprisoned, and bankrupt. Cimon paid the fine imposed on his father and strengthened his personal position by giving the hand of his sister to Callias, the leader of the wealthy Ceryces clan, and by taking a wife for himself from the Alcmeonid clan. He was elevated to power less by any support which these two clans may have given to him than by his own talents and personality. He was brave, direct, and genial. When men hesitated to leave Athens for Salamis, Cimon cheerfully led the way after dedicating his horse's bridle to Athena and taking a hoplite's shield from the temple. He won the confidence of the Athenians and of the Allies. He stood for a straightforward policy of war with Persia and friendship with Sparta. He led the conservative element in the state and supported the balanced constitution of Cleisthenes, which at this time was firmly guided by the Areopagus Council. An able diplomat and a daring general, he was appointed to command many allied operations, and he improved Athens' position as head of the Athenian Alliance by encouraging the allies to contribute money instead of ships. By 466 his policy had achieved the highest level of success which was ever attained while the dual hegemony of Sparta and Athens lasted in the Greek world.[3]

[1] Th. 1. 135-8. [2] 1. 93; 138. 3. [3] Arist. *Ath.* 28. 2; Plu. *Cim.* 4-16.

Thus a new factor developed in Greek history, a complete and undisputed thalassocracy within the Aegean Sea. At first it was exercised by an Alliance of Greek states. It suppressed piracy, protected its members, and stimulated seaborne trade. Pro-Persian governors were expelled, freedom was vindicated in foreign and home affairs, and prosperity returned to cities which had been burnt or pillaged by Persia. By 466 this thalassocracy was exercised virtually by one state, Athens, which within a single generation had outgrown her associates. Two policies were now open to Athens, that of Cimon and that advocated in the past by Themistocles. If the balance of power with Sparta continued, Athens and her Allies would enjoy peace and prosperity with neighbouring Greek states, but Athens was unlikely to make further conquests at the expense of Persia; for the Phoenician navy was still formidable and received strong support from Persia. If Athens broke with Sparta and sought to expand at the expense of other Greek states, she would have to switch her Alliance to a new objective and thereby change the basis of the original contract.[1]

[1] Th. 1. 18. 2.

CHAPTER 6

The Western Greeks 490–466

§ 1. *The Carthaginian invasion and the battle of Himera*

THE power built up by Hippocrates was extended by Gelon, an able commander of aristocratic birth, who set aside the young sons of Hippocrates and became tyrant of Gela himself. Between 490 and 485 he allied himself with Theron, tyrant of Acragas, married Theron's daughter Demarete, and gave his niece in marriage to Theron. He now controlled most of the south coast of Sicily and came to blows with the Carthaginians in the western sector. He asked the Greeks of the mainland for help against Carthage. He probably applied to Sparta and had hopes, like Dorieus, of extending the Greek holding on the North African coast as far as Emporia. But no help was given. He therefore attacked Syracuse c. 485 with the help of the aristocratic Gamoroi, who had been expelled during a democratic rising. The commons, who had enfranchised the serf class, the Kyllyrii, and then fallen out among themselves, offered no resistance to Gelon. Leaving his brother Hieron in charge of Gela, he transferred his court to Syracuse, which offered a far better port than Gela.

Gelon made Syracuse the most populous city in the Greek world by pouring into it half the Geloans, all the Camarinaeans, and the upper classes of Megara Hyblaea and Sicilian Euboea. The lower classes of these two towns were sold abroad into slavery, for Gelon held the poor in contempt. The great city was fortified with such skill that it resisted assault for nearly three centuries, and the forces of Gelon rose to 200 triremes, 20,000 hoplites, and brigades—each 2,000 strong—of heavy cavalry, light cavalry, archers, and slingers. His fleet, for which the rowers were recruited from the Syracusan commons, was probably of doubtful loyalty. But his army was very strong. The cavalrymen were the wealthy aristocrats whom Gelon favoured in his policy. They rode fine horses, bred in Sicily and especially at Gela. The infantry was stiffened by a large proportion of mercenary troops, who may have risen to 10,000 in number. To support so large an army and navy Gelon relied on spoil from Megara Hyblaea and Euboea and on the taxes of Syracuse, the richest commercial state in Sicily.

Meanwhile Theron of Acragas extended his influence northwards to Himera (Plate XII *c*), whence he expelled the tyrant Terillus, who fled to his son-in-law Anaxilas, tyrant of Rhegium. Terillus, however, was on friendly terms with Carthage, and Anaxilas felt that his control of the straits between Messana and Rhegium was threatened by the ambitions of Gelon. The two of them therefore invited Carthage to invade Sicily.[1]

[1] Hdt. 7. 153–6; Th. 1. 14. 2; 17; Arist. *Pol.* 1302ᵇ32; D.S. 11. 72. 3.

Late in 481 the envoys of the Greek Congress asked Gelon to join in resisting the Persian invasion. His demands for a position of command were

FIG. 20. Sicily and Magna Graecia

probably calculated to evoke a refusal; for he must have known that the
Carthaginians were preparing a large force, and he could not leave Syracuse
undefended. His purpose in sending Cadmus to Delphi was to secure his
flank without incurring the charge of medism. The Carthaginians were in-

formed of Xerxes' preparations by their own founders, the Phoenicians in Asia, and considered the time ripe in 480 to invade Sicily in response to the appeal of Terillus and Anaxilas. Later generations believed that Persia and Carthage had acted in concert; but it is unlikely that Persia feared any reinforcement of Greece from Sicily, or that Carthage wished to see Persia conquer Greece and perhaps advance upon Sicily.[1]

The Carthaginian fleet of 200 warships and numerous transports suffered loss in a storm during the crossing from Africa and then concentrated at Panormus on the north coast of Sicily. The army and navy then advanced together to Himera, whence the cargo vessels were sent off to fetch further supplies from Sardinia and Libya. The intention of the Carthaginian commander, Hamilcar, was to advance along the north coast and join forces with Anaxilas at Messana before attacking Syracuse. His total force probably exceeded 100,000 men. The Phoenicians of Carthage and west Sicily were accompanied by swarms of mercenary troops, who had been raised from the Carthaginian possessions in Libya, Iberia, Liguria, Sardinia, and Corsica. They represented the military strength of the western Mediterranean, powerful in infantry but weak in cavalry. It was the most formidable force that had ever invaded Sicily, and it aimed at the conquest of the island.[2]

At Himera, which was held by Theron with his Acragantine army, Hamilcar encamped in preparation for a siege. He beached his ships and protected them with a stockade, and he built a fortified camp for his army on the west side of the town. Gelon wisely decided to attack Hamilcar at Himera, before Hamilcar could join forces with Anaxilas of Rhegium. He therefore marched overland with 5,000 cavalry and some 50,000 infantry of all arms, broke the blockade of Himera and made a fortified camp on the east side of the town. Being much superior in cavalry, Gelon was able to round up the Carthaginian foragers and impose a blockade on Hamilcar. He then managed to enter Hamilcar's fortifications by exploiting a fortunate chance. Selinus, the Megarian colony in south-west Sicily, had allied with Carthage and received orders to send a force of cavalry to Hamilcar on a certain day. The courier reporting receipt of the orders was intercepted. So at dawn of the appointed day Gelon's cavalry presented themselves, and were admitted into the stockade by the Carthaginians. The cavalry at once set fire to the ships on the beach. In the ensuing confusion Hamilcar was killed, and Gelon's infantry advanced to the attack. The fighting was severe, neither side taking any prisoners. The Carthaginians were eventually driven back to a strong point, where lack of water compelled them to surrender at nightfall. The whole army was killed or captured. Carthage was so weakened that she paid an indemnity of 2,000 talents for peace and presented Gelon's wife, Demarete, with a golden crown. Seventy years were to pass before Carthage tried again to capture Sicily.[3]

[1] Hdt. 7. 157–64; Arist. *Poet.* 1459ª25; D.S. 11. 1.
[2] Hdt. 7. 165 (300,000 men); D.S. 11. 20.
[3] Hdt. 7. 166–7; D.S. 11. 21–22; 26. 2–3.

§ 2. *The effects of tyranny in Sicily*

The battle of Himera was so decisive that it won Gelon fame throughout the Greek world and popularity in Syracuse. The victors built temples at Himera, Acragas, and Syracuse and dedicated a statue of Zeus at Olympia. In emulation perhaps of the tripod commemorating the victory at Plataea, Gelon himself dedicated to Apollo at Delphi a golden tripod and a Victory with the inscription: 'dedicated to Apollo by Gelon, son of Deinomenes, the Syracusan; the tripod and the Victory were worked by Bion son of Diodorus, the Milesian.' Gratitude to the gods was also expressed in the beautiful coins of Leontini and Syracuse, the large silver decadrachms of Syracuse being called 'Demareteia' in memory of Demarete (Plate XII *b*). As a result of the victory Acragas extended her influence over the Phoenician cities Motya and Eryx, which adopted the eagle and crab of Acragas on their coinage, but the Phoenicians themselves were not expelled from Sicily and served as intermediaries of trade with the Carthaginian empire. Selinus and Rhegium made peace with the victors; Anaxilas married his daughter to Hieron and adopted the Attic standard of weight from Syracuse for the coinage of Rhegium. In 478 Gelon died, at the height of his reputation and at the dawn of a most prosperous period which was due to his victory and to his wise consolidation of the peace.[1]

Popular as he was at his death, Gelon had won and retained power as a tyrant, employing mercenary troops to destroy cities and enslave populations. At the new Syracuse which he had made his power was unconstitutional, whatever offices were voted to him and to members of his family. Courtiers might address him as king of Syracuse or ruler of Sicily, and he might describe himself as simply 'a man of Syracuse'; but the Deinomenids, like the Peisistratids, were usurpers of political liberty and faced a rising flood of opposition. Hieron, the brother and successor of Gelon, had much of his ability and ambition. In Sicily he destroyed Naxus and Catana, transplanting their populations in part to Leontini and in part to his new foundation Aetna. This city, situated to the south of Mt. Aetna, was intended to control the north part of the fertile plain. Its ruler was Hieron's son, Deinomenes, and the settlers were led by 5,000 Peloponnesian immigrants and 5,000 Syracusans. With Theron, the ruler of Acragas, Himera, and much of west Sicily until his death in 472, Hieron remained in close alliance. He found a field for expansion northwards, now that his father-in-law Anaxilas had been compelled to relax his grip on the Straits of Messana, and he had faithful allies in Locri and Cumae. In answer to an appeal from the latter his fleet sailed north and won a great victory over the Etruscans in the bay of Naples *c*. 474. Some of the spoils were dedicated at Olympia. Among them was a bronze helmet inscribed with the words 'Hieron, son of Deinomenes, and the Syracusans (dedicated) to Zeus the Etruscan spoils won at Cumae'. On the island of

[1] Paus. 6. 19. 7; *GHI* 17; *GC* 102.

Pithecusae he planted a colony of Syracusans, but the colonists fled after an earthquake. In these attempts to establish the influence of Syracuse in Italy Hieron was the forerunner of Dionysius.[1]

The first uprising against the tyrants was at Himera, where a son of Theron, Thrasydaeus, was a harsh ruler and the people appealed to Hieron *c.* 476. But Hieron betrayed the movement to Theron of Acragas, who massacred his opponents at Himera and restocked the city with Dorian immigrants. On Theron's death in 472, Thrasydaeus attacked Hieron and was defeated, the losses of both sides totalling 6,000. Acragas then entered the alliance of Hieron, whose power now extended from Cumae to west Sicily. In 467 Hieron died. He was succeeded by his brother Thrasybulus, who tried to quell opposition by harsh measures. In 466 the Syracusans rose in revolt. They obtained help from those who had been victims of the tyrants at Gela, Acragas, Himera, and Selinus, and also from the native Sicels. Thrasybulus concentrated his mercenaries and his partisans from Aetna and elsewhere in the eastern part of Syracuse and made sorties from Achradina and Ortygia, which he still held in Syracuse. But he suffered defeat by land and by sea, and finally withdrew to Locri in south Italy. Freedom and democracy were installed at Syracuse and throughout Sicily except at Messana, where the sons of Anaxilas held power until 461.[2]

Forty years of tyranny in Sicily had strengthened Hellenism in the West. The aggressive policy and the organizing skill of the tyrants had defeated the Sicels, Carthaginians, and Etruscans and had laid the basis for commercial expansion. Their coalitions and alliances gave to the Greek states a unified direction which would not have existed under the normal conditions of city-state separatism. For these services the greatest of the tyrants—Gelon, Hieron, and Theron—deserved the praises of Pindar, Bacchylides, and Simonides and the posthumous honours paid to them as 'founders' by their citizens. They fostered trade by imposing peace, promoting urbanization, and issuing fine coinages; in particular, the ascendancy of Syracuse in the economy of Sicily was confirmed, and the Attic standard of Syracusan coinage came to be adopted throughout the West. By birth and by inclination the tyrants were aristocratic, favouring their own class and resisting democratic trends, to the extent even of selling the poor into slavery. Gelon's saying 'the common people is a most thankless housemate' was typical of their outlook. Dorians themselves, they imported Dorian settlers from Greece and destroyed several of the Chalcidian cities in Sicily. But their methods sealed the fate of aristocracy. For, by transplanting whole populations and by enfranchising mercenaries in large numbers (Gelon, for instance, enfranchising 10,000 at Syracuse), the tyrants cut all the strands of local tradition which tied the people to their aristocracy. During this period a social and economic revolution was enacted which emancipated the poorer classes and enabled them finally to seize power.

[1] D.S. 11. 48–49; 51; Pi. *P.* 1. 72; *GHI* 22.   [2] D.S. 11. 53; 66–68; Arist. *Pol.* 1312^b10.

§ 3. *The Greek states of Italy*

In Italy the Greek states did not make a common front against the Italian peoples. Their own rivalries kept them divided. After the destruction of Sybaris in 510 Croton dominated the area between Caulonia and Metapontium for some thirty years. Rhegium looked to Taras for aid and Locri to Syracuse, while the Achaean colonies, allied with one another but weakened by the loss of Sybaris, maintained a precarious independence. Cumae, when threatened by Etruscan sea power, appealed not to her neighbours but to Hieron of Syracuse. These states were ruled by aristocratic governments, which were strengthened by the influence of Pythagoras and his followers. When Polycrates became tyrant at Samos, Pythagoras fled to Croton *c.* 530 and combined his philosophical and religious teaching with political activity; he and his followers played an important part in the campaign which ended in the destruction of Sybaris. His followers were aristocrats, organized in fraternities or clubs (*hetaireiai*), and in the period of Croton's ascendancy they found adherents in many Italiote states. The first democratic government to become firmly established was at Taras *c.* 473. There the Iapygians and their neighbours made common cause against Taras and her ally Rhegium, and won a great victory in which the aristocratic class at Taras was almost annihilated. The people of Taras defended the city successfully and then seized power.[1]

Although the Greek states did not extend their political control, the influence of Greek manners and commerce penetrated deep into the hinterland, especially into Campania. Etruria began to issue a coinage of which the standard was related to that of Cumae and Syracuse; and the Etruscan cities on the Adriatic coast adopted a standard related to that of Corcyra. The victories of Greek arms over Etruria facilitated the rise of Rome in Latium. Here a political union, which was lacking among the Greek states in Italy, was inaugurated *c.* 493 by the *foedus Cassianum* between Rome and the Latin League.

[1] Arist. *Pol.* 1303ᵃ3; D.S. 11. 52.

CHAPTER 7

Literature, Thought, and Art (546–466)

§ 1. *The contrast between Pindar and Xenophanes*

IN 546–466 the world of Greek states matured in power, prosperity, and culture. Hitherto individual states had contended successfully against ill-organized opposition. Now coalitions of states, led by Sparta, Gelon, Hieron, and Athens, withstood the well-organized empires of Persia, Carthage, and Etruria. They responded triumphantly to the challenge of external pressure. These coalitions not only offset an inherent weakness of the city-state, its smallness of scale, but also introduced more stable conditions into the Peloponnese and Sicily and later into the Aegean area. By a fortunate chance the latter part of this period was marked by an equilibrium or balance of power within the Greek world. The coalitions matched one another: Athens and the Ionians, Sparta and the Peloponnesians, Corinth and her colonies, Syracuse and Acragas. Within each coalition the leader was almost equivalent in power with its associates. Under such conditions prosperity grew apace. Except in the southern Peloponnese and north-west mainland a monetary economy·was established; it quickened trade and facilitated the accumulation of capital. The growth of Syracuse, Corcyra, Athens, and Chios and their ability to build large fleets were symptomatic of a general increase in the resources of the Greek states. In this development the maritime states forged ahead of the agricultural states. The coins of Athens, Corinth, and Aegina were issued in large denominations and circulated widely, whereas the Peloponnesian states issued only small coin for local dealings. Power and prosperity bred confidence. The victories of this age were rightly interpreted as the victories of Greek culture as well as of Greek arms. The hundreds of sovereign states which constituted the Greek world became more conscious of their common heritage and more confident of their institutions.

On the rising tide of prosperity the aristocracy still rode supreme but not secure. The aristocrats, too, responded to the challenge of the times. In many states they governed, and in others they took the lead in statecraft and in religion. In almost every state their ideals set the standard of social and religious life. They moved more freely than their successors beyond the orbit of their own city-state; for elsewhere they found a common stock of aristocratic tradition, to which the precepts of a Pythagoras or the exhortations of a Pindar made a universal appeal. In policy they were indeed nationalist, but they recognized the claims of a common Greek cause. Cleomenes, Gelon, and Cimon, for instance, had a degree of Panhellenism which was rare in subsequent statesmen. They worshipped not only the gods of their own city-state but also the gods of the Greek race, in whose honour the great festivals were held at Olympia, Delphi, Corinth, and Nemea. Aristocrats came from all parts of the Greek world to attend the festivals and compete in the games. The centre of their common worship was Zeus of Olympia, the king of the gods and the guardian of liberty.

The ideals of the aristocracy were expressed by the greatest genius of choral lyric poetry, Pindar, whose extant poems date from 498 to 446. To him and many of his contemporaries the mythological past was a reality. The gods and the heroes were no fantasies of poetic imagination. They moved in the living world. Gods and men were born of one mother, Earth; the gods were distinct in power, but men were related to the gods in intellect and in endowment. The heroes of the past participated in the actions of men. Theseus fought at the battle of Marathon. Phylacus and Autonoüs defended Delphi against the Persians; the images of the Aeacids and the Tyndarids, which led the forces of Aegina and Sparta, were visible symbols of an invisible presence.[1] The heroes of an aristocratic house inspired their descendants to supreme effort. Man's affinity with the divine was reaffirmed in each generation and not least in the generation of the Persian War by man's noblest acts. The talents of the individual—physical perfection, poetic understanding, or brilliance of speech—were given by the gods and inherited from his ancestors, and he must use them to the full in the pursuit of excellence (*arete*). But the gods also punished arrogance. Man must know himself and his own limitations, and he must not attempt to scale the gleaming heavens. His ambitions should be moderated by the quality of restraint (*sophrosyne*), which implied not passivity or caution but balance and discrimination. His highest endeavours were undertaken on behalf of the group to which he belonged. Victory in the games or in war was won for the family or for the state. And, if his services to the group ranked with those of his ancestors, the group might worship him after death as a hero. On such grounds were heroic honours paid to Miltiades in the Chersonese, Gelon at Syracuse, Hieron at Aetna, and the Greek dead on the battlefield of Plataea.

These ideals were strongest in the Dorian states. Pindar himself was a Dorian of Thebes, and most of his epinician odes were written for Dorian victors in the games. His predecessor, Corinna, the poetess of Tanagra, treated the local myths of Boeotia with a similar piety. The Ionians of the islands and East Greece were more sophisticated in intelligence and more individualist in outlook. They continued the tradition of personal poetry. They valued the legends of the past for their intrinsic beauty but not for their religious content. Simonides of Ceos, for example, depicted Danaë and her baby with grace and tenderness and commemorated the dead at Thermopylae with exquisite directness. If Simonides had a philosophy, it was that circumstances changed quickly and ruled man's character, so that men became evil in calamity. He and his countryman Bacchylides wrote epinician

---

[1] Plu. *Thes.* 35. 8; Hdt. 8. 39; 64; 5. 75. 2.

odes, which had a charming ease of narrative but lacked Pindar's moral and religious force. Anacreon of Teus was a frank individualist. 'Bring water, bring wine, lad, bring us flowery garlands, that I may spar with Love.' He laughed at life and age and death with the courage of complete agnosticism. A convert to the school of personal poetry was Ibycus of Rhegium, who had written choral lyrics in the West. He came to the court of Polycrates, tyrant of Samos. His love-poems were vivid and beautiful, and he inaugurated the genre of court-poetry by composing an ode which ranked the living Polycrates with the heroes of the Trojan War.[1]

The boldest thinker among the Ionian poets was Xenophanes, who fled from Colophon *c.* 545, roamed to and fro in the Greek world, and died in the West at Elea. In vigorous elegiacs he attacked the conventional ideas of his time. Olympic victories were of no service to the state, and Olympic victors deserved no public honours. The legends of the past were man-made fictions; the gods were created by man in his own image and were endowed by Homer and Hesiod with activities despicable in man—theft, adultery, deceit; if cows could draw, they would depict the gods in the image of cows. Having spurned the traditional beliefs, Xenophanes taught that God was a single entity, constant, unmoving, incorporeal, unlike man in form and mind, and that God saw, heard, and understood with all his being and swayed all material things by the effortless power of thought. In contrast to God all material things were created from earth and water—clouds, winds, and rivers, for instance, being created from the great sea—and man as a material being had no certain knowledge but only opinion on the subject of the divine nature. The contemporaries of Xenophanes were influenced more by his strictures than by his precepts, which seem to have severed any personal contact between God and man.[2]

§ 2. *Aeschylus, Pythagoras, and Ionian philosophers*

THUS between the Dorians and the Ionians there was a wide difference of outlook. For religious conservatism was antipathetic to free thinking, and corporate responsibility to the claims of individualism. Athens occupied an intermediate position between the two. In the past she had produced only one great poet, Solon, who championed both the rights of the individual and the claims of the state. In 534 the first Attic tragedy was produced, and Athens soon became the centre of Greek poetry. The keystone of Attic drama was religion. The plays were enacted at a state festival held in honour of the god Dionysus, and the themes were deeply concerned with the religious life of man and the state. At first the chorus played a predominant part. It spoke as the mouthpiece of corporate religion, and its utterances were expressed mainly in the choral lyrics which had developed under Dorian influence. As corporate religion declined and personal problems became more

[1] Simon. 13; 5; 11; 4; Anacr. 27; Ibyc. 6; 7; 5; 3.
[2] *Vorsokr.* 21 B 1. 21 f.; 2; 11; 15; 23–30; 34.

acute, the actors displaced the chorus in importance and the Ionian influence became stronger. From the evolution of Attic tragedy we learn much of the inner history of Athenian life and thought. The tragedians were themselves Athenians, and the people judged the plays and awarded the prize. Thus the plays which survive are representative of Athens' greatest poets and of the Athenian people's taste.

Aeschylus' lifetime (*c.* 525–456) spanned the generation of the Persian War, and he himself fought at Marathon and Salamis. This experience had a profound effect on his religious views. In the *Persae*, which was produced in 472, he ascribed the defeat of Persia not to the superior quality of the Greeks but to the working of the divine will. Xerxes was guilty of two offences. In the first place his attempt to bring Greece under the Persian yoke was contrary to the apportionment of power (*moira*) which was ordained for the family of nations. In the second place his personal arrogance excited the wrath of Zeus, the god of justice. The first offence caused suffering to the whole family of nations, Greek as well as Persian, and the second offence brought disaster to the group over which Xerxes ruled, Persia and her subjects. Thus contemporary events revealed two principles in accordance with which the supernatural powers directed the history of man: the principle of order, which stemmed from the proper apportionment of power, and the principle of justice, which was administered by Zeus. When these principles were infringed, suffering ensued for all members of the group.[1] The same ideas were set forth in the other extant plays, which dealt with the past history of men and gods as transmitted in the traditional legends.

In two great trilogies—groups of three plays, wherein the history of more than one generation was portrayed—Aeschylus dealt with the principle of order within a family group, and, since each family ruled a state, within the state itself. In the house of the Labdacidae, when Oedipus killed his father and married his mother, the disruption of order brought disaster to the family and pollution to the state. In the house of the Atreïdae, when Atreus killed the sons of his brother Thyestes, similar results ensued. The suffering entailed by these crimes affected the just and the unjust, Eteocles or Orestes as well as Polynices or Agamemnon, and also the citizens of their states. Less clear is the meaning of a third trilogy, of which only one play, the *Supplices*, survives. When the fifty maidens refused marriage and the fifty suitors threatened violence, the chorus of handmaidens reflected on the apportioned destiny of women—matrimony and motherhood.[2] Here, too, there was a principle of order, and any breach of it caused suffering to just and unjust alike. In these trilogies the principle of order and the principle of justice were distinct in character, and sometimes they operated in discord. Aeschylus therefore brought the supernatural powers upon the stage. He sought to explain the origin of the distinction and finally to reconcile the two principles in their working among mankind.

[1] *Pers.* 93; 181; 827. For these views see *StGH* 395–416=*JHS* 85.42 ff.   [2] *Supp.* 1047.

The principle of order was already accepted at an earlier stage of Greek religious thought. This principle was in the beginning, when the ordered universe came to be and the provinces of Earth, Underworld, and Sky were apportioned. It was primeval and impersonal. It was observed and safeguarded by Earth herself and her children, the spirits of the Underworld. It was anterior in time to the creation of the Gods of the Sky, and it operated both in the society of the gods and in the society of men. If the principle of order was infringed, suffering was inflicted by Earth and her children. They were impersonal, unseeing, and everlasting, and their will could not be thwarted by god or man. In the *Prometheus Vinctus* Aeschylus[1] described the evolution of the Gods of the Sky, who were personal, seeing, and immortal. As they had been born into existence, so they lived within the span of 'allteaching' Time. Zeus, the third ruler of the gods, was a harsh tyrant at first, but he learnt the lesson of moderation later and established the rule of justice. Prometheus, prompted by compassion, tried to raise man above his apportioned place in the order of the universe; for this error both Prometheus and man suffered. In the sequel Prometheus and Zeus were reconciled, and Zeus sent Heracles to benefit mankind. Thenceforth Zeus was just and benevolent in his dealings with gods and men. But he was not all-powerful. He could not alter the immortality of Prometheus or the place of man in the order of the universe; for these things had been ordained by the primeval powers.

Aeschylus reached the final phase of his religious thought in his latest trilogy, the *Oresteia*, produced in 458. An earlier trilogy, of which *The Seven against Thebes* alone survives, had shown the effects of murder within the family of the Labdacids, the ruling house of Thebes. When death followed death, the chorus of Theban maidens trembled in terror at the power of the Erinys, the destroyer of the family, a goddess not like the gods. For the Erinys was a spirit of the Underworld, an automatic agent of the primeval law, alien to the principle of benevolent justice which actuated Zeus. The sequel of the *Oresteia* portrayed a conflict between the will of the Erinyes and the will of Zeus. On the orders of Apollo, Orestes had avenged the murder of his father, Agamemnon, by murdering his mother. In this situation the primeval law ordained that Orestes must suffer; for suffering was his lot, whether he failed to avenge his father or murdered his mother. The principle of Zeus was different. By the standard of justice Orestes was innocent in motive and in act; for the act was ordered by Apollo, the son of Zeus. The case of Orestes was committed for trial to the Court of the Areopagus, over which the goddess Athena presided, and Orestes was acquitted. The conflict, however, was not resolved. For the will of Athena could not overrule the will of the Erinyes. But Zeus, working through the eloquence of Athena, persuaded the Erinyes to accept the verdict of acquittal and to be inspired with his benevolent purpose. They became the Eumenides, 'the kindly goddesses', administering the

---

[1] Despite doubts by modern scholars Aeschylus' authorship seems certain from the ancient *testimonia*.

primeval law in the spirit of benevolent justice. Thenceforth Apportionment (*moira*) and Zeus acted in unison towards mankind.[1]

In these plays Aeschylus presented his beliefs on the fundamental problems of human existence—the place of suffering, insanity, and war in the divine plan and the nature of divine intervention in human affairs. He recognized that violence within a group involves all its members, and that the sins of the father are visited on the children. These were the unavoidable facts of life, ordained by the primeval law of nature. He believed that they were used purposefully, by a benevolent deity, whose justice was revealed not in the life of individuals but in the life of state and family and mankind. Such a belief was acceptable to a society which valued the fate of the group more highly than the fate of the individual.

At the same time Aeschylus was not blind to the problem of the individual. He believed that in most situations the individual was free to choose his course of action but was unable to control the consequences of his act. Thus Xerxes and Agamemnon were free agents; in their own arrogance they chose a course which resulted in ruin to themselves, their families, and their states.[2] When the individual survived, he might reap from his suffering the lesson of moderation and understanding. But in some situations the individual's choice was limited to two alternatives, both disastrous, so that he had virtually no hope of escape. Such was the position of Cassandra and Eteocles and Orestes. Then they were free only to preserve their purity of motive, their self-respect, and their honour. As Eteocles went forth to die, he cried 'the gods have long since ceased to care for us'.[3] When Orestes was acquitted by an act of divine intervention, he gave thanks to the goddess Athena and to the enlightened city, Athens, whose court of law was acceptable to the gods. In later years it was not always so. The cry of Eteocles grew stronger and dominated the Attic theatre in the plays of Euripides. For him and to many of his contemporaries the individual was more important than the group.

The religious thought of Aeschylus is so profound that he seems at first sight to have outstripped the forms of contemporary belief. But this was not so. He believed in prophecy, in omens, and in dreams, which all revealed the will of the gods; in curses and in pollution, which evoked intervention by the gods; and in the injunctions of oracles, which were despite their ambiguity inspired. The gods of the upper world were anthropomorphic and numerous; the spirits of the underworld were as monstrous and terrifying as any medieval demon of Hell, with the difference that they were not evil but implacable. Within this environment of contemporary beliefs, which were held not academically but emotionally, Aeschylus won his way to the conception of a supreme and benevolent deity, who ruled the other gods of light, won the powers of darkness to his will, and carried mankind forward to a higher level of civilization and enlightenment.

---

[1] *A.* 161–82; *Eu.* 299–346; 1045–6.
[2] *Pers.* 739–52; *A.* 218–27.
[3] *Th.* 702.

While Aeschylus found a deeper meaning in the traditional beliefs, others followed Xenophanes' example in discarding them and formulating a new philosophy of religion. Foremost among the pioneers was Pythagoras, who founded a religious fraternity at Croton *c.* 530–510 and was influenced by Orphic doctrine. His precepts are the subject of controversy; for he left no writings, and his ideas survive only in the work of his followers. The Pythagoreans regarded the universe as a sphere; at its centre was fire, and the earth revolved around the fire. This fire was the seed from which the universe grew, the crust of earth hardening round the fire and the earth drawing breath from the outer air; thus the whole universe was a living organism, like any animal or plant. The fiery seed was the original unit, breathing in air and being itself an indivisible body or 'atom'. From this unit all things sprang, just as from the number One unlimited numbers spring, and from it the universe gained stability, each thing being separated from other things by interstices of air.

Within this cosmogony the Pythagoreans were primarily concerned with the soul as a harmonizing principle in man (*harmonia*). It corresponded to the soul of the living universe, and its highest function in life on earth was to contemplate the order revealed in the universe and especially in the heavenly bodies. For the contemplative pursuit of true knowledge (*philosophia*) brought man into converse with the divine. At death the soul survived. It migrated into a new body, human or animal. During its series of lives the soul was involved in good and evil, but in the course of time it might purify itself and return to the source from which it had originally come, there to rest in unity. The belief that the soul was a harmonizing principle was based on a study of arithmetic, geometry, and harmonics and on the conviction that soul, numbers, and forms were physical substances and not intellectual abstractions.

The philosophy of Pythagoras thus dealt with physical realities. He formulated for his followers a code of conduct, in which abstinence and contemplation played an important but not an overriding part. For the desirable state in man was a harmonious or well-proportioned tuning of his physical and spiritual characteristics, a tuning which contained the orthodox ideal of moderation (*sophrosyne*). His followers formed a closed order. They underwent initiation, preserved secrecy, and engaged in politics as promoters of aristocratic oligarchy. For the Pythagorean mystic and philosopher was also to be a man of action.

Pythagoreanism was pilloried at the beginning of the fifth century by Heraclitus of Ephesus, who rejected the previous concepts of rest and unity. To him the only constant was inconstancy. As the seasons flow, so all things flow ever-changing in the cycle of time; for, as summer changes into winter, so life changes into death, death into life, fire into air, air into water, and so on. But unity persists through the revolution of changes, because they balance one another. The world is a continuum of opposites which are really one. In this sense God is day and night, summer and winter, war and peace, satiety and hunger, and the universe is an everlasting fire, self-consuming, self-per-petuating, and self-changing. In so far as Heraclitus' philosophy impinged on earlier beliefs, it rejected the teachings of Homer and Pythagoras. The distinction of good and evil was man-made; the principle of restraint was not based on reality; and the soul was destructible. Aristocratic and dogmatic, Heraclitus claimed to have gained the ultimate truth by searching his own mind and by discerning therein the ordering principle which steered all things through all things in constant change. Heraclitus reached his view of the universe by carrying the evidence of the senses to their logical conclusion. This threw all earlier philosophies into the melting-pot. On the other hand his divination of the formula or plan (*logos*), which held all things together so as to constitute a universe, was entirely personal and subjective.[1]

His views were in turn attacked *c.* 485–450 by Parmenides of Elea, who disagreed also with many of Pythagoras' precepts. Parmenides boldly dismissed the evidence of the senses as misleading and unreal. As the probe of reality he substituted abstract reasoning (*noema*), and he claimed to have experienced the revelation of reality. Truth was a sphere, solid, stationary, and complete, devoid of movement, life, or plurality, timeless and continuous. To perceive Truth Parmenides was led beyond the gates of Day and Night, that is beyond the limits of the world; for Truth was perceptible to the reason and not to the senses. The world which was perceived by the senses was a seeming world which lacked reality. Nevertheless, Parmenides returned through the gates of Day and Night and described the seeming world. The sphere of Truth now became the sphere of the universe. It began to revolve and was occupied by pairs of opposites, such as light and dark, hot and cold, soft and hard, male and female, which were harmonized with one another by the agency of Eros, the procreative force. Thereby the plurality and the diversity of physical things came into seeming. In the teaching of Parmenides Truth and Seeming were incompatible and irreconcilable. The task of later philosophers was to seek a reconciliation between reasoning and observation.[2]

§ 3. *History, geography, medicine, and comedy*

THESE three great philosophers, like their predecessors of Miletus and Xenophanes of Colophon, were all Ionians and lived in the colonial areas, which had become more emancipated from their traditional faith and local loyalties than the Greeks of the mainland. Their reason operated without restraint from religion, although they used idioms of thought which were derived from religion. Their field of study, like that of Aeschylus, was the universe and mankind, but in their speculations the state and the family found no place. Anaximander, Anaximenes, and Heraclitus wrote in prose, which became increasingly the medium for rationalist expression. The Ionians turned their critical and inquiring minds also to the study of history and set down their

[1] *Vorsokr.* 22 B 76; 67; 30; 64; 42; 102; 41; 72.   [2] *Vorsokr.* 28 B 1–8; 12–13.

urbanization and democracy were more developed at Athens than in the Dorian states. Here comedy was presented at the state festival of Dionysus in January, perhaps for the first time in 486. Whereas Syracusan comedy was mainly a comedy of manners and beliefs, Attic comedy was probably marked from the outset by the personal and political invective which was so prominent in its later development.[1]

The art of painting pottery was stimulated by competition between Corinth, Athens, Laconia, East Greece, and other areas. As Athens became a richer centre of trade, she attracted potters and painters from other cities. Towards the middle of the sixth century she was producing such masterpieces as the François Vase by Clitias, and she outstripped her rivals in the next fifty years. Soon after 530 she introduced a new technique. Painters in the traditional style, which we call 'Black Figure', drew figures and ornaments in dark colour on the unpainted light-red clay and picked out silhouettes and details with incised lines. In 'Red Figure' the process was reversed. The figures and ornaments were unpainted, except that white was sometimes used to define silhouettes and details, and the rest of the surface was painted with lustrous black; thus the figures were reserved in the naturally red clay against a black background. By 500 Red Figure was dominant, except in the painting of the amphorae awarded at the Panathenaic Games, and Athens became the chief producer and exporter of fine pottery.

The period of competition produced many masterpieces of bold and imaginative drawing by such painters at Athens as Execias and Amasis. Greek legend provided the themes, portrayed in narrative sequences or in single studies. Vigorous or passionate action was represented with vivacity and emotional power, and a new delicacy of line was achieved in drawing the light folds of the Ionic dress, which was adopted at Athens under the tyranny. After 500, when the technique of Red Figure was mature, artists selected more subjects from contemporary life—dancing, drinking, wrestling and so on—and treated the traditional figures of mythology with a more animated realism and humour. The restrained strength inherited from the Black Figure style and a more subtle use of perspective and grouping brought Greek vase-painting to its zenith in the first half of the fifth century. At the same time wall-painting was becoming an accomplished art, and it offered a wider scope for artists in portraying scenes of heroic tradition or national achievement. Perhaps for this reason, or for lack of competition from other centres, Attic vase-painting declined in the second half of the fifth century, and was marked by grace and sentiment rather than by vigour and originality.

The long tradition of temple-building reached a high level in the sixth century. The excavations at Thermum in Aetolia have revealed an important stage. A primitive building, probably a temple of Apollo, known as 'Megaron B' (because it was built on the Mycenaean plan) and surrounded by stone

---

[1] *CGF* 1. 91–147; *Vorsokr.* 23 B 4–5; 12; Suid. *Epikharmos, Khionides*; *IG* 2. 2318, 2325; Arist. *Poet.* 1448ᵃ30; 1449ᵃ30.

bases for wooden pillars, was succeeded in the seventh century by a larger temple of similar plan, surrounded by a colonnade or 'peristyle' (see Fig. 21).

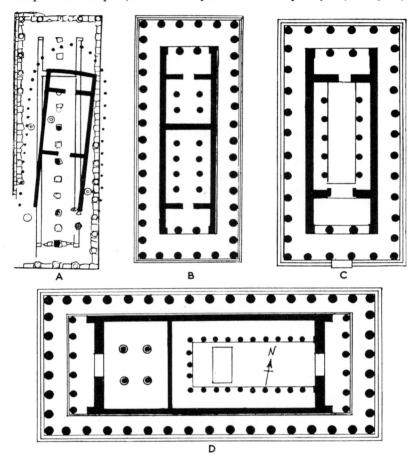

A. *Megaron B (in black) and the Temple of Apollo built above it at Thermum in Aetolia*
B. *The Temple of Apollo at Corinth*
C. *The Temple of Aphaea in Aegina*
D. *The Parthenon at Athens*

FIG. 21. Ground plans of Doric Temples

The columns were still of wood, the upper walls of mud-brick, and the metopes of terracotta, but the essential features of the Doric order were already formed. The same materials with a footing of stone were used in the Heraeum at Olympia and in Apollo's temple at Cyrene late in the seventh century, but the Temple of Athena Polias at Athens, Temple 'C' at Selinus, and the temples at Poseidonia (Paestum) were constructed entirely of stone in the mid-sixth century. The proportions of the temples changed; for now a greater width was given by the stylobate or stone base on which the colonnade was set. The Ionic order was represented by two temples with a double peristyle in east Greece—the Temple of Artemis at Ephesus, and that of Hera at Samos as planned probably by Polycrates in the second half of the sixth century. These temples were of great size, the stylobate measuring about 180 feet by 360 feet. They expressed the faith of the Greeks in their gods as magnificently as the cathedrals of medieval Europe.

From this age of experiment two of the classical orders of architecture emerged. The Temple of Apollo at Corinth, of which seven columns still stand, is an early example of the Doric order with a peristyle of six columns on the ends and fifteen columns on the flanks, a stylobate about 70 feet by 175 feet, a double cella containing a double row of columns, and a distyle *in antis*, that is two columns between the wall-ends of the cella (see Fig. 21). The columns were monoliths 21 feet high, thick and powerful, crowned with the simple splaying echinus of the Doric capital. The Temple of Apollo at Delphi, completed by 505 and embellished with marble by the Alcmeonids, was of similar size and plan. A fully developed Doric temple of classical style was built *c.* 490 to the goddess Aphaea in Aegina (see Fig. 21). The Ionic order with its more graceful column and capital was native to East Greece. It was rarely adopted on the mainland and in the West. The Temple of Zeus Olympius at Athens, as planned by Hipparchus, son of Peisistratus, had a double peristyle of the Ionic order, and the Treasuries of Cnidus and Siphnos at Delphi had Caryatids as columns. Some elements of the two orders were combined in the Throne of Apollo at Amyclae near Sparta in the latter part of the sixth century, but the experiment was not pursued. The fifth century saw the Doric order triumphant in the West and on the mainland.

Most temples of the period were built in limestone. Stucco was added to give a smoother finish, and frieze and cornice were painted with full colours, usually red and blue. Traces of colour survive, for instance, on the three-headed monster of limestone which watched Heracles wrestling with the Triton on the pediment of Athena's temple at Athens, the Hecatompedon. The straight lines of the temples were relieved by sculptures in the round or in relief. At first the figures on a pediment were isolated and statuesque, like those in a heraldic design: for instance the terrifying Gorgon and the lions of the temple of Artemis in Corcyra, and the Apollo and Heracles of the Siphnian Treasury at Delphi. Then the figures became members of a unified composition in the battle between gods and giants on the pediment of the Megarian Treasury at Olympia (*c.* 520–510). In the fifth century a remarkable impression of co-ordinated movement was given by goddess and warriors on the pediments of the Aphaea temple. The metopes below the pediment were similarly filled at first by a series of rather stiff figures, unrelated in design to each other; but those of the Athenian Treasury at Delphi (*c.* 510-500) were already rich in variety and designed as a whole. Complete harmony was achieved in the metopes of Temple 'E' at Selinus (475-450), where gods and heroes were shown in movement and repose. The continuous frieze made similar demands, which were well met in the frieze of the Siphnian Treasury at Delphi with the battle between gods and giants.[1]

Free standing statues of gods and men were usually sculptured in marble, which was occasionally used also in pedimental sculptures (for instance in the Aphaea temple). Many were painted with strong colours, such as survive on medieval French wooden statues. In 550-525 the earlier stiffness of pose was modified. Strength and grace were combined in the Peplos maiden from the Acropolis and the Attic gravestone of a youth (Plate V), and a greater variety of expression and an elaboration of decorative detail were visible in the Maidens (*korai*) dedicated at Athens in the last quarter of the century. Examples of Dorian art at this time from Sparta, Boeotia, and Aegina have a sturdy, rather severe strength and a formalized treatment of detail, which contrast with the richer and more animated style of Athens and Ionia.[2] The latest Maidens at Athens (500-480) combine the merits of both styles and have the serious calm of the classical period. The statues of gods, heroes, and athletic victors began to lose their archaic rigidity and became more natural in the modelling of curving flesh and muscle, as in the 'Strangford Apollo' (*c.* 510-500), and early in the fifth century the body of a Youth from the Acropolis was relaxed with the weight resting mainly on one hip.[3] Although sculptors were now capable of a realistic portrayal of the body, they preferred to keep the perfect proportion and the serene aloofness of idealized beauty in human form.

The same maturity of style and technical skill were apparent in the engraving of the dies between which the coins of the Greek states were struck. Syracuse, which began to coin after 530, produced some of the finest examples (Plate XI*j*). Metal-working received a fresh impetus *c.* 550, when the casting of bronze was perfected. More statuettes and life-size statues have survived intact in this medium than in limestone and marble, and they show the same development from stiffness to ease of stance. Early in the fifth century the warrior from Dodona is poised for action, about to strike. The statues of the tyrannicides at Athens, dedicated in 477, of which we have copies in stone, showed Harmodius and Aristogeiton striding forward. The charioteer at Delphi, who survives from a Syracusan chariot-group, stands serene and dignified in victory, his long chiton falling in graceful folds.[4] Most typical of the age is Zeus of Artemisium, recently recovered from the sea (Plate VI). He is a god supreme in strength and poise and beauty, about to cast his weapon in defence of Greece.

---

[1] Richter, *Sc.*, figs. 378-9, 76, 374, 382-3, 388-9, 406-9, 410-13, 418-19.
[2] Richter, *AGA*, figs. 123-5, 142, 151, 153, 236, 150.   [3] Richter, *Sc.*, figs. 28-30.
[4] Ibid., figs. 100, 565-6, 571-7, 162, 285. See Plate XII*d* for coin portraying the tyrannicides.

BOOK IV

THE GREAT WARS BETWEEN ATHENS AND SPARTA

(*c.* 466–404)

CHAPTER 1

Athens at War with Persia and Sparta

§ 1. *The democratic reform and rupture with Sparta*

THE danger of invasion by Persia was dispelled by victory at the Eurymedon and by troubles which followed the assassination of Xerxes in 465; for his successor, Artaxerxes, having murdered his elder brother, had to deal with risings in the empire and especially with the revolt of Bactria and later of Egypt. In the past this danger had held diverse elements together within the Greek world—at Athens the Areopagus Council and the Ecclesia, in the Aegean area Athens and her Allies, and on the mainland the two pillars of the Greek League, Athens and Sparta. A new situation now came into being. The initiative was seized by the democratic leaders at Athens. Within a few years they deposed the Areopagus, harnessed the Allies to the will of Athens, and broke finally with Sparta. Their policy dominated the history of the Greek states for the next sixty years.

The ascendancy of the Areopagus after the battle of Salamis rested less on constitutional prerogative than on ancient prestige and on recent services to the state. As the years passed, its ascendancy gradually weakened. The memory of its services dimmed, and the personal prestige of its members declined. In 487 the archons were appointed not by direct election of the people but through selection by lot; twenty years later the majority of the ex-archons in the Areopagus owed their membership to this procedure, and they were in consequence less influential than their predecessors had been. Their exceptional powers fostered suspicions of corruption—a common charge in Greek politics, which was probably often well founded—and their ascendancy was regarded as a threat to the personal liberty of the citizens. The opposition, led earlier by Themistocles and Aristides, was by 466 in the hands of Ephialtes and Pericles. The reputation of Ephialtes and Pericles for incorruptibility was impeccable and gave them a secure place in the confidence of the people. Ephialtes was an able constitutionalist and a fine speaker; Pericles, son of Xanthippus, was a young aristocrat of outstanding promise. At first they attacked individual Areopagites, impeaching them before the Heliaea on charges of corruption or of abuse of power, and in many cases secured their condemnation. Ephialtes and Pericles were appointed to generalships at least once in the period 465–463, and this indicated the increasing strength of their supporters. In summer 462 they attacked the most influential man in the state, Cimon, on a charge of corruption. But he, too, had a reputation for incorruptibility, and he was acquitted.[1] Shortly afterwards, when Cimon happened to be absent from Athens, Ephialtes and Pericles judged that the position of the Areopagus was sufficiently undermined, and thereupon carried a democratic reform through the Assembly.

The details of the reform are not known, but the effect is clear. The Areopagus Council was deprived of all its political powers, these powers being described as 'traditional' or 'acquired' in accordance with the bias of the reporter. Its jurisdiction as a court of law was reduced at this time, and again by Pericles later, until it dealt only with cases involving religious issues, such as murder or damage to the sacred olive trees.[2] By this step the Ecclesia and the Heliaea were set free from the check which had provided a balance in the Cleisthenic 'equality of rights' (*isonomia*), and the way was clear for full 'democracy' (*demokratia*), that is for the exercise of sovereignty by the majority in the state, the people (*demos*). The powers of the Areopagus were divided between the Council of the Five Hundred on the one hand and the Assembly and Heliaea on the other. The supervision of the magistrates, the hearing of charges of treason (*eisangelia*), and the power of summary arrest, fining, or execution under certain circumstances were bestowed upon the Council, which now became the chief executive organ of the people. Henceforth all decrees of state were enacted by decision of 'the Council and the Demos'.[3] The functions of the Areopagus as a court, dealing with certain charges, such as 'impiety', and hearing appeals, were transferred to the Heliaea. Later constitutionalists, such as Aristotle, saw in the Heliaea the secret of the people's rise to power and the lynch-pin of the people's sovereignty.[4] The supervisory and discretionary powers of the Areopagus were abrogated, and the Assembly of the people was henceforth restricted only by self-imposed limitations. Important among them was respect for the established laws, hitherto safeguarded by the Areopagus. Probably from 462 onwards, if a proposal or a decree was indicted as illegal, the Assembly held it in suspense and the proposer was liable to prosecution before the Heliaea on a charge of illegality (*graphe paranomon*). Thus, in the words of Plato the

---

[1] Arist. *Ath.* 25; Plu. *Cim.* 10–14; *Per.* 10.
[2] Arist. *Pol.* 1274ᵃ5; *Ath.* 25. 2; 27. 1; 35. 2; D.S. 11. 77. 6. For further reform by Pericles see p. 301.   [3] Arist. *Ath.* 25. 2; 45. 1–2.
[4] Arist. *Pol.* 1274ᵃ5; *Ath.* 9. 1 fin.

comic poet, Ephialtes 'poured out for the citizens a full and unadulterated draught of freedom'.[1]

To the reforms of Ephialtes and Pericles different party labels were attached. Some held that the reforms liberated the people from an 'oppressive and oligarchical' council, and others (including Aristotle) that they flattered the people 'as a tyrant'. When Cimon returned from overseas, he sought in vain to revoke the reforms and restore what Plutarch described as 'the ordered and aristocratic constitution' of Cleisthenes. Soon afterwards Ephialtes was assassinated by a Boeotian from Tanagra, whose suborners were never discovered.[2] In the *Oresteia*, produced in 458, Aeschylus emphasized the integrity and prestige of the Areopagus and warned the Athenians against the dangers of anarchy and strife.[3] As events proved, the people was firmly ensconced in power, and it turned to the problems of foreign policy with courage and energy and with a remarkable confidence in its strength.

As leader of the Athenian Alliance Athens had greatly increased her power since 477. On the advice of Themistocles and Cimon she kept her fleet at a battle strength of 200 triremes by laying down twenty hulls a year. The vast spoils won by the Alliance enriched her as hegemon to an unprecedented degree, and, as more and more allies contributed money instead of ships, the upkeep of her fleet fell less and less upon the Athenian treasury.[4] When the danger of Persian attack diminished, the interests of Athens and those of the Allies diverged. The Athenian state and the Athenians themselves, especially the thetes, benefited in power and in wealth from the continuation of the Athenian Alliance. The Allies, on the other hand, had now secured the independence from Persia for the sake of which they had entered the Alliance; and to them the price of membership—the provision of ships or tribute, the obligation to serve, and the cost of maintenance—became more and more irksome. The initiative now lay with Athens. She could either bring the interest of the allies more into line with her own interest by revising the price of membership and sharing the profits of victory, or widen the gap by holding the allies to their original bargain, although the conditions had altered. In 465 a test case arose. Thasos, the richest island in the north Aegean and the possessor of a strong fleet, seceded from the Athenian Alliance because she resisted Athens' claim to share in the commercial and mining interests of Thasos on the Thracian coast. Two issues were now at stake: whether Athens would permit a member to leave the Alliance, and whether Athens would invoke the other members to prosecute her private quarrel with Thasos.

The Athenian fleet under the command of Cimon attacked and defeated the Thasian fleet, capturing thirty-three ships, and then landed troops on the

[1] Plu. *Per.* 7 fin.
[2] Plu. 805d; Arist. *Pol.* 1274^{a}6; *Ath.* 25. 4; 29. 3; Plu. *Cim.* 15; *Per.* 10. 6.
[3] A. *Eu.* 526, 699, 977.
[4] D.S. 11. 43. 3; Plu. *Cim.* 9 fin.; 13 fin.; Th. 1. 99. 3; Arist. *Ath.* 24. 1.

island. At about the same time as the landing—late in 465—10,000 settlers, drawn both from Athens and from the allied states, were brought to the valley of the river Strymon in Thrace. There they secured possession of the strategic position known as 'The Nine Ways', Ennea Hodoi, the site later of Amphipolis, which controlled the passage from east to west across the Strymon and also the entry up the river into the hinterland. It was clear for all to see that Athens aimed at controlling for herself the rich resources of the Thracian coast in minerals, timber, and foodstuffs. But the Thracians united in alarm, and early in 464 they annihilated an Athenian force at Drabescus, whither it had advanced to cover the formation of the settlement at Ennea Hodoi. The whole enterprise thus ended in disaster. The Thracians attacked the Chersonese too, where Athens and her allies suffered casualties. Meanwhile in Thasos her troops won victories and invested the town in early summer 464, whereupon the Thasians made a secret appeal to Sparta to help them by invading Attica.[1]

Sparta had no obligations by treaty with Thasos. But as leader of the Spartan Alliance she had good reason to fear that Athens' power and ambition might some day threaten the maritime members of her Alliance. As self-appointed and generally accepted champion of liberty in the Persian War, she could condemn Athens for an act of imperialism and defend the liberties of Thasos by war. The rebels in Messenia, however, were still active. Perhaps on that account the Thasian appeal was not debated in the Assembly at Sparta, but the executive authorities gave a secret undertaking to Thasos that Sparta would invade Attica. The secret was kept for several years, but the invasion was prevented by a natural disaster in summer 464. A violent earthquake destroyed the town of Sparta and killed more than 20,000 persons. Casualties among the Spartiates, who lived normally in the town, were particularly heavy, and a large number of young men, who were training indoors, were killed when the roof collapsed. The Helots in the Eurotas plain gathered to attack their masters. Archidamus, the king, bade his trumpeter sound the call to arms, and the citizens, ceasing their search for relatives and possessions in the ruins, rallied round him and drove off the Helots. Shortly afterwards the Helots of Messenian descent rose as a body, won the support of two groups of Perioeci, and joined forces with the Messenian rebels, who had been holding out at Ithome since 469. Their combined forces overran Laconia and threatened to destroy Sparta.[2]

In her extremity Sparta turned to her Allies for help. A Spartiate, Pericleidas, came to Athens and sat as a suppliant, pale-faced in his scarlet cloak, before the altars of the city.[3] The citizens met in the Assembly to debate their reply. Ephialtes, regarding Sparta as a rival to Athens, advised them

---

[1] Th. 1. 100–1; 4. 102. 2; D.S. 11. 70. 1 and 5; Plu. *Cim.* 14; Hdt. 6. 45–47; 9. 75; Paus. 1. 29. 4; *IG* i.² 928 with *Hesp.* 25. 375. The chronology of 465-454 is much disputed; for the dates given here see *Historia* 4. 371.   [2] Th. 1. 101; Plu. *Cim.* 16. 4; D.S. 11. 63.
[3] Paus. 4. 24. 5–6; Ar. *Lys.* 1137–44 with Scholia.

not to yield to the appeal but to let Sparta's pride be trampled underfoot. Cimon, the advocate of the dual hegemony, urged them not to let Greece go lame and Athens lose her yoke-fellow. The Assembly chose the policy of generosity, and Cimon marched forth with a citizen force of 4,000 hoplites. Plataea, the faithful ally of Athens and of Sparta, sent one-third of her army, and Aegina, Mantinea, and others responded to the call. Their help saved Sparta from extinction. In 463 she passed to the offensive, and began a long blockade of the Messenian forces in the mountainous country of Ithome.[1]

The disaster at Sparta upset the balance of power in the Greek world. Argos extended her control over the lesser states in the Argolid, and Corinth began to press upon her neighbours, Cleonae and Megara. On his return from Laconia Cimon was reprimanded by Corinth for entering her territory without permission. The members of the Athenian Alliance realized that they could no longer look to Sparta for protection, and Athens was tempted to exercise a tighter control over them. On the double issue of relations with Sparta and of relations with the members of the Alliance the Areopagus and its leading general, Cimon, stood for the policy of moderation. The democratic leaders, Ephialtes and Pericles, regarded Sparta as an enemy to be destroyed and the members of the Alliance as satellites of Athens. In late summer 462 Thasos capitulated. Her walls were destroyed, her fleet confiscated, and her mint closed. Her gold-mine at Scapte Hyle and her other possessions on the mainland were ceded to Athens, and her immediate and future contributions to the Athenian Alliance were fixed in terms of money. Henceforth Thasos, deprived of the means of resistance, was a subject-state dependent on the will of Athens. Her fate was a warning to the members of the Alliance.[2]

The harsh terms which the Assembly imposed upon Thasos were probably inspired by the democratic leaders. When Cimon returned in triumph from Thasos, he was unsuccessfully impeached by Pericles and others on the charge that he had taken bribes from Alexander, king of Macedon, and therefore had abstained from attacking Macedonia. The charge revealed one of the democrats' ambitions, the annexation of part of Macedonia's territory. The acquittal of Cimon was a testimony to his personal influence and his reputation for incorruptibility. The trial was political in character. For at this time, in late summer 462, the pressure of the democratic leaders upon the Areopagus was reaching its height and the acquittal of Cimon, the staunch supporter of the Areopagus, was a set-back to their cause. In autumn 462 a second appeal for help came from Sparta, and the Assembly responded by sending Cimon, the advocate of alliance with Sparta, in command of an expeditionary force. During his absence Ephialtes and Pericles carried the reforms which ousted the Areopagus and placed the Assembly in full control.

The Spartans had conducted a long blockade of Ithome before appealing

[1] Plu. *Cim.* 16; Th. 2. 27. 2; 3. 54. 5; X. *HG.* 5. 2. 3.
[2] Plu. *Cim.* 17; Th. 1. 101. 3.

again to their allies, with whose help they now hoped to crush the cornered Messenians. The arrival of Cimon's force was particularly welcome, since the Athenians were famous for their skill in carrying field fortifications by assault. But on this occasion the Athenians did not show their usual dash. While they were in Messenia, they heard of the complete triumph of the democratic leaders at Athens, and they realized that their commander and the cause for which he was fighting were no longer in favour with the Assembly. The Spartan authorities were equally well informed. They suspected that so radical a reform at Athens would result in a change of policy towards Sparta, and at the moment they distrusted the Athenians on the spot as purveyors of revolutionary ideas and representatives of the Ionian peoples, who might even espouse the cause of the Messenians and the Helots. With a bluntness which betrayed their distrust the Spartans informed the Athenians that their services were no longer required and they should depart forthwith. The Athenians had no option. Before the eyes of the Spartan and Peloponnesian troops they marched out of the camp and returned in anger to Athens. There under the new democratic régime feeling was inflamed against Sparta and against the advocate of friendship with Sparta, Cimon. In the winter Athens, Argos, and Thessaly in their hostility to Sparta formed a tripartite alliance, and in spring 461 Cimon was ostracized. The period of co-operation between the two leading states of Greece was at an end.[1]

§ 2. *Athens' offensives on two fronts*

THE Athenian democracy now embarked on an ambitious foreign policy, to exploit simultaneously the weakness of Sparta and the weakness of Persia. In summer 460 the rebels at Ithome capitulated on condition of a safe conduct for the Messenians. In accordance with her new policy Athens afforded them a refuge. Shortly afterwards Megara, hard pressed by Corinth, absconded from the Spartan Alliance and concluded an alliance with Athens, who garrisoned Megara and Pegae and built Long Walls from Megara to Nisaea. By these measures Athens acquired a defensible port on the Corinthian Gulf and provided for the defence of Megara from the Saronic Gulf; and she now had her garrisons in position to bar the entry from the Isthmus into central Greece. The alliance of Athens with Megara engendered a bitter hatred between Athens and Corinth. For Corinth, and also Aegina and Epidaurus, were now pinched between Argos and the Athenian Alliance, at a time when Sparta was too exhausted to protect the members of the Spartan Alliance.[2]

To take advantage of Persia's weakness was more difficult. For Athens and her Allies could not challenge the full military strength of Persia. They

---

[1] Th. 1. 102; Plu. *Cim.* 14–16; 17; Paus. 4. 24. 6–7.

[2] Th. 1. 103. For Sparta's losses cf. Hdt. 9. 64. 2, and for their effects cf. Philochorus (*FGrH* 328 F 117) 'the disasters suffered by Sparta enabled Athens to seize the hegemony'.

could, however, damage the Phoenician fleet either by capturing its advanced bases in Cyprus or by carrying the war into its home waters off Lebanon and Palestine. The former policy was being pursued in 460, and 200 ships of the Athenian Alliance were operating in Cyprus. Meanwhile an insurrection was well under way in Lower Egypt, where a Libyan king, Inaros, had raised a force of Egyptians and mercenaries and had defeated the Persians on land and sea. He turned to Athens and her allies for aid, promising them great privileges if they liberated Egypt. The fleet of the Athenian Alliance was ordered to leave Cyprus. It sailed up the Nile and, joining the forces of Inaros, won a resounding victory. The Persian commander, Achaemenes, a son of Darius, was killed, and fifty of his ships were sunk or captured. On the Greek and Egyptian side the highest praise was due to Charitimides, the commander of the Athenian squadron of forty ships in the allied fleet. The Samian squadron alone took fifteen Phoenician ships. The victory rivalled that of the Eurymedon. But it was not decisive. The remainder of the Persian force and their Egyptian supporters held out in the fortress of Leukon Teichos. For six years the war continued in Egypt and drained the resources of Athens and her Allies. In the year 458, for instance, Athenians were killed in Egypt and in the approaches to Egypt along the coasts of Cyprus and Phoenicia.[1]

In the same year, 458, Athens began operations in the Saronic Gulf. A sea-borne landing at Halieis was defeated by Corinth and Epidaurus, but in a naval action off the island of Cecryphalea near Aegina the Athenians defeated the Peloponnesian fleet. At this stage war broke out between Athens and Aegina. In a great battle, at which the allies of each were present, the Athenians captured seventy ships, landed on the island, and laid siege to the town of Aegina. In order to aid the Aeginetans, Corinth and Epidaurus sent 300 hoplites into the island. The army of Corinth and her allies then invaded the Megarid, hoping either to relieve Aegina by forcing Athens to withdraw her troops from the island or to capture Megara and invade Attica. But an Athenian general, Myronides, marched out at the head of the reserve troops— the oldest and the youngest men under arms—held the enemy to an even battle in the Megarid and, twelve days later, sallied from Megara to engage a force of Corinthians, who, mocked by the older generation at Corinth, had entered the Megarid to set up a trophy. When the Corinthians were driven back, a detachment of their hoplites retreated into a *cul-de-sac*, of which the entry was closed off by the Athenian hoplites. The Corinthians were then destroyed to a man by the missiles of the Athenian light-armed troops. In western Sicily, too, Athens made an alliance with Segesta in 458/7. It was probably in March 457 that the casualties of the Athenian forces over the previous twelve months were officially recorded. An inscription is preserved which gives the names of 177 men of the tribe Erechtheis 'killed in action in Cyprus, Egypt, Phoenicia, Halieis, Aegina, and Megara in the same twelve-

[1] Th. 1. 104; 109; Hdt. 3. 12; 15; 7. 7; D.S. 11. 71; 74; Ctes. fr. 32; *Klio* 32. 289.

month'. These losses were indeed heavy. But Athens had not yet faced the military power of Sparta and Persia.[1]

In 457 an army of the Spartan Alliance, comprising 1,500 Lacedaemonians and 10,000 allies, began operations in central Greece. It is probable that Sparta and Athens were not formally at war. On their way north the Spartans avoided any clash with Athenian forces, hoping perhaps that the presence of so great an army near Attica would cause the Athenian state to negotiate for a peaceful settlement. The Spartan army marched probably through the Megarid, entered Boeotia, which was neutral, and settled a war between Doris and Phocis in favour of the former. Meanwhile, when the Spartan force was in Boeotia, the Athenians sent a squadron of fifty ships round the Peloponnese to Pegae. Its task was to attack transport vessels and prevent them mustering in the Gulf of Cirrha, so that the Peloponnesian force would be unable to return by sea. Moreover, as Athenian troops held Pegae and Megara, picketed the passes over Mt. Gerania towards the Isthmus, and were supported by the squadron at Pegae, retreat by land for the Peloponnesian force was hazardous. The Spartan commander, Nicomedes, decided to halt in Boeotia. Here he was able to conscript Boeotian hoplites and intrigue with some Athenians, who urged him to overthrow the democracy and put an end to the building of the Long Walls; for the last stage, the carrying of the walls down to the sea at Phalerum and at Peiraeus, was nearing completion and the city would soon be almost impregnable against attack by land.

When it became clear that Athens would not negotiate, Nicomedes prepared to fight a pitched battle, before Aegina was reduced by siege and before the Long Walls were finished. The Athenians meanwhile had mustered their full hoplite force, and had been joined by 1,000 Argives, by individual contingents from their other allies, and by a cavalry force of Thessalians. The hoplites alone numbered 14,000. They engaged the Spartan army at Tanagra on Boeotian soil. Victory was won by the Spartans, to whom the Thessalian cavalry deserted during the battle, but the losses on both sides were heavy. The depleted Peloponnesian force was no longer strong enough to attack Athens. It entered the Megarid, ravaged the territory, and passed unopposed into the Peloponnese. In this their first military operation outside Laconia and Messenia since the earthquake of 464 the reputation of the Spartan hoplites and of the Spartan Alliance was vindicated once more.[2]

Some two months later, *c.* August 457, Myronides led an Athenian army into Boeotia, defeated the forces of the Boeotians at Oenophyta, dismantled the walls of Tanagra near the Attic frontier, and established control over most of Boeotia and Phocis. Whereas Nicomedes had reconstituted the Boeotian League under the leadership of an oligarchic government at Thebes,

---

[1] Th. 1. 105–6; *IGA* 5 'dedicated by the Athenians from the Peloponnesians after the naval victory' may refer to the victory before the landing on Aegina; D.S. 11. 70. 2–3; 78; *GHI* 26. *GHI* 31 with *IG* i.[2] 20 and *TAPA* 75. 10.

[2] Th. 1. 107–8; D.S. 11. 79–80; Paus. 1. 29. 7–9; *GHI* 27; 28; *Hesp.* 14. 134; *AP* 7. 254.

Myronides disbanded the League, drove out the leading oligarchs, and set up democratic governments in all the states except Thebes, where a democracy came into power without his intervention but was soon overthrown. In Phocis and also in Opuntian Locris he took civilian hostages from the wealthy class and thereby favoured the rise of democratic leaders. It was probably during these operations that Naupactus was captured from the Ozolian Locrians and occupied as a colony by Athenian sympathizers from Opuntian Locris. Before the end of the year 457 the Long Walls of Athens were completed and Aegina capitulated. Her walls were dismantled, her fleet was surrendered, and her mint closed. She was compelled to become a member of the Athenian Alliance and to pay thenceforth a tribute which Athens dictated. Her allegiance was probably secured by the imposition of an Athenian garrison. The bulk of central Greece was now under Athens' control.[1]

In 456 Athens opened a vigorous offensive against the coasts of the Peloponnese. Tolmides, in command of fifty triremes and a picked force of marines numbering 1,000 men, ravaged the island of Cythera and the towns of Boeae and Methone on the south coast, burnt the dockyards of the Lacedaemonian fleet at Gytheum, won over the islands of Zacynthos and Cephallenia, and sailed into the Corinthian Gulf. There he captured a Corinthian colony, Chalcis, outside the narrows of Rhium and settled the Messenian troops in his fleet at Naupactus inside the narrows. This settlement was destined to play an important part in Athenian strategy. For the Messenians and the Naupactians maintained their independence on this narrow foreshore below the mountains, and they provided a safe base for the Athenian fleet in western waters. Sailing eastwards from Naupactus, Tolmides landed on the Peloponnesian coast and defeated the forces of Sicyon in battle. His fleet probably wintered at Naupactus and Pegae.

In 455 Tolmides operated in Boeotia. Pericles was given command of the western fleet, to which 1,000 marines were again allocated. He ravaged the northern coasts of the Peloponnese and won over all the cities of Acarnania, except Oeniadae at the mouth of the Achelous, which commanded the entry from the north-west into the Gulf. The operations of Tolmides and Pericles in the west, coupled with the Athenian control of the Saronic Gulf, pressed heavily upon the coastal peoples of the Peloponnese, especially Corinth and Sicyon, and aggravated the danger of a Helot rising in Laconia and Messenia. The sea power of Athens in Greek waters was now unchallenged, and its value as an offensive weapon was demonstrated.[2]

During these years the Athenian Alliance maintained considerable forces

[1] Th. 1. 108; *IG* i.² 18; D.S. 11. 78. 4; 81–83; Arist. *Pol.* 1302ᵇ29. The colony of Opuntian Locrians at Naupactus (*GHI* 24) was either founded some years before Athens captured Naupactus from the Ozolian Locrians (Th. 1. 103. 3) or in 457–456. If the latter is the case, the 'Naupactians' who joined the Messenians in making a dedication at Olympia (*GHI* 348) were the settlers from Opuntian Locris.

[2] Th. 1. 108. 5; D.S. 11. 84–85; Schol. Aeschin. 2. 75; Paus. 1. 27. 5.

in Egypt. Probably in 459 Persia sent an envoy, Megabazus, to Greece. He offered to subsidize an invasion of Attica, which would result in the withdrawal of the Athenian force from Egypt. Sparta, however, refused to medize. Artaxerxes thereupon equipped a large army and navy which invaded Egypt in spring 455, defeated the combined forces of the Egyptians and Greeks, and confined the Greek force to the island of Prosopitis, situated between a canal and two branches of the Nile. Here the Greeks were in a dangerous situation. For the Egyptians, apart from Inaros himself, made a separate peace, and all the supplies of the Greeks had to be brought by ship up the Nile. By strenuous efforts the expeditionary force held its ground for a period of eighteen months until midsummer 454, when the Persians diverted the waters of the canal and marched in to the assault. Only a few of the Greeks escaped across the desert to the colony at Cyrene; 6,000 surrendered and the rest were killed. Unaware of the disaster, a squadron of fifty ships, commanded by recently elected generals and carrying troops to relieve those at Prosopitis, put in to an eastern mouth of the Nile and was surprised by a Persian army and a Phoenician squadron. The majority were destroyed. The total loss of ships in both defeats probably exceeded 100 vessels. Such was the end of the great expedition of Athens and her Allies in Egypt.[1]

At this time in Greece an Athenian army, reinforced by contingents from her allies in Boeotia and Phocis, entered Thessaly and demanded the reinstatement of some supporters of Athens, who had been banished by the Thessalians after the battle of Tanagra. Pharsalus refused to accede to this demand. The movement of the Athenian army was restricted by the Thessalian cavalry, and it failed to take Pharsalus by storm. Soon after its return Pericles was dispatched with 1,000 marines to Pegae, where he manned the western fleet of 100 triremes and sailed for home waters. As he passed down the Gulf of Corinth, he gave a signal demonstration of Athenian power. He ravaged the territory of Sicyon, defeated a force of Sicyonians, transported some Achaean troops to Acarnania, and ravaged the territory of Oeniadae. In the winter of 454–453, when the Athenian fleets were assembled in the Aegean, Athens took a decisive step in her relations with her Allies. She transferred the great sum which lay in the Allied Treasury at Delos to the Acropolis at Athens, where it passed under the protection of Athena and into the control of the Ecclesia. The disaster in Egypt had thrown Athens on to the defensive,[2] and she had need of money to regain the initiative.

At this point we may review the policy of Athens in the years 461–454. It was based on the fact that she had greater resources than any Greek state. The citizen body, which had numbered some 30,000 adult males during the Persian War, rose towards 40,000 during these years of prosperity, when the

---

[1] Th. 1. 109–10; D.S. 11. 74. 5; 75; 77; 12. 3; Ctes. 33–34; Isoc. 8. 86 (putting the Greek loss at 200 ships).

[2] Th. 1. 111; D.S. 11. 83. 3–4; 88. 1–2; Plu. *Per.* 19 (giving 100 triremes, made up probably by 50 in 457 and 50 in 456).

state was still granting citizenship with liberality. Resident aliens, too, served in the armed forces, and cleruchs were in position overseas for service. As front-line troops she had between 10,000 and 12,000 hoplites, probably 300 cavalry, and numerous light-armed troops—archers, slingers, and skirmishers.[1] With light-armed troops serving as rowers and marines, she could man a fleet of nearly 200 triremes. These forces were available at Athens, because the population of Attica was freeborn. In most Dorian states the serfs predominated, and the citizens served in war as an *élite* and prosperous minority. Their manpower was therefore less, and the proportion of naval personnel to hoplites was lower than at Athens. Corinth, a commercial state of great prosperity, provided only forty ships at Salamis and 5,000 hoplites at Plataea; Sicyon, too, provided fifteen ships and 3,000 hoplites, and Sparta sixteen ships and 5,000 Spartiate hoplites.[2] As a naval power Athens had an outright superiority over the Peloponnesian states both in personnel and in hulls, so that in 460 her battle-fleet outnumbered the combined fleets of Corinth, Sicyon, and Sparta. As a military power she was superior in numbers of citizen hoplites to any one of the Peloponnesian states.

Athens set out to annihilate the fleets of her rivals. She succeeded brilliantly by striking before they could combine. Thasos and Aegina capitulated, and the squadrons of Corinth, Sicyon, and Sparta were crippled or destroyed by 455. As mistress of the Saronic and Corinthian Gulfs, she raided the coasts of the Peloponnese and gained the adherence of Achaea and probably Troezen.[3] Had she been at peace with Persia, she might have split the Spartan Alliance apart and imposed her will on the Peloponnese. But she chose to launch a major offensive against Persia at the same time.

In the Aegean Athens had great naval resources at her command. At the battle of Lade the Ionians alone had mustered some 350 triremes. In 460 Athens had many allies as well as the Ionians. She preferred to draw money from most of them, in order to maintain her own fleet; but Chios, Lesbos, and Samos had in the past manned 230 triremes, and other states provided oarsmen in large numbers.[4] In the years 460–455 the Aegean fleet of the Athenian Alliance was deployed against the naval strength of the Persian empire, recruited in the past from Cilicia, Cyprus, Phoenicia, and Egypt. When Athens and her Allies accepted the invitation of Inaros, they were already operating with 200 ships in Cyprus, and they now gained the adherence of the Egyptian fleet. They hoped therefore to destroy the residue of Persia's fleets. In this great naval programme the Athenian Alliance succeeded admirably. By 455 their fleet controlled the approaches to Egypt and the Nile Delta. In this theatre of war the Athenian squadron probably numbered some forty ships,[5] because her main fleet was occupied in destroying the navies of the Peloponnesians. However, so long as the Allies remained

---

[1] And. 3. 5; *IG* i.[2] 400; for Athenian numbers at Salamis, Plataea, Eurymedon, and Tanagra see above; Hdt. 1. 97; 8. 65. 1.   [2] Hdt. 8. 1; 9. 28.
[3] Th. 1. 115. 1.   [4] Hdt. 6. 8.   [5] Ctes. 32.

loyal to her, the Persian fleet was unlikely to offer a serious challenge to Greek supremacy on the high seas.

Athens embarked on the double offensive at a time when she had secured the alliance of three military powers, Argos, Thessaly, and Megara, and Sparta had been crippled by the earthquake and its aftermath. Nevertheless, Athens made no attempt to invade the Peloponnese and force a decisive battle. Her own hoplites were serving partly with the fleet and partly as garrison troops in the Megarid; and she probably was not confident that her Allies would put forth their whole strength against the Spartan Alliance. For her own part she improved her defences by building Long Walls at Athens and at Megara. On the other hand, Sparta was at first also on the defensive. Her force of Spartiates probably numbered little more than 3,000 and discontent was still rife in Messenia. She postponed her own declaration of war. Aegina, following her example, let Corinth and Epidaurus be worn down before her own turn came. In 457 the Spartan offensive was indecisive. After the Spartan withdrawal the Athenian defences were intact and Athens could continue her harassing of the Peloponnese. Her military policy was succeeding, despite the fact that her Allies on land were proving to be of little value.

In the east she did not challenge Persia on land until she had the military alliance of Inaros; then his army in co-operation with the Greek fleet and marines defeated a large Persian army and during five years was within an ace of liberating Egypt completely. In the *Persae*, produced in 472, Aeschylus had depicted the disasters which threatened to overthrow the Persian empire; then victory at the Eurymedon and the revolt of Egypt in 460 had seemed to afford a reasonable expectation that a dismemberment of the empire would ensue. This hope proved false. In the final test the Egyptian army was worsted, and the Egyptians made a separate peace with Persia. Athens, as leader of the Athenian Alliance, did not cut the losses and withdraw the fleet. As later at Syracuse, this persistence cost her dear.

In going to war Athens did not count only on her naval and military resources. Her democracy was a weapon of political warfare, capable of forming a bond of common interest with other states. At first it was effective. Argos changed from an aristocratic to a democratic constitution probably at the time of her alliance *c*. 461. Her popular Assembly and Council (alongside the older Council, 'The Eighty'), her popular Court, her five local tribes (alongside the older four ethnic tribes), and her institution of ostracism bore a very close resemblance to features of the Athenian constitution. It is likely, too, that Megara became democratic; there, too, ostracism was practised. In most of Boeotia and probably in Phocis and Locris democratic governments resulted not from free choice but from the intervention of Athenian armies;[1] and at Thebes, too, a democracy came into power. When in 455 Tolmides had to operate in Boeotia, these democratic governments threatened to become a liability.

[1] Th. 5. 47. 9; *FGrH* 306 F 3 (Deinias); Arist. *Pol.* 1302^{b}29; Schol. Ar. *Eq.* 855.

In 454 Athens realized that she could no longer maintain the double offensive. Her own losses had been severe, especially in the ranks of the hoplites, who bore the brunt of the fighting in Greece and in Egypt.[1] The position on the Greek mainland was hazardous. For Thessaly was hostile, Argos inactive, and her so-called allies, Megara, Boeotia, and Phocis, restless and apprehensive. Fortunately for Athens the Spartan Alliance still remained on the defensive. The danger was more acute in the Aegean. There the grounds for discontent had increased with the prosecution of the war. Athens' leadership was exacting, and her demands on the services of the Allies were increasing. Their losses had been particularly heavy at Drabescus and in Egypt where they supplied the bulk of the fleet, and their troops had been engaged against Aegina and at Tanagra. Although the war on the mainland was represented as a war between 'the Ionians and the Peloponnesians' on the spoils which Athens and Sparta dedicated, the members of the Athenian Alliance gained nothing from the destruction of the fleets of Aegina, Corinth, Sicyon, and Sparta and from the extension of Athens' power in central Greece.[2] The fate of Thasos had revealed the nature of Athens' ambitions, and the Allies came to realize that a victorious Athens might infringe the autonomy which the Athenian Alliance had been formed to preserve. The disaster in Egypt damaged the prestige of Athenian leadership, and the presence of a large and victorious Persian force in the south-east Mediterranean encouraged some of the Allies to embark on a struggle for liberation. In the winter of 454–3 a considerable number of them in East Greece revolted with the support of Persia.

§ 3. *Pericles' leadership and the Athenian empire*

DURING the years of victory and expansion, from 460 to 455, the honours of military command fell to Myronides, Tolmides, Leocrates, Charitimides, and others. Pericles was not in the first rank as a commander, and when he commanded in 455 he was probably deputizing for Tolmides. On the other hand, he succeeded Ephialtes as leader of the democrats. He deprived the Areopagus of further powers. He supervised the building of the Long Walls. Probably in 458 he issued the famous order to 'wipe out Aegina, the eyesore of the Peiraeus'. The democrats remained in the ascendant. In 458/457 they canvassed the support of the middle class by opening candidature for the archonships to members of the zeugite census, from which the hoplites were drawn.[3] In 457/456, when the intrigue of the oligarchs with Sparta had failed and the democracy extended its power in central Greece, Pericles proposed and carried the recall of Cimon from ostracism. He may have calculated that, if Cimon was present in Athens, Sparta would be inclined to hope for a

---

[1] Arist. *Ath.* 26. 1; *Pol.* 1303ᵃ9; Isoc. 8. 87.
[2] Th. 1. 99; 105. 2; *GHI* 27; *IGA* 5.
[3] Ar. *Lys.* 801; *Ec.* 303; Plu. *Per.* 13; 16; Arist. *Ath.* 26. 2.

peaceful settlement and Cimon would restrain the extremists in Athens. But, whatever his calculations, Pericles was sufficiently confident of his own pre-dominance to accept the presence of his former rival. When the disaster came in Egypt and secessions from the Athenian Alliance began, Pericles was appointed to the important task of demonstrating Athenian power in the west and bringing the main Athenian fleet into home waters. In the years which followed he was probably responsible for the consistent and shrewd policy of the state.[1]

Pericles had the initial advantage of noble birth, which gave him an entry into the highest circles of Athenian politics. His father Xanthippus, a member perhaps of the Buzygae clan, commanded the Athenian squadron at Mycale and left a considerable fortune; and his mother Agariste was a daughter of the Alcmeonid Cleisthenes, the opponent of tyranny and Sparta and the champion of the liberty of the people. Born *c.* 495, Pericles came of age with the rise of the Athenian Alliance, when the great days of the Greek League and of co-operation between Athens and Sparta were already waning. Throughout his career he opposed Sparta without remission, and he regarded the Athenian Alliance as the basis of Athens' own greatness. He insisted above all on the interests of his own city-state, and his insistence commended itself to the bulk of the people. In internal politics his devotion to the demo-cratic cause was guaranteed by his attacks on the Areopagus, on Cimon, and on Sparta. He was not suspected of aiming at tyranny, as Themistocles had been; for his probity of character and his impeccable reputation in the hand-ling of public money set him apart from the general run of politicians. His talents were outstanding. A brave soldier, a capable general, a moving orator, whose precise diction was combined with brilliant expression and spiritual force, he owed his influence above all to the sureness of judgement with which he calculated the elements in any military or diplomatic situation and foresaw the future development of Athens. His judgement was trained by education and experience. A pupil or associate of the leading thinkers of his day— Damon, Zeno, and Anaxagoras—his intellect was not clouded by any pre-conceptions or prejudices, secular or religious, and his experience bred in him a confidence and composure which reassured his followers. He was dependable personally and politically; as a general and as a politician his first thought was for the safety of his citizens. Above all, he filled them with a sense of their great destiny, and he did much to realize that destiny.[2]

In the political arena Pericles faced a strong opposition, led by Cimon and then by Cimon's successor, Thucydides, son of Melesias, who was finally ostracized in 443. The problems of domestic and foreign policy were closely interwoven. If democracy was to be carried farther, it was necessary to sub-sidize the lower class in the state. Money for this purpose could only be found by exploiting the leadership of Athens over her Allies; and such ex-

---

[1] Plu. *Per.* 16; 13 (Cratinus); 8; 10; *Cim.* 17; *FGrH* 115 F 88 (Theopompus).
[2] Plu. *Per.* 3-8; Schol. Ael. Arist. (Dind. 3. 473).

ploitation made it necessary to resist Sparta, so that Sparta could not intervene on the side of the discontented Allies. If democracy was modified, it
might be possible to achieve again the co-operation with the Allies and with
Sparta which had led up to the victory at Eurymedon.

The choice between these alternatives was taken in the years 454–451. The
disaster in 454 strengthened the hand of Cimon. There was much to recommend his policy of co-operation with the Allies and *rapprochement* with
Sparta. His open-handed generosity in undertaking public services and in
assisting his fellow-demesmen increased his popularity with all classes in the
state.[1] Pericles, however, carried through two reforms which made the
democracy more democratic: the Areopagus was further stripped of powers,
which, being judicial in character, were transferred to the Heliaea, and state-
pay was instituted for the jurymen, who had now to deal with an increasing
number of cases. The Heliaea was transformed into several courts (*dikasteria*).
The jurors for these were selected by lot from a panel of 6,000 citizens, who
had been chosen from all who had volunteered and served, 600 from each
tribe, for one year. To the democrat state-pay was justifiable on two grounds:
it gave an equal opportunity to every citizen, rich or poor, to serve in the
people's courts, and it provided a means of subsidizing many members of
the poorest class. At the same time it strengthened the position of the democratic leaders. For the bulk of the 6,000 jurors were prompted by their
material interest to support their paymaster, the democratic régime, and this
was especially so in time of war when the aged and poor tended to pre-
dominate among the jurors. Moreover, once the principle was established,
state-pay was introduced for other services, so that more and more citizens
came to have a vested interest in the continuance of democracy. Between 454
and 440 the number who benefited from some form of state-pay rose to a
total of some 20,000.[2] The reform of the Heliaea may have led to the re-
establishment in 453/452 of the thirty justices who went on circuit round the
demes. The introduction of state-pay provided one reason for an important
law proposed by Pericles in 451/450. In the past the son of an Athenian
citizen and a foreign woman had been eligible for citizenship. From 451/450
onwards citizenship was limited to those who were of citizen birth on both
sides. Thenceforth the state would be able to control the number of those
who were eligible to draw state-pay.[3]

The laws of Pericles which introduced state-pay and restricted citizenship
have been sharply criticized by later generations. Plato, for instance, believed
that state-pay made the Athenians 'idle, cowardly, talkative, and grasping',
and modern historians have maintained that the law on citizenship prevented
Athens from developing into a larger state. The first criticism was not true
so long as Pericles lived; the second criticism has more substance. But these

---

[1] Arist. *Ath.* 27. 3; Plu. *Cim.* 10; *Per.* 9; *FGrH* 115 F 89 (Theopompus); Nep. *Cim.* 4.
[2] Arist. *Pol.* 1274ᵃ8; *Ath.* 27. 3–4; Plu. loc. cit.; Arist. *Ath.* 24.
[3] Arist. *Ath.* 26. 3; Harp. *nautodikai*.

two laws should not be judged in isolation. They were intimately connected with the foreign policy of Athens; for the state could only provide pay continuously by taxing the Allies, and the discrimination against non-Athenian mothers was likely to apply for the most part to women of the allied states. Pericles intended to convert the Athenian Alliance into an Athenian empire. The revenues of empire were to contribute towards two objects—the working of the Athenian democracy and the maintenance of the Athenian forces. Thereby Athens was to become a city-state more after the Dorian than the Ionian model. The citizens would be an *élite* body, subsidized by the subject-peoples, and some of the able-bodied men would be liberated from civilian business for training and service in war, so that in the end Athens might prove stronger than Sparta. The policy of Pericles was expressed also by the dictum that he directed the state towards the exercise of naval power and thereby placed the whole constitution in the hands of the democratic leaders. His policy, like any policy, had its inherent defects; but, judged in the light of its results, it succeeded in securing an empire and in raising Athens to her zenith, although it failed to crush Sparta or unite the Greek world.[1]

In 454–451 Pericles no doubt envisaged the future trend of Athens' development, but he had at the time three immediate objectives—to outdo Cimon, to resist Sparta, and reduce the allied states which had revolted. His democratic reforms achieved the first objective. For three years Sparta and Athens took no action on land and then concluded a Five Years Truce, extending from 451 to 446; at the same time Argos made a Thirty Years Truce with Sparta and backed out of her alliance with Athens. These pacts postponed the solution of the second problem. In this field Pericles and Cimon perhaps co-operated; for Cimon negotiated the truce and received the command against Persia in 450, but Pericles and his followers kept their ascendancy in the internal politics of Athens. The Athenian forces were now free to restore order in the Aegean. They succeeded rapidly. Between 454 and 449 the number of Allies paying tribute increased from 135 to something between 155 and 173 states, and in 450 the fleet of Athens and her allies was able to take the offensive against Persia. The aim of Cimon in command of 200 triremes was to reassert Athens' thalassocracy in the eastern Mediterranean. Since their victory in 454 the Persians had captured Cyprus and confined the successor of Inaros, Amyrtaeus, to the swamps of the Delta, and in 450 large forces were at advanced stations in Cyprus and in Cilicia. Cimon won a great victory over the Persian fleet, detached a squadron of sixty ships to help Amyrtaeus in the Delta, and laid siege to the Phoenician base in Cyprus, Citium. During the winter Cimon died of disease and a famine caused the Athenians to raise the siege, but their forces won further victories over the Persian fleet and army off Salamis in Cyprus and probably on the coast of Cilicia. In the latter part of 449 Persia began to negotiate for peace, and the Greek forces withdrew from Cyprus and Egypt. It is possible that survivors

[1] Pl. *Grg.* 515c; Arist. *Ath.* 24. 3; 27. 1; 41. 2; *Pol.* 1275^{b}21; 1278^{a}34.

of the 6,000 Greeks who had been captured in Egypt in 454 were repatriated during the negotiations.[1]

The treaty of peace, concluded probably early in 448, has been named after Callias, who headed the plenipotentiaries of Athens, the hegemon of the Greek forces. At Susa he was perhaps helped by some envoys of Argos, who were renewing their pact of friendship with Artaxerxes. The treaty was concluded between Persia on the one hand and Athens and her Allies on the other. The terms are known to us only in a paraphrase of the main articles. 'All the Greek cities in Asia shall be autonomous. The Persian satraps shall not come within three days' journey of the coast, and no Persian warship shall sail the seas between Phaselis and Cyaneae. Athens shall not invade the territory of the Great King.'[2] By this treaty the Greeks in Asia were protected from Persia and the war with Persia was concluded, an achievement which marked the triumph of the pact entered into by Athens and the Ionians in 477 and brought its declared intention to an end; the Persian rule over Cyprus and Egypt was recognized and ensured against Athenian intervention; the sea power of Athens was recognized and her empire between Phaselis in Pamphylia and Cyaneae at the mouth of the Bosporus was ensured against Persian intervention; and the seas were open to merchant vessels of both nations, which were now at peace. The treaty marked the end of the Greek war against Persia and a stage in the consolidation of the Athenian empire.[3]

The conversion of the Athenian Alliance into an Athenian Empire was a gradual process, whereby more and more states lost their freedom of action and became subject to the will of Athens. By 454 some states were already in this position; for Carystus, Naxos, Thasos, Aegina, and perhaps others had been rendered defenceless and compelled to obey the commands of Athens. A second group of states, which was much the most numerous, had deprived themselves of the means to resist by contributing money to the Allied Treasury instead of ships to the Allied fleet; they were already intimidated, and they tended to cast their vote on the Allied Synod in accordance with the wish of Athens. A third group of states, which steadily diminished in number, still retained some guarantee of their autonomy in the fleets which they contributed to the allied cause; they could flout the will of Athens, although, as the example of Thasos showed, their chances of escape were small. The events of the years 460–454 revealed an important stage in the transition from Alliance to Empire. It was for the interests not of the Allies but of Athens that allied contingents fought against Aegina and against the land powers at Tanagra; their very participation proved that the Allied Synod was

[1] Th. 1. 112. 1–4; D.S. 12. 3–4; Plu. *Cim.* 18–19; the epigram in D.S. 11. 62. 3 probably refers to this victory in Cyprus; Ctes. 34–37.

[2] D.S. 12. 4. 5; Plu. *Cim.* 13; 19 (400 stades may refer to an article in the treaty which Diodorus paraphrases as three days' journey); *FGrH* 104 F 13 (Aristodemus); Isoc. 4. 120; Hdt. 7. 151; *FGrH* 115 F 153–4 (Theopompus, stating that a copy of the terms was forged); Paus. 1. 8. 2.

[3] Th. 3. 10. 4.

governed by the policy of Athens. These years also saw a rise in the naval strength of Athens and a decline in that of the Allies. While Athens destroyed or captured the fleets of the Aeginetans and Peloponnesians, the Allies bore the brunt of the fighting in Egypt and the greater part of the loss in the final disaster. As Thucydides expressed it, 'the Athenians no longer took an equal share in their joint campaigns, but yet found it easy to reduce those who revolted'.[1]

In the winter of 454–453 the Allied Treasury was transferred from the protection of Apollo at Delos to the protection of Athena at Athens. Early in the history of the Athenian Alliance such a step may have been proposed by Samos in the Allied Synod, but on the present occasion Athens probably acted at her own discretion. The transference itself might be justified on the ground that Delos was exposed to the danger of attack, because the Phoenician fleet was emboldened by the successes in Egypt and the seceding states offered advanced bases of operation. But the real significance of the transference was political. Henceforth Athens usurped control of the Allied Treasury, and at one bound her financial resources became enormous in relation to those of the few states who might still be regarded as autonomous. The 'Allied Treasury' ceased to exist as an independent fund; it became a department of Athenian finance, and probably in 450/449 a sum of 5,000 talents was transferred from it and later subsidized the building programme at Athens.[2] The Allied Synod ceased to meet. Decrees affecting the affairs of 'Athens and her Allies' were henceforth issued by the Athenian state. Now that she held all the reins of power in her own hands, Athens dispensed with the empty formality of consulting the wishes of her sometime Allies.

For some years the inactivity of Sparta gave Athens an opportunity to reassert her position of command throughout the Aegean. Between 454 and 449 the number of tribute-paying states rose approximately from 135 to something between 155 and 173. The additional states were probably of two classes: those which were compelled or persuaded to convert their contributions from ships to money, in order that they should lack the means to secede, and those which, having seceded, were forced to rejoin. The states in the former class were few, situated probably in Euboea and the Cyclades. By 448 the only ship-contributing states were Chios, Lesbos, and Samos, which acted as naval strong-points in the east Aegean and were accorded preferential treatment by Athens.[3] The states in the second class were much more numerous; they lay mainly in the south-east Aegean, and they included Miletus, Erythrae, and perhaps Colophon on the Ionian coast. The methods by which their allegiance was secured are recorded in several inscriptions which are probably to be dated within the period 453 to 449.

In Erythrae and Miletus Athens placed garrisons. Their presence might

[1] Th. 3. 10. 5; 1. 99. 2.
[2] Plu. *Per.* 12; *Arist.* 25; *ATL* 2. 61. D 13 (the date is doubtful).
[3] Arist. *Ath.* 24. 2.

be justified as a military measure in time of war, but they also served a political purpose. Athens sent out to these states and to Colophon Athenian 'commissioners' (*episkopoi*) or 'archons', whose activities were safeguarded by the military garrison. Their concern was to install a puppet or at least a compliant government in accordance with a decree of the Athenian state. At Erythrae the commissioners and the garrison commander selected by lot and installed the members of the Council for the first year of the new era, and the outgoing Councillors and the garrison commander installed their successors for succeeding years. The government there and at Colophon was then graced with the name of democracy. The Councillors were put under oath—the penalty for perjury being the execution of the Councillor and his sons—to be loyal to the democracy at Erythrae and to Athens and her Allies; not to revolt from the democracy of Athens or from her Allies; and not to expel any citizens or recall those in refuge with the Persians except on the approval of Athens and the democracy at Erythrae. By the terms of this oath the democratic régimes at Athens and Erythrae were linked together, Athens spoke in the name of herself and her Allies, and Athens dictated the policy of Erythrae in cases of political exile and recall. At Miletus a board of five Athenian magistrates 'co-operated' with the executive officials of the Milesian government, which was at first oligarchic but perhaps in 447 democratic in form, and imposed a similar oath of allegiance.[1]

Garrisons, commissioners, and governments sworn to an oath of loyalty were probably imposed on all states which seceded and were reduced. In individual cases special steps were taken. The Athenian commissioners, temporary in the first instance, sometimes became a regular board of political residents, 'archons', and an oath of obedience to the will of Athens was sometimes exacted from the people as well as from the Council. At Miletus two families and their descendants were outlawed for tyranny, probably at the request of Athens, and some judicial cases had to be referred to the Athenian courts for settlement. At Erythrae anyone sentenced to exile on a charge of murder was to be exiled from the territory of Athens and her Allies, and anyone guilty of betraying the city to tyrants was to be executed together with his sons. Athens also ordained that Erythrae should send envoys with offerings, of which the minimum value was specified, to the Great Panathenaic festival held every fourth year at Athens.[2]

In the transition from Alliance to empire an important part was played by Athenians who occupied strategic points in the Aegean area. Those at Sigeum, for instance, were commended for their services in 451/450 and were promised protection by Athens against any enemy in Asia. Others were at Scyros, Imbros, and Lemnos and in the Chersonese. Between 450 and 446 Athens planted settlements on the territory of her Allies for the first time—at Andros, Naxos, and probably Histiaea in Euboea—and also reinforced the

---

[1] *GHI* 29; *IG* i.² 11 (Erythrae); *IG* i.² 22, and *TAPA* 66. 177 (Miletus); 14–15 (Colophon).
[2] *IG* i.² 12, 13a; *GHI* 35 and [X.] *Ath.* 3. 11; *GHI* 29.

settlements perhaps at Lemnos and Imbros and certainly in the Chersonese. Such settlements acted as pickets of empire; for the settlers all acquired hoplite status, deterred their neighbours from revolting, and provided a *point d'appui* for the Athenian fleet. When a settlement was to be planted, Athens confiscated the best land, divided it into lots (*kleroi*), and gave each settler a lot so that he became a cleruch (*kleroukhos*); the numbers of such settlers at Andros, Naxos, and Histiaea were 250, 500, and probably 500, and they dispossessed populations three or four times as numerous. Many of the dispossessed persons became destitute; in a country so poor in fertile land they were faced with starvation or with emigration. The state from which the best land had been withdrawn was compelled to pay tribute in accordance with a new assessment of its diminished resources. No action by Athens roused deeper resentment among her subjects or shackled them more firmly than the planting of these cleruchies in their midst.[1]

Between 450 and 447 Athens made the use of Athenian silver currency and of Athenian weights and measures obligatory throughout the empire. All local currencies in silver had to be recalled from circulation and melted down; Attic coins were then issued, a slight loss in the exchange being carried by the recipients. The silver mints of the Allies were closed down and thereby the Athenian mint benefited. The flow of trade was facilitated throughout the Aegean and not least between Athens and her subjects. But in this measure, as in other measures after 454, the autonomy of the Allies was openly infringed.[2]

The statesman who inspired the establishment of the empire was Pericles. He was entrusted with the supervision of the Allied Treasury on its transference to Athens, and he proposed the diversion of 5,000 talents from it to the building fund. He advocated the policy of planting cleruchies, and he led the expedition to the Chersonese. It is probable that he exercised a dominating influence on the foreign policy of the state. For it was important to keep Athens' other enemies out of the field during the dangerous process of establishing the empire.

In the Far West Athens made alliances probably in 454/453 with Halicyae, Leontini, and Rhegium. These alliances were a diplomatic success for Athens: they represented her as a potential counterweight in Sicily against the naval power of Syracuse and might discourage Syracuse from coming to the help of Corinth. But the success was nullified by the consequences which sprang from the disaster in Egypt. In the Peloponnese Athens retained her footing in Achaea and Troezen and made a pact with Hermione, but she lost her main support when Argos concluded a Thirty Years Peace with Sparta in 451, thus renouncing her alliance with Athens.[3] In central Greece in 454/453 Athens concluded an alliance with Phocis, which as an enemy of Sparta, Thebes, and Thessaly was likely to remain loyal. She helped Phocis to assume

---

[1] *IG* i.[2] 32 and *Hesp.* 5. 360; Plu. *Per.* 11, 19, 23; D.S. 11. 88. 3 with Paus. 1. 27. 5 (probably Histiaea).   [2] *ATL* 2. 61. D 14; *Hesp.* Suppl. 8. 324.
[3] *GHI* 57, 58 (renewals of earlier treaties); *Hesp.* 2. 494 (Hermione); Th. 5. 28. 2.

control of Delphi and hoped thereby to enlist the religious authority of the Delphic Amphictyony in aid of her political sway over Boeotia and Locris. Sparta, however, upset this arrangement in autumn 449. She declared a Sacred War, ousted Phocis from control, and made the small state of Delphi autonomous. Thereby Sparta represented herself as the champion of religious and political liberty; her action did not violate the terms of her Five Years Truce with Athens, but at the same time it constituted a challenge to Athens' position in Central Greece. Athens took up the challenge in summer 447, restored the control of Delphi to Phocis, and re-affirmed her alliance with Phocis. During these abortive interchanges both Sparta and Athens engraved their right of precedence in consulting the oracle on the statue of a bronze wolf which stood in the sacred precinct.[1]

It was probably in 448, after the Spartan intervention at Delphi and before the Athenian riposte, that Pericles proposed a diplomatic offensive against Sparta. Twenty Athenian dignitaries were to be sent to all Greek states: from Thessaly and Ambracia in the north to Sparta in the south, to the Aegean islands from Lesbos to Rhodes, to the cities of the Thracian and Hellespontine coasts, as far as Byzantium, and of the Asiatic coasts, both Ionian and Dorian. They were to invite these states to attend a Panhellenic conference at Athens and discuss measures for restoring the temples burnt by the Persians, offering the sacrifices vowed in the crisis of the Persian War, securing the freedom of the seas for one and all, and establishing peace in the Greek world.

The occasion was well chosen, in that Persia had just recognized the freedom of the Greek states in Asia and the war between Persia and Greece had ended in a treaty of peace. But the times were too much out of joint for Athens to pose as peacemaker in the Greek world. The Aegean states which had accepted her leadership at the formation of the Athenian Alliance now saw in her imposition of garrisons, democracies, and cleruchies the acts of a tyrant state, while the states of the Greek mainland had suffered from repeated acts of Athenian aggression since 458. In recent years Pericles' own policy had stultified the apparent purpose of the invitation, and it is doubtful whether he expected a wide response. There were, of course, ulterior motives in the proposal. The great achievements of Athens against Persia were publicized in a manner which emphasized her service to the Greek gods and enlarged the pride of her people. The power of Athens was paraded before the Greek states. The freedom of the seas was indeed in her gift, and the prospects of peace for most Greek states depended directly on her will. If some of the Peloponnesian states were to yield to the power and the pretensions of Athens, she might extend her influence decisively and pin Sparta down in isolation. But when the envoys delivered the invitation, no response came from the Peloponnese. The Spartan Alliance stood firm, and the invitations to the other states were cancelled.[2]

[1] Th. 1. 112. 5; *GHI* 39; *FGrH* 328 F 34 (Philochorus); Plu. *Per.* 21.
[2] Plu. *Per.* 17 (based on the original decree); some place it in 446–445.

In the autumn of 447, when the Five Years Truce with Sparta had still one year to run, Pericles had triumphed over the opposition in Athens and over Persia in the Aegean. The empire was formed and the pickets were set at strategic points. He had lost none of Athens' allies or possessions on the mainland of Greece, and the forces of Athens were available to resist the Spartan Alliance. But in the winter of 447–446 the position began to change. Orchomenus, Chaeronea, and other cities in Boeotia were seized by the exiles whom Athens had expelled in setting up democratic governments. Early in 446 Tolmides with 1,000 Athenians and contingents from Athens' allies captured Chaeronea, placed a garrison in the city, and deported the men to be sold as slaves. As he withdrew he was attacked at Coronea by a combined force of exiles from Boeotia, Locris, and Euboea. Many of the Athenian troops, including Tolmides, were killed and the rest were captured. Athens then made terms. All Athenians were liberated, and the Athenian forces evacuated Boeotia.[1] The oligarchs returned to power in the Boeotian states, and cut the communications of Athens with Phocis and Locris. Shortly afterwards all the states in Euboea revolted from Athens. Pericles, in command of an Athenian army, crossed into the island. There he learnt that Megara had revolted with the help of Corinth, Sicyon, and Epidaurus and killed all the Athenian garrison troops, save such as found refuge in Nisaea; and that the Peloponnesians were about to invade Attica. Pericles brought his army back in haste to defend Athens, now almost surrounded by her enemies.

In the autumn of 446 the army of the Spartan Alliance under the command of the young king Pleistoanax advanced into the Megarid and was probably joined by a Boeotian force. The invaders then occupied the plain of Eleusis. The Athenian army was outmanœuvred. Three of the ten regiments were cut off at Pegae in the Megarid and had to make a détour via Boeotia to enter Attica. Meanwhile the invaders were ravaging the Thriasian plain. But, instead of engaging the Athenian army or crossing the ridge of Aegaleos to threaten the city, Pleistoanax suddenly withdrew. Pericles crossed at once to Euboea with 5,000 hoplites and fifty ships and overran the whole island. His quick success arrested the danger of further revolts in the Aegean and strengthened Athens' position in the negotiations with Sparta which were conducted by Athenian plenipotentiaries during the winter of 446–445.[2]

The Thirty Years Treaty brought the war to an end in midwinter 446–445. Under its terms Athens abandoned Achaea, Troezen, and the Megarid but retained her base at Naupactus. Aegina continued to be a tribute-paying member of the Athenian Alliance, but she was given by Athens a guarantee of autonomy. Delphi was probably declared an independent state. The Thirty Years Treaty was designed to ensure peace for thirty years. The negotiations were conducted on one side by Athens (her allies, Plataea in-

[1] Th. 1. 113; D.S. 12. 6; Plu. *Per.* 18; *CQ* 32. 80 (inscription); Paus. 1. 27. 5; 1. 29. 14.
[2] Th. 1. 114; D.S. 12. 7; Plu. *Per.* 22. 3; *GHI* 41 with *BSA* 49. 113; And. 3. 9.

cluded, being named in the treaty but not as contracting parties), and on the other side by 'Sparta and her Allies'. Thus Athens spoke alone for the block under her control; but Sparta and each of her Allies acted as sovereign states, sometimes called loosely 'the Peloponnesians' but comprising Megara and the reconstituted Boeotian League as well as all Peloponnesian states save Argos and Achaea. The contracting parties—Athens, and Sparta and her Allies—undertook not to commit aggression against one another for thirty years. Any state which was not named in the treaty as an ally either of Athens or of Sparta was free to become an ally of one or the other, with the exception of Argos which was debarred from alliance with either but was permitted to be on friendly terms with both. A state so entering the alliance of Athens or Sparta after the conclusion of the treaty became a party to the pact of non-aggression against the other group.

The clauses of the treaty are not known to us in detail, but the gist of some may be understood from the course of later events. All participants were to enjoy the freedom of the seas for purposes of trade, although this was perhaps expressed in general rather than specific terms. If any dispute should arise concerning the observance of the treaty, Athens on the one hand and Sparta and her Allies on the other hand agreed to submit the dispute to arbitration. The contracting states bound themselves by religious oaths to keep the treaty, and copies were inscribed at Olympia and perhaps at Delphi and the Isthmus, as well as at Athens and Sparta.[1]

In effect the Greek states returned to the balance of power between two groups, headed by Athens and Sparta, which had existed before they adopted a veiled hostility in 461. Great changes, however, had been brought about by the years of war. Previously the balance of power had been safeguarded by the alliance between the two leading states (*homaikhmia*) and by their common interest in the war against Persia. Now it rested on a pact of non-aggression, which was the product of suspended hostility and of the inability to defeat one another. No firm goodwill existed between Athens and Sparta, Boeotia, Corinth, and Megara, to say nothing of the 'allies' for whom Athens negotiated the treaty, and the bitter animosities of the past prejudiced the future.

The position of the two leading states had altered radically since the period when they were in alliance. Athens was no longer the leader of willing allies who formed a voluntary coalition. As the head of an empire, Athens ruled by force. Her own resources were now greater in wealth, ships, and naval personnel, and her military strength was not seriously weakened by losses in war. Nevertheless, her capacity for expansion was impaired. Her methods had alienated the land powers of central Greece and destroyed the confidence of her Allies in the Aegean. The moral ascendancy which she had gained in

---

[1] Th. 1. 115. 1 (Athens acting alone as in 421, cf. Th. 5. 18–19, and Sparta acting with her allies); 1. 23. 4 ('Peloponnesians'); 1. 35. 2; 44. 1; 67. 2 and 4; 78. 4; Paus. 5. 23. 4; *IG* i.² 18 with *BSA* 49. 21.

the war against Persia was dissipated by the war against the Greeks, and the fair fame of her democracy was smirched by acts of imperialist aggression. In the last resort the strength of the Athenian Alliance was now the strength of Athens alone.

Sparta had lost much of the prestige which she had enjoyed since 550 as leader of the Spartan Alliance. Her allies had been overrun or severely damaged by Athens, in particular Aegina, Boeotia, and the naval states of the Corinthian Gulf, and her armies had slight success in central Greece. In 446 the failure of Sparta to proceed with the invasion of Attica disillusioned her allies. The king Pleistoanax was fined, and his adviser, Cleandridas, was sentenced to death *in absentia*, the charges being that they had received bribes from Athens. The fact that thereafter Sparta chose to negotiate for peace rather than mount another invasion could be interpreted in various ways. Perhaps she lacked confidence in the strength of her Spartiate troops, so severely depleted by the earthquake and the Helots' Revolt, or she had no hopes of breaching the walls of Athens. It may have been thought that Sparta preferred in her own interest not to destroy Athens. For the pressure of Athenian naval power held the Spartan Alliance together, and the hoplite strength of Athens formed a counterweight to any ambitious land power in central Greece. Nevertheless, the treaty did much to restore Sparta's reputation. Every state on the Greek mainland and on Zacynthos and Cephallenia was enabled to determine its attitude towards the two great powers. Some remained neutral, several joined Sparta then or later, but only Plataea and Naupactus chose to maintain their alliance with Athens. In the last resort the strength of the Spartan Alliance was not the strength of Sparta alone but the combined strength of many states which stood together against Athenian aggression. Whatever her failings as a military leader, Sparta did not owe her leadership to force. In politics she favoured oligarchy, but she did not impose oligarchic governments on her associates by the use of garrisons and political residents. In a world which prized autonomy, Sparta's resistance to Athens endowed her leadership with a strong moral authority.

The foreign policy of Pericles was to consolidate and extend the empire and to maintain opposition to Sparta. He carried out the settlement of Euboea in 445. He treated Histiaea with special severity, because it had probably ejected the cleruchs and had killed the crew of an Athenian ship. The whole population was expelled, and the place was occupied as a colony by 1,000 settlers. The wealthy class at Chalcis, the Hippobotae, was expelled; and their lands—the richest in Euboea—were confiscated by Athens and divided into 2,000 lots. Of these some became a state-domain dedicated to Athena, and others were leased probably to non-Athenians, who paid rent and also taxes to Athens. Men and boys were taken as hostages from Chalcis, Eretria, and probably other cities and retained for some years in Athens. At Chalcis and Eretria every adult citizen was forced to take an oath to be loyal to the Athenian democracy on pain of disfranchisement and loss of property. In the case of Chalcis, if she obeyed the orders of Athens, the Athenian people undertook to treat her in accordance with peacetime conditions and legal procedure, save that any Chalcidian sentenced to death, exile, or disfranchisement at Chalcis was to have the right of appeal to the court at Athens. In addition, military measures were taken by the generals to prevent revolt. Euboea was indeed 'stretched on the rack by Pericles and Athens'.[1]

In Thrace Athens entered into friendly relations with Tereus, the founder of a strong kingdom of Odrysians, and planted a cleruchy at Brea *c.* 445, which the neighbouring members of the empire were obliged by treaty to protect. On this coast a joint settlement of 1,000 Athenians and of native Bisaltae was founded by Pericles, probably about this time. In the south Athens was on friendly terms with Psammetichus, the self-styled king of Egypt, who was in revolt from Persia: she received a generous gift of corn from him in 445/444.[2] Soon after the conclusion of the Thirty Years Treaty an invitation came to Athens and to Sparta from the survivors of Sybaris in south Italy, who asked for assistance in refounding their city. While Sparta refused, Athens accepted and sent out volunteers from Athens and from the Peloponnese. Before long they expelled the original Sybarites and founded a new city, named Thurii, probably in 443. For this new foundation Athens recruited volunteers from Greece. The population of Thurii was divided into ten tribes, of which three derived from Arcadia, Elis, and Achaea, three from the eastern areas of central Greece, and four from the Ionian peoples of the Aegean, including the Athenians, who provided the founders, Lampon and Xenocritus. Thurii soon became a prosperous state; it weathered attacks by Taras and in 433 joined Taras in founding a joint colony at Heraclea. Meanwhile a civil strife arose between the settlers, during which the leader-

---

[1] Th. 1. 114. 3; Plu. *Per.* 23; D.S. 12. 22 (1,000 settlers); *FGrH* 115 F 387 (Theopompus gives 2,000 settlers, the total perhaps of both acts of settlement); *GHI* 42; *IG* i.² 17; Hesych. *Eretriakos Katalogos*; Ael. *VH* 6. 1; And. 3. 9; Ar. *Nu.* 213.

[2] *GHI* 44; Plu. *Per.* 11 (the joint settlement being different from that at Brea); *FGrH* 328 F 119 (Philochorus); Plu. *Per.* 37._

ship of Athens in the colony was nullified and Apollo of Delphi was hailed as the founder. This great enterprise was initiated by Pericles. At the outset it demonstrated the ability of Athens to lead the Greek states in a joint under-taking which Sparta refused to sponsor. Athens provided the naval escort and the financial means. The pioneering leaders were Athenians, the first con-stitution was democratic, and Athena was the protectress of the city. The Greek thinkers who planned a model foundation were imbued with Attic culture—Lampon of Athens, a famous expounder of the sacred law, Hippo-damus of Miletus, the town-planner, Protagoras of Abdera, who drew up the code of civil law, and Herodotus of Halicarnassus, whose history was later to praise the Panhellenic spirit of Athens in the Persian Wars. The sequel at Thurii showed that the leadership of Athens was not acceptable, partly because the Greeks were divided against one another but principally because the conduct of Athens in the Aegean gave no grounds for confidence in her Panhellenic professions.[1]

By the end of 441 the net of Athens' influence was spread wide. Rhegium and Leontini were her allies,[2] the colony at Thurii was flourishing, Euboea was pinned down, and settlements were established on the coast of Thrace. Athens was at peace with the Peloponnesians, and her co-operation with them in founding Thurii redounded to her credit. In the east she was at peace with Persia, although her friendly relations with Psammetichus may have aroused the suspicions of the Great King. During the winter of 441–440 a war broke out between Samos and Miletus for possession of Priene, which lay between the Milesian territory and the Samian territory on the mainland. When the Milesians suffered a defeat they lodged complaints against Samos at Athens, and they were supported therein by some Samian individuals who wished to overthrow the constitution at Samos.

The response by Athens was regarded as a test case by the members of the Athenian Alliance. Under the terms of the original treaty in 478/477 the Allies of Athens were autonomous; they therefore had the right to go to war with one another, and Athens had no right to intervene as hegemon. Samos relied justifiably on her rights under the original treaty; for she had always contributed ships and supported Athens. Miletus had an in-ferior status; for she had been compelled to give an oath of loyalty and to install a democratic government, but at this time she was at least in name autonomous. Athens, however, did not pay any respect to the treaty of 478/477. She ordered Samos to suspend hostilities and to accept her arbitration. Samos was faced with the resignation of her autonomy and the acceptance of an arbiter whom she had no reason to regard as impartial. With great courage she refused. Her refusal had no doubt been anticipated by Athens. In the spring of 440 Pericles did not view the revolt of Samos with alarm, since Athens was at peace with Persia and with the Pelopon-

[1] D.S. 12. 10–23; Str. 263; Suid. *Thouriomanteis*; Plu. 812d; *GHI* 49.
[2] *GHI* 57, 58.

nesians, and he at once carried his proposal declaring war on Samos and set sail with forty ships. He took the island by surprise, imposed Athenian commissioners and an Athenian garrison, set up a democratic government, exacted a fine of eighty talents, seized 100 hostages—men and boys of the upper class—and deposited them at Lemnos. He then withdrew his fleet, having made a signal example of a state which presumed upon its rights as an autonomous associate of Athens.[1]

The Samians, however, were not cowed. Some of their leaders had escaped to the mainland. There they enlisted the alliance of the Persian satrap, Pissuthnes, and raised a body of 700 mercenary troops. Returning by night to Samos, they overpowered the democrats, liberated the hostages in Lemnos, and prepared to attack Miletus. They handed over their Athenian prisoners to Pissuthnes. At the same time Byzantium revolted and seized control of the Bosporus. If other states should follow their example and Persia support the action of Pissuthnes, there was a real danger that the eastern half of the empire would break away. Pericles sailed at once with sixty ships. He detached sixteen ships, some to keep watch off Caria, in case the Phoenician fleet came out, and others to call out the ships of Chios and Lesbos, before they were approached by the Samians; and he proceeded with the remainder to the island of Tragia, where he intercepted and defeated fifty Samian warships and twenty Samian transports on their way back from Miletus. His bold action limited the area of revolt. When forty ships came up from Athens and twenty-five from Lesbos and Chios, Pericles landed on the island, defeated the enemy, and invested the city. During the absence of sixty ships, with which Pericles sailed southwards on receiving a report that the Phoenician fleet was coming up in response to an appeal from Samos, the Samians made a sortie and defeated the investing force. For a fortnight they held the mastery of their own seas. Then Pericles returned. When he was reinforced by sixty ships from Athens and thirty from Chios and Lesbos, the Samians suffered defeat at sea and the city was invested again. In the ninth month of the siege, which lasted from *c.* August 440 to *c.* May 439, the Samians accepted the conditions offered by Athens that they should destroy their walls, give hostages, surrender their fleet, and pay in instalments the cost of the war, a sum of 1,276 talents. Byzantium then capitulated and resumed her tributary status.[2]

The Samian War made a deep impression on the Greek states. They realized, more clearly than ever before, that the Athenian empire was indeed a tyranny and that Athens would take great risks (greater perhaps in this instance than Pericles had calculated) in order to gratify her desire for power. The so-called allies of Athens saw that the fate of Samos set the seal on their own subjection; for the naval strength of Samos and the support of Pissuthnes had not availed against the fleet of Athens. Where Samos had failed, no other state was likely to succeed. Athens had been shaken by the war. The courage

[1] Th. 1. 115; D.S. 12. 27; Plu. *Per.* 24 init.; 25; Ar. *V.* 281 with Schol.
[2] Th. 1. 116–17; D.S. 12. 27–28; Plu. *Per.* 25–28; Isoc. 15. 111.

of the Samians at sea and under siege, combined with the possibility of Persian intervention, had constituted a very grave threat to the sea power of Athens. Her fears expressed themselves in an act of cruelty, the branding of captured Samians with the mark of the Samian state, an act which was repaid in kind by the Samians. Athens owed her success to the fact that she had a squadron of sixty ships in constant readiness, and Pericles used it with lightning speed. Before the Persians, if they should wish to intervene, or the Peloponnesians could decide on their course of action or begin to muster and man a fleet, the Samians were defeated and their dangerous break-out was contained. Even so Athens used some 200 ships, including those of Chios and Lesbos, and required nine months with new siege equipment to reduce Samos. During this siege the Peloponnesian states might have moved against Athens by land or by sea. They did in fact debate their policy at a meeting of the Peloponnesian Congress. Their votes were divided for and against intervention, and the majority were swayed by Corinth to make no move.[1]

In 440 Pericles had seen the danger of a simultaneous attack on Athens by Samos, Byzantium, Persia, and the Spartan Alliance. That the danger had passed was due partly to the holding power of the pacts with Persia and the Peloponnesians and partly to his own preparedness and generalship. In the future these pacts might not hold. Of the two great powers Pericles had more reason to fear Sparta and her Alliance. In the next few years he intensified his control of the empire, increased the preparedness of Athens, and endeavoured to weight the balance of power in favour of Athens by extending her net of alliances. In this policy he was fully supported by the Athenian people. They entrusted to him 'tribute of cities, and cities themselves to bind and to free, walls to build and walls to overthrow, treaties and rule and peace and prosperity too'. He was chosen to deliver the funeral speech, and he said probably of those who had fallen at Samos, at Byzantium, and in the Chersonese that the youth of Athens had passed away as the spring passes away from the year. He and his people held the initiative, and they used it with courage.[2]

In 439 the treaty with Samos was concluded, and the Samians were bound by an oath of loyalty to Athens and began to repay the great sum of 1,276 talents. In 437 or soon afterwards Pericles led a finely equipped fleet into the Black Sea. There he supported the interests of the Greek states, probably gained possession of Nymphaeum, a good port, and entered into a commercial alliance with Spartocus, the founder of a strong dynasty in the Crimea, which controlled the export of wheat from the hinterland. At Sinope on the south coast he left thirteen ships to help the citizens expel their tyrant; and later he proposed a decree for 600 Athenian 'volunteers' to occupy the lands of the tyrant. Another settlement was planted at Amisus, renamed Peiraeus, between Sinope and Trapezus. Later, in 435/434,

[1] Th. 2. 63; 8. 76. 4; Plu. *Per.* 26; 12; Th. 1. 40. 5; 41. 2; *GHI* 50 and *SEG* 10. 221.
[2] Teleclides fr. 42 in Plu. *Per.* 16; Arist. *Rhet.* 1365ª31, cf. Plu. *Per.* 8; *IG* i.² 943.

Athenian colonists occupied Astacus, a Megarian colony in the Propontis, which had been weakened by attacks from the hinterland. This expansion of Athenian sea power brought profit to Athens and to the states within her empire, and it strengthened the Greek colonies which held the shores of the Black Sea. At Sinope and at Amisus Athens may have infringed the nominal suzerainty of Persia, but the waters of the Black Sea were open to both parties under the Peace of Callias. Artaxerxes made no move.[1]

In 436 Athens defeated the Edonians at Ennea Hodoi and founded the important colony of Amphipolis on a hill which was washed on three sides by the river Strymon. The founder, Hagnon, fortified the city by building a wall on the landward side, and a bridge was soon constructed over the river. Amphipolis rapidly became a flourishing and populous city. It commanded the route from Macedonia to Thrace and the export of shipbuilding timber, minerals, and cereals from the neighbourhood. The Athenian element in the town formed a small minority, but Athenian dominance was ensured by her fleet, which had a naval base down river at Eïon. By this foundation Athens' control of the north Aegean waters was greatly strengthened. At the same time she alarmed her ally Perdiccas, the king of Macedonia, and Potidaea, a colony of Corinth, hitherto the strongest Greek city in the north-west Aegean.[2]

§ 2. *The disputes between Athens and some allies of Sparta*

At some time between 439 and 436 Athens sent a naval expedition into western waters. It sailed in response to an invitation from Acarnania and Amphilochia to assist in liberating Amphilochian Argos from some Ambracians who had been welcomed as joint settlers by the Amphilochians and then seized control of the city. The squadron, commanded by Phormion, sailed into the Ambraciote Gulf. The city was taken by assault, a group of Amphilochians and Acarnanians proceeded to occupy it, and the captured Ambracians were enslaved. Athens and Acarnania entered into an alliance.[3] As Ambracia, Amphilochia, and Acarnania were not allies of Sparta, the action of Athens was in accordance with the terms of the Thirty Years Treaty. At the same time Ambracia was a colony of Corinth, and any action by an Athenian fleet in the west was certain to arouse apprehension in Corinth. On this occasion, however, the fleets of Corinth and of her colonies were confident of their control in the Ionian Sea. Then in 435 an entirely new situation developed when Corinth came into conflict with her powerful colony, Corcyra.

The quarrel between Corinth and Corcyra grew out of a civil war in their joint colony, Epidamnus, which lay on the coast of Illyria to the north of

---

[1] *IG* i.² 65 and *DAT* 35; *IG* i.² 50 and *AFD* 54; Plu. *Per.* 20; *Luc.* 19. 6; *FGrH* 115 F 389 (Theopompus); 434 F 12 (Memnon).
[2] Th. 4. 102. 3; 106. 1; 108. 1; D.S. 12. 32. 3; Th. 1. 57. 2.   [3] Th. 2. 68. 6–8.

Corcyra. The democrats, in control of the town but hard pressed by the oligarchs, appealed in vain to Corcyra for aid but were accepted by Corinth, which sent a number of settlers overland with an escort of troops from Corinth and her colonies, Leucas and Ambracia. Corcyra then embraced the cause of the oligarchs and laid siege to Epidamnus. At this point Corinth enlarged the area of friction by offering a place in Epidamnus to any volunteers and by asking other states to assist in convoying the volunteers. Promises of vessels, troops, or money were received not only from Leucas and Ambracia but also from Megara, Thebes, Epidaurus, Hermione, Troezen, Phlius, Elis, and Pale in Cephallenia, states which were less interested in the fate of the volunteers than in the re-establishment of naval control in the Ionian Sea. While Corinth was making her preparations, Corcyra sought the advice of Sparta and Sicyon. They wished to avert a conflict. They therefore supported Corcyra in her proposal to Corinth that the dispute should be settled by arbitration. Corinth refused. In summer 435 a fleet of seventy-five Corinthian and allied ships set sail, engaged a Corcyraean fleet of eighty vessels, and suffered a decisive defeat. On the same day Epidamnus capitulated. The entire Corcyraean fleet, numbering 120 triremes, then carried its raids southwards as far as Elis. At Corcyra the Corinthian prisoners were put in fetters; all other prisoners taken in the naval action were executed, and the settlers introduced into Epidamnus by Corinth were sold as slaves. Corcyra was fully committed to war with a number of Peloponnesian states.[1]

For two years Corinth concentrated on the building of a great fleet. Whereas in 435 she had contributed thirty ships to the allied fleet and lost fifteen in the battle, by August 433 she manned ninety vessels with rowers whom she hired from Peloponnesian and Aegean states. Meanwhile Corcyra was isolated. Sparta and Sicyon did not intend to become involved, and their interests were on the side of the Peloponnesians. In 433, probably in June, Corcyra sent envoys to ask Athens for alliance, and Corinth, too, sent envoys to dissuade Athens from granting an alliance. So far as the letter of the Thirty Years Treaty was concerned, Athens was free to grant a defensive but not an offensive alliance to Corcyra; for Corcyra was not an ally of Sparta, and a defensive alliance between Athens and Corcyra would not break the pact of non-aggression between Athens and Corinth, a member of the Spartan Alliance. On the other hand, Athens had no obligations at all towards Corcyra and no immediate interests to protect in the west (for Acarnania and Naupactus were in no way involved). If Athens wished to preserve the Thirty Years Treaty, her course was clear: she would refuse the request of Corcyra. These and other considerations were expressed by the envoys of Corcyra and of Corinth. The Assembly debated the issue for two days. On the first day opinion favoured refusal. On the second day, swayed by the advice of Pericles, the people made a defensive alliance with Corcyra.[2]

[1] Th. 1. 24–30; D.S. 12. 30–31.   [2] Th. 1. 31–44; D.S. 12. 32–33. 2.

The defensive alliance of Athens with Corcyra opened up two possibilities. If Athens implemented the alliance to the full and reinforced the Corcyraean fleet of 120 ships with a large Athenian fleet, Corinth and her Peloponnesian supporters would either attack Corcyra and be worsted or seek other means of attacking Athens. In such a situation they were likely to be assisted by Sparta as leader of the Spartan Alliance, since the balance of naval power between Athens and the Peloponnesians, which formed a realistic basis of the Thirty Years Treaty, would be decisively overthrown. On the other hand, if Athens sent nominal help and watched the fleets of Corcyra and Corinth wear each other down, the balance of naval power would incline in favour of Athens, and Sparta as leader of the Spartan Alliance might not feel that her safety was immediately threatened. Pericles decided to send ten ships, a mere token of Athens' strength. The commanders were ordered to engage only if the Corinthians were on the point of landing on Corcyra or on territory owned by Corcyra.[1]

In August or September 433 a fleet of ninety Corinthian ships and sixty allied ships, supplied by Megara, Elis, Leucas, Ambracia, and Anactorium, engaged the Corcyraean fleet of 110 ships off Sybota and put seventy out of action. During the battle the Athenians and the Corinthians did not engage one another, but when the rout of the Corcyraeans was complete and a Corinthian landing on Corcyra was imminent they came to blows. Thereafter the Corinthians drew off to kill the Corcyraeans in the water and to secure the wrecks. It was late in the evening when they returned in order of battle. They were about to engage the remaining Corcyraean vessels and their Athenian allies, when they saw ships sailing up from the south which they realized must be an Athenian reinforcement. The Corinthians backed water and withdrew. As night fell, twenty Athenian ships, which had been sent out as an afterthought, came up and joined their compatriots. Next morning the Athenians and the Corcyraeans offered battle, but the Corinthians were now more concerned to make their escape. A parley followed in which the Corinthians accused the Athenians of aggression and the Athenians paraded their defensive alliance with Corcyra; anywhere else, they said, the Corinthians might sail without let or hindrance but not against the ally of Athens. The Corinthians then departed in despair. The seas they had once dominated were strewn with the wreckage of 100 triremes and the corpses of several thousand seamen—the result of the greatest battle fought at sea between Greek and Greek and between foundress and colony. By a combination of intelligent anticipation and fortunate coincidence the policy of Pericles had earned a signal success. The Athenian navy was intact. If war came, Athens need fear no rival in the west. And she had in Corcyra a strong base for operations against the Peloponnese and a staging-point on the passage to Italy and Sicily.[2]

[1] Th. 1. 45; Plu. *Per.* 29; *GHI* 55.
[2] Th. 1. 46–54; D.S. 12. 33. 3–4; for the battle *JHS* 65. 26 = *StGH* 486 ff.

Pericles' triumph was purchased at the risk of a general war. Corcyra had requested and Athens had granted the alliance with this contingency in mind. Corcyra insisted that her fleet and bases would be useful against the Peloponnesians; Pericles declared, probably on the second day of the crucial debate, that he saw the cloud of war blowing up from the Peloponnese, and the people were persuaded that such a war would come in any case. The Peloponnesian attitude had been different. Corinth had pointed out that, if the parties to the Thirty Years Treaty continued to respect one another's spheres of influence, the danger of war was remote. Even after the battle, when Athens withdrew her fleet from Corcyra, Corinth and her allies remained inactive. Sparta had used her influence to avert war between Corcyra and Corinth. She had made no move against Athens, and in the months after the battle she, too, was inactive. The Peloponnesians were still taking their stand on the letter and on the spirit of the Thirty Years Treaty.[1]

During the twelve months after the battle of Sybota Athens issued two decrees which aggravated the situation. The initiative was with her, and the timing was deliberate. One, the so-called 'Megarian decree', proposed by Pericles and enacted in summer 432, intensified economic sanctions against Megara, the ally of Corinth in the Corcyraean War. Some discrimination had probably been made late in 433 against the trade of Megara, but now she was excluded from every harbour and market of Athens and of the Athenian empire.[2] The second decree was an ultimatum to Potidaea, a colony of Corinth, which, in accordance with longstanding tradition, received magistrates annually from her foundress. Potidaea was ordered during the winter of 433-432 to demolish her defences on the seaward side, give hostages to Athens, dismiss the Corinthian magistrates, and receive no more in the future. The Potidaeans sent envoys to Athens, asking for a reconsideration of the matter, and prolonged discussions were held. When summer approached, Athens gave secret orders to Archestratus, the commander of a naval force destined for Macedonia, to seize hostages at Potidaea and raze the southern defences of the town. Meanwhile the Potidaeans, suspecting the designs of Athens, sent envoys to the Peloponnese, where with the support of Corinthian envoys they obtained a secret undertaking from the Gerousia and the Ephors that, if Athens attacked Potidaea, Sparta would invade Attica.

During these negotiations events moved rapidly in the hinterland of Potidaea. There Perdiccas, king of Macedonia, had been alienated by Athens' support of two rivals to his throne, Philip and Derdas. His intrigues were far-reaching: he urged Sparta to deploy the Spartan Alliance against Athens, Corinth to raise Potidaea in revolt, and the peoples of Chalcidice and Bottiaea to join with Potidaea in a general insurrection. In summer 432, when Archestratus reached the Thermaic Gulf, he found the Potidaeans,

---

[1] Th. 1. 33. 3; 36; 44. 2; Plu. *Per.* 29; Th. 1. 42. 2; 43. 1–2.

[2] Th. 1. 67. 4; Ar. *Ach.* 515–39; *Pax* 609; *FGrH* 328 F 121 (Philochorus); Plu. *Per.* 30–31; D.S. 12. 39. 4.

Bottiaeans, and Chalcidians in revolt, the last having evacuated their coast towns and settled within sight of Potidaea at Olynthus. Archestratus, having only thirty ships and 1,000 hoplites under his command, joined the forces of Philip and Derdas in an attack on Perdiccas and with the help of a second Athenian force compelled Perdiccas to make a pact of alliance with Athens. Meanwhile Potidaea was entered by 2,000 'volunteers', partly Corinthians and partly Peloponnesian mercenaries. Their commander, Aristeus, concluded a secret alliance on behalf of Corinth with the Bottiaean and Chalcidian states. He was then appointed to co-ordinate the defence of Potidaea and Olynthus. At the end of September 432 his forces were defeated on the Isthmus between the cities by the Athenians, who invested Potidaea from the north. Later it was walled off on the south and blockaded by sea.[1]

§ 3. *The negotiations which led to war*

A s soon as the Corinthians learnt of the defeat at Potidaea, they and their allies made a *démarche* at Sparta, accusing the Athenians of aggression and therefore of violating the Thirty Years Treaty. The Aeginetans, too, sent envoys secretly to complain that Athens had not respected the autonomy guaranteed to them under the treaty. The Spartan authorities then invited any state, allied or otherwise, to lodge complaints against the conduct of Athens. They called a meeting of their own Assembly, before which representatives of Corinth, Megara, and other states spoke, accusing Athens of aggression and hoping to stimulate Sparta into action. The Assembly was also addressed by some Athenian envoys, who, being at Sparta on other business, were permitted by the Spartan authorities to come forward; they emphasized the resilience and the strength of Athens, and urged Sparta not to break the terms of the treaty by declaring war, but to keep faith by submitting any dispute to arbitration. The representatives and the envoys then withdrew, and the Spartan Assembly debated the issue, being swayed particularly by the experienced king Archidamus and by the vigorous ephor Sthenelaïdas. The former advised the people to submit the dispute to arbitration and meanwhile to prepare urgently for a war which, if it came, was certain to last for many years. The latter stated that Athens had clearly committed aggression and broken the terms of the treaty, and that the gods would be on the side of Sparta in honouring her obligations to her Allies and attacking the aggressor. Sthenelaïdas then put the issue to the vote, not by the usual procedure of shouting 'yea' or 'nay' but by dividing the house. The great majority of the Spartiates voted that the terms of the treaty had been violated and Athens was guilty of aggression. The vote was reported to the representatives, and they were informed that Sparta was about to call a full meeting of the Allied Congress. Her first action, however, was to consult

[1] Th. 1. 56–65; 5. 30. 2; D.S. 12. 34; 37; for the chronology, which is disputed, see Th. 2. 2. 1 and Appendix 5.

Delphi. The god replied that a vigorous prosecution of the war would bring victory and he would be on their side, asked or unasked.[1]

Although the Spartans had not voted a declaration of war, they had committed themselves to war, provided always that the Congress of Allies voted in agreement. The steps which led to this decision had been delicate. The Gerousia and the Ephors had decided among themselves, when the envoys of Potidaea asked for help, to go to war with Athens on the ground that Athens was aggressive and must be stopped. But they were no autocrats. The Spartan people and, in addition, the Congress of Allies must vote with free judgement. The Gerousia and the Ephors had therefore allowed Corinth and others to press the case, and the Spartan people voted spontaneously and by a large majority for war. The chief motive which prompted the Gerousia and later the Assembly to take this decision was fear of Athens' growing power, which expressed itself not only in the accumulation of armaments but in the support of Corcyra, the oppression of Megara, and the ultimatum to Potidaea. By these actions Athens upset the balance of naval power and threatened the cohesion of the Spartan Alliance, from which the strength of Sparta in international politics derived. That Athens intended to do so was clear from her policy over the last thirty years. Other motives, to which Sthenelaïdas appealed, affected the Spartans—pride, animosity, resentment, and a sense of justice and of obligation to their allies—but the crowning motive was fear of ultimate defeat if they did not go to war.[2]

In October or November 432 the Congress of Allies met. The Corinthian delegates, who had canvassed the others in advance, were the most vehement. They claimed that by her acts of aggression Athens hoped to break the individual states of the Peloponnese piecemeal and impose her rule upon them all; let them unite in resistance to the aggressor and let them fulfil the will of the god of Delphi. The Spartans put the question to the vote, and the majority cast their vote for war. When hostilities began in 431, the Spartan state and the states of the Spartan Alliance were united in a cause which most men thought was the defence of freedom and justice.[3]

The Peloponnesians used the winter to prepare for war and to open a diplomatic offensive against Athens. If the offensive succeeded, war might be averted; if not, they would have a better *casus belli*. Sparta, as hegemon of the Spartan Alliance, ordered Athens to drive out the members of the Alcmeonid clan upon which Athena had laid her curse after the suppression of the conspiracy of Cylon. To this clan Pericles was related. The Spartans hoped not so much to bring about his exile as to undermine the influence of a statesman who opposed Sparta at every point. Athens riposted by ordering Sparta to rid herself of two 'curses', one laid on her by Poseidon for denying sanctuary to some Helots and the other by Athena for denying sanctuary to Pausanias. Sparta then indicated the terms on which war might be averted: cancellation of the Megarian decree, raising of the siege of Potidaea, and

[1] Th. 1. 67–87; 118. 3.   [2] Th. 1. 23. 6; 88; 118. 2.   [3] Th. 1. 119–125. 1.

restoration of autonomy to Aegina. When Athens refused to negotiate on these terms, three Spartan envoys delivered in the name of the Spartan Alliance an ultimatum which was designed rather for publicity than for negotiation: 'Sparta desires the peace to continue. If you respect the independence of the Greek states, there will be peace.'[1]

Upon receiving this ultimatum the Athenians met in the Assembly to make their final decision. The grounds on which they might hold the Peloponnesians guilty of aggression were the Corinthian attack at Sybota, the encouragement of Potidaea to revolt, the action of Peloponnesian 'volunteers' there, and latterly the harbouring of runaway slaves by Megara. At the same time the Athenians were intelligent enough to realize that such actions were caused by their own provocation. In the Assembly some speakers advised the people to cancel the Megarian decree, which the Spartans had hinted would suffice to avert war. Of those who said it was time to go to war Pericles was the most influential. He did not seek to justify the past actions of Athens by which she had improved her position without recourse to war. He concentrated on the hectoring tone of Sparta at the moment and insisted, as he had always done, that Athens must make no concession to the Peloponnesians. Athens had offered to submit any dispute to arbitration, and the offer still stood; if Sparta refused, the responsibility for war was hers. To yield to any of Sparta's demands now was to invite further demands. The alternative was war, and in war Athens had great advantages over the Peloponnesians. Confident in the wisdom of Pericles, the majority of the people voted in effect for war. Some of them may have believed that Sparta and the Spartan Alliance were aggressive. Most of them realized that Athens could only keep what she had won and add to her possessions by breaking the Spartan Alliance, which she had failed to do in 461–446. Moral considerations weighed little in a community which had deprived many states of liberty and treated recalcitrants with severity. Yet a minority, small but influential, still upheld the defeated principles of Cimon and his successor, Thucydides, the son of Melesias, and their ranks were to be swollen by the adversities of war. From the outset Athens was less united in spirit than Sparta, and her allies were enlisted by force rather than by goodwill.[2]

The Athenian people replied to the Spartan ultimatum as Pericles advised. Athens would accept no orders from Sparta, but was prepared to submit all complaints to arbitration in accordance with the procedure laid down by the Thirty Years Treaty. To this reply no answer was made. Diplomatic relations were at an end. Both sides waited until the first act of war should rend the uneasy peace.

[1] Th. I. 126–39.   [2] Th. I. 139. 3–144.

§ 4. *Athens and her empire in the time of Pericles*

WHEN the Treasury of the Allies was transferred from Delos to Athens, a new era began in the financial organization of the Athenian Alliance. In the past the Congress of Allies had controlled the Treasury, but after the winter of 454–453 Athens usurped this control and the Congress, atrophied as a financially independent body, ceased to meet at all. Athens was henceforth the financial capital of an empire. The Assembly decided, without consulting the so-called Allies, how the moneys should be disbursed, and it was sometimes in the form of loans to the Athenian state. The Council supervised and checked the annual income in revenue in the following manner. Each tribute-paying state sent up its money in a sealed container, for which a courier brought a corresponding seal or token. At Athens the container was checked against the seal in the presence of the Council, and the money was counted by the receiving officers of the Council, the *apodektai*. The sums of tribute were then passed to the Hellenotamiae, 'the Treasurers of the Greeks', who kept their original title as accountants of the tribute; they took a quota of one-sixtieth from the tribute (a mina from each talent) and paid it into the Treasury of the Sacred Monies of Athena, of which the keepers were called the Treasurers of the Goddess (*tamiai*). These transactions were checked by the state auditors, thirty *logistai*. The accounts were usually published on tablets of wood. But the records of the quota from 454/453 to 415/414 were inscribed on stone; many fragments of them have survived and are known for brevity as 'the Quota Lists' or less accurately 'the Tribute Lists'. The record may be missing for one year, either 449/448 or 447/446, but even so it is most unlikely that there was ever a cessation of tribute. For Athens had no reason to forgo the revenue which, apart from the niceties of book-keeping, passed into her own hands.[1]

After 454 the Council assessed the amount of tribute due from each state. It did so on the basis of a survey of each state's resources, the original survey having been made under the direction of Aristides.[2] The assessment was normally published at the Panathenaic Festival, when delegates of each state were present, and it covered the four years until the next Panathenaic Festival.[3] An appeal against an assessment could be lodged at Athens, where it was decided by a special court or by a panel of the Heliaea and, if necessary, referred back to the Council. The tribute was collected by the tributary state or, where a number of neighbouring states were small, by one state which was made responsible for a group (*synteleia*). Adjustments in these matters were made at the discretion of the Council. For example, in 453–449 Cherronesus

---

[1] *GHI* 30 (preamble); 51 and *ATL* 2. 46 (first decree of Callias); [X.] *Ath.* 3. 2 and 5; Teleclides fr. 42 in Plu. *Per.* 16; Poll. 8. 97; *GHI* 30, 38, 46, 56.

[2] Th. 5. 18. 5; Arist. *Ath.* 23. 5; Plu. *Arist.* 24.

[3] In *GHI* 56, in the year 434/433, several small states probably assessed their own tribute, and other states were registered by individual persons to pay tribute perhaps for services rendered or promised; the special conditions and the procedure are uncertain.

paid 18 talents for a group of states in the Chersonese, but later, when Pericles planted cleruchies in the area, the amount was scaled down to fit the diminished resources of the group and each member paid a separate assessment (*apotaxis*). All judicial cases concerning the tribute, whether initiated by an Athenian official or by a private informer who might be a citizen of the tributary state, were tried at Athens as the controller of the empire.

The payments of the tribute were due each year by a date in March when the Dionysiac Festival was held at Athens. The names were then recorded of those states which had paid and those which had defaulted. During the festival Athenian youths paraded, each carrying one talent of silver in a jar, and their number indicated the balance of tribute over expenditure for the past year. They were followed by hired attendants who carried notices of the valuations which had been set on the resources of each state for the assessment of the tribute. During the summer after the festival any arrears of tribute were exacted by Athenian warships, known as 'tribute-collectors' (*argyrologoi*).[1]

Athens drew other moneys from the empire. She received reparations from rebel states, such as Samos, and she acquired fines or realized the values of confiscated properties in cases where allies were tried in her courts. Rent, sometimes worth one-tenth of the produce, was paid on lands, such as those of the Hippobotae at Chalcis, which were leased out to cultivators. Colonies, such as Amphipolis, contributed moneys to Athens which were not included in the tribute. Spoils of war, including the sale or ransom-money of prisoners, were of considerable value, especially during the operations against Persia. After 434, and perhaps before that year, the temple funds of Apollo and Artemis at Delos were administered by Athenian officials, called Amphictyons, and these funds were probably drawn on by Athens in time of need.[2]

Precise figures for the revenues of Athens are given in the ancient sources. The study of the Quota Lists and other inscriptions concerning finance has enabled scholars to call these figures in question but not to disprove them. On the whole it is best to accept the figures and admit that we cannot fully account for them. The sum transferred from Delos to Athens was 8,000 talents, representing the balance of twenty-three years' contributions, of which the first year was assessed at 460 talents, and the profits of successful wars.[3] This sum, having been absorbed in practice into Athens' funds, became the bulk of the largest reserve ever accumulated on the Acropolis in the time of Pericles, namely 9,700 talents, probably in the years after the conclusion of the Thirty Years Treaty. Athens took loans from the reserve and repaid one

---

[1] Isoc. 8. 82.

[2] Th. 4. 108. 1 (Amphipolis); for spoils, &c., Plu. *Cim.* 9; 13. 6; *Per.* 9; D.S. 11. 88. 2; Th. 2. 13. 4 (cf. D.S. 12. 40. 2) gives the value of the dedicated spoils from Persia (probably one-tenth of the whole) together with festival equipment, &c., as some 500 talents; Th. 6. 62. 4 value of captives sold as slaves (cf. p. 391); *GHI* 53 and *IG* i.[2] 365 payments 'from a campaign' may refer to a balance due to spoils, &c.; *GHI* 54.

[3] D.S. 12. 38. 2, probably using and perhaps misapplying Ephorus.

of 3,000 talents probably in 434. By 431 the reserve stood at 6,000 talents; for there had been expenditure of 2,012 talents on the Propylaea and other buildings, probably including the Parthenon, and 1,000 talents or so on the initial stages of the siege of Potidaea. The tribute each year after 454 probably fell a little short of 400 talents, but this was not the only income from the empire; and in 431 the total revenue from 'the Allies' was 600 talents a year. In purchasing power one talent paid for the hull of a trireme in 483, and three talents may have represented the cost of commissioning a trireme for war in the middle of the century.[1]

Expenditure was incurred by Athens as head of the empire in building and maintaining ships and fortifications, paying troops and officials, and supporting war-orphans who paraded at the Dionysiac Festival. In time of peace the excess of income over expenditure was large, but in a large-scale and unprofitable war it disappeared. During the lifetime of Pericles the Athenians as a people and as individuals derived great benefits from the wealth of the imperial exchequer. The machinery of government, the fleet and the defences, the temples and the festivals were subsidized in the main from imperial revenues and accumulations. The state did indeed raise other funds by leasing the mines at Laurium and the sacred lands in Attica, by levying a tax on resident aliens, on non-Athenians coming to Athens, and on manumitted slaves, and by imposing tolls and dues on certain sales. But Pericles did not include these internal revenues in his summary of Athens' financial resources in 431, and Aristophanes rated them of less importance than the imperial revenues in 422; but they were probably about 400 talents a year. As individuals the Athenian thetes and zeugites had the chance of acquiring good land overseas as cleruchs, their military equipment being provided for them by the state. At home even before 440 state-pay for state-service, partly whole-time and more often part-time, was available for some 20,000 citizens from the imperial revenues and from taxes levied on non-citizens. During eight months of the year the crews of sixty triremes, totalling some 10,000 rowers, were in receipt of pay as well as 700 Athenian officials and a varying number of garrison troops overseas. At home 6,000 dicasts, 500 Councillors, 550 guards, 700 state-officials, and a standing force of archers, cavalry, and naval guards were in receipt of pay. In addition, employment was so readily available in the building of the Parthenon and the

---

[1] Th. 2. 13. 3 (the text is superior as Greek to the citation in Schol. Ar. *Pl.* 1193). The figure 9,700 is supported by other passages: Isoc. 15. 234 (born in 436) 10,000 talents deposited during the career of Pericles; Isoc. 8. 126 'without the temples' 8,000 talents at the end of Pericles' career ('the temples' appear separately in 15. 234); D. 3. 24 [D.] 13. 26 and later writers give 10,000 talents as the largest deposit, e.g. D.S. 12. 40. 2; 12. 54. 3; 13. 21. 3. These figures militate against the views in the *Athenian Tribute Lists* 3. 118 f. that the sum transferred from Delos was about 5,000 talents and the largest reserve never approached 9,700 talents. For the cost of the Propylaea, &c., see Harp. and Suid. *s.v.*, D.S. 12. 40. 2 and *SEG* 10. 257 (Athena Parthenos cost some 700 talents). Loans drawn from these funds probably earned interest (*GHI* 54, 64; cf. Th. 2. 13. 5 fin.).

Propylaea from 447 to 432, in the shipyards, and in the handicrafts that there was room in Athens and Attica for an increasing number of metics, foreigners, and slaves. During this period the Athenian citizens paid no direct taxes to the state, and in later and less prosperous days they saw in the extension of the empire the hope of receiving pay in abundance.[1]

The number of subject states in the empire was probably about 300. In the period 454–431 some 180 states figured on the Quota Lists, and some of these were paying as the leader of a group. In 425, when the Pontus district had been added, more than 300 states were nominated to bring tribute to Athens. In order to simplify the accounts, the states were listed under geographical districts, Ionia, Hellespont, Thrace, Caria, Islands, and in 425 Pontus and Acte, the last being the mainland opposite Lesbos and northwards to the mouth of the Hellespont. The states varied in size, interests, and accessibility; their political, judicial, and commercial relations with Athens were governed by a separate treaty in each case. Lesbos and Chios still contributed ships, regulated their own constitutions, and retained their possessions on the mainland. Remote states, such as Phaselis, paid tribute and received favoured treatment in commercial cases and perhaps in other respects. In general Athens treated the states of Asia Minor with moderation, lest they revolted to their neighbour Persia; no cleruchies were planted on their territories and the rate of tribute was less high than elsewhere. Her rule was severe in the islands, which formed the centre of the empire, and on the north shore of the Aegean, which was the chief source of shipbuilding timber and precious metals.[2]

From the existence of the empire the subject states received considerable benefits. They were protected from Persia and from pirates, and their trade prospered in time of peace. In the height of the peace Athens relaxed her restrictions on currency, permitted Thasos and Samos, for instance, to coin in silver, and restored to Thasos some of her mainland possessions. Yet economic interest counted for less in most Greek states than political independence. Pericles emphasized the cultural claims of Athens—'the School of Greece'—to rule over others. The allied delegates were present at the Dionysia and other festivals and saw the glorious temples on the Acropolis. But their admiration was soured by humiliation. The chief complaint against Athens was that she was a tyrant state, ruling others by force and robbing them of their autonomy. The citizens of the subject states resented Athens' support of democracy and encouragement of informers, the oath of loyalty, and the submission to Athenian courts of cases arising from murder or political accusations, quite apart from such exceptional measures as the imposition of garrisons and commissioners and the exaction of hostages. As

[1] Th. 2. 13. 3; Ar. *V.* 656 f.; 706 f.; X. *An.* 7. 1. 27 (400 talents); Arist. *Ath.* 24. 3; Plu. *Per.* 11–12; [X.] *Ath.* 1. 19; Th. 6. 24. 3.
[2] Ar. *V.* 707 exaggerates in putting the number of subject states at 1,000; *GHI* 46; 66; Arist. *Ath.* 24. 2; *GHI* 32.

states they had to send prescribed offerings to Athena at the Panathenaic Festival and to Demeter at Eleusis. Their citizens had to pay a fee to enter Athens and made a deposit, which they often lost, before bringing a case perforce into an Athenian court. Pericles had no illusions about their animosity towards Athens. It was too late to relax the strictness of her rule.[1]

As the empire developed, Athens became not only the political but also the commercial centre of the Aegean and thereby the leading market of exchange between East and West, drawing to herself the goods of Sicily, Italy, Cyprus, Egypt, Lydia, Pontus, and Peloponnese. The state controlled the traffic in shipbuilding timber, iron, copper, and tin, which were required for armaments, but otherwise put no restrictions on a free trade which expanded rapidly. A general peace reigned throughout the Mediterranean area between 446 and 431, and Greek products were in growing demand. In public and in private wealth Athens rivalled the great centres of the Bronze Age, Cnossus and Mycenae, in their prime, and far surpassed her contemporaries in the Greek world.[2]

Under the wise administration of Pericles the public wealth was conserved. The expenditure on state-pay, state-festivals, and state-buildings was well within the current resources of the exchequer, and the poorer class of citizens received only a modest payment for their services in the law courts and the fleet. Private wealth accumulated in the hands of the aristocratic families, which owned good land in Attica and had capital to invest at a high rate of interest, and in the hands of the *nouveaux riches* who speculated in commerce, mining, and contracting. From this class were drawn the 1,000 cavalrymen, the 400 trierarchs, and the holders of other unpaid posts in the public service, the *leitourgiai*. More significant was the growth of citizens in the middle class, which provided about 23,000 hoplites in 431 as compared with some 10,000 in 490. Prominent among them were the smallholders of Attic land, such as the demesmen of Acharnae who counted 3,000 hoplites among their number, some resident on their farms and others plying their business in Athens and the Peiraeus; the owners of shops, lodging-houses, and small workshops; and the master-craftsmen, shipwrights, masons, builders, smiths, and so forth. The lower class numbered 14,240 citizens in 445/444, when free corn was distributed; if the line of distribution was drawn between the zeugites and the thetes, then the thetes in 431 were not more than 16,000. They had many opportunities to earn modest pay from the state, and they supplemented their income by retailing, olive-picking, harvesting, ferrying, fishing, &c., rather than by regular labour.[3]

The upper and the middle classes were swollen by a large number of prosperous metics, who supplied some 6,000 hoplites. These resident aliens

---

[1] Th. 2. 41. 1 and 3; *IG* i.² 66; [X.] *Ath.* 1. 14; 16; 17; Ar. *V.* 659.
[2] [X.] *Ath.* 2. 7; 2. 11; D.S. 12. 26; Th. 1. 80. 3; 2. 38. 2; 2. 64. 3.
[3] Th. 2. 13. 6; 19. 2; 20. 4 (3,000 may be corrupt, but the figure has to be a 'great part of the state'); 31. 2; [X.] *Ath.* 1. 4; *FGrH* 328 F 119 (Philochorus); Plu. *Per* 37.

were debarred from owning land in Attica, they were subject to the metic tax (the penalty for a defaulter was enslavement), and they had no political rights. But in economic and social matters they enjoyed equal opportunities with the citizens, and they were regarded as an important part of the community. Many of them brought considerable wealth into Athens, and the bulk of them were engaged in handicrafts and in maritime commerce and promoted the trade of Athens. There were also less prosperous metics, of whom perhaps 3,000 served in the fleet. In addition there was a floating population of aliens, Greek and non-Greek, who visited Athens as 'allies', traders, seamen, and so forth.[1]

The number of slaves rose in proportion to the prosperity of the state. Slaves took part in skilled and unskilled labour and, being in private owner-ship, provided a field for investment, which yielded a return in the form of a part of their earnings (*apophora*). The mines at Laurium were worked by slave labour. The wealthy Nicias, for example, owned a gang of 1,000 slaves, whom he leased to a Thracian contractor at a clear return of an obol a head a day. Slaves worked in domestic service, in agriculture, in skilled crafts, and in the general field of unskilled labour. The state, too, owned slaves who acted as police, secretaries, clerks, messengers, labourers, and so forth. Apart from the mines, where conditions in Attica as elsewhere were bad, the treatment of slaves was generally humane. The slave had legal rights, was not distin-guished by his dress, and worked alongside the free man both citizen and metic. But, if he had to give evidence in a court of law, he did so after torture. Greeks were rarely kept in slavery; the household of a metic at Athens in 414 consisted of sixteen slaves from Thrace, Colchis, Lydia, Caria, Syria, Illyria, Scythia, and Malta. Manumission was not infrequent, and liberated slaves (*apeleutheroi*) were not segregated. Runaway slaves were common. The Acropolis was strengthened against those who sought sanctuary, and Athens accused Megara of harbouring Athenian slaves. During the Decelean War 20,000 escaped, most being skilled workers. The total number of slaves in Attica was probably of the order of 200,000 men, women, and children, a figure not far short of the serf population in Laconia and Messenia.[2]

The total population of Attica in 431 may be estimated approximately at 400,000 souls, the Athenians being 168,000, the resident aliens 30,000, the non-resident aliens 2,000, and the slaves 200,000. Of the Athenians perhaps 4,000 were in the two upper classes, 100,000 in the middle class, and 64,000 in the lower class. The wealth of the state and the activities of the aliens and slaves enabled the citizens to devote much of their time to affairs of state, in peace and in war, without serious detriment to the productive capacity and

[1] Th. 2. 31. 2 gives the ratio between hoplite and metic field forces; Ar. *Ach.* 508; [X.] *Ath.* 1. 12.

[2] [X.] *Ath.* 1. 10-12; 18; X. *Vect.* 4. 15; *GHI* 79; *IG* i.² 44; Th. 1. 139. 2; 7. 27. 5. Hop-lites and seamen both had slave attendants, cf. Paus 1. 29. 3; 32. 3 (Marathon); Th. 3. 17. 4; [X.] *Ath.* 1. 19. Gomme, *Population of Athens*, puts the slave total at 115,000.

commercial prosperity of Athens. The citizens were still deeply attached to the demes from which they derived their ancestry; there they buried their dead and carried out their family worship, and there the wealthy had their fine establishments. More than half of them lived outside the towns of Athens and Peiraeus, in which the aliens and perhaps half of the slave population were resident. As compared with Sparta and other states on the mainland, the population in the towns was large, and the size of the citizen population and the total population was exceptional. In this respect Athens had outgrown the dimensions of a city-state in which the citizens could know one another. In order to arrest the process Pericles had restricted citizenship to those who were of Attic parentage on both sides, and had dispatched a considerable number of citizens overseas as colonists.[1]

Prosperity set the hallmark of success on Athenian democracy. Even a hostile critic, the so-called 'Old Oligarch', whose pamphlet was probably written in 431–430, recognized the unshakeable position of the democracy in theory and in practice. The less wealthy element in the community, those who manned the fleet and held the empire, were responsible for the power and the prosperity of Athens, and they had the right to sway her policies. The democratic system was admirably designed to fulfil its purpose, namely, the supremacy of the people in the state and the supremacy of Athens over her subjects. Long experience had eased and perfected the working of the democratic government. The 500 Councillors, changing annually and appointed by lot, dealt with an astonishing amount of business: the preparation of agenda for the Assembly; the scrutinizing, directing, and preliminary auditing of all magistrates; the administration of state finance, buildings, festivals, docks, and naval and military establishments; the selection of citizens to undertake liturgies; the assessment and collection of tribute; and in time of war the preliminary decision on urgent matters of strategy and diplomacy.[2] They worked in full session or in committee with the assistance of the magistrates and a competent secretariat. The 1,400 magistrates at home and overseas, for the most part changing annually and appointed by lot, carried out the details of administration in a wide variety of fields. They worked often in committee, but each had to undertake responsibility and undergo an audit at the expiry of his office. The 6,000 Heliasts, selected by lot and often sitting in jury throughout the year, dealt with a wide range of cases affecting the Athenians and the Allies. Thus the citizens possessed an experience of the details of political and judicial administration which has never been paralleled in an ancient or a modern state. Moreover, this experience was spread through all classes in the citizen community by the use of the lot, the rotation of office, and the disregard of the property qualification except in the candidature for a few magistracies.

It was this wide and cumulative experience which enabled the Assembly

[1] Th. 2. 14–16; 65. 2; 1. 80. 3; 8. 66. 3; Plu. *Per.* 11. 5.
[2] [X.] *Ath.* 1. 1–2; 3. 1–6; 3. 9.

to exercise an informed control over all departments of policy in war and peace, at home and overseas. The procedure in introducing business, in debating policy, and in judging political cases was strictly defined. The quorum for taking certain important decisions was 6,000, and the presiding officer— a member of the Prytany of the Council who was selected by lot for the day— could at his discretion adjourn the meeting, if he thought the attendance was too small to justify a vote on an important issue. The citizens in the Assembly had generally held office as Councillor, Heliast, or magistrate and had themselves served overseas as magistrate, soldier, or sailor. They knew the details of their business and the personalities of the leading men. The level of power and prosperity to which they had lifted Athens by 431 was a proof of their political sagacity.

In the democratic system there was one apparent anomaly. In practice the most responsible magistracies were held by influential men of high birth, the military offices being filled by direct election and the financial offices being restricted to members of the wealthiest class; moreover there was no bar against continuous re-election. This anomaly enabled individual statesmen to establish their prestige and exert their leadership over the people. The most important officer of all, the *strategos ex hapanton* or general elected without reference to tribal representation, was the most popular man in the state for the post of general. Pericles was that officer in many years and in particular for the last fifteen years of his life. The other nine generals were elected with reference to tribal representation, so that each was the most popular man in his own tribe for the post. The ten generals, once elected, had equal powers, but the *strategos ex hapanton* had the highest prestige. From time to time Pericles was appointed to undertake special responsibilities, such as the supervision of the imperial treasury and of the funds for the statue of Athena, the general command of operations against Samos, and the delivery of funeral speeches on behalf of the state.[1]

The acknowledged leadership of Pericles gave stability to the policy of the Athenians. He curbed their exuberance in success and he encouraged them in adversity. Assured of his own position, he resisted their caprice and controlled their passions with an independence which sprang from his own patriotism, integrity, and will. His prestige was such that at times of crisis he ruled the state, and to this extent 'the democracy'—the domination by the majority—was in abeyance.[2] Therein he was not unique. Themistocles and Cimon before him, Demosthenes and Lycurgus after him, impressed their will upon the minds of the Athenians and won their allegiance. They were all freely elected and, if need was, freely deposed, and the allegiance was freely given. That Pericles held the leadership for so many years was due to his own personality and to the steadiness of the Athenian people, at a time when the middle class preponderated in the state and the conditions of life were eased

---

[1] Plu. *Per.* 16; D.S. 12. 38. 2; *FGrH* 328 F 121 (Philochorus); Plu. *Per.* 8; Th. 2. 34. 6. See *StGH* 372 f.

[2] Th. 2. 65. 8–9.

by a general prosperity. His closest friends and advisers received no such respect from the people. They were dubbed the new Peisistratidae. Damon was ostracized; Anaxagoras was accused of impiety and Phidias of embezzlement, and both fled from Athens. Their disgrace did not affect the position of Pericles in the years before the outbreak of war. In 431 he stood supreme in the people's favour.[1]

The influence of Pericles stemmed not only from his executive talents but also from his political ideals. In the spring of 430 he was chosen to speak at the state-funeral of those who had laid down their lives in the first year of the Peloponnesian War. Before the silent multitude he spoke of Athens' greatness. Her constitution was designed not to preserve the privilege of a class but to ensure equal rights for all citizens in the courts of law and in the administration of the state. Her principles were devoid of prejudice. Men were judged by their character and not by their circumstances. Freedom of speech, thought, and education was universal; for from individual and social freedom sprang true happiness, independence, and courage. A free society knew its own restraints and responsibilities. It respected the officers it had elected, the laws it had enacted, and the unwritten laws of honour. In conducting its affairs a democracy put its trust in the intelligence of the average citizen; discussion preceded action, and action was based on the will of the people. In foreign relations a democracy put up no barriers. It was open to the ideas of all the world, because it trusted in the spirit of its people to engage in the pursuit of beauty with moderation and in the pursuit of knowledge with manliness. In the Athenian citizen intelligence and action, deliberation and daring, private interest and public duty were in harmony, and from his versatility sprang the rich variety of Athenian civilization. Such was the ideal to which Pericles directed the eyes of his countrymen. Let them gaze upon the city, and their hearts would be filled with love of her. Life held no higher honour than to serve her, and death no finer justification than to have died for her.[2]

[1] Plu. *Per.* 16; 31–32; Arist. *Ath.* 27. 4; D.S. 12. 38–39; *FGrH* 328 F 121. Some put the trials of Anaxagoras and Phidias in 430. [2] Th. 2. 34–46; cf. E. *Suppl.* 404.

CHAPTER 3

Art, Literature, and Thought (466–431)

URING the central third of the fifth century Greek civilization attained an assurance of taste and judgement and a degree of intellectual courage which have never been equalled. It was an age of confidence, founded on victory over the barbarians, a balance of power in the Mediterranean, and an increasing material prosperity. It was an age of religious faith, especially in the states of the Greek mainland, where the roots of local worship were set deep and the centres of Panhellenic cults were situated. It was an age of intellectual enlightenment, engendered by the daring speculations of the Ionians and accelerated by the interchange of ideas under the favourable conditions of peace and prosperity. The extraordinary variety and versatility of the Greek genius in hundreds of city-states, each individual in character and each confident of its institutions, found expression in the building of temples comparable to the cathedrals of Europe, in attributing the origin of the universe to the interaction of atoms, in producing plays as poetic as those of Shakespeare, and in carrying every experiment in art, thought, and politics to its logical conclusion.

Great artists, like great thinkers, influenced one another in this period, and such masters as Polyclitus of Argos and Phidias of Athens were of universal importance in Greek art. In Polyclitus' bronze statues the vigorous tradition of the Peloponnesian school was employed to show the victorious athlete not in action but in repose. The powerful body of the Doryphorus (a youth holding a javelin) owes its remarkable suppleness and ease to the stance with one leg carrying the weight and the other leg relaxed. The Amazon and the Boy Athlete, each with the left arm resting on a short pillar, are wonderful examples of physical perfection at rest. There is in all three statues a serenity and calm which suggest a withdrawal of the spirit from the affairs of daily life. Polyclitus wrote a treatise in which he analysed the principles of proportion and composition, but his successors never achieved the harmonious balance of vigour and relaxation, of power and ease, of physical perfection and spiritual grace which marked his ideal representation of heroic man.[1]

Polyclitus carved a famous statue in gold and ivory of Hera at Argos, but Phidias was acknowledged to be the greatest sculptor of gods. His masterpieces were the colossal statues, 30 or 40 feet high, which were worshipped in the temples: the statue in gold and ivory of Zeus at Olympia, the statue in bronze of Athena Promachus ('the Defender') on the Acropolis, and the statue in gold and ivory of Athena Parthenus ('the Virgin') in the Parthenon.

[1] Richter, *Sc.*, figs. 645–9, 655; *Vorsokr.* 40.

The majesty and splendour of these statues, and particularly of the chryselephantine ones, are known mainly from descriptions by later writers who saw in them the highest expression of divinity. The Zeus of Phidias was regarded as 'the God of peace, the preserver of Greece when she was of one mind, not torn by civil war, the universal Father, Saviour and Guardian of mankind'. Such was the conception of the godhead evoked by the majesty of the statue: *adeo maiestas operis deum aequavit*. The Athena Promachus, erect on the Acropolis, her spear-tip and her helmet visible to sailors on the Saronic Gulf, guarded her city against attack as she had done at Marathon. And the Athena Parthenus, standing in the inner shrine of her own temple and holding Victory in her hand, received the offerings and the prayers of her citizens and her allies. These incomparable statues remained for centuries to come the finest representations of the God of the Greeks and the Goddess of Athens.[1]

To Zeus of Olympia and to Athena of Athens the finest temples of this period were dedicated. The austere grandeur of the Doric style was more in accord with the artistic and religious feelings of the age both in the Peloponnese and in Attica than the more decorative and gay Ionic style. The temple of Zeus, built probably between 468 and 456 in the conglomerate stone of Olympia and faced with white stucco, was of the normal plan with a peristyle of six columns on each façade and thirteen columns on each flank. The floor on which the columns rest, called the stylobate, is reached by ascending three steps. The overall dimensions, including the lowest step, are almost 100 feet wide and 220 feet long, and the original height was some 66 feet so that the temple, itself raised on a high platform of foundations, might dominate the Altis. Nowadays too little is standing for its proportions to be appreciated, but something of its beauty is visible in the marble sculptures from the pediments and the metopes (see Plate VII).

In the eastern pediment above the main entrance to the temple the preparations for the chariot-race between Pelops and Oenomaus are depicted with Zeus standing supreme in the centre. In the western pediment Apollo presides over the battle of Lapiths and Centaurs at the wedding of Peirithous and Hippodameia. The twelve metopes show the labours of Heracles, the hero of the Dorians. Strength and vigour are magnificently achieved in the western pediment, where the figures are caught in the throes of desperate action, and in the metopes, for instance in the strong neck and powerful body of a bull; but the composition of the eastern pediment is perhaps too symmetrical, too statuesque to combine grandeur and repose. The individual figures are superbly sculptured with strength and economy of line and at the same time with delicacy of detail, for instance Athena in her heavy Doric chiton. These sculptures are worthy forerunners of the sculptures of Phidias, even as the temple of Zeus at Olympia is of the Parthenon.[2]

---

[1] D. Chr. 12. 74; Paus. 5. 11; 1. 28. 2; 24. 5; Quint. *Inst.* 12. 10. 9.
[2] Paus. 5. 10. Richter, *Sc.*, figs. 390–3, 414, 355, 66, 115, 2, 133–4, 163, 191, 319.

The greatest statues of Phidias are known to us only by report, but his idea of style is visible to us in the marble sculptures of the Parthenon, executed under his direction by a group of sculptors during the years 447–433 (see Plate VIII). The pediments, of which few fragments remain, portrayed the birth of Athena and the contest between Athena and Poseidon for Attica; the metopes the battles of gods and giants, Amazons and Athenians, Centaurs and Lapiths, and the fall of Troy; and the Ionic frieze the procession of the Athenian people at the Panathenaic Festival in the presence of the gods. Past and present were united in glorification of Athena. The composition of these themes combines movement and repose with an amazing skill in perspective and boldness in execution. Nor is the strength of composition weakened in any way by the refinement of detail, which is carried to the highest possible degree of accuracy in representing, for instance, the texture of a horse's skin and muscle. The rendering of the drapery above all imparts a fluidity of line which makes the horsemen swing into motion and the Fates sink into rest. In comparison some of the sculptures at Olympia seem to be static and others to have caught a moment and not a continuance of action. On this great variety of subjects, poses, and details (extending in the Panathenaic procession for 523 feet) a unity has been imposed by the 'sublimity and precision' which were the characteristics of Phidias' style, and by the love of the artists themselves for Athena Polias, the goddess of the city, to whom the temple was dedicated.[1]

The Parthenon, so called later after the room which contained the statue of Athena Parthenus, was designed by Ictinus and Callicrates and built in the years 447–438, the sculptures being completed subsequently. Placed upon a platform of limestone, the temple dominated the Acropolis and the city of Athens, as it does today, so that the traveller's eye is drawn to it as soon as he sails into Attic waters or crosses a pass into the central plain. The Pentelic marble in which the temple is built, though not so white as it was, still shines resplendent in the sun, or gleams softly in the moon, so that the diffusion of light lifts and relieves the natural heaviness of the Doric order. The full colours, which once gave variety to the eye and distinction to architectural features, have long since disappeared, leaving traces only in the tone or surface of the marble. In the peristyle these colours were not applied below the level of the capitals but picked out in blue, red, or gold such details as the thin annulets, the triglyphs, and the taenia of the architrave. Colour also enriched the delicate sculptures of the metopes and the more massive figures of the pediments. The sculptures of the figures of the Panathenaic procession, which was carved inside the peristyle and was less conspicuous, were painted in colour against a blue background.

Although much of the delicate detail has disappeared with the passage of time, the sublimity of the building makes a tremendous impression. It is of

[1] Paus. 1. 24. 5; Plu. *Per.* 13; Demetr. *Eloc.* 14. Richter, *Sc.*, figs. 394-6, 69–71, 91, 292, 351, 622 (pediments); 415–16, 105, 131, 192 (metopes); 486, 488–9, 356, 291, 247 (frieze).

great size, 237 feet long by 110 feet wide including the bottom step, but its size is absorbed into the harmony of its proportions. The subtlety of the planning may be illustrated by noting some of the refinements which were employed to remove any optical illusion of overhang or of sag in so vast a building and to afford the intuitive pleasure of curves relieving straight lines. The surface of the upper step has a curvature, rising to $4\frac{5}{16}$ inches on the flanks and $2\frac{3}{8}$ inches on the façades, which is carried through the foundation below, the platform itself and the entablature, cornice, and tympanum above. The columns incline inwards by $2\frac{3}{8}$ inches and the walls on their outer surface incline in sympathy; so, too, most of the upper surfaces of the building have slight inclinations backward or forward. The face of each tapering column is not straight but curved convexly, to a maximum of $\frac{11}{16}$ inch. These are but a few examples of the masterly design and the meticulous craftsmanship which make this one of the most remarkable and exquisite buildings in the world.[1]

The Propylaea, designed by Mnesicles, was begun in 437 but never completed. As in the Parthenon, the material was Pentelic marble, fitted with doors and roof-beams of timber, and a sparing use was made of black limestone from Eleusis. The Propylaea enclosed the only entry to the Acropolis. The roadway was not stepped but sloping, in order to carry the wheeled vehicles of a procession. The portal for the roadway was 24 feet high and nearly 13 feet wide, and it was flanked on each side by two doorways of diminishing size in the main wall. These doorways were approached by four steps leading up to the stylobates, which each carried three Doric columns, supporting the outer or western façade, and then by five steps leading up to the threshold of the doorways. As the outer porch was so long, the marble roof was supported on six Ionic columns, three on the stylobate on each side of the road. The inner porch, supporting the eastern façade with three Doric columns on each side of the roadway, was much shorter and therefore needed no Ionic columns to support its continuous 'ceiling of white marble, unmatched for the beauty and size of its blocks'. The porches and the entries were themselves to have been flanked by two west wings, but the original plan was never completed. Even in its ruined state today the Propylaea forms a spacious and dignified entry, in which the strength of Doric and the grace of Ionic are harmoniously united. The skill with which the building is adapted to the exigencies of the site, and the technical refinements which rival those of the Parthenon, are almost forgotten in the general impression of majesty.[2]

Within the period 449–432 four temples, built in marble to the design of an unknown architect, were dedicated to Athena and Hephaestus on the hill west of the Agora, to Ares in the Agora, to Poseidon at Sunium, and to Nemesis at Rhamnus. These four temples have in common certain features of design such as the alignment of the third column on each flank of the peristyle with the antae of the porch in front of the cella. None of these temples rivals the Parthenon and the Propylaea, but they, too, are of the highest order in architectural design and in craftsmanship. The Hephaesteum has gained in dignity and grace through the excavating of the Agora, and the remains of the peristyle which still crown the extreme tip of Sunium's once 'wooded headland, washed by the waves of the sea' welcome the sailor as he enters the Saronic Gulf and sets his course for the city of Athens.[1]

At Olympia and in some of the metopes of the Parthenon themes of universal appeal in Greek religion were chosen. Such, too, were the subjects of the first great painter, Polygnotus of Thasos, whose mural paintings were seen by Pausanias at Athens, Plataea, and Delphi, portraying scenes from the *Iliad* and the *Odyssey*. He limited his colours to white, red, ochre, and black, used comparatively little shading and was very expressive of action and emotion. In the opinion of Aristotle Polygnotus in painting and Sophocles in drama portrayed men as better than we are and as revealing qualities of character; and the same might be said of Polyclitus in statuary.[2]

So universal was the interest in heroic themes and so deep the love of those values which were shared by many states in Greek lands that they became the main theme in the first great history composed in Greece. Herodotus of Halicarnassus wrote a history of the Persian wars in which he contrasted the culture of Greece and those of the non-Greek world. Born on the coastal fringe where Greek and Asiatic met, Herodotus travelled widely throughout the known world. Everything which he saw and heard was of absorbing interest to his inquiring mind—the burial rites of the Scythian kings, the fat-tailed sheep of Arabia, the origin of the Phoenicians, the circumnavigation of Africa, the colour of salt in Libya—and he arranged his rich and varied material in the traditional form of 'tales' (*logoi*) as evolved by his predecessors in Ionia, the 'logographers'. Just as 'Homer' surpassed the authors of epic 'lays' in his creation of a great epic poem, so did Herodotus surpass his predecessors by weaving his 'tales' into a historical pattern. His flowing prose possesses, even in translation, an unrivalled limpidity and charm, most suitable to a long story read aloud. Taking for his field the span of human memory and the frontiers of the known world, he composed his own 'tales' or adapted the 'tales' of his predecessors for particular areas, and he then imposed on the whole a unity, which derived not only from his own cast of mind but also from a central and dramatic theme, the conflict between West and East.

The quality of his mind has earned him the title 'the father of history'. Where others recorded, Herodotus inquired: why were priestesses at Dodona called 'doves', why did the Nile flood, why were the Scyths nomadic, why did Greece and Persia go to war? and so on. The meaning of 'history' (*historia*) is inquiry, and a written history is the result of inquiry. In this sense Herodotus began his work with the words: 'This is the result of the inquiry by Herodotus of Halicarnassus, that time should not blot out the past from

---

[1] Paus. 1. 8. 4; 1. 14. 6; S. *Aj.* 1218.
[2] Paus. 1. 18. 1; 1. 22. 6; 9. 4. 2; 10. 25–31; Arist. *Po.* 1448ᵃ; 1450ᵃ.

mankind nor fame be denied to great and wonderful deeds, accomplished by Greeks and non-Greeks, and in particular the reason why they went to war with one another.' Yet inquiry is not enough; for one needs standards of judgement in assessing the accuracy of the answer. Herodotus preferred to be his own observer, but he often had to rely on hearsay. Then he might give several variant accounts, and mark one account as more probable, but he did not fall into the error of supposing the more probable to be necessarily true. Sometimes he was over-credulous of events distant in time or space, sometimes he was swept off his feet by reports of huge numbers, but generally he showed a sturdy common sense matured by wide experience.

As the central theme of the Persian wars, and therefore of his history, he took the clash between two cultures, or rather between two groups of cultures, Greek and non-Greek, and this comprehensive view enriched his treatment and understanding. In political terms he saw the clash as one between the spirit of freedom and the exercise of despotism, and he fully realized the significance of the outcome for the future of the world. His final inquiry was into the ultimate causation of historical events. In the life of the individual he saw that chance played so important a part that no man should be called happy until death had put him beyond its grasp. In the lives of nations and of the great men who affect the destinies of nations Herodotus saw the hand of God at work—punishing excessive ambition, impious behaviour, and vain conceit. When God intervened in human affairs, He was jealous and disruptive; the thrones of the mighty were cast down, and the poor and the innocent were often crushed in the ruins. So, too, in the natural world the providence of God preserved a balance between the warring species. Faith and observation carried him no farther. He did not endeavour, as Aeschylus had done, to justify the works of God in terms of human justice.[1]

Of course there are defects in his history. Like his contemporaries, he believed in the efficacy of oracles, the significance of dreams, and the apparition of 'heroes'. A traveller himself and for long a man without a city, he had broadened his view of mankind, but he had not focused his attention on city-state politics. Therefore he appreciated the greatness of democracy at Athens, but he failed to understand the nature and motives of Cleisthenes' reforms.[2] Equally he was no general. He could describe equipment or grasp principles, but he could not understand or reconstruct the tactics employed in military and naval engagements. In the idiom of his day he used speeches to enliven narration and to convey judgements, but he did not imply that such speeches were replicas of what was actually said by Croesus or Xerxes. But these defects or peculiarities in modern eyes shrink into insignificance, when we consider the range of Herodotus' interest and originality, and the sureness and sanity of his judgements on men and on life.

As we see from Herodotus, travel was easier than it had ever been. The widespread peace, the safety of the seas, and the growth of trade encouraged

[1] Hdt. 1. 32; 34. 1; 3. 40. 2; 7. 46. 4; 3. 108. 2. [2] Hdt. 5. 69; 78.

men to exchange goods or ideas, especially with Athens, the centre of maritime commerce. Herodotus himself was a good example. He lived at Halicarnassus and Samos, stayed at Athens where he gave a recitation, probably in 445, and settled as a citizen at Thurii in 443. Such ease of communication was of particular benefit to the schools of philosophy. Anaxagoras, Empedocles, and Zeno, who were contemporary with Herodotus and Sophocles, knew and attacked one another's doctrines. At the time Anaxagoras exercised the greatest influence, because he settled and taught at Athens, and became a close friend and teacher of Pericles.

Anaxagoras of Clazomenae (*c.* 500–428) had original theories about matter and mind. Particles of matter, he argued, are infinitely divisible and infinitely diverse so that their range in number, size, and quality is limitless. A material object is formed of many particles of every sort; its individual character is due to the predominance of certain sorts of particles in its constituents. Thus in any material object there are particles of all sorts, so that 'all things are in all things', and 'a part of everything is in everything'. He was then able to explain 'birth', 'growth', and 'death' as simply stages in a process of arrangement and rearrangement of particles. However, he made one exception. The finest and purest substance, Mind (*nous*), is discrete, independent, and self-existent. Mind is present in some things, especially in man and other creatures which have 'soul' (*psyche*), but it is not present in all things. Where it is present, it exercises control.[1]

Proceeding from these definitions Anaxagoras stated his cosmogony. Matter was at first inert, an unseparated mixture, enveloped by the lower and upper strata of the atmosphere, which was itself limitless in extent. Mind was the prime mover of matter; at some small point in matter Mind set up a movement and the movement spread, increasing in speed and in the area affected. The movement was circular, so that centrifugal force threw the particles outwards and, as they cohered or separated, so objects were formed or changed. This process was still continuing; for Mind constantly initiates movement, which spreads into the infinite expanses of the universe (or into an infinite number of universes). Since Mind exercises control over everything in which it is present, Mind controls the infinite universe. Thus Mind is the initiating and controlling force, cognizant of the effects it creates.[2]

Anaxagoras did not import any religious ideas into his cosmogony. He was concerned with a materialistic explanation of the world, and it is possible, though not demonstrable, that he regarded Mind as a special form of matter. To him heat, cold, dryness, wetness, density, rarity, brightness, darkness were not abstractions but physical properties inherent in all things, so that a material object contained hot particles and cold particles, dry particles and wet particles, and so on. He relied on the evidence of the senses and noted the point on the scale where they ceased to record size, heat, and so on with accuracy. Regarding everything as material, he explained that sun, moon,

[1] *Vorsokr.* 59 B 3, 4, 6, 17, 11, 12.   [2] *Vorsokr.* 59 B 1, 12, 13, 14, 4.

and stars were formed of matter and moved on the circular course initiated by Mind; that the sun gave its light to the moon; and that eclipses and rainbows were due to physical causes (which he analysed correctly).[1]

Anaxagoras was probably tilting against Empedocles of Acragas (*c.* 493–433), who modified some of the views of Parmenides and Pythagoras. He postulated Earth, Water, Fire, and Air in finite quantities as the four elements, or 'roots', of which all things consisted, and Love and Strife as two continually active forces, which were perhaps envisaged as fluids or currents. In addition there was 'a strong decree' of fate (*aisa*)—which might nowadays be called a natural law—whereby Love and Strife ebbed and flowed.[2]

At some point in time, perhaps at the beginning of time, Love was dominant and Strife was at its lowest ebb. Then the four elements, contained in a finite sphere, were completely intermingled under the impulse of Love which was flowing among them, and the resultant homogeneous mixture was compacted into a unity. At this moment, when all was one, Strife was on the periphery of the sphere. Then Strife flowed back into the mass, disjoining what Love had joined, separating unity into disunity, and making the one into many, until Strife became dominant and Love sank to its lowest ebb. There were thus two extreme positions in the ebb-and-flow, one when Love was dominant and a homogeneous mixture ensued, and the other when Strife was dominant and the four elements were separated out into four disjoined parts. Except at the extreme positions, which were probably regarded as momentary phases in a cycle, the two forces Love and Strife were always flowing through the mixture, mingling and unmingling the hotch-potch of elements, as a painter mingles his pots of colours, and therewith Love and Strife made and unmade all things, as a painter makes and unmakes trees and men and gods with his colours.[3]

Empedocles' cosmology was probably intended to fit into a revealed religion of which he himself was the prophet. When created things were first created, Love was more powerful than Strife, so that men were innocent, animals gentle, and no blood was shed. Now, Strife being in the ascendant, evil, savagery, and slaughter abound. At the first creation men worshipped Love alone, to whom they made sacrifice of myrrh and frankincense and honey, not as now of blood, and the gods were created not in human form but as 'pure, ineffable mind darting with swift thoughts throughout the universe'. Intelligence in some form (*phronesis* or *noema*), which we may call the soul, was inherent in all things, implanted probably at the first creation, and Empedocles believed that these souls migrated from created object to created object during the age-long process of re-creation. 'I was once already', he wrote, 'boy and girl and thicket and bird and fish of the salty sea.'[4]

The migrant souls ranged over the whole gamut of created things, includ-

[1] *Vorsokr.* 59 B 21, 18, 19.   [2] *Vorsokr.* 31 B 6; 38–39; 16; 26, l. 2; 30.
[3] *Vorsokr.* 31 B 17; 13; 27; 21; 26; 35; 71; 23.
[4] *Vorsokr.* 31 B 130; 121; 128; 134; 110; 117.

ing the gods. Thus a god who stained his hands with blood or committed perjury was outcast for thrice ten thousand seasons to wander in all kinds of mortal forms over the rough paths of life. 'Such am I now', wrote Empedocles, 'outcast from heaven and a wanderer who put his trust in raging Strife.' As a god on earth he revealed the nature of the world to his followers, men and women, who honoured him with garlands at the great city by the yellow river Acragas.[1]

His cosmology and his religion have come down to us in fragments only from two poems, so that much is obscure. Yet their epic cadences convey the emotional force with which a great poet combated the cold logic of some natural philosophers, and his powerful ideas—especially the dualism of Love and Strife in the forms of Good and Evil, and the transmigration of souls— echoed down the ages at times when the theories of the Ionian physicist were no longer known. As a biologist and physiologist, too, Empedocles was an important figure. For he studied the eye and the heart, and he theorized about conception, respiration, and the circulation of the blood.

The problems of motion and the conceptions of the finite and the infinite, which were of such interest to Anaxagoras and Empedocles, were treated in a provocative manner by their contemporary, Zeno of Elea, whose teaching has survived only in the form of paradoxical statements. For example, in a handicap race between Achilles and a tortoise, Achilles never overtakes the tortoise because whenever he reaches the point where the tortoise has just been, it is in front; and, as an arrow in flight occupies at any given instant a space equal to itself, it is then at rest and not in flight. Zeno's statements, of which the first turned on an infinite subdivision of finite distance and the second on an indivisible instant of time, probably inspired Leucippus of Miletus, who visited Elea *c.* 450, to evolve the idea of indivisible units in infinite numbers in infinite space. His indivisible unit was called an 'atom' (*atomon*) and his space was called 'void' (*kenon*).[2]

The credit for developing Leucippus' hypothesis of the atom into an atomic theory of the universe is shared by his pupil Democritus of Abdera (*c.* 460–370). The atoms, infinite in shape and in number and situated in infinite void, were hurled about by an eddy and in consequence collided, cohered, and formed all material objects. Atoms are the only objective reality (*aletheia*) of nature (*physis*), and the only qualities of atoms are number, shape, and impenetrability. All other attributes of matter, such as colour, taste, and temperature, are due to man's fancy (*doxa*), which, being derived from the senses, is an adventitious and shadowy form of perception, founded on convention (*nomos*) and not on reality. The only genuine understanding in man is that of the intellect (*dianoia*), which conceives of the invisible and intangible atoms.[3]

In such a cosmology there was no room for Love or Strife and Good or

---

[1] *Vorsokr.* 31 B 115; 112.   [2] *Vorsokr.* 67 A 15.
[3] *Vorsokr.* 68 A 1, 44–45; 156; B 7; 9; 11.

Evil. The nearest thing to an initiating power in the creation of the world was an eddy in the void. The regulator of the chances and changes which make up human life on earth might be Chance or Necessity, but it could not be any supernatural person or thing. Leucippus preferred Necessity when he stated that 'nothing happens at random but all things of purpose and necessity' (*logos* and *ananke*),[1] but many after him chose Chance, the purposeless exploiter of coincidence. In assessing the importance of Leucippus and Democritus it should be emphasized that they were not scientists proceeding by observation and experiment and putting their theories to practical tests, but simply philosophers whose speculations were concerned with the nature of human thought as much as with the nature of the universe. Their theories, therefore, had far more impact on morality and religion than on engineering, which was in its infancy.

In this age of intellectual discovery Athens became the centre of art and philosophy. She was the pioneer of the new world. She carried the principles of liberty and equality to their logical conclusions in a constitution which was a model for others. But at the same time she was a centre of religion, where men worshipped Athena of Athens and the heroes of their demes, as they had done for generations. New and old were fused in the crucible of Attic Drama, of which the flame was religion because religion was the flame of life. In 458 the Athenian people, sitting on the hillside below the Acropolis, watched the great trilogy in which Aeschylus affirmed the majesty of Zeus, the son of Cronus, king of the gods. Perhaps for the first time scenery, painted by Agatharchus, was available for the production, and this scenery led Anaxagoras and Democritus to inquire into the theory of perspective. Religion and rationalism were soon to come into conflict. When they did so, a poet greater than Aeschylus was producing plays on the hillside and teaching the citizens that the greatest part of religion is understanding.[2]

Sophocles (*c.* 496–406) was a friend of Cimon, a Hellenotamias in the year of his successor's ostracism (443), a colleague of Pericles and later of Nicias as general, and an official adviser (*proboulos*) after the disaster in Sicily. He accepted and served the state, its democracy and its empire, as he accepted and served the orthodox religion of his day, not from traditionalism but from conviction. His salient quality was serenity, the fruit in him of courage and sensitivity, which brought him into peace with life and with death. For him the reality of God was unquestioned; His power ruled all life and controlled all happenings, and no man could evade His will.[3] Like Herodotus, with whom he had ties of friendship, Sophocles did not attempt to explain or explore the ways of God in terms of the universe; it was enough for him to observe the ways of God in relation to the state, the family, and the individual. There he accepted the traditional beliefs that, if the proper order within the family or state was disrupted, God's retribution followed—on Thebes and

---

[1] *Vorsokr.* 67 B 2.   [2] Vitr. 7 *praef.* 11; S. *Ant.* 1348.
[3] Ar. *Ra.* 82; S. *Tr.* 1276; *OT* 883; *Ph.* 1467.

the Labdacidae in *Oedipus Tyrannus*, *Oedipus at Colonus*, and *Antigone*—and that to execute this retribution He used human agents such as Deianeira in *Trachiniae* and Orestes and Electra in *Electra*.

The centre of Sophoclean tragedy was man, as citizen and as individual. Within God's overruling plan man had free will not to control his fate but to face his fate. Oedipus killed his father and married his mother in ignorance, but he tore out his eyes in knowledge by an act of free will. So, too, the situations which confronted Ajax, Antigone, Electra, and Philoctetes were not of their making, but each responded to the situation with freedom of will. Their response at its noblest was guided by the unwritten laws which Antigone invoked: 'laws immutable, unwritten, everlasting, not ordained today or yesterday, of origin unknown.' They are God's laws in contrast to Creon's edicts; they are what we may call the laws of conscience, but Sophocles called the laws of understanding; they represent at the same time the ideals established for men by God and the ideals accepted by Periclean Athens.[1] The characters in Sophocles' plays show man at his noblest, because they belong to a noble era in history, when men analysed the realities of life and faced them with open-eyed courage.

Sophocles' interest in man the citizen and man the individual differed from that of Aeschylus, who was concerned primarily with groups. Although he won his first victory in 468, the first extant plays, *Ajax* and *Antigone* (*c.* 441), belong to a period when Sophocles has already discarded the trilogy, introduced the third actor, diminished the amount of choral lyrics, and increased the importance of dialogue. These changes were consequent on the change of interest from group to individual, from divine laws to human reactions, from religious revelation to discussion of principles. In certain crises the laws of conscience guide a man—in helping the oppressed, in burying the dead, in shunning cowardice—but in most situations a man must reason out his course of action, deciding what is due to the state, the family, and himself and balancing right with right and wrong with wrong. Sophoclean dialogue is concerned above all with such decisions: the right of Ajax to commit suicide and the right of Agamemnon to deny him burial, the right of Creon to spurn the traitor Polyneices and the right of Antigone to bury her brother, the right of Oedipus as king, of Teiresias as priest, of Iocasta as mother-wife, or the problems which face Theseus, king of Athens, when the polluted and polluting Oedipus asks him for protection from the king of Thebes.

The Attic drama as developed by Sophocles was the perfect vehicle for the expression of his ideas. The chorus provided religious and social comments on actions which had religious and social consequences. Its beautiful lyrics contained a philosophy of man's existence, ranging from the glories of his achievement to the limitations of his lot. The characters were drawn not with detailed realism but in the bold lines which showed the qualities prompting their decisions—the proud spirit of Ajax, the love that was the strength of

[1] S. *OT* 1329–33; *OC* 521–5, 548; *Ant.* 369; 454; 1348.

Antigone, the impetuous determination of Oedipus, and the tenderness of Deianeira. The dialogue and also the messenger's speech, in which past action was reported, were in iambic verse, of which the rhythm and the diction were akin to those of ordinary speech; thereby the reality of the situations and the actions was enforced on the spectators. When Aristotle wrote the *Poetics*, he thought Sophocles was unrivalled in handling the well-known themes of Attic Tragedy. Sophocles more than any other filled the spectators with pity and fear as they re-lived those pieces of life in which men and women nobler than ourselves were carried onward by their own decisions to disaster. The supreme moment of tension was when the hero passed from ignorance to knowledge, from prosperity to adversity. This Sophocles managed with consummate artistry in the *Oedipus Tyrannus*.[1]

After the death of Sophocles at the age of ninety his last play, the *Oedipus at Colonus*, was produced. The aged Oedipus, once a famous man of courage and sensitivity, is now a blind beggar, an outcast from Thebes, a pariah among men. Yet his courage and his sensitivity are undimmed. He has come to accept what life, what God has done to him; and this he has learnt through suffering, through length of years, through self-respect, knowing himself in motive to be innocent of parricide and incest and in his revulsion justified in tearing out his eyes. The nobility of Oedipus the king is purified in Oedipus the old man.

The issue of the play turns on the final resting-place of the pariah. In response to that unwritten law which enjoined the protection of the weak on Periclean Athens, Theseus gave sanctuary to Oedipus. There by a miracle of God he passed from life to death, his destiny fulfilled. For he revealed that his tomb would ensure for Athens immunity from conquest by Thebes.

Life had brought sorrows, too, to the aged Sophocles. His beloved Athens was on the brink of collapse, her citizens had broken both written and unwritten laws in the passions of war; and God, who in most men's eyes had sent the plague and caused the eclipse of the moon at Syracuse, seemed to have turned His face away from Colonus. In the *Oedipus at Colonus* the chorus sang these lyrics: 'Not to be born is best, and, if one is born, to return thither whence one came with least delay is second best by far. For once he has passed youth with its passionate follies, man meets the blow of affliction and every weariness is there—envy, sedition, strife, war, and carnage. At last his lot is old age, disparaged, strengthless, unapproachable, friendless, wherein every ill of ills is one's companion.'[2] Such was Sophocles' cry of pain as he faced life to the end. But he did not despair. For in the *Oedipus at Colonus* he proclaimed his abiding faith in man, in Athens, and in God.

[1] Arist. *Po.* 1452ᵃ32.   [2] S. *OC* 1225.

CHAPTER 4

The First Part of the Peloponnesian War, 431–421[1]

§ 1. *The misfortunes of Athens 431–429*

SPARTA and her allies attained a higher level of prosperity during the years of peace than ever before, and in 431 they were a formidable adversary. Their hoplite forces far exceeded those of Athens and her allies. Sparta herself had an army of superb quality, which had grown up after the earthquake and the Helots' Revolt, and she had at her disposal the infantry of her allies—all the Peloponnesian states (except Argos and most of Achaea, which were neutral), Ambracia, Leucas, and Anactorium (which were colonies of Corinth), Megara, Boeotia, Locris, and Phocis. The last three provided cavalry also. Their full levies contained some 50,000 hoplites and larger forces of light-armed infantry, but these were available only for a short campaign, since the troops had to work their lands and raise foodstuffs. The naval strength of the Spartan Alliance had been severely damaged by the defection of Corcyra and by the losses of Corinth at the battle of Sybota. Sparta, Corinth with her colonies, and Megara, Sicyon, Pellene in Achaea, and Elis possessed 100 triremes or more, and they had some reserves of money for building and equipping a larger fleet. Their difficulty in time of war was to obtain the requisite timber and the trained oarsmen; for Athens controlled the supply of both in the Aegean area. The financial resources of the Spartan Alliance were far inferior to those of Athens, even if loans might be obtained from the temples of Olympia and Delphi. This mattered little in short campaigns and set battles, but siege-warfare and naval armaments were very expensive. If harvests were good, the states of the Peloponnese and of central Greece were self-supporting in essential foodstuffs, and the Peloponnesians hoped to import from Sicily, Crete, Cyrene, and Egypt. Their general trade overseas, however, was bound to suffer in the war, and this would weaken their financial and material resources in course of time.[2]

The strongest state in the Spartan Alliance was Sparta. Her indomitable hoplites, liberated for warfare by the labour of the Helots, ensured the Peloponnesian allies against any decisive defeat by land. Her qualities in war were summarized by Thucydides. Her constitution was stable and her people tenacious. They possessed a sanity of judgement which was unshaken by success or failure, and they had inherited a supreme self-confidence from their achievements in the past. They prided themselves more on their common

---

[1] In this chapter references to Thucydides are usually given without the prefix 'Th.'.
[2] 1. 19; 80. 3–4; 121. 3; 141; 2. 9; 3. 86. 4; 4. 53. 3; Plu. *Per.* 33. 4.

sense than on their intelligence. They were orderly, disciplined, and brave, and they were faithful to their own religious and moral standards. Uneasy though they were that they had rejected the Athenian offer to submit their disputes to arbitration, they felt that the God of Delphi was on their side and that the cause of liberation was just. The general goodwill of the Greek states fortified their resolution, and some of their allies were powerful states.[1]

Corinth was foremost in naval and commercial strength. She commanded the allegiance of all her colonies in the north-west except Corcyra. Chalcis, Astacus, Leucas, Anactorium, Ambracia, and Apollonia in Illyria sent offerings regularly to the Corinthian festivals, and some of them may have received like Potidaea political officials from Corinth. The solidarity of this colonial group was expressed in their fine currencies, which bore the national emblem, a Pegasus. When Aegina lost her independence in 457, the coins of Corinth and her colonies came second to those of Athens as an international currency, and they were particularly popular in Italy and Sicily. From the hinterland of the colonies in Epirus and Illyria she imported silver, timber, and hides, an important source of wealth now threatened by the war with Corcyra, and she had in the west her loyal and powerful colony Syracuse, which brought all the Dorian states in Sicily, except Camarina, on to the side of the Spartan Alliance.[2]

In central Greece the Boeotian League was the strongest ally. The geographical centre of the League was Thebes, and the Federal Council met and the Federal Treasury was placed on her acropolis, the Cadmea. The League's territory was divided into eleven cantons, each of which elected a general or 'Boeotarch', returned councillors and judges to the federal government, raised a contingent for the federal army, and contributed funds to the federal treasury. The cantons were equal units in the federal state, but they contained a varying number of political entities. Some cantons consisted of several small states and others of a single state, such as Tanagra. When the war broke out, a number of small states which had no fortifications looked to Thebes for protection and were granted the rights of a 'sympolity', whereby they retained their own citizenship but received the citizenship of Thebes. This Theban group made up two cantons, so that Thebes was able in 431 to influence the election of their two Boeotarchs. Thebes herself made up two cantons and returned two Boeotarchs. Thus her influence became dominant in the League. The Federal Council was divided into four separate Councils, of which one prepared the agenda and then sat in session with the other three. Decisions taken by a full session on a majority vote were binding on the member states. As regards the judicial and financial departments of the League we know only that the federal coinage, bearing the emblem of defence, the Boeotian shield, was minted at Thebes and bore her name from 446 onwards. Each member state was governed by an oligarchy in which those of hoplite

---

[1] 1. 84–85; 7. 18. 2; 2. 8. 4.
[2] D.S. 12. 30. 4; Th. 1. 38. 2–4; 3. 86. 2; *GC* 117 f.

census and above had equal rights and they alone possessed the political franchise. The League was welded together by fear of its powerful neighbour, Athens, and the oligarchs were loyal to Sparta. Their country was rich in cereals, and their cavalry and infantry forces were larger than those of any other ally of Sparta.[1]

The aim of the Spartan Alliance was to break the power of Athens and dissolve the Athenian empire. The strategic plan of Sparta was to offer a decisive battle and, if that offer was refused, to ravage Attica. At sea she could not as yet take the offensive. She instructed her allies to build ships and collect a specified sum of money for putting them into service. As some years would pass before the naval programme was fulfilled, they were meanwhile to avoid any engagement with the Athenian fleet. When their fleet was ready, they would enter the Aegean in strength and raise the subjects of Athens in revolt.[2]

Athens had an army in Attica which consisted of 1,200 cavalry, including mounted archers, 13,000 first-line hoplites, 16,000 reserve hoplites, and some thousands of light-armed troops, including 1,600 archers. She could also conscript hoplites and light-armed troops from her cleruchies, colonies, and allies. To these could be added the fine cavalry of her ally Thessaly. The strategy of Pericles, however, was not to engage the Peloponnesians in a pitched battle. He proposed to abandon Attica and move the flocks and herds to the islands. The reserve hoplites would defend the massive walls encircling Athens and the Peiraeus and the three Long Walls from Athens to Peiraeus and Phalerum, which made the city and suburbs into a single fortress with access to the sea. The first-line hoplites would be free to participate in a naval offensive. In 431 Athens had 300 triremes in commission, to which she could add the fleets of Lesbos, Chios, and Corcyra. Her own ships were manned by skilled seamen from Athens and the subject states, and her tactics in battle were far superior to those of the Peloponnesians. The navy would operate, as it had done in 458–454, forcing engagements at sea and making seaborne landings on the coasts of the Peloponnese; and, if occasion arose, it might establish fortified posts on enemy territory. In order to mount a wide offensive, Pericles had need of naval bases. These were available in Naupactus, Acarnania, and Zacynthos in the west and in the Cyclades in the east, except Melos and Thera, which were neutral. Pericles also had need of funds, since ships were expensive to maintain and the crews were in receipt of pay, quite apart from the cost of importing large quantities of foodstuffs into Athens. Here, however, he had great reserves—7,000 talents or more, apart from the gold on the statue of the goddess—and a current revenue of some 1,000 talents a year (600 from the empire and 400 from internal revenue) apart from any levies on wealth in private hands.[3]

[1] 4. 91; 5. 38; 3. 62. 3–5; *Hell. Oxy.* 11–12; *GC* 156.
[2] 1. 118. 2; 2. 7. 2 (the number 500 is probably corrupt); 2. 22. 3.
[3] 1. 143. 4–5; 2. 13. 2–9; 2. 7. 3; 2. 9. 4–5; X. *An.* 7. 1. 27; see above, p. 326, n. 1.

In adopting this strategy Pericles was guided by past experience. The Athenian army might hold its own in one battle, as it had done at Tanagra; but it could not face a series of battles; for Athens had no reserves of manpower, whereas the enemy had unlimited reserves. Moreover, Athens was not free to commit all her forces against the Peloponnesians. She had also to keep her empire in hand and be on guard against Persia and any large maritime land power. The disaster of 454 in Egypt had shown him the folly of dissipating Athens' strength in any third theatre of war. Experience had shown that a naval offensive against the Peloponnese was likely to wear down the enemy and force Sparta to sue for peace. If the terms were adverse to Sparta's allies, the Spartan Alliance was likely to split along the line of diverse interest, and Sparta would then be isolated and exposed. The Athenian empire might absorb the maritime states of the Peloponnese and administer the *coup de grâce* to Sparta. If the strategy of Pericles was defensive in Attica, it was offensive by sea. He aimed at complete victory over the Spartan Alliance and Sparta herself, the state against which he had consistently directed his policy.

The strategy of Pericles was realistic. It recognized the inferiority of Athenian land power and the superiority of Athenian finance and sea power. In a war of attrition which was likely to ensue, because neither side could strike a decisive blow at the other, Pericles' strategy involved Athens in no serious risks and gave an assurance of ultimate victory. In the judgement of Thucydides it was the correct strategy, despite the unforeseen disasters which fell later on the state. In 431 it was an unpopular strategy. To more than half the citizen body, and that the more well-to-do half, it meant the loss of their property in the countryside. To the younger generation it seemed reminiscent of the last great war against the Peloponnesians, unadventurous and indecisive. To the hoplite forces it grew to be a source of humiliation, and the disparity in numbers came to be regarded as a disparity in fighting quality. The opposition was led by Cleon, who advocated a more vigorous policy and set upon the elderly statesman. In 431 the authority of Pericles prevailed. His strategy was accepted by the Assembly. Its continuation depended not only on the chances of war but also on the chances of political leadership in Athens.[1]

On a dark night in March 431 the gates of Plataea were opened by a Plataean citizen to admit a force of 300 hoplites from Thebes. Their request, that Plataea enter the Boeotian League, was accepted, but as the night wore on the small number of the Thebans became known to the Plataeans, of whom the majority wished to preserve their alliance with Athens. Just before dawn the Plataeans attacked. Of the Thebans and their supporters 180 were taken prisoner, the rest falling in the battle. The main Theban force, which had intended to arrive at dawn but had been delayed by heavy rain, approached the wall of the town and was met by a Plataean herald. The two

[1] 1. 143. 5; 144. 1; 2. 13. 2; 65. 5, 7 and 13; Plu. *Per.* 33 fin. (Hermippus); [X.] *Ath.* 2. 1 (cf. 1. 2, 1. 15, 2. 2–5, 2. 14, and 2. 16, which reflect the ideas expressed by Pericles).

states, he declared, were at peace; if the Theban force withdrew, the Theban prisoners in Plataea would be liberated; if not, they would be executed. The Theban force then withdrew. The Plataeans executed their prisoners, maintaining later that the agreement had not been formally ratified, and sent a request to Athens for help. The Athenians placed a garrison in the town. The non-combatant population was evacuated and supplies were brought in, so that Plataea was ready to withstand a siege.[1]

Both sides regarded the incident at Plataea as an act of open war, because two participants in the Thirty Years Treaty had committed hostilities against one another. Athens and Sparta now made their final preparations. They approached the neutral Greek states, Persia, and other non-Greek powers for terms of alliance. In May the Spartan king, Archidamus, led the great army of the Spartan Alliance northwards from the Isthmus. His hoplites, representing two-thirds of the full levy, far outnumbered the infantry forces of Athens. Nevertheless, he proceeded with deliberate slowness, hoping to prolong the nervous tension at Athens and provoke the Athenians into an engagement. Before reaching the Attic frontier he sent a herald to the city, who was refused admission in accordance with a decree, proposed by Pericles, not to treat with Sparta once her army moved north of the Isthmus. As the herald departed, he spoke the long-remembered words: 'this day will be the beginning of great disasters for the Greeks'. Archidamus then delayed at the frontier fortress of Oenoe, which he failed to take by assault, and from there advanced in mid-June to Eleusis, where his soldiers destroyed the standing corn and the fruit trees. Meanwhile, in obedience to the orders of Pericles, the Athenians were bringing their women and children and possessions into the city and driving their flocks towards Euboea. When Archidamus advanced into the rich deme of Acharnae and his army lay within sight, the indignation in the city rose and the strategy of Pericles was bitterly criticized, especially by the younger men who wished to attack the enemy. Pericles, however, entrusted with sole charge of the operations, called no assembly of the people. He kept all his forces inside the walls, except a flying squadron of Athenian and Thessalian cavalry, until the Peloponnesians had ravaged the plain between Mt. Parnes and Mt. Pentelicus and withdrawn from view northwards to Boeotia. While they were still on Attic soil, Pericles passed to the naval offensive for which preparations had already been made.[2]

From late June until early autumn a fleet of 100 triremes, carrying 1,000 hoplites and 400 archers and reinforced by 50 Corcyraean ships and other allies in the west, operated continuously round the coast of the Peloponnese and in the approaches to the Gulf of Corinth. They began to close the net around Corinth by capturing two of her dependencies, Sollium and Astacus in Acarnania, and by winning over the large island of Cephallenia; and their sudden raids on the Peloponnesian coast were successful, except at Methone

[1] 2. 2–7. See Appendix 5.   [2] 2. 7–23; Ar. *Ach.* 65.

in Laconia, where a young Spartan officer named Brasidas broke through the Athenian force with a hundred Lacedaemonian hoplites, entered the walled town, and saved it from capture. Another fleet of thirty ships ravaged the coast of Locris, captured Thronium, and defeated the Locrian troops; the island of Atalante was then fortified and garrisoned as a naval base in the Euboean Channel, through which the convoys passed to Chalcidice. There the navy was supplying 3,000 Athenian hoplites who were blockading Potidaea and resisting attacks from the Chalcidians of Olynthus, now supported once again by Perdiccas of Macedonia. In this area Athens won a diplomatic success by gaining the alliance of Sitalces, the king of the Odrysian empire in Thrace, and through his agency the alliance of Perdiccas, to whom the Athenians restored Therma at the head of the Thermaic Gulf. They were thus able to isolate the Chalcidic peninsula. During the summer the whole population of Aegina was ejected and Athenian settlers occupied the island. In the autumn, when the Peloponnesians had gone home, an Athenian army of 13,000 hoplites and many light-armed infantry overran the Megarid, ravaging the countryside.[1]

In the first campaigning season of the war the preparedness of Athens proved of great advantage to her. Already in 433/432 building on the Acropolis had stopped so that money could be diverted to armaments and defences. In 431, when the Peloponnesians withdrew from Attica, 1,000 talents and 100 triremes were set aside as a reserve to be used only if the enemy attacked Attica by sea, and regular guard-posts were manned by the army and the navy. In addition Athens deployed more than 17,000 hoplites of her own and some 250 Athenian and allied triremes, of which the crews numbered some 45,000 men. Against this array of naval strength the Peloponnesians made no move, since their preparations were still under way; only in the winter, when the Athenian fleet had withdrawn, did a Corinthian fleet come out of the Gulf. With forty ships and 1,500 hoplites they recaptured Astacus but were unsuccesssful in a raid on Cephallenia. On land the Peloponnesians had failed to bring Athens to battle and had been inactive since the invasion; Sparta did no more than settle the Aeginetan refugees in Laconia. The initiative was firmly in the hands of Athens. In March 430 the people chose the statesman whom they considered most eminent in prestige and most wise in policy to deliver the funeral speech in honour of the fallen. The choice fell upon Pericles, and he delivered the speech which was recorded by Thucydides, who had already begun to takes notes for his history of the war.[2]

In early summer 430 the Peloponnesian army invaded and ravaged Attica for forty days. At the same time a terrible plague broke out in the crowded cities of Peiraeus and Athens, where the refugees from the countryside were

---

[1] 2. 25–32; Plu. *Per.* 34; Ar. *Ach.* 141; *SEG.* 10. 223.
[2] 2. 24; 3. 17 (whether this chapter is spurious or not, the numbers are about right); 1. 1; *GHI* 51.

squatting in shacks on waste land or in the precincts of the temples or in the fortifications themselves. Water-supplies were inadequate, especially in the Peiraeus, where the rain-tanks on which the people depended were soon fouled. Under such conditions the contagion spread apace. Medical skill was of no avail. Those who tended the sick were immediately infected. A prostrating melancholy was followed by a burning inflammation of the eyes, throat, and lungs, by coughing, ineffectual retching, and unquenchable thirst. Many died at this stage of the disease, on the sixth or eighth day of illness, and others succumbed to the final phase, ulceration of the stomach and diarrhoea. Men died like sheep; corpses accumulated in heaps and were burnt as chance offered. Of those who survived the disease many were afflicted with blindness, amnesia, or maimed extremities. Nothing protected men from its attack—not physical strength, nor piety nor wealth—and only those who had once survived the disease felt any security that they would live. Lawlessness and crime became general, as men quickly lost all respect for religious and social canons of behaviour. During the horrors of the plague the oracle of Apollo was recalled, that if the Spartans prosecuted the war with vigour the god would aid their cause. As the smoke rose from their farmsteads and the city stank with the dead, the citizens turned against Pericles who had instigated them to go to war. They tried to obtain suitable terms of peace from Sparta, but in vain.

In these dark days Pericles called upon the people to put loyalty to the state before the thought of their personal suffering. The greatness of Athens was not only of the past and the present but also of the future. Her spirit would again rise superior to distress and calamity, and her unimpaired sea power would carry her conquests to the ends of the world. The people rallied to his call and applied themselves vigorously to the war, but their personal animosity was not satisfied until they had put him on trial and fined him. Later they re-elected him general and reinstated him as their war-leader. In the autumn of 429 he died, a victim of the plague. His death alone may have been more harmful to the state than the loss of manpower which resulted from the prevalence of the disease in 430 and 429. For he could hold the people to his own cautious and intelligent strategy in the war, and even after the plague the strength of Athens was still sufficient, in the opinion of Thucydides, to secure victory over the Peloponnesians. The plague became virulent again in the winter of 427–6 and lasted through 426. When it ended, one third of Athens' first-line troops were dead and many others were maimed, while the casualties among the rest of the population were unnumbered. This calamity, paralleled only by the great earthquake at Sparta in 464, hardened the attitude of Athens and undermined her social morale as well as her power in war.[1]

When the plague was beginning at Athens and the Peloponnesians were

[1] 2. 17; 47–54; 59–65; 3. 87; Plu. *Per.* 34–38; the plague was probably typhus or measles, the former being more likely. *Gk. Lit. Pap.* n. 38 (referring probably to the trial of Pericles).

in Attica, a large force of 100 Athenian triremes, fifty Lesbian and Chian triremes, and a number of cavalry transports bore down on the eastern coast of the Peloponnese and ravaged the countryside with a striking force of 4,000 hoplites and 300 cavalry. The same force went on to Potidaea, where all attempts to assault the town were ineffective; moreover, as they had called in at Athens on the way, the troops carried the plague with them and a quarter of them died within forty days of their arrival. During the winter of 430–429 the supplies in Potidaea came to an end, and the defenders even had recourse to cannibalism before they sued for terms. They were allowed to depart with one garment for the men, two for the women, and some money for the journey, and they found refuge with their allies, the Chalcidians and the Bottiaeans. The blockade of Potidaea had cost Athens 2,000 talents and heavy casualties over a period of more than two years.

The revolt still continued in the Chalcidic peninsula. Athenian settlers occupied Potidaea and afforded a strong base for the operations of 429, which were conducted by 2,000 hoplites, 200 cavalry, and a force of light-armed infantry from Athens against the fortified city of Spartolus. But the Athenians were caught in the open by the fine Chalcidian cavalry and light-armed peltasts, who were equipped with a throwing spear and a leather shield. Under their continuous attacks the slow-moving Athenian hoplites, unable to come to grips, broke in a panic and withdrew to Potidaea, leaving 400 men and all their generals dead on the field of battle. In the autumn of 429 Sitalces came to Athens' aid with a huge army, estimated at 150,000 men, which included the most warlike peoples of his extensive empire. The Athenians had agreed to send ships and infantry to help him; but they made no move, fearing he would keep any area he conquered. For a month the Thracian hordes ravaged Chalcidice, Bottiaea, and Macedonia, opposed only for a short time by the heavy-armed Macedonian cavalry, which showed its superiority over the Odrysians and the Getae. Sitalces then withdrew, leaving the position unchanged, save that Perdiccas formed a marriage-alliance with Seuthes, the nephew and general of Sitalces. For the next four years Athens conducted no operations against Chalcidice.[1]

In 430 and 429, when Athens was suffering from the plague and concentrating her main effort against Chalcidice, the Peloponnesians had a chance to take the initiative. They were chiefly concerned to shake off the Athenian grip in the west. Two unsuccessful attempts were made in 430, one by 100 Peloponnesian ships and 1,000 hoplites against Zacynthos and the other by Ambracia against Amphilochian Argos. Athens replied in the winter of 430–429 by sending twenty triremes under the command of Phormion to Naupactus, where they attacked merchant ships passing through the narrows at Rhium. In 429 Ambracia and Sparta planned a combined operation in this theatre. They intended to conquer Acarnania, Cephallenia, Zacynthos, and

[1] 2. 56; 58; 70; 95–101; D.S. 12. 46. 7 (Athens sent 1,000 colonists to Potidaea); *SEG* 10. 223.

perhaps Naupactus, so that Athens would be deprived of intermediate bases in the west and her ally Corcyra would be isolated. With this end in view a Spartan commander, Cnemus, crossed the Corinthian Gulf with 1,000 Peloponnesian hoplites and made his way to Ambraciote territory. There he took under his command the hoplites of Ambracia, Leucas, and Anactorium and a large number of light-armed troops recruited from the hinterland, namely 1,000 Chaonians together with other Epirote tribesmen and 1,000 Orestians from the Macedonian side of the Pindus range. He did not wait for the arrival of 1,000 Macedonian infantry, who had been sent secretly by Perdiccas, then in name an ally of Athens. The squadrons of Ambracia, Leucas, and Anactorium had already mustered at Leucas for the attack by sea; there they awaited the coming of the main Peloponnesian fleet from Corinth, Sicyon, and other places in the Corinthian Gulf. Cnemus rashly decided to act at once. He marched towards the Acarnanian capital, Stratus, a fortified city. His large army proceeded in three separate columns, often out of sight of one another, and the Chaonians rushing impetuously ahead with the other Epirotes fell into an ambush and were routed. Their defeat disheartened the troops of Cnemus, who remained in their camp that day under the fire of the Acarnanian slingers and then withdrew to the walls of their ally, Oeniadae, where they broke up and dispersed homewards.[1]

Meanwhile, Phormion, who had refused the Acarnanian request for help, was waiting for the appearance of the main Peloponnesian fleet. When forty-seven triremes and many smaller vessels hove in sight heading along the south side of the Gulf, Phormion led his twenty triremes along the north shore and barred the crossing towards Acarnania. That night the Peloponnesians put out from Patrae, hoping to cross unobserved, but they were intercepted in the open waters west of Rhium (see Fig. 22). In the dim light before dawn they formed their warships into a circle, prows outward and sterns inward, and rested on their oars in the calm sea; inside the circle their five best warships were placed to reinforce the outer ring at any point and the smaller vessels were huddled together in the centre. Phormion did not intend to employ the customary boarding tactics of the Peloponnesians, which the Athenians had witnessed at the battle of Sybota; for he was out-numbered and he knew the enemy ships were heavy with infantry. He ordered his ships to await his signal for the attack and meanwhile to row in single column round and round the enemy circle, brushing close and feigning attack, so that the Peloponnesians backed water and gradually contracted their circle. When the wind for which Phormion was waiting blew out of the Gulf with the rays of the rising sun and ruffled the surface of the water, the stationary ships of the Peloponnesians were blown foul of one another in the confined space. Men leapt up to stave off the neighbouring vessels with poles, the air rang with shouts of abuse and the orders of the boatswains went un-heeded; even where the crews stayed at their oars, they found it difficult in

[1] 2. 66; 68; 80–82.

the rising sea to feather their oars, and their ships, not being under way, answered sluggishly to the sweeps which served as a rudder. At this juncture Phormion gave the signal and the Athenians rowed in to ram the enemy broadsides. Wherever they attacked, they crippled their opponents and chased the remainder in flight towards Patrae and Dyme. Without loss to themselves the Athenians captured twelve triremes during the pursuit and then returned to Naupactus, while the remnant of the Peloponnesian force sailed westward to Cyllene in Elis.

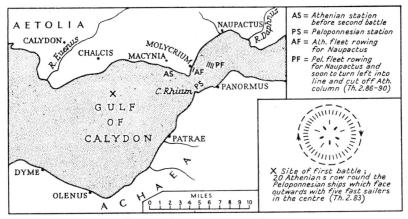

FIG. 22. Actions off Rhium in 429

There they found Cnemus and his Peloponnesians, who had been transported by the ships which had mustered at Leucas. The authorities at Sparta, informed of the humiliating defeat at sea, sent three commissioners, of whom one was Brasidas, with orders to muster more ships and attack Phormion. He meanwhile sent to Athens for reinforcements, but they had not arrived when seventy-seven Peloponnesian triremes, stripped for action, advanced to the narrows at Rhium and lay close inshore to their supporting land force on the Peloponnesian coast. Phormion placed his twenty ships inshore to the opposite coast, where the Messenian hoplites from Naupactus were in position, but westwards of the narrows, so that he had open waters for manœuvring.

After a delay of several days the Peloponnesian commanders formed their plan. As they lay closer than the Athenians to the now undefended naval base at Naupactus, they decided to sail northwards in the hope that Phormion would follow through the narrows to protect Naupactus. At dawn the Peloponnesian fleet rowed towards Naupactus in column, four ships abreast with the twenty fastest sailers leading. Phormion hastily embarked his men, rowed in single column inshore past the narrows and made course for Naupactus. Thereupon the Peloponnesian ships turned left into line and rowed full speed ahead across the narrow waters, hoping to trap the extended Athenian column close inshore and without sea-room for manœuvre. Nine of the ships they charged and damaged, but the other eleven escaped into more open water, where they were pursued by the twenty fastest sailers of the Peloponnesian fleet. Of these eleven ships ten reached Naupactus and came round head-on towards the enemy. But the eleventh was hotly pursued by the leading Peloponnesian ship, a Leucadian, which had outdistanced her fellows. As the Athenian ship drew near Naupactus, she suddenly doubled round a merchantman, which happened to be riding out offshore, and rammed the Leucadian amidships. This brilliant manœuvre caused the Peloponnesian ships to stop their eager pursuit; some indeed had run aground on the shallows and the others lost way and rested on their oars, a foolish thing to do when they were already at close quarters. The Athenian ships immediately charged and drove them off in disorder towards Rhium, capturing six vessels and recovering the nine of their own which had been damaged at the beginning of the engagement. The Peloponnesian fleet then disbanded. Soon afterwards Phormion was reinforced by a squadron of twenty ships.[1]

The brilliant victories of Phormion saved and strengthened the position of Athens in the north-west. During the winter he toured Acarnania, ejecting those who were suspected of Peloponnesian sympathies, and in spring 428 he returned in triumph to Athens. His victories raised the morale of plague-stricken Athens and dashed the hopes of Sparta at sea; for, if the Peloponnesians could not form an effective fleet in their home waters, they had little chance of forming one in the Aegean. After the second defeat by Phormion, in order to restore the confidence of their troops, Cnemus, Brasidas, and the other commanders planned a raid on the Peiraeus. The crews crossed the Isthmus, each man carrying his oar, thole-strap and cushion, and during the night they launched forty triremes which the Megarians had had in dry dock for two years. But, as the ships made water, the courage of the Peloponnesians sank. They ravaged Salamis instead. When the fire-signals flared up on the island, panic seized Peiraeus and Athens, but no attack developed. At dawn the Peloponnesians returned to Megara with spoil and prisoners, and the Athenians laid booms off the Peiraeus harbours and mounted guards against any surprise attack. Up to this time the Peloponnesians had done nothing in Aegean waters except send out single raiders against Athenian merchantmen off the Carian coast and execute any enemy or neutral seamen who were caught off the coasts of the Peloponnese. When the opportunity for naval action came in the Aegean, they were ill prepared and their methods had begun to alienate the sympathies of the islanders.[2]

In summer 429 Sparta employed her superiority on land to approach Plataea, the small state which had fought so heroically in the Persian War that the members of the Greek League had undertaken to protect her from

[1] 2. 83–92. See the model of a trireme in Plate IV.   [2] 2. 102–3; 93–94; 69; 67. 4.

aggression for all time. Archidamus offered to respect Plataea as a neutral, if she would renounce her alliance with Athens and withdraw from the war. The Plataeans were allowed to consult the Athenians, who urged them to preserve the alliance and promised to help them to the best of their ability. Plataea then refused the offer of Archidamus, and he felt himself justified in ordering an assault on the city. But every attempt was beaten back by the garrison of 400 Plataeans and 80 Athenians, for whom food was cooked by 110 Plataean women. The assault was abandoned, and by the autumn of 429 Plataea was invested with a double wall of mud-brick, within which a strong Peloponnesian and Boeotian garrison was stationed. Athens made no attempt to relieve the beleaguered town. If she could not save her own country-side, she could not hope to hold Plataea. On the other hand, the siege of Plataea, which was to extend over two years, exacted from the Peloponnesians a cost in money and in men which was quite disproportionate to the strategic value of the town.[1]

In 428 the Peloponnesians did not resume operations in the west. An Athenian fleet of thirty sail ravaged the coast of Laconia and detached twelve ships, which proceeded to Naupactus, joined the Acarnanians in an abortive attack on Oeniadae, and suffered heavy loss in a raid on Nericus near Leucas. In this theatre both sides had reached a stalemate: the Peloponnesians could not dislodge the Athenians, and the Athenians with only twelve ships and no active aid from Zacynthos, Cephallenia, and Corcyra were unable to impose any effective blockade on merchantmen sailing to the Peloponnese. In 428 the Peloponnesians ravaged Attica again and maintained the investment of Plataea, both actions being more damaging to Athenian morale than to Athens' military power. Athens herself was still too weak to take the initiative. In the south Aegean she had forced Thera to pay tribute, but she had failed to win over Cydonia in north-west Crete. The southern route was thus still open to Peloponnesian raiders and to merchantmen serving the Peloponnese. In Chalcidice Athens achieved little after the capture of Potidaea. Neither side had been able to enlist the support of Persia. The Peloponnesian envoys, who had set out in 430 to reach the court of the Great King, had been arrested in Thrace by Sitalces and delivered to the Athenians, who executed them without trial.[2]

§ 2. *Athens comes close to victory, 428–424*

THE general stalemate in all theatres of war was broken in June 428 by the revolt of Lesbos, the largest and richest island in the east Aegean. The organizer of the revolt was Mitylene. She was planning to unite the Lesbian cities under her political control and to build more ships, improve her fortifications, and bring in supplies of wheat and mercenary archers. But her plans were betrayed to Athens. Alarmed by memories of the Samian revolt, the Athenians proceeded promptly and cautiously to secure Methymna, the

[1] 2. 71–78.   [2] 3. 7; 3. 1; 2. 85. 5–6; 67; Hdt. 7. 137; *IG* i.[2] 216–17.

only state in the island which remained loyal to them, and to block the two harbours of Mitylene by establishing fortified naval bases on each side of the city. Meanwhile the Mitylenians sent envoys twice to Sparta, asking urgently for alliance and stressing the strength of the Mitylenian fleet. At the Olympic festival in August 428 they addressed the representatives of the Spartan Alliance. It was, they said, a unique opportunity for the Peloponnesians. Lesbos and Chios were the only states in the Athenian empire which possessed a fleet. If the Peloponnesians sent aid to Mitylene and at the same time attacked Athens by land and by sea, they would raise a general revolt in the Aegean and take advantage of Athens' weakness after the years of plague and of heavy financial outlay. The Spartan Alliance received Lesbos as an ally and undertook to act in accordance with the suggestions of the Mitylenian envoys. Sparta ordered two-thirds of the allied levies to muster for a second invasion of Attica and began to make preparations for the transportation of warships from the Corinthian to the Saronic Gulf. Their energy was not imitated by their allies. In the hills the Peloponnesians were still bringing in their harvest, having no Helots to do it for them, and they were tired of campaigning, year after year. So they mustered slowly and reluctantly. Meanwhile the Athenians made a fine display of vigour. They already had 70 ships at sea—30 rounding the Peloponnese and 40 blocking the harbours of Mitylene—but they manned another 100 ships with every available citizen below the level of the cavalry class and proceeded to ravage the eastern coast of the Peloponnese. The Spartans thereupon abandoned their plan of invading Attica. They issued orders to their allies to equip 40 ships for the sailing season of 427.

The dilatoriness of the Spartan Alliance and the energy of Athens sealed the fate of Mitylene. For, when the Spartans abandoned their plan, Athens threw 1,000 hoplites into the island and invested Mitylene by land and by sea. As provisions grew short and still no help came from the Peloponnese, the Mitylenian oligarchs found themselves in a desperate situation, and, on the advice of a Lacedaemonian, Salaethus, who had made his way into the city during the winter, they armed the common people with a view to making a sortie. But the people, with arms in their hands, grouped together and threatened to surrender the city to the Athenians. The oligarchs then surrendered to Paches, the Athenian commander, under an agreement that Mitylenian envoys should go to Athens and the Athenian people should decide the terms.

A week later forty-two Peloponnesian ships, commanded by the Spartan Alcidas, reached the Asiatic coast at Embatum without the knowledge of Paches. The Peloponnesians had invaded Attica in May and stayed on so that the Athenian forces were occupied in manning the walls. Meanwhile Alcidas had slowly and timorously led his squadron from Cape Taenarum via Delos, Icaria and Myconos to Embatum. Thence, instead of attacking Paches' army at Mitylene or seizing a base in Ionia with a view to raising a general revolt and enlisting the support of the Persian satrap, Pissuthnes, as his advisers suggested, Alcidas withdrew to Ephesus and then fled south-westwards for the Peloponnese, hotly pursued by the squadron of Paches. He crowned his craven withdrawal by butchering any seamen he captured, until the Samians warned him that he was making enemies of all who were friendly to the Peloponnesian cause. When Alcidas had gone, Paches ejected a medizing party which was in control at Notium and secured the place with Colophonian exiles and later with Athenian settlers. He then rounded up the instigators of the revolt in Lesbos and sent them with Salaethus to Athens, where the Mitylenian envoys awaited a hearing.

At Athens the people's nerve had been shaken by the news that the Peloponnesian fleet was out in the Aegean. When the danger passed, they were passionately angry. Salaethus was executed at once, and the Assembly met to decide the fate of Lesbos. Since the death of Pericles no statesman had gained the ascendancy, and the aspirants to power tended to comply with the mood of the people. On this occasion Cleon, a man whose vigour verged on violence, proposed and carried a resolution to execute every adult male in Mitylene and enslave the rest. A trireme departed with the order for Paches to act without delay. Next day the mood of the people changed and they repented of their cruel decision. The Assembly met again. Cleon defended the resolution of the previous day, on the grounds that in time of war an imperial power cannot afford to make concessions and must punish rebellion with death. His chief opponent, Diodotus, maintained that such terroristic methods would not prevent any subject-state from rebelling but only prolong its resistance to the bitter end, while the destruction of Mitylene would simply reduce the revenues of Athens. The voting was almost equal, but the proposal of Diodotus to rescind the previous resolution was carried by a narrow margin. A second trireme set off post-haste, the men eating as they rowed and sleeping in relays, and reached Mitylene harbour at the moment when Paches had read the order delivered by the first trireme and was about to put it into execution. Thus the walls of Mitylene were dismantled instead, their ships were surrendered and they were deprived of their possessions on the Asiatic coast. All the land on the island, except the territory of Methymna, was divided into 3,000 lots of which 300 were dedicated to the gods and the remainder allocated to support Athenian settlers; the Lesbians worked the land and paid 100 talents a year in rent. On the proposal of Cleon the instigators of the revolt, who had been held at Athens, were put to death. They numbered rather more than a thousand.[1]

Soon after the reduction of Lesbos supplies at Plataea ran out. The garrison numbered now some 200 Plataeans and twenty-five Athenians, apart from the women; for the remainder had made a brilliant escape during a stormy night in midwinter. Incapable of further resistance, the garrison surrendered to the

---

[1] 3. 2–6; 8–16; 18; 25–50; *GHI* 63 and *ATL* 2. 76; Arist. *Pol.* 1304ᵃ4. Some consider the figure 1,000 incorrect.

Spartan commander, on condition that they should receive a fair trial by a Spartan court. Five judges were sent from Sparta. They summoned the Plataeans and asked them only one question, whether they had rendered any service to the Spartan Alliance in the war. The Plataeans protested against this form of trial, and they were eventually allowed to speak of their services against the Persians and of their obligation to their ally, Athens. Theban representatives then addressed the judges, demanding vengeance for their citizens who had been killed as prisoners by the Plataeans at the beginning of the war. The Spartan judges summoned the Plataeans man by man and asked them the same one question. As each man answered that he had rendered no such service, he was taken off and executed. The Athenian prisoners, too, were put to the sword, and the women were enslaved. The town was later razed to the ground, and its lands were incorporated in those of Thebes.[1]

The massacre of the prisoners after the capitulation of Lesbos and Plataea was contrary to the general convention of Greek warfare. In the treatment of a conquered state practice varied: Sparta did not enslave her enemies except in the Messenian wars, whereas Argos and Athens did so on several occasions. Prisoners of war were normally exchanged, ransomed, or held until the conclusion of a treaty of peace. From the outset the Peloponnesian War had been marked by acts of brutality. The Plataeans slew their prisoners, the Spartans killed allied and neutral seamen, and the Athenians executed the Peloponnesians envoys whom Sitalces sent to them. The executions of prisoners from Mitylene and Plataea were more flagrant, in that they were masked by a form of judicial procedure and were decided in cold blood. Another evil aspect of the war was the embittering of civil strife between oligarchs and democrats, who were often able to call in the great powers. Epidamnus, Plataea, Mitylene, and Notium afforded examples.

In 427 a more terrible civil strife broke out in Corcyra, a state which might swing the balance of naval power in the west and was therefore of great importance to Athens and Sparta. Bloodshed began when the oligarchs, of whom five had been condemned by the democrats to pay a large fine, burst into the Council and assassinated sixty of their opponents. They had already seized power when a Corinthian trireme carrying some Spartan envoys arrived. Encouraged by their presence, the oligarchs attacked the democrats. During the fighting both sides began to arm the slaves, part of the town was burnt, and the democrats got the upper hand. At this juncture the Athenians arrived with twelve ships and 500 Messenian hoplites and managed to stop the fighting. A few days later a Peloponnesian fleet of fifty-three ships, commanded by Alcidas, to whom Brasidas was attached as an adviser, came up to Sybota on the coast of Epirus. When they advanced at dawn towards Corcyra, the Corcyraeans manned sixty vessels and sailed out in confusion. Two ships deserted at once; in others the crew fought among themselves; thirteen were captured by the Peloponnesians. But the Athenian ships held

[1] 3. 20–24; 52–68.

their own. They attacked the wing of the Peloponnesian fleet, which broke off and formed into a circle. The Athenians began to row round them, as they had done in the Gulf of Corinth, and then, when the rest of the Peloponnesian fleet came up, the Athenians backed water slowly in formation and the Peloponnesians did not dare to close with them. Next day Alcidas ravaged the southern promontory of the island. In Corcyra the democrats came to terms with the oligarchs, and between them they manned thirty ships. But that evening Alcidas learnt by fire-signal from Leucas that an Athenian fleet was sailing up from the south. He coasted along from Sybota to Leucas at night and escaped unobserved. When the Athenian fleet of sixty ships arrived, the democrats had begun to slaughter the oligarchs and their supporters, many of whom committed suicide rather than fall into their fellow-countrymen's hands. No sanctuary was respected, no human relationship revered. For a week, while the Athenian fleet lay in the harbour, the massacre proceeded. Even so a number of oligarchs escaped. Later they returned and waged a guerrilla war for two years, until the Athenian fleet again intervened.[1]

The protagonists, too, were feeling the strain of the war by 427. In the Peloponnese supplies were short. The second invasion of Attica in autumn 428 was postponed partly because the garnering of the harvest was of great importance; and the wellwishers of Sparta at this time were sending her wheat and raisins as well as money. The productivity of Attica and Athens had declined with the ravaging of her land and the effects of the plague. In 428 she exacted a capital levy (*eisphora*) from her wealthy citizens and metics, which realized 200 talents, and began to increase the tribute of her subjects.[2]

Although her financial reserves were running down, Athens made further efforts to attack by sea and cut off any source of supply or reinforcement for the enemy. In summer 427 Nicias took and garrisoned the island Minoa, from which the port of Megara, Nisaea, was effectively blockaded; and in summer 426 he ravaged Tanagra in Boeotia and the seaboard of Locris. His major operation that summer was an attack on the island of Melos, a friend of Sparta, with sixty ships and 2,000 hoplites. But the Melians refused to enter the Athenian empire. Late in 427 Athens sent twenty ships to Sicily, to help her allies Leontini and Rhegium in their war against Syracuse and the Dorian states, which were nominally in alliance with Sparta, and in summer 426 her forces captured Mylae and Messana, thus gaining control of the straits between Italy and Sicily. Further operations in the north-west were launched by an enterprising general, Demosthenes, with a squadron of thirty ships in summer 426. He raised large forces from Acarnania, Zacynthos, Cephallenia, and Corcyra, ravaged the territory of Leucas, and was about to invest the town of Leucas from the landward side, when the Messenians of Naupactus persuaded him to campaign in Aetolia.[3]

---

[1] 2. 103; 3. 70. 1; 69-85; for the killing of prisoners see E. *Heracl.* 962 f.
[2] 3. 13. 3; 19; Plu. *Arist.* 24; Ar. *Eq.* 313; 924.
[3] 3. 51; 91; 86; 90; 94; *GHI* 62 (Melos' gifts to Sparta).

Demosthenes entertained an ambitious plan, to subdue or win over all the peoples of central Greece up to the borders of Boeotia. The plan marked a departure from the strategy of Pericles. For Demosthenes proposed to undertake a new commitment on land, where the enemy had superior resources, and he no doubt envisaged an attack on Boeotia by the Athenian army. In this matter he may have counted on some support in Athens; for at about the same time in the summer of 426 when Nicias landed troops by sea to raid Tanagra, the full Athenian army marched out to join him in Boeotia. Demosthenes' plan failed miserably in Aetolia. The Corcyraeans and the Acarnanians refused to participate; the light-armed troops of his allies, the Ozolian Locrians, were slow to muster; and the Aetolian tribes combined with unexpected unanimity. After overrunning a few unfortified villages Demosthenes' force of hoplites and archers, which had not yet been joined by the Locrians, found themselves surrounded in wild country by a swarm of Aetolian mountaineers, armed with the throwing spear and the sling. Once the archers had shot their arrows, the Aetolians darted in and out and struck down the cumbrous hoplites with their missiles. The Athenians and their allies broke and fled. Perhaps half reached the coast, where the fleet awaited them. The Athenian survivors sailed for home, but Demosthenes stayed in Naupactus, being afraid to report his failure to the people. One lesson at least he had learnt, that an unsupported hoplite force was at the mercy of well-led skirmishers in hilly country. And to this lesson there was a corollary. Even if he had won over the tribes of Aetolia and entered Boeotia, their light-armed troops would have been at the mercy of the Boeotian cavalry and hoplites in the Boeotian plains.[1]

The failure of Demosthenes encouraged Sparta to undertake a campaign with the Aetolians against the Athenian possessions and allies in the northwest. In this same summer of 426 Sparta had founded a large and powerful colony at Heraclea in Trachis, where she had the support of the tribesmen of Trachis and of Doris. Her forces at Heraclea could close the pass of Thermopylae, and her allies in Doris lay athwart two routes, one from the Corinthian Gulf via Amphissa and the other from Boeotia via Phocis, which united at Cytinium in Doris before descending towards the Malian plain. If Sparta held both Cytinium and Heraclea in strength, she could cut the communications of Thessaly, an ally of Athens, with the south and perhaps push northwards to join hands with the Chalcidians and Bottiaeans. Heraclea also was close to the Euboean Channel. The colonists began to build docks, intending to attack Athenian shipping in the Channel and ravage Euboea. In the autumn of 426 they sent 500 hoplites to Delphi, whither a Peloponnesian force of 2,500 hoplites crossed under the command of a Spartan general, Eurylochus. Faced by so formidable an army, the Ozolian Locrians offered no resistance except at Oeneon and Eupalium, which were taken by assault. The Aetolians then helped Eurylochus to capture Molycrium and an open suburb of

[1] 3. 94–98.

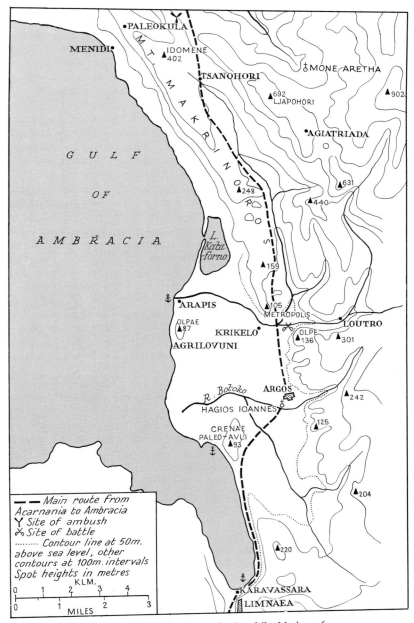

FIG. 23. The campaign in Amphilochia in 426

Naupactus. But Naupactus itself was saved by the prompt action of Demosthenes. For he had persuaded the Acarnanians to give him 1,000 hoplites, and he brought them by sea just in time to man the walls. As winter was at hand, Eurylochus passed on into west Aetolia and rested his troops. Meanwhile Ambracia was arming for a combined attack with Eurylochus upon Amphilochian Argos and Acarnania (Fig. 23).[1]

Aware of these preparations, the Acarnanians requested help from the commanders of twenty Athenian ships cruising off the Peloponnese and from Demosthenes who was at Naupactus. In the winter 3,000 hoplites from Ambracia occupied Olpae. The Acarnanians reinforced the garrison of Argos and occupied Crenae, hoping to intercept between these two points the army of Eurylochus as it came up by the main route from the south. He, however, made a detour, passed through the Acarnanian positions during the night and joined forces with the Ambraciotes. The combined army, numbering 6,000 hoplites and a few light-armed troops, encamped at Metropolis to the north of Argos and awaited the arrival of some reinforcements which had been summoned from Ambracia. Soon afterwards the twenty Athenian ships sailed into the Ambraciote Gulf, and Demosthenes came up with 200 Messenian hoplites and sixty Athenian archers. Being given precedence among the generals, Demosthenes pitched camp at Olpe which was close to Metropolis. His army was outnumbered and the proportion of hoplites to light-armed was smaller than in the army of Eurylochus; yet, if he waited, Eurylochus would be reinforced from Ambracia. He therefore offered battle. On the sixth day Eurylochus advanced to attack, himself commanding on the left wing. He was unaware that a force of some 300 Acarnanian hoplites and light-armed troops lay concealed in an advanced position outside his flank. As soon as he closed with the Messenians and the Athenians under Demosthenes' immediate command, the Acarnanians rose up, attacked his rear, and killed him and many of his men. Meanwhile the Ambraciotes and the Peloponnesians on the right wing had overcome their opponents and advanced towards Argos, but they then found themselves cut off by the victorious troops of Demosthenes and were driven in disorder to Olpae near the coast.

The successor of Eurylochus, a Spartan named Menedaïus, opened negotiations with Demosthenes and the Acarnanian commanders. His position was desperate. The remnants of his army held a waterless hill, and he was cut off by land and by sea. He entered into a secret agreement, whereby he and his Peloponnesians were to be passed through the enemy lines, leaving the Ambraciotes and the mercenary troops to their own devices. Meanwhile Demosthenes learnt that the reinforcements from Ambracia were on the march, and he sent troops northwards to occupy the passes and lay ambushes near Idomene. Menedaïus then moved his Peloponnesians in driblets into the plain, but his allies and his mercenary troops ran after them. The Acar-

[1] 3. 100–2; D.S. 12. 59. 5.

nanian soldiers, unaware of their commanders' agreement with Menedaïus, began to attack and a general *mêlée* ensued. The upshot was that Menedaïus and his Peloponnesians were eventually passed through the lines, and the allied and mercenary troops dispersed with some loss into the hills. Demosthenes then set off northwards, caught the Ambraciote reinforcements off their guard at dawn, and slew them almost to a man. For the Ambraciotes were unaware of the battle at Metropolis and its aftermath; they made no resistance at first to the Doric-speaking Messenians, whom they thought to be Ambraciotes; and, being mainly hoplites, they were outfought in the broken and wooded terrain by the light-armed forces of Demosthenes. Ambracia was almost completely stripped of its infantry, and Demosthenes proposed to attack its walls. But the Acarnanians refused. They had no wish to install an Athenian post in such close proximity to themselves. When the Athenian ships departed, Acarnania and Amphilochia formed a defensive alliance for a hundred years with Ambracia. Thereby the area ceased to be a theatre for active operations. During the winter Corinth succeeded in sending 300 hoplites overland to Ambracia and secured it against Athenian attack.[1]

These events damaged the prestige of Sparta and enhanced that of Demosthenes. Under his command a force, composed mainly of light-armed troops, had inflicted the first military defeat of the war on Peloponnesian and Ambraciote hoplites. Sparta abandoned the initiative in central Greece, where her colony at Heraclea was suffering under misrule by its Spartan magistrates and attacks from the Thessalians. She contented herself with an invasion of Attica in the spring of 425 and the dispatch of sixty Peloponnesian ships to Corcyra, where she hoped to overthrow the democrats. At Athens the people decided to reduce the rate of interest payable to Athena on loans of money for the war and to raise the tribute of her subjects to some 1,000 talents a year, apart from indemnities totalling some 200 talents.[2]

With these sums in prospect they equipped forty ships to sail round to Corcyra and then to reinforce the fleet in Sicilian waters, which had been making little headway. Demosthenes, who now held no office, was authorized by the people to accompany the expedition and to employ the troops against the Peloponnese, if he thought fit. It happened to be stormy when the fleet was off the Messenian coast, and the ships put in at Pylus, a rocky promontory on the seaward side of a sheltered harbour (see Fig. 24). Demosthenes wished to fortify the tip of the promontory, but the generals refused his request. When the bad weather continued, the troops relieved their boredom by raising a wall of rough stone and by strengthening it with clay, which they carried up on their backs, bending double and clasping their hands behind them. Six days later the weather cleared and the fleet sailed for Corcyra and Sicily, leaving Demosthenes with five ships at his strongpoint. The

---

[1] 3. 105–14; Polyaen. 3. 1. 2; *SIG* 81 (cf. *GHI* 65) and *IG* 2.[2] 403, 9. See *StGH* 471 ff.

[2] 4. 2; *GHI* 74; 66; Plu. *Arist.* 24; Ar. *Eq.* 839. The total sum is in dispute, some scholars putting the assessed total of tribute at *c.* 1,460 talents.

Spartans had taken no action while the forty ships lay at Pylus; for they were celebrating a festival at home, and their army was still in Attica. But, when Demosthenes remained there with his five ships, they recalled their army from Attica and their fleet from Corcyra, placed some infantry on the island of Sphacteria, which commanded the two entrances into the harbour, and made plans for closing them with blockships. Before carrying out these plans, they attempted to capture the position of Demosthenes by assault.

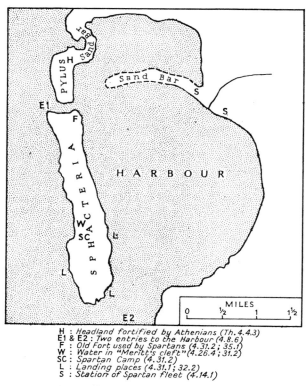

H : Headland fortified by Athenians (Th. 4.4.3)
E1 & E2 : Two entries to the Harbour (4.8.6)
F : Old Fort used by Spartans (4.31.2; 35.1)
W : Water in "Meritt's cleft"(4.26.4; 31.2)
SC : Spartan Camp (4.31.2)
L : Landing places (4.31.1; 32.2)
S : Station of Spartan fleet (4.14.1)

FIG. 24. Pylus as in 425

Demosthenes had sent off two of his five ships to recall the Athenian fleet from Zacynthos, and he had received a chance reinforcement in the shape of a Messenian thirty-oared vessel and a smaller boat, which had been operating as raiders and came to join him. The position had great natural strength, and Demosthenes' men—perhaps 1,000 in all, hoplites, archers, and sailors with improvised shields—beat off every attack with desperate courage and wounded the most conspicuous of the Spartan officers, Brasidas, whose shield was later dedicated with others to commemorate the Athenian victory. On the third day the Athenian fleet came up. Next morning the ships rowed through the two entrances, which the Spartans had not yet blocked, caught the enemy fleet unprepared and put it out of action. They then patrolled the waters round the island of Sphacteria, on which 420 Spartans with their attendant Helots were marooned.

The Spartan authorities then visited the scene and made an armistice, the chief conditions being that the Athenians permitted the delivery of rations to the men on the island and the Spartans placed their entire fleet of warships in Athenian hands. Spartan envoys then hastened to Athens and offered peace and alliance in exchange for the liberation of the men on the island. If Athens accepted, her empire would be safe from attack and the position of Sparta would be weakened. For Sparta had not consulted her allies; she was prepared to sacrifice their interests, abandon her crusade for liberty, and ally herself with the tyrant state. In such an alliance Athens would be far the stronger partner, and she could, if she wished, exploit by diplomatic means the superiority which the daring of Demosthenes had won for her. Pericles, had he been alive, might have persuaded the Assembly to accept the offer. But after six years of war the people wanted more solid gains, and Cleon spurred them on in their demands. On his proposal the Assembly made their reply: if Sparta handed over to Athens the men on Sphacteria, together with Nisaea, Pegae, Troezen, and Achaea, Athens would prolong the armistice and discuss terms in detail. When the envoys asked for a confidential meeting with Athenian representatives, Cleon demanded a public discussion. The Spartan envoys then returned home.

At Pylus the Athenian commanders alleged an infringement by Sparta of the terms of the armistice and kept the entire Spartan fleet of sixty vessels. Hostilities began again. The Athenian force encountered great difficulties, having nowhere to beach their ships and finding little water on the promontory. A few ships patrolled the waters round Sphacteria by day, and the whole fleet, raised by reinforcements to seventy sail, rode off the island by night. Despite their vigilance small boats and divers with skin bags brought food into the island for the hoplites and their attendants. Meanwhile Athens had to supply some 14,000 troops and oarsmen in this remote place. If the blockade was prolonged into the winter, the Athenian fleet would be unable to ride off the island and the long line of supply could not be maintained.

At Athens the Assembly repented of the intransigent attitude which Cleon had persuaded the people to adopt towards the Spartan envoys. When it was proposed to send Cleon and another to inspect the situation, Cleon retorted that action and not inspection was required; that, if the generals were men, they would easily capture the Spartans; and that, if he himself was in command, he would do so. Cleon's taunt was aimed at his rival, Nicias, the senior general present in the Assembly, but the taunt recoiled on his own head, when Nicias offered to resign and give the command to Cleon. Cleon then tried to withdraw. But, the more he withdrew, the louder the Assembly shouted at him 'Sail!'. In the end he sailed, naming Demosthenes alone as his colleague and taking a number of hoplites, peltasts, and archers. His claim, that he would capture the Spartans within twenty days or die in the attempt, was a cause of laughter in the Assembly. For the Athenians had such respect for the valour of a few hundred Spartan hoplites that they did not think it strange that their 14,000 men on the spot were unable to make an attack.

When Cleon reached Pylus, Demosthenes had made his preparations. A fire, started by chance and fanned by a wind, had burnt most of the cover on the island, so that Demosthenes had a better idea of the lie of the ground and of the number and dispositions of the Spartans. Landing at dawn and deploying his troops, he sent in his light-armed men to harass the Spartans and kept his hoplites out of reach. The Spartans, blinded by clouds of wood-ash and struck by javelins, arrows, and stones from every side, finally withdrew to a rough fort and fought valiantly, until some Messenians climbed the cliffs and turned the position. The Spartans then drew together, realizing that the end was near. But Cleon and Demosthenes called off their troops, and invited the Spartans to surrender. After obtaining orders from the Spartan command on the mainland to do nothing dishonourable and to decide for themselves, the Spartans surrendered. Within twenty days of his departure Cleon was back in Athens with 292 prisoners, of whom some 120 were Spartiates. He owed his success to his own political vigour and to the generalship of Demosthenes.[1]

The Athenian victory reduced the morale of Sparta to a low ebb. When the Athenians threatened to kill their prisoners if a Spartan set foot on Attic soil, the Spartans ceased to invade Attica. Having lost even that degree of initiative by land and stripped of their entire fleet, the Spartans were thrown back on the defensive. The Athenians pressed their advantage. They planted Messenians from Naupactus at Pylus, whence they raided inland and encouraged the Helots to desert. The fleet sailed on from Pylus to Corcyra, where it defeated the oligarchs with the help of the democrats. The survivors capitulated on condition that their fate was to be decided by the Athenian people. But on the grounds of a technical infringement the Athenian generals handed them over to the democrats, who butchered them to a man with the utmost cruelty. In the Aegean Nicias launched a large seaborne attack with eighty ships and some horse-transports against the Corinthian coast. During the night 2,000 Athenian hoplites and 200 Athenian cavalry landed together with a force of infantry drawn from Miletus, Andros, and Carystus. The Corinthians had been forewarned, but their forces were divided. In a hard-fought battle the Athenians were victorious. They then ravaged another part of Corinthia and the coast of Epidauria, captured the promontory of Methana,

[1] 4. 3–6; 8–23; 26–40; Ar. *Eq.* 54; 742; Spartan shields were dedicated at Athens, cf. Paus. 1. 15. 4, *Hesp.* 6. 347.

and built a wall across its narrow isthmus. There they left a garrison, which conducted raids into the adjoining territories of Epidaurus, Halieis, and Troezen. During the winter of 425-4 they rejected several offers of peace from Sparta, and they learnt by capturing a Persian agent and reading his dispatches for Sparta that the policy of Persia was still one of neutrality. They, too, sent an embassy to the court of the Great King. In the east Aegean their ships collected the tribute at the increased rate, and Chios, the only independent ally in the empire, obeyed the order to dismantle a recently built fortification.[1]

In summer 424 Nicias struck an effective blow at Laconia. He captured the Lacedaemonian island of Cythera and garrisoned it. From this naval base the Athenians intercepted the merchantmen which sailed from Egypt and Libya to Laconia, and Nicias raided the Laconian coast for a week without encountering much resistance. Later in the summer Athens endeavoured to capture Megara and cut off the Peloponnese from Boeotia and from central Greece. The Megarid had been ravaged twice a year since the beginning of the war, Nisaea was occupied by a Peloponnesian garrison under Spartan command, and the oligarchic exiles, having established themselves at Pegae, were attacking the Megarians in their fields. Under this strain the people proposed to receive back the oligarchic exiles. The democratic leaders then arranged to betray the city to Athens. Her forces arrived from Minoa at night—Demosthenes with light-armed troops and Hippocrates with 600 hoplites—and lay concealed outside the Long Walls linking Megara to Nisaea. Just before dawn the conspirators had a gate opened in the Long Walls, and Demosthenes and his men rushed in and cut off Megara from Nisaea. The next stage of the plot, whereby Megara was to be betrayed, broke down, and the Athenians, reinforced at dawn by 4,000 hoplites and 600 cavalry from Eleusis, spent the day walling off the Peloponnesian garrison in Nisaea. Next day in the evening the garrison capitulated. The Athenians then occupied Nisaea, broke down the inland end of the Long Walls, and prepared to blockade Megara (Fig. 19).

It so happened that Brasidas the Spartan was raising troops near Corinth when the news of the Athenian attack arrived. He sent a message at once to the Boeotians. They were to meet him on the second day before dawn at Tripodiscus in the Megarid. He reached the rendezvous first with some 4,000 hoplites, having marched during the night after the capitulation of the garrison at Nisaea. While it was still dark, he approached Megara but was refused admittance. At dawn a Boeotian force of 2,200 hoplites and 600 cavalry arrived, and Brasidas offered battle in a position of his choosing. The Athenian generals decided not to engage. Their troops were slightly outnumbered and they dared not face the risk of heavy losses; for Athens had small reserves of infantry, whereas their enemies' reserves were almost unlimited. When the Athenians withdrew into Nisaea, Megara opened her

[1] 4. 41-48; 50-51; Ar. *Eq.* 604.

gates to Brasidas. The oligarchs arrested about a hundred democrats, tried them in an open court on a charge of treason, and had them executed. The state was saved for the Spartan Alliance, and Brasidas withdrew to Corinth.[1]

At this point in the war Athens reached her highest level of success. The military and political prestige of Sparta was badly shaken. Spartiates had surrendered at Sphacteria. Sparta herself was weakened by revolts in Messenia and Laconia. She had failed to protect the members of her Alliance. Corinth had lost all her colonies in the Ionian and Aegean Seas except Leucas and Ambracia, and she only held these by sending out garrisons. Ever since 433 she had expended men, money, and ships to no avail. Megara was impoverished, and her very existence was threatened by the Athenian occupation of Nisaea. All states alike suffered from the ravaging of the coasts and the interception of merchant shipping. The Peloponnesian fleet had ceased to operate. The ring of blockade was closing; for Athens now held fortified posts at Pylus, Cythera, Methana, Nisaea, Minoa, Pteleum, and Atalante, and her fleets had bases in the west at Zacynthos, Cephallenia, Corcyra, Naupactus, and Acarnania, which had brought Oeniadae and Anactorium under its control. The strain of the long war split some of the states internally and weakened their ability to resist. Even in the states of Boeotia, which had suffered least, some democratic leaders were inviting Athens to intervene.[2]

Athens had paid a high price for her success. The plague had carried off a third of her population. The fighting had worn down her military strength: whereas 13,000 first-line hoplites took the field in 431, it is doubtful if 8,000 were available in 424. In view of her commitments this number of hoplites was already dangerously low. On the other hand, the fleet was superbly strong. It had lost only a few ships, and the crews of those were drawn in part from her subjects. The war had altered the balance of the classes in Athens. The upper and middle classes were now in the minority, and the control of the democratic constitution was in the hands of the poorer class. The war had also created a division of interest between the classes. The cavalry and the hoplites bore the brunt of the casualties. For they led the sea-borne landings, fought the battles, and conducted the sieges. The classes from which they were drawn suffered most through the ravaging of Attica, and they paid taxes in the form of liturgies and capital levies. Patriotic as they were, they wished to accept favourable terms from Sparta and put an end to the war. The thetes had suffered few casualties in battle. They paid no taxes. They received state-pay as a perquisite of empire, and they were naturally prompted by patriotic and by self-interested motives to extend the empire by prosecuting the war.[3] This division of interest between the two main groups in the state provided material for the writers of political comedy at Athens. In

[1] 4. 53–57; 66–74; for routes in the Megarid see *BSA* 49. 112 = *StGH* 431.
[2] 4. 40–41; 55; 42. 3; 49; 77. 2; 76. 2.
[3] Ar. *Eq.* 595; *Ach.* 225–32; *Eq.* 912; 924; *V.* 1303.

March 426 at the Great Dionysia, when the representatives of the Allies were present, Aristophanes portrayed the subjects of Athens as slaves working a treadmill and referred to the branding of the Samian prisoners. In February 425 at the City Dionysia he satirized the Athenian view of the causes of the war, stressed the longing of the farmers for the countryside of Attica, and attacked the leaders of the war-party. In February 424 he pilloried Cleon as a warmonger, who refused Sparta's offers of peace in order to confirm his own ascendancy in the state.[1] These were jests on the Attic stage, but they were barbed jests, aimed to strike at those who insisted on prolonging the war.

One result of the growing division of interest within the state was a distrust of the executive officials, who were drawn mainly from the upper class. Phormion was fined, probably at this time, on a charge of embezzlement. Demosthenes was afraid to face the people after his defeat in Aetolia. In summer 424 the Greek states in Sicily were persuaded by an able statesman of Syracuse, Hermocrates, to make peace among themselves and be rid of Athens' intervention. When the Athenian force returned, two generals were banished and a third fined, on the grounds that instead of reducing the whole of Sicily they had taken bribes. For the success of Athens in so many theatres of the war had filled the people with great ambitions and with an unjustified confidence. In two areas, however, they had not succeeded: in Chalcidice and Bottiaea, where the rebels were entrenched, and on the coast of Asia Minor, where the Samian and the Lesbian exiles had formed two centres of resistance. And on land their hoplite forces were not adequate to win a decisive victory over the enemy.[2]

§ 3. *Athenian defeats and the Peace of Nicias, 424–421*

IN the summer of 424, when the Athenian army returned from the Megarid, the generals accepted the overtures of some democrats in Boeotian cities, who asked for aid in order to establish a democratic régime throughout Boeotia. A three-sided attack was planned. Exiles from Orchomenus in north Boeotia, assisted by some Phocian supporters, were to seize Chaeronea near the frontier of Phocis and Boeotia. Demosthenes, sailing to Naupactus with forty ships, was to occupy Siphae on the south-west coast of Boeotia, which would be betrayed to him by the conspirators. The main Athenian army was to seize the sanctuary of Apollo at Delium in south-east Boeotia and to establish a fortified base there for the Boeotian insurgents. The three attacks were to be made on the same day, so that the Boeotian forces would be divided. At the beginning of November the plan was put into effect, the Athenians being unaware that the plot had been betrayed. Demosthenes arrived too early, a mistake having arisen in the timing, and Siphae was not

---

[1] Ar. *Babylonians* (cf. Schol. Ar. *Ach.* 378); *Acharnians* 509–56; 32 f.; *Equites* 44–79; 795–809. These plays were produced respectively in 426, 425, and 424.

[2] Schol. Ar. *Pax* 347; Paus. 1. 23. 10; Th. 3. 98. 5; 4. 58–65; 4. 7; 52; 75.

betrayed to him. Nor did anything happen at Chaeronea. Meanwhile Hippocrates was approaching Delium with the full levy of citizens, metics, and foreigners. After his arrival he spent two days in building temporary fortifications round the sacred precinct, and on the third day he sent the army off towards Attica, while he himself made final arrangements for garrisoning and fortifying the post. On this day the full force of the Boeotians, including detachments which had returned from Siphae and Chaeronea, was mustering out of sight at Tanagra. When they learnt that the Athenians were withdrawing towards Attica, ten of the Boeotarchs wished not to engage, but the eleventh Boeotarch, Pagondas of Thebes, who held the operational command on that day, decided to attack and inspired his men to follow him. It was late in the day when Pagondas detached a force to contain the Athenians at Delium and drew up his army in order of battle behind a ridge, where his dispositions could not be seen by the enemy. Of his 7,000 hoplites the Thebans on the right of the line were drawn up in files twenty-five men deep and the rest in files of the normal depth of eight men each. His wings were protected by 1,000 cavalry, 500 peltasts, and more than 10,000 light-armed troops.

Hippocrates, informed of the enemy's approach, left a garrison and 300 cavalry at Delium and rejoined his army. The light-armed troops had gone ahead homewards, but the cavalry and the hoplites were equal to the Boeotians in number. When Pagondas brought his line to the top of the ridge, he saw that Hippocrates had already drawn up his hoplites in the normal depth of eight men to a file with his cavalry on the wings and was halfway down the line, still exhorting his men to battle. Pagondas at once led the Boeotians downhill with the slope in their favour, having chosen a strip of ground where the flanks of his shorter line were protected by gullies. Hippocrates ordered his men to close at the double, in order to offset the impetus of the enemy. But the superior weight of the Theban formation on the right wing bore down the Athenians and finally broke their line. Meanwhile the Boeotians of the left wing and centre were being pushed back with considerable loss, but Pagondas sent from his wing two squadrons of cavalry, which passing unseen behind the ridge suddenly charged the victorious Athenians and threw them into a panic. The whole Athenian army then broke into flight. They were pursued by the Boeotian cavalry and by some Locrian cavalry, who had just arrived on the scene. The fall of night saved them from utter disaster. As it was, Hippocrates and 1,000 hoplites, with large numbers of light-armed troops and attendants, lay dead on the field of battle. Nevertheless, the Athenians reinforced the garrison at Delium. It was soon overwhelmed by a large force of Boeotians, Corinthians, Megarians, Malians, and Peloponnesians. Two hundred Athenians were taken prisoner, a number were killed in battle, and the remainder escaped to their ships.[1]

This was the only pitched battle of the Peloponnesian War in which the full

[1] 4. 76–77; 89–101; D.S. 12. 70. 5 (spoils); *SEG* 10. 81. 84 (Boeotian collaborators).

army of Athens was deployed. In itself the battle may not have seemed decisive; for the Boeotians lost some 500 hoplites, and their victory was due rather to the brilliant generalship of Pagondas than to any superiority in fighting quality over the Athenian hoplites. But the failure of the campaign at Delium was decisive in the strategy of the war. Athens recognized the truth of Pericles' advice, that she must not risk the resources of the state on land. Her strength lay on the sea and she must defeat the enemy from the sea. To the Boeotians and the Peloponnesians the loss in hoplites was not serious, since they had so large a margin of superiority. To Athens the loss of over 1,200 hoplites was crippling, because her resources in manpower were fully extended. And at this time Brasidas the Spartan had already opened an offensive in Chalcidice and Bottiaea, where Athens had failed to keep her subjects in hand.

The successes of Athens before the battle of Delium prompted the dispatch of Brasidas in the summer of 424, when Perdiccas of Macedonia and the rebels in Chalcidice, fearing they would be attacked, were asking for help. Sparta, too, was anxious to create a diversion. For the danger of insurrection in Laconia and Messenia was so great that the Spartan authorities organized the massacre of 2,000 leading Helots, recruited cavalry and archers to police the country, and tried desperately to prevent further raids and attacks on their territories. The authorities at Sparta therefore supported Brasidas when he offered to lead an army to Macedonia. They gave him 700 freed Helots (*neodamodeis*), trained as hoplites, and sufficient money to raise 1,000 hoplites in the Peloponnese. From Heraclea in Trachis, where he was joined by some Thessalian well-wishers, he marched at full speed through Thessaly, which was in alliance with Athens but not formally at war with Sparta, and he reached Dium in Pieria, before the Thessalians could raise a force to stop him. There he joined forces with Perdiccas, who provided the Peloponnesian army with half its supplies. Brasidas refused to be involved in a war against Perdiccas' neighbour to the west, Arrhabaeus of Lyncus, and he and the Chalcidians entered the territory of Acanthus, an important town on the east coast of Chalcidice. He did not ravage the ripe vineyards but persuaded the Acanthians to revolt from Athens. He undertook to respect their liberties in every respect, and he took the oaths of alliance with Acanthus on behalf of the Spartan government. Soon afterwards Stagirus revolted from Athens, and Brasidas opened negotiations with the people of Argilus. Their kinsmen in Amphipolis then formed a conspiracy to betray Amphipolis to him.

As the first successes of Brasidas coincided with the Athenian campaign in Boeotia, reinforcements were not sent to the two Athenian generals, Eucles at Amphipolis and Thucydides, the historian, who was at Thasos, the naval base. On a winter night, when snow was falling, Brasidas marched from the border of the Chalcidian territory, received Argilus into alliance, and forced the passage of the bridge over the Strymon. When dawn broke, his army held the southern suburb which lay outside the walls of Amphipolis, but the conspirators within the city were not able to open the gates. Eucles sent off a ship immediately to summon Thucydides to his aid. Meanwhile Brasidas exploited the confusion in Amphipolis by offering to liberate the prisoners he had taken, respect the property of the citizens, and grant a safe conduct without loss of property to anyone who preferred to leave the city. This offer was accepted. Brasidas entered Amphipolis a few hours before Thucydides with seven ships reached Eïon at the mouth of the Strymon. Brasidas then attacked Eïon without success, but three cities to the east of the Strymon—Myrcinus, Galepsus, and Oesyme—came over to his side.

The fall of Amphipolis had many repercussions. The revenues and the timber which Athens had drawn from this area were now available for Brasidas to start building a fleet. The subjects of Athens on the north shore of the Aegean and the adjacent islands began to plan revolt. The moderation and good faith of Brasidas were believed to be typical of Sparta, the proclaimed champion of liberty and autonomy. The Athenian people made a scapegoat of Thucydides. He was exiled for the loss of a city which he had done all in his power to save. During the winter, so far as the weather allowed, Athens reinforced her garrisons. But Brasidas reduced a number of small towns between Eïon and Chalcidice, captured Torone, and ejected the Athenian garrison. Meanwhile Brasidas' requests to Sparta for reinforcements were refused; for the aim of Sparta was to obtain terms of peace, and there was some jealousy of the successful commander. In March 423 Sparta and her allies concluded an armistice for one year with Athens, the terms being the *status quo* and the intention being to negotiate a treaty of peace.[1]

Two days after the signing of the armistice Scione on the promontory of Pallene in Chalcidice came over to Brasidas, who, being unaware of the armistice, received the city into alliance and was himself crowned by the citizens as the liberator of Greece. Some days later the armistice was reported, and the representatives of Athens refused to admit Scione as a beneficiary under its terms. Brasidas, who had already placed a garrison in Scione, argued the point, and the Spartan government offered to submit the matter to arbitration in accordance with the terms of the armistice. Athens refused. Cleon carried a proposal to execute the citizens of Scione, and an expedition was prepared. For the chief Athenian station in Chalcidice, Potidaea, was now threatened by the advance of Brasidas, and they feared that he might instigate a rising in the islands. Meanwhile Mende came over to Brasidas, who regarded the refusal of Athens to accept arbitration and some local incidents as breaches of the armistice. Athens extended her sentence of execution to include the citizens of Mende likewise. Brasidas thereupon removed the women and children from Scione and Mende, and sent a force of 800 men to assist in the defence of the two cities. Thus Chalcidice remained a theatre of war, although the armistice held elsewhere.

During summer 423 Perdiccas, who had gained nothing from the vic-

[1] 4. 78–88; 102–19.

tories of Brasidas, persuaded him to join in an attack on Arrhabaeus. After some initial success the Macedonian army panicked in the night and fled, leaving Brasidas far inland and exposed to attacks by the forces of Arrhabaeus and his Illyrian allies. He extricated the Greek army by brilliant generalship, marching in a square formation and himself commanding a picked force of assault troops. His men revenged themselves by pillaging the baggage train of Perdiccas, who with his usual duplicity proceeded to ally himself with Athens and brought some Bottiaean cities over to Athens. Brasidas was now cut off from the south. An army sent out from Sparta was prevented by the influence of Perdiccas from passing through Thessaly and turned back. A few Spartiates reached him, their aim being to view the situation and to install themselves as governors in the allied towns. Meanwhile Nicias, operating with a large force from Potidaea, had captured Mende and was investing Scione. Late in the winter Brasidas tried to take Potidaea by surprise but failed. He had now no means of relieving Scione.

In spring 422 the armistice expired. Athens was in no mood to treat for peace. Under Cleon's strict supervision the revenues from the tribute, the capital levies, taxes, and so forth came near to 2,000 talents in the current year.[1] A supreme effort could still be made. Cleon persuaded the people to appoint him to the command of 300 cavalry, 1,200 hoplites, and a large number of troops supplied by subject-states. Moving rapidly by sea he captured Torone by assault from two sides just before Brasidas came up to its support. He then sailed on to Eïon, captured Stagirus and Galepsus by storm, and instructed Perdiccas and a Thracian prince, Polles, to send him troops for an attack on Amphipolis. While he waited inactive at Eïon pending their arrival, his own men vented their discontent by comparing the experience and dash of Brasidas with the inexperience and sluggishness of Cleon. Indeed Cleon had acted hitherto with the speed which sea power made possible, and he had no reason to feel any inferiority in that respect. But now the discontent of the troops and the bravura of his personality prompted Cleon against his better judgement to make a reconnaissance in force before the walls of Amphipolis. In the meantime Brasidas was keeping the army of Cleon under observation from a post in the hills west of the Strymon. When he saw the army on the move, he anticipated the intention of Cleon and moved his force inside the city. In numbers it equalled the enemy, but the first-line hoplites were less numerous.

As Cleon approached the city from the south, all was quiet, the walls not manned and the gates closed. His column of march halted and turned left to face the east wall, while Cleon himself went ahead to gain a wider view. Inside the city Brasidas had massed his troops behind the east wall; the main body under a Spartan officer, Clearidas, stood behind the northerly gate and 150 picked hoplites under his own command behind the southerly gate. The Athenians could see into the city. They noticed Brasidas making sacrifices—

[1] Ar. *V*. 656-64.

usually a preliminary to battle—and some of them saw the hooves of horses and the feet of men in great numbers, just visible below the leaves of the gates. Cleon was informed and came to see for himself. He at once gave the order to retreat, hoping to withdraw before the enemy made a sortie. At first he turned the left of his line into column and started it off southwards in the direction of Eïon. Then, fearing the general withdrawal would be too slow, he turned his whole line into column and marched south, exposing the un-shielded right side of his men. As the Athenians hastened past his gate, Brasidas pointed to the bobbing spears and heads, assured his picked troops that the enemy would not stand their ground, opened the gate, and charged at the head of his men into the middle of the column. At the same time Clearidas issued from the other gate and struck at the end of the column. Most of the Athenians broke into flight, including Cleon who was killed. The best troops, who formed the rear of the column, fell back on to a hill and fought well, until they, too, were routed by the attacks of the cavalry and the peltasts. Some 600 Athenians were killed. Only seven of Brasidas' force fell, but one of the seven was Brasidas. He was buried in the city with military honours and acclaimed as the true founder of Amphipolis. Thereafter annual sacrifices and games were held in memory of him as a hero.[1]

After the defeat at Amphipolis in late summer 422 Athens ceased active operations and began to negotiate for peace. Almost a quarter of her hoplite force had fallen at Delium and in Chalcidice. Her financial reserves were wellnigh exhausted. The subject states saw in the success of Sparta at Amphipolis an encouragement to rise in revolt. Sparta was willing, indeed more willing than Athens, to negotiate for peace. The Spartan authorities had regarded the campaign in Chalcidice less as a crusade of liberation than as a means of alarming Athens. They wanted their men back before Sparta was called upon to face new dangers. For they suspected disaffection in the Spartan Alliance, and they were alarmed by the refusal of Argos to extend the Thirty Years Truce with Sparta, which ran out in 421, unless the terri-tory of Cynuria was ceded to her. Their aim was to obtain peace and, if possible, agreement with Athens, before the Spartan Alliance split and Argos entered the field. Death had removed the two war-leaders, Cleon and Brasidas. Their successors in the esteem of their countrymen, Nicias and Pleistoanax, both advocated peace.

After a series of conferences the terms of the so-called Peace of Nicias were drawn up. Athens on the one side and Sparta and her Allies on the other were to take an oath, binding for fifty years and renewable each year, not to perpetrate acts of war against one another and against the Allies of Athens but to submit any dispute to arbitration. They were to guarantee freedom of access to the national shrines and to safeguard the independence of the temple of Apollo at Delphi and of the state of Delphi. Prisoners were to be liberated. And both sides were to restore such places as they had cap-

---

[1] 4. 120–32; 135; 5. 2–3; 6–11; *IG* i. 42–43; *GHI* 68.

tured during the war. Finally, Athens and Sparta were to be entitled to make any changes in the terms, if they agreed between themselves. Concerning the places to be restored there was considerable dispute, and the final definition ran as follows. Athens gave up her claim to Plataea, but she retained possession of Nisaea. Sparta agreed to evacuate the cities in Chalcidice and Bottiaea on condition that their independence and their neutrality should be respected by Athens and her Allies, so long as they paid the tribute originally assessed by Aristides. Three cities, namely Scione, Torone, and Sermylium, were not included in this agreement. Athens could deal with them as she pleased. The places to be restored were enumerated, Athens ceding Pylus, Cythera, Methana, Pteleum, and Atalante and the Spartan Alliance ceding Amphipolis and Panactum, a frontier town recently captured by Thebes. These terms of peace were submitted by Sparta to the Congress of her Allies. A majority voting in favour, Sparta and her Allies severally took the oaths and made peace. But the Boeotian League, Megara, Corinth, and Elis refused to be bound by the majority vote and rejected the treaty. Their action was tantamount to withdrawal from the Spartan Alliance.[1]

Alarmed by this defection, Sparta approached Athens for a treaty of alliance. Shortly afterwards Sparta and Athens took an oath, binding for fifty years and to be renewed annually, to combine against anyone who invaded the territory of either and not to make a separate peace; in addition, Athens bound herself to aid Sparta in the event of a rising by the Helots. This alliance gave added meaning to the final clause in the Peace of Nicias, whereby Athens and Sparta had reserved the right to alter the terms, if they were in agreement. It was now clear that the two great powers intended to support one another during the dangerous process of restoring order within their separate spheres of influence.[2]

For practical purposes the ten years' war was ended. But the prospects of peace were not promising. The alliance between Athens and Sparta was an alliance of convenience and not of goodwill. Each had found the chink in the other's armour and been too exhausted to deal a further blow. It was probable that, when they recuperated and their allies were brought to heel, they would return to the attack on one another. In any case the Boeotian League, Megara, Corinth, and Elis and the emergence of Argos from her den of neutrality threatened the general peace at a time when both Athens and Sparta were still vulnerable.

§ 4. *The western Greeks 466–421 and Athenian intervention*

AFTER the expulsion of the tyrants there was a general rehabilitation of the Greek states. The mercenaries and the ex-mercenaries were expelled, often with much fighting, and took refuge mainly at Messana. The populations which the tyrants had transplanted returned to their original homes and

---

[1] 5. 14–22. 1; 30. 1 fin.   [2] 5. 22. 2–24; 29. 2–3; D.S. 12. 75. 1–5.

divided up the land. To prevent the rise of another tyrant Syracuse adopted the Athenian institution of ostracism under the name of 'petalism', in which names were written on an olive leaf and the victim was exiled for five years. Most of the states set up democratic constitutions. But the privileges of the pioneer families were still preserved, and in cases where the land was distributed they received favourable treatment.

The growing prosperity of the Sicilian states was threatened at sea by the navy of Etruria and on land by the vigorous native population, the Sicels. About 453 Syracuse inflicted a severe defeat on the Etruscans. With a fleet of sixty triremes her forces conquered Aethalia (Elba), overran Cyrnus (Corsica), and gained much booty from raids on the coast of Etruria. The leader of the Sicels, Ducetius, organized his people by imitating many Greek institutions. He founded a number of Sicel cities between 459 and 451, of which the most strongly fortified was Palice, and some of them began to issue coins in the Greek manner. As 'king of the Sicels' he formed the Sicels into a league, drew revenues from all the Sicel cities except Hybla, and organized a Sicel army. At first he co-operated with Syracuse. But in 451, when he began to encroach on the Greek area by capturing Aetna and attacking Motyum, Syracuse and Acragas joined forces against him. They were at first defeated, and Motyum fell to Ducetius. But in 450 the army of Syracuse defeated the Sicels, both sides suffering heavy losses, and the army of Acragas captured Motyum. Ducetius himself fled at night to Syracuse, where he took refuge as a suppliant at the altars of the state. The Syracusan people, respecting the sanctuary, sent him to Corinth, where provision was made for his well-being. In his absence the Sicel league collapsed.[1]

The success of Syracuse against Etruria and Ducetius whetted the ambition of the democracy. In 446 Syracuse attacked Acragas, the second city in Sicily, and in the course of the struggle brought Ducetius back to found a mixed colony of Greeks and Sicels at Cale Acte, where there was valuable timber for shipbuilding. Syracuse and her allies soon inflicted a severe defeat on Acragas and her allies, more than 1,000 Acragantines falling in battle. Ducetius tried to revive the power of the Sicels, but he died a natural death in 440. Syracuse and her allies proceeded to conquer the Sicels and enslaved the survivors of their last stronghold in the lowlands. She was now the greatest state in Sicily. She claimed hegemony over many Greek states, and she exacted tribute from the Sicel towns. Her wealth enabled her to double her force of cavalry, maintain a fleet of 100 triremes, and build up financial reserves. Her aim was to win the whole of Sicily. Her methods resembled those of Athens, whose ambitions had already made themselves felt in the West.[2]

By contracting alliances with Segesta in 458/457 and with Halicyae, Leontini, and Rhegium in 454/453 Athens ranged herself in opposition to

[1] D.S. 11. 72; 76; 78. 5; 86–87 (petalism); 88. 4–6; 90–92; *POxy* 4. 665.
[2] D.S. 12. 8; 29–30.

Syracuse, the leading Dorian state. Her colony at Thurii in south Italy was intended to offset the power of Taras, the daughter state of Sparta. When the Peloponnesian War broke out, Syracuse, Taras, and their satellites declared themselves on the side of the Spartan Alliance and facilitated the export of corn to the Peloponnese. They soon became involved in the war. For Syracuse and her Allies attacked Leontini and her friends, who included Camarina and Rhegium, and Athens sent out twenty ships in 427 to help them and enlisted the support of the Sicels. At first Syracuse and her allies— especially Locri in South Italy and Messana on the Sicilian side of the straits—suffered a number of defeats, but Syracuse soon rose to the occasion. She managed to hold her own against the Athenian ships by inviting attack close inshore and then throwing grappling-irons on to the enemy ships. When Athens sent out a reinforcement of forty ships in 425, even the allies of Athens began to fear that she had come to conquer. In the Conference of delegates, which was held at Gela in 424, Hermocrates of Syracuse persuaded the Sicilians to make peace with one another and to exclude Athens from their island. Once again Syracuse proved her power of leadership, when the independence of Sicily was threatened by a foreign invader.[1]

Unity in Sicily, however, was not achieved. Animosities between state and state were too deeply rooted. The conditions of war had aggravated the division between rich and poor, and this often led to civil war. At Leontini the democrats proposed to redistribute the land and the oligarchs called in Syracuse; Leontini then split, as Corcyra had done, into two groups which fought with one another. Messana, too, was racked by civil war, and one party surrendered the city for a time to Locri. In 422 Athens sent Phaeax as head of a diplomatic mission to Italy and Sicily, in the hope of forming a coalition against Syracuse. He was well received at Acragas, Camarina, and Locri and by the Sicels, but elsewhere he was unsuccessful. He returned home when the negotiations for the Peace of Nicias were being conducted. Meanwhile the quarrels of the Greek states were exposing them to attacks by their neighbours. In 421 Cumae, the outpost of Hellenism in the north, was destroyed, and the site was occupied by the Campanians.[2]

---

[1] *GHI* 31 with *IG* i.[2] 20 and *TAPA* 75. 10; *GHI* 57; 58; Th. 2. 7. 2; 3. 86; 88; 90; 99; 103; 115; 4. 1–2; 24–25; 58–65. [2] 5. 4–5; D.S. 12. 76. 4.

CHAPTER 5

The Second Part of the Peloponnesian War (421–404)

§ 1. *The uneasy peace, 421–416*

MANY members of the Spartan Alliance were disaffected, and Corinth took the initiative. She approached Argos, a powerful democratic state, which had enjoyed the advantages of neutrality and exemption from blockade during the war. On the suggestion of the Corinthian envoys, who were returning from the Congress of the Spartan Allies, the Argive Assembly elected twelve representatives and gave them full power to make a secret alliance with any Greek state except Athens and Sparta. If they wished to negotiate at all with Athens or Sparta, they were told to consult the Argive Assembly first. The Argive representatives then invited the Greek states to ally themselves with Argos. Their hope was to found an Argive coalition at the expense of the Spartan Alliance. The democratic states accepted first, Mantinea and Elis; for they had attacked their immediate neighbours during the war and now expected reprisals from Sparta. Corinth next joined Argos, and so did her allies, the Chalcidian states. Corinth and Argos then approached Tegea. But Tegea refused; for Tegea and Mantinea had recently been at war with one another. Megara and the Boeotian League declined all invitations, their oligarchic authorities distrusting the democratic government of Argos. Thus the Argive coalition consisted only of Mantinea, Elis, and Corinth together with the allies of Mantinea and the Chalcidian allies of Corinth. Their forces did not seem sufficient to challenge the combined forces of Sparta and Athens. The coalition therefore remained secret and unofficial.[1]

Sparta, however, was aware of the situation. In the summer of 421 she invaded and liberated Parrhasia, a district in south Arcadia over which Mantinea had imposed her rule. Argos did no more than place a garrison in Mantinea, being daunted by the fact that Sparta and Athens were in alliance. Sparta did all in her power to preserve the alliance with Athens. She liberated her Athenian prisoners. She withdrew her troops from Amphipolis, Chalcidice, and Bottiaea and tried to bring her recalcitrant allies into the treaty of peace. Athens liberated the Spartan prisoners of war, but she kept Pylus pending the restoration of Amphipolis and Panactum under the treaty. On further representations from Sparta she withdrew the Messenians and the runaway Helots from Pylus and placed an Athenian garrison there. But she would not do more, unless Sparta forced the recalcitrant members of her Alliance to subscribe to the Peace of Nicias. Sparta, she suggested, should

[1] 5. 27–31; 32. 3–7; 4. 134; D.S. 12. 75. 6–7.

threaten them with hostilities from Athens and Sparta. Such a step would have destroyed the Spartan Alliance, and the Spartan authorities were not prepared to do so.[1]

In the winter of 421–420, when it was clear that the alliance with Athens might break down, the new ephors at Sparta entered into secret negotiations with some executive officials of Corinth and the Boeotian League. They concocted the following plan. The Boeotian League was to give Panactum to Sparta, so that Panactum could be exchanged for Pylus; then the Boeotian League was to enter the coalition of Argos; finally, Corinth and the Boeotian League were to swing the Argive coalition into alliance with Sparta and into hostility with Athens. But the plan broke down, because the executive officials could not reveal its secret purpose to the governing body of the Boeotian League. Sparta then embarked on a second plan. In return for Panactum and the Athenians held as prisoners of war by Boeotia, Sparta concluded an alliance with the Boeotian League in February 420. As Boeotia was still technically at war with Athens (their relations being governed by a truce renewable every tenth day) and Sparta and Athens had bound themselves to make peace jointly, the action of Sparta endangered the alliance between Sparta and Athens. But Sparta hoped to save the alliance by giving Panactum and the prisoners to Athens in exchange for Pylus. This plan, too, miscarried. For the Boeotian League razed Panactum to the ground before giving it to Sparta. And Sparta herself was side-tracked by Argos. For Argos, fearing she would face a coalition of Sparta, Athens, and the Boeotian League, now sent envoys to Sparta to negotiate a Fifty Years Truce.[2]

At this stage Athens entered the game. Since the spring of 421 Athens had been operating in Chalcidice. Scione fell after a two years' siege in summer 421; the adult males were executed and the remainder were enslaved. This act of cruelty (as Diodotus had foreseen in 427) only stiffened the resistance of the other states in revolt. The Chalcidians even made headway, capturing two allies of Athens and an Athenian garrison; and Amphipolis persisted in her independence.[3] The Athenian people had accepted the Peace of Nicias with joy, hoping to be rid of the burden of war and to cultivate their farms in security, and they had acclaimed Nicias as the bringer of good fortune. But their hopes had not been fulfilled. Boeotia, Megara, and Corinth were still nominally at war with Athens, and they threatened her frontiers. Some Athenians were still prisoners in enemy hands. Panactum, Amphipolis, and the rebels in Chalcidice and Bottiaea had not been surrendered, and Sparta was violating the alliance with Athens by forming a separate alliance with the Boeotian League. Nicias now found himself in some disfavour. Nevertheless he adhered to his policy of preserving the peace and alliance with Sparta: thereby Athens was protected from attack; she could restore her strength and let Sparta flounder in the defection of her allies and the hostility of Argos. His policy had the merits of caution. He had good reason

---

[1] 5. 33; 35. 2–8.   [2] 5. 36–41.   [3] 5. 32. 1; 35. 1; 39. 1.

to suppose that Sparta would be unable to reconstitute the Spartan Alliance and at the same time avoid war with Argos; and then, if war broke out, Athens could take whichever side she pleased.

Nicias still commanded the affection of the Athenian people. He had all the personable qualities of conventional decency. He was a trusted general in the field; for he was capable, steady, and successful. His honesty and his patriotism were unquestioned. But as a politician he did not command the respect of the quick-witted and volatile Athenians. On the other hand, the radical democrats had been discredited by the failure of Cleon's aggressive policy and by his humiliating end. Men such as Cleon, Lysicles, and Eucrates were different in character and in method from the traditional type of statesman. They were of the people, and they paraded the fact in the vigorous vulgarity of their speeches before the Assembly. Their morals or their probity in financial matters might not be above suspicion, but they were masters in the art of oratory and repartee. Whereas Cleisthenes, Themistocles, and Pericles excelled in action and in words, Cleon and his fellows rose to power by words alone. In the Athenian democracy war favoured their rise. For war, being a violent master and moulding its pupils in its own image, created the turbulent feelings and the harsh resentments to which the popular orator could address his appeals. When peace came, a reaction set in against such leaders. Their place was taken by a wealthy young noble of brilliant intellect, Alcibiades, the son of Cleinias, versatile, persuasive, and ambitious. His policy was to discard the alliance of Sparta and win that of Argos, even at the risk of war with Sparta. Therein he followed in the footsteps of the democratic leaders of 462, Ephialtes and Pericles.[1]

While the Argive envoys were negotiating at Sparta for a Fifty Years Truce, Spartan envoys were receiving a cold reception at Athens. For they came not only to hand over the Athenians liberated by the Boeotian League but also to report the razing of Panactum and explain their separate alliance with the Boeotian League. Alcibiades thereupon sent privately to Argos, requesting the immediate dispatch of envoys from Argos, Mantinea, and Elis to propose alliance with Athens. Argos prepared to do so, and stopped negotiations with Sparta. But, before the arrival of any envoys from Argos, three Spartan envoys hastened to Athens and informed the Council that they had come with full powers to settle any points of dispute. Alcibiades was afraid that, when the Spartan envoys came before the Assembly, they might persuade the people to adhere to the alliance with Sparta. He therefore pledged his word to the envoys that he would arrange the cession of Pylus to Sparta, if they did not mention in the Assembly that they had full powers. During the meeting of the Assembly, when they made no mention of their full powers, Alcibiades turned upon them and led an outcry that the Spartans

---

[1] For Nicias see Th. 5. 16. 1; 7. 86. 5; Plu. *Nic.* 2 and 9. For Cleon Th. 3. 36. 6; 3. 82. 2; 5. 16. 1. For Alcibiades Th. 5. 43. 2; Plu. *Alc.* 1 and 10. For the change of leaders Th. 2. 65. 10; Arist. *Ath.* 28.

were inconsistent and double-faced; for they said one thing to the Council and another thing to the people. By this Themistoclean trick he would have got his way, had not an earthquake occurred and caused the Assembly to disband. Next day the Assembly met again. Nicias, who had shared the discomfiture of the Spartan envoys, maintained his policy of accommodation with Sparta and carried the people with him. He and others were then sent to Sparta. They demanded the cancellation of the alliance between Sparta and Boeotia, unless Boeotia signed the Peace of Nicias, the restoration of Amphipolis, and the rebuilding and restoration of Panactum. These demands Sparta refused to accept. She preferred the alliance of the Boeotian League, even at the risk of war with Athens.[1]

When Nicias reported Sparta's refusal, the Athenians were incensed. In July 420 Athens made an alliance with Argos, Mantinea, and Elis. The terms of the alliance were defensive. They promised to help one another against an invader and not to make a separate peace. In addition, they contracted to prevent the passage of any armed force through territories under their control, unless all parties agreed to permit such passage. Thus the four democratic states were grouped together, but the state which could have blocked passage through the Isthmus, Corinth, did not join them, although she was in defensive alliance with Argos. Neither Sparta nor Athens renounced the alliance with one another. Sparta was left with the rump of the Spartan Alliance in the Peloponnese and with the Boeotian League. Argos headed a considerable coalition. She was in alliance with Athens and on good terms with Persia. Behind the shield of the Argive coalition Athens was safe from attack by Sparta. She therefore waited to see whether Argos or Sparta would be the first to take the offensive.[2]

Despite some provocation Sparta took no strong action between July 420 and July 418. She twice paraded her forces on the frontier of Laconia, but on each occasion the sacrifices were unfavourable and they disbanded; during the winter of 419–418 she sent only 300 men to reinforce the garrison of Epidaurus, which lay on the flank of Argos. Even her ally Boeotia took advantage of her inactivity to occupy Heraclea in Trachis and dismiss the Spartan governor. The Argive coalition made no move either, except to exclude Sparta from the Olympic Games of 420. Alcibiades, who was elected general in 419, tried to bring Sparta and Argos to blows. He led an Athenian army twice into the Peloponnese and persuaded Argos to attack Epidaurus, which lay on the direct line of communications between Athens and Argos. In the winter of 419–418, when Sparta sent her 300 men to Epidaurus by sea, Argos complained that Athens had failed to intercept them. Alcibiades then persuaded the people to regard the Spartan move as a breach of the alliance with Athens and to garrison Pylus with some runaway Helots.

In midsummer 418 Sparta took the initiative. During the last three years

[1] 5. 42–46.   [2] 5. 46. 5–48.

she had dealt with her internal problems. When Brasidas' army of Neo-damodeis, originally 700 strong, returned from Chalcidice, the Helots who had served as attendants of the hoplites were enfranchised, and the whole force was settled at Lepreum, a place to which Elis laid claim. The restored prisoners were disfranchised for having surrendered at Sphacteria, but they were reinstated after a time. Thus the Spartan government restored the morale and the strength of the Spartan army. They also brought back Megara and Corinth into the Spartan Alliance; for these states, which distrusted both Athens and Argos and were unfavourably impressed by the operations of Argos against Epidaurus, sought the protection of their traditional champion. The route from Boeotia to the Peloponnese was now open, and the Spartan king, Agis, ordered the contingents of the Spartan Alliance to meet him at Phlius.[1]

The army which mustered at Phlius in midsummer 418 was the finest that Thucydides had ever known. The Lacedaemonian levy of Spartiates, Perioeci, Neodamodeis, and Helots was at its full strength, numbering 6,000 hoplites, thousands of light-armed troops, and some 400 cavalry. Of this levy the regular army, numbering nearly 5,000 hoplites, consisted only of Spartiates and Perioeci. The Spartiates (whose number is unknown to us) were all picked troops in the sense that they had been specially trained and kept under arms by the state. The regular army was organized in battalions, companies, and platoons, of which the full complements were approximately 600, 150, and 35 men, Spartiates and other personnel being mixed. The chain of command ran from the king with his staff of polemarchs through the battalion and company commanders to the platoon commanders, each trained for his specific duties. One battalion was drawn from Sciritis, a district near the Arcadian frontier, and it was specially trained to fight on the left of the line. The regular army was reinforced by the 'Brasideans', the enfranchised Helots trained by Brasidas. The Boeotian League's levy consisted of 5,000 hoplites (headed by a picked force of 300 Thebans), 5,000 light-armed troops, 500 cavalry, and 500 mounted infantry. Corinth sent 2,000 hoplites. There were also considerable forces from Megara, Sicyon, Pellene in Achaea, Phlius, Epidaurus, and Arcadia, the last headed by the fine infantry of Tegea. The supreme commander, Agis, thus had an army of some 20,000 hoplites, even more light-armed infantry, and a small force of cavalry under his command.

The Argive coalition disposed of some 6,000 Argive hoplites, headed by a picked force of 1,000 men; 3,000 hoplites from Elis and almost as many from Mantinea; and smaller forces from Cleonae and Orneae. Their full strength amounted perhaps to 16,000 hoplites and a larger number of light-armed troops, but they had no cavalry. If Athens could send her field army of some 6,000 hoplites and 1,000 cavalry, the combined forces of the Argive coalition and of Athens would be a match in numbers for the Spartan

[1] 5. 34; 49-57.

Alliance. But no Athenian troops had arrived at Argos when Agis set off from Sparta for Phlius.[1]

As the Spartan army was marching towards Phlius in order to join its allies, it was intercepted by the much superior forces of Argos, Elis, and Mantinea. The Argive commanders made the mistake of not engaging at once, and Agis slipped past during the night and reached Phlius. The Argive commanders then occupied the narrow valley just east of Nemea, blocking the main road from Phlius to Argos. They were in a strong position to withstand a frontal attack, and they still hoped troops would come from Athens. But Agis did not intend to fight on their terms. He divided his army into three columns. With the first column he marched by night along a difficult route, which lay to the west of the Nemea–Argos road, and descended behind the Argive army into the Argive plain, which he began to ravage after dawn. The second column, led by the Corinthians, set out at dawn by another track and cut the main road south of the Argive position. The third column, led by the Boeotians, started last, when it was already full day, and proceeded with the cavalry along the main road towards Nemea. Soon after dawn the Argive commanders received news that Agis was ravaging the Argive plain. They therefore marched southwards, broke through the second column, and entered the northern part of the Argive plain. Meanwhile the third column had not made contact, but it soon entered the Argive plain in the rear of the Argive force. The Argive commanders now found themselves cut off by three separate columns—Agis between them and Argos, the Corinthian column on the foothills, probably on the west side of the plain, and the Boeotian column in their rear. Their army was seriously outnumbered. It was cut off from its base and from any Athenian troops which might arrive by sea. If a pitched battle ensued, it would be encircled in the level plain by the enemy cavalry and light-armed troops.

One of the Argive generals, accompanied by an Argive who was acting as Spartan consul at Argos, crossed the plain and asked Agis for a conference. On their own authority they proposed to start negotiating a treaty of peace with Sparta and to submit any disputes to arbitration. Agis consulted one of the Spartan magistrates on his staff and accepted. He concluded a four months' armistice on the spot. His great army then withdrew to Nemea and broke up, his allies being indignant that the enemy had been released from the trap. Agis, however, had a political as well as a military objective in mind. His aim was to dissolve the Argive coalition, secure a truce with Argos, and isolate Athens. If the Argive general and the Argive consul carried out their proposal, Elis and Mantinea would perforce revert to the Spartan Alliance, their strength still unimpaired and their people not embittered by any losses.

---

[1] 5. 57–58; 64. 3; 66. 3–67. 1; 68. 2–3; 4. 55. 2. Brasideans and Neodamodeis are probably not included in Thucydides' numbering of the army at 5. 68. 3; their number can be estimated from Agis' orders at the Battle of Mantinea, where the transference of 1,200 men would have enabled his left wing to balance the enemy in numbers, and from D.S. 12. 76. 1.

But it turned out otherwise. The Argives were furious at the action of their general, but they still felt themselves bound by the agreement. Shortly afterwards 1,000 hoplites and 300 cavalry arrived from Athens. The Argive commanders intended to send them back, but the Elean and Mantinean generals, loth to find themselves isolated and at the mercy of Sparta, and Alcibiades, who was at Argos as an ambassador, prevailed upon the Argive commanders to set off and lay siege to Orchomenus in Arcadia. When Orchomenus capitulated, the Eleans wished to attack Lepreum. The other allies insisted on attacking Tegea. The Eleans then went home in disgust, and the Argives, Athenians, and Mantineans turned their forces towards Tegea.[1]

Meanwhile at Sparta Agis was criticized for having granted the armistice, and indignation rose when the fall of Orchomenus was reported. He was appointed again to command against the Argives, but he was saddled with ten Spartiates as advisers. He then marched from Sparta with all but the oldest and the youngest men. He was joined at Tegea by his Arcadian allies. Messengers went ahead to summon help from Corinth, Boeotia, Phocis, and Locris. The Spartans and Arcadians advanced from Tegea into Mantinean territory, where the Argive commanders had adopted a strong defensive position with a difficult uphill approach. Agis led his line forward to within a stone's throw and then withdrew; for the ground was unfavourable, and his allies might yet arrive from the Isthmus. The Argive commanders realized that their defensive tactics had lost them the chance of engaging the Spartans and Arcadians alone. Therefore they descended into the plain next day, their army already deployed in line of battle with the Mantineans on the right, 1,000 picked Argives next to them, and then the other Argives in the centre, and the troops of Cleonae, Orneae, and Athens on the left, the last supported by their cavalry. Their hoplites numbered nearly 10,000 in all. They caught the enemy marching in column and off his guard. But Agis issued orders at once. The column immediately swung into line of battle, Scirites and Neodamodeis on the left, Spartans in the centre, and Tegeans with a flanking force of Spartans on the right. During their deployment the troops sang the martial songs of Tyrtaeus and man exhorted man, conscious of their superior discipline. Then, marching in step to the tune of the flute, the solid line of men, shield close to shield and eight men deep, advanced slowly towards the enemy. The Argives and their allies had halted to hear the exhortations of their officers. They now advanced hastily and impetuously.

Before the lines clashed, an occurrence which was frequent in hoplite battles took place. The hoplite carried his shield on his left front; for it was attached to his left arm by metal bands just below the elbow and at the wrist. As he advanced, he tried to protect his unshielded right side by keeping as close as possible to his right-hand neighbour in the line. Thus the whole line, as it advanced, tended to edge to the right crabwise. On this occasion both lines advanced in this manner, so that the right wing of each line far over-

[1] 5. 58–62.

lapped the wing opposed to it. The Spartan line, being longer since their troops were rather more numerous, was about to overlap the Athenians on the Argive left wing by a wide margin, when Agis ordered the Scirites and Neodamodeis on his left wing to move out to their left and ordered two battalions on his right wing to move round into the gap opened up between the Neodamodeis and the centre. The Scirites and Neodamodeis executed the order, the two Spartan battalions did not. Thus the Spartan line split into two parts. Before they could rejoin, the Mantineans and the 1,000 picked Argives fell upon the Scirites and Neodamodeis and drove them back. But, as at the battle of Plataea, a tactical confusion was retrieved by the superb fighting quality of the Spartan troops. For their centre and right, and particularly the 300 Spartiates fighting beside the king, swept on in perfect order and overwhelmed all resistance. Indeed many of the Argives, Cleonaeans, Orneans, and Athenians did not dare to face their onslaught but fled in panic, trampling one another underfoot. Agis wheeled his right wing to take the Athenians in the flank, then pivoted his whole line and moved off to attack the victorious Mantineans and Argives on his left, who in their turn took to flight. The Spartans did not pursue far. Battles were still decided in terms of prestige rather than casualties, and the prestige of Sparta was demonstrated beyond any doubt. They remained in possession of the field, their losses trivial and those of the enemy exceeding a thousand.[1]

The complete vindication of Sparta's military supremacy had immediate effects. Sparta and Argos made a treaty of peace and alliance for fifty years, and the allies of both, whether inside or outside the Peloponnese, were invited to become participants. Provision was made for the inauguration of peace within the Peloponnese, for the exclusion of Athens from Peloponnesian affairs, and for arbitration in all matters of dispute. Mantinea then rejoined the Spartan Alliance, restoring the liberties of the states she had reduced to subjection. Early in 417 the Spartans strengthened the grip of the oligarchs in Sicyon and in Achaea. Then acting in collusion with the Argive *corps d'élite* of 1,000 hoplites, they overthrew the democracy at Argos and introduced an oligarchy. Perdiccas of Macedonia and the Chalcidian states accepted the invitation of Sparta and Argos and joined the coalition. Thus Sparta triumphed in the period of uneasy peace. For, although the democrats soon seized power again at Argos, disposed of some of their opponents with the assistance of Alcibiades, and inclined towards Athens, the other military powers of the mainland stood solidly on the side of Sparta.[2]

The failure of Athens to exploit the Peace of Nicias was a turning-point in the history of the Peloponnesian War. Pericles had foreseen the effects of the strategy which he had propounded at the outset. Athens had won the war of attrition. She had disrupted the Spartan Alliance by her diplomacy. But she had failed to execute the final stage and achieve the aim of the war, the destruction of Sparta and the extension of Athenian power on the mainland.

[1] 5. 63–74.   [2] 5. 75–84. 1.

Athens now turned elsewhere to expand her empire. In so doing she abandoned the strategy of Pericles, heedless of the fact that the situation in 416 was not radically different from the situation in 431. The Spartan Alliance was again intact, supported by Sicily in the west and by Macedonia and Chalcidice in the north. Athens had the friendship of a weakened Argos and a foothold at Pylus; but her own resources were diminished, the prestige of her army was lower, and the leadership of the state was divided. The advice of Pericles was as valid as ever—not to hazard the resources of the state in imperial expansion, so long as the Spartan Alliance was undefeated—and his words were still fresh in the memory of Thucydides the historian: 'I am more afraid of Athens' mistakes than of her enemy's plans.'[1]

§ 2. *The Sicilian expedition*

THE failure of Athens' policy in the Peloponnese brought discredit to its promoter, Alcibiades, and credit to its opponent, Nicias. The division between the two cut deeper into the general policy of the state. Alcibiades favoured war with Sparta, expansion of the empire, and strict control of the subject states; he set no limits to his own ambitions or to the ambitions of the people. He found his support largely in the lower class, which favoured adventure and looked for material gains, and in those of his own generation, the young men, who were averse to the cautious strategy of a Pericles or a Nicias. But his magnetic personality—his good looks, his persuasive oratory, his impetuous courage, his brilliance of ideas—appealed to all classes of the community, whether they agreed with his policy or not. Nicias wished to be at peace with Sparta, keep the empire intact, and treat the subject states with moderation; and the *status quo* met his own wishes and the plans he had for Athens. His policy was acceptable especially to the well-to-do, who would conserve their prosperity and farm their lands in Attica, and to those of the older generation who remembered the days of peace before 431. As the Assembly found itself divided, it had recourse to ostracism in the spring of 417. But Alcibiades and Nicias joined forces and urged their supporters to vote against Hyperbolus, a democratic agitator who had slandered both of them. When the people cast their ostraca, Hyperbolus was the victim. Thereafter the law of ostracism fell into disuse; for it had failed in its purpose, to decide between the policies of rival statesmen.[2]

The divided counsels of Athens had already cost her dear. Under Alcibiades' leadership she had made public her intention to attack Sparta and campaign in the Peloponnese. The alliance with Argos and her coalition, the attempt to build long walls at Patrae and at Rhium, the encouragement of Argos to attack Epidaurus, the occupation of a fort at Epidaurus, and the placing of Helots at Pylus bore no other interpretation. Yet, when the policy

[1] 1. 144. 1; 2. 65. 7; 5. 69. 1 fin.
[2] Plu. *Nic.* 11; *Alc.* 13; Th. 8. 73. 3; *FGrH* 115 F 96b (Theopompus); Ar. *Eq.* 1304.

was put to the test, Athens failed to prosecute it. Alcibiades was not elected general for the crucial year 418/417, and Athens was dilatory in sending even a small force to help Argos. By her indecision she incurred the risk of war with Sparta and lost the allies who could have given her a chance of military victory in such a war. In 417 she elected both Nicias and Alcibiades as generals. Nicias was to lead an expedition with the help of Perdiccas against Chalcidice and Amphipolis, but it was abandoned when Perdiccas changed sides. In the winter of 417–416 the fleet instituted a blockade of Macedonia. Alcibiades sailed early in 416 to Argos, where he took a number of political prisoners and confirmed the ascendancy of the democracy. In the same year Athens went to war with Corinth, and the Athenians and Helots at Pylus gained much booty at the expense of the Spartans. Another expedition sailed to Melos, a colony of Sparta, and demanded that it should enter the Athenian empire. These acts aggravated the chances of war with Sparta and the Spartan Alliance.[1]

The course of Athens' dealings with Melos was a warning to the Greek world. The small island had declared her neutrality at the beginning of the war, and she sent some gifts to Sparta but no troops. In 426 Athens ravaged her territory with large forces, and in 425 assessed her for a tribute of fifteen talents. But Melos preserved her neutrality. In 416 the forces of Athens arrived unheralded at Melos. There were thirty ships from Athens, six from Chios, and two from Lesbos, and some 3,000 troops, half Athenian and half allied. After effecting a landing the Athenian generals sent envoys to negotiate with the leaders of the oligarchic government of Melos. The envoys stated that Athens did not admit the neutrality of Melos: the island must enter the Athenian empire or face the consequences. An appeal by the Melians to international justice was dismissed. International justice, in the opinion of the Athenian envoys, existed only between states of equal power; the privilege of the strong was to treat the weak in the light of a different principle, that of expediency. The Melians refused to submit, fought gallantly under siege, and finally capitulated in the winter of 416–415, entrusting their fate to the verdict of the Athenian people. When the Assembly met, Alcibiades spoke in support of the proposal which was enacted: the adult males of Melos were slaughtered, the women and children were enslaved, and the island was occupied by 500 Athenians. The fate of Melos underlined the present policy of Athens. To be weak and to be neutral was to invite annihilation at the hands of the tyrant state.[2]

In the same winter Athenian envoys went to Sicily at the invitation of her ally Segesta, which was hard pressed in a war with Selinus, a Megarian colony allied to Syracuse. When they returned in the spring of 415, they brought sixty talents of silver and an erroneous report that Segesta had plenty of money to pay the costs of an Athenian expeditionary force. The

---

[1] 5. 52. 2; 53; 56. 3; 80. 3; 83. 4; 84. 1; 115. 2; cf. 6. 85. 1.
[2] 5. 84–114; 115. 4; 116. 2–4; *GHI* 76.

Assembly decided to send sixty ships under the command of Alcibiades, Nicias, and Lamachus, and met again to consider the fitting out of the force. Nicias took this opportunity to reopen the issue; for he was opposed to the expedition, and he did not wish to serve as one of its commanders.

Nicias argued that it was unsound strategy to disperse the forces of Athens. The Peloponnesians and the Boeotians stood ready to attack, the Chalcidians were still in revolt, Corinth and Perdiccas were already operating against Athens, Argos needed assistance, and the financial resources of Athens were already deeply committed. Sicily constituted no threat to Athens. Even if Athens conquered Sicily, she could not count on holding it; for the island was far off, and the population was numerous. Nicias also criticized Alcibiades, the chief advocate of the expedition, for his headstrong ambition and extravagant life. Alcibiades retorted that ambition and expenditure were honourable in an individual and in a state; they had won Athens her empire, and they would add new territories to it. By undertaking the expedition Athens would conquer Sicily and force the whole of Greece into submission, or else she would dock the power of Syracuse. When Nicias saw that Alcibiades was succeeding in his appeal to the adventurous spirit of the Athenians, he tried to alarm them by putting a high estimate on his requirements for the expeditionary force. But the Assembly was seized with an irrational enthusiasm for the enterprise. The majority of the people thought it would provide them with pay for the moment and pay in perpetuity, once Sicily was made subject. The younger generation welcomed the prospect of adventure and excitement; and even the older and more cautious thought the very size of the expedition would ensure its safety, if not its success. Those who had misgivings did not dare to voice them in an atmosphere of such enthusiasm. Nicias was compelled to name his figures for the expeditionary force. They were accepted in principle, and Alcibiades, Nicias, and Lamachus were authorized to proceed with the preparations.[1]

During the years of uneasy peace Athens had recovered from her financial exhaustion with remarkable speed. The imperial revenues were indeed reduced from the high level of 425–421, but they were still greater than at the outbreak of the war. As trade revived, the yield from indirect taxes rose, and money in private hands increased with the cultivation of Attica and the development of the mines. A considerable programme of public building was undertaken, and the state-pay remained at the same level, that of the dicasts, for instance, staying at the rate of 3 obols a day which Cleon had fixed. The money therefore was in hand for a vote of 3,000 talents towards the fitting out of the great expedition, and wealthy citizens spared no expense in performing their duties as trierarchs. In the latter part of June 415 the crews of 60 triremes and 40 troopships, 1,500 hoplites, 700 thetes armed as marines, and 30 cavalry assembled at the Peiraeus with their relatives and friends. After prayers on ship and on land the fleet put out to sea, raced under

[1] 6. 6; 8–26; cf. 6. 90.

oar to Aegina, and then set its course for Corcyra, where most of the forces which had been levied from the subjects of Athens or hired in friendly areas were already assembled. These numbered 34 triremes, 2,900 hoplites, and 1,300 archers, slingers, and light-armed troops. The armada sailed from Corcyra in three flotillas. It was accompanied by 30 supply vessels carrying corn and technicians, 100 smaller craft pressed into service, and many attendant vessels, packed with camp-followers. Never had such an expedition sailed the Mediterranean Sea since the Persian armada of Xerxes.[1]

While the expedition still lay in the Peiraeus, an act of sacrilege was committed in Athens. Most of the stone busts of Hermes, set upon square pillars at the doors of temples and houses, were mutilated during the night. It was generally thought to be an ill omen for the expedition, the work probably of some revolutionaries. Rewards were offered to anyone who would give information about this or any other act of impiety. Nothing was discovered about the mutilation of the Hermae, but informers reported two earlier acts of sacrilege, the mutilation of other statues and the burlesquing of the sacred ritual of the Mysteries, in which Alcibiades was named as the ringleader. Some colour was lent to this charge by the notorious wildness of Alcibiades and his young associates; for he was profligate, reckless, and irreligious. Moreover, his precocious talents and his boundless ambition led men to suspect that he aimed at seizing power and setting himself up as tyrant. His political enemies made capital out of these suspicions. When Alcibiades asked to be put on trial before he sailed, they managed to thwart him. For they intended to recall him for trial later, when he lacked the backing of those who were involved in the Sicilian expedition. He therefore sailed under a cloud of suspicion, which he was given no chance to disperse.[2]

These events revealed many of the faults in the Athenian democracy. The Assembly knew little of Sicily, its size or its military strength. Despite the successes of Syracuse and her allies in the Archidamian War and the united front which Hermocrates had formed, Alcibiades could declare that the Siceliote Greeks were a motley mob, incapable of concerted action and inferior as fighting men. When the Assembly decided to attack Syracuse, before it had defeated Sparta, it did so in the flush of an irrational enthusiasm. To send Nicias against his wish and to couple him with Alcibiades was an act of military folly, a compromise due to the political division within the state, when a clear-cut decision was essential. To send Alcibiades without

---

[1] The finances of Athens in 421–415 are disputed. Andoc. 3. 8 states that the annual tribute exceeded 1,200 talents and that 7,000 talents were deposited on the Acropolis. Extant quota-lists indicate that the figure for tribute is too high alone, but it may represent total annual income from the empire. Many scholars regard the figure of 7,000 talents as too high. Yet in 415 Athens put aside 3,000 talents for the Sicilian Expedition; she had the last reserve of 1,000 talents; and it is possible that she had other reserves to make a total of 7,000. For her financial recovery in 421–415 cf. Th. 6. 26. 2; for the 3,000 talents *GHI* 77 b 29; for forces employed in Sicily Th. 6. 30–32. 2; 42–43; 7. 16. 2; 20. 2; 31. 5; 35. 1; 42. 1; 57; 75. 5.

[2] 6. 27–29; 15. 3–4.

giving him a chance to clear himself was unfair to him and prejudicial to the command of the expedition. The political leaders of Athens, with the honourable exception of Nicias, were inspired by personal and sometimes corrupt motives, and they were more concerned with their own advancement than with the interests of the state. The people who chose them were little better. The salient qualities of the Athenian democracy in 415 were energy, opportunism, unscrupulousness, and instability.[1]

The citizens of Syracuse did not believe the rumour that Athens was about to make an attack. Hermocrates urged them in vain to take the initiative, rally the Sicels and the Greeks to their cause, and engage the Athenian expedition in south Italy. Meanwhile the great fleet was sailing from Corcyra to the heel of Italy. There the Greek cities shut their gates, and the fleet coasted down to Rhegium without acquiring a single ally. The disappointment of the Athenian generals was heightened by the news that Segesta had duped them and could not provide more than thirty talents towards their chest. They then held a council of war. Nicias proposed to settle affairs between Segesta and Selinus, make a display of force, and return home. Alcibiades favoured a diplomatic approach to the Sicels and Greeks of Sicily, in order to obtain a base—preferably Messana—and supplies, and later an advance on Syracuse if the need should arise. Lamachus urged an immediate attack on Syracuse; supplies would be got by pillage, Syracuse would be isolated, and her population intimidated. His plan was perhaps the best, but he could not convince either of the others. The deadlock was solved by Lamachus casting his vote in favour of Alcibiades' plan. A compromise was adopted. Messana was approached without success by Alcibiades, and half the battle-fleet sailed along the east coast of Sicily, reconnoitred the harbour and coast of Syracuse, and gained possession of Catana as a base in Sicily.[2]

Soon afterwards the state ship, the *Salaminia*, arrived to recall Alcibiades and some others for trial. For the agitation about the mutilation of the Hermae had continued in Athens until a prisoner turned informer and supplied a list of names. Although the name of Alcibiades was not among them, the people suspected him on many grounds and intended to put him to death. On their way home he and the others escaped at Thurii and crossed eventually to the Peloponnese. Nicias and Lamachus were now in sole command. They agreed to sail to the north coast of the island, where they captured a small port from the native Sicans, and sold their prisoners for 120 talents. These piratical methods damaged the prestige of Athens and enabled Syracuse to enlarge her coalition.[3]

When winter came, the Syracusan forces, reinforced by troops from Selinus, Gela, and Camarina, marched out to attack the Athenian base at Catana. An Athenian agent from Catana had encouraged them to make this

---

[1] 6. 1. 1; 17. 2–5; 12; 15. 2–3; 2. 65. 7, 10, 11.
[2] 6. 32. 3–41; 44. 2–52; 7. 42. 3.   [3] 6. 53; 60–62.

attack, and he informed the Athenians of the plan. They moved their whole army by night and landed unopposed in the Great Harbour of Syracuse. There they chose a position with a narrow front, and fortified it against attack by the Syracusan cavalry. On approaching Catana the Syracusans realized that the Athenian fleet had sailed. They hastened back to Syracuse, and formed their hoplites in a line of battle sixteen men deep, placing their 1,200 cavalry and their javelinmen on their right wing. Nicias and Lamachus placed half their hoplites in a line eight men deep and the other half behind them in a square formation, so that they could reinforce the front line wherever necessary and attack the enemy cavalry if it broke through. In the battle which ensued the Argives and Mantineans on the right wing and the Athenians in the centre of the front line outfought the enemy, but they were prevented by the Syracusan cavalry from pressing the pursuit. The Athenian victory heightened the prestige of the army, but it had no strategic effect. For the generals withdrew to Naxus and Catana for the winter and they failed to win over Messana and Camarina to their side.[1]

Nicias and Lamachus had achieved little in this first campaigning season. They were deficient in cavalry, allies, and money, without which they could neither move freely by land nor organize regular supplies. During the winter they sent to Athens for reinforcements, especially of cavalry and money, and they sought to make allies of the non-Greek peoples, the Sicels, Carthaginians, and Etruscans. By the early summer of 414 they had brought most of the Sicels into alliance by diplomacy or by force. From Athens they received 300 talents and 280 troopers, for whom mounts were obtained in Sicily. Preparations were now complete for landing again at Syracuse and blockading or assaulting the city. The Syracusans meanwhile had benefited by their experience in the battle. During the winter they equipped and trained their hoplites; and they replaced their fifteen generals by a board of three generals, including the able and determined Hermocrates, and entrusted full powers to them. They also sent envoys to the Peloponnese. Corinth promised help and sent envoys to Sparta to support the Syracusan envoys in their appeal. There they found Alcibiades, and his speech roused the Spartan Assembly to action. He depicted the aim of Athens in Sicily as he himself had conceived it: to conquer Sicily, south Italy, and Carthage, to build great fleets and raise native mercenaries in the west, and to blockade and assault the Peloponnese. He advised the Spartans to send out an able officer to conduct the defence of Syracuse, and themselves to establish a fortified post at Decelea in Attica, from which the supplies and land communications of Athens could be cut. The Spartans accordingly appointed Gylippus to conduct the defence of Syracuse and made preparations to invade Attica and fortify Decelea.[2]

In the early summer of 414 Nicias and Lamachus made their attempt on Syracuse. The defences were very strong (see Fig. 25). The old and new quar-

[1] 6. 63–71; 74; 75. 3–88. 2.   [2] 6. 88. 3–6; 72–73; 88. 7–10; 89–94.

ters of the city, built respectively on Ortygia and on the mainland, were both walled, and their walls were linked to form a single system of fortification. Ortygia, then an island joined by a mole to the mainland, dominated the entrance to the two harbours, the Lesser Harbour in which the Syracusan fleet lay behind a line of piles, and the Great Harbour where the beaches

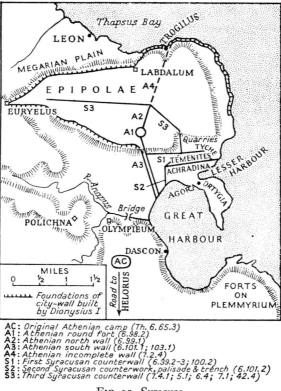

AC: *Original Athenian camp (Th. 6.65.3)*
A1: *Athenian round fort (6.98.2)*
A2: *Athenian north wall (6.99.1)*
A3: *Athenian south wall (6.101.1; 103.1)*
A4: *Athenian incomplete wall (7.2.4)*
S1: *First Syracusan counterwall (6.99.2-3; 100.2)*
S2: *Second Syracusan counterwork, palisade & trench (6.101.2)*
S3: *Third Syracusan counterwall (7.4.1; 5.1; 6.4; 7.1; 42.4)*

FIG. 25. Syracuse

were set with stakes to impede a landing. The fortified area on the main-land, known as Achradina, had been extended during the winter to include Temenites and now reached out towards Epipolae, a plateau overlooking the city and surrounded by steep scarps. The Athenians could invest Syracuse only from the western side, and for this purpose they must obtain possession of Epipolae. Hermocrates therefore made ready to man the approaches to Epipolae. But early one morning, when he was holding a review of his troops in the meadow south of Epipolae, the Athenians, having landed unobserved to the north of Epipolae at Leon, were already marshalling their army. They hastened to Epipolae, scaled it from the west at Euryelus, and defeated the Syracusans as they came into action piecemeal.

Once in possession of Epipolae the Athenians built a round fort, and from it began to carry one wall of investment northwards in the direction of Trogilus and then another southwards towards the Great Harbour. The Syracusans tried to prevent the progress of the southwards wall by constructing a counter-wall across its path. When this was captured by an assault force of 300 picked Athenians, they ran a palisade and a trench out into the marshy plain farther south. An assault on this palisade and trench was led by Lamachus, the round fort on Epipolae being held only by the camp-followers under Nicias, who was ill. The assault led to a general engagement between the two armies, in the course of which Lamachus was killed and an attack on the round fort was only staved off by Nicias setting fire to his dump of timber-trusses and siege-engines. At a critical moment in the battle the Athenian fleet, which had been instructed to move from its base at Thapsus, appeared in the Great Harbour, and the Syracusans withdrew into the city. It was now only a matter of time before the investment was complete and the city fell by blockade. The Athenians were further encouraged by receiving supplies from Italy, three penteconters from Etruria, and the accession of many Sicels to their side.[1]

The northern wall was already nearing completion and a double wall on the south was approaching the sea, when the Syracusans, who had deposed their generals and begun to negotiate with Nicias, were greatly heartened by the arrival of a Corinthian named Gongylus with a trireme. He brought the news that some ships from Corinth, Leucas, and Ambracia were on the way and that Gylippus was already in Sicily. Meanwhile Gylippus, who had crossed with four ships to Taras and then had sailed to Himera, was on his way overland at the head of a mixed army almost 3,000 strong, composed of his Peloponnesians, his allies at Selinus, Himera, and Gela, and some Sicels. He ascended Epipolae at Euryelus, as the Athenians had originally done, passed through an uncompleted part of the Athenians' northern wall and joined forces with the Syracusan army, which sallied forth to meet him. In failing to intercept Gongylus and Gylippus the Athenians committed a serious blunder, Nicias having underestimated their importance.[2]

Gylippus put new energy into the defence of Syracuse. He began to build a crosswall out from Temenites towards the uncompleted part of the Athenians' northern wall, and he protected it by attacking the Athenians. Finally, he managed to bring the Syracusan cavalry into action and defeated the Athenian army. Next night he carried his crosswall past the line of the northern wall and so saved Syracuse from the danger of circumvallation. Gylippus also succeeded in capturing Labdalum, a fortified base of supply, on the north side of Epipolae. Nicias then decided to move his main base south to Plemmyrium at the mouth of the Great Harbour. There he built three forts to

[1] 6. 75. 1; 96–103. 2.   [2] 6. 103. 4; 104; 7. 1–2.

protect the ships and the stores. But the seamen grumbled at the change: fresh water was some distance away, and the enemy cavalry attacked them outside their camp. He now controlled the round fort, the double wall from it to the Great Harbour, and the Great Harbour itself. The Syracusans held the egress north of the round fort, and their cavalry controlled the hinterland. Gylippus toured the rest of Sicily to obtain reinforcements, and twelve more ships, which Nicias tried in vain to intercept, sailed into the Lesser Harbour. The Syracusan navy began to practise within sight of the Athenian fleet, which was suffering from the wastage of its crews and from the lack of opportunity to careen the hulls of the vessels.

Nicias now saw the danger of the besiegers being besieged. He therefore sent out an urgent dispatch, which reached Athens early in the winter. He frankly stated the weakness of his position. His Athenian seamen were unruly, his foreign seamen were deserting in considerable numbers, and his fleet had lost its margin of superiority over the enemy. He depended for his supplies on the states in Italy, and these might any day change sides. In the coming spring the Syracusans would be reinforced from Sicily and the Peloponnese, and they would then become masters of the situation. Nicias advised the Athenians either to recall the expeditionary force or to send out another one, equally large and well supplied with money; in either event he asked to be relieved of his command in view of his illness. The Assembly decided to send out another force but not to relieve Nicias of his command. They appointed two generals to join him, Eurymedon, who sailed with ten ships in midwinter, and Demosthenes, who was to lead the main force in 413. Thus the Athenian people committed itself more deeply to the Sicilian enterprise, despite the fact that war on the home front was becoming more and more likely.[1]

While the main force was in Sicily, Athens undertook operations from her base in Macedonia, Methone, a member of the Athenian empire, to which Athens had accorded preferential treatment. In the winter of 416-415 her troops began to ravage Macedonia and later forced Perdiccas into alliance. In 414 he and a large force of Thracians joined Athens in an unsuccessful attack on Amphipolis. More of her energies went into the support of her ally, Argos, now at war with the Spartan Alliance. Both sides engaged in ravaging tactics, and in 414 the Argives persuaded an Athenian force of thirty ships to ravage the coast of Laconia. This was an act of war, which could not be justified by reference to the defensive alliance between Athens and Argos. The Athenian breaches of the peace and alliance with Sparta were now clear, and in addition Athens had refused to accept Sparta's request for arbitration of their differences. Corinth and her colony Syracuse were already pressing Sparta to invade Attica. The aggression of Athens against Melos and Sicily filled the allies of Sparta with alarm. Thus Sparta and her Alliance decided to renew the war of liberation. A more effective strategy was now possible.

[1] 7. 3-8; 10-16.

The idea of occupying a fortified post in Attica had been in the air in 432–431 and in 422–421; but, if such a post was to be maintained throughout the year and if regular operations were to be conducted in Attica, the Peloponnesians and Boeotians had to have a large margin of military superiority over the Athenian field-army. Such a margin first came into existence in 422, and it recurred when Athens was deeply engaged in Sicily. In accordance with Alcibiades' recommendation Sparta ordered her allies to provide iron, tools, and masons for the fortifying of Decelea, and to muster troops for Sicily. The war was to be fought on two fronts.[1]

Agis led the invading army into Attica in early spring 413, ravaged the borders of the plain, and fortified Decelea, which lay within sight of Athens, almost half-way between the city and the Boeotian border and on the main route towards Euboea. Meanwhile a considerable force of hoplites sailing in merchantmen set out across the open sea for Sicily; Sparta sent 600 Neodamodeis and Helots, Boeotia 300 men, Corinth 500, and Sicyon 200. Their departure was covered by a Corinthian fleet of 25 triremes, which engaged the Athenian squadron based at Naupactus. Two fleets were fitted out at Athens, 30 ships to collect Argive hoplites and raid the Laconian coast and 65 ships under Demosthenes' command to transport 1,200 Athenian hoplites and as many of their subjects as could be pressed into service. The two fleets were to operate together against Laconia. Demosthenes helped to select and fortify an isthmus opposite Cythera, and he then proceeded on his way to Sicily. The resources of Athens were now fully extended; for she had at least 225 ships at sea and 45,000 men in receipt of service pay.[2]

Even so her help arrived almost too late in Sicily. Gylippus and Hermocrates had encouraged the Syracusans to man their fleet and attack the enemy. Gylippus himself led his army at night into the vicinity of Plemmyrium. The Syracusan fleet attacked at dawn with two squadrons, one of 35 triremes operating in the Great Harbour and the other of 45 triremes sailing round from the Lesser Harbour. The Athenians quickly manned 60 ships and engaged the enemy squadrons before they could join forces. The fighting was bitter, and the men at the naval base were collecting on the shore to watch, when Gylippus suddenly assaulted and captured the three forts, inflicting heavy loss of life. At sea the Syracusans were at first victorious, but their ships soon fell foul of one another and the Athenians gained the upper hand. When the fleets disengaged, the Syracusans had lost 11 ships and the Athenians 3 ships. But the capture of the naval base at Plemmyrium was far more important. The gear of 40 triremes, the reserves of wheat, and many goods of value fell into the Syracusans' hands. As they now held the forts at Plemmyrium, their ships could threaten the entry into the Great Harbour from both sides. In order to intensify their blockade of the Athenians, they sent 12 ships to Italy and intercepted supplies of foodstuffs and timber at source.[3]

---

[1] *GHI* 61; Th. 6. 7; 95; 105; 7. 9; 18; 1. 142. 2; 5. 17. 2; 7. 66. 2.
[2] 7. 19–20; 26.   [3] 7. 21–25.

The success of the Syracusans brought them help from many states in Sicily, and Gylippus decided to attack again in July before reinforcements could arrive from Athens. The Syracusans cut down the bows of their ships and reinforced them with stay-beams, so that they could ram the Athenian ships bow on. For the Athenians, relying on their speed to outmanœuvre an enemy vessel and ram her broadside, built their ships with slender bows. In the open sea these tactics won them success, but on this occasion the engagement would take place in the confined waters of the Great Harbour. The Syracusan army moved first against the double wall of the Athenians, one force issuing from the city and another from Olympieum, and then their fleet of eighty ships sailed out against the seventy-five Athenian ships. No action occurred on that day or the day after. But on the following day the Athenian fleet attacked and the Syracusans, charging bow on, stove in the forepart of the enemy ships, sinking seven and disabling many more, while their javelinmen, being at close quarters, killed many of the oarsmen. The Athenian fleet was only saved from complete defeat by the foresight of Nicias; for he had protected his improvised harbour with merchantmen, anchored off the entrance and swinging from their yard-arms great masses of iron which could be dropped into any enemy vessel seeking to enter the harbour. Behind these merchantmen the battered Athenian fleet found refuge. The Syracusans were about to attack again, when Demosthenes sailed into the Great Harbour with seventy-three triremes, 5,000 hoplites, and swarms of light-armed troops, both Greek and barbarian.[1]

He decided to exploit the consternation into which the Syracusans were cast by the arrival of so vast an armament. His aim was to gain possession of Epipolae and complete the wall of circumvallation. He failed, however, to breach the long single wall built by Gylippus westward along Epipolae. He then delivered an attack by night from the west, where the entry at Euryelus was narrow. The spearhead of his large and mixed army surprised the enemy, captured the fort at the entry, and attacked the three fortified camps on the plateau. The victorious troops were rushing on impetuously and in disordered groups, when first the Boeotians and then other detachments of the Syracusan army rallied and counter-attacked. The Athenian troops then fell back in confusion, being for the most part ignorant of the terrain and unable to distinguish friend from foe in the hazy moonlight, and they were soon in headlong flight. Meanwhile more of their army were pushing their way up through the narrow entry and preventing the withdrawal of those who had been routed. The Syracusan forces, on the other hand, were operating on a broader front; they deployed in formation, made better use of their watchword, and knew which way they were facing. Their war-cries added to the turmoil. For to an Athenian ear they were indistinguishable from those of the Dorian troops on their own side, Argives, Corcyraeans, Rhodians, and others. In the end the army of Demosthenes was driven off the plateau, many

[1] 7. 36-42. 1.

falling to their death from the cliffs and many being killed at dawn by the Syracusan cavalry as they wandered lost in the plain.[1]

After this disaster Demosthenes proposed to withdraw the whole force by sea. Its military strength was impaired, and disease was rife in the camp. The army, he maintained, would be better employed at home in attacking Decelea. The fleet still held command of the Sicilian Sea, and could handle the evacuation without danger. Nicias was opposed to withdrawal. He said that the Syracusans might be on the verge of collapse, their finances exhausted, and their citizens disaffected. In his heart he was still undecided; and, being undecided, he preferred to risk his life in Sicily rather than in the people's court at Athens. Demosthenes and the third general, Eurymedon, then proposed to withdraw to Thapsus or Catana, where the army could forage for supplies and the navy operate in open waters, and meanwhile, if Nicias did not wish to decide on his own responsibility, a decision could be obtained from Athens. But Nicias persisted obstinately in his refusal to move, and the Athenian forces lingered where they were. Meanwhile, as August wore on, Gylippus increased his army by bringing in more troops from Sicily and collecting the Peloponnesians who had come via the African coast to Selinus. When Nicias became aware of their arrival, he withdrew his opposition, provided no open vote was taken, and the order for the evacuation was given. On the eve of sailing away, on 27 August 413, when the moon was full, an eclipse occurred. The soothsayers declared that the army must now wait 'thrice nine' days. The majority of the Athenians in the camp accepted their verdict, and Nicias, abandoning his indecision and making a necessity of his virtue, refused outright to move.[2]

Before the twenty-seven days were up, the Syracusans passed to the attack. They defeated the small force of Athenian cavalry and then captured eighteen ships in battle in the narrow waters. When the Syracusans began to close the mouth of the Great Harbour with an improvised boom of merchantmen and boats, the Athenian generals saw that they would be trapped without hope of obtaining supplies. They therefore manned every ship that would float, to the number of 110, driving as many troops as possible on board and exhorting them to fight for their lives and for the salvation of Athens, and sent them off under oar at full speed towards the gap in the boom. The Syracusans had posted their seventy-five ships partly in front of the gap and partly round the shores of the harbour, so that they could offset their inferiority in numbers by bringing all their ships into action on the flanks and front of the Athenian squadron. At first the Athenian ships charged right through to the boom which the sailors tried in vain to sever, but then the Syracusan ships closed in on all sides, ship crashing into ship, coxswains bellowing their orders, skirmishers hurling their missiles, and hoplites boarding the jammed and disabled vessels. From the shore the two armies watched the swaying conflict. The Athenians, their fate now in the balance, shouted in jubilation or in

[1] 7. 42. 2–44.   [2] 7. 45–50.

despair, each as he saw a particular piece of the action in the Great Harbour. At last the Athenian ships fled, hotly pursued by the Syracusans, and piled up on the beach, where the army was able to protect them. That evening, when the Syracusans sailed back to the city, Demosthenes persuaded Nicias that the best course was to resume the battle at sea next morning; for they still had more ships than the enemy. But the panic had gone too far. The sailors refused to row again, and the only alternative was to fight their way out by land.[1]

In Syracuse the victory was celebrated with wine and feasting in honour of Heracles. As the troops were not fit for action that night, Hermocrates sent a message, which duped Nicias into believing that the Syracusans already held the passes and the Athenians could not escape by night. When dawn came, the Athenian generals waited another day, and then the army of 40,000 men marched off, its dead unburied and its wounded abandoned. The Syracusans now held the passes towards Catana, and their cavalry and light-armed troops harassed the army incessantly as it fought its way across the plain. Five days passed and the Athenians had made little progress. Their supplies were now exhausted. They left fires burning that night and set off in the opposite direction. Demosthenes' division fell behind and was surrounded next day. He surrendered on condition that the lives of the men would be respected. Nicias' division was overhauled and surrounded on the following day, but it fought its way forward next day and reached water at the Assinarus river. As the Athenians broke ranks and rushed towards the water, tortured by thirst and eager to cross, the enemy hemmed them in and drove them against one another, so that many were trampled underfoot or impaled on their own spears. The top of the far bank, too, was lined by Syracusans, who threw their javelins into the confused mass of men in the hollow river bed, most of them drinking greedily. 'The Peloponnesians marched down and slaughtered them, especially those in the river, and the water was immediately spoiled, but all the same most of them were drinking it, bloody and muddy as it was, and even fighting for it.' When the dead lay there in piles, Nicias gave himself up to Gylippus and implored him to stop the massacre. Gylippus ordered the remnant to be taken alive. He wanted to keep Demosthenes and Nicias, but the Syracusans and Corinthians put them to death. The survivors, some 7,000 in number, were herded into a cramped quarry shaft at Syracuse, where many died of exposure, malnutrition, and disease. Seventy days later the Syracusans took out the allies of Athens and sold them as slaves, but they left the Athenians and any Greeks of Sicily and Italy to their fate.[2]

Meanwhile the Athenians at home had been feeling the strain of adversity. The regular garrison at Decelea and freebooters from Boeotia were stripping Attica of flocks, baggage-animals, and movable property. The mounts of the Athenian cavalry went lame on the rocky ground, and the city-walls had to

---

[1] 7. 51-72.   [2] 7. 73-87; Plu. *Nic.* 28-29.

be manned at all seasons, day and night. The city was now under blockade, and had to import all its supplies by sea at great expense. In an attempt to augment their dwindling resources the Athenians decided to impose a tax of 5 per cent. on all imports and exports within the empire instead of the tribute and screw more money out of their subjects. As their commitments increased, they relied less on their 'Allies' and more on barbarian mercenaries, whose atrocities, for instance at Mycalessus in Boeotia, where man, woman, and child were butchered, made Athens the object of a deeper hatred. Even at sea they suffered a defeat in the Gulf of Corinth at the hands of a smaller fleet of Corinthian ships, which had strengthened their bows for ramming head-on. When disaster came at Syracuse, it dealt a shattering blow to the power and the prestige of Athens. She lost in all more than 200 warships, the bulk being Athenian, and their complement of seamen, some 40,000, recruited mainly from the subject states; some 4,000 Athenian cavalrymen, hoplites, and light-armed men, and a considerably larger number of troops from the subject states, allies, and barbarian friends of Athens; and an enormous amount of money, weapons, and materials. All hope of expansion was at an end. Athens turned to fight for her life, and for the empire from which she derived much of her resources. She had the courage and resilience but not the unity among her citizens which had carried her to triumph in the Persian wars.[1]

§ 3. *Persia enters the war*

DURING the winter of 413–412 Sparta made preparations for the campaign which most men thought would end the war. Agis, setting out from Decelea, exacted money from allies and neutrals in central Greece, and the Spartan government ordered the building of an allied fleet of 100 triremes. Euboea, Lesbos, Chios, and Erythrae offered to revolt, and the two satraps in the coastal areas of Asia Minor promised assistance, Pharnabazus in the north and Tissaphernes in the south. The Spartans decided to support Chios, which had a navy of sixty ships, and to negotiate with Tissaphernes; but they and their allies were so dilatory that the Athenians learnt their plans and intercepted the first Peloponnesian squadron of twenty-one triremes, which did not dare to leave the coast of Epidaurus. Meanwhile Alcibiades, who had been urging on the Ephors at Sparta, and a Spartan commander, Chalcideus, sailed across with five ships and raised Chios, Erythrae, and Clazomenae, and later Miletus in revolt. Chalcideus then made an alliance on behalf of the Spartan Alliance with Darius, whereby 'the ancestral possessions of the Great King' were recognized as his and both parties undertook to combine against Athens. The revolt then spread to Lesbos, and four more triremes from the Peloponnese reached Chios. These triremes were units of the squadron which had broken through the Athenian blockade off the coast of

[1] 7. 27–30; 34; *Hell. Oxy.* 12. 4–5.

Epidaurus. They brought another Spartan, Astyochus, who took over the supreme command and reported that the main Peloponnesian fleet would soon arrive.[1]

While the Peloponnesians were slow to grasp the initiative, the Athenians pressed on with their preparations, building ships, economizing in the administration of the democracy, and fortifying Sunium to afford protection to their supply-ships. A board of ten elder statesmen, including Hagnon and the poet Sophocles, was appointed to act as advisory commissioners (*probouloi*) during the time of crisis. In the spring of 412 Athens had 27 triremes at Naupactus and 21 triremes in home waters, of which 7 were from Chios. Her first aim was to prevent her enemies from concentrating their squadrons; she succeeded in blockading one off the coast of Epidaurus, but she failed to stop another which sailed from Sicily to Corinth. When Chios revolted, Athens brought the reserve fund of 1,000 talents into use and manned the ships as fast as they came off the stocks.

In the east Aegean the island of greatest strategic value was Samos. It was situated on the shortest route from Greece to Ionia, on the line of communications from Sparta to Chios, and, when Miletus revolted, between the two chief areas of revolt. The first Athenian squadron, numbering only eight ships, secured the island. When the ships increased to thirty, some of the crews supported a violent revolution in Samos, which overthrew the upper classes and put the democrats in power. Athens granted full autonomy to Samos, hoping that this would encourage democrats in other subject states to remain loyal to her. The Athenians then blockaded Miletus, recaptured Mitylene and Clazomenae, and ravaged the island of Chios. Late in the summer forty-eight ships, including transports, and a hoplite force of 1,000 Athenians, 1,500 Argives, and 1,000 allies sailed from Athens and landed near Miletus. A detachment of Milesians and Peloponnesians made a sortie to join a Persian force of mercenary infantry and native cavalry under Tissaphernes, but they were defeated by the Athenians, who prepared to invest the city.[2]

At this juncture the main Peloponnesian fleet arrived. It consisted of thirty-three ships from the Peloponnese and twenty-two from Syracuse and Selinus. The Athenian commander, Phrynichus, prudently withdrew from Miletus to Samos, where the Athenian squadrons could concentrate for the winter of 412–411, which was now setting in. The Argive troops, who had suffered heavy losses at Miletus, went home disgruntled, and Argos ceased to take any active part in the war. During the winter both fleets were reinforced. The Peloponnesians received pay for their crews from Persia and augmented their funds by sacking Iasus and selling the population to Tissaphernes. Feeling themselves somewhat stronger, they made a second pact, in which

---

[1] 8. 2–3; 5–20; 23–26.

[2] 8. 1; 4; 10; 13; 15–17; 19–21; 23–26; Arist. *Pol.* 1299^{b}30–38; *FGrH* 328 F 138 (Philochorus).

Persia's claims were less strongly stated and Persia's obligation to pay all expenses was inserted. This pact, however, was rejected by Lichas, the spokesman of eleven Spartan commissioners, who came out to advise Astyochus. An open breach with Tissaphernes resulted, and during it the Spartans won over the important island of Rhodes, which cut the trade-route from Egypt to Athens. The Athenians meanwhile were doing their utmost to reduce Chios, but without success. At the same time they were covering the Hellespont, through which most of Athens' food-supply passed from the Black Sea. The balance of naval power was fairly even, and the Peloponnesians could only improve their position by entering again into alliance with Persia.[1]

Alcibiades, who had played so active a part in starting operations in the east Aegean, now incurred the distrust of the Spartans and the hatred of Agis, whose wife he had seduced at Sparta. He therefore transferred his counsels to the Persian side. At a meeting with the Great King and Tissaphernes he urged them to let the Greeks wear one another down; the Peloponnesian fleet should be kept on short pay, so that Sparta would be unable to add naval superiority to her military superiority. By parading his influence with the Persian court Alcibiades gave the impression to both sides that he could sway their destinies; for Athens and Sparta now realized that whoever disposed of Persian money and the Phoenician fleet would win the war. When, therefore, Alcibiades sent word to the Athenian trierarchs and leaders at Samos that, if an oligarchy was installed at Athens, he was willing to come back and use his friendship with Tissaphernes to their advantage, they adopted the suggestion with alacrity and sent some representatives to discuss the project with him. On their return a group of conspirators was formed, and the proposal was placed before the personnel of the fleet, who raised no objection; for they were tempted by the prospect of Persian subsidies. But at a private meeting Phrynichus, the general, expressed suspicion of Alcibiades and disbelief in his promises. The rest, however, proceeded with the plan and sent Peisander and some others to Athens to arrange for the introduction of oligarchy and the recall of Alcibiades. At Athens Peisander met with strong opposition, but he silenced it by arguing that the survival of the state was more important than any question of the constitution and this could only be achieved by gaining the alliance of Persia. He and ten others were then appointed to negotiate with Alcibiades and Tissaphernes for alliance. Their conditions were tacitly accepted by the Assembly: that an oligarchy would be set up at Athens and the sentence of death passed on Alcibiades would be revoked. Peisander also persuaded the Assembly to depose Phrynichus, whose hostility to Alcibiades might disrupt the impending negotiations.[2]

Peisander and his fellow envoys then set off for the court of Tissaphernes. There they met with a cruel disappointment. Alcibiades, who acted as

[1] 8. 27-44.   [2] 8. 45-54.

spokesman for Tissaphernes, suspected that Tissaphernes did not intend to transfer the aid of Persia from Sparta to Athens. He therefore raised the price of Persia's aid so high that the Athenian envoys broke off the negotiations. Tissaphernes then made a third and final pact with the Spartan Alliance in April 411. The two powers were to act jointly in making war and in concluding peace with Athens. Tissaphernes was to provide pay for the Peloponnesian fleet, until such time as the Phoenician fleet came into action; thereafter any monies provided by Tissaphernes were to be loans, repayable at the end of the war. 'All the territory of the King in Asia is to belong to the King, and he is to decide about his own lands as he pleases.' This pact remained in force until the end of the war. As it was based solely on considerations of expediency, neither side intended to honour it beyond the limits of expediency. Sparta promised indeed to sell the liberties of the Greek states in Asia (and the Athenian envoys had been willing to promise more for Persia's help), but the sale was nominal only, so long as the war continued, and the Peloponnesians began to draw subsidies from Persia at once.[1]

In the early summer of 411 the revolt spread to the Hellespont, where a Spartan officer, Dercyllidas, in co-operation with Pharnabazus, entered and occupied Abydus. Chios was still holding out despite the continued efforts of the Athenians, and the area from Miletus to Rhodes was mostly under Spartan control. Yet the Peloponnesian fleet, commanded by the timorous Astyochus, did not force an engagement with the Athenian fleet. Meanwhile the conspirators at Samos and at Athens were engaged in bringing the oligarchy into power, despite the fact that the ostensible object of the change —alliance with Persia—was no longer attainable. Their supporters in the armed forces at Samos were well organized and in control of the situation. The leaders were disappointed in their hopes of Persian money, but they devoted their private estates to the prosecution of the war, formed a plot to set an oligarchy over the Samians, and sent emissaries to impose oligarchies on other subject states. Peisander and others set off for Athens, and put oligarchies in power along the line of their route homewards.[2]

§ 4. *Oligarchy at Athens*

THE successive failures of the democracy and the crowning disaster at Syracuse made all sections of the people critical of democratic institutions. The active opponents of democracy were drawn mainly from the upper and middle classes, who had borne the entire burden of taxation and the bulk of the casualties until the disaster at Syracuse and naturally resented a system under which they had little say in the conduct of diplomacy and of war. They fell into two groups. The first and larger group wished to establish a moderate form of government, in which the well-to-do would administer the state with economy and prosecute the war with vigour. This group was not

---

[1] 8. 56–59; Athenian negotiations 8. 56. 4.   [2] 8. 55; 61–64.

organized within the political clubs. It had no precise programme for setting up 'a moderate oligarchy'. The other group wished above all to obtain power as oligarchic leaders; some of them were prepared in the last resort to impose a narrow oligarchy by violence and to collaborate with the enemy. They controlled the political clubs, which had existed as clandestine organizations and were now ready to come into the open. At the outset the two groups were held together by their dislike of democracy and by the prospect of winning the Persian alliance. Nevertheless, the large majority of the population still supported the ideas of democracy and would only tolerate a constitutional reform as a temporary expedient in order to obtain the alliance of Persia.[1]

When Peisander had first persuaded the Assembly to accept the idea of a change in the constitution, he had instructed the political clubs to concert their plans and take the preliminary steps for the overthrow of the democracy. While he was absent in Asia and Samos, the younger members of the party at Athens assassinated the democratic leader, Androcles, and some of his associates. All debates in the Council and in the Assembly were now controlled by the conspirators, who supplied the speakers and the content of their speeches. The programme which they preached was that of a moderate oligarchy: pay was to be given only to troops on active service, and the state was to be administered by those who were best fitted to finance and fight the war, their number being not more than 5,000. Anyone who spoke against this programme suffered the fate of Androcles, and no legal redress could be obtained; for the organs of the democratic government were becoming paralysed by a reign of terror. It was impossible in so large and crowded a city to estimate the number of the conspirators, and it was difficult to guess who they were. Indeed those put up to speak for the oligarchy were often people whom no one expected to be participants or sympathizers; and whether they were party men or not, they did much to further the revolution by making men afraid of one another and suspicious of their closest friends. Such was the situation towards the end of May when Peisander and his colleagues arrived with some trusty hoplites, trained in the subject states where they had already established oligarchic governments.[2]

Peisander and the others convened the Assembly at once. They did not reveal their failure to obtain alliance with Persia but proposed the election of ten men who were to draw up a constitution and report to the Assembly on a stated day. In the end the Assembly appointed twenty men over forty years of age and the ten elder statesmen, the *prouboloi*, who had been elected after the disaster in Sicily. They were instructed to pay particular attention to 'the ancestral laws' of Cleisthenes in drafting the new constitution. This suggested a moderation which was foreign to the aim of Peisander and his colleagues; for the drafters were in fact controlled by ten of their number who had full powers. On the stated day the Assembly was convened at Colonus outside

[1] 8. 48. 1; Arist. *Pol.* 1303ᵃ9; *Ath.* 26. 1; Isoc. 8. 87.   [2] 8. 54. 4; 65–66.

the walls of the city, where the danger of an attack by the enemy discouraged the faint-hearted from attending. On the recommendation of the ten drafters who had full powers, the constitutional safeguards of the democracy were formally abolished. On the proposal of Peisander the existing magistrates were deposed, and the members of a provisional government were appointed. The appointments were in the hands of a caucus: first five presidents were elected, then the five appointed a hundred, and the hundred co-opted three each. These, 'the Four Hundred,' were authorized to administer the state with full powers and to convene at their pleasure 'the Five Thousand'. The Five Thousand were as yet unnamed, but it was agreed that they should be the new electorate and the sovereign body in the constitution for the duration of the war. No dissentient voice being raised, the Assembly was then adjourned and the *coup d'état* was planned by the ringleaders. Ever since the Spartan occupation of Decelea the Athenians had manned the walls and remained under arms throughout the day and then gone home in the evening. One evening, therefore, the conspirators and the hoplites Peisander had brought from the islands stayed under arms near the Agora, while the Four Hundred entered the Council Chamber, each armed with a dagger and accompanied by 120 youths, who had been appointed executioners. There was no resistance. The members of the democratic Council departed. They were given any pay due to them.[1]

The Four Hundred were themselves controlled by the organizers of the conspiracy, a group probably of ten men with special powers. The most influential but not the most conspicuous was a brilliant lawyer, Antiphon, who had organized and directed the conspiracy. His chief assistants were Peisander, the spokesman of the conspirators, and Phrynichus the ex-general, who showed himself a courageous zealot. Another member of the group was an exceptionally able planner and orator, Theramenes, son of Hagnon, whose views were less extreme than those of the inner group. The Four Hundred disposed first of their opponents, killing a few and imprisoning or deporting the others, and then opened negotiations for peace with Agis at Decelea. But they showed no weakness towards the Peloponnesians. When Agis marched his army close to the walls, they inflicted some casualties on his troops. They then sent off two groups of envoys, one to Sparta to open official negotiations and the other to Samos to present their doings in a favourable light.[2]

Meanwhile the oligarchs' plot to install an oligarchy among the Samians had misfired. The Athenian troops, led by Thrasybulus and Thrasyllus, had taken the side of the Samian democrats, and then had heard exaggerated reports of atrocities committed by the Four Hundred at Athens. They thereupon set up a democratic government of their own, elected Thrasybulus,

---

[1] 8. 67; 69; Arist. *Ath.* 29. 2–5; 32. 1; *Rh.* 1419ᵃ28; Lys. 12. 65; *FGrH* 324 F 43 (Androtion); 328 F 136 (Philochorus); Schol. Ar. *Lys.* 421; Suid. *Probouloi.*

[2] 8. 68; 70–72; Arist. *Ath.* 32. 2–3; *Pol.* 1305ᵇ27; Lys. 12. 62–68.

Thrasyllus, and others as generals, and denounced the Four Hundred. The news of this counter-revolution reached the envoys of the Four Hundred when they were at Delos, and they decided to postpone their journey to Samos. In the meantime the democrats at Samos recalled Alcibiades on the proposal of Thrasybulus, who still thought that Alcibiades had his hand in the money-bags of Tissaphernes. He was at once appointed general and was at Samos when the envoys of the Four Hundred came on from Delos. They tried to make a good impression by saying that the troops at Samos would take their turn in due course as members of the Five Thousand. Their hearers were only prevented from seizing them and sailing to Athens by the intervention of Alcibiades. He sent a reply to Athens on his own authority: that the Four Hundred should be replaced by the democratic Council of Five Hundred, but that he had no objection to the setting up of the Five Thousand, provided they practised economy and sent money for the fleet. The Athenian state was now divided into two states, the Four Hundred holding the capital and the Democracy in possession of the main fleet. In preventing civil war between them Alcibiades rendered his finest service to the country of his birth.[1]

When the envoys of the Four Hundred delivered Alcibiades' message to Athens, it had the desired effect. The moderates, led by Theramenes and Aristocrates, were encouraged to press for the setting up of the Five Thousand, being inspired less by any political ideals than by the realization that the days of the oligarchy were numbered and the overthrowers of the Four Hundred might become the leaders of the democracy in time to come. The extremists now decided to admit the Spartans to the capital on any terms they could obtain. Their first envoys had never reached Sparta; for the crew of the state-ship, the *Paralus*, had arrested them and handed them over to the democracy at Argos. But they had sent others, and now they sent the leaders of the party, Antiphon, Peisander, Phrynichus, and others. During their absence the extremists pressed on with the fortification of Eëtionea, a breakwater from which a small force could command the entry into the Peiraeus. On their return Phrynichus was assassinated in the Agora of Athens, and then in September 411, when a Peloponnesian fleet appeared in the Saronic Gulf and raided Aegina, Aristocrates and Theramenes, who had assured themselves of the support of most of the hoplites, managed to demolish the fort at Eëtionea without coming to blows with the partisans of the Four Hundred.[2]

The linked fortifications of the city were now occupied by two armed forces, Athens by the extremists and the Peiraeus by the moderates. With the enemy close to them on land and on sea, 'cataloguers' were appointed to draw up the list of the Five Thousand, and both parties agreed to hold an Assembly in the theatre of Dionysus and bring about a reconciliation. But on the appointed day it was reported that a Peloponnesian fleet was sailing from Megara along the coast of Salamis, and the people rushed down to the

[1] 8. 73–77; 81–82; 86. 1–7.   [2] 8. 89–92.

Peiraeus to repel a landing. When the Peloponnesians sailed on towards Sunium, the Athenians manned their ships hastily and joined their patrol-ships in Euboea. Their squadrons of forty-two ships and thirty-six ships were in station at Oropus and at Eretria, some seven miles apart, when the Eretrians signalled to the Peloponnesians to attack; for they knew that the Athenian sailors had scattered to find food. The Peloponnesians caught them unprepared, destroyed twenty-two of the Athenian ships, and raised Euboea in revolt.[1]

This disaster left Athens exposed to attack. The Peloponnesians might have captured the Peiraeus or forced the fleet in the east Aegean to abandon its bases and return home. But they let the opportunity pass. At Athens the people deposed the Four Hundred and established the Five Thousand. The extremist leaders fled to Agis at Decelea, and one of them, having got posses-sion of the border town Oenoe, handed it over to Boeotia. From September 411 until June 410 the Five Thousand administered the capital. They passed motions recalling Alcibiades and other exiles, co-operated with the demo-cracy at Samos, and prosecuted the war with vigour. The revolutionary period, so disastrous to the liberties of many states, passed at Athens without serious bloodshed and without armed intervention by the enemy. The credit was due not only to such statesmen as Thrasybulus, Alcibiades, and Thera-menes but also to the moderation of the hoplite class at Athens and of the naval personnel at Samos.[2]

During the régime of the Four Hundred a constitutional programme for the Four Hundred was drafted but probably never put into effect. It is, how-ever, indicative of the aims of the extreme oligarchs. The Five Thousand, who existed only in theory as the bearers of the political franchise, were to elect candidates for the Council from those over thirty years of age, voting by tribes; from these candidates forty of each tribe were to be selected, perhaps by lot, to form the Council of Four Hundred 'in accordance with ancestral practice', a phrase which alluded probably to the Solonian Council of Four Hundred. The powers of the Council were to be very wide: to choose ten generals, appoint magistrates, conduct audits, and control legislation except in matters of civil law. Councillors and generals could be reappointed, other magistrates could not be. This programme was drafted at a time when the revolutionary Council of Four Hundred was already in power as a pro-visional body, and it was cited during the crisis of September 411. One clause implied that the generals then in office were the elected officers of the Five Thousand, and two clauses looked forward to the projected constitution of the Five Thousand.[3]

---

[1] 8. 93–95.   [2] 8. 96–98; Arist. *Ath.* 33; [Lys.] 20. 13.

[3] The significance of the decrees or documents cited in Arist. *Ath.* 29. 5–31 is disputed. They were probably inserted into the narrative in order to present the oligarchy in a more favourable light. For the interpretation in the text cf. Arist. *Ath.* 31; Th. 8. 72. 1; 92. 11; 93. 2; *GHI* 81. [Lys.] 20. 1–2 implies that the Four Hundred Councillors were elected by their tribesmen; if so, this happened after the seizure of power; but, as the speech is ten-dentious, the implication may be intended to mislead.

The programme for the constitution of the Five Thousand was probably drafted at the same time, and it was cited at Samos by the envoys of the Four Hundred. It may have formed the basis for the actual constitution of the Five Thousand, which was duly ratified after the fall of the Four Hundred. The 5,000 persons were to be listed by 100 officials (ten representing each tribe), and they were to be drawn from men over thirty years of age who belonged to the three upper property-classes. The 5,000 were then to be divided into four Councils, of which one was to act as an executive Council with legislative powers and the other three were to act as a consultative body, the choice of the executive Council being made annually by lot. The 5,000 were to hold a preliminary election of candidates and then a final election from them of the major military, financial, and administrative officials, all being elected from the personnel of the executive Council for the year. The minor officials were to be selected by lot from the personnel of the other three Councils. The executive Council was to meet every fifth day. It was to be convened by the nine archons, who were to fine absentees a drachma a session, unless absence was authorized by the Council. Procedure in the Council was carefully defined. The generals were given precedence for agenda of military importance, and five presidents took the votes. As it was anticipated that in time of war a plenary session of the three Councils would be difficult to convene, the members of the executive Council were to co-opt one man each for consultation, if need should arise. The executive Council was to pay special attention to matters of finance, and the Councillors were to receive no pay for their services.[1]

This programme probably drew its inspiration from the four Councils of 'the oligarchy with equal rights', which administered the states of the Boeotian League. In time of war it had great merits, which appealed to Thucydides and Aristotle. It conserved finances, centralized the administration, entrusted the direction of policy to the most responsible element in the community, and saved man-power for purposes of war. Since the 5,000 were little more than half of the Athenians of the requisite age who belonged to the upper classes, it was intended that the residue, who were on active service overseas, should in due course take their turn in the governing body of the state. With such a constitution Athens might have averted the final disaster which overtook her. But in 411-410 the democracy at Samos remained an independent entity, and, as it turned out, the lower class, which manned the fleet, claimed the decisive voice in affairs and swept the state onwards in the stream of full democracy.[2]

---

[1] Arist. *Ath.* 29. 5; 30; 33. 1 fin.; Th. 8. 86. 3; 97. 1. The 5,000 so listed were more or less those present in Athens (cf. Th. 8. 72. 1; 97. 1), and another 4,000 or so who were eligible were on overseas service, their names being listed but they themselves not participating in fact (cf. [Lys.] 20. 13). *IG* ii.² 12 (cf. *IG* i.² p. 297) probably refers to the five presidents and the executive Council of the Five Thousand; cf. [Plu.] 833d–e.

[2] 8. 72. 1 fin.; 86. 3; 97. 2; Arist. *Ath.* 33. 2; for the Boeotian League, p. 346.

§ 5. *The struggle for naval supremacy*

WHILE the oligarchic factions ruled at Athens, the democracy at Samos defended the empire. In the critical period of dissension the fleet at Samos was not attacked by the Peloponnesians. This was due to the incompetence of Astyochus, whose timorousness was characteristic of many Spartan commanders at sea; to the duplicity of Tissaphernes, who withheld pay and pretended to be about to bring up the 147 Phoenician ships from their base at

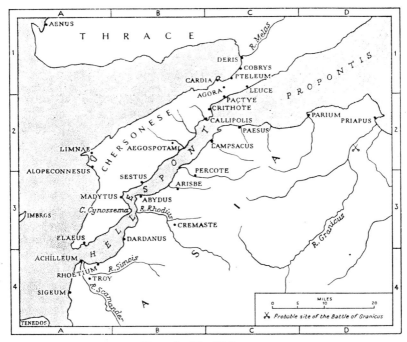

FIG. 26. The Hellespont

Aspendus in Pamphylia; and to the mutinous attitude of the allies of Sparta and of the citizens of Miletus, where the fleet lay inactive. Finally, Astyochus was replaced by Mindarus. In September 411 he decided to transfer his fleet to the rival paymaster, Pharnabazus. At that time the Peloponnesians had sixteen ships at Abydus in the Hellespont; in the north Aegean Byzantium was in revolt and Thasos was about to revolt. The Athenians had their main fleet at Samos (thirteen ships being absent with Alcibiades on a visit to Tissaphernes), a few ships at Lesbos, and a squadron of eighteen ships at Sestus in the Hellespont. When Mindarus reached Chios, the Athenian fleet moved from Samos to Lesbos; but Mindarus slipped through unobserved between the mainland and Lesbos, reached the Hellespont, and caught four of the Athenian squadron as it was sailing from Sestus for the open sea. Mindarus thus concentrated the Peloponnesian fleet of eighty-six sail in the Hellespont. The Athenian commanders, Thrasybulus and Thrasyllus, then brought up the main fleet and the survivors of the squadron from Sestus. They anchored at Elaeus with seventy-six ships.[1]

As Mindarus now controlled the passage through the Hellespont, Thrasybulus and Thrasyllus decided to attack. As their fleet rowed in single column up-stream along the shore of the Chersonese towards Sestus, the Peloponnesian fleet rowed in the same formation down-stream towards Dardanus. When the leading ships of the Peloponnesian column under the command of Mindarus passed the last Athenian ships under the command of Thrasybulus, the whole Peloponnesian column turned into line and charged across the narrow channel. As Mindarus' ships overlapped those of Thrasybulus and threatened to cut them off from the open sea and take them in the flank, Thrasybulus extended his formation down-stream, drawing upon the centre which became dangerously thin in ships. Meanwhile the leading Athenian ships under the command of Thrasyllus, having passed the angular promontory of Cynossema before turning into line, were out of sight and therefore unaware of Thrasybulus' manœuvre. The Peloponnesian centre then attacked the Athenian centre and drove many of their ships on to the coast. Meanwhile both wings of both fleets were hovering for an opportunity to attack; but, when the Peloponnesian centre lost its formation in the heat of victory, Thrasybulus suddenly attacked and routed the ships under Mindarus' command, swung his ships up-stream, and routed the disordered ships of the Peloponnesian centre. On the left of the Athenian line Thrasyllus' ships were already driving back the Syracusan ships opposite them, when the Syracusans saw the rout of their comrades and fled themselves. As the Peloponnesian troops held the Asiatic shore, the Athenians were unable to drive home their victory, but they had shown their superiority in fighting power over a larger fleet. The losses in the battle of Cynossema were almost equal, twenty-one Peloponnesian and fifteen Athenian ships, but the Athenians now sailed freely up the Hellespont, where they captured Cyzicus, which had revolted, and seized eight Byzantine ships.[2]

The news of this the first victory since the disaster at Syracuse caused jubilation at Athens, especially when the Peloponnesian squadron of fifty ships at Euboea was wrecked on its way to join Mindarus in the Hellespont. Alcibiades, too, reported that he had dissuaded Tissaphernes from bringing up the Phoenician fleet into the Aegean, had fortified Cos as a base in the

---

[1] 8. 64. 3–5; 78; 80–81; 83–85; 87; 96. 5; 99–103; for Thasos see J. Pouilloux, *Études Thasiennes* 3. 139–62.

[2] 8. 104–7; the number of the Peloponnesian fleets rests on a probable emendation; cf. D.S. 13. 45.

south, and was holding Samos with twenty-two ships. During the winter Alcibiades joined Thrasybulus and Thrasyllus. They won another victory, capturing thirty enemy hulls, and Thrasyllus sailed to Athens to report the victory and ask for reinforcements, which came out later under the command of Theramenes. In April or May 410 the Athenian fleet, now outnumbering the Peloponnesians, won a decisive victory in a battle off Cyzicus. Alcibiades, bringing up his ships in dirty weather, caught the Peloponnesian fleet of sixty ships outside the harbour, drove it ashore, and captured it. He then landed his troops, defeated the Peloponnesian and Persian troops, and captured Cyzicus. Athens' supremacy at sea was vindicated, and the Peloponnesian naval offensive was completely broken. The failure of Sparta was recorded in a dispatch sent by the adjutant of Mindarus, who had fallen in the battle. 'Ships lost; Mindarus dead; men starving; at a loss what to do.' It was three years before the Peloponnesians were able to muster another large fleet.[1]

The Athenian victories in the Hellespont made the restoration of democracy at Athens inevitable. The government of the Five Thousand did indeed prosecute the war with vigour, recall Alcibiades and others from exile on the advice of Theramenes, and support Alcibiades and the fleet at Samos. It held its own against Agis at Decelea, the Peloponnesian fleet at Euboea (until its withdrawal), and the Boeotians and Euboeans, who attempted to block the straits by a mole from Chalcis to the mainland. One fleet under the command of Theramenes was operating in the Aegean, raising money by raids on enemy territory, deposing extreme oligarchies established in subject states by the Four Hundred, and fining the oligarchic leaders. Another fleet under the command of Conon sailed to Corcyra in answer to an appeal from the democrats and intervened on their side in a further outbreak of civil war. Later Theramenes supported Archelaus (who had succeeded to the throne of Macedonia in 413) in an attack on Pydna, and he then joined Thrasybulus, to whom he accorded precedence of command. In the great victory of Cyzicus Theramenes and Thrasybulus each commanded a squadron, while Alcibiades held the supreme command. It thus happened that in 410 even before the victory at Cyzicus the commanders and the personnel of the fleets of the Five Thousand at Athens and of the Democracy at Samos were co-operating in action, Theramenes in the north Aegean and Thrasyllus in Athens. So, too, both governments needed revenues from their subjects, supported democracies in the subject and allied states and drew ship-building timber from Macedonia and foodstuffs from common sources. The leaders of the Five Thousand had all along foreseen the restoration of democracy at Athens, and they hoped to lead the democracy too. In the course of June 410 the governments of the Five Thousand at Athens and of the Democracy at Samos lapsed. Democracy was restored at Athens, and the state was unified.

---

[1] 8. 106. 5; 108; D.S. 13. 41; 45–47. 1; X. *HG* 1. 1. 1–23, whose account of the battle of Cyzicus is preferable to that of D.S. 13. 49–51.

Preparations were made to prosecute the war with vigour, and a picked force of 1,000 hoplites and 100 cavalry was formed to undertake special operations. Leaders of both groups were elected to boards such as the Hellenotamiae in 410/409. Thrasyllus became a general at Athens, Thrasybulus was sent out from Athens with a force of cavalry and hoplites, and Alcibiades continued to conduct operations in the Hellespont with Thrasybulus and Theramenes.[1]

There was, however, a residue of animosity, particularly in the lower class at Athens, which had been deprived of the political franchise and of state-pay for a year. The first official prytany of the restored Democracy was marked by every citizen taking an oath: 'I will kill with my own hand anyone who overthrows the democracy at Athens, holds office under an undemocratic régime, seeks to establish a tyranny, or collaborates with a tyrant. The slayer of any such person shall be regarded by me as clean in the sight of gods and spirits.' The assassin of Phrynichus was now publicly honoured and made an Athenian citizen. There was still some suspicion of Alcibiades as a would-be tyrant, and men remembered the solemn curse which had been laid upon him for impiety. Alcibiades himself did not come back to Athens. He could no longer offer the people his good offices with Tissaphernes; for he had been arrested by Tissaphernes early in 410, and only escaped a month later by eluding his guards. But he was elected to office each year, because he was unrivalled as a general and diplomat. In foreign policy the division of interest between the classes was accentuated by the hardships of war. The moderates were prepared to make peace on favourable terms, but the democrats still hankered after victory. Their ebullient spirit was shown in refusing the offers of peace on the basis of a *status quo* which Sparta made after the battle of Cyzicus. This refusal was due especially to Cleophon, an extreme democrat like Cleon, who carried his motion in the Assembly before the democratic Council entered office in July 410. He and others led the attack in the law courts on members of the Four Hundred, such as Critias (who went as an exile to Thessaly), and on many others who were less deeply implicated. Their rancour weakened the state at a time when unity and goodwill were needed to resist their enemies.[2]

In the Aegean both sides were crippled by lack of money. Athens melted down silver and gold objects in the temples to issue an emergency coinage. Athens and Sparta alike placed governors and garrisons in subject or allied states and exacted contributions for the war. Alcibiades imposed a 10 per cent. toll on cargoes passing through the Bosporus. Thrasyllus, commanding a fleet of fifty ships equipped at Athens, raided the Asiatic coast for booty in 409 and lost 400 men. In 408 Alcibiades won much booty and large indem-

---

[1] 8. 97. 3; D.S. 13. 38; 42; Plu. *Alc.* 27; 33; D.S. 13. 47. 3–49. 2; And. 2. 11–12; Th. 8. 89. 3–4; *GHI* 83. 35; D.S. 13. 52. 1; 64. 1–3.

[2] And. 1. 96–98; *GHI* 86; Th. 6. 15. 3–4; X. *HG* 1. 1. 9–10; D.S. 13. 52–53; Plu. *Alc.* 27–28; *FGrH* 328 F 139 (Philochorus, sub 411/10); Arist. *Ath.* 28. 4; Lys. 30. 7; Arist. *Rh.* 1375[b] fin.; And. 1. 75–76.

nities from Chalcedon and Pharnabazus, and in 407 he took 100 talents by raiding the coast of Caria.[1] Such desperate methods aroused the hostility of the Persian Court. Meanwhile at Athens state-pay was introduced on the earlier system, and Cleophon instituted the two-obol payment (*diobelia*) to the poor. The Peloponnesians received sufficient subsidies from Pharnabazus to keep their footholds in Ionia and the Hellespont, and to maintain a garrison in Byzantium from 410 until the winter of 408–407, when the city was betrayed at night to Alcibiades' army. On the mainland Sparta captured Pylus, and the Megarians captured Nisaea in winter 409–408. The Athenians avenged the loss by inflicting a defeat on the Megarian army, which was then strengthened by Spartan troops; but to engage in a further land battle was to hazard the small resources of the state. The indecisive war of attrition was prolonged by Persia, Pharnabazus granting Alcibiades a local armistice in 408 and the Court receiving envoys from both sides. In March 407 Darius sent a viceroy, his younger son Cyrus, to take control of all the coastal area and to support Sparta. On his way Cyrus met some Athenian envoys. In order to keep the new policy secret, he kept them in custody for three years and then released them.[2]

In the spring of 407 Alcibiades reached the zenith of his success, and began to move towards Athens, collecting his loot worth 100 talents and reconnoitring Gytheum, the naval base of Sparta in Laconia. As he approached home waters after eight years of absence, he learnt that the generals elected for 407/406 included himself, Thrasybulus, who had just reduced Thasos, and Conon, who had held office under the Five Thousand. On a festival day late in May he sailed into the Peiraeus at the head of his squadron. Crowds assembled to see the most able Athenian of the day, some with admiration or affection and others with suspicion or detestation. At first he stood motionless on the quarter-deck; then, when he saw his friends there to escort him, he landed and walked up to the city. Once more his persuasive oratory charmed the Council and the Assembly. He was absolved from the curse laid upon him. He was granted supreme command of the Athenian forces. The triumphant cruise of his squadron from Byzantium round the Aegean had revived the dreams of a great empire in the minds of the citizens, and now they gave him the honour of leading the state-procession, which followed the Sacred Way to Eleusis for the first time since the occupation of Decelea. Towards autumn 407 he sailed off in command of 100 ships, 150 cavalry, and 1,500 hoplites. He hoped to regain full control of the empire.[3]

[1] Ar. *Ra.* 720 with Schol.; X. *HG* 1. 1. 22; 1. 2. 1–13; 1. 3. 2–4; 8; 1. 4. 8; D.S. 13. 64. 2–4; 66. 3–4, 6.

[2] Arist. *Ath.* 28. 3; *GHI* 83; 92; X. *HG* 1. 3. 14–22 and D.S. 13. 65. 5–67 (Byzantium); X. *HG* 1. 2. 18 and D.S. 13. 64. 5–7 (Pylus); D.S. 13. 65. 1–2 and *PSI* 1304ᵃ (Megara); X. *HG* 1. 3. 8–9; 12–13; 1. 4. 1–7 (Cyrus).

[3] X. *HG* 1. 4. 8–21; D.S. 13. 68. 2–69. 3; Plu. *Alc.* 33. The remark in X. *HG* 1. 4. 10, that Alcibiades was still 'in exile', is rhetorically effective, but it is shown to be incorrect by the sources cited on p. 412, n. 1 above. Decrees proposed by Alcibiades: *GHI* 88; 89.

The secret of Cyrus' appointment had been well kept. Before Alcibiades sailed, a new Spartan commander, Lysander, had crossed via Rhodes to Ephesus. There he assembled seventy ships, won the confidence of Cyrus, and received money to pay a higher wage than Athens for mercenary seamen. He then summoned reinforcements from Chios, equipped ninety ships, and awaited his opportunity. The main fleet lay at Notium under the command of Alcibiades' deputy Antiochus. Alcibiades himself, who had failed to reduce Andros and wished now to concentrate the squadrons of Athens, was on his way with the pick of his hoplites to meet Thrasybulus at Phocaea. He had instructed Antiochus not to attack the fleet of Lysander. Nevertheless, Antiochus provoked a battle. He sailed with ten fast ships past the Peloponnesian station, but his own ship was overhauled and sunk. Lysander, who had been informed by deserters of Alcibiades' absence, quickly launched his entire fleet in pursuit of the other Athenian ships and caught the main fleet as it issued in disorder from Notium. The Athenians lost twenty-two ships. The battle fell early in 406. Thereafter Lysander refused to face the more numerous fleet mustered by Alcibiades, but he captured Delphinium, the strong-point on Chios which the Athenians had held for five years. Complaints against Alcibiades were lodged at Athens by his own seamen and by allies whose territory he had been ravaging. Elections were held in the spring to appoint ten generals for the Attic year 406/405. Alcibiades was not among them. A special decree was passed by which his command was transferred at once to Conon. Rather than face an Athenian court he fled in self-imposed exile to his private fortress in the Chersonese.[1]

Conon reduced the number of ships in commission to seventy, hoping to increase their efficiency. He was soon faced by a new Spartan admiral, Callicratidas, who refused to toady to Cyrus for subsidies and enlisted support rather from the Greek states in Asia. In June 406 Callicratidas with a fleet of 140 ships caught Conon's fleet at sea, pursued it into the harbour at Mitylene, and captured thirty vessels, the crews escaping to the shore. The remainder were blockaded, and the news was only brought to Athens by a trireme which raced its way through the enemy. Soon afterwards another general, Diomedon, coming up to relieve Conon, lost ten of his twelve ships when Callicratidas suddenly attacked. The crisis was now grave. The Assembly decided to issue an emergency coinage in gold and enfranchise a number of metics, foreigners, and slaves; and it was probably now that Athens sought help from the Carthaginians, who were invading Sicily. Within a month the city manned 110 ships, many of the cavalry serving as marines to make up the complements, which totalled some 22,000 men. The Samians then contributed ten ships and the subject states were impressed to serve on other vessels. In August Callicratidas learnt that an Athenian fleet of more than 150 triremes was approaching. He left Eteonicus and 50 ships to maintain the

---

[1] X. *HG* 1. 5. 1–17; D.S. 13. 69. 4–72. 2; 73. 3–74; *PSI* 1304[b]2 (battle of Notium); Plu. *Lys.* 4.

blockade at Mitylene and sailed with 120 ships to Cape Malea, whence he saw the fires of the Athenian fleet at the Arginusae islands, some twelve miles distant. He took the bold decision to sail at midnight, in order to surprise the Athenian fleet at dawn, but a violent thunderstorm broke over the fleet and dawn found him still sailing towards the islands. The Athenian fleet, its crews fresh after a night's rest, put out to sea to fight the greatest battle between Greek and Greek since the battle of Sybota.[1]

The eight generals in command of the Athenian fleet realized that on this occasion the enemy fleet was superior in seamanship and tactical skill. In order to prevent their line being pierced by single ships, which could then turn to ram them broadside, they drew up the wings in a double line and formed their centre in single line, shielded by an island of the Arginusae group. Callicratidas divided his fleet into two flotillas, each in single line, and attacked both the Athenian wings. He himself commanded a group of 10 Spartan ships on the right wing. He was killed early in the action, nine of the Spartan ships were sunk, and the whole of the right wing broke and fled southwards. The left wing fought on under the command of a Theban general, Thrasondas. At last this flotilla fled too. Of the Athenian fleet 13 ships were sunk and 12 disabled, and of the Peloponnesian fleet 75 ships were sunk. The Athenian commanders detached 47 ships under two ship-captains, Theramenes and Thrasybulus, and some other officers to pick up the Athenian survivors and corpses, while they sailed off for Mitylene, hoping to catch Eteonicus and his 50 ships. But a gale sprang up from the north. They put back, and during the night Eteonicus escaped to Chios. Meanwhile in the rough sea the survivors and the 12 disabled ships had not been saved. It was reckoned that some 20,000 Greeks had lost their lives.[2]

The energy shown by Callicratidas at sea was emulated by Agis at Decelea. Early in 406 he attempted to break into Athens. He delivered a night attack with 14,000 hoplites, 14,000 light-armed men, and 1,200 cavalry. The outposts were taken by surprise, but the walls were manned in time. The Athenian army came out and offered battle close to the walls, where they were covered by fire from above. Agis refused to engage under such conditions, and the Athenians did not advance. This incident shook the nerve of the people, and more night duty was demanded of the army.

Athens' victory at Arginusae was overshadowed by a casualty list of 5,000 men. The news aroused deep resentment, which was exploited by Archedemus, the leading democrat and the administrator of the *diobelia*. He indicted one of the generals, Erasinides, in a people's court, for peculation in the Hellespont and also for the conduct of his command. Erasinides was imprisoned and the Council decided to arrest the other generals. Two of them fled. The other five were arrested—Aristocrates, Diomedon, Lysias,

---

[1] X. *HG* 1. 5. 18–1. 6. 28; D.S. 13. 76–79. 7; 97; *FGrH* 328 F 141 (Philochorus); Ar. *Ra.* 720. For negotiations with Carthage, see p. 471 below.
[2] X. *HG* 1. 6. 29–38; D.S. 13. 98–100. 6.

Pericles, son of the statesman, and Thrasyllus, who had led the democracy at Samos in 411—and brought before the Assembly. The ship-captains who had failed to save the men in the water—Theramenes, Thrasybulus, and others—blamed the generals bitterly, but the generals' defence of their action and the support of eyewitnesses would probably have led to their acquittal, had it been possible to take a vote before nightfall. Some days passed, during which the Athenians celebrated the Apatouria, a festival of the phratries, and the relatives mourned their dead. Feeling was more hostile to the generals when the Assembly met again, and there were many present in black clothes with their heads shaven in grief.

At this meeting the Council had to recommend the procedure for the trial. Callixenus, who was inspired by the friends of Theramenes, proposed an immediate vote for or against the execution of the generals collectively. Those who indicted the proposal as illegal, and pointed out too that at least one general was in the water himself when the orders were given, were shouted down and silenced; for many cried out that it was monstrous to prevent the People from doing what it pleased. Some of the prytany-members of the Council then refused to conduct the voting as it was illegal; but they too were intimidated and retracted, all except Socrates, who insisted on acting in accordance with the law. A counter-proposal, that the generals be tried individually, was lost on a second count. The procedure proposed by Callixenus was then put into effect. The six generals were condemned collectively and executed without delay.

On this occasion the Athenian people, meeting in mass assembly and exposed to the influence of hysteria and jobbery, overrode both the written and the unwritten laws on which Pericles had based his claim that the democracy was a model for the world. The horrors of war and the possibility of defeat had sapped the integrity of the Athenian citizens and embittered their feelings. Later they repented of what they had done, and they instituted proceedings against those who had deceived them. Yet to make amends was impossible. The critics of democracy now had a stronger case. They were supported by men of principle, who preferred to stand aside from such a degradation of politics. The Athenian courts, too, were no longer regarded as impartial; for the rich were often victimized, and the jurors were bribed *en masse* by Anytus, a general who had been held responsible for the loss of Pylus in 409/408.[1]

After the battle of Arginusae the Spartans offered terms. They proposed to evacuate Decelea and then make peace on the *status quo*. But Athens, led by Cleophon, refused to negotiate unless Sparta evacuated all the cities in the Athenian empire. The Spartans, returning to the attack, were pressed by their allies to appoint Lysander to the command of the Peloponnesian fleet. As their laws forbade them to appoint the same man twice to the supreme

---

[1] D.S. 13. 72. 3–73. 2; X. *HG* 1. 7. 1–35; D.S. 13. 101–3; Plat. *Apol.* 32b; X. *Mem.* 1. 1. 18; 4. 4. 2; Arist. *Ath.* 34. 1; 27. 5; *FGrH* 328 F 142 (Philochorus).

command, they had recourse to a legal fiction and appointed Aracus admiral and Lysander second-in-command with authority over the fleet. Lysander obtained generous subsidies from his friend Cyrus, mustered a fleet of some 200 sail, and moved his forces by land and by sea to the Hellespont, where he took Lampsacus by assault and followed the example of Callicratidas in liberating all free-born prisoners. An Athenian fleet of 180 ships under the command of Conon and Philocles moved forward in August to Aegospotami, an open beach opposite Lampsacus, where the channel was two miles wide. The Athenians were anxious to force an engagement at once, in order to open the passage for the corn-ships bound from the Black Sea for Athens. On four successive days they crossed the channel at dawn and offered battle in the waters outside Lampsacus, but Lysander kept his fleet under oar inside the harbour. In the afternoon of each day, when the Athenian fleet withdrew to Aegospotami and the crews foraged on shore for an evening meal, Lysander sent his fastest ships to watch what was happening and kept the rest of his fleet in readiness until they returned. On the fourth day Alcibiades came down from his fortress and advised the Athenian generals to move the fleet to Sestus; but they paid no heed, and he rode away. On the fifth day both fleets acted as before; but this time, as soon as the Athenian crews disembarked and scattered, the fast ships of Lysander in mid-channel hoisted a shield aloft as a signal. Lysander led his fleet at full speed across the channel. The Athenians were surprised even more completely than at Oropus in 411. Eight ships under Conon and the state-vessel, the *Paralus*, made good their escape. The other 171 ships were captured, empty or half-manned, and the camp was overwhelmed by the Peloponnesian infantry.[1]

When Lysander had assembled the prisoners in tens of thousands, he summoned his allied commanders to decide their fate. The cruelties of the Athenian state were recalled. Only recently the crews of two triremes, from Corinth and from Andros, had been thrown over a cliff at the command of Philocles, and the Assembly had ordered its commanders to cut off the right hand of any captured seaman. Lysander accepted the decision of his allies. He executed all Athenian prisoners to the number of some 3,000, except a general, Adeimantus, who had spoken against the Assembly's orders. The other prisoners were liberated. From then on, as Lysander swept across the Aegean, he sent all Athenian prisoners and cleruchs to Athens to swell the population in the beleaguered city, and he reinstated the dispossessed inhabitants of Melos, Aegina, and other states. By November 405 his fleet was blockading the Peiraeus, and the Peloponnesian armies under the Spartan kings, Agis and Pausanias, lay encamped outside the city.[2]

Xenophon described the scene at Athens after the battle of Aegospotami. 'It was night when the *Paralus* arrived and reported the disaster, and lamentation passed from the Peiraeus along the Long Walls to the city as each man told

[1] Arist. *Ath.* 34. 1; X. *HG* 2. 1. 1–29; D.S. 13. 104–6.
[2] X. *HG* 2. 1. 30–32; 2. 2. 1–2; 5–9; Plu. *Alc.* 37.

his neighbour. That night nobody slept, not only in grief for the dead but rather for themselves, as they expected to be treated as they had treated the people of Melos, Histiaea, Scione, Torone, Aegina and many other places.' Next day they met in the Assembly and decided to prepare for the defence of the city. When the blockade started, an amnesty was granted to all disfranchised citizens, and the Athenian franchise was conferred on the Samian democrats, who alone had not joined Sparta.

During December supplies of food began to give out. The people asked for peace if they could retain their walls and become allies of Sparta, but the Ephors demanded the demolition of part of the Long Walls. Cleophon then carried a decree to put to death anyone who proposed the acceptance of such terms. The people next appointed Theramenes to negotiate with Lysander. He stayed away for three months, during which time many died of starvation and Cleophon was executed for desertion, the charge being brought by members of an oligarchic club. When Theramenes returned, he and nine others were appointed with full powers to arrange the terms of surrender. They presented themselves before the Congress of the Spartan Alliance.[1]

The representatives of Corinth, Thebes, and other states proposed a sentence of *andrapodismos*, that is to say massacre of the adult males and enslavement of the women and children, which Athens had perpetrated at Melos and elsewhere. But Sparta refused to destroy the city which had served Greece so nobly in the Persian wars. The envoys returned with terms which the Athenian people accepted with relief—demolition of the Long Walls and the Peiraeus fortifications, surrender of the fleet save twelve vessels, evacuation of the empire, recall of exiles, and obedience to Sparta in all matters of foreign policy. In April 404 Lysander sailed into the Peiraeus, and his troops began to demolish the Long Walls with great enthusiasm to the music of flutes, 'believing that day to inaugurate the freedom of Greece'.[2]

Thus the war ended in the total defeat of Athens. In the judgement of Thucydides defeat was due to the errors of the Athenian people and the leaders whom the people chose, errors caused by the selfish interests of the people, their factions, and their leaders. Strength, courage, and initiative they had in abundance, but they lacked the solidarity, self-denial, and discipline which could have carried them to victory. The Spartan Alliance triumphed not only because Athens made mistakes. Its members, great and small, endured adversity with tenacity and fought to the death in the cause of freedom, a cause inspired less by material self-interest than by patriotic idealism. Its leader, Sparta, was often slow to act and unimaginative in strategy, but she made fewer of those mistakes which Thucydides judged to be so often decisive in war. Above all, she possessed the self-control, the moderation in success, and the sanity in adversity, which enabled her to lead a team of headstrong states and to maintain her military supremacy. The Greek world reaped little but evil from the Peloponnesian War. Its ability

[1] X. *HG* 2. 2. 3–4; 10–18; And. 1. 73–79; *GHI* 96.   [2] X. *HG* 2. 2. 19–23.

to resist the outside powers was deeply, perhaps fatally, impaired. Its future was overshadowed by hatreds between state and state, which war had embittered, and by factions within individual states, which put reprisals before patriotism. Yet in the fourth century the Greek states, and not least Athens, rose to the political and cultural problems of their age with an amazing resilience.[1]

[1] Th. 1. 144. 1; 2. 65. 7, 10–12; 1. 68. 1; 84; 2. 64. 6 fin.

CHAPTER 6

The Cultural Crisis in the Peloponnesian War

WHEN a democracy is at war, oratory becomes of greater importance, because more vital issues are debated and more stirring leadership is demanded. This was doubly so at Athens. For the people at mass meetings not only decided policy but also tried all magistrates, so that a politician without oratory lacked the means of carrying conviction and of escaping condemnation. Cimon and Pericles, both great orators, had been trained in the school of family tradition, but at the beginning of the war oratory was becoming a marketable art which could be sold to many would-be politicians or advocates. Protagoras of Abdera, who visited Athens about 450, taught the art of rhetoric for a fee, and others, such as Prodicus of Ceos and Hippias of Elis, followed his example. In the democratic states of Sicily Corax started the study of oratory as a technique, and Tisias and Gorgias were already famous exponents of this technique when they visited Athens in 427 as members of an embassy from Leontini. Their eloquence amazed the Athenian people. Tisias taught at Athens, Isocrates being one of his pupils, and Gorgias won a Panhellenic reputation by delivering prize speeches at Delphi and Olympia and by giving lessons at high fees.[1]

Corax, Protagoras, and Gorgias revolutionized Greek prose. Whereas Herodotus and his predecessors aimed at a flowing narrative and the political pamphleteer known as the 'Old Oligarch' wrote with an air of simplicity, the innovators aimed at the sublimity and precision which appealed to the taste of the day in architecture, sculpture, and painting. Their prose was consciously artistic. It appropriated those devices of poetry which stir emotion and sway belief: diction, rhythm, assonance, metaphor, and high flights of thought. When married to depth and sincerity of understanding, it attained great power, for instance in the pages of Thucydides and sometimes in the Assembly and Law Courts. Whatever its defects may have been through straining for effect and for novelty, this style set a standard for prose which persisted to the end of the Roman empire.

A stately style, however, was not enough. Precision of meaning was required. The niceties of grammar and language were taught by Prodicus and the semantics of diction by Protagoras. The order of words, the formal arrangement of arguments, and the principles of reasoning were carefully studied.[2] When meaning commands the centre of attention, the problems of the meaning of meaning become urgent. Prodicus, Antiphon, and others felt

---

[1] D.S. 12. 53; fragments of Gorgias' prize speeches survive.
[2] *Vorsokr.* 84. A 19; ridiculed in Pl. *Phdr.* 266–7.

competent to deal with them. For they were philosophers as well as rhetoricians, and they were abreast of the theories propounded by Anaxagoras, Zeno, Empedocles, Leucippus, and Democritus. Thus they became not only purveyors of oratory but also purveyors of wisdom, 'sophists' as they were called, and their particular brand of wisdom came from a group which tended to be rationalist in method and agnostic in belief.

The sophists found a ready market in wartime Athens. As no education was provided by the state, children in the past had been taught at home in their demes or in their town houses, and there were no special facilities for higher education. The younger generation, uprooted from their demes and crowded in the city, turned readily to the sophists and scorned their parents for their ignorance of rhetoric and of the new wisdom. The versatility of the sophists tended to conceal the dangers of their influence. Many of them were polymaths, like the philosophers whom they emulated. Protagoras taught ethics, politics, metaphysics, and mathematics, drafted the laws of Thurii at its foundation, and disputed the nature of knowledge with Democritus. Hippias investigated early history, compiled lists of the Olympic victors, and discussed mathematics, astronomy, poetry, and music. So too among philosophers Democritus wrote not only on physics, mathematics, and astronomy but also on psychology, logic, music, and poetry. A wealth of new ideas poured into a city which was always fond of novelty.

As philosophers remarked, 'much learning does not teach sense'. People were apt to remember the wrong thing, to seize on the destructive scepticism and not on the constructive thinking of the sophists. Gorgias argued that if any thing exists it is unknowable and incommunicable, and Protagoras argued that the senses are the criterion of reality and that therefore 'man is the measure of all things'. Thus truth was relative to each man's outlook. Protagoras himself said he could not know whether gods did or did not exist. From such arguments it was a short step to the position of the agnostic hedonist, but it was not a step which all the sophists took. Having knocked down divine sanctions for morality, Protagoras set up human sanctions in the form of state laws enacted by good lawgivers, and maintained that the state taught men to practise virtue. Yet those whose faith in divine sanctions is shattered do not *ipso facto* transfer their faith to man-made laws. Hippias, indeed, and Antiphon regarded man-made law as a despot and welcomed all men as related by nature and fellow-citizens of the universe. Thrasymachus claimed that 'justice is the interest of the stronger' and the laws of a democracy therefore protected the interest of the majority and those of an oligarchy that of the minority. Two apt pupils in sophistry went farther. Callicles proclaimed that might was right, and Critias that religion was invented by a shrewd man who knew the belief of others therein to be in his own interest.[1]

While sophistry was a solvent of traditional belief, the influences of war

[1] *Vorsokr.* 68 A 114; 80 B 1; 4; 82 B 3; 88 B 25 fin.; 87 B 44, fr. A 2. 26, fr. B 2. 10; Pl. *Prt.* 326c–e; 328b–c; 337c; *R.* 338c; *Grg.* 483c.

tended in the same direction. The evacuation of Attica, the terrors of the plague, and the disaster at Syracuse loosened the strands of religious belief, and the rigours of war and defeat made some men question the right of the state to make such demands. Philosophy too, having defined its cosmogony and disposed of any deity, turned to man as the microcosm and studied his personal psychology. The shift of interest from the group to the individual upset the traditional relation between the state and the citizen. A new basis for belief was needed. A philosopher like Democritus might provide it to his followers at Abdera when he taught that goodness is a state of the soul, dependent on self-respect and not on social convention; that the wrongdoer is more unhappy than the wronged; and that the source of happiness is not wealth but uprightness.[1] But the Athenians needed a more practical demonstration, and some of them found it in the first Athenian to make a mark in the field of philosophy or sophistry.

Socrates of Athens (469–399) studied the macrocosm of the universe before he turned to the microcosm of man, and developed the art of dialectic before he began to teach his compatriots. He was no sophist in the technical sense of taking fees for his lessons or professing to impart the secrets of success. As a master of cross-examination and of irony he outdid all sophists. Yet his philosophical technique resembled theirs in that he questioned the basic assumptions of his hearers in all matters of religion, ethics, and belief. He professed to know that he knew nothing; but he knew the object of his own search in life, namely to serve God and persuade others to serve God by subordinating all material considerations, even life itself, to the claims of goodness, truth, and understanding for the perfection of the soul. His teaching influenced the ideas of men. But his personality and his conduct influenced the outlook of some far more profoundly. He so clearly lived by principle, not for himself but for others. Because Athens had brought him up, he served her courageously in battle and he upheld her laws against the clamour of the people after Arginusae. But his ultimate obedience was not to Athens. It was to his inner soul, to the absolute goodness which his intellect comprehended, and to the voice of God which spoke within him when his intellect was silent. In Socrates the higher loyalty to God did not clash with the loyalty to the Athens which he loved, the Athens of the peace rather than the Athens of the war.[2]

The mission of Socrates in some ways resembled that of Euripides of Athens (*c.* 485–406), who used the medium of Attic drama to question the assumptions of the orthodox in society and in religion. His first production was in 455. Of the nineteen extant plays *Alcestis* (438), *Medea* (431), and *Hippolytus* (428) show that he was already interested in the psychology of women before the full impact of the war was felt.

In the Greek states a marriage was arranged not after a period of courtship,

---

[1] *Vorsokr.* 68 B 34; 40; 45; 62; 264 (his teaching probably fell mainly in 430–390).
[2] P. *Ap.* 29d–30b; *Cri.* 50a; X. *Mem.* 1. 1. 4.

but by the heads of the two families; and, as the girl took a dowry with her, the heads of the families were concerned more with matters of property than of the heart. After marriage affection doubtless developed in most cases; but emphasis was placed rather on family feeling than on a passionate attachment between man and woman. Such passion, being the opposite of 'moderation' (*sophrosyne*), was held to be 'folly' (*aphrosyne*), wherein Aphrodite turned one's mind to madness. In Sophocles' play Antigone is actuated by family affection; so too is Haemon, her betrothed, until Creon taunts him; and the Chorus sing of love (*eros*) as a maddening force. In the *Trachiniae* Deianeira is reasonable when she learns that Heracles has taken a paramour; for she sees that he has lost his reason and is a sick man. In Greek civilization men had no less high a regard for women than in any other civilization, and this is nowhere clearer than in Sophocles' portrayal of such women as Antigone, Electra, Tecmessa, and Deianeira. But they were highly regarded for their loyalty and their fortitude rather than for any amorous passion.[1]

The *Alcestis* was a substitute for the satyric drama which was submitted with three tragedies by a competitor at the dramatic festival. It was written, therefore, in a lighter vein than a tragedy, but the humour, as often in Euripides' plays, is mordant. Admetus, having been promised extension of his life if anyone would die for him, asked his parents, who refused, and his wife Alcestis, who consented. The play opens on the day appointed for her death with a scene between Apollo and Death. Alcestis, best of all women in devotion to her husband, is dying, and a slave-girl tells a chorus of old men that Alcestis has prayed for her children, wept upon her marriage bed, and said good-bye to the slaves. Alcestis, Admetus, and their two little children appear on the stage, where she dies after entrusting the children to him and gaining his promise not to marry again. In the remainder of the play Admetus' selfishness is made clear by a bitter quarrel between him and his aged father, as they stand over the corpse of Alcestis. Both are mean in their anger: the father calls his son a murderer and Alcestis a fool, and the son curses and disowns his parents. When the funeral rites have been completed, Admetus returns; he now realizes his mistake and grieves for Alcestis and for himself. At the end of the play Heracles brings Alcestis back from death. Euripides has presented a traditional story in a new and realistic light with children, slaves, funeral rites, and sordid squabbling; with a noble wife and a self-centred husband; and with a happy ending thanks to a miracle, which religious tradition supplies.

In the *Medea* the passionate love for Jason, which made Medea earlier bring about the death of her own brother, is the motive of her actions throughout the play. Now that Jason is deserting her to marry the daughter of Creon, her love has turned to hatred. Jason's defence is hypocritical, and Creon brutally banishes Medea and her children. The contrast between their callousness and Medea's passionate nature makes us feel sympathy for her,

[1] S. *Ant.* 791; *Tr.* 543.

despite the further murders she contrives. The play is entirely realistic, except for the miracle of Medea's escape in a supernatural chariot. The slaves are afraid of Medea, the children appear upon the stage alive and dead, and the Messenger's speech reports the grisly details of death. In *Hippolytus* our sympathies are better balanced. There is nobility in Phaedra and in Hippolytus. She, ashamed of her passion for her stepson, intends to die. He, loathing passion in her and indeed in all women, does not tell his father Theseus, because he has bound himself by an oath to keep her passion secret. The characterization of both is excellent. Phaedra's innate purity of mind causes a deep revulsion against herself and leads to suicide, but not before her passion, turned to hatred, has prompted her to accuse Hippolytus of assault and encompass his death. Hippolytus, too, is passionate in his love of an ascetic purity, which is personified in the celibate goddess Artemis and symbolized in his mystic love of wild nature, so that his icy harshness towards Phaedra and his obstinate steadfastness in his oath are both convincing. For this play and those that were produced with it Euripides won one of his five victories.[1]

In these plays the centre of interest is not in any divine overruling, nor in the principles of right action, but in the personalities of individual people, set against the realistic background of daily life and portrayed 'as they are' and not 'as they ought to be'. Euripides, like Protagoras, took mankind as the measure of life, and found the springs of tragedy in the nature of individual men and women. When Phaedra lay pining, the chorus sang of 'woman's difficult temperament, in which two sources of irresistible pain are wont to be conjoined, motherhood and passion'. In Alcestis, Medea, and Phaedra, as young mothers of young children, the intensity of their suffering was due to love of their children, stronger in the mother than in the father, and passionate devotion to a man, whether husband or another. The strain of suffering imposed upon Medea and Phaedra resulted in the disintegration of their personality. The tragedy in *Medea* is enacted in the heart and mind of Medea, where a great intensity of love is warped into a murderous and ruthless hate.[2]

As the war progressed, Euripides presented the effects of human suffering not as the ennobling of an Oedipus but as the degradation of an Orestes; the realities of rapine, rape, and murder in the sack of Troy and the enslaving of the *Troades*; and the despair of Hecuba, once Queen of Troy, who did not find release like Polyxena in death but became a murderess herself. Yet Orestes, the women of Troy, and Hecuba herself once upheld the standards of humanity. Had circumstances been different, they might have died with the heroism of an Eteocles, a Polyxena, or a Macaria. Other men and women, more fortunate in life than they, were base and mean, but they, having been cast in a finer mould, were more sensitive to honour and to pain. Their humanity at its best and at its worst was rooted in themselves, not dependent

---

[1] E. *Hipp.* 1296-1309; 1390. [2] Arist. *Po.* 1460ᵇ32; E. *Hipp.* 161.

on the religious beliefs or social conventions of any particular age. Because Euripides probed the depths of human psychology, his plays have a timeless quality which influenced Seneca and, through Seneca, Shakespeare and Racine.

In the opinion of later critics Euripides excelled in presenting 'passion and madness' on the stage, and he was the most tragic of the tragedians because his plays ended in complete disaster. To his contemporaries he was a controversial figure, because the medium of his art was not the secular theatre of later times but the religious festival of Dionysus. His realism may have given a sharper edge to the details of life's terrors than Sophocles' plays did. But what was his religious message? To this question his attitude was as quizzical as that of Socrates. Whereas Sophocles in his plays and Herodotus in his history wrote of the divine element almost as an absolute power of which there are temporal manifestations or nomenclatures, Euripides returned to the galaxy of Homeric gods and introduced them, sometimes wrangling, upon the stage of human life—Apollo and Thanatos in *Alcestis*, Aphrodite and Artemis in *Hippolytus*, Poseidon and Athena in *Troades*, Hermes and Athena in *Ion*, and so on. Such archaism was not due to a sincere belief in religion but was a convenience of dramatic technique, whereby the secular treatment of a religious story could be attached to the religious tradition. Sometimes a discord was deliberately struck between the secular treatment and the religious tradition, so that the tragedian's disbelief became apparent.[1]

In the *Electra* Euripides showed the type of brother and sister who would kill their mother for personal reasons rather than for religious motives. At the last moment Orestes, degenerate though he is, scruples to do the deed, and cries out that in ordering him to kill his mother Apollo ordered a stupidity. 'Where Apollo is stupid,' interjects Electra, 'who are wise?' Their mother done to death, they both realize their guilt and stand appalled at the result of Apollo's orders. Do men know better than the gods in whom they put belief? Two gods, the Dioscuri, appear hovering over the stage to foretell the future and end the play, with the cryptic remark about their master Apollo that he is wise but his orders to Orestes were not wise. In *Orestes*, where the murder has occurred before the play begins, Orestes knows that no man, not even Agamemnon, would think it right for a man to murder his mother; yet Apollo did so, and Orestes blames Apollo. The same censure appears in several plays: 'Gods should be wiser than men' and yet 'Aphrodite has ruined her and me and all this house; she is surely no god but something greater than a god.' 'Zeus sent the ghost of Helen to Troy, in order to cause strife and bloodshed among men.' 'Would that men's curses could smite the gods!'[2]

These passages show that Euripides was an unbeliever in terms of orthodox religion. Whether he believed in 'something greater than a god' or in something behind Chance is not discernible; for the elemental forces which are at

[1] E. *Hec.* 547 (Polyxena); *Heracl.* 591 (Macaria); Longin. 15. 3; Arist. *Po.* 1453ᵃ26.
[2] E. *El.* 971; 1245; 1302; *Hipp.* 120; 359; 1415; *El.* 1282.

play in *Hippolytus* and in *Bacchae* do not emerge into any more intelligible form. He certainly believed that humanity is capable of finer ideals than orthodox religion attributed to the gods. When his Chorus could sing in the orchestra of the Dionysiac theatre 'I give little credence to this tale . . . stories that terrify men are useful to ensure their worship of gods', the day was approaching when religion and drama were divorced and the great age of Attic Drama came to an end.[1]

The advanced views of the sophists, the quizzical methods of Socrates, and the realistic posturings of Euripides provided a butt for the greatest writer of Attic Comedy, Aristophanes of Athens (*c.* 450–*c.* 385). His wartime plays reflect the immense vitality and vivacity of the Athenians, and the outspokenness of his attacks on leading politicians show what importance they attached to freedom of speech. His humour was as varied as the winds—witty, earthy, punning, fantastic, suggestive, intellectual, bawdy, puerile—and it played upon an endless variety of characters in the streets and festivals of Athens—orators, slaves, generals, prostitutes, philosophers, statesmen, fishwives, and footpads. His sense of fun sprang from a *joie de vivre* which inspired the most charming of lyrics—the songs of the clouds or the birds or the mystics—and revelled in the kaleidoscope of human situations. For these reasons his humour is more fresh today than that of any playwright before Shakespeare and of many since.[2]

Attic Comedy, presented in honour of Dionysus, was intimately associated with the religion of the city-state. Aristophanes, and no doubt other playwrights too, had a didactic mission to fulfil, not only through the medium of humour and satire, but also by the plain speaking which occurred in the *Parabasis*, when the poet addressed the audience through the words of the Chorus. 'Demeter, queen of the sacred rites, inspire me to say much indeed in fun but much in earnest too,' sing the Chorus in the *Frogs*, 'so that my fun and mockery may be worthy of thy festival and win the ribbon of victory.' As the mouthpiece of the people's conscience, Aristophanes denounced with virulence anything unworthy of the state. In the *Babylonians* (produced in 426), of which fragments survive, the cruelty of Athens towards her subjects was compared to the cruelty of Darius towards the Babylonians, and the Chorus represented the Allied states treading a mill as slaves and among them Samos 'branded with letters'—for in 440 Athens had branded Samian prisoners-of-war. For this cruelty Aristophanes attacked the magistrates and above all Cleon, the advocate of massacre at Mitylene, who responded by prosecuting him unsuccessfully on a charge of treasonable action. In *Acharnians* (425) and *Knights* (424), which both won first prize, he denounced the tribe of demagogues, Pericles and Cleon included, as war-mongers, pricked a bubble of self-justification by putting the enemy's case for going to war, and pilloried the people for choosing such scoundrels as 'a cattle-dealer' (Eucrates) and 'a leather-seller' (Cleon) to mislead and intimidate them.[3]

[1] E. *El.* 743.   [2] Ar. *Nu.* 275; *Av.* 209; *Ra.* 324.   [3] Ar. *Ra.* 386; *Ach.* 509; *Eq.* 125.

With equal candour he berated the people for their corruptness, their litigiousness, and their ingratitude. In the *Clouds* (423) he exposed the impostures practised by the sophists, choosing as his target the greatest, though the least representative of them, Socrates the Athenian. He ridiculed Euripides mercilessly for producing princes in rags, piffling prologues, loose women, quibbling sophisms, and jingling lyrics, but he paid him the quasi-compliment of parodying his plays. He expended a lot of his wit on the women of Athens, but in the *Lysistrata* he enrolled them on his side in the crusade for peace—peace for Athens and the Allies and all Greece. In the *Birds* (414), when war had begun again, his leading characters sought peace elsewhere by founding a city of birds, 'Cloud-cuckoo-land', but in the *Lysistrata* (411) he made a direct appeal for peace at Athens before it was too late.

To interpret the serious purpose behind a comic poet's humour is always difficult. But it is less so in the case of Aristophanes, because he accepted the traditional role of the poet in Old Comedy—to give the best advice to the people. 'It was for you and the islands', he cried, 'that I persisted always in the fight' against Cleon. By the same standard, in the *Frogs*, he judged Aeschylus and Euripides as tragedians whose function was 'to teach men and teach them good, not shameful things'. As an artist he probably preferred Euripides but as a citizen he preferred Aeschylus, because his themes were more honourable and his advice to the State was better. So too with Socrates. Aristophanes and Socrates may have been close friends, but as a poet Aristophanes judged the philosopher by his value to the state. The Socrates of the *Clouds* was meant to be physically identical with the real Socrates, and the parody of his methods as a teacher was not meant to disguise the real effect of his teaching, which was, in Aristophanes' opinion, that young Athenians, including young aristocrats, lost faith in the gods of the City and of Greece, and were turned by the art of dialectic into jugglers with black and white, with right and wrong. In 405 when Athens was fighting for her life and Aristophanes gave the palm to Aeschylus, he added 'it is better not to sit by Socrates and chatter, sacrificing the finest traits of Tragedy and abandoning the art of the Muses'. By Aristophanes, as the sincere adviser of Athens, Euripides and Socrates stood condemned not as persons, but as preachers of an individualism which was breaking down the unity of the city-state. By 405 Euripides had left Athens and died in Macedonia, and Alcibiades and other pupils of Socrates were in exile. In 399 Aristophanes' charges against Socrates were to be correctly interpreted, but they were to be enforced against the person of Socrates with a severity which he cannot have condoned.[1]

The Athens which Aristophanes loved was the Athens of the war with all her virtues and her faults, her gaiety and her spirit. The Athens of which he sometimes dreamed was a finer Athens, violet-crowned for her victory over Persia and queen of a willing Greece; but he was a practical man with a

---

[1] Ar. *Pax* 759; *Ra.* 1053, 1078, 1435, 1501, 1530; Pl. *Smp.* 221B; Ar. *Nu.* 101, 112, 423, 818, 1477; *Ra.* 1491; Pl. *Ap.* 18B; 19C.

practical mission for the Athens of his day. He urged the Athenians to abide by right principles (*to dikaion*) in their policy towards the Allies and Greece, towards the old and the weak, and towards one another within the city. What Sophocles taught in tragedy, Aristophanes taught in comedy—adherence to the unwritten laws of which Pericles spoke in the Funeral Speech. In terms of practical politics he was no academic pacifist, but he advised peace in the true interests of Athens and of Greece; he did not want to disband the empire, but he urged a liberal treatment of the Allies; he was no enemy of democracy, but he demanded a democracy free from war-mongering, injustice, and cruelty. As the war drew towards its close, Aristophanes, like Sophocles, maintained his faith in Athens and expressed his love for her in the finest of his plays, the *Frogs*, produced in 405. Thereafter he continued to write plays, but his faith in Athens was less bright.[1]

As the city-state is represented in tragedy by Sophocles and in comedy by Aristophanes, so it is in history by Thucydides of Athens (*c.* 460–*c.* 400). His life centred in the city-state, and he studied city-states at war. As a man he loved Athens, and he served her, until she exiled him in 424 for failing as general to save Amphipolis from Brasidas. As a historian he revealed his love of Athens in the Funeral Speech, but he wrote with exemplary impartiality. In him art and science were married more happily than in any other writer of contemporary history. The world of small states, into which he gave a unique insight, has indeed passed, probably for ever, from the range of human experience. But the deductions which he made about man in politics and in war are as true today as when he wrote.

As an artist Thucydides achieved in his own style the sublimity and precision at which Gorgias aimed. He used some of Gorgias' figures, such as the jingle in rhyme or rhythm of parallel clauses and the construction of balanced antitheses, but he used them to enforce his meaning with colour and vigour. In narration he was the pioneer of the periodic style, where a single sentence comprehended at one view the points relevant to a situation and forced them into a reasoned relationship one to another. At the same time he has great speed, as he sweeps his reader on to each salient point and employs vivid tenses to throw actions into bold relief. In reflection and in analysis he has a roughness and a stringency in diction and phrasing which arise from his determination to define and enforce his meaning: 'Thus every form of depravity developed because of the factions in the Greek world, and the directness which constitutes the chief part of nobility was destroyed by derision, and the fact that men were opposed to one another in policy counted for much in lack of trust.'

The same qualities appear in the speeches, especially when he strives to plumb the depths of meaning. 'Retaliation does not succeed in accordance with right, just because it is wronged, nor is right a surety, just because it is confident, but the incalculable factor of the future is for the most part deci-

---

[1] Ar. *Eq.* 1325–34; *Ach.* 500; for later plays see p. 584.

sive, and yet, while it is the most treacherous factor of all, it proves itself most salutary because, facing it with equal fears, we proceed against one another rather with forethought.' The refinements of his diction and word-order cannot be appreciated in translation. It must be enough to note that he studied the effect not only of hiatus between individual words, but also of the juxtaposition of 'smooth' and 'rough' consonants at the end and beginning of adjacent words. Each word, like each block in the Parthenon, was deliberately shaped and fitted to give a precise effect in meaning and in sound.[1]

In addition to the technical qualities of 'firmness, astringency, condensation, severity, and gravity' in his style, the critic Dionysius of Halicarnassus emphasized 'his terrifying intensity, and above all his power of striking the emotions'. For Thucydides had not only the artist's skill in describing the brave departure of the expeditionary force for Syracuse, but also the artist's sensitivity in conveying the sufferings of the survivors, who rushed into the river Assinarus or finally perished in the quarries of Syracuse. Dionysius described Thucydides' power in terms which Aristotle had used in defining the qualities of Attic Tragedy, and especially those of Sophoclean Tragedy. The similarity is striking. It lies in their common outlook as artists, not in any sharing of literary technique. Sophocles does not condemn the cruelty of Creon to Antigone any more than Thucydides condemns that of the Corcyraean democrats to their countrymen. They both make us relive it and condemn it. So too in describing a sudden change of situation, a reversal of fortune, as Aristotle later called it, Thucydides observed himself and conveyed to us the dramatic force of the disaster to Ambracia, the Athenian lodgement at Pylus, or the Athenian defeat in the Great Harbour.[2]

Science records facts accurately, selects those relevant to its inquiry, and determines their interrelation and, if possible, their causation. Thucydides applied this method of science to history. 'I thought it proper', he wrote, 'to record the facts of the war, not from chance information nor from my own impression, but in accordance with the most accurate investigation possible of each particular, not only in the situations of which I heard from others, but also in those at which I was present myself.' At the same time he discounted any partisanship, whether in others or in himself. His selection of those facts alone which were relevant to his inquiry was carried out with strict economy, when he surveyed the past history of Greece. Having stripped away from the heroic tradition all romantic and chivalrous elements, he deduced from the residue of historical fact that no Greek state or group of states, until and including the fall of the tyrants, rivalled the protagonists of the Peloponnesian War in power and enterprise. Moreover, in a summary of Athens' growth since the Persian wars, he marked each step on the road to power and each instance of enterprise in policy up to the immediate ante-

---

[1] Longin. 25; Th. 3. 83. 1; 4. 62. 4; D. H. *Comp.* 22 (106–110) cf. 20 (90 f.); Demetr. 2. 72.
[2] D.H. *Th.* 24 (= *Ep. Amm.* 2. 2. fin.); Th. 6. 32; 7. 84. 2; 7. 87; 3. 113; 4. 12. 3; 7. 55–56.

cedents of the war. Thus he selected in both cases those facts which were relevant to an inquiry into the nature of power and policy in the world of Greek city-states.[1]

Besides recording the facts of the war, Thucydides included some speeches by statesmen, diplomats, and generals which revealed the psychological aspects of power and the motives of policy. As the actual words could not be reproduced, he warned his readers that the speeches contained not only the general sense of what was actually said, but also the arguments which he himself thought most appropriate to each occasion and speaker. Thus we have two elements in the speeches, the arguments of the speakers and arguments supplied by Thucydides. The proportion varies from speech to speech, and in some speeches one or another element may be absent. For example, the Corcyraeans spoke at Athens for and the Corinthians spoke against an alliance between Corcyra and Athens. Each speech contains an analysis of the advantages which the course they advocate would give to Athens, and the two together enable us to see more clearly the issues of power and policy which were involved at the time. Again, after the isolation of the Spartans at Sphacteria, the Spartans sued for peace. Their speech contains an analysis of the benefits which will accrue from making a generous peace when Athens has a momentary advantage. Here too we see the issue in greater depth. Whether these analyses come ultimately from Thucydides himself or from the Corcyraean, Corinthian, and Spartan speakers, they deepen our understanding and they do so in a dramatic and artistic manner which carries conviction. Who indeed can read the Melian dialogue and remain untouched, intellectually and emotionally, by the issues which beset a small and innocent state faced by a brutal and powerful aggressor?[2]

In addition Thucydides described the interrelation of events, and sometimes he expressed his own views of their causation. After recounting the facts and the policies involved in the events which preceded the outbreak of the war, Thucydides gave the speeches of Corinthians, Athenians, and Spartans, which revealed the effect of those events on the leading states and their reactions to them. He depicted the national psychology of each state in the crisis of decision, just as Sophocles and Euripides depicted the psychology of each protagonist. By the same method he showed the interrelation between statesman and people at Athens in the Funeral Speech, between policy and policy in the words of Archidamus and Sthenelaïdas, Cleon and Diodotus, Nicias and Alcibiades. In his narrative too he showed the interrelation of plague, morality, and power; of faction, morality, and disintegration; and of failure or success abroad and national attitudes at home. So might a physiologist analyse the interplay of forces, the strains and stresses, physical and mental, in a human body, but the precise causation of a particular disease might elude him.

---

[1] Th. 1. 22. 2–3 (cf. 1. 1. 3; 1. 20. 3–21. 1); 1. 17 fin.; 19 fin.
[2] Th. 1. 22. 1; 1. 32–43; 4. 17–20; 5. 85–113.

Historians have attributed wars to a variety of causes, economic forces, geographical factors, rival ideologies, religions, or races. Thucydides regarded these as attendant circumstances (*tychai*) or variable contingencies (*syntychiai*), like time, tide, or weather, outside man's power to control but not usually decisive. Some historians have attributed wars to divine will, whether benevolent or malevolent, driving men forward into battle. Thucydides placed the responsibility squarely on the shoulders of men. 'The real cause, in my view,' he stated, 'was Athens' power and Sparta's fear, which compelled them to go to war.' A situation had developed in which two nations with certain psychological characteristics were to be involved in conflict as inevitably as Creon and Antigone, or Jason and Medea. This situation was of men's making. Wise statesmen and nations, if they had wished to avoid conflict, would have prevented the situation from developing to this crucial stage. Men, in his belief, make history by the exercise of free will towards one another. An understanding of human nature is therefore of vital importance. Thucydides believed that in some basic respects human nature was and would be constant: in the instinct to dominate one who yields, to defend oneself against an intruder, to keep what one has gained by force for reasons of prestige, self-interest, and fear. Wise statesmen and nations will take these instincts into account, both in others and in themselves, and wield their power or regulate their policy accordingly. In particular they will realize the nature and the effects of war. If men use their intelligence (*gnome*), they will perceive that neither might nor right will ensure victory; that confidence in divine intervention is not based on an intelligent observation of history; that the implications of going to war and the hazards of war itself are unpredictable; that wars are decided more by errors of judgement than by margins of strength; and that the violence of prolonged wars provokes passion, brutality, and disintegration.[1]

'It will be sufficient', wrote Thucydides, 'if my history is judged useful by those who wish to have a clear understanding not only of what has happened, but also of what will happen again at some time and on such or similar lines in accordance with human nature.' He was correct in his prognosis. The basic qualities of human nature remain constant, the attendant circumstances of war are similar, and the effects of prolonged wars on civilized peoples are the same. 'It is only from the past that one can judge the future', said Churchill at the conclusion of another war. He, like Thucydides, believed that man's intelligence can dominate history and make the whole world 'safe and clean'. It is a message of hope, like that of Sophocles in the *Oedipus Coloneus*. Thucydides had seen man triumph in the city-state of Pericles, where a great statesman of vision, integrity, and intelligence had led a great-hearted people, and in the political situation before the war, when power and justice had been combined in a harmonious peace. He lived to see triumph

[1] Th. 4. 64. 1; 3. 82. 2; Livy *caelestes ita velle*; Tacitus *ira deum*; Th. 1. 23. 6; 1. 76. 2–3; 4. 61. 5; 5. 105. 2; 4. 62. 4; 5. 104–5; 1. 78. 1–2; 4. 18. 4; 2. 65. 11–13; 3. 82. 2.

turn to failure, the Greek world distraught, Athens prostrate. The history of that experience was written with an intellectual clarity and an emotional force which no chronicler of past events can hope to recapture.[1]

Antiphon of Athens (*c.* 480–411) laid the foundations of Attic oratory as a literary genre. He practised and taught the art of composing speeches calculated to convince the people in the assembly or in the law-courts (but his defence of his conduct as a leader of the oligarchic revolution did not save him from execution). In the manner of Tisias, he studied the principles of arguing not from definite evidence but in terms of probability, intention, and so on. Model speeches in groups of four, two prosecuting and two defending in hypothetical cases, were used for instructing pupils in these principles of argument. Three such groups called the *Tetralogies* have survived under the name of Antiphon but may have been written by a non-Athenian of his time. His influence on the oratorical prose of the next century was important.[2]

As Democritus and Thucydides viewed physical and political phenomena without religious or philosophical preconceptions, so Hippocrates of Cos (*c.* 460–*c.* 400) viewed the human body and thus laid the foundations of medical theory. Among the treatises of the Hippocratic corpus a few can probably be dated to his lifetime in view of their outlook and their style. One of them, *The Sacred Disease*, a treatise on epilepsy, contains the following passage: 'This disease is, in my opinion, no whit more sacred than other diseases but is of the same nature and causation as they; it is also curable, no less than they, . . . provided it is not at too virulent a stage for the remedies which are applied. Its origin, like theirs, is in heredity . . . and its cause lies in the brain, as is the case too with all the most serious diseases.' Such emancipation from the religious or philosophical view of disease, coupled with the precise observation practised by the Cnidian school of medicine and the importance attached to prognosis by the Coan school, made a considerable advance possible in the understanding of the nature and the causes of diseases and in their treatment.[3]

In this period important strides were made in the field of geometry, mathematics, and astronomy. Pythagoras and his followers had laid the main foundations by understanding the properties of parallels, using geometrical areas to express arithmetical addition or subtraction, evolving a theory of numbers, detailing some solid figures, and approximating to the square root of two. Democritus, the perfecter of the 'atomic' theory, began the study of solid geometry and was successful in calculating the volumes of pyramids and cones. In 'the Great Year' he probably integrated the lunar and the solar years, and in physical geography he postulated that the earth's flat surface was not circular but elongated to a form one and a half times as long as it was broad. The greatest influence in this field came from a contemporary of

---

[1] Th. 1. 22. 4; Churchill in world broadcast, 13 May 1945; Th. 2. 65. 5–8; 1. 144. 4; 1. 76. 3.   [2] Antiph. *Fr.* 1 (his defence); Th. 8. 68. 1–2.

[3] Hp. *Morb. Sacr.* 1. 1.

Socrates, Hippocrates of Chios, who spent much of his life in Athens. His Book of Elements summarized and carried further the study of geometry, especially that of the circle. He concluded that the areas of circles are to one another as the squares on their diameters, and investigated the quadrature of lunes. The sophist Hippias of Elis discovered the use of the quadratrix for trisecting an angle, and Theodorus of Cyrene, also a contemporary of Socrates, proved the irrationality of the square root of three, five, seven, and so on to seventeen in geometrical terms. Although their theories may have contributed to the skill of architects and surveyors, the mathematicians and the geometers were held by the public to be probing into the supernatural, like Socrates in the *Clouds*.[1]

Apart from the prosecution of Anaxagoras for 'impiety' (the date of which is uncertain), the danger of a conflict between rationalism and democracy had been averted by the genius of Pericles. In 430 he boasted with truth that the Athenians loved wisdom, tolerated one another's views, and obeyed the laws of the democracy. This happy state was due to his position as the champion of rationalism and the leader of democracy, and to the success of his policy, which gave the citizens prosperity and confidence. After his death a rift appeared, and with the deterioration of conditions it widened, until rationalism and democracy were at loggerheads. This antagonism, so dangerous to the health of both, was rooted in the religious beliefs and the educational conditions of the time.

The point of friction did not lie in the observance of state religion. Even an agnostic like Protagoras would have approved the paying of one's dues to Athena. During the war years state religion flourished. A beautiful little temple in Ionic style was built to Athena Nike (Victory) on the Acropolis in the years 427–424, and a parapet of exquisitely sculptured slabs was added later in the century. Below the Acropolis Nicias dedicated a small temple near the theatre to Dionysus, and a statue in gold and ivory was placed there. At the Hephaesteum statues in bronze of Athena and Hephaestus were made by Alcamenes during the peace of Nicias. The chief building of the war years was the Erechtheum on the Acropolis. Although work stopped at the time of the Sicilian Expedition, it was completed about 406–405. The plan had to fit the exigencies of the site, which was cramped and on two levels, and the effect is less grand than that of the Propylaea. On the other hand it has many beauties and graces in the Ionic tradition: the door-frames in marble are magnificently decorated and the detail of the Caryatid Maidens is charming. Overseas a Doric temple of Apollo was dedicated by Nicias at Delos in 417. The expenditure of so much skill and treasure on statues, temples, and furnishings such as a gold lamp in the Erechtheum is an eloquent tribute to the sincerity of Athenian worship in time of war.

Family religion, on the other hand, suffered. For centuries its ceremonies had been held at the shrines in the demes, but with the evacuation of the

[1] Heath, *MGM* and Thomas, *GMW* 1. 228.

countryside they were discontinued for long periods. The effect was serious, because the average Athenian derived his or her stability more from this side of personal religion than from the Eleusinian Mysteries or Orphic rites. Family traditions, such as respect for parents and the marriage-bond, were correspondingly weakened. Family land, hitherto inalienable, came on to the market under the stress of economic need. The standards of the younger generation were further shaken by the strain of the plague, the revolution, and the long war. At this point the new learning brought a disruptive influence to bear; for it questioned the conventional codes of conduct. 'What is shameful but the thinking makes it so?' said a Euripidean character. Such ideas, broadcast in a city where free living and prostitution by non-Athenian courtesans were common enough in high society, threatened the traditional standard of morality and aroused hostility especially among Athenian women.[1]

A third stratum of religious belief, which we usually label 'superstition', was much less tangible. Its outer manifestations were faith in oracles and omens, such as eclipses or prodigies, and divination by stars or entrails. Its inner force was fear of offending the unseen, incomprehensible powers of darkness which rose up in days of trouble, a fear most potent in the form of the 'miasma', a pollution incurred by an act of sacrilege, bringing disaster upon the whole state until the perpetrator was made a scapegoat. Such a miasma, incurred by Oedipus, was dramatized by Sophocles, probably in a year of plague, and the vitality of the belief is apparent from some of the *Tetralogies* attributed to Antiphon. Foreign religions of an equally primitive character, such as the Dionysiac rites in Macedonia (dramatized in the *Bacchae*), or the licentious worship of the Thracian goddesses Bendis and Cotytto, came into Athens with the slaves and metics and gained adherents among the citizens. With this stratum of belief the rationalists knew no compromise. To them the sun was a fiery mass of ore bigger than the Peloponnese, the moon a land of mountains and gorges, but to the superstitious they represented the eye of God and its closure held the army at Syracuse for a fatal month. To them a one-horned ram had a defect in its brain, but to the superstitious its deformity portended the fall of a statesman. To them disease was explicable as a physical phenomenon, but to the superstitious disease in a man was sent by heaven, just as disaster in a state might be the effect of a miasma not yet purged.[2]

The gap between rationalism and religion in a modern democracy is narrowed by universal education. In Athens state education was lacking, and during the war family education was weakened, especially in its moral aspect. All citizens were literate, whether they learnt at home or at a private school, but only the well-to-do could afford the higher education given by the sophists. Yet all citizens were exposed to the influx of new ideas. They heard them in the plays of a Euripides, in the pleadings of an Antiphon, or in the oratory of a Gorgias, and they discussed them with quick-witted avidity in

[1] Th. 2. 16; E. *Fr.* 19.   [2] D.L. 2. 8 (Anaxagoras); Plu. *Per.* 6.

the crowded city. In answer to an increasing demand there was a rapid expansion of the trade in books, and in 405 Aristophanes assumed that his audience knew the latest fashionable treatise. Their powers of memory too were highly developed by judging plays, politicians, or prisoners at a single hearing. Athenians in Sicily entertained their captors by reciting long passages by heart from the plays of Euripides. Yet quickness of wit was no substitute for a general education, when it was a question of accommodating old religious beliefs to new secular ideas. An antagonism grew up, and it was exacerbated by the horrors of plague, defeat, and revolution.[1]

Most dangerous of all, the antagonism was exploited by politicians. The more primitive beliefs were held by the poorer class of citizens, whose material and political interests were protected by the democracy and the demagogues. The Athenian exponents of the new wisdom, for reasons of finance and fashion, were mainly young and wealthy men who prided themselves on their superiority of birth and of intellect; and the political form which their sense of superiority demanded was not democracy, but oligarchy. A second Pericles might have held both groups together in a common loyalty and a common enlightenment. Nicias, the outstanding man of Pericles' social class, lacked the intellectual ability to lead the young aristocrats and the spiritual qualities to fire the people as a whole. The political successors of Pericles, men such as Cleon and later Cleophon, were of a different stamp. Their oratory was violent and emotional, not dignified and intellectual, and they appealed to the more primitive passions and beliefs of the less well-to-do class from which they themselves originated.

There was much truth in Aristophanes' gibes that Cleon's path to power was paved with oracles. Indeed oracle-mongering soon became a necessary technique. Nicias paraded his sincere belief in oracles and omens, kept his own diviners, and attributed his military successes to his lucky star. Alcibiades employed diviners to discredit those approved by the state and advance his own cause. Cleon's use of oracles was a part of his plan to exploit the reaction against the new ideas and discredit his political opponents. Cleon himself prosecuted Euripides on a charge of 'impiety', perhaps in 426, and his followers probably inspired a demonstration against him by women at the Thesmophoria. At this time Euripides stood out as the Athenian exponent of such ideas, whereas his friends the atheistic philosophers Diagoras and Protagoras were foreigners. In the years after the plague Aristophanes scoffed at both sides, demagogues like Cleon and Eucrates and new-thinkers like Euripides and Socrates.[2]

A greater crisis came when Athens embarked on the expedition to Sicily. Then Alcibiades personified all that the extreme democrats loathed. He was a young aristocrat turned demagogue; a more adroit manipulator of such

[1] A. *Ra.* 1114 (for books cf. A. *Av.* 1288; Eupolis *Fr.* 304; D.L. 9. 52); Plu. *Nic.* 29.
[2] A. *Eq.* 61, 109, 997; Plu. *Nic.* 4; 13. 1; *Pap. Oxyr.* 9, pp. 152–3 (= Satyrus); D.L. 9. 54.

demagogic techniques as mob-oratory, oracle-mongering, and ostracism; and a statesman capable perhaps of combining democracy and enlightenment: He was vulnerable at a vital point, because he had been a pupil of Socrates and was reputed to have parodied the Mysteries. The mutilation of the Hermae gave the extreme democrats their chance. The sacrilege, they claimed, was an evil omen for the expedition, and the perpetrators were among those who, contemptuous alike of religion and democracy, meant to establish oligarchy or tyranny by force. Alcibiades' name was mentioned, and in due course he was condemned to death on a charge of 'impiety'. Diagoras 'the atheist' fled on the same charge. His books were burnt in public and a price was put on his head. Many leading people were imprisoned or executed. Protagoras fled, probably at this time. The answer to the heresy-hunt was revolution in 411. The extremists among the oligarchs were intellectuals, several being associates of Socrates, and they took their revenge on the demagogues. When the democracy was restored, Euripides went to live in Macedonia. The first act of Alcibiades in 407 was to deny any sacrilege in the past and to escort the procession of the Eleusinian Mysteries. But the very day of his arrival was counted as an omen against him, and his opponents soon secured his downfall. Aristophanes' words of moderation in 405, advising Athens to use the talents of 'the Lion' Alcibiades, went unheeded.[1]

Thus in the dark days of the war the rift became a chasm. Extremists on one side who posed as intellectual leaders had seized power by revolutionary methods. Extremists on the other side who posed as champions of democracy had exploited the superstitious fears of the people. Both were impostors. The true spirit of enlightenment and the true spirit of democracy demanded a grasp of principle and a sense of moderation, which had been ousted by the violent conditions of war and faction. Unless the chasm could be bridged when peace came, enlightenment and democracy were likely to follow separate paths, and the city-state would never be again, as it had been under Pericles, the focal point of intellectual and democratic progress.

[1] Th. 6. 27. 3; 29. 3; 60. 1–2; D.S. 13. 6. 7 (cf. Th. 7. 60. 4 with A. *Av.* 1073 in support of the date in D.S. for Diagoras' flight); D.L. 9. 52; X. *HG* 1. 4. 12; Plu. *Alc.* 36. 1–4; A. *Ra.* 1432.

BOOK V

THE PERIOD OF TRANSIENT HEGEMONIES
(404–354)

CHAPTER 1

The Hegemony of Sparta, 404–386

§ 1. *The political problems of the period*

VICTORIOUS in two great wars, Sparta found the initiative firmly in her hands. In theory she could revert to the policy of inactivity and isolationism which had once been imposed on her by the power of Athens. In practice she was drawn on, as later Athens and Thebes were drawn on, by the principle that the victor dominates the vanquished, the strong dominates the weak, a principle which Thucydides believed to be inherent in human nature.

In 404 the victor was faced by problems of the utmost gravity. Most of the Greek states were torn by faction and animosity, and many like Corcyra were ruined spiritually and economically. To restore confidence within the Greek states true leadership was required. The hope had been expressed by Thucydides that Sparta would provide such leadership after defeating Athens. 'Thereafter Sparta herself will live free from fear, and the whole of Greece will accept from her a leadership which rests not on might but on goodwill.' A similar hope might have been placed in Syracuse, that she would lead the Siceliote Greeks towards unity.[1] But the Greek world was no longer self-contained, no longer safe from foreign aggression. Persia and Carthage were pressing upon the Greeks, and later Macedon and Rome did likewise. Leadership must also look outwards and lead the Greeks against their enemies. Sparta herself had undertaken to sell the Greeks of Ionia to Persia, in order to draw Persian gold and win the war. Medism was indeed freely practised by individual states for their own ends, but a leader who put the friendship of Persia before the liberty of the Greeks in Ionia was unlikely to command a following based on goodwill. Thus Sparta faced a double problem, to set the Greek world in order and to withstand Persia.

---

[1] Th. 6. 92. 5 fin.; 8. 2. 4; 4. 64. 5.

If Sparta and her successors failed to solve the problem, it is easy to censure them. At the worst they sank to a combination of medism and imperialism which was condemned in their own generation.[1] But the fault was not exclusively theirs. Other city-states failed to follow them in their worthwhile policies or to experiment seriously with such ideas as federal union. The Greek world of city-states was suffering from a political *malaise* which rendered them incapable not only of leading one another but of following a leader. In this period the city-state was put to its crucial test as a political form. Its citizens were approaching a stage of intellectual emancipation and capitalist development, when the traditional city-state was unable to satisfy their intellectual and material requirements and therefore laid less claim to their full-hearted loyalty. Attempts to modify it were made in political theory by Plato and Aristotle and in political practice by Syracuse, Thebes, and Olynthus. If the Greek states had lived in isolation, they might have worked out their salvation along the lines of federation, in which important developments were made. But the outer world was pressing upon them. States of a more primitive character but of stronger qualities, such as Macedon and Rome, arose quite independently of the city-state and proved superior to it in generating military and financial power.

The period which we are about to study has sometimes been labelled a period of decline. Nothing could be farther from the truth. Greek civilization ran with as strong a current as ever. It was an age of bold experiments in politics, philosophy, literature, and art. The civilization which led Macedon and Rome captive and through them influenced the modern world was predominantly a fourth-century civilization. It is true that the traditional container of this civilization, the sovereign city-state, was beginning to crack under the ferment of new ideas from within and under the pressure of stronger forces from outside. The same may be said of the traditional container of our European civilization, the sovereign national state. In both cases the container is of less importance than the content, and in the civilization of the fourth century many of the most fruitful ideas in human history came to birth.

§ 2. *The problems and the resources of Sparta*

SPARTA fought the Peloponnesian War in the name of liberty, and the day of final victory was greeted as the dawn of liberty in Greece.[2] Liberty is indeed a simple and acceptable slogan. But liberty in politics, both within a state and between states, is a complex relationship which is rarely achieved in practice. This was already apparent in the closing years of the war. Then Sparta contracted to sell the liberties of the Greeks in Asia Minor, in exchange for the Persian subsidies which alone enabled her to preserve the liberties of herself and her allies from Athens. When the war ended in triumph, Sparta was faced by her first dilemma. If she fulfilled her contract with Persia, she would belie her pretensions as a liberator and lose the respect of the Greeks;

[1] Isoc. 4. 128.   [2] Th. 1. 139. 3; 4. 85. 1; X. *HG* 2. 2. 23.

if she did not, she must expect war with Persia and for the purposes of war she must retain her naval power in the Aegean and her military bases in Asia Minor. At first she enjoyed a respite, because Cyrus made no move against the Greek states in Ionia, but the respite was to be shortlived. Her second dilemma was to determine the quality of liberty in the states of the Aegean which might help her most in a war with Persia. There many had already earned the gratitude of Sparta by helping to overthrow the puppet governments of Athens, and their leaders had been duly installed in power during the period of military government. Thus in states such as Thasos, Byzantium, Chios, and Miletus oligarchies of an extreme type were established before the war was over, and Spartan governors, called 'harmosts', were using their troops to support the oligarchs in exacting reprisals from the democrats.[1] What was she to do when victory was complete? If she withdrew her forces from the Aegean, widespread faction and confusion would ensue. If she kept them there, she must support her own partisans and continue to exact the financial levies which she needed to keep her fleet in commission.

The problems which faced Sparta in Asia Minor and in the Aegean in 404 were handled by her experienced commander, Lysander. An able and ambitious man, he had concentrated the means to victory in his own person: he commanded the favour and the gold of Cyrus, the confidence of the allied seamen in the great fleet, and the loyalty of the oligarchs in the Aegean whom he had organized into political clubs.[2] When he won the war, his prestige and his power were unique. In the portico which was built at Delphi in commemoration of the battle of Aegospotami a statue of Lysander being crowned by Poseidon was placed before the statues of the other commanders and beside those of the gods; it was dedicated by Lysander himself, 'who set the wreath of victory on unsacked Sparta, the citadel of Greece, the country of beautiful dances, his fatherland'.[3] At Samos, when he expelled the democrats in September 404, the restored oligarchs honoured him by renaming the Heraea, or festival of Hera, 'the Lysandreia'. In October he brought to Sparta the fruits of his victories—the prows of some 200 warships, the fleet surrendered by Athens, 470 talents of silver, a quantity of spoils, and the crowns which the liberated states had conferred upon him. The splendour of his homecoming to Sparta late in 404 excelled even that of Alcibiades to Athens in 407. Despite the Spartan law against reappointment, he had been appointed to the supreme command as navarch for 404/403. During this year, when the influence of Lysander dominated the Ephors, the policy of Sparta was made clear to the Greek states: in the Aegean to support extreme oligarchies (often 'decarchies', in which ten men exercised full powers), to install Spartan harmosts and garrisons, and to exact an annual tribute of some 1,000 talents; in Sicily to support Dionysius, the tyrant of Syracuse; and in Asia to collaborate with Cyrus and, through the agency of

---

[1] Th. 8. 64. 5; X. *HG* 1. 1. 32; 1. 3. 15; 2. 2. 1-2; D.S. 13. 65. 3-4.
[2] D.S. 13. 70. 4; X. *HG* 1. 6. 4; 2. 1. 6-7.   [3] *GHI* 94; 95; Paus. 10. 9. 7-10.

Pharnabazus, to bring about the assassination of Alcibiades. As hegemon by sea Sparta was already following in the wake of imperial Athens.[1]

Meanwhile Sparta had to consider her relations with her Allies. Boeotia, Corinth, Megara, Syracuse, and other states had provided the bulk of the manpower and the shipping, and they had suffered heavy losses. In particular the Spartan Alliance, and not Sparta alone, had defeated Athens. It had been held together by fear or hatred of Athens as much as by the leadership of Sparta. As soon as peace was concluded in 404, it tended to fall apart, as it had done in 421. The settlement which Sparta made with Athens in 404 may have been inspired by the principle that generosity to an enemy makes for a more lasting peace. But at the same time it was a settlement to which the leading members of the Spartan Alliance did not subscribe; and they observed that Athens and her former subjects became dependent on Sparta in foreign policy, paid tribute to Sparta, and were controlled by pro-Spartan governments. The spoils of war were delivered up to Sparta, not divided among the victorious Allies. These causes of discontent were aggravated by the memory of such Spartan leaders as Astyochus and by fear of Sparta's intentions in the future. Thebes and Corinth showed their independence by harbouring men who had been banished by the pro-Spartan governments and by disobeying the order of Sparta to supply contingents in 403 for an invasion of Attica. Thus within a year of victory the hegemony of Sparta by land ceased to rest on any vestiges of goodwill.[2]

Victory had placed within the grasp of Sparta that hegemony by land and by sea which she had exercised during the Persian wars and had been advised by Hetoemaridas *c.* 474 to abandon on the ground that the hegemony on both elements was not in her true interests. Were her resources now such that she could exercise hegemony by land and by sea? The prestige of Sparta as a military power stood high in 404. Her hoplites had not been defeated in regular battle; her commanders—Brasidas, Agis, Gylippus, Clearchus, Callicratidas, and Lysander—had acquitted themselves with distinction in the field; and her troops overseas, mainly Perioeci and Neodamodeis, had shown fine fighting qualities. Her fleet was small but efficient; it had held the post of honour and had attacked with vigour in the naval actions of the war. The prestige of her constitution was remarkable. Sparta was one of the few participants in the war which had not suffered from party-strife. Her stability and efficiency were envied not only by the oligarchs who aped Spartan manners, but also by others who disliked her policy. The orator Lysias hardly exaggerated when he spoke at the Olympic festival: 'Sparta is justly acclaimed as the leader of Greece because of her innate worth and military skill. Unique in her immunity from invasion, faction, or defeat, she trusts for her defence not in walls but in her unchanging institutions.'[3]

[1] Plu. *Lys.* 18; D.S. 14. 10–11; 14. 13. 1; Arist. *Pol.* 1271ᵃ38.
[2] Th. 4. 19. 2–3; X. *HG.* 2. 4. 30; D.S. 14. 6. 3; Justin 5. 10.
[3] D.S. 11. 50. 6; Lys. 33. 7.

Yet the long war had imposed a great strain on Sparta. The Spartiate hoplites in 404 were probably some 3,000 in number, whereas in 479 they had been about 5,000; the Spartiate element in the Lacedaemonian army, originally one half of the hoplite strength, sank to a third in 371; and the army itself was repeatedly reinforced by the creation of separate brigades of Neodamodeis. During and after the war her officers frequently abused the powers which were suddenly entrusted to them. Gylippus was condemned for peculation; Clearchus ruled harshly at Byzantium; Callibius struck Athenian citizens in the street; and many other harmosts, undermined by the flattery of their partisans, behaved like petty tyrants. When they returned home, often with reluctance, they resented the austerity and the discipline of Spartan life. Lysander himself was suspected of planning to overthrow the dual monarchy at Sparta. When Sparta set out to rule an empire, some weaknesses in her constitution became more apparent. All political and financial responsibilities were concentrated in the hands of the Kings, the Gerontes, who were over sixty years of age, and the annually changing board of five Ephors. Friction between King and King or between Kings and Ephors produced some instability in the policy of the state. The controlling hand of the Gerousia had some of the defects of old age; for, as Aristotle observed, there is an old age of the mind as well as of the body. Slowness, conservatism, and lack of imagination were to prove more harmful qualities in an imperial state than in the leader of a defensive coalition.[1]

More serious than any of these defects was the progressive corruption of Spartan institutions. The experience of war and of empire gave point to the Delphic oracle: 'love of money and nothing else will destroy Sparta'. In theory the Spartiate system rested on an agricultural economy, which was cut off from outside traffic by its iron currency and was maintained internally by serf labour. And in theory individual Spartiates were more or less equally well-to-do, so long as they retained their original estates (*kleroi*). In practice, despite the law which forbade the private ownership of coined money, gold and silver found their way into private hands at Sparta. This quickly upset the basic equality of the Spartiates, and led to the disfranchisement of those who fell into debt and failed to contribute to their messes (*syssitia*). In late 398 a serious rising was organized by Cinadon, a disfranchised Spartiate or 'Inferior' (*hypomeion*). He planned to raise the Inferiors, Perioeci, Neodamodeis, and Helots against their masters, the Spartiate Equals (*homoioi*). Numbers were about twenty to one in his favour, but the Ephors suppressed the plot by arresting Cinadon and his fellow-conspirators. Yet they did not check the rate of disfranchisement. When many Equals had fallen in battle and two fifths of the estates had passed into the hands of women under the Spartan law of inheritance, the shortage of Spartiates became acute. It thus happened that, as Sparta's commitments increased, her fully franchised

[1] Th. 4. 81. 2–3; D.S. 13. 106. 8–9; 66. 6; Plu. *Lys.* 15; X. *Lac. Pol.* 14; D.S. 14. 13; Arist. *Pol.* 1270ᵇ35.

population declined. During the fourth century it became more and more dangerous to send Spartiates abroad; for they were required to hold down the subject-population at home. Yet, when they were invaded by a foreign foe, all classes in the state except some of the Helots combined in defence of Laconia.[1]

Despite her defects Sparta remained the dominant state in Greece for almost forty years. Her power had a stabilizing influence, if only in the sense that it prevented other states from disturbing an uneasy peace. Her methods became increasingly repressive. She favoured separatism in an age which was groping its way towards federalism, and she supported agricultural oligarchy in a society which was becoming increasingly mercantile and monetary in its economy. Her culture remained backward in an age of individualism and intellectual sophistication, so that she could never claim of herself, as Pericles claimed of Athens, that her subjects need not blush to submit to her rule. When her empire collapsed, Isocrates could assert with some justice that Sparta had inherited a false tradition of leadership. Yet in 338, when the other Greek states bowed to the power of Macedon, Sparta alone defended her independence as the citadel of Greece, the most perfect and the most anti-quated example of the Dorian city-state.[2]

§ 3. *Oligarchy and civil war in Attica*

IN the moment of victory Sparta reversed the acts of her enemy. Aegina, Melos, Scione, and other victims of Athenian violence were reconstituted as states, the territories appropriated by Athens were restored to the original owners, and the exiles whom the pro-Athenian democracies had expelled were reinstated in their homes. The sacred island of Apollo, Delos, was liberated from Athenian occupation, and the temples were administered by the Delians. The Messenians whom Athens had planted at Naupactus and in Cephallenia were expelled; they fled to Sicily and Cyrene. In the liberated states there was a natural swing towards an oligarchical form of government, prompted partly by antipathy to the pro-Athenian democrats and partly by the knowledge that Lysander favoured such governments. This swing was soon arrested by the atrocities which the extreme oligarchs or 'decarchs' committed with the support of Spartan governors and garrisons. At Miletus, for instance, some 800 'democrats' were massacred with the connivance of Lysander. The Spartan governors themselves caused a revulsion of feeling; for they acted harshly and sometimes tyrannically towards those whom they claimed to have liberated. At Byzantium the Spartan harmost Clearchus, who was sent to assist the oligarchs, raised a force of mercenary soldiers and set himself up as tyrant; he refused to take orders from Sparta, and, when a Spartan force drove him out, he became the organizer and commander of

[1] Arist. *Fr.* 544; X. *HG* 3. 3. 5–11; Arist. *Pol.* 1270ª23; 1271ª29.
[2] Th. 2. 41. 3; Isoc. 4. 18.

Cyrus' mercenaries. Within a year of her final victory the political methods of Sparta were deeply resented. The first open challenge to her policy came from Athens.[1]

At Athens also there was at first a swing towards an oligarchical form of government. The most influential statesman at Athens, Theramenes, the negotiator of the peace, was a moderate oligarch of established reputation. The restored exiles, headed by Critias, a friend of Theramenes, were on good terms with Sparta and particularly with Lysander. In the misery of defeat the people were willing to accept an oligarchical government as a *modus vivendi* with the victors, and they made no move to help the democratic leaders when they were arrested at the instigation of the leading oligarchs, a caucus of five self-styled 'Ephors'. A provisional government was formally established in the summer of 404, probably at the beginning of the Attic year in July. In an assembly at which Lysander himself spoke, the proposal of Dracontides was ratified, namely that thirty men should be appointed to draft 'the ancestral laws' as the basis for a permanent constitution and meanwhile to direct the administration. The Thirty were then appointed, ten being nominated by Theramenes, ten by the Ephors, and ten by those present in the Assembly. They in turn detailed 500 men to serve as Councillors and certain others to act as magistrates—in particular, ten governors of the Peiraeus and eleven controllers of the state prison—selecting them in each case from a panel of candidates chosen from the 'One Thousand', who were probably a nominated body. To keep up the appearance of constitutional procedure, the Thirty repealed the laws of Ephialtes which had deposed the Areopagus Council from power, annulled the people's courts, and began a revision of the legal code. The Thirty themselves, exercising full powers and using 300 'whip-bearers' to execute their will, controlled the entire administration and were justly named the Thirty Tyrants.[2]

As in 411, so in 404 the oligarchs were drawn from two camps. The extremists, either restored exiles or clandestine members of the political clubs, were headed by Critias, who had made his mark as one of the Four Hundred and had spent his years of exile as a democratic agitator in Thessaly. Their views and their methods were exemplified by two sayings of Critias, 'the finest constitution is that of Sparta' and 'all changes of constitution involve bloodshed', and they certainly put the interests of the party before those of the state. The moderates, who had served among the Five Thousand and under the restored democracy, were led by Theramenes, who had ousted the extremists in 411 and brought the Five Thousand into power. But on this occasion the extremists, counting on the whiphand of Lysander, took control of the situation. They disposed of the democratic leaders by putting them on

---

[1] Plu. *Lys.* 14; 19; *GHI* 99; X. *HG* 2. 2. 9; D.S. 14. 34.

[2] Lys. 12. 43; 12. 71; Arist. *Ath.* 34. 3; 35. 1–2 ('from the One Thousand' may be corrupt); X. *HG.* 2. 3. 2 and 11; D.S. 14. 3–4; Plu. *Lys.* 15. The chronology is disputed; see p. 446, n. 3 for the dates given here.

trial in the Council of Five Hundred and demanding an open vote from the Councillors.[1] As their rule grew harsher and opposition increased, the Thirty obtained a Spartan harmost, Callibius, and a garrison, and proceeded to kill their opponents without the formality of a trial. Under pressure from Theramenes, they listed those who were to possess the political franchise up to a maximum of Three Thousand apart from the Knights. They then disarmed the other citizens and denied them any right of appeal.

In October 404, when Theramenes protested at the rising number of executions, he was impeached before the Council of Five Hundred by Critias, who had set the stage by introducing an armed band of young assassins into the Council House and by posting the Spartan garrison in the forecourt. To the charges that he was truly nicknamed 'the Buskin'—a boot which fitted either foot—and that he was now betraying the oligarchs for the second time, Theramenes replied with such spirit that the Councillors openly showed their approval of his words. Critias then moved forward his assassins, struck Theramenes off the list of the Three Thousand, and in the name of the Thirty condemned him to death. Before the eyes of the terrorized Council Theramenes was torn from the sanctuary of the altar by Satyrus, the leader of the Police Commissioners, and was dragged across the Agora to drink the deadly cup of hemlock. As he tossed the dregs to the ground, he proposed a mocking toast 'to the fair Critias'. In the manner of his death Theramenes showed himself to be more than a time-serving politician. He died a martyr to the dictum that in an age of revolution moderate and patriotic citizens are destroyed.[2]

Within the next eight months or so the Thirty executed 1,500 and banished 5,000 of their fellow-countrymen. Their excesses proved to be their undoing. The exiles and the fugitives found a welcome at Thebes, Megara, Elis, and Argos, and there they began to plan their return with active help from the Theban leaders, Ismenias and Androcleides. In the course of the winter, perhaps in January 403, Thrasybulus of Stiria, who had led the Athenian democrats at Samos in 411, set off from Thebes with seventy exiles and seized the fortress of Phyle, which is situated on the barren slopes of Mt. Parnes, on the Attic side of the Boeotian frontier. There he held out until his force rose to 700 men, whereupon he descended into the plain and defeated a patrol of Athenian and Spartan troops in a surprise attack before dawn. Probably in May 403, he moved at night into the Peiraeus, where large numbers of refugees were already concentrated. Critias immediately led out the Spartan garrison troops, the Athenian cavalrymen, and the hoplites who had been listed as the Three Thousand, to assault the position of the democrats on the hill of Munychia. Foolishly attacking uphill in close formation on a narrow road, Critias and his leading files were overwhelmed by stones and javelins. The victorious democrats respected the corpses of their fellow-

---

[1] Arist. *Ath.* 34. 3; X. *HG* 2. 3. 32 and 34; Lys. 13. 35-37.

[2] X. *HG* 2. 3. 13-56; Arist. *Ath.* 28. 4; 32. 2; 33. 2; 34. 3; 36-37; Th. 3. 82. 8.

countrymen, and their spokesman in a loud voice issued a solemn proclamation inviting all Athenians to unite and put an end to mutual slaughter.

The invitation was rejected by the oligarchs, who expected Sparta to intervene on their behalf. But it split them into two camps. The extremists withdrew to Eleusis and Salamis. Their implacable spirit was expressed in the

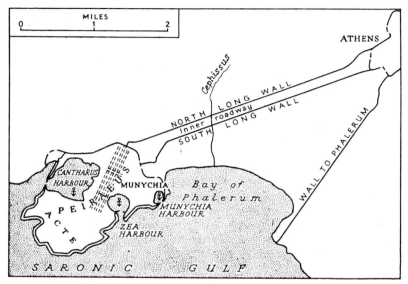

FIG. 27. Peiraeus and the Long Walls

epitaph they composed for Critias and his men: 'Here lie the brave men who checked for a time the arrogance of the damned democracy at Athens.' The moderates concentrated their forces in the city, where the Acropolis was occupied by the Spartan garrison. They elected their own leaders, a board of Ten, who together with the commanders of the cavalry conducted the defence of the city. Meanwhile Thrasybulus and the democrats consolidated their position at the Peiraeus.[1]

As the summer of 403 advanced and the Spartans made no move, Thrasybulus and his men brought siege-engines forward to the walls of the city. Their well-wishers in other states even helped them to raise some mercenary troops. The Thirty at Eleusis and the Ten at Athens therefore redoubled their appeals to Sparta. There the star of Lysander was already waning. His policy of supporting extreme oligarchies was criticized, his chosen lieutenants Clearchus and Thorax were found guilty of treason and embezzlement, and

---

[1] X. *HG.* 2. 4. 1–24; Plu. *Lys.* 27 fin.; *Hell. Oxy.* 12. 1; Arist. *Ath.* 37–38. 1 (where the order of events is confused); D.S. 14. 32–33·.5; Schol. Aeschin. 1. 39 (epitaph).

he himself was the object of complaints from Greek and Persian alike. For some months the Spartans did no more than lend money to the Ten, who were at least protecting the Spartan garrison on the Acropolis. Finally, *c.* August 403, Lysander prevailed. A loan of 100 talents was made to the Thirty and the Ten. Lysander was appointed to command by land and his brother, Libys, the new navarch, sailed into the Saronic Gulf. After assembling a force of Peloponnesian mercenaries at Eleusis, Lysander blockaded the democrats at Peiraeus. The desperate venture on which Thrasybulus had embarked at Phyle seemed certain to end in disaster.[1]

During the absence of Lysander the two Kings of Sparta, Agis and Pausanias, combined against him. They convinced a majority of the recently elected Ephors and called out the levy of the Spartan Alliance. Pausanias himself took command, and he was accompanied by two Ephors sympathetic to his views. On entering Attica he superseded Lysander and with the help of Athenian cavalry inflicted a minor defeat on the democratic forces. He then sent secret instructions to Thrasybulus and his colleagues in the Peiraeus, urging them to sue for terms, and at the same time advised the citizens at Athens to come to terms with the democrats at the Peiraeus. His plan succeeded admirably. He sent forward to Sparta an embassy from the democrats at Peiraeus and two moderate individuals from the party at Athens. He followed them up with a report that a second and conciliatory board of Ten, having replaced the first board of Ten, had put the city in the hands of Sparta and had urged the democrats to surrender the fortifications of the Peiraeus. Convinced by these signs of moderation, the Spartan Assembly sent a commission of fifteen Spartiates to Athens, with instructions to assist Pausanias in bringing the war to a conclusion. They set up two separate states in Attica, one at Eleusis, where the Thirty could be joined by any sympathizers, and the other at Athens, where Pausanias had done his best to bring the moderates and the democrats together. When both states had sworn to keep peace with one another, repay the debts to Sparta, and follow her in matters of foreign policy, Pausanias disbanded the levy of the Spartan Alliance. He had defeated Lysander in the field of foreign policy; he had prevented the reimposition of a tyrannical oligarchy which had already brought the name of Sparta into disrepute; and he had won some gratitude from the moderate party at Athens.[2]

When Pausanias departed in late September 403, the democrats marched in arms from the Peiraeus to the Acropolis. There they paid sacrifice to Athena in gratitude for the salvation of the city and for their own home-coming.[3] The three-sided civil war, aggravated by the invocation of Sparta, had

[1] X. *HG.* 2. 4. 25–29; Plu. *Lys.* 19–21; D.S. 14. 33. 5.

[2] Arist. *Pol.* 1271ᵃ38; *Ath.* 38; X. *HG.* 2. 4. 29–39; Plu. *Lys.* 21; D.S. 14. 33. 6.

[3] March of the democrats on 12 Boedromion, i.e. late Sept. 403/402 (Plu. 349ᵈ; Arist. *Ath.* 39. 1). Expedition of Pausanias in Sept. and that of Libys as navarch in succession to Lysander in Aug. 403 (D.S. 14. 10 Lysander navarch 404/403). Battle of Munychia in May/June 403 (X. *HG.* 2. 4. 25 mentioning 'fruit'). Excesses of the Thirty during the previous

split family and state in rancorous hatreds, which in many cases stemmed from the dark days of the Decelean War. The lines of cleavage had followed the divisions of the classes: the extreme oligarchs had found their main support in the Knights, the moderates in the propertied 'hoplite' class of the Three Thousand, and the democratic leaders in the rank and file of the unpropertied or dispossessed. In September 403 Athens stood on the brink of the chasm into which Corcyra and many other states had fallen. But she was saved from disaster by the forceful leadership of moderate and democratic statesmen and, above all, by the self-restraint of the people, who might have used revolutionary methods to enforce a redistribution of property.[1]

The moderates and the democrats combined at once in honouring the principles of the agreement under which Pausanias had brought them together: respect for the rights of property, legal procedure for the trial of criminal acts, such as murder, and complete amnesty for all other acts of the civil war. Every citizen of the state at Athens took an oath to observe the amnesty. Thrasybulus exhorted his followers to abide by the laws, and Archinus, a leader of the moderates, brought about the execution of the first man who tried to infringe the amnesty. A commission of twenty men, elected by a joint assembly of the moderates and the democrats in Athens, was empowered to draft the terms of the constitution and in the interim to direct the administration in accordance with the laws of Solon and the judicial code of Draco, the two great legislators who had experienced the evils of civil war.

During the archonship of Euclides (403/402) the democracy of Ephialtes and Pericles was reaffirmed in all its essentials. Past verdicts of the democratic courts in regard to property and debt were upheld as valid. The Periclean law requiring Athenian parentage on both sides for admission to citizenship was re-enacted, and an attempt by Thrasybulus to enfranchise metics and slaves who had supported him in the civil war was defeated by Archinus. On the other hand, an attempt by Phormisius to disfranchise some 5,000 citizens who held no landed property—probably dispossessed cleruchs for the most part—was unsuccessful, and the rights of the thetic class were thus confirmed. Rhinon, leader of the second board of Ten in Athens, was elected one of the generals for 403/402, and the democrats assisted in repaying to Sparta the debt which had been incurred by the first board of Ten. After a short period, during which plated coins were issued,

---

eight months, i.e. from *c*. Sept. 404, in which the death of Theramenes may be placed (X. *HG*. 2. 4. 21 and 2. 4. 1, cf. Arist. *Ath*. 37. 2). Occupation of Phyle 'when the winter of 404/403 had already set in', *c*. Jan./Feb. 403 (Arist. *Ath*. 37. 1). Establishment of the Thirty and their officials, including the eponymous archon, probably coincided with the opening of the Attic year 404/403 in July 404 (Arist. *Ath*. 35. 1; X. *HG*. 2. 3. 1, which, though probably interpolated, may be correct, and D.S. 14. 3. 1.).

[1] X. *HG*. 2. 4. 2, 4, 8, 10, 26–27, 31 and 3. 1. 4, and Arist. *Ath*. 38. 2 (for the Knights); X. *HG*. 2. 4. 2, 10, 23 and Arist. *Ath*. 36. 1, 38. 1 with 39. 6 (for the Three Thousand); Arist. *Ath*. 40. 3 fin. (for redistribution of property).

Athens began to emerge from her economic distress and feel her strength returning.[1]

The state at Eleusis, which was safeguarded by the terms of Pausanias' settlement, was faced by even greater difficulties. Its leaders had been expressly excluded from the amnesty which the moderates and the democrats formed between themselves. As the Thirty, the Eleven, the Ten governors of the Peiraeus, and the first board of Ten at Athens could be held responsible for their past acts, unless they submitted themselves to audit and were cleared, there was no chance for them to re-enter the state at Athens. At the outset anyone could migrate to Eleusis within twenty days of registering his wish to do so, but Archinus foreclosed this period and thereby prevented many from joining the oligarchs. The two states were sealed off from one another by a complete ban on movement, except for the celebration of the Mysteries at Eleusis, to which the citizens from Athens were admitted. The state at Eleusis had to repay its debt to Sparta; it relied on the wealth of its own members, but its hopes of maintaining that wealth were remote. When it began to rearm in 401, the democrats marched out in full force. The generals of the Eleusis forces were invited to a conference and treacherously killed. Their followers agreed to dissolve their own state and join the state at Athens. An amnesty was granted to them, and it was honoured. Athens was again a united state.[2]

The terrible sufferings of these years left their mark. Political concord did not put an end to personal animosities. Hatred and fear of oligarchy in any form were so intense in the restored democracy that the word 'oligarch' became a term of abuse on the lips of an orator or a lawyer. The courts were busy with cases in which allusion to a man's record in the civil war was a commonplace, and the apprehension felt by the poor sapped the moderation of the restored democracy. The prejudice against the extreme oligarchs spread to the social and intellectual circles from which they had sprung— aristocratic, free-thinking, and outspoken. Their intellectual association with the Sophists, and not least with the Athenian Socrates, was more widely known than understood by the average citizen, who was less interested in the niceties of philosophical discussion than in the practice of traditional religion.

In 399 Socrates was prosecuted on a charge of impiety 'for not worshipping the gods whom the city worships, for introducing religious innovations, and for corrupting the young men'. The prosecutor, Meletus, was supported by the moderate democrat, Anytus. He proposed the penalty of death. Socrates was found guilty by a majority of 60 votes in a court of probably 501 jurors. It was then open to Socrates to propose an alternative penalty. After declaring that he deserved free meals for life in the Prytaneum, he proposed ironically a small fine. The court had to choose between the two proposals.

[1] Arist. *Ath.* 39; 40. 1–2; X. *HG.* 2. 4. 40–42; Andoc. 1. 81; 87; 90; Schol. Aeschin. 1. 39; D.H. *Lys.* 32.   [2] X. *HG.* 2. 4. 43; Arist. *Ath.* 40. 4.

It condemned him to death by a larger majority than before. A month later, contemptuous of physical death and confident of spiritual survival, Socrates drank the cup of hemlock as the last rays of the sun were lingering on Mt. Hymettus. As a man he surpassed all men in justice, in honesty of thought, and in probity of conduct. As a citizen he obeyed the laws but not the dictates of those in power, whether they were the People during the trial of the generals after the battle of Arginusae or the Thirty Tyrants who ordered him to arrest a fellow-citizen. In equity Socrates was innocent. In Attic law he was guilty of the charge preferred against him, and he refused stubbornly to accept the mitigation of sentence which the law allowed to him. He died a martyr to his faith, that the individual is to be guided by his own intellect in every field of human life. His martyrdom inspired the greatest philosophers of antiquity. In their eyes it discredited the restored democracy of Athens. Yet his death was due more to the general defects of man-made law in society than to the institutions of any single polity.[1]

§ 4. *Sparta at war with Persia*

IN September 403 Sparta modified the policy of Lysander. She now announced her support of 'ancestral constitutions',[2] by which she meant moderate rather than democratic constitutions. The change was one of degree and not of principle; for she did not withdraw her governors and garrisons from all the former dependencies of Athens. Her aim too was still the same, to keep Attica divided and to make the Aegean states dependent upon herself. Eleusis and Athens had to repay the loans which Sparta had made, and the Aegean states had to pay tribute to Sparta; as dependents of Sparta, they were not admitted to membership of the Spartan Alliance but were tied to Sparta in all matters of foreign policy. Their position was the same as that of the 'Allies' of Athens in the second half of the fifth century. They were in fact subject-states in a Spartan empire.

The members of the Spartan Alliance were in theory sovereign states. Their alliance with Sparta was voluntary, defensive, and reciprocal. Each ally possessed one vote in the Congress of Allies, which was free to reject any proposal of the Spartan Assembly and to initiate its own proposals. In the past Sparta had been careful to move when she had not only a majority vote in the Congress but also the support of the leading members of the Alliance. But in making her settlement with Athens in 404 she disregarded the opposition of Thebes, Corinth, and others. Again in 403, when Pausanias invaded Attica, he did so despite the opposition of Thebes and Corinth, which refused to send contingents. In both cases Sparta probably obtained a majority vote in favour of her policy from the Congress of Allies, but she did so at the cost of estranging the strongest members. During the régime of the Thirty at Athens Sparta forbade any Greek state to admit Athenian exiles; this edict

[1] Pl. *Ap.*; *Phd.* 116e; *Ep.* 7. 324e; X. *Ap.*   [2] X. *HG.* 3. 4. 2 and 7.

may have been authorized by a majority vote in the Congress of Allies, but it was opposed and disobeyed by Thebes, Corinth, and Megara. Even if Sparta's conduct in these cases respected the letter of the constitution, it certainly contravened the purpose of the Alliance, the defence of allied interests. For Sparta was simply strengthening her own grip on a subject-state in her incipient empire, and Thebes, Corinth, and Megara had no desire to encourage this process.

If Sparta wished to obtain a majority vote in the Congress rather than attune her policy to the real strength of the Alliance, she could usually do so by favouring or intimidating the small states. The more imperialistic she became, the more eager she was to break up any great state into a number of small states, even at the price of weakening the strength of the Alliance. Early in 400, her own power being already augmented by her control of Athens and other subject-states, she decided to make an example of Elis. On her own initiative Sparta demanded that Elis should liberate some small states which she had reduced to the status of Perioeci, and pay her contribution towards the cost of the Peloponnesian War. When Elis refused, Sparta declared war and Agis led an army into her territory. But an earthquake occurred, and this was later interpreted as an unfavourable omen. Agis therefore withdrew. Elis, however, canvassed support from states which were ill disposed towards Sparta, and in 399 Sparta again declared war. This time she obtained a declaration of war from the Congress of Allies. Boeotia and Corinth, however, refused to send contingents. Sparta with the levy of the other members of the Alliance and with a contingent from Athens ravaged and looted the rich territory of Elis, but did not attack the unwalled town. The wealthy oligarchic party, on which Sparta counted, tried but failed to seize power, and in early summer 398 the democratic leaders of Elis accepted Sparta's terms, namely the surrender of her fleet, the demolition of two fortresses, the liberation of some eight small states, and the conclusion of an alliance with Sparta. This war had much in common with the war of Athens against Thasos in 465–463. It terrorized the members of the Alliance inside the Peloponnese and alarmed those which were farther afield.[1]

In central Greece Boeotia had consistently opposed the imperialistic policy of Sparta, and in 399 Aetolia had sent 1,000 picked hoplites to·help Elis. Here Sparta counted on the support of Athens and Phocis and on her fortified base at Heraclea in Trachis. In 399 she sent a force northwards, which executed 500 citizens of Heraclea and evicted the tribesmen round Mt. Oeta. Farther north she had the strong Chalcidian League as an ally. These points lay on the overland route to Asia Minor, which now became of great importance to her.[2]

---

[1] X. *HG.* 3. 2. 21–31; D.S. 14. 17. 4–12; 34. 1 (under 402/401 and 401/400). Xenophon's chronology is preferred in the text; Diodorus, then, gave too early a date for the beginning and end of the war, and consequently for the death of Agis.

[2] D.S. 14. 17. 9; 38. 4–5.

When Darius died in 405/404, Artaxerxes Mnemon succeeded to the throne and left his brother Cyrus as viceroy in Asia Minor. Cyrus, however, had designs on the throne himself. As he wished to make use of the Greeks, he did not ask Sparta to implement the agreement of 412, whereby Sparta had recognized Persia's suzerainty over the Greek cities in Asia Minor; and in spring 401, when he marched southwards with an army, he informed the Spartan government that he intended to attack Artaxerxes, and requested their co-operation. The implications of the request were clear. If Sparta's policy was to implement the agreement of 412 and abandon the Greek cities to Persia, she would be unwise to support Cyrus. If on the other hand she intended to defend Ionia and go to war with Persia, she would lose nothing by supporting Cyrus. The Ephors decided to co-operate, and in summer 401 the Spartan navarch with a squadron of thirty-five ships appeared off Cilicia, where he enabled Cyrus to turn the coastal passes and enter Syria. Unofficially Sparta was now at war with Persia.[1]

Cyrus had under his command a native army and a force of 13,000 Greek mercenaries, drawn mainly from the Peloponnese and commanded by a Spartan, Clearchus. At Cunaxa, where the Euphrates draws close to the Tigris, the decisive battle was fought. The Greeks routed the entire left wing of the Persian army without suffering a single casualty, but in the centre Cyrus fell and his native army fled. The revolt was over, and the Greeks found themselves alone in the heart of a hostile empire. In open warfare too they proved their superiority over the troops of the East; for despite the treacherous seizure of their commanders they fought their way out through Jezireh, Kurdistan, and Armenia to the plateau of Erzerum, where the deep snow diverted them towards the Black Sea. Misled by a native guide, they wandered lost in the wild mountains of Armenia and fought on through hostile tribesmen, until they reached the holy mountain above the Greek city of Trapezus. As the army approached the top of the pass, Xenophon, who was commanding the rearguard, heard loud shouts ahead and galloped forward. He expected another attack by the enemy, but it was his own men shouting *thalassa, thalassa*, 'the sea, the sea'. On the spot they raised a great cairn of stones, and a week later they were celebrating their escape with sacrifices and games at Trapezus. In spring 399 they enlisted in the service of Sparta; for she was then officially at war with Persia.[2]

The exploits of the 'Ten Thousand', so brilliantly publicized by Xenophon, heightened the Greek contempt for barbarian arms and conveyed a false impression of the strength of the Persian empire. The Greek hoplite was indeed unsurpassed in a pitched battle of heavy infantry, and Artaxerxes did not forget the charge of the Greek brigade at Cunaxa; but the strength of Persia lay in her cavalry, her wealth, and her fleets whenever she had need of sea power. Sparta too was deceived. When Artaxerxes ordered his satrap Tissaphernes to occupy the Greek cities, Sparta took up the challenge and sent an

---

[1] X. *HG.* 3. 1. 1; *Anab.* 1. 4. 2.   [2] X. *Anab.*; *JHS* 83, 16; *HG.* 3. 1. 6; D.S. 14. 19–31.

expeditionary force to protect Ionia. Its commander, Thibron, arrived in 400 with a levy of 4,000 infantry from the Spartan Alliance, 1,000 Neodamodeis from Laconia, and 300 Athenian cavalry, whom the democratic leaders of Athens were now happy to dispatch; to these he added conscripts from the Greek cities, and in 399 he enlisted 6,000 seasoned troops, the survivors of the Ten Thousand. At sea Sparta had a large fleet, and her control of Aegean waters was undisputed. In 397 she allied herself with Egypt, then in revolt from Persia, and was promised supplies of wheat and gear for her fleet. Nothing on this scale had been attempted by the Greeks since the Athenian adventure in Egypt; its very size was likely to be its weakness, because Persia could not afford to regard the action of Sparta as another frontier incident.

The general strategy of the expedition was directed from Sparta by the Ephors. They instructed Thibron and his successor, Dercyllidas, to invade Caria; and a successful invasion of Caria might have won the Carians to their side and secured for Sparta the harbours which any Persian fleet would try to use for an advance into the Aegean. Such a policy was obvious to anyone who had studied the campaigns of the Ionians, Cimon, and Cyrus. But the Ephors, being perhaps jealous of their powers, did not give Thibron and Dercyllidas the means of executing this policy. A united command was essential, if the fleet was to transport or supply the army in its advance along the Carian seaboard; but the Ephors placed the fleet and the army under independent commanders. Lacking any control over the navy, the generals led their army northwards and ravaged the satrapy of Pharnabazus. As they could not bring the Persian cavalry to battle or capture any large city, because they had no siege-train, they gained nothing but loot and enmity from their actual or potential allies. Dercyllidas rendered a good service to Hellenism by defeating the Bithynians and fortifying the neck of the Chersonese in 399–398, but his operations were irrelevant to the main issue of the war.

In 397 the Ephors issued joint orders to Dercyllidas and the navarch, Pharax, that they must attack Caria. Pharnabazus and the satrap in the south, Tissaphernes, at once combined their land forces in order to protect a small Persian fleet of forty ships, which lay at Caunus in Caria under the command of an Athenian *émigré*, Conon. Even so Dercyllidas and Pharax did not conduct an amphibious operation. No sooner did Dercyllidas move into Caria than Tissaphernes and Pharnabazus moved towards Ionia and lured him back from Caria. The two armies faced one another at last, but Dercyllidas was as afraid of the Persian cavalry as the Persians were of the Greek infantry. An armistice was concluded, pending negotiations at a higher level. Meanwhile Pharax with 120 ships blockaded Conon at Caunus, but he had not enough troops to engage the Persian army, which was supporting Conon. Outwitted, he withdrew to Rhodes.[1]

As the winter of 397–396 approached, Sparta hoped for a settlement with Persia on the lines which Dercyllidas and Tissaphernes proposed, namely

[1] X. *HG.* 3. 1. 1–3. 2. 20; D.S. 14. 35–36–37. 4; 38. 2–3 and 6–7; 39; 79. 4–5.

that Persia would recognize the independence of the Greek cities in Asia, and that Sparta would evacuate her harmosts and garrisons from them. Her sea power was intact, and the Persian fleet was much inferior in numbers. Heraclea in Trachis had been strengthened, Elis in the Peloponnese punished, and the conspiracy of Cinadon in Laconia suppressed. In the West she had the alliance of Dionysius, the powerful tyrant of Syracuse. Her power seemed more imposing than it had ever been. But it was sapped by widespread discontent. Boeotia and Corinth were recalcitrant. Envoys from Athens to Persia had been intercepted and executed in 397. The Aegean islanders and the Greeks in Asia were so lukewarm that many had deserted from Dercyllidas during his advance on Caria. In Sparta itself a dynastic crisis had followed the death of Agis (summer 398). His son Leotychidas was disqualified on the charge that he was really the bastard of Alcibiades, and the lame Agesilaus, a brother of Agis, was elected king through the baleful influence of Lysander, who hoped to return to power.[1]

During the winter of 397–396 a Syracusan sailor on a merchantman which put into a Phoenician port saw ships of war concentrating and many others being built. He took the first boat for Greece and reported at Sparta what he had seen. The Spartans had no doubt that Persia intended to deploy this fleet in the Aegean and prise them out of Asia; for the Great King had dropped the negotiations which Tissaphernes had initiated, and he had appointed the Greek captain, Conon, to be admiral of the fleet. Sparta and her Alliance, therefore, decided to redouble their efforts and defeat Persia in Asia before the new fleet was ready for action. Their decision was mainly inspired by Lysander, who had unrivalled experience of amphibious operations in the Hellespont and Ionia. He believed that the Greek fleet would prove far superior, especially as Persia no longer commanded the services of Egypt, and that the Greek army would surpass the exploits of the Ten Thousand.[2] If Sparta emulated the strategy of Cimon and moved with large naval and military forces into Caria and Cilicia, she could defeat the Persian fleet or confine it to Phoenician waters. In his calculations the doubtful factor was not the vulnerability of Persia but the solidarity of the Greeks. For in the course of the last seven years the conduct of Sparta had been such that her claim to champion the cause of Greek freedom in Asia, true though it was, rang hollow in the ears of the Aegean states.

The importance of the expedition was shown by the appointment of one of the Spartan kings, Agesilaus, to command by land. He was given a staff of thirty Spartiates, headed by Lysander himself, and an army from the mainland consisting of 2,000 Neodamodeis from Laconia and 6,000 hoplites from the members of the Spartan Alliance. To these were added Dercyllidas' army of more than 10,000 seasoned infantry and the resources of the Greek states in Asia, so that his total force of infantry fell not far short of that which

---

[1] X. *HG.* 3. 3. 1–4; Plu. *Lys.* 22; *Hell. Oxy.* 2. 1.
[2] X. *HG.* 3. 4. 1–2; Plu. *Lys.* 23.

Alexander of Macedon later led into Persia. Agesilaus had only a small force of cavalry, whereas Alexander's superiority lay in cavalry; but with at least a hundred triremes in commission and large reserves in the Aegean states, he had a naval superiority which enabled him to turn any coastal position by landing in the enemy's rear. The fact, for example, that Tissaphernes' cavalry held the plain of the Maeander between Agesilaus' base at Ephesus and Caria should not have deterred Agesilaus from moving by sea into Caria, a country unsuitable for cavalry.[1]

In spring 396, while the expeditionary force was mustering at Geraestus in Euboea, Agesilaus, like Agamemnon, was offering sacrifices at Aulis, when some Boeotian horsemen appeared and told him in the name of the Boeotarchs to desist. When he sailed away, they threw his offerings into the sea. The fact that Thebes, Corinth, and Athens did not provide any contingents showed that the home front was far from united in support of Agesilaus. In Asia Agesilaus made a truce with Tissaphernes, the satrap responsible for Caria, dismissed Lysander from the command of the staff and sent him to the Hellespont, where he showed his value by winning over a Persian noble, Spithridates, and then overran much of Pharnabazus' satrapy in the north, until his weakness in cavalry forced him to withdraw. During the winter of 396–395 Agesilaus recruited cavalry from the Greek states in Asia, and trained a fine army of hoplites, peltasts, javelin-men, and archers, to such good effect that early in 395 he won a notable victory over the Persian cavalry near the river Pactolus and captured seventy talents' worth of loot in their camp. This victory cost Tissaphernes his head; but his successor, Tithraustes, an even more able diplomatist, paid Agesilaus 30 talents to attack the satrapy of Pharnabazus instead of Caria. When Agesilaus was near Cyme on the march northwards, he received fresh instructions from the Spartan government. He was to take command by sea, as well as by land, and to appoint his own navarch, in order that amphibious operations might be undertaken presumably in the area of strategic importance, Caria and Cilicia. Agesilaus appointed as navarch his brother-in-law, Peisander, and instructed the island and coastal states to provide naval reinforcements. Soon 120 new triremes were available, supplementing those already in commission. During the rest of the normal campaigning season and throughout the winter Agesilaus raided far and wide in the satrapy of Pharnabazus and acquired a vast amount of booty. But he failed to win over Pharnabazus, and he lost his ally Spithridates by quarrelling over the division of the spoil.[2]

The strategy of Agesilaus in 396 and 395 was popular with his army but fatal to the outcome of the war. For, while he left Caria and Cilicia in peace, the Persian fleet was passing from weakness to strength. In 396 it is probable that the Persian fleet was crippled by dissension between the various squad-

---

[1] X. *HG.* 3. 4. 2; 12; D.S. 14. 79. 1–2.
[2] X. *HG.* 3. 4. 3–4; 3. 5. 5; Paus. 3. 9. 1–3; X. *HG.* 3. 4. 5–28; 4. 1. 1–41; *Hell. Oxy.* 6–8; 16–17; D.S. 14. 79. 2–3; 80.

rons—Greek, Cilician, Cyprian, and Phoenician, the last being particularly galled by the appointment of Conòn to the supreme command. In the summer of 395 Conon gained a notable success. He advanced his base to the mainland south-east of Rhodes, and instigated a rising by the democrats in Rhodes. They assassinated the pro-Spartan oligarchs and opened their harbour to his fleet. Establishing himself there, he intercepted a convoy of supply-ships from Egypt and brought up additional squadrons from Phoenicia and Cilicia. Pay, however, was lacking for his crews, and during the absence of Conon, who went to Tithraustes and probably to Babylon in pursuit of money, the Cypriote squadron mutinied and set up a rival commander at Caunus. On Conon's return fighting ensued at Caunus and at Rhodes. By the end of 395 Conon reasserted his authority by executing a hundred or so ringleaders and distributing arrears of pay to his men. In spring 394, when Agesilaus was planning a great raid into the hinterland, Conon's fleet was ready to assume the offensive in the Aegean.[1]

Meanwhile in Greece the anti-Spartan leaders at Thebes, Ismenias and Androcleides, having organized strong parties in Thebes and in some states of the Boeotian League, fomented a war between Phocis and Locris in summer 395, and then persuaded the Boeotian League to accept the Locrian request for help. When the Phocians appealed to Sparta, the Ephors ordered Boeotia not to invade Phocis, but to submit the dispute to arbitration by the Spartan Alliance. At the instigation of Ismenias the Boeotian League refused to comply, invaded Phocis, and ravaged Phocian territory in late summer 395. Sparta and her Alliance thereupon declared war and began to muster their forces for an invasion of Boeotia. It was probably during the negotiations between the Boeotian League and Sparta that an agent of Persia, the Rhodian Timocrates, distributed largess to the anti-Spartan leaders at Thebes, Corinth, and Argos and informed the anti-Spartan leaders at Athens (who did not accept his money) that the Persian fleet was about to launch an offensive. His visit raised the hopes of Thebes and Athens, and in late summer or autumn 395 Athens entered into a defensive alliance 'for all time' with the Boeotian League and separately with Locris.[2]

No sooner were these alliances concluded than the Spartan offensive

[1] *Hell. Oxy.* 4; 10; 14; 15; D.S. 14. 79. 6–8; 81. 4–6. The chronology of naval affairs depends upon the sequence of the Spartan navarchs, whose command ran probably from c. August to August: Pharax 398/397 (*Hell. Oxy.* 2. 1; D.S. 14. 79. 4; X. *HG.* 3. 2. 12–14); Archelaïdas 397/396 (*Hell. Oxy.* 4. 2; Polyaen. 2. 8); Pollis 396/395 (*Hell. Oxy.* 4. 2; 14. 1); Cheiricrates 395 (*Hell. Oxy.* 14. 1; 17. 4); Peisander, superseding Cheiricrates in autumn 395 (X. *HG.* 3. 4. 29). Conon's fleet was active already in 398/397 (*Hell. Oxy.* 2. 1; X. *HG.* 3. 2. 12–14; D.S. 14. 39 and 79, placing several years of operations under two years 399/398 and 396/395); the fragments of *Hell. Oxy.* 4. 2 date probably to c. Aug. 396, and the rising in Rhodes to before c. Aug. 395, when Cheiricrates succeeded Pollis, but in the same year as the war between Phocis and Boeotia (*Hell. Oxy.* 10 and 14. 1).

[2] *Hell. Oxy.* 11. 1; 12. 1–2; 13; cf. 2. 2–3; X. *HG.* 3. 5. 1–5; D.S. 14. 81. 1; Plu. *Ages.* 15; Paus. 3. 9. 8 states that the Athenians Cephalus and Epicrates took Persian gold; *GHI* 101; 102.

opened. A simultaneous invasion had been planned. Lysander was to operate from Phocis, and Pausanias was to march up from the Peloponnese. Lysander, however, arrived first at the head of an army which he had raised from Heraclea and her neighbours in Trachis and from Phocis and Orchomenus (for Orchomenus had seceded from the Boeotian League). Without waiting for Pausanias he attacked Haliartus, was caught between the defenders of the town and a Theban army, and together with many of his men fell fighting under the walls of the town. The main body retreated to a strong position and beat off a Theban attack. But many of Sparta's allies fled during the night. When Pausanias came up with his army from Plataea, he found that an Athenian army had already arrived to reinforce the Boeotian levy and that he was heavily outnumbered in cavalry. He called a meeting of his senior officers. They were more anxious to recover the bodies of Lysander and his men than to fight a pitched battle. When the Boeotians refused to hand over the dead unless Pausanias promised to withdraw, he gave his consent and the Spartan forces departed.[1]

On his return Pausanias was impeached for his conduct of the campaign. He was condemned to death but escaped to Tegea, where he lived in exile. He had sacrificed the prestige of Sparta in central Greece without striking a blow, and the consequences of his folly were soon apparent. Corinth (which had refused to send a contingent with Pausanias), Argos, Acarnania, Leucas, Ambracia, Euboea, and the Chalcidian League joined the insurgents during the winter. A Spartan garrison at Pharsalus in Thessaly was overwhelmed, and Heraclea in Trachis was betrayed to the Boeotians, who killed the Spartan prisoners and gave the town to the neighbouring tribes. With their help the Boeotians then invaded Phocis and defeated a Spartan and Phocian army. As she expected that the Peloponnese would be invaded by the confederate forces, Sparta decided early in 394 to recall Agesilaus and the bulk of his army. The war undertaken for the liberty of the Greek states in Asia was thereby abandoned. The chief reasons for its failure were the lack of a combined command by land and by sea, the incompetence of Thibron, Dercyllidas, and Agesilaus, the political aggressiveness of Sparta, the adroit use by Persia of her gold, and the readiness of Thebes, Corinth, Athens, and Argos to medize.[2]

Those who condemned medism had every right to condemn Thebes, Corinth, Athens, and Argos on this occasion. It was true that Sparta and Athens were equally ready to medize when they were locked in the desperate strife of the Peloponnesian War, but in 395 Sparta was fighting to preserve the independence of Ionia when the medizing states stabbed her in the back. It was to their shame that they did not follow the example of Sparta *c.* 459 when she rejected the offers of Megabazus.

---

[1] X. *HG.* 3. 5. 17–25; Plu. *Lys.* 28–29; D.S. 14. 81.
[2] D.S. 14. 82–83. 1; X. *HG.* 4. 2. 1–2 ; Plu. *Cim.* 19.

§ 5. *The Corinthian War and the King's Peace*

IN early summer 394 the confederates opened the 'Corinthian War'. They had a unique opportunity of striking at Sparta, while the army of Agesilaus was marching back from Asia. Having assembled at Corinth, they lost precious time in debating whether a river is smaller at its source. Meanwhile the Spartans were already on the move. They collected the contingents of Mantinea and Tegea, and were mustering their forces at Sicyon, while the confederates still lingered on in Corinthia, discussing priorities of command and dispositions for battle. The Spartan force numbered some 20,000 hoplites, drawn from all parts of the Peloponnese except Phlius, which pleaded a truce in time of festival; 6,000 of them were Spartans under Aristodemus, who had supreme command of the whole army. In addition there were 600 Spartan cavalry, 300 Cretan archers serving as mercenaries, and a number of light-armed troops. The confederates mustered some 24,000 hoplites (Argos providing 7,000, Athens 6,000, Boeotia 5,000, Corinth 3,000, and Euboea 3,000), and they had about 1,500 cavalry and a larger number of light-armed troops than their opponents. In the preliminary skirmishing the Spartans manoeuvred the confederates into a defensive position beside the river Nemea, where the ground was unsuitable for cavalry, while they themselves held the plain on which the pitched battle between the hoplite forces ensued. The confederates had no one commander-in-chief, but the command, and with it the position of honour on the right of the line, was held each day by a different contingent. On a day in June or July, when the Boeotians were holding the right wing and the Athenians on the left wing were facing the dreaded Spartans, the Boeotians gave the order to attack.[1]

All hoplite lines tended to advance crabwise towards their right front, each man trying to keep his unshielded right flank as close as possible to his neighbour. On this occasion the tendency was exaggerated by the action of the Boeotians. Having massed their men to the unusual depth of more than sixteen men, they led off to their right front and drew the whole line slantwise with them. The Athenians on the left wing, afraid to open a gap, were compelled to follow the general movement. The Spartans, quick to see their opportunity, led off to the right, so that their own troops on the extreme right wing overlapped the Athenians and immediately wheeled round to take them in the flank and rear. The rest of the Spartan line, except for the brigade from Pellene in Achaea, was overwhelmed by the superior numbers of the enemy and fled, hotly pursued by the confederates. But the Spartans themselves, having inflicted heavy losses on the six tribal regiments of the Athenians whom they had encircled, wheeled their whole contingent in perfect formation and attacked each contingent of the confederates in the flank as it returned from the pursuit, first the Argives, then the Corinthians, and finally

[1] X. *HG.* 4. 2. 9-18.

the Boeotians. In the opening phase of the battle the allies of Sparta lost about 1,000 men, while the confederates in the end lost almost 3,000 men. The Spartans claimed they had lost only eight men. The outcome of the battle proved once again the remarkable superiority of the Spartan hoplite under a competent commander.[1]

The confederates now passed to the defensive (for they held Corinthia firmly) and prepared to attack Agesilaus on his march through central Greece. Having left 4,000 men to defend the Greek states in Asia, Agesilaus had meanwhile crossed the Hellespont and held a review of his troops before beginning his march through Thrace and Macedonia. At Amphipolis he learnt of Sparta's victory at Nemea. In Thessaly he inflicted a defeat on the cavalry of the Thessalians, who were allied with the Boeotians. In Trachis and Phocis he collected contingents from his allies and reinforced his own Neodamodeis with half a Spartan brigade which had been acting as garrison in Orchomenus, and with a complete Spartan brigade which had been sent by sea from Sicyon.

On 14 August 394, as he was preparing to invade Boeotia, the sun was partially eclipsed. On this day Agesilaus received the news that the fleet of Peisander had been defeated at Cnidus and Peisander killed. Agesilaus told the army that Peisander's fleet had won a great victory, and he then led his men into Boeotia. There, in the plain by Coronea, they drove back and defeated the forces of Boeotia, Argos, Athens, Corinth, Euboea, Locris, and Aeniania. The Thebans alone distinguished themselves. For at the initial onset they overwhelmed the Orchomenians and pursued them to the camp. When the Thebans began to return, Agesilaus did not wait, as Aristodemus had done at the battle of Nemea, to take them in the flank, but closed his ranks to meet them face to face. Locking their shields one against another, the hoplites 'pushed, fought, killed, and were killed'. In weight, spearmanship, and stamina the Thebans in their deep formation more than held their own. The bulk of them broke their way through the Spartans and joined the confederates in a defensive position on Mt. Helicon. Apart from this significant episode the battle of Coronea proved once again the superiority of Spartan arms. Twenty-three years were to pass before any enemy dared to face their regular army in a pitched battle.[2]

In the long war which followed Agesilaus was the outstanding military commander on the Spartan side. He was very popular with citizens and mercenaries alike. He led his men in battle and was wounded at Coronea. He excelled in the arts of subterfuge, ambush, and rapid raids, and he had returned from his last campaign in Asia with 1,000 talents' worth of loot. As the other king, Agesipolis, son of Pausanias, was young and less popular, Agesilaus commanded the Spartan armies for many years and acquired a

---

[1] X. *HG.* 4. 2. 18–23; 4. 3. 1; D.S. 14. 83. 2; Lys. 16. 15; *GHI* 104–5.

[2] X. *HG.* 4. 3. 1–19 (the eclipse gives a fixed point for chronology); Plu. *Ages.* 16–19; D.S. 14. 83. 3–4; 84. 1–2.

degree of experience and prestige which rarely fell to the lot of an annually elected general in other states. When he had brought his army home by sea from central Greece, he addressed himself to the task of breaking a way through the Isthmus. In Greek warfare the arts of defence were far superior to those of assault. The massive walls of Corinth and Acrocorinth were impregnable. The two parallel walls running down from Corinth to Lechaeum on the Corinthian Gulf blocked the route towards the Isthmus, but they were betrayed by some oligarchic sympathizers in Corinth, perhaps in 392. Entering these walls, the Spartans drove off a counter-attack, breached the walls, and garrisoned Sidus and Crommyon in north Corinthia. Recaptured and rebuilt by the Athenian army, these walls were again breached in 391 by Agesilaus, who overran north-western Corinthia in 390, taking much booty and placing a garrison in Oenoe. Even so, Corinth and Argos threatened his lines of communication, and in the very moment of his success in north-western Corinthia a Spartan brigade (*mora*) was almost annihilated near Lechaeum. Agesilaus then withdrew. His garrisons at Oenoe, Sidus, and Crommyon soon fell, and, although Lechaeum was held, he abandoned the attempt to break through the Isthmus. In 389 he crossed the Gulf and ravaged Acarnania, which made peace and alliance with Sparta in 388 rather than face a second invasion. The land war thus became a stalemate.[1]

In these operations Sparta made considerable use of mercenary troops, partly because she wished to conserve her citizen forces but mainly because mercenaries were more serviceable. The heavy-armed hoplite was slow and cumbrous in open warfare. The mercenary peltast with his light shield, javelin, and dagger was more nimble than the hoplite. His equipment was improved in the fourth century by an Athenian mercenary captain, Iphicrates, who lengthened the javelin and made the dagger into a short sword fit for hand-to-hand fighting. In the past a hoplite force, when unaccompanied by other infantry and attacked by peltasts or skirmishers, had suffered heavily, for example in Aetolia, Sphacteria, and Attica. Now Iphicrates' band of peltasts proved their worth in an action near Lechaeum. A brigade of Spartan hoplites was returning to Lechaeum ahead of its escorting cavalry force, when the peltasts swarmed round them, striking at the flanks, giving way before every charge, and hurling their javelins until 250 hoplites lay dead. In Acarnania too a force led by Agesilaus was severely mauled by Acarnanians armed as peltasts. Thereafter Sparta used her citizen hoplites mainly for major campaigns. They were at their best in ravaging the Argolid under Agesilaus in 391 and under Agesipolis in 388.[2]

On the confederate side Corinth and Argos bore the brunt of the fighting and the losses. The Boeotians were rarely in action after the battles of Nemea

[1] X. *HG.* 4. 3. 20–21; 4. 4. 1–18; 4. 5–6; 4. 7. 1; D.S. 14. 86; 91. 2. The chronology of the war is not certain in detail.

[2] X. *HG.* 4. 4. 14; 4. 5. 11–17; D.S. 15. 44; Nep. *Iph.* 1; Arr. *Tact.* 3; X. *HG.* 4. 6. 7–11; 4. 4. 19; 4. 7; D.S. 14. 97. 5.

and Coronea. The Athenians, whose hoplites had suffered so heavily in the battle of Nemea, supplied only mercenary peltasts under Iphicrates. In addition to their victory over the Spartan brigade these peltasts raided parts of Arcadia and attacked Sicyon and Phlius successfully; but after 390 (by which time Athens was protected by her new Long Walls) they were withdrawn for service overseas. The strain of war soon split Corinth into two factions. In 392 with the connivance of Argos, Athens, and Boeotia the democratic faction set upon their opponents during a sacred festival and murdered 120 of them at the altars and in the temples. This act of impiety caused a revulsion of feeling, which saved the survivors of the oligarchic faction from a similar fate. The democratic leaders of Corinth then merged their state with Argos, probably by an act of isopolity, whereby the citizens of Corinth and Argos had reciprocal rights in each other's state, but Argos became the dominant partner by virtue of her size. The oligarchic leaders in Corinth then betrayed the Long Walls to Sparta, fled from Corinth, and served with the Spartans as garrison-troops at Lechaeum. Probably in 389 Argos took the further step of annexing Corinth, which thus ceased to exist as an independent state. Argos herself suffered severely. She sustained several defeats in battle, and her territory was devastated. But her democratic government held firm, and the state was united by its age-long rivalry with Sparta. The Boeotian League, protected on land by Argos and Corinth and at sea by Athens, was free to strengthen its position in central Greece. Having failed as yet to force Orchomenus back into membership of the League, the Boeotians were less eager for peace than the other confederates in 387.[1]

In the war at sea Persia's money played the dominant part. Ample funds enabled Conon to man a large squadron with Greek *émigrés* and Greek mercenary seamen. In the decisive battle of Cnidus in August 394 this Greek squadron led the Persian fleet into action and itself overwhelmed the Spartan fleet. While Peisander died fighting on his flagship, the vessels of his allies fled for Cnidus. Of the fleet of eighty-five triremes all but thirty-five were captured or sunk. Once again, as Callicratidas said during the Decelean War, Persia was helping the Greeks to destroy one another. Her fleet sailed the Aegean Sea in security for the first time since the battle of Mycale. Pharnabazus and Conon toured the island and maritime states in the east Aegean, expelling the Spartan harmosts and garrisons, and on the advice of Conon promised to respect the autonomy of the Greek states. By means of this political propaganda and a discriminating use of her gold Persia intended to exercise a remote control over the states of Greece and prevent the rise of any single power which might unite Greece and attack Persia. Persia was content with this negative aim; for she did not intend to police the unruly states of Greece herself.[2]

[1] X. *HG.* 4. 4. 1–6; 4. 5. 1; 4. 8. 34; D.S. 14. 86. 1; 91. 3; 92. 1; And. 3. 26–27.
[2] X. *HG.* 4. 3. 10–12; 4. 8. 1–2; D.S. 14. 83. 4–7; Nep. *Con.* 4; Plu. *Lys.* 6 fin.

On the way back to Greece, Agesilaus had sent Dercyllidas from Amphipolis to the Hellespont to defend the interests of Sparta. Dercyllidas concentrated all Spartan and allied troops at Sestus and Abydus, which controlled the shortest crossing over the Hellespont, won the support of the citizens for the defence of the Straits, and withstood an attack delivered by Conon with forty ships and by Pharnabazus' army, which had marched overland from Ephesus to invade the territory of Abydus. As the aim of Pharnabazus was not to lead an army of invasion across the Straits but to damage the power of Sparta, he switched his offensive to the west Aegean in the spring of 393. Having manned a considerable fleet with Greek mercenary seamen, he and Conon sailed through the Cyclades to Melos, and occupied it as an advanced base. After ravaging the coasts of Laconia and Messenia Pharnabazus captured Cythera, placed an Athenian governor in the island, and sailed on to the Isthmus, where he exhorted the confederates to show their loyalty to the Great King and gave their leaders handsome baksheesh. With the permission of Pharnabazus, who returned home, Conon sailed under the Persian flag into the Peiraeus. By a lavish expenditure of Persian funds and by employing the crews of his eighty triremes as labourers he expedited the re-fortification of the Peiraeus and the reconstruction of the Long Walls (Fig. 27). These great works, begun in 394 before the battle of Cnidus, were finally completed about 391 with the help of Boeotia and other allies.[1]

In 392 the Persian subsidies became effective. Thebes issued an electrum coinage with the infant Heracles strangling the snake and the Boeotian shield on the reverse. These devices proclaimed the war of liberation and the principle of federalism. They were adopted by Rhodes, Cnidus, Iasus, Samos, Ephesus, and Byzantium, which formed a coalition and issued a common coinage, and later by Lampsacus, Cyzicus, Zacynthos, and Croton (Pl. XII e). The prestige of the Boeotian League under the leadership of Thebes stood high, and the principle of federalism probably inspired some of the Aegean states to resist the renascent imperialism of Athens. Corinth was enabled by Persian gold to launch a fleet and contest the control of the Corinthian Gulf with Sparta. But Sparta still had financial reserves, derived from the tribute and from Agesilaus' loot. She maintained her fleet in the western waters, and captured Rhium at the narrows of the Gulf. Her able admiral, Teleutias, a brother of Agesilaus, drove the Corinthians off the Gulf, probably early in 391, and his success enabled Agesilaus to pass to the offensive in Corinthia and Acarnania. Athens, however, gained most from the aid of Persia. For Conon, enrolling and paying Athenian seamen to serve under the Persian flag, was in fact reconstituting the Athenian fleet and furthering the interests of Athens in the Aegean. She endeavoured to strengthen her position overseas by diplomacy. In 393 she paid honour to Dionysius, the tyrant of Syracuse, to Evagoras, king of Salamis in Cyprus, and to Carpathos in the south-east Aegean, and she formed an alliance on equal terms with Eretria

[1] X. *HG.* 4. 8. 3–10; D.S. 14. 84. 3–5; 85. 2–4; *GHI* 107.

in 394/393. During 392 Lemnos, Imbros, and Scyros were reoccupied by Athenian cleruchs, and her influence was probably re-established at Delos.[1]

Late in 392 Sparta sent an envoy, Antalcidas, to open negotiations with Tiribazus, the successor of Tithraustes, for the conclusion of peace with Persia. The terms Antalcidas suggested were the cession of the Greek states in Asia to the Great King and a guarantee of autonomy for all other Greek states. Athens too sent envoys, and at her request Boeotia, Corinth, and Argos did likewise. Tiribazus presided over a conference of angry delegates; for all except the Spartans opposed the principle of autonomy, which meant for Athens the loss of her three cleruchies, for Thebes the dissolution of the Boeotian League, and for Argos the loosening of her grip on Corinth. Tiribazus favoured Sparta and supplied Antalcidas with money, so that she might hold her own at sea against Athens, but his policy was not endorsed by the Great King, who sent a pro-Athenian viceroy, Strouthas, to supervise the war at sea. Conon, however, who had been detained by Tiribazus, was cast into prison by the Great King and died subsequently in Cyprus. Persia had had enough of his double-dealing and viewed with alarm the personal position which he had built up, like Alcibiades and Lysander before him, as the dispenser of the Great King's favours and moneys. Statues of him had been set up, for instance, at Erythrae, Samos, Ephesus, and Athens, and he had helped to introduce democracies into the liberated states in place of the ruling oligarchies.[2]

Having failed to swing Persia over to her side, Sparta tried in the winter of 392/391 to negotiate a general peace independently of Persia. She proposed that all states should be autonomous, with the proviso that Athens should keep Lemnos, Imbros, and Scyros and the Boeotian League should be recognized, Orchomenus remaining independent. This was a shrewd attempt to break up the alliance of her enemies; for, if Thebes and Athens agreed, then Argos would either surrender Corinth or else fight on alone. Athens, however, refused to negotiate on these terms. Her hopes were now set on winning the mastery of the seas.[3]

Since the restoration of democracy in 403 the moderate leaders had exerted a strong influence in the Assembly. Anytus and others, for instance, had defeated the untimely desire of the democratic leaders to embroil Athens in war with Sparta *c.* 397. The bold policy of alliance with the Boeotian League in 395 had been sponsored by Thrasybulus of Stiria, the friend of Thebes and the leader of the democrats in 403, and he probably had the support of all parties in the war of liberation from Sparta, at least until the end of 392. In the Aegean Athens' policy was one of moderation; alliance on equal terms was made with Eretria, and no state had a better claim than Athens to

---

[1] *GC* 157 (the date of the federal coinage of Rhodes, &c., is disputed); X. *HG.* 4. 8. 10–12; 15; *GHI* 103; 108–10.

[2] X. *HG.* 4. 8. 12–17; D.S. 14. 85. 4; D. 20. 70; *GHI* 106; Paus. 6. 3. 16.

[3] Andoc. 3; *FGrH* 328 F 149b (Philochorus).

Lemnos, Imbros, and Scyros. When Sparta offered peace in 392/391, the propertied classes as a whole supported the moderate leaders in their desire to accept the Spartan terms. But the poorer citizens, who formed the majority in the state, gave their support to the policy of the democratic leaders, Thrasybulus, Cephalus, and Epicrates, who proposed to regain the Chersonese, the cleruchies, and the assets lost overseas in the Peloponnesian War. At the moment the situation in the Aegean was inviting. Neither Sparta nor Persia had a fleet in the Aegean. Persia indeed was friendly to Athens, and Evagoras, Strouthas, and Pharnabazus were willing to help her. The democracies which had come into power in Rhodes, Samos, Ephesus, Mitylene, and other states were well disposed towards Athens. If she could offer naval protection to such states, she might win their active co-operation. But to build a navy she needed a year at least and, above all, money, which she tried to raise by imposing capital levies on her wealthy class.[1]

Sparta, aware of her danger, made good use of the year 391. While Dercyllidas held on in the Hellespont, she resumed the policy of attacking Persia in Ionia and thus enlisted the help of many Greek states in the east. Her generals, Thibron and Diphridas, regained Ephesus as a base of operations and met their financial needs by raiding the hinterland; her admiral, Teleutias, won over Samos, cut off the democrats in Rhodes, and captured ten Athenian ships on their way to Evagoras in Cyprus.[2]

In spring 390 Athens opened her naval offensive by sending out forty ships under Thrasybulus. He won spectacular successes in the north Aegean, where he was practically unopposed. As Euboea, Boeotia, and Thessaly were friendly, his lines of communication were assured, and he obtained alliances with Thasos, two kings in Thrace (Amadocus and Seuthes), and Samothrace, which together with the cleruchies in Lemnos, Imbros, and Scyros gave him control of the north-east route towards the Hellespont. Leaving Dereyllidas at Abydus on his flank, Thrasybulus entered Byzantium, which was betrayed to him by the democratic faction, and established friendly relations with Chalcedon. He was now master of the Bosporus and the Propontis; for the Thracian kings on the European shore and Pharnabazus on the Asiatic shore were his allies. But he had not dislodged the tenacious Dercyllidas from his bases in the Hellespont, Sestus and Abydus.[3]

Athens, however, either could not or would not support the fleet of Thrasybulus out of her own resources. He therefore imposed a 10 per cent. tax on goods passing out of the Black Sea and a 5 per cent. tax on imports and exports which had been levied in the latter days of the Athenian Empire. Meanwhile at Athens the people began to use their revenues for state-pay. In some of the Allied states he placed garrisons, and in general he supported democratic governments. These steps made it clear to Persia and the Aegean

---

[1] *Hell. Oxy.* 1–2; X. *HG.* 3. 5. 16; Andoc. 3. 15; Ar. *Ec.* 197 (produced in 392); Lys. 28. 2–5; X. *HG.* 4. 8. 4 fin.   [2] X. *HG.* 4. 8. 17–24; D.S. 14. 97. 1–4; 99. 1–3.
[3] X. *HG.* 4. 8. 25–27; 5. 1. 7; D.S. 14. 94. 2; D. 20. 59–60; *GHI* 114.

states that Athens aimed at establishing a second Athenian empire. Late in 390 or early in 389 Thrasybulus moved south from the Hellespont. In Lesbos, where all the cities except Mitylene were held by Sparta, he won over some cities and gained enough booty from the others to pay his troops. Obtaining reinforcements from Mitylene and Chios, he collected money by threats or by raids as far afield as Aspendus beside the river Eurymedon. There, however, he was killed during reprisals for freebooting (389). His energy in these years won Athens her greatest successes; his methods alienated many potential allies; and his failure to concentrate on attacking Dercyllidas was a serious error of strategy.[1]

Throughout 389 and 388 the small fleets of Athens and Sparta fought on indecisively in the Hellespont, in Rhodes, and in the Saronic Gulf, where the Spartans, based on Aegina, did much damage to Athenian shipping. Both sides used mercenary soldiers as marines, were desperately short of funds, and obtained money by exactions or by raids. The Athenians failed to show their previous superiority at sea and dissipated their resources by sending ships to Oeniadae in Acarnania. More daring feats were performed by the Spartans: Gorgopas and Teleutias, for instance, conducted a successful night attack and a dawn raid on the Peiraeus.

As the war on sea and on land was now a stalemate, Sparta made another attempt to swing Persia over to her side. She sent her navarch, Antalcidas, to negotiate in the winter of 388/387. Artaxerxes had good reason to revise his policy. In 391 Evagoras, having conquered most of Cyprus, had revolted and instituted a blockade of the Asiatic coast in alliance with Egypt. In the same year Athens, whom Persia was supporting, had sent a squadron of ten ships to help Evagoras, and Sparta, whom Persia was opposing, had intercepted them. In 388 Athens allowed Evagoras to hire the services of an Athenian mercenary captain, Chabrias, and some peltasts, and in addition placed some Athenian hoplites and triremes under his command. They served with great distinction against Persia. Artaxerxes was clearly backing the wrong side. If he could negotiate a peace in Greece, he would put an end to Athens' intervention in Cyprus and to Sparta's attacks in Asia, obtain access to the market of Greek mercenary soldiers and seamen, and be able to concentrate on suppressing Evagoras.[2]

In spring 387 Antalcidas reported that he had gained the alliance of Persia for such time as Athens and her confederates refused to accept Artaxerxes' conditions for a general peace. Supported and subsidized by Tiribazus, Antalcidas marched overland to Abydus, outmanoeuvred the Athenian commanders in the Hellespont, and assembled a fleet of eighty ships, of which twenty had been sent from Sicily and Italy by Dionysius and others had been manned with the assistance of Persian satraps. He now controlled the Hellespont, as Lysander had done in 405, and a second Spartan fleet blockaded

---

[1] Ar. *Ec.* 815; 825; X. *HG.* 4. 8. 28–30; D.S. 14. 94. 3–4; 99. 4–5; Arist. *Ath.* 41. 3.
[2] X. *HG.* 4. 6. 14; 4. 8. 31–39; 5. 1. 24; D.S. 14. 98.

Athens from Aegina. In autumn 387 Tiribazus summoned envoys from the Greek states to hear the terms which Artaxerxes proposed for the settlement of Greek affairs: all states in Asia, including the two islands Clazomenae and Cyprus, were to be subject to Persia, and all states in Greece, both large and small, were to be autonomous, except that Lemnos, Imbros, and Scyros were to belong to Athens. Tiribazus then read out the ultimatum of Artaxerxes that Persia, aided by any state willing to accept these terms, would attack any dissentient state 'by land and by sea, with ships and money'.[1]

The envoys returned to Greece and reported these terms to their states. All accepted them, save Thebes, which asked to sign on behalf of the Boeotian League. Agesilaus refused to grant her request. In spring 386 he called up the levy of the Spartan Alliance. Thebes acquiesced. Thereupon the oaths to the King's Peace were taken by all Greek states, including Corinth and each state in Boeotia separately, and Corinth received back her oligarchs from exile and re-entered the Spartan Alliance. The third great war was at an end. Where Athens had failed twice, Sparta had succeeded. Her rule extended over the states of the Greek peninsula and islands, exhausted by generations of war and torn by internal dissensions. Her success was due not to her superior strength but to the support of Persia. The Great King was the real victor in the war.[2]

[1] X. *HG*. 5. 1. 25–31; D.S. 14. 110; Polyaen. 2. 24; *GHI* 116.
[2] X. *HG*. 5. 1. 32–36.

The Autocratic Methods of Dionysius and of Sparta (386–368)

§ 1. *The zenith of the Spartan empire*

W HEN the Greek states made peace, many mercenary soldiers and seamen found employment in the service of Artaxerxes or Evagoras. Persia was already almost excluded from the waters of the southeastern Mediterranean. From the Greek states in Cyprus Evagoras manned seventy triremes, and his army comprised 6,000 citizens and many mercenaries; from Tyre and other Phoenician cities he drew twenty triremes, from Egypt money, corn, and troops, and from disaffected rulers in the Persian empire, such as Hecatomnos, ruler of Caria, a further supply of troops. The Persian commanders, Orontes and Tiribazus, selected Ionia as their base. There they assembled their army and fleet (the latter probably manned to a great extent by Greek seamen), moved into Cilicia, and crossed thence into Cyprus. During two years of fighting Evagoras raised his fleet to some 200 ships, of which Egypt supplied fifty. He nearly overcame the invading forces by cutting off their sea-borne supplies, but in a great battle at sea off Citium Evagoras was defeated by the Persian admiral, Glos, and his capital, Salamis, was invested. During the siege Evagoras received further help from Egypt and sent envoys to Sparta, seeking alliance against Persia. Soon afterwards, probably in 382, he came to terms with Orontes, the Persian commander. But Glos, the Persian admiral, then turned against his master. With the great fleet and the war-chest of Persia in his control he obtained the alliance of Egypt and of Sparta. He was master of the seas for a short time before he was assassinated. His successor, Tachos, founded a city on the coast between Cyme and Clazomenae, but his early death put an end to the enterprise. The men who followed Glos and Tachos came from Ionia, Pisidia, Caria, and other maritime areas, which so often produced pirates or mercenaries in troubled times. The power of Persia at sea and in Greece had this in common, that it was based on the willingness of Greek soldiers, sailors, and statesmen to accept her wages and fight against one another.[1]

During the Corinthian War every leading state on the mainland had medized. With Persia's aid the confederates had forced Sparta to abandon the war of liberation in Ionia, and with Persia's aid Sparta had forced the confederates to submit to her will, sacrificing in the process the Ionians, whom she could no longer defend. Political theorists, such as Isocrates, and

---

[1] *FGrH* 115 F 103 (Theopompus); D.S. 14. 110. 5; 15. 2–4; 8–9; 18; Isoc. 4. 134.

ordinary men lamented the disunity of Greece and the perfidy of the leading states, especially Sparta, which set Greek fighting against Greek and made Persia the arbiter of Greek affairs. Practical politicians, dealing with the everyday needs and ambitions of their states, saw no danger in medizing; the Great King's money, they felt, was much as other men's money, except that it was more plentiful and in a harder currency. The two viewpoints are reflected in one of Plutarch's anecdotes. When a Greek commented on the Peace of Antalcidas 'alas for Greece when we find the Spartans medizing', Agesilaus replied 'nay, rather say the Medes are laconizing'. The fact that Sparta claimed to be the champion of autonomy and the leader of the Greek states at the very time when she was surrendering Ionia to Persia was certainly one cause of her unpopularity. But the chief cause was the aggressive imperialism which she had shown towards the Greek states in general.[1]

The King's Peace gave Sparta an opportunity to change her policy. Agesipolis advised a moderate and just interpretation of its terms, which might perpetuate the general peace and restore the prestige of Sparta. Agesilaus, however, intended to dominate Greece. His policy was one of frank imperialism and he was inspired with a deep hatred of Thebes and a distrust of democracy. As ambitious as Cleomenes and as ruthless as Lysander, he held a firmer place than either in the affections of the Spartan people. Ten years of warfare had shown him to be an ardent patriot, a dashing soldier, and a loved commander. Now his bellicosity and his bluffness appealed to the militarist strain in the Spartan character, and he carried his people forward in a policy which Agesipolis and Agesipolis' young successor, Cleombrotus, were to resist in vain.[2]

To dominate Greece Sparta relied on military force and political intervention. When her military commitments increased, perhaps in 382, she sharpened her military weapon for the purposes of repression. She persuaded the Congress of Allies to provide money instead of men (the rate was one Aeginetan drachma a day for a cavalry trooper and half a drachma for a hoplite) or, if an Ally insisted on providing men, to levy fines for any cases of desertion. With the money Sparta hired mercenaries, who were under her immediate control and had no political scruples. There were many opportunities for political intervention. In the name of the King's Peace Sparta restored the exiled oligarchs to Corinth and other states, where they promptly seized power and got rid of their opponents. Then in the name of their states the oligarchs voted as Sparta wished in the Congress of Allies. Such methods, however, were not always applicable. Some states remained recalcitrant, and Sparta decided to discipline them one by one, before they could combine against her.[3]

---

[1] Isoc. 4. 120–5; X. *HG.* 4. 2. 5; Plu. *Artax.* 22.

[2] D.S. 15. 19. 4; 15. 5. 1; 15. 31. 3; *FGrH* 115 F 321 (Theopompus); X. *HG.* 5. 1. 33; Plu. *Ages.* 20.

[3] X. *HG.* 5. 2. 20–22; D.S. 15. 31. 2–3; X. *HG.* 5. 2. 9 fin.; D.S. 15. 5. 2–3.

In the Peloponnese Mantinea and Phlius were obstinately democratic. In 385 Sparta required Mantinea to raze her walls, on the pretext that she had been remiss in her service during the Corinthian War. Mantinea refused. Her appeals to democratic Argos and Athens for help were unanswered. After a long siege, which ended in 384 when a river was diverted by the Spartans and washed away part of the mud-brick walls, Mantinea accepted the terms which Sparta offered: the demolition of all defences, the splitting up of Mantinea into the five autonomous village-communities out of which it had been formed, and the participation of these villages as states in the Spartan Alliance. By the intercession of the exiled Spartan king, Pausanias, whose son Agesipolis was in command, the democratic leaders were allowed to depart. Oligarchical governments then took power in the villages. At Phlius Sparta demanded the restoration of the oligarchic exiles. The demand was obeyed, the property of the oligarchs being returned to them and all disputes being submitted to arbitration. But in autumn 381 the oligarchs came to Sparta and some of their sympathizers complained of maltreatment. Agesilaus, who had friends among them, brushed aside all offers from the democrats of Phlius and demanded the surrender of the acropolis. His demand refused, he laid siege to the city, arming the oligarchs and their sympathizers against their fellow-citizens. The city fell as a result of famine in 379, and Agesilaus was empowered at his own request to dictate the settlement. He placed the city under a garrison for six months, empanelled fifty oligarchs and fifty sympathizers as judges, and gave them authority to try and execute any citizen of Phlius. An extreme oligarchy then ruled over the crippled state.[1]

In central Greece Thebes and Athens were Sparta's most dangerous rivals. At Thebes Ismenias and Androcleides, the democratic leaders, were still holding their own against the restored oligarchs, who were led by Archias and Leontiades. At Athens the moderate party had regained its influence. Both states were careful to give Sparta no pretext for intervention. But Sparta was anxious to weaken the states which had supported Thebes and Athens in the Corinthian War, and in 382 she found an opportunity to attack one of them, the Chalcidian League. Founded early in the Peloponnesian War and consolidated by its struggles against Athens and Macedonia, the League had expanded during the fourth century and had developed a progressive constitution on the initiative of Olynthus. This city, like Mantinea, was itself a 'sympolity', that is a group of settlements originally independent which formed a single state with a common Olynthian citizenship. It was also the administrative centre of the larger 'sympolity', formed by most of the cities in Chalcidice with a common Chalcidian citizenship, and known as 'the state of the Chalcidians' (*to koinon ton Khalkideon*). This state had a federal government with sovereign powers and a federal coinage, while the member-states retained their individual citizenships and regulated their internal affairs. In

[1] X. *HG.* 5. 2. 1–10; 5. 3. 10–17 and 21–25; D.S. 15. 5. 3–5; 12.

382 Olynthus and probably the other member-states were democratic, and they proposed to strengthen their sympolity by granting at least some aspects of isopolity to one another, namely equal and reciprocal rights of inter-marrying without loss of citizenship and of holding property in each other's state. If this proposal had been implemented, the Chalcidian League would have progressed farther towards becoming a completely federal state than the Leagues of central Greece, and particularly the Boeotian League, from which it may have drawn its first inspiration.[1]

In its foreign policy the Chalcidian League had formed a defensive alliance with Amyntas, king of Macedonia. When Amyntas' kingdom was overrun by the Illyrians, he entrusted some of his cities to the League. These and others, including Pella, became members of the League, which then refused to restore them to Amyntas. He therefore appealed to Sparta for aid. At the same time the League tried to compel two Greek cities, Acanthus and Apollonia, to join its membership. They too appealed to Sparta. The League was on friendly terms with Thebes and Athens, and it possessed an abundance of shipbuilding timber, which was of particular importance to Athens. When the envoys of Acanthus and Apollonia visited Sparta and said that the Chalcidian League had decided to seek the alliance of Thebes and Athens, the Ephors were filled with alarm. They let the envoys state their case before the Spartan Assembly and the Congress of Allies, which both voted in favour of war against Olynthus, the most influential state in the League. When the levy was called out, the Theban government prohibited any Theban citizen from serving against Olynthus. The first expeditionary force, exceeding 10,000 in number, was severely defeated by the cavalry, peltasts, and hoplites of Olynthus. A second and larger force was sent out in 381 under Agesipolis, who was accompanied by a staff of thirty Spartiates. With the help of Thessalian and Macedonian cavalry Agesipolis isolated and invested Olynthus. During the siege Agesipolis died of fever, but his successor in command starved Olynthus into surrender. In 379 the League was dissolved. The individual states made treaties with Sparta under which they were compelled, as Athens had been in 404, to follow Sparta in any war she might undertake.[2]

In 382, when the main body of the first expeditionary force lay encamped outside Thebes on its way north, its commander, Phoebidas, was approached by Leontiades, the leader of the oligarchic faction, who offered to betray the acropolis to him. Phoebidas accepted, garrisoned the Cadmea, and arrested Ismenias. The pro-Spartan oligarchs seized power. Three hundred supporters of Ismenias fled to Athens. At Sparta the Ephors and the Assembly resented the initiative shown by Phoebidas, but Agesilaus defended his assault on an allied state in time of peace on the grounds that it was expe-

---

[1] X. *HG*. 5. 2. 12 and 18–19; *GC* 198.

[2] *GHI* 111; D.S. 14. 92. 3; 15. 19. 2–3; *POxy*. 1. 36 nr. 13 (Thebes' alliance with the Chalcidians *v.* Amyntas, probably during the Corinthian War); X. *HG*. 5. 2. 11–24; 37–43; 3. 1–9; 18–19; 26; D.S. 15. 19. 3; 20. 3; 21–23. 3.

dient. Phoebidas was fined by a Spartan court but not cashiered. Ismenias was tried before a court of the Spartan Alliance, found guilty on a charge of medism, and condemned to death.[1]

In 379 the Spartan empire seemed to be even stronger than it had been in 395 on the eve of the Corinthian War. The Congress of Allies, now obedient to the will of Sparta, was rarely consulted. Most of the states were governed by pro-Spartan oligarchies. Elis, Mantinea, and Phlius had been weakened, and the Boeotian League and the Chalcidian League were completely dissolved. In the Peloponnese Argos was isolated. In central Greece Spartan garrisons held Plataea, Thebes, Thespiae, and Heraclea, and farther north Sparta had the alliance of Thessaly, Macedonia, and Molossia in Epirus, which she had helped to stave off an Illyrian invasion. At sea Sparta and her Allies had no rival. In the west Dionysius of Syracuse was her friend, and in the east she was supported at least nominally by Persia. But her rule rested on fear alone. Her cynical policy, which set expediency before every other consideration, had lost her any claim to respect. Her interpretation of 'the autonomy of the Greek states', which she had sworn to respect under the King's Peace, was epitomized in an old saying of Lysander: 'We cheat boys with dice and men with oaths.' The structure of her empire rested on insecure foundations. The oligarchic governments she supported were themselves minority governments. The military levy of the Spartan Alliance was no longer dependable. The use of mercenary troops was double-edged; for they would serve any paymaster. In the last resort Sparta's strength was now the strength not of the Spartan Alliance but of the Spartan state, and that had been gradually undermined by loss in war and by the decay of her institutions.[2]

§ 2. *The career of Dionysius I*

THE defeat of the Athenian Expedition in 413 enhanced the prestige of Syracuse and strengthened her influence in Sicily. Nevertheless, the exigencies of war had strained her material resources and her political unity. In the moment of victory the treatment of the Athenian prisoners was debated in the Syracusan Assembly, much as that of the Mitylenean prisoners had been debated in the Athenian Assembly. The architect of victory, Hermocrates, urged moderation on the principle that 'a generous use of victory is greater than victory itself'; but the leader of the extreme democrats, Diocles, proposed and carried the motion that the prisoners should be sent to the quarries. For the moment the moderate democrats were still in power. They honoured their alliance with Sparta, and sent a squadron under their leader Hermocrates to continue the war in the Aegean. During his absence his opponents obtained power. They established an extreme democracy on the Athenian model, the

[1] X. *HG.* 5. 2. 25–36; D.S. 15. 20. 1–3; Plu. *Pelop.* 6; *Ages.* 24.
[2] X. *HG.* 5. 3. 27; D.S. 15. 23. 3–5; 15. 1. 3–4.

lot being used for the selection of magistrates and the annual generals being raised from three to ten, and they drafted a new code of laws, named after Diocles, which was widely copied by other states in Sicily. That the political institutions of Syracuse developed like those of Athens is not surprising. She too was a large and prosperous state which possessed naval power and imperial revenues, and her people possessed initiative, resilience, and aggressiveness. Yet the Syracusans lacked the important ingredient which had made Athens great in internal politics—moderation. One of the first acts of the extreme democracy was to banish Hermocrates and his leading officers. Another was to go to war with her Chalcidian neighbours.[1]

At the invitation of Segesta, which was at war with Selinus, an ally of Syracuse, some mercenary troops were sent by Carthage to defend the town. When these troops inflicted a defeat on Selinus, Syracuse was invoked and decided, if necessary, to challenge Carthage. Probably in 409 Carthage began to muster an army of citizen troops, native Libyans, and European mercenaries under the command of the suffete Hannibal, a grandson of the Hamilcar who had been killed at the battle of Himera in 480. In spring 408 Hannibal landed at Lilybaeum, collected the forces of his Greek and native allies in Sicily, carried Selinus by assault, and massacred the population. He then outwitted Diocles, the commander of the Syracusan and allied relief force, and captured Himera, where he avenged the death of Hamilcar by torturing and executing 3,000 prisoners. In autumn 408 he returned triumphant to Carthage, leaving mercenary troops to garrison the extended territory of Carthage in Sicily. During the winter of 408/407 Hermocrates arrived in Sicily with five triremes and a thousand mercenaries and enlisted a number of survivors from Selinus and Himera. By raiding and pillaging Carthaginian territory he won booty and fame; under the walls of Himera he retrieved the bones of some Syracusan dead, whom Diocles had abandoned, and he sent them to the Syracusans, who, he hoped, would recall him from banishment. They exiled Diocles, but did not recall Hermocrates, who tried to force his way into the city. In an affray with the democrats Hermocrates was killed. His followers were killed or exiled, except a few who shammed dead or were reported dead. Among the latter was a young officer of twenty-three, named Dionysius.[2]

Meanwhile Carthage, encouraged by her easy successes at Selinus and Himera, decided to conquer the whole of Sicily. Her generals, Hannibal and Himilco, were already in touch with Athens, in the hope that she would prevent Sparta and Corinth from coming to the aid of Syracuse. Large forces of mercenaries were raised in Spain, the Balearic Isles, and Campania to stiffen the levies of Carthaginian and African troops. Near the deserted site of Himera a new city called Thermae was founded as a base for future operations. In 406 an army of some 120,000 men landed and advanced upon Acragas, a city second only to Syracuse in size and wealth. The Acragantines,

[1] D.S. 13. 19. 4; 33; 34. 6; Plu. *Nic.* 28; Th. 6. 20. 3–4; 7. 55. 2; 8. 96. 5; X. *HG.* 1. 1. 27.
[2] D.S. 13. 43–44; 54–63; 75.

supported by Greek mercenaries under the command of a Spartan, Dexippus, and by Campanian mercenaries, withstood the assault of the Carthaginians and were then relieved by an allied force of 30,000 infantry, 5,000 cavalry, and thirty ships. This force had been recruited from Syracuse, Gela, Camarina, Messana, and south Italy and was commanded by Daphnaeus, a Syracusan general. Hannibal died, the victim of plague, and Himilco's army was itself besieged. But through the carelessness of the Greek commanders Himilco intercepted a convoy of corn-ships, won over the Campanian mercenaries, and blockaded Acragas. The troops from south Italy went home in disgust. In December 406 Daphnaeus and his colleagues suddenly ordered the evacuation of Acragas by night. At dawn the Carthaginians entered the city, butchered everyone they found, and spent the winter there undisturbed. In spring 405 Himilco razed Acragas to the ground and advanced on Gela.[1]

Great numbers of refugees were now squatting in the ruins of Leontini and in the outskirts of Syracuse and other cities, where they spread rumours of treachery and reports of Carthaginian atrocities. In this atmosphere of despair and distrust Dionysius, who had distinguished himself at Acragas by his personal courage and leadership, saw his opportunity. Appearing now in the guise of a democratic agitator, he inflamed the people's resentment against the generals, had them deposed, and was himself elected one of their successors. But he was too shrewd to rely on the people's favours. He obtained the recall of his former associates, the supporters of Hermocrates, and set off with them and a picked band of mercenaries to Gela, where terror and dissension were rife. There too he played the demagogue, confiscated the property of the rich, and used the proceeds to pay the mercenaries, who gave their loyalty to him as a reliable paymaster.

On his return to Syracuse he accused his colleagues of treachery, contrasting his own energy with their inactivity. The people thereupon appointed Dionysius sole general with absolute powers (*strategos autokrator*). The Carthaginian onslaught was imminent, and men remembered that Gelo the autocrat had saved Sicily at Himera. Dionysius immediately doubled the pay of the mercenaries, recruited 1,000 refugees to form his personal bodyguard, and filled the posts of military command with his supporters, dismissing the Spartan Dexippus and sending him home. He then married the daughter of Hermocrates, who, like himself, belonged to a distinguished family, and persuaded the people to execute Daphnaeus and their other leaders. In April 405, when Himilco laid siege to Gela, Dionysius was master of Syracuse.[2]

Dionysius' first campaign ended in disaster. Abandoning his plan of blockading the Carthaginians outside Gela, he launched a concerted attack on their fortified camp but failed to co-ordinate the movements of his troops. The allied contingents from south Italy, the Syracusans, and the Geloans went into action, but Dionysius and his mercenaries did not engage at all.

---

[1] D.S. 13. 79. 8; 80–81; 85–91; *Harvard Studies in Classical Philology*, suppl. vol. 1 (1940), 247.   [2] D.S. 13. 91–96; Arist. *Pol.* 1305ᵃ27.

The shattered army fell back inside the walls, and he ordered his men to evacuate Gela during the night. The civil population fled, the Italiote Greeks marched off towards the Straits of Messana, and the Syracusan cavalry prepared to kill Dionysius during the withdrawal to Syracuse. But, when they saw him protected by a large force of mercenaries, they rode on to Syracuse, captured his headquarters there, maltreated his wife, and raised the citizens against him. Meanwhile Dionysius was arranging for the evacuation of Camarina. When news reached him, he made a forced march of some 45 miles with 700 picked mercenaries, burnt down the gate at Achradina at midnight, and killed most of his opponents in the city. At daybreak the main body of his mercenaries and the army of the Siceliote Greeks arrived. They found Dionysius master of the situation. His Syracusan opponents fled to Aetna. The Greeks of Gela and Camarina went on to Leontini and severed their connexion with Dionysius. He and Syracuse were left alone to face the army of Himilco. At this moment fortune favoured Dionysius. Plague spread among the ranks of the enemy and reduced its fighting strength by half. A Carthaginian herald came to Syracuse and offered terms which Dionysius was only too glad to accept. West Sicily, including the native Elymi and Sicans, was to be Carthaginian; Selinus, Himera, Acragas, Gela, and Camarina were to remain unfortified and pay tribute to Carthage; Leontini, Messana, and all Sicel communities were to be autonomous. Thus in 405 Carthage subjugated most of Sicily and dictated terms for the rest. But force was her only title to rule, and force was the weapon which Dionysius proceeded to forge against her.[1]

For thirty-eight years Dionysius ruled Syracuse. In time of war he held unrestricted powers as commander of the armed forces (*strategos autokrator*). He, his brothers Leptines and Thearidas, and his brother-in-law Polyxenus, and later he and his sons, were the heads of the state, and with them foreign powers negotiated. The magistrates, the council, and the commanders of the armed forces of Syracuse appended their oaths to diplomatic contracts but merely as executors of the tyrant's wishes. In Syracuse his power was based on the mercenary troops who garrisoned the fortified citadel of Ortygia; there he amassed armaments and kept sixty warships in a locked harbour. He hired soldiers and sailors, Greek and barbarian, in great numbers, and he rewarded them liberally with booty. He settled veterans on the lands of Greek cities, such as Catana, which he dispossessed. As his most dangerous enemies were the mercenary soldiers of Carthage, he tried to win them over by high wages, and he crucified all Greek mercenaries whom he captured in Carthaginian service. He could trust the population of Syracuse only when the choice lay between the tyranny of Carthage and the tyranny of Dionysius. In 404, when the people rose with the support of Messana and Rhegium and cornered him in Ortygia, he lulled them into false confidence by agreeing to withdraw,

---

[1] D.S. 13. 108–14; the article in the Carthaginian terms that Syracuse should be subject to Dionysius (D.S. 13. 114. 1) is probably apocryphal.

hired the services of a band of Campanian cavalry, and routed the citizen forces. Thereafter he kept the bulk of the population disarmed and under strict supervision. He endeavoured to form a party of supporters by re-distributing much of the landed property in Syracuse and by benefiting the poorer citizens and the liberated slaves; but these 'new citizens', as his opponents dubbed them, were probably a minority in the state. His power thus rested ultimately on his mercenaries. To maintain them he needed more money than Syracuse could supply. Therefore one of the chief objects of his foreign policy was to obtain revenue and loot.[1]

The terms of the Carthaginian treaty were calculated to isolate Syracuse; for Carthage guaranteed the autonomy of the Sicels, of the refugees at Leontini, and of Messana, the mistress of the Straits. While the plague raged in Africa, Dionysius was able to disregard Carthage. He attacked the Sicel towns Herbessus and Herbita, gained by treachery the Chalcidian cities of Naxus and Catana, which were in alliance against him, and intimidated Leontini into surrender. His policy towards the conquered peoples varied. The Sicels usually became tributary subjects or allies; for they were good fighting material. The Chalcidians were sold in the slave-market. The mixed population of Leontini was removed to Syracuse and enfranchised. The fortifications of the swollen city were extended and strengthened by a labour-gang of 60,000 citizens; Epipolae was included in the circuit and a strong fortress was built at Euryelus, so that Syracuse became more than twice as large as Athens and even more impregnable (Fig. 25). In order to drive the Syracusan exiles farther afield and secure control of the Straits, which were of great importance to the naval power of Syracuse, Dionysius won the alliance of Messana by a gift of territory and the goodwill of Locri in Italy by marrying the daughter of a leading Locrian. Rhegium, however, the neighbour of Locri, refused his matrimonial advances and became his bitter enemy. In Greece he enlisted the friendship of Sparta. Early in his rule he was helped by a Spartan emissary, Aristus, to catch some of his opponents, and through her good offices he was able to recruit Peloponnesian mercenaries.[2]

During the years of peace with Carthage Dionysius was manufacturing armaments. The core of his field army consisted of mercenaries, both Greek and barbarian, numbering 10,000 or 20,000 as occasion demanded; they formed specialist units of cavalry, hoplites, peltasts, engineers, and techni-cians. In time of war he called out the levies of the Greek and Sicel cities of east Sicily. His armourers produced the equipment appropriate to each arm and nationality in his service and built up a reserve in Ortygia. The techni-cians invented the 'catapult'(*katapeltes*) or large mechanically-strung bow, of which the arrows could pierce a light shield (*peltes*) or a leather screen at a

---

[1] *GHI* 108; 133; 136; D.S. 14. 7–9; 10. 4; 15. 3; 53. 4; 65. 2–3; 66. 5; Polyaen. 5. 2. 11; 14; Cic. *Rep.* 3. 43 *nihil populi et unius erat populus.*
[2] D.S. 14. 7. 6; 14–16. 1; 18; 44. 2–7; 10. 2–3.

range of 200 yards. They also adopted and developed all the devices of siege-craft. The army was commanded not by annually changing magistrates but by Dionysius and his staff of mercenary captains. Realizing the importance of amphibious operations in a war against Carthage, Dionysius set his ship-wrights to build a fleet with the timber which he felled on Mt. Aetna or imported from Italy, floating it in the form of rafts to the docks at Syracuse. His battle-fleet numbered 200 ships, with a reserve of a hundred hulls; the largest units were the 'quinqueremes' (so called because five men rowed to each sweep), which Dionysius' shipwrights invented, and then came quadri-remes, triremes, and smaller vessels. The ships were manned half by mercenary seamen and half by citizens, and the fleet was commanded by Leptines, the brother of Dionysius. The forces of Dionysius were thus more imposing and stronger in cavalry, siegecraft, and warships than those de-ployed by Sparta against Persia. As yet, however, they lacked experience, discipline, and cohesion.[1]

Carthage, although weakened by the effects of the plague, was still a for-midable power. Her best troops were the infantry and cavalry of Carthage and her African dependencies; to these she added levies from her subjects in Spain and Sardinia and large numbers of mercenaries, hired mainly in the western Mediterranean. Her fleet had a long tradition, and, when brought up to full strength, outnumbered the fleet of Dionysius. Her revenues, based on taxation and trade, enabled her to maintain a large army and fleet without endangering her national economy. Her morale had been heightened by the great victories of Hannibal and Himilco, and her citizens showed more tenacity than the subjects of Dionysius.

In 398 Dionysius delivered an ultimatum to Carthage, that unless Carthage evacuated all Greek cities in Sicily Syracuse would declare war. Carthage rejected the ultimatum and began to rearm. Dionysius had counted on her unpreparedness; he had at least a year in which to liberate Sicily and occupy the western ports. His propaganda was enthusiastically received by the Greeks under Carthaginian rule; they rose against their masters and repaid massacre with massacre. During his march westwards Dionysius armed the Greeks and Sicels, and reached Motya with 80,000 infantry, 3,000 cavalry, and almost 200 warships. Motya was a strongly fortified town which lay on a small island, separated by shallow water from the west coast of Sicily. Dionysius stationed his fleet and his convoy of supply ships in the bay of Motya and began to build a causeway out to the island. Meanwhile he attacked the five cities which alone remained loyal to Carthage but failed to capture any of them by assault. Before the causeway to Motya could be completed, Himilco struck two blows by sea from Carthage. His object was to destroy the merchantmen; for Dionysius relied on them to supply his huge army, which was more than 200 miles from its base. A squadron of ten fast triremes entered the harbour of Syracuse at night and sank almost every

[1] D.S. 14. 41. 2–6; 42–43; 44. 1–2; 58. 2.

merchantman afloat. Himilco himself with 100 ships made a surprise attack at dawn in the bay of Motya; he sank or burnt a number of merchantmen, but his attack upon the Greek warships which lay on shore was foiled by the covering fire of Dionysius' catapultists, archers, and slingers. The Greeks then transported their ships on rollers across the peninsula to the open sea, and Himilco sailed back to Carthage. Motya now had little hope of relief.[1]

The causeway was quickly completed. Dionysius brought up the battering-rams—long wooden beams tipped with bronze and wielded on men's shoulders—and, while the rams pounded the masonry of the circuit-wall, the defenders were driven off the parapets by the missiles of the catapultists, archers, and slingers, who shot from apertures in wooden towers, six stories high, which were moved forward on wheels. The defenders countered by swinging long yard-arms out from the parapets and suspending from them men who dropped flaming bundles of tow and pitch on to the towers. The circuit-wall was at last breached, but it proved to be only the first line of defence. Fighting from the tops of their high houses and barricading the narrow alleys, the Carthaginians beat off the repeated attacks, which were delivered on gangways run out from the movable towers. During a night-attack by picked troops, who erected scaling ladders on the rubble of collapsed houses, the Greeks finally broke into the inner city and overwhelmed the Carthaginians by weight of numbers. Dionysius tried in vain to stop a general massacre, which would only diminish the amount of ransom-money he could exact. The city was looted and the survivors sold into slavery. The heroic defence of Motya was not in vain. The season was already far advanced, and Dionysius was unable after the loss of his merchant fleet to maintain his large army in the field any longer. He left a garrison, composed mainly of Sicels, to hold Motya, ordered Leptines to lay siege to Segesta and Entella, and disbanded the rest of his army. He had won a remarkable success at Motya. A strongly fortified site had fallen not by the traditional methods of invest-ment and blockade, which Athens had employed at Potidaea and Sparta was to employ at Mantinea and Phlius, but by a determined assault with the aid of artillery. Yet he had not deprived Carthage of a bridge-head in Sicily.[2]

In 397 a well-planned counter-attack by superior forces on land and sea deprived Dionysius of his hard-won gains. Himilco recaptured Eryx and Motya and won over the Sicans to his side. He then advanced along the north coast, and sent his powerful fleet ahead to capture Messana. Dionysius mean-while retired from his advanced position near Segesta; for his line of supply was in jeopardy. As he retreated towards Syracuse the Sicels deserted him and joined Carthage. Cast upon his local resources, Dionysius mustered only 30,000 infantry, 3,000 cavalry, and 180 ships, of which a third were manned by liberated slaves, and then moved his whole force from Syracuse to Catana. There, while the army of Himilco was perforce marching inland of

---

[1] D.S. 14. 46. 1–5; 47–50; Polyaen. 5. 2. 6.   [2] D.S. 14. 51–53.

Mt. Aetna, which was in eruption, the Greek fleet forced an engagement with the unsupported Carthaginian fleet under the command of Mago, while Dionysius' army lined the shore. The admiral, Leptines, foolishly brought the Greek squadrons into action piecemeal. His own squadron was quickly surrounded and the Carthaginians employed the boarding tactics which favoured their superior numbers. More than 100 Greek ships were lost, and more than 20,000 men were killed. Soon afterwards Himilco advanced on Syracuse. The sails of his fleet—250 warships and large numbers of merchantmen— covered the waters of the Great Harbour, and his army occupied an open suburb outside Achradina. Neither ship nor man emerged from the fortifications of Syracuse. Himilco then encamped his army for the winter, choosing the low ground beside the Great Harbour. His merchantmen were dispatched to Sardinia and Libya to bring up supplies, and his men built three forts, at Polichna, Dascon, and Plemmyrium (Fig. 25).[1]

In 396 Dionysius' appeals for help were answered by Sparta. Her admiral, Pharacidas, arrived in command of thirty triremes, drawn from the Peloponnese and south Italy. Discontent was rife in Syracuse. The citizens were plotting a revolt, but the mercenaries stood by the tyrant. Pharacidas restored some unity of purpose by declaring that his orders were to help Dionysius against Carthage and not Syracuse against Dionysius. At this juncture a deadly plague wrought havoc in the Carthaginian camp; men died in agony, generally on the sixth day of the disease, and no remedy was efficacious. The Greeks, seeing in the plague the will of the gods whose temples Himilco had outraged, were greatly inspirited. At dawn they delivered an attack by land and sea, which was planned by Dionysius and brilliantly executed. The bulk of the Carthaginian fleet was destroyed, and the forts at Dascon and Polichna were captured. But Himilco's encampment was strongly fortified and he still held the fort at Plemmyrium, which controlled the exit from the Great Harbour. A few days passed, during which the Greeks made no attempt to storm the encampment, and then Himilco slipped away at night, taking forty triremes manned by his citizen troops. The Sicels in his army escaped to the hills. The remainder surrendered or were captured by Dionysius, who enlisted some Iberian mercenaries and sold the rest as slaves.[2]

The enemies of Dionysius alleged that Himilco had paid Dionysius 300 talents on condition that he allowed the Carthaginians to escape. The allegation is almost certainly untrue. For Himilco, controlling the exit from the Great Harbour, could escape under cover of darkness, whenever he pleased, and he had every reason to distrust the wily Dionysius and conceal rather than reveal his plan of escape. The motive which his enemies ascribed to Dionysius was that he believed the Syracusan people to be reconciled to his tyranny by their fear of Carthage and therefore did not intend to drive the Carthaginians out of Sicily. This is false reasoning. For the proximity of the Carthaginians in 405, 404, and 396 prompted the Syracusans to revolt or plan

[1] D.S. 14. 54–63.   [2] D.S. 14. 63. 4; 64–75.

revolt against Dionysius. Moreover, Dionysius himself had done his utmost in 398 to expel the Carthaginians from Sicily, and he could not have regarded the escape of Himilco as ending the war.[1]

Carthage was checked temporarily by her losses at Syracuse and by a widespread revolt of the Libyans, who, enraged by Himilco's desertion of their troops, seized Tunis and besieged Carthage. But the rebels received no support from the Greeks and were soon subdued. On the other hand, the power of Dionysius was severely crippled by his campaigns. The loss of ships, equipment, and men was the more serious because he had spent his treasure and lacked the financial reserves of a great state. His mercenaries were discontented, and he replaced a large number of them more cheaply with slaves whom he liberated and armed. His failure to defend the Greeks who had revolted at his instigation had lost him their goodwill. The Sicels had altered the balance of military power by transferring their allegiance to Carthage; for they were fine fighters, and their hill towns controlled the routes through Sicily. During the recent campaigns both sides had tried to found strongly fortified bases on their lines of communication. Carthage had founded Lilybaeum near Motya, Thermae near Himera, and Tauromenium near Naxus, the last as a centre of Sicel resistance to the Greeks. Dionysius now planted settlements at Entella, Adranum, and Aetna, settled 10,000 mercenaries at Leontini, established Locrians at Messana, and founded Tyndaris near by for Messenian refugees from Greece. He then conducted several campaigns against the Sicels, forcing some into subjection and gaining the alliance of others, notably Agyris, tyrant of Agyrium, but he failed to capture Tauromenium during an attack in midwinter. In 393 Mago landed in Sicily with sufficient money to raise a large army and bring the Sicels back to his side. He advanced towards Messana but was defeated and driven back. In 392 he advanced through the interior with an army of 80,000 men, ran short of supplies when faced by the combined forces of Dionysius and Agyris, and made terms of peace whereby the Sicel states and in particular Tauromenium were abandoned to Dionysius. The Greek states on the coasts of central Sicily were probably recognized by both sides as autonomous and independent.[2]

Dionysius was now free to turn towards his bitter enemy, Rhegium, which harboured the Syracusan exiles and contested the control of the Straits. Already in 393 he had attacked Rhegium without success, and the Italiote states had then formed a coalition to defend their liberties. In 390 Dionysius renewed his attack, but was repulsed by the Italiotes; so he allied himself to the Lucanians of the hinterland and sent his fleet to their support. Caught between two fires, the Italiotes lost 10,000 men in battle with the Lucanians and were outfought in 389 by Dionysius, who granted generous terms and let 10,000 prisoners go free as a token of his goodwill. The states in the toe of Italy were now isolated. Dionysius was determined to add them to his

[1] D.S. 14. 75. 1–4; 15. 74. 3.   [2] D.S. 14. 76–78; 88; 90. 2–4; 95–96.

dominions. He made terms of peace with the Rhegines, who paid 300 talents and surrendered their fleet of seventy ships, and he then destroyed Caulonia and Hipponium, deporting their populations to Syracuse and giving their territories to Locri. In 388 he deliberately picked a quarrel with Rhegium and laid siege to the city. Ten months later, in 387, the 6,000 Rhegines who survived were forced by famine to surrender. All who could not purchase their liberty for a mina of silver were sold into slavery. Their commander, Phyton, was scourged until Dionysius' own troops protested; then Phyton and his family were done to death by drowning. Dionysius' ambition was at last fulfilled. He began to build a wall across the neck of the peninsula from sea to sea, in order to enclose his conquests.[1]

Dionysius now controlled both sides of the Straits, and in the Ionian Sea his fleet was unrivalled. Inspired by the exiled king of the Molossi, Alcetas, who was a refugee at his court, Dionysius sent a supply of arms and 2,000 troops to the Illyrians, who burst into Epirus and slaughtered 15,000 Molossians. Sparta intervened to expel the Illyrians, but Alcetas had regained his throne and opened the ports of Epirus to the fleet of Dionysius. Farther north, where the Illyrians were his allies, he planted a colony at Lissus on the mainland, joined the Parians in colonizing the islands of Pharos and Issa, and sent settlers to Hadria, which is probably to be identified with the city at the mouth of the Po. Syracusan exiles, maintaining their hostility towards the tyrant, colonized Ancona, which had a fine port on the Italian coast. The object of Dionysius was to gain some hold on the trade-routes leading from Greece to Italy and from the Mediterranean into the Adriatic, which in the past the Corinthian colonies and especially Corcyra had controlled. Small though his settlements were, he probably raised revenue by exactions which were akin to piracy, and at the same time he protected Sicilian traders who entered the Adriatic Sea. On the other side of the Italian peninsula he used his sea power to profitable effect in 384 by raiding Agylla in Etruria, where he rifled a temple and took prisoners and property to the value of 1,500 talents.[2]

In 383, his finances being now restored, Dionysius tried to raise the states of west Sicily and provoked Carthage to declare war. The Carthaginian Mago delivered offensives both in Sicily and in Italy, where the Italiote states became his allies. Dionysius won a great victory at Cabala, an unidentified place in Sicily, and demanded from Carthage the complete evacuation of Sicily and an indemnity for the cost of the war. The Carthaginians returned to the attack and inflicted a decisive defeat on the Siceliotes, in which more than 14,000 men, including Leptines, were killed. On this occasion the Carthaginians took no prisoners. Peace was made, probably in 378, Dionysius paying an indemnity of 1,000 talents and Carthage extending her domain to the river Halycus, so that Thermae and part of the territory of Acragas came under her

[1] D.S. 14. 87; 90. 4–7; 91. 1; 100–8; 111–12; Str. 261.
[2] D.S. 15. 13–14; *FGrH* 115 F 128c (Theopompus); Str. 226; 241; *SIG* 141.

rule. Meanwhile on the second front in Italy Dionysius made an alliance with the Gauls; they were raiding in central and south Italy and provided him with valiant mercenaries. It was perhaps after the conclusion of peace with Carthage that he captured Croton and failed to take Thurii. These extensive wars were followed by a long period of recuperation. Finally in 368 he undertook his last campaign with 300 triremes, 30,000 infantry, and 3,000 cavalry against the Carthaginians. As in 398, so now Carthage was weakened by the effects of a plague and revolts in Libya and Sardinia. Being at first unopposed, Dionysius gained Selinus, Entella, and Eryx and laid siege to Lilybaeum. But the strong Carthaginian garrison held firm, and Dionysius, deceived by a false report of a great fire in the docks at Carthage, sent the bulk of his fleet back to Syracuse. The enemy fleet then made an unexpected attack on Drepanum, his naval base, and captured most of the 130 triremes he had retained in the west. A truce was concluded during the winter, and in 367 Dionysius died a natural death. His successor Dionysius II finally made peace with Carthage on the previous terms, the Halycus river forming the frontier between Greek Sicily and Carthaginian Sicily.[1]

The career of Dionysius showed for the first time what an autocrat could achieve in an age of developed capitalism. By confiscating outright or by taxing heavily the accumulated resources of the rich states in east Sicily, he amassed within six years a most formidable array of armaments, and, when he had expended much of these resources, he found a new field to exploit by similar methods in south Italy. In moments of crisis he seized temple treasures, imposed severe capital levies (*eisphorai*), and perhaps devalued his coinage;[2] but, once his power was firmly based, he encouraged commercial enterprise and he raised Syracuse to a position of unrivalled supremacy in the trade of Sicily and south Italy. In the last phase of his rule, when Syracuse reached the zenith of her material prosperity, her leadership in the Greek West resembled that of Athens in the Aegean during the fifth century, albeit on a smaller scale. She was the capital of an empire, comprising two thirds of Sicily and the toe of Italy, which lay athwart the trade routes leading into the western Mediterranean. She was the centre of commercial exchange between Greece, Italy, and Carthage, and her coinage was the strongest currency in the West, both in silver and, after 387, in electrum. She became the largest fortified city in Greek lands, with a population exceeding half a million souls, and she possessed a navy of 300 to 400 ships, which controlled the Sicilian Sea and protected her traders in the Ionian and Adriatic Seas.[3]

Yet the prosperity of Syracuse did not alter the fact that Dionysius rose to power and remained in power as a military autocrat, the commander of mercenary soldiers and not the leader of a political party or united state. The

---

[1] D.S. 15. 15–17; 24; 73; Justin 20. 5; Ael. *VH* 12. 61.
[2] D.S. 13. 81. 4–84 (wealth of Acragas); 14. 53. 2; 65. 2; Ael. *VH* 1. 20; Arist. *Pol.* 1313[b] 26; [Arist.] *Oec.* 2. 20.
[3] *GC* 188; Isoc. 3. 23; D.S. 2. 5. 6; 14. 42. 5; Plu. *Dio* 14.

mercenaries, who were so readily available in the fourth century, served the tyrant not only as assault troops and naval personnel but also as police and guards. They were indispensable to his régime. In order to secure their services, he issued a gold coinage *c.* 406 and thereafter a fine silver coinage of decadrachms; being in competition with Carthage, he adopted the popular Punic emblems, the palm-tree and the prancing horse, and she in turn issued copies of his silver decadrachms.[1] In war he used his mercenaries to good effect. He led them with conspicuous courage, being wounded in action several times. He was tenacious and resourceful but not outstanding as a general, a brilliant organizer of amphibious operations, and a pioneer among the Greeks in siegecraft, in naval construction, and in the co-ordination of specialized units. He surpassed the great mercenary captains of the Greek homeland in this war-ridden century.

Although Dionysius created a great city, a powerful army and navy, and a considerable empire, he did not create a unified state. By pouring a mixed population into Syracuse he deprived it of the cohesion which made it a city-state, and he substituted for the ties of blood the common bond of political servitude. However much he endeavoured to legitimize his position by proclaiming himself a liberator, by preserving some forms of constitutionalism, and by placing the name of Syracuse or the emblem of Sicily, the *triskeles*, on his coins (Plate XII*g*), the Greeks of Syracuse and of the subject states were not reconciled to the loss of their political liberty. His empire was bound together only by the fetters of steel which he had forged as a manipulator of men and money. His success was a personal success. He had few counsellors and friends, he lived in fear of treachery, and he deposed his brother, Leptines, and banished his supporter, Philistus, the historian. To buttress his régime he looked farther afield—to Sparta, the tyrant state of Greece, and to Athens, when her sea power revived. In Greece he sought the fulfilment of an ambition which his enemies ridiculed, the ambition to be acclaimed a tragedian. At the Olympic festival of 384 his verses were publicly mocked, and they were described by a visiting poet at his court as 'tragic'. It was perhaps to compensate for his thwarted ambition that he had statues of himself set up in the guise of Dionysus, the god of tragedy. But in the end his ambition was gratified by the Athenian people, who made him an Athenian citizen and awarded him the first prize at the Dionysiac festival of 367.[2]

Whatever the true merits of his tragedies may have been, his political achievement aroused great interest in Greece. Plato and Aristippus came to Syracuse to study this example of one-man power, and both suffered harsh treatment at his hands. Lysias, speaking at the Olympic festival of 384, urged the Greeks to unite and to liberate Sicily. Isocrates, who had no illusions

---

[1] *GC* 128; 186.

[2] D.S. 16. 5. 4; Pl. *Ep.* 7. 331d; *GHI* 108; 133; 136; D.S. 15. 23. 5; 15. 6–7; 15. 74; D. Chr. 37. 21.

about the character of his rule, hailed him as a saviour of Hellenism and urged him to unite Greece against Persia.[1]

The great merit of Dionysius was indeed that he succeeded, when others might have failed, in saving Greek Sicily from conquest by Carthage. Yet he was by no means an idealistic champion of Hellenism. He had no scruples in using Sicels, Lucanians, and Illyrians to destroy Greek states and in picketing his domains with Campanian, Iberian, and Gallic mercenaries. The antipathy between Greek and Carthaginian was only one of the hatreds which he exploited in pursuit of personal power. He set poor against rich, slave against master, mercenary against citizen, even to the extent of forcing the wives of his victims to marry his minions,[2] and he played upon the hostility between Dorian and Chalcidian, Greek and Sicel, or state and state. By fostering revolution and by uprooting populations he destroyed the moral no less than the material foundations of numerous city-states. By enfranchizing slaves and by planting settlements of mercenaries he brought about a mixture of races which tended to lower the standards of Hellenism. His personal example was malignant; he was perfidious, vindictive, and cruel, and he recognized no secular or religious restraint. If his military power saved Greek Sicily from conquest, his political methods did it more damage than those of any other Siceliote.

§ 3. *The war of liberation 379–374*

LATE on a December evening in 379 seven Theban exiles, walking among a group of labourers, passed undetected through the gates of Thebes. Their leader, Melon, had hatched a plot with Phillidas, the secretary of the three Theban polemarchs. That evening the polemarchs were celebrating the end of their year of office by feasting and drinking, and it was late in their revels that Phillidas introduced the seven Theban exiles disguised as women. Melon and his companions promptly assassinated the polemarchs. During the night they surprised and killed Leontiades and other pro-Spartan leaders, and by dawn their supporters inside the city were in arms. At the same time a group of exiles, led by Epaminondas and Gorgidas, arrived from the Attic frontier; they were followed later by an Athenian force under the command of two Athenian generals, both privy to the plot. The Spartan commander of the garrison in the Cadmea, which numbered 1,500 men, had sent a dispatch to Sparta during the confusion of the first night. He now took a decision, for which he was later executed, to evacuate Thebes on condition of a safe conduct. He met the Spartan relief force at Megara. Its commander, the young king Cleombrotus, marched through the northern Megarid, skirting the Attic frontier, where Chabrias with an Athenian force held Eleutherae, and carried the pass above Plataea to descend into Boeotia. Joining the Spartan garrison

---

[1] Plu. *Dio* 5; Lys. 33; Isoc. *Ep.* 1; *Phil.* 65; *Arch.* 44–45.
[2] D.S. 14. 66. 5; Polyaen. 5. 2. 20.

at Thespiae, he entered the territory of Thebes, made no attack upon the city, and soon afterwards withdrew, following the difficult route along the coast from Creusis to Aegosthena (Fig. 19). But a third of the army remained at Thespiae under the command of a Spartan officer, Sphodrias, whose orders were no doubt to isolate Thebes. For Cleombrotus seems to have acted in the expectation that a change of heart would occur in the Theban people and Athens would think twice about intervening.[1]

At Athens the demonstration of Sparta's power had an immediate effect. When Cleombrotus disregarded the force under Chabrias at Eleutherae, the Athenians paraded their neutrality by condemning to death the two generals who had given their support to the exiles. There is no doubt that Athens would have left Thebes to her fate, had not Sphodrias and his army appeared suddenly at dawn in the Thriasian plain between Eleusis and Athens, pillaged the houses, and retired to Thespiae. His intention had clearly been to seize the Peiraeus and threaten Athens. It was thought at the time that Cleombrotus had prompted him, or that the Theban leaders had bribed him, but it is probable that Sphodrias was inspired by personal ambition to emulate the exploit of Phoebidas, who had seized the Cadmea in time of peace. Some Spartan envoys, who happened to be at Athens, assured the Athenians that his action was irresponsible and that he would be executed. But, although Sphodrias disobeyed the summons to present himself for trial at Sparta, he was acquitted thanks to the influence of Agesilaus. This flagrant breach of international usage drove Athens into alliance with Thebes. She decided to send an army of 5,000 infantry and 200 cavalry under the command of Chabrias to assist in the defence of Thebes.[2]

At Sparta the conduct of the war was entrusted to Agesilaus. He decided to concentrate his attack upon Thebes. His personal hatred for the city was one of his motives; but at the same time he realized the importance of preventing Thebes from reconstituting the Boeotian League, which at the turn of the century had boasted a powerful army of 11,000 hoplites and 1,100 cavalry, and he hoped by defeating Thebes to isolate and win over Athens. For this crucial campaign he reorganized the system of military assessments which were made upon the land powers in the Spartan Alliance. Ten districts were defined, each being responsible for one army group: two districts were drawn from Arcadia, and one each from Lacedaemonia, Elis, Achaea, Corinth-Megara, the smaller states of the north-east Peloponnese, Acarnania, Phocis-Locris, and, lastly, the states of Chalcidice. Each district might, if it wished, provide money instead of men, and with this money Sparta could hire mercenaries who were particularly valuable for service throughout the year as garrison troops. In the latter part of 378 Agesilaus invaded Boeotia with 1,500 cavalry and more than 18,000 hoplites, a force equivalent, on the equation of one cavalryman with four hoplites, to some 25,000 men and probably

[1] X. *HG.* 5. 4. 2–18; Plu. *Pel.* 7–13; D.S. 15. 25–27.
[2] X. *HG.* 5. 4. 19–34; Plu. *Pel.* 14; D. S. 15. 29. 5–7; 32. 2.

representing five-sixths of the full levy; for Sparta contributed five of her six regular brigades or *morai*. In a pitched battle on the plain Agesilaus was confident of success, but he found the Thebans and Athenians holding the strong defences which they had prepared on a ridge outside Thebes. He was not prepared to assault this position; for the Spartans were notoriously unskilful in attacking such defences and he was impressed by the fine discipline of Chabrias' mercenaries. In addition, he was alarmed by the disaffection among his own allied troops. He therefore ravaged Theban territory and withdrew, leaving his garrisons in some of the Boeotian cities to harass Thebes. In 377 he invaded again with the same army, ravaged more extensively, but failed to force a pitched battle. In 376, when Agesilaus was ill, Cleombrotus proved unable to carry the passes over Mt. Cithaeron. Boeotia was now safe from invasion, and Thebes could deal with the Spartan garrisons singly.[1]

While the Theban forces avoided a pitched battle with the great armies of invasion, they gradually gained an ascendancy over the Spartan garrisons in Boeotia. In the winter of 378–377, for instance, they defeated the garrison at Thespiae, killing Phoebidas and routing his mercenaries. In 375 the Sacred Band, consisting of 300 picked hoplites, won a remarkable victory at Tegyra. Encountering two Spartan brigades, which were returning to their base at Orchomenus, the Sacred Band, although heavily outnumbered, adopted a compact formation, forced a way through the enemy, and routed them in disorder. For the first time in Greek warfare Spartan hoplites suffered defeat at the hands of a smaller number of hoplites. The prestige of the Theban commander, Pelopidas, and of the Theban hoplites was now firmly established. By 374 Orchomenus was the only ally left to Sparta in Boeotia. During these years of war against Sparta the Theban democracy counted upon the support of the democratic parties in the Boeotian states, which resented the narrow oligarchies imposed upon them by Sparta. As each state was liberated, a pro-Theban democracy came into power. Thus the ground was gradually prepared for the reconstitution of the Boeotian League on a democratic basis with Thebes the liberator occupying the key position in its structure.[2]

Federalism had always been the source of Boeotia's strength. During the Peloponnesian War the federal government of Boeotia consisted of four Councils of Boeotian delegates (see above, p. 346). At the turn of the century the federal system grew tighter, and the federal government became a single Council of 660 members, sitting at the Cadmea of Thebes. The Councillors were elected by the eleven cantons of the League to hold office for one year, each canton returning sixty members. Thus government by proportional representation was achieved; for the cantons were equal in electoral and military strength. Thebes and her dependencies comprised four cantons, that is four elevenths of the Boeotian electorate; for some states, such as Plataea, were subject to her. Rule by a Council marked the League as oligarchical in

---

[1] D.S. 15. 31–34. 2; X. *HG*. 5. 4. 35–59; Plu. *Ages.* 26; Polyaen. 2. 1. 2.
[2] X. *HG*. 5. 4. 42–46; Plu. *Pel.* 15–18.

character. The member-states too were at that time oligarchical; for the political franchise was limited to those who owned property above a fixed valuation. When the League was re-forming between 376 and 374, it did so on a democratic basis, in sympathy with the development towards democracy among its member-states. The franchise was therefore extended to all Boeotians without distinction of class, and they met at Thebes in the 'General Assembly of the Boeotians' (*koine synodos* or *damos ton Boioton*). The Assembly was the sovereign body in the constitution of the League. It decided all matters of policy. The federal magistrates, namely councillors, generals, justices, and financial officers in charge of the federal mint, were elected by the Boeotians on a cantonal basis and held to account by the General Assembly. The number of cantons was reduced to seven. Orchomenus, which with Hysiae had comprised two cantons, was still outside the League; Plataea became subject again to Thebes, and Thespiae and Tanagra, which had fought for the Spartans, were made subject to Thebes. With her larger number of dependencies Thebes now represented three-sevenths of the electorate, and in addition her citizens could attend the General Assembly more easily than the citizens, for instance, of Chaeronea. Her prestige too lent weight to her opinions, particularly on the board of the federal generals, the seven Boeotarchs, who made their decisions on a majority vote; there the authority of the great Theban commanders Pelopidas and Epaminondas often prevailed. Because Thebes had a preponderant influence in the League, the strength of the national federal state of Boeotia was often measured by that of Thebes. The League did not advance to the further phase of federalism which had been envisaged by the Chalcidian League, namely the interchange of reciprocal rights between the member-states which was known as 'isopolity', and it always contained within itself an unhealthy element, the swelling growth of states made subject to Thebes. But, despite these weaknesses, the democratic Boeotian League enshrined a new principle, which raised Boeotia to greatness and inspired other states to follow her example.[1]

During the winter of 378–377, when Thebes was pinned down by Spartan garrisons in Boeotia, Athens began, in the interest of the common struggle, to form the Second Athenian Alliance. The policy of recovering the empire had been discredited by the Peace of Antalcidas. In 386–380 she initiated a new policy, which was reflected in the *Panegyricus*, a pamphlet composed at this time by Isocrates. The fundamental principle was that she should treat her Allies as equals and not as subjects. The situation in the Aegean was favourable to her enterprise: Sparta and Persia stood for the imperialistic principle, and neither was concerned to suppress piracy and protect maritime trade. In 384 a defensive alliance, on terms of equality and within the framework of the King's Peace, was concluded between Athens and Chios; the signatories

---

[1] See pp. 346 and 461 above; *Hell. Oxy.* 11; 12. 2; D.S. 15. 80. 2; *IG* 7. 2408; Paus. 9. 13. 6; Isoc. 14. 8–9; X. *HG.* 5. 4. 63; 6. 1. 1; *GC.* 158; Arist. *Pol.* 1321ᵃ29 shows that at Thebes the humblest occupations excluded some from the franchise. See Plate XII *f*.

undertook to respect each other's 'freedom and autonomy and to observe the covenanted peace to which Persia, Athens, Sparta, and other Greek states had bound themselves by oath'. Similar alliances were contracted with Byzantium and with Methymna in Lesbos; there too Mitylene and in the north the Odrysian king, Hebryzelmis, entered into friendly relations with Athens, and in 378 Thebes became an equal ally of Athens.

In March 377 Athens announced to the Greek states the charter of the Second Athenian Alliance, which has been preserved in an important inscription. The invitation ran as follows. 'Any Greek or non-Greek state, provided it is not subject to Persia, may become an ally of Athens and her Allies on conditions of freedom and autonomy, preserving its chosen form of constitution, receiving neither garrison nor governor, paying no tribute, and enjoying the same terms as Chios, Byzantium, and the other allies.' Freedom and autonomy were defined in terms which implied a contrast with the actions of Sparta. The object of the Alliance was clearly stated in terms of hostility to Sparta—'that Sparta may leave the Greek states in peace, in enjoyment of liberty and autonomy, and in secure possession of their territory'. As Athens intended not to pick a quarrel with Persia but rather to drive a wedge between Persia and Sparta, the object of the Alliance was further defined—'and that the peace and friendship covenanted by the Greek states and Persia may be valid and lasting'. For her own part Athens renounced all claims to property in the territory of a state entering the Alliance, cancelled any records of discrimination against any such state, and undertook not to acquire property in the territory of any such state either by public or by private act. The contract between the members was a defensive alliance by land and by sea, and anyone proposing to abrogate the contract or the terms of the contract was to be liable to punishment.[1]

The name of the Alliance was 'The Athenians and the Allies'. Its constitution too resembled that of its predecessor, founded a century before. The policy of the Alliance was decided by agreement between two separate bodies, the Athenian State and the Council of the Allies (*to koinon* or *to synedrion ton symmakhon*). Each deliberated independently of the other, and each passed its resolutions to the other via the Athenian Council. The Athenian State conducted its deliberations in its own Assembly, except when it delegated its authority to the Athenian Council. The Council of the Allies, sitting at Athens, was attended by the delegates of the Allied states, who elected from their own number a president, probably at the beginning of every session. Each Allied state, regardless of its size, cast one vote. Resolutions were adopted on a majority vote, and were binding on all the Allied states. If on a specific matter the resolution of the Athenian State and the resolution of the Council of Allies were at odds, no action was taken by the Alliance as a whole; for the two bodies were equal in power, and a dead-lock between them

---

[1] Isoc. 4. 104; *GHI* 118; 121–2; 123 (the restoration which describes the King's Peace as a 'general peace' is not accepted in the text); D.S. 15. 28. 2–5; 29. 7–8.

could not be broken. If the resolutions were in agreement, the matter was thereby decided for the Alliance as a whole. The actual wording of the decision for the purposes of record might be in the name of the Council of the Allies, or of the Athenian Assembly, or of the Athenian Council, this being a matter not of principle but of convenience.[1]

When a decision was taken, it was enacted by the executive authority, Athens, to which the Allied states had entrusted the hegemony at the formation of the Alliance. The powers of the executive authority were no doubt carefully defined; they included the supreme command, the mustering of ships, men, and money, and the conduct of preliminary negotiations in the field. In one case, which may have been a unique exception to the general rule, the supreme command on land was not held by Athens; for in 377–375 Thebes evidently commanded the operations in Boeotia. On official embassies of the Alliance one or more delegates of the Council of the Allies accompanied the delegates of Athens. The executive powers entrusted to Athens were wielded mainly by her own generals, who were restricted by the terms of the Charter of the Alliance (for instance, they could not place a garrison on the territory of an Allied state, unless the Council of the Allies gave formal approval) and by the ability of an Ally to seek redress through the Council of the Allies.[2]

The finances of the Alliance were recruited from the two separate bodies. The Athenian State allocated and administered grants in money and ships from its own resources, such grants being considerably larger than those contributed by any one Allied state. The Council of Allied States assessed the resources of each Allied state and, probably in consultation with the Athenian State, fixed the amounts in money alone or in both money and ships which were to be paid by each Allied state in order to meet the needs of the occasion. The amounts in money were called 'contributions' (*syntaxeis*), a term chosen by Callistratus to contrast with the ill-famed word 'tribute' (*phoros*), which was common to the past empire of Athens and the present empire of Sparta. The 'contributions' were paid into the Allied Treasury, from which the Council of Allied States made disbursements at its discretion. The ships supplied by an Allied state had their own captains but were placed under the command of Athens as hegemon.[3]

The Alliance also provided courts of justice. The judicial delegates of Athens and of the Council of the Allies were to try those who proposed to abrogate or alter the terms of the contract of alliance. This joint court was competent to impose the penalty of death or to banish a delinquent from the territory of the Alliance. The Council of the Allies sitting alone was to try any Athenian who acquired property in the territory of an Allied state,

[1] D.S. 15. 28. 3–4; *GHI* 126, ll. 19 and 23; 133, l. 11; 144, l. 12; Accame, *La Lega Ateniense* 230 (inscription).

[2] D.S. 15. 28. 4; Aeschin. 2. 20; *GHI* 124, l. 25.

[3] X. *HG.* 6. 2. 9; *CIA* 2, 17, l. 45; 65, l. 15; 62; Harp. s.v. *suntaxis*; [D.] 49. 49.

and the penalty in such a case was confiscation of the property by the Council.[1]

In its relations with outside powers the Alliance acted as one body. If a state wished not only to ally with the Alliance but also to enter the Alliance, both Athens and the Council of the Allies had to approve; and the entering state had to swear to accept the majority decisions of the Council of the Allies in matters of war, peace, and so forth, and to renounce the right of making war or peace, unless it was in accordance with the resolution of Athens and the Council of the Allies. If a state wished to make alliance or peace with the Alliance but not to enter the Alliance, both Athens and the Council had to consent. As a corollary, a member-state of the Alliance, whether Athens or another, was probably not free to make a separate alliance with an outside power; for there was a danger that, as a result of so doing, the member-state might have occasion to invoke the Alliance's contract of defensive alliance and involve the Alliance in commitments beyond its control.[2]

The Second Athenian Alliance was not a federal body. There was no federal citizenship and no federal government. It was a military alliance, constructed to defeat Sparta and to safeguard liberty and autonomy on the principles of collective action and collective security. Like the military alliance in the Corinthian War of 395–387, it required a plan of organization, which, in view of its continuing existence, may be termed a constitution. In March 377, when Athens and her Allies issued their programme, the constitution was comprehensive and progressive. It provided for deliberative, executive, financial, judicial, and diplomatic functions. In the eyes of a political theorist such a constitution might seem a first step towards a permanent federal system. But from first to last the Alliance was military in character and in purpose, and its terms were essentially realistic. To defeat Sparta Athens needed allies and she attracted them by offering liberal terms. On their side the Allies were ineffective unless they had the advantage of Athens' power and leadership; therefore they conceded to her the right of veto in framing policy and the full executive authority in action. Both parties to the Alliance shouldered a risk—Athens that her Allies might not contribute enough to the common cause, and the Allies that Athens might abuse her position as hegemon—, but the Alliance was formed in an atmosphere of concord, urgency, and optimism.

Between 377 and 374 the Alliance grew apace. A religious centre for it was provided at Delos, where an Athenian board took control of the temples but respected the autonomy of the Delian community. The first recruits—several Euboean states, Peparethos, Sciathos, Maronea in Thrace, and Perinthus in the Propontis—lay on the corn-route to the Black Sea, which was of supreme importance to Athens and at this time also to Thebes. In 376 Sparta, unable to enter Boeotia, switched her offensive against Athens. A fleet of sixty ships, based on Aegina, blockaded the approaches to the Saronic Gulf, but in

[1] *GHI* 123, l. 51; l. 41.   [2] *GHI* 127; 144, l. 12; 147, l. 12.

September 376 it was decisively defeated by a larger Athenian fleet off Naxos. Most of the Cyclades now joined the Alliance. In 375 the Alliance did not concentrate its forces against the Spartan base at Aegina but divided them into two fleets, one under the command of Chabrias winning new adherents along the Thracian coast, and the other under the command of Timotheus sailing into the Ionian Sea to win over Corcyra, Cephallenia, Acarnania, and Alcetas, king of Molossia. While continuing her raids from Aegina, Sparta manned a fleet of fifty-five ships in the west, which engaged Timotheus off Alyzia in Acarnania but suffered a reverse (*c.* June 375); thereafter, as Timotheus received reinforcements from Corcyra, Sparta lost the initiative. By the summer of 374 Athens and her Allies were the leading sea power in the Aegean and Ionian Seas.[1]

The meteoric success of the Second Athenian Alliance was due to a combination of circumstances. The military prowess of the renascent Boeotian League protected Attica from invasion by Sparta and enabled Athens to concentrate on naval warfare. The tyrannical methods of Sparta had engendered such fear and hatred in the small states that only a few, such as Histiaea in Euboea, remained loyal to her. As soon as Thebes and Athens challenged Sparta, the democratic parties in the other states became more active and swung towards the Athenian Alliance, which could offer more immediate protection than the Boeotian League. Athens, too, made a supreme effort which justified her position as hegemon. She helped Thebes both directly in Boeotia and indirectly by operating in Euboea and then drawing the attack of Sparta to the west. She honoured her obligations under the Charter of the Alliance, notably at Corcyra, where Timotheus was invoked by the democratic party but did not tamper with the constitution. Her generals were capable— Callistratus, the statesman behind the Charter of the Alliance, Chabrias and Iphicrates, who had gained experience as mercenary commanders, and the young and able Timotheus, son of Conon—and her troops outfought the Spartan forces at Naxos and Alyzia. A new board of ten Naval Commissioners, elected each year, was instituted in 377/376 to take charge of all naval preparations. Above all, she taxed herself heavily by raising repeated levies on the capital which had accumulated in private hands during the years of peace. A proposal to conscript 20,000 hoplites and 500 cavalry and to equip 200 ships was not fully realized; but the fact that the ships on her naval list rose from some 100 in 377/376 to 283 in 357/356 showed her spirit in these eventful years.[2]

The efforts of the Alliance imposed a severe strain on Athens. In order to raise the capital levies more rapidly in 378/377, the state valued all private property above a line which was probably drawn through the lower part of the hoplite class. The total capital available for taxation under this schedule

[1] *GHI* 123, l. 79; 124; 125; 126 and *Hesperia* 9. 321; 127; D,S. 15. 30; 34. 3–36; X. *HG.* 5. 4. 60–66; Plu. *Phoc.* 6; Nep. *Timoth.* 2; Polyaen. 3. 10. 4, 6, 12, 13, 16, 17; 3. 11. 2, 11.
[2] D.S. 15. 30; X. *HG.* 5. 4. 64; D.S. 15. 29. 7; Plb. 2. 62. 6; *IG* ii.² 1604, 1611.

amounted to some 6,000 talents, and the capitalists themselves were divided up into 100 groups, called 'Symmories', each worth 60 talents. When the state demanded a percentage of the taxable capital as a levy (*eisphora*), each Symmory was responsible for providing its own contribution. Probably in 374 payment was expedited by making the three richest men in each Symmory advance their Symmory's contribution as a prepayment (*proeisphora*) which they could later regain from their fellow taxpayers. We do not know how much money was raised by capital levies during the years 377 to 374. To judge from the levy of 200 talents raised in 428 B.C. and from the size of the Athenian forces in these years, the total sum is more likely to have been in hundreds than in tens of talents. The incidence of the tax caused distress to the capitalist classes, of which the wealthiest also carried the burden of the trierarchies and other liturgies. Even so the proceeds were not sufficient to cover the cost of the campaigns undertaken by Timotheus and Chabrias.[1]

At the end of 375 Thebes was ready to pass to the offensive. The Boeotian cities, except Orchomenus, had entered the Boeotian League or submitted to Thebes, and the Theban hoplites had defeated the Spartans at Tegyra. The moment seemed favourable to Theban expansion in central Greece. The hands of Athens, her traditional rival, were tied by her alliance and by the war with Sparta. In the north a new power had arisen, Jason, tyrant of Pherae, who commanded a strong force of cavalry and a band of 6,000 picked mercenaries. As an ally of Thebes, he had clashed with Sparta in a struggle to secure Histiaea in Euboea and he had sent corn to Thebes during the Spartan invasions of Boeotia. At the end of 375 the only obstacle to his unification of Thessaly was Polydamas of Pharsalus, a close friend of Sparta, who relied on the support of the Spartan garrison at Heraclea in Trachis. In the spring of 374, no doubt in collusion, Thebes invaded Phocis and Jason delivered an ultimatum to Polydamas. Phocis and Polydamas appealed to Sparta, who found herself too widely committed to add Jason to her active enemies; she therefore sent a large army under Cleombrotus across the Corinthian Gulf to support Phocis but reluctantly refused the appeal of Polydamas. Cleombrotus' presence put Thebes on the defensive, but Jason secured the submission of Polydamas and the path was clear for him to be elected ruler (*tagos*) of all Thessaly.[2]

These developments in central Greece alarmed Athens as well as Sparta. Her relations with Thebes were already strained because Thebes had ceased to pay her contributions to the Council of Allies, and the establishment of the

---

[1] Plb. 2. 62. 6–7; *FGrH* 323 F 8, 328 F 41, 46; D. 50. 8–9; Poll. 8. 130; D. 22. 44, where some regard the 300 talents as paid in the archonship of Nausinicus (378/377), others as the total of all *eisphorai* from 378 to 355, and others emend to 1,300 talents. The second interpretation gives an average yield of 13 talents a year, i.e. a levy of 0·2 per cent., which is trivial in relation to actual and proposed *eisphorai* of 200 talents (Th. 3. 19; D. 3. 4), a levy by Dionysius of 20 per cent. per annum (Arist. *Pol.* 1313^{b}27), and the size of Athens' fleets in these years. X. *HG.* 5. 4. 66; Isoc. 15. 109; 120.

[2] X. *HG.* 5. 4. 56–57; D.S. 15. 30; X. *HG.* 6. 1. 1–19; 6. 2. 1. For the *tagos* see p. 142.

Boeotian League, the subjugation of Plataea, and the attack on Phocis were all developments contrary to the traditional policy of Athens. At the moment Thebes was indeed her ally, but Athens had no wish to see her neighbour become the dominant partner in the alliance. Her own objective in the war was already gained; her sea power was unchallenged and she needed a pause for financial recuperation. Therefore she opened negotiations with Sparta for peace on the terms of a *status quo*, whereby the Second Athenian Alliance was to be recognized and Thebes, if she wished to benefit by the peace, would do so as a member-state of that Alliance. In July 374 peace on these terms was concluded. Athens was jubilant. A statute of Timotheus was set up, and an annual sacrifice on the anniversary of this peace was decreed in perpetuity. For the old balance of power in Greece seemed to have been struck again with Athens dominant by sea and Sparta controlling the Peloponnese.[1]

§ 4. *The overthrow of Sparta*

THE peace was of short duration. The swing towards democracy was gathering force; it tempted Athens and alarmed Sparta. When Timotheus was informed of the peace and recalled homewards, he landed some democratic *émigrés* on Zacynthos, where they established a stronghold on the coast and proceeded to attack the oligarchs. Sparta protested to Athens, but the Athenian Assembly decided to espouse the cause of the Zacynthian democrats. The decision was fatal to the newly-established balance of power. Athens deliberately chose the course of aggression in the hope of gaining supremacy in Greece, and Sparta had no option but to continue the war.

In the winter and spring of 374/373 Sparta sent fleets to Zacynthos and Corcyra. Lacking the money to equip a fleet for their relief, Athens sent a force of 600 mercenary peltasts overland into Epirus, whence they were ferried across by night to Corcyra, and Timotheus was ordered to seek new recruits and contributions for the Alliance in the Aegean. He won over Jason of Pherae, now ruler of all Thessaly and influential in Epirus, whose resources were advertised at 8,000 cavalry, 20,000 hoplites, and countless peltasts and may in practice have been half as numerous. Amyntas of Macedon allied himself with Athens, and many states joined the Athenian Alliance. Yet this did not solve the financial problem. In autumn 373 Timotheus' fleet lay idle at the mouth of the Saronic Gulf, his coffers empty and his allied seamen disgruntled. He was prosecuted by Callistratus and Iphicrates, acquitted thanks to the support of Jason and Alcetas, and superseded in the command by Iphicrates. But money was still lacking, until Callistratus, Iphicrates, and Chabrias imposed further capital levies and special taxes. When Iphicrates arrived with seventy ships in 372, the Spartan fleet withdrew. In order to obtain food for his men Iphicrates had to hire out his sailors as labourers in Corcyra. At this time Athenian officials with garrison troops

[1] X. *HG.* 6. 2. 1; Isoc. 15. 109; *GHI* 128; Aeschin. 3. 243; Nep. *Timoth.* 2.

were placed in Cephallenia to keep control of it and the adjacent islands and mainland.[1]

The folly of Athens was now apparent. Her finances did not justify a bid for supremacy, and she was straining the loyalty of her Allies by political intervention and by financial mismanagement. Her relations with Thebes in particular were deteriorating. In 373/372, although Thebes supplied a contingent of ships for Timotheus' fleet and a Theban was elected president of the Council of Allies, Thebes destroyed Plataea and deprived Thespiae of her political independence. The refugees from Plataea were welcomed at Athens and were granted equal rights under a decree of isopolity. This action increased the annoyance of Thebes, which had already been excited by Athens' seizure of Oropus some years earlier. Jason's actions also alarmed Athens; for he had withdrawn from the Athenian Alliance but remained in alliance with Thebes.[2] The leading statesman at Athens, Callistratus, persuaded the people to negotiate for peace with Sparta and to inform Thebes of their intention in advance. At this juncture the Great King re-entered the diplomatic field. He was still endeavouring to reduce the revolt in Egypt and had need of Greek mercenary captains and soldiers. His envoys were present at a peace conference convened at Sparta in summer 371, to which the warring states sent delegates. The following terms were proposed by Sparta and supported by Persia and Athens. The Greek states were to be independent, all garrisons were to be withdrawn, and a general disarmament was to be carried out; if any state infringed the proposed terms, the other signatories to the peace would not be under oath to intervene, but any state that wished could aid the victim of aggression. These terms were approved, and officers were appointed to supervise the withdrawal of garrisons. Sparta took the oath to the peace treaty on behalf of herself and her Alliance; Athens and the member-states of her Alliance, Thebes included, took the oath separately and individually; then followed other states singly. This procedure implied the recognition of the Spartan Alliance and the Athenian Alliance by Persia as the chief guarantors of the peace. In addition, the claim of Athens that certain places should be regarded as her possessions was conceded; among them were the Chersonese and Amphipolis, the latter with the consent of Amyntas, king of Macedon, who was present.[3]

On the day after the oaths were taken, the Theban delegates asked to substitute the word 'Boeotians' for 'Thebans' in the peace treaty, in order that the Boeotian League might be recognized. In proposing the word 'Thebans' Sparta had probably acted in collusion with Athens, since both sympathized

[1] X. *HG.* 6. 2. 2–38; D.S. 15. 45–46. 3; 47; X. *HG.* 6. 1. 19; *GHI* 123, l. 111; 129; [D.] 49. 9–24; *Hesperia* 9. 323.

[2] [D.] 49. 14; *AJA* 40. 461; X. *HG.* 6. 3. 1; D.S. 15. 46. 4–6; Isoc. 14; Paus. 9. 1. 8; *Hesperia* 8. 3 (inscription honouring Thrasybulus of Collytus) may concern relations with Thebes.

[3] X. *HG.* 6. 3. 2–18; D.S. 15. 50. 4 (15. 38 probably refers to the Peace of 371); D. 9. 16; Aeschin. 2. 32.

with Plataea, Thespiae, and Phocis and both feared the rise of the Boeotian League. Therefore Agesilaus, the spokesman of Sparta, refused the Theban request: 'Thebes', he said, 'must either abide by the oath she had taken or else ask to have her name deleted from the treaty.' The Theban delegates, headed by Epaminondas, asked to have the name of Thebes deleted. Thus Thebes severed herself from the Athenian Alliance and exposed herself to the possibility of an attack supported by Persia, Sparta, Athens, and any other state which wished to act.

The Conference was then dissolved. Athens implemented the terms by recalling Iphicrates and restoring any states she had detached from the Spartan Alliance since the taking of the oaths. Both Athens and Sparta then withdrew their garrisons and armed forces, except that Cleombrotus, who commanded the Spartan army in Phocis, still maintained his position. The Assembly at Sparta held a debate to determine what orders should be issued to Cleombrotus. Prothous proposed that the army should be disbanded and the peace solemnized by a dedication at the temple of Apollo at Delphi, and that thereafter, if any state refused to recognize the autonomy of another state, action should be taken. But the Assembly preferred immediate action. Cleombrotus was ordered to attack Thebes, unless she agreed to disband the Boeotian League.[1]

For Thebes the King's Peace of 371 was a repetition of the King's Peace of 386. To flout it was all the more dangerous because the Spartan Alliance might combine with the Athenian Alliance to enforce the disbanding of the Boeotian League. The danger of such a combination was averted for the moment by the precipitate decision of the Spartan Assembly, a decision based on the immediate tactical advantages of the situation. For Cleombrotus' army in Phocis was able to act before Jason could intervene or the Boeotian League could muster its full levy. Within three weeks of the signing of the peace Cleombrotus, having marched via Creusis on the Corinthian Gulf, reached the plain of Leuctra, some ten miles from Thebes, before he found his way barred by a Boeotian force. His own army of some 1,000 cavalry and 10,000 hoplites outnumbered the Boeotians, who mustered perhaps 600 cavalry and 6,000 hoplites.[2] After preparing camp in a strong natural position, Cleombrotus moved his army into the plain at midday, and deployed his men, invigorated by a dram of wine, in their normal order of battle. He himself, his staff, and his Spartans over 2,000 strong held the right wing, his allies held the centre and left wing, and his cavalry formed a screen in front of the whole line. In 377 the Thebans had relied on holding prepared positions and avoided a set battle, but on this occasion Epaminondas persuaded his fellow Boeotarchs to commit their well-trained army to the attack. Having permitted the faint-hearted Thespian troops to withdraw, he placed his best troops, headed by the Sacred Band under the command of Pelopidas, on the

[1] X. *HG.* 6. 3. 19–6. 4. 3; D.S. 15. 50. 5; Plu. *Ages.* 27–28.
[2] See Appendix 6.

left wing in a mass formation fifty men deep and ordered his centre and right wing to delay their advance, so that the line would be *en échelon* at the time of onset.

The battle opened when the Boeotian cavalry, far superior in quality, drove their opponents back in confusion on to the Spartan line. Prompt behind them came the massive spearhead of the Theban infantry, led at the double by Pelopidas against Cleombrotus and his staff, who were caught in the act of extending their line towards their right front to outflank the enemy. Cleombrotus himself fell mortally wounded, but in the first sway of the hand-to-hand fighting his body was recovered by his officers; then they too and the whole of the Spartan right wing were overwhelmed by the weight of hoplites under Epaminondas' own command. When half the Spartans, including 400 Spartiates, had fallen, the remainder broke and fled to the camp, accompanied by the allied contingents of the centre and left wing, who had not engaged at all. The surviving Spartiates wished to renew the battle rather than admit defeat. But their allies were disaffected, and they therefore concluded a truce to take up the dead. The Boeotians set up a trophy on the field of battle. Thus Epaminondas proved his theory that, if the head of the serpent is severed, its body is useless, and the Boeotians showed themselves under his leadership to be the finest hoplites in Greece.[1]

The news of the disaster reached Sparta during the last day of the Festival of the Gymnopaediae. The Ephors ordered the festival to proceed as usual, informed the next of kin of their bereavement, and forbade any mourning. On the following day every available man up to the age of sixty was called to the colours, and Archidamus, the son of Agesilaus, who was ill, marched north, collecting the contingents of the Allies—Tegea, Mantinea, Corinth, Sicyon, Achaea, and others. At Aegosthena he met the survivors of the battle of Leuctra. Meanwhile a garlanded envoy from Thebes had carried the news of the victory to the Athenian Council and asked for the assistance of Athens. The Councillors did not conceal their chagrin, and the Theban envoy withdrew, his request unanswered. Thebes had applied also to her ally Jason. He marched at speed through the hostile territory of Phocis with his cavalry and his mercenaries but refused to join the Boeotians in an attack on the camp of the Spartan army at Leuctra. He had no wish to strengthen Boeotia unduly. Instead he negotiated an armistice to cover the withdrawal of the Spartan army, which made a forced march by night to Creusis and thence along the coast road to Aegosthena. Faced by the demoralized survivors of the battle and appalled by the heavy loss in Spartiates, Archidamus turned back to Corinth and disbanded his army. The Boeotian League had at last asserted its independence triumphantly.[2]

During the winter of 371–370 the Greek states began to adjust themselves

---

[1] X. *HG*. 6. 4. 4–15; D.S. 15. 55–56 (incorrect for the campaign but of value for the battle); Plu. *Pel.* 20–23; Polyaen. 2. 3. 2, 3 and 15; Paus. 9. 13. 3–12; *GHI* 130.

[2] X. *HG*. 6. 4. 16–26; Plu. *Ages.* 29.

to the changed situation. Athens, hoping to make political capital out of Sparta's defeat, summoned a conference of all states which wished to maintain the King's Peace of 371. She proposed to make the Athenian Alliance the chief guarantor of the Peace and invited all states participating in the peace to contract a defensive alliance with the Athenian Alliance and follow the decisions of the Athenian Alliance in the event of war. By this proposal Athens did not invite the mainland states to enter the Athenian Alliance as members. She intended rather, with the support of Persia, to make the Athenian Alliance the moderator of a general peace among the Greek states. At the best Athens might thereby attract the members of the Spartan Alliance to herself and keep Thebes out of the diplomatic field, and at the worst she might find she was involving the Athenian Alliance in the defence of states which had few interests in common with the maritime states of the Aegean. In the event all states in the Peloponnese, except Sparta and Elis, and perhaps some states outside the Peloponnese accepted the invitation and formed a defensive alliance with the Athenian Alliance, which itself comprised some seventy states. This was a great triumph, but it was only a diplomatic triumph at a time when armed action was to be decisive.[1]

Sparta now tasted the bitterness of her defeat. In Tegea and Mantinea, and probably in Corinth, Megara, Sicyon, Phlius, and Phigalia, the democrats rose in revolt against the pro-Spartan oligarchs. Some of the risings failed, but in spring 370 Mantinea became one city again under democratic government and helped the democrats of Tegea to seize power and form an Arcadian League, which soon entered into alliance with Elis and Argos. Thus the Peloponnese split into two factions. At Sparta the people turned to the aging Agesilaus for guidance and authorized him to reform their constitution. Agesilaus, however, made no reforms. For the survivors of Leuctra he suspended the law whereby the Spartiate survivors of a military defeat were reduced to the rank of Inferiors, but he took no steps to increase the number of Spartiates for the future. His courageous and unimaginative conservatism condemned Sparta to fight for her existence with a force of some 800 Spartiates and their dependants.[2]

North of the Isthmus the Boeotian League and Jason of Thessaly were uneasy allies. For, after settling affairs at Leuctra, Jason attacked a city in Phocis, paraded his strength in Locris, and captured the Spartan colony, Heraclea, whose territory he gave to the Malians and Oetaeans. Jason's power now extended from Macedonia and Epirus, where Amyntas and Alcetas were perforce his allies, to the gate of Greece at Thermopylae. He proclaimed his intention of presiding over the Pythian Games at Delphi in the summer of 370, and he ordered the mobilizing of his armed forces, to ensure that his presidency would be unopposed. His picked mer-

---

[1] X. *HG*. 6. 5. 1–3; D.S. 15. 30. 2; Aeschin. 2. 70.

[2] X. *HG*. 6. 5. 3–9; 7. 2. 2–3; D.S. 15. 40 (antedated by D.S.), 58; Plu. *Ages*. 30; *Agis* 5 probably refers to a later time.

cenaries alone numbered 6,000, his Thessalian cavalry exceeded 3,000, and
he could raise large numbers of infantry from Thessaly and from his allies.
But in 370 the tyrant was assassinated, and the power of his united Thessaly
soon collapsed in the incompetent hands of his successors. Jason had the
same unscrupulous ability and restless ambition as Dionysius I. If he had
lived and succeeded, he, too, might have posed as a liberator of Greece; for he
talked of attacking Persia. As it was, he set an example for ambitious in-
dividualists in his own rise to power, his use of mercenaries, and his plans to
exploit the authority of Delphi for secular purposes.[1]

The Boeotian League consolidated its success before Jason died. On the
advice of Epaminondas Thebes did not destroy Orchomenus but granted it
membership of the Boeotian League, and alliances were concluded with
Phocis, Ozolian Locris, and Aetolia. After Jason's death Opuntian Locris,
Malis, Heraclea, Euboea, and Acarnania joined the Boeotian Coalition, of
which the Boeotian League was the head. With the exception of Athens the
vigorous, if backward, states of central Greece stood solid behind Thebes,
when an invitation reached her late in 370 to invade the Peloponnese.[2]

The Peloponnese was a scene of violent turmoil throughout the year 370.
Argos weakened herself by an internal revolution, in which a democratic mob
bludgeoned 1,200 opponents to death, and then joined Elis in supporting the
Arcadian League against Sparta. The League itself was formed by exiling the
leaders of the other faction at Tegea, and they invoked Sparta, which sent out
Agesilaus with an army. At the same time the League applied force to two
recalcitrant Arcadian cities, Orchomenus and Heraea, which obtained some
help from Phlius and Corinth. In this fighting, where there were so many
blatant breaches of 'autonomy', Athens and her Allies did not intervene to
honour the defensive alliance made in the winter of 371–370, although the
Arcadian group of allies asked her to do so. The Arcadians therefore invited
the Boeotians to assist them against Sparta, and an alliance between the two
Leagues was concluded for the purpose.[3]

The Peloponnesian winter was not severe for the Boeotians and their
allies, and contrary to all precedent they entered the Peloponnese in midwinter 370–369. At the request of Arcadia, Argos, and Elis they did not depart
after reducing Orchomenus and Heraea but marched southwards, where an
Arcadian contingent captured a pass leading into Laconia. The great army,
headed by Epaminondas and Pelopidas as Boeotarchs and comprising some
40,000 hoplites and almost as many skirmishers and marauders, descended
into the vale of Lacedaemon and followed the left bank of the swollen
Eurotas, until they gazed at Sparta across the river. The town was unwalled

[1] X. *HG.* 6. 4. 20–32 (cf. 6. 1. 19); D.S. 15. 57. 2; 60; X. *HG.* 6. 1. 5, 12; Isoc. 5. 119;
8. 118.
[2] D.S. 15. 57. 1; X. *Ages.* 2. 24; *HG.* 6. 5. 23. For the chronology here see Appendix
7.
[3] D.S. 15. 57. 3–59; 62. 1–3; X. *HG.* 6. 5. 6–22; *Ages.* 2. 23; D. 16. 12.

and the Spartiates a mere 800 or so in number, but Agesilaus liberated and armed 6,000 Helots to aid the defence. When the columns of smoke rose from the burning villages, the Spartans, like the Athenians in 431, wished to attack, but Agesilaus held them back.

Epaminondas then led his army south to cross the Eurotas at Amyclae and probed the southern defences of the town in an unsuccessful cavalry action. Thereafter he withdrew south, ravaging and looting as far as Gytheum, the Spartan naval base, which he failed to capture by assault. The invasion lasted some three months, during which help reached Sparta from Corinth, Phlius, Sicyon, Epidaurus, Troezen, Hermione, Halieis, and Pellene in Achaea, and the invading army dwindled as the Peloponnesians absconded, laden with their loot. Epaminondas departed in April 369, easily eluding the army of Sparta's new ally, Athens, which with the Corinthians tried to hold the Isthmus.[1] In early summer 368 Epaminondas returned with an army of 600 cavalry and 7,000 infantry. By a surprise attack before dawn his Thebans carried the western end of the Isthmus defences, now held by a force of some 20,000 men from Sparta, Athens, Corinth, and Pellene, and joined their allies in the Peloponnese. There they forced Sicyon and Pellene to enter the Boeotian Coalition, and then ravaged the territories of Epidaurus and Corinth before departing through the Isthmus.[2]

During these two campaigns Epaminondas completed the downfall of Sparta as a great power. Defeat at Leuctra had shattered the hitherto invincible reputation of the Spartan hoplites in a set battle, but Epaminondas now broke the economic basis of the Spartan state by liberating Messenia and building a strongly fortified capital at Messene. The invasion of Laconia also enabled many of the Helots and Perioeci to escape, but the ravaging tactics of his Peloponnesian allies made liberation for the rest less palatable than their previous condition. In addition his invasions enabled the Arcadian League to consolidate its power and to build in 368 a federal centre in south Arcadia at Megalopolis, a strongly fortified city at the head of the Alpheus. Throughout the rest of her history Sparta was hemmed in by Messene, Megalopolis, Tegea, and Argos, and the Alliance she had led for two centuries was broken for ever.[3]

Enlightened imperialism has many merits. Spartan imperialism in the fourth century had none, and Isocrates was right in saying that the traditional claim of Sparta to exercise leadership in Greece rang false in the ears of his contemporaries. If she produced a *Pax Peloponnesiaca*, it was a peace brought about not by contentment but by repression, treachery, and brutality. For she banned from her domain those progressive features of democracy and federalism which might have brought prosperity and strength to the Greek states.

---

[1] X. *HG*. 6. 5. 23–32; 49–52; 7. 2. 2; D.S. 15. 62. 4–65; X. *Ages*. 2. 24; Plu. *Ages*. 31–32; *Pel*. 24–25; Polyaen. 2. 1. 14, 15, 27, and 29.

[2] X. *HG*. 7. 1. 15–22; D.S. 15. 68–69.

[3] D.S. 15. 66. 1–2; 72. 4; Plu. *Pel*. 24; *Ages*. 34; Paus. 4. 26–27; 8. 27. 1–8; *GC* 166.

She prostituted the principles of autonomy and independence by promoting party strife and maintaining minorities, whose methods were more akin to despotism than government. Her statesmen and officers employed treachery in peace and in war. Her governors were rapacious, cruel, and perfidious, and their power in the subject-states rested on political desperadoes and mercenary soldiers. When her empire fell, it left a legacy of hatred and dissension which could only be assuaged by liberal and moderate statesmanship.[1]

[1] X. *HG.* 6. 3. 7–9; Isoc. 4. 18; 110–17; 126–8.

CHAPTER 3

The Collapse of the Leading Powers

§ 1. *Boeotia at the height of her power*

WITH the collapse of Sparta the declared object of the Athenian Alliance was achieved. If Athens had been content to maintain the freedom of the seas and leave the land powers of the Peloponnese to work out their own salvation, she would have won the support of the maritime states in the Aegean Sea and brought prosperity to herself and to them. For the Charter of the Alliance was in accord with the aspirations of the smaller states, and its initial success was as much due to this fact as to the unpopularity of Sparta. But Athens aspired to more than the control of the Aegean Sea. Jealousy and fear of her immediate neighbour, Thebes, certainly sharpened her ambition to control the Greek world, but the ambition had already been revealed by her political intervention in Zacynthos in 374 and by her attempt in 371 to bring all the Greek states into her web of alliances. When Laconia was invaded, Athens allied with Sparta, not so much from generosity towards her fallen rival as from the desire to strengthen her own power. At the same time she espoused the friends of Sparta—Dionysius the tyrant, Persia, Phlius, Epidaurus—and the pro-Spartan oligarchs of Corinth, and it was difficult for her to represent these alliances as being consonant with her claim to be fighting 'for the freedom of the Greeks'.

The troops of Athens, Sparta, and their allies, including 2,000 Iberian and Celtic mercenaries sent by Dionysius, were no match for the army of Epaminondas in 368. After his departure from the Peloponnese the Arcadian League, led by Lycomedes, proposed to dominate the Peloponnese on its own account, and Athens found herself fighting against Arcadia rather than against Boeotia. In winter 368 an agent of Persia, Philiscus, summoned the chief belligerents to Delphi and tried to negotiate a general peace. This Athens favoured (indeed she made Philiscus an Athenian citizen), but her ally, Sparta, refused to recognize the independence of Messenia. Philiscus then engaged a contingent of 2,000 mercenaries to help Sparta, and Dionysius sent a second force of mercenaries in spring 367. These troops were of no service to Athens but enabled Sparta to win the 'Tearless Battle' against the Arcadians, in which Sparta suffered no casualties and her victory was greeted with tears of joy. Thus Athens' entanglement in Peloponnesian affairs brought her no advantage, and her participation simply imposed a strain on the loyalty and credulity of her Alliance.[1]

[1] X. *HG.* 7. 1. 23–32; D. 23. 141; D.S. 15. 70. 1–2; 72. 3; Plu. *Ages.* 33; *GHI* 131, l. 41.

Boeotia rather than Athens was hailed as the liberator by the states of the mainland. Her democracy, too, was more like theirs; for democracy, like a chameleon, takes its colour from its background, which in the mainland states was an agricultural rather than a mercantile economy. But, most important of all, Boeotia stood for a new and potent form of political organization, a close-knit federal system with a democratic basis. Under the leadership and inspiration of Epaminondas the Boeotian League was stamped with the hall-mark of success, and it had shown moderation by granting equal member-ship to Orchomenus.

The example of the Boeotian League, and perhaps the prompting of Epaminondas, inspired the efficient organization of the Aetolian League (*to koinon ton Aitolon*), of which the salient features were a sovereign democratic Assembly, an administrative Council, and a cantonal system for electoral and military purposes. At this time, too, a League of the Western Locrians was probably formed. Farther west, the Acarnanian League (*to koinon ton Akarnanon*), having existed since the fifth century as a loose tribal federation, had developed a closer organization in resisting the attacks of Agesilaus. After the victory at Leuctra the Acarnanian League transferred its allegiance from Athens to Boeotia, and joined in the invasion of the Peloponnese. There the Arcadian League was consolidated under the guidance of Epaminondas. Its federal Assembly (*koine synodos*), which was called 'The Ten Thousand', had sovereign powers. The Council was administrative, and met at Tegea and perhaps also at Mantinea and Megalopolis by turns. The magistrates, for instance the *damiorgoi*, were elected on a cantonal basis. The member-states adopted democratic constitutions, and the Arcadian League was democratic in colouring, even if the name of its federal Assembly indicates some limitation of democratic rights in accordance with a property-qualification.[1]

During the years after the battle of Leuctra Boeotia formed a Coalition of states on the basis of a defensive alliance—Aetolia, Acarnania, Phocis, East and West Locris, Euboea, Heraclea, Malis, and for a time Arcadia. The Coalition probably had its administrative centre at Delphi. The details of its organization are unknown, but the allied delegates were competent to pass decrees of banishment from allied territories. When the Coalition decided to go to war, the hegemony or executive command was entrusted to Boeotia and the allied contingents were bound to obey the Boeotarchs in the field. Farther north Jason of Thessaly was nominally an ally of Boeotia, and after his death Thessalian cavalry and peltasts served under Epaminondas in the first invasion of the Peloponnese. In 368, when Epaminondas returned to the Peloponnese, Pelopidas went north with an army. In answer to an appeal from the Thessalian cities he liberated Larisa from the troops of Alexander of Macedon, the son and successor of Amyntas, and he restrained Alexander of Pherae, who had murdered Jason's brother, Polyphron. He followed up his

[1] D.S. 15. 57. 1; *GHI* 137; Lerat, *Les Locriens de l'ouest* i. 133 (inscription); Th. 2. 81. 1; 3. 105. 1; X. *HG*. 4. 6. 4; Plu. *Pel*. 24; X. *HG*. 6. 5. 6–9; D.S. 15. 59; *GHI* 132; *GC* 165.

success by arbitrating between Alexander of Macedon and a pretender, Ptolemy, and concluded an alliance with the former.

It was probably at this time that Pelopidas organized the Thessalian League (*to koinon ton Thessalon*) on the Boeotian model with a general Assembly, a cantonal division into four tetrarchies, and a number of federal magistrates, including the delegates (*hieromnemones*) who represented Thessaly on the Amphictyonic Council. The League had a President (*archon*) with wide powers, inherited from the long tradition of the Ruler of Thessaly (*tagos*). The Thessalian League, which soon disposed of strong forces of cavalry and infantry, became a member of the Boeotian Coalition. But Alexander of Pherae probably took no part in either.[1]

In 367 Boeotia was again engaged in the north. There Alexander of Macedon was murdered by Ptolemy, and Alexander of Pherae attacked the Thessalian League. This time Pelopidas and Ismenias were sent as envoys, but Pelopidas found that the Athenian commander in the north Aegean, Iphicrates, had intervened to support Ptolemy. Pelopidas won over Ptolemy, who entered into an offensive and defensive alliance with Boeotia and sent hostages to Thebes, including Philip, son of Amyntas. But Alexander of Pherae treacherously seized Pelopidas and Ismenias during a truce, imprisoned them, and obtained an alliance with Athens. Boeotia replied at once by sending an army of 600 cavalry and 8,000 infantry, which arrived before a force of 1,000 infantry and thirty ships, sent by Athens, reached Alexander. In the Thessalian plains the Boeotians failed to force a battle. They were harassed by the cavalry of Alexander, until Epaminondas, who was serving in the ranks, was raised to the command and extricated them. Later in 367 Epaminondas returned to the attack, forced Alexander to release Pelopidas and Ismenias, but did not reduce him to impotence.[2]

The steady growth of Boeotian power prompted Sparta and Athens to send envoys to Persia in 367 in the hope of winning Persia's active support. Sparta had spent the wages provided by Philiscus and saw no hope of defeating Arcadia without further subsidies. Athens was alarmed, not only by her failure to make headway against Boeotia in the Peloponnese and in the north, but also by the growing discontent among the members of the Athenian Alliance. Her attempts to seize Amphipolis were reminiscent of the imperialism shown by Athens in the fifth century, and the Chalcidian League had seceded from the Athenian Alliance. She had added to the list of her allies on the mainland Alexander of Pherae, a dastardly and blood-thirsty tyrant, and even set up a statute of him as a benefactor; and in 367 she allied herself with 'Dionysius and his descendants for all time', tying her faith to the tyrannical rulers of Syracuse. To the states of the Aegean islands and coasts these alliances, following on those with Sparta and Sparta's allies, could only give cause

[1] X. *HG.* 7. 1. 22; 7. 5. 4; 7. 1. 39; Plu. *Pel.* 26; X. *HG.* 6. 4. 33–34; 7. 3. 11; D.S. 15. 67. 3–4; *GHI* 147; *IG* ii². 175.

[2] D.S. 15. 71; 75. 2; Plu. *Pel.* 27–29; Aeschin. 2. 27–29; Paus. 9. 15. 1–2.

for alarm; their object was not to safeguard autonomy and liberty, but to increase the power of Athens in a struggle for supremacy. If her Allies in the Aegean were restless, Athens had need of Persia's support to keep them in control.

The Spartan envoys were closely followed by those of Athens, Boeotia, Arcadia, Elis, and Argos. In a symposium at Susa the envoys of the six states paid their compliments to the Great King, who did not disguise his preference for Pelopidas, the envoy of Boeotia. The Great King then had his orders read out to the company: peace on the basis of autonomy and liberty was to be concluded, and in particular Sparta was to recognize the independence of Messene, and Athens that of Amphipolis; furthermore, Athens was to beach her fleet. The initiative of Sparta had indeed acted like a boomerang. Her envoy, Antalcidas, committed suicide and Timagoras, an Athenian envoy, was executed on his return. The peace came to be called the Peace of Pelopidas.[1]

In spring 366 Thebes invited the Greek states to a conference, at which the Great King's emissary read out his rescript. The enemies of Thebes rejected the terms, and they were joined by Lycomedes of Arcadia. Sparta sent off Agesilaus to earn subsidies in the service of Ariobarzanes, a satrap who raised the standard of revolt in Asia Minor. Athens, alarmed by the order to beach her fleet, sent mercenaries into Corinthia to oppose the Boeotians. In early summer 366 her irritation was heightened by the loss of Oropus, a town on the Boeotian frontier which she had seized in 374; now the exiles from Oropus captured the town and delivered it to Thebes, and none of Athens' allies were willing to help her regain it. The failure at Susa, the lack of success in the Peloponnese, and the loss of Oropus caused an attack on Callistratus and Chabrias, who were prosecuted for treason but acquitted; nevertheless, this attack presaged a change in policy. In summer 366 she entered into a defensive alliance with Arcadia; but, to have the best of both worlds before this alliance was made public, the Athenian Assembly instructed Chares to occupy Corinth, at present her ally, and install a democratic government. The plot, however, was bungled. Corinth, Phlius, and Epidaurus thereupon made peace with Boeotia (summer 366). Sparta, aided only by Dionysius II of Syracuse, fought on against Arcadia, the new ally of Athens.[2]

The strain of waging war continuously since 378 had its effect also at Athens. The Athenian people grew distrustful of their leaders and punished them for policies which the Assembly itself had adopted, and the well-to-do classes resented the continued exactions (*eisphorai*), which *inter alia* were required to help Sparta or Arcadia. The ultimatum issued by the Great King caused further alarm, because the discontent among the Aegean members of the Athenian Alliance might now be exploited by Persia and Thebes.

In 366 Athens reinstated Timotheus. She gave him command of a force of

---

[1] X. *HG.* 7. 1. 33–40; Plu. *Pel.* 30–31; D.S. 15. 76. 3; D. 19. 137; 23. 150; *GHI* 136.
[2] Isoc. 14. 20 and 37 (Oropus); X. *HG.* 7. 4. 1; D.S. 15. 76. 1; Plu. *Dem.* 5; Arist. *Rhet.* 1, p. 1364[a]19; X. *HG.* 7. 4. 2–12 (Arcadia and Corinth), cf. D.S. 14. 92. 2.

thirty ships and 8,000 mercenary peltasts, and ordered him to support Ariobarzanes, the satrap in revolt, but not to rupture relations with the Great
King. Athens may have received money from Ariobarzanes, on whom she
conferred her citizenship, but Timotheus limited his action to attacking
Samos, which was held by a Persian protégé, Cyprothemis. After a blockade
of ten months, during which Timotheus supported his troops by looting,
Samos fell and its best land was occupied by cleruchs. Timotheus then captured Sestus and Crithote in the Chersonese, to which cleruchs were sent out
from Athens. In 364, with the aid of Perdiccas, king of Macedon, he captured Potidaea, Torone, and other cities in Chalcidice and, at Perdiccas' expense, Pydna and Methone on the coast of Macedonia. Cleruchs were sent
out to Potidaea, probably in 364. For these operations Timotheus drew the
'contributions' (*syntaxeis*) of the Allies in the Thracian area, but his actions
were entirely contrary to the spirit of the Charter. In promising to liberate
the Greek states and to respect the autonomy of her Allies, Athens had undertaken a clear and solemn obligation. It was a mere quibble to argue that, because Samos, Potidaea, Sestus, and Crithote were not already members of the
Athenian Alliance, Athens was entitled to subjugate them and seize their land
for her own citizens to occupy as cleruchs. The imperialistic policy of Athens
was now apparent to the Greek world, and her methods in diplomacy and in
war were comparable to those of pirates.[1]

Boeotia, too, had been at war since 378. As she fought her campaigns with
citizen troops and maintained only a small navy, she was under less financial
stress than Athens, but the citizens themselves were in danger of becoming
exhausted. The strain was revealed in the changeable attitude of the Boeotian
Assembly towards their leaders. In 369 Epaminondas and Pelopidas were impeached but acquitted on the charge of having exceeded their year of office
as Boeotarchs during the first invasion of the Peloponnese, and after the
second invasion Epaminondas was not elected Boeotarch for 367. The probable reason for their dissatisfaction was that Epaminondas pursued a liberal
policy; for he did not acquire territory or impose garrisons, he did not
practise political intervention at Sicyon but left the oligarchs in power, and
he pursued a policy of reconciliation with Orchomenus and with the Boeotian
émigrés who fell into his hands. Nevertheless, when the Greek states refused
to accept the terms of the Peace sponsored by Boeotia and Persia, the Boeotian Assembly accepted the policy advocated by Epaminondas, namely to enforce the terms by war on land and sea.

While preparations for building a fleet were put in train, Epaminondas as
Boeotarch invaded the Peloponnese early in 366. By a concerted operation
with Argos he broke through the defences south of the Isthmus, which were
held by Spartan and Athenian forces, and joined his Peloponnesian allies,
Argos, Arcadia, Messene, Sicyon, and Elis. He now marched into Achaea

---

[1] D. 16. 2; X. *Vect.* 3. 7; Isoc. 15. 108–12; D. 2. 14; 15. 9; Dein. 1. 14; Polyaen. 3. 10. 9,
14. Arist. *Rhet.* 2, p. 1384ᵇ32; [Arist.] *Oec.* 1350ᵃ23; 1351ᵃ18.

and prevailed on the Achaean cities to join the Boeotian Coalition. This gave Boeotia control of both shores of the Gulf of Corinth, and facilitated her entry by sea into the Peloponnese.[1]

The Achaeans at this time had a well-established federal organization. Early in the century they had used their federal system to incorporate new territory at Calydon in Aetolia, making the Calydonians Achaean citizens. Subsequently they had acquired Naupactus from Aetolia and Dyme from Elis. At this time there were Achaean garrisons in these three cities. Epaminondas now restored these cities to his allies, Aetolia and Elis. The Achaean League had an oligarchic basis, and in the past the oligarchs in the cities and the League itself had been faithful to Sparta. In 366 Epaminondas did not seek to change the constitutional basis of the League; he issued orders that the oligarchs were not to be exiled and that no revolutionary change of city-constitutions should be made. This step was a wise one; for it emphasized a community of interest in upholding the federal principle and not the partisan spirit of democracy as opposed to oligarchy. But the allies of Boeotia, especially Arcadia, and the opponents of Epaminondas attacked his settlement of affairs in Achaea, arguing that the oligarchs would revert to a pro-Spartan policy. They gained their point at Thebes, and Epaminondas' settlement was reversed. Boeotian governors with garrisons were sent to occupy the Achaean cities, democratic governments were installed, and oligarchic leaders were exiled. But the Achaeans had no stomach for an imposed democracy. The exiles returned, and the Achaean League rescinded the alliance with Boeotia and renewed its alliance with Sparta. Arcadia now found herself between two fires.[2]

At Sicyon, too, the arrangements which Epaminondas had made were overthrown with the connivance of his allies, Arcadia and Argos. There Epaminondas had left the oligarchs in power, but an ambitious oligarch, Euphron, having ensured the presence of Arcadian and Argive troops, proclaimed a democracy in Sicyon. He then had himself elected as one of the new generals and his son appointed as commander of the mercenaries in the city. By seizing temple treasures and private property he was able to engage more mercenaries, kill or banish his fellow-generals, and establish himself as tyrant. This situation was accepted by Boeotia as a *fait accompli*, but the Boeotian League placed an officer and a garrison in Sicyon.

At first Euphron co-operated with the Boeotian officer in an abortive attack on Phlius, but the Arcadians distrusted him and tried to eject him from Sicyon. However, Euphron occupied the harbour of Sicyon with his mercenary troops and joined the Spartan group of allies. Athens supplied him with some more mercenaries, and he won the town but not the acropolis, which was still held by the Boeotian garrison. Euphron then decided on the bold policy of proceeding to Thebes and trying to re-enter the Boeotian Coali-

---

[1] X. *HG.* 7. 1. 41–44; D.S. 15. 57; Paus. 9. 15. 2 and 4.
[2] X. *HG.* 4. 6. 1; 7. 1. 42–43; D.S. 15. 49. 2–3; 15. 75. 2.

tion, but, while he was speaking to the Council of the Boeotian League on the Cadmea, he was assassinated by some political opponents who had followed in his tracks. The Council pardoned the assassins, and the Boeotians recaptured the harbour at Sicyon. But the methods which the Boeotians had employed against the advice of Epaminondas in Achaea and at Sicyon brought them into discredit. They resembled those practised by Sparta and Athens.[1]

In 365 neither Athens nor Boeotia sent troops to the Peloponnese, but in 364 Boeotia responded to an appeal from the Thessalians for help against Alexander of Pherae, the ally of Athens. Pelopidas was about to march with some 7,000 citizen troops when an eclipse of the sun occurred on 13 July; as this was taken to be an adverse omen, the citizen force was withheld, but Pelopidas set off with 300 volunteer cavalrymen and joined the army of the Thessalians, which was strong in cavalry. The decisive battle was fought at Cynoscephalae. Alexander posted his much superior force of heavy infantry on rising ground in the foothills. Pelopidas sent his infantry forward to attack, and during their advance he led a cavalry charge, which defeated the enemy cavalry in the plain. Pelopidas then wheeled the victorious cavalry and prepared to attack the enemy infantry in flank and rear. But his own infantry were now losing ground, and there was a danger that Alexander's infantry would re-form to face the cavalry onslaught. Pelopidas therefore rallied his infantry and led them against the right wing, where Alexander stood in command of his picked mercenaries. Outstripping his men, Pelopidas engaged the enemy alone. He fell mortally wounded in the moment of victory, as his cavalry scattered the enemy line and killed 3,000 men during the long pursuit.

In Pelopidas Boeotia lost her most popular leader—an able diplomat, a devoted supporter of Epaminondas, a brilliant general who co-ordinated his cavalry and his infantry, a superb commander of the Sacred Band or of the Thessalian cavalry. At his death the Thessalian troopers cut the manes of their horses in mourning for the liberator, and the Thessalian League set up a statue of him at Delphi. His death was avenged in autumn 364, when a Boeotian army of 700 cavalry and 7,000 infantry confined Alexander to Pherae and compelled him to submit to the orders of the Boeotian League and supply troops at its command. Thebes now dominated central Greece. Her position was acknowledged by Delphi, which in 363/362 granted her the right of precedence in consulting the oracle.[2]

In summer 363 Epaminondas launched the naval offensive against Athens. The small fleet of Boeotia had been increased by the addition of 100 new triremes, built with timber supplied probably from Macedonia and Thessaly. Negotiations had been made in advance with Byzantium, Chios, and Rhodes, the strongest naval powers among Athens' Allies. Epaminondas, therefore, set sail for the Bosporus, a vital point on the corn-route from the Black Sea to Athens. The Athenian fleet avoided any engagement, and Epaminondas'

[1] X. *HG.* 7. 1. 44–46; 7. 2. 11–15; 7. 3. 1–12; D.S. 15. 70. 3.
[2] Plu. *Pel.* 31–35; D.S. 15. 80–81; Nep. *Pel.* 5; *Rev. Arch.* 1939, p. 126; *SIG* 3. 176.

force of 100 triremes reached Byzantium. It is probable that Chalcedon, and perhaps other states in the Propontis and Hellespont, revolted from Athens at this time and joined Byzantium in attacking the corn-ships of Athens. Ceos, too, revolted and entered into close relations of isopolity with Histiaea in Euboea. Epaminondas returned unscathed, having shaken the confidence and the prestige of Athens.[1]

During his absence a plot was betrayed in which some Theban exiles and 300 leading men of Orchomenus planned to overthrow the democracy at Thebes. The Assembly of the Boeotian League decided to exact the full punishment for treachery, the terrible fate of *andrapodismos*: all males were killed, the women and children were enslaved, and the city was razed. On his return Epaminondas protested against the cruelty of his compatriots.[2]

Meanwhile the Peloponnese was in turmoil. In 365 Elis and Arcadia went to war for the possession of Triphylia. The oligarchic leaders of Elis obtained help from Achaea and Sparta, while Arcadia drew assistance from the democratic states, Messene, Argos, Thebes, and even Athens. In July 364 the armed forces of Arcadia, aided by Argos and Athens, occupied Olympia and enabled the Pisatans to conduct the Olympic Festival, despite the heroic efforts of the troops of Elis and Achaea, who fought their way into the sacred precincts. The Arcadian leaders celebrated their victory by appropriating some temple monies, in order to pay the 5,000 Eparitoi, who formed the regular army of the Arcadian League. This act of sacrilege split the Arcadian League into two camps, led by Tegea, to which many of the guilty leaders belonged, and by Mantinea, which denounced their action. The rank and file, too, regarded the matter of pay as a political counter; for the democrats demanded pay to ensure equal opportunity for themselves, and the oligarchs opposed it for that very reason. The dispute was aggravated by the fact that the leaders of Tegea as democratic federalists sympathized with Boeotia, and the leaders of Mantinea as oligarchic separatists sympathized with Sparta.

In 363 the General Assembly of the Arcadian League condemned the appropriation of the temple monies. It abolished pay for the Eparitoi, instructed Thebes not to send troops to Arcadia, unless invited, and negotiated an armistice with Elis as a preliminary to making peace. The Mantinean party was now in control of the Arcadian League. The oaths solemnizing the armistice were taken at once by the interested parties, including a Theban officer who commanded 300 Boeotian hoplites at Tegea. That evening with his connivance the Tegeate leaders arrested as many of their opponents as they could find, but the next day the Theban officer lost his nerve and liberated them. He withdrew to Thebes, pursued by complaints from Arcadia. Epaminondas replied that the Arcadian League had infringed its treaty with the Boeotian League by negotiating a separate peace with Elis, and he announced his intention of entering Arcadia in order to assert Boeotia's interests. His warning finally split the Arcadian League. Tegea, Megalopolis, and other cities

[1] D.S. 15. 78. 4–79; Isoc. 5. 53; *GHI* 141.   [2] D.S. 15. 79. 2; Paus. 9. 15. 3.

The Collapse of the Leading Powers

declared for Epaminondas. Mantinea and her supporters invoked the aid of Elis, Achaea, Athens, and Sparta. While the members of Mantinea's coalition were deciding that each state should hold the supreme command in its own territory, Epaminondas led his army, drawn from Boeotia, Locris, Euboea, Malis, Aeniania, and Thessaly, through the Isthmus into the Peloponnese, where his allies from Argos and Sicyon awaited him.[1]

First in the field in 362, Epaminondas kept the initiative throughout the campaign. While his enemies were still dispersed, he tried to strike at them individually. At Nemea he laid an ambush for the Athenians in case they came overland; but they went by sea. At Tegea, where he picked up his Arcadian and Messenian contingents, he dumped his supplies and treated the fortified city as a base for mobile warfare. He now lay between Mantinea and Sparta. Those of the enemy who were already at Mantinea held a strong defensive position. Therefore, when he learned that the main body of the Spartan army under Agesilaus' command was at Pellene on the way to Mantinea, he decided to strike at the open city of Sparta, now devoid of defenders. Marching by night some thirty-five miles over the mountains to the east of Pellene, his mobile column descended upon Sparta soon after dawn, only to find that Agesilaus, informed by a deserter, had managed to throw some troops into the city. Desperate street fighting ensued, before the main body of Agesilaus' army entered the city. Epaminondas disengaged his forces about noon. Anticipating that the Spartan vanguard at Mantinea and Sparta's allies there would now be marching via Asea and Pellene to the relief of Sparta, Epaminondas left his camp-fires burning that evening and marched back over the mountains by night to Tegea, whence he sent his cavalry forward to surprise Mantinea, now devoid of defenders. But chance, which is often decisive in war, was against him. A full brigade of Athenian cavalry, newly arrived from the north and still in the saddle, clashed with the Theban and Thessalian cavalry in the outskirts of the town and repelled their attack.[2]

The forces of Mantinea, Sparta, Athens, Elis, and Achaea now managed to assemble at Mantinea. Where the plain narrows to a width of one mile, their army of 20,000 hoplites formed a solid line, some twelve men deep, with its flanks protected by the steep hillsides (see Fig. 28). The Mantineans, with whom lay the chief command, held the right of the line and the Spartans came next to them; their forces covered the road to Mantinea, which afforded the best route for retreat. The left wing was held by the Athenians, behind whom there was a cup in the hills which offered no exit. The troops in the line could obtain welcome shade from the June sun by falling out and entering a wood in their rear. The cavalry, 2,000 strong, was placed on the wings, in advance of the infantry. The position was well chosen. It blocked Epaminondas' route northwards; it could not be turned from either flank, and in a

---

[1] X. *HG.* 7. 4. 12–5. 5; D.S. 15. 77–78. 3; 82. 1–4; Paus. 8. 8. 10.
[2] X. *HG.* 7. 5. 6–17; D.S. 15. 82. 5–84. 3; Plb. 9. 8; Plu. *Ages.* 34; *Moral.* 346c; Polyaen. 2. 3. 10.

frontal attack all along the line the superior numbers of Epaminondas' army, comprising 30,000 hoplites and 3,000 cavalry, could not be made effective.

Epaminondas planned an attack in mass on the enemy's strongest point, the right wing, and a holding movement on the enemy's left wing. If his attack succeeded, he would cut the road of escape to Mantinea, unhinge the

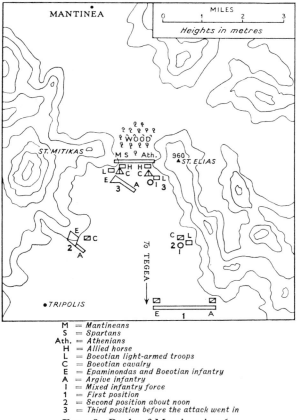

M	= *Mantineans*
S	= *Spartans*
Ath.	= *Athenians*
H	= *Allied horse*
L	= *Boeotian light-armed troops*
C	= *Boeotian cavalry*
E	= *Epaminondas and Boeotian infantry*
A	= *Argive infantry*
I	= *Mixed infantry force*
1	= *First position*
2	= *Second position about noon*
3	= *Third position before the attack went in*

Fig. 28. Battle of Mantinea in 362

enemy line, and drive it back into the cup behind the Athenian wing. In executing this plan the chief problem was to escape the enemy's observation, lest he should reinforce his right wing. During the morning Epaminondas manoeuvred in the plain, where his forces were fully visible, the helmets of the cavalry and the burnished shields of the infantry shining in the sun. The line, of which the left was held by the Thebans and the right by the Argives, formed column to the left and marched westwards to the foot-hills, where the leading companies grounded arms and the succeeding companies began to form up in depth behind them. It was now noon, and the clouds of dust raised by the cavalry as they manœuvred in front of the line hid the massing of Epaminondas' infantry. The Mantineans and the Spartans, expecting no attack that day, fell out into the shade to take their midday meal. Thereupon Epaminondas sounded the advance. His left wing, massed like the bow of a ship, bore down upon the enemy right as it hastily re-formed. His cavalry in a deep wedge, 1,600 strong and mingled with light-armed slingers and javelin-men, crashed into the enemy cavalry, which was drawn up in files of six with no admixture of infantry. Behind his cavalry marched the deep block of Boeotian hoplites, picked men marching shoulder to shoulder with Epaminondas at their head.

On his right the rest of the line was advancing *en échelon*, the right wing still far distant from the enemy. On the other side of the plain the battle had already started. For Epaminondas had sent forward a brigade of Theban cavalry, reinforced with light infantry, to engage the Athenian cavalry, and also a group of heavy and light infantry to seize some foot-hills and outflank any advance by the Athenian infantry. The Theban cavalry dispersed the Athenian cavalry, and then pinned down the Athenian infantry by harassing tactics. These operations discouraged the enemy from trying to reinforce his right wing. Indeed the Theban cavalry were so effective that a squadron of Elean cavalry was sent to reinforce the Athenians.

Meanwhile the massed attack overwhelmed first the cavalry and then the infantry of the Mantineans and the Spartans, who broke and fled. The leading Boeotian troops, cavalry and infantry mingled, raced through and swung right to seal off the rest of the enemy force. But behind them Epaminondas had fallen, mortally wounded. The news of his death paralysed the army, which halted in mid-battle. The enemy made good their escape. The leading Boeotian troops, who had advanced in ignorance of his death, reached the rear of the enemy's left wing, before they were cut to pieces by the retreating Athenians.

Thus passed the moment for a victory which could well have been decisive both in war and in politics. The coalition smashed, the individual states would have come to terms with the Boeotian victor, and it is doubtful if Athens could have retained her grip on her recalcitrant empire. The supremacy of Boeotia seemed to be assured beyond dispute in the minutes before Epaminondas died, and with him died the prospects of his country. After the battle peace was concluded, a peace which inaugurated a period of 'even greater confusion and indecision in the Greek world'. On this note Xenophon closed his history.[1]

The genius of Epaminondas in war was fully displayed in his last campaign. He so welded and led the forces of several states that they were capable of remarkable endurance and of precise co-ordination. In skill and speed of

[1] X. *HG.* 7. 5. 18–27; D.S. 15. 84. 4–87; Paus. 8. 11; Polyaen. 2. 3. 14; Arr. *Tact.* 11. 2.

manoeuvre, in tactical planning, and in concerted use of cavalry, infantry, and light-armed troops he far surpassed his predecessors. He was rivalled only by the great Macedonian commanders, who, like him, struck at the heart of the enemy in order to gain not merely the glory of martial prestige but the full effect of complete victory. In his lifetime he made the Boeotian plain 'the dancing-floor of Ares' and the Boeotian people the most formidable weapon of war on land and on sea. The revolution which Epaminondas and Pelopidas worked in the technique of war was observed by a young hostage at Thebes, Philip, soon to be king of Macedon.

The genius of Epaminondas in politics is debatable. Some have censured him for destroying the Spartan Alliance and for shaking the Athenian Alliance, but no statesman in the fourth century could have hoped to change the international situation without attacking those two organs of imperialism. If he had lived to reap the fruits of military victory, he would, like Philip of Macedon after the battle of Chaeronea, have shown his plan for the Greek states. The plan alone contained the clue to Epaminondas' greatness, but it died with him. We must judge him from his unfinished work. Part of his epitaph survives: 'by our counsels Sparta was shorn of her glory, sacred Messene received her children at last, Megalopolis was crowned with walls by Theban prowess, and all Greece was free and independent'; but it is a record rather of his achievements than of his spirit. True federalism in his view was liberal and magnanimous. Therefore he condemned the use of force against Orchomenus, he left the oligarchs in power in Achaea, and he spared those Boeotian exiles who fell into his hands. His policy was not to divide and rule in the manner of Sparta and Athens, but to combine and lead. The Boeotian League, the Arcadian League, the Aetolian League, the Western Locrian League, the Thessalian League, and the Achaean League were treated as self-governing entities. They might reject his leadership, but, when they accepted it, they were stronger than a congeries of divided subjects. Epaminondas' vision of a coalition of self-governing Leagues may have been Utopian, but it is probable that it inspired Timoleon in Sicily and Philip in Greece.

The character of Epaminondas attracted the attention of his biographers. An adherent of the Pythagorean philosophy, he was portrayed as devout, generous, unselfish. Nevertheless in the eyes of history he must be judged as a statesman. He may have had a finer vision of international politics than Pericles; but he lacked Pericles' power in a democracy to dominate the people. Above all he lacked the material; for the Boeotians might make fine soldiers, but they could not grasp the essence of his policy. Instead, they destroyed Orchomenus; they antagonized the Achaean League; and they showed a cruelty which sprang in part from a lack of education and culture. This deficiency Epaminondas may have realized when he called on the Thebans 'to bring the Propylaea of Athens to the forecourt of the Cadmea'. But it remained a deficiency which he could not make good. The decline of Boeotia after his death showed in the sphere of politics and war the truth of the dictum that he alone was of more value than the state in which he lived: *unum hominem pluris quam civitatem fuisse.*[1]

§ 2. *The decline of the Boeotian League and the Athenian Alliance*

AN immediate effect of the standstill at Mantinea was that, whereas nothing had been decided, many thousands of men had faced death and been saved. It was perhaps in revulsion from war that during the winter of 362 a League of City-States was formed. All mainland states, with the exception of Sparta, which refused to recognize the independence of Messenia, tied themselves by oath to observe a 'general peace and alliance', undertaking to settle disputes by negotiation and to defend one another against aggression. The aim of the League was to end war between member and member, to enable each member to attain prosperity and strength, and to speak with one voice for all members in foreign affairs. In order to implement its Charter, the League required a practical organization. The details unfortunately are not known to us. A congress of delegates, with one vote to each state, presumably met at fixed times to deliberate; at the outset its recommendations are not likely to have been binding on the member-states. A federal court was certainly formed, and a federal financial chest was probably instituted. For the first time since 481 the majority of Greek states thus voluntarily formed a federal system, however loose, in which they styled themselves 'the Greeks' and took common action. Then it was formed in war to repulse Persia. Now it was formed in peace to preserve peace.

Only one decision of the League has survived. It concerns an invitation which the satraps made, asking the Greeks to join in their revolt against Persia. The League replied by emphasizing its solidarity and announcing its neutrality, and it added a warning that it would show a common front to any aggressor, whether the Great King himself or another. This reply revealed the limitations of the League. It lacked the initiative and the energy to attack Persia, liberate the Greeks in Ionia, and gain new fields for expansion. Rather it tied itself to the *status quo*. Therefore it remained static, not dynamic, and its members were interested in keeping what they possessed, not in helping the dispossessed.[2]

Even so a League of States with such a Charter may be effective if its strongest members give a strong lead. On the other hand, if they concern themselves with forming coalitions within the League, the days of the League are numbered. In 361 Athens alone was in a position to lead the League against Persia. Yet in the course of that year she made two alliances, one with Arcadia, Achaea, Elis, and Phlius and the other with the Thessalian

---

[1] D.S. 15. 57. 1; 15. 79. 3–6; Paus. 9. 15. 3–6; X. *HG.* 7. 1. 42; Plu. *Tim.* 36; Aeschin. 2. 105; Str. 401 (Ephorus); Nep. *Epam.* 10. 4.

[2] D.S. 15. 89. 1–2; 94; Plu. *Ages.* 35. 3–4; Plb. 4. 33. 8; *GHI* 145 (sometimes dated earlier).

League, in which her aim was to extend her own power at the expense of Thebes. Boeotia thereupon sent her armed forces into Arcadia, in order to maintain her grip on Megalopolis. So far as practical politics were concerned, the League of City-States was still-born. Yet in the history of political ideas its very birth was of the greatest significance.[1]

The collapse of the League meant that the struggle between Boeotia and Athens, involving so many other states, was unresolved. Boeotia was too exhausted to undertake an offensive, except in the Peloponnese, where she kept control of Megalopolis, and she found herself losing ground in central Greece. In Thessaly Athens split the unity which Boeotia had imposed, and left her the less dependable portion, Alexander of Pherae. In Euboea, where the governments in the cities were pro-Theban, risings occurred early in 357. Both Thebes and Athens sent troops into the island, and after a month of fighting the Thebans were driven out and Athens obtained control of the whole island. This set-back heightened Thebes' fear lest Phocis, too, should leave the Boeotian Coalition in central Greece.

In 362 Phocis had refused to send a contingent to Mantinea on the ground that her alliance with Boeotia was defensive only, and in 357 Philomelus and other Phocians who were engaged in party-strife looked towards Athens. But in summer 357 Athens was crippled by the outbreak of the Social War (p. 515 below). Thebes seized the chance to regain Thessaly and dragoon Phocis by passing a resolution through the Amphictyonic Council, in April 356, which demanded the payment of fines previously laid on Sparta for seizing the Cadmea and on Philomelus and others for cultivating sacred land. This political use of a religious organ outraged the people of Phocis, who elected Philomelus sole general (*strategos autokrator*) to meet the emergency. In June 356, after consulting Archidamus, king of Sparta, he seized Delphi, expunged the resolution passed against him by the Amphictyonic Council, and claimed on the authority of Homer that Phocis was occupying 'rocky Pytho' by ancestral right.[2]

At first Boeotia treated Philomelus as an individual. But during the summer her troops made no headway against Philomelus, who defended Delphi with 5,000 mercenary soldiers, and in the winter he not only secured the approval of the Phocian assembly for his action but also obtained the alliance of Sparta, Athens, and probably Achaea. As soon as Athens admitted defeat in the Social War, Thebes treated Philomelus as the representative of the Phocian state. She was confident now of obtaining the support of the Thessalian peoples, who commanded a majority of the votes on the Amphictyonic Council. On her initiative in October 355 the Amphictyonic Council formally declared a 'Sacred War' against Phocis, that is to say a war on behalf of

---

[1] *GHI* 144; 147; D.S. 15. 94.

[2] D.S. 16. 7. 2; D. 8. 74; Aeschin. 3. 85; X. *HG.* 7. 5. 4; D.S. 16. 23–24; Arist. *Pol.* 1304ᵃ10; Paus. 10. 2. 1–3; Il. 2. 517. The chronology is disputed; for that given in the text see *JHS* 57. 44 = *StGH* 486 ff.

the god of Delphi in which no prisoners were to be taken and no mercy shown to the vanquished. Such conditions meant war to the death. Philomelus, therefore, appropriated the temple monies of Delphi, raised more than 10,000 soldiers, and defeated first the armies of Boeotia and Locris and then a Thessalian army of 6,000 men in spring 354. Thereafter Thessaly ceased to assist Boeotia. The Boeotian Coalition had completely collapsed, and the finest citizen army in Greece was being broken down in a war of attrition against mercenaries.[1]

During 362 the Athenian Assembly faced a choice which was of supreme importance to Athens and to the Greek states. Although Epaminondas did not repeat his naval offensive, he had revealed the deficiencies of Athens' sea power and the discontent of her Allies. Nevertheless, Athens did not moderate her policy. Early in 362 she forced Ceos to rejoin the Alliance on terms inferior to those of the Charter: a pro-Athenian democracy was imposed at Iulis, the anti-Athenian party was banished, Athenian commissioners were empowered to obtain arrears of contributions 'by any method they think fit', and lawsuits involving sums over 100 drachmae in which an Athenian was concerned were to be tried in the Athenian courts. These terms, following upon the planting of cleruchies, made it clear to her Allies that Athens intended to convert her Alliance into an empire; for they had not forgotten the methods employed in 454 and in 390. On the other hand, the saving of her army at Mantinea and the 'general peace and alliance' in summer 362 made possible a return to the policy which Athens had followed in 371, namely to rally the Greek states to unity round the Athenian Alliance. Even now, if Athens showed a liberal spirit, the magnetic qualities of her Alliance might revive (as recently as 364 Heraclea in Pontus had asked Athens for help), and she and her Allies might make the League of City-States a reality and lead it against Persia, as Isocrates had been advocating since the King's Peace of 386. The choice for Athens was still open. On her decision hinged the destiny of the Greek states.[2]

In 362–361 Callistratus, the liberal founder of the Athenian Alliance, was condemned to death *in absentia*; Aristophon, who later advocated reconciliation with Thebes, stood his trial and escaped conviction by two votes; the cleruchies at Samos and Potidaea were reinforced; and within the framework of the League of City-States an alliance was concluded between the Athenian Alliance and the anti-Theban group in the Peloponnese. The die was cast. The chief problem was finance. In 454/453, when Athens embarked on a similar policy, she had had the vast resources of the Delian treasury at her disposal. Now she was practically penniless. A captain in the fleet of 362/361 described his crew as deserting when they realized that 'his purse was empty, the Treasury was remiss, the Allies bankrupt, and the generals corrupt'. Under the circumstances the sovereign people resembled those gamblers whom

[1] D.S. 16. 25; 27–30; Aeschin. 3. 118; Isoc. 5. 54–55.
[2] *GHI* 142; Justin 16. 4.

Callistratus described: 'if they win a single success, they double the stakes and in most cases end in complete impoverishment.'[1]

During the years 362 to 358 circumstances favoured Athens. Boeotia was exhausted, and Athens gained allies against her in the Peloponnese and in the Thessalian League. Alexander of Pherae caused trouble by ravaging Tenos and Peparethos and by raiding the money-market in the Peiraeus. One general, Leosthenes, failed against him, anticipated conviction and fled, like Callistratus, to Macedonia. His successor, Chares, a democratic leader, 'avoided the enemy and maltreated the allies'. In 358 Alexander of Pherae was murdered by his wife. Meanwhile Chares sailed to Corcyra, where he intervened in party politics and supported the oligarchs in a massacre. This resulted in the secession of Corcyra and the collapse of Athens' influence in the west. A more vital area for her trade was the northern Aegean. There Timotheus failed to capture Amphipolis, which was supported by the Chalcidian League and by Perdiccas of Macedon; his successor, Callisthenes, failed too, and was executed by Athens; Timotheus tried again but was forced to burn his fleet on the river Strymon in 360 rather than let it fall into enemy hands. However, in 359 Perdiccas was killed and Macedonia was overrun by the Illyrians. Athens had already intrigued in the hinterland with Menelaus the Pelagonian, and she now supported Argaeus, a pretender to the Macedonian throne; when he was defeated, she came to terms with his victor, Philip, who removed the Macedonian garrison from Amphipolis in 358.[2]

More pressing still was the situation in the Bosporus and the Hellespont. In 362 Byzantium, Chalcedon, and Cyzicus raided Athenian corn-ships proceeding from the Black Sea, and in 360 Cotys, king of Thrace, captured Sestus and threatened Crithote and Elaeus, Athens' last footholds in the Chersonese. However, in 359 Cotys was murdered. Athens supported a pretender to the throne against Cotys' son, Cersebleptes,.and thereby caused the Thracian kingdom to be split between Berisades, Amadocus, and Cersebleptes, who then agreed to cede Sestus to Athens but dishonoured his agreement. By the end of 358 Athens, in alliance with Berisades and Amadocus, was again at war with Cersebleptes. During these years six Athenian generals failed in the Chersonese, and lack of funds drove them to commit acts of brigandage, such as the sack of Stryme, which were rivalled by those of the mercenary commanders, Iphicrates, Athenodorus, and Charidemus, whom the Thracian princes employed.

On the Asiatic side of the Hellespont Athens was on good terms with Ariobarzanes, the leader of the Satraps' Revolt, to whom she granted her citizenship. Soon after the failure of the Satraps' Revolt Artaxerxes Mnemon died (winter 359/358), and the satraps of Ionia and Hellespontine Phrygia, Orontes and Artabazus, rose against his successor, Artaxerxes Ochus. Farther south

---

[1] Hyperid. 3.1 col. 18; D. 18. 102; Schol. Aeschin. 1. 53; 1. 64; *GHI* 146; 144; [D.] 50. 15.
[2] *GHI* 147; D.S. 15. 95; Polyaen. 6. 2; Aen. Tact. 11. 13; D. 23. 150; Aeschin. 2. 29; Polyaen. 3. 10. 8; *GHI* 143; D.S. 16. 2. 6; 3. 3; 3. 5.

the satrap of Caria, Mausolus, remained loyal to Artaxerxes Ochus. His capital, Halicarnassus, was in close touch with Rhodes and other members of the Athenian Alliance.[1]

Thus during the years 362 to 358 Athens was fully extended in her efforts to prevent any strong power from arising on the coasts of the Aegean—in central Greece, in Macedonia, in Thrace, or in Asia Minor—and to gain control of strategic bases, such as Amphipolis and the Chersonese. The deaths of potentates—Alexander, Perdiccas, Cotys, Artaxerxes—seemed to help her in the gamble for power, but at the end of 358 she was still engaged, like Sisyphus, in pushing back a stone which was too heavy for her.

In 357 several crises occurred. Euboea, revolting from Boeotia, invited and received Athenian help; and the Euboean cities entered the Athenian Alliance, each city sending its own representative to the Congress of Allies. Fighting had just ended in Euboea in the spring when envoys arrived from Amphipolis and from Macedonia. The Amphipolitans offered to surrender their city to Athens, because they were being attacked by Philip. The envoys from Macedonia brought a letter from Philip in which he asked for Athens' friendship and proposed to give Amphipolis to Athens. Because Athens wished to use her troops in the Chersonese, she made a secret pact with Philip, whereby she would give him Pydna, her ally, in exchange for Amphipolis. Her mercenary force under the command of Chares proceeded direct from Euboea to the Chersonese, where an agreement was concluded with the mercenary commanders of the Thracian kings. Under this agreement the Greek cities in the Chersonese, except Cardia, were to join the Athenian Alliance but pay tribute to the Thracian kings as well as contributions to Athens. Next came the news in early summer that Chios, Rhodes, and Cos, with the support of Byzantium and Mausolus of Caria, had overthrown their democratic governments and revolted from the Athenian Alliance.

The Social War (357–355), as it was called, began with a rapid move by an Athenian fleet under the command of Chares. He intercepted help sent by the confederates to Chios and then blockaded Chios town by land and sea. In midsummer the Athenian fleet was decisively defeated, and Chabrias, acting as commander, was killed. Chares withdrew to the Hellespont, where he began operations against Byzantium, now joined by Perinthus and Selymbria. In autumn Philip captured Amphipolis, granted it independence, and permitted, or perhaps prompted, its government to banish some partisans of Athens. During the winter he captured and kept Pydna, made an alliance with the Chalcidian League against Athens, and displaced Athens as the ally of the Thessalian League, while Cersebleptes discarded his agreement to cede the Chersonese.[2]

[1] [D.] 50. 6; D. 23. 158 f.; [D.] 50. 21; D. 23. 179 f.

[2] *GHI* 153; 154; Aeschin. 3. 85 and D.S. 16. 7. 2 (Euboea); D. 22. 14; D.S. 16. 8. 2–3 (Amphipolis); D. 1. 8; [D.] 7. 27; D. 2. 6; *FGrH* 115 F 30 (Theopompus); *GHI* 151; D. 23. 173 (Chersonese); D.S. 16. 7. 3–4 (the Social war lasted 'three years', 358/357–356/355; cf. 16. 22. 2 and *Hesperia*, 8. 14); 16. 21. 1; D. 15. 3, 19, 26; *GHI* 155; *GHI* 150 (Amphipolis); D.S. 16. 14 (Thessaly).

In 356, while Chares held on in the Chersonese with sixty ships, the rebels with 100 sail ravaged the Athenian islands of Lemnos and Imbros. In their hatred of democracy they foolishly attacked some islands which might otherwise have joined in the revolt, and then laid siege to Samos, which was defended by the cleruchs. Athens placed governors and garrisons in some of the Cyclades, but she failed to act with speed. The hulls were there (for she had 283 ships on her naval list in 357/356) but neither the money nor the volunteers to man them. She had introduced in 357 the system of boards (*symmories*) into the trierarchy, in order to accelerate the equipping of the fleet, but even so she did not man another sixty ships until the summer. Commanded by Chares, Timotheus, and Iphicrates, the grand fleet of 120 ships faced the rebels at Embata in the channel between Chios and the mainland. The weather was stormy. Timotheus and Iphicrates refused to engage. Chares, attacking alone, was defeated (autumn 356). Thus the war at sea was lost decisively. During the year, too, Thebes attacked the Phocians at Delphi, and Philip captured Potidaea, expelled the cleruchs, and gave it to the Chalcidian League. An Athenian relief force reached Potidaea too late, and a coalition of native powers which Athens raised against Philip was defeated in summer 356.

Unwilling to admit defeat, Athens made her last throw. The plan was to join Artabazus, the satrap in revolt, draw pay for her mercenaries from him, and then ask the Great King to buy her neutrality by recalling Mausolus from operations in the Aegean. The first part of this ingenious plan succeeded. Chares' mercenary armies won a great victory for Artabazus, who paid a handsome subsidy, and Chares reported to Athens that he had won a second battle of Marathon. But the second part failed. Artaxerxes Ochus demanded the withdrawal of Athens' forces from Asia; if his demand was rejected, the Phoenician fleet would enter the Aegean in support of Mausolus and his allies. Athens evacuated Asia at once, and, although some orators advocated continuing the war, the wiser counsels of statesmen such as Eubulus prevailed. In summer 355 Athens made peace with the rebels and recognized their independence.[1]

Thus Athens' second attempt to win an extensive empire and dominate the Greek world ended in failure and exhaustion. The rump of the Athenian Alliance remained with her—Euboea, the Cyclades, and a few islands and mainland ports in the north Aegean—and paid some 45 talents a year in contributions. Her treasury was so bankrupt that the courts of the Heliaea were closed. The name of Athens, as one of her orators said, was associated not with the glorious leadership of Greece but with Myonnesos, the nest of pirates. Her only allies on the mainland were Phocis, against whom the Sacred War was declared in autumn 355, and Sparta, pinned down by continuous warfare with the Messenians and Arcadians.[2]

---

[1] *Hesp.* 8. 12 (Chersonese); D.S. 16. 21–22. 2; *GHI* 152; 156; *IG* ii². 1611 (naval list): *IG* ii². 1612, l. 227 (ships before Embata); D. 4. 35 (Potidaea); 6. 20; Schol. D. 3. 28, 33.

[2] D. 18. 234; Aeschin. 2. 72.

§ 3. The trend to anarchy in Sicily

THE disintegration of the Boeotian Coalition and the Athenian Alliance was less disastrous than that of Dionysius' empire in the west. Beside that man of iron his son was a man of straw. Amiable, unpractical, and interested in philosophical speculation, Dionysius II at the age of nearly thirty longed for a life of peace and popularity, which was incompatible with the maintenance of a military autocracy. On his accession to power he opened the prisons and remitted taxes. He soon made peace with Carthage and the Lucanians, and he refounded two cities which his father had destroyed, Rhegium and Naxus. In Apulia he planted two naval posts to safeguard the entry into the Adriatic Sea from piracy, and in 366 he continued his father's policy, but only for the moment, by sending troops to help Sparta and Athens.

Left to himself and wisely advised, Dionysius II might have preserved the empire in peace and prosperity, but his amiability and inexperience exposed him to family intrigues, which were complicated by his father's polygamy. Dionysius had two younger half-brothers, Hipparinus and Nysaeus, and through his step-mother an uncle, Dion, who was also his brother-in-law, having become the second husband of the first of Dionysius' triad of sisters, 'Virtue', 'Equity', and 'Prudence'. Whereas his nephews were inexperienced, Dion had wielded power as administrator and commander under their father, and he felt himself competent to guide the hands of young Dionysius, whom he regarded as quite contemptible. With a view to improving the young ruler or at least making him more receptive of his uncle's admonitions, Dion persuaded Dionysius to invite Plato to his court.[1]

On his previous visit to Syracuse in 389 Plato had formed a close friendship with Dion, for whose intellect, character, and experience he had a high regard. In accepting Dionysius' invitation in 366 he may have been influenced by Dion's wishes, but his chief motive was to put his philosophical precepts into political practice by converting the young tyrant into a philosopher-king. For the Director of the Academy it was a courageous decision; he knew that the Greek world would watch the impact of 'intelligence on the great power' and that the innumerable subjects of Dionysius might be affected by his influence with their ruler. At first all went well. Dionysius meekly accepted Plato as his political and philosophical adviser; for the great man drew no worldly distinction between politics and philosophy. But the courtiers of Dionysius became alarmed. They engineered the recall of Philistus, a strong-minded supporter of the tyranny, in order to offset the influence of Plato and Dion and preserve the military autocracy in working order. They had no doubt that Dion was using Plato as a stalking-horse to promote his own rise to power either through the resignation or the subservience of Dionysius. In order to discredit Dion, they showed to Dionysius a letter in which Dion asked the Carthaginian authorities not to negotiate with

[1] D.S. 16. 5; Plu. *Dion* 1–10; Arist. *Pol.* 1312ª4.

Syracuse unless he was present. This request was held to be treasonable, perhaps justifiably as later events were to suggest, and Dionysius sent Dion into honourable exile with full enjoyment of his vast property.[1]

Once Dion had gone, no one objected seriously to Plato staying. For he now withdrew from day-to-day politics, concentrated on cultivating Dionysius' mind, and tried to reconcile Dionysius with Dion. When little success attended his efforts, he departed for Athens, having gained the affection and the interest of Dionysius. For five years Dionysius went his own way, learning to rule with a firm hand and determined to deal with a mounting opposition. In 361 Plato returned to Syracuse, having been prevailed upon by Dion and others to accept the repeated invitations of Dionysius. He found the tyrant less malleable in the field of philosophy, since Aristippus and other sophists had been expounding their doctrines, and more suspicious of Plato's motives because Plato tried to obtain the recall of Dion. After some recriminations Plato returned to Athens, the only result of his visit having been that Dionysius confiscated Dion's property in Sicily, married his wife 'Virtue' to a favourite, Timocrates, and made it clear Dion would never be recalled.[2]

Among Plato's companions on this visit was a close friend of Dion, the philosopher Speusippus, who took advantage of the tyrant's hospitality to probe the strength of the opposition. On his return Speusippus urged Dion to use force where philosophy had failed. Plato, who knew what was afoot, neither informed Dionysius nor encouraged Dion. In August 357 Dion sailed direct across the Sicilian Sea with 1,500 mercenaries, leaving Heraclides, an exiled democratic leader, to follow later with reinforcements. He landed at Heraclea Minoa in Carthaginian territory, where he was a close friend of the commander. At the time Dionysius was in Italy, and Philistus was sailing off the Italian coast to intercept any ships coming by the coastal route. Dion marched on Syracuse, collecting supporters at Acragas, Gela, and Camarina, and instructing his agents in the city to spread rumours of his strength. The governor, Timocrates, fled in panic, and such mercenaries as remained loyal to the tyrant withdrew into the citadel of Ortygia. The city lay open for the liberators, who marched, garlanded with flowers, into the city and proclaimed Dion and his brother Megacles generals with full powers in the new republic. The populace celebrated their liberty for a week by hunting down the toadies of the tyrant.

The fighting, however, was still to come. Dionysius returned to Ortygia and secured the loyalty of the mercenaries by paying high wages; they broke into the city to loot, and they intercepted the city's supplies by sea. When Heraclides arrived with a fleet, he won a naval victory and blockaded Dionysius in Ortygia (summer 356). Meanwhile Dion, who, like most intellectuals, favoured oligarchic government, had lost his popularity with the Syracusans, among whom the extreme democrats were becoming influential. Heraclides,

[1] Plato *Ep.* 316c; 315e–316a; Plu. *Dion.* 11–14; D.S. 16. 6. 1–4.
[2] Plato *Ep.* 316d; 317b.

jealous of Dion, joined the democrats and drove Dion out of Syracuse. At this point Dionysius, who had slipped out of Ortygia, sent a force of Campanian mercenaries into the city, who looted and slaughtered for two days and nights before Dion returned to take control, this time being appointed sole commander with unrestricted powers (*strategos autokrator*). After further conflicts with Heraclides and with a Spartan adventurer, Pharax, who tried to make capital out of the turmoil in Sicily, Dion finally occupied Ortygia in 355, when the mercenaries departed under treaty to join Dionysius at Locri.[1]

Syracuse, free at last, was already weakened by two years of anarchy, party strife, and mercenary warfare. Dion was now suspected of aiming at tyranny himself, and he put an end to Heraclides' intrigues by having him murdered. When Dion was trying to establish an aristocratic constitution in 354, he was himself murdered by the agents of Callippus, a Platonic philosopher, who established himself as autocrat and attacked Catana. In 352 Hipparinus, Dion's nephew and Dionysius' half-brother, seized power in Syracuse and was succeeded on his death by Nysaeus, his brother. In 347 Dionysius himself drove Nysaeus out of Syracuse. The embittered tyrant ruled the city with such cruelty that the people invoked the aid of a Syracusan, Hicetas, who was influential at Leontini. In 344 Hicetas, who was on terms of close alliance with the Carthaginians, defeated Dionysius and drove him back into Ortygia. In 343 the Carthaginian fleet sailed into the Great Harbour, and the days of Greek independence in Sicily seemed to be numbered.[2]

The experiences of Syracuse since the arrival of Dion were repeated in most cities throughout the empire of Dionysius. Liberation meant the end of organized government. Party-strife, tyranny, and anarchy ensued. Many large cities were seized by adventurers, employing barbarian mercenaries, who then attacked neighbouring cities to extend their power. The plight into which Sicily was falling was described in a Platonic letter as a vicious circle leading to disaster. 'There is never any end, but what seems to be an end always links on to a new beginning, so that this circle of strife is likely to destroy utterly both factions, those of tyranny and democracy alike, and the Greek tongue will almost die out of Sicily as it becomes a province of Carthage or Italy.' In 344, when Timoleon came to save Sicily from this fate, grass was growing in the streets of Syracuse, and of the other Greek cities some were abandoned as the result of war, while others were in the control of barbarian mercenaries who lacked a paymaster.[3]

In Italy, where the power of Dionysius had kept the Greek cities together and driven back the barbarians, the collapse of the empire had similar consequences. The vigorous Italian peoples, who supplied so many mercenary soldiers to the Sicilian adventurers, began to press more strongly into the rich coastal areas occupied by the Greek colonies. In 356 the city of Terina was

[1] Plu. *Dion.* 22–50; D.S. 16. 6. 5; 9–13; 16–20; Nep. *Dion.* 7.
[2] Plu. *Dion.* 51–58; D.S. 16. 31. 7; 36. 5; 45. 9.
[3] Plato *Ep.* 353d; Plu. *Timol.* 1.

stormed and destroyed by a Lucanian tribe, the Bruttii, a tough pastoral people, who formed a League for the purposes of war. Later Sybaris, Hipponium, and other cities fell singly to their assault and ceased to exist.[1]

Of these calamities the ultimate cause was the corruption of political life through fifty years of autocracy, which stifled political responsibility, transplanted populations, disarmed the Greeks, and imported barbarian mercenaries. The fruits of corruption were anarchy, strife, and demoralization on a terrifying scale. The impulse that caused the collapse of the autocracy was provided by Dion, whose cause was supported publicly, if not by Plato himself, by leading members of the Academy. Dion, however, lacked the statesmanlike qualities which were required to save Sicily from anarchy; for, although his motives may have been philosophically admirable, he was a rigid advocate of intellectual and political aristocracy, a ruthless despiser of the proletariat, and in his relations with Heraclides both weak and treacherous.

Plato's part in the Sicilian catastrophe is not above criticism. The gravest charge against him is that he misjudged Dion as a man and miscast him as a statesman. Plato's dabbling with Dionysius had little practical consequence, and the rule of Dionysius during the first ten years may have been the more humane for Plato's influence and ideals. But Plato's attitude towards Dion, admirable as it may have been in terms of personal loyalty, was mischievous in its political consequences. When Plato realized what the consequences would be, namely revolution and violence of which he disapproved on intellectual grounds, he did not take an open or public stand against Dion but withdrew on to the personal plane, trying to reconcile Dion and Dionysius when hopes of reconciliation were futile. A defence of Plato has come down to us in an open letter which was probably written soon after his death, when interest in Sicily was still lively. In this letter the practical issues were avoided by a philosophical digression, and the idealistic assessment of Dion was maintained to the end.[2] But Plato himself must have been more deeply touched by the deterioration of Dion and more bitterly disillusioned by the results of Dion's actions, for which in the imperfect world of practical politics he must bear some responsibility.

[1] D.S. 16. 15; Str. 5. 1. 4; Justin, 23. 1.

[2] Plato *Ep.* 7; the woolliness of the historical setting in Sicily, as in the last part of *Ep.* 8, affords good grounds for believing the letter not to be authentic, although many Platonists think it genuine.

CHAPTER 4

The Social and Economic Background to the Troubles of Greece

THE lifetime of Xenophon *c.* 430–354 coincided with a period of political frustration. No state was able to impose its leadership for long on the rest of Greece, and yet without such leadership the Greek states fought almost incessantly. Peace existed only when one or two powers were supreme, Athens and Sparta during the peace of Nicias and then Sparta alone. The attempt in 362/361 to ensure a self-imposed peace by forming a League of City-States failed signally. In 355, when Xenophon wrote the *Revenues* and Isocrates the *Peace*, they both advised Athens to make terms with all the Greek states and lead a movement for peace. Xenophon advised Athens to act as an intermediary not only between states but also between factions in individual states. Such a policy was sensible, but it meant sacrificing the immediate interests of Athens in favour of Thebes. After 355 Athens proved unequal to the task. The failure of the Greek states in general to work out their political salvation calls for some investigation.[1]

As Thucydides noted, an imperialist state requires a considerable margin of superiority in fighting power and in financial reserves. During the fourth century Sparta, Athens, and Thebes lacked that margin. Sparta's hoplites had to compete with mercenary troops and then with the intensively trained Theban hoplites. Even at sea Athens found rivals in Boeotia, Thessaly, and Caria, and on land Thebes found herself challenged by Thessaly, Arcadia, and even Phocis. The reason was not that Sparta, Athens, and Thebes were weaker than they had been in the fifth century. Sparta and Thebes were certainly wealthier in the fourth century, and Athens had as many ships of war in her docks as ever before. The reason was rather that the other states in Greece had grown stronger. In the fifth century Athens and Syracuse had been almost unique in their democracy and their prosperity. In the fourth century a social and economic revolution put most states in Greece and Sicily into the company of Athens and Syracuse. 'Ships of war, numbers of men, revenues of money, abundance of general equipment, and everything else by which a city-state gauges its strength', said Demosthenes in 341, comparing his generation with that of the Persian wars, 'these all the Greeks today possess in number and in quantity far beyond the Greeks of those days.'[2]

Prosperity, based on commerce and capitalism, spread to the Greek

[1] X. *Vect.* 5. 8; Isoc. 8. 16.
[2] Th. 1. 9. 1–2; 18. 2 fin.; 141. 5; 7. 55. 2 (Syracuse and Athens); D. 9. 40.

colonies and beyond them to such areas as the Mediterranean coast of Spain, the interior of Sicily, the shores of the Adriatic Sea, the Balkans, and south Russia. The wealth of Massilia and her colonies, Sicily under Dionysius, Panticapaeum in the Crimea under Spartocus, Caria under Mausolus, and Cyprus under Evagoras, all contributed to the general flow of prosperity throughout the Mediterranean area. The leading states of the Greek mainland had diplomatic relations with distant powers. Thebes, for instance, was on friendly terms with Carthage as well as Persia. During the first half of the fourth century many signs of national and international commerce and capitalism made their appearance: commercial treaties, commercial representation, monetary pacts, trading privileges, banking, arbitration, marine insurance, mortgaging, and so on. Traffic in goods, slaves, and mercenaries ranged from Spain to Iran, from Russia to Cyrene, and passed through the Greek peninsula as its central bridge. Persia's interest in Greek politics was not altruistic. Peace in Greece quickened the flow of inter-continental trade, especially in regard to Greek mercenary soldiers, of whom fifty thousand or more were in Persia's service between 336 and 330. Great fortunes were to be made by merchants. Commercial profits ran as high as 30 per cent. on cargoes to the Crimea, and the normal rate of interest on loans was 12 per cent. Greeks who had made money abroad as mercenaries or merchants returned to enrich their own states. It was indeed an age of potential plenty (*aphthonia*). A small state like Megara, well situated to trade by land and sea, was proverbial for her prosperity because she remained neutral.[1]

Culture, too, was widely diffused. Euripides' plays were in demand in Sicily; he produced the *Bacchae* in Macedonia, and after his death his plays were popular wherever there were Greek communities. In the past philosophers and sophists had travelled mainly to Athens, where progressive ideas were exchanged. In the fourth century they ranged the Greek world and were present in any city of the Peloponnese. New ideas were distributed by the sophists and the book-trade, so that a more uniform culture was steadily developing. Capitalism carried in its wake Attic commercial law, the Attic alphabet of twenty-four letters (adopted by Athens from Miletus in 403), and the Attic literary dialect. In the writings of the Athenian *émigré* Xenophon and the Arcadian mercenary captain, Aeneas 'Tacticus', a modification of the Attic literary dialect appeared, which was later to become the *lingua franca* (*koine*) of the Greek-speaking world. Of this rapid development in prosperity and in culture Athens was the centre. In 380 Isocrates claimed that her influence was such that 'the name Greek is no longer a mark of race but of outlook and is accorded to those who share our culture rather than our blood'.

At the same time the outward form of Greek cities became more standardized. When Aeneas wrote *On the Defence of Fortified Positions* (*c.* 357–356)

---

[1] *IG* 7. 2407 (Carthage); *GHI* 111, l. 10, 114, l. 18, 141 (commercial); 112 (monetary); 113 (arbitration); 115, 163, 167 (Spartocids); 139, 155 (Sidon and Caria); Isoc. 8. 117 (Megara); mercenaries p. 665 below.

any city of moderate size had a theatre, a civic centre, and open spaces for a stadium or gymnasium. It was protected by fine massive walls and laid out with care. At Halicarnassus, for instance, Mausolus copied the semi-circular plan of Rhodes, which centred on its harbour and market. At Olynthus the new part of the city was laid out on the gridiron plan, which Hippodamus had employed at Miletus, Thurii, and the Peiraeus in the fifth century. This was 'the modern fashion' in the middle of the fourth century. The civic centre (*agora*) was the heart of the Greek city. There the administrative, social, and political sides of life tended to concentrate; temples, altars, fountains, and gardens were at hand, shops might be there or booths for special market-days, and processions, festivals and addresses were to be seen and heard. The Agora at Athens provided a model. After the Persian wars it was gradually rebuilt. At about 350 one looked down from the Hephaesteum on the following scene (see Fig. 14, p. 188). The Strategeion for the generals, the Tholos for the prytaneis, the Bouleuterion for council meetings, and the old Bouleuterion, used as a record office. Beyond them the statues of the eponymous heroes on a high base, where public notices were posted. To the left the temple of Heavenly Aphrodite and the sanctuary of Demos and the Graces; then the temple of Apollo Patroüs, patron of the Attic phratries, and facing a statue of Zeus on a round pedestal a long Stoa, where the *archon basileus* and the Areopagus Council sat. Beyond them the altar of the Twelve Gods and the Eschara or sacrificial hearth. To the north the Stoa of the Herms and the Stoa Poikile, where philosophers and others walked below the mural paintings of Polygnotus and other artists. Across the Panathenaic Way the temple of the daughters of Leos. To the south the South-west Fountain House and the long sanctuary of Theseus, where the hero's bones were re-interred *c*. 475; and beyond it the nine-spouted fountain, the Enneakrounos, built by Peisistratus, and the Mint of the Athenian state.[1]

The building of fortifications, civic centres, and entire cities such as Messene and Megalopolis could only have been undertaken in a time of exceptional prosperity. There was much wealth, too, in private hands. Timotheus and Meidias built houses which were humorously described as 'towers' or 'over-shadowers', and the well-to-do at Olynthus, for instance, constructed a new residential quarter of roomy houses. 'Rich men' had 'fine arms, good horses, magnificent houses and establishments, and rich women expensive clothes and gold jewelry.' At Athens Meidias had 'many maid-servants', and Plato remarked *c*. 375 that in any state a rich man's household would have fifty slaves or more. This new wealth was not concentrated in one or two cities but was widely spread. A Thessalian noble, Polydamas, could make up a deficit in public revenue from his own pocket; Dion of Syracuse had sufficient wealth, when in exile, to finance an expedition; a Phocian before the Sacred

[1] Isoc. 4. 50; Aen. Tact. 1. 9; 22. 4; Arist. *Pol.* 1331^{a}12; ^{b}1–13; Vitr. 2. 8. 11; Arist. *Pol.* 1267^{b}23, 1330^{b}24 (Hippodamus); Arist. *Pol.* 1331^{a}24, ^{b}1 (Agora); Aen. Tact. 17. 5; D. 18. 169.

War owned more than 1,000 slaves; and a metic laid out the market at Aegina at his own expense.[1]

This wave of prosperity certainly caused an increase in the number of slaves in Greek lands. Until the nineteenth century slaves were in many countries a normal adjunct of wealth, and their number was largely a matter of locality and trade. Slavery was endemic in Greece. Sparta, Argos, and other Dorian states had reduced the earlier population to serfdom, but elsewhere the majority of slaves were imported and owned as personal chattels. Well-to-do citizens in the non-Dorian states had probably had small numbers of slaves from early times. In Boeotia, for instance, a small farmer who worked his own land (*autourgos*) had in Hesiod's day a slave to follow him as he ploughed, and others at work in the fields. Greek colonists often acquired slaves in vast numbers. Syracuse, Corcyra, and Byzantium used slave labour to cultivate their lands. Chios, wealthy herself and able to raid the Asiatic coast, had a higher proportion of slaves to citizens than any state except Sparta, where it was probably about 10 to 1. At Athens in the late fifth century privately owned slaves were engaged in every variety of occupation and formed a feature of daily life in the plays of Euripides and Aristophanes. Some were used in unskilled occupations such as mining, Nicias, for example, owning 1,000 who were let out for this work, but most of them were probably artisans skilled in a handicraft (*cheirotechnai*); for this type formed a majority of the 20,000 slaves who, according to Thucydides, ran away in the Decelean War. Sometimes Athens, like Corcyra and Sparta, made slaves serve in the fleet and probably attend on the hoplites. During the fourth century there were larger numbers of slaves than ever before in most parts of the mainland, and the method of treating them became an issue of great interest.[2]

In the fourth century slaves were assumed to be in plentiful supply. As Euripides remarked, slavery was a natural function in a barbarian, not in a Greek, and the slaves were nearly always barbarians. In the *Laws* Plato planned to have in his state a sufficiency of slaves in number and quality to help in every kind of task. Aristotle remarked that 'states are bound to have a population of slaves in large numbers and of resident aliens and foreigners', and in his ideal state he proposed to have all agricultural labour conducted by slaves, some state-owned and some privately owned (as in Laconia and Crete at that time). Xenophon in 355 proposed that Athens should eventually acquire three slaves to each adult citizen and let them out as mining labour. These suggestions were not intended to be Utopian but practical. In the states records of slaves, as of other sections of the population, were certainly

[1] A. *Pl.* 180; D. 21. 158; X. *Vect.* 4. 8; *Mem.* 3. 11. 4; Pl. *R.* 578d; X. *HG.* 6. 1. 3; Athen. 6. 272 with Arist. *Pol.* 1304ᵃ12; D. 23. 211.

[2] Hdt. 7. 155 (Syracuse); Th. 3. 73 (Corcyra); 8. 40. 2 (Chios: cf. Polyaen. 3. 9. 23); Athen. 6. 271c (Byzantium); Hes. *Op.* 470, 502, 573, 597, 608; Th. 7. 27. 5 and *Hell. Oxy.* 12. 4 (Decelean War); Th. 1. 55. 1 (more than three slaves to one citizen in the Corcyraean losses); Plu. *Nic.* 28. 2, Isoc. 8. 48 (Athens); Athen. 6. 271 f. (Sparta); X. *Vect.* 4. 14–17; P. *Lg.* 776c–778a; Arist. *Pol.* 1259ᵃ38; 1259ᵇ22; 1326ᵃ18; 1330ᵃ26; X. *Oec.* 5. 16.

kept, because the ownership and purchase of slaves were liable to tax, and slaves were entered as a form of capital on the assessment for a capital levy (*eisphora*); Athens and Thebes had regulations about runaway slaves, and a record of such runaways was no doubt the basis of Thucydides' statement about them in the Decelean War. The figure given by Hyperides for the number of adult male slaves from the silver-mines and elsewhere in Attica in 338 was 150,000. It may be an inflated figure, but it cannot be a wild exaggeration. Athens had then enjoyed seventeen years of almost continuous peace, and the mines were being exploited on so large a scale that individuals won fortunes as high as 300 talents from that source alone, whereas Nicias' fortune from all sources was only 100 talents.[1]

Prosperity, however, did not bring peace to the fourth century. It simply enabled states to recover with amazing speed and embark on another war. 'Of all states,' said Xenophon, 'Athens is naturally fitted to increase her wealth in time of peace.' Many cities did likewise. The spate of war was almost continuous from 431 to 351, between state and state and between faction and faction within individual states. The result for Greece as a whole was enfeeblement. Ionia was lost to Persia, some Aegean islands to Mausolus, the Chersonese to Cersebleptes, some cities in Thrace to Philip, some parts of south Italy to the Bruttii, and much of Greek Sicily to Carthage. In Greece itself every city was as heavily fortified as in Mycenaean times, and coalitions were formed and dissolved as readily as they had been then. In the shifting sea of alliances and counter-alliances Athens tried to gain stability by making pacts with dominant parties of her own political shade in other states, rather than with the states themselves; but neither she nor they kept loyal to them. Expediency and faithlessness ruled supreme in inter-state politics. Aeneas Tacticus assumed that within any city at war the danger of revolution by an opposing party was grave and imminent. Faction, often generated spontaneously, was stimulated by hostile powers. The horrors of the revolution at Corcyra spread, as Thucydides said of his own lifetime, 'to almost all the Greek world', and the wheel of revolution was kept revolving in the fourth century by the rise and fall of imperialist powers.[2]

The turmoil in and between the Greek states was ultimately due to the failure of the city-state as a political form to meet the spiritual, social, and economic needs of the citizens. Towards the end of the Peloponnesian War at Athens political democracy and intellectual enlightenment were already at loggerheads. The trial and the death of Socrates in 399 perpetuated the division. The philosophers of the fourth century took to heart the terrible indictment made by Socrates in his speech of defence. 'A man who really fights for the right must lead a private, not a public life, if he intends to survive for

---

[1] E. *IA*. 1400; P. *Lg*. 776c–778a; Arist. *Pol*. 1259^{a}38; ^{b}22; [Arist.] *Oec*. 2. 1350^{a}13 shows that each citizen had more than two slaves *c*. 385; Poll. 8. 130; Isoc. 17. 49; Plu. *Nic*. 14. 6; Hyp. *Fr*. 29 (cf. X. *Vect*. 4. 42 for slaves of this type).

[2] X. *Vect*. 5. 2; *GHI* 127; Th. 3. 82. 1; Aen. Tact. 1. 6; 10. 3.

even a little time.' Plato was the adviser not of Athens but of Dionysius, and the intellectuals acted not as leaders but as critics of Athenian democracy. During the fourth century a different type of literature and art developed, drawing its inspiration less from the state than from the individual. Philosophy was concerned primarily with the soul; tragedy, pursuing the psychological drama of Euripides and lacking spiritual force, declined rapidly; comedy, losing its political interest, changed into a social comedy of manners. The lyrical quality, inspired by the Periclean intensity of emotional and religious feeling for the enlightened democracy, disappeared from tragedy and comedy. Oratory took its place, the oratory of the defendant in a lawsuit, the politician facing the jury, and the statesman facing the people. These tendencies in philosophy and literature were also apparent in the art of the period, where portraiture came into vogue.

Once the state lost its catholicity of appeal, the citizens tended to become more self-interested. 'You leave the Assembly,' said Aeschines to the Athenians, 'not after deliberating but after dividing the surplus like shareholders.' In Greek states generally there was a sharp division between the interests of those who had property and those who had none, and it was the clash between them which led to revolution. The causes of faction were envy according to Democritus, and acquisitiveness and ambition according to Thucydides, both emphasizing human responsibility, while the economist's viewpoint was expressed by Plato in the middle of the fourth century: 'there must not be severe poverty in any section of the citizen body nor yet opulence; for either breeds faction, which may more correctly be called disruption.' The causes of war between state and state were much the same: acquisitiveness and ambition in the citizens as a whole, and the economic requirements of a state or of a class in a state. In 425 the Athenians 'grasped after more', and from then on the motive of acquisitiveness emerged repeatedly. In 355 Xenophon reported a politician's diagnosis in economic terms: 'the poverty of the majority compels us to be aggressive rather than honourable in our dealings with other states.'[1]

When the labouring or wage-earning class contains a large number of slaves, the social gulf between those who own property and those who do not tends to widen. Wealth (*euporia*) and poverty (*aporia*) in the fourth century meant the possession or the lack of capital (*ousia*) rather than an ability to earn high or low wages. Even the smallest capitalist tended to look down on the wage-earning citizen who had to engage in a vulgar occupation (*banausia*). For capital gave leisure, and 'one needs leisure', said Aristotle, 'to develop excellence and to participate in politics'. If one had no capital, one could not have leisure. One became a wage-earner like a skilled slave, and was on the level of the labouring class (*chernetikon*). In their ideal states Plato and Aristotle put all their citizens above this level by giving them two forms of

[1] P. *Ap.* 32a; Aeschin. 3. 251; Ar. *Ec.* 206; *Vorsokr.* 66 B 245; Th. 3. 82. 8; P. *Lg.* 744d; Th. 4. 21. 2; X. *Vect.* 1. 1 (cf. Isoc. 8. 6–7; Arist. *Pol.* 1320ᵃ33).

capital holding, land and slaves. The Athenians tried to give land in cleruchies to those who lacked sufficient capital at home. Failing cleruchies, the democratic leaders gave state-pay to poor citizens. Aristotle condemned this method, because state-pay was insufficient to lift the poor citizen above the level of the wage-earner. Instead, 'surplus revenue should be distributed in lump sums to the poor (*aporoi*), enough to purchase a plot of land or to provide capital (*aphorme*) for trading or farming . . . so that they may have a lasting prosperity (*euporia*)'. 'This', said Aristotle, 'is, I consider, the division in a state: the rich (*euporoi*) and the poor (*aporoi*).' The division, as we should say, was between the capitalist and the non-capitalist. Aristotle therefore had no use for a dole, which only subsidized the wages of a citizen. He believed that all citizens (or as many as possible) should have some capital.[1]

Slaves in most states worked alongside of free men, whether as artists or clerks, as hands on a boat or as harvesters winnowing grain. There were no large factories, but some workshops employed fifty or sixty hands, for instance in making knives or bedsteads. Usually an owner put slaves to work on his own account, or else he hired them out to others and took a part of the proceeds (*apophora*). In consequence the wages of citizen labour, competing openly with those of servile labour, remained low and barely kept pace with the rising cost of bread. At the same time the demand for citizen labour diminished as more capitalists owned their own slaves. Socially, too, a scorn of manual work (*banauson ergon*) grew up among citizens. In the fifth century it is not so noticeable, but in the latter half of the fourth century 'the best State', said Aristotle, 'will not make a citizen a manual worker, because the bulk of manual labour is today slave or foreign.' Such was the case at Thebes. Politically, the poor citizen was assured of his franchise, provided the constitution was a democracy and the state gave him pay for carrying out his political duties. Therefore the poorer citizens in Athens fought with ferocity for democracy and often for an aggressive foreign policy as well.[2]

In a thinly peopled continent such a state of affairs would have been less serious. But the city-states were far more tightly packed in Greece than national states in Europe. The peninsula suffered from an excess of population, due partly to natural increase and partly to the import of slaves. Phlius, certainly an extreme case, had about five times as many hoplites in the fourth century as in 479. The increase in population could not be absorbed by the countryside, although cultivation was more intensive and skilful in the fourth century than ever before, and it tended to concentrate in the cities where politics were more heated. Old cities grew larger (Athens, for instance, containing almost half the citizen population *c.* 330, as compared with rather over a third *c.* 430) and new cities arose in Arcadia, Messenia, Thessaly, and Sicily. Even so a considerable surplus of citizens, lacking regular employment, became impoverished, and they and their families moved off as vagrants looking

[1] Arist. *Pol.* 1329ª1; 1291ᵇ25; P. *Lg.* 744e; Arist. *Pol.* 1330ª6–32; 1320ª30; 1291ᵇ8.
[2] Arist. *Pol.* 1337ᵇ8; 1278ª7; 1321ª29 (Thebes); Isoc. 8. 130.

for a livelihood. 'It is easier', said Isocrates in 356 with no wild exaggeration, 'to raise a bigger and better force from the floating population than from the citizen population.' In most of Greece overpopulation increased the need for imported food-stuffs, especially cereals, which came principally from Sicily, Thessaly, south Russia, and Egypt. Thus states became more dependent on commercial treaties with other states or, failing treaties, on force in the form of war. The Second Athenian Alliance grew rapidly because it gave protection to trade as well as freedom from political persecution.[1]

Thus the city-state as a political form was no longer self-sufficient. It was ceasing to command spiritual loyalty from the more enlightened citizens; it was failing to unite the classes; and it gave no guarantee of economic security. Its shortcomings were the causes of dissension within and war without. Dionysius produced a temporary solution by fusing several city-states into one cosmopolitan state, Jason by re-creating the *tageia*, Megara by maintaining neutrality, while others tried the well-worn path of imperialism under the guise of a coalition. But no one state or group of states gave lasting stability to the Greek world, and in 354 the empire of Dionysius, the Athenian Alliance, and the Boeotian Coalition in Central Greece were all collapsing.

Athens still led the Greek world in culture and stability. Her position was more fortunate than that of any other state because she was in peacetime the centre of Greek trade and indeed almost of world trade. Throughout the century the volume of goods passing through the Peiraeus, often for reshipment, increased steadily. The size of the citizen population can be roughly estimated. During a prosperous period, such as 370–365, there were 1,200 in the richest class, about 15,000 in the hoplite class, and perhaps 20,000 in the thetic class, making a total of adult male citizens approaching 40,000. In 394 the figure was 'over 30,000' and in 322 about 31,000, these lower figures being due to losses in war and to emigration respectively. The class-structure varied with economic conditions. Between 365 and 357, when cleruchies were planted, the well-to-do classes may have outnumbered the thetic class. At other times they did not. The number of resident aliens varied vastly with economic conditions. At a guess one might say there were 8,000 metics in 360. They were liable to pay taxes, including a residence tax, and to serve in the forces. They were usually well-to-do; some were very wealthy and their wealth included slaves. The size of the slave-population *c*. 360 is a subject of controversy. It was probably not less than 200,000, which gave a ratio of approximately one slave to one free. For the rough total of men, women, and children in the citizen body was 160,000, in the metic population 24,000, and in the passing foreigners (*xenoi*) a few thousands. The total estimated population of some 400,000 may be compared with the figure of 200,000 given by Diodorus for Acragas in 406.[2]

---

[1] *Ep.* 9. 9; Isoc. 5. 96, 120; 4. 168; 8. 24; X. *Oec.*, e.g. 16. 12 (triple rotation of crops); Aen. Tact. 10. 12.

[2] Isoc. 4. 42; X. *Vect.* 1. 6; D.S. 13. 90. 3; for army figures see p. 661; Gomme, *The*

The peacetime revenue of Athens came from the exploitation of trade and its by-products. She levied a 2 per cent. *ad valorem* tax on cargoes passing through the Peiraeus, a 2 per cent. purchase tax in Attica, harbour-dues and tolls, and taxes on metics, slaves, and prostitutes. She also drew rents from public properties, including 4 per cent. of the silver mined at Laurium, and the fines and confiscations imposed by her law-courts. The revenue was more than enough in time of peace, and then no direct taxes were levied on the citizens at all. In 355, when Xenophon advised her how to improve her position, he suggested the same means: to attract more metics, foreigners, and ship-captains, build more state lodging-houses, and work the mines on a larger scale by buying three slaves to each citizen, that is some 120,000 slaves, and hiring them out as labour in the mines. He said correctly that Athens could provide plenty of relief for impoverished citizens, restore her docks, walls, and temples, and build up reserves, if only she kept at peace. In war the position changed radically. The three top classes were liable to pay a capital tax (*eisphora*) and serve in the forces; the richest also paid large sums as trierarchs, cavalrymen, prepayers of tax, and so on. At the same time conditions of war disrupted trade and drove away the metics, so that revenues dropped rapidly. 'Athens is now deserted', said Isocrates in 355, 'by the merchants, foreigners, and metics who in time of peace will throng her.' Because in war Athens burnt the financial candle at both ends, she ran out of money in war as quickly as she regained it in peace.[1]

As the thetes paid nothing in war or peace and were paid for rowing in the fleet, they lost nothing financially by going to war and, if the empire were reconstituted, they might rise into the hoplite class as cleruchs. Since the thetes were usually the majority in the democracy, it is not surprising that they opted so often for war and sought to turn an Athenian Alliance into an Empire. In 415 'the great crowd and the soldiery expected to win pay for the moment and to acquire the power which would supply them with pay for ever'. In 393 Aristophanes described the atmosphere in Athens on the verge of another new venture. 'Let's launch the fleet (an orator cries); the poor vote "Aye", the rich men and the farmers vote "No".' In 355 Xenophon summarized the attitude of the people to their Second Alliance as one of aggression, caused by the poverty of the majority.[2]

The division of interest between the well-to-do and the poor modified the spirit and the working of the Athenian constitution. Respect for the law and especially for the 'unwritten laws' was weakened by the people's determination to exercise its will and to govern by decree rather than by legislation. The

Population of Athens, gives the following for 323: citizens 112,000, metics 42,000, slaves 104,000, total 258,000. Estimates based on the incomplete evidence for corn-import and corn-consumption are most hazardous.

[1] Poll. 8. 130; X. *Vect.* throughout, e.g. 4. 19; *IG* ii.² 1579; Isoc. 8. 21. The taxation of the rich at Athens was, of course, far less severe than the modern system of super-tax and death duties.

[2] Th. 6. 24. 3; Ar. *Ec.* 197; X. *Vect.* 1. 1.

charge of 'illegality' (*graphe paranomon*), designed to protect established law, was blunted by over-use; it is said to have been advanced unsuccessfully against Aristophon no less than seventy-five times. The charge of 'treason' (*eisangelia*), intended to protect the state when legal processes were not appropriate, was so cheapened by ridiculous misuse that it was employed against men who paid a higher fee to some flute-girls than the legal tariff. Both charges were taken direct to the people in the Assembly. At some time before 355 a new procedure was introduced in order to safeguard the principle of precedent in the law. A panel of jurors from the Heliaea, as numerous as 1,001, were appointed at the Assembly's pleasure as *nomothetae* to try all past and current laws and make alterations in accordance with their findings. Here again the people became the source and the judge of law.[1]

The executive authorities were steadily weakened. The Council lost its right of execution, of trying charges of 'treason', and of rejecting candidates for office on its scrutiny. In these matters the Assembly or the Heliaea had the final say. The Council's powers of conducting diplomatic negotiations and dealing with finance were cut down to the advantage of the Assembly. The senior magistrates were viewed with suspicion by the people, and many were executed, banished, or fined by the Heliaea. For them the people had no mercy. Callistratus, charged with 'treason' for 'not giving the best advice to the people', escaped death by flight in 361 and returned *c*. 355 as a suppliant at the altar of the Twelve Gods, whence he was removed and executed. In 356 Iphicrates, threatening to use his mercenaries in the court, was acquitted on a charge of treason, whereas Timotheus was fined the enormous sum of 100 talents. Political eminence was very dangerous for any major magistrate or even for a Councillor. The tacit assumption that the People was never wrong meant that its policy must be right, and its executants were responsible for any failure.[2]

'The people', wrote Aristotle, 'has made itself master of everything; all administration is conducted by decrees of the Assembly and decisions of the Courts, in which the people is sovereign.' In such direct government by the people political leadership was of paramount importance. Whereas Pericles had been general, financier, and orator, his successors were seldom versatile. The generals tended to be specialists, who served abroad as mercenary captains if they became unpopular or unemployed at home. The financiers, too, specialized in a subject which became increasingly important in the conduct of the state, and some of them were also capable speakers. The orators specialized in persuading the people in the Assembly or in the Courts to accept their point of view. The most unscrupulous among them were the sophists of politics, able to prove black white and selling this ability to any patron; they were often employed by mercenary generals, foreign powers, contractors,

---

[1] Hyp. 3. 3; Arist. *Ath.* 59. 2; D. 24. 20–27; Arist. *Pol.* 1292ᵃ4.
[2] Arist. *Ath.* 45. 1 and 3; 59. 2; Hyp. 3. 1 and Lycurg. 1. 93 (Callistratus); Polyaen. 3. 1. 15, 29.

cavalry commanders, and so on. Even those who had pretensions to the title of statesmen had to pander at first to the people's wishes, in order to establish any influence at all. Unless they held an administrative office, the orators were not easily impeachable, however criminal the policy they advocated. The blame for disaster fell upon those who carried out the policy.[1]

'Be assured,' said a character of Aristophanes, addressing Wealth, 'you all alone are responsible for failure and success; even in war those only win who have you at their side.' Money meant mercenaries and all states, even Sparta, used them to release citizen troops or supplement them in battle. Athens was an employer on a large scale; armies of 7,000 or 8,000 mercenaries served her, and these in the Social War alone cost 1,000 talents. The Athenian hoplites were willing to serve only in nearby areas, and in training and discipline were inferior to the mercenaries. The cavalry, although composed of Athenians who supplied their own mounts, cost the state 40 talents a year. Fortifications, fleets, docks, arsenals, and armaments consumed much revenue. New ships were probably built each year. In addition, state-pay increased. Those who attended the Assembly received at the beginning of the century 1 obol, and in the second half of the century 6 obols at ordinary meetings and 9 obols at the chief meetings. The dicasts, who also received state-pay, were more fully employed than in the past, and every magistrate received a small salary. It was a sign of financial exhaustion that the Heliaea was closed in 355 and again in 348.[2]

Some other modifications were made in the constitution as established in 403. Perhaps in 378/377 nine presidents (*proedroi*) were chosen by lot, one from each tribe except the tribe represented in the prytany, in order to preside at the meetings of the Assembly and the Council; and probably in 366/365 a secretary (*grammateus*) of the prytany was selected by lot for the whole year in addition to the 'Secretary of the Council', who was elected month by month. The aim of the new arrangements was no doubt a more efficient administration. The most important innovations dealt with finance. Such were the Symmories, concerned with the capital levy and later with the trierarchy, and the Board of Naval Commissioners. The co-ordinating authority in the field of finance was the Council until 354, when the Commissioners of the Theoric Fund (*to theorikon*) were empowered to supervise the expenditure of other departments. The distribution of monies to enable the poorest citizens to attend state festivals and functions had been a form of relief for the poor in the fifth century and was an important one during hard times in the fourth century. Probably in 358 the Theoric Fund was formed as a special fund to provide money regularly, and Commissioners of the Fund were appointed. Elected by the people for a four-year spell, from one Panathenaic Festival to the next, the Commissioners were an exception to the normal rule

---

[1] Arist. *Ath.* 41. 2 fin. (cf. *Pol.* 1299ᵇ39; 1317ᵇ2); *FGrH* 115 F 105 (Theopompus on generals); Isoc. 8. 9 f.; 129; X. *Eq. Mag.* 1. 8.

[2] A. *Pl.* 181; Isoc. 15. 111; 7. 9; 8. 44; D. 4. 21; Polyaen. 3. 9. 32 and X. *Eq. Mag.* 9. 3 (mercenaries' training); D. 22. 14; Arist. *Ath.* 41. 3; 62. 2.

of the democracy that officials were appointed by lot for one year only. Their exceptional powers, too, soon enabled them to 'control almost all the administration of the State'.[1]

In 354 the Chief Commissioner of the Theoric Fund was Eubulus, a capable politician, who had proposed the motion for peace in 355. He and his successors conducted a far-sighted financial policy. Its mainstay was a law, passed probably during his tenure of office (354/350), that all surplus revenue must go into the Theoric Fund. This law gave the poorer citizens a financial interest in preserving peace; for, should Athens undertake a major war, the surplus would have to go not to the Theoric Fund but to the Military Fund (*stratiotikon*). In most ways it was an admirable measure. The people were now less sharply divided than when rich and poor had had opposing interests with regard to peace and war. Financial economy could be enforced in all departments. Preparations for war were made with the money which the Assembly allocated in their budget to the Military Fund. The law simply put a brake on going to war. Nor could the brake be easily removed. For someone must propose that the Assembly should appoint *nomothetae* to reconsider this law like any other on the statute book. In this there was a danger. At any moment when there was a need to go to war the vested interests of peace might prove too strong.[2]

The Athenian democracy of this period was severely criticized as an example of 'extreme democracy' by those who preferred a more moderate or even a non-democratic type of constitution. The heirs of Thucydides and Aristophanes were Plato, Isocrates, Xenophon, Theopompus, and Aristotle, who condemned the follies of an Assembly or a Heliastic Court swayed by rhetoric and tempted by the lure of imperialism. But the city of Athena had many outstanding qualities. It gave its citizens freedom in politics, speech, education, law, and business. It fed its poor, and it gave them self-respect. It conducted the relations of daily life with humanity (*philanthropia*) towards the metics and slaves, who were admitted to many forms of family and state worship and received protection under the law. It led the world in culture, commerce, and capitalism. In the working of its constitution there were many factors which made for moderation. The Councillors and the dicasts were men of over thirty years of age. In normal times most of them came from the hoplite class, because the pay for office was not sufficient to attract many members of the thetic class, and the Assembly was attended mostly by those who had the leisure and therefore the means to do so. It was only at times of financial depression that the poor predominated as dicasts,[3] and in critical debates that the poorest class attended the Assembly in sufficient numbers to take control. The inherited experience of generations, combined with strict rules of procedure, enabled the Athenians to conduct their affairs in a way which still served as a model for other states in the fourth century.

[1] Arist. *Ath.* 44. 2; 54. 3; 43. 1; 47. 2; Poll. 8. 113; Aeschin. 3. 24.
[2] D. 3. 10.   [3] Isoc. 8. 130.

BOOK VI

THE RISE AND EXPANSION OF MACEDON

CHAPTER 1

Macedon Wins a Place among the Greek Powers (359–346)

§ 1. *The re-establishment of the larger Macedonian state*

IN terms of geography Macedonia may be divided into two parts. Lower Macedonia comprises the coastal plain, through which two great rivers, the Axius and the Haliacmon, flow into the Thermaic Gulf. The plain is ringed by hills except towards the east. Beyond the hills lie the extensive plateaux of Upper Macedonia, which are themselves enclosed by high mountain ranges except towards the east. The mountain ranges are pierced by only a few passes: the Vale of Tempe between Mt. Olympus and Mt. Ossa, and the pass of Oloösson between Mt. Olympus and the Pindus range; two passes from the districts Orestis and Lyncus over the main Balkan range into Illyria; a pass between the Balkan range and Mt. Paíkon, and another between Mt. Paíkon and Mt. Cercine, both leading into Paeonia. Thus except towards the east, where the river Strymon is the first continuous barrier, Upper Macedonia is well defended by a circle of mountains. In terrain Lower Macedonia has good agricultural land and a flat coast. Upper Macedonia is predominantly pastoral land with some fine arable tracts. In climate they are both continental, not Mediterranean, and their combined area is far greater than that of any Greek canton, even Thessaly. The modern population, excluding that of Chalcidice (78,000), is 1,140,000, whereas that of Boeotia is 106,000.

Lower Macedonia is the centre from which four continental routes radiate. Southwards one passes through the Vale of Tempe on the main road towards the Isthmus and the Peloponnese. Northwards the valley of the Axius leads towards the central Danube basin. Westwards the gap in the Balkan range in Lyncus gives access to Illyria and the Adriatic coast, where the two Greek colonies Epidamnus and Apollonia were situated. Eastwards a depression between the Chalcidic peninsula and Mt. Cercine leads to the river Strymon, whence a route proceeds through Thrace to Byzantium on the Bosporus. Invading peoples have usually followed the last three routes, coming from Paeonia, Illyria, and Thrace and converging upon Lower Macedonia. The people of Greece, unaccustomed to the continental climate, were attracted more by the Chalcidic peninsula and to a lesser degree by the coastal plain. Thus Macedonia may be described as a geographical entity, continental in character, ringed round by mountains and strategically placed in the Balkan area.

The people are of mixed race. The 'Macedonian language' of today is the name given to a particular dialect, based on Bulgarian, which is spoken in part of Yugoslav Macedonia. Physically the Macedonians are sturdier in build than the southern Greeks, and their hard life as peasants and highlanders has made them more remarkable for dourness than vivacity.

The mountains still carry the vestiges of virgin forests, which were much more extensive in antiquity, when pitch and timber of all kinds were important exports. The plains with their swamps and lakes provide pasture for great herds of horses, cattle, and sheep, and the large tracts of alluvial soil grow enough cereals to permit of export. Orchards, vineyards, and rose-gardens caused the slopes below Naoussa to be called the Garden of Midas. A small amount of gold is still washed from the river Lydias, and silver was once mined to the north and west of Macedonia. For ancient shipping the best ports were on the Chalcidic peninsula. Pydna had a harbour, Methone and Therma had roadsteads, and Pella, fifteen miles inland, was reached by river and by a lake, which has now silted up.

In antiquity Macedonia contained people of various origins. At the end of the Bronze Age a residue of Greek tribes stayed behind in southern Macedonia. Perhaps in the seventh century one of these, the 'Macedones', occupied Aegae and expanded into the coastal plain of Lower Macedonia, which became the kingdom of 'Macedon'; their descendants were the Macedonians proper of the classical period, and they worshipped Greek gods, especially Zeus and Heracles. The other Greek tribes became intermingled in Upper Macedonia with Illyrians, Paeonians, and Thracians, and the Thracians especially had their own orgiastic religions, such as that portrayed in the *Bacchae*. Southern Greeks planted city-states on the peninsula of Chalcidice and a few on the Macedonian coast. In the early fifth century the royal house of Macedon, the Temenidae, was recognized as Greek by the presidents of the Olympic games. Their verdict was and is decisive; for modern critics adduce no evidence. It is certain that the kings considered themselves to be of Greek descent from Heracles, son of Zeus. The royal house of Lyncus in Upper Macedonia claimed descent from the Bacchiadae, who fled from Corinth about 657. The great wealth of another royal house has been revealed by the gold masks and furniture discovered in tombs of the late sixth century of Trebenishte near Lake Lychnitis. The Temenidae and Bacchiadae certainly spoke Greek. They also spoke the language of their people, 'Macedonian', a strong dialect of very early Greek which was not intelligible to contemporary Greeks. The Macedonians in general did not consider themselves Greeks, nor were they considered Greeks by their neighbours.[1]

The royal house of Macedon claimed a traditional suzerainty over the cantons of Upper Macedonia, just as the Spartan kings did over Lacedaemonia. In the fifth century this suzerainty was of a Homeric type, loosely exercised over individual tribes, which had their own royal houses and served the Macedonian kings in war as their nominal subjects. But it caused Thucydides to regard the areas of Upper and Lower Macedonia as one kingdom, 'Macedonia'. The kingship was 'an hereditary kingship with defined prerogatives', similar to those of the Heroic Age in Mycenaean Greece. It was hereditary to the Temenid house and each successor in the line was elected king by the Macedonian people. He was the personification of the state. His name stood for the state in diplomatic documents and on the coinage, first minted after the Persian wars (Plate XI *l*). He owned all land, held supreme command in war, was judge, priest, and treasurer, and could delegate his powers during absence abroad. Cases of treason in which the king was a litigant were tried by the Macedonian people, and a king could be deposed by their vote. The Macedonians owed him personal service in war and in peace, paid taxes, and rendered him other dues on land and property. Leading families, originally of pastoral groups and then of a settled society, had a personal 'kinship' and a special status with the king. From them the king selected his 'Companions' (*hetairoi*). They attended his court in peace and fought by his side in war, owing him as complete a loyalty as the Myrmidon 'companions' owed to Achilles in the Trojan War. From the Companions the king recruited his Council. Socially the Macedonians were on easy terms with their king. They wore the same dress and spoke to him with frankness.[2]

In the fourth century the institutions of Macedonia were more akin to those of Molossia in Epirus and of Illyria, Paeonia, and Thrace than to those of the Greek city-states. The Macedonian kings attracted Greek culture to their court and encouraged the economic development of their country by trading with Greek states, but their realm remained impervious to the political effects of Greek influence. As a middle class arose, a new group, the 'Foot-Companions' (*pezetairoi*), was formed from it to wait upon the king and receive honours second only to those of his Companions. As villages changed into towns and Pella became the largest city in Macedonia, the urban centres remained administrative units under the throne and did not emerge as independent political entities. The Macedonians themselves had little love for the Greeks who had settled in city-states on their coast and in

---

[1] Hdt. 1. 56. 3; Th. 2. 99; Hdt. 8. 137–9; 5. 22; Isoc. 5. 105 (Heracles); Str. 326 (Lyncestae); Plu. *Alex.* 51. 6; Kalléris, *Les Anciens Macédoniens* i, has a glossary of Macedonian words; Th. 4. 124. 1 fin.; *Vorsokr.* 85 B 2 (Thrasymachus). Population figures for 1951 in *The Statesman's Year Book.*

[2] Th. 2. 99; Plu. *Alex.* 15. 3; Arr. *An.* 1. 7. 5; D. 18. 235; Plu. *Alex.* 42. 2. (as judge); Arr. *An.* 3. 26–27 (treason); 1. 16. 5 (taxes); Il. 1. 179; Arr. *An.* 2. 6. 2 (council); Plb. 5. 27. 6.

Chalcidice, nor for the imperialistic powers, Sparta, Thebes, and Athens, which treated Macedonia as a pawn in the game of power politics. They had been formed into a compact people by pressure from the Greeks as much as from their barbarian neighbours.

The military organization of Macedonia owed much to the last of several able kings, Archelaus (413–399), who built straight roads and fortified strongholds throughout the land. The chief arm was the heavy cavalry led by the king and his Companions. The cavalrymen wore cuirasses, had stronger horses than those usually bred in Greece, and showed themselves superior to the Thracian troops in battle. Archelaus began to develop some heavy infantry, but in the dynastic troubles after his death the infantry seem to have lost importance. The weakness of Macedonia in relation to its neighbours became clear during the reign of Amyntas (393–370). Soon after his accession the Illyrians overran his kingdom. He gave some territory to the powerful Chalcidian League as the price of its neutrality, and soon regained his throne with the help of Thessaly. He then concluded a defensive alliance with the Chalcidian League, which bound both parties to a common policy towards some neighbouring states. When the Chalcidian League was expanding *c.* 382, the Illyrians again broke into Upper Macedonia, and the Chalcidians proceeded to annex most of Lower Macedonia. On this occasion the Chalcidian League was disbanded by Sparta. When it re-formed, Amyntas entered into alliance with Athens *c.* 373 and took part in the abortive negotiations for peace among the Greek states in 371.[1]

It was probably the eldest son of Amyntas, Alexander (370–368), who formed the 'Foot Companions'. The establishment of a regular hoplite force in Macedonia was a sign of economic and social progress in the country. When Alexander was assassinated by Ptolemy (368–365), Thebes and Athens contended for influence in Macedonia. When Ptolemy was displaced by Amyntas' eldest surviving son, Perdiccas (365–359), the Athenian Timotheus seized Methone and Pydna on the Macedonian coast, and forced Perdiccas to accept an alliance against the Chalcidian League and Amphipolis. At this time Timotheus won Torone and Potidaea from the Chalcidian League, but he failed then and later to capture Amphipolis. In 362 Perdiccas changed sides and sent troops to help Amphipolis against Athens. In 359 Perdiccas attacked the Illyrians and suffered an overwhelming defeat, in which he and 4,000 Macedonians were killed. By such desperate changes of alliance did the Macedonian kings strive with varying success to maintain the safety of their realm.[2]

In early summer 359 the Macedonian people elected as king the infant son of Perdiccas, Amyntas, and as regent Philip, brother of Perdiccas, who was

---

[1] Th. 2. 100. 2 and 5 (the larger Macedonian horse may have been bred from Nesaean horses captured in the Persian wars, Hdt. 7. 40. 3; its heavy build is portayed on Macedonian coins); X. *HG.* 5. 2. 12; 38; D.S. 14. 92; 15. 19. 2; *GHI* 111; 129; Aeschin. 2. 32.

[2] *FGrH* 72 F 4 (Anaximenes), referred by some to Alexander I; Aeschin. 2. 26–33.

twenty-two years old. Philip, having spent the years 367–364 as a hostage at Thebes, where he knew Epaminondas and Pelopidas, was already conversant with contemporary methods in diplomacy and war. The kingdom for which he now became responsible was in danger of dismemberment. Lyncus was lost to Illyria. Pelagonia, an adjacent canton, had recently contracted an independent alliance with Athens, and its prince, Menelaus, who was expelled about 362, received refuge and citizenship at Athens. The record of the *theorodokoi* (who welcomed missions to and from the shrine at Epidaurus) shows that the following places in Macedonia were independent in the reign of Perdiccas: Pydna, Methone, and Aenea on the coast; Calindoea in Mygdonia, represented by a Pausanias; and Apollonia and Argilus on the approaches to Amphipolis. The Pausanias at Calindoea was probably the Pausanias who was one of several pretenders to the throne in 359. He received backing from Berisades, king of western Thrace. Three half-brothers of Philip—Archelaus, Arrhidaeus, and Menelaus—probably hoped for support among the Macedonians. Argaeus, who had at one time displaced Amyntas, the father of Philip, was supported by Athens. In addition, the Paeonians were preparing to emulate the Illyrians and overrun Macedonia. Philip's only allies were the Chalcidian League, always ready to grab land from Macedonia, and Amphipolis, which troops sent by Perdiccas were helping to defend against Athens.[1]

Philip struck at once to keep his enemies divided. He bought off Berisades, who then killed Pausanias. He engineered the assassination of Archelaus, whose brothers later found refuge with the Chalcidian League. He paid a *danegeld* to the Paeonians, so that they should not invade. He withdrew his troops from Amphipolis, and started to train his Macedonian infantry in the manner which he had learnt at Thebes. In late summer, when Argaeus, with 3,000 mercenary hoplites from Athens, marched inland from the Athenian base at Methone and an Athenian general with a considerable fleet lay in the Thermaic Gulf, Philip did not prevent him from reaching Aegae (Vergina). He knew that the people would remain faithful, and he wished to demonstrate the fact to Athens. When Argaeus turned back, Philip attacked, defeated his troops, and surrounded the survivors on a hill. On condition that Argaeus and any Macedonians with him were surrendered, Philip let the others depart without ransom, sent envoys to Athens to renounce any claim on his part to Amphipolis, and asked for a treaty of peace. At this time Athens was his most dangerous enemy. Fortunately for Philip her interests were centred rather on Amphipolis and the Chersonese than on Macedonia. Athens, therefore, made peace with Philip, probably in the winter, hoping no doubt to bring him on to her side in the war against the Chalcidian League and Amphipolis.[2]

Secure from attack by sea, Philip invaded Paeonia in summer 358, won a great victory, and made the Paeonians subject to his authority. He turned

[1] Just. 7. 5. 2 (Philip at Thebes); *GHI* 143; 148; *IG* 4². i. 94–95 (*theorodokoi*); D.S. 16. 2; Just. 7. 4. 5.   [2] D.S. 16. 3–4. 1; Polyaen. 4. 2. 10, 17.

next on the Illyrians, the common enemies of all Macedonian and Paeonian cantons, and invaded Lyncus with an army of 600 cavalry and 10,000 infantry. The Illyrian king, Bardylis, recalling his own decisive victory a year before, now offered peace on the *status quo* and persisted in keeping the Macedonian soil he had won. Philip decided to engage the Illyrian army of 500 cavalry and 10,000 selected infantry, which lay in an open plain. Because he was outclassed in cavalry, Bardylis formed his infantry into a square. Adopting the tactics of the great Theban generals, Philip in person led his finest infantry forward, delaying the advance of his centre and left wing, and ordered the cavalry on his right to charge in, on the flank and rear of the enemy, as soon as an opening appeared. The spearhead of his infantry smote the left corner of the Illyrian square, stove it in, and spread confusion into the flank and rear, where his heavy cavalry galloped in to the attack. This concentrated onslaught shattered the left half of the Illyrian square. The army fled across the wide plain, hotly pursued by the cavalry, and 7,000 men had been slain before the survivors reached the hills. Bardylis sued for terms. Philip made peace on condition that Bardylis ceded all territory up to Lake Lychnidus; and he later received in marriage Audata, an Illyrian princess. By this victory his infantry as well as his cavalry proved their superiority over the troops of the Balkan kings.[1]

The defeat of Illyria relieved Epirus from pressure, and the gratitude of the Molossian royal house was marked by the marriage of Philip with the princess Olympias, daughter of Neoptolemus, who became the queen in Philip's household. For it was probably now that the Macedonians deposed the child Amyntas and elected Philip as King Philip II of Macedon. In spring 357 Philip laid siege to Amphipolis. He knew that Athens was already fighting in Euboea and had more vital interests in the Chersonese than at Amphipolis; therefore, when the Amphipolitans offered their city to Athens in return for an effective garrison, Philip proposed to Athens that he would give her Amphipolis in exchange for her ally on his coast, Pydna. Athens accepted his proposal, and the two states signed a secret pact. The fact that Philip had some understanding with Athens deterred the Chalcidian League from attacking him, lest her own coasts be attacked from the Athenian bases at Potidaea and Torone. While Athens lost the battle of Chios and concentrated her resources against the rebels in the Hellespontine area, Philip pressed on with the siege of the city which had defied so many Athenian generals. In late summer the Chalcidian League, realizing that he might succeed, asked Athens for peace and offered alliance against Philip. At this time Athens' situation in the east Aegean was too critical for any diversion of her forces. The Chalcidian offer was refused, and in autumn Philip's battering-rams breached the walls of Amphipolis. The victor declared Amphipolis independent, to the surprise and pleasure of the Chalcidian League, and the Amphipolitan democracy exiled the leading partisans of Athens. Philip at

[1] D.S. 16. 4. 2–7; Front. *Strat.* 2. 3. 2.

once attacked Pydna, where a pro-Macedonian party opened the gates and surrendered the city. The secret pact was thereby broken, and Athens had lost her bargaining counter as well. She declared war on Philip. But her hands were tied by the Social War, and Philip began to negotiate for an alliance with the Chalcidian League, now the strongest power in the north-west Aegean.[1]

In winter 357–356 during the negotiations with the Chalcidian League, the Aleuadae of Larisa appealed to Philip for help against the sons of Alexander, who now ruled over Pherae. Philip welcomed the opportunity to defend liberty against tyranny. He sent sufficient help to earn the gratitude of Larisa, where he married a Thessalian lady, Philinna, and became a close friend of the Larisean spokesman, Cineas. His gain was at the expense of Athens, the ally hitherto of the Thessalian League, but in spring 356 Thebes took control and carried the whole of Thessaly with her in passing the Amphictyonic sentence against Phocis.[2]

Since its dissolution by Sparta in 379, the Chalcidian League had regained its strength. While Athens was at the height of her power, the League had maintained the independence of Amphipolis and lost only Potidaea and Torone. As chief exporter for Macedonia and Paeonia, and also for western Thrace during Athens' numerous attacks on Amphipolis, the cities of the League had become very prosperous. Its armed forces rivalled those of Macedon in reputation (for it had 1,000 cavalry and 10,000 hoplites), and its ships, if supported by Athens, could blockade the Thermaic Gulf. It could raise allies in the hinterland against Philip, strike rapidly at his capital, and sever his communications through Anthemus with Amphipolis. In winter 357 both Athens and Philip were suing for alliance with the League. Because the future of Macedonia was now at stake, Philip offered the rich area Mygdonia to the Chalcidian League and promised to help in freeing Potidaea from Athens. A defensive alliance between Macedon and the League was concluded on these terms with the blessing of Apollo, who prophesied that the pact would be in the interests of the two parties, and copies were set up at Delphi, at Olynthus in the Temple of Artemis, and at Dium in that of Zeus of Olympus. Macedonia and the League were now formally at war with Athens. So the treaty of alliance contained an undertaking not to negotiate separately with her. Safeguarded by this alliance, Philip captured Potidaea in spring 356, let the Athenians depart without ransom, and handed the town to the League. Athens had sent a force to the relief of Potidaea, which arrived too late, and she now began to organize a coalition of powers in the hinterland to attack Macedonia.[3]

The appeasement of the Chalcidian League enabled Philip to advance beyond Amphipolis to Crenides, which asked for help against the Thracians.

[1] Just. 7. 6. 10; D.S. 16. 8. 2; D. 1. 8; [D.] 7. 27; D. 2. 6; *FGrH* 115 F 30 (Theopompus); *GHI* 150; D. 1. 5 (Pydna).

[2] Polyaen. 4. 2. 19; D.S. 16. 14. 1–2; *FGrH* 115 F 34–35.

[3] D.S. 16. 8. 3–5; *GHI* 158; D. 6. 20; 4. 35; 23. 107.

He fortified the town, strengthened it by planting settlers there, renamed it Philippi, under which title it continued to issue coins, and acquired control of the gold and silver mines on Mt. Pangaeum. This advance increased the hostility of Cetriporis, king of western Thrace, who with Lyppeus, king of Paeonia, and Grabus, king of Illyria, entered into an alliance with Athens in July 356, in order to defeat Philip and wrest from him Crenides and other places. Athens, however, was mustering her strength before the disastrous naval battle at Embata. Without her help, or that of the Chalcidian League, the three kings were defeated piecemeal. In August 356 Philip received three items of good news on the same day: his general Parmenio had defeated the Illyrians, Olympias had borne a boy, Alexander, and his horse had won a race at the Olympic Games. Cetriporis, too, fell under his sway, and in early summer 355 the Athenian base, Neapolis, was isolated and in danger. Before the end of 355 he held the territory of Abdera and Maronea on the Thracian coast. Athens was now weakened by her collapse in the Social War, and in midwinter 355 Philip undertook the very dangerous operation of attacking Methone, the last Athenian base on his coast. For if Athens and the Chalcidian League combined, they could overrun Lower Macedonia. But the League held to its alliance. An Athenian relief force arrived in summer 354 to find that the city had been carried by a desperate assault.[1]

In the years 359–354 Philip won the devotion of the Macedonian army. He led his men in the attack against Bardylis and in the siege of Methone, where an arrow deprived him of the sight of his right eye, and his generalship in battle and in siege-warfare was vindicated by success. Thus a great citizen army was being built at a time when the Greek states relied mainly upon mercenaries. In diplomacy Philip outwitted his adversaries. By quick and bold decisions he played off Athens against the Chalcidian League and the Chalcidian League against Athens, so that he kept his potential enemies divided and advanced his own interest. By leaving Amphipolis and Philippi autonomous and showing generosity to the inhabitants, he encouraged those who might aid him in other cities. In Thessaly he espoused the cause of liberty against the tyrants of Pherae, and at Delphi he was on friendly terms with the authorities, until the shrine was seized by Philomelus. Even when he was at war with Athens, he tried to avoid embitterment. For he released her mercenaries in 359, let her agents go free from Amphipolis and her colonists from Potidaea, and did not enslave the people of Methone, who were allowed to depart with one garment apiece.[2]

Although Philip had liberated Macedonia and lulled the Chalcidian League into alliance by 354, his power was by no means consolidated within the areas

---

[1] D.S. 16. 8. 6–7; Harp. s.v. *Datos*; St. Byz. s.v. *Philippoi*; *GC* 200; D.S. 16. 22. 3; *GHI* 157; Plu. *Alex*. 3. 8; *GHI* 159; Polyaen. 4. 2. 22 (Maronea); D.S. 16. 31. 6 (cf. 34. 4–5); *IG* ii.² 130; *FGrH* 115 F 52 (Theopompus).

[2] D. 6. 20 shows that, if Potidaea was 'andrapodized' (D.S. 16. 8. 5, where the reading is uncertain), the Chalcidians so treated the native Potidaeans.

under his authority. The cantons of Upper Macedonia had a long tradition of independence and lagged behind Lower Macedonia in prosperity. Philip's aim was to weld the whole of Macedonia into one kingdom. In order to engage the loyalty of the royal house of Elimia, he married one of its members, Phila, and his general policy was to enrol the aristocracy of the cantons among his Companions. To this end, too, he chose young nobles to be pages at his court. It is probable that he built military roads, as Archelaus had done, founded some cities, such as Heraclea Lynci to commemorate his victory over Bardylis, and strengthened others, as he did Philippi. These roads not only enabled him to exploit his strategic position in the centre of the Balkans by speed of manoeuvre. They, and the cities built on them, also facilitated the development of trade. Pella was already a thriving port. It was perhaps there that Callistratus, in exile from Athens, sold the harbour dues for 40 talents *c.* 360. The capture of Pydna and Methone finally removed the last middlemen from the Macedonian coast. The alliance of Macedonia and the Chalcidian League was of great economic benefit to both parties and accelerated the development of Upper Macedonia. Above all, the mines on Mt. Pangaeum soon yielded 1,000 talents of gold and silver ore a year. Abandoning the archaic Persian standard in coinage, he adopted the Thracian standard in silver and the Attic standard in gold, so that Macedonia could trade freely within the orbits of Thrace and Athens, and especially with the Chalcidian League, where the same standards were in force. His coins soon had a wide circulation. The emblems included the heads of Heracles Zeus of Olympus, a horse and rider who is probably Philip, and the racehorse ridden by a boy jockey at the Olympic Games (Plate XII *h*).[1]

In the past the predecessors of Philip had gained and lost territories, but he built for permanence. As his conquests grew, he incorporated some of them into Macedonia as king's land won by the spear; and he created new Macedonian citizens by granting holdings therein, sometimes to the natives and sometimes to Greeks whom he wished to include in his entourage. The land of Methone, for instance, was divided up in this way, but the city with its autonomous tradition was destroyed. Thus he developed the national territorial state, capable unlike the Greek city-state of expanding its territory and its citizenship by incorporation. Farther afield, where the time was not yet ripe for incorporation, he left the local systems in force: Amphipolis and Philippi remained autonomous, and Lyppeus in Paeonia and Cetriporis in western Thrace ruled as vassal-kings. In 354, when these great changes were being made in the life of Upper Macedonia, there was still considerable friction which might be exploited by an outside power. The successes of Philip in his foreign policy had not yet made Macedonia into a centralized and united state, when he was tempted by the situation in Greece to intervene in the Sacred War.

[1] X. *HG.* 5. 2. 38 (Derdas of Elimia independent); Arr. *An.* 4. 13. 1 (Pages); [Arist.] *Oec.* 2. 1350ᵃ16 (Callistratus); *GC* 200.

§ 2. *Philip in Thessaly and Thrace*

In 354 Philomelus exploited his strategic position athwart the main route between his chief enemies, Thessaly and Boeotia. By defeating the Thessalian army in the spring, he not only prevented his enemies from joining forces but put Thessaly out of the war for a year. Boeotia was now surrounded by her enemies; for Athens, Euboea, and, across the Gulf, Achaea were in League with Phocis, and Locris was exhausted after two defeats at the hands of Philomelus. During the summer Boeotia could make no headway. Meanwhile in Thessaly the tyrants of Pherae went to war with the cities of the Thessalian League. As neither side could expect help from Boeotia, they looked elsewhere, the League to Philip and the tyrants to Athens. In late summer, after the fall of Methone, Philip laid siege to Pagasae, the port of Pherae, and Athens sent a naval force to its relief. Again Philip was too quick for Athens. In autumn 354 he captured Pagasae and also controlled the passes of Tempe and Oloösson. Pherae was now isolated.[1]

In late autumn 354 Philomelus was defeated and killed by the Boeotians at Neon in Phocis. The bulk of the Phocians and their mercenaries escaped into the foot-hills of Parnassus, and faction broke out again in the Phocian state. Boeotia decided to send her general, Pammenes, with 5,000 men to help Artabazus, the satrap in revolt, in order to replenish her finances; he departed early in 353, and Boeotia was confident of giving Phocis the *coup de grâce* with the rest of her forces when the snows left the mountains. On his way Pammenes met Philip at Maronea in Thrace in spring 353, where Cersebleptes, king of eastern Thrace, was under pressure not only from Philip but also from Athens. Pammenes then negotiated a pact of non-aggression between Philip and Cersebleptes, which confirmed the friendship between Thebes and Philip and secured Pammenes a passage through Thrace to Asia. Soon afterward Athens concluded an alliance with Amadocus, the king of central Thrace.[2]

In spring 353 Boeotia found herself cheated of her hopes. By executing all prisoners taken in the Sacred War, she had driven the Phocians to desperation. They united under an able leader, Onomarchus, who hired more mercenaries, subsidized friends abroad, and invited any friendly state to send representatives to Delphi as 'wardens of the temple-fabric' (*naopoioi*). Athens, Locris, Megara, Epidaurus, Sparta, Corinth, and Phocis sent funds for the rebuilding of the Temple, which had been destroyed in 373–372. Their participation was of more political than practical value, but Onomarchus had the troops to force East and West Locris into acquiescence by capturing Thronium and threatening Amphissa, re-found Orchomenus, and pin down the depleted forces of Boeotia. In Thessaly, too, Onomarchus used bribery; for if he could swing the states of Thessaly on to his side, he would possess

---

[1] D.S. 16. 30. 4–31. 2; 31. 6; D. 1. 9; 4. 35; *FGrH* 115 F 78 (Theopompus); Polyaen. 4. 2. 19.   [2] D.S. 16. 31. 3–5; 32. 1–2; 34. 1–2 (Pammenes); D. 23. 183.

a crushing superiority over Boeotia on the Amphictyonic Council and on the field of battle. The Thessalian cities, however, invoked the help of Philip against the tyrants of Pherae and Crannon, and in summer 353 Philip defeated the combined forces of the tyrants and Phayllus, the brother of Onomarchus, who was supporting them with 7,000 Phocian mercenaries. Onomarchus, however, marched north with his full force in the autumn, defeated the combined army of Philip and his Thessalian allies, and drove Philip out of Thessaly with heavy loss to his Macedonian troops. On his return to Phocis Onomarchus defeated the Boeotian army and captured Coronea.[1]

The power of Onomarchus, *strategos autocrator* of Phocis, based upon Delphi's gold, mercenary troops, and his allies' goodwill, reigned supreme from Mt. Olympus to the Gulf of Corinth and threatened to extinguish Boeotia, the only unbeaten signatory of the Amphictyonic decree which had declared the Sacred War. His allies, too, had successes in 353. Sparta defeated Argos at Orneae and proposed that all territories in Greece should revert to their original owners, so that Phocis would keep Delphi, Sparta recover Messenia, Athens regain Oropus, and Thebes lose control over Orchomenus, Thespiae, and Plataea. Athens at last gained a foothold in the Chersonese, where Chares captured Sestus, massacred the adult males, and sold the rest of the population into slavery, and forced Cersebleptes into making an alliance and ceding all the cities of the Chersonese, except Cardia.[2]

Philip, however, had withdrawn, 'like a ram, to butt the harder'. Early in 352 he laid siege to Pherae. When its tyrants appealed to Onomarchus and Athens for aid, Philip persuaded the Thessalian League to put its forces under his command. In the spring Onomarchus came north with 500 cavalry and 20,000 infantry, and a considerable Athenian fleet under Chares sailed in support of him. The intention of Onomarchus and Chares was presumably to reach the foot-hills east of Phthiotic Thebes; there the Athenians would disembark, and their joint forces would march through hilly country to collect the fine cavalry and the mercenaries of Pherae, before engaging the enemy. Philip had meanwhile assembled a Macedonian and Thessalian army of 3,000 cavalry and over 20,000 infantry outside Pherae, and his intention was to engage before Onomarchus could join his allies and strengthen his cavalry arm. When news of Onomarchus' approach was received, Philip left Pherae during the night, probably deceiving its defenders into expecting an attack at dawn, and hastened into the plain south of Phthiotic Thebes, where he caught the army of Onomarchus near the coast. Before the Athenian fleet could disembark its troops, Philip attacked Onomarchus. As soon as the infantry lines were engaged, the Thessalian and Macedonian cavalry assaulted the flank of the enemy and drove them to the shore, where many threw off

---

[1] D.S. 16. 32. 3–33; 35. 1–3; *Fouilles de Delphes* 3. 5. 79 f. and 3 fasc. *Chronologie delphique* 13 (*naopoioi*); for chronology see *JHS* 57. 62 = *StGH* 518; Polyaen. 2. 38. 2.

[2] D.S. 16. 34. 3–4; D. 16, e.g. 4 and 16.

their armour and swam out to the Athenian ships. Of the Phocian army more than 6,000 were killed in battle, and 3,000 prisoners were taken. In accordance with the precedent set by the Greek belligerents of the Sacred War, the prisoners were put to death by hanging or drowning, and the victorious Macedonians and Thessalians, crowned with wreaths of laurel, gave thanks to Apollo, the god of Delphi.[1]

An immediate result of the victory of the 'Crocus Field', as it has been called, was the capitulation of Pherae and other cities, from which the tyrants and their 2,000 mercenaries withdrew under safe conduct. Philip then helped the Thessalian League to put its house in order. Pharcadon and Tricca, which were at war with their neighbours, were defeated and the former was destroyed, the western plain of Thessaly was pacified, and now or later Gomphi, from which a pass led to the Gulf of Ambracia, was renamed Philippi and received some Macedonian settlers. Philip also acquired some strongpoints in Perrhaebia and Magnesia, which strengthened his control of the passes of Oloösson and Tempe, and placed some troops in Pagasae to safeguard the freedom of Pherae. The Thessalian League accepted Philip as commander of its forces, and granted him the market and harbour dues of the country. In midsummer 352 he led his Macedonian and Thessalian troops towards Thermopylae.[2]

After the battle of the Crocus Field Phayllus succeeded Onomarchus. He rallied his supporters in other states by further subsidies of gold. Sparta sent 1,000 men and Achaea 2,000 men, and the 2,000 mercenaries of the Thessalian tyrants joined him. He suffered several minor defeats in Boeotia, before the movement of Philip towards Thermopylae drew him northwards. Then Athens, too, sent 400 cavalry and 5,000 hoplites by sea to help in the defence of Thermopylae and prevent Philip from joining forces with Boeotia. Faced by this coalition of Phocis' allies Philip withdrew. He had no wish to break his army against a strong defensive position, or to dissipate his fame as the champion of Apollo. His energy, however, was not exhausted. In November 352 he was besieging Heraeum Teichos near the shore of the Propontis at the invitation of Byzantium, Perinthus, and Amadocus, who were at war with Cersebleptes. By spring 351 Cersebleptes was defeated. He ceded some disputed territories to Philip's allies, and surrendered his son to Philip as a hostage. Philip himself drew his frontier at the river Hebrus, and established friendly relations with Cardia on the neck of the Chersonese. The Bosporus was now controlled by his ally Byzantium, which had annexed Chalcedon and Selymbria. Athens meanwhile received overtures for friendship and alliance from the Chalcidian League in autumn 352, which were meant to be secret

---

[1] D.S. 16. 35. 3–6 (the 'chance' presence of Chares' fleet is unlikely; the word probably reflects an attempt to exculpate Athens); *FGrH* 115 F 249 (Theopompus); Polyaen. 4. 2. 20 (probably on the eve of the battle); Paus. 10. 2. 5; Justin 8. 2. 3.

[2] D.S. 16. 37. 3; 38. 1; D. 1. 13; Polyaen. 4. 2. 18; St. Byz. s.v. *Philippoi*; Isoc. 5. 21; *FGrH* 115 F 81, 82 (Theopompus).

but became known; she also voted to dispatch an expeditionary force to the Chersonese. On his return from Thrace in spring 351 Philip told the Chalcidian leaders the story of the lady, Insolence, who was always pursued by her jealous husband, War. This sufficed to terminate the overtures, which constituted a breach of the Chalcidian alliance with Philip in 357/356, and a report that Philip was ill caused the Athenians to reduce the size of their expedition to the Chersonese.[1]

After the withdrawal of Philip the Sacred War degenerated into guerrilla operations in central Greece and resulted in the ravaging of East Locris, Phocis, and north Boeotia. Phayllus fell ill in 351 and was succeeded by Phalaecus, who discontinued the meetings of the *naopoioi* and sent troops into the Peloponnese. There Sparta had attacked Megalopolis and precipitated a major war. She obtained 150 cavalry from the exiled tyrants of Pherae and 3,000 infantry from Phalaecus, while Megalopolis was supported by the full levies of Argos, Sicyon, and Messene and later by 500 cavalry and 4,000 infantry from Boeotia. Several battles were fought before Archidamus, the king of Sparta, gained a convincing victory and forced Megalopolis to sign an armistice, probably in summer 351. The Phocians and the Boeotians then returned to continue the Sacred War in their own territories.[2]

During the years 355 to 351 Athens showed unusual restraint in her foreign policy. Invitations to attack Boeotia in her weakness, raise Rhodes in revolt from Persia, intervene in central Thrace, and join one side or the other in wars in the Peloponnese were all refused. Expeditions were sent out to help Methone, Neapolis, and Pagasae, to oppose Philip in Thessaly and again at Thermopylae, and to win the Chersonese, where cleruchs were established at Sestus in 353/352. Athens let her allies fight for her in some of the wars to which she was committed: the Phocians and the tyrants of Pherae in the theatres of the Sacred War, Amadocus in central Thrace, and later Cersebleptes in eastern Thrace. She made an alliance with Locris and attempted to do so with the Chalcidian League.

The general policy in these years was inspired by Eubulus, Chief Commissioner of the Theoric Fund, and his supporters, among whom was Aeschines, a powerful orator. His aims showed a proper sense of priorities: financial recuperation, resistance to Philip, control of the Chersonese, and non-intervention elsewhere. The proposal to defend Thermopylae was made by Diophantus, the assistant of Eubulus, and the negotiations with the Chalcidian League were probably handled by Eubulus. His steady policy restored the trade and finances of Athens; the revenues rose to some 400 talents in 347/346 and the contributions of the Allies rose from 45 talents in 354 to 60 talents. Most of the surplus was used in laying down new triremes and improving the docks and fortifications. In 353/352 Athens had 349 ships on

[1] D.S. 16. 37; 38. 1–2; D. 4. 17; Schol. Aeschin. 2. 86 (Heraeum Teichos); D. 3. 4; 15. 26 (Byzantium); 23. 109 (Chalcidian League); *FGrH* 115 F 101, 127 (Theopompus).

[2] D.S. 16. 38. 3–39. 7; Paus. 8. 27. 9.

her naval list, and by 349 recent armaments had cost 1,500 talents. The cleruchy at Samos was reinforced in 352/351. The amount of wealth in private hands increased rapidly so that the mines were developed on a large scale and a capital levy (*eisphora*) of 60 talents was voted in 352/351. This stable policy in 354–350 was only achieved by liberal disbursements from the Theoric Fund for festivals and relief, but it did not result in a lack of military effort or a preference for pacificism, whenever the real interests of Athens were at stake.[1]

In these years Demosthenes (384–322) commenced his career as a politician. He was already an accomplished orator, having prosecuted his guardians, who had squandered his inheritance, and then taken part in two political cases in 355 and 354. In his first public speech (*On the Symmories*), delivered in 354, he opposed an offensive against Persia, which was being advocated in the Assembly. At this time Athens was in the doldrums, and Persia was raising large forces. Demosthenes therefore argued that Athens lacked the financial resources for such an operation; she should rather prepare against the enemies she already had. He took the opportunity to suggest a reform in the system of raising money for the trierarchies by means of boards (*symmoriai*), and he outlined a more efficient method of manning the fleet at short notice. This sensible speech, which agreed with the policy of Eubulus at the time, was followed in later years by two speeches in which he recommended an offensive policy. In the latter part of 353 Sparta and Megalopolis were at enmity, and both asked Athens for an alliance, which would involve her in war in the Peloponnese; Sparta could offer the aid of Elis and Phlius, Megalopolis that of the other Peloponnesian states. In his speech (*For the Megalopolitans*) Demosthenes advised Athens to join Megalopolis against Sparta, in order to maintain a balance of power in the Peloponnese and detach Megalopolis from her alliance with Thebes. Had his advice been followed, Athens would have alienated her ally Sparta, spent her resources in an unimportant theatre, gained no help from her new allies in any area outside the Peloponnese, and exacerbated her relations with Thebes. In 351 the exiled democrats of Rhodes asked Athens to liberate Rhodes from an oligarchy which was supported by Caria. Demosthenes (*For the Liberty of the Rhodians*) urged Athens to do so; he argued that Caria would not retaliate, Persia should be forced to reveal her attitude, and democrats should be helped against oligarchs. This policy was of a piece with his policy for the Peloponnese. Both advocated methods which had led to the collapse of the Second Athenian Alliance.[2]

The policies advocated towards Megalopolis and Rhodes showed a complete disregard of the menace from Macedon. Two explanations are possible. Either Demosthenes lacked the intelligence to appreciate the menace, or he

---

[1] *IG* ii.² 1613, l. 297 (Sestus); *IG* ii.² 148 (Locris); *FGrH* 115 F 166 (Theopompus); D. 18. 234; *IG* ii.² 1613 (naval list); D. 3. 28; *FGrH* 328 F 154 (Philochorus); D. 3. 4 (*eisphora*); *FGrH* 115 F 99; D. 4. 35.

[2] D. 14. 5, 9, 11, 36; D. 16. 4–6, 30–31; D. 15. 11, 13, 19.

chose to disregard it in order to push his own policy. The latter is much the more probable. His aim, in fact, was as much to unseat Eubulus, who opposed these policies, and bring himself to the fore, as to embroil Athens in war. By the very nature of politics in the Assembly a politician could only gain prominence by attacking those already in favour, and in such attacks politicians used arguments and advocated policies which appealed to the past traditions of Athens. The opposition of Demosthenes to Eubulus was indeed apparent in a law-court speech (*Against Aristocrates*) delivered in summer 352, which touched on policy in Thrace. Demosthenes advised alliance with the minor princes in Thrace, so that the country would be divided and Athens hold the balance of power. Such a policy was unrealistic, not only because it under-estimated Philip's strength but also because it over-estimated Athens' ability to apply military power in an inland and mountainous area. Demosthenes' aim, however, was rather to obtain a condemnation, and incidentally to attack Eubulus and his supporters.[1]

In 351 and 350 Athens saw little of Philip, and her fears were somewhat allayed. Events in the East commanded attention. Artabazus, who had been helped by Chares in 356–355 and Pammenes in 353–352, fled with his mercenary captain, Memnon of Rhodes, to Philip's court, probably in winter 352–351. Artaxerxes Ochus, who had recruited large forces, invaded Egypt probably in 351. He was severely defeated by the Egyptians, whose mercenaries were commanded by Diophantus of Athens and Lamius of Sparta. A series of revolts then broke out in Cyprus and Phoenicia, and Artaxerxes employed Phocion of Athens and 8,000 mercenaries under the general command of Idrieus, satrap of Caria, to reduce Cyprus in 350. In 351/350 he paid a subsidy of 300 talents to Thebes, which was in need of funds for the Sacred War. At this time the Athenian commanders in the Chersonese were on friendly terms with Orontes, satrap of Mysia, who later, *c.* 349, revolted from Artaxerxes and controlled north-west Asia Minor. The Athenian hold on the Hellespont was thus strengthened, and Persia was to be occupied by the Phoenician revolt until 345.[2]

§ 3. *The clash between Macedon and Athens in Chalcidice*

MEANWHILE Philip extended his sway westwards. Probably in 351 he reduced the Illyrians west and south-west of Lake Lychnitis, except those near the Adriatic coast, and left their king to rule as his vassal. This area, which included the rich plains of the lakeland, paid him tribute and supplied fine light-armed troops, and fortified posts were built in it to secure his communications toward Epirus. There his brother-in-law Alexander was heir to the Molossian throne, for which Arybbas acted as regent. In 350 Philip

[1] D. 23. 207–10 (attacking Eubulus and his supporters).
[2] D.S. 16. 52. 3 (Artabazus); 40. 6 (Egypt); 48. 2; D. 15. 5; D.S. 16. 42. 7; 46. 1 (Phocion); 40. 2 (Thebes); cf. *GHI* 160. The chronology in D.S. is very confused.

entered Epirus, removed Alexander to his own court, and annexed Parauaea, through which the passes ran from the upper Aous valley to Macedonia. He also campaigned in Paeonia and probably extended his realm northwards. In north Thessaly he tightened his control over Pagasae and Magnesia, probably in the winter of 350–349, and despite protests from the Thessalians he continued to take for himself the market and harbour dues of Thessaly. In the east he probably came to terms with Persia at this time, whereby Artabazus and Memnon returned home and relations of friendly neutrality were established between Macedon and Persia. The fleet which he was gradually enlarging raided Lemnos, Imbros, and Scyros from the Thracian coast, probably in 351, and captured Athenian corn-ships off Euboea from bases in Thessaly. On one occasion his triremes landed troops at Marathon and captured a state-galley there on its way to a festival at Delos. By 349 he felt strong enough to undertake the most dangerous operation still awaiting him, the conquest of the Chalcidian League, which offered a base of operations for his enemies.[1]

In Athens the activities of Philip were frequently debated in the Assembly. Demosthenes' *First Philippic* was delivered in such a debate, probably in 350. He gave a fine analysis of Philip's speed and resilience, comparing him to a deft boxer whose blows are always parried too late, and urged Athens to attack Philip in Macedonia before he attacked her in Attica. The problem, however, was how to attack. Demosthenes proposed to maintain a mobile force of 2,000 infantry and 200 cavalry with ten warships and some transports, based on Lemnos, Thasos, and Sciathos, which should raid the Macedonian coast and blockade Philip's ports. This operation, costing some ninety talents a year, would have had little chance of success as an offensive measure; for Athens had no base inside the Thermaic Gulf, and Macedonia did not live on imports. He also proposed to have fifty ships and a citizen force of some 10,000 men ready to sail from the Peiraeus at short notice. If it was practicable, this measure, already suggested in his speech *On the Symmories*, was a sensible one. The speech made a stirring appeal to the people to fight in person and to avoid procrastination. The test came in 349. In the summer, when some Macedonian sympathizers, probably paid by Philip, were influential in Olynthus and had just banished a democratic leader, Apollonides, to whom Athens gave her citizenship, Philip ordered the leaders of the Chalcidian League to surrender two pretenders to his throne, his half-brothers Arrhidaeus and Menelaus. The decision for the Chalcidian League now lay between appeasement, followed ultimately by absorption into Macedon, and independence, followed at once by war. The League refused to surrender Arrhidaeus and Menelaus, and asked Athens for assistance.

In the *First Olynthiac* Demosthenes urged Athens to attack her powerful enemy at once by sending a defensive force to protect Chalcidice and an

[1] D. 1. 13; 4. 48; Isoc. 5. 21; D. 1. 12 with Schol. (Thessaly); 2. 11; Arr. *An.* 2. 14. 2 (Persia); D. 4. 34; [D.] 59. 3; Aeschin. 2. 72.

offensive force to raid Macedonia. He hinted at the need, but did not make the proposal, to repeal the law governing the Theoric Fund and apply all surplus revenue to the Military Fund, where it would be needed to wage a major war. Another orator, Demades, opposed this policy. His attitude was revealed by his epigram, uttered perhaps on this occasion, that the Theoric Fund was as vital to the democracy as glue to a book (because it kept the people united). The Assembly made an alliance with the League, and sent to Olynthus 2,000 peltast mercenaries and thirty-eight triremes under Chares. Soon afterwards Demosthenes delivered the *Second Olynthiac*, in which he argued that Philip was not too strong an enemy for Athens to attack and that his power, being based on injustice, was bound to decay. He depicted Philip as a dissolute tyrant, the Companions as footpads and toadies, and the Macedonian people as discontented. This misrepresentation, so strange after the *First Olynthiac*, may have been designed to encourage the Athenians, but it is doubtful if it imparted the sense of urgency which Demosthenes and the occasion required. The *Third Olynthiac* made a powerful attack on the people and their leaders and called for the appointment of *nomothetae* to repeal the law of the Theoric Fund. 'At present the politicians hold the purse-strings and control everything, while you, the people, enervated and bereft of funds and allies, play the part of their menial attendants, grateful for any festival money they distribute among you.' During the winter, when the situation had worsened, Apollodorus proposed not the appointment of *nomothetae* but the immediate allocation of surplus monies. In the Assembly no one opposed him, but the proposal was obstructed as being illegal, and later he was fined a talent.[1]

The three Olynthiac speeches were delivered before November or December, when Philip opened hostilities. Sailing conditions then were so bad that Athens could not send further aid. Some cities in Chalcidice fell by treachery, others by storm, and the promontory of Pallene was occupied by the Macedonians. Philip himself was diverted to Pherae, where one of the exiled tyrants, Peitholaus, now an Athenian citizen, had re-established himself. He drove out Peitholaus before January 348. Late in that month, in accordance with Philip's plans, a rising started in Euboea against the pro-Athenian tyrant of Eretria, Plutarchus, who asked Athens for help. Phocion, sent in command of a small force of picked citizen troops, fell back on the defensive, as the rising spread and Macedonian mercenaries entered the island from Thessaly. Nevertheless, he won a victory at Tamynae, let his Greek captives go free, and garrisoned the narrow waist of the island in early April. At this time the full citizen levy reached the island, and Phocion was recalled. His successor failed dismally. Early in July Athens paid fifty talents to recover Athenian prisoners of war and recognized the independence of all Euboea except Carystus.[2]

During the winter the Macedonians advanced in Chalcidice and the League

[1] Suid. s.v. *Demades*; Plu. *Moral.* 1011b; *FGrH* 328 F 49–51 (Philochorus); [D.] 59. 3–5.
[2] D.S. 16. 52. 9; Plu. *Phoc.* 12–14; Aeschin. 3. 87; D. 21. 132.

asked again for help. A squadron of Athenian cavalry 150 strong was detached from Euboea, and Charidemus was sent from the Chersonese with 4,000 peltasts and eighteen triremes, probably in April, having received money and supplies from Orontes, the satrap of Mysia in revolt from Persia, on whom Athens conferred her citizenship. During the summer Philip defeated the Olynthians in two battles and laid siege to the city. A third request by Olynthus, asking for citizen troops and not mercenaries, was made in early July. Athens dispatched a citizen force of 300 cavalry and 2,000 hoplites with eighteen triremes and the necessary transports. In August, while the Etesian winds were delaying the expedition, Philip forced an engagement, during which the Olynthian cavalry, 500 strong, deserted under its commanders, and the city fell before the Athenian fleet arrived. By Philip's order Olynthus was razed to the ground and the people were sold into slavery for having broken their oath as his allies—a treatment less severe than Sestus had received at the hands of Athens—and some of the other cities in Chalcidice were deprived of their fortifications. The Chalcidic peninsula was now effectively incorporated in the Macedonian realm, and from some cities the people may have been transplanted to the hinterland.[1]

In these operations Philip kept the initiative by careful timing. He waited for bad weather before he attacked; then he divided his enemies by promoting the rising in Euboea; and he used his full strength just before the Etesian winds began to blow. He played upon Athens' tendency to procrastinate, exploited the jealousies of the states in Chalcidice and of the parties in each state, and used bribery as much as force to win cities to his side. For Athens the results were disastrous. She had lost the last chance of striking at Macedonia; she had lost Euboea too, so that the pass of Thermopylae was turned and Philip might have access now to Boeotia. In face of this danger Eubulus sent envoys, including Aeschines, to summon the Greek states to a congress and unite them against their common foe. There was no response. Athens, weakened by a double defeat and committed to the losing side in the Sacred War, faced the future alone.[2]

Recriminations followed at Athens. Chares, the commander of the last relief force, stayed away. Another general, Hegesileos, a nephew of Eubulus, was fined heavily. Demosthenes condemned the conduct of the war against Philip. Athens, he held, had been slow to act, and she had been side-tracked into sending an army to Euboea, a policy he alone had opposed at the time. His first criticism was sound, his second not necessarily so. For, if Chalcidice was vital for offence, Euboea was vital for defence; and communications with Chalcidice would be threatened, if Euboea were in hostile hands. The col-

---

[1] *FGrH* 328 F 49–51; *IG* ii.[2] 207; D.S. 16. 53; Suid. s.v. *Karanos*; D. 9. 56, 66; 19. 267; Hyperid. *Fr.* 76; D. 3. 26 exaggerating the destruction in Chalcidice.

[2] The chronology depends on *FGrH* 328 F 49–51; 156; D. 19. 266; 21. 197; 39. 16; Aeschin. 2. 12; and on the fracas between Demosthenes and Meidias at the Dionysia in March 348; Aeschin 3. 58 and D. 19. 10 (Aeschines' mission).

lapse of Chalcidice was due more to treachery in Chalcidice, and especially Olynthus, and to the incompetence of Athens' mercenary captains than to lack of troops. The Chalcidian League had 1,000 cavalry and over 10,000 hoplites. In all Athens sent 6,000 or 10,000 mercenaries, 2,000 or 4,000 citizen hoplites, 450 citizen cavalry, and 50 or 70 triremes—that is over 20,000 men. Some arrived late, most saw little action, and it is doubtful if any citizen troops at all were in Olynthus when it fell. Money, too, was available to finance these expeditions, and the wealthy made voluntary contributions (*epidoseis*) to help in Euboea and Chalcidice. In addition, the full levy of citizens served in Euboea, only to be defeated because Phocion was recalled and his successor was incompetent. The failure of Athens was due to deeper causes than the decision, whether right or wrong, to send troops into Euboea. Athens lacked speed, courage, and determination. For this the fault lay as much with the citizens in the Assembly as with any political leaders.[1]

§ 4. *Philip brings the Sacred War to an end*

DEMOSTHENES emerged with credit. He had called for the qualities which Athens had failed to show, and he had foreseen the danger of defeat in both theatres. But it was clear to him, as it was to Eubulus and Aeschines, that Athens' only policy now was to make peace with Philip and extricate herself from the Sacred War. For the time being, therefore, he joined forces with them. In summer and autumn 348 Philip expressed a desire for peace with Athens. Philocrates, a supporter of Eubulus, proposed that Philip be encouraged to send envoys to Athens; and Demosthenes defended Philocrates, when the impeachment of this proposal was under trial in the winter. Demosthenes, as a Councillor in 347–346, proposed in autumn 347 the award of a crown to Aristodemus for his report that Philip wanted not only peace but alliance with Athens. Meanwhile the Sacred War continued indecisively. Phocis deposed Phalaecus from his command for embezzlement and appointed three generals, who ravaged Boeotia from their bases in Orchomenus, Coronea, and Corsiae. The Boeotians appealed to Philip, who sent a few troops early in 347, and they won a minor victory at Abae that autumn. During the winter the Phocian generals made secret offers to Sparta and Athens, who promised to send help, while the Boeotians approached Philip again but received only verbal assurances.[2]

It was probably in February 346 that a Spartan army of 1,000 hoplites, led by their king, Archidamus, and part of an Athenian fleet of fifty triremes, commanded by Proxenus, arrived to take over the fortifications near Thermopylae in accordance with the secret offers of the three Phocian generals. They hoped to keep Philip out and settle the Sacred War by giving the *coup de grâce* to Thebes. But at the last moment the plan miscarried. In northern Phocis Phalaecus had regained control, and he refused to surrender the fortifications.

[1] D. 19. 290; 5. 5; different numbers are given in D. 19. 266 and *FGrH* 328 F 49–51.
[2] Aeschin. 2. 12–18; D.S. 16. 56–58.

Therefore the Spartans and Athenians had no alternative but to withdraw. Their attempt to outmanoeuvre Philip was now manifest. An embassy of ten Athenians, proposed by Philocrates and including him, Demosthenes, and Aeschines, hastened north to Macedonia.[1]

At this time Philip's intentions were by no means clear to Athens. After the fall of Olynthus he might have taken advantage of her exhaustion and isolation to force the pass of Thermopylae or else use Euboea as a bridge, join hands with his allies, the Boeotians, defeat Phocis, and then lead them against his and their enemy, Athens. Yet all he had done between summer 348 and February 346 was to ask Athens for peace and alliance and give the minimum of help to Thebes, on whose side the Thessalian allies of Philip had originally entered the Sacred War. For Philip's inactivity two explanations were possible: either he really wished to make alliance with Athens and act as an arbitrator rather than as a partisan in the Sacred War, or else he intended to lull Athens into a false sense of security, end the war without her intervention, and then attack her. As the Athenian envoys went north, they passed Philip's general, Parmenio, encamped outside Halus, a city in southern Thessaly friendly to Athens and situated on the main route towards Thermopylae. At Pella Philip received them with kindness, gave them a written statement that, if Athens made not only peace but also alliance, he would benefit her, and promised not to invade the Chersonese during the period of negotiations. Late in March the envoys returned. On Demosthenes' proposal he and his colleagues were crowned and banqueted, and the Assembly met on two consecutive days in mid April to discuss the question of peace and alliance between Athens and Philip. At the time of the meetings Philip's own envoys were in Athens.[2]

The first day's debate opened with a proposal of the Allied Synod that a treaty of peace be made with Philip, containing a moratorium of three months, within which any Greek state might sign as one of Athens' allies. Demosthenes and Aeschines supported this proposal, but Philocrates made a counter-proposal, which they opposed, that a treaty of peace and alliance be made between Philip and the Athenian Alliance, and that Phocis and Halus be expressly excluded from the treaty. That evening Philip's envoys probably said that the proposal of the Allied Synod was unacceptable. On the second day Philocrates put forward his proposal again, stressing the enmity of Thebes and Megara towards Athens. Aeschines probably spoke in support of him. Aristophon advocated the breaking off of all negotiations. At the end of a stormy meeting Eubulus said the only alternative to Philocrates' proposal was war, and that meant the conversion of the Theoric Fund into a Military Fund, a capital levy, and personal service. Demosthenes, the renowned opponent of Philip, sat silent on an occasion when silence meant acquiescence in the pro-

---

[1] D.S. 16. 59. 1; Aeschin. 2. 132; D. 19. 322; the month of Phalaecus' action was September or February, and the latter suits Athens' haste in sending envoys.

[2] D. 19. 163; Aeschin. 2. 82.

posed peace and alliance. With a bad grace the people accepted Philocrates' proposal. Terms of peace and alliance were drafted and approved by the Assembly, Cersebleptes being excluded from the list of Athens' allies by the ruling of Demosthenes, who was President of the Assembly on the occasion. The peace confirmed the *status quo* with regard to territory and allies, and the alliance included a mutual undertaking to suppress piracy and maintain the freedom of the seas. The oaths of Athens and her Allies were given in the presence of the Macedonian envoys.[1]

The Athenian envoys who went to receive the oaths of Philip and his allies reached Pella in May. Philip was then in Thrace, subjugating Cersebleptes, who was not a signatory to the peace, but respecting the Chersonese in accordance with his promise, and he returned in June to find envoys from Athens, Thebes, Phocis, Euboea, and Sparta. He could still take his pick among the Greek states not only of central Greece, but also of the Peloponnese, where Argos, Megalopolis, and Messene, the friends of Thebes, asked for his help in their war against Sparta. However, on behalf of himself and his allies Philip took the oath to the treaty of peace and alliance with Athens and her Allies in July at Pherae, where his armed forces were already assembling. The envoys hurried back to Athens. In the Council meeting Demosthenes charged his colleagues with misconduct. In the Assembly a letter from Philip was read in which he repeated that he would benefit Athens. Aeschines said this sentiment was sincere. Demosthenes disagreed. When Philocrates interjected 'Demosthenes drinks water, I drink wine', the people laughed at the pessimism of Demosthenes. The Assembly extended the alliance to Philip's descendants and expressed readiness to act against any Phocians who refused to surrender Delphi.

Philip twice asked Athens to send troops to Thermopylae and join him in putting an end to the Sacred War. His request was refused on the advice of Demosthenes and Hegesippus, who said Philip meant to seize Athens' troops as hostages, and ten envoys set off to report this refusal to their ally Philip. On their way they learnt that Phalaecus had already capitulated on 17 July, on condition of a safe conduct for himself and 8,000 mercenaries. They hurried back at once with the news, which threw the city into a panic. Attica was evacuated and the fortresses manned. For, if Demosthenes' interpretation of Philip's aim was correct, he would now lead his forces and those of Boeotia against Attica. A fourth embassy, including Aeschines but not Demosthenes, set off to make the best of an awkward situation and found that the whole of Phocis had capitulated. Philip protested at Athens' unfriendly attitude and called a meeting of the Amphictyonic Council to impose terms on Phocis.[2]

---

[1] Details of the debate were disputed by Demosthenes and Aeschines in their speeches *De Falsa Legatione*, and are so today. Firm points are in Aeschin. 3. 69; 2. 82; 3. 73; [D.] 7. 14; 12. 2; *FGrH* 115 F 164–6 (Theopompus).

[2] Isoc. 5. 74 (Peloponnese); Aeschin. 2. 90; 137; D. 19. 158 (treaty); 46; 125 (panic); D.S. 16. 59.

At the Council meeting the representative of the Oetaeans proposed to massacre all Phocian males and sell the rest as slaves. This proposal was in accord with the practice of both sides in the Sacred War. Thebes so treated the people of Orchomenus and Coronea, over whom she had now a free hand. Aeschines, representing Athens, disassociated the Phocian people from their leaders and advised mercy. The decision lay with Philip; for he controlled the votes of the Thessalian peoples, which formed a majority on the Council. The Phocian towns were split into villages, arms were surrendered, and an indemnity of sixty talents, payable annually to the temple, was imposed on Phocis. She was excommunicated, and her two votes on the Amphictyonic Council were transferred to Philip. Athens' privilege of consulting the oracle first—a privilege granted by Philomelus—was now given to Philip. The Council also arranged for the future of the shrine, outlined a programme for peace and concord (*homonoia*) among the members of the Amphictyony, and elected Philip president of the forthcoming Pythian Games of September 346. When these resolutions by the Amphictyony were reported to Athens, the Assembly refused to send delegates to the Pythian Games. An embassy from the Amphictyonic Council, fortified with a letter from Philip, asked Athens to apologize and send envoys. After a stormy debate, in which Aeschines was shouted down and Demosthenes gained a hearing, the people accepted Demosthenes' advice to make an apology and send envoys. After presiding at the Pythian Games Philip departed to Macedonia.[1]

The policy of Philip emerged clearly from these transactions. Whereas it was in his power to massacre the Phocians and lead Thessaly, Boeotia, and Megara against Attica, he preferred to end hostilities with Athens, and allay the interstate hatreds of the participants in the Sacred War. His actions showed a sincere desire to liberate the shrine of Apollo and induce a settlement of Greek affairs·under his own leadership. Above all he sought the co-operation of Athens rather than that of Boeotia. The policy of Philocrates and Aeschines was to cô-operate with Philip. They divined correctly, in the course of the negotiations, that he intended to treat Phocis leniently and not align himself with Boeotia against Athens. So far as their personal motives were concerned, they were probably patriotic as well as ambitious; and if their policy continued to prevail in Athens, they would be the leaders of the people. Demosthenes, too, knew that war with Philip in the years 348–346 would be fatal. Therefore he wanted peace but not alliance. Because he also divined Philip's intentions correctly, he was prepared to frustrate any move towards implementing an alliance, even at the risk of offering Philip an opening for war, which he believed Philip would not take. In this Demosthenes was patriotic. He had a more profound understanding of politics than Philocrates and

[1] Aeschin. 2. 142; D. 19. 325; D.S. 16. 60 (Amphictyonic decree); *GHI* 172; D. 19. 128; D. *De Pace*, probably composed after the debate, represents his views.

Aeschines; for he realized the truth of Thucydides' saying that, if one state yields, the other dominates, and that therefore an effective alliance between Philip and Athens would end in Philip dominating his ally, even as the alliance between Philip and Chalcidice had ended. At the same time Demosthenes was ambitious. If the policy of Philocrates and Aeschines prevailed, he would have no future; for he had risen to prominence as the bitter enemy of Philip, and henceforth patriotic as well as personal motives inflamed his enmity.

CHAPTER 2

Macedon Gains Control of the Greek States 346–336

§ 1. *The diplomatic struggle*

WHEN Philip was about to intervene in the Sacred War, Isocrates published his pamphlet the *Philippus*. Realizing the strength of the Macedonian monarchy and believing Philip to be a man of culture and intelligence, he urged him to unite the Greek states and lead them against Persia. Isocrates wrote not as an Athenian politician but as an academic observer of the Greek scene, who realized the exhaustion of the leading Greek states and the social and economic dangers of further strife between them. He appealed to Philip, as a descendant of Heracles, to prove himself a benefactor of Greece by showing the generosity and goodwill which alone could bring the states into unity and concord (*homonoia*). Athens, he thought, would join Philip willingly in a crusade against Persia, if only she could put aside the demagogues and see her true interest. The ultimate objective of Isocrates—unity and concord among the Greek states—was emphasized in the programme of the Amphictyonic Council which Philip inspired in August 346. During the next few years he waited for Athens to decide her policy towards him.[1]

In his speech *On the Peace* Demosthenes hinted that those who had advised the people were corrupt, and he arranged for Timarchus to charge Aeschines with misconduct when the envoys underwent their scrutiny before the auditors. But Aeschines parried by prosecuting Timarchus. Early in 345 Timarchus was disfranchised for immorality, Demosthenes not even speaking in his defence, and Aeschines reaffirmed his confidence in Philip's promises to benefit Athens. At this time, and also later, Athens complained to Philip that he had taken some towns from Cersebleptes; she asked him to restore them and admit Cersebleptes as a beneficiary of the peace and alliance. Philip replied with justice that he had captured these places before the alliance with Athens; that they were not Athens' concern; and that Athens herself had excluded Cersebleptes from the peace and alliance. He expressed his goodwill and, as a token of it, made an offer, which was refused, to cut a canal through the neck of the Chersonese for the benefit of Athens. Demosthenes, however, and others continued to accuse Philip of bad faith in regard to Cersebleptes, and their accusations must have gained some credence with the people. In autumn 344 Demosthenes was appointed head of a mission to counteract Philip's influence with Argos, Arcadia, and Messenia, but the only

---

[1] Isoc. 5. 29, 106–15, 154 (Philip); 73, 129 (Athens); D.S. 16. 60. 3.

results were protests from Argos and Messenia, the erection of statues of Philip in Argos and Arcadia, and a protest from Philip at such conduct in an ally.[1]

In reply to Philip's protest Demosthenes delivered his *Second Philippic*, declaring Philip to be the enemy of Athens, resuscitating claims to Amphipolis and Potidaea, and attributing the fall of Phocis to the corruption by Philip of Athenian envoys. Prosecutions of Philocrates and Proxenus followed. Philocrates fled and was condemned to death on a charge, preferred by Hyperides, that he had not advised the people correctly, having taken bribes. Proxenus was sentenced to a heavy fine through the activity of Demosthenes. Between autumn 344 and spring 343 Philip made two attempts to improve relations with Athens. A discontented party in Delos asked the Delphic Amphictyony to liberate the temple of Delian Apollo from Athens. The Assembly elected Aeschines, but the Areopagus appointed Hyperides in his place to present the Athenian case. The custody of the temple was awarded to Athens, the decision being no doubt inspired by Philip, whose friend Cottyphus of Pharsalus presided over the Amphictyonic Council from autumn 346 onwards. Next, a mission of envoys from states allied with Philip, headed by Python of Byzantium, made an official protest on his behalf at Athens. Aeschines, said Demosthenes, supported Python, whereas he and Hegesippus opposed him. Philip offered to review the treaty of peace and alliance and extend the peace to other Greek states. The Assembly thereupon appointed Hegesippus, a bitter opponent of Philip, to lead a mission to Macedonia. On behalf of Athens Hegesippus demanded that the clause establishing the *status quo* in 346 should be amended to read that 'each should have his own possessions'—an amendment which was intended to give Athens every city she had ever claimed. Philip refused to discuss the amendment, and the question of admitting other Greek states to the peace of 346 was dropped.[2]

At the time of Python's visit envoys from the Great King were in Athens. Their request to renew the traditional friendship between Persia and Athens was coldly received; for Athens replied that friendship was always there if Persia refrained from attacking Greek cities. It is possible that Persia may have been angling for an alliance against Philip, which Athens in her isolation would not have dared to accept; but it is more probable that Artaxerxes Ochus, who was about to invade Egypt, wanted to raise soldiers and sailors, as he succeeded in doing from his friends Thebes and Argos.

In summer 343 Demosthenes charged Aeschines with misconduct on the embassy of 346. Their two speeches, *On the False Legation*, delivered before 1,501 jurors, so distorted the facts of the involved negotiations of the embassy that the jurors must have been guided mainly by political and personal con-

---

[1] Aeschin. 1. 169; D. 6. 30; [D.] 7. 40; D. 6. 19–27; 19. 261.

[2] D. 6. 6, 17, 34–36; Hyperid. 3. 29 (Philocrates); D. 19. 280 and schol. to 290 (Proxenus); D. 18. 134 (Delos); 136; [D.] 7. 18, 26, 30 (Python).

siderations. Aeschines escaped death by thirty votes. The support of Eubulus and Phocion was an important factor, and Demosthenes overreached himself in making so scurrilous an attack that the jury cut him short. But the trials of Philocrates, Proxenus, and Aeschines showed that politically Demosthenes' star was in the ascendant. Later in 343 he and Hegesippus were appointed members of another mission to canvass support in the Peloponnese against Philip.[1]

While the struggle raged between Aeschines and Demosthenes, the Athenians knew themselves to be in imminent danger, whether war was provoked by Demosthenes or declared by Philip. Euboea, Boeotia, and Megara were hostile. She was not only isolated by land and vulnerable by sea, but she was also an immediate neighbour of the allies of Macedon. She prepared desperately for war. Cephisophon, the successor of Aeschines' brother as Chief Commissioner of the Theoric Fund in 346, practised strict economy and provided generously for the Military Fund, over which a special officer, 'the Treasurer', was appointed by election for a four-year spell. In 346/345 the roll of citizens was drastically revised in the demes; many were disfranchised, and their property was confiscated. Much money was spent on the navy. A naval arsenal, financed in part by a recurring capital levy of ten talents a year since 347/346, was being built at Zea, and 300 triremes were fully equipped for active service in 343. Fear of Philip's agents, so vividly portrayed by Demosthenes, caused the people to invest the Areopagus Council with special powers of security, which were invoked by Demosthenes against Proxenus and others. To a special point of danger, the Chersonese, which protected part of the corn-route from the Crimea, Athens sent a further contingent of cleruchs and tried to re-establish Cersebleptes as a buffer against Philip, but in vain. Golden crowns were conferred in 346 on the Spartocid rulers of the Crimean Bosporus for promising to export wheat to Athens. An alliance was made with the democracy of Mitylene in Lesbos (which had probably ejected a tyrant with Athens' help), and the tyrant of Methymna in Lesbos remained on good terms with Athens. The Cyclades honoured Athens for her protection in 348–346, and Thasos accorded Athens a base for her mercenary troops *c.* 343.[2]

Philip meanwhile confirmed his supremacy in the central Balkans by crossing the watershed of the river Axius and invading Dardania, in which the Morava, a tributary of the Danube, rises. Then he invaded Illyria and probably carried his conquests through the wild and mountainous country towards the plain of Scodra.[3] While pursuing the Illyrian king, Pleuratus, he and 150 Companion cavalrymen were wounded in a fierce engagement. These great

---

[1] Did. *in D.* 8. 8; D.S. 16. 44. 1–2 (Persia); Plu. *Dem.* 15.

[2] *IG* ii.² 223 C 5; 1443, l. 13; Arist. *Ath.* 43. 1; Schol. Aeschin. 1. 77 (revision of roll); *FGrH* 324 F 52 (Andronion); *IG* ii.² 1627, b. 352 (arsenal); 244, l. 13 and 505, l. 14; D. 19. 89; Din. 1. 62–63 (Areopagus); D. 8. 6 (Chersonese); *GHI* 167–8; 170–1; *IG* ii.² 1441; Plu. *Mor.* 845 f.   [3] See my article in *BSA* 61. 245.

campaigns safeguarded the frontiers of the Macedonian state, which he was developing into a prosperous and unified kingdom. After capturing Chalcidice he issued in great numbers the famous gold 'Philippics', which bore the Chalcidian device, the head of Apollo, and on the reverse a chariot drawn by two horses (Plate XII*i*). Their circulation throughout the Mediterranean countries and central Europe, and eventually to Britain, bears testimony to the great wealth of Philip's kingdom and the adjacent areas under his authority. Upper Macedonia was planted with cities, in which the vagrant shepherds of the uplands and peoples transplanted from the lowlands combined to establish law and order, and the rich plains were scientifically cultivated. Trade, urbanization, and improved communications raised the whole standard of life and created a reservoir of sturdy and settled peasants. The encouragement of local loyalties within the Macedonian army, the promotion of the gifted to the privileged ranks of the Companions or Foot-Companions, and the magnetic personality of Philip himself were creating the 'one kingdom and one people' which was to be inherited by Alexander and the Successors.[1]

In autumn 344 Philip entered Thessaly. He expelled the tyrants who had seized power in some leading cities (such as Simus in Larisa) and tried to subjugate their neighbours. In some of these cities governing committees of ten, 'decadarchies', were installed by Philip, and either now or in 342 the former administrative divisions of Thessaly, the 'tetrarchies', were revived, so that local administration under the League was conducted in districts rather than in cities. Thus the ambitious city-states within the League were checked, and they ceased to issue their own coinages. The country was organized as a unity and used the coinage of Macedon. The Thessalian people elected Philip 'archon' of the League for life, either now or in 342; as such, he controlled the mobilization of troops and the raising of taxes, and he commanded the Thessalian forces in time of war. Demosthenes claimed that the Thessalians had been treacherously enslaved by Philip, whereas Isocrates congratulated Philip on making a just settlement in the interest of the Thessalian people.[2] Whichever view was taken by Athenians, Thessaly remained loyal to Philip and Alexander, and the country enjoyed both peace and prosperity. A Macedonian garrison, which Philip placed in Pherae as a protection against the exiled tyrants, also safeguarded his control of the road southwards, where the small tribes of Achaea Phthiotis and the Spercheus valley entered into alliance with him. The eastern end of the Thermopylae passage was guarded by a Thessalian garrison at Nicaea, which had been allocated by the Amphictyonic Council to Thessaly in 346. This city, like Echinus on the north shore of the Maliac Gulf, which was at this time independent, had been claimed unsuccessfully by Thebes in 346; for Philip did not trust her with an area so

---

[1] Justin 8. 6: 'ex multis gentibus nationibusque unum regnum populumque constituit'; Did. *in D.* 12. 64 (Illyria); D.S. 16. 69. 7; Arr. *An.* 7. 9. 2–4; *GC.* 201.

[2] D.S. 16. 69. 8; Arist. *Pol.* 1306ª31; D. 6. 22; 9. 26; *FGrH* 115 F 208–9 (Theopompus); Just. 9. 3. 2; Isoc. *Ep.* 2. 20.

important to himself. The Aetolian League, too, made alliance with Macedon. At Delphi golden statues of Apollo and Philip were dedicated by the Amphictyony some time after 346. Amphictyonic honours were bestowed *c.* 344 on his friends in the Peloponnese, Megalopolis and Messenia, and Sparta was deprived of her traditional vote. In Megara some leading citizens opened negotiations with Philip, and a revolution in Elis, for which Demosthenes held Philip responsible, brought an oligarchy into power, probably late in 344. The democratic exiles from Elis, employing the surviving mercenaries of the Sacred War, were defeated later by the Eleans and their allies, the Arcadians. The Eleans executed half of the 4,000 mercenaries taken alive, and the Arcadians sold half as slaves.[1]

In the winter of 343–342 Philip entered Epirus. He expelled Arybbas the regent, since he refused to cede the throne of Molossia to Alexander, the brother-in-law of Philip, and extended Alexander's kingdom to the Ambraciote Gulf by conquering and incorporating the Greek cities of Cassopia—Pandosia, Boucheta, and Elatria. At the same time he probably strengthened the control of the Molossian king over the tribes of central and northern Epirus, carrying out the same policy there as in Macedonia. His operations alarmed two Greek cities, Ambracia and Leucas. Their foundress, Corinth, appealed for help to Athens, where Arybbas and his son had taken refuge and been granted Athenian citizenship. At this time Speusippus, nephew and successor of Plato, congratulated Philip by letter and advanced an incident from the life of Heracles as a reason for his descendant to lay claim to Ambracia.[2]

In the *De Pace* Demosthenes had stated that Thessaly and Thebes had supported Philip solely from motives of self-interest, and he suggested that in different circumstances self-interest might equally well disunite them. With Thebes he saw no hope of *rapprochement* in these years. He did not scruple to denounce the Thebans as cruel and stupid and extol Athens for harbouring Boeotian and Phocian refugees. Indeed relations were so embittered that Athens reinforced her garrisons on the Boeotian frontier early in 343. But, because he had a deep understanding of city-state politics, he foresaw that reaction against the growing power of Philip was bound to come in many Greek states. The appeal of Corinth and her allies in winter 343–342 marked the turning-point. Athens at once sent citizen troops to Acarnania, and Philip withdrew from the vicinity of Ambracia; for he was not yet ready to force a passage into Greece. During the winter of 343–342 Demosthenes, Hegesippus, and other envoys sought alliances. In Thessaly they failed, but in the Peloponnese they had considerable success. Alliances were made with Corinth and her colonies, Ambracia, Leucas, and Corcyra, and with the

---

[1] [D.] 7. 32; D.S. 16. 69. 8; D. 6. 22; *SIG* 222, 223; Athen. 13. 591b; Did. *in D.* 4. 1; D. 19. 294–5; 260; D.S. 16. 63. 4.

[2] [D.] 7. 32; *FGrH* 115 F 206–7 (Theopompus); Justin 8. 6. 4; D.S. 16. 72. 1; *GHI* 173; *FGrH* 69 F 2 (Antipatrus).

Achaean League, which feared that Philip's ally, the Aetolian League, might attack Naupactus. Friendly relations were established with Cephallenia, Argos, Messenia, and most of Arcadia, and in June 342 an alliance was concluded with Messenia. Thereby Athens alienated Sparta, but she gained a grip on the western flank of Greece.[1]

After withdrawing from Ambracia Philip offered once again to review his treaty with Athens and submit any differences to arbitration. The speech *On the Halonnese*, which survives from a debate on this offer, is clearly that of an agitator, probably Hegesippus, who feared any acceptance of Philip's approaches. Athens, the saviour of Greece, he asserted, must never submit her authority to any arbitrator at the request of 'an upstart from Pella'. Philip had offered to 'give' her a rocky islet, Halonnesos, which he had just freed from pirates. The offer was an insult. Philip must 'give back' what was at all times an Athenian possession. Such counsels prevailed. Negotiations lapsed early in 342, and Philip prepared for his next move.

Hitherto Athens had not pitted her citizen troops in any considerable numbers against Macedon; for she had sent mercenaries as combatant troops to Macedonia, Chalcidice, and Thrace. The personal animosity which springs from the shedding of citizen blood was lacking, so that Philip still had hopes of bringing about a change of heart and of political leadership in Athens by exerting indirect pressure. He planned, therefore, to acquire control of the Bosporus and cut off Athens' food supply from the Black Sea. To this end he embarked on a campaign in Thrace. At the same time the changing situation on the Persian side of the Straits made him anxious to consolidate his power in western Thrace. Artaxerxes Ochus, having crushed the revolt in Phoenicia in 345, had invaded Egypt in 343 with a huge army, which included 10,000 Greek troops from Thebes, Argos, and Ionia. The Egyptian forces of Nectanebo, although stiffened by 20,000 Greek mercenaries, were completely defeated, and Nectanebo fled to Ethiopia. Mentor of Rhodes, the victorious commander of Persia's mercenaries, was sent as viceroy in 342 to restore order in Asia Minor, where the ruler of Atarneus, Hermias, had created his own principality, comprising the mainland opposite Lesbos and part of the Troad, and had entered into close relations with Philip. Mentor caught Hermias by treachery and sent him to Artaxerxes, who interrogated him about Philip's plans before putting him to death. The power of Persia now extended again to the Hellespont, and the chances of Persia helping Athens against Macedon grew greater. Philip's first task, therefore, was to consolidate his grip on Thrace as far as the Bosporus. Thereafter he could act with confidence agaiint Athens or Persia, whether they combined or not.[2]

---

[1] D. 5. 15–23. D.'s hopes of winning Thebes are often dated earlier, but see D. 5. 18; 6. 9–12, 19; 14. 33; 16. 4–5, 25, 31; 18. 36, 43, 188; 19. 81; 20. 109. D. 19. 326 and 54. 3 (garrisons); D. 9. 34, 72 (Corinth); 48. 24 (Acarnania); 9. 72 (Peloponnese); Schol. Aeschin. 3. 83; *IG* ii.² 224–5.

[2] *GHI* 165 (Hermias); D.S. 16. 52. 1–8; Did. *in D.* 4. 60; 6. 51; 8. 26.

Philip campaigned in the hinterland of Thrace throughout the summer and winter of 342. Cersebleptes perished, Teres submitted, and the old Odrysian kingdom passed completely under the control of Macedon. The king of the Getae, who held the plains of the lower Danube, gave to Philip his daughter's hand and a rich dowry. In his new territories Philip founded military colonies and built roads. Philippopolis controlled the great plain of the upper Hebrus, and Cabyle (which the Greeks called 'Poneropolis') the trade route into the Danube basin. The Greek cities which lay at the terminals of this trade route, Apollonia and Odessus on the Black Sea and Aenus on the Aegean coast, made alliance with Philip, and the whole area ultimately benefited from the pacification of the marauding Thracian tribes. But his successes in Thrace alarmed his allies, Byzantium and Perinthus, and the Athenian cleruchs in the Chersonese.[1]

The commander of Athens' mercenary troops in the Chersonese, Diopeithes, forced merchant-ships to pay 'benevolence money' for unmolested passage through the Hellespont, as his predecessors had been wont to do, and he also raided the adjacent parts of Thrace for loot. In spring 342 he attacked Cardia, Philip's ally on the narrow neck of the Chersonese, which asked for and received a Macedonian garrison. When Diopeithes committed further acts of aggression and held Philip's envoy to ransom for nine talents, Philip protested to Athens early in 341 and offered to accept arbitration in all matters affecting Cardia. In the Assembly Demosthenes delivered two speeches of great power, *On the Chersonese* and the *Third Philippic*, which showed he was determined to commit Athens to the arbitrament of war, however weak her *casus belli* might be. He denounced Philip as the aggressor and enemy of Athens, claimed Diopeithes was 'defending' the Thracians, and urged the people to cudgel to death any advocate of peace. Granted his premiss, that Philip was determined to 'annihilate' Athens, Demosthenes was right in pressing for war, though he warned the people war would cost them 'trouble, toil, and treasure', and in regarding anyone who advocated a policy of appeasement as guilty of treason. In the *Third Philippic* especially he urged Athens to fight not only for her own sake, but also, as in the Persian wars, for the liberty of Greece. His opponents, having different premisses, regarded him as a war-mongering demagogue, intent on securing power at whatever cost. The decision lay with the Athenian people. They refused Philip's offers and chose Demosthenes as their leader. Although they did not yet declare war, they made preparations for war. Reinforcements were sent to Diopeithes and garrisons to Proconnesos and Tenedos at either end of the Hellespont. Demosthenes obtained alliances with Byzantium and Abydus, and Hyperides with Chios and Rhodes. Money was supplied by Persia to Diopeithes, probably as the result of negotiations between Athens and Persia. For in the *Third Philippic* Demosthenes had advocated such a course, and the Athenians, like the Thebans, Argives, and Spartans in the

[1] D.S. 16. 71. 1–2; Str. 320 fin.; *FGrH* 115 F 110 (Theopompus).

fourth century, had come to regard 'medism' as a commonplace in the political game.[1]

Nearer home Athens had two successes. As an ally of Byzantium she gained sympathy at Megara, the foundress of Byzantium, and she now received a secret approach from some Megarian democrats. An Athenian army, commanded by Phocion, made a sudden descent on Megara, installed a democracy before Boeotia could intervene, and began to link Megara to Nisaea with Long Walls (*c.* May 341). In Euboea an agent of Philip, named Callias, who was in control of Chalcis, betrayed the town to Athens. A force of Athenians and Megarians, assisted by Callias, captured Oreus in June 341 and Eretria later in the summer. Democracies came into power in the Euboean cities, which banded together for purposes of war and allied themselves with Athens and her Allies but did not themselves become members of the Athenian Alliance. In March 340 the allies of Athens attended a congress, at which they agreed in principle to contribute men and money for a war against Philip, and Demosthenes was crowned with a gold wreath for his services to the state.[2]

Athens saw fit to take these actions without denouncing the treaty of alliance. Philip now took advantage of her ambiguous attitude and openly flouted her power at sea. In summer 340, probably in late July, when the Etesian winds were due, he sailed up the Hellespont, landing troops on the coast of the Chersonese to prevent any attack on his fleet, which was carrying his siege-train. He disembarked near Perinthus and laid siege to the city, which, though his ally, had probably refused to co-operate with him in Thrace. On the orders of Artaxerxes the Persian satraps sent mercenaries and supplies into Perinthus. Byzantium, too, provided her best troops. The Macedonians hurled sharp missiles from catapults against the defenders, brought up battering-rams, towers 120 feet high, and scaling-ladders, and drove tunnels under the walls. They soon broke into the town, but they were driven out again after fierce fighting among the tall, close-packed houses. Philip then divided his army, which had been reinforced by land to a total of some 30,000 men, and began a simultaneous attack on Byzantium, the ally of Athens.[3]

§ 2. *The invasion of Greece*

ALTHOUGH Philip's attack on Byzantium did not constitute a breach of his treaty of peace and alliance with Athens (for Byzantium had not been a signatory on Athens' side in 346), Philip chose to end the uneasy peace at this point by sending a letter to Athens. In it he announced his intention to retaliate for actions taken by Athens in contravention of the treaty of peace and

---

[1] D. 8. 24 ('benevolences'); 8. 3, 7, 8, 39, 48, 60, 61; 9. 20, 28, 29, 70; Schol. Aeschin. 3. 83; Arist. *Rh.* 1386ª13 (Diopeithes); D. 9. 71; [D.] 10. 34.

[2] Plu. *Phoc.* 15; *FGrH* 103 F 19 (Charax); 328 F 159–60 (Philochorus); Schol. Aeschin. 3. 85, 103; D.S. 16. 74. 1; Aeschin. 3. 95; *IG* ii.[2] 230; D. 18. 83; Plu. *Dem.* 17.

[3] *FGrH* 328 F 53–56 (Philochorus on Perinthus, &c.); Paus. 1. 29. 7; D.S. 16. 74. 2–76. 4; Arr. *An.* 2. 14. 5.

alliance: slave-raiding in Thrace by Diopeithes, torturing a Macedonian envoy, selling into slavery the crews of merchantmen bound for Macedonia, raiding the coast of Thessaly, negotiating for alliance with Persia against Macedon, and refusing every offer of arbitration. Thereupon the Assembly decided to destroy the record of the treaty and 'to man the fleet and expedite the other measures of war'. Thus the democracy made up its mind at last. Procrastination had enabled Philip to take the initiative again, pass his fleet through waters Athens claimed to control, and lay siege to Perinthus and Byzantium. But the threat to the corn-trade from the Black Sea affected most of the Greek states, so that Athens could now rally many of them to her side in a general cause.[1]

Philip made the first move. A convoy of 230 merchantmen was assembling under Athenian naval protection to pass through the Straits, when the Macedonians suddenly sailed in, seized all enemy vessels, and released the rest (*c.* September 340). Athens now ordered Chares, who had succeeded Diopeithes, to relieve Byzantium with his squadron of forty ships. But the Byzantines, distrusting him and his mercenaries, refused to admit him. Another squadron, to which wealthy Athenians, including Demosthenes and Hyperides, supplied ships at their own expense, set sail under the command of Phocion and Cephisophon in late autumn, and the Byzantines entrusted Phocion with a share in the defence of the city. Members of the Athenian Alliance provided contingents; Chios, Rhodes, Cos, and Persia assisted Byzantium; and Ephialtes, who had been sent to Persia as an envoy, returned to Athens with the alliance of Persia and a large sum of money to finance the war. On a moonlit night in late winter the Macedonians delivered a final assault on Byzantium, but the barking of dogs roused the defenders in time, and Philip's army then broke off the siege. His fleet, however, was bottled up in the Black Sea. He arranged for a dispatch alleging that Thrace was in revolt to fall into the hands of the Athenians, who thereupon set sail for the Thracian coast. Meanwhile their allies were lulled into inactivity by Philip's offer of negotiation, and his fleet slipped safely through the Bosporus and Hellespont into the open sea.[2]

Philip probably made peace with Perinthus and Byzantium, which had no desire to fall into Persia's hands, before he turned northwards to deal with a Scythian king, Ateas, whose tribes had migrated southwards through the gap between the southern Carpathians and the Black Sea and defeated the Triballi and Getae on the lower Danube. Ateas, too, may have had designs on Byzantium; but he had first asked Philip for help and later rejected his conditions. When Ateas proved so evasive, Philip claimed the right to dedicate a statue of Heracles at the mouth of the river. This right Ateas denied him. Philip summoned Alexander from Macedonia, where he had been acting

---

[1] [D.] 12 (contains the substance, if not the actual words); *FGrH* 328 F 55.

[2] *FGrH* 328 F 162 with commentary for dating; D.S. 16. 77. 2–3; *GHI* 175 and *IG* ii.² 232–5; Plu. *Phoc.* 14; *Mor.* 848e (Ephialtes); Front. *Strat.* 1. 4. 13.

as his deputy, to join the expedition and gain experience in war, and challenged the Scythian host in the plains near the Danube. Using some of his cavalry to defend the rear of his infantry against encirclement, he attacked the Scythians and inflicted a decisive defeat upon them. While he was returning with the loot, which included hordes of captives—men, women, and children—, cattle, and brood-mares, Philip was refused passage by the Triballi. He fought his way through their territory, but he was wounded in the thigh and the Macedonians lost most of their booty. On his return to Pella late in the summer the situation was ripe for him to continue the war against Athens.[1]

At Athens there was great rejoicing over Philip's withdrawal from Byzantium. Under Demosthenes' leadership the state was now becoming better organized for war. His proposal to place a heavier share of the cost of fitting out triremes on to the 300 wealthiest men in Athens was adopted, and he himself was appointed to the special post of 'Commissioner of the Fleet'. In midsummer 339 he persuaded the people at last to divert all surplus revenue from the Theoric Fund to the Military Fund, and Lycurgus, a supporter of Demosthenes, became its Chief Commissioner.[2] Philip, however, intended to attack Athens not by sea but by land, and his influence had already been exerted at Delphi to split the Greek land-powers.

On the Amphictyonic Council representatives of the belligerents sat side by side, discussing international arrangements. In April 339 the delegates of West Locris proposed that a fine of fifty talents be imposed on Athens for improper procedure in rededicating spoils captured 'from Persia and Thebes, when they fought against Greece'. This proposal put Athens in a quandary. Refusal would heighten the insult to Thebes and might provoke the declaration of a Sacred War against Athens, whereas acceptance of the fine would be a grave humiliation for her. The Athenian delegates asked one of their number, Aeschines, to reply. When he began to speak, a Locrian shouted out that Athens should be excommunicated for her share in the last Sacred War. Aeschines countered by accusing the Locrians of Amphissa of sacrilege in having recently tilled sacred land and levied tolls at Cirrha, the harbour of Delphi. His counter-attack succeeded so well that rioting and bloodshed ensued between Amphissa and Delphi, and further consideration of the Locrians' behaviour was postponed until a special meeting in May–June. Aeschines had done well to avert the danger of Athens insulting Thebes. But neither he nor anyone else could prevent Philip from using his influence with a majority of the states on the Amphictyonic Council. At the special meeting a Sacred War was declared against the Locrians of Amphissa. To this meeting Thebes and, on the advice of Demosthenes, Athens did not send any representatives, nor did they take part in the abortive operations against

---

[1] D.S. 16. 77. 3 (the peace with Athens is fictitious); Just. 9. 2–3; Front. *Strat.* 2. 4. 20; 2. 8. 14; *FGrH* 493 F 6 (Aristocratus); Did. *in D.* 13. 3.

[2] Aeschin. 3. 222; *FGrH* 328 F 56 (Philochorus).

Amphissa. At the next regular meeting in early September 339, which both Thebes and Athens attended, Cottyphus of Pharsalus, who was presiding, carried the Amphictyonic Council with him and offered the command of the Amphictyonic forces to Philip. The offer was at once accepted.[1]

The decision of the Amphictyonic Council alarmed Boeotia. Although she was an ally of Philip, she resented his control of the Amphictyony and in this dispute was moved also by her traditional friendship for West Locris. Moreover, during Philip's campaign against the Scythians, Thebes had expelled a Macedonian garrison from Nicaea. This and other differences between them were still under negotiation when Philip marched south with his Macedonian and Thessalian forces (*c.* November 339). As the Theban garrison at Nicaea blocked the exit from the pass of Thermopylae, he crossed the mountains to Cytinium in Doris, whence one road led to Amphissa and another to Phocis, which was still unfortified and disarmed. After sending forward envoys of his Amphictyonic allies to ask Thebes to give Nicaea to the East Locrians, in whose territory it lay, he advanced rapidly to Elatea, where he cut the direct route between Nicaea and Thebes and threatened Boeotia.

The news that Philip was at Elatea, two days' march from Attica, reached Athens in the evening and threw the city into commotion. At dawn the Assembly was seated on the Pnyx. Demosthenes rose first to speak. He suggested that Boeotia might be won over to Athens' side by an offer of alliance on generous terms, backed by a display of Athens' will to mobilize her forces. Demosthenes himself, who was Theban representative (*proxenus*) at Athens, other envoys, and the generals were dispatched to Thebes. There they found that the Thebans had prevaricated with the envoys of Philip's Amphictyonic allies about Nicaea, and that the Assembly of the Boeotian League was about to be addressed by a second embassy, composed of delegates from Philip, Thessaly, and other Amphictyonic states. This second embassy asked the Boeotians as allies of Philip and as members of the Amphictyonic League either to act with his army or to grant free passage into Attica. The Athenian envoys asked the Boeotians for alliance against Philip, and offered to give Boeotia command of the armies, share command of the navies, pay two thirds of the expenses, and support the authority of the Boeotian League over all cities in Boeotia. As an earnest of their determination, the Athenian citizen troops stood under arms near the Boeotian frontier. The Assembly of the Boeotians voted in favour of alliance with Athens. For the Boeotians the decision was one of the highest courage; it involved them in another Sacred War, and it meant the breaking of their oath as allies of Macedon. For the Athenians it was the first hope of salvation, and for Demosthenes it was a personal triumph.[2]

---

[1] The chronology is disputed, and some place all the meetings between April and September 339. Aeschin. 3. 113–31; D. 18. 143–52; *SIG* 249, l. 46.

[2] *FGrH* 328 F 56b (Philochorus); 135 F 20 (Marsyas); 115 F 328 (Theopompus); D. 18. 168 f.; Aeschin. 3. 140; D.S. 16. 84–85. 4.

The combined forces of Boeotia and Athens fortified the entries from Phocis, especially at Parapotamii, and Athens sent 10,000 mercenaries, commanded by Chares, to serve under a Boeotarch and hold the pass leading from Amphissa to Cytinium. Philip built counter-fortifications at Elatea, Cytinium, and Thermopylae. During the winter, although some skirmishes occurred, both sides maintained a defensive strategy and sent embassies to the other states. Achaea, Corinth, Megara, Euboea, Acarnania, Leucas, and Corcyra joined Boeotia and Athens, while the others decided to remain neutral. Philip rebuilt the fortifications of the Phocians, who set up again their federal state with the approval of the Amphictyonic Council in spring 338. The Phocian payment to Delphi of 30 talents was reduced thereafter to 10 talents, thanks to Philip. He also made overtures of peace to Boeotia and Athens. They were rejected largely through the influence of Demosthenes, who threatened the Boeotarchs as well as the Athenians with summary action, if these overtures were discussed at all in their Assemblies. Thus the allied front held firm. Demosthenes received a golden crown at the Dionysiac Festival of March 338, and an Athenian fleet under Phocion sailed in the spring to attack Macedonian shipping in the north Aegean.[1]

In midsummer 338 Philip exploited the division of the main Greek armies at Amphissa and Parapotamii, which were two days' march apart. He arranged for the commanders of the mercenaries at Amphissa to capture a false dispatch which stated that a revolt in Thrace was causing him to withdraw part of his army. He then withdrew his troops from Cytinium. The Greek commanders assumed that Philip would not be so stupid as to use again the trick which he had employed to extricate his fleet from the Black Sea, and they relaxed their guard of the pass. Philip led a large force through the pass at night, destroyed the force of 10,000 mercenaries, and captured Amphissa. The position of the allies was now turned. When a Macedonian column passed through Delphi and ravaged the Boeotian plains near Lebadea, the Greek army fell back hastily from Parapotamii to Chaeronea. Philip again made overtures for peace to Athens and Boeotia. Phocion, who had returned to Athens, advised acceptance, but Demosthenes and others obtained a refusal by both states. Philip thereupon captured Naupactus, which he gave to the Aetolian League, left a small force covering Delphi, and concentrated his army for a decisive battle at Chaeronea, probably on 2 August 338.[2]

The Macedonian army was the most experienced and the most intensively trained in Europe. The heavy cavalry, led by the Companions and reinforced on this occasion by Thessalian cavalry, wore protective armour, carried shield, sword, and lance (*sarissa*) for fighting at close quarters, and each squadron employed a wedge-shaped formation, invented by Philip. The light

---

[1] *IG* 9. 1. 316 (Thermopylae); *GC* 202; Aeschin. 3. 148; Plu. *Dem.* 18. 3; *Phoc.* 14. 8 (cf. 16. 1).

[2] Polyaen. 4. 2. 8, 14; Plu. *Phoc.* 16. 1–3 (Philip's offer is usually equated with the earlier one in Aeschin. 3. 148 and Plu. *Dem.* 18. 3); *FGrH* 115 F 235 (Theopompus).

cavalry wore lighter armour, and were equipped, like most Greek cavalry, with two spears or javelins for skirmishing and a sword. The infantry of the line, the 'Foot Companions', were equipped almost as heavily as Greek hoplites, but carried a spear or pike which was twice as long as the hoplite's

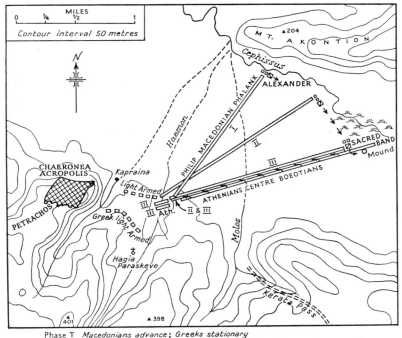

Phase I̱ *Macedonians advance; Greeks stationary*
Phase Ī̲Ī *Philip retreats, his centre and left advancing; Athenians, Centre and Boeotians advance to left front, but the Sacred Band stands firm*
Phase Ī̲Ī̲Ī *Alexander charges, the centres engage, and Philip drives the Athenian wing up the Haemon valley*

FIG. 29. The Battle of Chaeronea

spear. The formation in which the infantry fought—the 'phalanx'—was usually more open and deeper than the Greek hoplite line; it allowed a front of at least three feet for each man, had ten men in a file, and was capable of flexible manoeuvre. The spears of the leading lines probably varied in length, the longest being about 13 feet, so that at least three spearheads could be presented by any one file to the front line of the enemy. Peltasts and light-armed infantry were employed as mobile covering troops outside the phalanx. At Chaeronea Philip had at least 2,000 cavalry and 30,000 infantry, the latter being the full strength of the Macedonian field army; for he probably did not use the Greek hoplites of his allies in this battle of prestige between Macedonian and Greek.

The position adopted by the Greek army of some 35,000 infantry was a strong one, extending from the bank of the Cephissus river to the foot-hills east of the walled acropolis of Chaeronea (see Fig. 29). The Boeotian hoplites, some 12,000 in number, formed the right wing, the Sacred Band being on the extreme right; the Athenian hoplites, some 10,000 strong, held the left wing; and the allied hoplites, stiffened by some 5,000 mercenaries, held the centre. The line, two miles long, lay obliquely across the plain; if Philip's army advanced into the broad wedge of open ground and was defeated, the Athenians could swing into the plain and throw the enemy back towards the Cephissus, and at the same time, if the Greek line was broken, most of the troops could escape via the Kérata pass to Lebadea. The Greek line stood solid, eight men deep except on the extreme right, where the Sacred Band was in massed formation, and its left wing was linked by light-armed troops with the strong fortress of Chaeronea. The Greek cavalry, approximately equal in number to the Macedonian cavalry, was held in reserve.

Philip knew that the Boeotians were seasoned troops and the Athenians, having had only one month's regular fighting in the last twenty-four years, were very inexperienced. For political purposes he wished to break the Boeotian army and capture as many Athenian citizens as possible. The tactical problem was to create a gap in the Greek line, into which his squadrons of heavy cavalry could charge; for they were unable to attack a solid line of spearmen. At dawn Philip placed Alexander and his staff officers in command of the heavy cavalry on the extreme left of his phalanx. He posted a strong force of light-armed troops on his right flank. He himself at the head of the king's own battalions, the 'Hypaspists', led the extreme right of the phalanx forward first, so that his line advanced obliquely in relation to the Greek line. The Hypaspists therefore reached the Athenian position before the other battalions came within distance of engaging the Greek centre and right wing. He then 'retired step by step', marching the Hypaspists backwards towards his right rear, until he reached slightly rising ground in the plain; during this retreat the right wing of the phalanx 'was contracted and his men were protected by a hedge of spears', and the remainder of the phalanx and the cavalry were still advancing. The Athenians thought victory was within their grasp. They advanced impetuously towards their left front in pursuit of Philip's wing, and the whole Greek line began to move towards its left to keep contact, except on the extreme right where the Sacred Band in their massed formation stood still near the bank of the Cephissus. Inevitably a gap opened between the hoplite line and the extreme right wing, and into this gap Alexander charged at the head of the Companion cavalry. At the same time Philip ordered the Hypaspists to charge the Athenians, whose line had become extended and disordered by their impetuous advance, and his troops drove them into a pocket in the hills, where 1,000 men were killed and 2,000 captured. On the other side of the battlefield the Sacred Band, encircled by Alexander's cavalry, was annihilated. As the centres engaged, the Macedonian battalion on the left entered the gap behind Alexander's cavalry and rolled up the Greek line from its flank. The whole Greek line then broke. Philip ordered his cavalry not to pursue the fleeing enemy. The victory was already as complete as he wished to make it.[1]

Thebes capitulated at once. The Boeotian League was disbanded; Thespiae, Plataea, and Orchomenus were restored; and Thebes, reduced to a single city-state, was compelled to receive back her exiles. An oligarchy of 300 Thebans was installed, the democratic leaders were executed or banished by the oligarchs, and a Macedonian garrison occupied the Cadmea. Theban prisoners of war, if not ransomed, were sold into slavery, and relatives had to buy back the Theban dead. Her fate was hard, but not as hard as that she had inflicted on Orchomenus and Coronea. At Athens preparations were made to defend the city to the last. As Chares stayed away, Charidemus was appointed general in place of Lysicles, who was condemned to death for being among the fugitives. His prosecutor, Lycurgus, and Hyperides organized the defences, the latter proposing to arm all fit slaves and state prisoners, and Demosthenes, who was appointed corn-commissioner, set sail to obtain money and supplies, especially from Persia. At this stage the Areopagus Council intervened. It deposed Charidemus, and Phocion was elected in his place. Philip then sent an Athenian prisoner of war, the orator Demades, to express his willingness to negotiate, and Phocion, Aeschines, and Demades were appointed to treat with Philip. The following terms of peace were offered. Philip undertook not to send any troops into Attica or ships of war into the Peiraeus. Athens was to dissolve the Athenian Alliance, retain possession of Lemnos, Imbros, Scyros, Delos, and Samos, and receive Oropus at the expense of Thebes. Athens was to become the ally of Macedon. These terms were accepted. The Athenian prisoners of war were restored without ransom, and the ashes of the dead were brought to the city by a military escort, led by Alexander, Antipater, and Alcimachus.[2]

§ 3. *The settlement of Greece and the assassination of Philip*

DEMOSTHENES' contention, that Philip intended to 'destroy' Athens, was thus disproved. Philip's claim, that he wanted her co-operation, was justified by his attitude as her victor in war. In a surge of gratitude the Athenians gave their citizenship to Philip and Alexander, and resolved to set up a statue of

---

[1] For Greek cavalry armour and weapons see X. *Eq.* 12. For Philip's tactics see *Klio* 31 (1938) 201 ff. and *StGH* 534 ff. Polyaen. 4. 2. 2, 7; D.S. 16. 85. 5–86; Plu. *Alex.* 9. 2–4; *Dem.* 19. 2; *Pel.* 18. 7; Paus. 7. 6. 5; D. 18. 264; Plu. *Mor.* 894a; Just. 9. 3. 9; Arr. *Tact.* 12. 6 (phalanx); 16. 6 (wedge-formation of cavalry). The Lion of Chaeronea probably marks the tomb of 254 Macedonians who fell under Philip's own command.

[2] D.S. 16. 87–88. 2; Plu. *Mor.* 848 f.; *Phoc.* 16. 4; Plb. 5. 10; Just. 9. 4; Arist. *Ath.* 62. 2.

Philip in the Agora. At the same time Demosthenes was chosen to deliver the Funeral Speech in honour of the dead. In the weeks after the battle Isocrates wrote a letter to Philip. A year before, he had written the *Panathenaicus*, singing the praises of the Athens he loved, 'the Athens of the violet crown' which had saved Greece. Now he urged Philip 'to put an end to the madness and the imperialism (*pleonexia*) with which the Greeks have treated one another, reconcile and bring them into concord (*homonoia*), and declare war on Persia'. He rejoiced that he had lived so long (he was now ninety-eight), because he thought his dreams of Greek unity were on the eve of fulfilment. He died before they were realized.

In central Greece Philip arranged that the Amphictyonic Council should reduce the fine imposed on Phocis from sixty talents to ten talents a year and treat Amphissa, the latest victim of a Sacred War, with such leniency that a statue of Philip was probably dedicated at Delphi by the grateful Amphisseans. From central Greece Philip passed into the Peloponnese, where he was honoured by all states except Sparta, which refused him entry. He marched through Laconia to Gytheum, as Epaminondas had once done, and awarded some of Sparta's territory to Argos, Messenia, and the Arcadian League, which he had just re-formed. After arbitrating in other territorial disputes, he invited the Greek states to attend a conference in late autumn. All, save Sparta, accepted, and their delegates received a manifesto from Philip, in which he outlined his plans for promoting the interests of Greece. During the winter the manifesto was discussed throughout the country, while Philip withdrew his army to Macedonia, leaving garrisons probably at Corinth, Chalcis, and Ambracia as well as at the Cadmea.[1]

In spring 337 the settlement of the Greek states—the 'Greek League' or the 'League of Corinth', as it is now called—was finally ratified by the congress at Corinth and sworn to by each state. All mainland states south of Olympus, except Sparta, and many island states became members of a federal union, which styled itself 'The Greeks'. They undertook to observe a general peace; use military sanctions in accordance with the principle of collective security against any violator of the peace; respect the liberty and autonomy of each member-state under its existing constitution, which could only be changed by constitutional processes; refrain from executions, redistribution of landed property, and other subversive measures contrary to current laws; and suppress all brigandage and piracy. The aim of this undertaking was to arrest the cycle of inter-state wars and internal revolutions in individual states. The organ of government in the federal union was 'the Council of the Greeks', its members being recruited by election in each state in numbers proportionate to its military and naval strength. The list of members, which has survived as an appendix to the Charter, is defective. Some were city-states, others were tribal units forming one group (for instance those round

---

[1] Paus. 1. 9. 4; Isoc. *Ep.* 3; *BCH* 73. 259 (Str. 419 and 427 seems to be mistaken in saying Amphissa was destroyed); Plb. 9. 28. 6; 18. 14; D.S. 16. 89. 1–2; Plu. *Phoc.* 16. 5.

the Spercheus valley), and the number of votes so held by states and tribal groups was probably 100 or more at the outset. The decisions of the Council, passed by a majority vote, were binding on all members. Its competence covered all departments of federal affairs: declaration of war and peace, levying of contingents, supplies, and taxes, trial of offenders against the federal contract, power of banishment from federal territory, appointment of arbitrators to settle disputes and of executive officials to safeguard the general peace. The Council was to meet at the centres of Greek religion—Delphi, Olympia, Nemea, and the Isthmus—and five presidents for each session were to be selected by lot from the Councillors.

The closest parallel to this settlement was the League of City-States, formed in 362/361 within the memory of Philip. The federal union was more strongly centralized (for its resolutions were binding on all members, and the principle of one vote for each state was abandoned), but it was in the direct line of Greek federal developments during the fourth century. The League of City-States had failed, because it lacked leadership and remained static. At its first regular meeting in summer 337 the federal union entered into an offensive and defensive alliance for all time with the Macedonian state, defined as 'Philip and his descendants'. It then made a joint declaration of war on Persia, to avenge the sacrilege committed by Xerxes on the temples of the Greek gods, and unanimously elected Philip 'Hegemon', with full powers of command over its forces by land and sea, 'as a benefactor of Greece'. Once war was declared on Persia, the link between Greece and Macedon lay in the person of Philip. Operations of war were conducted 'in accordance with the resolutions of the Council and the orders of the Hegemon', and the Hegemon or his deputy acted as Chairman at the sessions of the Council. Thus the Greek states, reminded of the union in 481 which had enabled them to defeat the Persians, now embarked on a religious crusade which might liberate their kindred in Ionia and remove the shame of so many settlements imposed by the Great King.[1]

On the declaration of war Philip obtained approval for keeping his garrisons in Thebes, Chalcis, Ambracia, and Corinth, and called up the contingents of the Greek states. In spring 336 a vanguard of at least 10,000 men, commanded by Parmenio and Attalus and supported by a fleet, crossed the Hellespont, and the main body of the army was to follow under Philip's command in the autumn. In Asia Minor Mentor, the Viceroy, had died, and his brother Memnon had succeeded only to his military authority. At Susa the commander of the Palace Guard, Bagoas, having poisoned Artaxerxes Ochus in 338, and his son Arses in 336, was himself poisoned by Darius Codomannus (*c.* May 336). The invading army was welcomed by Cyzicus and other Greek cities, which revolted from Persia. The Ephesians set up a statue

[1] *GHI* 177, 179, 183, 192; *IG* 4.² 1. 68; [D.] 17. 8, 10, 15, 16, 19; D.S. 16. 89. 3; Plb. 3. 6. 12; 9. 33. 7; Arr. *An.* 2. 14. 4; 3. 24. 5; 7. 9. 5; Just. 9. 5. Some details are much disputed.

of Philip in the temple of Artemis, and Pixodarus, the satrap of Caria, offered the hand of his daughter to Arrhidaeus, a son of Philip. Meanwhile at Athens prosecutions and counter-prosecutions were laid by the supporters and the opponents of co-operation with Macedon. In internal affairs Lycurgus strove to restore the state's finances. In 337 Demosthenes was elected Chief Commissioner of the Theoric Fund, which was once more absorbing the surplus monies, and he obtained the Assembly's approval for undertaking repairs and fortifications at the Peiraeus. Early in 336 a proposal by Ctesiphon to confer a gold crown on Demosthenes at the Dionysia was impeached as illegal by Aeschines, and Alcimachus, a Macedonian general, was honoured by the Assembly. When a contingent of cavalry and triremes was required for the campaign against Persia, Phocion persuaded the Assembly to send it without demur. When it was reported that Philip's daughter Cleopatra was to marry Alexander of Molossia in July 336, the Athenians sent a gold crown to Philip and reported their willingness to surrender to him anyone who, having plotted to take his life, was being harboured in the city. Thus the democracy continued to oscillate between opposition and co-operation.[1]

In the Macedonian monarchy polygamy was probably a traditional practice. Amyntas, the father of Philip, had had at least six sons by two marriages and thereby secured the succession within the royal house. Philip had six wives but only two sons, the first-born of Olympias, Alexander, and a son of Philinna, Arrhidaeus, who suffered from epilepsy. Olympias, being herself of royal Greek blood, was the queen, and Alexander was marked out as the heir. If Philip and Alexander should be killed in the forthcoming campaign in Asia, neither Arrhidaeus nor Amyntas, the son of Perdiccas, for whom Philip had at first acted as regent, was worthy of the throne. It was probably in the hope of begetting another son that Philip married Cleopatra, niece of a Macedonian noble, Attalus, in 337. The marriage, however, caused estrangement with Olympias and Alexander, who left the court but were recalled by Philip in 336, and it was a mark of reconciliation that Olympias' daughter, Cleopatra, was to be married to Alexander of Molossia. During the wedding celebrations Philip, unaccompanied by the royal guards, was entering the theatre at Aegae, when he was assassinated by a young noble, Pausanias, who was actuated by a personal grudge rather than by any political motive. The body of the king, who was in his forty-sixth year, was laid to rest in the royal tomb of the Macedonian kings, and his son Alexander was acclaimed by the people 'King of Macedon'.[2]

The military and diplomatic achievements of Philip were clear to his contemporaries. They had seen his kingdom rise from weakness to a strength

[1] D.S. 16. 91. 1–2; 17. 5. 3–5; Polyaen. 5. 44. 4; Plu. *Alex.* 10. 1; D. 18. 113, 248; *GHI* 180; Plu. *Phoc.* 16. 6.

[2] *FHG* 3. 161 (Satyrus, fr. 4, 'Philip always married for war', understood the political character of a monarch's marriages better than Theopompus, fr. 27, who thought of Philip's wives, like Hyperides' famous mistresses, as a sign of incontinence). Arist. *Pol.* 1311^b2; D.S. 16. 91–94; Plu. *Alex.* 9. 5–10.

which had never been equalled in the history of Europe. Isocrates believed that in comparison with such an achievement the conquest of Persia was a less difficult task. Theopompus, the historian, who lived to see the conquest of Persia, wrote that Europe had never produced such a man as Philip, son of Amyntas, and that all Europe would become his if he continued to observe the same principles in his policy. Those who criticized his treatment of Greece did not deny his success in the Balkans, where he formed a bulwark against the nomadic peoples of northern Europe which was to hold firm for several centuries. The greater Macedonian state was his creation. Without disrupting its institutions or draining its manpower, but rather by strengthening and extending both, he made its authority supreme from the Adriatic to the Black Sea and from the Danube to the borders of Laconia. Despite the speed with which the nation had grown, it had the strength to carry the strain of Alexander's campaigns in Asia and to remain the central bastion in the Balkans.[1]

The army was the people in arms, devoted in loyalty to their king and supported by the basis of economic prosperity which he had built. In the early years of his reign he used mercenary troops freely, but towards the end only in specialist units. The Companions, who formed his staff and his heavy cavalry, were unsurpassed in efficiency and in prowess. The squadrons, recruited from individual districts in his realm, rivalled one another in their territorial loyalties, and the distinguished service of individuals was rewarded by promotion to the privilege of membership of the staff or of the Royal Guard (*agema*). The Foot Companions, or heavy infantry of the phalanx, were similarly organized, the king's own battalions, the Hypaspists, forming the *corps d'élite*. The ancillary units of light cavalry, infantry fighting in conjunction with cavalry, peltasts, javelin-throwers, slingers, engineers, sappers, commissariat, and surveyors were expert in conducting mountain warfare in the Balkans and sieges of strongly fortified cities. Philip himself led whichever arm had the stiffest task. He was wounded organizing the siege of Methone and commanding the Companion cavalry in Illyria, and he led the infantry against Bardylis and at Chaeronea. The army which Alexander inherited had been trained in the perils of war and had proved itself almost invincible in battles against Illyrian infantry, Greek hoplites, and Scythian cavalry.[2]

Philip was said to have prided himself more on his diplomacy than on his military victories. He employed duplicity and bribery, as his contemporaries did, and he employed them more successfully. In warfare he could be as cruel in executing the mercenaries of Onomarchus or in destroying Olynthus as Thebes or Athens were in dealing with Orchomenus or Sestus, but he showed a higher standard of humanity towards Phocis and Amphissa and a greater

---

[1] Isoc. *Ep.* 3. 5; *FGrH* 115 F 27, 256 (Theopompus).
[2] D. 1. 22 (mercenaries); *FGrH* 115 F 249; Polyaen. 4. 2. 18; Plb. 8. 9–10 and *FGrH* 115 F 224–5 (Companions); D.S. 17. 9. 3 (training); Polyaen. 4. 2. 10.

generosity towards Athens. The range of his statesmanship was shown not only in the organization of his own kingdom but also in his handling of neighbouring peoples, both Greek and barbarian. While the territory between Lake Lychnidus and the river Nestus was incorporated in Macedonia, he left Illyrian and Thracian tribes under vassal kings and developed their resources by founding colonies. In Epirus he strengthened the kingdom of Molossia and extended its realm, but the association was cemented only by ties of marriage. In Thessaly, where he was faced with a civilization equal to that of Macedon, the political bond was one of association on equal terms; for Thessaly not only elected him *archon* of its League, but also became, unlike Macedon, a member of the Greek League. In all these areas he favoured urban development but not city-states. For Greece he found a different solution. The man who tried so patiently to win the co-operation of Athens, and stopped his cavalry from pursuing at Chaeronea, did not intend, as his enemies claimed, to destroy the Greek city-states but to pacify them and win their collaboration against Persia. He may have been trying to achieve the impossible. Yet the Charter of federal union revealed a deep insight into the causes of anarchy in the Greek states, and Philip at the height of his career had more prudence and probably more regard for Greece than Alexander was to show in his youth.[1]

The centre of the whole structure was one man who acted in several distinct capacities: King of Macedon, king over vassal kings in the Balkans, *archon* of the Thessalian League, *hieromnemon* on the Amphictyonic Council, *hegemon* of the Greek League in time of war. The personality and the aims of Philip are therefore of the greatest historical importance. In some respects they are enigmatic. Demosthenes, Aeschines, Theopompus, and Isocrates differed in their interpretation. Each judged him primarily as Greek judging Greek. Demosthenes saw him, like Epaminondas of Thebes, endangering the ambitions of Athens, and Isocrates cast him, like Dionysius or Archidamus, as the leader of a Panhellenic crusade against Persia. Philip was certainly more than a capable barbarian from Pella. His court was Greek in manners. He brought Hellenization to the Balkan lands, and would have done the same to Asia, if he had lived and defeated Persia. His plan to pacify the Greek states and provide scope for their surplus populations in Asia was conceived in the interest of Greece as well as of Macedon. He was reputed to be interested in Greek thought, he employed Aristotle to teach Alexander, and he admired 'the Attic graces' of the city of Athena. If we judge him as a Greek of the fourth century, he was certainly an enlightened conqueror of other states, but it may be that we should regard him rather in the context of the Macedonian monarchy.[2]

---

[1] Polyaen. 4. 2. 9; Str. 323 fin. (Nestus); Plb. 5. 10. 1 (on Philip's treatment of Athens).

[2] Philip did not use the title of king in dealing with the Greek states or on his coins. The constitution of Macedon was described as 'the kingdom of Philip and his descendants' in contrast to the republics of Greece in the Charter of the League (*GHI* 177). His charm as a

The Macedonian kings had much in common with the Mycenaean kings portrayed in the *Iliad*. They, too, were 'sprung from Zeus'. For Philip claimed to be a descendant of Heracles, the son of Zeus. He put the head of Heracles on his earliest coins, named his first city-foundation Heraclea, and dedicated a statue of Heracles at the mouth of the Danube. He worshipped Zeus at Dium, dedicated a treasury to Zeus at Olympia, defended Apollo's shrine at Delphi, and placed the heads of Zeus and Apollo on his coins. It is significant that Isocrates asked Philip as a descendant of Heracles to consider all Greece his fatherland. The Homeric qualities of Philip—qualities which are better known to us in Alexander—were a will for power, a desire for glory, a passionate, generous, and emotional nature, which caused him to weep over the brave men of the Sacred Band who lay dead at Chaeronea. If Philip had the simple faith of the Heroic Age and believed himself to be in truth a descendant of Zeus, called, like Heracles, to benefit mankind, then the springs of his personality and his policy, as of Alexander's, are to be found in a deep religious conviction.[1]

§ 4. *The Western Greeks, 345–322*

IN the period 400–348 great changes took place in Italy, which were later to affect the Greek cities of the West. The southwards pressure of the tribal peoples of central Europe, which probably caused the Illyrians, Paeonians, Thracians, Getae, and Scythians to threaten the settled areas of the Balkans, brought the Gauls over the Alps into the area north of the Po at the beginning of the fourth century. Wedged between the realm of Etruria and the territory of the Veneti at the head of the Adriatic Sea, the Gauls advanced down the centre of Italy, forcing the Etruscans back to the foot-hills of the Apennines and to the Adriatic coast of Umbria. Rome took advantage of this pressure on the Etruscans to capture Veii (396) and acquire the southern tip of Etruria (391). It was before the attack on Veii that Rome first sent envoys to Greece, to consult the oracle at Delphi; and after it she dedicated a gold bowl at Delphi, in the Treasury of Massilia, with whom she was on friendly terms. But the Roman advance was halted for a time by the Gauls, who sacked Rome *c*. 391 and carried their raids into Campania and Apulia.

A generation of intensive warfare followed. From it Rome emerged triumphant. In 358 she inflicted a severe defeat on the Gauls, forced the Aequi and Hernici into alliance, and drove the Volsci back from the coastal plains. In 354 she compelled some recalcitrant states to rejoin the Latin League, and made an alliance with the Samnites. In 351 her annexation of southern

Greek impressed Greek envoys; his least Greek characteristic was his fondness of liquor on festive occasions, which gave rise to many good stories, such as his drunken chanting of the preamble of an Attic decree in the name of his enemy *Demosthenes Demosthenous Paeanieus* (Plu. *Dem.* 20; cf. D. 19. 308; Aeschin. 2. 52; D.S. 16. 87).

[1] Isoc. 5. 29 (enlightenment); 5. 105, 109, 111, 115, 127 (Heracles); Isoc. *Ep.* 3. 4 (love of glory); Plb. 18. 14. 14; Plu. *Mor.* 178a, 179c; Plb. 9. 29 and 9. 33 (for contrasting views of Philip). For coins see Plate XII *h* and *i*.

Etruria was confirmed by a treaty of peace with Tarquinii and Falerii. These successes aroused the interest of Carthage. In 348 Rome and her allies concluded with Carthage and her allies a treaty of friendship, which regulated conditions of trade and piracy in the maritime areas controlled by the signatories. The Carthaginians were excluded from Roman and allied territory save that they could trade at Rome, and the Romans and their allies were excluded from Sardinia and Africa but could trade at Carthage or in the Carthaginian part of Sicily.[1]

In the same period Carthage was acquiring an empire in Spain, where her rivals in trade were Greek colonies founded by Massilia. Her main ambition in 348, when she made her treaty with Rome, was to conquer Greek Sicily and control the Straits of Messana. For this purpose the capture of Syracuse was essential. When Hicetas in 345/344 invited Carthage to help in expelling Dionysius from Ortygia, the Carthaginians prepared to occupy Syracuse and conquer the Greek cities, now weakened by continuous warfare since 357. They were not deterred by the fact that Hicetas had previously sent envoys to Corinth; for Greece was then overshadowed by the power of Macedon.

When Hicetas and the aristocrats of Syracuse asked Corinth for help, they wanted a liberator who would not turn into a tyrant. The Corinthians chose Timoleon, who had proved his detestation of tyranny *c.* 365 by arranging the assassination of his brother, then tyrant of Corinth. A letter arrived soon afterwards from Hicetas to discourage Corinth from intervening, because he had just invoked the aid of Carthage. Nevertheless, Timoleon set sail in 344 with ten ships and 700 mercenaries, mostly veterans of the Sacred War. He was intercepted by a Carthaginian squadron at Rhegium, but slipped away to Tauromenium in Sicily, where he was welcomed by Andromachus, father of the later historian, Timaeus. He was soon invited to intervene in a party struggle at Adranum. But Hicetas, who had now confined Dionysius to Ortygia, the citadel of Syracuse, arrived at Adranum as a rival participant with a much stronger force. Timoleon suspected with good reason that Hicetas was a would-be tyrant; he therefore attacked Hicetas without warning and defeated his troops. This success won Timoleon the support of a rival of Hicetas, a Campanian *condottiere* called Mamercus, who was tyrant of Catana; and he was put (probably by Mamercus) into touch with Dionysius, whose enmity towards Hicetas and Carthage gave an interest in common to the tyrant and the liberator. An agreement was concluded, whereby Timoleon would help in the defence of Ortygia and Dionysius would share Catana as a base. In autumn 344, some fifty days after Timoleon's arrival in Sicily, his lieutenant, Neon, was in Ortygia, collaborating with Dionysius' 2,000 mercenaries against Hicetas and Carthage. Dionysius and Timoleon probably acted together for some months, but in summer 343 Dionysius left the Sicilian scene and retired to Corinth.

[1] Scyl. 17 (Etruria); Appian *Ital.* 8 (Veii); D.S. 14. 93; Plb. 3. 24 (Carthage); D.S. 16. 69. 1; Livy 7. 27. 2.

In spring 343 Carthage, having control of the seas round Sicily, sent a large army and 150 ships under Mago to occupy Syracuse. He blockaded Ortygia by land and sea and posted a squadron in south Italy to intercept any aid from Greece. As Timoleon managed to send fishing smacks with supplies to Ortygia in stormy weather, Mago and Hicetas set off to attack his base at Catana, but in their absence Neon made a sortie and captured Achradina. By hard fighting Neon and Timoleon both held out until a force of ten ships and 2,000 hoplites, sent by Corinth, evaded the Carthaginian squadron in south Italy, joined Timoleon at Catana, and enabled him to capture Messana which was friendly to Carthage. Meanwhile a quarrel had arisen between Mago and Hicetas, and it was accentuated when Mago heard that the Greek mercenaries of Hicetas were conversing with those of Neon during a truce. Mago, perhaps suspecting treachery, sailed away to western Sicily, where he was censured by his government and committed suicide. Timoleon arrived next day at Syracuse with 4,000 men, and Hicetas removed his mercenaries to Leontini. In autumn 343 Syracuse was at last liberated from the double menace of tyranny and Carthaginian occupation, and on Timoleon's orders the citizens demolished the citadel, palace, and tombs of the tyrants.[1]

Timoleon enjoyed almost two years of respite from Carthaginian attack, during which he made little progress against the crop of tyrants in the Siceliote cities but strengthened Syracuse by recalling exiles, attracting settlers, and revising her constitution. He came to terms with Hicetas and borrowed mercenaries from him, before Carthage returned to the attack. As her army of some 70,000 men included the finest citizen troops of Carthage, known as 'The Sacred Band', and a squadron of chariots, and was supported by a large fleet, based at Lilybaeum, it is clear that the aim of the expedition was to annex the Greek part of Sicily. Timoleon could raise only 12,000 troops, of whom 3,000 were Syracusans, some came from Corinth and her colonies, and the rest were mercenaries, and he had no fleet to challenge that of Carthage. With great courage he invaded Carthaginian territory. He lost 1,000 mercenaries who mutinied on the march, but his initiative succeeded in drawing the Carthaginians inland, probably towards Entella. There, perhaps more by luck than by design, he caught the Carthaginian army in the act of crossing the river Crimisus. Before the main body could get across, he attacked the vanguard, led by the Sacred Band and the chariots, just as a thunderstorm broke overhead and a gale of wind drove the hail into the faces of the enemy. His cavalry galloped past the chariots and attacked the wing of the Sacred Band, just as his hoplites in a massed formation delivered a frontal attack. The enemy were driven into the river, which was quickly becoming a raging torrent, the Sacred Band was annihilated, and the supporting Spanish, Gallic, Italian, and African mercenaries suffered heavy casualties. Timoleon's victory was crowned by capturing the Carthaginian camp with its treasure

[1] Arist. *Pol.* 1306ᵃ23; Plu. *Tim.* 3–13; 16. 1; D.S. 16. 65–70. 3; *FGrH* 255. 4 (P. Oxy. 12). The chronology of Timoleon's career is uncertain.

intact (*c.* May 341). Some panoplies were sent to Corinth to commemorate the victory of Corinthian arms over Carthage.[1]

Timoleon's success against Carthage caused Hicetas, Mamercus, and other tyrants to form a coalition against him and obtain help from Carthage, which now for the first time recruited many Greek mercenaries. In 339 Timoleon made peace with Carthage; he accepted the river Halycus as his boundary, on condition that Carthage withdrew her aid from the tyrants. Warfare, conducted on both sides with mercenaries, continued until 337 when the last tyrants were suppressed and the Campanian mercenaries of Aetna were expelled. In order to mark the end of a terrible chapter in the history of Sicily, Hicetas, Mamercus, and all other tyrants who fell into Timoleon's hands were publicly done to death.[2]

Between 342 and 336 Timoleon recruited settlers from Greece, Italy, and Sicily to repeople the cities. Syracuse received at least 40,000 men, Agyrium 10,000, and they probably extended their citizenship to one another by an act of *isopolity*. Gela, Acragas, and other cities rose again from their ashes. The settlers in the Siceliote cities, numbering with their families some hundreds of thousands, give striking evidence of the floating population in Greek lands. At Syracuse coinage had not been issued probably for some ten years. From 342 onwards Timoleon minted silver coins bearing a Pegasus for Syracuse and Leontini, and after the victory of the Crimisus an issue in gold and silver depicting the head of Zeus the Liberator (Plate XII*j*). A bronze issue had the head of a warrior which may portray Timoleon as the second founder of Syracuse. In order to prevent any recurrence of tyranny at Syracuse, Timoleon and his Corinthian advisers abolished extreme democracy and established a mixed constitution. The senior civil magistrate was the priest of Olympian Zeus (*amphipolos*), chosen by a process of election by vote and selection by lot from the members of three families; a Council of 600 members, drawn probably from the well-to-do classes, conducted all departments of civil administration; and the Assembly discussed and decided questions of major importance only. Military affairs were entrusted to an elected panel of generals, who, in the event of war against people of another race, were under oath to obtain a generalissimo from Corinth. Although details of the constitution are uncertain, its purpose was clearly to avoid class strife by giving all classes a share in government. Similar constitutions were perhaps set up throughout Greek Sicily, except at Tauromenium, and the city-states were organized into some form of League under the leadership of Syracuse.[3]

Having completed his mission of liberation, Timoleon retired from public life. His sight failed, and he died within a few years at Syracuse, where the

---

[1] Plu. *Tim.* 22. 3–29; D.S. 16. 70. 4–6; 72. 2–73; 77. 4–81. 2; *Hesp.* 21. 13.

[2] Plu. *Tim.* 30–34; D.S. 16. 81. 3–82. 4.

[3] Plu. *Tim.* 23; 35; 39. 3 (settlers); D.S. 16. 83. 2, 5; 83. 1; Plu. *Tim.* 24. 3; 38. 2; 39. 3–4 (constitution); D.S. 16. 70. 5; 82. 4, 6; Nep. *Tim.* 3; *GC* 191.

citizens laid his ashes in the Agora and instituted games in his memory. An admirer of Epaminondas, Timoleon was a sincere idealist who upheld the liberal traditions of the city-state. He was a brilliant commander of mercenary troops, who used the methods of duplicity and violence for a higher purpose than his rivals. His triumph over tyrants and Carthaginians saved Sicily from self-destruction by party-strife and from annexation by a foreign power. The constitution and the League which he devised were intended to keep Sicily safe in the future, but they could only be made effective by a change of spirit in the Siceliotes and by a change of social conditions in the Siceliote cities. For the neighbouring powers sought not the co-operation of the Siceliotes but the annexation of their lands.[1]

In south Italy the raids of the Lucanians and Messapians caused Taras to appeal for help to her mother-city, Sparta, which sent out an army and a fleet *c.* 343 under one of her kings, Archidamus, the son of Agesilaus. Taras, once so powerful, was weakened by the luxury and indolence of her citizens, who relied mainly on mercenary troops for defence against the Italian tribes. Archidamus fell in battle in 338—on the very day, it was said, of the battle at Chaeronea. The Tarentines refused him burial, probably because he was believed to have taken bribes from the Phocians at Delphi. The Spartans dedicated a statue of him at Olympia, and severed relations with the Tarentines. In 334 Taras applied for help to Alexander of Molossia.[2]

With the help of Philip the Molossian king had enlarged the Molossian state and acquired allies, of which he was commander in war (*hegemon*). The 'Molossi', like the 'Macedones', were probably of Greek origin, and their royal house claimed descent from Neoptolemus, son of Achilles. The territory of the Molossi extended down to the Gulf of Ambracia, where the small city-states in Cassopia were subject to Alexander's authority. The tribes in northern Epirus, partly Greek and partly Illyrian in descent, provided excellent troops, and the country had a larger free population than any city-state. On the Greek mainland there was no opportunity to expand, but the conquest of southern Italy would afford land for settlers and control the entry to the Adriatic Sea. Alexander crossed to Taras with a large army of cavalry and infantry, took command of the levy of the Italiote League, and attacked the Italian tribes. By conquering Messapia and allying himself with the Peucetii, he protected the Greek cities on the Adriatic coast. By cutting off the Bruttii from the Lucanians, he captured Consentia, liberated Terina, and fought his way through Lucania to the bay of Salerno. He was now near the border of Campania and came into contact with Rome (*c.* 332).

After the treaty with Carthage Rome was faced by a revolt of the Latin states. In 340, when the last rebels were defeated, Rome adopted a new policy

---

[1] Plu. *Tim.* 37–39; D.S. 16. 90. 1.
[2] D.S. 16. 61. 4; 88. 3; *FGrH* 115 F 232–3 (Theopompus); Str. 280; Paus. 3. 10. 5; 6. 4. 6. *FGrH* 115 F 382; *GDI* 1334–5; *GC* 195; Aeschin. 3. 242; Str. 280; Livy 8. 17, 24; Just. 12. 2–3. 1.

which was soon to make her the strongest power in central Italy. Hitherto she had led the states of the Latin League as a military coalition, much as Sparta had once led the states of the Peloponnese, but now she disbanded the Latin League and bound each state directly to herself by separate and usually generous treaties. To some states she gave full Roman citizenship, thereby enlarging her citizen body as no Greek state had done except Syracuse under Dionysius, and to others she gave lesser rights. In Campania, too, she disbanded the Campanian League and granted to Cumae, for instance, Roman *civitas sine suffragio*. At the same time she strengthened her control of Latium and Campania by planting military colonies. Her progressive policy alarmed the Samnites. They joined forces with the Lucanians, and threatened to disrupt her settlement in Latium and Campania. When Alexander appeared near the border of Campania, Roman statecraft rose to the occasion. She concluded with Alexander a treaty of friendship and peace, wherein Alexander probably undertook not to invade Campania and Rome not to send ships into the bay of Taras.

Alexander defeated the Lucanians and Samnites in rapid campaigns and took civilian hostages, whom he sent to Epirus. His authority now spanned the southern part of Italy, and he was probably in alliance with Syracuse. His army had proved its superiority over some of the toughest Italian tribes, and he possessed sufficient wealth to issue gold and silver coins, which were minted at Taras and Metapontium and in Epirus. But, whereas Rome was building a nation by extending her citizenship, Alexander of Molossia was leading Greek cities which had strong traditions of separatism. His very success was the sign for revolt. Taras and other city-states broke away from the Italiote League, and Alexander moved the capital of the remaining members from Heraclea to Thurii. During a battle in central Lucania, when he was leading his cavalry across a river, a Lucanian deserter struck him down with a javelin (330). Their king slain and their allies split, the Epirotes departed from Italy, and Rome soon took the offensive against the weakened Samnites.

In Sicily and Italy the Greek cities were entering upon a moral decline. War and faction had weakened them economically and socially, and the influx of Sicels and mercenaries into the cities had led to a fusion of races which was hardly affected by fresh immigration from the motherland. When the city-states were united by Timoleon or by Alexander, they were so far superior in fighting power and in financial resources that they could defeat Carthaginians and Italians alike. But time and again their political disunity squandered the superior resources at their disposal. Meanwhile the influences of Hellenism spread far into the Italian peninsula, not only affecting the art of Etruria, as it had done for centuries, but also awakening the Italian peoples to a new understanding of political and military organization. In the West, as in the East, Aristotle's dictum, that Greece could conquer the world, if only she could achieve political unity, was still true in 330, but the sands of her superiority were fast running out.[1]

---

[1] Arist. *Pol.* 1327[b]33.

CHAPTER 3

The Intellectual Background of the Fourth Century

THE antagonism between philosophy and government at Athens was not due to the democracy. It would have arisen no less inevitably under an autocracy or an oligarchy. The truth was rather that the city-state, although it remained for long a condition of men's thinking, was ceasing to be the centre of their loyalties. New and vital interests were springing into prominence with a vigour which was never equalled throughout antiquity. Men found an absorbing subject of inquiry and portraiture in the individual man and his qualities: his intellectual capacity and his religious perception—combined perhaps in a philosopher-king or a constitutional monarch—his inner psychology, his moral sense, and his response to education. Man's potentialities were studied in a wider setting than the contemporary city-state. His mind soared into a world of ideas so untrammelled by political considerations that only ambition or conscience could make a philosopher become a ruler. Anthropology, geography, and ethnology became once again subjects of inquiry. Now that books were more readily available, scholarship developed rapidly. As the sum of human knowledge increased, it was encompassed by the great schools of philosophy which had supreme confidence in the power of the human mind. It was as if man's intellect had burst the walls of the city-state to shed its light upon a wider world.

In historical writing there was no heir to Thucydides. A comparable concentration on war and politics in the city-state was found only in such specialized fields as the study of tactics by Aeneas, of political action by Demosthenes, and of political theory by Aristotle. Writers of contemporary history blazed new trails. Xenophon of Athens (*c.* 430–354), who spent most of his adult life in exile, wrote a brilliant account of military adventure in the *Anabasis*. His memoirs covered the range of his interests in cavalry, hunting, estate-management, kingship, Athens' revenues, the character and trial of Socrates, the constitution of Sparta, and the life of Agesilaus. In the *Hellenica*, which covered the years 411 to 362, his personal sympathies for oligarchy and Sparta were as patent as in his lesser works. He had an eye for exciting events and colourful personalities. We gain a vivid impression of the scenes after the battle of Arginusae or the trial of Theramenes, and of the quick-witted Agesilaus, the vigorous Jason, or the unscrupulous Euphron. Yet his mind was superficial. There was no analysis of political development, which might have given a central theme, and no deeper reason was advanced for the rise of Thebes than the prompting of an anonymous supernatural power, a *daimonion*. Theopompus of Chios (*c.* 378–*c.* 305), whose works survive only in fragments, studied as a wealthy youth in the school of Isocrates at Athens and was thrice exiled from Chios as an oligarchic leader. His histories were based on industrious research. He included digressions on geography, ethnology, politics, and morals. But his chief interest was in personality, and his criterion was personal morality, so that oligarchs as well as democrats incurred the censure of this *scriptor maledicentissimus*. The title of his major work, the *Philippica*, was an acknowledgement of the fact that individuals were ousting the city-states from the forefront of historical events.[1]

Ephorus of Cyme in Asia Minor (*c.* 405–330) wrote a universal history with Greece as its centre. His narrative of Greek affairs ran from the Return of the Heracleidae to the beginning of Philip's reign, and was continued by his son Demophilus down to the end of the Sacred War, while the narrative of Persian affairs ended with Persia's intervention at the siege of Perinthus. Fragments alone survive, but his work was used by many later authors whose writings are extant. Ephorus was more deeply influenced than Theopompus by his teacher, Isocrates. Panhellenism and federal developments played a more prominent part than personality in his interpretation of the fourth century. His emphasis on 'general peace' (*koine eirene*), transmitted through the narrative of Diodorus Siculus, led him to see the culmination of events in the unification of Greece by Philip. A scholar rather than a man of affairs, Ephorus undertook the enormous task of synthesizing the work of his predecessors and created the general structure of ancient history. In dealing with the earliest traditions he had an academic tendency to prune and rationalize, and gave a misleading clarity to much that Herodotus, for instance, had wisely left opaque. When he wrote of later times, he showed a good understanding of naval tactics, but he was so ignorant of land warfare that his descriptions of battles and sieges were mere exercises in rhetorical writing. He showed great erudition in studying the origins of cities and the geography of the world, but he did not travel as Herodotus had done. The massive bulk of his material was arranged by topics, not by archon-years. He passed moral judgements which were less stringent than those of Theopompus, and he had a marked sympathy for Epaminondas. A fragment of a history known as the work of the Oxyrhynchus Historian, whether he was Theopompus, Ephorus or a Boeotian writer, Daïmachus, affords a valuable idea of the thorough and careful study of politics, topography, and chronology which marked the work of the great fourth-century historians.[2]

In their approach to history Theopompus and Ephorus owed much to a fifth-century figure, Hellanicus of Lesbos, who studied mythology, chronology, and local history and paid special attention to ethnology. His most famous work, the *Atthis* or local history of Athens, appeared *c.* 402. In it he dated the first king of Athens to 1796 (which we should call the beginning of

[1] X. *HG.* 6. 4. 3; 7. 4. 3 (*daimonion*); Nepos, *Alcib.* 11. 1; Plb. 8. 9–11 (on Theopompus).
[2] Plb. 9. 1. 4; 12. 25 F; 12. 28. 10; D.S. 4. 1. 2; 5. 1. 4; 16. 1 (based on a proem by Ephorus); 16. 76. 5.

the Middle Bronze Age), and the fall of Troy probably to 1240; he related the career of Theseus in considerable detail and brought his narrative down to the closing years of the Peloponnesian War. Hellanicus was followed by a large number of local historians. Ctesias of Cnidus, who was doctor to the Great King *c*. 405–397, wrote histories of Persia and of India, which contained absurd fantasies and romantic stories, typical of the later Greek novels, but were accepted as authoritative in his own day. On the mainland of Greece the most famous local history was the *Atthis* of Androtion. While he was in exile, he published *c*. 342 a systematic study of Athens from the beginning down to 346 and gave attention especially to the historical period. In the West a history of Sicily by Philistus of Syracuse (*c*. 430–355) was outstanding. He, too, wrote in exile and devoted almost half of his history to the tyranny of Dionysius, whose reputation he endeavoured to defend. These local historians, whose works survive only in fragments, provided material for many later writers.

While history flourished, poetry declined. The lyrical joy in life which sprang from the idealism and religious faith of fifth-century Athens disappeared with the changing conditions of the fourth century. Tragedy did not evolve beyond the stage to which the great tragedians had carried it. Euripides' plays were produced more and more in the numerous theatres of the Greek world as interest grew in individual psychology, romantic themes, and secular problems. The plays of Agathon, a younger contemporary of Euripides, were also popular. He treated choral lyrics as picturesque interludes in a play of realistic action and invented some of his plots without regard to any mythological tradition. Many tragedies were written in the fourth century, but the verdict of posterity has condemned them to oblivion.

In Comedy two plays survive from the fourth century, both written by Aristophanes. In *Women in Parliament* (*c*. 392) the Athenian women occupy the Pnyx. They are tired of men in politics, so self-seeking and quarrelsome and so vacillating in foreign policy, and they proclaim a New Order of share-and-share-alike in husbands and young men too, provided the slave girls and prostitutes are put out of business. Praxagora, the successful female demagogue, shows signs of becoming a powerful general who will imperil the liberties of the new communistic order. In *Wealth* (388), when it is proposed to restore the sight of the blind god 'Wealth', the harridan Poverty is outraged. She is responsible for the blessings of democracy; she keeps men decent, honest, and brave, while Wealth turns them into crooks and sycophants. The political flavour is still present in these plays, but it has lost its astringency. 'Rule by women' and 'wealth by merit' are portrayed more for their social effects than for their political consequences. The characters—the idle city-dweller, the honest countryman, the witty onlooker, the love-sick youth, the lubricious hag, the cynical priest, and the huckster Hermes—derive less from the political scene at Athens and more from the social manners of the fourth-century city. The New Order is a parody not so much of democracy as of the philosophical ideas which Plato was then propounding and later published in his *Republic*. The situations are nearer to realistic human life—the swindle of faith-healing in the temple of Asclepius, and the parody of a sophisticated love-song in a fashionable city. In *Women in Parliament* Aristophanes claimed that he was tapping a new source in Comedy, which yielded laughter rather than satire. The direct exhortation by the poet has gone; the Chorus has become so insignificant in its utterances that the text of *Wealth* provides at times no lyrics but just the entry 'a bit by the Chorus'. Tradition relates that in his old age Aristophanes wrote two plays with no choral lyrics or political satire, and that these plays contained the good-natured burlesque and the neatness of plot which were destined to mark the revival of comedy by Menander. In a famous couplet Plato bade farewell to the most creative poet of the age: 'The Graces sought a shrine that would not fall; they found the heart of Aristophanes.'[1]

Oratory flourished in the unsettled conditions of the fourth century. Private life was riddled with litigation, while public men advocated policies in the Assembly and fought for their lives, like gladiators, in the people's courts. As litigants spoke in person, they often hired a professional orator to compose their speeches for them. Such a writer was Lysias, a metic at Athens, who was active *c*. 403–380. Departing from the rather stilted style of Antiphon, he developed a persuasive limpidity of expression which was close to colloquial diction, and a sufficiently flexible style to fit the personality of the litigant. Another metic, Isaeus, whose extant speeches were delivered in the period *c*. 390–353, combined the merits of Lysias' style with a greater versatility in depicting the personality of his litigants and a more vigorous exposition of close argument. Beside these two Andocides, who spoke himself in court *c*. 410–390, was an amateur of natural genius, especially in the dramatic force of his narration, and he bequeathed an example of directness and vividness to the great political orators who lived in the age of Philip and Alexander. No other period has yielded such a galaxy of gifted speakers. Demosthenes, Aeschines, Hyperides, Hegesippus, Lycurgus, Demades, and the speechwriter Dinarchus were the models of the Roman orators and through them of European and American orators. Supreme among them was Demosthenes. His art was as meticulously studied as that of Thucydides in diction, rhythm, and antithesis. His evocation of emotion in his audience was achieved by a wide variety of effects, from which humour alone was lacking. The intensity of his feeling, the vigour of his argument, and the speed of his narrative assail the mind of the modern reader with such force that he is constrained, often against his better judgement, to accept Demosthenes' point of view.

The superb quality of Attic Oratory was rivalled by that of written prose. Whereas Xenophon wrote with a natural charm and ease, Isocrates (436–338) laid the foundations of a studied artistic prose. After a short career as a speech-

---

[1] Ctesias, see *POxy.* 22. nr. 233a. Ar. *Ec.* 557; 1155 (for novelty); *Life* 10 and Platonius *Diff. Com.* 1. 8 for connexion with New Comedy.

writer, he turned *c.* 392 to the teaching of oratory and developed his own talent as a political essayist. He used the artistic effects of Gorgias, but with a more sparing hand; for metaphor, poetic words, balanced clausulae, and rhythmical endings were set within a medium which had much of the apparent simplicity of Lysias. He developed a periodic style which had more balance, smoothness, and amplitude than that of Thucydides, but tended in its mellifluousness to become monotonous. He combined dignity with precision, and clarity with embellishment. His works became the model for stately prose, whether cast in the form of essay, encomium, or open letter, and influenced the styles of Ephorus, Theopompus, Lycurgus, and in due course Cicero. Equally influential was his arrangement of the subject-matter in a manner calculated to carry conviction. His theme, for instance in the *Panegyricus*, published in 380, was expounded in accordance with a carefully balanced plan. This part of his teaching encouraged Ephorus and Theopompus to write history by subject rather than in an annalistic form, and orators to pay more attention to the exposition of their argument.

A less stately but more charming style was employed in the 'dialogue', which represented conversations, actual or imaginary, in a literary setting. Xenophon incorporated such conversations in his portrayal of the great Cyrus and in his memoirs of Socrates, but they excelled more in conversational ease than in dramatic force. The master of dialogue was Plato. In his hands the characters live, their arguments are cogent, and the thrill of intellectual discovery is re-experienced. Few passages in prose or poetry are as moving as the close of the *Phaedo*, or as beautiful as Diotima's description of love in the *Symposium*. His style is amazingly versatile. He describes a scene, paints a character, sets out a disputation, and expresses a spiritual belief with equal charm; for in every mood his writing has a 'noiseless current and grandeur', unmatched by subsequent writers of dialogues. Aristotle, too, was famed for his dialogues (which have not survived). In many of their longest works Plato and Aristotle made more use of consecutive exposition, which excels in clarity of definition and logic. Few ages have achieved so much in prose as that of Isocrates, Plato, Lysias, Xenophon, Demosthenes, and Aristotle.

As the claim of the city-state and the appeal of orthodox religion grew weaker, men began to lose the sense of their vocation. Uncertain of their own ideals, they relied more on formal education than on family training to give a standard of conduct to their children. During the Peloponnesian War there were several forms of education. The sophists offered technical education, especially in law and politics, for the ambitious. At Athens Socrates discussed the theoretical basis of knowledge and conduct. Sparta continued to give her traditional form of state-education to all her citizens. In the fourth century the sophists plied their trade throughout the Greek world, spreading often a specious philosophy of superficial knowledge and of self-interest. Socrates had many successors, and the versatility of his genius was apparent in the diversity of their views. The Spartan system of education found many admirers; for, unlike most states, Sparta was almost immune from party-strife, revolution, or tyranny. An interesting combination of Socrates' influence and Spartan education appeared in Xenophon's *Education of Cyrus* (*Cyropaedia*), a mixture of history and fiction, which attributed to sixth-century Persia an idealized form of Spartan education. Xenophon wanted boys to learn justice and honour, because the shamelessness which results from the lack of them is at the root of all moral and political wrongs; and he intended at the same time to produce good citizens of a military society.

The first school of higher education, analogous to a modern university, was founded at Athens by Isocrates. His aims were moral and practical. He regarded grammar, arithmetic, disputation, and literature as basic subjects for preliminary training, and he set the pupils, who came to him at university age for three or four years, not to study the theoretical basis of knowledge but to learn the art of expounding what they knew in speech and writing. He did not advance any theory of ethics, but he accepted the highest standards of traditional morality. He advocated the claims not of individual ambition nor of city-state politics, but of Greece as a whole; for he sincerely believed that the highest interests of individuals and of city-states lay in the advancement of Hellenic unity. He gave close supervision to his students' work, and he set an example by speaking and writing himself on Panhellenic topics. Because Isocrates took fees, his critics classed him with the sophists, but his writings show that he taught from conviction, had a high sense of personal and national honour, and was concerned with the political and social troubles of his age. His pupils, he hoped, would bring a more enlightened statesmanship into politics.

The greatest of Socrates' followers, Plato (*c.* 429–347), founded the Academy *c.* 387. He expounded a theory of knowledge, which he held to be the true basis of wisdom, conduct, and politics, and thereby created an intellectual religion in place of orthodox piety. At the same time he endeavoured to incorporate his intellectual religion into a training for life in the city-state. Elementary and secondary education, he believed, should train the child by imitation and habituation towards the practice and understanding of good principles. Because the models for imitation must be perfect, Plato expelled from his *Republic* those poets and those forms of music which were unworthy. When the faculty of reason dawns, it should gradually take control of the appetitive and wilful sides of the personality or 'soul'. When there is a 'harmony' in the soul, an understanding of principles develops; but this understanding is at first based only on instruction and observation. The final fruit of education is a knowledge of the world of abstract Ideas. The contemplation of this world is the highest function of the philosopher. When he applied this type of education to his ideal state in the *Republic*, he assumed that it would grade the citizens in classes by their abilities; and these classes would undertake the duties for which they were fitted, as rulers, warriors, and workers. The citizens would have no family life and no private property. Their children would be reared by state-nurses; learn music, literature, and gymnastics of the proper types; complete two years of military training; and then, if fit for it, undergo a course of higher education. The subjects in the course were to be Theory of Number, Plane and Solid Geometry, Astronomy, and Harmonics. Only a few selected students would go on to study Philosophy, which leads to the contemplation of the absolute. These few would become the rulers of the state not from preference but from a sense of duty.

In the *Republic* Plato expounded the nature of virtue and justice first and gave his plan of an Ideal State only in outline. In the *Laws*, on which he was engaged probably from *c.* 360 until his death, he was concerned primarily with politics of a practical kind and therefore with a more detailed system of education, which is in some respects different. Children were to stay with their family until the age of six, and attend from the age of three a nursery school under women teachers. After the age of six the boys and girls were to be segregated in separate dormitories, but undergo, as far as possible, the same course of education in state schools, controlled by the Minister of Education and staffed by expert teachers, who were to be recruited from other states. In the event of misbehaviour by a child, the teacher and the child were both to receive corporal punishment. Attendance at school was to be compulsory on the ground that 'the child is even more the property of the state than of the parents'. Physical education by dancing and wrestling and mental education by music were to lead on to the study of literature, arithmetic, geometry, and astronomy, all aspects of the curriculum having been censored by the Minister of Education. Women were to play an equal part with men in the state, participating in games and warfare, and associating freely in all activities, provided that social conscience upheld a high standard of sexual behaviour. Women magistrates were to supervise the nursery schools and advise married couples during the first ten years of marriage, and women as well as men were to have public meals organized by the state. In the state of the *Laws* organized religion was to play an important part, because true understanding comes from two sources, religious observation and intellectual education. The supreme board of control, in a state remarkable for innumerable boards, was to be recruited from persons eminent in virtue, piety, geometry, and astronomy. These are indeed the rulers of the *Republic* under a different constitution.

The state for which Plato devised this scheme of education was to be a city-state on the Spartan model: in economy not urbanized and not maritime but agricultural; in population restricted to a constant figure of 5,040 citizen families; in labour dependent entirely on a subject population; and in capitalism so controlled that the richest citizen family was no more than four times richer than the poorest. The citizen-class, possessing two inalienable estates to each family, enjoyed sufficient leisure for education and politics. In its constitution Plato wished to combine the merits of monarchy and democracy. The Laws themselves were to be the rulers. On the other hand, the magistrates were to be the people's representatives, and the people were to become so just and so intelligent that all laws would be willingly obeyed.

Aristotle of Stagirus (*c.* 385–322), who was a member of the Academy for the last twenty years of Plato's life and opened a rival institute at the Lyceum in 335, put a similar faith in the value of education for the city-state. As man is unique in the conscious direction of his activities, the task of the statesman is to direct the city-state towards the right life. He takes for his chief assistant the educator, who trains the citizen's mind to understand what is right and the citizen's will to do what is right. For Aristotle, too, state-education was to be compulsory and universal for the members of the citizen class, and the subjects of study were to be similar to those outlined by Plato in the *Republic* and the *Laws*. The right life is a double life of good citizenship in the light of practical wisdom, and of contemplation which is the quintessence of philosophy. Aristotle's ideal state also follows the Spartan pattern in its economy, class-structure, and insulation from contemporary commerce and capitalism; and it, too, has a mixed constitution. The political aim of the educator is to make the citizen's good judgement coincide with that of the good legislator who imprints the personality or 'soul' of the whole state upon its parts.

Whereas Isocrates envisaged a modification of city-state autonomy within a wider framework and devised his course of education accordingly, Plato and Aristotle both regarded the city-state, and indeed in material terms the Spartan type of city-state (although they criticized Sparta's institutions and aims), as the highest form of man's political existence. At first sight their conservatism seems strange. Yet they observed correctly that the Greek city-state had produced the finest achievements of civilized man, and their faith in its potentialities for the future was still unshaken. The limitation in size was necessary, so that all citizens should be members of one body by knowing one another and knowing their rulers. Their attempts to infuse the city-state with a new religion seems stranger still. For the highest initiates become contemplatives, not men or women of action, and yet they have to be the rulers of the city-state. To us an intellectual religion of such a range seems to be a universal religion above questions of race or politics. To Plato it may have been so. But to Aristotle the Greek alone was capable of such perception 'by nature'. For both of them the highest intellectual understanding was within the range only of the intellectual aristocrat. For this reason the political methods of their ideal states are to us illiberal but to them necessary. Our belief in universal education as a potential equalizer is a tenet of political democracy; their belief in an intellectual aristocracy made necessary an authoritarian régime by intellectual oligarchs. Plato and Aristotle ventured to believe that the other citizens would be capable of accepting that authority without demur, but they never overcame the fundamental difficulty of making their contemplatives willing to act as rulers or legislators or committee-men. For their highest loyalty was to an intellectual religion which had outgrown the limits of the city-state.

The basis of Plato's philosophy was Socrates' dictum that virtue is knowledge. His early dialogues put previous theories of knowledge to the test and found them wanting. Because perception is based on recognition, knowledge is represented (especially in the *Phaedo*) as 'recollection' by the soul of the non-material world of absolutes, with which the soul was conversant, before it entered the body, and will again become conversant, when it sheds the body. The aim of education is to free the highest quality of the soul, its intellectual perception, from the distracting pull of its associates, appetite and will, and thereby to attain the true happiness and end of man in the contemplation of the absolute. The world of ideas is non-material. Yet it is the cause of the material world, and its principles are apparent to those who understand the movements of the material world, especially those of the heavenly bodies. Supreme in the world of ideas is 'the good and the beautiful'. 'No mortal man', said Plato at the end of the *Laws*, 'will ever become a true worshipper of God, unless he accepts our two statements—that the soul is anterior to all things which participate in generation, and that the soul is immortal and sovereign over all material bodies—and in addition perceives the Mind of the universe among the constellations.'

Aristotle, whose father was a doctor, had a more biological approach. A seed already contains the actuality of the final product, whether it be an individual sheep or oak tree; the seed is the activator, matter the medium, growth the activity, and the actuality envisaged in the seed is the end (or final form) of the object. Similarly with a man-made object, whether it be a bowl or a tragedy, the man is the activator, the metal or the words are the medium, growth or 'making' the activity, and the completed object the end. All four components are required for production and are in this sense 'causes'; and there is a correlation or overlap between them, in that the final form is immanent in the seed or in the man's mind and conditions the growth or making. As the actuality of the eye is a seeing organ, so the actuality of the individual man is an intelligent and moral being. This actuality has been immanent in him from the beginning as his 'soul' or 'form'.

Man's 'soul' or 'form' is unique in one respect. Other animals, and also the human infant, desire what appears to them good by sense-perception. Man stores up his sense-perceptions in memory and draws deductions from them; but he has also intuitive reason. It is intuitive reason which grasps the universal principles that are the guiding lines of morality and understanding. The intuitive reason, Aristotle believed, is divine and non-material; and though it is immanent in an individual man as part of his soul, it can exist without body or soul and contemplate its own understanding. Similarly in the universe, which consists of fifty-four concentric spheres with our earth in the centre and a fifty-fifth sphere enveloping all, there are several intelligences (divine like human intuitive reason) which activate the rotatory movements of the spheres, and the 'unmoved mover', God, who is the 'good' or 'desire' of the universe, directs its movements by attraction and exists only in self-contemplation. To the process of life and motion in the universe and in the species of nature there is neither beginning nor end, and God alone is motionless and unmoved.

It is, of course, impossible to sketch even the barest outlines of the two greatest philosophies of antiquity in a few sentences. Nor can one summarize the immense services of the Academy and the Lyceum to learning in every field. The *Laws* of Plato, for instance, rest on detailed research into the theory and practice of Attic law, which was to form the basis of Hellenistic law and affect Roman law. The *Politics* of Aristotle, together with memoranda on 158 Greek constitutions (the *Athenaion Politeia* is the only survivor) and on non-Greek institutions, provided the foundation of later political theory and precept. The systematic studies of zoology by Aristotle, botany by Theophrastus, and musicology by Aristoxenus (both his pupils) started the scientific method of observation, classification, and deduction. Important progress was made in mathematics, geometry, and mechanics by Plato's friend Archytus of Taras, Theodorus of Cyrene, Theaetetus, Eudoxus, and Menaechmus. Aesthetics, ethics, psychology, literary criticism, chronology, geography, and many other subjects excited the fresh curiosity of the Greek mind in this age of extraordinary vitality.

A revolt against the sophistication of life and the demands of the city-state was led by Antisthenes of Athens (*c.* 455–360), an admirer of Socrates, and Diogenes of Sinope (*c.* 400–*c.* 325). They accepted the interrelation of knowledge, virtue, and happiness but sought the ideal conditions for happiness in a return to primitivism and self-sufficiency. They rejected all social distinctions and other features of city-state life as based on convention, scorned orthodox religion as a fabrication of lies, and studied early legends and animal life in order to arrive at a true understanding of natural law. The individual was free and self-sufficient when he was master of his passions, secure in his intelligence, impervious to social or religious demands, and satisfied with the poverty of a mendicant. Diogenes was content with a tub for shelter. Because he reduced his physical needs to a minimum by asceticism and satisfied them with a simplicity which paid no regard to social conventions, he received the name of 'the dog' and his followers that of 'followers of the dog', Cynics. They propagated their faith zealously by preaching and writing, and fragments survive of poems by Crates of Thebes (*c.* 365–285). He wrote of a haven untouched by the tides of contemporary life, where garlic, thyme, figs, and crusts of bread suffice and no man comes in war to win riches or glory, and he found his own home and city not in any walled tower but in the whole wide earth.

Another admirer of Socrates, Aristippus of Cyrene, was an advocate of individualism who scorned the tenets of society and religion and found happiness in an enlightened hedonism. Little is known of his philosophy, except that it influenced Epicurus in the Hellenistic period.[1]

Sculpture and painting, even more refined in technique than in the fifth century, found new sources of inspiration in a naturalistic and humanistic treatment of new and traditional themes. In the statue of Peace with the child

[1] *PPF* 10 F 4, 15 (Crates).

Wealth, sculptured in marble by Cephisodotus of Athens to commemorate the peace of 374 or 371, her head is turned towards the playful child in an expression of tenderness. The same lightness of stance and gentleness of feeling recur in the Hermes and child Dionysus by Praxiteles of Athens (*floruit* 364), of which the marble original was found in the Heraeum at Olympia (Plate IX). The human rather than the divine side is stressed in these representations of the anthropomorphic gods. The artists are content to portray the grace of the human body and the emotion in human relations, without striving for the majesty and grandeur of the divine. The texture of the skin and the softness of the curves in the Hermes and Dionysus have a new realism of treatment and perfection of finish. Praxiteles' most famous statue was the nude Aphrodite of Cnidus, laying her drapery on a water jar by her side and standing in graceful relaxation. To Pliny it was the finest statue in the world, and Lucian admired 'the melting expression of her eyes, and their bright joyfulness'. Although the subject is the Goddess of Love, the conscious pose and realistic setting remind one of the human model, Phryne the courtesan, among whose lovers was Praxiteles. His statues of the boy Apollo killing a lizard, the boy Eros, and the girl Artemis of Anticyra express the serenity of youth, and the gilded statue of Phryne at Delphi was among the early portraits in Greek sculpture.[1]

Scopas of Paros, who rivalled Praxiteles in fame, represented stronger emotions in scenes of action—Amazons in battle, Maenads in ecstasy, and Love in attitudes of yearning and desire. Fine portraits were executed of Isocrates and Philip by Leochares, of Plato by Euphranor, and of Seleucus by Bryaxis. Four artists—Scopas, Leochares, Bryaxis, and Timotheus—are best known from the sculptural remains of the Mausoleum, built at Halicarnassus after the death of Mausolus in 353. The portrait statues of Mausolus and Artemisia are good examples of Aristotle's dictum that the artist renders the individual likeness but makes the subject more beautiful than he is; for realism is still restrained by an artistic and intelligent idealism. The same characteristics appear in the friezes, where the battle of Amazons and Greeks is depicted with great boldness and force of composition and a new intensity of emotion.

Their style reached its acme in Lysippus of Sicyon (*fl.* 328), who excelled in portraiture and battle scenes. He gave his figures an appearance of greater height by making the head smaller and the body more slender and firm. He developed a new canon of proportions to replace the rather square stance of earlier statuary with a greater use of the third dimension, as in the Youth with a scraper (*Apoxyomenus*) held with both arms extended. He himself claimed that earlier artists represented men as they were, and he represented them as they appeared to the eye; and that he acknowledged no artist but Nature herself as his model. His portraits of Alexander in bronze caught the

---

[1] Richter, *Sc.*, figs. 499, 659–63 (Peace); 170, 444, 664–5, 667 (Hermes); 668–72 (Aphrodite); 673–5 (Apollo); Pliny, *NH* 36. 20; Lucian, *Erotes* 13; *Eikones* 6 (Aphrodite).

inclination of the head in repose and the melting expresssion of the eyes so truly that the king would permit no other artist to model his likeness. Hunting scenes and battle scenes, containing portraits of Alexander and the Companions in action, were no less famous. None of these scenes survive, but those on the Sarcophagus of Alexander reflect his influence (Plate X).

Painting, too, reached its acme in this century with Apelles of Colophon, whose qualities as an artist resembled those of Praxiteles and Lysippus. His most famous painting was of Aphrodite Anadyomene rising from the sea and wringing out her hair in a human pose, like Aphrodite of Cnidus standing by the water jar. His portraits of Philip and Alexander and his self-portrait were much admired, and his naturalistic realism is delightfully described in a mime by Herodas, where a girl exclaims before a picture by Apelles: 'If I pinch this naked boy, he will show the bruise; for his flesh lies warmly pulsing on the panel. And the ox and the man leading him and the girl following and the hook-nosed man and the fellow with his hair standing up have all the look of living day. I almost shrieked for fear the ox would hurt me.'[1]

The magnificent temple of Apollo the Succourer, situated on a mountain ridge at Bassae in Arcadia, was built during the Peloponnesian War. It was in Doric style with fewer refinements than the Parthenon, but it contained new features in the engaged Ionic columns, of which two had Corinthian capitals, and one free-standing Corinthian column inside the cella. The engagement of columns and the Corinthian style were developed further, *c.* 350, in the large Doric temple of Athena Alea at Tegea, which rivalled the Erechtheum in the exquisite detail of ornament and the Parthenon in the refinements of its construction. The evolution of the Corinthian capital was a Dorian achievement, and this capital became a characteristic feature of Greco-Roman architecture. The fourth century also produced the Temple of Zeus at Nemea, the sixth Temple of Apollo at Delphi, and those of Asclepius and Artemis at Epidaurus. Great skill was shown in the building of circular *tholoi*, or rotundas, where the inner cella is surrounded by an inner and an outer circle of columns, Corinthian and Doric respectively, at Delphi and Epidaurus. The circular Philippeum at Olympia, begun by Philip and completed by Alexander, was surrounded by Ionic columns, and the inner wall of the cella was decorated by engaged Corinthian columns. In Sicily and Italy troubled conditions brought the building of temples to an end. The enforced peace gave prosperity to Asia Minor. Great temples in Ionic style were built at Ephesus to Artemis (the stylobate measuring 343 by 164 feet), and at Didyma near Miletus to Apollo (359 feet by 168 feet). Their splendour was not matched by any novelty in design, except in the sculptured column-drums at Ephesus. Priene and Sardis also built temples, and the huge Mausoleum at Halicarnassus ranked as one of the seven wonders of the world.

[1] Arist. *Po.* 1454^{b}9 (portrait painters); Richter, *Sc.*, figs. 228, 313–14, 697–702, 720–2, 729–30, 735 (Mausoleum); 739, 742–3 (Apoxyomenus); 176, 399, 400, 748 (Sarcophagus of Alexander); Pliny, *NH* 34. 61–65 (Lysippus); Plu. *Alex.* 4. 2; Herodas 4. 56.

Secular buildings rivalled the temples in grandeur: Philon's arsenal at Athens, some 400 feet long; the Thersilion or Assembly-hall of the Arcadian League at Megalopolis, 218 feet by 173 feet with a roof carried throughout on stone columns; and the Leonidaeum or residential quarters at Olympia, 263 feet by 243 feet in area, the rooms surrounding an inner court with a Doric peristyle and the outer colonnade consisting of 138 Ionic columns. Similar, no doubt, were the great buildings of Dionysius of Syracuse, forerunners of Agathocles' 'sixty-couch' palace. Finest of all surviving buildings of the fourth century are the stone theatre at Epidaurus (*c.* 350), where the semi-circular auditorium is 387 feet in diameter, and that at Athens (*c.* 330) with a seating capacity of some 17,000 persons. Both are still used for the production of plays and have remarkable acoustic qualities. The Panathenaic stadium at Athens, 850 feet long in 'poros' stone, was also built under the financial régime of Lycurgus. No less typical of the fourth century are the massively constructed and artistically finished fortification-walls, towers, and gateways (which sometimes use the arch) of innumerable cities throughout Greece, Sicily, and south Italy. Notable among them are those at Messene which withstood the assaults of Sparta.

These fortifications are an indication of the fear which was a mark of the fourth century. Brigandage, piracy, marauding mercenaries, and war after war forced many men to live in walled cities or in watch-towers or forts. As faith in orthodox religion declined, fear drove those who found little solace in philosophy or humanism into deeper forms of superstition. The oracular utterances of Delphi and Dodona, the soothsayers and the interpreters of omens had a lively vogue, for instance with the soldiers of Timoleon. Some, like Xenophon, had a vague faith in an anonymous divine power. 'If anyone is surprised', he said, 'at my advice to work with God, his surprise will diminish if he is often in peril; . . . for the Gods reveal the future in sacrifices, omens, voices, and dreams.' Others, like Timoleon, worshipped Chance and reckoned themselves 'lucky'. The Mystery religions, especially Orphism, attracted a greater following than ever throughout the Greek world. But the strongest tendency in this age of growing individualism was to see divine power in the strong man, to regard a Lysander or a Philip 'as a god'. Occasionally there were outbursts of superstitious fear, such as had occurred in the Peloponnesian War. One split the Arcadian League, another the Phocian state. It may have contributed to the condemnation at Athens of Aristotle, who only escaped execution by retiring to Chalcis (323); and it caused the persecution at Athens of his memory and of philosophers on the charge of 'impiety' in 306. Even in the capital of Greek culture, where intellectual enlightenment and artistic skill flourished, there were strong undercurrents of political and social animosity and of superstitious panic which threatened to undermine the fabric of civilization. The Macedonian monarchy was founded on a more primitive but robust religion. The Temenid kings were admirers of Greek culture; Alexander endowed the first great library, that of Aristotle, and his scientists collected information for Aristotle and others during the campaigns in the East. They sought, as Pericles had done, to bring political power and intellectual enlightenment into unity but in a wider world than that of the city-state.[1]

[1] Brigandage, &c.: [*D.*] 12. 2–3; 17. 19; D.S. 16. 62–63; Plu. *Tim.* 1. 3; 22. 6. Faith and chance: X. *Eq. Mag.* 9. 8; Plu. *Tim.* 16; 21. 3–4; 30. 5; 8. 1 (omens, &c.); 12. 6; 26.

CHAPTER 4

Alexander and the Greeks defeat Persia, 336–330

§ 1. *Alexander asserts his authority in Europe*

ALEXANDER'S qualities at the age of twenty in administration, hunting, and war were already known to the Macedonian people. He had been trained for kingship as a Royal Page, King's Deputy, Commander of the Companion cavalry at Chaeronea, and leading envoy at Athens. He had fought against Thracians and Illyrians in 340 and founded his first city, 'Alexandria', in Thrace. On the assassination of Philip, Alexander immediately sat on the royal throne, his supporters congregated round him, and in due course he was elected King. The assassin had been killed, and three rivals to the throne, who were perhaps accused of complicity in the assassination, were executed after the state funeral: two princes of the Macedonian royal house, and Amyntas, son of Perdiccas, for whom Philip had at first acted as regent. Later Olympias, who resembled Clytemnestra in ruthless ferocity, killed the infant daughter of Cleopatra and compelled the mother to commit suicide. Olympias acted without the knowledge of Alexander, who expressed his disapproval. As Alexander and his half-brother Arrhidaeus were now the only males in the royal line, Parmenio advised the king to beget an heir before embarking on the conquest of Persia. Alexander, who a year earlier had wished to marry the daughter of Pixodarus, failed to follow this excellent advice.[1]

When Philip was murdered, Alexander addressed the envoys of the Greek states who were present, and bade them remember the goodwill and the treaty of alliance between Macedon and the Greek League. The news of Philip's assassination delighted his opponents. Demosthenes, who received early information, pretended that Zeus and Athena, appearing to him in a dream, had prophesied some happy event; when the event was known, he put on a garland of flowers, and the Assembly voted a crown to the assassin. Secret negotiations were opened with Attalus, one of the Macedonian generals in Asia Minor, and with several Greek states in which the anti-Macedonian party was strong. A Thessalian army blocked the narrow Vale of Tempe, while Ambracia expelled its Macedonian garrison and became a democracy. Thebes and others published their intention to annul the Greek League. Meanwhile Alexander was on the march with a Macedonian army. He turned the Thessalian position by cutting steps up the precipitous face of Mt. Ossa and led his men over the mountainside into Thessaly, where the Thessalian

---

[1] D.S. 17. 2; Plu. *Alex.* 10. 8; Just. 9. 7. 12; D.S. 17. 16. 2; St. Byz. *Alexandreiai.*

League gave way and elected him *archon* for life. The Amphictyonic Council at Thermopylae recorded its wish that he become the *hegemon* of the Greek League's forces, and Ambracia accepted his generous offer of a free pardon. When he pitched camp outside Thebes, the Athenians took refuge behind their walls and sent an embassy to apologize. Demosthenes, who had been elected to serve, turned back half-way. Before the envoys arrived, Thebes had capitulated. Alexander accepted the apology of Athens, convened the Council of the Greek League, and announced his intention of continuing the policy of his father. He did not propose to punish Thebes and the other recalcitrant states. The Council then elected him *hegemon* of its forces for the further prosecution of the war against Persia and confirmed the regulations which he put forward. Athens and other states conferred honours upon him, and accepted their obligation under the terms of the Greek League to provide contingents. Alexander returned with his army and arranged for the assassination of Attalus, whose treasonable negotiations with Demosthenes were now known. Before he crossed to Asia, all male members of Attalus' family were put to death in accordance with the Macedonian law of treason. During the remainder of his life no one in Macedonia conspired against the throne.[1]

In spring 335 Alexander conducted his first campaign as commander of the army which Philip had trained to a superb pitch of efficiency. His aim was to reassert Macedon's authority in the Balkans and in particular to punish the Triballi, who had attacked Philip during the remarkable campaign of 339. Alexander left Antipater in Macedonia and Parmenio in Asia; for he intended to show his own ability as a general in terrain where he had served under Philip's command. The army included the best heavy infantry, the Hypaspists in three battalions of 1,000 men each, of which the senior battalion was the Guard (*agema*); some battalions of the phalanx, each numbering 1,500 men; a battalion of Agrianian light infantry and one of archers, each 1,000 strong, and some skirmishers; at least two squadrons of Companion cavalry, each some 200 strong; and light cavalry from Upper Macedonia and the subject peoples, perhaps 2,000 in all. He marched rapidly by the road through Philippopolis towards Mt. Haemus, where he found his way barred, probably at the Kajan pass on the trade-route from Aenus to the Danube estuary, by a large force of Thracians escorting a caravan of merchandise. The enemy held a steep escarpment, from which they prepared to launch their heavy wagons on to the Macedonian infantry. Alexander ordered the phalangites to open their ranks and let the wagons through, or, where space was not available, to crouch forming a 'testudo', or covering with their shields, so that they should pass over their backs. His tactics were successful, and the wagons caused no

---

[1] The continuity of the alliance is inferred from the general practice of the age, the phrase in the Charter of the League 'the kingdom of Philip and his descendants' (*GHI* 177, l. 11), and the mention of 'the peace and the alliance' in Arr. *An.* 3. 24. 5. D.S. 17. 2–5. 2; Polyaen. 4. 3. 23 (the steps were known as 'Alexander's ladder'); Plu. *Dem.* 22; *Phoc.* 16. 8; Aeschin. 3. 160; *GHI* 183; Arr. *An.* 1. 1. 1–3; Curt. 6. 11. 20 (law of treason).

casualties. Then, while the archers gave a covering cross-fire, he led the Hypaspists and Agrianians to the assault and carried the pass with heavy loss to the Thracians.[1]

When he entered the territory of the Triballi between Mt. Haemus and the Danube, the king of the Triballi took refuge on an island in the river but sent part of his army back to cut Alexander's lines of communication. Alexander retraced his steps and found the enemy holding a strong position at the mouth of a glen. He sent forward a screen of archers and slingers to harass the Triballi. When they retaliated by charging, the archers and slingers retreated and drew the enemy into open ground, where they were engaged on either flank by the Macedonian cavalry and on their front by a line of cavalry with the phalanx massed in support. The heavily armed cavalry, whose chargers were trained to rear and strike with their hooves, spread terror among the tribesmen. Three thousand Triballi fell, and the remainder fled. At the Danube, Alexander was joined by a fleet which he had sent through the Black Sea and up the river, but he failed to force a landing on the island. 'A strong desire' (*pothos*), which is mentioned now and later by Arrian, the historian of Alexander's campaigns, impelled him to cross the Danube. Collecting native dug-outs and improvising floats from tent-skins stuffed with hay, he ferried 1,500 cavalry and 4,000 infantry across by night, surprised an army of the Getae which fled, and razed their town to the ground. The king of the Triballi then submitted.

These victories of Alexander established the authority of Macedon along the line of the Lower Danube, where the independent tribes paid homage to him. Envoys came from the Celts who had established themselves between the territory of the Veneti and the Middle Danube, and Alexander concluded a treaty of friendship and alliance with them. On the bank of the great river he sacrificed to Zeus and Heracles and the river-god 'Ister', before he turned westwards. The campaigns of Philip and Alexander against the Thracians, Scyths, Getae, and Triballi, like those of Marius and Caesar, protected civilization from the migrating peoples of central Europe.[2]

During the march, probably over the Shipka pass, towards Agriania and Paeonia news reached Alexander that the Illyrians of king Cleitus, son of Bardylis, were in revolt and that the Taulantii farther west and the Autariatae to the north were planning to join them. Detaching the king of Agriania to ravage the territory of the Autariatae, Alexander surprised Cleitus at Pelium, a strongly fortified town surrounded by wooded hills, but the Taulantii came up on the following day. His army was heavily outnumbered by the Illyrians, who held both the town and the surrounding hills with cavalry, heavy infantry, javelin-men, and slingers, but by rapid and orderly manoeuvres the

[1] Arr. *An.* 1. 4–13; D.S. 17. 8. 1; Plu. *Alex.* 11. 3–5. For the campaign see *JHS* 94.66 ff.

[2] Dug-outs—logs hollowed out to form boats—are still used in Albania. Arr. *An.* 1. 2–4. The frontier of civilization was not advanced beyond the Danube until the campaigns of Trajan.

Macedonian infantry succeeded in escaping from the impasse without loss. The enemy then attacked while his army was crossing the river Eordaicus. The Hypaspists led the phalanx in formation through the water and secured the further bank, while Alexander with the Companion Cavalry, Agrianians, and archers, fought a rear-guard action and protected the last sections by covering fire from his siege-catapults and from the archers, who shot from mid-stream. Later Alexander recrossed the river by night with the Hypaspists, Agrianians, archers, and two battalions of infantry and at dawn surprised the combined forces of the enemy in bivouac. Victory was completed by the Companion cavalry under Alexander, who pursued as far as the mountain strongholds of the Taulantii. The western frontier of Macedonia was now secure, the pressure of the Taulantii on Epirus was eased, and Alexander, who had set out in the spring merely as the successor of Philip, was accepted in August as a commander of equal brilliance.[1]

During his absence from Macedonia rumours that he had been killed in action encouraged his opponents in the Greek states. Demosthenes obtained 300 talents from Darius, which the Assembly officially refused to accept but Demosthenes used to promote action. He helped some Theban exiles at Athens to return to Thebes and supplied them with arms, bought with Darius' gold. There they caught two officers of the Macedonian garrison unawares, killed them, and told the Theban Assembly that Alexander was dead. The Thebans then laid siege to the Cadmea. Athens voted to send an army to Thebes, manned her fleet, and sent an embassy to ask Persia for alliance, as Thebes probably did; the Peloponnesian states, when asked by Thebes and Demosthenes to send help, did not comply, except that an Arcadian force came as far as the Isthmus and turned back. The news reached Alexander at Pelium. By forced marches through the highlands of Pindus and then down the upper Peneus valley he reached Pelinna in Thessaly on the seventh day, and encamped seven days later outside Thebes, where he was joined by a Macedonian army under Antipater and by troops from Phocis, Plataea, and other Boeotian cities hostile to Thebes. For three days he waited to see if Thebes would sue for terms, but the returned exiles, whose policy was to restore the Boeotian League, persuaded the Theban Assembly to keep quiet.

On the fourth day the assault began. The Thebans, having built stockades to confine the garrison in the Cadmea, manned their field defences outside the city walls. Part of the Macedonian infantry managed to penetrate these defences, and Alexander sent in the Agrianians and archers as well. When the Thebans began to master them and committed more of their troops, Alexander charged with the rest of the phalanx. The Theban forces broke and fled, and the Macedonians entered the gates on the heels of the fugitives. Fierce fighting ensued in the streets, during which the Greeks supporting Alexander were more conspicuous than the Macedonians in slaughtering their traditional enemies. By the evening of the same day all resistance was at

[1] Arr. *An*. i. 5–6. The Illyrians sacrificed boys, girls, and rams before the battle.

an end. Six thousand Thebans lay dead, and over 30,000 were taken prisoner. Of the Macedonians 500 were killed. As the revolt of Thebes was an act of treachery in the war declared by the Greek League against Persia, Alexander referred the matter to the Council of the League, as whose *hegemon* he had acted. After enumerating the Theban acts of medism in the past, the Council decided to garrison the Cadmea, raze the city, sell the men, women, and children of the citizen population into slavery, banish any surviving Thebans from Greek soil, and allot the lands of Thebes to her neighbours. The decision was executed by Alexander. Except for the temples and the house of Pindar, which he spared, no remnant was left of what had been for forty years the strongest military state in Greece.[1]

The responsibility for the elimination of Thebes by *andrapodismos* lay formally with the League but morally with Alexander. When Phocis, Amphissa, and Thebes had capitulated, Philip had spared them. In 336 Alexander had himself influenced the Greek League to pardon Thebes, Ambracia, and other states. He could have done so again in 335, but he preferred to make a terrible example of her. A militarist might indeed argue that after committing treachery against Macedon three times Thebes merited the customary punishment of the fourth century; and that, if Thebes survived and the Greek states rose during the absence of Macedonian forces in Asia, she and they might threaten the very existence of Macedon. However, this argument is not convincing. Sparta had shown at Mantinea, and Philip in Phocis, that a state could be rendered impotent by less harsh methods. Macedon's military power was sufficiently demonstrated to the Greek states by capturing in one day a city which withstood Sparta's attack for years and by inflicting 6,000 casualties. As an act of deliberate policy the destruction of Thebes after her surrender weakened the possibility of that co-operation between Macedon and the Greek states which Philip had hoped to achieve not only by his statesmanship in the period 346 to 336 but also by a joint expedition against Persia.

After 335 the Greek League was regarded by the Greek states not as a political link between a union of Greek states and Macedon but as the vehicle of Alexander's control, which commanded the obedience not of loyalty but of fear. The expedition against Persia ceased to be in any true sense a joint operation, capable of preserving the pride of the Greek states; for it was launched from a background of discontent. Thus in the history of Greece the destruction of Thebes was to prove a more decisive event than the sack of Persepolis. The Greeks themselves turned a blind eye on their share in an act which Alexander later regretted. In encouraging Thebes, attacking her, or voting for her destruction they showed the lack of principle and humanity which had characterized much of their policy since the beginning of the century. Indeed Athens and Thebes had set the precedent for *andrapodismos* and surpassed it

---

[1] Arr. *An.* 1. 7–9; D.S. 17. 8–14; Plu. *Alex.* 11. 6–12; Polyaen. 4. 3. 12; Just. 11. 3. 7–11; Plb. 38. 2. 13. The number of prisoners, common to D.S. and Plu. *Alex.*, is compatible with her military strength (see Appendix 6).

by slaughtering all males in some states. But their actions did not justify Alexander in stooping to their methods and abandoning the chance of eventual reconciliation.

At Athens the spirit of resistance collapsed. An embassy, headed by Demades, brought Alexander a letter (which he is said to have thrown away in disgust) congratulating him on the defeat of Thebes; he demanded the surrender of those responsible for abetting Thebes—among them Demosthenes and Lycurgus. The Assembly sent a second embassy, headed by Phocion, who advised Alexander to turn his hand against Persia rather than Greece, and persuaded him to be content with the expulsion of the general Charidemus (who later entered the service of Persia). The Arcadian League executed those who had advised the dispatch of troops towards Thebes, and other states apologized and received back their exiles in accordance with the terms of the Greek League. During the winter, while Alexander was in Macedonia, the members of the Greek League provided their contingents for the invasion of Persia, Demosthenes' opposition being overruled at Athens. Except in Thessaly, which was loyal to him, the demands of the *hegemon* were modest. From the other states he took perhaps 7,000 hoplites, whom he intended to use for less responsible duties, a few cavalry, and a naval force of 160 triremes. Their presence gave colour to his claim that Macedon and Greece were engaged in a crusade of vengeance for the sacrilege committed by Xerxes against the gods they worshipped in common. At the same time he left half the Macedonian infantry in Macedonia under Antipater. For the danger that Persia might instigate a rising by the Greek states was now too real to be disregarded.[1]

§ 2. *The campaigns in Asia Minor*

PERSIA had been at war with the allied powers, Macedon and Greece, since 337. The satraps had failed to break Parmenio's control of the Asiatic side of the Hellespont, and Darius had not manned the Phoenician fleet to support the satraps in Ionia and encourage Athens to join Thebes in her revolt. The short-sighted policy of Darius left the initiative with Alexander. The national arm of Persia was cavalry, well trained and well mounted but less suitably equipped. Even the finest cavalry, which wore armour of mail, used javelins and relied on scimitars for close fighting. The average Persian trooper wore turban, quilted tunic, and trousers, whereas the Macedonian wore helmet and cuirass, and he fought with javelins and scimitar against the cornelwood spear and sword of the heavy Macedonian trooper or the lance and sword of the lancer. Persia had relied mainly on Greek mercenary hoplites since the battle of Cunaxa, and the hordes of native infantry which she could raise in her empire were much inferior in quality. Alexander, counting on the striking power of a comparatively small army, took almost the full strength of the

[1] Arr. *An.* 1. 10: D.S. 17. 15; Plu. *Alex.* 13; *Dem.* 23; *Phoc.* 17; Din. 1. 10.

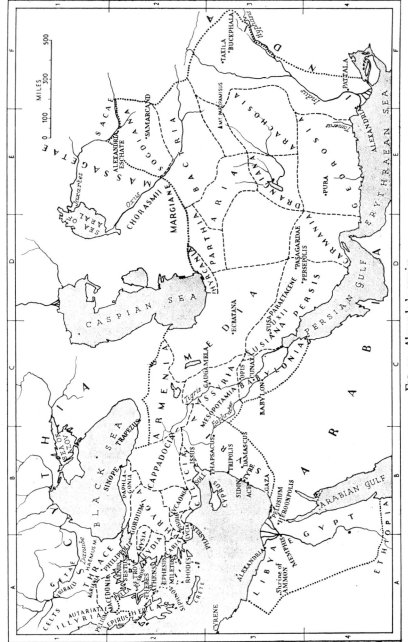

FIG. 30. Alexander's empire

Macedonian and Thessalian cavalry but only a part of the infantry available in Macedon's empire and in Greece.

The organization and the approximate numbers of the army which opened the campaign in Asia Minor were as follows. The heavy cavalry comprised 1,800 Companions and 1,800 Thessalians; the former, commanded by Philotas, son of Parmenio, consisted of the Royal Squadron, 300 strong under the command of Cleitus, and seven squadrons of 150 to 200 men each. The lancers and light horse from parts of Upper Macedonia, Paeonia, and Thrace, perhaps 1,400 strong, and the Greek League and Greek mercenary cavalry, 500 strong, brought the total cavalry force to a little over 5,000 men. The heavy infantry were 24,000 in number, half being Macedonian and half Greek, each armed in their traditional manner. Nicanor, son of Parmenio, commanded the three battalions of Hypaspists, each 1,000 strong; and the six territorial battalions had 1,500 men each. The Greek League hoplites may have numbered 7,000 and the Greek mercenary hoplites 5,000. Ancillary units, totalling some 8,000 men—Agrianian javelinmen, archers, peltasts, slingers, surveyors, sappers, and siege-engineers—were drawn mainly from the Balkan dependencies of Macedon but included Greeks serving as mercenaries. The General Staff, headed by Parmenio, and the entourage of Alexander were drawn from the ranks of the King's Companions. The secretariat under Eumenes of Cardia, who kept the records day by day (*ephemerides*), dealt with routine administration and intelligence. The medical service was led by Greek doctors. The commissariat organized supplies for an army of almost 40,000 men and at least 6,000 war-horses and the transport of a siege-train. In the Balkans baggage-animals were used, but the Macedonian military road to the Hellespont and the Persian imperial roads in Asia made it possible there to use wheeled transport. Whereas Xerxes' huge army had needed to lay supply-dumps in advance and use sea transport, Alexander relied on rapid movement and quick victories to gain him new areas from which supplies could be requisitioned. Therefore he crossed into Asia with one month's stock of provisions. In fact he did not need more, and his small reserve of 70 talents in cash made it impolitic to purchase more than was necessary.

At sea Alexander had a small Macedonian fleet, which was perhaps stationed primarily on the Macedonian coast and in the Hellespontine area. The main fleet, supplied by the Greek League, contained 160 triremes, of which twenty were Athenian, and supply vessels and transports in addition. Persia could have raised thrice as many warships from Cyprus, Phoenicia, Egypt, and other maritime satrapies, but in spring 334 she had no large fleet in the Aegean Sea. Money Persia had in abundance. Although Alexander had little cash in hand, the mines under his control were very productive and his coinage was of the finest quality. By abandoning the Chalcidian standard and adopting the Attic standard in silver, as Philip had done in gold, he tied his economy to that of the Aegean world. The new 'Alexander-types' in gold with the head of Athena and on the reverse a Victory with a naval mast, and in silver with Heracles and on the reverse Zeus of Olympus, emphasized the Macedonian and Hellenic aspects of the war against Persia and prophesied victory. It is probable that the Greek League had a federal chest, too, for meeting naval expenses.

The expeditionary force marched from Pella to Sestus in twenty days, a distance covered by Xerxes in some three months. While Parmenio organized the crossing over the Hellespont, Alexander sacrificed at the Tomb of Protesilaus, the first hero who fell in the expedition of Agamemnon, and on shipboard sacrificed to the Nereids and Poseidon, whose wrath had cost Agamemnon's army such suffering. Landing on Asiatic soil, he sacrificed to Zeus, Athena, and Heracles. At Troy, where his ancestors Heracles and Achilles had fought and Neoptolemus, son of Achilles, had killed Priam, Alexander sought to propitiate Athena as goddess of Troy and also Priam by sacrifices, and he and his friend Hephaestion placed wreaths on the tombs of Achilles and Patroclus. From the Temple of Athena, where he dedicated his armour, he took a shield, a sacred relic of the Trojan War, which his body-guard thereafter carried into battle. Thus Alexander marked the beginning of a personal and national crusade, which for him at least was imbued with a religious zeal. Four days later his vanguard of cavalry made contact with the Persian army, which was under a multiple command. Memnon of Rhodes had advised the other generals and the satraps to retreat, scorching the earth as they went, so that Alexander would run short of supplies, but they were determined to fight a battle, relying on their 20,000 cavalry, which had been recruited from many of the inland satrapies of the empire.[1]

Alexander, aware that the Persian cavalry might attack him in open country, was marching with his army ready for action; behind the vanguard came the lancers and 500 light-armed infantry and then the phalanx in twice the normal depth with squadrons of heavy cavalry on both flanks and the baggage train close behind. The Persians, however, had adopted a defensive position on the far bank of the river Granicus, which was steep but with a narrow foreshore beside the water; the cavalry in an extended line held the top of the bank, and the infantry, consisting of almost 20,000 mercenaries, was in line behind them on level ground. Alexander prepared to engage at once. Although the initial difficulty of crossing the river was serious, he saw that the Persian disposition wasted their great superiority in numbers of cavalry and made no use at all of their infantry. If he attacked with his whole line, he would overlap the Persian cavalry line and he hoped also to punch a hole through that line with his best troops. He therefore drew up his army on his bank with the Thessalian, Greek, and Thracian cavalry on the left under Parmenio; the infantry battalions in the centre with the Hypaspists on the right; and a powerful right wing formed by the Lancers, Paeonian cavalry, Companion cavalry,

---

[1] For numbers see Arr. *An.* 1. 11. 3; D.S. 17. 17. 3; Plu. *Mor.* 327d; Plb. 12. 19. *AJP* 56. 362, ll. 149–54 (coinages); *GC* 204. Arr. *An.* 1. 11. 3–12; D.S. 17. 17–18; Plu. *Alex.* 15; Just. 11. 5. For the Lancers as Macedonians see Arr. *An.* 1. 2. 5; 2. 8. 9.

archers, and Agrianians in that order from left to right. The squadron of Socrates, whose turn it was to head the order of battle for the day, was the left-hand squadron of the Companion cavalry, next to the Paeonians. Alexander and his body-guard stationed themselves near Socrates' squadron. The Persian commanders, seeing Alexander resplendent in a white-winged helmet, concentrated their best cavalry opposite him.

When the bugles sounded, the squadron of Socrates rode first into the river, then the Paeonian cavalry, the Lancers, and the adjacent battalion of Hypaspists. As they began to cross in close formation, they kept moving obliquely towards the right, lest the rest of the right wing, which was beginning to enter the water, should be outflanked on the extreme right. As Socrates' squadron and the cavalry on his left approached the other bank, the Persian cavalry hurled javelins from the top and some of them, led by Memnon, rode down to the foreshore. Many of the leading cavalry were killed or wounded, as they strove to gain the foreshore, but Alexander and the Companion cavalry were now at hand and forced a landing. The struggle was at close quarters, like a battle of hoplites, and the stouter spears and protective armour of the Macedonian cavalry began to tell as they pressed on in massed formation. Alexander pushed ahead, unhorsed Mithridates, a son-in-law of Darius, and was nearly cut down himself. The stoutness of his helmet and the speed of Cleitus in coming to his aid alone saved him, and then the main mass of cavalry began to come up, and, intermingled with the Agrianians, who attacked the enemy's horses, forced their way through the enemy line. The cavalry on his left then pushed back the enemy centre, and the Thessalian cavalry on the left wing defeated their opponents. The cavalry battle was over with the loss of 1,000 Persian cavalry and some ninety Macedonian horsemen. When the Persian cavalry fled, the infantry were exposed to attack on all sides. As most of them were Greek mercenaries, Alexander showed no mercy, and only 2,000 prisoners were taken.[1]

After the battle, Alexander visited his wounded men and listened to their exploits. Of his Greek prisoners he released any Thebans and sentenced the others to hard labour for treachery to the Greek League. He sent 300 panoplies as an offering to Athena, goddess of Athens, to be dedicated with the words 'taken from the barbarians of Asia by Alexander, son of Philip, and the Greeks, save Sparta'. The victory opened the way into Asia Minor. Alexander marched through the coastal area, detaching troops to occupy Sardis and other cities which joined him, and replaced the pro-Persian oligarchy at Ephesus with a democracy, which he restrained from carrying out the usual massacre of its opponents. He was now at the terminal of the Persian main road leading to Susa, but his immediate concern was with the Persian navy of 400 sail, which was now at sea and approaching Miletus. Alexander reached Miletus first. His fleet blocked the entrance to the harbour and he took the city by storm, while the Persian fleet lay nearby off Cape Mycale. At this

[1] Arr. *An.* 1. 13–16. 3; D.S. 17. 19–21; Plu. *Alex.* 16; Just. 11. 6. For the battle see *JHS* 100.73 ff.

point Alexander disbanded most of the Greek fleet, declaring that he would defeat the Persian fleet on land by capturing its continental bases. As he had to leave the islands unprotected, the Persian fleet occupied Samos and later Chios. Alexander used the ships he still had, including twenty Athenian triremes, to transport his siege-train to Halicarnassus, which was bravely defended by Memnon and the satrap of Caria, Orontopates, with a strong garrison of mercenaries. When the city was about to fall after many assaults, Memnon escaped by sea and Orontopates fled inland, where he continued to resist until 332. As it was now midwinter 334–333, Alexander sent some recently married Macedonians home on leave, ordered Parmenio to move his base into Phrygia, and himself campaigned in Lycia and Pamphylia as far as Perge. Thence, turning inland, he fought his way through Pisidia to Phrygia, where he met Parmenio at Gordium.[1]

In 336 the forces of Parmenio and Attalus had invaded Asia Minor in the name of Macedon and the Greek League to free the Greek cities from Persian rule. They had expelled the representatives of Persian rule, who were usually tyrants or oligarchs, from Chios, Lesbos, and Ephesus. In 334 when Alexander liberated Ephesus again, he expelled the oligarchs and issued a directive to his general Alcimachus to depose oligarchies, set up democracies, restore their laws, and remit the tribute (*phoros*), payable in the past to Persia, in the Aeolian and Ionian cities. At Priene, where he had dedicated a temple of Athena Polias, a letter from 'King Alexander' emphasized the 'liberty and autonomy' given to the Prieneans, and the liberated cities in the islands and on the mainland issued coinage and made treaties as autonomous states. Yet their liberty was under some restraint. For Alexander did not permit the democrats to massacre their opponents at Ephesus or elsewhere; and later in 332 the sentence passed at Eresus in Lesbos by the democracy against some tyrants had to be confirmed by Alexander. For his aim was reconciliation and concord (*homonoia*). Nor did he install democracies everywhere. At Rhodes an oligarchy remained in power, probably because it had not been actively pro-Persian. Since the Charter of the Greek League placed restraints on party-strife in its member-states, Alexander, as *hegemon* of the League during the war, was acting in accordance with the spirit and probably the letter of the Charter.[2]

The island-states became members of the Greek League, making covenants with 'Alexander and the Greeks', and therefore were liable for contributions (*syntaxeis*) towards the conduct of the war. Chios, for instance, had to send twenty ships to 'the fleet of the Greeks' in 332 and traitors were delivered to the Greek League for trial. There is not sufficient evidence to determine

[1] Arr. *An.* 1. 16. 4–29; D.S. 17. 21. 7–28; Plu. *Alex.* 17–18. 1.

[2] D.S. 16. 91. 2; 17. 24. 1; *GHI* 191, l. 6 (liberation; the reference to Philip is probably as liberator; 'Alexander and the Greeks'). Arr. *An.* 1. 17. 10 (Ephesus); 1. 18. 2 (Alcimachus); *GHI* 184–6 (Priene); 191, l. 99 (Eresus); *OGI* 2, ll. 29 and 31 (*homonoia*); 223, l. 23 (Erythrae); *AJP* 56. 361, l. 6 (Colophon).

whether the Greek cities of the Asiatic mainland entered the Greek League. It is probable that they did not. Effective representation on the League Council would have been difficult and their numbers would have made the Council unwieldy. Their problems, too, were tied up with the neighbouring lands over which the League had no jurisdiction, and some cities and villages were of mixed Greek and barbarian blood. The Greek cities on the Asiatic mainland in any case had to pay contributions (*syntaxeis*) towards the conduct of the war, unless Alexander chose to exempt a city, for instance Priene. When a city misbehaved, he imposed harsher conditions. Ephesus was ordered to devote the Great King's tribute to the temple of Artemis. Aspendus had not only to pay an indemnity but also, like a non-Greek community, to render 'tribute (*phoros*) to Macedon'.[1]

In the native areas Alexander took over the Persian system of administration with small but important changes. The land owned by the Great King now became the land of Alexander, King of Macedon (he tended to use the royal title in Asia, where it was customary, but not in Greece). He claimed it by right of conquest for himself and his country, Macedon, and not for the Greek League. The native peoples paid him the tribute (*phoros*) due in the past to Darius, and were subject to the authority of Alexander and his satraps. In Caria, where the queen-mother Ada adopted Alexander as her son, he made her satrap. Elsewhere he appointed Macedonians from the ranks of the Companions, but in one case at least he divided the powers which had been concentrated in one man's hands under the Persian system. At Sardis, the capital of the Lydian satrapy, his governor wielded civil powers and commanded a small body of troops; another officer dealt with all matters of finance; and a third commanded the garrison in the citadel. The mints which he set up at Lampsacus and Sardis, where he captured Persian treasure, and later at Tarsus and Miletus, were under his own financial officers. Although the political and economic status of the native inhabitants remained as before, Alexander came as a liberator from oppression. For he restored to them the right of practising their own religion and using their native customs, which Persia had often suppressed. He told the villagers to return in confidence to their farms, and he did not permit his army to ravage and loot during the advance. His reputation as a clement conqueror went before him into Syria, Phoenicia, Cyprus, and Egypt.[2]

In regulating the relations between the Greek cities and the native peoples Alexander disregarded the advice of Isocrates and Aristotle to treat the barbarians as helots or cattle. He did not extend the territories of the Greek cities, except for merit, or make more natives subject to their rule, but he acted as an impartial arbitrator between the two parties, for instance at Phaselis and

---

[1] Arr. *An.* 2. 2. 2 (Tenedos; Arr. *An.* 2. 1. 4 is less precise in wording); *GHI* 192 (Chios); 185, l. 15 (Priene); Arr. *An.* 1. 17. 10 (Ephesus), 1. 27. 4 (Aspendus). As *hegemon* Alexander gave back her *syntaxeis* to Mitylene later (Curt. 4. 8. 13).

[2] Arr. 1. 17. 1, 7; 23. 4, 7; 27. 4; *GHI* 185, ll. 11–12 (tribute); *SIG* 302 (King's land).

Aspendus. He encouraged Colophon to build her walls, planned a canal at Erythrae, ordered the rebuilding of Smyrna, and set his Thracian troops to build a military road. The development of Asia Minor, which he planned, was to be in the interest of both Greek and barbarian. As an act of military government, he placed garrisons, wherever he wished, to preserve the peace and resist Persia, and he removed many of them when the need passed. As his father had done in Europe, Alexander was building his peacetime organization as his army swept forward. His regulations in Asia Minor and the treaties (*synthekai*) which were set up in the cities in 334–333 were still valid under the Successors.[1]

At Gordium Alexander saw the chariot of Gordius, founder of the Phrygian monarchy, and was informed of the oracle that any man who loosed the knot binding the yoke to the pole would rule over Asia. Alexander succeeded where all had failed, either by an impetuous sword-cut or by pulling out the pole-pin. But the fulfilment of the oracle seemed far from certain at that time. For the Persian fleet under the able Memnon, who had been given supreme command of the coastal areas by Darius, had captured Chios by treachery from within and was blockading Mitylene in Lesbos. Memnon then died, but his successor Pharnabazus won over Mitylene and Tenedos, and sent ships as far as Siphnos in the Cyclades. With Greek mercenaries, Persian money, and agents in the Greek cities he might have raised Greece in revolt; but he acted with treachery towards Mitylene and set up tyrants again. His policy contrasted so unfavourably with that of Alexander that he received little support in the Aegean, and Darius unwisely recalled the Greek mercenaries for service in Asia. Even so Alexander gave orders for a Greek fleet to be collected in the Hellespont to safeguard his lines of communication, while Antipater sent out a squadron to expel the Persians from Siphnos. Darius endeavoured to have Alexander assassinated by Alexander Lyncester, a senior general. But the plot was detected by Parmenio, and Alexander was placed under arrest. Alexander the king fell ill in late summer with a violent fever. Parmenio reported in a letter that his doctor was in Persia's pay, whereupon Alexander gave the letter to the doctor and at the same time drank the medicine he had prepared. This illness occurred at Tarsus, whither he had advanced from Gordium; for he knew that Darius had mustered a great army at Babylon and was on the march westwards.[2]

§ 3. *The conquest of Syria and Egypt*

WHEN Alexander had recovered from his illness, he reduced part of Cilicia, held games at Soli, stopped a civil war at Mallus, and, treating the city as Greek, remitted the tribute. There he learnt that Darius' army was in north

---

[1] Isoc. *Ep.* 3. 5; Arr. *An.* 1. 24. 6; 26. 1; 27. 4; Pliny *N.H.* 5. 116–18; Curt. 4. 8. 13 (later gift of land to Mitylene).

[2] Arr. *An.* 2. 1–4; D.S. 17. 29–32. 2; Plu. *Alex.* 18–19; Just. 11. 7–8; Curt. 3. 1. 14–24.

Syria (near Aleppo), and pressed on round the head of the Gulf to Issus, where he left his sick, and then to Myriandrus (Iskanderun). A heavy storm prevented him crossing southwards over the pass near Antioch into Syria,

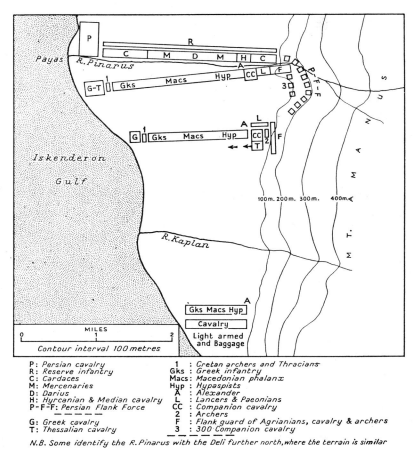

P: Persian cavalry
R: Reserve infantry
C: Cardaces
M: Mercenaries
D: Darius
H: Hyrcanian & Median cavalry
P-F-F: Persian Flank Force

G: Greek cavalry
T: Thessalian cavalry

1 : Cretan archers and Thracians
Gks : Greek infantry
Macs: Macedonian phalanx
Hyp : Hypaspists
A : Alexander
L : Lancers & Paeonians
CC : Companion cavalry
2 : Archers
F : Flank guard of Agrianians, cavalry & archers
3 : 300 Companion cavalry

N.B. Some identify the R.Pinarus with the Deli further north, where the terrain is similar

FIG. 31. The Battle of Issus

and then he learnt to his surprise that Darius had abandoned the wide plains of Syria, which suited his superiority in numbers, and descended by an inland pass to the head of the Gulf, so that he was now on Alexander's route from Cilicia. Darius reached Issus first, mutilated and killed the Macedonian sick, and camped beside the dry bed of the river Pinarus between the rocky spurs of Mt. Amanus and the sea. Alexander, who knew the ground between

Myriandrus and Issus, led his army back in the hope of engaging Darius in narrow ground, where the superior numbers of the Persian army would be less effective. Early on a November morning in 333 Alexander's army marched in column and then gradually deployed into line, as it neared the Pinarus river. His army was again at full strength, some 30,000 foot and 5,000 horse; for 3,000 Macedonian infantry, 2,000 other infantry, and 650 cavalry from Macedonia, Thessaly, and Elis had joined him in Phrygia and Cilicia.

Darius sent forward cavalry and light infantry to screen the deployment of his army (Fig. 31). The Greek mercenary hoplites, perhaps 30,000 strong, who formed the centre, and Persians trained as peltasts (Cardaces) on either side of the Greeks lined the north bank of the river-bed and strengthened it with palisades. Darius was in the centre. Units of cavalry were in position on each wing. On the left flank Persian infantry of inferior quality were posted in a line which bent forward through the foot-hills so as to attack Alexander's flank, if he attempted a frontal engagement. Once again the Persians left Alexander the initiative. His army advanced as if on a parade ground, the deployed phalanx leading with the Hypaspists on the right near the foot-hills and Parmenio commanding the left wing near the coast. When the ground widened, Alexander, knowing Darius was likely to hold the centre with his best infantry, began to deploy his cavalry, which had marched behind the phalanx. The Greek cavalry he sent to Parmenio; the rest he placed in massed formation on the right wing with a screen of light cavalry and archers in advance. He also posted at a right-angle to his line a force of Agrianians, archers, and cavalry which, advancing more slowly, drove back the Persian infantry on the foot-hills. Thus Alexander was poised for a powerful attack with his right wing, as at the Granicus river.

At this point Darius recalled his screen of cavalry and infantry. The cavalry rode off to either wing, but, finding little room on the left wing, the main bulk of the cavalry settled down in a deep mass on the right wing opposite Parmenio. Darius, whose chariot and entourage were in the centre, and Alexander on the right of his centre could now see each other's dispositions. Alexander saw at once that Darius' plan was to break through near the coast and drive the Macedonian line towards the hills; he therefore sent the Thessalian cavalry to support Parmenio, but with orders to pass unseen behind the phalanx, lest Darius change his plan and transfer some cavalry to the left wing opposite Alexander. He saw, too, that his right wing, as it advanced, was in danger of being overlapped. He therefore withdrew 300 Companion cavalry from his deep formation, and sent them unseen by Darius to replace the flank-guard of Agrianians, archers, and cavalry, whom he quickly swung forward to lengthen his right wing just before he reached the enemy. Darius made no counter-move but kept his army stationary.

In order to keep his men in line, Alexander advanced slowly until they came within range of the Persian archers. Then he led the charge of the Infantry Guard, followed on his right by the Cavalry Guard and on his left by the

Hypaspists and part of the phalanx. But the centre of the Macedonian phalanx, endeavouring to keep contact with its own right, opened up a gap into which the Greek mercenaries of the Persian centre charged with great effect. Meanwhile on the left by the coast the Persian heavy cavalry charged. However, Alexander's forces on his right wing and right centre broke down all opposition. The phalanx battalions, swinging left, took the Greek mercenaries in the flank and mowed them down. Darius led the flight, and Alexander swung his cavalry across the battlefield to the left wing. There the Persians broke and, in full flight, rode one another down to avoid encirclement. The pursuit lasted until nightfall. Darius escaped, leaving his chariot and weapons; but his mother, wife, and son were captured in the Persian camp and the baggage-train and treasure at Damascus were later collected by Parmenio. When Alexander was told that the womenfolk were lamenting for Darius, he sent Leonnatus to tell them Darius was alive and they would be treated with the respect due to royalty. Next day, despite a thigh wound, he visited the wounded, who numbered over 4,000, and buried the 450 dead. The number of Persian casualties is not known.

The battle of Issus was closely contested. The Greek mercenaries, fighting with a racial hatred for the Macedonians, achieved a break-through and 10,000 escaped as a body; of them 2,000 rejoined Darius and the rest took ship from Syrian Tripolis to join the fleet of Pharnabazus. The Persian heavy cavalry nearly achieved a second break-through. It was only the final changes made by Alexander in his order of battle, the excellence and speed of the Companion cavalry, and the efficiency of its flank-guard which turned the battle into a decisive victory. One important result was that the Greek mercenaries in general abandoned Persia. Many thousands more crossed the seas to Greece during the winter, and the final battle was fought by Darius with a diminished force of Greeks. The provinces west of the Euphrates were now open to Alexander, but he continued to advance down the coast, in order to defeat the Persian fleet on land. During the march he refused Darius' offer to cede Asia Minor and make a treaty of friendship and alliance, declaring that Persia had first committed aggression in Europe at Perinthus, and ordered Darius to address him henceforth as 'King of Asia'.[1]

All the Phoenician cities on the coast of Lebanon welcomed Alexander except Tyre. Because the island-fortress of Tyre was considered impregnable and her fleet commanded the sea, the Tyrians professed friendship but would not commit themselves to his side. For Alexander it was co-operation or war. In order to put their friendship to the test, as Philip had done with King Ateas, Alexander asked to enter Tyre and sacrifice to Heracles, with whom the Greeks identified the Phoenician god Melcart. The Tyrians refused, and Alexander undertook the siege of Tyre. He attempted first to build a mole out to the island. When it came under attack from the walls and warships, he

---

[1] Arr. *An.* 2. 5–14; D.S. 17. 32–39; Plu. *Alex.* 20–21; Just. 11. 9; Curt. 3. 2–13; Plb. 12. 17–22. See Appendix 8 and *HA* 94–110.

placed two towers on the end of the mole, but these were destroyed by fire-ships. He therefore decided to collect a fleet at Sidon. The news of his victory at Issus and the surrender of the other Phoenician ports had caused the fleet of Pharnabazus to break up. Squadrons from Rhodes, Lycia, Cilicia, Cyprus, and Phoenicia joined Alexander, and with some 220 warships he controlled the coastal waters and blockaded the entries to the harbour of Tyre. The besieged fought with ingenuity and ferocity, killing every prisoner they took, but in the seventh month of the siege Alexander, commanding the Hypaspists, and Coenus, leading a battalion of the phalanx, landed from transports and stormed two sections of the walls. The troops poured into the city and avenged their compatriots by widespread massacre. All survivors, except the Tyrian king, his entourage, and some envoys from Carthage, were sold into slavery. Thus Tyre suffered the fate of Thebes. Alexander sacrificed to Heracles and garrisoned the island as a naval base (July 332).[1]

During the siege Darius offered to cede all territory west of the Euphrates and pay 10,000 talents, if Alexander would restore the women of the royal family, marry his daughter, and conclude a treaty of friendship and alliance. When the terms were read to the Staff, it is said that Parmenio remarked 'Were I Alexander, I should accept, and end the war without running further risks', and that Alexander replied 'Were I Parmenio, I should accept, but being Alexander I shall reply as follows.' He then announced his rejection of any offer which did not give him the whole of the Persian empire. There were many arguments of common sense in favour of Parmenio's advice. As yet, Alexander had conquered only the coastal areas of the great territories west of the Euphrates, and Antigonus as commander in Asia Minor had already fought three battles to keep the lines of communication open. These territories would suffice for settling the surplus population of Greece and form an economic unit with the Balkans. Nor was Greece yet pacified and secure. For after the battle at Issus Greek envoys sent to Darius by Athens and Sparta had been captured and kept by Alexander, and Athens had recently instituted military training for her young men (*ephebia*). Pharnabazus, too, had given to Agis, king of Sparta, money, ships, and the 8,000 Greek mercenaries from Tripolis to force Crete on to the Persian side, and cut sea-communications between Greece and Tyre. These signs meant more than the gold crown sent by the Council of the Greek League in honour of the victory at Issus. More important were the fact that Asia west of the Euphrates was defensible, as Rome was to show later, by a power based in the Mediterranean and the expectation that the future interests of Macedon and Greece might be better served by expansion westwards against the European peoples, with some of whom Alexander the Molossian was already at war. Alexander's reply sprang from the impulsive force of his genius. When he had conquered Darius, resistance would die behind him, and the eastern limits of the Persian empire,

[1] Arr. *An.* 2. 15–24; D.S. 17. 40–47; Plu. *Alex.* 24–25. 3; Just. 11. 10. 6–14; Curt. 4. 1. 1–15; 4. 2–4; Polyaen. 4. 3. 3–4.

he thought, were close to the edge of inhabited Asia. He was just twenty-four. Later, when the Persian empire was conquered, he might turn his armies into the western Mediterranean, but for the present he intended to drive towards the East. His decision was one of the most crucial in the history of civilization.[1]

From Tyre Alexander marched south, receiving the formal submission of the inland peoples of Palestine, and laid siege to Gaza, which held out for two months. The defenders fought to the last man; the women and children were sold as slaves. A week later, when the army and fleet reached Pelusium, the Persian satrap of Egypt surrendered without fighting. The Egyptians welcomed Alexander as their liberator. He gave them religious freedom, sacrificed to their gods, and was invested by the priests as Pharaoh of Egypt (November 332). By the western mouth of the Nile he founded a new city, Alexandria, which with its two harbours was to be the centre of Mediterranean commerce with Egypt. The city, which he planned with a Greek architect, was to be Greek in character with temples to the Greek gods, city-walls, Council-house, Agora, and so on, and its institutions were to be Greek. In the adjacent native town, Rhacotis, he built a temple to Isis as a token of his interest in Egyptian religion; and he sacrificed to the gods of Greece and Egypt at Memphis. During the winter a 'strong desire' (*pothos*) moved him to visit the famous shrine of Zeus Ammon in an oasis of the western desert, where he entered the shrine alone and said the answer of the god was in accordance with his desire. The fact that Alexander the Pharaoh was acclaimed 'Son of Re' and may have been addressed as such by the priest of 'Amon-Re', who to the Greeks was 'Zeus Ammon', caused rumours to spread that Alexander was more than man. Yet he himself gave no sign that deification was more than a political convenience within the frontiers of Egypt. In order to lessen the danger of a *coup d'état* in so rich and defensible a country, he appointed six governors: two Macedonians with military powers, two Greeks and two Egyptians with civil powers. He put the garrisons of Pelusium and Memphis and the fleet of the Nile area under independent Macedonian commanders, and the supervision of all finance in the hands of one of the Greek governors, Cleomenes of Naucratis. After receiving Cyrene into alliance, he returned in spring 331 to Tyre where his army was mustering for the march to the East.[2]

For the first time in history the coastal lands of the eastern Mediterranean from Cape Malea to Cyrene were under a single control. Where Athenian sea power and Persian land and sea power had failed, the Macedonian army had succeeded under the brilliant generalship of Alexander. But it was far

[1] Arr. *An.* 2. 25. 1–3; Plu. *Alex.* 29. 7; Curt. 4. 5. 1–8 (confused with the earlier offer of Darius). Curt. 4. 1. 34 (Antigonus); Arr. *An.* 2. 13. 4 (Agis); D.S. 17. 48; Curt. 4. 1. 38. Arr. *An.* 2. 15. 2 (Greek envoys). *IG* ii.² 1156 (first ephebic list yet known, in 334/333).

[2] Arr. *An.* 2. 25. 4–27 (Gaza); D.S. 17. 48. 7; Curt. 4. 6. 7–31. Arr. *An.* 3. 1–5 (Egypt); D.S. 17. 49–52; Plu. *Alex.* 26–27; Curt. 4. 7–8. 9; Just. 11. 11. The inner harbour was like the lake of Pella and Lake Cercinitis.

more than an achievement of arms. Alexander aimed at the unification of diverse peoples by giving them a common interest in the religious, social, and economic benefits of the peace which he imposed. Many native peoples, unaccustomed to political liberty, attached greater importance to the religious freedom which he brought and saw in his work the hand of their own god— Jehovah, Melcart, or Re. So wrote Zechariah of the fall of Tyre. 'And Tyrus did build herself a stronghold and heapeth up silver as the dust and fine gold as the mire of the streets; behold, the Lord will cast her out; and he will smite her power in the sea, and she shall be devoured with fire.' By Greek and Oriental standards he was merciful and tolerant; for he pardoned where military considerations permitted, and he restored the social rights and legal codes of Greek and non-Greek alike. Within the areas under his control trade was stimulated not only by the foundation of 'Alexander-cities' in the Troad, at Myriandrus, and in Egypt, but also by the issue of Alexander's coinages from Persian treasure. He established mints in Asia, some before and others after his departure for the east: at Lampsacus, Sardis, and Miletus in western Asia Minor, at Side and Tarsus in southern Asia Minor; at Alexandria ad Issum (Myriandrus) and Damascus in Syria; and at Sidon, Ace, Aradus, and Byblus in Phoenicia. The leading cities of Cyprus later adopted the Attic standard and the coin-types of Alexander. New opportunities for trade brought Orientals to Greece and Greeks to the Orient, where Alexander's interest and Greek enterprise brought about an economic revival. The year 333 was rightly adopted by Sidon as the first year of a new era.[1]

At Tyre Alexander made final arrangements for the eastern Mediterranean. He appointed one senior financial officer for Phoenicia and another for Asia Minor, gave Harpalus charge of his treasury, and replaced some of his satraps. Naval operations were to be started against the Spartans in Crete and against pirates off the Lycian coast, and he allocated Phoenician and Cyprian ships as reinforcements to the Macedonian and Greek navies. Requests by several Greek states were granted: Athenians captured at the battle of the Granicus were liberated, and Macedonian garrisons were withdrawn from Rhodes and Chios. Most of the pro-Persian tyrants who had been captured in the islands were sent to their cities for trial, but some from Chios he left under guard in Egypt. Antipater in Macedonia received money and help from the commander of the Macedonian fleet in the south Aegean, in case Sparta should make headway in the Peloponnese. After holding games and a dramatic festival and sacrificing to Heracles, Alexander led his army, reinforced by drafts from Macedonia and her dependencies and by groups of Greek mercenaries, towards Mesopotamia, where the last great battle for the Persian empire was to be fought.[2]

[1] Zechariah 9. 3; *GC* 207.
[2] Arr. *An.* 3. 2. 7; 3. 6; Plu. *Alex.* 29; Curt. 4. 3. 11–16.

§ 4. *The defeat of Persia*

FOR the defence of his empire Darius no longer had access to the market of Greek mercenary hoplites. He still had a considerable number of them, perhaps 6,000, but he could only support them with the Persian Royal Guard, probably 10,000 in number like 'the Immortals' of Xerxes, which had been trained for hoplite warfare. His weakness in heavy infantry was offset by strength in cavalry, recruited from the hill countries between Cappadocia and Bactria and reinforced by his Scythian allies, the Sacae. The heavy cavalry was particularly formidable. Even under the cramped conditions at Issus it had almost overwhelmed the Thessalians; and after the experience gained at the Granicus and Issus the king had introduced longer spears and swords to match the Macedonian arms. He called up even greater numbers of good light-armed cavalry than before. He had, too, a new weapon, 200 chariots armed with scythes, which were designed to break the enemy formation and open gaps for his heavy cavalry to exploit. With an army of 40,000 cavalry, some 16,000 heavy infantry, and swarms of light infantry Darius advanced to Gaugamela, east of Nineveh (Mosul), where a plain seven miles wide was enclosed between foot-hills on the north and uneven ground near the Tigris (see Fig. 32). The ground in front of the position where he intended to fight was levelled to make fairways for the chariots; and fields of 'caltrops'—spikes set to cripple horses—were sown at appropriate points. The place was well chosen for a cavalry battle, in which his superior numbers could surround the enemy. While he waited for Alexander, he drew supplies from Media and the environs of Babylon. He had already sent out a mobile force under Mazaeus to the bank of the Euphrates, with orders to delay Alexander's advance and scorch the ground in his path.

By recruiting Greek mercenary cavalry and infantry and obtaining further drafts from Macedonia, Alexander had maintained his infantry strength at 40,000 and raised his cavalry to 7,000, all being first-line troops. He relied on the tactical skill of his cavalry squadrons to offset the superior numbers of the enemy. The Thessalians were trained to manoeuvre in lozenge-shaped formations and the Macedonians in wedge-shaped formations, so that they could wheel or employ shock tactics with equal rapidity. At Issus, for example, the manoeuvring of the Thessalian heavy cavalry had averted disaster. When the army set out from Tyre, Parmenio with the vanguard had begun to bridge the Euphrates at Thapsacus. When Alexander arrived, Mazaeus withdrew. Crossing by two bridges, Alexander crossed northern Mesopotamia unimpeded, brought his heavy baggage-train across the fast-flowing Tigris by a ford (near Abu Wajnam), and halted for four days near Nineveh to rest his men. Soon after dawn he crossed the ridge by the plain of Gaugamela, set his army to fortify a camp, and reconnoitred the plain with his cavalry. That night his army slept, but the troops of Darius, having no fortifications, stood under arms.

On 1 October 331 Alexander drew up his army at a distance of some three miles from the enemy, detailing some Thracian infantry to guard the baggage-train and prisoners, who included the women of the royal family. The vital task for Alexander was to move his heavy infantry across the plain to within striking distance of the enemy line. In case the hordes of Persian

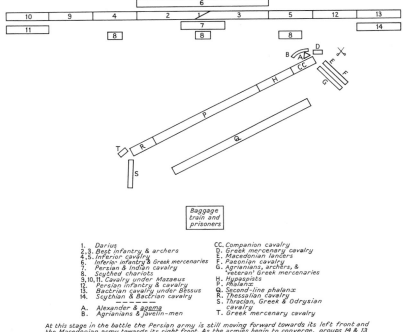

1. Darius
2,3. Best infantry & archers
4,5. Inferior cavalry
6. Inferior infantry & Greek mercenaries
7. Persian & Indian cavalry
8. Scythed chariots
9,10,11. Cavalry under Mazaeus
12. Persian infantry & cavalry
13. Bactrian cavalry under Bessus
14. Scythian & Bactrian cavalry

A. Alexander & *agema*
B. Agrianians & javelin-men

CC. Companion cavalry
D. Greek mercenary cavalry
E. Macedonian lancers
F. Paeonian cavalry
G. Agrianians, archers, & 'veteran' Greek mercenaries
H. Hypaspists
P. Phalanx
Q. Second-line phalanx
R. Thessalian cavalry
S. Thracian, Greek & Odrysian cavalry
T. Greek mercenary cavalry

At this stage in the battle the Persian army is still moving forward towards its left front and the Macedonian army towards its right front. As the armies begin to converge, groups 14 & 13 ride out first to be engaged by D & F. ✗ marks the point where 12 & E then engaged one another

FIG. 32. The Battle of Gaugamela

cavalry surrounded his infantry in the open plain, he adopted an order of battle which could either be contracted into a rectangle or be extended into a longer line. The phalanx, forming the centre with the Hypaspists on the right, was followed at some distance by a thinner line of infantry which could face about, if necessary. The Thessalian and allied cavalry on the left and the Companion cavalry on the right continued the line of the phalanx. On either flank he posted a flank-guard at an oblique angle, which could either advance into line or fall back to form the short side of a rectangle, as occasion demanded. The flank-guard on the left consisted of Greek, Thracian, and Odrysian cavalry. The flank-guard on the right was a double one, light-armed cavalry from Macedonia and Paeonia in advance, and half of the Agrianians with archers and Greek mercenaries behind them. In front of the left end of the line he placed a body of Greek mercenary cavalry, and in front of the right end the Royal Guard of cavalry (*agema*) headed by himself; in front of him there was a screen of Agrianians, archers, and javelin-men; and to the right of them a body of Greek mercenary cavalry.

Having deployed the army in front of that of Darius and with a much shorter line than his, Alexander began to march towards the Persians with his right advanced and his left delayed, so that the line was moving on a slant; moreover he directed his advance towards his right front, in the direction of the uneven ground near the Tigris. His aim was to draw the Persians off their prepared ground and then to strike their left centre with the powerful troops on the right-hand part of his line—the Companion cavalry and the Hypaspists. The danger was that the Persian cavalry would surround both flanks and halt his advance before the Hypaspists and the phalanx were within charging distance of the enemy centre.

In advance of the Persian centre there were fifty chariots and good cavalry. Behind them was Darius in a chariot, with the Royal cavalry guard, his own entourage, the Greek mercenaries, the Persian Guard of infantry, and Mardian archers. Behind Darius a second line was formed by infantry of inferior quality. On either side of the centre he placed cavalry and infantry, with 50 chariots in advance on the right and 100 on the left. The wings were heavy with first-class cavalry. Mazaeus commanded the right. Bessus on the left had an advanced force of Scythian and Bactrian cavalry, a supporting body of Bactrian and other cavalry, and a linking force of Persian infantry and cavalry. Darius' plan was to disrupt the Macedonian phalanx with his chariots, outflank it with both powerful wings of cavalry, and use his centre mainly as a pivot from which his wings would advance. Thus he intended to win by envelopment, whereas Alexander aimed at penetration.

The oblique march by Alexander threatened to outflank the Persian left. Therefore Darius began to move his massive army, keeping his line straight and marching forward towards his left front; at the same time he pushed his left wing forward, in order that it should swing forward, outflank, and stop the Macedonians. While the infantry lines were still at a considerable distance from one another, the advanced force of Scythian and Bactrian cavalry began to outflank Alexander's right wing. He ordered the Greek mercenary cavalry to charge their flank. When the enemy repulsed the Greeks, he committed his Paeonian cavalry, supported by Greek mercenaries, and they drove back the Scythians and Bactrians. Meanwhile the phalanx was advancing steadily. The main body of Bactrian cavalry under Bessus now joined the battle; it pushed the Paeonians and mercenaries back on to the flank of the main line. But they rallied, and, although less heavily armed, their shock tactics in compact units pushed the Bactrians and Scythians back from the line. At this moment, before the Macedonians were clear of the fairways, Darius launched his chariots. Some caused horrible carnage with their sharp scythes, but most were caught by the Agrianians and javelin-men in front of Alexander and others passed through the phalanx which opened ranks, as at the Shipka pass, and continued to advance. Alexander's right flank was now threatened with encirclement by the Persian cavalry mixed with infantry, as well as by the Bactrians and Scythians, but the Hypaspists were now almost within striking distance. Therefore he committed the Macedonian Lancers under Aretes. Their charge, supported by the Agrianians of the flank-guard, cleared Alexander's right front. The left centre of Darius was now close at hand. It was already losing its formation when the charge of the Lancers and the Agrianians broke off the left wing and created a gap. Alexander wheeled his line half-left, and charged into the gap at the head of the Royal Guard in a wedge-shaped formation. He was followed by the Companion cavalry, and on his left by the Hypaspists and four phalangite battalions, which engaged the Persian centre.

Meanwhile the Persian right wing of heavy cavalry had at last charged the Thessalians under Parmenio and brought the left wing to a halt. The fifth and sixth phalangite battalions stood firm to protect the flank of the Thessalians, and a large gap opened as the rest of the phalanx advanced with Alexander. Indian and Persian cavalry from the Persian centre galloped into this gap, pierced the second line of infantry, and broke into the baggage-train, where they attacked the Thracian infantry and tried to liberate the women of the royal family. There were now four theatres of action—the baggage-train, both wings, and the Persian centre—and clouds of dust obscured the scene. Alexander's charge into the Persian left centre and the infantry attack on the centre were decisive. The heavy cavalry struck deep into the flank towards Darius, the bristling phalanx directed their pikes at the faces of the Persians, the Great King fled headlong in his chariot, and the whole centre broke. On the right wing the Macedonians drove the Bactrians back, and Bessus seeing Darius in flight rode off with his cavalry. The pursuit of the centre had just begun, when a message reached Alexander from Parmenio, asking for help. Alexander wheeled the Companion cavalry left and set off across the battle-field. By this time the fight in the baggage-train was finished; for the second line of the phalanx had faced about and taken the Indians and Persians in disorder from the rear and driven them off. These Indian and Persian cavalry, returning as they had come, joined forces with some Parthian cavalry of the Persian right centre. Clouds of dust obscured their vision when they collided head-on with Alexander's cavalry as he rode to help Parmenio. A desperate engagement, with no possibility of manoeuvre, resulted in the loss of sixty Macedonians, but Alexander forced his way through to the Thessalians, who were fighting magnificently. Their opponents, too, fled, and the great pursuit began. It continued without a halt until nightfall. Parmenio captured the Persian camp, where some Indian elephants were stabled, and Alexander, resuming the pursuit at midnight, captured the treasure and the royal chariot at Arbela but not Darius himself.[1]

[1] Arr. *An.* 3. 7–15; D.S. 17. 53–61; Plu. *Alex.* 31–34; Curt. 4. 9–16; Just. 11. 13–14. 5; Polyaen. 4. 3. 6, 17. See Appendix 8 and *HA* 137–48.

The Great King fled to Media with the Royal Guard of cavalry, part of the Bactrian cavalry, a few of the Royal Guard of infantry, and 2,000 Greek mercenaries who came up later. The rest of his army suffered terrible losses, and great numbers were taken prisoner. Persia's imperial army was finally and decisively defeated. Alexander's losses were considerable, particularly in warhorses. Advancing towards Babylon, he received the surrender of the city from Mazaeus, who had commanded the right wing at Gaugamela. Alexander was acclaimed King of Babylon, paid sacrifice to Marduk, the Babylonian god, and ordered the restoration of Marduk's temple, which Xerxes had destroyed. He appointed Mazaeus satrap with civil powers, and put Macedonians in charge of troops and finance. Meanwhile Philoxenus, whom he had sent ahead, reported the surrender of Susa and the capture of the Royal Treasury. Alexander advanced to Susa, took over the bullion, and found among the treasure the bronze statues of Harmodius and Aristogeiton, the tyrannicides, which he sent to Athens. He issued orders that all tyrants in Greece should be expelled in the name of autonomy and that Plataea, which had been the scene of Greece's victory over Persia a century and a half before, should now be rebuilt. At Susa he appointed a Persian satrap, a Macedonian military governor, and a Macedonian garrison-commander; reorganized his army with new drafts from Macedonia; and sent a large sum of money to Antipater at Pella for the conduct of operations against Sparta. It was now winter, and Alexander paused to hold games and a torch race in the Macedonian fashion.[1]

In Europe a rising by an Odrysian king, aided at first by a disloyal general of Macedon and encouraged by Athens, had drawn Antipater's army into Thrace. This rising and the absence of Alexander in the East seemed to Agis, king of Sparta, who had received Persian subsidies, to provide an opportunity for mastering the Peloponnese and breaking away from Macedon's control. He asked Athens for help. A debate was held at which an extant speech, *On the Treaty with Alexander*, may perhaps have been delivered. Its arguments that Macedon had violated the terms of the Charter of the Greek League seem to have little truth. Demosthenes supported the request of Agis. Demades defeated it by arguing as Theoric Commissioner that war would mean the people sacrificing all Theoric monies. In early 331 Agis, aided by Elis and much of Arcadia and Achaea, defeated a Macedonian army and laid siege to Megalopolis with 2,000 cavalry and 20,000 infantry, of whom half were mercenaries. Antipater soon entered the Peloponnese with a larger army, drawn from Macedonia and his Greek allies, and in autumn 331 Sparta was defeated with heavy losses on both sides. Agis himself fell fighting. Antipater sent fifty Spartans as hostages to Alexander, and referred the rebellion to the Greek League's Council. The Council asked Alexander as *hegemon* to decide. In spring 330 at Persepolis, where he ended the crusade against Persia, he pardoned everyone except the ringleaders, ordered Elis, Arcadia, and Achaea as

[1] Arr. *An.* 3. 16; D.S. 17. 64–66; Plu. *Alex.* 35–36; Curt. 5. 1–2; Just. 11. 14. 6–8.

rebels to pay 120 talents to Megalopolis, and made Sparta join the Greek League.[1]

From Susa Alexander advanced into Persia. He overran the Uxii with two mobile columns, carried the 'Persian Gates' by a night march round the enemy's flank, and captured Persepolis, Pasagardae, and later Ecbatana (summer 330). He marked the end of the crusade of vengeance by firing the Palace of Xerxes at Persepolis, and by sending home the Thessalians and the other troops of the Greek League with generous gratuities. On hearing the news the Greek League continued Alexander's tenure of office as *hegemon* for life. But he did not ask that any League troops should be sent to join him.

Although Alexander was very conciliatory towards Athens, the people still vacillated. The politicians fought to and fro in the law courts. In 330 Lycurgus sued Leocrates for having left Athens after the battle of Chaeronea. His speech *Against Leocrates* shows the attitude of his party towards Macedon. He wrote of those who fell at Chaeronea. 'They alone in all Greece had the freedom of Greece in their bones; for they died as Greece fell into slavery. With their bodies the freedom of Greece was buried.' Leocrates escaped death by a narrow margin. Later in 330 Aeschines brought Demosthenes into the courts by his speech *Against Ctesiphon*, to which Demosthenes replied with his famous speech *On the Crown*. Aeschines failed to gain even a fifth of the votes and chose to leave Athens, never to return. Alexander's hopes of co-operation with Athens were receding, even as his conquests carried him farther to the East.[2]

---

[1] D.S. 17. 62–63; 73. 5; *GHI* 193; [D.] 17; Plu. *Dem.* 24. 1; *Mor.* 818e; Aeschin. 3. 165; Din. 1. 34; Curt. 6. 1.

[2] Arr. *An.* 3. 17–18; 19. 5; D.S. 17. 67–72; Plu. *Alex.* 37–38; Curt. 5. 3–8; Lycurg. 1. 50; *GHI* 197; 205 B 6.

CHAPTER 5

Alexander's Eastern Conquests, 330–323

§ 1. *The subjugation of the eastern satrapies*

NOW that he had captured the capital cities of the Persian empire and acquired 180,000 talents of treasure—worth a hundred million pounds or more—Alexander had several courses of action open to him. He could withdraw to the Euphrates line, leaving the military and economic strength of Persia broken; he could stop, as Trajan was to do later, content with the control of the rich plains of Mesopotamia; or he could go on to conquer the rest of the Persian empire. Alexander took the third course. He had already decided against the first, and he knew that the second would not give him a defensible frontier. For the Persian empire resembled Macedonia herself, in that its rich plains were exposed to the attacks of the vigorous mountain peoples of the north and its furthest provinces formed a barrier against pugnacious nomadic peoples. Alexander had indeed claimed during the siege of Tyre to be 'King of Asia' and 'master of all Darius' possessions'. On Alexander's lips this claim was more than a taunt. It was confirmed at Arbela when he was proclaimed 'King of Asia'; then, too, he inscribed a dedication to Athena of Lindus with the words 'having become master of Asia'. His courtesy to the women of the Persian royal family was inspired by policy as well as chivalry. Alexander addressed Sisygambis, the queen mother, as if she were his adopted mother (just as he had treated Ada of Caria when she adopted him), and he granted her request that he should spare the Uxii. He now intended to become the King of Asia in actual fact, just as he had become Pharaoh of Egypt and King of Babylon. In that capacity he restored the tomb of Cyrus, his predecessor as King of Asia.[1]

Alexander received the tribute of his subjects as King of Asia. He was, of course, still King of Macedon; but he no longer claimed tribute in that capacity, as he had at first done in Asia Minor. The bullion of Persia was converted by Alexander into coinage. About 331 the Persian griffin appeared as an emblem on Alexander's coins, minted in Phoenicia; and a large mint at Babylon began *c.* 329 to issue Alexander-coins with the title 'King', that is King of Asia (not King of Macedon, for his Macedonian coins lacked the title). As King of Asia he appointed the Persian Mazaeus to be Satrap of Babylon. He intended to harness the Persian governing class to help in administering his empire; for the co-operation of the Greek states was not forth-

---

[1] Arr. *An.* 2. 14. 9; Plu. *Alex.* 34. 1 ('King of Asia'); *Chron. Lind.* 38 (line 103); Arr. *An.* 3. 17. 6 (Sisygambis); Curt. 5. 2. 20; Arr. 3. 16. 4 (Babylon); Arr. 6. 29. 8 (Cyrus).

coming, and Macedonian manpower was already severely strained. At Ecbatana he reorganized the control of his conquests and his long lines of communication. The trusted Parmenio was ordered to collect together all the bullion of Persia and hand it over to Harpalus as royal treasurer. Parmenio was then to campaign in Hyrcania and protect Alexander's communications in Media. Philoxenus was put in charge of sea-communications between Asia Minor and Macedonia, and Menes of those between Syria and Macedonia.

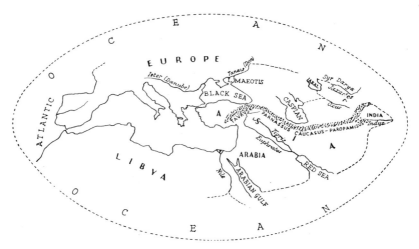

FIG. 33. The Greek idea of the inhabited land masses of the world

These arrangements were necessary, because Alexander was about to engage in arduous campaigns in the north-east of the empire.[1]

Alexander's conquests in Asia, which were even more rapid than those of Cyrus and Cambyses, were won by similar means—aristocratic cavalry, fine infantry, and a policy of religious toleration. When he entered the interior, he struck the rock of Persia's national strength. From summer 330 to spring 327 the Macedonians, led by him in person, campaigned continuously summer and winter alike, throughout great areas of mountainous country, such as they had rarely experienced even in the central Balkans. The pursuit of Darius was pushed so hard by Alexander that his picked force covered 400 miles in eleven days and fifty miles in the final night to find Darius stabbed by Bessus, who had deposed him and assumed the throne. A Macedonian gave water to Darius, but he died before Alexander came up (July 330). He suffered no dishonour at the hands of his conqueror. For Alexander accorded him a royal funeral at Persepolis and educated his son at Susa, probably intending him to

[1] Arr. *An.* 1. 27. 4 and 3. 17. 6 (tribute); *GC* 210; Arr. *An.* 3. 18. 11 (on Asiatics accepting Alexander); 3. 19. 7 (Parmenio).

become ruler of Persia. The last Greek mercenaries, 1,500 in number, surrendered; those who had served Persia before the ratification of the League of Corinth and the alliance of Greece with Macedon in 337 were allowed to go home, and the rest had to enter the service of Alexander. Greek envoys from Athens, Sparta, and Sinope, who had been with Darius, also surrendered. The Athenians and Spartans were imprisoned. As Sinope was not a member of the Greek League, her envoys went free. The pursuit of Bessus was delayed by a widespread revolt in Aria and Arachosia, but in 329 Bessus was handed over by a noble, Spitamenes. In the winter Alexander prosecuted Bessus for treason in killing Darius and rebelling against himself before a tribunal of Medes and Persians. Bessus was found guilty. His nose and ears were cut off as Persian law decreed, and he was done to death by the Persian nobles.[1]

The punishment of Bessus did not end the war. Spitamenes led an even more formidable revolt, but he was driven into the territory of his allies, the Massagetae, who cut off his head, sent it to Alexander, and submitted to his rule (summer 328). Paraetacene was still held by rebels. In the snows of midwinter Alexander laid siege to the fastness of one of the Sogdian leaders, Oxyartes, which was known as 'the Sogdian Rock' and considered impregnable. In response to his call for volunteers 300 Macedonian mountaineers scaled a precipice with ropes and iron pegs. Thirty fell to their death; but when the rest appeared on a peak above the fortress, the garrison surrendered. Alexander fell in love with one of the captives, Roxane, daughter of Oxyartes, who was famed for her beauty, and announced his intention of marrying her. Oxyartes then surrendered, and helped Alexander. The wedding of Alexander and Roxane was celebrated at the fortress of another leader, Chorienes, who had been terrified into surrender by a further feat of mountaineering. The marriage also served a political purpose; for the honour paid to the Sogdian nobility and the continuation of Oxyartes and Chorienes in their commands brought the last revolts to an end in spring 327.[2]

In 330 Alexander first encountered some opposition in the ranks of the Macedonian army. The men wished to return home. While Alexander was determined to conquer the mountainous areas of the Persian empire, they greeted the death of Darius as marking the end of the campaign. For practical purposes they were the Macedonian people. He therefore convened them as an Assembly and put his case. They agreed to fight on. Alexander's Persian policy aroused serious opposition among his Companions. Because he appointed Persians to office and claimed their loyalty in his capacity as King of Asia, he dealt with his Persian subjects in an Asian manner. When Darius was dead, Alexander wore Persian dress of an unostentatious kind on Persian

---

[1] For Cyrus see pp. 176 f. above; Plu. *Alex.* 43 (death of Darius); Arr. *An.* 3. 23. 8; 3. 24. 4 (mercenaries); 4. 7. 3 (trial of Bessus); D.S. 17. 83. 8.

[2] Arr. *An.* 4. 18. 4 (Sogdian Rock); 4. 19. 5 (Roxane); Plu. *Alex.* 47. 7; Curt. 8. 4. 25. The ritual of the wedding was probably Macedonian.

occasions. Later he tried Bessus and punished him in Persian fashion, and the Persian Roxane was his queen. The most vital aspect of the Persian monarchy was the 'kinship' of the king with the Persian aristocrats. As his 'kin' they formed his entourage and received from him land and authority; they tried traitors; they fought as his Royal Guard of cavalry and served him as ministers, satraps, or generals. Alexander's honouring of Sisygambis and Darius' son entitled him to claim this 'kinship', and after his marriage with Roxane and the conquest of the hinterland the claim was acknowledged by the Persian nobles. In him they saw 'the King of the lands of all Peoples', invested with divine right by Ahura-Mazda, and they prostrated themselves in obeisance before him.[1]

In theory Alexander's policy was intelligible to his Macedonian Companions. The institutions of Macedon were very similar: the nobles of Macedonia were the 'kin' of the king, received lands and authority from him, and served him in similar capacities; and the Macedonian Assembly tried traitors in its traditional manner. Yet the Macedonians were more ready to see the differences than the similarities. In particular the differences were stressed by the Greeks who served among the Companions and in the army. They had always regarded the Persian monarchy as the antithesis of Greek liberty in politics and religion. Above all, prostration (*proskynesis*) was misunderstood; for it implied to a Greek, and probably to a Macedonian also, the worship of a god. Alexander endeavoured to counter the latent opposition of the Companions by parading the truth, that he was himself a Macedonian, untouched by the Persian manners which he adopted only for reasons of policy. He marched with the Macedonians over snow-bound mountains and arid deserts; he was wounded twice in Bactria; and he hunted and drank with his Companions as he had done in Europe. Noble youths were brought from Macedonia to join the corps of Pages and in due course to be his Companions. He consulted the Council of Companions, addressed the Macedonian Assembly, and used the Macedonian seal on all documents of the Macedonian state. In his inner beliefs he was purely Macedonian. Games, sacrifices, and religious worship were conducted 'in the ancestral manner', and Alexander's Macedonian court was untouched by the priestly lore of Egypt, Babylon, or Persia. The king was the descendant of Zeus, the founder of his house, and he had cried aloud to this Zeus for help at the battle of Gaugamela. The *Iliad* was always with him. He was *diogenes*, 'of divine descent', and the obeisance of priests or nobles in the Orient was of no religious significance to the descendant of Heracles and Achilles.[2]

The strain of disagreement weakened the loyalty of some Companions and made Alexander suspicious, with disastrous consequences. In autumn 330 a conspiracy was reported to Philotas, son of Parmenio and commander of the

---

[1] D.S. 17. 74. 3; Plu. *Alex.* 47. 1; 45 (Persian dress); Arr. *An.* 7. 6. 2; Curt. 6. 8. 25 (Assembly).

[2] Plu. *Alex.* 28. 1; 45; 47. 5 (Persian dress); 33. 1 (at Gaugamela); Curt. 5. 1. 41 (Pages).

Companion cavalry; he kept silence, and Alexander heard of it from another source. The conspiracy was quashed, Philotas and others were brought by Alexander before the Macedonian assembly, and Philotas alone was found guilty of treason and executed. By the Macedonian law of treason his male relatives shared the sentence of death. Parmenio had served Philip and Alexander brilliantly, and had lost his other two sons in Alexander's battles. He was now in command of a strong Macedonian army controlling Alexander's lines of communication. It seemed too dangerous to exempt Parmenio from the rigour of the law; for he might lead a revolt. Alexander's emissaries, outstripping the news of Philotas' execution, killed Parmenio and read the king's orders to Parmenio's troops. At this time, too, Alexander Lyncestes, who had been arrested in 333 as a pretender, was brought before the Assembly, tried, and condemned to death.[1]

In autumn 328 at Samarcand Alexander and his Companions were drinking at a banquet when Cleitus, who had saved his life at the Granicus, began to taunt Alexander with his Persian practices. Cleitus was an older man, one of the contemporaries of Philip (who would have been fifty-three years of age, had he lived), and he represented those who had least sympathy for the young king's policy. When Cleitus mocked Alexander as 'son of Ammon, not Philip' and ridiculed the Persian prostrations before their white-smocked monarch, Alexander lost his temper and reached for his dagger, but found that a guardsman had removed it. When he shouted in the Macedonian dialect for the Guard, there was no response and Alexander seized a pike from a guardsman. Meanwhile the friends of Cleitus had hustled him out of the room; but Cleitus re-entered by another door as Alexander was shouting 'Cleitus', called out 'Here is Cleitus, Alexander', and was transfixed by Alexander's pike. He died at once. Alexander lay for three days in desperate remorse, refusing all food and attention, until his Companions broke into his room and made him resume his duties.[2]

In spring 327 Alexander tried to bridge the gap between the Macedonians and the Persians. After the death of Darius he had appointed as a Macedonian Companion a brother of Darius, who was already the leader of the Persian 'kin'. Now he proposed that the Macedonian Companions should prostrate themselves in the presence of the Median and Persian 'kin', who would follow suit. Hephaestion, Alexander's closest friend, led the way and was followed by the Macedonians, but Callisthenes of Olynthus, the chronicler, who was of Greek blood, refused to comply. Alexander never made the attempt again. But his animosity towards Callisthenes flared up, when a conspiracy was detected among some of the Pages whom Callisthenes taught. The boys confessed their guilt, were tried by the Macedonian Assembly, and executed in the traditional manner by stoning. Callisthenes, arrested at the time as an accomplice, was later put to death. Whether he was innocent or guilty, is not

---

[1] Arr. *An.* 3. 26; D.S. 17. 79; Plu. *Alex.* 48; Curt. 6. 7 and 7. 3. 4 (for law of treason see 6. 11. 20 and 6. 10. 30).   [2] Arr. *An.* 4. 8; Plu. *Alex.* 50; Curt. 8. 1. 19.

known; but the leaders of Aristotle's Peripatetic school, to which Callisthenes had belonged, wrote later of Alexander with the same venom which Demosthenes had used against Philip.[1]

The army, too, became a cause of controversy. Alexander had won his great battles with the army of Philip, based on the Macedonian elements which had prevailed at Chaeronea. Already at the capture of Miletus Alexander had found it advisable to recruit Greek mercenaries, and he needed them even more after the death of Darius. Troops from his Balkan dependencies became more prominent in the drafts sent out by Antipater: Illyrians and Odrysians, as well as Thracians, Paeonians, and Agrianians, fought at Issus and Gaugamela and served in the Iranian mountains. The casualties due to wounds, sickness, and exhaustion, especially in the winter campaigns, and the constant demand for garrisons to man the fortresses captured by Alexander and to protect old and new cities remained in excess of the flow of reinforcements from Europe. In autumn 330 Lydians began to serve as mercenaries, and Persians from the hill-country as subjects. Early in 327 Alexander ordered the training in Greek speech and Macedonian arms of 30,000 Asian youths—a number as great as that of the infantry in the army of 338–334.

The organization, too, of the army was modified to meet the needs of mountain warfare in 330–327. The squadrons of the Companion cavalry were split into two companies, each of 100 men. The death of Philotas and then of Cleitus caused changes in the general command of the Companion cavalry, which was henceforth shared by Alexander and Hephaestion. Specialized Iranian troops were employed for mountain warfare in large numbers as horsed javelin-men and archers; and a new unit was formed of mounted men trained to fight both as cavalry and hoplites. The Macedonians of the original army still remained the *élite*, but they were no longer almost the entire strength of the army.[2]

The king had no central organ of government which carried out administration during his absence. He at the head of his troops was the government, and he alone; for the generals, the satraps, and the Companions, who formed his Council, were subordinates. He dealt with a great amount of correspondence, writing not only to Olympias and Antipater, to his satraps and commanders between Egypt and Uzbek in Turkestan,.but also to the Greek states, where some of his directives were engraved on stone and still survive. The vast task of organizing the economic health of the empire was brilliantly achieved by minting a fine coinage, driving roads into the hinterland, and founding new towns for commercial as well as military purposes. The Alexander-cities (for instance at Herat in Aria, Ghazni in Arachosia, Merv in Margiane, and Chodjend in Sogdiana) had a Greek lay-out and municipal

---

[1] Arr. *An.* 4. 10. 5; Plu. *Alex.* 47. 9 (Hephaestion); 53; Curt. 8. 5. 5.

[2] Arr. *An.* 1. 19. 6 (Greek mercenaries); 3. 24. 5; Curt. 3. 10. 10 (Illyrians, &c.); 4. 13. 31; 4. 21. 10 (winter campaigns); Curt. 6. 6. 35 (Lydians); Plu. *Alex.* 47. 6 (Persian youths); Curt. 8. 5. 1; Arr. 3. 16. 11; 3. 24. 1; Poll. 1. 132.

institutions of a Greek type. At Chodjend, known as Alexandria Eschate, Greek mercenaries, Macedonians unfit for active service, and native tribesmen joined together as the first settlers. In such cities, small as some of them were, the co-operation of Macedonian, Greek, and Persian began to come about in answer to practical needs, as it was doing at the higher level of Alexander's entourage and army.[1]

§ 2. *The invasion of India*

'EUROPE, Asia, and Libya', wrote Theopompus in the *Philippica*, 'are islands around which Ocean flows.' Whether the world was a flat table or a sphere (as Aristotle taught), its inhabited surface was divided into these three 'islands', or continents as we should say, by the river Tanaïs (Don), the river Nile, and the Straits of Gades (Gibraltar). In the fifth century Herodotus asserted that the Mediterranean, the Atlantic outside the Straits of Gades, and the 'Red Sea' (our Persian Gulf) were all one sea, that is part of circumambient Ocean. And he reported that Libya had been circumnavigated and that a Greek captain, Scylax, sent by Darius I down the river Indus, had sailed in thirty months to the Arabian Gulf (our Red Sea). In the fourth century Herodotus' stories may have been forgotten or disbelieved, but the idea persisted, as it had done since the Late Bronze Age at latest, that Ocean flowed round the three 'islands'.[2]

The outer edges of the three islands were not known. Hecataeus had believed the whole land area to be round, but Aristotle thought it was elliptical, the proportion of length to breadth being five to three. The outer lands were supposed to be desert or steppe, where only nomadic peoples, or none at all, could live. Thus Libya was bounded on the south by desert and on the west (in Morocco) by nomads; Europe on the north by nomads—Scythians and others; and Asia by nomads—Scythians or Massagetae—on the north and by sands on the east and south. In Europe two great rivers, Tartessus and Ister (Danube), were thought to rise in 'Pyrene' (our Pyrenees); as to Libya there was doubt whether the upper Nile flowed from the west or from the east; and the course of the upper Tanaïs was entirely unknown. The central feature of Asia was a mountain mass, extending from Cilicia and called in its sections Taurus, Parnassus, Caucasus, and Paropamisus. North of this mass lay the Caspian Sea and a great river, probably the Jaxartes (though Herodotus confused it with the Araxes), across which lived the Massagetae. This river had many mouths at its delta, and one of them entered the Caspian Sea (the others were probably thought to enter the Ocean). At the eastern end of the whole mountain mass lay India, the last inhabited land (*eschate*). On crossing

---

[1] Plu. *Alex.* 42; *GHI* 185, 191–2, 201–2; Arr. *An.* 4. 1. 3; 4. 4. 1 (Alexandria Eschate); 22. 5; 24. 7.

[2] *FGrH* 115 F 75 C 2 (Theopompus); Arr. *An.* 3. 30. 8–9; Hdt. 1. 203; 4. 42–44.

the last ridge, said Aristotle, one sees 'the outer sea', that is Ocean (see Fig. 33).[1]

When Theopompus said Philip might become 'the king of all Europe', he was not exaggerating. The Danube was near the rim of Europe, and beyond it lay the nomad tribes and the steppes. When Alexander reached the Danube,

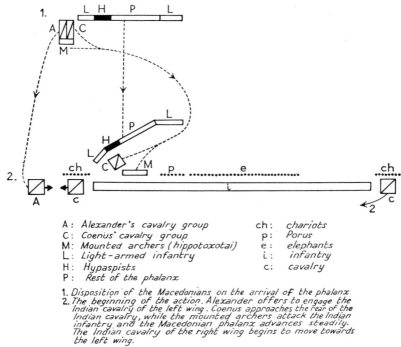

A : Alexander's cavalry group   ch : chariots
C : Coenus' cavalry group   p :   Porus
M : Mounted archers (hippotoxotai)   e :   elephants
L : Light-armed infantry   i :   infantry
H : Hypaspists   c :   cavalry
P : Rest of the phalanx

1. Disposition of the Macedonians on the arrival of the phalanx
2. The beginning of the action. Alexander offers to engage the Indian cavalry of the left wing. Coenus approaches the rear of the Indian cavalry, while the mounted archers attack the Indian infantry and the Macedonian phalanx advances steadily. The Indian cavalry of the right wing begins to move towards the left wing.

FIG. 34. The Battle of the Hydaspes

'the strong desire' moved him to cross the river and the Getae fled from the river into 'the desert'; and the alliance with the Veneti extended his influence along the Danube to the point beyond which Europe began to grow narrower. When Alexander, having crossed the river Oxus, reached the river Jaxartes, which he thought might be the upper Tanaïs, he was visited by envoys from two groups of Scythians, living on different sides of the Tanaïs, one in 'Asia' and the other in 'Europe'. He founded Alexandria Eschate as a base for 'the invasion of Scythia, should it ever come', and sent envoys to seek alliance and

---

[1] Hdt. 1. 201 (Massagetae); 202–3 (Caspian); 4. 40–41 (India); Arist. *Meteor.* 350ᵃ18 (Parnassus and India); 362ᵇ21; Arr. *An.* 5. 3. 3.; 5. 26. 1; 7. 5; D.S. 18. 5. 2; Curt. 7. 3. 19. Aristotle's views are probably derived in part from Alexander's discoveries.

spy out the land of the European Scythians. These envoys returned with
Scythian envoys, who offered Alexander 'friendship and alliance' and the
hand of the king's daughter. Alexander accepted the alliance but not the offer
of marriage. Another visitor was Pharasmanes, king of the Chorasmii, who
offered to guide and aid Alexander in an expedition to subdue the peoples as
far as the Black Sea. With him Alexander made an alliance. It was not oppor-
tune then, he said (winter 329–328), to invade towards the Black Sea, because
his attention was on India. Once he had subdued the Indians, he would hold
'all Asia', return towards Greece, and invade the Black Sea area with a navy
and army from the Propontis. Pharasmenes could co-operate with him then.[1]

In fact a Macedonian army had previously been sent across the Danube
into Scythian territory, but had been defeated. As Alexander thought that he
was near Ocean when he reached the Jaxartes, and that, if the Jaxartes was the
upper Tanaïs, it led to the Black Sea, a campaign westwards seemed practicable. But the Caspian's extent was unknown, and he may have heard also of
the Sea of Aral with its fresh-water fish. It was believed that one branch of
the Oxus or of the Jaxartes flowed into the Caspian Sea (as the Oxus may
have done at some unknown date, at Kara Bogaz). The Caspian Sea was then
either an inland sea, perhaps with the Tanaïs flowing out of it again into the
Maeotid Lake (Sea of Azov), or an arm of Ocean. In 323 Alexander felt 'the
strong desire' (*pothos*) to explore the Caspian Sea and ascertain which of
the two it was, and a naval expedition was prepared.[2]

Alexander's misconceptions about Europe and Asia explain why he decided
to invade India and took ship-wrights and crews with his army. If India jutted
eastwards into Ocean, he could turn either northwards by Ocean to the rim of
Europe and perhaps enter the Caspian Sea or else southwards to explore a
route along the rim of Asia. Because he thought of India as a relatively small
peninsula and of Arabia (which he knew in southern Palestine to be desert) as
similar, the statement he made to Pharasmanes was a true one; for if he
mastered India he would also be the master of all Asia. This belief, rather
than a tradition that Darius I had once held India, inspired Alexander to
attempt a conquest, which was also an exploration and would, he thought,
open up sea-communications for his empire.

The army which set out in early summer 327 included many contingents
from the peoples of Asia but was headed by the Macedonian units and
Balkan troops. Surveyors and scientists accompanied Alexander on this as on
other campaigns, and large numbers of camp-followers came with the army,
which was far larger than that which had invaded Asia in 334. His base in
Bactria was entrusted to a Macedonian satrap, with 3,500 cavalry and 10,000

[1] *FGrH* 115 F 256; Arr. *An.* 1. 3. 5; 1. 4. 4; 3. 30. 7 (Tanaïs); Plu. *Alex.* 45. 6; Arr. *An.*
4. 1. 1; 4. 15 (Scythians and Pharasmanes).

[2] Just. 12. 2. 16; Curt. 10. 1. 44; Hdt. 1. 202 fin.; Arist. *Meteor.* 350ᵃ21; Plu. *Alex.* 44;
Arist. *Meteor.* 354ᵃ3 (two separate seas, perhaps Caspian and Aral); Str. 509 fin.; Curt. 7. 3.
19–21; 6. 4. 19 (connecting Caspian Sea and Ocean off India by a northern valley or sink);
Arr. *An.* 7. 16. 2.

infantry. Crossing the great range of Paropamisus (Hindu Kush), he descended towards the Cabul river, a tributary of the Indus, and accepted the aid of Taxiles, the ruler of the valley. Dividing his army, he sent Hephaestion with Taxiles and the baggage-train through the Khyber Pass to bridge the Indus, while he set off in November to reduce the hill tribes on the north. In bitter fighting Alexander was wounded twice. At Massaga he slaughtered 7,000 Indian mercenaries who had come from beyond the Indus, and captured Aornus, a mountain fastness, by remarkable feats of climbing and engineering. He then joined Hephaestion and sacrificed by the Indus; the river had been bridged and some boats had been built in sections by the shipwrights. In spring 326 Alexander crossed to an Indian town, Taxila, where Taxiles increased Alexander's train of elephants and told him of a hostile coalition by the rulers of Cashmir and the Punjab, Abisares and Porus. Before advancing farther, Alexander organized his Indian satrapies, placed a garrison at Taxila, raised 5,000 Indian troops, and divided up his Companion cavalry, so that except for the Guard (*agema*), which he kept under his own command, there were four hipparchies headed by Companions but consisting mainly of Persian and other horse.[1]

At the river Hydaspes (Jhelum) Porus held the far bank with a large army and many elephants (see Fig. 34). Alexander brought up his boats in sections from the Indus, made rafts and floats with skins full of chaff, and boldly crossed before dawn with part of his army at a point higher up the river. A detachment under Craterus was to cross only if the bank was clear of the elephants; for they terrified the cavalry horses. Detachments of mercenary cavalry and infantry under their own commanders lay between Alexander's point of crossing and Craterus; they were to cross as soon as the Indian army was engaged by Alexander. His own force, consisting of 5,000 cavalry and 6,000 infantry, surprised and defeated a group of Indian cavalry and chariots under Porus' son. Porus himself left some elephants to hinder Craterus from crossing, and drew up his army on a sandy plain with a line of 200 elephants in front; then 30,000 infantry forming a line behind the elephants but extending beyond them on either side; and on the wings a total of 300 chariots and 4,000 cavalry. As Alexander's cavalry was not trained to face elephants, he could only attack the wings or rear of the Indians and leave the elephants to his infantry. The phalanx was drawn up with the Hypaspists under Seleucus on the right. The archers, Agrianians, and javelin-men formed a curtain on either wing, that on the left wing being advanced. Seleucus was ordered not to attack until he saw that the Indian cavalry and infantry were thrown into confusion by Alexander's group of cavalry. He divided his cavalry into three groups. The mounted archers, 1,000 in number, were to make a frontal attack on the Indian infantry of the left wing between the elephants and the cavalry. Coenus, leading two hipparchies of cavalry, was

---

[1] Plu. *Alex.* 66. 2 and Curt. 8. 5. 4 give 120,000 men for the army, which is not reliable, since Arrian gives no total. Arr. *An.* 4. 22. 3–5. 8. 3. For the battle see *HA* 204 ff. See *CQ* 30. 466 for hipparchies.

to make a feint towards the Indian right wing. Alexander with two hipparchies, Iranian and Scythian cavalry was to manoeuvre on the flank of the Indian cavalry on the left wing; then, if the Indian cavalry turned left to face him, Coenus was to wheel and attack the Indians in the flank and rear.

The first stage of Alexander's plan worked well. The Indian cavalry moved out left to face him, was attacked by Coenus, and formed a second front against him. At this point Alexander charged and broke the Indian cavalry who were pushed back to their infantry; but Porus, having ordered the cavalry round from his right wing, had turned his elephants and infantry into column towards the left and was approaching Alexander's cavalry. The Macedonian infantry under Seleucus now came into action, taking advantage of any gaps in the Indian column, and increased the disorder of the Indian left wing. While the infantry, greatly helped by the Agrianians and javelin-men, contained the elephants, Alexander's cavalry, passing to the rear, defeated the Indian cavalry who had arrived from the other wing, and drove them into the *mêlée* too. There the elephants, trained to trample, gore, and pick up the enemy, did much damage to the Macedonian infantry, but in the end their mahouts were killed and the wounded beasts backed 'like ships' into the Indian ranks. The phalangites, forming a dense mass with locked shields at Alexander's order, charged against the enemy and broke them into flight. Meanwhile the mercenary troops and finally the force under Craterus had crossed the Hydaspes and joined the fight and pursuit. The Indian losses were very heavy. The Macedonians lost some 250 cavalry and probably 700 infantry, killed or maimed; and the fear inspired by the elephants remained with them. Porus, himself a giant, rode off wounded on a huge elephant, but Alexander persuaded him to come back and asked his wish. When Porus replied 'Treat me like a king', Alexander confirmed him as ruler of his kingdom.[1]

Alexandria Nicaea and Alexandria Bucephala, named after his war-horse Bucephalas which died there, were founded one on either bank of the Hydaspes. Games were held, and sacrifices made to the gods; Alexander himself sacrificed to Helius, the sun-god, whose rising place he thought he was approaching. With part of the army he pressed on towards 'the end of India'. He crossed two rivers with difficulty in the monsoon rains, fought a desperate battle with heavy losses against the Cathaei at Sangala, and reached a third river, the Hyphasis (Beas). The country beyond was not desert but fertile, and another great river, the Ganges, was said to lie to the east. At this point the army mutinied. The troops were weary in body and spirit. Year after year they had marched and fought, and now there was no end to this 'India' which contained more and more elephants and warriors the farther east one

---

[1] Arr. *An.* 5. 8. 4–5. 19. 3; D.S. 17, 87–89; Plu. *Alex.* 60; Curt. 8. 13. 5–14; Polyaen. 4. 3. 9, 22; Frontin. *Strat.* 1. 4. 9. Alexander had left some of the phalanx units on garrison duty, and Arrian twice gives the number of his troops at the opening of the action (5. 8. 5 *fin.*; Just. 15. 1; 18. 3). A coin commemorating the victory is shown in Plate XII *k*.

went. Harangues by Alexander were of no avail. He stayed in his tent for three days, and silence reigned in the camp. On the fourth day he sacrificed. The omens were unfavourable for crossing, and he gave the order to turn back. The *anabasis* was at an end.[1]

On the bank of the river the army built twelve altars and made a thank-offering for the victories which had attended their arms. During the march back to the Hydaspes Alexander gave his new territories to Porus, received the submission of Abisares, and fixed the amount of tribute to be paid by these two vassal kings. At Alexandria on the Acesines some veteran mercenaries and Indians were settled, Alexandria and Bucephala on the Hydaspes were completed, and large reinforcements and medical supplies arrived from Macedonia. On finding crocodiles and beans of an Egyptian type in the Indus basin Alexander had at first imagined the Indus to be the upper Nile, the great river being the equivalent in the south of the Tanaïs in the north. Later he had learnt that the Indus entered the sea, and he decided this sea must be the Ocean. When 1,000 ships had been built, Alexander sacrificed to the river-gods, to the Macedonian gods, to Poseidon, and to Oceanus himself, and the army and fleet started the journey southwards (November 326). In the upper valley of the Indus he had dealt mainly with peoples of Indo-European stock, but as he moved south he encountered the religious fanaticism of the Brahmans, who inspired the Dravidian peoples to a more tenacious resistance. Alexander was determined to clear the Indus route down to the sea, and he used the harsher methods of massacre and enslavement wherever the tribes refused to accept his rule. During a campaign against the Malli Alexander and three others led the assault against a fortress and were isolated inside the walls. Alexander was wounded by an arrow which pierced his chest. When he had been carried out unconscious on his shield, the rumour grew that he was dead. The army was in despair, until he was shown to them on a boat and raised his hand in greeting; then they cheered him to the echo.[2]

§ 3. *The return and death of Alexander*

IN July 325 the expedition arrived at Pattala, where the apex of the Indus delta then lay, and Alexander set the troops to excavate a large harbour and build docks. For he was confident of finding a sea-route to the 'Red Sea' (Persian Gulf) and linking Persia and India together. As much of India as he had conquered was already organized in satrapies and several Alexander-cities had been built and populated, and his vassal kings acted as buffer states towards the east. Part of the army under Craterus had started westwards by an inland route with the baggage-train. Alexander sailed out into the sea,

---

[1] Arr. *An.* 5. 19. 4–28; D.S. 17. 90–94; Plu. *Alex.* 62; Curt. 9. 1–9. 3. 19.

[2] Arr. *An.* 5. 29–6. 13; D.S. 17. 95–99. 4; Plu. *Alex.* 62. 8–63; Curt. 9. 3. 20–9. 6. 2; Just. 12. 9. 5.

sacrificed to Poseidon, and flung the sacrificial gold cup into the waves. In September Nearchus started with the fleet from another Alexander-city (Karachi); his orders were to explore and map the coast, so that a regular route might be established for the future. Alexander took the residue of the army and marched near the coast, reducing the native peoples and laying dumps for the fleet, which had been delayed by adverse winds. At Ora he founded another Alexandria and left Leonnatus with part of the army, while he pressed on with some 10,000 men and many camp-followers. Behind him in India many Macedonians lay dead, and among them his infant son, Heracles, whom Roxane had borne to him during the campaign.[1]

When Alexander reached the river Tomerus (Hingol), he had to turn inland of the mountains and soon entered the torrid Gedrosian desert. The guides lost the way. The baggage animals had to be eaten, the army could only march at night when the heat abated, and those who fell out were left to die. Alexander himself dismounted and led his men on foot; he had his own baggage destroyed, and he refused water unless there was enough for all. Most of the soldiers reached Pura, where they rested, but many of the camp-followers perished in the desert. The crews of Nearchus' fleet also suffered from lack of food and water, as they followed the coast. At one point they charged a school of whales. At another they landed to find aborigines who ate fish raw and lived in whalebone huts. But they came at last to the mouth of the 'Red Sea' (Persian Gulf) and anchored after a voyage of eighty days at the estuary of the Amanis river. From there Nearchus went inland to find Alexander. When they met and Nearchus said the fleet was safe, Alexander wept and gave thanks to Zeus of the Greeks and to Ammon of the Libyans. For he had begun to lose hope. After a feast to celebrate the reunion of the fleet and the army, they proceeded to the head of the Gulf and thence up the Tigris to Susa, which they reached in spring 324. There, too, was Leonnatus, and Alexander crowned him and Nearchus with golden crowns.[2]

The long absence of Alexander had encouraged some of the satraps and generals to abuse their powers. He arrested and executed four Persian satraps and three generals, and ordered all satraps to disband any mercenary armies which they had enlisted. Macedonians were appointed to the vacant satrapies; one of them, Peucestas, satrap of Persia and Susiana, adopted Persian dress and won the devotion of the Persian people. Harpalus, who had lived luxuriously on the treasure of Alexander, fled into the Aegean with a fleet, 6,000 mercenaries, and 5,000 talents. On the advice of Demosthenes Athens refused him entry into the Peiraeus, but in summer 324 she let him enter with two triremes and held him under arrest. Soon afterwards he escaped, and the Areopagus instituted an inquiry to ascertain who had received bribes from him. In Egypt Cleomenes had oppressed the native merchants, monopolized

---

[1] Arr. *An.* 6. 14–22; D.S. 17. 100–5. 2; Plu. *Alex.* 66; Curt. 9. 6. 3–9. 10. 7; Just. 12. 10. 6.

[2] Arr. *An.* 6. 23–7. 5; D.S. 17. 105. 3–106; Plu. *Alex.* 67; Curt. 9. 10. 8–10. 1. 16.

the export of grain, and sold it at exorbitant prices, making himself a fortune stated to amount to 8,000 talents. For the present Alexander took no action, lest he should revolt and fortify the Egyptian frontier. Although these abuses were disheartening, Alexander's stern measures in the eastern satrapies put an end to them, and he showed his determination to safeguard the interests of his subjects.[1]

During the rest of 324 Alexander devoted himself to the organization of his eastern empire. Although he knew his policy was unpopular with the Macedonians, he was determined to associate the best elements of the Iranian aristocracies with the Macedonian Companions and to develop an army drawn from the warlike peoples of the empire. At Susa Alexander and eighty of his Companions were married at a mass wedding with Asian ritual to daughters of the Persian and Median aristocracy, Alexander taking as his second wife Barsine, the eldest daughter of Darius, and Hephaestion her sister, Drypetis. After this public demonstration of affiliation and friendship the 30,000 Persian youths who had been undergoing military training were paraded before him at Susa in Macedonian formations. Greater numbers of Iranian cavalry were recruited; as had been done in India, these were drafted into the existing Hipparchies, and some noble youths were taken into the Royal Guard of cavalry (*agema*). Any Macedonian soldiers who had taken Asiatic concubines received financial help if they were in debt. Their marriages were made official, and Alexander presented wedding gifts to the couples, who exceeded 10,000 in number. Thus Alexander sought to encourage a mutual respect between the two races at the administrative and military levels, but he knew that his action would arouse resentment among the older Macedonians.[2]

In summer 324 he assembled his Macedonian troops at Opis and announced the discharge of all whose age or wounds rendered them unfit for military service. He had already paid the personal debts of the whole army, and now he would give them a generous gratuity and assist them to return to Macedonia. An uproar broke out; for the pride of the soldiers was offended and they thought he wished to be rid of them and use Asiatics in their stead. Some shouted that he should dismiss the entire army and 'go campaigning with his father', Ammon of Libya. Alexander and his officers sprang into the crowd, seized thirteen ringleaders, and had them marched off. In silence Alexander mounted the platform again. He reminded the Macedonians of the services which Philip and he had rendered to their country; of his labour and his wounds and his gifts to them; and of his readiness to be as they were in his way of life, in war and in peace. Now that they all wished to go home, let them all go and tell the Macedonian people the truth, that they had deserted their king. In silence he left them and stayed two days in his palace,

---

[1] Arr. *An.* 6. 27–30; 7. 4. 1; D.S. 17. 106. 2–3; 108. 4 (Harpalus); Plu. *Alex.* 68–69. 5; Curt. 9. 10. 19; 10. 1. 1; 10. 1. 36; 10. 2. 1 (Harpalus); [D.] 56. 7 (Cleomenes).

[2] Arr. *An.* 7. 4. 4; 7. 6. 1; D.S. 17. 107. 6; 108; Plu. *Alex.* 70. 3; Just. 12. 10. 9.

unvisited and unseen. Then he sent for the leading Persians, gave them high military commands, and allowed those whom he had declared his 'kin' to kiss him. At the news of this the Macedonians rushed to the palace and threw down their weapons as suppliants. When Alexander came out, a senior member of the Companion cavalry expressed the grievance of them all, that Alexander called the Persians his 'kinsmen' and permitted them to kiss him, but not the Macedonians. 'But I consider all of you my kinsmen', cried Alexander, and they crowded round him, kissing him and shouting for joy. Then they took up their arms and returned to the camp.[1]

At Opis Alexander held a feast of reconciliation, attended by 9,000 persons, Macedonians and Iranians alike, all chosen for their prestige or qualities, and solemnized by Greek seers and Persian priests (the Magi). They drank from a loving-cup and poured the same libations, and Alexander prayed for concord between Macedonians and Persians and for their sharing of the empire. After the feast all Macedonians who were unfit for service and wished to return home received a gratuity from Alexander, and left behind their sons by Asiatic wives who, with any orphans, were to be trained at Alexander's expense in Macedonian ways and in due course to enter the army. The departing soldiers, some 10,000 in number, set off under Craterus, who was to take charge of Macedonia. Antipater was instructed to bring out Macedonian reinforcements, and meanwhile Alexander proceeded to fill the gaps in his Macedonian units with Persians at all levels, including the Royal Guard of Infantry. In 323 he advanced to the final stage of re-forming the army. At Babylon he received 20,000 more Persians, groups of Iranian archers and slingers, a Carian and a Lydian contingent, and some cavalry probably from the Balkans. He now mixed the nationalities so that a section of sixteen men contained four Macedonian phalangites and twelve men of other races armed as archers or javelin-men. The section leader was a Macedonian, and the Macedonians received higher pay; but otherwise the nationals from different parts of the empire were to fight side by side and receive equal honour.[2]

Alexander intended to hold his Eastern empire with a relatively small army, in which perhaps 2,000 cavalry and 13,000 infantry were to be European. The large army which assembled at Babylon in spring 323 was about to undertake a major campaign. During the winter of 324–323 timber from the Lebanon and naval gear from Cyprus had been transported to Thapsacus; there warships had been built and floated down the Euphrates to Babylon, where a basin for 1,000 ships had been dug and ship-yards had been made. Crews were brought from Phoenicia and Syria to serve in the eastern fleet. Part of the naval force was to open up the sea-route to India, and colonize the coast and islands of the Persian Gulf; for Alexander hoped

[1] Arr. *An.* 7. 5; 7. 8–11. 7; D.S. 17. 109. 2; Plu. *Alex.* 71; Curt. 10. 2. 10; Just. 12. 11. 1.
[2] Arr. *An.* 7. 11. 8–12; 7. 23. 1–4; D.S. 17. 110. 2 (the 20,000 Persians are additional to the 30,000 'Epigoni' of D.S. 17. 108. 1); Plu. *Alex.* 70.

to make this area a second Phoenicia as the emporium between the Indus valley and Mesopotamia. Part of the force, however, was to establish a sea-route to the Arabian Gulf (our Red Sea) by exploring the Arabian peninsula, which had been reconnoitred by three separate expeditions from Babylon and one from Heroönpolis (Suez) but had not yet been circumnavigated. Alexander hoped, no doubt, to take his army to Egypt in 323. The 'strong desire' urged him, too, to explore the Hyrcanian Gulf (Caspian Sea). Shipwrights were sent to build warships there and his officers were to discover whether the Caspian Sea opened into the Ocean and gave sea-connexion with India from the north, or gave access to the Black Sea (along the river Tanaïs); for in the past he had told Pharasmanes that he might invade the areas round the Black Sea in collaboration with Pharasmanes' army. Embassies now came to him from Libya, Etruria, Bruttium, and Lucania. His fame had spread far and wide and the world expected that his forces would soon be campaigning in the west. For he seemed to those around him to be already 'lord of every land and sea'.[1]

Experience had shown that Alexander could not rely on the co-operation of the Greek states in his rule over the East. Even the Greek mercenaries whom he had used, for instance as garrison troops in Bactria, were trying to return home; others recruited by his satraps had been disbanded at his order and were returning to Greece in 324, where 6,000 mercenaries had been brought already by Harpalus (who was killed in 324). The mercenaries were symptomatic of the political strife in the Greek states, which Philip and Alexander had hoped to check by means of the Greek League. The majority were exiles; and other exiles had sought refuge in Asia Minor, for instance the Samians driven out by Athens to make room for her cleruchs in Samos. These exiles were a threat to the peace inside and outside Greece, and Alexander decided that they should all be restored, except criminals and those Thebans who had been banished by the Greek League. Although evidence is lacking, it has been thought that he consulted the Greek states and arranged the principles governing the exiles' religious status, property-rights, and so forth, before any announcement was made. But he did not work through the Greek League Council; for its membership was limited and its business was the Common Peace. Although Aetolia and Athens thought at first of resisting (for it would mean to Athens the loss of Samos), the consent of the Greek states was obtained and later their envoys crowned Alexander for his action. The announcement was made to the Greeks in his army and to the assembled exiles (more than 20,000 were present) at the Olympic Festival in July/August 324. Some inscriptions which survive show the principles and details laid down by Alexander in order to obtain concord (*homonoia*) among the citizens. In the event of resistance his deputy as *hegemon*, Antipater, was authorized

---

[1] Curt. 10. 1. 19; 10. 2. 8; Arr. *An.* 7. 15. 4; 16. 1; 19. 3; 23. 5; Plu. *Alex.* 68. If some of the mixed units of infantry were intended for service in Asia, the figures in Curtius suggest an infantry army for Asia of some 50,000 men.

to use force. For Alexander meant to put an end to violent party-strife, as he had tried to do after the fall of Thebes and in Asia Minor. He also gave some instructions, of which the details are not known, concerning the Assemblies of the Achaean and Arcadian Leagues.[1]

In 324, probably after the recall of the exiles, Alexander requested the Greek states to pay him 'godlike honours'. He wished to emphasize his services to Greece and to the Greek gods. He had avenged Greece on Persia, rebuilt Plataea in accordance with the oath taken by the Greeks in 479, and given 10,000 talents for the rebuilding of the Greek temples. He had carried the worship of the Greek gods to the banks of the Jaxartes and the Indus and to the southern Ocean, opened a wide field for Greek colonization, founded Greek temples in his new cities, and given to the Greek states a period of peace and concord, which had been rivalled only under the Thirty Years Treaty in 446–431. He asked now for the recognition of his services without prescribing any particular form of 'godlike honour'. Demosthenes ridiculed the request by saying 'let him be son of Zeus and Poseidon too, if he wishes', and Demades was fined ten talents for proposing to call him a god. Sparta passed the pithy decree 'Since Alexander wants to be a god, let him be a god'. From Demosthenes and Sparta, the most obstinate enemies of Macedon, such a reaction was to be expected, but there were many states and many people who had a real gratitude for the peace, prosperity, and prospects which Alexander's conquests had made possible. Just as most states had welcomed the recall of the exiles, so in 323 the Greek states sent envoys wearing crowns—the mark of a sacred mission—to pay honour to Alexander as though they were honouring a god.[2]

Some have thought that Alexander sought 'deification' for political purposes, in the belief that he could establish in Greece the divine autocracy which he exercised as Pharaoh in Egypt. Such a view is unsound. Alexander did not ask to be a specific god at all. His autocracy in Egypt was based not only on a long tradition but also on an organized cult and priesthood which were entirely lacking in Greece; and there is no sign that he tried to harness Delphi or Olympia to any cult of Alexander or even put his own head on his coins. Alexander asked only for the divine honours which many Greeks were willing to grant to him, as in the past to Lysander and Dion. To the irreligious such honours were only a compliment, but to the religious they expressed gratitude to the gods for inspiring a man to do outstanding service to mankind. Such gratitude had been shown by the Ephesians in instituting a cult of 'Zeus Philippios' and by the Syracusans in honouring the memory

[1] D.S. 17. 99. 5 (Bactria); Hyp. 1. 18; Din. 1. 81; 103; *SIG* 312, l. 11; *Michel* 417, l. 9; D.S. 17. 109; 18. 8; Curt. 10. 2. 4; Just. 13. 5. 2; Plu. *Mor.* 221a; *GHI* 201–2. Alexander wanted all Greek states to recall their exiles. An appeal to the Greek League would affect only its members and not the numerous Greek states on the coast of Thrace and in Asia. See *HA* 249 ff.

[2] Ael. *V.H.* 2. 19; 5. 12; Hyp. 1. 31; Din. 1. 94; Plb. 12. 12b; Athen. 6. 251b; Arr. *An.* 7. 23. 2.

of Timoleon. The ill-starred Callisthenes had in the past tried to stimulate the worship of Alexander as a god by saying that the sea had retreated before him in Pamphylia, the oracle at Miletus had attributed his birth to Zeus, and the priest of Zeus Ammon had greeted him 'son of Zeus'. But these were the flatteries of a courtier who seems to have exercised no influence over the king. Alexander certainly used contemporary religious beliefs in Egypt, Babylon, Persia, India, and elsewhere, and he was not averse to using them in Greece if they supported his position. But his political standing in Greece was as *hegemon* of the Greek League, and his request for divine honours sprang rather from his own beliefs than from any political designs.[1]

In the year after his return from India in spring 324 Alexander was mainly engaged in the immense task of organizing his empire, reforming the army, developing a navy to open up maritime trade with India and later Egypt, regulating conditions in Greece, and in many other matters. His own way of life did not alter. The 'strong desire' (*pothos*) moved him to sail into the Persian Gulf, and on this journey he removed the artificial weirs on the Tigris to improve navigation. Later he sailed on the Euphrates and planned to improve the irrigation of Mesopotamia, and other important works were projected, such as the draining of Lake Copaïs in Boeotia. He visited the plain of Nysa, where the cavalry chargers of Persia were bred, arranged for Indian cattle to be sent to Macedonia to improve the European stock, and conducted a winter campaign against the Cossaei, who practised brigandage. During the winter his dearest friend, Hephaestion, died at Ecbatana, and for three days Alexander lay fasting in his grief. Mourning was proclaimed throughout the empire, as it had been for Alexander the Molossian, and Alexander obtained the approval of the oracle of Zeus Ammon for paying honours to Hephaestion as a hero. No one was appointed to command Hephaestion's hipparchy, a pyre was built at Babylon, and games were organized to commemorate him.[2]

In 323 Alexander marched from Ecbatana to Babylon. He disregarded the warnings of the Chaldaean priests not to enter the city (for he suspected their motives), and made his plans for naval exploration and assembled the army and navy at Babylon for his next campaign. There, too, the envoys from Greece came wearing crowns, the reply from the oracle of Zeus Ammon was reported, and the funeral of Hephaestion was held. The naval contingents practised their manoeuvres, boat-races were held, and on the eve of their departure Alexander arranged for the army and navy units to make sacrifice; and he himself sacrificed in the traditional manner. That night he spent feasting with his Companions, and next morning he fell ill with a fever.[3] Nevertheless, he continued with his preparations for departure, issued orders for the march, and was carried out to conduct sacrifices daily, although the

[1] *FGrH* 124 F 14, 31 (Callisthenes); D.S. 17. 102. 4.
[2] Arr. *An.* 7. 1. 1; 7. 7. 6; 7. 21. 6; 7. 13. 1; Plu. *Alex.* 72. 4; Arr. *An.* 7. 14 (Hephaestion); 7. 23. 6.
[3] Arr. *An.* 7. 16. 5 (Chaldaeans); 7. 23. 6 (Hephaestion); 7. 24. 4–7. 26 (illness and death).

fever was not abating. At last he was too ill to be moved any more. When the officers came to the palace, he could not speak to them. Forty-eight hours later he was still speechless. Then the soldiers began to file through his room, and he greeted each man, moving his head with difficulty and bidding them farewell with his eyes. All night his Companions stayed with him. In the morning they told him that the god whom they had consulted had replied that it would be better for Alexander not to be brought into the temple but to remain where he was. Shortly afterwards he died, on 13 June 323.

§ 4. *The achievement of Alexander*

IN his illness Alexander's thoughts were of what mattered to him most, war and religion. He was incomparable as warrior, captain, and general. 'Nothing in the field of war', said Arrian, 'was beyond the power of Alexander.' If he was planning to add the civilized fringes of the Mediterranean Sea to his empire (as he may have intended), such plans were far from impracticable. The man who at the age of thirty-two had defeated every race he met from the Adriatic to the Indus could have gone on to conquer Carthage and Rome. It is true that he thought the inhabited surface of the earth to be smaller than it was, and he may have therefore envisaged 'a world-empire'. If he had lived another thirty years, he could have founded an empire in which Macedonia and Greece lay at the centre and not on the periphery. In any event he would not have ceased to conduct campaigns and explore the seas of Ocean. As Arrian said, he was insatiable in his thirst for conquest.[1]

In statesmanship, too, he was incomparable. No man in history has combined such vast conquests with the power to weld them into a pacified and unified entity. His ideals were high—to bring to his subjects religious freedom, racial tolerance, political concord, economic prosperity, and peaceful conditions of life. In general his methods of warfare were more humane than those of his contemporaries, but at times he was as harsh as they—at Thebes, Tyre, Gaza, and in the Brahman areas of India—because he judged it necessary in order to implement his purposes. He rose above the nationalism of Isocrates and Aristotle in his respect for the religious practices, social customs, and political rights of all in his realm, whom no governor was permitted to persecute so long as they recognized Alexander as king. On the other hand he did not try to abolish national distinctions or fuse races. The equal association of Macedonians and Iranians in government, marriage, and warfare was designed for the purposes of administration and conquest and not for any philosophical or religious ends. In consequence it was attempted only at the higher social levels of the Indo-European peoples. The seventy new cities which he founded or proposed to found served the same purposes; for as centres of Greco-Macedonian culture they were to spread a new way of life, in education, economics, and military training, among the higher

[1] Arr. *An.* 7. 15. 3; 7. 1. 4; 7. 19. 6; the plans of Alexander in D.S. 18. 4 are perhaps fictitious, but the fiction is based on probability.

strata of the indigenous societies. His economic measures in coinage, trade, and maritime commerce and his development of natural resources brought fresh inspiration and prosperity to the Mediterranean peoples as well as to those of the East. He inaugurated a new age which would have been much richer if he had lived and left an heir.[1]

The administrative centre of the empire was Alexander. In carrying out his task, he commanded the service and the loyalty of his Companions and kinsmen—Macedonians, Greeks, and Persians. Philip and Alexander had trained the Macedonians as Royal Pages, Companion cavalrymen, generals, financiers, and administrators; and a new generation was being trained in Alexander's court, in Macedonia, and in the new cities. In the years after his death many of the Companions were to show their strength of will and their qualities of leadership, but during his lifetime they were dominated by his will.[2] He grasped at once those essentials of imperial administration which became clear to the Roman Republic only after generations of bloodshed—responsibility for the conquered peoples and respect for their institutions; separation of civil, military, and financial powers in provincial administration; inclusion of other nationals in the governing and military classes; suppression of piracy, brigandage, and civil war, and defence of the frontiers by an army in which auxiliary troops of other nationalities were included either as parallel units or even within the cadres of the imperial army; prosperity based on economic planning for overland and sea-borne commerce; and every subject's right of appeal to Alexander. The offices which he held were many and he incorporated several nationalities in his person.[3] He was *hegemon* for life of the Greek League and recipient of 'godlike honours'; hereditary King of Macedon, subject to the power of the Macedonian Assembly; Pharaoh of Egypt, son of Amon-Re; King of Babylon by grace of Ahura-Mazda; King of Asia as Cyrus had been; suzerain of vassal kings from Illyria to India; ally of Cyrene, Cyprian kings, Pharasmanes, and many others. But those offices were united in the magnetic personality of their holder. Alexander was the heart of the empire in a more vital sense than even Augustus was to be of the Roman empire.

In personality Alexander had many qualities in common with his father: personal courage, generalship, quickness of decision, intellectual perception, and religious faith. From his mother, Olympias, he inherited a stronger will for power and a more passionate nature than even Philip had had. He found his inspiration in the Heroic Age. In boyhood he emulated Achilles, his own ancestor; in manhood he sacrificed to Priam and laid a wreath on Achilles' grave; and throughout his campaigns he had the *Iliad* at his side. Like Philip,

---

[1] Arr. *An.* 6. 27. 5; Plb. 18. 3. 5 (methods of warfare; cf. 5. 10. 9); 5. 10. 6 (respect for religious practices); Plu. *Mor.* 328d–329a (seventy city-foundations; some believe the number to have been exaggerated).   [2] Plb. 8. 10. 5 (on the Companions).
[3] *GC* 213 (a coin, issued at Babylon, refers to many of his offices: cf. Plate XII *k*).

he revered Heracles, the ancestor of the Temenidae, who had suffered all his labours in the service of mankind. Throughout his life he sacrificed to Heracles, and he named his only son and two at least of his cities after him. His belief in Greek myths was not academic but personal and vital. He lived as Achilles and Heracles had lived—brave, wilful, passionate, and magnanimous—and he, too, sought to win 'the fame of men' by his prowess in war and his labours on man's behalf. When his officers once urged him not to lead his men in war, he was moved to anger 'by his spirit in battle and his passion for glory', and he approved the comment of a Boeotian soldier that man is born to noble deeds and to the suffering that attends noble deeds. Such was his conception of life, based upon the intense and direct emotions which made him march with his men into the Gedrosian desert, weep at the meeting with Nearchus and at the reconciliation after the mutiny, grieve desperately for Hephaestion, and think of his soldiers as he lay dying. As in Achilles, so in Alexander passion led him to commit dreadful acts in the killing of Cleitus and the murder of Parmenio, and to shut himself off from his men at the Hyphasis and at Opis. Yet such are the qualities which inspire valour in battle and command love among men.[1]

During his lifetime many Asiatics believed him to be a god on earth, and afterwards their belief in his divine origin and epic qualities gave birth to the 'Alexander Romance', of which the effects still live in the hero of Islam 'Iskander Dhulcarnein' (Alexander of the Two Horns) and in the figure of Alexander on the coins of Albania. The tragedy of his life was that few Macedonians approved of his ideals in government, and the triumph was that he forced them to follow by the power of his will. His intellect was Greek in its love of Greek culture, its daring speculation and amazing versatility. It may have been shaped by Aristotle when Alexander was a boy of fifteen, but it quickly outgrew his teaching. His temperament was Macedonian in its passion, its generosity, and its response to the 'strong desire' (*pothos*). The origin of his power was a religious faith which sprang from Greek and Macedonian sources. In health and in sickness he sacrificed to the gods of Greece and Macedon. He believed himself to be of divine descent on both sides, from Heracles, son of Zeus, and Achilles, son of Thetis. At the Temple of Zeus Ammon this belief may have been confirmed; for thereafter he showed a special regard for the temple, and his friends believed it was his wish to be buried there and not at Aegae in Macedonia. He may have felt in 324 that his deeds justified his claim to emulate Achilles and Heracles, and therefore he sought from the Greeks the recognition which they alone could give, by according him 'godlike honours' as a Greek.[2]

[1] Arr. *An.* 7. 14. 4 (Achilles); *An.* 6. 13. 4 (words of the Boeotian soldier, with which the speech in 5. 26. 4 is in keeping); Plu. *Mor.* 331c; 334d.

[2] Ammon was identified with Zeus by Pindar (*P.* 4. 16) and Herodotus 2. 55; Arr. *An.* 3. 3. 1 (Ammon and Heracles); 6. 19. 4; *Ind.* 18. 11; 35. 8; *An.* 7. 14. 7; 7. 23. 6. The 'pothos' figures in Arr. *An.* 1. 3. 5; 2. 3. 1; 3. 1. 5; 3. 3. 1; 4. 28. 4; 5. 2. 5; 7. 1. 1; 7. 16. 2; *Ind.* 20. 1. For Romance literature see *POxy* 1798 and for his outlook compare that of Pindar, p. 274 above.

At two moments in his life he revealed the meaning of his religious faith. At the battle of Gaugamela when he addressed the Greek troops, he raised his right arm to heaven and prayed to the gods that, if he was in truth descended from Zeus, they would aid and support the Greeks. His prayer, he believed, was answered then and later. At Opis, when he held the feast of reconciliation, he urged the Macedonian and Iranian leaders to regard the inhabited earth as their fatherland and good men as their kindred. For he himself, he said, had been sent from the gods as a governor and mediator in the world, to mingle the lives and institutions of men as in a loving-cup. His faith was indeed like that of 'the divine Odysseus, who was as a father to the peoples over whom he ruled', and it is a faith that does not die.[1]

---

[1] Plu. *Alex.* 33. 1 (cf. Arr. *An.* 1. 26. 2; 3. 3. 4–5); *POxy.* 1798, fr. 44 says Alexander invoked Thetis also at Gaugamela; Plu. *Mor.* 329c (Plutarch's words, although overlaid with the Cynic idea of the brotherhood of man in 329a, preserve the essence of Alexander's prayer); Od. 5. 11. For a portrait of him see Plate XII *l*.

CHAPTER 6

The Splitting of the Empire and Antipater's Occupation of Greece, 323–321

§ 1. *The first war of the Successors*

WHEN Alexander realized his illness was fatal, he had already lost the power of speech. All he could do was give his ring to Perdiccas. On the day after his death a Council was convened of the king's closest Companions and Commanders. In their presence Perdiccas placed the ring upon the throne. As Roxane was expecting a child, Perdiccas proposed that if the child proved to be a boy he should be king; meanwhile they should wait. The decision, however, lay with the Macedonians, who represented the people of Macedon, and the proposal was passed on to them. The cavalry supported Perdiccas, but the infantry opposed him; they wanted not the child of a Persian woman but the son of Philip, Arrhidaeus, now renamed Philip Arrhidaeus. The army nearly came to blows, the cavalry forming under Perdiccas and the infantry under Meleager; but bloodshed was averted by Eumenes, and a compromise was reached, that Philip should be king and Roxane's child, if a boy (as it proved to be, in August 323), should share the throne. As Philip was incapable of ruling, Craterus was to be his head of state in Macedonia; Perdiccas was to command the army in Asia, with Meleager as his second-in-command; and Antipater was to continue as general in Macedonia. A purification of the Macedonian army was then enacted in a plain, where Perdiccas took advantage of his control of the cavalry and the elephants to intimidate the infantry, seize Meleager's supporters, and do him and them to death. Perdiccas immediately summoned the Council again, which allocated the commands of the satrapies in accordance with his wishes. Only six days had passed since the death of Alexander. The body was embalmed, and it was decided to take it to Macedonia for burial in the tombs of the Kings.[1]

The prestige of Alexander and his Macedonians was such that the Asiatic peoples did not rise in revolt. But he left behind him several hundred thousand experienced troops—Macedonian, Greek, and Asiatic—, a number of capable and ambitious generals, and large quantities of treasure in different parts of the empire. For the moment Perdiccas held the reins of power, because he commanded the bulk of the army, which acted as the Macedonian people, and he controlled the movements of the king, Philip III. His first task

---

[1] Curt. 10. 6–10; D.S. 17. 117. 3; 18. 2–4. As the authenticity of Alexander's plans in D.S. 18. 4 is doubtful, they are omitted from the text.

was to halt the discontented Greek mercenaries who had collected in Bactria and were on the march homewards, an army estimated at 3,000 cavalry and 20,000 infantry. They were intercepted by a large Macedonian army, compelled to surrender by a superior force of Macedonian and Asiatic cavalry, and then treacherously massacred by the Macedonians. The most vulnerable part of the empire was in Asia Minor, where Ariarathes, the independent ruler of Cappadocia, threatened the lines of communication with Europe. Perdiccas, therefore, ordered two generals, Antigonus and Leonnatus, who had armies in Asia Minor, to combine with Eumenes and conquer Cappadocia. Both of them refused to obey. The Lamian War, which pinned down Antipater in Greece and drew off Leonnatus to his death in Thessaly, made it more imperative to secure the route to Europe, and in spring 322 Perdiccas took the main army and Philip III from Babylon and overran Cappadocia, putting Ariarathes to death. He then persuaded the army to recognize him as the executive agent of the two kings, Philip III and Alexander IV. But he still had to impose his will on the generals.

His enemies combined against him. Antipater and Craterus, who were bringing the Lamian War to an end, had more than 40,000 men under their command; Antigonus took charge of part of Antipater's fleet and landed in Caria; and Ptolemy, the governor of Egypt, had a strong army and navy. Perdiccas divided his forces. One army under Eumenes drew off Craterus and defeated him in Asia Minor, while Antipater marched southwards to help Ptolemy. Perdiccas reached Egypt first with his main army and the two kings, but he failed to force a passage of the Nile and lost many men in the river. The army then mutinied, killed Perdiccas in his tent, and offered his position to Ptolemy (June 321). The offer was refused in favour ultimately of Antipater, the general of Philip and colleague of Parmenio. He held the army and the empire together by force of arms and the vigour of his personality until his death early in 319, and then the empire split finally and irrevocably.

Ptolemy had a deeper insight into the situation than any of the generals. He obtained Egypt from Perdiccas, got rid of Cleomenes, annexed Cyrene, and attracted Macedonians and Greeks to his service. When the corpse of Alexander was being taken in 322 from Babylon to Macedonia, Ptolemy had the *cortège* diverted at Damascus to Egypt, where a magnificent tomb was built at Alexandria; there an official cult of Alexander was observed, and the kinship of the Ptolemies with the Argeadae was stressed. By 321 Egypt was a separate kingdom, capable of withstanding Perdiccas and disobeying Antipater. It was the prototype of the Hellenistic monarchy, in which a Macedonian king ruled mainly with Macedonian and Greek administrators and soldiers and Greek cities developed a municipal and cosmopolitan character within an autocratic state. Alexandria soon became the centre of a new form of Greek culture, which has bequeathed to us the pastoral idylls of Theocritus, the scholarly poems of Callimachus, and the artificial epic of Apollonius Rhodius. The monarchy of the Ptolemies was also the most long-lived. The last of the Ptolemies, the son of Cleopatra and Julius Caesar, named Ptolemy Caesar, was killed on the order of Octavian in 31 B.C., but the new form of Greek culture lived on as a civilizing force in the Roman Empire.

§ 2. *The Lamian War*

OF all who knew Alexander the Greeks of the mainland were least impressed by the spell of his personality. In their eyes he was the Macedonian, the sacker of Thebes, the king whose authority was wielded by the capable but ruthless hands of Antipater. They had not co-operated in Alexander's campaigns with any sincerity, and they did not think at all in terms of Greco-Macedonian civilization. Many individuals and some classes were grateful for the peace which Macedon had brought and for the economic benefits and opportunities afforded by the expansion of Macedon's power; and this gratitude was voiced by the restored exiles and the state-envoys at Babylon. Alexander's presence in Greece, coupled with his generosity and interest in Greek welfare, might have turned the scales towards a reconciliation. But events turned out otherwise, and the rivalry of the generals seemed to offer a chance of breaking away from the authority of Antipater.

The Athenian people had little idea of Alexander's power. They were persuaded only with difficulty to pay divine honours to Alexander and accept the restoration of the exiles. Demosthenes and Demades at first advised resistance, and Demosthenes was appointed leader of the embassy which was sent to the Olympic Festival in 324. But closer acquaintance with the situation caused him to advise acceptance, and Demades also changed his mind. Hyperides, however, remained in opposition. Before the death of Alexander, the Areopagus Council reported to the Assembly that some of the lost treasure of Harpalus had found its way into the pockets of Demosthenes, Demades, and others. The Assembly appointed ten orators, led by Hyperides, to prosecute the accused persons. Demosthenes and Demades were found guilty of receiving twenty talents each. Demosthenes was imprisoned, until he should pay a fine of fifty talents, and Demades was disfranchised but remained at liberty. The guilt of Demosthenes can hardly be in doubt. His motives may have been public rather than personal (as in 336–335); but even if this was believed to be the case, Demosthenes could hardly have been acquitted while Alexander, the owner of the stolen money, was still alive. He escaped from prison, settled at Calauria, and appealed in vain for pardon.

The news of Alexander's death came early to Leosthenes, an Athenian in mercenary service, who commanded 8,000 mercenaries—refugees from Asia—at Taenarum in south Laconia. Leosthenes negotiated secretly at Athens with the Council, which gave him fifty talents and some arms and sent envoys to Aetolia. When the death of Alexander was beyond dispute, Hyperides supported a proposal in the Assembly to organize a rising against

Macedon, and Demosthenes sent messages to the same effect from Calauria. The richer classes and the cautious Phocion opposed the proposal, but the poorer citizens decided with enthusiasm to protect 'the general freedom of Greece' and expel any Macedonian garrisons. The financial genius of Lycurgus (who had died in 324) had raised the resources of the state to a higher level than they had reached in 431; the annual revenue was 1,200 talents, and 18,000 talents had been amassed in reserve funds. The nominal strength of the fleet was 400 ships, and the young men had been undergoing military training since 334 at least. Athens had spent large sums not only on civic buildings but also on defensive works. The Assembly therefore resolved to man 240 warships and send out of Attica an expeditionary force of 500 cavalry, 2,000 mercenaries, and citizen hoplites under forty years of age from seven tribes—the actual number who marched later being 5,000.[1]

The decision of Athens did not command the support of all classes. The period of peace and prosperity had not been used to improve the condition of the poorer classes, as Aristotle had advised; it is likely rather that the gulf between rich and poor widened, as the possibilities of speculation increased for the wealthy and the cost of cereals rose for the poor. The apprehensions of the poor had been seen in a decree, passed in 336, which pronounced dire punishments against any Athenian, or any member of the Areopagus Council, who initiated or countenanced the overthrow of the democracy in favour of tyranny or oligarchy. Athenian morale had been shaken by defeat at Chaeronea, and the danger of a mercenary commander or a Macedonian agent attempting a *coup d'état* seemed considerable. At the same time the majority held by the poorest class in the Assembly may have diminished somewhat since 338; for many of the poor had probably gone to Asia or Egypt for employment, and others had sailed in 325/324 to found a colony on the Adriatic coast. As events were to prove, Athens now lacked sufficient manpower to send out a fleet of 240 ships. But party feeling ran high, and the democratic leaders called for war, as they had so often done, without making a clear assessment of the chances of success. A number of Athenians and metics—among them Aristotle—were prosecuted on a charge of sympathy with Macedon, and were condemned or fled from Attica. When the die was cast, the Assembly voted a sum of fifty talents to Demosthenes, so that he could pay his fine, and recalled him to Athens.[2]

In October 323 Leosthenes led an army of mercenaries to Aetolia, received 7,000 troops from the Aetolian League, and was joined by Phocis and Locris. He then occupied Thermopylae. The Athenian army set out to join him; but its way was barred by the Boeotians, who were supported by some

---

[1] D.S. 18. 8; Hyp. 1. 31; 6. 3, 21; Din. 1. 1; Plu. *Dem.* 25–27; *Phoc.* 23; Paus. 1. 29. 16 (finances); Plu. *Mor.* 842 f.; *GHI* 204 (ephebic oath).

[2] *GHI* 196, l. 4 (corn shortage); *Hesp.* 21. 355 (tyranny decree); *GHI* 200 (colony); Athen. 697a (Aristotle); Euseb. *Praep. Evang.* 15. 2 (esp. § 11). The charge of impiety was probably made in 306.

Macedonians and Euboeans, and Leosthenes had to send help to enable the Athenians to break through. Meanwhile Athenian envoys toured the Greek states to raise a coalition. Antipater was in a weak position, having sent so many reinforcements to Alexander, and he sent urgent requests for help to Craterus, then in Cilicia with the 10,000 Macedonian veterans, and to Leonnatus, satrap of Phrygia by the Hellespont. But before the coalition forces could grow, Antipater marched south with 600 cavalry and 13,000 infantry, perhaps supported by a fleet of 110 triremes which had recently returned to Macedonia on convoy duty, and called up the troops of Thessaly. But, as he neared Thermopylae, the Thessalian cavalry deserted. With their aid Leosthenes' army of 22,500 men defeated Antipater and drove him to take refuge behind the strong walls of Lamia. The coalition was now joined by most of the hill tribes of central Greece, Leucas, and Carystus; but the Athenian fleet failed to win over the rest of Euboea or cut communications between Macedonia and Asia. Argos, Sicyon, Elis, and Messenia declared for the coalition, but the other Peloponnesian states and the islands took no active part.

The members of the coalition described the war as 'the Greek War'. They set up a council of command, each contingent having its own commander, and accepted Leosthenes as commander-in-chief of the army. Leosthenes held the initiative on land, but he failed to take Lamia by assault and put it under blockade. When negotiations were offered, Leosthenes demanded unconditional surrender and Antipater refused. As winter set in, the Aetolians went home to conduct some political business and Leosthenes was killed in a skirmish during their absence. His successor in the general command, Antiphilus, an Athenian, was less capable of holding the allied forces together. Meanwhile Athens was still unsuccessful at sea. The Macedonians even raided Rhamnus on the coast of Attica, whence Phocion drove them off, and the Athenian fleet sailed into the Hellespont but won no allies. The Macedonian commander in Thrace, Lysimachus, was pinned down by a rising of the Odrysians, but the way was still open for reinforcements from the East.

In spring 322 Leonnatus brought his army across the Straits, raised its strength to 2,500 cavalry and 20,000 infantry in Macedonia, and marched into Thessaly. Antiphilus still lay outside Lamia. The Aetolians had not rejoined him, and his forces numbered 3,500 cavalry and 22,000 infantry. He raised the siege, attacked Leonnatus alone in the plain, and used his superiority in cavalry to defeat the army of Leonnatus, who was among the slain. The Macedonians, however, were able to manoeuvre in the hills, where they were soon joined by the army of Antipater and withdrew to Macedonia. There Antipater waited for the arrival of Craterus with a third army. The Greek fleet could alone save the situation now. But a second Macedonian fleet under Cleitus won a decisive victory off Abydus, controlled the Straits, and joined forces with the fleet of Antipater. The Athenian fleet of 170 ships was now outnumbered.

In summer 322 the Athenian fleet fought at Amorgos and suffered defeat. The war at sea was virtually ended, and Athens was threatened with blockade. In September Craterus joined Antipater, who took command of the combined forces—5,000 cavalry, more than 40,000 heavy infantry, and 3,000 light infantry, of whom a thousand were Persians. The Greek army had been dwindling, as contingents kept going home, and numbered 3,500 cavalry and 25,000 infantry for the decisive battle at Crannon in Thessaly. Antiphilus placed his fine cavalry in front of his infantry line, hoping to defeat the enemy cavalry and surround the infantry; but, as soon as the cavalry forces engaged, Antipater led the phalanx into the attack and drove the Greek infantry line back to rougher ground, where the cavalry could not come to their aid. Neither side suffered heavy losses. But the Greeks had been outmanœuvred; they could hold the rough ground with field defences, but could not leave it. On the following day Antiphilus and the commander of the Thessalian cavalry treated for peace. Antipater refused to negotiate with the coalition as a whole, and Antiphilus broke off negotiations. Antipater then proceeded to capture the cities in Thessaly and made peace on generous terms with state after state, until only Athens and Aetolia were left at war.[1]

As the Aetolians went home to defend their country, Athens found herself hopelessly outclassed by land and sea. She was in a weaker position than in 338 or 335, and she had to deal not with Philip and Alexander, who had wanted reconciliation and co-operation, but with a Macedonian general who was determined to end her powers of resistance. Antipater concentrated his forces in Boeotia. Athens restored the franchise to Demades, and sent him, Phocion, and others to sue for peace. Antipater offered not to invade Attica in force, if Athens surrendered unconditionally. His offer was accepted by the Assembly. In mid-September 322, at the commencement of the Eleusinian Mysteries, a Macedonian garrison marched past the city to occupy Munychia. Oropus was transferred from Athens to Boeotia. The future of Samos was referred to Perdiccas, who expelled the Athenian cleruchs and restored the Samians. Athens had to pay a war indemnity, and an oligarchic government was installed by Antipater, who required the political franchise to be restricted to owners of twenty minae. Their number proved to be 9,000. The remainder, numbering 22,000, were to lose all political rights. The orators responsible for advising Athens to go to war were to be surrendered to Antipater. On the proposal of Demades the Assembly passed sentences of death for treason on Hyperides, Demosthenes, and others, who had already fled from the city. The sentences were carried out by Antipater's men. Demosthenes was found in the temple of Poseidon at Calauria. He took poison, tried to leave the temple, lest death pollute its precincts, and fell

[1] D.S. 18. 11–17; Just. 13. 5; 13. 6. 9; *FGrH* 156 F 1 (Arrian); *IG* ii.² 398; 493; Plu. *Demetr.* 11. 3 (Amorgos); *FGrH* 239 B 9 (Marmor Parium); Plu. *Phoc.* 23–25. Hyp. 6 *Epitaphios* was delivered in honour of Leosthenes.

dead beside the altar. The freedom of Athens thus ended even more tragically in 322 than in 404.[1]

Antipater went on from Athens to the Peloponnese, where pro-Macedonian parties took power in the states. An Athenian orator, Dinarchus, was installed at Corinth as Macedonian governor with authority over the Peloponnese. His moderation was indeed praised, but his presence marked the establishment of a Macedonian Protectorate. The Aetolians resisted more stubbornly than Athens. Their citizen army of 10,000 men withdrew into the mountains and fought off an army thrice their size. Antipater decided to starve them out during the winter of 322–321, but the movements of Perdiccas in Asia distracted him. He granted moderate terms to the Aetolian League, and brought the Lamian War to a conclusion.[2]

§ 3. *Different ideas of freedom*

THE freedom of the individual may be absolute in the mind or soul, because it is based on self-respect. The freedom of the citizen, which is based on political self-expression, is relative to the needs and rights of other citizens. And the freedom of a state, which is based on self-government, is relative to the needs and rights of other states. At Athens, for instance, the citizen class enjoyed political freedom, except in 404–403, until the end of the Lamian War, and the Macedonians enjoyed political freedom until Rome imposed a settlement in 197. The leading states of Greece in the fourth century down to 338 interpreted freedom in inter-state politics as the right to dominate weaker states by imposing puppet governments, garrisons, tribute, and in extreme cases *andrapodismos*. Sparta, Athens, and Thebes were less concerned with self-government than with 'hegemony', the exercise of control over other states. But at the same time a different conception of freedom was developing, under which states were free to co-operate and conduct their own affairs without imposing or receiving puppet governments, garrisons, and tribute. The larger federal states, the Second Athenian Alliance at its inception, and the League of City-States in 362/361 realized this new idea in a wide field. Philip carried it farther after his victory at Chaeronea. He gave to the Greek states a charter of freedom and self-government, conditioned by co-operation and respect for others, and Alexander followed his example in 336. Garrisons were indeed placed in some citadels; but this measure was approved by the Council of the Greek League as the self-governing organ of the whole.

[1] D.S. 18. 18; Plu. *Phoc.* 25–28; *Dem.* 28–30; *FGrH* 156 F 9 (Arrian); Plb. 9. 29. The figure 9,000 agrees well enough with the figure for the Lamian War, assuming metic hoplites were included in D.S. 18. 11. 3. The disfranchised appear as 22,000 in D.S. 18. 18. 5 and 12,000 in Plu. *Phoc.* 28. 7. Of these figures one is a textual or factual error; the number of ships manned, whether 240 as planned or 170 at Amorgos, requiring respectively some 40,000 or 30,000 men, shows that 22,000 is the correct figure, and this accords well with the figure of 21,000 citizens in 313, as considerable emigration occurred between 322 and 313 (see Appendix 6).   [2] D.S. 18. 24–25; Suid. *Deinarchos.*

In 335 Thebes claimed the earlier form of freedom, the right to dominate the other states in Boeotia. Because she persisted in this claim, her 'Boeotarchs' refused Alexander's offer of terms. The *andrapodismos* of Thebes·was voted by the Council of the Greek League and particularly by those states on the Council which had suffered from Thebes' exercise of freedom in the past. In the Lamian War Athens and Aetolia claimed to be fighting for 'the freedom of the Greek states'. They might have received general support, if men had assumed that the Macedonian generals intended to discard the policy of Philip and Alexander and that Athens and Aetolia were advocating a freedom of co-operation and respect for other states. In fact few responded. They had such cases as Samos in mind, and they feared a return to the earlier exercise of freedom by Athens. They preferred the freedom of co-operation, which Philip and Alexander had extended to them.

Historians may rate one form of freedom more highly than the other, in the light of the value they attach to military strength, humane methods, economic prosperity, artistic genius, social justice, or such ideals as pacifism, 'democracy', or federalism. The statesman is faced by a more immediate and practical task, to preserve the well-being of his state in a world of other states, which requires not only a definition of well-being but also an understanding of other states. The Theban statesmen of 335 certainly failed to understand the power of Alexander, and they may have misjudged the feeling of the Greek states. The Athenian statesmen of 338–323 were not unanimous. Phocion and others believed that the well-being of Athens under the conditions of the time lay in co-operation with the Greek League and Macedon. Demosthenes, Hyperides, and others hankered after the earlier form of freedom for Athens, with dominion over others, and they considered that contemporary conditions in the world of states offered a reasonable chance of success. In 323 their calculations proved false. Their cause did not command general support. They misjudged their own strength. Lack of unity at home, weak discipline in the field, dependence on mercenaries, and readiness to admit defeat made them much inferior to the power of Macedon. It is far from certain that Demosthenes has a higher claim to the title of statesman than Phocion in the years from 338 to 322.

In times of crisis a democracy often produces a leader who reflects its own qualities with some degree of magnification. Such a leader was Demosthenes throughout his career: unscrupulous in his ambition, rancorous in his animosities, cynical in regard to others, clamorous for his own rights, gifted with artistic genius and intellectual acumen but not martial prowess, trusting less in strength than in 'good luck', determined to assert the traditional 'freedom' of Athens and prepared to accept himself and impose on others any sacrifice for the fulfilment of his aim. His early speeches reveal in all frankness his conception of freedom for Athens, which was or appeared to be practicable in the contemporary world. Between 350 and 338 he fought for that freedom with tenacity, courage, and ingenuity, and he judged to a hair's breadth how far he could drive Philip without provoking open war. He differed from Eubulus, Aeschines, and Phocion in his interpretation of Philip's ultimate purpose and in his idea of freedom, but his policy may have been based on a deeper insight into the ultimate effects of Macedonian supremacy in the world of his time. When Philip did not deprive Athens of self-government, nor even of her fleet or army or finances, Demosthenes and his supporters were unable to re-orientate themselves. 'The philanthropy of Philip thereafter', he cried, 'was a hypocritical mask, and you gained the advantages of it, lucky people—but I pass to other matters.'[1] In 330, when Lycurgus said the freedom of Greece was buried with the dead at Chaeronea, he spoke of Demosthenes' and his idea of freedom, not of freedom within the framework of the Greek League.

Between 338 and 322 Demosthenes faced a new world, because the power of Macedon could no longer be denied. The choice was either co-operation with the Greek League's type of freedom and the conquest of Persia or resistance to the Greek League and Macedon with the gravest risk of disaster. Demosthenes advised the leaders of Thebes and the people of Athens to adopt resistance in 335. The sack of Thebes followed, but 'philanthropy' was shown towards Athens then and later. Demosthenes still advised resistance, at first with more caution than his less well-informed followers among the people, but finally in 323 with the same courage and foolhardiness as they. This time there was no 'philanthropy' towards Demosthenes and Athens. Antipater chose to interpret Macedon's victory and Macedon's freedom as Sparta had done in 404, but even so not as Athens had done towards Melos, Sestus, or Samos.

In these years a greater issue than Athens' field of freedom was decided. Philip adopted the new idea of freedom, with its principles of self-government and co-operation, and extended it to the Greek states. Alexander sought to establish it in the East. Some military safeguards were necessary in each case during the initial stages of their policy; for the world is not changed instantaneously by new ideas and methods. Each was close to success, when death intervened. Greece and Macedon were akin in blood and culture; if they had combined under the leadership of Philip as *hegemon* of the Greek League and king of Macedon, the Greco-Macedonian era might have been a reality rather than a catchword for the historian. If Alexander had lived, the co-operation of Macedon and Asia might have prospered, and his genius might even have realized the co-operation of Macedon and Greece which would have withstood the arms of Rome. The actuality was otherwise. In 322 the generals abandoned the policy of Philip and Alexander. Antipater, as deputy of Alexander in 331, had referred the case of the rebels to the Council of the Greek League. In 322 he disregarded it. The League was as dead as the policy which had brought it to birth. Antipater's treatment of Athens and the installation of a Macedonian governor in the Peloponnese marked the end of the freedom which the Greeks as a race had enjoyed for more than a thousand years.

[1] D. 18. 231.

APPENDIX 1

Short Bibliography of the Archaeological Evidence for Book I

GENERAL. *The Cambridge Ancient History*[2] I–IV; E. Vermeule, *Greece in the Bronze Age*; P. Warren, *The Aegean Civilizations*.

ARCADIA. E. J. Holmberg, *The Swedish Excavations at Asea in Arcadia*.

ARGOLIS. H. Schliemann, *Mycenae*; *Tiryns*; A. J. B. Wace, *Mycenae*; *BSA* 25 and 48–52; G. E. Mylonas, *Mycenae and the Mycenaean Age*: *Hesperia* 23–27 (Lerna); A. W. Persson, *The Royal Tombs at Dendra near Midea*; C. W. Blegen, *Prosymna*; W. Taylour, *The Mycenaeans*.

ATTICA. *The Athenian Agora*; H. A. Thompson and R. E. Wycherley, *The Agora of Athens*; C. W. Blegen in *Athenian Studies to W. S. Ferguson*; W. Kraiker and K. Kübler, *Kerameikos*; Sp. Marinatos in *AAA* 3. 153 f. and 349 f. (Marathon); Sp. Iakovides, *Perati*; V.R.D'A. Desborough, *Protogeometric Pottery*.

BOEOTIA. H. Goldman, *Excavations at Eutresis*; H. Bulle, *Orchomenos*.

CHALCIDICE. G. E. Mylonas, *Olynthus*.

CORINTHIA. C. W. Blegen, *Korakou*; *Zygouries*; T. J. Dunbabin, *JHS* 68. 59; H. Payne, *Perachora*; *Hesperia* 29; S. S. Weinberg in *Corinth* VII.

CRETE. Sir Arthur Evans, *Palace of Minos*; *Scripta Minoa*; J. D. S. Pendlebury, *Archaeology of Crete*; R. W. Hutchinson, *Prehistoric Crete*; H. T. Bossert, *Altkreta*; P. Demargne, *La Crète dédalique* and, with H. Gallet de Santerre, *Mallia*; K. Branigan, *The Foundations of Palatial Crete*; S. Marinatos and M. Hirmer, *Crete and Mycenae*; S. Hood, *The Minoans*.

CYPRUS. E. Gjerstad, *The Swedish Cyprus Expedition*; *Opuscula Archaeologica* 3.107; E. Sjöqvist, *Problems of the Late Cypriot Bronze Age*.

EPIRUS. N. G. L. Hammond, *Epirus*, and *Migrations and Invasions in Greece*.

ITHACA. *BSA* 32 f.

LACONIA. R. M. Dawkins, *The Sanctuary of Artemis Orthia*; *BSA* 55, 67, 76, 79.

LESBOS. W. Lamb, *Excavations at Thermi in Lesbos*.

LEUCAS. W. Dörpfeld, *Alt-Ithaka*; *BSA* 69 and 70.

MACEDONIA. W. A. Heurtley, *Prehistoric Macedonia*; N. G. L. Hammond, *History of Macedonia* I; M. Andronikos, *Vergina* I.

MELOS. T. D. Atkinson, *Excavations at Phylakopi* (*JHS* Suppl. Papers 4).

MESSENIA. C. W. Blegen and M. Rawson, *The Palace of Nestor at Pylos in Western Messenia*; N. Valmin, *Swedish Messenia Expedition*.

RHODES. *Opuscula Archaeologica* 6; *Clara Rhodos*.

TARSUS. H. Goldman, *Tarsus*.

THESSALY. A. J. B. Wace and M. S. Thompson, *Prehistoric Thessaly*.

TROY. H. Schliemann, *Ilios*; C. W. Blegen, *Troy*; J. M. Cook, *The Troad*.

UGARIT. C. F. A. Schaeffer, *Ugaritica*.

LANGUAGE AND DIALECTS. M. G. F. Ventris and J. Chadwick, *Documents in Mycenaean Greek*;[2] L. R. Palmer, *Mycenaean Greek Texts*; C. D. Buck, *Greek Dialects*; *CAH*[2] I. 2. 824; II. 1. 582; II. 2. 805; III. 1. 850.

WEAPONS. H. L. Lorimer, *Homer and the Monuments*; A. M. Snodgrass, *Early Greek Armour*; *Early Greek Arms and Weapons*.

GEOGRAPHY. Maps 1–6a in N. G. L. Hammond, *Atlas of the Greek and Roman World in Antiquity*.

Chronology in the Thirteenth and Twelfth Centuries

§ 1. GREEK authors gave different dates for the Trojan War and events on either side of it. Herodotus probably put it *c.* 1280–1260 (2. 145. 4: Heracles 900 years before his time *c.* 1350–1330, Penelope's son roughly 800 years *c.* 1250–1230; the Dorian invasion of Laconia four generations after Heracles *c.* 1190–1170; cf. the Pseudo-Herodotean life of Homer 538 f. putting the fall of Troy in 1270). Thucydides put it *c.* 1220–1200 (5. 112. 2 Dorians occupied Melos 700 years before 416, *c.* 1116; 1. 12. 3 Dorian invasion eighty years after the fall of Troy, and the occupation of Melos probably came quickly after the invasion of Laconia). Theopompus gave the same date approximately as Thucydides (*FGrH* 115 F 205: Trojan War 500 years before accession of Gyges *c.* 710, i.e. *c.* 1210), and so did Dicaearchus, a disciple of Aristotle. Democritus, Ephorus, Thrasyllus, Timaeus, and many Alexandrian scholars put Troy's fall in 1194 or 1184, and Ephorus and others still later (references in F. Jacoby, *Marmor Parium* 146 f.).

It is very likely that these dates were based on genealogies, such as those of the Spartan kings (Hdt. 7. 204 and 8. 131). The interpretation of genealogies depends on the time allowed for a generation. Herodotus seems to have allowed forty years to a generation in his reckoning for the Trojan War (elsewhere he allowed thirty-three years, e.g. 2. 142. 2). Later historians probably realized this was excessive; for the Spartan kings from Alcamenes and Theopompus to Leonidas, Leotychidas, and Demaratus give an average generation of thirty-three years, the Mermnadae of Lydia thirty-four years, and the Alcmeonidae about the same (*CQ* 6, p. 47). In settled times men normally married in their thirties (Hes. *Op.* 697–705; Sol. fr. 19. 9; Pl. *R.* 460e; *Lg.* 705b); and in unsettled times earlier, if we judge from the Macedonian kings *c.* 485–323 with a generation of twenty-seven years. For the period 1300–1200 I have reckoned in my text on the basis of a thirty-year generation. When we judge between the dates given by Herodotus and Thucydides, we prefer Thucydides, because his estimate is lower than forty years and he may have had other data (his 'sixty years' and 'eighty years' after the fall of Troy for the invasion by the Boeotians and the Dorians can hardly be based on genealogical reckoning). It is therefore best, on this part of the evidence, to put the fall of Troy *c.* 1200.

§ 2. Precise information comes from Egyptian and Hittite documents which can be dated to years B.C.: raids on Egypt in 1221, 1194, and 1192, &c., and a raid on Cyprus *c.* 1225 by 'Attarissiyas, the man of Ahhiyava'. If he is Atreus, then the sack of Troy by his son Agamemnon must have been *c.* 1200 and cannot have been before 1210 at the earliest. If he is not Atreus, we fall back on the raids, of which the first came mainly from Libya and the others in 1194 and 1192 were delivered chiefly by migrating peoples from the north, who probably destroyed the Hittite empire *c.* 1200. The entry of the raiders into Asia Minor was evidently due to the fall of Troy, and the Greek tradition of the wanderings of the heroes returning from Troy fits the period of raids. Among the successors of the Hittites were the Phrygians, coming from Europe after the Trojan War (Hdt. 7. 73; Xanthus *FHG* 1. 37, 8); Herodotus 1. 7 placed their arrival *c.* 1221, but his inflated chronology should probably be reduced to a date after 1200.

§ 3. Herodotus links the Cadmeid genealogy and the Heraclid genealogy at 6. 52, where Argea, wife of Aristodemus, leader of the Dorians invading Laconia, is sister of Theras, who on going to Thera joined his kinsmen left there eight generations earlier by Cadmus on his way to Thebes (4. 147). The names supplied by Herodotus in the Cadmeid genealogy (5. 59 and 6. 52) and in the Heraclid genealogy (6. 52 and 7. 204) agree with the eight generations of 4. 147 and the contemporaneity of Laius and Amphitryon at 5. 59. If we calculate as in § 1 and put the manhood of Theras in the generation 1130–1100, then Cadmus' visit with his grown-up nephew to Thera and Cadmus' coming to Thebes were in the generation *c.* 1370–1340. Herodotus gives us not only the data for the date of Cadmus but also the following points: Cadmus came from Phoenicia; Cadmus brought 'Phoenician letters' with him; Cadmus founded a dynasty at Thebes; and his dynasty was ousted by the Epigoni in the generation of Laodamas (5. 61) *c.* 1220–1190 on the same system of calculation. The discovery (reported in *ILN*, 28 November 1964, p. 860) in a burnt layer, dated to 'the end of the Late Helladic III B period' by its pottery, in the palace of Cadmus at Thebes of cylinder seals with cuneiform inscriptions, some being dated to the reign of King Burraburrias II of the Kassite dynasty in 1367–46, confirms the date of Cadmus, his origin, his chosen place, the 'Cadmean letters', and the fall of his dynasty *c.* 1220–1190. The sceptic might regard confirmation of any one point as coincidental, but he cannot—or should not—so regard the confirmation of five points; for this uniquely fine collection of cylinder seals was clearly a royal heirloom, brought by Cadmus and lost in the sack by the Epigoni.

§ 4. Archaeological dating is very approximate in this period when objects from Egypt are rare in the Aegean and chronological deductions have to be made from the stylistic development of pottery, &c. The destruction of Troy VII A came before the end of L.H. III B, which most archaeologists place somewhere between 1230 and 1180. The presence of L.H. III B pottery at Ugarit and other Syrian sites which were destroyed by the great raids *c.* 1192 (p. 72 above) shows that L.H. III B was in vogue there at the time. When the Philistines settled in south Palestine at an unknown interval after *c.* 1191, in which year they were defeated on the Egyptian border, their pottery showed the influence of L.H. III C pottery; thus L.H. III C may have begun *c.* 1180. This date suits the foundation of Tarsus (pp. 73–74 above), where pottery of the transitional period L.H. III B–L.H. III C was found. The latter part of L.H. III B, which includes the sack of Thebes, the sack of Troy, and the founding of Tarsus during the return from Troy, may then be put *c.* 1220 to 1180. On the whole, then, it is best to accept the view of Thucydides and the evidence of the Egyptian and Hittite records and date the sack of Troy *c.* 1200.

List of Colonies from the Eighth to the Sixth Century

THE dates of foundation are in most cases approximate. Where another date is given in brackets, it means the date of the refoundation of a colony.

Colonies of the Black Sea and its approaches

Colony	Foundress	Date of foundation
Abydus	Miletus	675
Amisus	Miletus, Phocaea	8th century (560)
Apollonia Pontica	Miletus, Phocaea, ? Rhodes	609
Apollonia Rhyndacia	Miletus	
Arisbe	Miletus, Mitylene	
Artace	Miletus	
Astacus	Megara	712
Bisanthe	Samos	
Bizone	Ionians and natives	
Borysthenes	Miletus	
Byzantium	Megara	660
Callatis	(1) Miletus	
—	(2) Heraclea Pontica	Late 6th century
Cerasus	Sinope	
Chalcedon	Megara	676
Chersonesus	Megara	5th century
Cius	Miletus	628
Colonae	Miletus	
Cotyora	Sinope	
Cromna	Sinope	
Crouni	Ionians and natives	
Cytorus	Sinope	
Cyzicus	Miletus	756 (676)
Dascylium	Miletus	
Dioscurias	Miletus	Late 6th century
Heraclea Pontica	(1) Miletus	560
	(2) Megara	
Heraeum Teichos	Samos	
Istrus	Miletus	656
Lampsacus	Phocaea	654
Mesembria	Megara	6th century
Miletopolis	Miletus	
Myrlea	Colophon	
Niconium	Miletus	
Odessus	Miletus	560
Olbia	Miletus	644
Ophiousa	Miletus	
Paesus	Miletus	
Panticapaeum	Miletus	600

Colonies of the Black Sea and its approaches—contd.

Colony	Foundress	Date of foundation
Parium	Paros, Erythrae, ? Miletus	710
Perinthus	Samos	601
Phanagoria	Teus	540
Phasis	Miletus	6th century
Pityus	Miletus	
Priapus	Miletus	
Proconnesos	Miletus	675
Ptereum	Sinope	
Selymbria	Megara	7th century
Sinope	Miletus	770 (657, 630)
Theodosia	Miletus	600
Tieum	Sinope	630
Tomis	Miletus	6th century
Trapezus	Miletus	756
Tyras	Miletus	656

Colonies of the north Aegean

Colony	Foundress	Date of foundation
Abdera	(1) Clazomenae	654
	(2) Teus	540
Acanthus	Andros	655
Aenus	Aeolians	
Alopeconnesos	Aeolians	
Argilus	Andros	654
Cardia	Miletus, Clazomenae	
Datum	Thasos	
Dicaea	Eretria	
Galepsus	Thasos	654
Limnae	Miletus	
Madytus	Aeolians	
Maronea	Chios	
Mende	Eretria	730
Methone	Eretria	730
Neapolis	Thasos	
Oesyme	Thasos	654
Potidaea	Corinth	600
Sane	Andros	655
Scapte Hyle	Thasos	Late 6th century
Scione	Achaea	700
Sestus	Aeolians	
Stagirus	Andros	655
Stryme	Thasos	
Thasos	Paros	710
Torone	Chalcis	710

Colonies of north-west Greece and Illyria

Colony	Foundress	Date of foundation
Ambracia	Corinth	*c.* 625
Anactorium	Corinth, Corcyra	*c.* 625
Apollonia Illyrica	Corinth	*c.* 600
Boucheta	Elis	
Chalcis	Corinth	*c.* 700
Corcyra	(1) Eretria	8th century
	(2) Corinth	733
Corcyra Nigra	Cnidus	6th century
Elatria	Elis	
Epidamnus	Corcyra	627
Leucas	Corinth	*c.* 625
Macynia	Corinth	*c.* 700
Molycrium	Corinth	*c.* 700
Oeniadae	Corinth	*c.* 700
Oricum	Eretria	730
Pandosia	Elis	
Sollium	Corinth	*c.* 625

Colonies in Italy, Sicily, and the West

Colony	Foundress	Date of foundation
Acrae	Syracuse	663
Acragas	Gela	580
Agathe	Massilia	
Alalia	Phocaea	560
Alonis	Massilia	
Antipolis	Massilia	
Callipolis	Taras	
Camarina	Syracuse	598
Casmenae	Syracuse	643
Catana	Naxos	729
Caulonia	Achaea	675–650
Croton	Achaea	708
Cyme (Cumae)	Chalcis, Cyme, Eretria	757
Dicaearchia	Samos	531
Elea	Phocaea	535
Emporium	Massilia	
Gela	Rhodes, Crete	688
Hemeroscopium	Massilia	
Himera	Zancle	649
Hipponium	Locri	
Hydruntum	Taras	
Ischia	Chalcis, Eretria	Early 8th century
Lametini	Croton	
Laüs	Sybaris	
Leontini	Naxus	729

List of Colonies from Eighth to Sixth Century
Colonies in Italy, Sicily, and the West—contd.

Colony	Foundress	Date of foundation
Lipara	Cnidus	580–576
Locri Epizephyrii	Locris	673
Maenace	Massilia	
Massilia	Phocaea	600
Medma	Locri	*c.* 575
Megara Hyblaea	Megara	728
Metapontium	Achaea	690–680
Mylae	Zancle	716
Naxus	Chalcis	734
Neapolis	Cyme	
Nicaea	Massilia	
Olbia	Massilia	
Petelia	Croton	
Poseidonia (Paestum)	Sybaris	700
Pyxus	Sybaris	7th century
Rhegium	Chalcis	730–720
Rhode	(1) Rhodes	
	(2) Emporium	
Scidrus	Sybaris	7th century
Scylletium	Croton	
Selinus	Megara Hyblaea	628
Siris	Colophon	680–670
Sybaris	Achaea	720
Syracuse	Corinth	733
Taras	Sparta	706
Tauroeis	Massilia	
Temesa	? Sybaris	
Terina	Croton	6th century
Theline	Massilia	
Zancle	Cyme, Chalcis	730

Colonies and Emporia in the south-west Mediterranean

Colony	Foundress	Date of foundation
Amorgos	Naxos, Samos, Miletus	7th–6th centuries
Apollonia Cyrenaica	Cyrene	*c.* 560
Barca	Cyrene	*c.* 570
Celenderis	Samos	6th century
Cyrene	Thera	*c.* 630
Euesperides	Cyrene	6th century
Milesion Teichos	Miletus	Late 7th century
Nagidus	Samos	6th century
Naucratis		*c.* 610
Phaselis	Rhodes, Crete	*c.* 688
Poseidium		*c.* 750
Side	Cyme (Aeolian)	*c.* 750

The Date of the Earliest Coinages

Xenophanes (*fl. c.*550) attributed the first coins to Lydia (Pollux 9. 83), correctly, as a Lydian lion appears on them. The evolution from dumps to coins is clear from those found, all of electrum, at the Artemisium at Ephesus: plain, 'incused' and 'striated' dumps and stamped coins. They were in the temple's foundation deposit together with objects which were dated in general to the seventh century but a few to as late as 590 (*JHS* 71. 85 f.; 156 f.). The first temple was built *c.* 645. If the deposit was closed then for ever, the objects have been wrongly dated after 645 (*AJA* 86. 343 f. argues so). As we cannot exclude the possibility that the foundation-deposit was reinforced for the building of the second temple on the site (see *Ann. Liv.* 24. 26 for re-use of Basis A blocks from collapsed walls), it seems best to date the objects to *c.* 700–600. Since half were dumps, we might postulate a use of dumps for commercial exchange (e.g. at Samos; see *GC* 30) until 650. This postulate is supported by a remarkable but often forgotten hoard in Crete, dated to before 650, which included ingots and dumps of gold and one of silver (*JHS* 64. 86). If the ancients regarded dumps as coins, the literary tradition is correct that Midas and Gyges of Lydia coined first, reigning *c.* 700–652 (Pollux 3. 87; Heraclid. Pont. 11. 3). The prior claim of Pheidon, coining in Aegina (Strabo 358, 376; *Marm. Par.* 45; *EM* 613), may be rejected in favour of Herodotus who mentioned weights and measures only (6. 127).

Coins in the modern sense started in Lydia (and at the Artemisium) probably after but not long after 650 and were adopted in Ionia and then by Aegina *c.* 625. Corinth followed perhaps *c.* 610 and Athens *c.* 600. Strong literary evidence connects Solon with coinage *c.* 594–592: the 16th *Axon* = Ruschenbusch T8 and F8, and *Ath. Pol.* 10, based presumably on the use of Solon's *Axones* by Androtion and Aristotle (see *StGH* 165 f. arguing against C.M. Kraay). If Athens coined then, we avoid the unlikely sequence that backward tribes in Thrace coined from *c.* 560 (and Peisistratus there in exile) and Athens did not coin until *c.* 540 (*CAH*[2] 3.3.379). One cause of error has been too tight an interpretation of coin-hoards, which provide a *terminus ante quem* but do not show how long objects in a hoard had been in use.

Date of the Attack on Plataea in 431

THE date in March is uncertain. It depends not on the 'two months' of 2. 2. 1, which is incorrect and probably an intrusive *marginale*, nor on the time of the harvest, which in 431 may have been early or late (2.19.1); but on the third *decad* of the moon (2. 4. 2), which gives us a choice of 28 February to 9 March or 28 March to 7 April 431, and the meaning of 'at the beginning of spring' (2. 2. 1), which was determined not by the variable civil calendar but by observation each year. Hippocrates (*Vict.* 3. 1) defines the end of winter by the spring equinox, which we can fix to a precise day, 24 March, but Thucydides—presumably making his own observation in most years—could place within a bracket of several days, perhaps our 20 to 27 March. This period for the beginning of spring and (in Thucydides' terminology) of summer fits the eclipse of 21 March 424 (4. 52. 1), the probable dates of Elaphebolion 14, *c.* 24 March 423 (4. 117. 1 and 118. 12), and of the city Dionysia on Elaphebolion 13, *c.* 30 March 421 (5. 20. 1), and the lapse of probably some 95 days between the winter solstice of 412 on 24 December (8. 39. 1) and 'the end of the winter' (8. 60. 3 with 8. 44. 4 = 80 days and, say, 15 days for events from 8. 39. 1 to 8. 44. 4), which brings us to 29 March 411. All these events are said by Thucydides to have fallen at the turn of the year, so that we shall probably be correct in putting the attack on Plataea late in March 431, and the end of the war immediately after *c.* 30 March 421, which fits Thucydides' statement that the war lasted 'just ten years with a difference of a few days' (5. 20. 1, translation by Jowett). The battle at Potidaea then fell *c.* late September 432 (2. 2. 1) and the invasion of Attica about mid-June near midsummer, the time of harvest in 431 being later than usual nowadays (2. 19. 1). In 1953 there was a late harvest: it began in the plain on 13 May and was then delayed until the period 27 May to 10 June, when the corn was mostly cut, but some corn was still standing on 28 June.

Army Strengths of Sparta, Boeotia, and Athens in the Fourth Century

THE nominal establishment of the army of the Spartan Alliance in early 371 was probably as follows: Spartan cavalry 600 (X. *HG*. 4. 2. 16), Spartan hoplites 3,600 in six brigades or 'morai' with platoons or 'enomotiai' at 36 men (X. *Lac. Pol.* 11. 4; X. *HG*. 4. 5. 12; 6. 4. 12), allied contingents 10,000 (X. *HG*. 5. 2. 20). At Leuctra Cleombrotus had four Spartan brigades, that is two-thirds of the Spartan army. However, the men between fifty-five and sixty years of age and those holding office were not present (X. *HG*. 6. 1. 1; 6. 4. 17), so that the actual strength of the four brigades may have been some 2,100 men. If we allow a similar proportion of two-thirds for the allied contribution, he had some 6,600 allies and probably the complete levy of the Phocians. Thus the total figure given in Plu. *Pel.* 20, namely 1,000 cavalry and 10,000 hoplites, is reasonable. The Spartiates in this force numbered some 700 (X. *HG*. 6. 4. 15); thus the Spartiates formed about one-third of the Spartan army in the battle, and we can estimate the total number of Spartiates of military age at some 1,200 men. In the battle 400 Spartiates fell (X. *HG*. ibid.; *Ages*. 2. 24), and this was about one-third of the total number of Spartiates of military age.

The nominal strength of the Boeotian League at the turn of the century was 1,100 cavalry and 11,000 first-line hoplites (*Hell. Oxy*. 11. 4). In 394 at Nemea the League, excluding Orchomenus, sent 5,000 hoplites (X. *HG*. 4. 2. 17). In 378, when Sparta held many places in Boeotia, 1,500 cavalry and 7,000 hoplites defended Thebes against Agesilaus (D.S. 15. 26). At Leuctra Diodorus Siculus gives the figure 6,000 for the full force of Thebes and the available Boeotians (15. 52. 2); this figure probably represents the hoplites, and the cavalry should be added. The tendency was to underestimate the numbers in order to magnify the victory (Frontin. 4. 2. 6), but the figure in Diodorus may be nearly right, because the full Boeotian levy had not concentrated and the Thespian contingent withdrew. In 364 the Boeotian League voted to send 7,000 men to Thessaly (Plu. *Pel.* 31. 4; D.S. 15. 80. 2), and the Boeotian League put 13,000 men in the field against Phocis in 355–354 (D.S. 16. 30. 4). At the height of her power *c.* 365 Boeotia probably had at least 13,000 hoplites and 1,500 cavalry.

Athens sent 6,000 hoplites and 600 cavalry to Nemea in 394 (X. *HG*. 4. 2. 17) and 6,000 hoplites and a considerable force of cavalry to Mantinea in 362 (D.S. 15. 84. 2); and expeditionary forces of similar size went out from Attica in 379/378 and in 352 (D.S. 15. 26. 2; 16. 37. 3). It is unlikely that these forces represented the full strength of Athens' army, even in 394 when Boeotia sent about half of her forces. In 369 Athens sent the full force

(X. *HG.* 6. 5. 49) of the 'young men' (D.S. 15. 63. 2) numbering 12,000, while the older men no doubt held the Boeotian and Megarian frontiers. Even at the time of Tanagra in 457 it is doubtful if Athens had quite so many hoplites serving outside Attica, but in 369 men under fifty years of age had not fought in the Peloponnesian War, and there had been few major battles in the fourth century. Athens, then, probably had at least 15,000 first-line hoplites in 369. The following points support this estimate. Xenophon writing *c.* 365 (*Eq. Mag.* 7. 3) reckoned the Athenian hoplites at 'not less' than those of Boeotia (cf. *Mem.* 3. 5. 2). Athens in the optimism of 378/377 hoped to equip 20,000 hoplites (D.S. 15. 29. 7). Polybius 2. 62 put her actual strength in 378 at 10,000 hoplites and 100 triremes (the latter figure is confirmed by *IG* ii.² 1604). As the hoplite strength varied with financial prosperity, so did the cavalry strength: 600 at Nemea in 394 (X. *HG.* 4. 2. 17), 500 in 378 (D.S. 15. 26. 2; 29. 7), 1,000 laid down by law before *c.* 365 and 800 at that time (X. *Eq. Mag.* 1. 2; 9. 3), and 1,000 in 354 (D. 14. 13). The cavalry strengths of Athens and Boeotia after the destruction of Orchomenus, which had 300 cavalry (D.S. 15. 79. 3), were fairly comparable in number (X. *Eq. Mag.* 7. 1).

At Embata the 120 ships were rowed mainly by the citizens (Isoc. 8. 48) and needed some 20,000 oarsmen.

The Chronology of 370–362

THE chronology of the years 370–362 is disputed. The dates given in the text are based on the following considerations. (1) Epaminondas was Boeotarch in 370; his year of office ended in late December, but he retained command illegally until about April 369 when he returned and was impeached (Plu. *Pel.* 25. 2; X. *HG.* 5. 4. 4; Paus. 9. 14. 5). It is clear that he was not Boeotarch in 369 either before his trial or after it (Plu. *Pel.* 25. 2, 5, 6). In 368 Epaminondas as Boeotarch invaded the Peloponnese for the second time, but he was deposed on his return and was not elected Boeotarch for 367 (D.S. 15. 72. 1–2). (2) During the year after Epaminondas' first invasion, that is in the year commencing in spring 369 (X. *HG.* 7. 1. 1), Athens and Sparta contracted a formal alliance, and they received help from Dionysius during Epaminondas' second invasion. Dionysius sent help twice and his son sent help once, the occasions probably being in consecutive years (X. *HG.* 7. 1. 20; 7. 1. 28; 7. 4. 12); as the mercenaries had wages for five months and departed at the end of the summer on the first occasion (D.S. 15. 70. 1), they arrived about May. In May 369 Epaminondas was in Boeotia either on trial or just acquitted; but in May 368 his second invasion of the Peloponnese was well under way (X. *HG.* 7. 1. 15–20). The forces from Syracuse came, therefore, in 368, 367, and 366 (cf. Tod, *GHI* 133, 136). (3) Pelopidas was in Thessaly during Epaminondas' second invasion (Plu. *Pel.* 26. 1), i.e. in 368; he was a prisoner in 367 when Epaminondas served in the ranks (Plu. *Pel.* 28; D.S. 15. 71. 6), and he was released in summer 367. The mission to Susa, the invasion of Achaea, and the seizure of Oropus came before June 366, since the last event is dated to the archon year 367/366 (Schol. Aeschin. 3. 85); and the separate peace made by Corinth, &c., with Thebes was negotiated 'about the time of the arrival' of help from Dionysius II (X. *HG.* 7. 4. 12), say in midsummer 366, which agrees with the note that the peace was 'more than five years after Leuctra' (D.S. 15. 76. 3). (4) Pelopidas' plan to invade Thessaly with the Boeotian army is dated by the solar eclipse which occurred on 13 July 364 (Plu. *Pel.* 31. 3; D.S. 15. 80. 2). Boeotia had not the resources in manpower to plan a naval enterprise with a complement of 17,000 men in the same summer; therefore Epaminondas' naval expedition was in 363 (D.S. 15. 78. 4 puts plan and execution in 364/363).

Battles of Issus and Gaugamela, and Greek Mercenaries in Persian Service

A T Issus the total numbers are uncertain. Callisthenes in Polybius (12. 18. 2) gives 30,000 cavalry on Darius' right wing, 30,000 Greek mercenaries, and no number for the Cardaces; these were all in the first line, and other troops were behind and on the advanced left wing. The given numbers are credible, because Darius clearly had more cavalry and more Greek mercenaries than at the Granicus. All sources agree that his good troops were too cramped in space for them to be effective against Alexander's 35,000 men, who did have space. At Arr. *An.* 2. 9. 3 I take the word 'all' to refer to the left-wing troops just mentioned in Arrian's preceding sentence. Darius at first meant to take command on his left centre or left wing, but he moved to the centre, probably because the ground on his left was not very good for cavalry. When the attack came, Darius had posted his Hyrcanian and Median cavalry near the left end of his line (Arr. *An.* 2. 8. 10–11; 2. 9. 1; Curt. 3. 9. 5). In the centre he was protected by his Royal Cavalry Guard, probably 3,000 strong (Curt. 3. 9. 4). When Alexander's Infantry Guard broke through the enemy infantry, the Companion Cavalry exploited the gap and swung left to take the cavalry round Darius in the flank (D.S. 17. 34. 2–4; Curt. 3. 11. 8). The defeat of the Persian Royal Cavalry Guard was regarded as critical in Diodorus' account (17. 34. 9). More important, the first break in the enemy line was achieved by Alexander's Infantry Guard charging 'at the double' (Arr. *An.* 2. 10. 3). The Cardaces were probably on both sides of the Greek phalanx, which was itself opposite to the Macedonian phalanx (Plb. 12. 18. 6; Arr. *An.* 2. 8. 6), and also on the left wing beyond the Hyrcanian and Median cavalry; this explains Arrian's phrase 'here and there' (*An.* 2. 8. 6) instead of 'on both sides' (as at Arr. *An.* 3. 11. 7). See *HA* 94–110.

At Gaugamela the Persian order of battle was captured. Arr. *An.* 3. 8. 6 gives 40,000 cavalry, Curt. 4. 12. 13 (cf. 4. 9. 3) 45,000, either from the order of battle or subsequent information; as 2,000 Greek mercenaries rejoined after the battle, their number was much more before the battle (the 2,000 with Mazaeus at Thapsacus were only a part, probably mounted to withdraw rapidly). For the Macedonian lancers (*sarissophoroi* or *prodromoi*; probably 'the cavalry from upper Macedonia' of Arr. *An.* 1. 2. 5) under command of Aretes see Arr. *An.* 3. 12. 3; 3. 14. 1; Curt. 4. 15. 13 and 18 (disregarding the baggage). At Arr. *An.* 3. 13. 4 fin. 'the Macedonians' is a general term as opposed to 'Persians' (cf. 3. 14. 5 fin.), and the last word *taxis* refers to the Macedonian line. In Arr. *An.* 3. 12. 4, at the end of the first sentence, 'they' are the Scythians and Bactrians, who are to be charged as they bend round the Macedonian right wing and expose their flank. For cavalry formations and the *epikampe* or pincer-movement see Arr. *Tact.* 16 and 26. 7, and Curt. 3. 11. 14.

In Artaxerxes Ochus' reign some 20,000 Greek mercenaries were involved in Cyprus and Phoenicia (D.S. 16. 42. 2, 7, 9) and at least 34,000 in the Egyptian campaign (D.S. 16. 44. 4; 47. 6), apart from those employed in the fleets and in other satrapies. In 336 Memnon held up and later defeated the Macedonian vanguard of 10,000 men with a superior force, probably composed mainly of mercenaries (D.S. 17. 7. 3 and 10, one corps of 5,000; Polyaen. 5. 44. 4), and at the Granicus the mercenaries were not far short of 20,000, of whom 2,000 were captured and sent to Macedonia (Arr. *An.* 1. 12, 8; 14. 4; 16. 6; 29. 5); and there were also garrisons (1. 19. 6) and mercenary seamen and soldiers with the fleet of 400 sail (1. 18. 5; 1. 19. 11 a ship from Iasus), from which more than 8,000 infantry were sent to Darius by Pharnabazus (2. 2. 1; 2. 13. 2 when the ships were too many for their depleted numbers). These 8,000 were among the 30,000 at Issus (Callisthenes in Polyb. 12. 18. 2) but not among those at Gaugamela, who numbered perhaps 6,000 as 2,000 escaped. In 330 the last of them, 1500, surrendered. Thus in pitched battles Darius probably used some 50,000 mercenaries (Curt. 5. 11. 5), and his satraps employed many others in the fleet and in garrisons.

Three Royal Tombs at Aegae

THE identification of Aegae with Vergina, proposed by Hammond, in *Ancient Macedonia* (ed. B. Laourdas) 1. 64 f. and *History of Macedonia* 1. 156 f., was confirmed by the three indisputably royal tombs excavated by M. Andronikos. Hammond argued that the occupants were Amyntas III and members of his family in Tomb I, Philip II and a Getic or Scythian wife in Tomb 2, and Alexander IV in Tomb 3 (*GRBS* 19. 331–50; *Philip II, Alexander the Great and the Macedonian Heritage*, ed. W. L. Adams and E. N. Borza, 111–27). Analysis of the bones has demonstrated that the man in Tomb 2 had had a severe injury to his right eye-socket, such as appears on two miniature ivory heads from the tomb. Since Philip II was blinded in the right eye by a catapult bolt (*FGrH* 115 F 52 and 135/6 F 16), the identification is certain (*JHS* 104. 60–78). The bones in Tomb 3 are of a boy aged between 12 and 14, i.e. of Alexander IV, the only possible candidate (*ob*. 310/309). The shrine beside Tomb 1 was for worship of its occupant as a god. Amyntas III was so worshipped at Pydna (*Schol.* ad D. 1. 5).

Objects in Tombs 2 and 3 are masterpieces of workmanship in gold, silver, iron and ivory, and the frescoes in all three tombs are of an excellence totally unexpected for that period. The Macedonian court already outstripped Athens as the centre of fine art and was initiating developments in portraiture, painting, architecture and craftmanship, which were to be the marks of the subsequent 'Hellenistic', or rather 'Graeco-Macedonian', age.

INDEX

References in brackets are to the maps; thus 11^b3 = Fig. 11 in the grid square B3.

PLATES

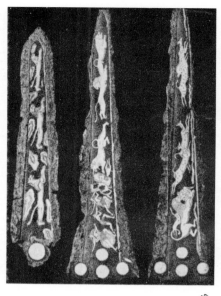

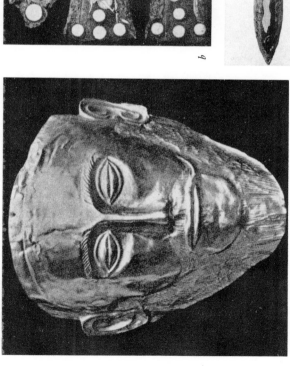

PLATE II

c

b

a

a. DEATH MASK OF A MYCENAEAN KING (*c.* 1550). A life-size mask, in gold foil hammered into relief, found in Shaft Grave V at Mycenae. National Museum, Athens

b. DAGGERS FROM A ROYAL GRAVE AT MYCENAE (*c.* 1550). Bronze blades, about a foot long, with gold studs and gold inlay; the top one shows lions running, and the lower two, being the sides of one blade, show men hunting lions and lions hunting deer. Found in Shaft Grave IV. National Museum, Athens

c. HAFTED DAGGER FROM PYLUS (*c.* 1500). Gold haft and bronze blade inlaid in gold, silver and niello with stalking leopards. Found in Shaft Grave II inside a Tholos Tomb near Pylus. National Museum, Athens

PLATE III

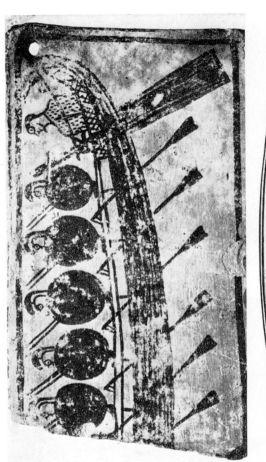

WARSHIPS OF THE COLONIZING PERIOD

a. After-part of a ship with marines on the side-decks, steersman and oars (oarsmen to be imagined). From a Proto-Attic plaque found at Sunium; *c.* 690. National Museum, Athens

b. A thirty-oared boat (triaconter) with side-rails and no deck. From the François Vase of Attic Black Figure style found in Etruria; *c.* 570. Florence Museum

PLATE IV

a. HOPLITES GOING INTO ACTION. The first two ranks, marching with the piper between them, and one end of the enemy's first rank showing on the right. From the Chigi vase of Proto-Corinthian style found at Veii; *c.* 650–640. Villa Giulia, Rome

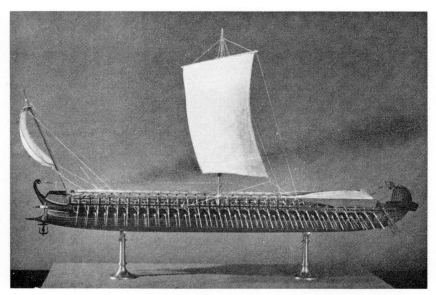

b. MODEL OF A FIFTH-CENTURY TRIREME. Length 120 feet, beam at water line 14 feet, draught 3 feet, displacement 82 tons, crew 200; this model, having side rails and no deck, represents a ship of the time of the Peloponnesian War. By C. Busley, Deutsches Museum, Munich

PLATE V

a. THE PEPLOS KORE (*c*. 540–530). Marble statue, almost four feet high, with traces of the original paint. Acropolis Museum, Athens

b. HEAD OF A YOUTH (*c*. 530–520). From an Attic gravestone of marble with traces of red colour, portraying the youth as an athlete. Metropolitan Museum, New York

PLATE VI

ZEUS OF ARTEMISIUM (*c*. 475). Bronze statue, nearly seven feet high, of Zeus casting a spear; commemorates the actions against the Persians off Artemisium. Found on the sea-bed there. National Museum, Athens

PLATE VII

HEAD OF APOLLO and CENTRAL PART OF THE WEST PEDIMENT AT OLYMPIA (*c.* 465–460). Apollo (the marble statue is ten feet high) presides over the battle between the Lapiths and the Centaurs. Sculpture in Olympia Museum; model in Altes Museum, Berlin

PLATE VIII

RIDERS IN THE PANATHENAÏC PROCESSION (c. 442–438). Carved in marble on the west frieze of the Parthenon. *In situ*

PLATE IX

HERMES WITH THE CHILD DIONYSUS (*c.* 343). Marble statue, seven feet high, by Praxiteles; found in the Heraeum at Olympia. Olympia Museum

PLATE X

THE ALEXANDER SARCOPHAGUS (c. 325–300). A hunting scene in marble (nine feet long) with many traces of colour; Alexander is portrayed on the left-hand horse. Found at Sidon; in the Constantinople Museum

DESCRIPTION OF PLATES XI AND XII

PLATE XI

a. Electrum dump, punched and striated, seventh century (p. 131)

b. Electrum stater of Ionia, inscribed above the stag 'I am the emblem of Phanes', seventh century (p. 132)

c. Silver didrachm 'turtle' of Aegina, seventh century (p. 132)

d. Silver stater 'foal' of Corinth, *c*. 600, the ♀ under Pegasus being the archaic Κ (pp. 133 f.)

e. Silver didrachm of Athens with oil-amphora inside a shield-circle, *c*. 590 (p. 160)

f. Silver Tetradrachm of Athens, issued perhaps for Panathenaic Festivals, *c*. 520 (p. 182)

g. Gold daric of Persia, portraying the Great King, fifth century (p. 177)

h. Silver three-obol piece of Phocis, sixth century (p. 196)

i. Silver didrachm recording alliance of Boeotian League and Chalcis, *c*. 506 (p. 197)

j. Silver tetradrachm of Syracuse with head of Artemis Arethusa, *c*. 510 (p. 286)

k. Silver tetradrachm of Chersonese, with head of Athena and the lion revealing Miltiades' sympathy with the Ionians, *c*. 495 (p. 208)

l. Silver octadrachm of Alexander I, King of Macedon, with a trooper on a charger of heavy build, *c*. 478–454 (pp. 535 f.)

PLATE XII

a. Silver tetradrachm of Athens, the olive-leaves on Athena's helmet and the waning moon by the owl's neck serving to commemorate the Battle of Marathon, *c*. 485 (p. 217)

b. Silver decadrachm 'Demareteion' of Syracuse, Arethusa being wreathed with bay leaves to commemorate the victory at Himera, *c*. 479 (p. 270)

c. Silver didrachm of Himera, showing its control by the crab of Acragas, *c*. 482 (p. 267)

d. Electrum stater of Cyzicus, the device of Harmodios and Aristogeiton showing the influence of Athens above the tunny-fish of Cyzicus, *c*. 420 (pp. 184 and 286 n.)

e. Silver tridrachm of Ephesus, commemorating a coalition inspired by Thebes from which Heracles strangling the snake is taken, *c*. 390 (p. 461)

f. Silver didrachm of the Boeotian League, Epaminondas being the Boeotarch responsible for this issue, *c*. 370 (p. 485)

g. Silver tetradrachm of Syracuse, the triskeles advancing Dionysius' claim to be 'Ruler of Sicily', *c*. 380 (p. 481)

h. Gold half-stater of Philip, King of Macedon, with head of Heracles, probably minted at Philippi, *c*. 356 (pp. 541, 576)

i. Gold stater 'Philippic', with the head of Apollo adopted from Olynthus, *c*. 348 (pp. 559, 576)

j. Silver stater of Timoleon's Syracuse, with head of Zeus Eleutherios and Corinthian Pegasus, *c*. 340 (p. 579)

k. Silver decadrachm commemorating the Battle of the Hydaspes, with Alexander wearing Macedonian cloak, Persian head-dress and Greek arms, and Porus on an elephant, *c*. 323 (p. 631)

l. Silver tetradrachm of Lysimachus, portraying Alexander the Great, with Athena on the reverse, *c*. 300

PLATE XI

a

b

c

e

d

f

g

i

h

k

j

l

PLATE XII

a
b
c
d
e
f
h
g
i
j
k
l